Collins

WORLDATLAS

ILLUSTRATED EDITION

contents

map symbols

SETTLEMENTS

Population	National Capital	Administrative Capital	Other City or Town
over 10 million	BEIJING ✪	Karachi ◉	New York ◉
over 5 million	JAKARTA ✫	Tianjin ◉	Nova Iguaçu ◉
1 million to 5 million	KĀBUL ✸	Sydney ⊙	Kaohsiung ⊙
500 000 to 1 million	BANGUI ✡	Trujillo ◎	Jeddah ◎
100 000 to 500 000	WELLINGTON ✿	Mansa ⊙	Apucarana ⊙
50 000 to 100 000	PORT OF SPAIN ✿	Potenza ○	Arecibo ○
10 000 to 50 000	MALABO ✿	Chinhoyi ○	Ceres ○
under 10 000	VALLETTA ✿	Ati ○	Venta ○

Built-up area

BOUNDARIES

- International boundary
- Disputed international boundary or alignment unconfirmed
- Administrative boundary
- Ceasefire line

MISCELLANEOUS

- National park
- Reserve or Regional park
- ✿ Site of specific interest
- Wall

LAND AND SEA FEATURES

- Desert
- Oasis
- Lava field
- *1234* Volcano _height in metres_
- Marsh
- Ice cap or Glacier
- Escarpment
- Coral reef
- *1234* Pass _height in metres_

LAKES AND RIVERS

- Lake
- Impermanent lake
- Salt lake or lagoon
- Impermanent salt lake
- Dry salt lake or salt pan
- *123* Lake height _surface height above sea level, in metres_
- River
- Impermanent river or watercourse
- Waterfall
- Dam
- Barrage

RELIEF

Contour intervals and layer colours

metres

6000
5000
4000
3000
2000
1000
500
200
0
below sea level
0
200
2000
4000
6000

- *1234* Summit _height in metres_
- *-123* Spot height _height in metres_
- *123* Ocean deep _depth in metres_

TRANSPORT

- Motorway (tunnel; under construction)
- Main road (tunnel; under construction)
- Secondary road (tunnel; under construction)
- Track
- Main railway (tunnel; under construction)
- Secondary railway (tunnel; under construction)
- Other railway (tunnel; under construction)
- Canal
- ✈ Main airport
- ✈ Regional airport

SPOT

Space Shuttle

IKONOS

SATELLITE IMAGERY - The thematic pages in the atlas contain a wide variety of photographs and images. These are a mixture of terrestrial and aerial photographs and satellite imagery. All are used to illustrate specific themes and to give an indication of the variety of imagery available today. The main types of imagery used in the atlas are described in the table below. The sensor for each satellite image is detailed on the acknowledgements page.

Main satellites/sensors

SATELLITE/SENSOR NAME	LAUNCH DATES	OWNER	AIMS AND APPLICATIONS	WEB ADDRESS	ADDITIONAL WEB ADDRESSES
Landsat 4, 5, 7	July 1972-April 1999	National Aeronautics and Space Administration (NASA), USA	The first satellite to be designed specifically for observing the Earth's surface. Originally set up to produce images of use for agriculture and geology. Today is of use for numerous environmental and scientific applications.	geo.arc.nasa.gov ls7pm3.gsfc.nasa.gov	asterweb.jpl.nasa.gov earth.jsc.nasa.gov earthnet.esrin.esa.it
SPOT 1, 2, 3, 4, 5 (Satellite Pour l'Observation de la Terre)	February 1986-March 1998	Centre National d'Etudes Spatiales (CNES) and Spot Image, France	Particularly useful for monitoring land use, water resources research, coastal studies and cartography.	www.cnes.fr www.spotimage.fr	earthobservatory.nasa.gov eol.jsc.nasa.go modis.gsfc.nasa.gov
Space Shuttle	Regular launches from 1981	NASA, USA	Each shuttle mission has separate aims. Astronauts take photographs with high specification hand held cameras. The Shuttle Radar Topography Mission (SRTM) in 2000 obtained the most complete near-global high-resolution database of the earth's topography.	science.ksc.nasa.gov/shuttle/countdown www.jpl.nasa.gov/srtm	seawifs.gsfc.nasa.gov topex-www.jpl.nasa.gov visibleearth.nasa.gov www.rsi.ca
IKONOS	September 1999	Space Imaging	First commercial high-resolution satellite. Useful for a variety of applications mainly Cartography, Defence, Urban Planning, Agriculture, Forestry and Insurance.	www.spaceimaging.com	www.usgs.gov

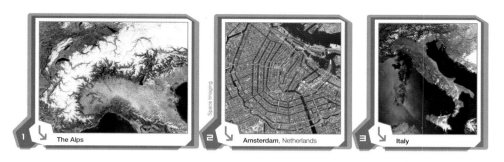

1 The Alps   2 Amsterdam, Netherlands   3 Italy

Space Imaging

EUROPE

COUNTRIES		area sq km	area sq miles	population	capital	languages	religions	currency
ALBANIA		28 748	11 100	3 164 000	Tirana	Albanian, Greek	Sunni Muslim, Albanian Orthodox, Roman Catholic	Lek
ANDORRA		465	180	94 000	Andorra la Vella	Spanish, Catalan, French	Roman Catholic	Euro
AUSTRIA		83 855	32 377	8 069 000	Vienna	German, Croatian, Turkish	Roman Catholic, Protestant	Euro
BELARUS		207 600	80 155	10 106 000	Minsk	Belorussian, Russian	Belorussian Orthodox, Roman Catholic	Belarus rouble
BELGIUM		30 520	11 784	10 276 000	Brussels	Dutch (Flemish), French (Walloon), German	Roman Catholic, Protestant	Euro
BOSNIA-HERZEGOVINA		51 130	19 741	4 126 000	Sarajevo	Bosnian, Serbian, Croatian	Sunni Muslim, Serbian Orthodox, Roman Catholic, Protestant	Marka
BULGARIA		110 994	42 855	7 790 000	Sofia	Bulgarian, Turkish, Romany, Macedonian	Bulgarian Orthodox, Sunni Muslim	Lev
CROATIA		56 538	21 829	4 657 000	Zagreb	Croatian, Serbian	Roman Catholic, Serbian Orthodox, Sunni Muslim	Kuna
CZECH REPUBLIC		78 864	30 450	10 250 000	Prague	Czech, Moravian, Slovak	Roman Catholic, Protestant	Czech koruna
DENMARK		43 075	16 631	5 343 000	Copenhagen	Danish	Protestant	Danish krone
ESTONIA		45 200	17 452	1 361 000	Tallinn	Estonian, Russian	Protestant, Estonian and Russian Orthodox	Kroon
FINLAND		338 145	130 559	5 183 000	Helsinki	Finnish, Swedish	Protestant, Greek Orthodox	Euro
FRANCE		543 965	210 026	59 670 000	Paris	French, Arabic	Roman Catholic, Protestant, Sunni Muslim	Euro
GERMANY		357 028	137 849	81 990 000	Berlin	German, Turkish	Protestant, Roman Catholic	Euro
GREECE		131 957	50 949	10 631 000	Athens	Greek	Greek Orthodox, Sunni Muslim	Euro
HUNGARY		93 030	35 919	9 867 000	Budapest	Hungarian	Roman Catholic, Protestant	Forint
ICELAND		102 820	39 699	283 000	Reykjavik	Icelandic	Protestant	Icelandic króna
IRELAND, REPUBLIC OF		70 282	27 136	3 878 000	Dublin	English, Irish	Roman Catholic, Protestant	Euro
ITALY		301 245	116 311	57 449 000	Rome	Italian	Roman Catholic	Euro
LATVIA		63 700	24 595	2 392 000	Riga	Latvian, Russian	Protestant, Roman Catholic, Russian Orthodox	Lats
LIECHTENSTEIN		160	62	33 000	Vaduz	German	Roman Catholic, Protestant	Swiss franc
LITHUANIA		65 200	25 174	3 682 000	Vilnius	Lithuanian, Russian, Polish	Roman Catholic, Protestant, Russian Orthodox	Litas
LUXEMBOURG		2 586	998	448 000	Luxembourg	Letzeburgish, German, French	Roman Catholic	Euro
MACEDONIA (F.Y.R.O.M.)		25 713	9 928	2 051 000	Skopje	Macedonian, Albanian, Turkish	Macedonian Orthodox, Sunni Muslim	Macedonian denar
MALTA		316	122	393 000	Valletta	Maltese, English	Roman Catholic	Maltese lira
MOLDOVA		33 700	13 012	4 273 000	Chişinău	Romanian, Ukrainian, Gagauz, Russian	Romanian Orthodox, Russian Orthodox	Moldovan leu
MONACO		2	1	34 000	Monaco-Ville	French, Monegasque, Italian	Roman Catholic	Euro
NETHERLANDS		41 526	16 033	15 990 000	Amsterdam/The Hague	Dutch, Frisian	Roman Catholic, Protestant, Sunni Muslim	Euro
NORWAY		323 878	125 050	4 505 000	Oslo	Norwegian	Protestant, Roman Catholic	Norwegian krone
POLAND		312 683	120 728	38 542 000	Warsaw	Polish, German	Roman Catholic, Polish Orthodox	Złoty
PORTUGAL		88 940	34 340	10 049 000	Lisbon	Portuguese	Roman Catholic, Protestant	Euro
ROMANIA		237 500	91 699	22 332 000	Bucharest	Romanian, Hungarian	Romanian Orthodox, Protestant, Roman Catholic	Romanian leu
RUSSIAN FEDERATION		17 075 400	6 592 849	143 752 000	Moscow	Russian, Tatar, Ukrainian, local languages	Russian Orthodox, Sunni Muslim, Protestant	Russian rouble
SAN MARINO		61	24	27 000	San Marino	Italian	Roman Catholic	Euro
SERBIA AND MONTENEGRO		102 173	39 449	10 522 000	Belgrade	Serbian, Albanian, Hungarian	Serbian Orthodox, Montenegrin Orthodox, Sunni Muslim	Yugoslav dinar, Euro
SLOVAKIA		49 035	18 933	5 408 000	Bratislava	Slovak, Hungarian, Czech	Roman Catholic, Protestant, Orthodox	Slovakian koruna
SLOVENIA		20 251	7 819	1 983 000	Ljubljana	Slovene, Croatian, Serbian	Roman Catholic, Protestant	Tólar
SPAIN		504 782	194 897	39 924 000	Madrid	Castilian, Catalan, Galician, Basque	Roman Catholic	Euro
SWEDEN		449 964	173 732	8 823 000	Stockholm	Swedish	Protestant, Roman Catholic	Swedish krona
SWITZERLAND		41 293	15 943	7 167 000	Bern	German, French, Italian, Romansch	Roman Catholic, Protestant	Swiss franc
UKRAINE		603 700	233 090	48 652 000	Kiev	Ukrainian, Russian	Ukrainian Orthodox, Ukrainian Catholic, Roman Catholic	Hryvnia
UNITED KINGDOM		244 082	94 241	59 657 000	London	English, Welsh, Gaelic	Protestant, Roman Catholic, Muslim	Pound sterling
VATICAN CITY		0.5	0.2	472	Vatican City	Italian	Roman Catholic	Euro

DEPENDENT TERRITORIES		territorial status	area sq km	area sq miles	population	capital	languages	religions	currency
Azores		Autonomous Region of Portugal	2 300	888	242 000	Ponta Delgada	Portuguese	Roman Catholic, Protestant	Euro
Faroe Islands		Self-governing Danish Territory	1 399	540	47 000	Tórshavn	Faroese, Danish	Protestant	Danish krone
Gibraltar		United Kingdom Overseas Territory	7	3	27 000	Gibraltar	English, Spanish	Roman Catholic, Protestant, Sunni Muslim	Gibraltar pound
Guernsey		United Kingdom Crown Dependency	78	30	63 000	St Peter Port	English, French	Protestant, Roman Catholic	Pound sterling
Isle of Man		United Kingdom Crown Dependency	572	221	77 000	Douglas	English	Protestant, Roman Catholic	Pound sterling
Jersey		United Kingdom Crown Dependency	116	45	87 000	St Helier	English, French	Protestant, Roman Catholic	Pound sterling

Ganges Delta, India

Cyprus, eastern Mediterranean

Indian subcontinent

ASIA

COUNTRIES		area sq km	area sq miles	population	capital	languages	religions	currency
AFGHANISTAN		652 225	251 825	23 294 000	Kābul	Dari, Pushtu, Uzbek, Turkmen	Sunni Muslim, Shi'a Muslim	Afghani
ARMENIA		29 800	11 506	3 790 000	Yerevan	Armenian, Azeri	Armenian Orthodox	Dram
AZERBAIJAN		86 600	33 436	8 147 000	Baku	Azeri, Armenian, Russian, Lezgian	Shi'a Muslim, Sunni Muslim, Russian and Armenian Orthodox	Azerbaijani manat
BAHRAIN		691	267	663 000	Manama	Arabic, English	Shi'a Muslim, Sunni Muslim, Christian	Bahrain dinar
BANGLADESH		143 998	55 598	143 364 000	Dhaka	Bengali, English	Sunni Muslim, Hindu	Taka
BHUTAN		46 620	18 000	2 198 000	Thimphu	Dzongkha, Nepali, Assamese	Buddhist, Hindu	Ngultrum, Indian rupee
BRUNEI		5 765	2 226	341 000	Bandar Seri Begawan	Malay, English, Chinese	Sunni Muslim, Buddhist, Christian	Brunei dollar
CAMBODIA		181 000	69 884	13 776 000	Phnom Penh	Khmer, Vietnamese	Buddhist, Roman Catholic, Sunni Muslim	Riel
CHINA		9 584 492	3 700 593	1 279 557 000	Beijing	Mandarin, Wu, Cantonese, Hsiang, regional languages	Confucian, Taoist, Buddhist, Christian, Sunni Muslim	Yuan, HK dollar*, Macau pataca
CYPRUS		9 251	3 572	797 000	Nicosia	Greek, Turkish, English	Greek Orthodox, Sunni Muslim	Cyprus pound
EAST TIMOR		14 874	5 743	779 000	Dili	Portuguese, Tetun, English	Roman Catholic	United States dollar
GEORGIA		69 700	26 911	5 213 000	T'bilisi	Georgian, Russian, Armenian, Azeri, Ossetian, Abkhaz	Georgian Orthodox, Russian Orthodox, Sunni Muslim	Lari
INDIA		3 065 027	1 183 414	1 041 144 000	New Delhi	Hindi, English, many regional languages	Hindu, Sunni Muslim, Shi'a Muslim, Sikh, Christian	Indian rupee
INDONESIA		1 919 445	741 102	217 534 000	Jakarta	Indonesian, local languages	Sunni Muslim, Protestant, Roman Catholic, Hindu, Buddhist	Rupiah
IRAN		1 648 000	636 296	72 376 000	Tehrān	Farsi, Azeri, Kurdish, regional languages	Shi'a Muslim, Sunni Muslim	Iranian rial
IRAQ		438 317	169 235	24 246 000	Baghdād	Arabic, Kurdish, Turkmen	Shi'a Muslim, Sunni Muslim, Christian	Iraqi dinar
ISRAEL		20 770	8 019	6 303 000	Jerusalem	Hebrew, Arabic	Jewish, Sunni Muslim, Christian, Druze	Shekel
JAPAN		377 727	145 841	127 538 000	Tōkyō	Japanese	Shintoist, Buddhist, Christian	Yen
JORDAN		89 206	34 443	5 196 000	'Ammān	Arabic	Sunni Muslim, Christian	Jordanian dinar
KAZAKHSTAN		2 717 300	1 049 155	16 027 000	Astana	Kazakh, Russian, Ukrainian, German, Uzbek, Tatar	Sunni Muslim, Russian Orthodox, Protestant	Tenge
KUWAIT		17 818	6 880	2 023 000	Kuwait	Arabic	Sunni Muslim, Shi'a Muslim, Christian, Hindu	Kuwaiti dinar
KYRGYZSTAN		198 500	76 641	5 047 000	Bishkek	Kyrgyz, Russian, Uzbek	Sunni Muslim, Russian Orthodox	Kyrgyz som
LAOS		236 800	91 429	5 530 000	Vientiane	Lao, local languages	Buddhist, traditional beliefs	Kip
LEBANON		10 452	4 036	3 614 000	Beirut	Arabic, Armenian, French	Shi'a Muslim, Sunni Muslim, Christian	Lebanese pound
MALAYSIA		332 965	128 559	23 036 000	Kuala Lumpur/Putrajaya	Malay, English, Chinese, Tamil, local languages	Sunni Muslim, Buddhist, Hindu, Christian, traditional beliefs	Ringgit
MALDIVES		298	115	309 000	Male	Divehi (Maldivian)	Sunni Muslim	Rufiyaa
MONGOLIA		1 565 000	604 250	2 587 000	Ulan Bator	Khalka (Mongolian), Kazakh, local languages	Buddhist, Sunni Muslim	Tugrik (tögrög)
MYANMAR		676 577	261 228	48 956 000	Rangoon	Burmese, Shan, Karen, local languages	Buddhist, Christian, Sunni Muslim	Kyat
NEPAL		147 181	56 827	24 153 000	Kathmandu	Nepali, Maithili, Bhojpuri, English, local languages	Hindu, Buddhist, Sunni Muslim	Nepalese rupee
NORTH KOREA		120 538	46 540	22 586 000	P'yŏngyang	Korean	Traditional beliefs, Chondoist, Buddhist	North Korean won
OMAN		309 500	119 499	2 709 000	Muscat	Arabic, Baluchi, Indian languages	Ibadhi Muslim, Sunni Muslim	Omani riyal
PAKISTAN		803 940	310 403	148 721 000	Islamabad	Urdu, Punjabi, Sindhi, Pushtu, English	Sunni Muslim, Shi'a Muslim, Christian, Hindu	Pakistani rupee
PALAU		497	192	20 000	Koror	Palauan, English	Roman Catholic, Protestant, traditional beliefs	United States dollar
PHILIPPINES		300 000	115 831	78 611 000	Manila	English, Pilipino, Cebuano, local languages	Roman Catholic, Protestant, Sunni Muslim, Aglipayan	Philippine peso
QATAR		11 437	4 416	584 000	Doha	Arabic	Sunni Muslim	Qatari riyal
RUSSIAN FEDERATION		17 075 400	6 592 849	143 752 000	Moscow	Russian, Tatar, Ukrainian, local languages	Russian Orthodox, Sunni Muslim, Protestant	Russian rouble
SAUDI ARABIA		2 200 000	849 425	21 701 000	Riyadh	Arabic	Sunni Muslim, Shi'a Muslim	Saudi Arabian riyal
SINGAPORE		639	247	4 188 000	Singapore	Chinese, English, Malay, Tamil	Buddhist, Taoist, Sunni Muslim, Christian, Hindu	Singapore dollar
SOUTH KOREA		99 274	38 330	47 389 000	Seoul	Korean	Buddhist, Protestant, Roman Catholic	South Korean won
SRI LANKA		65 610	25 332	19 287 000	Sri Jayewardenepura Kotte	Sinhalese, Tamil, English	Buddhist, Hindu, Sunni Muslim, Roman Catholic	Sri Lankan rupee
SYRIA		185 180	71 498	17 040 000	Damascus	Arabic, Kurdish, Armenian	Sunni Muslim, Shi'a Muslim, Christian	Syrian pound
TAIWAN		36 179	13 969	22 548 000	T'aipei	Mandarin, Min, Hakka, local languages	Buddhist, Taoist, Confucian, Christian	Taiwan dollar
TAJIKISTAN		143 100	55 251	6 177 000	Dushanbe	Tajik, Uzbek, Russian	Sunni Muslim	Somoni
THAILAND		513 115	198 115	64 344 000	Bangkok	Thai, Lao, Chinese, Malay, Mon–Khmer languages	Buddhist, Sunni Muslim	Baht
TURKEY		779 452	300 948	68 569 000	Ankara	Turkish, Kurdish	Sunni Muslim, Shi'a Muslim	Turkish lira
TURKMENISTAN		488 100	188 456	4 930 000	Ashgabat	Turkmen, Uzbek, Russian	Sunni Muslim, Russian Orthodox	Turkmen manat
UNITED ARAB EMIRATES		83 600	32 278	2 701 000	Abu Dhabi	Arabic, English	Sunni Muslim, Shi'a Muslim	United Arab Emirates dirham
UZBEKISTAN		447 400	172 742	25 618 000	Tashkent	Uzbek, Russian, Tajik, Kazakh	Sunni Muslim, Russian Orthodox	Uzbek som
VIETNAM		329 565	127 246	80 226 000	Ha Nôi	Vietnamese, Thai, Khmer, Chinese, local languages	Buddhist, Taoist, Roman Catholic, Cao Dai, Hoa Hao	Dong
YEMEN		527 968	203 850	19 912 000	Şan'ā'	Arabic	Sunni Muslim, Shi'a Muslim	Yemeni rial

*Hong Kong dollar

DEPENDENT AND DISPUTED TERRITORIES		territorial status	area sq km	area sq miles	population	capital	languages	religions	currency
Christmas Island		Australian External Territory	135	52	2 000	The Settlement	English	Buddhist, Sunni Muslim, Protestant, Roman Catholic	Australian dollar
Cocos Islands		Australian External Territory	14	5	632	West Island	English	Sunni Muslim, Christian	Australian dollar
Gaza		Semi-autonomous region	363	140	3 433 000*	Gaza	Arabic	Sunni Muslim, Shi'a Muslim	Israeli shekel
Jammu and Kashmir		Disputed territory (India/Pakistan)	222 236	85 806	13 000 000				
West Bank		Disputed territory	5 860	2 263			Arabic, Hebrew	Sunni Muslim, Jewish, Shi'a Muslim, Christian	Jordanian dinar, Israeli shekel

*includes occupied West Bank

4 **Victoria Falls**, Zambia/Zimbabwe   5 **Madagascar**   6 **Sinai Peninsula**, Egypt

AFRICA

COUNTRIES		area sq km	area sq miles	population	capital	languages	religions	currency
ALGERIA		2 381 741	919 595	31 403 000	Algiers	Arabic, French, Berber	Sunni Muslim	Algerian dinar
ANGOLA		1 246 700	481 354	13 936 000	Luanda	Portuguese, Bantu, local languages	Roman Catholic, Protestant, traditional beliefs	Kwanza
BENIN		112 620	43 483	6 629 000	Porto–Novo	French, Fon, Yoruba, Adja, local languages	Traditional beliefs, Roman Catholic, Sunni Muslim	CFA franc*
BOTSWANA		581 370	224 468	1 564 000	Gaborone	English, Setswana, Shona, local languages	Traditional beliefs, Protestant, Roman Catholic	Pula
BURKINA		274 200	105 869	12 207 000	Ouagadougou	French, Moore (Mossi), Fulani, local languages	Sunni Muslim, traditional beliefs, Roman Catholic	CFA franc*
BURUNDI		27 835	10 747	6 688 000	Bujumbura	Kirundi (Hutu, Tutsi), French	Roman Catholic, traditional beliefs, Protestant	Burundian franc
CAMEROON		475 442	183 569	15 535 000	Yaoundé	French, English, Fang, Bamileke, local languages	Roman Catholic, traditional beliefs, Sunni Muslim, Protestant	CFA franc*
CAPE VERDE		4 033	1 557	446 000	Praia	Portuguese, creole	Roman Catholic, Protestant	Cape Verde escudo
CENTRAL AFRICAN REPUBLIC		622 436	240 324	3 844 000	Bangui	French, Sango, Banda, Baya, local languages	Protestant, Roman Catholic, traditional beliefs, Sunni Muslim	CFA franc*
CHAD		1 284 000	495 755	8 390 000	Ndjamena	Arabic, French, Sara, local languages	Sunni Muslim, Roman Catholic, Protestant, traditional beliefs	CFA franc*
COMOROS		1 862	719	749 000	Moroni	Comorian, French, Arabic	Sunni Muslim, Roman Catholic	Comoros franc
CONGO		342 000	132 047	3 206 000	Brazzaville	French, Kongo, Monokutuba, local languages	Roman Catholic, Protestant, traditional beliefs, Sunni Muslim	CFA franc*
CONGO, DEMOCRATIC REP. OF		2 345 410	905 568	54 275 000	Kinshasa	French, Lingala, Swahili, Kongo, local languages	Christian, Sunni Muslim	Congolese franc
CÔTE D'IVOIRE		322 463	124 504	16 691 000	Yamoussoukro	French, creole, Akan, local languages	Sunni Muslim, Roman Catholic, traditional beliefs, Protestant	CFA franc*
DJIBOUTI		23 200	8 958	652 000	Djibouti	Somali, Afar, French, Arabic	Sunni Muslim, Christian	Djibouti franc
EGYPT		1 000 250	386 199	70 278 000	Cairo	Arabic	Sunni Muslim, Coptic Christian	Egyptian pound
EQUATORIAL GUINEA		28 051	10 831	483 000	Malabo	Spanish, French, Fang	Roman Catholic, traditional beliefs	CFA franc*
ERITREA		117 400	45 328	3 993 000	Asmara	Tigrinya, Tigre	Sunni Muslim, Coptic Christian	Nakfa
ETHIOPIA		1 133 880	437 794	66 040 000	Addis Ababa	Oromo, Amharic, Tigrinya, local languages	Ethiopian Orthodox, Sunni Muslim, traditional beliefs	Birr
GABON		267 667	103 347	1 293 000	Libreville	French, Fang, local languages	Roman Catholic, Protestant, traditional beliefs	CFA franc*
THE GAMBIA		11 295	4 361	1 371 000	Banjul	English, Malinke, Fulani, Wolof	Sunni Muslim, Protestant	Dalasi
GHANA		238 537	92 100	20 176 000	Accra	English, Hausa, Akan, local languages	Christian, Sunni Muslim, traditional beliefs	Cedi
GUINEA		245 857	94 926	8 381 000	Conakry	French, Fulani, Malinke, local languages	Sunni Muslim, traditional beliefs, Christian	Guinea franc
GUINEA-BISSAU		36 125	13 948	1 257 000	Bissau	Portuguese, crioulo, local languages	Traditional beliefs, Sunni Muslim, Christian	CFA franc*
KENYA		582 646	224 961	31 904 000	Nairobi	Swahili, English, local languages	Christian, traditional beliefs	Kenyan shilling
LESOTHO		30 355	11 720	2 076 000	Maseru	Sesotho, English, Zulu	Christian, traditional beliefs	Loti, S. African rand
LIBERIA		111 369	43 000	3 298 000	Monrovia	English, creole, local languages	Traditional beliefs, Christian, Sunni Muslim	Liberian dollar
LIBYA		1 759 540	679 362	5 529 000	Tripoli	Arabic, Berber	Sunni Muslim	Libyan dinar
MADAGASCAR		587 041	226 658	16 913 000	Antananarivo	Malagasy, French	Traditional beliefs, Christian, Sunni Muslim	Malagasy franc
MALAWI		118 484	45 747	11 828 000	Lilongwe	Chichewa, English, local languages	Christian, traditional beliefs, Sunni Muslim	Malawian kwacha
MALI		1 240 140	478 821	12 019 000	Bamako	French, Bambara, local languages	Sunni Muslim, traditional beliefs, Christian	CFA franc*
MAURITANIA		1 030 700	397 955	2 830 000	Nouakchott	Arabic, French, local languages	Sunni Muslim	Ouguiya
MAURITIUS		2 040	788	1 180 000	Port Louis	English, creole, Hindi, Bhojpurī, French	Hindu, Roman Catholic, Sunni Muslim	Mauritius rupee
MOROCCO		446 550	172 414	30 988 000	Rabat	Arabic, Berber, French	Sunni Muslim	Moroccan dirham
MOZAMBIQUE		799 380	308 642	18 986 000	Maputo	Portuguese, Makua, Tsonga, local languages	Traditional beliefs, Roman Catholic, Sunni Muslim	Metical
NAMIBIA		824 292	318 261	1 819 000	Windhoek	English, Afrikaans, German, Ovambo, local languages	Protestant, Roman Catholic	Namibian dollar
NIGER		1 267 000	489 191	11 641 000	Niamey	French, Hausa, Fulani, local languages	Sunni Muslim, traditional beliefs	CFA franc*
NIGERIA		923 768	356 669	120 047 000	Abuja	English, Hausa, Yoruba, Ibo, Fulani, local languages	Sunni Muslim, Christian, traditional beliefs	Naira
RWANDA		26 338	10 169	8 148 000	Kigali	Kinyarwanda, French, English	Roman Catholic, traditional beliefs, Protestant	Rwandan franc
SÃO TOMÉ AND PRÍNCIPE		964	372	143 000	São Tomé	Portuguese, creole	Roman Catholic, Protestant	Dobra
SENEGAL		196 720	75 954	9 908 000	Dakar	French, Wolof, Fulani, local languages	Sunni Muslim, Roman Catholic, traditional beliefs	CFA franc*
SEYCHELLES		455	176	83 000	Victoria	English, French, creole	Roman Catholic, Protestant	Seychelles rupee
SIERRA LEONE		71 740	27 699	4 814 000	Freetown	English, creole, Mende, Temne, local languages	Sunni Muslim, traditional beliefs	Leone
SOMALIA		637 657	246 201	9 557 000	Mogadishu	Somali, Arabic	Sunni Muslim	Somali shilling
SOUTH AFRICA, REPUBLIC OF		1 219 090	470 693	44 203 000	Pretoria/Cape Town	Afrikaans, English, nine official local languages	Protestant, Roman Catholic, Sunni Muslim, Hindu	Rand
SUDAN		2 505 813	967 500	32 559 000	Khartoum	Arabic, Dinka, Nubian, Beja, Nuer, local languages	Sunni Muslim, traditional beliefs, Christian	Sudanese dinar
SWAZILAND		17 364	6 704	948 000	Mbabane	Swazi, English	Christian, traditional beliefs	Emalangeni, S. African rand
TANZANIA		945 087	364 900	36 820 000	Dodoma	Swahili, English, Nyamwezi, local languages	Shi'a Muslim, Sunni Muslim, traditional beliefs, Christian	Tanzanian shilling
TOGO		56 785	21 925	4 779 000	Lomé	French, Ewe, Kabre, local languages	Traditional beliefs, Christian, Sunni Muslim	CFA franc*
TUNISIA		164 150	63 379	9 670 000	Tunis	Arabic, French	Sunni Muslim	Tunisian dinar
UGANDA		241 038	93 065	24 780 000	Kampala	English, Swahili, Luganda, local languages	Roman Catholic, Protestant, Sunni Muslim, traditional beliefs	Ugandan shilling
ZAMBIA		752 614	290 586	10 872 000	Lusaka	English, Bemba, Nyanja, Tonga, local languages	Christian, traditional beliefs	Zambian kwacha
ZIMBABWE		390 759	150 873	13 076 000	Harare	English, Shona, Ndebele	Christian, traditional beliefs	Zimbabwean dollar

*Communauté Financière Africaine

DEPENDENT AND DISPUTED TERRITORIES		territorial status	area sq km	area sq km	population	capital	languages	religions	currency
Canary Islands		Autonomous Community of Spain	7 447	2 875	1 695 000	Santa Cruz de Tenerife, Las Palmas	Spanish	Roman Catholic	Euro
Madeira		Autonomous Region of Portugal	779	301	243 000	Funchal	Portuguese	Roman Catholic, Protestant	Euro
Mayotte		French Territorial Collectivity	373	144	171 000	Dzaoudzi	French, Mahorian	Sunni Muslim, Christian	Euro
Réunion		French Overseas Department	2 551	985	742 000	St-Denis	French, creole	Roman Catholic	Euro
St Helena and Dependencies		United Kingdom Overseas Territory	121	47	6 000	Jamestown	English	Protestant, Roman Catholic	St Helena pound
Western Sahara		Disputed territory (Morocco)	266 000	102 703	268 000	Laâyoune	Arabic	Sunni Muslim	Moroccan dirham

Canberra, Australia 1

New Zealand 2

Mount Cook, New Zealand 3

OCEANIA

COUNTRIES		area sq km	area sq miles	population	capital	languages	religions	currency
AUSTRALIA		7 682 395	2 966 189	19 536 000	Canberra	English, Italian, Greek	Protestant, Roman Catholic, Orthodox	Australian dollar
FIJI		18 330	7 077	832 000	Suva	English, Fijian, Hindi	Christian, Hindu, Sunni Muslim	Fiji dollar
KIRIBATI		717	277	85 000	Bairiki	Gilbertese, English	Roman Catholic, Protestant	Australian dollar
MARSHALL ISLANDS		181	70	53 000	Delap-Uliga-Djarrit	English, Marshallese	Protestant, Roman Catholic	United States dollar
MICRONESIA, FEDERATED STATES OF		701	271	129 000	Palikir	English, Chuukese, Pohnpeian, local languages	Roman Catholic, Protestant	United States dollar
NAURU		21	8	13 000	Yaren	Nauruan, English	Protestant, Roman Catholic	Australian dollar
NEW ZEALAND		270 534	104 454	3 837 000	Wellington	English, Maori	Protestant, Roman Catholic	New Zealand dollar
PAPUA NEW GUINEA		462 840	178 704	5 032 000	Port Moresby	English, Tok Pisin (creole), local languages	Protestant, Roman Catholic, traditional beliefs	Kina
SAMOA		2 831	1 093	159 000	Apia	Samoan, English	Protestant, Roman Catholic	Tala
SOLOMON ISLANDS		28 370	10 954	479 000	Honiara	English, creole, local languages	Protestant, Roman Catholic	Solomon Islands dollar
TONGA		748	289	100 000	Nuku'alofa	Tongan, English	Protestant, Roman Catholic	Pa'anga
TUVALU		25	10	10 000	Vaiaku	Tuvaluan, English	Protestant	Australian dollar
VANUATU		12 190	4 707	207 000	Port Vila	English, Bislama (creole), French	Protestant, Roman Catholic, traditional beliefs	Vatu

DEPENDENT TERRITORIES		territorial status	area sq km	area sq miles	population	capital	languages	religions	currency
American Samoa		United States Unincorporated Territory	197	76	72 000	Fagatogo	Samoan, English	Protestant, Roman Catholic	United States dollar
Cook Islands		Self-governing New Zealand Territory	293	113	20 000	Avarua	English, Maori	Protestant, Roman Catholic	New Zealand dollar
French Polynesia		French Overseas Territory	3 265	1 261	241 000	Papeete	French, Tahitian, Polynesian languages	Protestant, Roman Catholic	CFP franc*
Guam		United States Unincorporated Territory	541	209	162 000	Hagåtña	Chamorro, English, Tapalog	Roman Catholic	United States dollar
New Caledonia		French Overseas Territory	19 058	7 358	224 000	Nouméa	French, local languages	Roman Catholic, Protestant, Sunni Muslim	CFP franc*
Niue		Self-governing New Zealand Territory	258	100	2 000	Alofi	English, Polynesian	Christian	New Zealand dollar
Norfolk Island		Australian External Territory	35	14	2 000	Kingston	English	Protestant, Roman Catholic	Australian Dollar
Northern Mariana Islands		United States Commonwealth	477	184	79 000	Capitol Hill	English, Chamorro, local languages	Roman Catholic	United States dollar
Pitcairn Islands		United Kingdom Overseas Territory	45	17	51	Adamstown	English	Protestant	New Zealand dollar
Tokelau		New Zealand Overseas Territory	10	4	1 000		English, Tokelauan	Christian	New Zealand dollar
Wallis and Futuna Islands		French Overseas Territory	274	106	15 000	Matā'utu	French, Wallisian, Futunian	Roman Catholic	CFP franc*

*Franc des Comptoirs Français du Pacifique

Bora Bora, French Polynesia 4

Uluru (Ayers Rock), Australia 5

Sydney, Australia 6

Space Imaging

The Pentagon, Washington DC, USA `7`

Panama Canal, Panama `8`

Cuba, Caribbean Sea `9`

NORTH AMERICA

COUNTRIES		area sq km	area sq miles	population	capital	languages	religions	currency
ANTIGUA AND BARBUDA		442	171	65 000	St John's	English, creole	Protestant, Roman Catholic	East Caribbean dollar
THE BAHAMAS		13 939	5 382	312 000	Nassau	English, creole	Protestant, Roman Catholic	Bahamian dollar
BARBADOS		430	166	269 000	Bridgetown	English, creole	Protestant, Roman Catholic	Barbados dollar
BELIZE		22 965	8 867	236 000	Belmopan	English, Spanish, Mayan, creole	Roman Catholic, Protestant	Belize dollar
CANADA		9 970 610	3 849 674	31 268 000	Ottawa	English, French	Roman Catholic, Protestant, Eastern Orthodox, Jewish	Canadian dollar
COSTA RICA		51 100	19 730	4 200 000	San José	Spanish	Roman Catholic, Protestant	Costa Rican colón
CUBA		110 860	42 803	11 273 000	Havana	Spanish	Roman Catholic, Protestant	Cuban peso
DOMINICA		750	290	70 000	Roseau	English, creole	Roman Catholic, Protestant	East Caribbean dollar
DOMINICAN REPUBLIC		48 442	18 704	8 639 000	Santo Domingo	Spanish, creole	Roman Catholic, Protestant	Dominican peso
EL SALVADOR		21 041	8 124	6 520 000	San Salvador	Spanish	Roman Catholic, Protestant	El Salvador colón, United States dollar
GRENADA		378	146	94 000	St George's	English, creole	Roman Catholic, Protestant	East Caribbean dollar
GUATEMALA		108 890	42 043	11 995 000	Guatemala City	Spanish, Mayan languages	Roman Catholic, Protestant	Quetzal, United States dollar
HAITI		27 750	10 714	8 400 000	Port-au-Prince	French, creole	Roman Catholic, Protestant, Voodoo	Gourde
HONDURAS		112 088	43 277	6 732 000	Tegucigalpa	Spanish, Amerindian languages	Roman Catholic, Protestant	Lempira
JAMAICA		10 991	4 244	2 621 000	Kingston	English, creole	Protestant, Roman Catholic	Jamaican dollar
MEXICO		1 972 545	761 604	101 842 000	Mexico City	Spanish, Amerindian languages	Roman Catholic, Protestant	Mexican peso
NICARAGUA		130 000	50 193	5 347 000	Managua	Spanish, Amerindian languages	Roman Catholic, Protestant	Córdoba
PANAMA		77 082	29 762	2 942 000	Panama City	Spanish, English, Amerindian languages	Roman Catholic, Protestant, Sunni Muslim	Balboa
ST KITTS AND NEVIS		261	101	38 000	Basseterre	English, creole	Protestant, Roman Catholic	East Caribbean dollar
ST LUCIA		616	238	151 000	Castries	English, creole	Roman Catholic, Protestant	East Caribbean dollar
ST VINCENT AND THE GRENADINES		389	150	115 000	Kingstown	English, creole	Protestant, Roman Catholic	East Caribbean dollar
TRINIDAD AND TOBAGO		5 130	1 981	1 306 000	Port of Spain	English, creole, Hindi	Roman Catholic, Hindu, Protestant, Sunni Muslim	Trinidad and Tobago dollar
UNITED STATES OF AMERICA		9 809 378	3 787 422	288 530 000	Washington DC	English, Spanish	Protestant, Roman Catholic, Sunni Muslim, Jewish	United States dollar

DEPENDENT TERRITORIES		territorial status	area sq km	area sq miles	population	capital	languages	religions	currency
Anguilla		United Kingdom Overseas Territory	155	60	12 000	The Valley	English	Protestant, Roman Catholic	East Caribbean dollar
Aruba		Self-governing Netherlands Territory	193	75	108 000	Oranjestad	Papiamento, Dutch, English	Roman Catholic, Protestant	Arubian florin
Bermuda		United Kingdom Overseas Territory	54	21	64 000	Hamilton	English	Protestant, Roman Catholic	Bermuda dollar
Cayman Islands		United Kingdom Overseas Territory	259	100	41 000	George Town	English	Protestant, Roman Catholic	Cayman Islands dollar
Greenland		Self-governing Danish Territory	2 175 600	840 004	56 000	Nuuk	Greenlandic, Danish	Protestant	Danish krone
Guadeloupe		French Overseas Department	1 780	687	435 000	Basse-Terre	French, creole	Roman Catholic	Euro
Martinique		French Overseas Department	1 079	417	388 000	Fort-de-France	French, creole	Roman Catholic, traditional beliefs	Euro
Montserrat		United Kingdom Overseas Territory	100	39	3 000	Plymouth	English	Protestant, Roman Catholic	East Caribbean dollar
Netherlands Antilles		Self-governing Netherlands Territory	800	309	219 000	Willemstad	Dutch, Papiamento, English	Roman Catholic, Protestant	Netherlands guilder
Puerto Rico		United States Commonwealth	9 104	3 515	3 988 000	San Juan	Spanish, English	Roman Catholic, Protestant	United States dollar
St Pierre and Miquelon		French Territorial Collectivity	242	93	7 000	St-Pierre	French	Roman Catholic	Euro
Turks and Caicos Islands		United Kingdom Overseas Territory	430	166	18 000	Grand Turk	English	Protestant	United States dollar
Virgin Islands (U.K.)		United Kingdom Overseas Territory	153	59	25 000	Road Town	English	Protestant, Roman Catholic	United States dollar
Virgin Islands (U.S.A.)		United States Unincorporated Territory	352	136	124 000	Charlotte Amalie	English, Spanish	Protestant, Roman Catholic	United States dollar

SOUTH AMERICA

COUNTRIES		area sq km	area sq miles	population	capital	languages	religions	currency
ARGENTINA		2 766 889	1 068 302	37 944 000	Buenos Aires	Spanish, Italian, Amerindian languages	Roman Catholic, Protestant	Argentinian peso
BOLIVIA		1 098 581	424 164	8 705 000	La Paz/Sucre	Spanish, Quechua, Aymara	Roman Catholic, Protestant, Baha'i	Boliviano
BRAZIL		8 547 379	3 300 161	174 706 000	Brasília	Portuguese	Roman Catholic, Protestant	Real
CHILE		756 945	292 258	15 589 000	Santiago	Spanish, Amerindian languages	Roman Catholic, Protestant	Chilean peso
COLOMBIA		1 141 748	440 831	43 495 000	Bogotá	Spanish, Amerindian languages	Roman Catholic, Protestant	Colombian peso
ECUADOR		272 045	105 037	13 112 000	Quito	Spanish, Quechua, other Amerindian languages	Roman Catholic	US dollar
GUYANA		214 969	83 000	765 000	Georgetown	English, creole, Amerindian languages	Protestant, Hindu, Roman Catholic, Sunni Muslim	Guyana dollar
PARAGUAY		406 752	157 048	5 778 000	Asunción	Spanish, Guaraní	Roman Catholic, Protestant	Guaraní
PERU		1 285 216	496 225	26 523 000	Lima	Spanish, Quechua, Aymara	Roman Catholic, Protestant	Sol
SURINAME		163 820	63 251	421 000	Paramaribo	Dutch, Surinamese, English, Hindi	Hindu, Roman Catholic, Protestant, Sunni Muslim	Suriname guilder
URUGUAY		176 215	68 037	3 385 000	Montevideo	Spanish	Roman Catholic, Protestant, Jewish	Uruguayan peso
VENEZUELA		912 050	352 144	25 093 000	Caracas	Spanish, Amerindian languages	Roman Catholic, Protestant	Bolivar

DEPENDENT TERRITORIES		territorial status	area sq km	area sq miles	population	capital	languages	religions	currency
Falkland Islands		United Kingdom Overseas Territory	12 170	4 699	2 000	Stanley	English	Protestant, Roman Catholic	Falkland Islands pound
French Guiana		French Overseas Department	90 000	34 749	176 000	Cayenne	French, creole	Roman Catholic	Euro

The current pattern of the world's countries and territories is a result of a long history of exploration, colonialism, conflict and politics. The fact that there are currently 193 independent countries in the world – the most recent, East Timor, only being created in May 2002 – illustrates the significant political changes which have occurred since 1950 when there were only eighty two. There has been a steady progression away from colonial influences over the last fifty years, although many dependent overseas territories remain.

The shapes of countries and the pattern of international boundaries reflect both physical and political processes. Some borders follow natural features – rivers, mountain ranges, etc – others are defined according to political agreement or as a result of war. Many are still subject to dispute between two or more countries, and many remain undefined on the ground.

High-resolution satellite image of **Vatican City**, the world's smallest country by both population and area.

ABBREVIATION KEY

A.	ANDORRA	**HUN.**	HUNGARY	**ROM.**	ROMANIA
AL.	ALBANIA	**ISR.**	ISRAEL	**S.**	SERBIA AND MONTENEGRO
ARM.	ARMENIA	**JOR.**	JORDAN	**SL.**	SLOVENIA
AUST.	AUSTRIA	**L.**	LUXEMBOURG	**SLA.**	SLOVAKIA
AZER.	AZERBAIJAN	**LAT.**	LATVIA	**SUR.**	SURINAME
B.	BURUNDI	**LEB.**	LEBANON	**SW.**	SWITZERLAND
BEL.	BELGIUM	**LITH.**	LITHUANIA	**TAJIK.**	TAJIKISTAN
B.H.	BOSNIA-HERZEGOVINA	**M.**	MACEDONIA	**TURKM.**	TURKMENISTAN
BULG.	BULGARIA	**MOL.**	MOLDOVA	**U.A.E.**	UNITED ARAB EMIRATES
CR.	CROATIA	**NETH.**	NETHERLANDS	**U.K.**	UNITED KINGDOM
CZ.R.	CZECH REPUBLIC	**N.Z.**	NEW ZEALAND	**U.S.A.**	UNITED STATES OF AMERICA
EST.	ESTONIA	**R.**	RWANDA	**UZBEK.**	UZBEKISTAN
GEOR.	GEORGIA	**R.F.**	RUSSIAN FEDERATION		

FACTS

◇ The longest single continuous land border stretches for 6 416 kilometres between Canada and the USA

◇ Both China and the Russian Federation have borders with 14 different countries

◇ Vatican City, the smallest independent country, was created in 1929 as an enclave within Rome, the capital of Italy

◇ All countries of the world are members of the United Nations except Taiwan and Vatican City

Satellite image of **Dili**, capital of East Timor, the world's newest independent country.

World extremes

COUNTRIES			
Largest country (area)	Russian Federation	17 075 400 sq km	6 592 849 sq miles
Smallest country (area)	Vatican City	0.5 sq km	0.2 sq miles
Largest country (population)	China	1 279 557 000	
Smallest country (population)	Vatican City	472	
Most densely populated country	Monaco	17 000 per sq km	34 000 per sq mile
Least densely populated country	Mongolia	2 per sq km	6 per sq mile

CAPITALS			
Largest national capital (population)	Tōkyō, Japan	26 444 000	
Smallest national capital (population)	Vatican City	480	
Most northerly national capital	Reykjavik, Iceland	64° 08'N	
Most southerly national capital	Wellington, New Zealand	41° 18'S	
Highest national capital	La Paz, Bolivia	3 630 m	11 909 ft

The earth's physical features, both on land and on the sea bed, closely reflect its geological structure. The current shapes of the continents and oceans have evolved over millions of years. Movements of the tectonic plates which make up the earth's crust have created some of the best-known and most spectacular features. The processes which have shaped the earth continue today with earthquakes, volcanoes, erosion, climatic variations and man's activities all affecting the earth's landscapes.

The total topographic range of the earth's surface is nearly 20 000 metres, from the highest point Mount Everest, to the lowest point in the Mariana Trench. Major mountain ranges include the Himalaya, the Andes and the Rocky Mountains, each of which give rise to some of the world's greatest rivers. In contrast the deserts of the Sahara, Australia, the Arabian Peninsula and the Gobi cover vast areas and each provide unique landscapes.

Greenland, the world's largest island, located almost entirely within the Arctic Circle.

FACTS

Approximately 10% of the earth's land surface is permanently covered by ice

The Pacific Ocean is larger than all the continents' land areas combined

The world's highest waterfall, 980 metres high, is Angel Falls, Venezuela

52% of the earth's land surface is below 500 metres

The mean elevation of the earth's land surface is 840 metres

Lake Baikal is the world's deepest lake with a maximum depth of 1 637 metres

height	depth
< 0m	
0-200m	
200-500m	
500-1000m	
1000-2000m	
2000-3000m	0-200m
3000-4000m	200-2000m
4000-5000m	2000-4000m
5000-6000m	4000-6000m
> 6000m	>6000m

The world's longest river, the **Nile**, flowing through Egypt into the Mediterranean Sea.

World's physical features

HIGHEST MOUNTAINS

Mt Everest, China/Nepal	8 848 m	29 028 ft
K2, China/Jammu and Kashmir	8 611 m	28 251 ft
Kangchenjunga, India/Nepal	8 586 m	28 169 ft
Lhotse, China/Nepal	8 516 m	27 939 ft
Makalu, China/Nepal	8 463 m	27 765 ft

LONGEST RIVERS

Nile, Africa	6 695 km	4 160 miles
Amazon, South America	6 516 km	4 049 miles
Yangtze, Asia	6 380 km	3 965 miles
Mississippi-Missouri, North America	5 969 km	3 709 miles
Ob'-Irtysh, Asia	5 568 km	3 460 miles

LARGEST LAKES

Caspian Sea, Asia/Europe	371 000 sq km	143 244 sq miles
Lake Superior, North America	82 100 sq km	31 699 sq miles
Lake Victoria, Africa	68 800 sq km	26 564 sq miles
Lake Huron, North America	59 600 sq km	23 012 sq miles
Lake Michigan, North America	57 800 sq km	22 317 sq miles

LARGEST ISLANDS

Greenland, North America	2 175 600 sq km	840 004 sq miles
New Guinea, Oceania	808 510 sq km	312 167 sq miles
Borneo, Asia	745 561 sq km	287 863 sq miles
Madagascar, Africa	587 040 sq km	226 657 sq miles
Baffin Island, North America	507 451 sq km	195 928 sq miles

Earth's dimensions

Mass	5.974 X 10²¹ tonnes
Total area	509 450 000 sq km / 196 699 746 sq miles
Land area	148 721 936 sq km / 57 421 861 sq miles
Water area	360 728 064 sq km / 139 277 885 sq miles
Volume	1 083 207 X 10⁶ cubic km / 259 911 X 10⁶ cubic miles
Equatorial diameter	12 756 km / 7 927 miles
Polar diameter	12 714 km / 7 901 miles
Equatorial circumference	40 075 km / 24 903 miles
Meridional circumference	40 008 km / 24 861 miles

Earthquakes and volcanoes hold a constant fascination because of their power, their beauty, and the fact that they cannot be controlled or accurately predicted.
Our understanding of these phenomena relies mainly on the theory of plate tectonics. This defines the earth's surface as a series of 'plates' which are constantly moving relative to each other, at rates of a few centimetres per year. As plates move against each other enormous pressure builds up and when the rocks can no longer bear this pressure they fracture, and energy is released as an earthquake. The pressures involved can also melt the rock to form magma which then rises to the earth's surface to form a volcano.

The distribution of earthquakes and volcanoes therefore relates closely to plate boundaries. In particular, most active volcanoes and much of the earth's seismic activity are centred on the 'Ring of Fire' around the Pacific Ocean.

FACTS

Over 900 earthquakes of magnitude 5.0 or greater occur every year

An earthquake of magnitude 8.0 releases energy equivalent to 1 billion tons of TNT explosive

Ground shaking during an earthquake in Alaska in 1964 lasted for 3 minutes

Indonesia has more than 120 volcanoes and over 30% of the world's active volcanoes

Volcanoes can produce very fertile soil and important industrial materials and chemicals

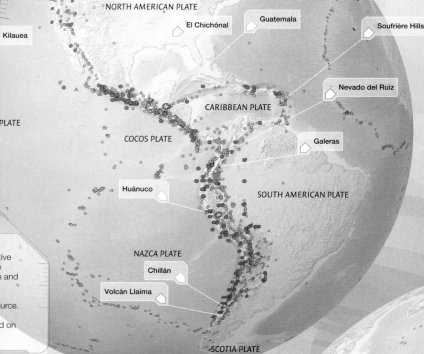

Mt St Helens
NORTH AMERICAN PLATE
El Chichónal
Guatemala
Soufrière Hills
Kilauea
Nevado del Ruiz
CARIBBEAN PLATE
PACIFIC PLATE
COCOS PLATE
Galeras
Huánuco
SOUTH AMERICAN PLATE
NAZCA PLATE
Chillán
Volcán Llaima
SCOTIA PLATE

- ⊕ Deadliest earthquake
- ● Earthquake of magnitude 7.5 or greater
- ○ Earthquake of magnitude 5.5 – 7.4
- ♨ Major volcano
- ▲ Other volcano

Distribution of earthquakes and volcanoes

Earthquakes

Earthquakes are caused by movement along fractures or 'faults' in the earth's crust, particularly along plate boundaries. There are three types of plate boundary: constructive boundaries where plates are moving apart; destructive boundaries where two or more plates collide; conservative boundaries where plates slide past each other. Destructive and conservative boundaries are the main sources of earthquake activity.

The epicentre of an earthquake is the point on the earth's surface directly above its source. If this is near to large centres of population, and the earthquake is powerful, major devastation can result. The size, or magnitude, of an earthquake is generally measured on the Richter Scale.

Ech Chélif
SOUTH AMERICAN PLATE

Deadliest earthquakes, 1900–2002

YEAR	LOCATION	DEATHS
1905	**Kangra**, India	19 000
1907	west of **Dushanbe**, Tajikistan	12 000
1908	**Messina**, Italy	110 000
1915	**Abruzzo**, Italy	35 000
1917	**Bali**, Indonesia	15 000
1920	**Ningxia Province**, China	200 000
1923	**Tōkyō**, Japan	142 807
1927	**Qinghai Province**, China	200 000
1932	**Gansu Province**, China	70 000
1933	**Sichuan Province**, China	10 000
1934	**Nepal/India**	10 700
1935	**Quetta**, Pakistan	30 000
1939	**Chillán**, Chile	28 000
1939	**Erzincan**, Turkey	32 700
1948	**Ashgabat**, Turkmenistan	19 800
1962	northwest **Iran**	12 225
1970	**Huánuco Province**, Peru	66 794
1974	**Yunnan** and **Sichuan Provinces**, China	20 000
1975	**Liaoning Province**, China	10 000
1976	central **Guatemala**	22 778
1976	**Hebei Province**, China	255 000
1978	**Khorāsan Province**, Iran	20 000
1980	**Ech Chélif**, Algeria	11 000
1988	**Spitak**, Armenia	25 000
1990	**Manjil**, Iran	50 000
1999	**Kocaeli (İzmit)**, Turkey	17 000
2001	**Gujarat**, India	20 000

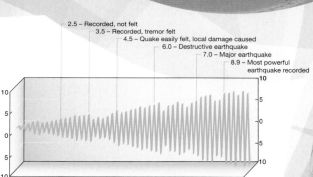

2.5 – Recorded, not felt
3.5 – Recorded, tremor felt
4.5 – Quake easily felt, local damage caused
6.0 – Destructive earthquake
7.0 – Major earthquake
8.9 – Most powerful earthquake recorded

Earthquake magnitude – the Richter Scale

The scale measures the energy released by an earthquake. It is a logarithmic scale: an earthquake measuring 5 is ten times more powerful than one measuring 4.

Extensive damage caused by a major earthquake centred on **Kocaeli (İzmit), Turkey** in August 1999.

Lava flow from **Mt Etna, Sicily, Italy** threatens the town of Zafferana Etnea.

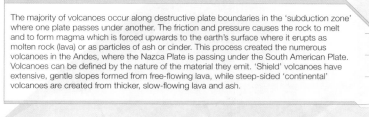

Major volcanic eruptions, 1980–2002

VOLCANO	COUNTRY	DATE
Mt St Helens	USA	1980
El Chichónal	Mexico	1982
Gunung Galunggung	Indonesia	1982
Kilauea	Hawaii	1983
Ō-yama	Japan	1983
Nevado del Ruiz	Colombia	1985
Mt Pinatubo	Philippines	1991
Unzen-dake	Japan	1991
Mayon	Philippines	1993
Galeras	Colombia	1993
Volcán Llaima	Chile	1994
Rabaul	Papua New Guinea	1994
Hekla	Iceland	2000
Mt Etna	Italy	2001
Nyiragongo	Democratic Republic of Congo	2002

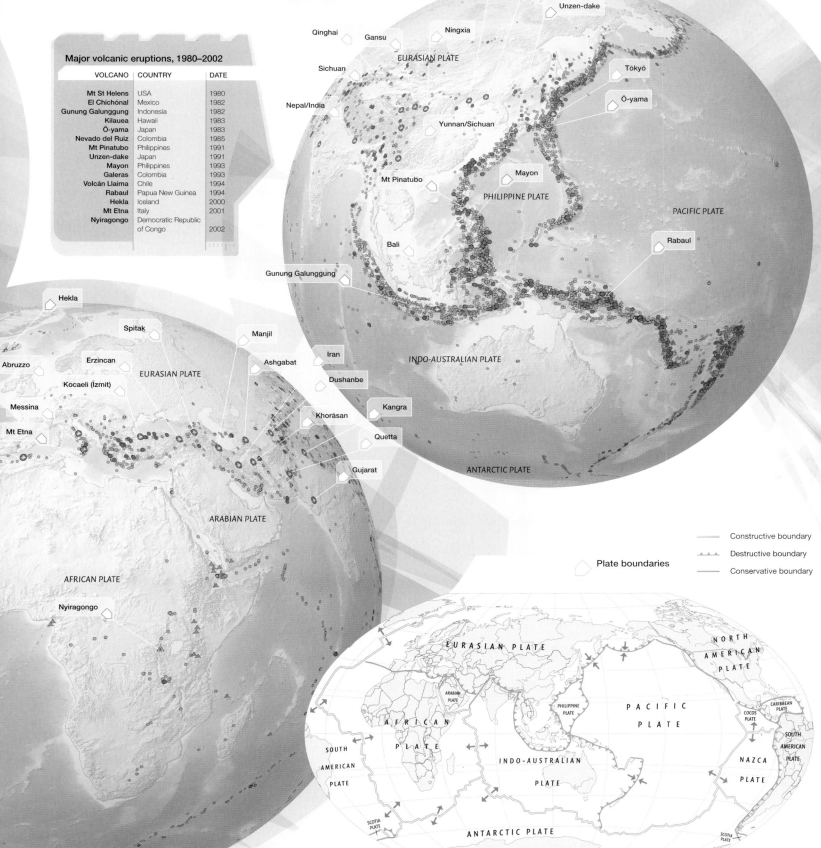

Plate boundaries

⎯⎯ Constructive boundary

▲▲▲ Destructive boundary

⎯⎯ Conservative boundary

The climate of a region is defined by its long-term prevailing weather conditions. Classification of Climate Types is based on the relationship between temperature and humidity and how these factors are affected by latitude, altitude, ocean currents and winds. Weather is the specific short term condition which occurs locally and consists of events such as thunderstorms, hurricanes, blizzards and heat waves. Temperature and rainfall data recorded at weather stations can be plotted graphically and the graphs shown here, typical of each climate region, illustrate the various combinations of temperature and rainfall which exist worldwide for each month of the year. Data used for climate graphs are based on average monthly figures recorded over a minimum period of thirty years.

world statistics: see pages 150–156

Cyclone Tropical storm Dina, January 2002, northeast of Mauritius and Réunion, Indian Ocean.

Weather extremes

Highest recorded temperature	**57.8°C/136°F** Al'Azīzīyah, Libya (September 1922)
Hottest place - annual mean	**34.4°C/93.6°F** Dalol, Ethiopia
Driest place - annual mean	**0.1mm/0.004 inches** Atacama Desert, Chile
Most sunshine - annual mean	**90%** Yuma, Arizona, USA (over 4000 hours)
Lowest recorded temperature	**-89.2°C/-128.6°F** Vostok Station, Antarctica (July 1983)
Coldest place - annual mean	**-56.6°C/-69.9°F** Plateau Station, Antarctica
Wettest place annual mean	**11 873 mm/467.4 inches** Meghalaya, India
Greatest snowfall	**31 102 mm/1 224.5 inches** Mount Rainier, Washington, USA (February 1971 - February 1972)
Windiest place	**322 km per hour/200 miles per hour** (in gales) Commonwealth Bay, Antarctica

FACTS

- Arctic Sea ice thickness has declined 4% in the last 40 years
- 2001 marked the end of the La Niña episode
- Sea levels are rising by one centimetre per decade
- Precipitation in the northern hemisphere is increasing
- Droughts have increased in frequency and intensity in parts of Asia and Africa

Climate change

In 2001 the global mean temperature was 0.63°C higher than that at the end of the nineteenth century. Most of this warming is caused by human activities which result in a build up of greenhouse gases, mainly carbon dioxide, allowing heat to be trapped within the atmosphere. Carbon dioxide emissions have increased since the beginning of the industrial revolution due to burning of fossil fuels, increased urbanization, population growth, deforestation and industrial pollution.

Annual climate indicators such as number of frost free days, length of growing season, heat wave frequency, number of wet days, length of dry spells and frequency of weather extremes are used to monitor climate change. The map highlights some events of 2001 which indicate climate change. Until carbon dioxide emissions are reduced it is likely that this trend will continue.

1. Warmest winter recorded in **Alaska and Yukon**.
2. Third warmest year on record in **Canada**.
3. Severe rainfall deficit in **northwest USA**.
4. Costliest storm in US history was tropical storm **Alison**.
5. Extreme summer drought in **Central America**.
6. Strongest hurricane to hit Cuba since 1952 was **Michelle**.
7. End of **La Niña** episode.
8. Severe flooding in **Bolivia**.
9. Normal rainy season hit by drought in **Brazil**.
10. Longer lasting ozone hole than previous years in **Antarctica**.
11. Worst flooding since 1997 in **southwest Poland and Czech Republic**.
12. Temperatures 1°–2°C above average for 2001 in **Europe and Middle East**.
13. Severe November flooding in **Algeria**.
14. Continued drought in area around **Horn of Africa**.
15. Widespread minimum winter temperatures near -60°C in **Siberia and Mongolia**.
16. 1998 drought continues in **Southern Asia**.
17. Severe drought and water shortages in **Northern China, Korean Peninsula and Japan**.
18. Extensive flooding in September caused by Typhoon **Nari**.
19. Severe flooding August to October in **Vietnam and Cambodia**.
20. Severe flooding causes more than 400 deaths when four tropical cyclones, **Durian, Yutu, Ulor and Toraji** made landfall in July.
21. Major flooding in February on **Java**.
22. Driest summer on record in **Perth**.
23. Cooler and wetter than normal in **Western Australia**.
24. One of the driest summers recorded in **New Zealand**.
25. Severe flooding February to April in **Mozambique, Zambia, Malawi and Zimbabwe**.

Legend:
- Temperature above average
- Temperature below average
- Rainfall above average
- Rainfall below average
- Paths of storms
- 25 Indicator of climate change

Evidence of climate change during 2001

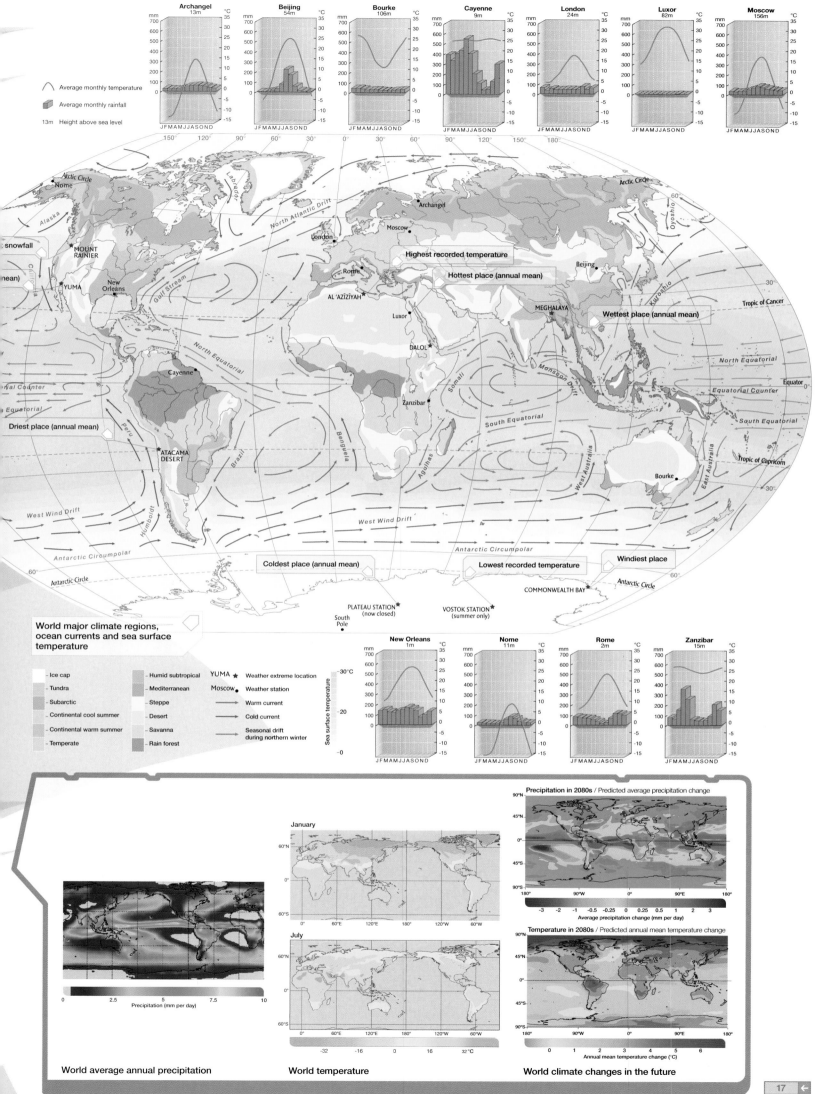

World major climate regions, ocean currents and sea surface temperature

World average annual precipitation

World temperature

World climate changes in the future

The oxygen- and water- rich environment of the earth has helped create a wide range of environments. Forest and woodland ecosystems form the predominant natural land cover over most of the earth's surface. Tropical rainforests are part of an intricate land-atmosphere relationship that is disturbed by land cover changes. Forests in the tropics are believed to hold most of the world's bird, animal, and plant species. Grassland, shrubland and deserts collectively cover most of the unwooded land surface, with tundra on frozen subsoil at high northern latitudes. These areas tend to have lower species diversity than most forests, with the notable exception of Mediterranean shrublands, which support some of the most diverse floras on the earth. Humans have extensively altered most grassland and shrubland areas, usually through conversion to agriculture, burning and introduction of domestic livestock. They have had less immediate impact on tundra and true desert regions, although these remain vulnerable to global climate change.

Snow and ice, Spitsbergen, Svalbard, inside the Arctic Circle.

Urban, La Paz, Bolivia.

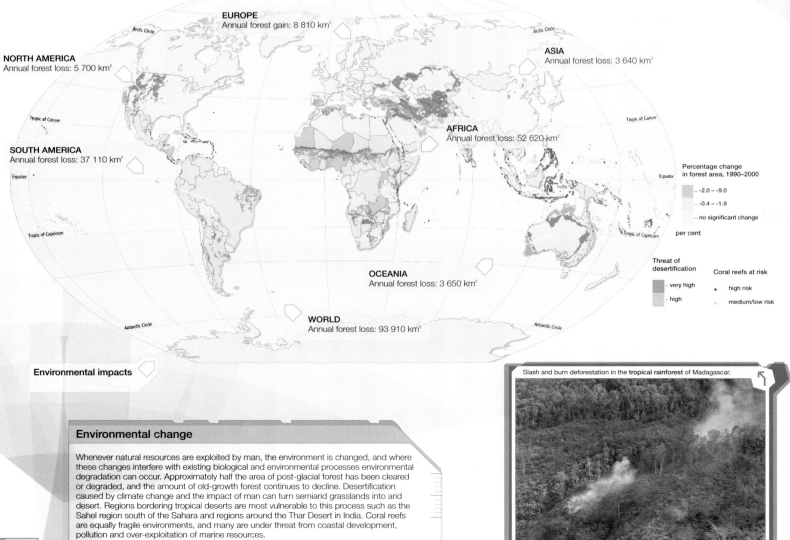

NORTH AMERICA
Annual forest loss: 5 700 km²

EUROPE
Annual forest gain: 8 810 km²

ASIA
Annual forest loss: 3 640 km²

SOUTH AMERICA
Annual forest loss: 37 110 km²

AFRICA
Annual forest loss: 52 620 km²

OCEANIA
Annual forest loss: 3 650 km²

WORLD
Annual forest loss: 93 910 km²

Percentage change in forest area, 1990–2000

-2.0 – -9.0
-0.4 – -1.9
no significant change

per cent

Threat of desertification

very high
high

Coral reefs at risk

high risk
medium/low risk

Environmental impacts

Slash and burn deforestation in the **tropical rainforest** of Madagascar.

Environmental change

Whenever natural resources are exploited by man, the environment is changed, and where these changes interfere with existing biological and environmental processes environmental degradation can occur. Approximately half the area of post-glacial forest has been cleared or degraded, and the amount of old-growth forest continues to decline. Desertification caused by climate change and the impact of man can turn semiarid grasslands into arid desert. Regions bordering tropical deserts are most vulnerable to this process such as the Sahel region south of the Sahara and regions around the Thar Desert in India. Coral reefs are equally fragile environments, and many are under threat from coastal development, pollution and over-exploitation of marine resources.

Barren/Shrubland, Death Valley, California, United States of America.

Legend

Evergreen needleleaf forest	Savanna
Evergreen broadleaf forest	Grassland
Deciduous needleleaf forest	Permanent wetland
Deciduous broadleaf forest	Cropland
Mixed forest	Urban and built-up
Closed shrubland	Cropland/Natural vegetation mosaic
Open shrubland	Snow and Ice
Woody savanna	Barren or sparsely vegetated
	Water bodies

Arctic Circle

Tropic of Capricorn

Antarctic Circle

World land cover
Map courtesy of IGBP, JRC and USGS

FACTS

◇ Land covers less than one-third of the total surface of the planet

◇ There are an estimated 44 000 parks and protected areas covering about 10% of the world's land surface

◇ Degraded soils have lowered global agricultural yields by 13% since 1945

◇ The oceans have lost 27% of their coral in the past 50 years

◇ Over 1% (1.23 million km²) of tropical forests are lost every year, mainly for food production

Land cover

The land cover map shown here was derived from data aquired by the Advanced Very High Resolution Radiometer sensor on board the polar orbiting satellites of the US National Oceanic and Atmospheric Administration. The high resolution (ground resolution of 1km) of the imagery used to compile the data set and map allows detailed interpretation of land cover patterns across the world. Important uses include managing forest resources, improving estimates of the earth's water and energy cycles, and modelling climate change.

Agricultural demands for water, and climate change have caused dramatic shrinking of the **Aral Sea.**

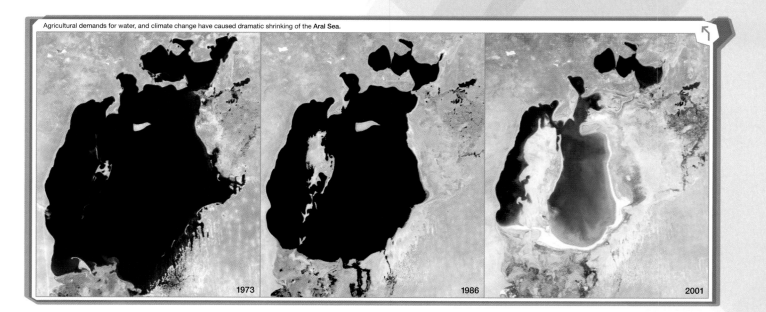

1973   1986   2001

After growing very slowly for most of human history, world population more than doubled in the last half century. Whereas world population did not pass the one billion mark until 1804 and took another 123 years to reach two billion in 1927, it then added the third billion in 33 years, the fourth in 14 years and the fifth in 13 years. Just twelve years later on October 12, 1999 the United Nations announced that the global population had reached the six billion mark. It is expected that another three billion people will have been added to the world's population by 2050.

One important factor in population growth is fertility rate – the average number of children born to each woman. The world's average fertility rate has fallen from five in 1950 to less than three today. Europe's total fertility rate is now down to 1.3. Despite this, developed countries still continue to have high growth rates. The burden on agricultural land and resources in general is increasing from population growth, poorer regions in particular are having to tackle the social and economic implications of increasing population.

world statistics: see pages 150–156

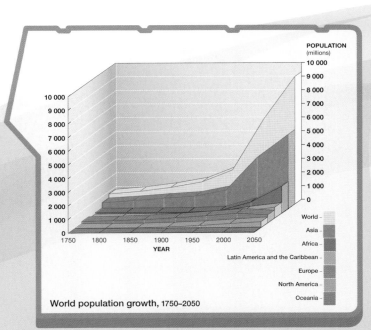

World population growth, 1750–2050

FACTS

The world's population is growing at an annual rate of 77 million people per year

Today's population is only 5.7% of the total number of people who ever lived on the earth

India's population reached 1 billion in August 1999

More than 90% of the 70 million inhabitants of Egypt are located around the River Nile

It is expected that in 2050 there will be more people aged over 60 than children aged less than 14

NORTH AMERICA
Total population **319 925 000**
Population change **0.88%**

LATIN AMERICA AND THE CARIBBEAN
Total population **534 223 000**
Population change **1.42%**

Kuna Indians inhabit this congested island off the north coast of Panama.

Arctic Circle

Tropic of Cancer

Antarctic Circle

World population distribution
Population density, continental populations (2002) and continental population change (2000–2005)

over 2 500	over 1 000
1 250 – 2 500	500 – 1 000
625 – 1 250	250 – 500
250 – 625	100 – 250
125 – 250	50 – 100
62.5 – 125	25 – 50
12.5 – 62.5	5 – 25
2.5 – 12.5	1 – 5
0 – 2.5	0 – 1
uninhabited	uninhabited

inhabitants (per sq mile) | inhabitants (per sq km)

Population distribution

The world's population in mid-2002 had reached 6 211 million, over half of which live in six countries: China, India, USA, Indonesia, Brazil and Pakistan. Over 80% (5 015 million) of the total population live in less developed regions. As shown on the population distribution map, over a quarter of the land area is uninhabited or has extremely low population density. Barely a quarter of the land area is occupied at densities of 10 or more persons per square km, with the three largest concentrations in east Asia, the Indian subcontinent and Europe accounting for over half the world total.

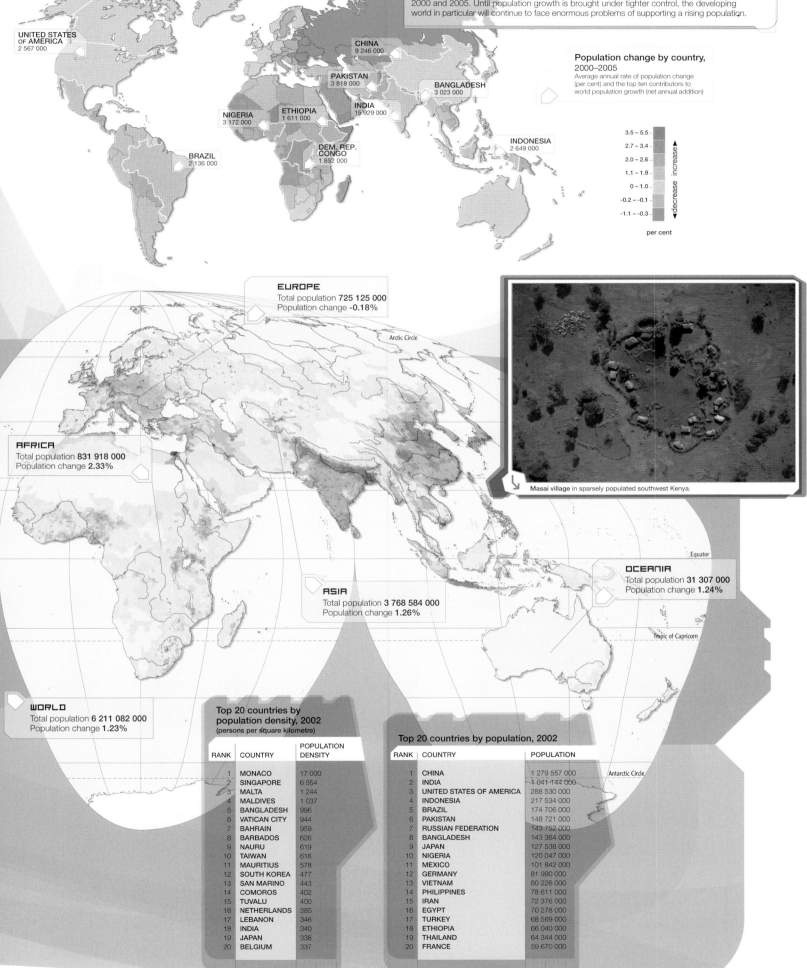

World population change

Population growth since 1950 has been spread very unevenly between the continents. While overall numbers have been growing rapidly since 1950, a massive 89 per cent increase has taken place in the less developed regions, especially southern and eastern Asia. In contrast, Europe's population level has been almost stationary and is expected to decrease in the future. India and China alone are responsible for over one-third of current growth. But most of the highest rates of growth are to be found in Sub-Saharan Africa with Liberia and Sierra Leone experiencing the highest percentage increases in population between 2000 and 2005. Until population growth is brought under tighter control, the developing world in particular will continue to face enormous problems of supporting a rising population.

UNITED STATES OF AMERICA 2 567 000

CHINA 9 246 000

PAKISTAN 3 818 000

BANGLADESH 3 023 000

INDIA 15 929 000

NIGERIA 3 172 000

ETHIOPIA 1 611 000

BRAZIL 2 136 000

DEM. REP. CONGO 1 852 000

INDONESIA 2 649 000

Population change by country, 2000–2005
Average annual rate of population change (per cent) and the top ten contributors to world population growth (net annual addition)

	per cent
3.5 – 5.5	▲ increase
2.7 – 3.4	
2.0 – 2.6	
1.1 – 1.9	
0 – 1.0	
-0.2 – -0.1	
-1.1 – -0.3	▼ decrease

EUROPE
Total population 725 125 000
Population change -0.18%

Arctic Circle

AFRICA
Total population 831 918 000
Population change 2.33%

Masai village in sparsely populated southwest Kenya.

Equator

ASIA
Total population 3 768 584 000
Population change 1.26%

OCEANIA
Total population 31 307 000
Population change 1.24%

Tropic of Capricorn

WORLD
Total population 6 211 082 000
Population change 1.23%

Antarctic Circle

Top 20 countries by population density, 2002
(persons per square kilometre)

RANK	COUNTRY	POPULATION DENSITY
1	MONACO	17 000
2	SINGAPORE	6 554
3	MALTA	1 244
4	MALDIVES	1 037
5	BANGLADESH	996
6	VATICAN CITY	944
7	BAHRAIN	959
8	BARBADOS	626
9	NAURU	619
10	TAIWAN	616
11	MAURITIUS	578
12	SOUTH KOREA	477
13	SAN MARINO	443
14	COMOROS	402
15	TUVALU	400
16	NETHERLANDS	385
17	LEBANON	346
18	INDIA	340
19	JAPAN	338
20	BELGIUM	337

Top 20 countries by population, 2002

RANK	COUNTRY	POPULATION
1	CHINA	1 279 557 000
2	INDIA	1 041 144 000
3	UNITED STATES OF AMERICA	288 530 000
4	INDONESIA	217 534 000
5	BRAZIL	174 706 000
6	PAKISTAN	148 721 000
7	RUSSIAN FEDERATION	143 752 000
8	BANGLADESH	143 364 000
9	JAPAN	127 538 000
10	NIGERIA	120 047 000
11	MEXICO	101 842 000
12	GERMANY	81 990 000
13	VIETNAM	80 226 000
14	PHILIPPINES	78 611 000
15	IRAN	72 376 000
16	EGYPT	70 278 000
17	TURKEY	68 569 000
18	ETHIOPIA	66 040 000
19	THAILAND	64 344 000
20	FRANCE	59 670 000

The world is becoming increasingly urban but the level of urbanization varies greatly between and within continents. At the beginning of the twentieth century only fourteen per cent of the world's population was urban and by 1950 this had increased to thirty per cent. In the more developed regions and in Latin America and the Caribbean seventy per cent of the population is urban while in Africa and Asia the figure is less than one third. In recent decades urban growth has increased rapidly to nearly fifty per cent and there are now 387 cities with over 1 000 000 inhabitants. It is in the developing regions that the most rapid increases are taking place and it is expected that by 2030 over half of urban dwellers worldwide will live in Asia. Migration from the countryside to the city in search of better job opportunities is the main factor in urban growth.

world statistics: see pages 150–156

Level of urbanization and the world's largest cities

NORTH AMERICA
84.5% urban

New York

Largest city in North America

Mexico City

Largest city in South America

LATIN AMERICA AND THE CARIBBEAN
75.8% urban

São Paulo

3-D perspective view of the greater city region of **Los Angeles**, California, USA.

Major city growth, 1975–2015

Million inhabitants

2015
2000
1975

per cent urban
80 – 100
60 – 80
40 – 60
20 – 40
0 – 20

World percentage urbanization

City population (millions)
over 20
10 – 20
5 – 10
2.5 – 5

FACTS

Cities occupy less than 2% of the earth's land surface but house almost half of the human population

Urban growth rates in Africa are the highest in the world

Antarctica is uninhabited and most settlements in the Arctic regions have less than 5 000 inhabitants

India has 32 cities with over one million inhabitants; by 2015 there will be 50

London was the first city to reach a population of over 5 million

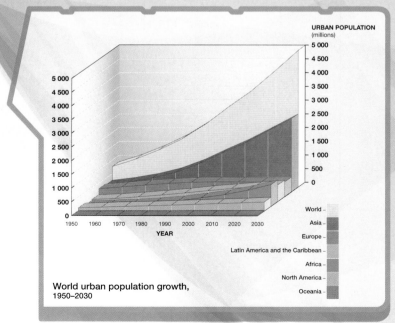

URBAN POPULATION (millions)

World urban population growth, 1950–2030

YEAR

World
Asia
Europe
Latin America and the Caribbean
Africa
North America
Oceania

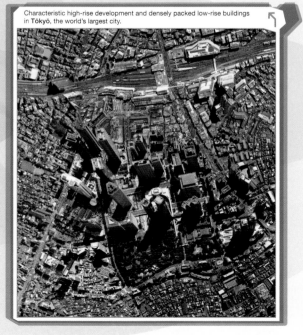

Characteristic high-rise development and densely packed low-rise buildings in Tōkyō, the world's largest city.

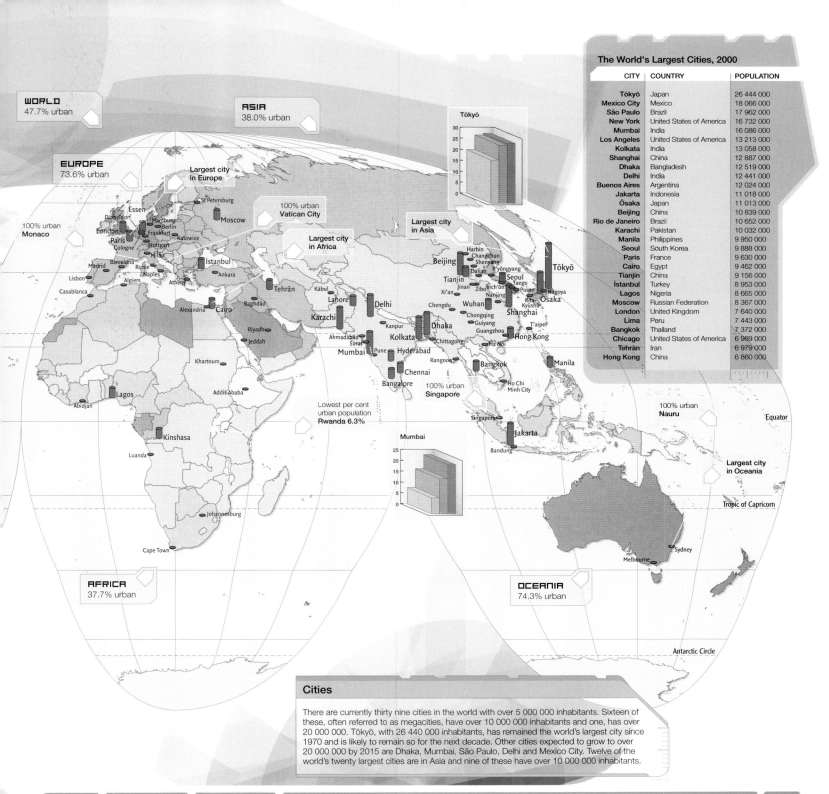

WORLD
47.7% urban

EUROPE
73.6% urban

100% urban
Monaco

ASIA
38.0% urban

Largest city
in Europe

100% urban
Vatican City

Largest city
in Asia

Largest city
in Africa

Tōkyō

Lowest per cent
urban population
Rwanda 6.3%

100% urban
Singapore

100% urban
Nauru

Equator

Largest city
in Oceania

Tropic of Capricorn

Mumbai

AFRICA
37.7% urban

Antarctic Circle

OCEANIA
74.3% urban

The World's Largest Cities, 2000

CITY	COUNTRY	POPULATION
Tōkyō	Japan	26 444 000
Mexico City	Mexico	18 066 000
São Paulo	Brazil	17 962 000
New York	United States of America	16 732 000
Mumbai	India	16 086 000
Los Angeles	United States of America	13 213 000
Kolkata	India	13 058 000
Shanghai	China	12 887 000
Dhaka	Bangladesh	12 519 000
Delhi	India	12 441 000
Buenos Aires	Argentina	12 024 000
Jakarta	Indonesia	11 018 000
Ōsaka	Japan	11 013 000
Beijing	China	10 839 000
Rio de Janeiro	Brazil	10 652 000
Karachi	Pakistan	10 032 000
Manila	Philippines	9 950 000
Seoul	South Korea	9 888 000
Paris	France	9 630 000
Cairo	Egypt	9 462 000
Tianjin	China	9 156 000
İstanbul	Turkey	8 953 000
Lagos	Nigeria	8 665 000
Moscow	Russian Federation	8 367 000
London	United Kingdom	7 640 000
Lima	Peru	7 443 000
Bangkok	Thailand	7 372 000
Chicago	United States of America	6 989 000
Tehrān	Iran	6 979 000
Hong Kong	China	6 860 000

Cities

There are currently thirty nine cities in the world with over 5 000 000 inhabitants. Sixteen of these, often referred to as megacities, have over 10 000 000 inhabitants and one, has over 20 000 000. Tōkyō, with 26 440 000 inhabitants, has remained the world's largest city since 1970 and is likely to remain so for the next decade. Other cities expected to grow to over 20 000 000 by 2015 are Dhaka, Mumbai, São Paulo, Delhi and Mexico City. Twelve of the world's twenty largest cities are in Asia and nine of these have over 10 000 000 inhabitants.

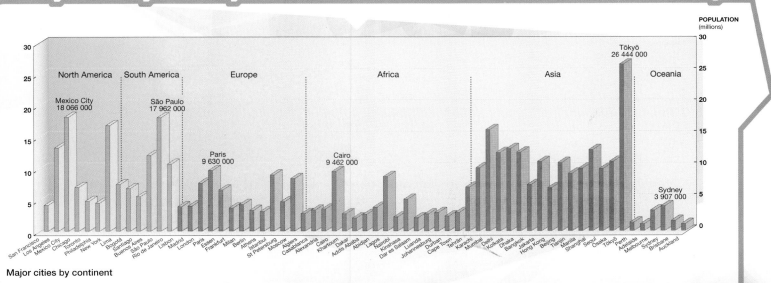

Major cities by continent

Increased availability and ownership of telecommunications equipment since the beginning of the 1970s has aided the globalization of the world economy. Over half of the world's fixed telephone lines have been installed since the mid-1980s and the majority of the world's internet hosts have come on line since 1997. There are now over one billion fixed telephone lines in the world. The number of mobile cellular subscribers has grown dramatically from sixteen million in 1991 to over one billion in 2001.

The internet is the fastest growing communications network of all time. It is relatively cheap and in 2001 linked 141.3 million host computers globally. Its growth has resulted in the emergence of hundreds of Internet Service Providers (ISPs) and internet traffic is now doubling every six months. In 1993 the number of internet users was estimated to be just under ten million, by 2001 the figure had risen to over half a billion.

Fibre-optic cables can carry enormous amounts of data and information and have been crucial to the growth of global telecommunications.

Internet users per 1 000 inhabitants

- over 200
- 150 – 200
- 100 – 149
- 10 – 99
- 0 – 9
- no data

Major interregional internet routes

- 0.0 – 0.9
- 1.0 – 4.9
- 5.0 – 24.9
- 25.0 – 125.0

∘ London

Internet hub cities, 2001

Internet users and major Internet routes

The Internet

The Internet is a global network of millions of computers around the world, all capable of being connected to each other. Internet Service Providers (ISPs) provide access via 'host' computers, of which there are now over 140 million. It has become a vital means of communication and data transfer for businesses, governments and financial and academic institutions, with a steadily increasing proportion of business transactions being carried out on-line. Personal use of the Internet – particularly for access to the World Wide Web information network, and for e-mail communication – has increased enormously and there are now estimated to be over half a billion users worldwide.

Top 20 Internet Service Providers (ISPs)

INTERNET SERVICE PROVIDER	WEB ADDRESS	SUBSCRIBERS (000s)
AOL (USA)	www.aol.com	20 500
T-Online (Germany)	www.t-online.de	4 151
Nifty-Serve (Japan)	www.nifty.com	3 500
EarthLink (USA)	www.earthlink.com	3 122
Biglobe (Japan)	www.biglobe.ne.jp	2 720
MSN (USA)	www.msn.com	2 700
Chollian (South Korea)	www.chollian.net	2 000
Tin.it (Italy)	www.tin.it	1 990
Freeserve (UK)	www.freeserve.com	1 575
AT&T WorldNet (USA)	www.att.net	1 500
Prodigy (USA)	www.prodigy.com	1 502
NetZero (USA)	www.netzero.com	1 450
Terra Networks (Spain)	www.terra.es	1 317
HiNet (Taiwan-China)	www.hinet.net	1 200
Wanadoo (France)	www.wanadoo.fr	1 124
AltaVista	www.microav.com	750
Freei (USA)	www.freei.com	750
SBC Internet Services	www.sbc.com	720
Telia Internet (Sweden)	www.telia.se	613
Netvigator (Hongkong SAR)	www.netvigator.com	561

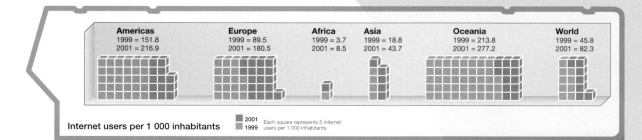

Americas	Europe	Africa	Asia	Oceania	World
1999 = 151.8	1999 = 89.5	1999 = 3.7	1999 = 18.8	1999 = 213.8	1999 = 45.8
2001 = 216.9	2001 = 180.5	2001 = 8.5	2001 = 43.7	2001 = 277.2	2001 = 82.3

Internet users per 1 000 inhabitants

- 2001
- 1999

Each square represents 5 internet users per 1 000 inhabitants.

Satellite communications

International telecommunications use either fibre-optic cables or satellites as transmission media. Although cables carry the vast majority of traffic around the world, communications satellites are important for person-to-person communication, including cellular telephones, and for broadcasting. The positions of communications satellites are critical to their use, and reflect the demand for such communications in each part of the world. Such satellites are placed in 'geostationary' orbit 36 000 km above the equator. This means that they move at the same speed as the earth and remain fixed above a single point on the earth's surface.

Cellular mobile subscribers per 100 inhabitants

- over 40
- 15 – 39.9
- 5 – 14.9
- 1.5 – 4.9
- 0.5 – 1.4
- 0 – 0.4
- no data

- ○ In service
- ● Inclined orbit
- ○ Planned

Geostationary communications satellites

Mobile phone subscribers and communications satellites

FACTS

Luxembourg has the world's highest density of telephone lines per person with more telephones than Bangladesh – a country with more than 300 times as many people.

Fibre-optic cables can now carry approximately 20 million simultaneous telephone calls

The first transatlantic telegraph cable came into operation in 1858

The internet is the fastest growing communications network of all time and now has over 140 million host computers

Sputnik, the world's first artificial satellite, was launched in 1957

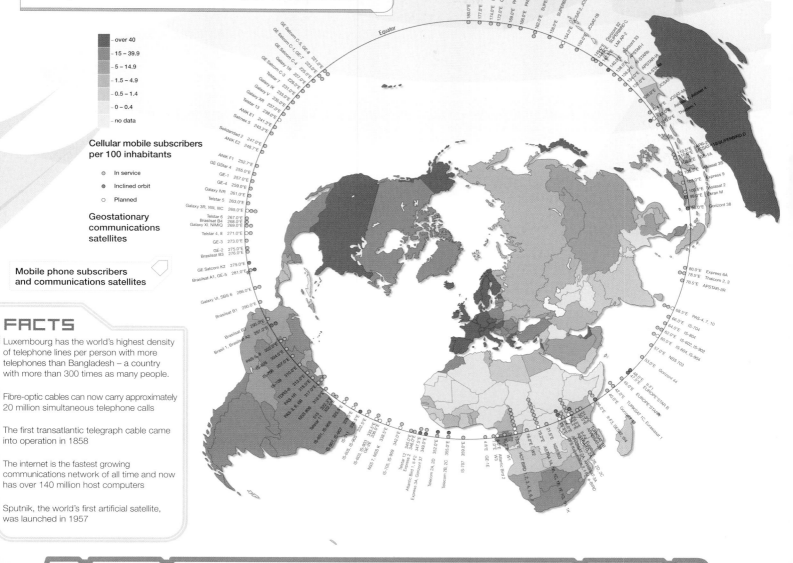

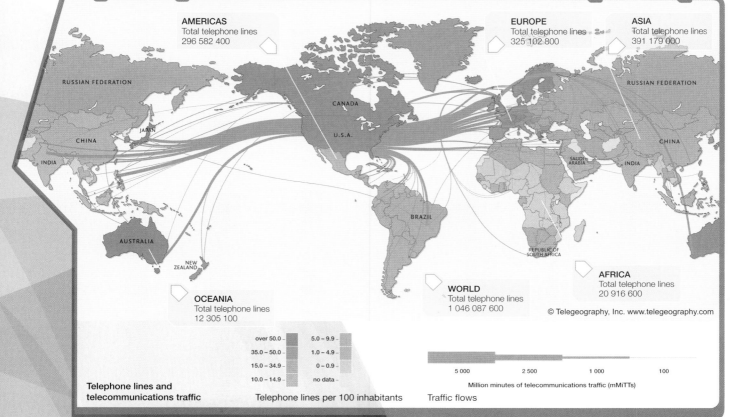

AMERICAS
Total telephone lines
296 582 400

EUROPE
Total telephone lines
325 102 800

ASIA
Total telephone lines
391 179 000

OCEANIA
Total telephone lines
12 305 100

WORLD
Total telephone lines
1 046 087 600

AFRICA
Total telephone lines
20 916 600

© Telegeography, Inc. www.telegeography.com

Telephone lines and telecommunications traffic

Telephone lines per 100 inhabitants

- over 50.0
- 35.0 – 50.0
- 15.0 – 34.9
- 10.0 – 14.9
- 5.0 – 9.9
- 1.0 – 4.9
- 0 – 0.9
- no data

Traffic flows

5 000   2 500   1 000   100

Million minutes of telecommunications traffic (mMiTTs)

Countries are often judged on their level of economic development, but national and personal wealth are not the only measures of a country's status. Numerous other indicators can give a better picture of the overall level of development and standard of living achieved by a country. The availability and standard of health services, levels of educational provision and attainment, levels of nutrition, water supply, life expectancy and mortality rates are just some of the factors which can be measured to assess and compare countries.

While nations strive to improve their economies, and hopefully also to improve the standard of living of their citizens, the measurement of such indicators often exposes great discrepancies between the countries of the 'developed' world and those of the 'less developed' world. They also show great variations within continents and regions and at the same time can hide great inequalities within countries.

world statistics: see pages 150–156

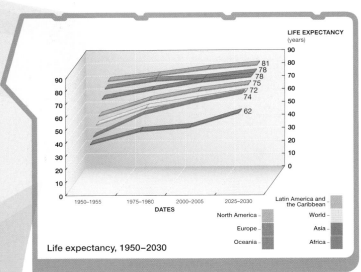

Life expectancy, 1950–2030

LIFE EXPECTANCY (years)

North America
Europe
Oceania
Latin America and the Caribbean
World
Asia
Africa

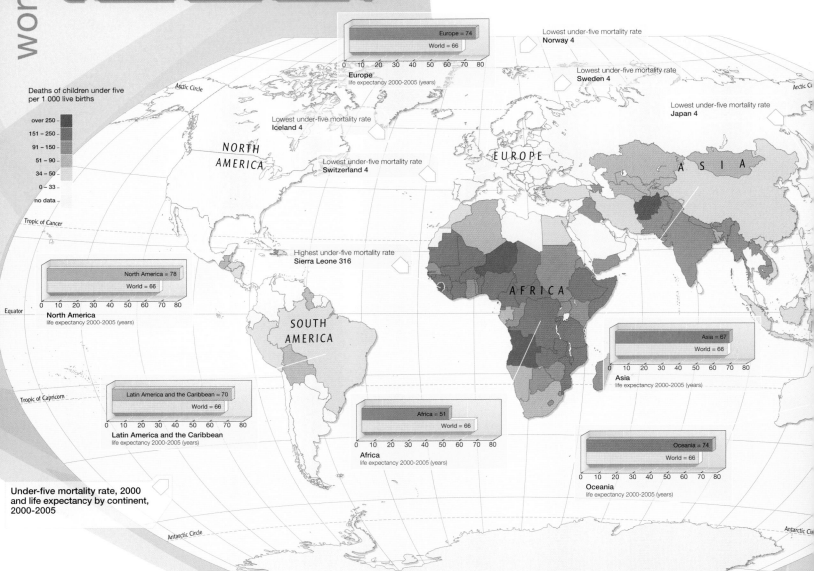

Deaths of children under five per 1 000 live births

over 250
151 – 250
91 – 150
51 – 90
34 – 50
0 – 33
no data

Europe = 74
World = 66
Europe
life expectancy 2000-2005 (years)

Lowest under-five mortality rate
Norway 4

Lowest under-five mortality rate
Sweden 4

Lowest under-five mortality rate
Japan 4

Lowest under-five mortality rate
Iceland 4

Lowest under-five mortality rate
Switzerland 4

Highest under-five mortality rate
Sierra Leone 316

North America = 78
World = 66
North America
life expectancy 2000-2005 (years)

Asia = 67
World = 66
Asia
life expectancy 2000-2005 (years)

Latin America and the Caribbean = 70
World = 66
Latin America and the Caribbean
life expectancy 2000-2005 (years)

Africa = 51
World = 66
Africa
life expectancy 2000-2005 (years)

Oceania = 74
World = 66
Oceania
life expectancy 2000-2005 (years)

Under-five mortality rate, 2000 and life expectancy by continent, 2000-2005

FACTS

Of the 10 countries with under-5 mortality rates of more than 200, 9 are in Africa

Many western countries believe they have achieved satisfactory levels of education and no longer closely monitor levels of literacy

Children born in Nepal have only a 12% chance of their birth being attended by trained health personnel, for most European countries the figure is 100%

Over 5 million people die each year from water-related diseases such as cholera and dysentery

Measuring development

Measuring the extent to which a country is 'developed' is difficult, and although there have been many attempts to standardize techniques there is no universally accepted method. One commonly used measure is the Human Development Index (HDI), which is based on a combination of statistics relating to life expectancy, education (literacy and school enrolment) and wealth (Gross Domestic Product – GDP).

At the Millennium Summit in September 2000, the United Nations identified eight Millennium Development Goals (MDGs) which aim to combat poverty, hunger, disease, illiteracy, environmental degradation and discrimination against women. Forty eight indicators have been identified which will measure the progress each country is making towards achieving these goals.

Health and education

Perhaps the most important indicators used for measuring the level of national development are those relating to health and education. Both of these key areas are vital to the future development of a country, and if there are concerns in standards attained in either (or worse, in both) of these, then they may indicate fundamental problems within the country concerned. The ability to read and write (literacy) is seen as vital in educating people and encouraging development, while access to safe drinking water is a fundamental requirement in maintaining satisfactory levels of basic health. Currently over 1.2 billion people drink unclean water and expose themselves to serious health risks.

Domestic use of **untreated water** in Kathmandu, Nepal.

91 – 100
66 – 90
51 – 65
31 – 50
0 – 30
no data

Access to safe water, 2000
Percentage of population with access to improved drinking water

per cent

Lowest under-five mortality rate
Singapore 4

Tropic of Cancer

Equator

Tropic of Capricorn

OCEANIA

96 – 100
86 – 95
66 – 85
41 – 65
0 – 40
no data

per cent

Literacy rate, 2002
Percentage of population aged 15–24 with at least a basic ability to read and write

UN Millennium Development Goals
From the Millennium Declaration, 2000

Goal 1	Eradicate extreme poverty and hunger
Goal 2	Achieve universal primary education
Goal 3	Promote gender equality and empower women
Goal 4	Reduce child mortality
Goal 5	Improve maternal health
Goal 6	Combat HIV/AIDS, malaria and other diseases
Goal 7	Ensure environmental sustainability
Goal 8	Develop a global partnership for development

http://www.un.org/millenniumgoals/index.html

Human Development Index (HDI), 2002

TOP 10

RANK	COUNTRY
1	NORWAY
2	SWEDEN
3	CANADA
4	BELGIUM
5	AUSTRALIA
6	USA
7	ICELAND
8	NETHERLANDS
9	JAPAN
10	FINLAND

BOTTOM 10

RANK	COUNTRY
164	MALI
165	CENTRAL AFRICAN REPUBLIC
166	CHAD
167	GUINEA-BISSAU
168	ETHIOPIA
169	BURKINA
170	MOZAMBIQUE
171	BURUNDI
172	NIGER
173	SIERRA LEONE

Outdoor education at a school in Bahia state, northeast Brazil.

The globalization of the economy is making the world appear a smaller place. However, this shrinkage is an uneven process. Countries are being included in and excluded from the global economy to differing degrees. The wealthy countries of the developed world with their market-led economies, access to productive new technologies and international markets, dominate the world economic system. Great inequalities exist between and also within countries. There may also be discrepancies between social groups within countries due to gender and ethnic divisions. Differences between countries are evident by looking at overall wealth, levels of debt and the flow of aid. Although aid makes a vital contribution to many of the world's poorer countries, the benefits are often greatly reduced by the burden of debt.

world statistics: see pages 150–156

The City, London, the world's largest financial centre.

Rural homesteads, Sudan – most of the world's poorest countries are in Africa.

FACTS

The City, one of 33 London boroughs, is the world's largest financial centre and contains Europe's biggest stock market

Half the world's population earns only 5% of the world's wealth

During the second half of the 20th century rich countries gave over US$1 trillion in aid

For every £1 in grant aid to developing countries, more than £13 comes back in debt repayments

On average, The World Bank distributes US$30 billion each year between 100 countries

- High-income economies
- Latin America and the Caribbean
- East Asia and Pacific
- Europe and Central Asia
- South Asia
- Middle East and North Africa
- Sub-Saharan Africa

World Gross National Income: 31 500 010 US$ millions

Regional distribution of wealth

Debt and aid

To assist them in development programmes, many countries borrow huge amounts of money from agencies such as the World Bank. Changes in the world's economy have created conditions in which it is virtually impossible for these countries to repay their loans. The total debt need not be a problem if the country can make its repayments or 'service' the debt. Problems arise where the debt service ratio (total debt service as a percentage of exports of goods and services) is high. A country with a debt service ratio of 50% needs to spend half of its income on debt repayments.

Overseas Aid is the provision of funds or services at non-commercial rates for development purposes. The Development Assistance Committee (DAC) of the Organization for Economic Co-operation and Development (OECD) is one of the key forums in which the major donors work together to increase their effectiveness in supporting sustainable development. The United Nations and DAC have set a target for countries to donate 0.7% of their GNI as aid. By 2000 only 5 countries had reached that target.

Gross National Income

HIGHEST

RANK	COUNTRY	US$ MILLIONS 2001
1	UNITED STATES	9 900 724
2	JAPAN	4 574 164
3	GERMANY	1 947 951
4	UNITED KINGDOM	1 451 442
5	FRANCE	1 377 389
6	CHINA	1 130 984
7	ITALY	1 123 478
8	CANADA	661 881
9	SPAIN	586 874
10	MEXICO	550 456

LOWEST

RANK	COUNTRY	US$ MILLIONS 2001
1	SOLOMON ISLANDS	253
2	DOMINICA	224
3	COMOROS	217
4	VANUATU	212
5	GUINEA-BISSAU	202
6	TONGA	154
7	PALAU	132
8	MARSHALL ISLANDS	115
9	KIRIBATI	77
10	SÃO TOMÉ AND PRÍNCIPE	43

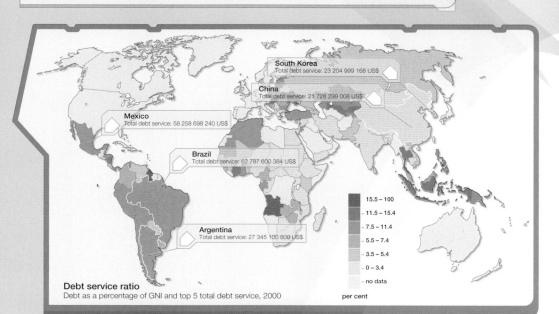

South Korea
Total debt service: 23 204 999 168 US$

China
Total debt service: 21 728 299 008 US$

Mexico
Total debt service: 58 258 698 240 US$

Brazil
Total debt service: 62 787 600 384 US$

Argentina
Total debt service: 27 345 100 800 US$

15.5 – 100
11.5 – 15.4
7.5 – 11.4
5.5 – 7.4
3.5 – 5.4
0 – 3.4
no data

Debt service ratio
Debt as a percentage of GNI and top 5 total debt service, 2000

per cent

Tropic of Cancer
Equator
KIRIBATI
Tropic of Capricorn

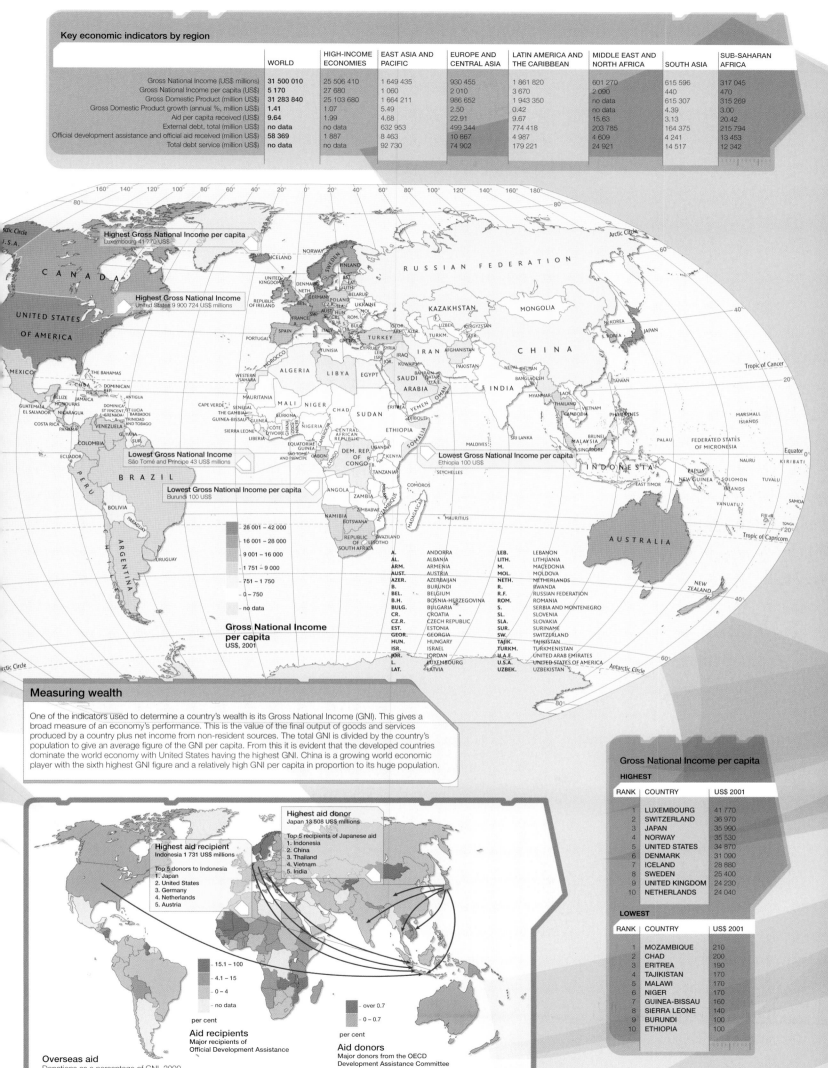

Key economic indicators by region

	WORLD	HIGH-INCOME ECONOMIES	EAST ASIA AND PACIFIC	EUROPE AND CENTRAL ASIA	LATIN AMERICA AND THE CARIBBEAN	MIDDLE EAST AND NORTH AFRICA	SOUTH ASIA	SUB-SAHARAN AFRICA
Gross National Income (US$ millions)	31 500 010	25 506 410	1 649 435	930 455	1 861 820	601 270	615 596	317 045
Gross National Income per capita (US$)	5 170	27 680	1 060	2 010	3 670	2 090	440	470
Gross Domestic Product (million US$)	31 283 840	25 103 680	1 664 211	986 652	1 943 350	no data	615 307	315 269
Gross Domestic Product growth (annual %, million US$)	1.41	1.07	5.49	2.50	0.42	no data	4.39	3.00
Aid per capita received (US$)	9.64	1.99	4.68	22.91	9.67	15.63	3.13	20.42
External debt, total (million US$)	no data	no data	632 953	499 344	774 418	203 785	164 375	215 794
Official development assistance and official aid received (million US$)	58 369	1 887	8 463	10 867	4 987	4 609	4 241	13 453
Total debt service (million US$)	no data	no data	92 730	74 902	179 221	24 921	14 517	12 342

Highest Gross National Income per capita
Luxembourg 41 770 US$

Highest Gross National Income
United States 9 900 724 US$ millions

Lowest Gross National Income
São Tomé and Príncipe 43 US$ millions

Lowest Gross National Income per capita
Burundi 100 US$

Lowest Gross National Income per capita
Ethiopia 100 US$

Gross National Income per capita
US$, 2001

- 28 001 – 42 000
- 16 001 – 28 000
- 9 001 – 16 000
- 1 751 – 9 000
- 751 – 1 750
- 0 – 750
- no data

A.	ANDORRA	LEB.	LEBANON
AL.	ALBANIA	LITH.	LITHUANIA
ARM.	ARMENIA	M.	MACEDONIA
AUST.	AUSTRIA	MOL.	MOLDOVA
AZER.	AZERBAIJAN	NETH.	NETHERLANDS
B.	BURUNDI	R.	RWANDA
BEL.	BELGIUM	R.F.	RUSSIAN FEDERATION
B.H.	BOSNIA-HERZEGOVINA	ROM.	ROMANIA
BULG.	BULGARIA	S.	SERBIA AND MONTENEGRO
CR.	CROATIA	SL.	SLOVENIA
CZ.R.	CZECH REPUBLIC	SLA.	SLOVAKIA
EST.	ESTONIA	SUR.	SURINAME
GEOR.	GEORGIA	SW.	SWITZERLAND
HUN.	HUNGARY	TAJIK.	TAJIKISTAN
ISR.	ISRAEL	TURKM.	TURKMENISTAN
JOR.	JORDAN	U.A.E.	UNITED ARAB EMIRATES
L.	LUXEMBOURG	U.S.A.	UNITED STATES OF AMERICA
LAT.	LATVIA	UZBEK.	UZBEKISTAN

Measuring wealth

One of the indicators used to determine a country's wealth is its Gross National Income (GNI). This gives a broad measure of an economy's performance. This is the value of the final output of goods and services produced by a country plus net income from non-resident sources. The total GNI is divided by the country's population to give an average figure of the GNI per capita. From this it is evident that the developed countries dominate the world economy with United States having the highest GNI. China is a growing world economic player with the sixth highest GNI figure and a relatively high GNI per capita in proportion to its huge population.

Highest aid recipient
Indonesia 1 731 US$ millions

Top 5 donors to Indonesia
1. Japan
2. United States
3. Germany
4. Netherlands
5. Austria

Highest aid donor
Japan 13 508 US$ millions

Top 5 recipients of Japanese aid
1. Indonesia
2. China
3. Thailand
4. Vietnam
5. India

Aid recipients
Major recipients of Official Development Assistance

- 15.1 – 100
- 4.1 – 15
- 0 – 4
- no data

per cent

Aid donors
Major donors from the OECD Development Assistance Committee

- over 0.7
- 0 – 0.7

per cent

Overseas aid
Donations as a percentage of GNI, 2000

Gross National Income per capita

HIGHEST

RANK	COUNTRY	US$ 2001
1	LUXEMBOURG	41 770
2	SWITZERLAND	36 970
3	JAPAN	35 990
4	NORWAY	35 530
5	UNITED STATES	34 870
6	DENMARK	31 090
7	ICELAND	28 880
8	SWEDEN	25 400
9	UNITED KINGDOM	24 230
10	NETHERLANDS	24 040

LOWEST

RANK	COUNTRY	US$ 2001
1	MOZAMBIQUE	210
2	CHAD	200
3	ERITREA	190
4	TAJIKISTAN	170
5	MALAWI	170
6	NIGER	170
7	GUINEA-BISSAU	160
8	SIERRA LEONE	140
9	BURUNDI	100
10	ETHIOPIA	100

Geo-political issues shape the countries of the world and the current political situation in many parts of the world reflects a long history of armed conflict. Since the Second World War conflicts have been fairly localized, but there are numerous 'flash points' where factors such as territorial claims, ideology, religion, ethnicity and access to water and resources can cause friction between two or more countries which may develop into wider conflict.

Military expenditure can take up a disproportionate amount of a country's wealth – Eritrea, with a Gross National Income (GNI) per capita of only US$190 spends over twenty seven per cent of its total GNI on military activity. There is an encouraging trend towards wider international cooperation, mainly through the United Nations (UN) and the North Atlantic Treaty Organization (NATO), to prevent escalation of conflicts and on peacekeeping missions.

FACTS

- There have been nearly 70 civil or internal wars throughout the world since 1945
- The Iran-Iraq war in the 1980s is estimated to have cost half a million lives
- The UN are currently involved in 15 peacekeeping operations
- It is estimated that there are nearly 20 million refugees throughout the world
- Over 1 600 UN peacekeepers have been killed since 1948

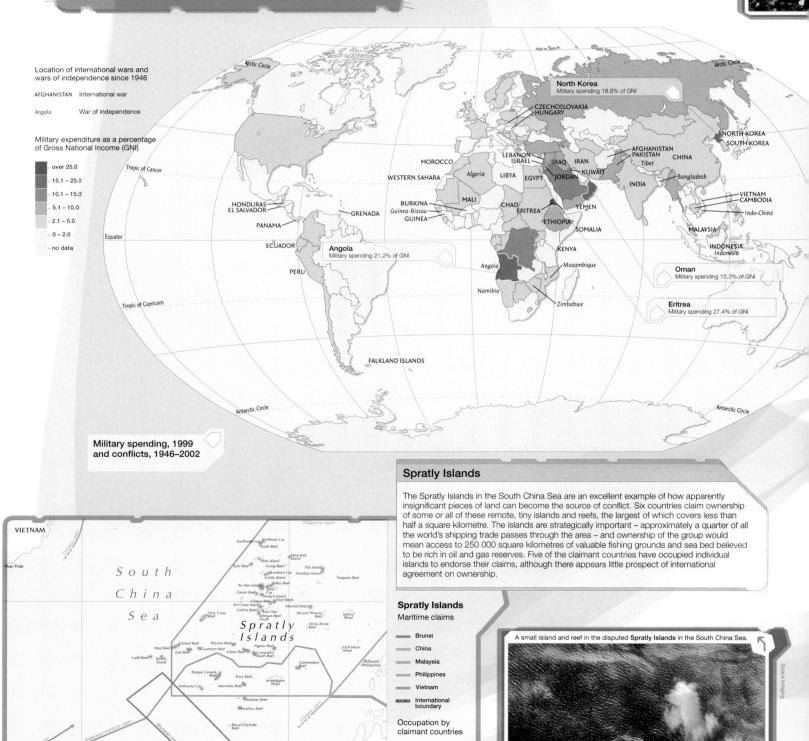

Location of international wars and wars of independence since 1946

AFGHANISTAN International war

Angola War of independence

Military expenditure as a percentage of Gross National Income (GNI)

- over 25.0
- 15.1 – 25.0
- 10.1 – 15.0
- 5.1 – 10.0
- 2.1 – 5.0
- 0 – 2.0
- no data

North Korea
Military spending 18.8% of GNI

Angola
Military spending 21.2% of GNI

Oman
Military spending 15.3% of GNI

Eritrea
Military spending 27.4% of GNI

Military spending, 1999 and conflicts, 1946–2002

Spratly Islands

The Spratly Islands in the South China Sea are an excellent example of how apparently insignificant pieces of land can become the source of conflict. Six countries claim ownership of some or all of these remote, tiny islands and reefs, the largest of which covers less than half a square kilometre. The islands are strategically important – approximately a quarter of all the world's shipping trade passes through the area – and ownership of the group would mean access to 250 000 square kilometres of valuable fishing grounds and sea bed believed to be rich in oil and gas reserves. Five of the claimant countries have occupied individual islands to endorse their claims, although there appears little prospect of international agreement on ownership.

Spratly Islands
Maritime claims

- Brunei
- China
- Malaysia
- Philippines
- Vietnam
- International boundary

Occupation by claimant countries

- China
- Malaysia
- Philippines
- Taiwan
- Vietnam

A small island and reef in the disputed **Spratly Islands** in the South China Sea.

Albanian refugees from **Kosovo**, Yugoslavia near the Macedonian border in 1999.

The Balkans

The Balkans has a long history of instability and ethnic conflict. The former country of Yugoslavia in particular has a very complex ethnic composition and the 1990 Yugoslav elections uncovered serious divisions. Over the next three years, four of the six Yugoslav republics – Croatia, Slovenia, Bosnia-Herzegovina and Macedonia – each declared their independence. The civil war continued until 1995 when the Dayton Peace Accord was established. In Kosovo, direct Serbian rule was imposed on the mainly Muslim Albanian population. Support grew for independence and in 1998 and 1999 the Serbs reacted through 'ethnic cleansing'. Many Kosovans were killed and thousands were forced to flee their homes. After NATO intervention, a settlement was reached in June 1999, although tensions between communities remain high.

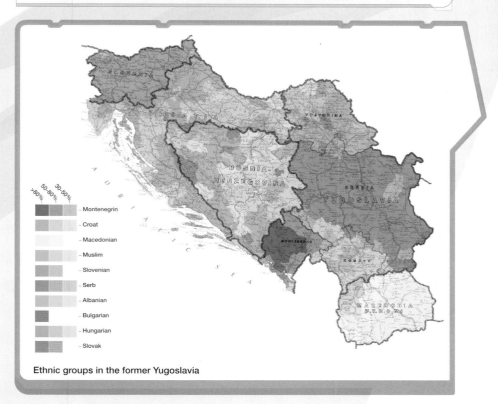

>80% 50-80% 30-50%

- Montenegrin
- Croat
- Macedonian
- Muslim
- Slovenian
- Serb
- Albanian
- Bulgarian
- Hungarian
- Slovak

Ethnic groups in the former Yugoslavia

—·—·— International boundary

—x—x— Disputed International boundary

········· Ceasefire line

———— British Mandate Boundary 1922-1948

———— Israel Boundary 1948

///// Land occupied by Israel 1967

 □ Main Palestinian towns

Middle East politics
Changing boundaries in Israel/Palestine, 1922–2003

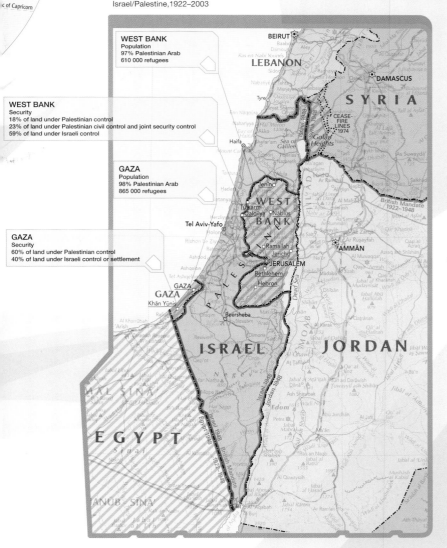

WEST BANK
Population
97% Palestinian Arab
610 000 refugees

WEST BANK
Security
18% of land under Palestinian control
23% of land under Palestinian civil control and joint security control
59% of land under Israeli control

GAZA
Population
98% Palestinian Arab
865 000 refugees

GAZA
Security
60% of land under Palestinian control
40% of land under Israeli control or settlement

Security fence along the **Egypt/Gaza** border near Rafiah.

The Middle East

The on-going Israeli/Palestinian conflict reflects decades of unrest in the region of Palestine which, after the First World War, was placed under British control. In 1947 the United Nations (UN) proposed a partitioning into separate Jewish and Arab states – a plan which was rejected by the Palestinians and by the Arab states in the region. When Britain withdrew in 1948, Israel declared its independence. This led to an Arab-Israeli war which left Israel with more land than originally proposed under the UN plan. Hundreds of thousands of Palestinians were forced out of their homeland and became refugees, mainly in Jordan and Lebanon. The 6-Day War in 1967 resulted in Israel taking possession of Sinai and Gaza from Egypt, West Bank from Jordan, and the Golan Heights from Syria. These territories (except Sinai which was subsequently returned to Egypt) remain occupied by Israel – the main reason for the Palestinian uprising or 'Intifada' against Israel. The situation remains complex, with poor prospects for peace and for mutually acceptable independent states being established.

Europe, the westward extension of the Asian continent and the second smallest of the world's continents, has a remarkable variety of physical features and landscapes. The continent is bounded by mountain ranges of varying character – the highlands of Scandinavia and northwest Britain, the Pyrenees, the Alps, the Carpathian Mountains, the Caucasus and the Ural Mountains. Two of these, the Caucasus and Ural Mountains define the eastern limits of Europe, with the Black Sea and the Bosporus defining its southeastern boundary with Asia.

Across the centre of the continent stretches the North European Plain, broken by some of Europe's greatest rivers, including the Volga and the Dnieper and containing some if its largest lakes. To the south, the Mediterranean Sea divides Europe from Africa. The Mediterranean region itself has a very distinct climate and landscape.

Iceland in winter, one of Europe's largest islands.

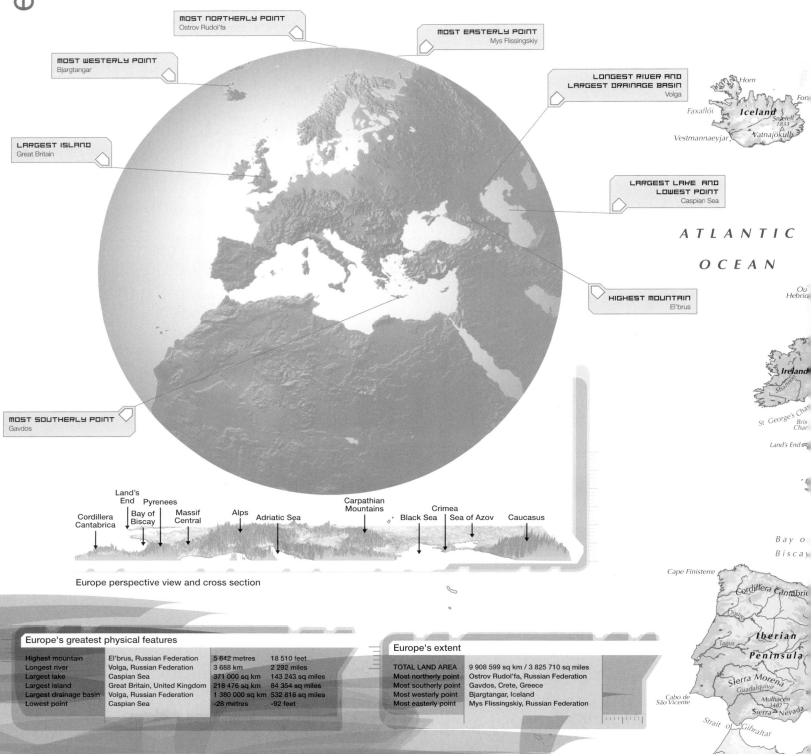

MOST NORTHERLY POINT
Ostrov Rudol'fa

MOST EASTERLY POINT
Mys Flissingskiy

MOST WESTERLY POINT
Bjargtangar

LONGEST RIVER AND LARGEST DRAINAGE BASIN
Volga

LARGEST ISLAND
Great Britain

LARGEST LAKE AND LOWEST POINT
Caspian Sea

HIGHEST MOUNTAIN
El'brus

MOST SOUTHERLY POINT
Gavdos

Europe perspective view and cross section

Cordillera Cantabrica · Land's End · Bay of Biscay · Pyrenees · Massif Central · Alps · Adriatic Sea · Carpathian Mountains · Black Sea · Crimea · Sea of Azov · Caucasus

ATLANTIC OCEAN

Horn · Iceland · Faxaflói · Snæfell 1833 · Vatnajökull · Vestmannaeyjar · Fon

Ou Hebrid · Ireland · Shannon · St George's Chan · Bris Chan · Land's End

Bay o Biscay

Cape Finisterre · Cordillera Cantabric · Douro · Tagus · Iberian Peninsula · Sierra Morena · Guadalquivir · Cabo de São Vicente · Mulhacén 3482 · Sierra Nevada · Strait of Gibraltar · A F

Europe's greatest physical features

Highest mountain	El'brus, Russian Federation	5 642 metres	18 510 feet
Longest river	Volga, Russian Federation	3 688 km	2 292 miles
Largest lake	Caspian Sea	371 000 sq.km	143 243 sq miles
Largest island	Great Britain, United Kingdom	218 476 sq.km	84 354 sq miles
Largest drainage basin	Volga, Russian Federation	1 380 000 sq.km	532 818 sq miles
Lowest point	Caspian Sea	-28 metres	-92 feet

Europe's extent

TOTAL LAND AREA	9 908 599 sq km / 3 825 710 sq miles
Most northerly point	Ostrov Rudol'fa, Russian Federation
Most southerly point	Gavdos, Crete, Greece
Most westerly point	Bjargtangar, Iceland
Most easterly point	Mys Flissingskiy, Russian Federation

The Danube, Europe's second longest river, flows north and east to the Romanian coast of the Black Sea through a large delta.

Caucasus, mountain range marking the boundary of Europe and Asia, contains Europe's highest peak, El'brus.

Jan Mayen

Barents Sea

North Cape

Varanger Halvøya

Poluostrov Rybachiy

Ostrov Kolguyev

Novaya Zemlya

Cheshskaya Guba

Poluostrov Kanin

Usa

Pechora

Ural Mountains

Vesterålen

Lofoten

Lappland

Inarijärvi

Kola Peninsula

Timanskiy Kryazh

Ekostrovskaya Imandra

Ozero

White Sea

Dvinskaya Guba

Mezen

Scandinavia

Vestfjorden

Kem

Ozero Topozero

Luleå

Dvinskaya Guba

Severnaja Dvina

Vychegda

Kama

Norwegian Sea

Boknafjorden

Galdhøpiggen 2470

Ume

Indals

Gulf of Bothnia

Lake Onega

Ozero Beloye

Kamskoye Vodokhranilishche

Faroe Islands

Shetland

Cape Wrath

Orkney

Moray Firth

Grampian Mountains

Åland Islands

Lake Ladoga

Rybinskoye Vodokhranilishche

Kuybyshevskoye Vodokhranilishche

Volga

Vänern

Vättern

Gulf of Finland

Hiiumaa

Saaremaa

Lake Peipus

Ozero Il'men

Valdayskaya Vozvyshennost'

Volga

North Sea

Skagerrak

Kattegat

Öland

Gotland

Gulf of Riga

Baltic Sea

British Isles

Irish Sea

Jutland

Zealand

Fyn

Lolland

Bornholm

Gulf of Gdańsk

Central

Russian

Upland

Great Britain

Pennines

Cambrian Mountains

Thames

East Frisian Islands

Ijsselmeer

North European Plain

Weser

Wisła

Bug

Pripet Marshes

Kyyivs'ke Vodoskhovyshche

Don

Tsimlyanskoye Vodokhranilishche

Volga

English Channel

Channel Islands

Maas

Rhine

Elbe

Oder

Wisła

Seine

Marne

Moselle

Ardennes

Böhmer Wald

Erzgebirge

Sudety

Kremenchuts'ka Vodoskhovyshche

Dnieper

Kakhovs'ke Vodoskhovyshche

Don

Loire

Saône

Vosges

Rhine

Danube

Inn

Tisza

Danube

Carpathian Mountains

Dniester

Ozero Manych-Gudilo

ASIA

Jura

Lake Constance

Vienne

Lake Geneva

Mont Blanc 4808

Alps

Dolomites

Lake Garda

Lake Balaton

Mureşul

Dnieper

Gulf of Taganrog

Sea of Azov

Stavropol'skaya Vozvyshennost'

Caspian Sea

Massif Central

Gironde

Rhône

Po

Sava

Transylvanian Alps

Karkinits'ka Zatoka

Crimea

El'brus 5642

Caucasus

Pyrenees

Aneto 3404

Ebro

Golfe du Lion

Ligurian Sea

Cap Corse

Corsica

Isola d'Elba

Apennines

Dinaric Alps

Adriatic Sea

Sava

Drava

Danube

Balkan Mountains

Rhodope Mountains

Black Sea

Golfo de Valencia

Balearic Islands

Ibiza

Minorca

Majorca

Formentera

Sardinia

Capo Carbonara

Tyrrhenian Sea

Vesuvius 1281

Isole Lipari

Monte Etna 3323

Sicily

Golfo di Taranto

Strait of Otranto

Pindus Mts

Thasos

Limnos

Lesbos

Chios

Sea of Marmara

Aegean Sea

Bosporus

Mediterranean Sea

Sicilian Channel

Malta

Ionian Sea

Ionian Islands

Peloponnese

Evvoia

Andros

Kythira

Krytiko Pelagos

Crete

Dodecanese

Rhodes

Karpathos

CA

FACTS

The Danube flows through 7 countries and has 7 different name forms

Lakes cover almost 10% of the total land area of Finland

The Strait of Gibraltar, separating the Atlantic Ocean from the Mediterranean Sea and Europe from Africa, is only 13 kilometres wide at its narrowest point

The highest mountain in the Alps is Mont Blanc, 4 808 metres, on the France/Italy border

The predominantly temperate climate of Europe has led to it becoming the most densely populated of the continents. It is highly industrialized, and has exploited its great wealth of natural resources and agricultural land to become one of the most powerful economic regions in the world.

The current pattern of countries within Europe is a result of numerous and complicated changes throughout its history. Ethnic, religious and linguistic differences have often been the cause of conflict, particularly in the Balkan region which has a very complex ethnic pattern. Current boundaries reflect, to some extent, these divisions which continue to be a source of tension. The historic distinction between 'Eastern' and 'Western' Europe is no longer made, following the collapse of Communism and the break up of the Soviet Union in 1991.

Paris, the capital of France and Europe's largest capital city with 9 630 000 residents.

Space Imaging

LEAST DENSELY POPULATED COUNTRY
Iceland

MOST NORTHERLY CAPITAL
Reykjavik

LARGEST CAPITAL
Paris

SMALLEST COUNTRY (AREA AND POPULATION)
Vatican City

LARGEST COUNTRY (AREA AND POPULATION)
Russian Federation

FACTS

The European Union currently has 15 members: Austria, Belgium, Denmark, Finland, France, Germany, Greece, Italy, Luxembourg, Netherlands, Portugal, Republic of Ireland, Spain, Sweden, UK

10 countries will join the European Union in 2004: Cyprus, Czech Republic, Estonia, Hungary, Latvia, Lithuania, Malta, Poland, Slovakia, Slovenia

Europe has the 2 smallest independent countries in the world – Vatican City and Monaco

Vatican City is an independent country entirely within the city of Rome, and is the centre of the Roman Catholic Church

HIGHEST CAPITAL
Andorra la Vella

SMALLEST CAPITAL
Vatican City

MOST DENSELY POPULATED COUNTRY
Monaco

MOST SOUTHERLY CAPITAL
Valletta

Reykjavik ICELAND

ATLANTIC

OCEAN

REPUBLI OF Dub IRELAND

Bres

Bay o
Biscal

Azores
(Portugal)

Cape Finisterre   A Coruña
Bilbao

Oporto
Salamanca

Lisbon   Madrid

SPAIN

Cabo de
São Vicente   Seville   Córdoba

Cádiz   Cartag
Málaga

Str. of
Gibraltar   Gibraltar

Bosporus, Turkey, a narrow strait of water which separates Europe from Asia.

Europe's countries

Largest country (area)	Russian Federation	17 075 400 sq km	6 592 812 sq miles
Smallest country (area)	Vatican City	0.5 sq km	0.2 sq miles
Largest country (population)	Russian Federation	143 752 000	
Smallest country (population)	Vatican City	480	
Most densely populated country	Monaco	17 000 per sq km	34 000 per sq mile
Least densely populated country	Iceland	3 per sq km	8 per sq mile

Europe (excluding Russian Federation) percentage of total population and land area

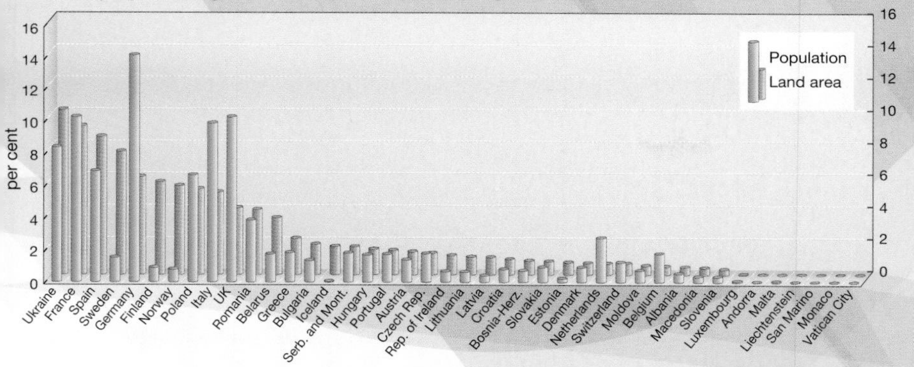
per cent
16
14
12
10
8
6
4
2
0
Population
Land area
Ukraine
France
Spain
Sweden
Germany
Finland
Norway
Poland
Italy
UK
Romania
Belarus
Greece
Bulgaria
Iceland
Serb. and Mont.
Hungary
Portugal
Austria
Czech Rep.
Rep. of Ireland
Lithuania
Latvia
Croatia
Bosnia-Herz.
Slovakia
Estonia
Denmark
Netherlands
Switzerland
Moldova
Belgium
Albania
Macedonia
Slovenia
Luxembourg
Andorra
Malta
Liechtenstein
San Marino
Monaco
Vatican City

Belgrade, the capital of Serbia and Montenegro, stands at the junction of the Danube, Europe's second longest river, and the Sava river.

Europe's capitals

Largest capital (population)	Paris, France	9 630 000	
Smallest capital (population)	Vatican City	480	
Most northerly capital	Reykjavík, Iceland	64° 39'N	
Most southerly capital	Valletta, Malta	35° 54'N	
Highest capital	Andorra la Vella, Andorra	1 029 metres	3 376 feet

Jan Mayen (Norway)
Barents Sea
North Cape
Ostrov Kolguyev
Vorkuta
Murmansk
Kola Peninsula
White Sea
Lappland
Norwegian Sea
SWEDEN
FINLAND
NORWAY
RUSSIAN FEDERATION
Archangel
Syktyvkar
Faroe Islands (Denmark)
Trondheim
Gulf of Bothnia
Petrozavodsk
Lake Onega
Lake Ladoga
Perm'
Kirov
Izhevsk
Naberezhnyye Chelny
Ufa
Shetland
Bergen
Orkney
Oslo
Stockholm
Åland Islands
Turku
Helsinki
Gulf of Finland
Tallinn
St Petersburg
Vologda
Yaroslavl'
Kazan'
Nizhniy Novgorod
Lake Peipus
ESTONIA
Vänern
Vättern
Skagerrak
Kattegat
Gotland
Gulf of Riga
Riga
LATVIA
Moscow
Ul'yanovsk
Samara
Orenburg
Edinburgh
North Sea
Ålborg
DENMARK
Öland
Baltic Sea
UNITED KINGDOM
Malmö
Copenhagen
LITHUANIA
Vitsyebsk
Smolensk
Tula
Penza
Saratov
Leeds
Manchester
Bornholm
RUS. FED.
Vilnius
Kaliningrad
Minsk
Mahilyow
Gdańsk
Hrodna
Białystok
BELARUS
Voronezh
NETHERLANDS
Hamburg
Bremen
Bydgoszcz
Homyel'
The Hague
Amsterdam
Rotterdam
Berlin
Poznań
Warsaw
Brest
Chernihiv
Belgorod
Volgograd
London
Essen
Leipzig
Łódź
Kiev
Kharkiv
English Channel
Brussels
Bonn
GERMANY
Wrocław
POLAND
Rivne
Guernsey
Jersey
BELGIUM
LUXEMBOURG
CZECH REPUBLIC
Prague
Katowice
UKRAINE
Luxembourg
Frankfurt am Main
Kraków
L'viv
Donets'k
Astrakhan'
ASIA
Kirovohrad
Dnipropetrovs'k
Rennes
Paris
Stuttgart
Brno
SLOVAKIA
Rostov-na-Donu
Orléans
Strasbourg
Munich
Vienna
Bratislava
Košice
Chernivtsi
Nantes
Dijon
Zürich
LIECHTENSTEIN
Salzburg
Budapest
Chişinău
Mykolayiv
Odesa
Sea of Azov
Stavropol'
Bern
Vaduz
AUSTRIA
HUNGARY
Iaşi
MOLDOVA
Caspian Sea
FRANCE
SWITZERLAND
Szeged
ROMANIA
Crimea
Novorossiysk
Krasnodar
Groznyy
Geneva
Lyon
SLOVENIA
Ljubljana
Zagreb
Simferopol'
El'brus 5642
Caucasus
Bordeaux
Milan
Venice
Trieste
CROATIA
Timişoara
Braşov
Turin
BOSNIA-HERZEGOVINA
Belgrade
Craiova
Bucharest
Constanţa
Toulouse
Genoa
Bologna
Black Sea
Marseille
MONACO
Florence
SAN MARINO
Sarajevo
SERB. AND MONT.
Niš
Pleven
Varna
Andorra la Vella
ANDORRA
Adriatic Sea
Split
BULGARIA
Sofia
Burgas
Zaragoza
ITALY
Podgorica
Plovdiv
Edirne
Corsica
Vatican City
Rome
Skopje
TURKEY
Bosporus
Barcelona
Tirana
MACEDONIA
İstanbul
Bari
Balearic Islands
Minorca
Naples
ALBANIA
Thessaloniki
Valencia
Palma de Mallorca
Majorca
Ibiza
Sardinia
Larisa
Aegean Sea
Cosenza
GREECE
Mediterranean Sea
Messina
Palermo
Athens
Sicily
Syracuse
Ionian Sea
Dodecanese
Rhodes
MALTA
Valletta
Crete
AFRICA

europe
northern europe

Conic Equidistant Projection

1:7 500 000

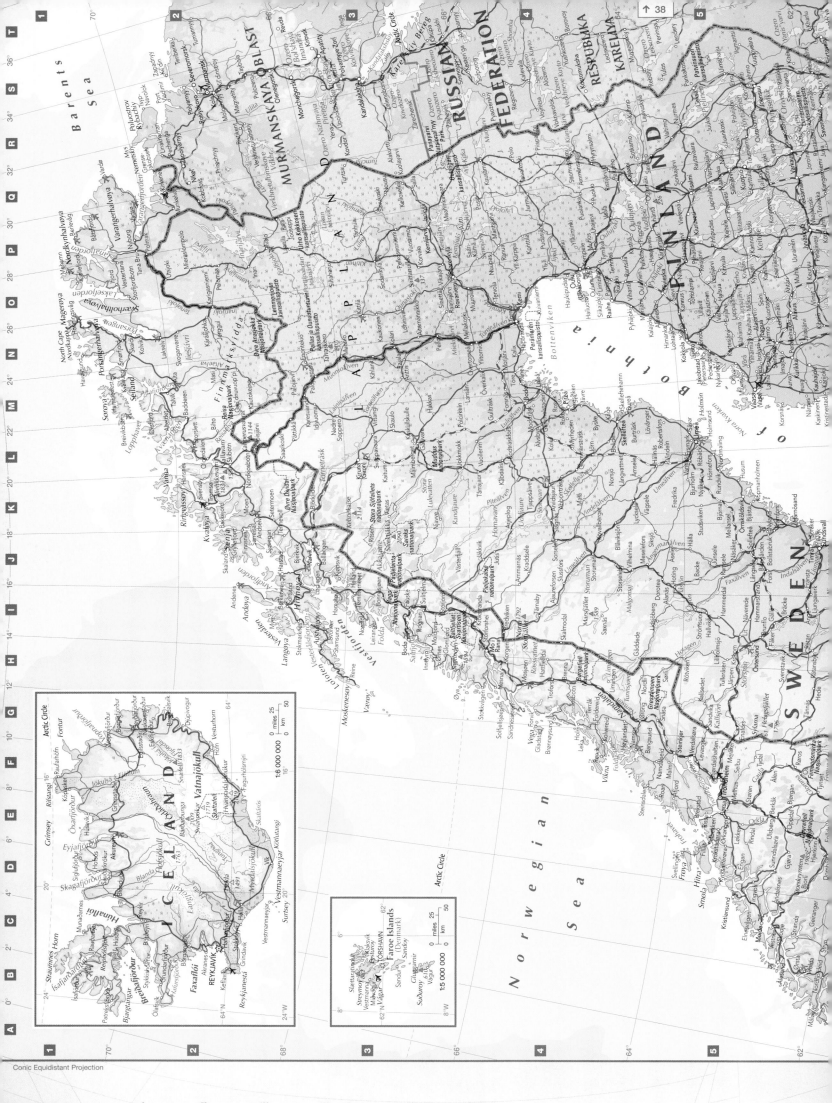

Conic Equidistant Projection

1:5 000 000

Conic Equidistant Projection

1:5 000 000

0   50   100   150 miles

0   50   100   150   200   250 km

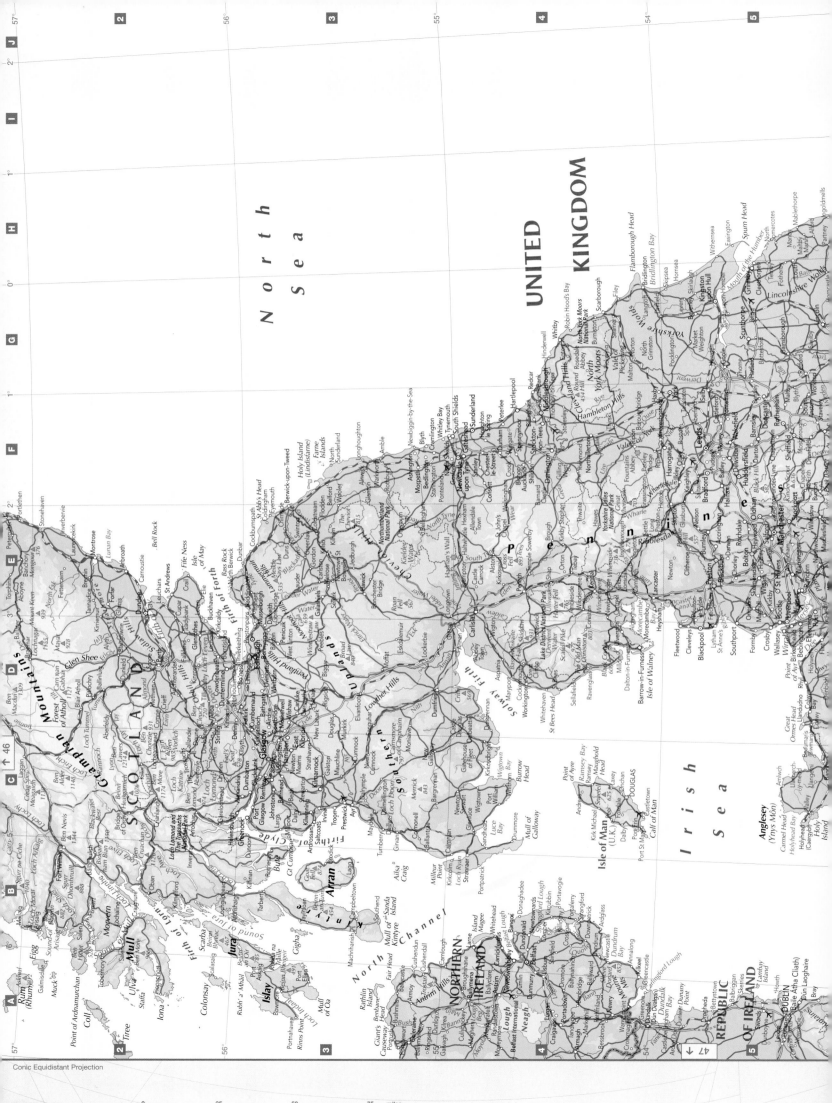

Conic Equidistant Projection

1:2 000 000

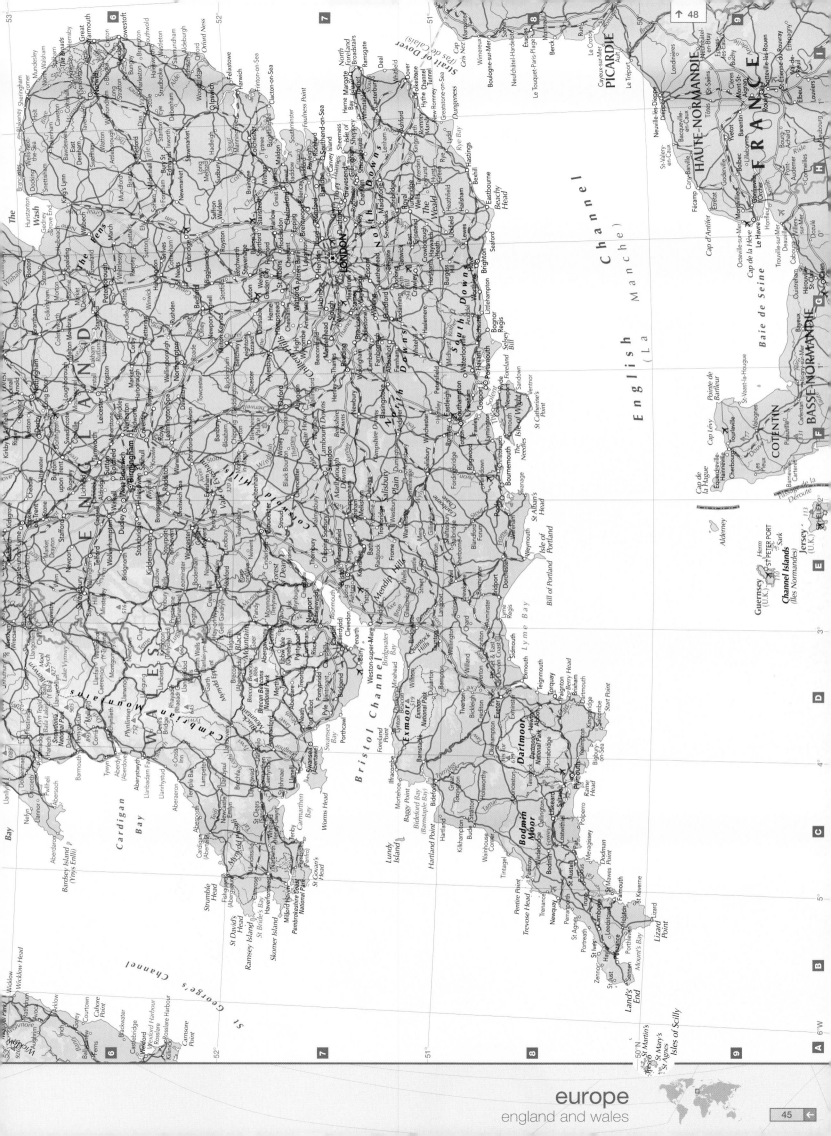

europe
scotland

1:2 000 000

Conic Equidistant Projection

← 46

← 47   ↓ 44

North
Sea

UNITED
KINGDOM

ENGLAND

NETHERLANDS

BELGIUM

FRANCE

LUXEMBOURG

PICARDY

HAUTE-
NORMANDIE

ÎLE-DE-FRANCE

CHAMPAGNE-
ARDENNE

LORRAINE

Conic Equidistant Projection

48   1:2 000 000

0   25   50   75   miles
0   25   50   75   100   125 km

ATLANTIC

OCEAN

REPUBLIC OF IRELAND

UNITED KINGDOM

NETHERLANDS

GERMANY

BELGIUM

LUX.

English Channel (La Manche)

Channel Islands (U.K.)

Bay of Biscay

FRANCE

SWITZERLAND

Mar Cantábrico

Gulf of Gascony (Golfe de Gascogne)

Cordillera Cantábrica

Pyrenees

ANDORRA LA VELLA

ANDORRA

PORTUGAL

SPAIN

MADRID

Barcelona

Balearic Islands (Islas Baleares)

Minorca (Menorca)

Ibiza (Eivissa)

Majorca (Mallorca)

Formentera

Sierra Morena

LISBON

Golfo de Valencia

Valencia

Corsica (Corse) (France)

Ajaccio

ITALY

ROME

Ligurian Sea

MONACO

Marseille

Toulon

Golfe du Lion

Mediterranean

Sardinia (Sardegna) (Italy)

Cagliari

Tyrrhenian Sea

Golfo de Cádiz

Strait of Gibraltar

Gibraltar (U.K.)

Tangier (Tanger)

Ceuta

Melilla (Spain)

ALGIERS (Alger)

Oran

TUNIS

TUNISIA

Sicily (Sicilia)

Trapani

Marsala

Sicilian Channel

RABAT

Casablanca

MOROCCO

Moyen Atlas

Haut Atlas

Anti Atlas

Atlas Mountains

Hauts Plateaux

Atlas Saharien

Atlas Tellien

ALGERIA

Hammada du Drâa

Grand Erg Occidental

Grand Erg Oriental

TRIPO (Ṭarābu)

Plateau du Tademaït

Jabal Nafūsah

Al Ḥamādah al Ḥamrā'

Conic Equidistant Projection

→ 50

1:10 000 000

0   100   200   300   400 miles

0   100   200   300   400   500   600 km

europe
france

Conic Equidistant Projection

1:5 000 000

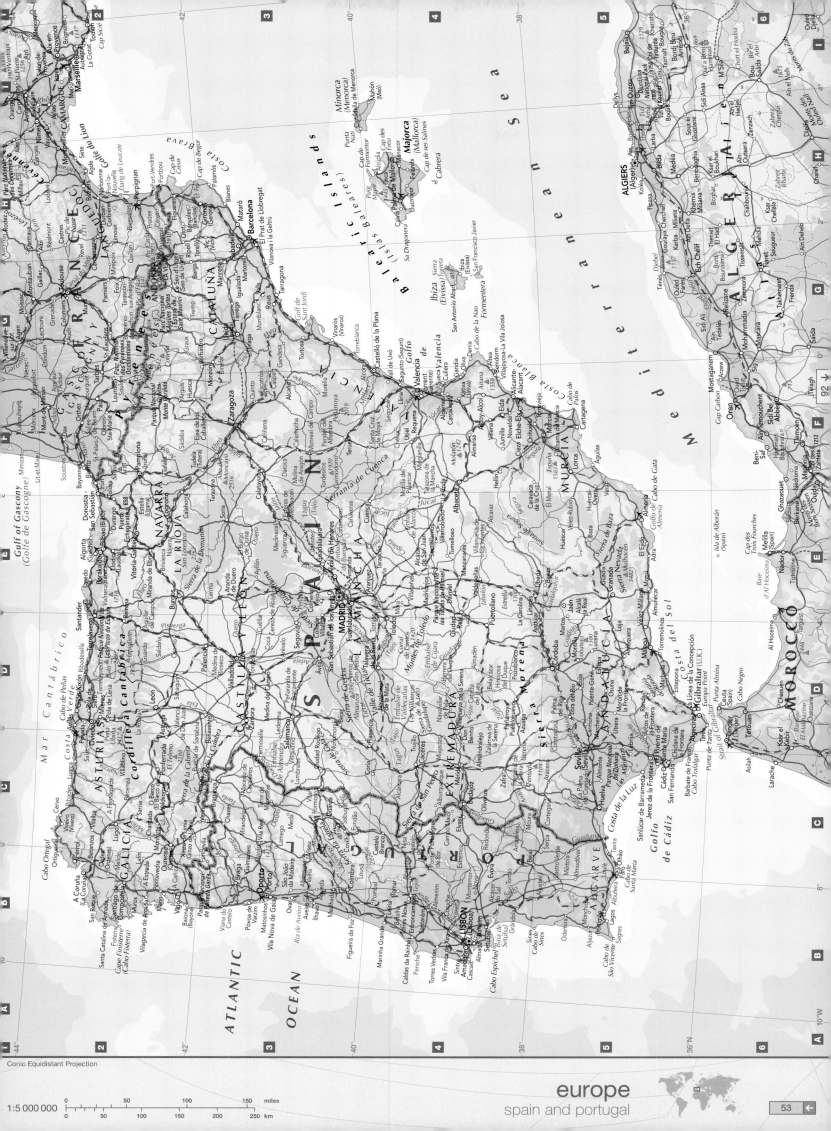

1:5 000 000

Asia is the world's largest continent and occupies almost one-third of the world's total land area. Stretching across approximately 165° of longitude from the Mediterranean Sea to the easternmost point of the Russian Federation on the Bering Strait, it contains the world's highest and lowest points and some of the world's greatest physical features. Its mountain ranges include the Himalaya, Hindu Kush, Karakoram and the Ural Mountains and its major rivers – including the Yangtze, Tigris-Euphrates, Indus, Ganges and Mekong – are equally well-known and evocative.

Asia's deserts include the Gobi, the Taklimakan, and those on the Arabian Peninsula, and significant areas of volcanic and tectonic activity are present on the Kamchatka Peninsula, in Japan, and on Indonesia's numerous islands. The continent's landscapes are greatly influenced by climatic variations, with great contrasts between the islands of the Arctic Ocean and the vast Siberian plains in the north, and the tropical islands of Indonesia.

Ice and snow covered peaks of the volcanic mountains on the Kamchatka Peninsula, northeast Russian Federation.

FACTS

- 90 of the world's 100 highest mountains are in Asia

- The Indonesian archipelago is made up of over 13 500 islands

- The height of the land in Nepal ranges from 60 metres to 8 848 metres

- The deepest lake in the world is Lake Baikal, Russian Federation, which is over 1 600 metres deep

- The 3 Gorges Dam, currently under construction in China, will create a reservoir 620 kilometres long

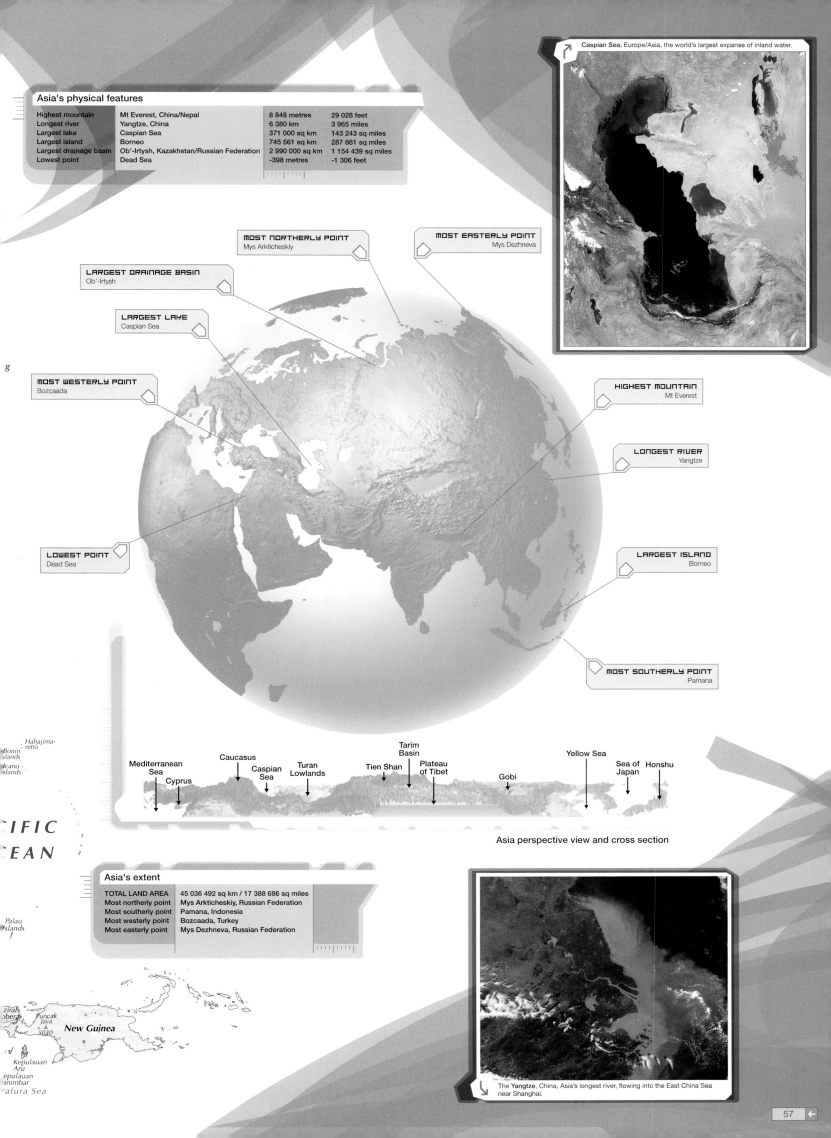

Asia's physical features

Highest mountain	Mt Everest, China/Nepal	8 848 metres	29 028 feet
Longest river	Yangtze, China	6 380 km	3 965 miles
Largest lake	Caspian Sea	371 000 sq km	143 243 sq miles
Largest island	Borneo	745 561 sq km	287 861 sq miles
Largest drainage basin	Ob'-Irtysh, Kazakhstan/Russian Federation	2 990 000 sq km	1 154 439 sq miles
Lowest point	Dead Sea	-398 metres	-1 306 feet

Caspian Sea, Europe/Asia, the world's largest expanse of inland water.

MOST NORTHERLY POINT
Mys Arkticheskiy

MOST EASTERLY POINT
Mys Dezhneva

LARGEST DRAINAGE BASIN
Ob'-Irtysh

LARGEST LAKE
Caspian Sea

MOST WESTERLY POINT
Bozcaada

HIGHEST MOUNTAIN
Mt Everest

LONGEST RIVER
Yangtze

LOWEST POINT
Dead Sea

LARGEST ISLAND
Borneo

MOST SOUTHERLY POINT
Pamana

Mediterranean Sea
Cyprus
Caucasus
Caspian Sea
Turan Lowlands
Tien Shan
Tarim Basin
Plateau of Tibet
Gobi
Yellow Sea
Sea of Japan
Honshu

Hahajima-rettō
Bonin Islands
Icano Islands

Asia perspective view and cross section

Asia's extent

TOTAL LAND AREA	45 036 492 sq km / 17 388 686 sq miles
Most northerly point	Mys Arkticheskiy, Russian Federation
Most southerly point	Pamana, Indonesia
Most westerly point	Bozcaada, Turkey
Most easterly point	Mys Dezhneva, Russian Federation

Palau Islands

zira oberg
Puncak Jaya
5030
New Guinea

Kepulauan Aru
epulauan animbar
rafura Sea

CIFIC
EAN

The Yangtze, China, Asia's longest river, flowing into the East China Sea near Shanghai.

With approximately sixty per cent of the world's population, Asia is home to numerous cultures, people groups and lifestyles. Several of the world's earliest civilisations were established in Asia, including those of Sumeria, Babylonia and Assyria. Cultural and historical differences have led to a complex political pattern, and the continent has been, and continues to be, subject to numerous territorial and political conflicts – including the current disputes in the Middle East and in Jammu and Kashmir.

Separate regions within Asia can be defined by the cultural, economic and political systems they support. The major regions are: the arid, oil-rich, mainly Islamic southwest; southern Asia with its distinct cultures, isolated from the rest of Asia by major mountain ranges; the Indian- and Chinese-influenced monsoon region of southeast Asia; the mainly Chinese-influenced industrialized areas of eastern Asia; and Soviet Asia, made up of most of the former Soviet Union.

Timor island in southeast Asia, on which East Timor, the world's newest independent state, is located.

FACTS

Over 60% of the world's population live in Asia

Asia has 12 of the world's 20 largest cities

East Timor is Asia's newest independent country – founded in May 2002

The Korean peninsula was divided into North Korea and South Korea in 1948 approximately along the 38th parallel

Asia's countries

Largest country (area)	Russian Federation	17 075 400 sq km	6 592 812 sq miles
Smallest country (area)	Maldives	298 sq km	115 sq miles
Largest country (population)	China	1 279 557 000	
Smallest country (population)	Palau	20 000	
Most densely populated country	Singapore	6 554 per sq km	16 975 per sq mile
Least densely populated country	Mongolia	2 per sq km	5 per sq mile

MOST NORTHERLY CAPITAL
Astana

LARGEST COUNTRY (AREA)
Russian Federation

LEAST DENSELY POPULATED COUNTRY
Mongolia

LARGEST CAPITAL
Tōkyō

LARGEST COUNTRY (POPULATION)
China

HIGHEST CAPITAL
Thimphu

SMALLEST COUNTRY (POPULATION)
Palau

SMALLEST CAPITAL
Koror

MOST SOUTHERLY CAPITAL
Dili

SMALLEST COUNTRY (AREA)
Maldives

MOST DENSELY POPULATED COUNTRY
Singapore

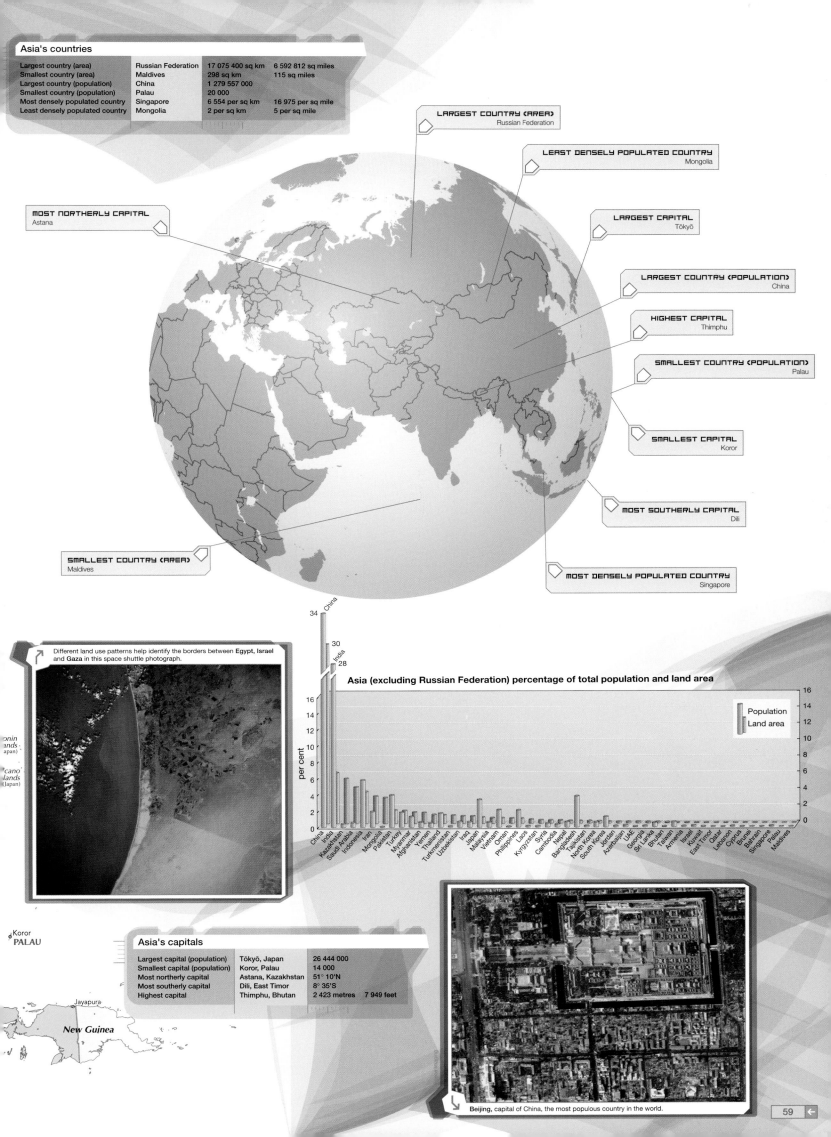

Different land use patterns help identify the borders between **Egypt**, **Israel** and **Gaza** in this space shuttle photograph.

Asia (excluding Russian Federation) percentage of total population and land area

per cent

Population
Land area

China, India, Kazakhstan, Saudi Arabia, Indonesia, Iran, Mongolia, Pakistan, Turkey, Myanmar, Afghanistan, Yemen, Thailand, Turkmenistan, Uzbekistan, Iraq, Japan, Malaysia, Vietnam, Oman, Philippines, Laos, Kyrgyzstan, Syria, Cambodia, Nepal, Bangladesh, Tajikistan, North Korea, South Korea, Jordan, Azerbaijan, UAE, Georgia, Sri Lanka, Bhutan, Taiwan, Armenia, Israel, Kuwait, Qatar, Lebanon, Cyprus, Brunei, Bahrain, Singapore, Palau, Maldives

Koror
PALAU

Jayapura

New Guinea

Asia's capitals

Largest capital (population)	Tōkyō, Japan	26 444 000	
Smallest capital (population)	Koror, Palau	14 000	
Most northerly capital	Astana, Kazakhstan	51° 10'N	
Most southerly capital	Dili, East Timor	8° 35'S	
Highest capital	Thimphu, Bhutan	2 423 metres	7 949 feet

Beijing, capital of China, the most populous country in the world.

asia
northern asia

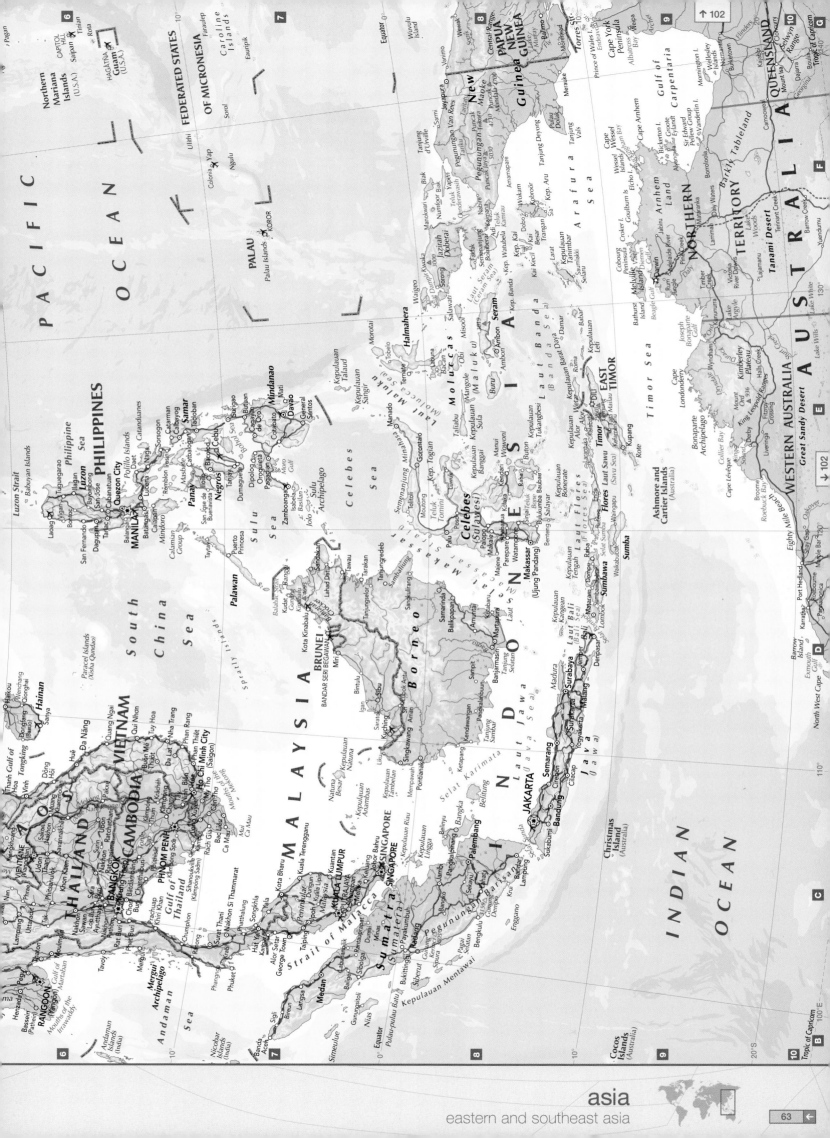

asia

eastern and southeast asia

Albers Conic Equal Area Projection

1:15 000 000

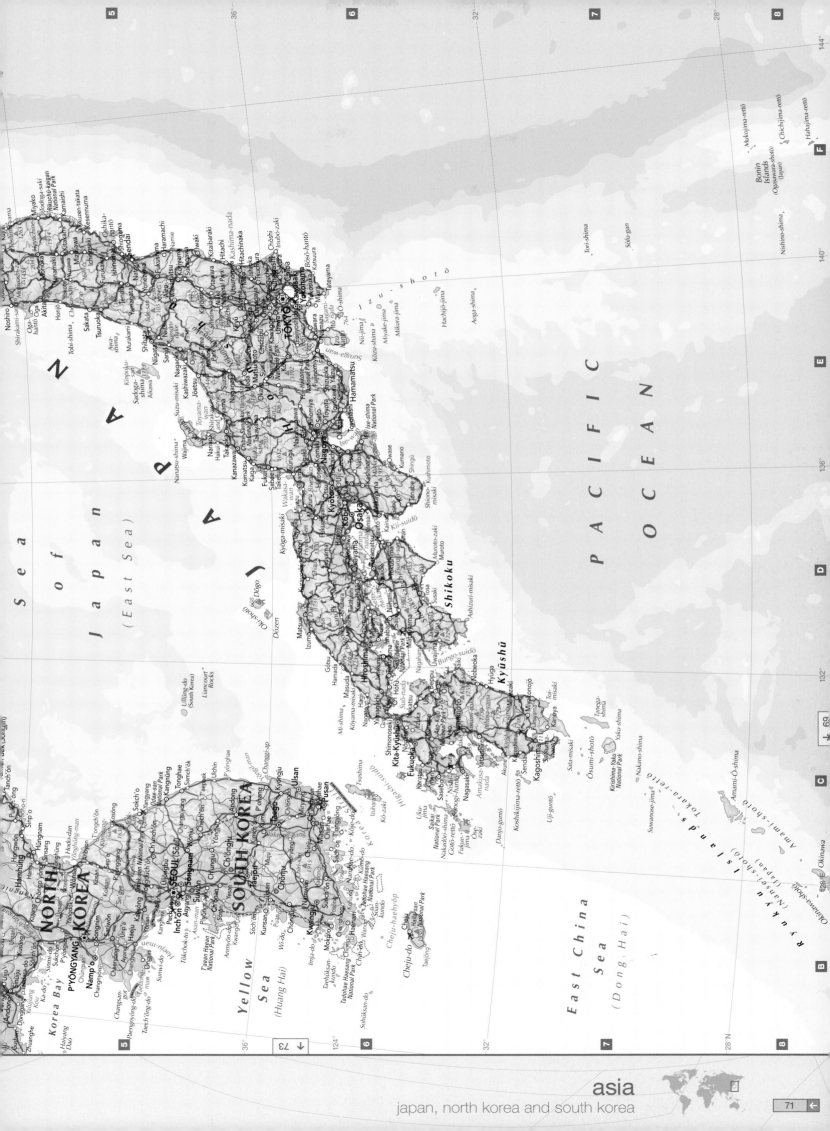

asia

japan, north korea and south korea

Yellow Sea
(Huang Hai)

SHANXI

SHANDONG

HENAN

JIANGSU

ANHUI

HUBEI

THREE GORGES
DAM PROJECT

Wuhan

East
China Sea
(Dong Hai)

ZHEJIANG

Shanghai

SHANGHAI

Hangzhou

Ningbo

Nanchang

HUNAN

JIANGXI

Changsha

Hengyang

FUJIAN

Fuzhou

Guilin

ZHUANGZU ZIZHIQU

GUANGDONG

Guangzhou

Dongguan

Shenzhen
(Bao'an)

Hong Kong

MACAU

HONG KONG

Taiwan Strait

T'AIPEI

TAIWAN

Kaohsiung

Tropic of Cancer

HAINAN

Hainan

Haikou

South
China Sea

GUANGDONG
Shenzhen

SHENZHEN SPECIAL
ECONOMIC ZONE
Deep Bay
(Shenzhen Wan)

Crooked Island
Mirs Bay
(Tai Pang Wan)
Double Island

HONG KONG

Tsuen
Wan

Kowloon Peninsula

Kowloon

Hong Kong

Hong Kong
Island

Lantau Island
(Tai Yue Shan)

South China
Sea

1:700 000

miles

km

Albers Conic Equal Area Projection

1:20 000 000

0		200		400		600 miles
0	200	400	600	800	1000 km	

← 51

← 93

↓ 94

Albers Equal Area Conic Projection

1:13 000 000

| 0 | 100 | 200 | 300 | | 400 | 500 miles |
| 0 | 100 | 200 | 300 | 400 | 500 | 600 | 700 | 800 km |

Administrative divisions in India
numbered on the map:

1. DADRA AND NAGAR HAVELI (C5)
2. DAMAN AND DIU (B5, C5)

Conic Equidistant Projection

1:7 000 000

asia
southern india and sri lanka

1:7 000 000

Conic Equidistant Projection

Administrative divisions in India
numbered on the map:

1. DADRA AND NAGAR HAVELI (B1)
2. DAMAN AND DIU (A1, B1)
3. PONDICHERRY (C4)

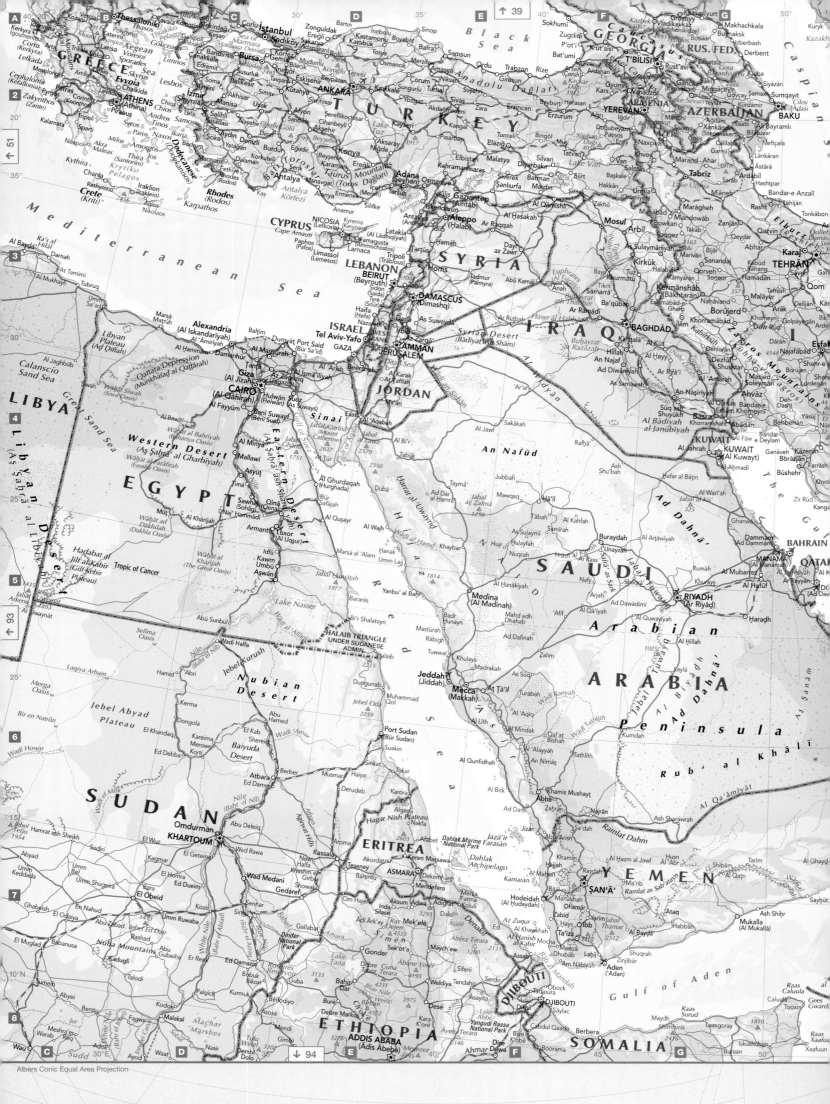

Albers Conic Equal Area Projection

1:13 000 000

Some of the world's greatest physical features are in Africa, the world's second largest continent. Variations in climate and elevation give rise to the continent's great variety of landscapes. The Sahara, the world's largest desert, extends across the whole continent from west to east, and covers an area of over nine million square kilometres. Other significant African deserts are the Kalahari and the Namib. In contrast, some of the world's greatest rivers flow in Africa, including the Nile, the world's longest, and the Congo.

The Great Rift Valley is perhaps Africa's most notable geological feature. It stretches for nearly 3 000 kilometres from Jordan, through the Red Sea and south to Mozambique, and contains many of Africa's largest lakes. Significant mountain ranges on the continent are the Atlas Mountains and the Ethiopian Highlands in the north, the Ruwenzori in east central Africa, and the Drakensberg in the far southeast.

The confluence of the Ubangi and Africa's second longest river, the **Congo**.

Africa's physical features

Highest mountain	Kilimanjaro, Tanzania	5 892 metres	19 331 feet
Longest river	Nile	6 695 km	4 160 miles
Largest lake	Lake Victoria	68 800 sq km	26 564 sq miles
Largest island	Madagascar	587 040 sq km	226 656 sq miles
Largest drainage basin	Congo, Congo/Dem. Rep. Congo	3 700 000 sq km	1 428 570 sq miles
Lowest point	Lake Assal, Djibouti	-152 metres	-499 feet

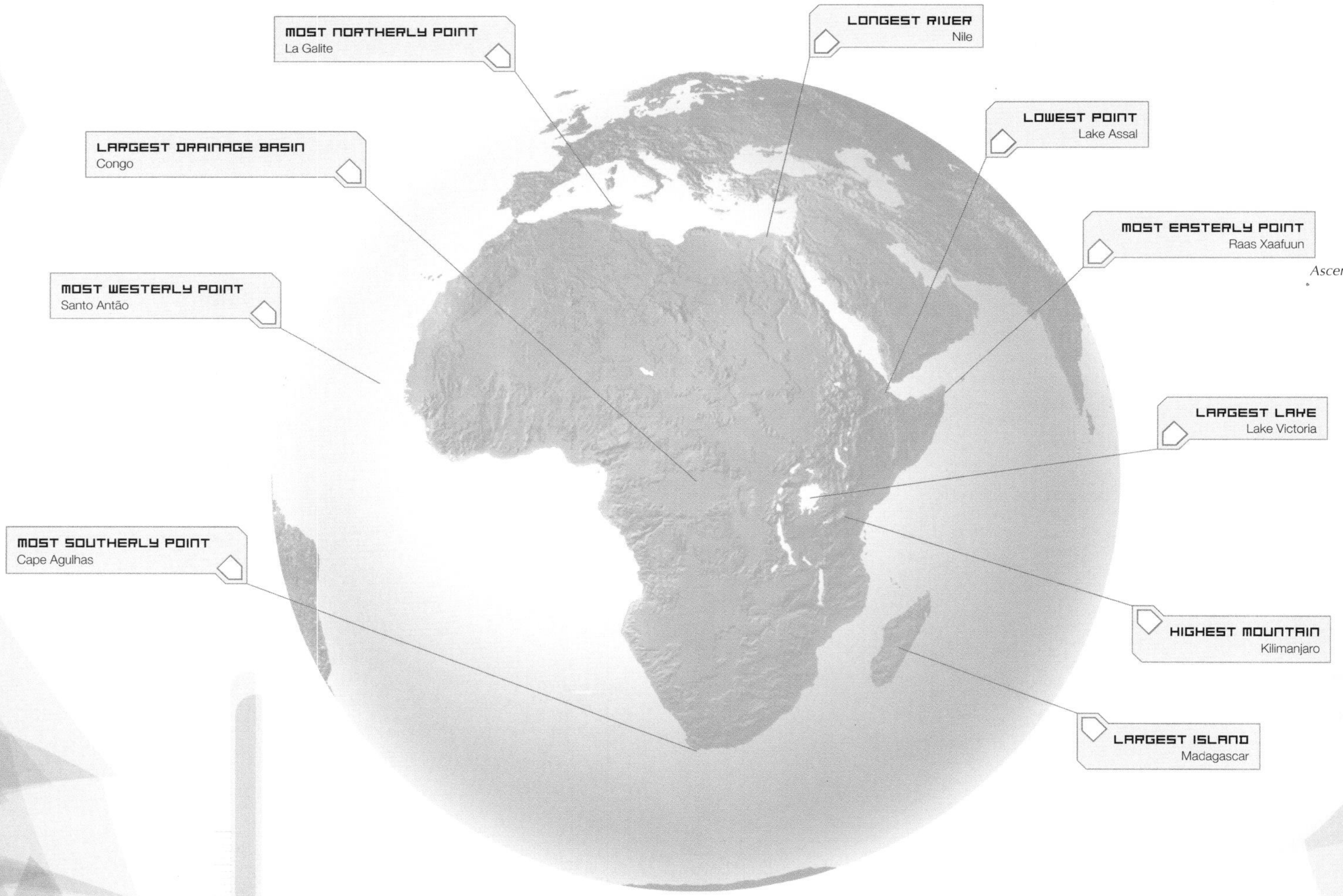

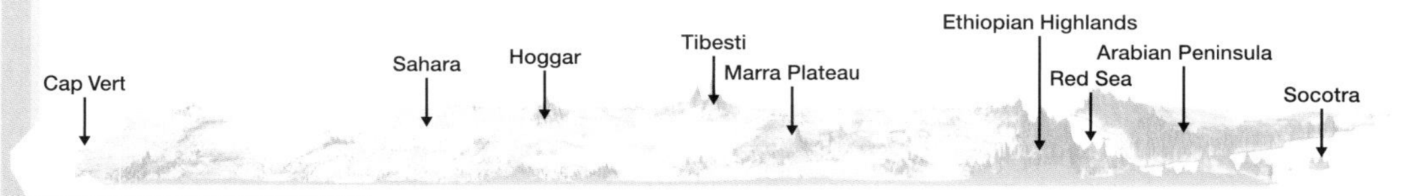

Madeira

Canary Islands
Tenerife
Gran
Canaria

Akchâr

Aou

Cape Verde Santo
Antão
Boa
Vista
Ilhas dos
Cabo Verde
Fogo Santiago   Cap Vert
Sénégal
Gambia
Fouta
Djallon

MOST NORTHERLY POINT
La Galite

LONGEST RIVER
Nile

LARGEST DRAINAGE BASIN
Congo

LOWEST POINT
Lake Assal

MOST WESTERLY POINT
Santo Antão

MOST EASTERLY POINT
Raas Xaafuun

Ascension

LARGEST LAKE
Lake Victoria

MOST SOUTHERLY POINT
Cape Agulhas

HIGHEST MOUNTAIN
Kilimanjaro

LARGEST ISLAND
Madagascar

Cap Vert Sahara Hoggar Tibesti Marra Plateau Ethiopian Highlands Red Sea Arabian Peninsula Socotra

Africa perspective view and cross section

Lake Victoria, Africa's largest lake, and Lake Albert lie within Africa's Great Rift Valley.

Kilimanjaro, Kenya/Tanzania, the highest point in Africa at 5 892m.

FACTS

The Atlas Mountains are part of the same geological system as the Alps

The floor of the Great Rift Valley varies from nearly 400m below sea level to over 1 800m

The Suez Canal, linking the Mediterranean Sea to the Red Sea is 163 kilometres long and opened in 1869

The Sahara desert covers 9 million square kilometres, approximately 30% of Africa's total land area

Lake Assal in Djibouti is the saltiest lake in the world

Africa's extent

TOTAL LAND AREA	30 343 578 sq km / 11 715 655 sq miles
Most northerly point	La Galite, Tunisia
Most southerly point	Cape Agulhas, South Africa
Most westerly point	Santo Antão, Cape Verde
Most easterly point	Raas Xaafuun, Somalia

africa countries

Africa is a complex continent, with over fifty independent countries and a long history of political change. It supports a great variety of ethnic groups, with the Sahara creating the major divide between Arab and Berber groups in the north and a diverse range of groups, including the Yoruba and Masai, in the south.

The current pattern of countries in Africa is a product of a long and complex history, including the colonial period, which saw European control of the vast majority of the continent from the fifteenth century until widespread moves to independence began in the 1950s. Despite its great wealth of natural resources, Africa is by far the world's poorest continent. Many of its countries are heavily dependent upon foreign aid and many are also subject to serious political instability.

Cape Verde, North Atlantic Ocean, a small group of islands lying 500 kilometres off the coast of west Africa.

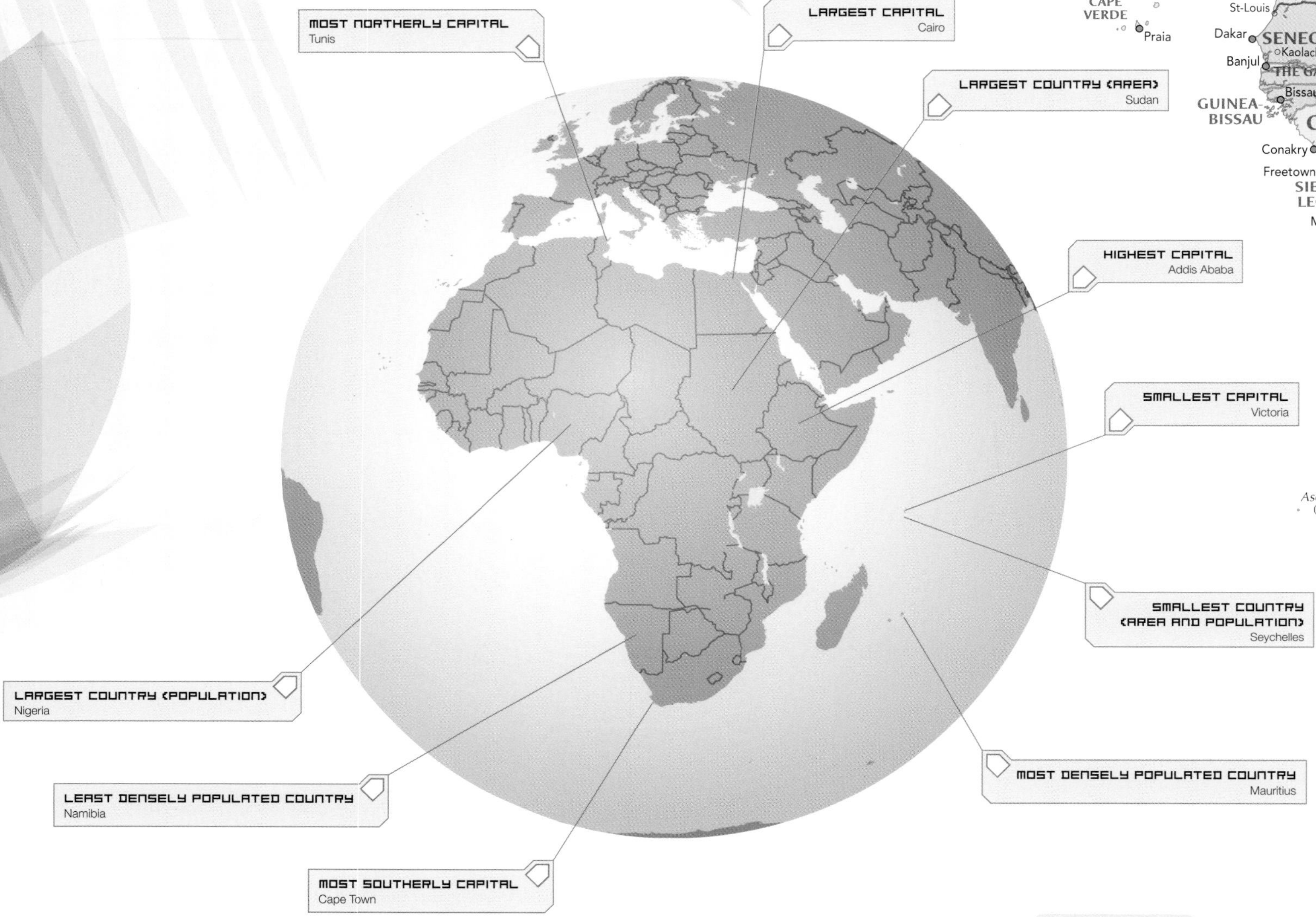

Madeira (Portugal)

Canary Island (Spain)

Laâyoune

WESTERN SAHARA

Nouâdhibou

MAURITANI
Nouakchott

St-Louis
Dakar
Kaolack
Banjul
THE GAMBIA
Bissau
GUINEA-BISSAU
GUINEA
Conakry
Ka

Freetown
SIERRA LEONE
Monrovia
LIBER

CAPE VERDE
Praia

MOST NORTHERLY CAPITAL
Tunis

LARGEST CAPITAL
Cairo

LARGEST COUNTRY (AREA)
Sudan

HIGHEST CAPITAL
Addis Ababa

SMALLEST CAPITAL
Victoria

Ascension (U.K.)

SMALLEST COUNTRY (AREA AND POPULATION)
Seychelles

LARGEST COUNTRY (POPULATION)
Nigeria

MOST DENSELY POPULATED COUNTRY
Mauritius

LEAST DENSELY POPULATED COUNTRY
Namibia

MOST SOUTHERLY CAPITAL
Cape Town

Africa percentage of total population and land area

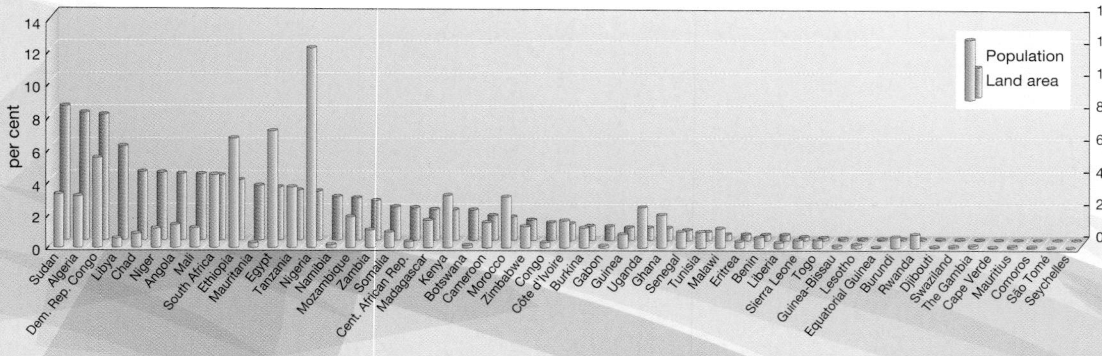

per cent

Population
Land area

Sudan, Algeria, Dem. Rep. Congo, Libya, Chad, Niger, Angola, Mali, South Africa, Ethiopia, Mauritania, Egypt, Tanzania, Nigeria, Namibia, Mozambique, Zambia, Somalia, Cent. African Rep., Madagascar, Kenya, Botswana, Cameroon, Morocco, Zimbabwe, Congo, Côte d'Ivoire, Burkina, Gabon, Guinea, Ghana, Uganda, Senegal, Tunisia, Malawi, Eritrea, Benin, Liberia, Sierra Leone, Togo, Guinea-Bissau, Lesotho, Equatorial Guinea, Burundi, Rwanda, Djibouti, Swaziland, The Gambia, Cape Verde, Mauritius, Comoros, São Tomé, Seychelles

FACTS

Africa has over 1 000 linguistic and cultural groups

Only Liberia and Ethiopia have remained free from colonial rule throughout their history

Over 30% of the world's minerals, and over 50% of the world's diamonds, come from Africa

9 of the 10 poorest countries in the world are in Africa

Cairo, capital of Egypt and the largest city in Africa with 9 462 000 inhabitants.

Cape Town, legislative capital of the Republic of South Africa and the most southerly African capital city.

Africa's countries

Largest country (area)	Sudan	2 505 813 sq km	967 494 sq miles
Smallest country (area)	Seychelles	455 sq km	176 sq miles
Largest country (population)	Nigeria	120 047 000	
Smallest country (population)	Seychelles	83 000	
Most densely populated country	Mauritius	578 per sq km	1 497 per sq mile
Least densely populated country	Namibia	2 per sq km	5 per sq mile

Africa's capitals

Largest capital (population)	Cairo, Egypt	9 462 000	
Smallest capital (population)	Victoria, Seychelles	30 000	
Most northerly capital	Tunis, Tunisia	36° 46'N	
Most southerly capital	Cape Town, Republic of South Africa	33° 57'S	
Highest capital	Addis Ababa, Ethiopia	2 408 metres	7 900 feet

1

B   Ouguta   Whitehandvei   C   Onjati 18   D   Xanagas Ishootsha   E   Okwa   22°   F   24°
Ebony   Okahandie   Gross Batien   2050   Omitara   Buitepos   Charles Hill   Mamuno   Okwa   Kumchuru

ERONGO   Okahandja   KHOMAS   Gobabis   OMAHEKE   Kule   GHANZI   BOTSWANA   Central Kalahari Game Reserve
Hentiesbaai   Arandis   Usakos   16°   WINDHOEK   Witvlei   Ncojane   Takatshwaane   Moratswa

National   Rossing   Swakop   Aris   2485   Doreenville   Gross Ums   Kgomofatshe   Palamakoloi   2
West Coast   Swakopmund   Khomas Highland   Bergland   Dordabis   Pan   Kang   Khutse
Tourist Recreation   Wortel   Leonardville   Ukwi   Ukwi Pan   One   Game Reserve
Area   Walvis Bay   Rehoboth   Aminuis   Hukuntsi   Tsetseng   Moreswe   Salajwe

Tropic of Capricorn   Heide   Derm   Kalahari   Lokgwabe   Tshane   Pan   KWENENO

Namib-   Nauchas   Solitaire   Tsumis Park   Hoachanas   Lidfontein   Dutlwe   Takatokwane
Nauklift   Remhoogte Pass   Büllsport   Narib   Stampriet   KGALAGADI   Kokong   Kgoro Pan   Mabutsane
Game   1992   Kuis   Hardap   Saldbrunn   Aranos   Dimpho   Khokhowe Pan   Sekoma   Jwaneng
Park   HARDAP   Nananib   Hardap   Mariental   Pan   Mpaathutlwa   Makopong   Werda   SOUTHER

24°   HARDAP   Plateau   Ebenerde   Desert   Pan   Bosoboggllo   Moselebe
Maltahöhe   Gibeon   Gochas   Gemsbok   Pan
NAMIBIA   Bossiesvlei   Witbooisvlei   National Park

Fischersbrunn   Awasib   Twee Rivier   Auob   Kalahari   Terra Firma   3
Meobbaai   Mountains   Brukkaros   Koës   Gemsbok   Pomfret   Senlac   Tosca   Molopo
Schwarzrand   National   Omaweneno   NORT
14°   Mountains   Park   Tshabong   Morokweng

Dolphin Head   Tiraz   Hammeringhausen   Berseba   Gemsbokplem   Montrose
Mountains   GREAT NAMAQUALAND   Wasser   Kolonkwang   Severn   Vryburg   Stel
26°   Hottentots Bay   2040   Mooifontein   Rietfontein   Khuis   Moshaweng   Huhudhi
Hottentots Point   Keetmanshoop   Hakseen   Bokspits   Kopnieskraal   Lowane   Tsineng

Diaz Point   Lüderitz   Schakalskuppe   Goageb   Gobas   Aroab   Pan   Kuruman   Kathu
Kolmanskop   Grasplatz   Seeheim   Naute Dam   Kopnieskraal   Van Zylsrus   Hotazel   Kuruman   Pudimoe   Taung
Elizabeth Point   Aus   Sandverhaar   Gawachab   Molopo   Groot-Aar   Olifantshoek   Gakarosa   GRIQUALAND WEST   4
Elizabeth Bay   Huib-Hoch   KARAS   2202   Pan   Eenzamheid   1855   Danielskuil   Tlhakalatlou   Ikhutse
Possession   Plateau   Little   Groot Karas Berg   Pan   Ditloung   Lohatla   Sishen   Postmasburg   Lime Acres   Barkly
Island   Pomona   Konkiep   Karas Berg   Boichoko   Campbell   Kimberley   West

Cape Dernberg   1556   Klein   Kums   Severn   Koegrabie   Griquatown   Douglas   Bongani   Ritchie
Chamais Bay   Rosh Pinah   Huns Mountains   Karas   Langklip   Upington   Grootdrink   Koffiefon
Grünau   Ai-Ais   Kanus   Ariamsvlei   Augrabies Falls   Pabalelo   Grblershoop   VaalbosRED
Ai-Ais Hot Springs   Karasburg   Kokerboom   National Park   Keimoes   Kleinbegin   National   Galeshewe   5
28°   Richtersveld   and Fish River   Warmbad   Augrabies   Kakamas   Park
National Park   Canyon Park   Onseepkans   Augrabies   Koes   Koedoesrand   Hopetown
Oranjemund   Orange   Pella   Pofadder   Kenhardt   Putsonderwater   Strydenburg   Luckhoff
Alexander Bay   Eksteenfontein   Koegabie   Orange
Bay   Lekkersing   Marydale   Hopetown
Wreck Point   Aggeneys   Lubbeskolk   Geel   De Aar

Port Nolloth   Steinkopf   Vloer   Kakop Hills   Priesk   E Thembini   Copperton   Omdraaisvlei   Petrusville
McDougall's Bay   NAMAQUALAND   Concordia   NORTHERN   Vanderkl
6   Nababeep   Goegap Nature Reserve   Groot Vloer   De Naawte   Vosburg   Britstown   Vandkl
Kleinsee   Buffels   Springbok   CAPE   Vanwyksvlei   Hanov
Komaggas   1550   Verneuk   Copperton   Philipst
30°   Namaqua   Kamieskroon   Pan   OF
National Park   Brandvlei   SOUTH AFR
Hondeklipbaai   Wallekraal   Kamiesberge   Flaminksvlei   Kareeberge   Carnarvon   Victoria West   Richmond   Hanover
Garies   Loeriesfontein   Sak   Williston   Masinyusane

ATLANTIC   Hardeveld   Nieuwoudtville   Calvinia   Great Karoo   Ongers   Nqupo
Bitterfontein   Rivier   Fraserburg   Murraysburg   Kwanonz
Nuwerus   Kootjieskolk   Sterling   Toorberg   1200
Koekenaap   Great Karoo   Nuweveldberge   1966   Dubergpas   Graaf-Reinet
OCEAN   Lutzville   Doring   Sutherland   Karoo   Beaufort West   Nature Reserve   2280
6   Klawer   Tankwa-Karoo   Roggeveld   National Park   Aberdeen
Vredendal   Vanrhynsdorp   National Park   Komsberg   Merweville   Jansen
32°   Lambert's Bay   Klawer   Wuppertal   Roggeveldberge   Beervlei   Willowmore
Baboon Point   Sandveld   Hantam   Nuweveldberge   Dam   Steytlerville   Cocksc
Elandsvlei   Dwyka   Prince Albert Road   De Rust   Baviaanskloofberge
Cape St Martin   St Helena   Citrusdal   Koue   Laingsburg   WESTERN CAPE   Prince Albert
Cape Columbine   Bay   Oliphants   Kouebokkeveld   Groot Swartberge   2325   Cango Caves   Uniondale
Vredenburg   Veldrif   Groot   2250   Touwsrivier   2325   Little   Oudtshoorn   Dysselsdorp   Tsitsikamma Forest
Saldanha   Hopefield   Porterville   Prince Alfred   Matroosberg   Ceres   Zoar   Karoo   Oudtshoorn   and Coastal
Saldanha Bay   West Coast   Moorreesburg   Hamlet   Zweletemba   Montagu   Olifants   George   National Park
National Park   Malmesbury   Tulbagh   Worcester   Swartbergpas   Uniondale   Knysna   Kruisfon
7   Atlantis   Wolseley   Robertson   Warmwaterberg   Joubertina   Plettenberg Bay
Durbanville   Wellington   Paarl   McGregor   Barrydale   Langeberg   Groot Brak   Cape Seal
Bellville   Stellenbosch   Somerset West   Grabouw   Swellendam   Riversdale   Stilbaai   Mossel Bay
CAPE TOWN   Khayelitsha   Strand   Caledon   Bontebok   Riversdale   Mossel Bay   Kanonpunt
Cape of Good Hope   Somerset   Protem   National Park   Port Beaufort   St Sebastian
Nature Reserve   False   Hawston   Swellendam   Bay
Cape of Good Hope   Bay   Hermanus   De Hoop
Walker Bay   Nature Reserve   Waenhuiskrans
8   Danger Point   Bredasdorp
Quoin Point   Struis Bay   Cape Agulhas

A   14°E   B   16°   C   18°   D   20°   E   22°   F   24°

Lambert Azimuthal Equal Area Projection

1:5 000 000   0 100 200 300 miles   0 100 200 300 400 500 km

Oceania comprises Australia, New Zealand, New Guinea and the islands of the Pacific Ocean. It is the smallest of the world's continents by land area. Its dominating feature is Australia, which is mainly flat and very dry. Australia's western half consists of a low plateau, broken in places by higher mountain ranges, which has very few permanent rivers or lakes. The narrow, fertile coastal plain of the east coast is separated from the interior by the Great Dividing Range, which includes the highest mountain in Australia.

The numerous Pacific islands of Oceania are generally either volcanic in origin or consist of coral. They can be divided into three main regions of Micronesia, north of the equator between Palau and the Gilbert islands; Melanesia, stretching from mountainous New Guinea to Fiji; and Polynesia, covering a vast area of the eastern and central Pacific Ocean.

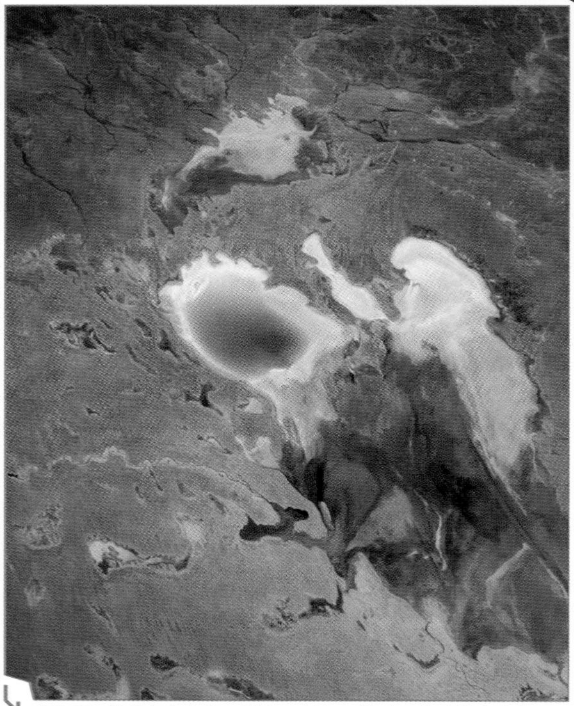

Lake Eyre, South Australia, Oceania's largest lake and the lowest point in Australia.

New Caledonia (bottom) and **Vanuatu** (right) in the southern Pacific Ocean.

ASIA

Northern Mariana Islands
Pagan
Saipan
Tinian
Rota
Guam

Wake Island
Taongi

Marshall Islands

M i c r o n e s i a

Enewetak
Bikini
Rongelap
Ratak Chain
Ralik Chain
Wotje
Kwajalein
Ailinglapalap
Majuro

Yap
Gaferut
Pikelot
Hall Islands
Chuuk
Pohnpei

C a r o l i n e   I s l a n d s

Mortlock Islands
Kosrae

Butaritari
Abaiang
Tarawa
Gilbert Islands
Nonouti
Beru
Nikunau
Tabiteuea
Onotoa
Arorae
Kingsmill Group

Kapingamarangi

Nauru

Banaba

Nanumea
Nanumanga
Nui
Nukufetau
Funafuti
Nukulaelae
Niutao
Tuvalu
Vaite

Admiralty Islands
New Hanover
New Ireland
Bismarck Arch.
Bismarck
Tauu Islands
Nukumanu Islands

M e l a n e s i a

Puncak Jaya 5030
New Guinea
Mount Wilhelm 4509
Bismarck Sea
New Britain
Bougainville I.
Choiseul
Santa Isabel
Solomon Islands
Nukumanu Islands

Niulakita

Mount Victoria 4073
Solomon Sea
New Georgia Islands
Malaita
Santa Cruz Islands

Owen Stanley Ra.
D'Entrecasteaux Islands
Guadalcanal

Rotuma
Îles de H

Arafura Sea
Gulf of Papua
Torres Strait
Cape York
Louisiade Archipelago
Rennell
San Cristobal

Banks Islands

Vanua Levu
Fiji

Melville Island
Bathurst Island
Cape Arnhem
Cape York Peninsula
Espiritu Santo
Malakula
Ambrym
Viti Levu
Kadavu
Ko
Gа

Timor Sea
Cape Londonderry
Arnhem Land
Gulf of Carpentaria
Mitchell
Wellesley Islands
Great Barrier Reef
Coral Sea
Éaté
Îles Loyauté
Erromango
Tanna
Anatom
Ono-i-L

Cape Léveque
Kimberley Plateau
Lake Argyle
Barkly Tableland
Gregory Range
Flinders
Nouvelle Calédonie
Île des Pins
Hunter Island

INDIAN OCEAN

Eighty Mile Beach
Great Sandy Desert
Barrow Island
North West Cape
Hamersley Range
Ashburton
Gibson Desert
Macdonnell Ranges
Uluru 867
Musgrave Ranges
Simpson Desert
Lake Eyre

A u s t r a l i a

Great Dividing Range

Norfolk Island
Raoul Is
Kermade
Island

Cape Inscription
Great Victoria Desert
Nullarbor Plain
Lake Torrens
Darling
Lachlan
Murray
Mount Kosciuszko 2229

Lord Howe Island

North Cape
Great Barrie Island

Great Australian Bight
Kangaroo Island

New Zealand
North Island

T a s m a n   S e a

Aoraki
Southern Alps
South Island

Cape Leeuwin
King Island
Bass Strait
Flinders Island
Tasmania
South East Cape

Stewart Island
Snares Islands
Bounty Islands
Antipodes Islands
Auckland Islands

Campbell Island

Macquarie Island

S O

Oceania's extent

TOTAL LAND AREA (includes New Guinea and Pacific Island nations)	8 844 516 sq km / 3 414 868 sq miles
Most northerly point	Eastern Island, North Pacific Ocean
Most southerly point	Macquarie Island, South Pacific Ocean
Most westerly point	Cape Inscription, Australia
Most easterly point	Isla Sala y Gómez, South Pacific Ocean

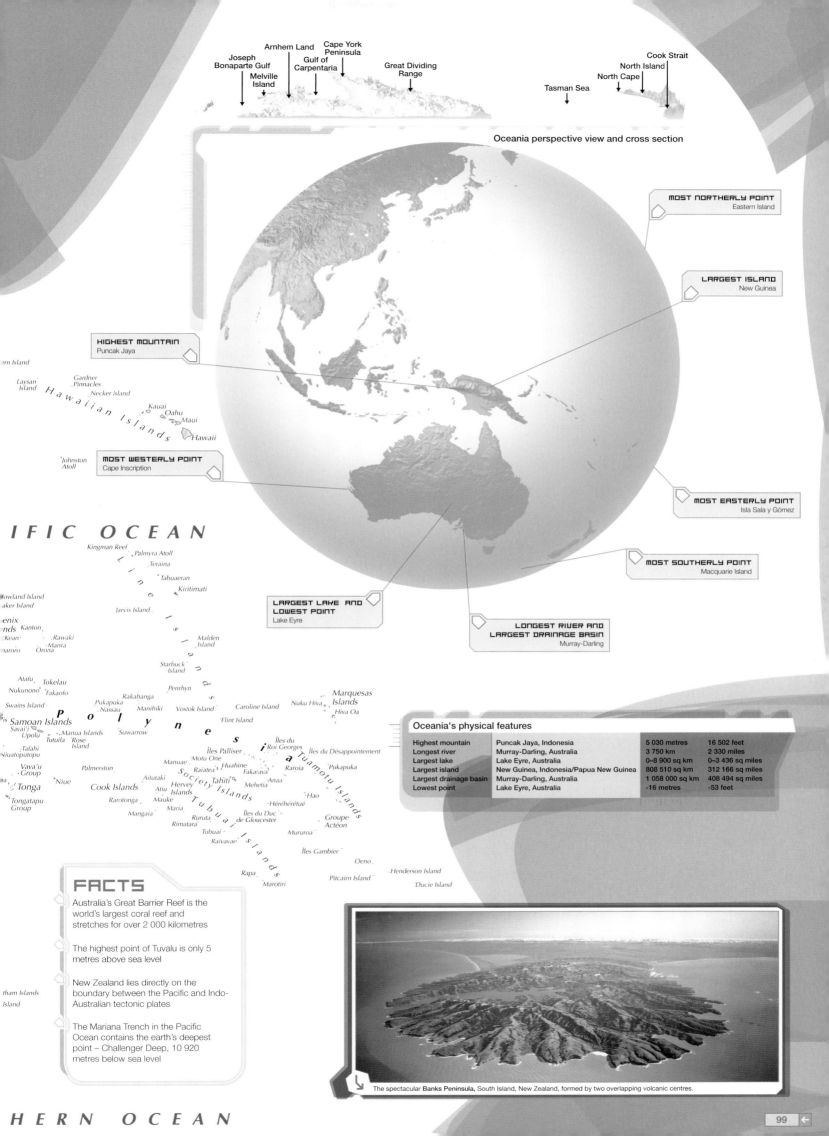

Oceania perspective view and cross section

Joseph Bonaparte Gulf
Melville Island
Arnhem Land
Gulf of Carpentaria
Cape York Peninsula
Great Dividing Range

Tasman Sea
North Cape
North Island
Cook Strait

MOST NORTHERLY POINT
Eastern Island

LARGEST ISLAND
New Guinea

HIGHEST MOUNTAIN
Puncak Jaya

MOST WESTERLY POINT
Cape Inscription

MOST EASTERLY POINT
Isla Sala y Gómez

MOST SOUTHERLY POINT
Macquarie Island

LARGEST LAKE AND LOWEST POINT
Lake Eyre

LONGEST RIVER AND LARGEST DRAINAGE BASIN
Murray-Darling

rn Island

Laysan Island

Gardner Pinnacles

Necker Island

Kauai
Oahu
Maui
Hawaii

Hawaiian Islands

Johnston Atoll

IFIC OCEAN

Kingman Reef
Palmyra Atoll
Teraina
Tabuaeran
Kiritimati

Line Islands

owland Island
aker Island

Jarvis Island

Malden Island

enix
ckean
naroro
Kanton
Rawaki
Manra
Orona

Starbuck Island

Atafu
Tokelau
Nukunono
Fakaofo

Swains Island

Penrhyn

Rakahanga
Pukapuka
Nassau
Manihiki

Vostok Island

Caroline Island

Nuku Hiva

Marquesas Islands

Hiva Oa

Flint Island

is
Samoan Islands
Savai'i
Upolu
Manua Islands
Tutuila
Rose Island

Polynesia

Suwarrow

Îles du Roi Georges
Îles du Désappointement

Motu One

Manuae
Palmerston

Vava'u Group
Niuatoputapu
Tafahi

Huahine
Raiatea
Tahiti
Mehetia

Fakarava
Anaa

Raroia
Pukapuka

a
Tonga
Niue
Cook Islands

Aitutaki
Atiu
Mauke

Hervey Islands
Society Islands

Hao

Hérehérétué

Tongatapu Group

Rarotonga
Mangaia
Maria

Îles du Duc de Gloucester

Ruruta
Rimatara
Tubuai

Tubuai Islands

Groupe Actéon

Mururoa

Raivavae

Îles Gambier

Oeno

Rapa
Marotiri

Pitcairn Island

Henderson Island

Ducie Island

Oceania's physical features

Highest mountain	Puncak Jaya, Indonesia	5 030 metres	16 502 feet
Longest river	Murray-Darling, Australia	3 750 km	2 330 miles
Largest lake	Lake Eyre, Australia	0–8 900 sq km	0–3 436 sq miles
Largest island	New Guinea, Indonesia/Papua New Guinea	808 510 sq km	312 166 sq miles
Largest drainage basin	Murray-Darling, Australia	1 058 000 sq km	408 494 sq miles
Lowest point	Lake Eyre, Australia	-16 metres	-53 feet

FACTS

◊ Australia's Great Barrier Reef is the world's largest coral reef and stretches for over 2 000 kilometres

◊ The highest point of Tuvalu is only 5 metres above sea level

◊ New Zealand lies directly on the boundary between the Pacific and Indo-Australian tectonic plates

◊ The Mariana Trench in the Pacific Ocean contains the earth's deepest point – Challenger Deep, 10 920 metres below sea level

tham Islands
Island

The spectacular **Banks Peninsula,** South Island, New Zealand, formed by two overlapping volcanic centres.

oceania countries

Stretching across almost the whole width of the Pacific Ocean, Oceania has a great variety of cultures and an enormously diverse range of countries and territories. Australia, by far the largest and most industrialized country in the continent, contrasts with the numerous tiny Pacific island nations which have smaller, and more fragile economies based largely on agriculture, fishing and the exploitation of natural resources.

The division of the Pacific island groups into the main regions of Micronesia, Melanesia and Polynesia – often referred to as the South Sea islands – broadly reflects the ethnological differences across the continent. There is a long history of colonial influence in the region, which still contains dependent territories belonging to Australia, France, New Zealand, the UK and the USA.

Wellington, capital of New Zealand and the most southerly national capital in the world.

Tasmania, a small Australian island state, separated from the mainland by the Bass Strait.

FACTS

Over 91% of Australia's population live in urban areas

The Maori name for New Zealand is Aotearoa, meaning 'land of the long white cloud'

Auckland, New Zealand, has the largest Polynesian population of any city in Oceania

Over 800 different languages are spoken in Papua New Guinea

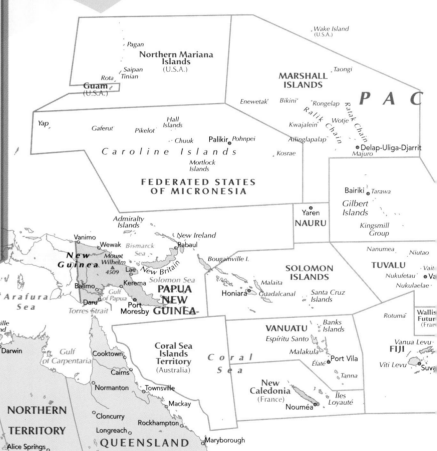

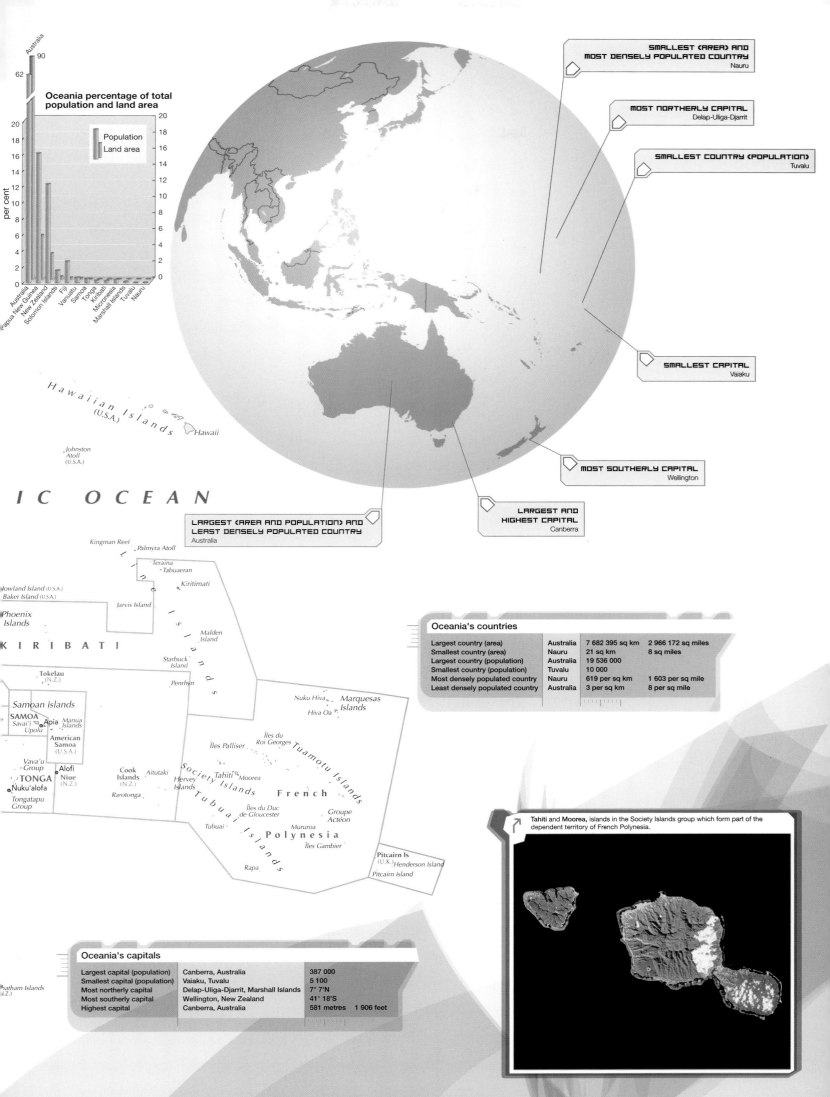

Oceania percentage of total population and land area

per cent

Population
Land area

Australia 90, 62

Australia, Papua New Guinea, New Zealand, Solomon Islands, Fiji, Vanuatu, Samoa, Tonga, Kiribati, Micronesia, Marshall Islands, Tuvalu, Nauru

SMALLEST (AREA) AND MOST DENSELY POPULATED COUNTRY
Nauru

MOST NORTHERLY CAPITAL
Delap-Uliga-Djarrit

SMALLEST COUNTRY (POPULATION)
Tuvalu

SMALLEST CAPITAL
Vaiaku

MOST SOUTHERLY CAPITAL
Wellington

LARGEST AND HIGHEST CAPITAL
Canberra

LARGEST (AREA AND POPULATION) AND LEAST DENSELY POPULATED COUNTRY
Australia

Hawaiian Islands (U.S.A.)
Hawaii

Johnston Atoll (U.S.A.)

IC OCEAN

Kingman Reef
Palmyra Atoll
Teraina
Tabuaeran
Kiritimati
Howland Island (U.S.A.)
Baker Island (U.S.A.)
Jarvis Island
Phoenix Islands
Line Islands
Malden Island
K I R I B A T I
Starbuck Island
Tokelau (N.Z.)
Penrhyn
Nuku Hiva
Hiva Oa
Marquesas Islands
Samoan Islands
SAMOA
Savai'i
Upolu
Apia
Manua Islands
American Samoa (U.S.A.)
Îles Palliser
Îles du Roi Georges
Tuamotu Islands
Vava'u Group
Alofi
Niue (N.Z.)
TONGA
Nuku'alofa
Tongatapu Group
Cook Islands (N.Z.)
Aitutaki
Rarotonga
Society Islands
Tahiti
Moorea
Hervey Islands
Îles du Duc de Gloucester
Groupe Actéon
French
Tubuai
Tubuai Islands
Mururoa
Polynesia
Îles Gambier
Pitcairn Is (U.K.)
Henderson Island
Rapa
Pitcairn Island

Chatham Islands (N.Z.)

Oceania's countries

Largest country (area)	Australia	7 682 395 sq km	2 966 172 sq miles
Smallest country (area)	Nauru	21 sq km	8 sq miles
Largest country (population)	Australia	19 536 000	
Smallest country (population)	Tuvalu	10 000	
Most densely populated country	Nauru	619 per sq km	1 603 per sq mile
Least densely populated country	Australia	3 per sq km	8 per sq mile

Oceania's capitals

Largest capital (population)	Canberra, Australia	387 000	
Smallest capital (population)	Vaiaku, Tuvalu	5 100	
Most northerly capital	Delap-Uliga-Djarrit, Marshall Islands	7° 7'N	
Most southerly capital	Wellington, New Zealand	41° 18'S	
Highest capital	Canberra, Australia	581 metres	1 906 feet

Tahiti and **Moorea**, islands in the Society Islands group which form part of the dependent territory of French Polynesia.

OCEAN

INDONESIA

Celebes Sea
Borneo
Equator
Celebes (Sulawesi)
Makassar (Ujung Pandang)

NEW GUINEA
PAPUA
New Guinea
PORT MORESBY
Torres Strait

EAST TIMOR

INDIAN OCEAN

Arafura Sea

AUSTRALIA

WESTERN AUSTRALIA
Great Sandy Desert
Gibson Desert
Great Victoria Desert
Perth

NORTHERN TERRITORY
Tanami Desert
Darwin
Arnhem Land
Kimberley Plateau
Barkly Tableland

QUEENSLAND
Simpson Desert
Cape York Peninsula
Brisbane

SOUTH AUSTRALIA
Nullarbor Plain
Adelaide

NEW SOUTH WALES
Sydney
CANBERRA
A.C.T.

VICTORIA
Melbourne

Great Australian Bight

TASMANIA
Hobart

Gulf of Carpentaria
Coral Sea Islands Territory
Great Barrier Reef

Lambert Azimuthal Equal Area Projection
1:20 000 000

miles
0 200 400 600

km
0 200 400 600 800 1000

NAURU

YAREN
Nauru

Banaba
(Ocean Island)

Aranuka

Howland Island (U.S.A.)
Baker Island (U.S.A.)

Nonouti
Tabiteuea
Beru
Nikunau
Onotoa
Kingsmill Group
Tamana
Arorae

K I R I B A T I

Phoenix
Islands
Kanton
McKean
Rawaki
Nikumaroro
Orona
Manra

Tauu
Islands
Nukumanu
Islands

Ontong
Java Atoll
Choiseul
Roncador
Reef
Santa
Isabel
Buala

**SOLOMON
ISLANDS**

w. Georgia Sound
N. Georgia
New
Georgia
Islands
Florida
Islands
Malu'u
Maramasike
Malaita
Arawu
Ulawa Island

Guadalcanal
Kirakira
Santa
Ana
San Cristobal
(Makira)

Rennell

Nanumea
Nanumanga
Niutao

Nui

Nukufetau

TUVALU
Funafuti
VAIAKU

Nukulaelae

Niulakita

Nanumea

Vaitupu

Tokelau
(New Zealand)
Atafu
Nukunono
Fakaofo

Swains Island

Pukapuka
(Danger Islands)
Nassau

al Sea

Indispensable
Reefs

Duff
Islands
Nupani
Swallow Islands
Ndeni
Santa Cruz Islands
(Solomon Islands)
Utupua
Vanikoro
Islands
Tikopia
Cherry
Island

Torres Islands

Uréparapara

Rotuma
(Fiji)

Wallis and
Futuna Islands
(France)
Îles
Wallis
MATA'UTU

SAMOA

American
Samoa
(U.S.A.)
Savai'i
Upolu
APIA
Manua
Islands
Tutuila
FAGATOGO
Rose
Island

Suwarrow

Mitre
Island

Banks
Islands
Vanua Lava
Santa María Island

Îles de Hoorn

Espíritu Santo
Mount
Tabwémasana
1879
Aoba
Maéwo
Pentecost Island
Norsup
Ambrym
Malakula
Epi
Émaé
Shepherd
Islands

VANUATU

Récifs
d'Entrecasteaux
PORT VILA
Éfaté

Grand Passage
Grand Récif
de Cook
Îles Chesterfield
(France)
Îles Belep
Récif des
Français
Koumac

Erromango
Tanna
Futuna
361
Anatom
(Aneityum)

Nouvelle Calédonie
Ouvéa
Lifou
Îles Loyauté
(France)
Tadin
Maré

New Caledonia
(France)
Bourail
Yaté
Île des Pins

NOUMÉA

Grand Récif
du Sud

Hunter
Island
100

Great Sea Reef
Vanua Levu
Yasawa
Group
Labasa
(Lambasa)
Bligh
Water
Tomanivi
Victoria
Koro
Lautoka
Taveuni
Northern
Lau Group

FIJI
Viti Levu
SUVA
Koro
Sea
Gau
Lakeba
Kadavu Passage
Moala
Southern
Lau Group
Kadavu
Matuku
Kabara
Vatoa

Ceva-i-Ra
(Conway Reef)

Doi
Ono-i-Lau

Vava'u
Group

ALOFI
Niue
(New Zealand)

Palmerston

Niuafo'ou
210
Tafahi
Niuatoputapu

Cook Islands
(New Zealand)

Tofua
500
Ha'apai
Group

TONGA
NUKU'ALOFA
Tongatapu
Group

Ata

Minerva Reefs

Tropic of Capricorn

P A C I F I C   O C E A N

Norfolk Island
(Australia)
KINGSTON

Lord Howe Island
(Australia)

Raoul Island

Kermadec Islands
(New Zealand)
Macauley Island
Curtis Island

Havre Rock
L'Espérance Rock

an Sea

an Sea

Three Kings
Islands
North
Cape
Cape
Maria van Diemen
Awanui

Whangarei
North Island
Great Barrier Island

Takapuna
Auckland
Manukau

Hamilton
Tauranga
Tokoroa
East Cape
Te Kuiti
Taupo
Whakatane
New
Plymouth
Mount
Gisborne
Mount Taranaki
(Mount Egmont)
Mount
Ruapehu
Wairoa
Mahia Peninsula

**NEW
ZEALAND**

Hawera
Wanganui
Napier
Hastings
Cape Farewell
Palmerston North

Cape Farewell
Tasman
Bay
Levin
Masterton
Nelson
Picton
Lower Hutt
WELLINGTON

**South
Island**
Westport
Blenheim

Hokitika
Greymouth

Aoraki
(Mount Cook)

Southern Alps
Christchurch
Banks Peninsula

Mount
Aspiring
Ashburton
Timaru

Mount
Cook
3830
Queenstown
Oamaru

Cape Providence
Mount
Christina
2502

Gore

Invercargill
Dunedin

Stewart Island
Foveaux Strait
South West Cape

Snares
Islands

Chatham Islands
(New Zealand)

Chatham Island

Waitangi
Pitt Island

Bounty Islands
(New Zealand)

Auckland Islands
(New Zealand)

Antipodes Islands
(New Zealand)

Lambert Azimuthal Equal Area Projection

1:8 000 000

oceania
western australia

Rossel Island
Tagula Island
The Calvados Chain
Tagula
Misima Island
Bonvouloir Islands
Conflict Group
Daloloia Group
Louisiade Archipelago
East Numanuma
ala
Mount 3676 Suckling
Amau
Gadaisu
Wedau
Suau
Mount Maganda

PAPUA
NEW GUINEA

Hood Point

Ashmore Reefs

Eastern Fields

C o r a l   S e a

Coral Sea Islands Territory
(Australia)

Diane Bank

Willis Group
Moore Reef
Magdelaine Cays
Herald Cays
Holmes Reef
Flora Reef
Coringa Islands
Malay Reef
Diamond Islets
Tregosse Islets and Reefs
Abington Reef
Lihou Reef and Cays
Carola Cay
Marion Reef
Paget Cay

Kenn Reef
Frederick Reef
Wreck Reef
Cato Island and Bank
Tropic of Capricorn

Saumarez Reef
Hixson Cay
Swain Reefs

Capricorn Channel
Capricorn Group
Bunker Group
Curtis Channel

Sandy Cape
Fraser Island National Park
Bundaberg
Burrum Ra.
Monto

G   r   e   a   t   B   a   r   r   i   e   r   R   e   e   f

Osprey Reef
Shark Reef
Bougainville Reef

Great Barrier Reef Marine Park
(Far North Section)

Raine Island

Cooks Passage
Second Three Mile Opening
First Three Mile Opening

Magnetic Passage
Gratton Passage

Bowling Green Bay
Cape Upstart National Park
Abbot
Bowen

Hook Reef
Whitsunday Island National Park
Whitsunday Group / Lindeman Group
Cape Conway National Park

Repulse Bay
Mackay

Great Barrier Reef Marine Park (Capricorn Section)

Townshend Island
Warginburra Peninsula
Percy Isles
Bell Cay

Cape Palmerston National Park

Yeppoon
Keppel Bay
Curtis Island
Gladstone

Rockhampton
Mount Morgan
Raglan
Biloela
Thangool
Jambin
Goovigen

1 : 8 000 000

Lambert Azimuthal Equal Area Projection

0   100   200   300 miles
0 100 200 300 400 500 km

G u l f

o f

C a r p e n t a r i a

A r a f u r a   s e a

Boucaut Bay
Maningrida
Ramingining
Elcho Island

Wessel Islands
Cape Wessel
Marchinbar Island
Cape Arnhem
Guluwuru Island

Nhulunbuy
Gapuwiyak
Caledon Bay
Cape Grey
Cape Shield

Mount Alexander
Numbulwar

Groote Eylandt
Cape Beatrice
Vanderlin Island

Sir Edward Pellew Group

Maria Island
Limmen Bight
Bing Bong
Cape Crawford

Arnhem
Land

Bulman Gorge
Bulman
Mainoru
Wilton

Ngukurr
Roper Bar
Nutwood Downs
Hodgson Downs
Minamia

Parsons Range
Roper

Walker
Wilton

Borroloola
Robinson River

Broadmere
Benmara

Wollogorang
Calvert Hills

NORTHERN
TERRITORY

Barkly Tableland

Anthony Lagoon
Brunette Downs
Alroy Downs
Tarrabool Lake

Cape York

Thursday Island
Prince of Wales Island
Badu Island
Moa Island

Endeavour

Cape York
Jardine River National Park

Shelburne Bay
Cape Grenville

Cullen Point
Mapoon
Weipa
Andoom
Aurukun
Pera Head
Albatross Bay
Wordbook Point

Iron Range National Park
Portland Roads

Cape Direction

Cape York Peninsula

McIlwraith Range

Birthday Mountain
Coen
Rokeby
Archer Bend National Park
Rokeby National Park

Edward
Holroyd

Pormpuraaw
Wallaby Island

Kowanyama

Mitchell and Alice Rivers National Park

Cape Keer-weer
Kendall

Cape Melville
Saddle Hill
Starcke National Park
Cape Flattery
Cape Bedford
Cooktown

Finders Group National Park
Cape Melville National Park
Princess Charlotte Bay
Lakefield National Park

Palmerville
Laura
Musgrave
Fairview
Almaden

Lakefield National Park
Port Douglas
Mossman
Cairns

Daintree National Park
Cape Tribulation National Park

Clifton Beach
Mount Finnigan
Bloomfield

Mareeba
Mossman
Dimbulah

Cape Van Diemen
Mornington Island
Wellesley Islands
South Wellesley Islands
Tarrant Pt
Kangaroo Pt
Karumba

Nicholson
Doomadgee

Westmoreland

Gregory Downs
Riversleigh
Lawn Hill National Park

Burketown
Inverleigh
Leichhardt
Gregory

Normanton
Glenore

Croydon
Georgetown

Forsayth

Einasleigh
Mount Surprise

Undara Volcanic
The Lynd Junction

Greenvale

Charters Towers
Homestead
Pentland
Torrens Creek
Prairie

Hughenden

Mount Isa
Cloncurry
Duchess
Dajarra
Phosphate Hill

Julia Creek
Malbon
Kuridala
Kamilaroi
Quamby

Richmond
Maxwelton

Winton
Corfield

Longreach
Ilfracombe
Isisford

Muttaburra
Aramac
Barcaldine
Jericho
Alpha

Emerald
Capella
Clermont
Blackwater

Dysart
Moranbah
Middlemount

Springsure
Rolleston

Tambo
Blackall

Jericho
Alpha

Camooweal
Austral Downs
Lake Nash

Urandangi
Headingly

Boulia
Bedourie

Diamantina National Park

Birdsville

Windorah

Jundah

Stonehenge

Blackwater
Duaringa
Dingo
Bluff

Expedition Range National Park

Buckland Tableland
Carnarvon National Park

Isla Gorge National Park
Cracow
Theodore

Simpson Desert
Simpson Desert National Park

G r e a t   D i v i d i n g   R a n g e

Q U E E N S L A N D

S i m p s o n

Connors Range
Denham Range
Leichhardt Range
Clarke Range
Eungella National Park

Drummond Range
Expedition Range
Carnarvon Range
Warrego Range

Gregory Range
Selwyn Range
Swords Ra.
Kirby Ra.
Lochern National Park
Welford National Park
Tregole National Park

oceania
eastern australia

oceania
southeast australia

1:5 000 000

Lambert Azimuthal Equal Area Projection

North America, the world's third largest continent, supports a wide range of landscapes from the Arctic north to sub-tropical Central America. The main physiographic regions of the continent are the mountains of the west coast, stretching from Alaska in the north to Mexico and Central America in the south; the vast, relatively flat Canadian Shield; the Great Plains which make up the majority of the interior; the Appalachian Mountains in the east; and the Atlantic coastal plain.

These regions contain some significant physical features, including the Rocky Mountains, the Great Lakes – three of which are amongst the five largest lakes in the world – and the Mississippi-Missouri river system which is the world's fourth longest river. The Caribbean Sea contains a complex pattern of islands, many volcanic in origin, and the continent is joined to South America by the narrow Isthmus of Panama.

North America's longest river system, the Mississippi-Missouri, flows into the Gulf of Mexico through the **Mississippi Delta**.

MOST NORTHERLY POINT
Kap Morris Jesup

MOST EASTERLY POINT
Nordøstrundingen

HIGHEST MOUNTAIN
Mt McKinley

LARGEST ISLAND
Greenland

MOST WESTERLY POINT
Attu Island

LARGEST LAKE
Lake Superior

LOWEST POINT
Death Valley

LONGEST RIVER AND
LARGEST DRAINAGE BASIN
Mississippi-Missouri

MOST SOUTHERLY POINT
Punta Mariato

Chukchi Sea

Bering Strait

Seward Peninsula

Norton Sound

Pribilof Islands

Nunivak Island

Andreanof Islands

Aleutian Islands

Fox Islands

Unalaska Island

Bristol Bay

Iliamna Lake

Alaska Range

Mount McKinley

6194

Unimak Island

Alaska Peninsula

Aleutian Range

Kodiak Island

Gulf of Alaska

Alexander Archipelago

Dixon Entrance

Queen Charlotte Islands

Cape B

Coast Ranges

Rocky Mountains

Great Plains

Lake Michigan

Lake Huron

Lake Erie

Chesapeake Bay

Appalachian Mountains

Long Island

Cape Cod

Nova Scotia

PACIFIC OCEAN

North America perspective view and cross section

North America's physical features

Highest mountain	Mt McKinley, USA	6 194 metres	20 321 feet
Longest river	Mississippi-Missouri, USA	5 969 km	3 709 miles
Largest lake	Lake Superior, Canada/USA	82 100 sq km	31 699 sq miles
Largest island	Greenland	2 175 600 sq km	839 999 sq miles
Largest drainage basin	Mississippi-Missouri, USA	3 250 000 sq km	1 254 825 sq miles
Lowest point	Death Valley, USA	-86 metres	-282 feet

North America's extent

TOTAL LAND AREA (including Hawaiian Islands)	24 680 331 sq km / 9 529 076 sq miles
Most northerly point	Kap Morris Jesup, Greenland
Most southerly point	Punta Mariato, Panama
Most westerly point	Attu Island, USA
Most easterly point	Nordostrundingen, Greenland

The Grand Canyon, Arizona, USA, the world's largest and most spectacular land canyon.

FACTS

Devon Island, Canada, is the world's largest uninhabited island

Canada has the longest coastline of any country in the world

Lake Superior is the world's largest freshwater lake

Over 320 000 square kilometres of the USA is protected for conservation purposes

The Yucatán peninsula, Mexico, divides the Gulf of Mexico from the Caribbean Sea.

North America has been dominated economically and politically by the USA since the nineteenth century. Before that, the continent was subject to colonial influences, particularly of Spain in the south and of Britain and France in the east. The nineteenth century saw the steady development of the western half of the continent. The wealth of natural resources and the generally temperate climate were an excellent basis for settlement, agriculture and industrial development which has led to the USA being the richest nation in the world today.

Although there are twenty three independent countries and fourteen dependent territories in North America, Canada, Mexico and the USA have approximately eighty five per cent of the continent's population and eighty eight per cent of its land area. Large parts of the north remain sparsely populated, while the most densely populated areas are in the northeast USA, and the Caribbean.

Washington DC, a leading international political centre and capital city of the United States.

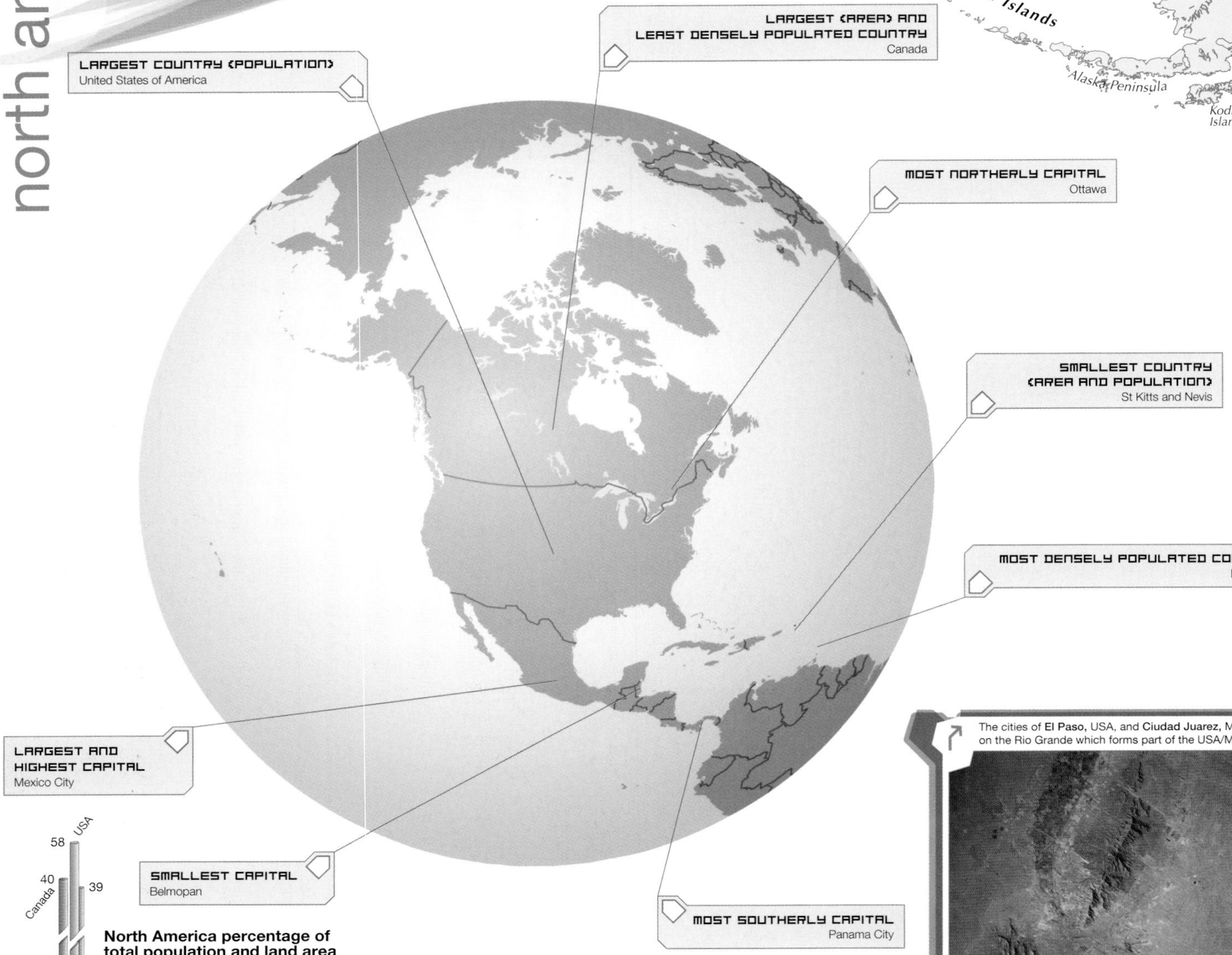

LARGEST COUNTRY (POPULATION)
United States of America

LARGEST (AREA) AND LEAST DENSELY POPULATED COUNTRY
Canada

MOST NORTHERLY CAPITAL
Ottawa

SMALLEST COUNTRY (AREA AND POPULATION)
St Kitts and Nevis

MOST DENSELY POPULATED COUNTRY
Barbados

LARGEST AND HIGHEST CAPITAL
Mexico City

SMALLEST CAPITAL
Belmopan

MOST SOUTHERLY CAPITAL
Panama City

Point Hope
Bering Strait
St Lawrence Island
Nome
Yukon
U.S
ALASK
Mount McKinley 6194
Anchorage
Valdez
Alaska Peninsula
Kodiak Island
Gulf of Alaska
Alexande Archipelago
Queen Charlotte Islands
Aleutian Islands

The cities of **El Paso**, USA, and **Ciudad Juarez**, Mexico, are located on the Rio Grande which forms part of the USA/Mexico border.

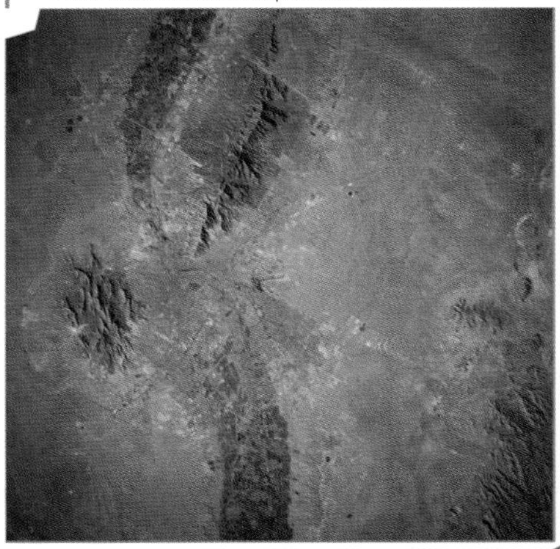

North America percentage of total population and land area

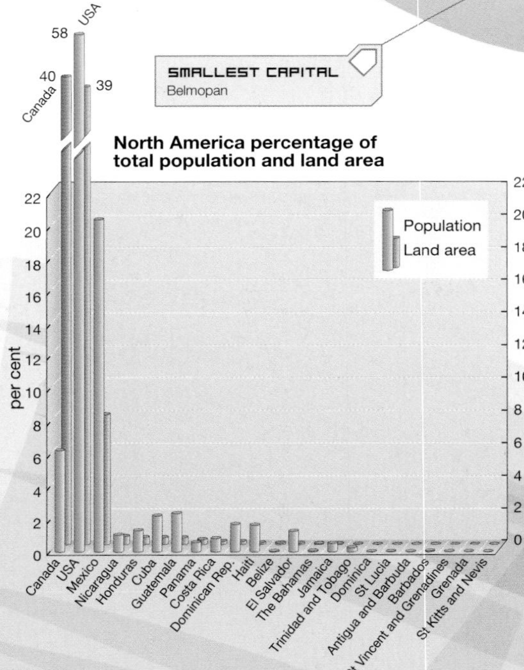

Population
Land area

Canada 40
USA 58
39

per cent

Canada
USA
Mexico
Nicaragua
Honduras
Cuba
Guatemala
Panama
Costa Rica
Dominican Rep.
Belize
Haiti
El Salvador
The Bahamas
Jamaica
Trinidad and Tobago
Dominica
St Lucia
Antigua and Barbuda
Barbados
St Vincent and Grenadines
Grenada
St Kitts and Nevis

North America's countries

Largest country (area)	Canada	9 970 610 sq km	3 849 653 sq miles
Smallest country (area)	St Kitts and Nevis	261 sq km	101 sq miles
Largest country (population)	United States of America	288 530 000	
Smallest country (population)	St Kitts and Nevis	38 000	
Most densely populated country	Barbados	626 per sq km	1 621 per sq mile
Least densely populated country	Canada	3 per sq km	8 per sq mile

North America's capitals

Largest capital (population)	Mexico City, Mexico	18 066 000
Smallest capital (population)	Belmopan, Belize	9 000
Most northerly capital	Ottawa, Canada	45° 25'N
Most southerly capital	Panama City, Panama	8° 56'N
Highest capital	Mexico City, Mexico	2 300 metres 7 546 feet

The Bahamas, a chain of islands in the North Atlantic Ocean, lying southeast of Florida, USA. It is a former British colony which gained independence in 1973.

FACTS

The Panama Canal, opened in 1914, cut the journey between the Atlantic and the Pacific by over 14 000 km

Mexico City is the highest city in North America and houses approximately 18% of Mexico's population

The state of Alaska was bought by the USA from Russia in 1867

The territory of Nunavut is Canada's newest administrative division, created in 1999 from the eastern part of Northwest Territories

Lambert Conformal Conic Projection

1:16 000 000

north america
western canada

north america
eastern canada

Lambert Conformal Conic Projection

1:12 000 000

Lambert Conformal Conic Projection

1:7 000 000

north america
western united states

Lambert Conformal Conic Projection

1:7 000 000

north america
central united states

States in the U.S.A.
numbered on the map:

1. CONNECTICUT (F3)
2. DELAWARE (F4)
3. MASSACHUSETTS (F3)
4. RHODE ISLAND (G3)

Lambert Conformal Conic Projection

1:7 000 000

miles
0   100   200

0   100   200   300   400 km

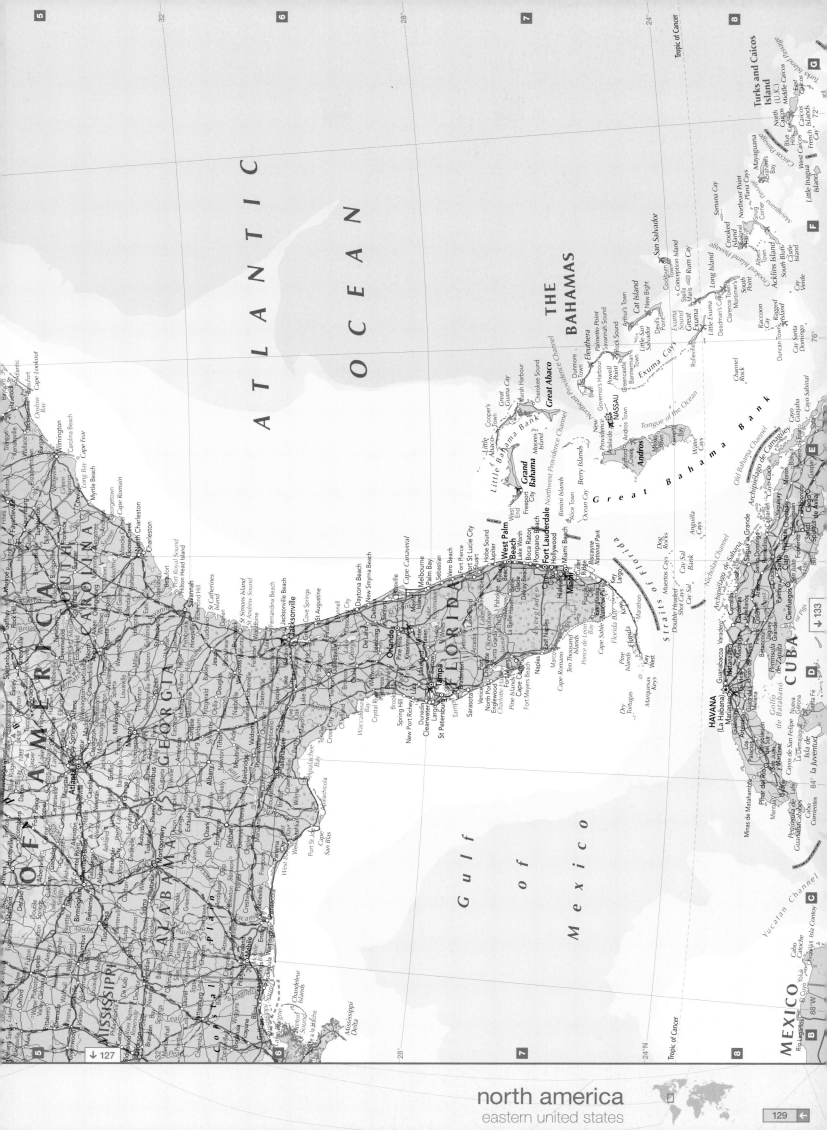

north america
eastern united states

Lambert Conformal Conic Projection

1:3 500 000

0   50   100   150   200 km
0   50   100 miles

South America is a continent of great contrasts, with landscapes varying from the tropical rainforests of the Amazon Basin, to the Atacama Desert, the driest place on earth, and the sub-Antarctic regions of southern Chile and Argentina. The dominant physical features are the Andes, stretching along the entire west coast of the continent and containing numerous mountains over 6 000 metres high, and the Amazon, which is the second longest river in the world and has the world's largest drainage basin.

The Altiplano is a high plateau lying between two of the Andes ranges. It contains Lake Titicaca, the world's highest navigable lake. By contrast, large lowland areas dominate the centre of the continent, lying between the Andes and the Guiana and Brazilian Highlands. These vast grasslands stretch from the Llanos of the north through the Selvas and the Gran Chaco to the Pampas of Argentina.

South America's largest lake, **Lake Titicaca,** high in the Andes on the border between Bolivia and Peru.

Andes

Selvas

Planalto do Mato Grosso

Bahia de São Marcos

Cabo de São Roque

South America perspective view and cross section

MOST NORTHERLY POINT
Punta Gallinas

MOST WESTERLY POINT
Galapagos Islands

LARGEST LAKE
Lake Titicaca

HIGHEST MOUNTAIN
Cerro Aconcagua

LARGEST ISLAND
Isla Grande de Tierra del Fuego

MOST SOUTHERLY POINT
Cape Horn

LONGEST RIVER AND LARGEST DRAINAGE BASIN
Amazon

MOST EASTERLY POINT
Ilhas Martin Vas

LOWEST POINT
Península Valdés

South America's physical features

Highest mountain	Cerro Aconcagua, Argentina	6 959 metres	22 831 feet
Longest river	Amazon	6 516 km	4 049 miles
Largest lake	Lake Titicaca, Bolivia/Peru	8 340 sq km	3 220 sq miles
Largest island	Isla Grande de Tierra del Fuego, Argentina/Chile	47 000 sq km	18 147 sq miles
Largest drainage basin	Amazon	7 050 000 sq km	2 722 005 sq miles
Lowest point	Península Valdés, Argentina	-40 metres	-131 feet

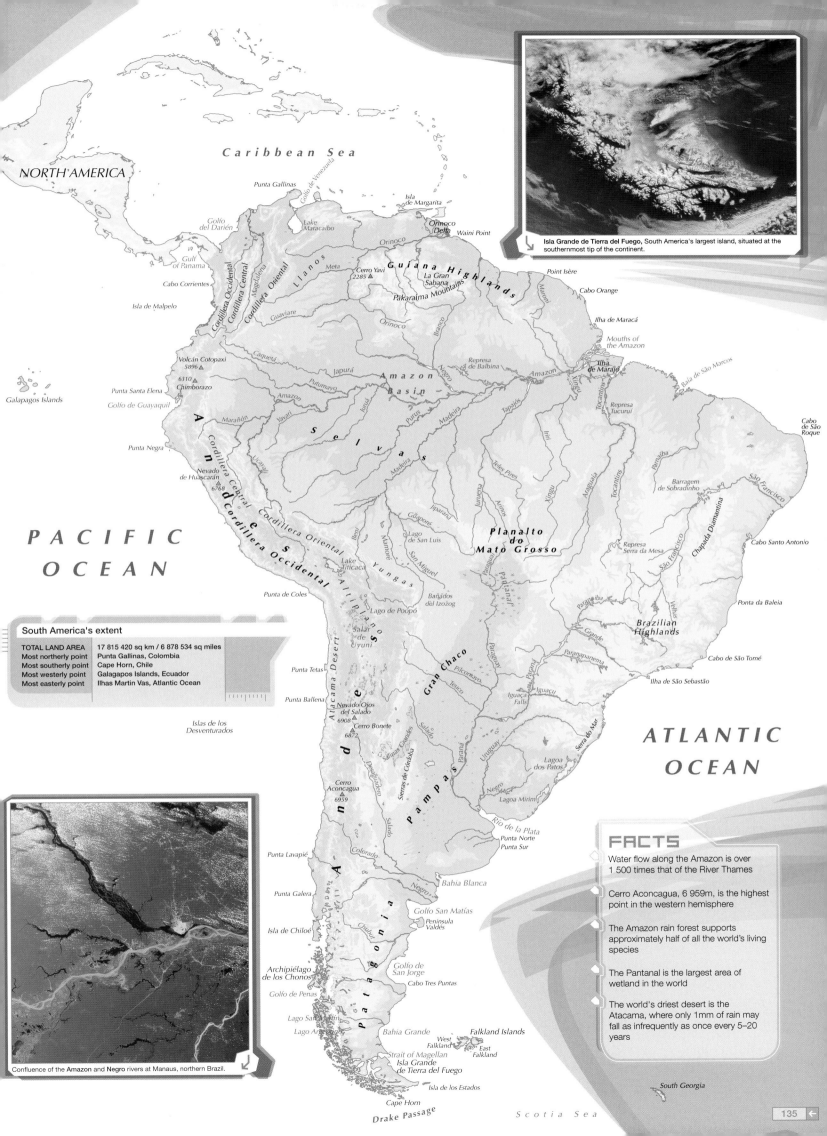

NORTH AMERICA

Caribbean Sea

PACIFIC OCEAN

ATLANTIC OCEAN

Isla Grande de Tierra del Fuego, South America's largest island, situated at the southernmost tip of the continent.

Confluence of the **Amazon** and **Negro** rivers at Manaus, northern Brazil.

South America's extent

TOTAL LAND AREA	17 815 420 sq km / 6 878 534 sq miles
Most northerly point	Punta Gallinas, Colombia
Most southerly point	Cape Horn, Chile
Most westerly point	Galagapos Islands, Ecuador
Most easterly point	Ilhas Martin Vas, Atlantic Ocean

FACTS

Water flow along the Amazon is over 1 500 times that of the River Thames

Cerro Aconcagua, 6 959m, is the highest point in the western hemisphere

The Amazon rain forest supports approximately half of all the world's living species

The Pantanal is the largest area of wetland in the world

The world's driest desert is the Atacama, where only 1mm of rain may fall as infrequently as once every 5–20 years

French Guiana, a French Department, is the only remaining territory under overseas control on a continent which has seen a long colonial history. Much of South America was colonized by Spain in the sixteenth century, with Britain, Portugal and the Netherlands each claiming territory in the northeast of the continent. This colonization led to the conquering of ancient civilizations, including the Incas in Peru. Most countries became independent from Spain and Portugal in the early nineteenth century.

The population of the continent reflects its history, being composed primarily of indigenous Indian peoples and mestizos – reflecting the long Hispanic influence. There has been a steady process of urbanization within the continent, with major movements of the population from rural to urban areas. The majority of the population now live in the major cities and within 300 kilometres of the coast.

Rio de Janeiro, third largest city in Brazil and the capital until 1960 when the status of capital was transferred to Brasilia.

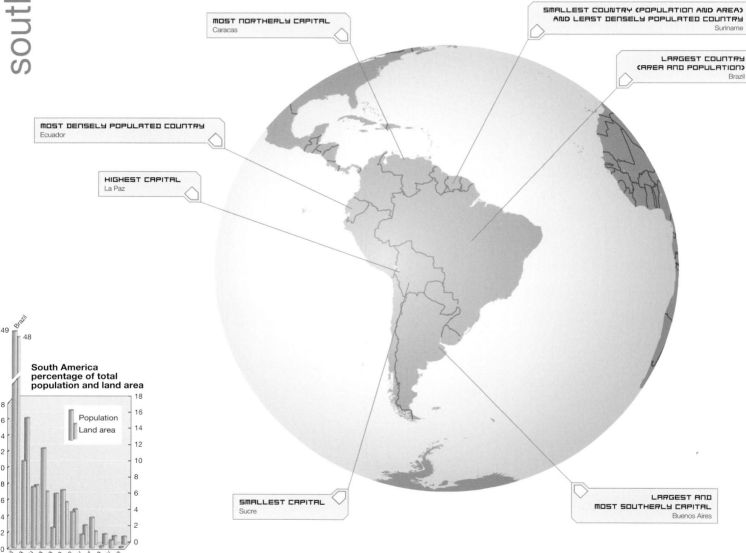

MOST NORTHERLY CAPITAL
Caracas

SMALLEST COUNTRY (POPULATION AND AREA) AND LEAST DENSELY POPULATED COUNTRY
Suriname

LARGEST COUNTRY (AREA AND POPULATION)
Brazil

MOST DENSELY POPULATED COUNTRY
Ecuador

HIGHEST CAPITAL
La Paz

SMALLEST CAPITAL
Sucre

LARGEST AND MOST SOUTHERLY CAPITAL
Buenos Aires

South America percentage of total population and land area

Population
Land area

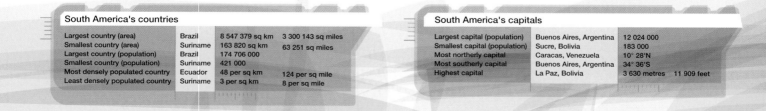

South America's countries

Largest country (area)	Brazil	8 547 379 sq km	3 300 143 sq miles
Smallest country (area)	Suriname	163 820 sq km	63 251 sq miles
Largest country (population)	Brazil	174 706 000	
Smallest country (population)	Suriname	421 000	
Most densely populated country	Ecuador	48 per sq km	124 per sq mile
Least densely populated country	Suriname	3 per sq km	8 per sq mile

South America's capitals

Largest capital (population)	Buenos Aires, Argentina	12 024 000
Smallest capital (population)	Sucre, Bolivia	183 000
Most northerly capital	Caracas, Venezuela	10° 28'N
Most southerly capital	Buenos Aires, Argentina	34° 36'S
Highest capital	La Paz, Bolivia	3 630 metres 11 909 feet

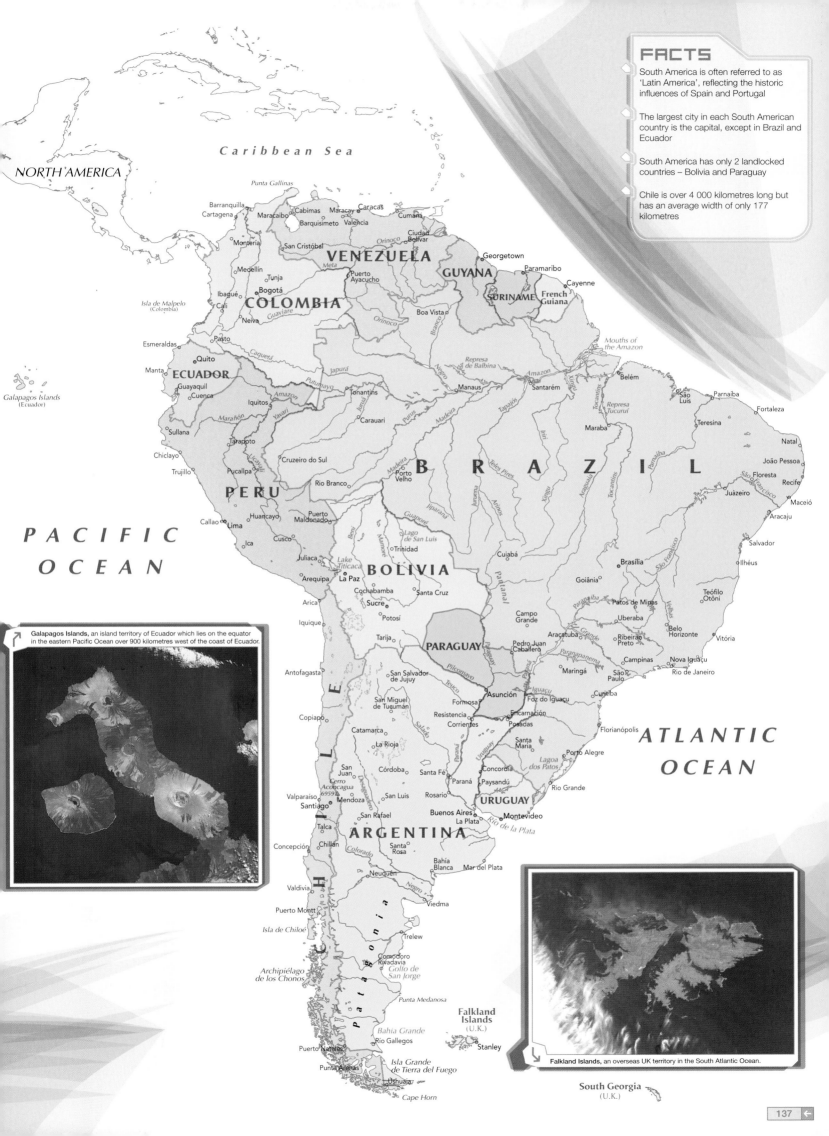

Galapagos Islands, an island territory of Ecuador which lies on the equator in the eastern Pacific Ocean over 900 kilometres west of the coast of Ecuador.

Falkland Islands, an overseas UK territory in the South Atlantic Ocean.

NICARAGUA
MANAGUA
León
Jinotepe
Granada
Rivas
Lake
Managua

COSTA RICA
SAN JOSÉ
Puerto Limón
Cabo Santa Elena
Península
de Nicoya
Bahía de Coronado
Península
de Osa
Puerto Armuelles

Isla de Coco
(Costa Rica)

PANAMA
PANAMA CITY
David
Santiago
Chitré
Colón
El Porvenir
Gulf of
Panama
Golfo de
Chiriquí
Isla de
Coiba
Punta
Mariato
Península
de Azuero
Punta
Mala

Islas del Maíz
(Corn Islands)
Punta de Perlas
Bluefields (Nicaragua)
Punta del Mono
Costa de Mosquitos

Isla de
Providencia
(Colombia)
Islas de San Andrés
(Colombia)

Isthmus of Panama
Golfo de
Darién
Golfo de
Morrosquillo

Cabo
Corrientes
Golfo de
Cupica

COLOMBIA
BOGOTÁ
Medellín
Manizales
Pereira
Armenia
Tulua
Buga
Cali
Palmira
Buenaventura
Popayán
Pasto
Florencia
Quibdó
Mutis
Cartagena
Barranquilla
Santa Marta
Ciénaga
Maicao
Riohacha
Valledupar
Sincelejo
Montería
Turbo
Caucasia
Magangué
Mompós
Ocaña
Cúcuta
Bucaramanga
Pamplona
San Cristóbal
Tunja
Chiquinquirá
Ibagué
Villavicencio
Neiva
Yopal
San José
del Guaviare
Mitú
El Dorado
Tres Esquinas
Ipiales
Tumaco
Ibarra
Tulcán
Mocoa
Puerto Leguizamo

Parque Nacional
Paramillo
Parque Nacional
Los Katíos
Parque Nacional
de Darién
Sierra Nevada
de Santa Marta
Parque Nacional
Perijá
Parque Nacional
Sierra Nevada
el Cocuy
Parque Nacional
La Macarena
Parque Nacional
Sumapaz
Parque Nacional
Cordillera
de los Picachos
Parque Nacional
Farallones de Cali
Parque Nacional
La Paya

Península de la Guajira
Golfo de
Venezuela

VENEZUELA
CARACAS
Maracaibo
Cabimas
Maracay
Valencia
Barquisimeto
Valera
Mérida
Barinas
San Cristóbal
Guanare
San Carlos
Acarigua
San Fernando
de Apure
Puerto Ayacucho
Ciudad Guayana
Ciudad
Bolívar
El Tigre
Maturín
Cumaná
Barcelona
Puerto Cabello
San Felipe
Coro
Punto Fijo
El Dorado
La Gran
Sabana
Achaguas
Elorza
Arauca

GRENADA
ST GEORGE'S
PORT OF SPAIN
TRINIDAD AND TOBAGO
Isla de Margarita
Porlamar
Los Testigos
Isla La Tortuga
Isla Blanquilla
Isla Orchila
Islas Los Roques
ORANJESTAD
Aruba
(Neth.)
Bonaire
(Neth.)
WILLEMSTAD
Curaçao
Netherlands
Antilles

Serranía
de Imataca
Orinoco
Delta
Gulf of
Paria

Sierra de Guampi
Cerro Yaví 2285
Cerro
Marahuaca
Pico da
Neblina
Cerro
Duida

Parque Nacional
Canaima
Angel
Falls
Parque Nacional
Jaua Sarisariñama
Parque Nacional
Cinaruco Capanaparo
Parque Nacional
El Tuparro
Parque Nacional
Duida-Marahuaca
Parque Nacional
Serranía de la Neblina
Parque Nacional
Parima-Tapirapecó
Parque Nacional
do Pico da Neblina
Parque Nacional
do Rio Branco

Pakaraima Mountains
Guiana Highlands

Llanos

ECUADOR
QUITO
Guayaquil
Cuenca
Ambato
Portoviejo
Manta
Machala
Loja
Esmeraldas
Ibarra
Latacunga
Riobamba
Babahoyo
Salinas
Tena
Macas
Cañar
Azogues
Nueva Loja

Volcán
Cayambe
Volcán
Cotopaxi 5896
Chimborazo 6310
Volcán
Sangay

Parque Nacional
Yasuní
Parque Nacional
Sangay
Parque Nacional
Podocarpus

Galápagos Islands
San Salvador (Islas Galápagos)
(Ecuador)
Isla Fernandina
Isla Isabela
Isla
Santa Cruz
Isla
San Cristóbal
Isla
Santa María
Puerto
Baquerizo Moreno
Equator
90°
90°W
1:14 000 000
0   miles   100
0   km   150

PERU
LIMA
Callao
Trujillo
Chimbote
Piura
Chiclayo
Cajamarca
Iquitos
Pucallpa
Huánuco
Cusco (Cuzco)
Arequipa
Tacna
Ica
Nazca
Puno
Juliaca
Cerro de Pasco
Huancayo
Huaraz
Ayacucho
Abancay
Tarapoto
Moyobamba
Chachapoyas
Sullana
Talara
Paita
Tumbes
Catacaos
Sechura
Pisco
Chincha Alta
Huacho
Machu Picchu
Sicuani

Nevado de Huascarán 6768
Yerupaja 6634
Cordillera Blanca
Cordillera Negra
Cordillera Occidental
Cordillera Oriental
Cordillera Central

Parque Nacional
Huascarán
Parque Nacional
Abiseo
Parque Nacional
Cordillera Azul
Parque Nacional
Manu
Parque Nacional
Bahuaja-Sonene

Lake
Titicaca

BOLIVIA
LA PAZ
SUCRE
Santa Cruz
Cochabamba
Oruro
Potosí
Tarija
Trinidad
Riberalta
Cobija
Puerto Maldonado
Altiplano
Nevado Illampu 6402
Nevado Sajama 6542

Parque Nacional
Alto Madidi
Parque Nacional
Isiboro Sécure
Parque Nacional
Carrasco
Parque Nacional
Noel Kempff Mercado
Parque Nacional
Amboró
Parque Nacional
Kaa-Iya
Bañados
del Izozog

CHILE
Arica
Iquique
Antofagasta
Tocopilla
Calama
Chuquicamata
San Pedro
de Atacama
Desierto de Atacama
Salar de
Atacama
Salar de
Uyuni

ARGENTINA
Orán

BRAZIL
Rio Branco
Porto Velho
Cruzeiro do Sul
Manacapuru
Leticia
Tabatinga
Benjamin Constant
Manaus
Coari
Lábrea
Humaitá
Ariquemes
Ji-Paraná
Vilhena

Amazon
Rio Negro
Rio Madeira
Rio Juruá
Rio Purus

Serra do Divisor
Serra do Mucajaí
Serra Parima
Serra Tulu-Tulai
Serra Curuena

Parque Nacional
Amacayacu
Parque Nacional
da Serra do Divisor
Parque Nacional
do Jaú
Parque Nacional
Pacaás Novos

**PACIFIC
OCEAN**

Equator

Tropic of Capricorn

Lambert Azimuthal Equal Area Projection

ATLANTIC

OCEAN

BRAZIL

south america
northern south america

south america
southern south america

1:14 000 000

Lambert Azimuthal Equal Area Projection

MATO GROSSO

TOCANTINS

BAHIA

GOIÁS

DISTRITO FEDERAL

★ BRASÍLIA

B R A Z I L

MINAS GERAIS

Belo Horizonte

SÃO PAULO

RIO DE JANEIRO

Nova Iguaçu

Rio de Janeiro

Niterói

São Paulo

Santo André

Santos

PARANÁ

Curitiba

SANTA CATARINA

Florianópolis

RIO GRANDE DO SUL

to Alegre

Tropic of Capricorn

A T L A N T I C

O C E A N

Lambert Azimuthal Equal Area Projection

1:7 000 000

0   100   200   300   400 km
0   100   200   300   400 miles

Between them, the world's oceans and polar regions cover approximately seventy per cent of the earth's surface. The oceans contain ninety six per cent of the earth's water and a vast range of flora and fauna. They are a major influence on the world's climate, particularly through ocean currents. The Arctic and Antarctica are the coldest and most inhospitable places on the earth. They both have vast amounts of ice which, if global warming continues, could have a major influence on sea level across the globe.

Our understanding of the oceans and polar regions has increased enormously over the last twenty years through the development of new technologies, particularly that of satellite remote sensing, which can generate vast amounts of data relating to, for example, topography (both on land and the seafloor), land cover and sea surface temperature.

The oceans

The world's major oceans are the Pacific, the Atlantic and the Indian Oceans. The Arctic Ocean is generally considered as part of the Atlantic, and the Southern Ocean, which stretches around the whole of Antarctica is usually treated as an extension of each of the three major oceans.

One of the most important factors affecting the earth's climate is the circulation of water within and between the oceans. Differences in temperature and surface winds create ocean currents which move enormous quantities of water around the globe. These currents re-distribute heat which the oceans have absorbed from the sun, and so have a major effect on the world's climate system. El Niño is one climatic phenomenon directly influenced by these ocean processes.

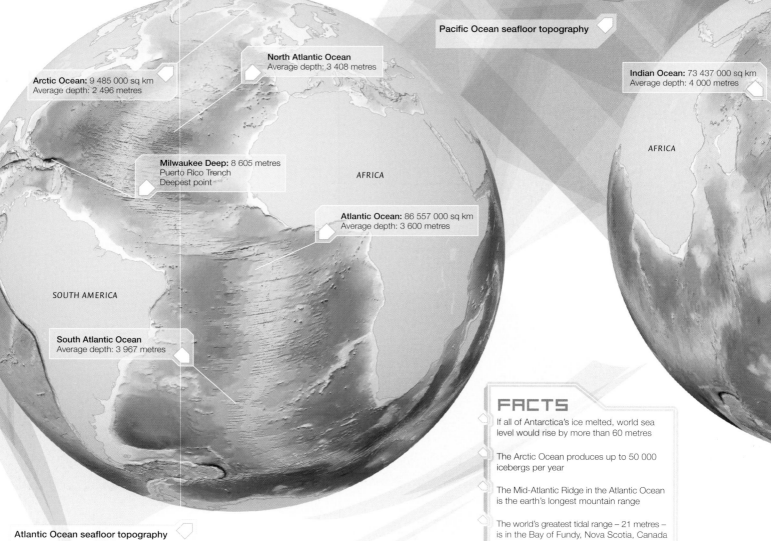

North Pacific Ocean
Average depth: 4 573 metres

NORTH AMERICA

Challenger Deep: 10 920 metres
Mariana Trench
Deepest point

Pacific Ocean
World's largest ocean: 166 241 000 sq km
Average depth: 4 200m

South Pacific Ocean
Average depth: 3 935 metres

AUSTRALIA

Pacific Ocean seafloor topography

North Atlantic Ocean
Average depth: 3 408 metres

Arctic Ocean: 9 485 000 sq km
Average depth: 2 496 metres

Indian Ocean: 73 437 000 sq km
Average depth: 4 000 metres

AFRICA

Milwaukee Deep: 8 605 metres
Puerto Rico Trench
Deepest point

AFRICA

Atlantic Ocean: 86 557 000 sq km
Average depth: 3 600 metres

SOUTH AMERICA

South Atlantic Ocean
Average depth: 3 967 metres

Atlantic Ocean seafloor topography

FACTS

If all of Antarctica's ice melted, world sea level would rise by more than 60 metres

The Arctic Ocean produces up to 50 000 icebergs per year

The Mid-Atlantic Ridge in the Atlantic Ocean is the earth's longest mountain range

The world's greatest tidal range – 21 metres – is in the Bay of Fundy, Nova Scotia, Canada

The Circumpolar current in the Southern Ocean carries 125 million cubic metres of water per second

Sea ice concentration in the Arctic Ocean, February 2000. Purple indicates a concentration of more than 90%.

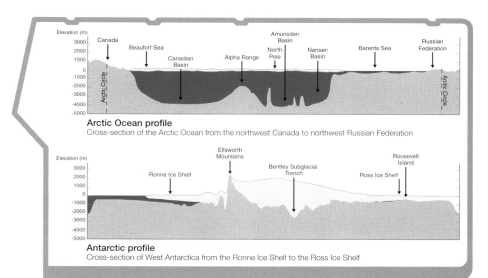

Arctic Ocean profile
Cross-section of the Arctic Ocean from the northwest Canada to northwest Russian Federation

Antarctic profile
Cross-section of West Antarctica from the Ronne Ice Shelf to the Ross Ice Shelf

Polar regions

Although a harsh climate is common to the two polar regions, there are major differences between the Arctic and Antarctica. The North Pole is surrounded by the Arctic Ocean, much of which is permanently covered by sea ice, while the South Pole lies on the huge land mass of Antarctica. This is covered by a permanent ice cap which reaches a maximum thickness of over four kilometres. Antarctica has no permanent population, but Europe, Asia and North America all stretch into the Arctic region which is populated by numerous ethnic groups. Antarctica is subject to the Antarctic Treaty of 1959 which does not recognize individual land claims and protects the continent in the interests of international scientific cooperation.

ASIA

Java Trench: 7 125 metres
Deepest point

AUSTRALIA

Southern Ocean
Average depth: 3 239 metres

ANTARCTICA

Indian Ocean seafloor topography

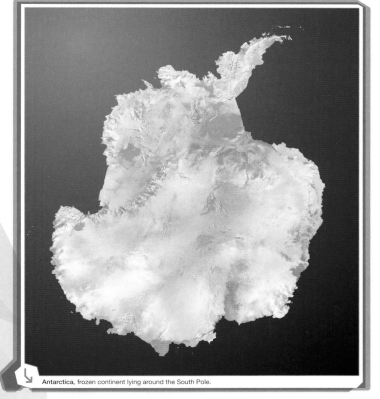

Antarctica, frozen continent lying around the South Pole.

The island of **Novaya Zemlya**, Russian Federation, prevents the Kara Sea (right) from being affected by the warming influence of the Gulf Stream in the Atlantic Ocean and the Barents Sea (left).

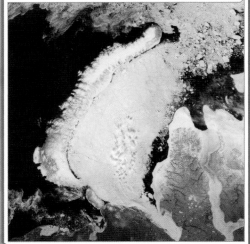

Antarctica physical features

Highest mountain: Vinson Massif	4 897 m	16 066 ft
Total land area (excluding ice shelves)	12 093 000 sq km	4 669 292 sq miles
Ice shelves	1 559 000 sq km	601 954 sq miles
Exposed rock	49 000 sq km	18 920 sq miles
Lowest bedrock elevation (Bentley Subglacial Trench)	2 496 m below sea level	8 189 ft below sea level
Maximum ice thickness (Astrolabe Subglacial Basin)	4 776 m	15 669 ft
Mean ice thickness (including ice shelves)	1 859 m	6 099 ft
Volume of ice sheet (including ice shelves)	25 400 000 cubic km	10 160 000 cubic miles

Lambert Azimuthal Equal Area Projection

144

1:50 000 000

0   500   1000   1500 miles

0   500   1000   1500   2000   2500 km

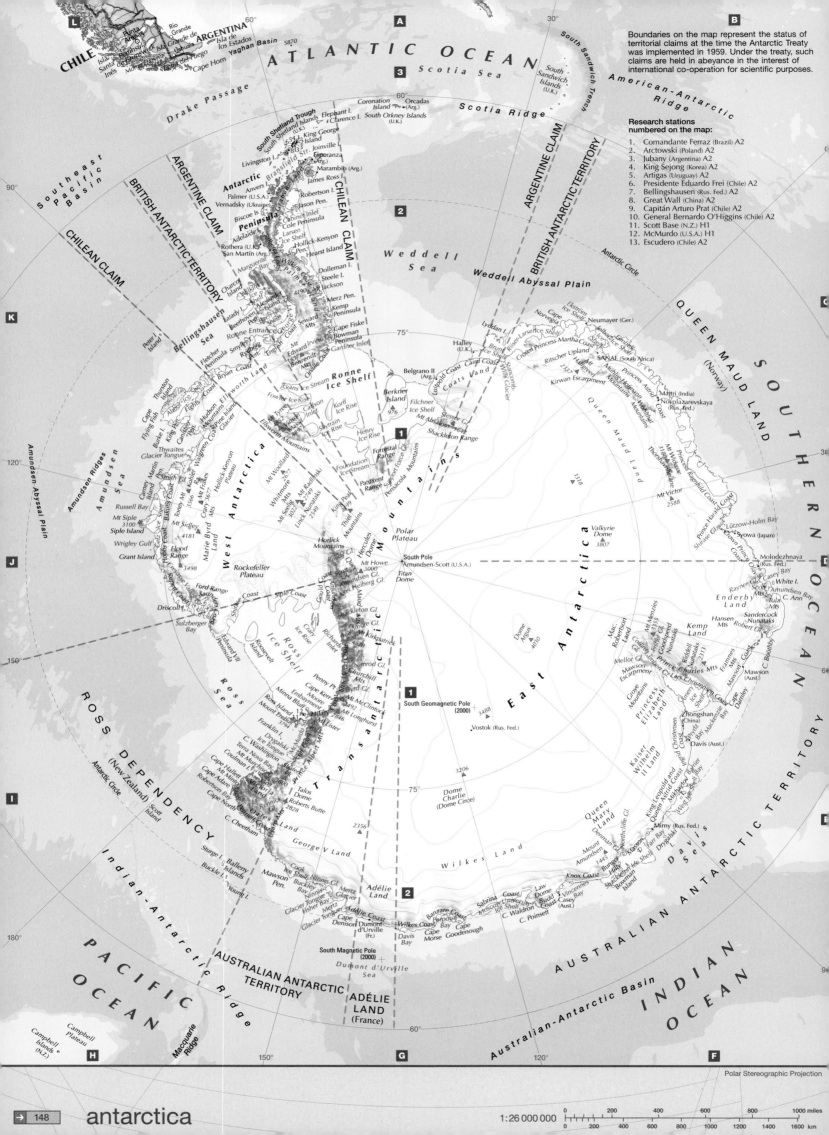

world statistics

	POPULATION						ECONOMY					
	total population	population change (%)	% urban	total fertility	population by age (000s) 0–14	population by age (000s) 65 or over	2050 projected population	total Gross National Income (GNI) (US$M)	GNI per capita (US$)	total debt service (US$)	debt service ratio (% GNI)	aid receipts (% GNI)	military spending (% GNI)
WORLD	**6 211 082 000**	**1.2**	**47.7**	**2.7**	**1 814 525**	**418 420**	**9 322 251 000**	**31 500 010**	**5 170**	**...**	**...**	**...**	**2.3**
AFGHANISTAN	23 294 000	3.7	22.3	6.8	9 466	619	72 267 000	...	...	...	...	...	...
ALBANIA	3 164 000	0.6	42.9	2.3	939	184	3 905 000	4 236	1 230	27 000 000	0.7	8.5	1.3
ALGERIA	31 403 000	1.8	57.5	2.8	10 554	1 248	51 180 000	50 355	1 630	4 466 500 096	8.8	0.3	4.0
ANDORRA	94 000	4.1	92.2	...	...	...	193 000						
ANGOLA	13 936 000	3.0	34.9	7.2	6 326	373	53 328 000	6 707	500	1 204 499 968	25.4	8.1	21.2
ANTIGUA AND BARBUDA	65 000	0.3	37.1	...	...	...	73 000	621	9 070			1.5	...
ARGENTINA	37 944 000	1.2	88.3	2.4	10 265	3 592	54 522 000	260 994	6 960	27 345 100 800	9.9		1.6
ARMENIA	3 790 000	0.1	67.2	1.1	898	327	3 150 000	2 127	560	43 000 000	2.2	11.2	5.8
AUSTRALIA	19 536 000	1.0	91.2	1.8	3 927	2 346	26 502 000	383 291	19 770	...	...	...	1.8
AUSTRIA	8 069 000	-0.1	67.4	1.2	1 343	1 256	6 452 000	194 463	23 940				0.8
AZERBAIJAN	8 147 000	0.6	51.8	1.5	2 330	546	8 897 000	5 283	650	180 900 000	3.7	2.9	6.6
THE BAHAMAS	312 000	1.2	88.9	2.3	90	16	449 000					0.1	...
BAHRAIN	663 000	1.7	92.5	2.3	180	19	1 008 000	...	...	...	...	...	8.1
BANGLADESH	143 364 000	2.1	25.6	3.6	53 190	4 291	265 432 000	49 882	370	789 699 968	1.7	2.4	1.3
BARBADOS	269 000	0.4	50.5	1.5	55	28	263 000	...	...	...	...	...	0.5
BELARUS	10 106 000	-0.4	69.6	1.2	1 904	1 357	8 305 000	11 892	1 190	232 200 000	0.8	0.1	1.3
BELGIUM	10 276 000	0.1	97.4	1.5	1 771	1 744	9 583 000	239 779	23 340	...	...	...	1.4
BELIZE	236 000	1.9	48.1	2.9	87	10	392 000	718	2 910	66 100 000	8.6	1.9	1.6
BENIN	6 629 000	2.8	43.0	5.7	2 907	172	18 070 000	2 349	360	76 700 000	3.6	10.6	1.4
BHUTAN	2 198 000	2.6	7.4	5.1	891	88	5 569 000	529	640	6 600 000	1.3	11.6	...
BOLIVIA	8 705 000	2.2	62.9	3.9	3 300	334	16 966 000	8 044	940	661 600 000	8.2	5.8	1.8
BOSNIA-HERZEGOVINA	4 126 000	1.1	43.4	1.3	753	393	3 458 000	5 037	1 240	334 000 000	7.2	16.2	4.5
BOTSWANA	1 564 000	0.5	49.4	3.9	649	44	2 109 000	5 863	3 630	68 000 000	1.3	0.6	4.7
BRAZIL	174 706 000	1.2	81.7	2.2	49 077	8 760	247 244 000	528 503	3 060	62 787 600 384	11.0	0.1	1.9
BRUNEI	341 000	1.8	72.8	2.5	105	11	565 000	...	...	...	...	...	4.0
BULGARIA	7 790 000	-1.0	67.4	1.1	1 252	1 282	4 531 000	12 644	1 560	1 189 200 000	10.2	2.7	3.0
BURKINA	12 207 000	3.0	16.9	6.8	5 617	375	46 304 000	2 395	210	54 700 000	2.5	14.0	1.6
BURUNDI	6 688 000	3.0	9.3	6.8	3 023	182	20 219 000	692	100	21 400 000	3.2	13.8	7.0
CAMBODIA	13 776 000	2.4	17.5	4.8	5 749	367	29 883 000	3 329	270	31 400 000	1.0	12.6	4.0
CAMEROON	15 535 000	2.1	49.7	4.7	6 411	545	32 284 000	8 723	570	561 900 032	6.8	4.7	1.8
CANADA	31 268 000	0.8	78.9	1.6	5 882	3 875	40 407 000	661 881	21 340	...	...	...	1.4
CAPE VERDE	446 000	2.1	63.5	3.2	168	20	807 000	596	1 310	16 100 000	2.9	17.0	0.9
CENTRAL AFRICAN REPUBLIC	3 844 000	1.6	41.7	4.9	1 599	150	8 195 000	1 006	270	14 100 000	1.5	7.9	2.8
CHAD	8 390 000	3.1	24.1	6.7	3 663	247	27 732 000	1 597	200	26 300 000	1.9	9.6	2.4
CHILE	15 589 000	1.2	86.1	2.4	4 328	1 090	22 215 000	66 915	4 350	6 162 599 936	9.0	0.1	3.0
CHINA	1 279 557 000	0.7	36.7	1.8	316 838	87 428	1 462 058 000	1 130 984	890	21 728 299 008	2.0	0.2	2.3
COLOMBIA	43 495 000	1.6	75.5	2.6	13 806	1 993	70 862 000	82 017	1 910	5 170 599 936	6.6	0.2	3.2
COMOROS	749 000	2.9	33.8	5.0	304	19	1 900 000	217	380	2 700 000	1.3	9.3	...
CONGO	3 206 000	3.0	66.1	6.3	1 396	101	10 744 000	2 171	700	42 800 000	1.9	1.5	3.5
CONGO, DEMOCRATIC REPUBLIC OF	54 275 000	3.3	30.7	6.7	24 846	1 465	203 527 000	...	...	24 800 000	...	...	14.4
COSTA RICA	4 200 000	2.0	59.5	2.7	1 302	205	7 195 000	15 332	3 950	649 900 032	4.4	0.1	0.5
CÔTE D'IVOIRE	16 691 000	2.1	44.0	4.6	6 745	495	32 185 000	10 259	630	1 020 300 032	11.8	3.7	0.8
CROATIA	4 657 000	0.0	58.1	1.7	840	658	4 180 000	20 366	4 550	2 437 400 064	13.0	0.3	3.3
CUBA	11 273 000	0.3	75.5	1.6	2 377	1 072	10 764 000	...	...	...	...	...	1.9
CYPRUS	797 000	0.8	70.2	1.9	181	90	910 000	...	...	...	...	...	3.4
CZECH REPUBLIC	10 250 000	-0.1	74.5	1.2	1 686	1 421	8 429 000	54 108	5 270	4 773 499 904	9.5	0.9	2.3
DENMARK	5 343 000	0.2	85.1	1.7	971	798	5 080 000	166 345	31 090	...	...	...	1.6
DJIBOUTI	652 000	1.0	84.2	5.8	273	20	1 068 000	572	890	13 500 000	2.4	12.5	4.3
DOMINICA	70 000	-0.1	71.4	...	...	...	72 000	224	3 060	10 200 000	4.3	6.4	...
DOMINICAN REPUBLIC	8 639 000	1.5	66.0	2.7	2 805	359	11 960 000	18 955	2 230	520 800 000	2.8	0.3	0.7
EAST TIMOR	779 000	3.9	7.5	3.9	317	20	1 410 000	...	...	...	...	...	...
ECUADOR	13 112 000	1.7	63.4	2.8	4 278	594	21 190 000	15 952	1 240	1 276 099 968	10.3	1.2	3.7
EGYPT	70 278 000	1.7	42.7	2.9	24 004	2 808	113 840 000	99 406	1 530	1 813 400 064	1.8	1.3	2.7
EL SALVADOR	6 520 000	1.8	61.5	2.9	2 235	312	10 855 000	13 088	2 050	373 700 000	2.9	1.4	0.9
EQUATORIAL GUINEA	483 000	2.8	49.3	5.9	200	18	1 378 000	327	700	5 300 000	1.1	...	3.2
ERITREA	3 993 000	4.2	19.1	5.3	1 608	106	10 028 000	792	190	3 300 000	0.5	25.3	27.4
ESTONIA	1 361 000	-1.1	69.4	1.2	247	200	752 000	5 255	3 810	427 600 000	9.3	1.4	1.5
ETHIOPIA	66 040 000	2.4	15.9	6.8	28 414	1 859	186 452 000	6 767	100	139 400 000	2.2	11.1	8.8
FIJI	832 000	1.1	50.2	3.0	271	28	916 000	1 755	2 130	30 100 000	2.1	2.0	2.0
FINLAND	5 183 000	0.1	58.5	1.6	933	773	4 693 000	124 171	23 940	...	...	...	1.4
FRANCE	59 670 000	0.4	75.5	1.8	11 098	9 462	61 833 000	1 377 389	22 690	...	...	...	2.7
GABON	1 293 000	2.5	82.3	5.4	494	72	3 164 000	3 990	3 160	467 900 000	11.0	0.3	2.4
THE GAMBIA	1 371 000	2.4	31.3	4.8	525	40	2 605 000	440	330	18 600 000	4.5	12.4	1.3
GEORGIA	5 213 000	-0.5	56.5	1.4	1 077	680	3 219 000	3 097	620	116 900 000	3.8	5.3	1.2

	SOCIAL INDICATORS						ENVIRONMENT				COMMUNICATIONS				
infant mortality rate	life expectancy		literacy rate (%)	access to safe water (%)	doctors per 100 000 people	forest area (%)	annual change in forest area (%)	protected land area (%)	CO_2 emissions	telephone lines per 100 people	cellular phones per 100 people	internet connections per 1 000 people	international dialling code	time zone
	M	F												
83	**63.9**	**68.1**	...	**82**	...	**29.6**	**-0.2**	**6.4**	...	**17.2**	**15.6**	**82.3**	...	...
257	43.0	43.5	...	13	...	2.1	...	0.3	0.0	...	...	...	...	+4.5
31	70.9	76.7	98.2	97	129	36.2	-0.8	2.9	0.5	5.0	8.8	2.5	355	+1
65	69.9	73.3	90.4	89	85	0.9	1.3	2.5	3.6	6.0	0.3	1.9	213	+1
7	...	...	...	100	...	...	...	...	...	43.8	30.2	89.7	376	+1
295	44.5	47.1	...	38	8	56.0	-0.2	6.6	0.5	0.6	0.6	4.4	244	+1
15	...	...	...	91	114	20.5	...	...	5.0	47.4	31.8	65.2	1 268	-4
21	70.6	77.7	98.6	...	268	12.7	-0.8	1.8	3.8	21.6	18.6	80.0	54	-3
30	70.3	76.2	99.8	...	316	12.4	1.3	7.6	0.9	14.0	0.7	142.1	374	+4
6	76.4	82.0	...	100	240	20.1	-0.2	7.0	17.7	52.0	57.8	372.3	61	+8 to +11
5	75.4	81.5	...	100	302	47.0	0.2	29.2	7.9	46.8	80.7	319.4	43	+1
105	68.7	75.5	...	78	360	13.1	1.3	5.5	4.9	11.1	8.0	3.2	994	+4
18	65.2	73.9	97.4	97	152	84.1	...	...	6.1	40.0	19.7	55.0	1 242	-5
16	72.1	76.3	98.6	...	100	...	14.9	...	29.1	24.7	42.5	198.9	973	+3
82	60.6	60.8	52.1	97	20	10.2	1.3	0.7	0.2	0.4	0.4	1.1	880	+6
14	74.5	79.5	...	100	125	4.7	...	...	5.9	46.3	10.6	37.4	1 246	-4
20	62.8	74.4	99.8	100	443	45.3	3.2	6.3	6.0	27.9	1.4	41.2	375	+2
6	75.7	81.9	...	...	395	22.2	-0.2	2.8	9.9	49.3	74.7	280.0	32	+1
41	73.0	75.9	98.2	92	55	59.1	-2.3	20.9	1.8	14.4	11.6	73.8	501	-6
154	52.5	55.7	55.5	63	6	24.0	-2.3	6.9	0.1	0.9	1.9	3.9	229	+1
100	62.0	64.5	...	62	16	64.2	...	21.2	0.5	2.0	...	3.6	975	+6
80	61.9	65.3	96.3	83	130	48.9	-0.3	14.2	1.5	6.2	9.0	14.6	591	-4
18	71.3	76.7	...	...	...	44.6		0.5	1.2	11.1	5.7	11.1	387	+1
101	38.7	37.4	89.1	95	24	21.9	-0.9	18.0	2.4	9.3	16.7	15.4	267	+2
38	64.7	72.6	93.0	87	127	64.3	-0.4	4.4	1.8	21.8	16.7	46.6	55	-2 to -5
7	74.2	78.9	99.5	...	85	83.9	-0.2	...	17.1	24.5	28.9	104.5	673	+8
16	67.1	74.8	99.7	100	345	33.4	0.6	4.5	5.7	35.9	19.1	74.6	359	+2
198	47.0	49.0	36.9	42	3	25.9	-0.2	10.4	0.1	0.5	0.6	1.7	226	GMT
190	39.8	41.4	66.1	78	...	3.7	-9.0	5.3	0.0	0.3	0.3	0.9	257	+2
135	53.6	58.6	80.1	30	30	52.9	-0.6	15.8	0.1	0.3	1.7	0.7	855	+7
154	49.3	50.6	94.4	58	7	51.3	-0.9	4.4	0.1	0.7	2.0	3.0	237	+1
6	76.2	81.8	...	100	229	26.5	...	9.1	15.5	65.5	32.0	435.3	1	-3.5 to -8
40	67.0	72.8	89.2	74	17	21.1	9.3	...	0.3	14.3	7.2	27.5	238	-1
180	42.7	46.0	69.9	70	4	36.8	-0.1	8.2	0.1	0.3	0.3	0.5	236	+1
198	45.1	47.5	69.9	27	3	10.1	-0.6	9.0	0.0	0.1	0.3	0.5	235	+1
12	73.0	79.0	99.0	93	110	20.7	-0.1	18.7	4.1	23.9	34.0	200.2	56	-3
40	69.1	73.5	98.2	75	162	17.5	1.2	6.2	2.5	13.8	11.2	26.0	86	+8
30	69.2	75.3	97.2	91	116	47.8	-0.4	8.2	1.7	17.1	7.6	27.0	57	-5
82	59.4	62.2	59.0	96	7	4.3	-4.3	...	0.1	1.2	...	3.4	269	+3
108	49.6	53.7	97.8	51	25	64.6	-0.1	4.5	0.6	0.7	4.8	0.2	242	+1
207	51.0	53.3	83.7	45	7	59.6	-0.4	4.3	0.1	0.0	0.3	0.1	243	+1 to +2
12	75.0	79.7	98.4	95	141	38.5	-0.8	14.2	1.4	23.0	7.6	93.4	506	-6
173	47.7	48.1	67.6	81	9	22.4	-3.1	5.2	0.9	1.8	4.5	4.3	225	GMT
9	70.3	78.1	99.8	...	229	31.9	0.1	7.4	4.5	36.5	37.7	55.9	385	+1
9	74.8	78.7	99.8	91	530	21.4	1.3	17.2	2.2	5.1	0.1	10.7	53	-5
7	76.0	80.5	99.8	100	255	18.6	3.7	...	7.9	64.3	46.4	221.6	357	+2
5	72.1	78.7	...	...	303	34.1	...	15.8	11.5	37.4	65.9	136.3	420	+1
5	74.2	79.1	...	100	290	10.7	0.2	32.0	10.1	72.3	73.7	447.2	45	+1
146	...	...	85.7	100	14	0.3	...	...	0.6	1.5	0.5	5.1	253	+3
16	...	...	...	97	49	61.3	-0.7	...	...	29.1	1.6	77.8	1 767	-4
48	64.4	70.1	91.7	86	216	28.4	...	31.3	2.5	11.0	14.7	21.5	1 809	-4
...	49.2	50.9	...	...	...	34.3	-0.6	...	...	...	...	...	670	+9
32	68.3	73.5	97.5	85	170	38.1	-1.2	42.6	2.2	10.4	6.7	25.4	593	-5
43	68.2	71.9	71.3	97	202	0.1	3.3	0.8	1.7	10.3	4.3	9.3	20	+2
40	67.7	73.7	89.0	77	107	5.8	-4.6	0.2	1.0	9.3	12.5	8.0	503	-6
156	52.4	55.6	97.4	44	25	62.5	-0.6	0.0	0.6	1.5	3.2	1.9	240	+1
114	51.1	53.7	72.0	46	3	13.5	-0.3	4.3	...	0.8	...	2.6	291	+3
21	65.8	76.4	99.8	...	297	48.7	0.6	11.1	12.1	35.2	45.5	300.5	372	+2
174	42.8	43.8	57.2	24	...	4.2	-0.8	5.0	0.0	0.5	0.0	0.4	251	+3
22	68.1	71.5	99.2	47	48	44.6	-0.2	1.1	0.9	11.0	9.3	18.3	679	+12
5	74.4	81.5	...	100	299	72.0	...	5.5	10.4	54.8	77.8	430.3	358	+2
5	75.2	82.8	...	...	303	27.9	0.4	13.5	6.3	57.4	60.5	263.8	33	+1
90	53.1	55.1	...	86	...	84.7	...	2.7	2.4	3.0	20.5	13.5	241	+1
128	45.7	48.5	60.0	62	4	48.1	1.0	2.0	0.2	2.6	3.2	13.5	220	GMT
29	69.5	77.6	...	79	436	43.7	...	2.8	1.0	15.9	5.4	4.6	995	+4

	POPULATION						ECONOMY					
	total population	population change (%)	% urban	total fertility	population by age (000s)		2050 projected population	total Gross National Income (GNI) (US$M)	GNI per capita (US$)	total debt service (US$)	debt service ratio (% GNI)	aid receipts (% GNI)	military spending (% GNI)
					0 – 14	65 or over							
GERMANY	81 990 000	0.0	87.7	1.3	12 739	13 453	70 805 000	1 947 951	23 700	...	...	...	1.6
GHANA	20 176 000	2.2	36.4	4.2	7 901	627	40 056 000	5 731	290	471 800 000	9.4	11.5	0.8
GREECE	10 631 000	0.0	60.3	1.2	1 598	1 862	8 983 000	124 553	11 780	...	...	...	4.7
GRENADA	94 000	0.3	38.4	...	...	...	105 000	368	3 720	12 000 000	3.2	4.7	...
GUATEMALA	11 995 000	2.6	39.9	4.4	4 965	404	26 551 000	19 559	1 670	438 000 000	2.3	1.4	0.7
GUINEA	8 381 000	1.5	27.9	5.8	3 592	226	20 711 000	3 043	400	133 000 000	4.5	5.0	1.6
GUINEA-BISSAU	1 257 000	2.4	32.3	6.0	521	43	3 276 000	202	160	6 200 000	3.1	37.7	2.7
GUYANA	765 000	0.2	36.7	2.3	233	38	504 000	641	840	115 600 000	17.5	16.3	0.8
HAITI	8 400 000	1.6	36.3	4.0	3 305	302	13 982 000	3 887	480	41 700 000	1.0	5.4	...
HONDURAS	6 732 000	2.3	53.7	3.7	2 682	216	12 845 000	5 922	900	578 099 968	10.0	7.8	0.7
HUNGARY	9 867 000	-0.5	64.8	1.2	1 689	1 460	7 486 000	48 924	4 800	7 945 900 032	18.0	0.6	1.7
ICELAND	283 000	0.7	92.7	1.9	65	33	333 000	8 201	28 880	...	...	...	...
INDIA	1 041 144 000	1.5	27.9	3.0	337 921	50 096	1 572 055 000	474 323	460	9 694 000 128	2.1	0.3	2.5
INDONESIA	217 534 000	1.2	42.1	2.3	65 232	10 221	311 335 000	144 731	680	18 771 900 416	13.2	1.2	1.1
IRAN	72 376 000	1.4	64.7	2.8	26 302	2 364	121 424 000	112 855	1 750	3 438 200 064	3.3	0.1	2.9
IRAQ	24 246 000	2.7	67.4	4.8	9 554	659	53 574 000	...	...	...	...	...	5.5
IRELAND, REPUBLIC OF	3 878 000	1.0	59.3	2.0	820	431	5 366 000	88 385	23 060	...	...	...	1.0
ISRAEL	6 303 000	2.0	91.8	2.7	1 706	596	10 065 000	...	...	...	...	...	8.8
ITALY	57 449 000	-0.1	67.1	1.2	8 216	10 396	42 962 000	1 123 478	19 470	...	...	...	2.0
JAMAICA	2 621 000	0.9	56.6	2.4	810	186	3 816 000	7 264	2 720	643 400 000	9.2	0.2	0.8
JAPAN	127 538 000	0.1	78.9	1.3	18 694	21 826	109 220 000	4 574 164	35 990	...	...	...	1.0
JORDAN	5 196 000	2.8	78.7	4.3	1 968	137	11 709 000	8 786	1 750	669 200 000	8.0	6.8	9.2
KAZAKSTAN	16 027 000	-0.4	55.8	2.0	4 364	1 109	15 302 000	20 146	1 360	1 839 500 032	10.8	1.2	0.9
KENYA	31 904 000	1.9	34.4	4.2	13 331	869	55 368 000	10 309	340	481 000 000	4.7	5.0	1.9
KIRIBATI	85 000	1.3	38.6	...	...	...	138 000	77	830	...	...	21.8	...
KUWAIT	2 023 000	2.6	96.1	2.7	599	42	4 001 000	...	...	...	...	...	7.7
KYRGYZSTAN	5 047 000	1.2	34.3	2.3	1 670	297	7 538 000	1 386	280	173 200 000	14.2	17.8	2.4
LAOS	5 530 000	2.3	19.7	4.8	2 256	184	11 438 000	1 650	310	41 900 000	2.5	17.1	2.0
LATVIA	2 392 000	-0.6	59.8	1.1	421	357	1 744 000	7 719	3 260	561 600 000	7.8	1.3	0.9
LEBANON	3 614 000	1.6	90.1	2.2	1 089	212	5 018 000	17 585	4 010	1 821 200 000	10.5	1.2	4.0
LESOTHO	2 076 000	0.7	28.8	4.5	799	85	2 478 000	1 127	550	65 800 000	5.7	3.7	2.6
LIBERIA	3 298 000	5.5	45.5	6.8	1 244	83	14 370 000	...	...	700 000	...	...	1.2
LIBYA	5 529 000	2.2	88.0	3.3	1 795	179	9 969 000	...	...	...	...	...	...
LIECHTENSTEIN	33 000	1.1	21.5	...	...	...	39 000	...	...	...	...	...	...
LITHUANIA	3 682 000	-0.2	68.6	1.2	719	494	2 989 000	11 401	3 270	906 000 000	8.1	0.9	1.3
LUXEMBOURG	448 000	1.2	91.9	1.8	81	63	715 000	18 550	41 770	...	...	...	0.8
MACEDONIA (F.Y.R.O.M.)	2 051 000	0.3	59.4	1.5	460	203	1 894 000	3 445	1 690	161 300 000	4.6	7.7	2.5
MADAGASCAR	16 913 000	2.8	30.1	5.7	7 143	481	47 030 000	4 170	260	92 700 000	2.4	8.1	1.2
MALAWI	11 828 000	2.2	15.1	6.3	5 239	332	31 114 000	1 778	170	58 700 000	3.5	24.9	0.6
MALAYSIA	23 036 000	1.7	58.1	2.9	7 575	918	37 850 000	86 510	3 640	5 967 200 256	7.2	0.1	2.3
MALDIVES	309 000	3.0	28.0	5.4	127	10	868 000	578	2 040	19 900 000	3.8	4.7	...
MALI	12 019 000	2.9	30.9	7.0	5 235	454	41 724 000	2 280	210	97 200 000	4.3	15.6	2.3
MALTA	393 000	0.4	91.2	1.8	79	48	400 000	...	...	...	...	...	0.8
MARSHALL ISLANDS	53 000	...	66.0	...	...	...	85 000	115	2 190	...	...	56.6	...
MAURITANIA	2 830 000	3.0	59.1	6.0	1 176	84	8 452 000	974	350	100 300 000	11.0	23.3	4.0
MAURITIUS	1 180 000	0.8	41.6	1.9	298	72	1 426 000	4 592	3 830	553 299 968	12.7	0.5	0.2
MEXICO	101 842 000	1.4	74.6	2.5	32 770	4 671	146 652 000	550 456	5 540	58 258 698 240	10.4	...	0.6
MICRONESIA, FEDERATED STATES OF	129 000	2.4	28.6	...	...	...	269 000	258	2 150	...	...	39.5	...
MOLDOVA	4 273 000	-0.3	41.4	1.4	993	400	3 577 000	1 399	380	135 400 000	10.0	9.1	0.5
MONACO	34 000	0.9	100.0	...	...	...	38 000	...	...	...	...	...	...
MONGOLIA	2 587 000	1.1	56.5	2.3	892	96	4 146 000	962	400	29 200 000	3.1	23.7	2.1
MOROCCO	30 988 000	1.8	56.1	3.0	10 355	1 238	50 361 000	34 555	1 180	3 332 699 904	10.3	1.3	4.3
MOZAMBIQUE	18 986 000	1.8	33.3	5.9	8 037	591	38 837 000	3 747	210	87 500 000	2.5	24.8	2.5
MYANMAR	48 956 000	1.2	28.1	2.8	15 806	2 193	68 546 000	...	...	87 000 000	...	...	7.8
NAMIBIA	1 819 000	1.7	31.4	4.9	768	66	3 663 000	3 520	1 960	...	...	4.4	2.9
NAURU	13 000	2.3	100.0	...	...	...	26 000	...	...	...	...	...	...
NEPAL	24 153 000	2.3	12.2	4.5	9 455	859	52 415 000	5 879	250	99 700 000	1.8	7.2	0.8
NETHERLANDS	15 990 000	0.3	89.6	1.5	2 902	2 165	15 845 000	385 401	24 040	...	...	...	1.8
NEW ZEALAND	3 837 000	0.7	85.9	2.0	867	441	4 439 000	47 632	12 380	...	...	...	1.2
NICARAGUA	5 347 000	2.6	56.5	3.8	2 162	155	11 477 000	...	...	300 200 000	14.2	25.7	1.2
NIGER	11 641 000	3.6	21.1	8.0	5 401	218	51 872 000	1 953	170	28 300 000	1.6	11.5	1.2
NIGERIA	120 047 000	2.6	44.9	5.4	51 300	3 471	278 788 000	37 116	290	1 009 299 968	2.7	0.5	1.6
NORTH KOREA	22 586 000	0.7	60.5	2.1	5 902	1 315	28 038 000	...	...	...	...	...	18.8
NORWAY	4 505 000	0.4	75.0	1.7	883	687	4 880 000	160 577	35 530	...	...	...	2.2
OMAN	2 709 000	3.3	76.5	5.5	1 119	63	8 751 000	...	...	864 099 968	...	...	15.3

SOCIAL INDICATORS						ENVIRONMENT				COMMUNICATIONS				
infant mortality rate	life expectancy		literacy rate (%)	access to safe water (%)	doctors per 100 000 people	forest area (%)	annual change in forest area (%)	protected land area (%)	CO_2 emissions	telephone lines per 100 people	cellular phones per 100 people	internet connections per 1 000 people	international dialling code	time zone
	M	F												
5	75.0	81.1	...	...	350	30.7	...	26.9	10.1	63.5	68.3	364.3	49	+1
102	56.0	58.5	92.1	73	6	27.8	-1.7	4.6	0.2	1.2	0.9	1.9	233	GMT
6	75.9	81.2	99.8	...	392	27.9	0.9	3.6	8.1	52.9	75.1	132.1	30	+2
26	...	...	...	95	50	14.7	0.9	...	1.9	32.8	6.4	52.0	1 473	-4
59	63.0	68.9	80.3	92	93	26.3	-1.7	16.8	0.9	6.5	9.7	17.1	502	-6
175	48.0	49.0	...	48	13	28.2	-0.5	0.7	0.2	0.3	0.7	1.9	224	GMT
215	44.0	46.9	60.9	56	17	60.5	-0.9	0.0	...	1.0	...	3.3	245	GMT
74	58.0	66.9	99.8	94	18	78.5	-0.3	0.3	2.2	9.2	8.7	109.2	592	-4
125	50.2	56.5	66.2	46	8	3.2	-5.7	0.3	0.2	1.0	1.1	3.6	509	-5
40	63.2	69.1	84.2	88	83	48.1	-1.0	6.0	0.8	4.7	3.6	6.2	504	-6
9	67.8	76.1	99.8	99	357	19.9	0.4	7.0	5.8	37.4	49.8	148.4	36	+1
4	77.1	81.8	...	...	326	0.3	2.2	9.5	7.6	66.4	82.0	679.4	354	GMT
96	63.6	64.9	74.1	84	48	21.6	0.1	4.4	1.1	3.4	0.6	6.8	91	+5.5
48	65.3	69.3	98.0	78	16	58.0	-1.2	10.1	1.2	3.7	2.5	18.6	62	+7 to +9
44	68.8	70.8	94.8	92	85	4.5	...	5.1	4.7	16.0	2.7	6.2	98	+3.5
130	63.5	66.5	45.3	85	...	1.8	...	<0.1	3.7	...	...	...	964	+3
6	74.4	79.6	...	...	219	9.6	3.0	0.9	10.3	48.5	72.9	233.1	353	GMT
6	77.1	81.0	99.5	...	385	6.4	4.9	15.5	10.1	47.6	80.8	230.5	972	+2
6	75.5	81.9	99.8	...	554	34.0	0.3	7.3	7.2	47.1	83.9	275.8	39	+1
20	73.7	77.8	94.5	92	140	30.0	-1.5	0.1	4.3	19.7	26.9	38.5	1 876	-5
4	77.8	85.0	...	...	193	64.0	...	6.8	9.0	59.7	58.8	454.7	81	+9
34	69.7	72.5	99.5	96	166	1.0	...	3.3	3.0	12.7	14.4	40.9	962	+2
75	59.6	70.7	...	91	353	4.5	2.2	2.7	8.2	11.3	3.6	6.2	7	+4 to +6
120	48.7	49.9	95.8	57	13	30.0	-0.5	6.0	0.3	1.0	1.6	16.0	254	+3
70	...	...	...	48	...	38.4	...	...	0.3	4.0	0.5	25.0	686	+12 to +14
10	74.9	79.0	93.1	...	189	0.3	3.5	1.5	26.3	24.0	24.8	101.5	965	+3
63	64.8	72.3	...	77	301	5.2	2.6	3.5	1.3	7.7	0.5	10.6	996	+5
105	53.3	55.8	73.3	37	24	54.4	-0.4	0.0	0.1	0.9	0.5	1.8	856	+7
21	65.7	76.2	99.8	...	282	47.1	0.4	12.5	3.2	30.8	27.9	72.3	371	+2
32	71.9	75.1	95.6	100	210	3.5	-0.4	0.5	3.9	19.5	21.3	85.8	961	+2
133	37.5	35.1	91.1	78	5	0.5	...	0.2	...	1.0	1.5	2.3	266	+2
235	54.6	56.7	71.7	...	...	31.3	-2.0	1.2	0.1	...	...	...	231	GMT
20	70.7	74.8	97.0	72	128	0.2	1.4	0.1	7.2	10.9	0.9	3.6	218	+2
11	...	...	...	...	...	46.7	1.2	...	...	...	...	...	423	+1
21	67.6	77.7	99.8	...	395	31.9	0.2	9.9	4.2	31.3	25.3	67.9	370	+2
5	74.6	80.9			272	...	...	...	18.0	78.3	96.7	226.6	352	+1
26	71.4	75.8	...	...	204	35.6	...	7.1	6.1	26.4	10.9	34.3	389	+1
139	52.5	54.8	81.5	47	11	20.2	-0.9	1.9	0.1	0.4	0.9	2.1	261	+3
188	39.6	39.0	72.5	57	...	27.2	-2.4	8.9	0.1	0.5	0.5	1.7	265	+2
9	70.6	75.5	97.9	...	66	58.7	-1.2	4.6	5.4	19.9	30.0	239.5	60	+8
80	68.3	67.0	99.2	100	40	3.3	...	...	1.3	10.1	6.8	37.0	960	+5
233	51.1	53.0	69.9	65	5	10.8	-0.7	3.7	0.1	0.4	0.4	2.6	223	GMT
6	75.9	81.0	98.7	100	261	n.s.	...	...	4.7	53.0	35.4	252.6	356	+1
68	...	...	...	...	...	...	...	...	...	6.0	0.1	12.9	692	+12
183	50.9	54.1	49.6	37	14	43.9	...	1.7	1.2	0.7	0.3	2.6	222	GMT
20	68.4	75.8	94.3	100	85	7.9	-0.6	...	1.5	25.6	25.0	131.7	230	+4
30	70.4	76.4	97.2	88	186	28.9	-1.1	3.4	3.9	13.7	21.7	36.2	52	-6 to -8
24	...	...	...	...	...	21.7	-4.5	...	...	8.3	...	33.8	691	+10 to +11
33	62.8	70.3	99.8	92	350	9.9	0.2	1.4	2.3	15.4	4.8	13.7	373	+2
5	...	...	...	100	...	...	...	...	...	...	...	...	377	+1
78	61.9	65.9	99.6	60	243	6.8	-0.5	11.5	3.3	4.8	7.6	15.6	976	+8
46	68.3	72.0	69.6	80	46	6.8	...	0.7	1.2	3.9	15.7	13.2	212	GMT
200	37.3	38.6	62.8	57	...	39.0	-0.2	6.0	0.1	0.4	0.8	0.7	258	+2
110	53.8	58.8	91.4	72	30	52.3	-1.4	0.3	0.2	0.6	0.0	0.2	95	+6.5
69	48.9	49.0	92.3	77	30	9.8	-0.9	12.9	0.0	6.6	5.6	25.2	264	+2
30	...	...	...	...	...	...	...	...	...	...	...	...	674	+12
100	60.1	59.6	62.8	88	4	27.3	-1.8	7.6	0.1	1.3	0.1	2.5	977	+5.75
5	75.6	81.0	98.3	100	251	11.1	0.3	5.7	10.4	62.1	73.9	329.2	31	+1
6	75.3	80.7	...	...	218	29.7	0.5	23.4	7.9	47.1	62.1	280.7	64	+13
45	67.2	71.9	72.3	77	86	27.0	-3.0	7.0	0.7	3.1	3.0	9.9	505	-6
270	45.9	46.5	24.4	59	4	1.0	-3.7	7.7	0.1	0.2	0.0	1.1	227	+1
184	52.0	52.2	88.5	62	18	14.8	-2.6	3.3	0.1	0.4	0.3	1.8	234	+1
30	62.5	68.0	...	100	...	68.2	...	2.6	10.3	...	...	...	850	+9
4	76.0	81.9	...	100	413	28.9	0.4	6.5	7.6	72.0	82.5	596.3	47	+1
14	70.2	73.2	98.5	39	133	0.0	5.3	16.1	8.8	9.0	12.4	45.8	968	+4

	POPULATION					ECONOMY					
	total population	population change (%)	% urban	total fertility	population by age (000s)	2050 projected population	total Gross National Income (GNI) (US$M)	GNI per capita (US$)	total debt service (US$)	debt service ratio (% GNI)	aid receipts (% GNI)	military spending (% GNI)
					0 – 14	65 or over							
PAKISTAN	148 721 000	2.5	33.4	5.1	59 021	5 195	344 170 000	59 637	420	2 856 600 064	4.8	1.1	5.9
PALAU	20 000	2.1	69.3	…	…	…	39 000	131	6 730	…	…	…	…
PANAMA	2 942 000	1.4	56.5	2.4	…	…	4 262 000	9 532	3 290	928 400 000	9.9	0.2	1.4
PAPUA NEW GUINEA	5 032 000	2.2	17.6	4.3	1 929	117	10 980 000	3 026	580	304 500 000	8.3	7.2	1.1
PARAGUAY	5 778 000	2.5	56.7	3.8	2 173	191	12 565 000	7 345	1 300	330 000 000	4.4	1.1	1.1
PERU	26 523 000	1.6	73.1	2.6	8 567	1 238	42 122 000	52 147	2 000	4 305 299 968	8.3	0.8	2.4
PHILIPPINES	78 611 000	1.9	59.4	3.2	28 395	2 670	128 383 000	80 845	1 050	6 736 699 904	8.5	0.7	1.4
POLAND	38 542 000	-0.1	62.5	1.3	7 395	4 685	33 370 000	163 907	4 240	10 290 299 904	6.6	0.9	2.1
PORTUGAL	10 049 000	0.1	65.8	1.5	1 672	1 563	9 006 000	109 156	10 670	…	…	…	2.1
QATAR	584 000	1.5	92.9	3.3	151	9	831 000	…	…	…	…	…	10.0
ROMANIA	22 332 000	-0.3	55.2	1.3	4 095	2 986	18 150 000	38 388	1 710	2 340 800 000	6.4	1.2	1.6
RUSSIAN FEDERATION	143 752 000	-0.6	72.9	1.1	26 123	18 170	104 259 000	253 413	1 750	11 670 700 032	4.9	0.7	5.6
RWANDA	8 148 000	2.1	6.3	5.8	3 370	200	18 523 000	1 884	220	35 000 000	2.0	18.3	4.5
SAMOA	159 000	0.3	22.3	4.2	65	7	223 000	260	1 520	8 500 000	3.6	11.6	…
SAN MARINO	27 000	1.1	90.4	…	…	…	30 000	…	…	…	…	…	…
SÃO TOMÉ AND PRÍNCIPE	143 000	1.8	47.7	…	…	…	294 000	43	280	4 400 000	10.1	79.5	1.0
SAUDI ARABIA	21 701 000	3.1	86.7	5.5	8 735	602	59 683 000	…	…	…	…	…	14.9
SENEGAL	9 908 000	2.5	48.2	5.1	4 176	236	22 711 000	4 726	480	228 000 000	5.3	9.8	1.7
SERBIA AND MONTENEGRO	10 522 000	-0.1	51.7	1.6	2 113	1 381	9 030 000	…	…	177 400 000	2.1	…	5.0
SEYCHELLES	83 000	1.3	64.6	…	…	…	145 000	…	…	17 400 000	3.0	3.0	…
SIERRA LEONE	4 814 000	4.5	37.3	6.5	1 949	128	14 351 000	726	140	42 600 000	6.9	29.0	3.0
SINGAPORE	4 188 000	1.7	100.0	1.5	878	291	4 620 000	…	…	…	…	…	4.8
SLOVAKIA	5 408 000	0.1	57.6	1.3	1 054	615	4 674 000	20 028	3 700	2 590 000 128	13.8	0.6	1.8
SLOVENIA	1 983 000	-0.1	49.1	1.1	316	277	1 527 000	19 447	9 780	…	…	0.3	1.4
SOLOMON ISLANDS	479 000	3.3	20.2	5.3	200	12	1 458 000	253	580	9 100 000	3.2	24.0	…
SOMALIA	9 557 000	4.2	27.9	7.3	4 209	211	40 936 000	…	…	…	…	…	…
SOUTH AFRICA, REPUBLIC OF	44 203 000	0.8	57.7	2.9	14 734	1 545	47 301 000	125 486	2 900	3 859 599 872	3.1	0.4	1.5
SOUTH KOREA	47 389 000	0.7	82.5	1.5	9 740	3 305	51 561 000	447 698	9 400	23 204 999 168	5.1	…	2.9
SPAIN	39 924 000	0.0	77.8	1.1	5 874	6 767	31 282 000	586 874	14 860	…	…	…	1.3
SRI LANKA	19 287 000	0.9	23.1	2.1	4 976	1 186	23 066 000	16 294	830	737 500 032	4.6	1.7	4.7
ST KITTS AND NEVIS	38 000	-0.7	34.2	…	…	…	34 000	283	6 880	19 600 000	7.1	1.4	…
ST LUCIA	151 000	1.1	38.0	2.5	47	8	189 000	628	3 970	40 300 000	6.0	1.6	…
ST VINCENT AND THE GRENADINES	115 000	0.6	56.0	…	…	…	138 000	312	2 690	15 400 000	4.9	2.0	…
SUDAN	32 559 000	2.3	37.1	4.5	12 474	1 071	63 530 000	10 346	330	61 000 000	0.6	2.3	4.8
SURINAME	421 000	0.4	74.8	2.1	127	23	418 000	709	1 690	…	…	…	1.8
SWAZILAND	948 000	0.9	26.7	4.4	385	32	1 391 000	1 388	1 300	23 600 000	1.6	1.0	1.5
SWEDEN	8 823 000	-0.1	83.3	1.3	1 609	1 541	7 777 000	225 894	25 400	…	…	…	2.3
SWITZERLAND	7 167 000	-0.1	67.3	1.4	1 194	1 147	5 607 000	266 503	36 970	…	…	…	1.2
SYRIA	17 040 000	2.5	51.8	3.7	6 612	507	36 345 000	16 608	1 000	343 600 000	2.2	1.0	7.0
TAIWAN	22 548 000	0.7	36.7	…	…	…	…	…	…	…	…	…	…
TAJIKISTAN	6 177 000	0.7	27.7	2.9	2 397	279	9 763 000	1 051	170	87 500 000	9.3	15.3	1.3
TANZANIA	36 820 000	2.3	33.3	5.0	15 800	857	82 740 000	9 198	270	216 700 000	2.4	11.2	1.4
THAILAND	64 344 000	1.1	20.0	2.0	16 742	3 282	82 491 000	120 872	1 970	14 016 499 712	11.6	0.5	1.7
TOGO	4 779 000	2.6	33.9	5.4	2 004	142	11 832 000	1 279	270	29 600 000	2.5	5.5	1.8
TONGA	100 000	0.4	33.0	…	…	…	125 000	154	1 530	4 100 000	2.6	12.1	…
TRINIDAD AND TOBAGO	1 306 000	0.5	74.5	1.5	323	86	1 378 000	7 249	5 540	500 200 000	7.5	…	1.4
TUNISIA	9 670 000	1.1	66.2	2.1	2 809	554	14 076 000	20 051	2 070	1 900 000 000	10.2	1.2	1.8
TURKEY	68 569 000	1.3	66.2	2.3	20 021	3 847	98 818 000	168 335	2 540	21 135 800 320	10.5	0.2	5.3
TURKMENISTAN	4 930 000	1.9	44.9	3.2	1 783	202	8 401 000	5 236	950	…	…	0.7	3.4
TUVALU	10 000	1.3	53.2	…	…	…	16 000	…	…	…	…	…	…
UGANDA	24 780 000	3.2	14.5	7.1	11 466	586	101 524 000	6 286	280	159 300 000	2.6	13.1	2.3
UKRAINE	48 652 000	-0.9	68.0	1.1	8 840	6 849	29 959 000	35 185	720	3 660 699 904	11.9	1.7	3.0
UNITED ARAB EMIRATES	2 701 000	1.7	87.2	2.9	678	71	3 709 000	…	…	…	…	…	4.1
UNITED KINGDOM	59 657 000	0.2	89.5	1.6	11 272	9 359	58 933 000	1 451 442	24 230	…	…	…	2.5
UNITED STATES OF AMERICA	288 530 000	0.9	77.4	1.9	61 507	34 831	397 063 000	9 900 724	34 870	…	…	…	3.0
URUGUAY	3 385 000	0.7	92.1	2.3	827	430	4 249 000	19 036	5 670	1 313 100 032	6.8	0.1	1.3
UZBEKISTAN	25 618 000	1.4	36.6	2.3	9 022	1 163	40 513 000	13 780	550	898 700 032	12.1	1.4	1.7
VANUATU	207 000	2.5	22.1	4.3	83	6	462 000	212	1 050	2 200 000	1.0	20.4	…
VATICAN CITY	472	…	100.0	…	…	…	1 000	…	…	…	…	…	…
VENEZUELA	25 093 000	1.8	87.2	2.7	8 227	1 075	42 152 000	117 169	4 760	5 846 099 968	4.9	0.1	1.4
VIETNAM	80 226 000	1.3	24.5	2.3	26 070	4 178	123 782 000	32 578	410	1 303 200 000	4.2	5.4	…
YEMEN	19 912 000	4.1	25.0	7.6	9 188	423	102 379 000	8 304	460	221 400 000	3.0	3.5	6.1
ZAMBIA	10 872 000	2.1	39.8	5.7	4 850	307	29 262 000	3 336	320	185 600 000	6.7	28.7	1.0
ZIMBABWE	13 076 000	1.7	36.0	4.5	5 709	403	23 546 000	6 164	480	471 400 000	6.6	2.6	5.0

	SOCIAL INDICATORS					ENVIRONMENT				COMMUNICATIONS				
infant mortality rate	life expectancy M	life expectancy F	literacy rate (%)	access to safe water (%)	doctors per 100 000 people	forest area (%)	annual change in forest area (%)	protected land area (%)	CO_2 emissions	telephone lines per 100 people	cellular phones per 100 people	internet connections per 1 000 people	international dialling code	time zone
110	61.2	60.9	58.7	90	57	3.1	-1.5	4.7	0.7	2.4	0.6	3.5	92	+5
29	...	...	...	79	...	76.1	...	...	...	...	...	...	680	+9
26	...	...	97.0	90	167	38.6	-1.6	18.8	2.1	14.8	20.7	31.7	507	-5
112	56.8	58.7	76.9	42	7	67.6	-0.4	<0.1	0.5	1.4	0.2	28.1	675	+10
31	68.6	73.1	97.3	78	110	58.8	-0.5	3.4	0.9	5.1	20.4	10.6	595	-4
50	67.3	72.4	97.1	80	93	50.9	-0.4	2.7	1.1	7.8	5.9	115.0	51	-5
40	68.0	72.0	98.8	86	123	19.4	-1.4	4.8	1.0	4.0	13.7	25.9	63	+8
10	69.8	78.0	99.8	...	236	29.7	0.2	9.1	8.3	29.5	26.0	98.4	48	+1
6	72.6	79.6	99.8	...	312	40.1	1.7	6.6	5.5	42.7	77.4	349.4	351	GMT
16	69.4	72.1	95.3	...	126	0.1	9.6	...	85.7	27.5	29.3	65.6	974	+3
22	66.5	73.3	99.7	58	184	28.0	0.2	4.6	4.1	18.3	17.2	44.7	40	+2
22	60.0	72.5	99.8	99	421	50.4	...	3.1	9.8	24.3	3.8	29.3	7	+2 to +12
187	40.2	41.7	84.9	41	...	12.4	-3.9	13.8	0.1	0.3	0.8	2.5	250	+2
26	66.9	73.5	99.8	99	34	37.2	-2.1	...	0.8	5.6	1.7	16.7	685	-11
6	...	...	...	...	...	...	...	...	...	...	...	...	378	+1
75	...	...	...	...	47	28.3	...	...	0.5	3.6	...	60.0	239	GMT
29	71.1	73.7	93.6	95	166	0.7	...	2.3	14.4	14.5	11.3	13.4	966	+3
139	52.5	56.2	52.9	78	8	32.2	-0.7	11.1	0.4	2.5	4.0	10.4	221	GMT
20	70.9	75.6	...	98	...	28.3	-0.1	3.3	...	22.9	18.7	56.2	381	+1
17	...	...	...	...	132	66.7	...	...	2.5	26.7	55.2	112.5	248	+4
316	39.2	41.8	...	57	7	14.7	-2.9	1.1	0.1	0.5	0.6	1.4	232	GMT
4	75.9	80.3	99.8	100	163	3.3	...	4.7	21.0	47.1	72.4	605.2	65	+8
9	69.8	77.6	...	100	353	45.3	0.9	22.1	7.1	28.8	39.7	120.3	421	+1
5	72.3	79.6	99.8	100	228	55.0	0.2	5.9	7.4	40.1	76.0	300.8	386	+1
25	67.9	70.7	...	71	14	88.8	-0.2	0.0	0.4	1.6	0.2	4.3	677	+11
225	47.4	50.5	...	...	...	12.0	-1.0	0.3	0.0	...	...	...	252	+3
70	42.5	42.3	91.8	86	56	7.3	-0.1	5.4	8.3	11.4	21.0	70.1	27	+2
5	71.8	79.1	99.8	92	136	63.3	-0.1	6.9	7.8	47.6	60.8	510.7	82	+9
5	75.4	82.3	99.8	...	424	28.8	0.6	8.4	6.3	43.1	65.5	182.8	34	+1
19	69.9	75.9	97.1	77	36	30.0	-1.6	13.3	0.4	4.3	3.8	7.9	94	+6
25	...	...	...	98	117	11.1	-0.6	...	2.5	56.9	3.1	51.6	1 869	-4
19	71.1	76.4	...	98	47	14.8	-4.9	...	1.3	...	...	...	1 758	-4
25	...	...	...	93	88	15.4	-1.4	...	1.4	22.0	2.1	30.9	1 784	-4
108	57.6	60.6	79.1	75	9	25.9	-1.4	3.4	0.1	1.4	0.3	1.8	249	+3
33	68.5	73.7	...	82	25	90.5	...	4.5	5.2	17.6	19.1	33.0	597	-3
142	35.8	34.8	91.2	...	15	30.3	1.2	...	0.4	3.1	6.5	13.7	268	+2
4	77.6	82.6	...	100	311	65.9	...	8.1	5.5	73.9	79.0	516.3	46	+1
4	75.9	82.3	...	100	323	30.3	0.4	25.7	5.9	71.8	72.4	404.0	41	+1
29	70.6	73.1	88.3	80	144	2.5	...	0.0	3.3	10.9	1.2	3.6	963	+2
...	...	...	...	...	...	...	...	...	...	57.3	96.6	349.0	886	+8
73	65.2	70.8	99.8	60	201	2.8	0.5	4.1	0.8	3.6	0.0	0.5	992	+5
165	50.1	52.0	91.6	68	4	43.9	-0.2	14.6	0.1	0.4	1.2	8.3	255	+3
29	67.9	73.8	99.0	84	24	28.9	-0.7	13.8	3.2	9.4	11.9	55.6	66	+7
142	51.1	53.3	77.4	54	8	9.4	-3.4	7.6	0.2	1.0	2.0	10.7	228	GMT
21	...	...	...	100	...	5.5	...	...	1.2	9.9	0.1	10.2	676	+13
20	72.5	77.2	99.8	90	79	50.5	-0.8	6.0	17.4	24.0	17.3	92.3	1 868	-4
28	70.8	73.7	94.3	80	70	3.1	0.2	0.3	2.4	10.9	4.0	41.2	216	+1
45	68.0	73.2	96.9	82	121	13.3	0.2	1.3	3.2	28.5	30.2	37.7	90	+2
70	63.9	70.4	...	...	300	8.0	...	4.1	5.7	8.0	0.2	1.7	993	+5
53	...	...	...	...	...	...	...	...	...	...	...	...	688	+12
127	45.3	46.8	80.3	52	...	21.0	-2.0	7.9	0.1	0.3	1.4	2.7	256	+3
21	62.7	73.5	99.9	98	299	16.5	0.3	1.6	7.0	21.2	4.4	11.9	380	+2
9	74.1	78.4	91.5	...	181	3.8	2.8	...	32.4	39.7	72.0	339.2	971	+4
6	75.7	80.7	...	100	164	11.6	0.6	20.4	9.2	58.8	78.3	399.5	44	GMT
8	74.6	80.4	...	100	279	24.7	0.2	13.1	19.8	66.5	44.4	499.5	1	-5 to -10
17	71.6	78.9	99.3	98	370	7.4	5.0	0.3	1.8	28.3	15.5	119.0	598	-3
67	66.8	72.5	99.7	85	309	4.8	0.2	1.8	4.5	6.6	0.3	5.9	998	+5
44	67.5	70.5	...	88	12	36.7	0.1	...	0.3	3.4	0.2	27.4	678	+11
...	...	...	...	...	...	...	...	...	...	...	...	...	39	+1
23	70.9	76.7	98.2	83	236	56.1	-0.4	35.4	6.7	11.2	26.4	52.8	58	-4
39	66.9	71.6	97.3	77	48	30.2	0.5	3.0	0.6	3.8	1.5	4.9	84	+7
117	60.7	62.9	67.8	69	23	0.9	-1.9	0.0	0.9	2.2	0.8	0.9	967	+3
202	42.6	41.7	89.1	64	7	42.0	-2.4	8.5	0.2	0.8	0.9	2.4	260	+2
117	43.3	42.4	97.6	83	14	49.2	-1.5	7.9	1.2	1.9	2.4	7.3	263	+2

Definitions

INDICATOR	DEFINITION
POPULATION	
Total population	Interpolated mid-year population, 2002.
Population change	Percentage annual rate of change, 2000–2005.
% urban	Urban population as a percentage of the total population, 2001.
Total fertility	Average number of children a women will have during her child-bearing years, 2000–2005.
Population by age	Population in age groups 0–14 and 65 or over, in thousands, 2000.
2050 projected population	Projected total population for the year 2050.
ECONOMY	
Total Gross National Income (GNI)	The sum of value added to the economy by all resident producers plus taxes, less subsidies, plus net receipts of primary income from abroad. Data are in U.S. dollars (millions), 2001. Formerly known as Gross National Product (GNP).
GNI per capita	Gross National Income per person in U.S. dollars using the World Bank Atlas method, 2001.
Total debt service	Sum of principal repayments and interest paid on long-term debt, interest paid on short-term debt and repayments to the International Monetary Fund (IMF), 2000.
Debt service ratio	Debt service as a percentage of GNI, 2000.
Aid receipts	Aid received as a percentage of GNI from the Development Assistance Committee (DAC) of the Organization for Economic Co-operation and Development (OECD), 2000.
Military spending	Military-related spending, including recruiting, training, construction, and the purchase of military supplies and equipment, as a percentage of Gross National Income, 1999.
SOCIAL INDICATORS	
Infant mortality rate	Number of deaths of children aged under 5 per 1 000 live births, 2000.
Life expectancy	Average life expectancy, at birth in years, male and female, 2000–2005.
Literacy rate	Percentage of population aged 15–24 with at least a basic ability to read and write, 2002.
Access to safe water	Percentage of the population with sustainable access to sources of improved drinking water, 2000.
Doctors	Number of trained doctors per 100 000 people, most recent year figures obtained.
ENVIRONMENT	
Forest area	Percentage of total land area covered by forest.
Change in forest area	Average annual percentage change in forest area, 1990–2000.
Protected land area	Percentage of total land area designated as protected land.
CO_2 emissions	Emissions of carbon dioxide from the burning of fossil fuels and the manufacture of cement, divided by the population, expressed in metric tons, 1998.
COMMUNICATIONS	
Telephone lines	Main telephone lines per 100 inhabitants, 2001.
Cellular phones	Cellular mobile subscribers per 100 inhabitants, 2001.
Internet connections	Internet users per 1 000 inhabitants, 2001.
International dialling code	The country code prefix to be used when dialling from another country.
Time zone	Time difference in hours from Greenwich Mean Time.

Main statistical sources

SOURCE	WEB ADDRESS
United Nations Statistics Division	unstats.un.org/unsd
World Population Prospects: The 2000 Revision and World Urbanization Prospects: The 2001 Revision, United Nations Population Division	www.un.org/esa/population/unpop
United Nations Population Information Network	www.un.org/popin
United Nation Development Programme	www.undp.org
Organisation for Economic Cooperation and Development	www.oecd.org
State of the World's Forests 2001, Food and Agriculture Organization of the United Nations	www.fao.org
World Development Indicators 2002, World Bank	www.worldbank.org/data
World Resources 2000–2001, World Resources Institute	www.wri.org
International Telecommunication Union	www.itu.int

Introduction to the index

The index includes all names shown on the reference maps in the atlas. Each entry includes the country or geographical area in which the feature is located, a page number and an alphanumeric reference. Additional entry details and aspects of the index are explained below.

Name forms

The names policy in this atlas is generally to use local name forms which are officially recognized by the governments of the countries concerned. Rules established by the Permanent Committee on Geographical Names for British Official Use (PCGN) are applied to the conversion of non-roman alphabet names, for example in the Russian Federation, into the roman alphabet used in English.

However, English conventional name forms are used for the most well-known places for which such a form is in common use. In these cases, the local form is included in brackets on the map and appears as a cross-reference in the index. Other alternative names, such as well-known historical names or those in other languages, may also be included in brackets on the map and as cross-references in the index. All country names and those for international physical features appear in their English forms. Names appear in full in the index, although they may appear in abbreviated form on the maps.

Referencing

Names are referenced by page number and by grid reference. The grid reference relates to the alphanumeric values which appear on the edges of each map. These reflect the graticule on the map – the letter relates to longitude divisions, the number to latitude divisions.

Names are generally referenced to the largest scale map page on which they appear. For large geographical features, including countries, the reference is to the largest scale map on which the feature appears in its entirety, or on which the majority of it appears.

Rivers are referenced to their lowest downstream point – either their mouth or their confluence with another river. The river name will generally be positioned as close to this point as possible.

Alternative names

Alternative names appear as cross-references and refer the user to the index entry for the form of the name used on the map.

For rivers with multiple names - for example those which flow through several countries - all alternative name forms are included within the main index entries, with details of the countries in which each form applies.

Administrative qualifiers

Administrative divisions are included in entries to differentiate duplicate names - entries of exactly the same name and feature type within the one country - where these division names are shown on the maps. In such cases, duplicate names are alphabetized in the order of the administrative division names.

Additional qualifiers are included for names within selected geographical areas, to indicate more clearly their location.

Descriptors

Entries, other than those for towns and cities, include a descriptor indicating the type of geographical feature. Descriptors are not included where the type of feature is implicit in the name itself, unless there is a town or city of exactly the same name.

Insets

Where relevant, the index clearly indicates [inset] if a feature appears on an inset map.

Alphabetical order

The Icelandic characters Þ and þ are transliterated and alphabetized as 'Th' and 'th'. The German character ß is alphabetized as 'ss'. Names beginning with Mac or Mc are alphabetized exactly as they appear. The terms Saint, Sainte, etc, are abbreviated to St, Ste, etc, but alphabetized as if in the full form.

Numerical entries

Entries beginning with numerals appear at the beginning of the index, in numerical order. Elsewhere, numerals are alphabetized before 'a'.

Permuted terms

Names beginning with generic geographical terms are permuted - the descriptive term is placed after, and the index alphabetized by, the main part of the name. For example, Mount Everest is indexed as Everest, Mount; Lake Superior as Superior, Lake. This policy is applied to all languages. Permuting has not been applied to names of towns, cities or administrative divisions beginning with such geographical terms. These remain in their full form, for example, Lake Isabella, USA.

Gazetteer entries and connections

Selected entries have been extended to include gazetteer-style information. Important geographical facts which relate specifically to the entry are included within the entry in coloured type.

Entries for features which also appear on, or which have a topical link to, the thematic pages of the atlas include a reference to those pages.

Abbreviations

admin. dist.	administrative district	IL	Illinois	plat.	plateau
admin. div.	administrative division	imp. l.	impermanent lake	P.N.G.	Papua New Guinea
admin. reg.	administrative region	IN	Indiana	Port.	Portugal
Afgh.	Afghanistan	Indon.	Indonesia	pref.	prefecture
AK	Alaska	Kazakh.	Kazakhstan	prov.	province
AL	Alabama	KS	Kansas	pt	point
Alg.	Algeria	KY	Kentucky	Qld	Queensland
AR	Arkansas	Kyrg.	Kyrgyzstan	Que.	Québec
Arg.	Argentina	l.	lake	r.	river
aut. comm.	autonomous community	LA	Louisiana	reg.	region
aut. reg.	autonomous region	lag.	lagoon	res.	reserve
aut. rep.	autonomous republic	Lith.	Lithuania	resr	reservoir
AZ	Arizona	Lux.	Luxembourg	RI	Rhode Island
Azer.	Azerbaijan	MA	Massachusetts	Rus. Fed.	Russian Federation
b.	bay	Madag.	Madagascar	S.	South, Southern
Bangl.	Bangladesh	Man.	Manitoba	S.A.	South Australia
B.C.	British Columbia	MD	Maryland	salt l.	salt lake
Bol.	Bolivia	ME	Maine	Sask.	Saskatchewan
Bos.-Herz.	Bosnia-Herzegovina	Mex.	Mexico	SC	South Carolina
Bulg.	Bulgaria	MI	Michigan	SD	South Dakota
c.	cape	MN	Minnesota	sea chan.	sea channel
CA	California	MO	Missouri	Serb. and Mont.	Serbia and Montenegro
Cent. Afr. Rep.	Central African Republic	Moz.	Mozambique	Sing.	Singapore
CO	Colorado	MS	Mississippi	Switz.	Switzerland
Col.	Colombia	MT	Montana	Tajik.	Tajikistan
CT	Connecticut	mt.	mountain	Tanz.	Tanzania
Czech Rep.	Czech Republic	mts	mountains	Tas.	Tasmania
DC	District of Columbia	N.	North, Northern	terr.	territory
DE	Delaware	nat. park	national park	Thai.	Thailand
Dem. Rep. Congo	Democratic Republic of Congo	N.B.	New Brunswick	TN	Tennessee
depr.	depression	NC	North Carolina	Trin. and Tob.	Trinidad and Tobago
des.	desert	ND	North Dakota	Turkm.	Turkmenistan
Dom. Rep.	Dominican Republic	NE	Nebraska	TX	Texas
E.	East, Eastern	Neth.	Netherlands	U.A.E.	United Arab Emirates
Equat. Guinea	Equatorial Guinea	NH	New Hampshire	U.K.	United Kingdom
esc.	escarpment	NJ	New Jersey	Ukr.	Ukraine
est.	estuary	NM	New Mexico	U.S.A.	United States of America
Eth.	Ethiopia	N.S.	Nova Scotia	UT	Utah
Fin.	Finland	N.S.W.	New South Wales	Uzbek.	Uzbekistan
FL	Florida	N.T.	Northern Territory	VA	Virginia
for.	forest	NV	Nevada	Venez.	Venezuela
Fr. Guiana	French Guiana	N.W.T.	Northwest Territories	Vic.	Victoria
F.Y.R.O.M.	Former Yugoslav Republic of Macedonia	NY	New York	vol.	volcano
g.	gulf	N.Z.	New Zealand	vol. crater	volcanic crater
GA	Georgia	OH	Ohio	VT	Vermont
Guat.	Guatemala	OK	Oklahoma	W.	West, Western
HI	Hawaii	OR	Oregon	WA	Washington
H.K.	Hong Kong	PA	Pennsylvania	W.A.	Western Australia
Hond.	Honduras	Para.	Paraguay	WI	Wisconsin
i.	island	P.E.I.	Prince Edward Island	WV	West Virginia
IA	Iowa	pen.	peninsula	WY	Wyoming
ID	Idaho	Phil.	Philippines	Y.T.	Yukon Territory

1

3-y Severnyy Rus. Fed. 37 S3
5 de Outubro Angola see Xá-Muteba
9 de Julio Arg. 140 D5
25 de Mayo Buenos Aires Arg. 140 D5
25 de Mayo La Pampa Arg. 140 C5
26 Bakı Komissarı Azer. 87 H3
70 Mile House Canada 116 F5
100 Mile House Canada 116 F5
150 Mile House Canada 116 F4

A

Aabenraa Denmark see Åbenrå
Aachen Germany 48 G4
Aalborg Denmark see Ålborg
Aalborg Bugt b. Denmark see Ålborg Bugt
Aalen Germany 49 K6
Aalesund Norway see Ålesund
Aaley Lebanon see Aley
Aalst Belgium 48 E4
Aanaar Fin. see Inari
Aarhus Denmark see Århus
Aarlen Belgium see Arlon
Aars Denmark see Års
Aarschot Belgium 48 E4
Aasiaat Greenland 115 M3
Aath Belgium see Ath
Aba China 72 D1
Aba Dem. Rep. Congo 94 D3
Aba Nigeria 92 D4
Abacaxis r. Brazil 139 G4
Ābādān Iran 84 C4
Ābādeh Iran 84 D4
Ābādeh Ţashk Iran 84 D4
Abadla Alg. 50 D5
Abaeté Brazil 141 B2
Abaetetuba Brazil 139 I4
Abagnar Qi China see Xilinhot
Abaiang atoll Kiribati 146 H5
Abajo Peak U.S.A. 125 I3
Abakaliki Nigeria 92 D4
Abakan Rus. Fed. 68 G2
Abakanskiy Khrebet mts Rus. Fed. 68 F2
Abalak Niger 92 D3
Abana Turkey 86 D2
Abancay Peru 138 D6
Abariringa atoll Kiribati see Kanton
Abarkūh, Kavīr-e des. Iran 84 D4
Abarqū Iran 84 D4
Abarshahr Iran see Neyshābūr
Abashiri Japan 70 G3
Abashiri-wan b. Japan 70 G3
Abasolo Mex. 127 D7
Abau P.N.G. 106 E1
Abaya, Lake Eth. 94 D3
Ābaya Hāyk' l. Eth. see Abaya, Lake
Ābay Wenz r. Eth. 94 D2 see Blue Nile
Abaza Rus. Fed. 68 G2
Abba Cent. Afr. Rep. 94 B3
Abbasabad Iran 84 D3
'Abbāsābād Iran 84 E2
Abbasanta Sardinia Italy 54 C4
Abbatis Villa France see Abbeville
Abbe, Lake Djibouti/Eth. 82 F7
Abbeville France 48 B4
Abbeville AL U.S.A. 129 C6
Abbeville GA U.S.A. 129 D6
Abbeville LA U.S.A. 127 E6
Abbeville SC U.S.A. 129 D5
Abbey Canada 117 I5
Abbeyfeale Rep. of Ireland 47 C5
Abbey Town U.K. 44 D4
Abborrträsk Sweden 40 K4
Abbot, Mount Australia 106 D4
Abbot Ice Shelf Antarctica 148 K2
Abbotsford Canada 116 F5
Abbott NM U.S.A. 123 G5
Abbott VA U.S.A. 130 E5
Abbottabad Pak. 85 I3
'Abd al 'Azīz, Jabal hill Syria 87 F3
'Abd al Kūrī i. Yemen 82 H7
'Abd Allah, Khawr sea chan. Iraq/Kuwait 84 C4
Abd al Ma'asīr well Saudi Arabia 81 D4
Ābdānān Iran 84 B3
Abdollāhābād Iran 84 D3
Abdulino Rus. Fed. 37 Q5
Abéché Chad 93 F3
Abellinum Italy see Avellino
Abel Tasman National Park N.Z. 109 D5
Abengourou Côte d'Ivoire 92 C4
Åbenrå Denmark 41 F9
Abensberg Germany 49 L6
Abeokuta Nigeria 92 D4
Aberaeron U.K. 45 C6
Aberchirder U.K. 46 G3
Abercorn Zambia see Mbala
Abercrombie r. Australia 108 D4
Aberdare U.K. 45 D7
Aberdaron U.K. 45 C6
Aberdaugleddau U.K. see Milford Haven
Aberdeen Australia 108 E4
Aberdeen Hong Kong China 73 [inset]
Aberdeen S. Africa 96 G7
Aberdeen U.K. 46 G3
Aberdeen U.S.A. 126 D2
Aberdeen Lake Canada 117 L1
Aberdovey U.K. see Aberdyfi
Aberdyfi U.K. 45 C6
Aberfeldy U.K. 46 F4
Aberford U.K. 44 F5
Aberfoyle U.K. 46 E4
Abergavenny U.K. 45 D7
Abergwaun U.K. see Fishguard
Aberhonddu U.K. see Brecon
Abermaw U.K. see Barmouth
Abernathy U.S.A. 127 C5
Aberporth U.K. 45 C6
Abersoch U.K. 45 C6
Abertawe U.K. see Swansea
Aberteifi U.K. see Cardigan
Aberystwyth U.K. 45 C6
Abeshr Chad see Abéché
Abez' Rus. Fed. 37 S2
Āb Gāh Iran 85 E5
Abhā Saudi Arabia 82 F6
Abhar Iran 84 C2
Abiad, Bahr el r. Sudan/Uganda 82 D6 see White Nile

▶Abidjan Côte d'Ivoire 92 C4
Former capital of Côte d'Ivoire. 4th most populous city in Africa.

Abijatta-Shalla National Park Eth. 94 D3
Ab-i-Kavīr salt flat Iran 84 E3
Abilene KS U.S.A. 126 D4
Abilene TX U.S.A. 127 D5
Abingdon U.K. 45 F7
Abingdon U.S.A. 130 D5
Abington Reef Australia 106 E3
Abinsk Rus. Fed. 86 E1
Abiseo, Parque Nacional nat. park Peru 138 C5
Abitau Lake Canada 117 J2
Abitibi, Lake Canada 118 E4
Ab Khūr Iran 84 E3
Abminga Australia 105 F6
Abnūb Egypt 86 C6
Åbo Fin. see Turku
Abohar India 78 C3
Aboisso Côte d'Ivoire 92 C4
Aboite U.S.A. 130 C3
Abomey Benin 92 D4
Abongabong, Gunung mt. Indon. 67 B6
Abong Mbang Cameroon 92 E4
Abou Déia Chad 93 E3
Abovyan Armenia 87 G2
Aboyne U.K. 46 G3
Abqaiq Saudi Arabia 84 C5
Abraham's Bay Bahamas 129 F8
Abramov, Mys pt Rus. Fed. 38 I2
Abrantes Port. 53 B4
Abra Pampa Arg. 140 C2
Abreojos, Punta pt Mex. 123 E8
'Abri Sudan 82 D5
Abrolhos Bank sea feature S. Atlantic Ocean 144 F7
Abruzzo, Parco Nazionale d' nat. park Italy 54 E4
Absalom, Mount Antarctica 148 B1
Absaroka Range mts U.S.A. 122 F3
Abtar, Jabal al hills Syria 81 C2
Abtsgmünd Germany 49 J6
Abū aḑ Ḑuhūr Syria 81 C2
Abū al Ḩusayn, Qā' imp. l. Jordan 81 D3
Abū'Alī i. Saudi Arabia 84 C5
Abū al Jirāb i. U.A.E. 84 D5
Abū 'Āmūd, Wādī watercourse Jordan 81 C4
Abū 'Arīsh Saudi Arabia 82 F6
Abu 'Aweigīla well Egypt see Abū 'Uwayqilah
Abu Deleiq Sudan 82 D6

▶Abu Dhabi U.A.E. 84 D5
Capital of the United Arab Emirates.

Abū Du'ān Syria 81 D1
Abu Gubeiha Sudan 82 D7
Abū Ḩafnah, Wādī watercourse Jordan 81 D3
Abu Haggag Egypt see Ra's al Ḩikmah
Abū Ḩallūfah, Jabal hill Jordan 81 C4
Abu Hamed Sudan 82 D6

▶Abuja Nigeria 92 D4
Capital of Nigeria.

Abū Jifān well Saudi Arabia 84 B5
Abū Jurdhān Jordan 81 B4
Abū Kamāl Syria 87 F4
Abu Matariq Sudan 93 F3
Abumombazi Dem. Rep. Congo 94 C3
Abu Musa i. The Gulf 84 D5
Abū Mūsā, Jazīreh-ye i. The Gulf see Abu Musa
Abunã r. Bol. 138 E5
Abunã Brazil 138 E5
Ābune Yosēf mt. Eth. 82 E7
Abū Nujaym Libya 93 E1
Abū Qa'ṭūr Syria 81 C2
Abū Rawthah, Jabal mt. Egypt 81 B5
Aburo mt. Dem. Rep. Congo 94 D3
Abu Road India 75 G4
Abū Rujmayn, Jabal mts Syria 81 D2
Abu Rûtha, Gebel mt. Egypt see Abū Rawthah, Jabal
Abū Sawādah well Saudi Arabia 84 C5
Abu Simbil Egypt see Abū Sunbul
Abū Sunbul Egypt 82 D5
Abū Ṭarfā', Wādī watercourse Egypt 81 A5
Abut Head hd N.Z. 109 C6
Abū 'Uwayqilah well Egypt 81 B4
Abu Zabad Sudan 82 C7
Abū Ẓabī U.A.E. see Abu Dhabi
Abūzam Iran 84 C4
Abū Zanīmah Egypt 86 D5
Abu Zenîma Egypt see Abū Zanīmah
Abyad Sudan 82 C7
Abyaḑ, Jabal al mts Syria 81 C2
Abyār al Hakīm well Libya 86 A5
Abydos Australia 104 B5
Abyei Sudan 82 C8
Abyssinia country Africa see Ethiopia
Academician Vernadskiy research station Antarctica see Vernadsky
Academy Bay Rus. Fed. see Akademii, Zaliv
Acadia prov. Canada see Nova Scotia
Acadia National Park U.S.A. 128 G2
Açailândia Brazil 139 I5
Acamarachi mt. Chile see Pili, Cerro
Acampamento de Caça do Mucusso Angola 95 C5
Acandí Col. 138 C2
A Cañiza Spain 53 B2
Acaponeta Mex. 132 C4
Acapulco Mex. 132 E5
Acapulco de Juárez Mex. see Acapulco
Acará Brazil 139 I4
Acaraú Brazil 139 J4
Acaray, Represa de resr Para. 140 E3
Acari, Serra hills Brazil/Guyana 139 G3
Acarigua Venez. 138 E2
Acatlan Mex. 132 E5
Accho Israel see 'Akko
Accomac U.S.A. 131 H5
Accomack U.S.A. see Accomac

▶Accra Ghana 92 C4
Capital of Ghana.

Accrington U.K. 44 E5
Ach r. Germany 49 L6
Achacachi Bol. 138 E7
Achaguas Venez. 138 E2
Achalpur India 78 D5
Achampet India 80 C2
Achan Rus. Fed. 70 E2
Achayvayam Rus. Fed. 61 S3
Acheng China 70 B3
Achhota India 80 D1
Achicourt France 48 C4
Achill Rep. of Ireland 47 C4
Achillbeg Island Rep. of Ireland 47 C4
Achill Island Rep. of Ireland 47 B4
Achiltibuie U.K. 46 D2
Achim Germany 49 J1
Achinsk Rus. Fed. 60 K4
Achit Rus. Fed. 37 R4
Achit Nuur l. Mongolia 76 H2
Achkhoy-Martan Rus. Fed. 87 G2
Achna Cyprus 81 A2
Achnasheen U.K. 46 D3
Acıgöl l. Turkey 55 M6
Acıpayam Turkey 55 M6
Acireale Sicily Italy 54 F6
Ackerman U.S.A. 127 F5
Ackley U.S.A. 126 E3
Acklins Island Bahamas 129 F8
Acle U.K. 45 I6

▶Aconcagua, Cerro mt. Arg. 140 B4
Highest mountain in South America.
south america 134–135

Acopiara Brazil 139 K5
A Coruña Spain 53 B2
Acqui Terme Italy 54 C2
Acra U.S.A. 131 H2
Acragas Sicily Italy see Agrigento
Acraman, Lake salt flat Australia 107 A7
Acre r. Brazil 138 E6
Acre Israel see 'Akko
Acre, Bay of Israel see Haifa, Bay of
Acri Italy 54 G5
Ács Hungary 43 Q7
Actaeon Group is Fr. Polynesia see Actéon, Groupe
Actéon, Groupe is Fr. Polynesia 147 K7
Acton Canada 130 E2
Acton U.S.A. 124 D4
Acungui Brazil 141 A4
Acunum Acusio France see Montélimar
Ada MN U.S.A. 126 D2
Ada OH U.S.A. 130 D3
Ada OK U.S.A. 127 D5
Ada WI U.S.A. 130 B2
Adabazar Turkey see Sakarya
Adaja r. Spain 53 D3
Adalia Turkey see Antalya
Adam Oman 83 I5
Adam, Mount hill Falkland Is 140 E8
Adamantina Brazil 141 A3
Adams IN U.S.A. 130 C4
Adams KY U.S.A. 130 D4
Adams MA U.S.A. 131 I2
Adams NY U.S.A. 131 G2
Adams, Mount U.S.A. 122 C3
Adams Center U.S.A. 131 G2
Adams Lake Canada 116 G5
Adams Mountain U.S.A. 116 D4
Adam's Peak Sri Lanka 80 D5
Adams Peak U.S.A. 124 C2

▶Adamstown Pitcairn Is 147 L7
Capital of the Pitcairn Islands.

'Adan Yemen see Aden
Adana Turkey 81 B1
Adana prov. Turkey 81 B1
Adana Yemen see Aden
Adapazarı Turkey see Sakarya
Adare Rep. of Ireland 47 D5
Adare, Cape Antarctica 148 H2
Adavale Australia 107 D5
Adban Afgh. 85 H2
Ad Dabbah Sudan see Ed Debba
Ad Dabbīyah well Saudi Arabia 84 C5
Ad Dafīnah Saudi Arabia 82 F5
Ad Dahnā' des. Saudi Arabia 82 G5
Ad Dakhla W. Sahara 92 B2
Ad Damir Sudan see Ed Damer
Ad Dammām Saudi Arabia see Dammam
Addanki India 80 C3
Ad Dār al Ḩamrā' Saudi Arabia 82 E4
Ad Darb Saudi Arabia 82 F6
Ad Dawādimī Saudi Arabia 82 F5
Ad Dawḩah Qatar see Doha
Ad Dawr Iraq 87 F4
Ad Daww plain Syria 81 C2
Ad Dayr Iraq 87 G5
Ad Dibdibah plain Saudi Arabia 84 B5
Ad Diffah plat. Egypt see Libyan Plateau

▶Addis Ababa Eth. 94 D3
Capital of Ethiopia.

Addison U.S.A. 131 G2
Ad Dīwānīyah Iraq 87 G5
Addlestone U.K. 45 G7
Addo Elephant National Park S. Africa 97 G7
Addoo Atoll Maldives see Addu Atoll
Addu Atoll Maldives 77 D12
Ad Duwayd well Saudi Arabia 87 F5
Ad Duwaym Sudan see Ed Dueim
Ad Duwayris well Saudi Arabia 84 C6
Adegaon India 78 D5
Adel GA U.S.A. 129 D6
Adel IA U.S.A. 126 E3

▶Adelaide Australia 107 B7
State capital of South Australia.

Adelaide r. Australia 104 E3
Adelaide Bahamas 129 E7
Adelaide Island Antarctica 148 L2
Adelaide River Australia 104 E3
Adele Island Australia 104 C3
Adélie Coast Antarctica 148 G2
Adélie Land reg. Antarctica 148 G2
Adelong Australia 108 D5
Aden Yemen 82 F7
Aden, Gulf of Somalia/Yemen 82 G7
Adena U.S.A. 130 E3
Adenau Germany 48 G4
Adendorf Germany 49 K1
Aderbissinat Niger 92 D3
Aderno Sicily Italy see Adrano
Adesar India 78 B5
Adhan, Jabal mt. U.A.E. 84 E5
Adh Dhāyūf well Saudi Arabia 87 G6
'Adhfā' well Saudi Arabia 87 F5
'Ādhirīyāt, Jibāl al mts Jordan 81 C4
Adi i. Indon. 65 I7
Ādī Ārk'ay Eth. 82 E7
Adige r. Italy 54 E2
Ādīgrat Eth. 94 D2
Adilabad India 80 C2
Adilcevaz Turkey 87 F3
Adin U.S.A. 122 C4
Adīrī Libya 93 E2
Adirondack Mountains U.S.A. 131 H1
Ādīs Ābeba Eth. see Addis Ababa
Adi Ugri Eritrea see Mendefera
Adıyaman Turkey 86 E3
Adjud Romania 55 L1
Adlavik Islands Canada 119 K3
Admiralty Island Canada 115 H3
Admiralty Island U.S.A. 116 C3
Admiralty Island National Monument - Kootznoowoo Wilderness nat. park U.S.A. 116 C3
Admiralty Islands P.N.G. 65 L7
Ado-Ekiti Nigeria 92 D4
Adok Sudan 82 D8
Adolfo L. Mateos Mex. 123 E8
Adolphus U.S.A. 130 B5
Adonara i. Indon. 104 C2
Adoni India 80 C3
Adorf Germany 49 M4
Adorf (Diemelsee) Germany 49 I3
Ado-Tymovo Rus. Fed. 70 F2
Adour r. France 52 D5
Adra Spain 53 E5
Adramyttium Turkey see Edremit
Adramyttium, Gulf of Turkey see Edremit Körfezi
Adrano Sicily Italy 54 F6
Adrar Alg. 92 C2
Adrar hills Mali see Ifôghas, Adrar des
Adraskand r. Afgh. 85 F3
Adré Chad 93 F3
Adrian MI U.S.A. 130 C3
Adrian TX U.S.A. 127 C5
Adrianople Turkey see Edirne
Adrianopolis Turkey see Edirne
Adriatic Sea Europe 54 E2
Adua Eth. see Ādwa
Adunara i. Indon. see Adonara
Adusa Dem. Rep. Congo 94 C3
Aduwa Eth. see Ādwa
Adverse Well Australia 104 C5
Ādwa Eth. 94 D2
Adycha r. Rus. Fed. 61 O3
Adyk Rus. Fed. 39 J7
Adzhiyan Turkm. 84 D2
Adzopé Côte d'Ivoire 92 C4
Aegean Sea Greece/Turkey 55 K5
Aegina i. Greece see Aigina
Aegyptus country Africa see Egypt
Aela Jordan see Al 'Aqabah
Aelana Jordan see Al 'Aqabah
Aelia Capitolina Israel/West Bank see Jerusalem
Aelönlaplap atoll Marshall Is see Ailinglapalap
Aenus Turkey see Enez
Aerzen Germany 49 J2
Aesernia Italy see Isernia
A Estrada Spain 53 B2
Afabet Eritrea 82 E6
Afanas'yevo Rus. Fed. 38 L4
Affreville Alg. see Khemis Miliana
Afghānestān country Asia see Afghanistan
▶Afghanistan country Asia 85 G3
asia 6, 58–59
Afgooye Somalia 94 E3
'Afīf Saudi Arabia 82 F5
Afiun Karahissar Turkey see Afyon
Åfjord Norway 40 G5
Aflou Alg. 50 E5
Afmadow Somalia 94 E3
Afogados da Ingazoira Brazil 139 K5
A Fonsagrada Spain 53 C2
Afonso Cláudio Brazil 141 C3
Āfrēra Terara vol. Eth. 82 F7
Africa Nova country Africa see Tunisia
'Afrīn Syria 81 C1
'Afrīn, Nahr r. Syria/Turkey 81 C1
Afşin Turkey 86 E3
Afsluitdijk barrage Neth. 48 F2
Afton U.S.A. 122 F4
Afuá Brazil 139 H4
'Afula Israel 81 B3
Afyon Turkey 55 N5
Afyonkarahisar Turkey see Afyon
Aga Germany 49 M4
Agadès Niger see Agadez
Agadez Niger 92 D3
Agadir Morocco 92 C1
Agadyr' Kazakh. 76 D2
Agalega Islands Mauritius 145 L6
Agana Guam see Hagåtña
Agara Georgia 87 F2
Agartala India 79 G5
Agashi India 80 B2
Agate Canada 118 E4
Agathe France see Agde
Agathonisi i. Greece 55 L6
Agats Indon. 65 J8
Agatti i. India 80 B4
Agboville Côte d'Ivoire 92 C4
Ağcabädi Azer. 87 G2
Ağdam Azer. 87 G3
Ağdaş Azer. 87 G2
Agdash Azer. see Ağdaş
Agde France 52 F5
Agdzhabedi Azer. see Ağcabädi
Agedabia Libya see Ajdābiyā
Agen France 52 E4
Aggeneys S. Africa 96 D5
Aggteleki nat. park Hungary 43 R6
Aghil Pass China/Jammu and Kashmir 78 D1
Agiabampo Mex. 123 F8
Agiguan i. N. Mariana Is see Aguijan
Ağın Turkey 86 E3
Aginskoye Rus. Fed. 68 G1
Aginum France see Agen
Agios Dimitrios Greece 55 J6
Agios Efstratios i. Greece 55 K5
Agios Georgios i. Greece 55 J6
Agios Nikolaos Greece 55 K7
Agios Theodoros Cyprus 81 B2
Agiou Orous, Kolpos b. Greece 55 J4
Agirwat Hills Sudan 82 E6
Agisanang S. Africa 97 G4
Agnes, Mount hill Australia 105 E6
Agnew Australia 105 C6
Agnibilékrou Côte d'Ivoire 92 C4
Agnita Romania 55 K2
Agniye-Afanas'yevsk Rus. Fed. 70 E2
Agra India 78 D4
Agrakhanskiy Poluostrov pen. Rus. Fed. 87 G2
Agram Croatia see Zagreb
Ağrı Turkey 87 F3
Agria Gramvousa i. Greece 55 J7
Agrigan i. N. Mariana Is see Agrihan
Agrigento Sicily Italy 54 E6
Agrigentum Sicily Italy see Agrigento
Agrihan i. N. Mariana Is 65 L3
Agrinio Greece 55 I5
Agropoli Italy 54 F4
Agryz Rus. Fed. 37 Q4
Ağsu Azer. 87 H2
Agua, Volcán de vol. Guat. 132 F6
Água Clara Brazil 140 F2
Aguadilla Puerto Rico 133 K5
Agua Escondida Arg. 140 C5
Agua Fria r. U.S.A. 125 G5
Agua Fria National Monument nat. park U.S.A. 125 G4
Aguanaval r. Mex. 127 C7
Aguanga U.S.A. 124 E5
Aguanus r. Canada 119 J4
Aguapeí r. Brazil 141 A3
Agua Prieta Mex. 123 F7
Aguaro-Guariquito, Parque Nacional nat. park Venez. 138 E2
Aguascalientes Mex. 132 D4
Agudos Brazil 141 A3
Águeda Port. 53 B3
Aguemour reg. Alg. 92 D2
Aguié Niger 92 D3
Aguijan i. N. Mariana Is 65 L4
Aguilar U.S.A. 123 G5
Aguilar de Campóo Spain 53 D2
Águilas Spain 53 F5

▶Agulhas, Cape S. Africa 96 E8
Most southerly point of Africa.

Agulhas Basin sea feature Southern Ocean 145 J9
Agulhas Negras mt. Brazil 141 B3
Agulhas Plateau sea feature Southern Ocean 145 J8
Agulhas Ridge sea feature S. Atlantic Ocean 144 I8
Ağva Turkey 55 M4
Agvali Rus. Fed. 87 G2
Ahaggar plat. Alg. see Hoggar
Āhangarān Iran 85 F3
Ahar Iran 84 B2
Ahaura N.Z. 109 C6
Ahaus Germany 48 H2
Ahipara Bay N.Z. 109 D2
Ahiri India 80 D2
Ahklun Mountains U.S.A. 114 B4
Ahlen Germany 49 H3
Ahmadabad India 78 C5
Aḩmadābād Iran 85 E3
Aḩmad al Bāqir, Jabal mt. Jordan 81 B5
Ahmadī Iran 84 E5
Ahmadnagar India 80 B2
Ahmadpur East Pak. 85 H4
Ahmar mts Eth. 94 E3
Ahmar Mountains Eth. see Ahmar
Ahmedabad India see Ahmadabad
Ahmednagar India see Ahmadnagar
Ahorn Germany 49 K4
Ahr r. Germany 48 H4
Ahram Iran 84 C4
Ahrensburg Germany 49 K1
Āhtäri Fin. 40 N5
Ahtme Estonia 41 O7
Ahu China 73 H1
Āhū Iran 84 C4
Ahun France 52 F3
Ahuzhen China see Ahu
Ahvāz Iran 84 C4
Ahwa India 80 B1
Ahwāz Iran see Ahvāz
Ai-Ais Namibia 96 C4
Ai-Ais Hot Springs and Fish River Canyon Park nature res. Namibia 96 C4
Aichwara India 78 D4
Aid U.S.A. 130 D4
Aidin Turkm. 84 D2
Aigialousa Cyprus 81 B2
Aigina i. Greece 55 J6
Aigio Greece 55 J5
Aigle de Chambeyron mt. France 52 H4
Aigües Tortes i Estany de Sant Maurici, Parc Nacional d' nat. park Spain 53 G2
Ai He r. China 70 B4
Aihua China see Yunxian
Aihui China see Heihe
Aijal India see Aizawl
Aikawa Japan 71 E5
Aiken U.S.A. 129 D5
Ailao Shan mts China 72 D3
Aileron Australia 104 F5
Ailinglabelab atoll Marshall Is see Ailinglapalap
Ailinglapalap atoll Marshall Is 146 H5
Ailly-sur-Noye France 48 C5
Ailsa Craig Canada 130 E2
Ailsa Craig i. U.K. 46 D5
Aimangala India 80 C3
Aimorés, Serra dos hills Brazil 141 C2
Aïn Beïda Alg. 54 B7
'Aïn Ben Tili Mauritania 92 C2
'Ain Dālla spring Egypt see 'Ayn Dāllah
Aïn Defla Alg. 53 H5
Aïn Deheb Alg. 53 G6
Aïn el Hadjel Alg. 53 H6
'Ain el Maqfi spring Egypt see 'Ayn al Maqfī
Aïn el Melh Alg. 53 I6
Aïn Mdila well Alg. 54 B7
Aïn-M'Lila Alg. 50 F4
Aïn Oussera Alg. 53 H6
Ain Salah Alg. see In Salah
Aïn Sefra Alg. 50 D5
Ainsworth U.S.A. 126 D3
Aintab Turkey see Gaziantep
Aïn Taya Alg. 53 H5
Aïn Tédélès Alg. 53 G6
Aïn Temouchent Alg. 53 F6
'Ain Tibaghbagh spring Egypt see 'Ayn Tabaghbugh
'Ain Timeira spring Egypt see 'Ayn Tumayrah
'Ain Zeitûn Egypt see 'Ayn Zaytūn
Aiquile Bol. 138 E7
Air i. Indon. 67 D7
Airaines France 48 B5
Airdrie Canada 116 H5
Airdrie U.K. 46 F5
Aire r. France 48 E5
Aire, Canal d' France 48 C4
Aire-sur-l'Adour France 52 D5
Air Force Island Canada 115 K3
Airpanas Indon. 104 D1
Aisatung Mountain Myanmar 66 A2
Aisch r. Germany 49 L5
Aishihik Canada 116 B2
Aishihik Lake Canada 116 B2
Aisne r. France 48 C5
Aïssa, Djebel mt. Alg. 50 D5
Aitamännikkö Fin. 40 N3
Aitana mt. Spain 53 F4
Aït Benhaddou tourist site Morocco 50 C5
Aiterach r. Germany 49 M6
Aitkin U.S.A. 126 E2
Aiud Romania 55 J1
Aix France see Aix-en-Provence
Aix-en-Provence France 52 G5
Aix-la-Chapelle Germany see Aachen
Aix-les-Bains France 52 G4
Aiyina i. Greece see Aigina
Aiyion Greece see Aigio
Aizawl India 79 H5
Aizkraukle Latvia 41 N8
Aizpute Latvia 41 L8
Aizu-wakamatsu Japan 71 E5
Ajaccio Corsica France 52 I6
Ajanta India 80 B1
Ajanta Range hills India see Sahyadriparvat Range
Ajaureforsen Sweden 40 I4
Ajax Canada 130 F2
Ajayameru India see Ajmer
Ajban U.A.E. 84 D5
Aj Bogd Uul mt. Mongolia 76 I3
Ajdābiyā Libya 93 F1
a-Jiddet des. Oman see Ḩarāsīs, Jiddat al
'Ajlūn Jordan 81 B3
'Ajman U.A.E. 84 D5
Ajmer India 78 C4
Ajmer-Merwara India see Ajmer
Ajnala India 78 C3
Ajo U.S.A. 125 G5
Ajo, Mount U.S.A. 125 G5
Ajrestan Afgh. 85 G3
Akademii, Zaliv b. Rus. Fed. 70 E1
Akademii Nauk, Khrebet mt. Tajik. see Akademiyai Fanho, Qatorkŭhi
Akademiyai Fanho, Qatorkŭhi mt. Tajik. 85 H2
Akagera National Park Rwanda 94 D4
Akalkot India 80 C2
Akama, Akra c. Cyprus see Arnauti, Cape
Akamagaseki Japan see Shimonoseki
Akan National Park Japan 70 G4
Akaroa N.Z. 109 D6
Akas reg. India 72 B3
Akāshat Iraq 87 E4
Akbarābād Iran 87 I5
Akbarpur Uttar Pradesh India 78 E4
Akbarpur Uttar Pradesh India 79 E4
Akbaytal, Pereval pass Tajik. 85 I2
Akbaytal Pass Tajik. see Akbaytal, Pereval
Akbez Turkey 81 C1
Akçadağ Turkey 86 E3
Akçakale Turkey 81 D1
Akçakoca Turkey 55 N4
Akçakoca Dağları mts Turkey 55 N4
Akçakoyunlu Turkey 81 C1
Akçalı Dağları mts Turkey 81 A1
Akchâr reg. Mauritania 92 B3
Akchi Kazakh. see Akshiy
Akdağlar mts Turkey 55 M6
Akdağmadeni Turkey 86 D3
Akdere Turkey 81 A1
Akelamo Indon. 65 H6
Åkersberga Sweden 41 K7
Akersloot Neth. 48 E2
Aketi Dem. Rep. Congo 94 C3
Akgyr Erezi hills Turkm. see Akkyr, Gory
Akhali-Afoni Georgia see Akhali Ap'oni
Akhali Ap'oni Georgia 87 F2
Akhḑar, Al Jabal al mts Libya 93 F1
Akhḑar, Jabal mts Oman 84 E6
Akhisar Turkey 55 L5
Akhnoor Jammu and Kashmir 78 C2
Akhsu Azer. see Ağsu
Akhta Armenia see Hrazdan
Akhtarīn Syria 81 C1
Akhtubinsk Rus. Fed. 39 J6
Akhty Rus. Fed. 87 G2
Akhtyrka Ukr. see Okhtyrka
Aki Japan 71 D6
Akiéni Gabon 94 B4
Akimiski Island Canada 118 E3
Akishma r. Rus. Fed. 70 D1
Akita Japan 71 F5
Akjoujt Mauritania 92 B3
Akkajaure l. Sweden 40 J3
Akkerman Ukr. see Bilhorod-Dnistrovs'kyy
Akkeshi Japan 70 G4
'Akko Israel 81 B3
Akkol' Akmolinskaya Oblast' Kazakh. 76 D1
Akkol' Atyrauskaya Oblast' Kazakh. 39 K7
Akku Kazakh. 76 E1
Akkul' Kazakh. see Akkol'
Akkuş Turkey 86 E2
Akkyr, Gory hills Turkm. 84 D1
Aklavik Canada 114 E3
Aklera India 78 D4
Ak-Mechet Kazakh. see Kyzylorda
Akmeņrags pt Latvia 41 L8
Akmeqit China 78 D1
Akmola Kazakh. see Astana
Akmolinsk Kazakh. see Astana
Akobo Sudan 93 G4
Akobo Wenz r. Eth./Sudan 94 D3
Akokan Niger 92 D3
Akola India 80 C1
Akom II Cameroon 92 E4
Akonolinga Cameroon 92 E4
Akordat Eritrea 82 E6
Akören Turkey 86 D3
Akot India 78 D5
Akpatok Island Canada 119 I1
Akqi China 76 E3
Akra, Jabal mt. Syria/Turkey see Aqra', Jabal al
Akranes Iceland 40 [inset]
Åkrehamn Norway 41 D7
Akréréb Niger 92 D3

Akron CO U.S.A. 126 C3
Akron IN U.S.A. 130 B3
Akron OH U.S.A. 130 E3
Akrotiri Bay Cyprus 81 A2
Akrotirion Bay Cyprus see Akrotiri Bay
Akrotiriou, Kolpos b. Cyprus see Akrotiri Bay
Akrotiri Sovereign Base Area military base Cyprus 81 A2
▶Aksai Chin terr. Asia 78 D2 Disputed territory (China/India).
Aksaray Turkey 86 D3
Aksay China 76 H4
Aksay Kazakh. 37 Q5
Ak-Say r. Kyrg. 83 M1
Aksay Rus. Fed. 39 H7
Akşehir Turkey 55 N5
Akşehir Gölü l. Turkey 55 N5
Akseki Turkey 86 C3
Aksha Rus. Fed. 69 K2
Akshiganak Kazakh. 76 B2
Akshiy Kazakh. 76 E3
Akshukur Kazakh. 87 H2
Aksu China 76 F3
Aksu Kazakh. 76 E1
Aksu r. Tajik. see Oqsu
Aksu r. Turkey 55 N6
Aksuat Kazakh. 76 F2
Aksu-Ayuly Kazakh. 76 D2
Aksubayevo Rus. Fed. 39 K5
Āksum Eth. 82 E7
Aktag mt. China 79 F1
Aktas Dağı mt. Turkey 87 G3
Aktau Kazakh. 74 E2
Akto China 85 J2
Aktobe Kazakh. 74 E1
Aktogay Karagandinskaya Oblast' Kazakh. 76 E2
Aktogay Vostochnyy Kazakhstan Kazakh. 76 E2
Aktsyabrski Belarus 39 F5
Aktyubinsk Kazakh. see Aktobe
Akulivik Canada 115 K3
Akune Japan 71 C6
Akure Nigeria 92 D4
Akuressa Sri Lanka 80 D5
Akureyri Iceland 40 [inset]
Akusha Rus. Fed. 39 J8
Akwanga Nigeria 92 D4
Akxokesay China 79 G1
Akyab Myanmar see Sittwe
Akyatan Gölü salt l. Turkey 81 B1
Akyazı Turkey 55 N4
Akzhaykyn, Ozero salt l. Kazakh. 76 C3
Ål Norway 41 F6
'Alā, Jabal al hills Syria 81 C2
Alabama r. U.S.A. 129 C6
Alabama state U.S.A. 129 C5
Alabaster AL U.S.A. 129 C5
Alabaster MI U.S.A. 130 D1
Al 'Abṭīyah well Iraq 87 G5
Alaca Turkey 86 D2
Alacahan Turkey 86 E3
Alaçam Turkey 86 D2
Alaçam Dağları mts Turkey 55 M5
Alacant Spain see Alicante-Alacant
Alaçatı Turkey 55 L5
Aladağ Turkey 86 D3
Ala Dağlar mts Turkey 87 F3
Ala Dağları mts Turkey 86 D3
Al 'Adam Libya 86 A5
Al Aflāj reg. Saudi Arabia 84 B6
Alag Hu l. China 72 C1
Alagir Rus. Fed. 87 G2
Alagoinhas Brazil 141 D1
Alahärmä Fin. 40 M5
Al Aḥmadī Kuwait 84 C4
Alai Range mts Asia 85 H2
Ālaivān Iran 84 D3
Alājah Syria 81 B2
Alajärvi Fin. 40 M5
Al 'Ajrūd well Egypt 81 B4
Alakanuk U.S.A. 114 B3
Al Akhḍar Saudi Arabia 86 E5
Alakol', Ozero salt l. Kazakh. 76 F2
Ala Kul salt l. Kazakh. see Alakol', Ozero
Alakurtti Rus. Fed. 40 Q3
Al 'Alamayn Egypt 86 C5
Al 'Alayyah Saudi Arabia 82 F6
Alama Somalia 94 E3
Al 'Amādīyah Iraq 87 F3
Alamagan i. N. Mariana Is 65 L3
Alamaguan i. N. Mariana Is see Alamagan
Al 'Amārah Iraq 87 G5
'Alam ar Rūm, Ra's pt Egypt 86 B5
'Alāmarvdasht watercourse Iran 84 D4
Alamdo China 72 B2
Alameda U.S.A. 124 B3
'Alam el Rûm, Râs pt Egypt see 'Alam ar Rūm, Ra's
Al Amghar waterhole Iraq 87 G5
Al 'Āmirīyah Egypt 86 C5
Alamo GA U.S.A. 129 D5
Alamo NV U.S.A. 125 F3
Alamo Dam U.S.A. 125 G4
Alamogordo U.S.A. 123 G6
Alamo Heights U.S.A. 127 D6
Alamos Sonora Mex. 123 F7
Alamos Sonora Mex. 123 F8
Alamos r. Mex. 127 C7
Alamos, Sierra mts Mex. 123 F8
Alamosa U.S.A. 123 G5
Alamos de Peña Mex. 123 G7
Alampur India 80 C3
Alan Myanmar see Myede
Alanäs Sweden 40 I4
Åland is Fin. see Åland Islands
Aland r. Germany 49 L1
Aland India 80 C2
Al Andarīn Syria 81 C2
Åland Islands Fin. 41 K6
Alandur India 80 D3
Alanson U.S.A. 130 C1
Alanya Turkey 86 D3
Alaplı Turkey 55 N4
Alappuzha India see Alleppey
Alapuzha India see Alleppey
Al 'Aqabah Jordan 81 B5
Al 'Aqīq Saudi Arabia 82 F5
Al 'Arabiyah as Sa'ūdīyah country Asia see Saudi Arabia
Alarcón, Embalse de resr Spain 53 E4
Al 'Arīsh Egypt 81 A4
Al Arṭāwīyah Saudi Arabia 82 G4
Alas, Selat sea chan. Indon. 104 B2
Alaşehir Turkey 55 M5
Alashiya country Asia see Cyprus
Al Ashmūnayn Egypt 86 C6
Alaska state U.S.A. 114 D3
Alaska, Gulf of U.S.A. 114 D4
Alaska Highway Canada/U.S.A. 116 A2
Alaska Peninsula U.S.A. 114 B4
Alaska Range mts U.S.A. 114 D3
Älät Azer. 87 H3
Alat Uzbek. 85 F2
Alatau Shankou pass China/Kazakh. see Dzungarian Gate
Al Atwā' well Saudi Arabia 87 F5
Alatyr' Rus. Fed. 39 J5
Alatyr' r. Rus. Fed. 39 J5
Alausí Ecuador 138 C4
Alaverdi Armenia 87 G2
'Alavī Iran 84 C3
Alavieska Fin. 40 N4
Alavus Fin. 40 M5
Alawbum Myanmar 66 B1
Alawoona Australia 107 C7
Alay Kyrka Toosu mts Asia see Alai Range
Al 'Ayn Oman 84 E6
Al 'Ayn U.A.E. 84 D5
Alayskiy Khrebet mts Asia see Alai Range
Al 'Azīzīyah Iraq 87 G4
▶Al 'Azīzīyah Libya 51 G5 Highest recorded shade temperature in the world.
Al Azraq al Janūbī Jordan 81 C4
Alba Italy 54 C2
Alba U.S.A. 130 C1
Al Bāb Syria 81 C1
Albacete Spain 53 F4
Al Badī' Saudi Arabia 84 B6
Al Bādiyah al Janūbīyah hill Iraq 87 G5
Alba Iulia Romania 55 J1
Al Bahrayn country Asia see Bahrain
Al Bajā' well U.A.E. 84 C5
Albājī Iran 84 C4
Al Bakhrā well Saudi Arabia 84 B5
Albanel, Lac l. Canada 119 G4
▶Albania country Europe 55 H4 europe 5, 34–35
Albany Australia 105 B8
Albany r. Canada 118 E3
Albany GA U.S.A. 129 C6
Albany IN U.S.A. 130 C3
Albany KY U.S.A. 130 C5
Albany MO U.S.A. 126 E3
▶Albany NY U.S.A. 131 I2 State capital of New York.
Albany OH U.S.A. 130 D4
Albany OR U.S.A. 122 C3
Albany TX U.S.A. 127 D5
Albany Downs Australia 108 D1
Albardão do João Maria coastal area Brazil 140 F4
Al Bardī Libya 86 B5
Al Bārīdah hills Saudi Arabia 81 D5
Al Baṣrah Iraq see Basra
Al Baṭḥa' marsh Iraq 87 G5
Al Bāṭinah reg. Oman 84 E5
Albatross Bay Australia 106 C2
Albatross Island Australia 107 [inset]
Al Bawīṭī Egypt 86 C5
Al Bayḍā' Libya 82 B3
Al Bayḍā' Yemen 82 G7
Albemarle U.S.A. 129 D5
Albemarle Island Galápagos Ecuador see Isabela, Isla
Albemarle Sound sea chan. U.S.A. 128 E5
Albenga Italy 54 C2
Alberche r. Spain 53 D4
Alberga Australia 107 A5
Alberga watercourse Australia 107 A5
Albergaria-a-Velha Port. 53 B3
Albert Australia 108 C4
Albert France 48 C5
Albert, Lake Dem. Rep. Congo/Uganda 94 D3
Albert, Parc National nat. park Dem. Rep. Congo see Virunga, Parc National des
Alberta prov. Canada 116 H4
Alberta U.S.A. 131 G5
Albert Kanaal canal Belgium 48 F4
Albert Lea U.S.A. 126 E3
Albert Nile r. Sudan/Uganda 93 G4
Alberto de Agostini, Parque Nacional nat. park Chile 140 B8
Alberton S. Africa 97 I4
Alberton U.S.A. 122 E3
Albert Town Bahamas 129 F8
Albertville Dem. Rep. Congo see Kalemie
Albertville France 52 H4
Albertville U.S.A. 129 C5
Albestroff France 48 G6
Albi France 52 F5
Albia U.S.A. 126 E3
Al Biḍah des. Saudi Arabia 84 C5
Albina Suriname 139 H2
Albino Italy 54 C2
Albion CA U.S.A. 124 B2
Albion IL U.S.A. 126 F4
Albion IN U.S.A. 130 C3
Albion MI U.S.A. 130 C2
Albion NE U.S.A. 126 D3
Albion NY U.S.A. 131 F2
Albion PA U.S.A. 130 E3
Al Biqā' valley Lebanon see El Béqaa
Al Bi'r Saudi Arabia 86 E5
Al Birk Saudi Arabia 82 F6
Al Biyāḍh reg. Saudi Arabia 82 G5
Alborán, Isla de i. Spain 53 E6
Ålborg Denmark 41 F8
Ålborg Bugt b. Denmark 41 G8
Albro Australia 106 D4
Al Budayyi Bahrain 84 C5
Albufeira Port. 53 B5
Al Buḥayrāt al Murrah lakes Egypt see Bitter Lakes
Albuquerque U.S.A. 123 G6
Al Burayj Syria 81 C2
Al Buraymī Oman 84 D5
Al Burj Jordan 81 B5
Alburquerque Spain 53 C4
Albury Australia 108 C6
Al Buṣayrah Syria 87 F4
Al Busayṭā' plain Saudi Arabia 81 D4
Al Bushūk well Saudi Arabia 84 B4
Alcácer do Sal Port. 53 B4
Alcalá de Henares Spain 53 E3
Alcalá la Real Spain 53 E5
Alcamo Sicily Italy 54 E6
Alcañiz Spain 53 F3
Alcántara Spain 53 C4
Alcantara Lake Canada 117 I2
Alcaraz Spain 53 E4
Alcázar de San Juan Spain 53 E4
Alcazarquivir Morocco see Ksar el Kebir
Alchevs'k Ukr. 39 H6
Alcobaça Brazil 141 D2
Alcoi Spain see Alcoy-Alcoi
Alcoota Australia 104 F5
Alcora Spain 53 F3
Alcova U.S.A. 122 G4
Alcoy Spain see Alcoy-Alcoi
Alcoy-Alcoi Spain 53 F4
Alcúdia Spain 53 H4
Aldabra Islands Seychelles 95 E4
Aldan Rus. Fed. 61 N4
Aldan r. Rus. Fed. 61 N3
Alde r. U.K. 45 I6
Aldeboarn Neth. see Oldeboorn
Aldeburgh U.K. 45 I6
Alder Creek U.S.A. 131 H2
Alderney i. Channel Is 45 E9
Alder Peak U.S.A. 124 C4
Aldershot U.K. 45 G7
Al Dhafrah reg. U.A.E. 84 D6
Aldingham U.K. 44 D4
Aldridge U.K. 45 F6
Aleg Mauritania 92 B3
Alegre Espírito Santo Brazil 141 C3
Alegre Minas Gerais Brazil 141 B2
Alegrete Brazil 140 E3
Alegros Mountain U.S.A. 125 I4
Aleksandra, Mys hd Rus. Fed. 70 E1
Aleksandriya Ukr. see Oleksandriya
Aleksandro-Nevskiy Rus. Fed. 39 I5
Aleksandropol Armenia see Gyumri
Aleksandrov Rus. Fed. 38 H4
Aleksandrov Gay Rus. Fed. 39 K6
Aleksandrovsk Rus. Fed. 37 R4
Aleksandrovsk Ukr. see Zaporizhzhya
Aleksandrovskiy Rus. Fed. see Aleksandrovsk
Aleksandrovskoye Rus. Fed. 87 F1
Aleksandrovsk-Sakhalinskiy Rus. Fed. 70 F2
Aleksandry, Zemlya i. Rus. Fed. 60 F1
Alekseyevka Akmolinskaya Oblast' Kazakh. see Akkol'
Alekseyevka Vostochnyy Kazakhstan Kazakh. see Terekty
Alekseyevka Amurskaya Oblast' Rus. Fed. 70 B1
Alekseyevka Belgorodskaya Oblast' Rus. Fed. 39 H6
Alekseyevka Belgorodskaya Oblast' Rus. Fed. 39 H6
Alekseyevskaya Rus. Fed. 39 I6
Alekseyevskoye Rus. Fed. 38 K5
Aleksin Rus. Fed. 39 H5
Aleksinac Serb. and Mont. 55 I3
Alèmbé Gabon 94 B4
Ålen Norway 40 G5
Alençon France 52 E2
Alenquer Brazil 139 H4
Alenuihaha Channel HI U.S.A. 123 [inset]
Alep Syria see Aleppo
Aleppo Syria 81 C1
Alert Canada 115 L1
Alerta Peru 138 D6
Alès France 52 G4
Aleşd Romania 55 J1
Aleshki Ukr. see Tsyurupyns'k
Aleşkirt Turkey see Eleşkirt
Alessandria Italy 54 C2
Alessio Albania see Lezhë
Ålesund Norway 40 E5
Aleutian Basin sea feature Bering Sea 146 H2
Aleutian Islands U.S.A. 114 A4
Aleutian Range mts U.S.A. 114 C4
Aleutian Trench sea feature N. Pacific Ocean 146 I2
Alevina, Mys c. Rus. Fed. 61 Q4
Alevişik Turkey see Samandağı
Alexander U.S.A. 126 C2
Alexander, Kap c. Greenland see Ullersuaq
Alexander, Mount hill Australia 106 B2
Alexander Archipelago is U.S.A. 116 B3
Alexander Bay b. Namibia/S. Africa 96 C5
Alexander Bay S. Africa 96 C5
Alexander City U.S.A. 129 C5
Alexander Island Antarctica 148 L2
Alexandra Australia 108 B6
Alexandra N.Z. 109 B7
Alexandra, Cape S. Georgia 140 I8
Alexandra Channel India 67 A4
Alexandra Land i. Rus. Fed. see Aleksandry, Zemlya
Alexandreia Greece 55 J4
Alexandretta Turkey see İskenderun
Alexandria Afgh. see Ghaznī
Alexandria Canada 131 H1
▶Alexandria Egypt 86 C5 5th most populous city in Africa.
Alexandria Romania 55 K3
Alexandria S. Africa 97 H7
Alexandria Turkm. see Mary
Alexandria U.K. 46 E5
Alexandria IN U.S.A. 130 C3
Alexandria KY U.S.A. 130 C4
Alexandria LA U.S.A. 127 E6
Alexandria VA U.S.A. 131 G4
Alexandria Arachoton Afgh. see Kandahār
Alexandria Areion Afgh. see Herāt
Alexandria Bay U.S.A. 131 H1
Alexandria Prophthasia Afgh. see Farāh
Alexandrina, Lake Australia 107 B7
Alexandroupoli Greece 55 K4
Alexis r. Canada 119 K3
Alexis Creek Canada 116 F4
Aley Lebanon 81 B3
Aleyak Iran 84 E2
Aleysk Rus. Fed. 68 E2
Alf Germany 48 H4
Al Farwānīyah Kuwait 84 B4
Al Fas Morocco see Fès
Al Fatḥah Iraq 87 F4
Al Fāw Iraq 87 H5
Al Fayyūm Egypt 86 C5
Alfeld (Leine) Germany 49 J3
Alfenas Brazil 141 B3
Alford U.K. 44 H5
Alfred ME U.S.A. 131 J2
Alfred NY U.S.A. 131 G2
Alfred and Marie Range hills Australia 105 D6
Al Fujayrah U.A.E. see Fujairah
Al Fuqahā' Libya 93 E2
Al Furāt r. Iraq/Syria 81 D2 see Euphrates
Alga Kazakh. 76 A2
Ålgård Norway 41 D7
Algarrobo del Aguilla Arg. 140 C5
Algarve reg. Port. 53 B5
Algeciras Spain 53 D5
Algemesí Spain 53 F4
Algena Eritrea 82 E6
Alger Alg. see Algiers
Alger U.S.A. 130 C1
▶Algeria country Africa 92 C2 2nd largest country in Africa. africa 7, 90–91
Algérie country Africa see Algeria
Algermissen Germany 49 J2
Algha Kazakh. see Alga
Al Ghāfāt Oman 84 E6
Al Ghammās Iraq 87 G5
Al Ghardaqah Egypt see Al Ghurdaqah
Al Ghawr plain Jordan/West Bank 81 B4
Al Ghayḍah Yemen 82 H6
Alghero Sardinia Italy 54 C4
Al Ghurdaqah Egypt 82 D4
Al Ghuwayr well Qatar 84 C5
▶Algiers Alg. 53 H5 Capital of Algeria.
Algoa Bay S. Africa 97 G7
Algoma U.S.A. 130 B1
Algona U.S.A. 126 E3
Algonac U.S.A. 130 D2
Algonquin Park Canada 131 F1
Algonquin Provincial Park Canada 131 F1
Algorta Spain 53 E2
Algueirao Moz. see Hacufera
Al Habakah well Saudi Arabia 87 F5
Al Ḥabbānīyah Iraq 87 F4
Al Ḥadaqah well Saudi Arabia 84 B4
Al Ḥadd Bahrain 84 C5
Al Hadhālīl plat. Saudi Arabia 87 F5
Al Ḥadīdīyah Syria 81 C2
Al Ḥadīthah Iraq 87 F4
Al Ḥadīthah Saudi Arabia 81 C4
Al Ḥaḍr Iraq see Hatra
Al Ḥafār well Saudi Arabia 87 F5
Al Ḥaffah Syria 81 C2
Al Haggounia W. Sahara 92 B2
Al Ḥajar al Gharbī mts Oman 84 E5
Al Ḥajar ash Sharqī mts Oman 84 E6
Al Ḥamād plain Asia 86 E5
Al Ḥamādah al Ḥamrā' plat. Libya 92 E2
Alhama de Murcia Spain 53 F5
Al Ḥamar Saudi Arabia 84 B6
Al Ḥamīdīyah Syria 81 B2
Al Ḥammām Egypt 86 C5
Al Ḥanākīyah Saudi Arabia 82 F5
Al Ḥanīsh al Kabīr i. Yemen 82 F7
Al Ḥaniyah esc. Iraq 87 G5
Al Ḥariq Saudi Arabia 84 B6
Al Ḥarrah Egypt 86 C5
Al Ḥarūj al Aswad hills Libya 93 E2
Al Hasa reg. Saudi Arabia 84 C5
Al Ḥasakah Syria 87 F3
Al Hawi salt pan Saudi Arabia 81 D5
Al Ḥawjā' Saudi Arabia 86 E5
Al Ḥawṭah reg. Saudi Arabia 84 B6
Al Ḥayy Iraq 87 G4
Al Ḥayz Egypt 86 C5
Al Ḥazīm Jordan 81 C4
Al Ḥazm Saudi Arabia 86 E5
Al Ḥazm al Jawf Yemen 82 F6
Al Ḥibāk des. Saudi Arabia 83 H6
Al Ḥijānah Syria 81 C3
Al Ḥillah Iraq see Hillah
Al Ḥillah Saudi Arabia 82 G5
Al Ḥinnāh Saudi Arabia 94 E1
Al Ḥinw mt. Saudi Arabia 81 D4
Al Ḥirrah well Saudi Arabia 84 C6
Al Ḥishah Syria 81 D1
Al Ḥismā plain Saudi Arabia 86 D5
Al Ḥiṣn Jordan 81 B3
Al Hoceima Morocco 53 E6
Al Ḥudaydah Yemen see Hodeidah
Al Ḥufrah reg. Saudi Arabia 86 E5
Al Hufūf Saudi Arabia 82 G4
Al Ḥūj hills Saudi Arabia 86 E5
Al Husayfīn Oman 84 E5
Al Huwwah Saudi Arabia 84 B6
Ali China 78 D2
'Alīābād Afgh. 85 H2
'Alīābād Golestān Iran 84 D2
'Alīābād Hormozgan Iran 84 D4
'Alīābād Khorāsān Iran 85 F4
'Alīābād Kordestān Iran 84 B2
Alīābād, Kūh-e mt. Iran 84 C3
Aliağa Turkey 55 L5
Aliakmonas r. Greece 55 J4
Alibag India 80 B2
Äli Bayramlı Azer. 87 H3
Alicante Spain see Alicante-Alacant
Alicante-Alacant Spain 53 F4
Alice r. Australia 106 C2
Alice watercourse Australia 106 D5
Alice U.S.A. 127 D7
Alice, Punta pt Italy 54 G5
Alice Springs Australia 105 F5
Alice Town Bahamas 129 E7
Aliceville U.S.A. 127 F5
Alichur Tajik. 85 I2
Alichur r. Tajik. 85 I2
Alick Creek r. Australia 106 C4
Alifu Atoll Maldives see Ari Atoll
Al Ifzi'iyyah i. U.A.E. 84 C5
Aliganj India 78 D4
Aligarh Rajasthan India 78 D4
Aligarh Uttar Pradesh India 78 D4
Alīgūdarz Iran 84 C3
Alihe China 70 A2
Alījūq, Kūh-e mt. Iran 84 C4
'Alī Kheyl Afgh. 85 H3
Al Imārāt al 'Arabīyah at Muttaḥidah country Asia see United Arab Emirates
Alimia i. Greece 55 L6
Alindao Cent. Afr. Rep. 94 C3
Alingsås Sweden 41 H8
Aliova r. Turkey 55 M5
Alipura India 78 D4
Alipur Duar India 79 G4
Alirajpur India 78 C5
Al 'Irāq country Asia see Iraq
Al 'Īsāwīyah Saudi Arabia 81 C4
Al Iskandarīyah Egypt see Alexandria
Al Iskandarīyah Iraq 87 G4
Al Ismā'īlīyah Egypt 86 D5
Aliveri Greece 55 K5
Aliwal North S. Africa 97 H6
Alix Canada 116 H4
Al Jafr Jordan 81 C4
Al Jāfūrah des. Saudi Arabia 84 C5
Al Jaghbūb Libya 86 B5
Al Jahrah Kuwait 84 B4
Al Jamalīyah Qatar 84 C5
Al Jarāwī well Saudi Arabia 81 D4
Al Jauf Saudi Arabia see Al Jawf
Al Jawb reg. Saudi Arabia 84 C6
Al Jawf Libya 93 F2
Al Jawf Saudi Arabia 87 E5
Al Jawsh Libya 92 E1
Al Jaza'ir country Africa see Algeria
Al Jaza'ir Alg. see Algiers
Aljezur Port. 53 B5
Al Jībān reg. Saudi Arabia 84 C5
Al Jil well Iraq 87 F5
Al Jilh esc. Saudi Arabia 84 B5
Al Jithāmīyah Saudi Arabia 87 F6
Al Jīzah Egypt see Giza
Al Jīzah Jordan 81 B4
Al Jubayl hills Saudi Arabia 84 B5
Al Jubaylah Saudi Arabia 84 B5
Al Jufra Oasis Libya 93 E2
Al Julayqah well Saudi Arabia 84 C5
Aljustrel Port. 53 B5
Al Juwayf depr. Syria 81 C3
Al Kahfah Al Qaṣīm Saudi Arabia 82 F4
Al Kahfah Ash Sharqīyah Saudi Arabia 84 C5
Alkali Lake Canada 116 F5
Al Karak Jordan 81 B4
Al Kāẓimīyah Iraq 87 G4
Al Khābūrah Oman 84 E6
Al Khalīl West Bank see Hebron
Al Khāliṣ Iraq 87 G4
Al Khārijah Egypt 82 D4
Al Kharj reg. Saudi Arabia 84 B6
Al Kharrārah Qatar 84 C5
Al Kharrūbah Egypt 81 A4
Al Khaṣab Oman 84 E5
Al Khatam reg. U.A.E. 84 D5
Al Khawkhah Yemen 82 F7
Al Khawr Qatar 84 C5
Al Khizāmī well Saudi Arabia 84 C5
Al Khums Libya 93 E1
Al Khunfah sand area Saudi Arabia 86 E5
Al Khunn Saudi Arabia 94 E1
Al Kifl Iraq 87 G4
Al Kir'ānah Qatar 84 C5
Al Kiswah Syria 81 C3
Alkmaar Neth. 48 E2
Al Kūbrī Egypt 81 A4
Al Kūfah Iraq 87 G4
Al Kumayt Iraq 87 G4
Al Kuntillah Egypt 81 B5
Al Kusūr hills Saudi Arabia 81 D4
Al Kūt Iraq 87 G4
Al Kuwayt country Asia see Kuwait
Al Kuwayt Kuwait see Kuwait
Al Labbah plain Saudi Arabia 87 F5
Al Lādhiqīyah Syria see Latakia
Allagadda India 80 C3
Allahabad India 79 E4
Al Lajā lava field Syria 81 C3
Allakaket U.S.A. 114 C3
Allakh-Yun' Rus. Fed. 61 O3
Allanmyo Myanmar see Myede
Allanridge S. Africa 97 H4
Allapalli India 80 D2
'Allāqī, Wādī al watercourse Egypt 82 D5
'Allâqi, Wâdi el watercourse Egypt see 'Allāqī, Wādī al
Allardville Canada 119 I5
Alldays S. Africa 97 I2
Allegan U.S.A. 130 C2
Allegheny r. U.S.A. 130 F3
Allegheny Mountains U.S.A. 130 D5
Allegheny Reservoir U.S.A. 131 F3
Allen, Lough l. Rep. of Ireland 47 D3
Allendale U.S.A. 129 D5
Allendale Town U.K. 44 E4
Allende Coahuila Mex. 127 C6
Allende Nuevo León Mex. 127 C7
Allendorf (Lumda) Germany 49 I4
Allenford Canada 130 E1
Allenstein Poland see Olsztyn
Allensville U.S.A. 130 B5
Allentown U.S.A. 131 H3
Alleppey India 80 C4
Aller r. Germany 49 J2
Alliance NE U.S.A. 126 C3
Alliance OH U.S.A. 130 E3
Al Lībīyah country Africa see Libya
Allier r. France 52 F3
Al Lihābah well Saudi Arabia 84 B5
Allinge-Sandvig Denmark 41 I9
Al Liṣāfah well Saudi Arabia 84 B5
Al Lisān pen. Jordan 81 B4
Alliston Canada 130 F1
Al Līth Saudi Arabia 82 F5
Al Liwā' oasis U.A.E. 84 D6
Alloa U.K. 46 F4
Allons U.S.A. 130 C5
Allora Australia 108 F2
Allur India 80 D3
Alluru Kottapatnam India 80 D3
Alma Canada 119 H4
Alma MI U.S.A. 130 C2
Alma NE U.S.A. 126 D3
Alma WI U.S.A. 126 F2
Al Ma'ānīyah Iraq 87 F5
Alma-Ata Kazakh. see Almaty
Almada Port. 53 B4
Al Madāfi' plat. Saudi Arabia 86 E5
Al Ma'danīyāt well Iraq 87 G5
Almaden Australia 106 D3
Almadén Spain 53 D4
Al Madīnah Saudi Arabia see Medina
Al Mafraq Jordan 81 C3
Al Maghrib country Africa see Morocco
Al Maghrib reg. U.A.E. 84 D6
Al Mahākik reg. Saudi Arabia 84 C6
Al Mahdum Syria 81 C1
Al Maḥḥā depr. Saudi Arabia 86 E6
Al Maḥwīt Yemen 82 F6
Al Majma'ah Saudi Arabia 84 B5
Al Malsūnīyah reg. Saudi Arabia 84 C5
Almalyk Uzbek. 76 C3
Al Manādir reg. Oman 84 D6
Al Manāmah Bahrain see Manama
Al Manjūr well Saudi Arabia 84 B6
Almanor, Lake U.S.A. 124 C1
Almansa Spain 53 F4
Al Manṣūrah Egypt 86 C5
Almanzor mt. Spain 53 D3
Al Mariyyah U.A.E. 84 D6
Al Marj Libya 93 F1
Almas, Rio das r. Brazil 141 A1
Al Maṭarīyah Egypt 86 D5
▶Almaty Kazakh. 76 E3 Former capital of Kazakhstan.
Al Mawṣil Iraq see Mosul
Al Mayādīn Syria 87 F4
Al Mazār Egypt 81 A4
Almaznyy Rus. Fed. 61 M3
Almeirim Brazil 139 H4
Almeirim Port. 53 B4
Almelo Neth. 48 G2
Almenara Brazil 141 C2
Almendra, Embalse de resr Spain 53 C3
Almendralejo Spain 53 C4
Almere Neth. 48 F2
Almería Spain 53 E5
Almería, Golfo de b. Spain 53 E5
Al'metievsk Rus. Fed. see Al'met'yevsk
Al'met'yevsk Rus. Fed. 37 Q5
Älmhult Sweden 41 I8
Almina, Punta pt Spain 53 D6
Al Mindak Saudi Arabia 82 F5
Al Minyā Egypt 86 C5
Almirós Greece see Almyros
Al Mish'āb Saudi Arabia 84 C4
Almodôvar Port. 53 B5
Almond r. U.K. 46 F4
Almont U.S.A. 130 D2
Almonte Spain 53 C5
Almora India 78 D3
Al Mu'ayzīlah hill Saudi Arabia 81 D5
Al Mubarrez Saudi Arabia 82 G4
Al Muḍaibī Oman 83 I5
Al Muḍairib Oman 84 E6
Al Muḥarraq Bahrain 84 C5
Al Mukallā Yemen see Mukalla
Al Mukhā Yemen see Mocha
Al Mukhaylī Libya 82 B3
Al Munbaṭiḥ des. Saudi Arabia 84 C6
Almuñécar Spain 53 E5
Al Muqdādīyah Iraq 87 G4
Al Mūrītānīyah country Africa see Mauritania
Al Murūt well Saudi Arabia 87 E5
Almus Turkey 86 E2
Al Musannāh ridge Saudi Arabia 84 B4
Al Musayyib Iraq 84 B3
Al Muwaqqar Jordan 81 C4
Almyros Greece 55 J5
Almyrou, Ormos b. Greece 55 K7
Alnwick U.K. 44 F3
▶Alofi Niue 103 J3 Capital of Niue. oceania 8, 100–101
Aloja Latvia 41 N8
Alon Myanmar 66 A2
Along India 79 H3
Alongshan China 70 A2
Alonnisos i. Greece 55 J5
Alor i. Indon. 104 D2
Alor, Kepulauan is Indon. 104 D2
Alor Setar Malaysia 67 C6
Alor Star Malaysia see Alor Setar
Alost Belgium see Aalst
Aloysius, Mount Australia 105 E6
Alozero Rus. Fed. 40 Q4
Alpen Germany 48 G3
Alpena U.S.A. 130 D1
Alpercatas, Serra das hills Brazil 139 J5
Alpha Australia 106 D4
Alpha Ridge sea feature Arctic Ocean 149 A1
Alpine AZ U.S.A. 125 I5
Alpine NY U.S.A. 131 G2
Alpine TX U.S.A. 127 C6
Alpine WY U.S.A. 122 F4
Alpine National Park Australia 108 C6
Alps mts Europe 52 H4
Al Qa'āmīyāt reg. Saudi Arabia 82 G6
Al Qaddāḥīyah Libya 93 E1
Al Qadmūs Syria 81 C2
Al Qaffāy i. U.A.E. 84 D5
Al Qāhirah Egypt see Cairo
Al Qā'īyah Saudi Arabia 82 F5
Al Qā'īyah well Saudi Arabia 84 B5
Al Qalībah Saudi Arabia 86 E5
Al Qāmishlī Syria 87 F3
Al Qar'ah Libya 86 B5
Al Qar'ah well Saudi Arabia 84 B5
Al Qar'ah lava field Syria 81 C3
Al Qardāḥah Syria 81 C2
Al Qarqar Saudi Arabia 81 C4
Al Qaryatayn Syria 81 C2
Al Qaṣab Ar Riyāḍ Saudi Arabia 84 B5
Al Qaṣab Ash Sharqīyah Saudi Arabia 84 C6
Al Qaṭīf Saudi Arabia 84 C5
Al Qaṭn Yemen 82 G6
Al Qaṭrānah Jordan 81 C4
Al Qaṭrūn Libya 93 E2
Al Qayṣūmah well Saudi Arabia 87 F5
Al Qumur country Africa see Comoros
Al Qunayṭirah Syria 81 B3
Al Qunfidhah Saudi Arabia 82 F6
Al Qurayyāt Saudi Arabia 81 C4
Al Qurnah Iraq 87 G5
Al Quṣaymah Egypt 81 B4
Al Quṣayr Egypt 82 D4
Al Quṣayr Syria 81 C2
Al Quṣīyah Egypt 86 C6
Al Qūṣūrīyah Saudi Arabia 84 B6
Al Quṭayfah Syria 81 C3
Al Quwayī' Saudi Arabia 84 B6
Al Quwayīyah Saudi Arabia 82 G5
Al Quwayrah Jordan 81 B5
Al Rabbād reg. U.A.E. 84 D6
Alroy Downs Australia 106 B3
Alsace admin. reg. France 49 H6
Alsace reg. France 52 H2
Alsager U.K. 45 E5
Al Samīt well Iraq 87 F5
Alsask Canada 117 I5
Alsatia reg. France see Alsace
Alsek r. U.S.A. 116 B3
Alsfeld Germany 49 J4
Alsleben (Saale) Germany 49 L3
Alston U.K. 44 E4
Alstonville Australia 108 F2
Alsunga Latvia 41 L8
Alta Norway 40 M2
Alta, Mount N.Z. 109 B7
Altaelva r. Norway 40 M2
Altafjorden sea chan. Norway 40 M1
Alta Floresta Brazil 139 G5
Altai Mountains Asia 68 F3
Altamaha r. U.S.A. 129 D6
Altamira Brazil 139 H4

Anzio Italy 54 E4
Aoba i. Vanuatu 103 G3
Aoga-shima i. Japan 71 E6
Aokal Afgh. 85 F3
Ao Kham, Laem pt Thai. 67 B5
Aomen China see Macau
Aomen Tebie Xingzhengqu aut. reg. China see Macau
Aomori Japan 70 F4
Ao Phang Nga National Park Thai. 67 B5

▶Aoraki mt. N.Z. 109 C6
Highest mountain in New Zealand.

Aôral, Phnum mt. Cambodia 67 D4
Aorangi mt. N.Z. see Aoraki
Aosta Italy 54 B2
Aotearoa country Oceania see New Zealand
Aouk, Bahr r. Cent. Afr. Rep./Chad 93 E4
Aoukâr reg. Mali/Mauritania 92 C2
Aoulef Alg. 92 D2
Aozou Chad 93 E2
Apa r. Brazil 140 E2
Apache Creek U.S.A. 125 I5
Apache Junction U.S.A. 125 H5
Apaiang atoll Kiribati see Abaiang
Apalachee Bay U.S.A. 129 C6
Apalachicola U.S.A. 129 C6
Apalachicola r. U.S.A. 129 C6
Apalachin U.S.A. 131 G2
Apamea Turkey see Dinar
Apaporis r. Col. 138 E4
Aparecida do Tabuado Brazil 141 A3
Aparima N.Z. see Riverton
Aparri Phil. 146 E4
Apatity Rus. Fed. 40 R3
Apatzingán Mex. 132 D5
Ape Latvia 41 O8
Apeldoorn Neth. 48 F2
Apelern Germany 49 J2
Apennines mts Italy 54 C2
Apensen Germany 49 J1
Apex Mountain Canada 116 B2
Api mt. Nepal 78 E3
Api i. Vanuatu see Epi
Apia atoll Kiribati see Abaiang

▶Apia Samoa 103 I3
Capital of Samoa.

Apiacas, Serra dos hills Brazil 139 G6
Apiaí Brazil 141 A4
Apishapa r. U.S.A. 126 C4
Apiti N.Z. 109 E4
Apizolaya Mex. 127 C7
Aplao Peru 138 D7
Apo, Mount vol. Phil. 65 H5
Apoera Suriname 139 G2
Apolda Germany 49 L3
Apollo Bay Australia 108 A7
Apollonia Bulg. see Sozopol
Apolo Bol. 138 E6
Aporé Brazil 141 A2
Aporé r. Brazil 141 A2
Apostle Islands U.S.A. 126 F2
Apostolens Tommelfinger mt. Greenland 115 N3
Apostolos Andreas, Cape Cyprus 81 B2
Apoteri Guyana 139 G3
Apozai Pak. 85 H4
Appalachian Mountains U.S.A. 130 D5
Appalla i. Fiji see Kabara
Appennino mts Italy see Apennines
Appennino Abruzzese mts Italy 54 E3
Appennino Tosco-Emiliano mts Italy 54 D3
Appennino Umbro-Marchigiano mts Italy 54 E3
Appingedam Neth. 48 G1
Applecross U.K. 46 D3
Appleton MN U.S.A. 126 D2
Appleton WI U.S.A. 130 A1
Apple Valley U.S.A. 124 E4
Appomattox U.S.A. 131 F5
Aprilia Italy 54 E4
Aprunyi India 72 B2
Apsheronsk Rus. Fed. 87 E1
Apsheronskaya Rus. Fed. see Apsheronsk
Apsley Canada 131 F1
Apt France 52 G5
Apucarana Brazil 141 A3
Apucarana, Serra da hills Brazil 141 A3
Apulum Romania see Alba Iulia
Aq"a Georgia see Sokhumi
'Aqaba Jordan see Al 'Aqabah
Aqaba, Gulf of Asia 86 D5
'Aqaba, Wâdi el watercourse Egypt see 'Aqabah, Wādī al
'Aqabah, Birkat al well Iraq 84 A4
'Aqabah, Wādī al watercourse Egypt 81 A4
Aqadyr Kazakh. see Agadyr'
Aqdoghmish r. Iran 84 B2
Aqköl Akmolinskaya Oblast' Kazakh. see Akkol'
Aqköl Atyrauskaya Oblast' Kazakh. see Akkol'
Aqmola Kazakh. see Astana
Aqqan China 79 F1
Aqqikkol Hu salt l. China 79 G1
Aqra', Jabal al mt. Syria/Turkey 81 B2
'Aqran hill Saudi Arabia 81 D4
Aqsay Kazakh. see Aksay
Aqsayqin Hit terr. Asia see Aksai Chin
Aqshī Kazakh. see Akshiy
Aqshuqyr Kazakh. see Akshukur
Aqsū Kazakh. see Aksu
Aqsūat Kazakh. see Aksuat
Aqsū-Ayuly Kazakh. see Aksu-Ayuly
Aqtaū Kazakh. see Aktau
Aqtöbe Kazakh. see Aktobe
Aqtoghay Kazakh. see Aktogay
Aquae Grani Germany see Aachen
Aquae Gratianae France see Aix-les-Bains
Aquae Sextiae France see Aix-en-Provence
Aquae Statiellae Italy see Acqui Terme
Aquarius Mountains U.S.A. 125 G4
Aquarius Plateau U.S.A. 125 H3
Aquaviva delle Fonti Italy 54 G4
Aquidauana Brazil 140 E2
Aquiles Mex. 123 G7
Aquincum Hungary see Budapest
Aquiry r. Brazil see Acre
Aquisgranum Germany see Aachen
Aquitaine reg. France 52 D5
Aquitania reg. France see Aquitaine
Aqzhayqyn Köli salt l. Kazakh. see Akzhaykyn, Ozero
Ara India 79 F4
Āra Ārba Eth. 94 E3
Arab Afgh. 85 G4
Arab, Bahr el watercourse Sudan 93 F4
'Arab, Khalîg el b. Egypt see 'Arab, Khalīj al
'Arab, Khalīj al b. Egypt 86 C5
'Arabah, Wādī al watercourse Israel/Jordan 81 B5
Arabian Basin sea feature Indian Ocean 145 M5
Arabian Gulf Asia see The Gulf
Arabian Peninsula Asia 82 G5
Arabian Sea Indian Ocean 83 K6
Araç Turkey 86 D2
Araça r. Brazil 138 F4
Aracaju Brazil 139 K6
Aracati Brazil 139 K4
Aracatu Brazil 141 C1
Araçatuba Brazil 141 A3
Aracena Spain 53 C5
Aracruz Brazil 141 C2
Araçuaí Brazil 141 C2
Araçuaí r. Brazil 141 C2
'Arad Israel 81 B4
Arad Romania 55 I1
'Arādah U.A.E. 84 D6
Arafura Sea Australia/Indon. 102 D2
Arafura Shelf sea feature Australia/Indon. 146 E6
Aragarças Brazil 139 H7
Aragón r. Spain 53 F2
Araguaçu Brazil 141 A1
Araguaia r. Brazil 141 A1
Araguaia, Parque Nacional de nat. park Brazil 139 H6
Araguaiana Brazil 141 A1
Araguaína Brazil 139 I5
Araguari Brazil 141 A2
Araguari r. Brazil 139 H3
Araguatins Brazil 139 I5
Arai Brazil 141 B1
'Arâif el Naga, Gebel hill Egypt see 'Urayf an Nāqah, Jabal
Araiosos Brazil 139 J4
Arak Alg. 92 D2
Arāk Iran 84 C3
Arak Syria 81 D2
Arakan reg. Myanmar 66 A2
Arakan Yoma mts Myanmar 66 A2
Arakkonam India 80 C3
Araks r. Armenia see Araz
Araku India 80 D2
Aral China 76 F3
Aral Kazakh. see Aral'sk
Aral Tajik. see Vose

▶Aral Sea salt l. Kazakh./Uzbek. 76 B2
3rd largest lake in Asia.

Aral'sk Kazakh. 76 B2
Aral'skoye More salt l. Kazakh./Uzbek. see Aral Sea
Aralsor, Ozero l. Kazakh. 39 K6
Aral Tengizi salt l. Kazakh./Uzbek. see Aral Sea
Aramac Australia 106 D4
Aramac Creek watercourse Australia 106 D4
Aramah plat. Saudi Arabia 84 B5
Aramberri Mex. 127 D7
Aramia r. P.N.G. 65 K8
Aran r. India 80 C2
Aranda de Duero Spain 53 E3
Arandai Indon. 65 I7
Aranđelovac Serb. and Mont.. 55 I2
Arandis Namibia 96 B2
Arang India 79 E5
Arani India 80 C3
Aran Island Rep. of Ireland 47 D3
Aran Islands Rep. of Ireland 47 C4
Aranjuez Spain 53 E3
Aranos Namibia 96 D3
Aransas Pass U.S.A. 127 D7
Arantangi India 80 C4
Aranuka atoll Kiribati 103 H1
Aranyaprathet Thai. 67 C4
Arao Japan 71 C6
Araouane Mali 92 C3
Arapaho U.S.A. 127 D5
Arapgir Turkey 86 E3
Arapiraca Brazil 139 K5
Arapis, Akra pt Greece 55 K4
Arapkir Turkey see Arapgir
Arapongas Brazil 141 A3
Araquari Brazil 141 A4
'Ar'ar Saudi Arabia 87 F5
Araracuara Col. 138 D4
Araranguá Brazil 141 A5
Araraquara Brazil 141 A3
Araras Brazil 139 H5
Ararat Armenia 87 G3
Ararat Australia 108 A6
Ararat, Mount Turkey 87 G3
Araria India 79 F4
Araripina Brazil 139 J5
Aras Turkey 87 F3
Aras r. Turkey see Araz
Arataca Brazil 141 D1
Arauca Col. 138 D2
Arauca r. Venez. 138 E2
Aravalli Range mts India 78 C4
Aravete Estonia 41 N7
Arawa P.N.G. 102 F2
Araxá Brazil 141 B2
Araxes r. Asia see Araz
Arayıt Dağı mt. Turkey 55 N5
Araz r. Azer. 87 H2
also spelt Araks (Armenia), Aras (Turkey), formerly known as Araxes
Arbailu Iraq see Arbīl
Arbat Iraq 87 G4
Arbela Iraq see Arbīl
Arberth U.K. see Narberth
Arbīl Iraq 87 G3
Arboga Sweden 41 I7
Arborfield Canada 117 K4
Arborg Canada 117 L5
Arbroath U.K. 46 G4
Arbuckle U.S.A. 124 B2
Arbu Lut, Dasht-e des. Afgh. 85 F4
Arcachon France 52 D4
Arcade U.S.A. 131 F2
Arcadia FL U.S.A. 129 D7
Arcadia LA U.S.A. 127 E5
Arcadia MI U.S.A. 130 B1
Arcanum U.S.A. 130 C4
Arcata U.S.A. 122 B4
Arc Dome mt. U.S.A. 124 E2
Arcelia Mex. 132 D5
Archangel Rus. Fed. 38 I2
Archer r. Australia 63 G9
Archer Bend National Park Australia 106 C2
Archer City U.S.A. 127 D5
Arches National Park U.S.A. 125 I2
Archipiélago Los Roques nat. park Venez. 138 E1
Ärçivan Azer. 87 H3
Arckaringa watercourse Australia 107 A6
Arco U.S.A. 122 E4
Arcos Brazil 141 B3
Arcos de la Frontera Spain 53 D5
Arctic Bay Canada 115 J2
Arctic Institute Islands Rus. Fed. see Arkticheskogo Instituta, Ostrova
Arctic Mid-Ocean Ridge sea feature Arctic Ocean 149 H1

▶Arctic Ocean 149 B1
poles 142–143

Arctic Red r. Canada 114 E3
Arctowski research station Antarctica 148 A2
Arda r. Bulg. 55 L4
also known as Ardas (Greece)
Ardabīl Iran 84 C2
Ardahan Turkey 87 F2
Ardakān Iran 84 D3
Årdalstangen Norway 41 E6
Ardara Rep. of Ireland 47 D3
Ardas r. Bulg. see Arda
Ard aş Şawwān plain Jordan 81 C4
Ardatov Nizhegorodskaya Oblast' Rus. Fed. 39 I5
Ardatov Respublika Mordoviya Rus. Fed. 39 J5
Ardee Rep. of Ireland 47 F4
Ardennes plat. Belgium 48 E5
Ardennes, Canal des France 48 E5
Arden Town U.S.A. 124 C2
Arderin hill Rep. of Ireland 47 E4
Ardestān Iran 84 D3
Ardglass U.K. 47 G3
Ardila r. Port. 53 C4
Ardlethan Australia 108 C5
Ardmore U.S.A. 127 D5
Ardnamurchan, Point of U.K. 46 C4
Ardon Rus. Fed. 87 G2
Ardrishaig U.K. 46 D4
Ardrossan U.K. 46 E5
Ardvasar U.K. 46 D3
Areia Branca Brazil 139 K4
Arel Belgium see Arlon
Arelas France see Arles
Arelate France see Arles
Aremberg hill Germany 48 G4
Arena, Point U.S.A. 124 B2
Arenas de San Pedro Spain 53 D3
Arendal Norway 41 F7
Arendsee (Altmark) Germany 49 L2
Areopoli Greece 55 J6
Arequipa Peru 138 D7
Arere Brazil 139 H4
Arévalo Spain 53 D3
Arezzo Italy 54 D3
'Arfajah well Saudi Arabia 81 D4
Argadargada Australia 106 B4
Arganda Spain 53 E3
Argel Alg. see Algiers
Argentan France 52 D2
Argentario, Monte hill Italy 54 D3
Argentera, Cima dell' mt. Italy 54 B2
Argenthal Germany 49 H5

▶Argentina country S. America 140 C5
2nd largest country in South America. 3rd most populous country in South America.
south america 9, 136–137

Argentine Abyssal Plain sea feature S. Atlantic Ocean 144 E9
Argentine Basin sea feature S. Atlantic Ocean 144 F8
Argentine Republic country S. America see Argentina
Argentine Rise sea feature S. Atlantic Ocean 144 E8
Argentino, Lago l. Arg. 140 B8
Argenton-sur-Creuse France 52 E3
Argentoratum France see Strasbourg
Argeș r. Romania 55 L2
Arghandab r. Afgh. 85 G4
Argi r. Rus. Fed. 70 C1
Argolikos Kolpos b. Greece 55 J6
Argos Greece 55 J6
Argos U.S.A. 130 B3
Argostoli Greece 55 I5
Arguis Spain 53 F2
Argun' r. China/Rus. Fed. 69 M2
Argun Rus. Fed. 87 G2
Argungu Nigeria 92 D3
Argus Range mts U.S.A. 124 E4
Argyle Canada 119 I6
Argyle, Lake Australia 104 E4
Argyrokastron Albania see Gjirokastër
Ar Horqin Qi China see Tianshan
Århus Denmark 41 G8
Ariah Park Australia 108 C5
Ariamsvlei Namibia 96 D5
Ariana Tunisia see L'Ariana
Ariano Irpino Italy 54 F4
Ari Atoll Maldives 77 D11
Aribinda Burkina 92 C3
Arica Chile 138 D7
Arid, Cape Australia 105 C8
Arigza China 72 C1
Arīḩā Syria 81 C2
Arīḩā West Bank see Jericho
Arikaree r. U.S.A. 126 C3
Arima Trin. and Tob. 133 L6
Ariminum Italy see Rimini
Arinos Brazil 141 B1
Aripuanã Brazil 139 G6
Aripuanã r. Brazil 138 F5
Ariquemes Brazil 138 F5
Aris Namibia 96 C2
Arisaig U.K. 46 D4
Arisaig, Sound of sea chan. U.K. 46 D4
'Arīsh, Wādī al watercourse Egypt 81 A4
Aristazabal Island Canada 116 D4
Arixang China see Wenquan
Ariyalur India 80 C4
Arizaro, Salar de salt flat Arg. 140 C2
Arizona Arg. 140 C5
Arizona state U.S.A. 123 F6
Arizpe Mex. 123 F7
'Arjah Saudi Arabia 82 F5
Arjasa Indon. 64 F8
Arjeplog Sweden 40 J3
Arjuni India 78 E5
Arkadak Rus. Fed. 39 I6
Arkadelphia U.S.A. 127 E5
Arkaig, Loch l. U.K. 46 D4
Arkalyk Kazakh. 76 C1
Arkansas r. U.S.A. 127 F5
Arkansas state U.S.A. 127 E5
Arkansas City AR U.S.A. 127 F5
Arkansas City KS U.S.A. 127 D4
Arkatag Shan mts China 79 G1
Arkell, Mount Canada 116 C2
Arkenu, Jabal mt. Libya 82 B5
Arkhangel'sk Rus. Fed. see Archangel
Arkhara Rus. Fed. 70 C2
Arkhipovka Rus. Fed. 70 D4
Árki i. Greece see Arkoi
Arklow Rep. of Ireland 47 F5
Arkoi i. Greece 55 L6
Arkona Canada 130 E2
Arkona, Kap c. Germany 43 N3
Arkonam India see Arakkonam
Arkport U.S.A. 131 G2
Arkticheskogo Instituta, Ostrova is Rus. Fed. 60 J2
Arkul' Rus. Fed. 38 K4
Arlang, Gora mt. Turkm. 84 D2
Arles France 52 G5
Arlington S. Africa 97 H5
Arlington NY U.S.A. 131 I3
Arlington OH U.S.A. 130 D3
Arlington SD U.S.A. 126 D2
Arlington VA U.S.A. 131 G4
Arlington Heights U.S.A. 130 A2
Arlit Niger 92 D3
Arlon Belgium 48 F5
Arm r. Canada 117 J5
Armadale Australia 105 A8
Armagh U.K. 47 F3
Armant Egypt 82 D4
Armavir Rus. Fed. 87 F1

▶Armenia country Asia 87 G2
asia 6, 58–59

Armenia Col. 138 C3
Armenopolis Romania see Gherla
Armeria Mex. 132 D5
Armidale Australia 108 E3
Armington U.S.A. 122 F3
Armit Lake Canada 117 N1
Armori India 80 D1
Armour U.S.A. 126 D3
Armoy U.K. 47 F2
Armstrong r. Australia 104 E4
Armstrong Canada 118 C4
Armstrong, Mount Canada 116 C2
Armstrong Island Cook Is see Rarotonga
Armu r. Rus. Fed. 70 E3
Armur India 80 C2
Armutçuk Dağı mts Turkey 55 L5
Armyanskaya S.S.R. country Asia see Armenia
Arnaoutis, Cape Cyprus see Arnauti, Cape
Arnaud r. Canada 119 H2
Arnauti, Cape Cyprus 81 A2
Årnes Norway 41 G6
Arnett U.S.A. 127 D4
Arnhem Neth. 48 F3
Arnhem, Cape Australia 106 B2
Arnhem Land reg. Australia 104 F3
Arno r. Italy 54 D3
Arno Bay Australia 107 B7
Arnold U.K. 45 F5
Arnold's Cove Canada 119 L5
Arnon r. Jordan see Mawjib, Wādī al
Arnprior Canada 131 G1
Arnsberg Germany 49 I3
Arnstadt Germany 49 K4
Arnstein Germany 49 J5
Arnstorf Germany 49 M6
Aroab Namibia 96 D4
Aroland Canada 118 D4
Arolsen Germany 49 J3
Aroma Sudan 82 E6
Arona Italy 54 C2
Arorae i. Kiribati 103 H2
Arore i. Kiribati see Arorae
Aros r. Mex. 123 F7
Arossi i. Solomon Is see San Cristobal
Arqalyq Kazakh. see Arkalyk
Arquipélago da Madeira aut. reg. Port. 92 B1
Arrabury Australia 107 C5
Arrah India see Ara
Arraias Brazil 141 B1
Arraias, Serra de hills Brazil 141 B1
Ar Ramādī Iraq 87 F4
Ar Ramlah Jordan 81 B5
Ar Ramthā Jordan 81 C3
Arran i. U.K. 46 D5
Ar Raqqah Syria 81 D2
Arras France 48 C4
Ar Rass Saudi Arabia 82 F4
Ar Rastān Syria 81 C2
Ar Rayyān Qatar 84 C5
Arrecife Canary Is 92 B2
Arretium Italy see Arezzo
Arriagá Mex. 132 F5
Ar Rifā'ī Iraq 87 G5
Ar Rihāb salt flat Iraq 87 G5
Ar Rimāl reg. Saudi Arabia 94 F1
Arrington U.S.A. 131 F5
Ar Riyāḍ Saudi Arabia see Riyadh
Arrochar U.K. 46 E4
Arrojado r. Brazil 141 B1
Arrow, Lough l. Rep. of Ireland 47 D3
Arrowsmith, Mount N.Z. 109 C6
Arroyo Grande U.S.A. 124 C4
Ar Rubay'iyah Saudi Arabia 84 B5
Ar Rummān Jordan 81 B3
Ar Ruq'ī well Saudi Arabia 84 B4
Ar Ruşāfah Syria 81 D2
Ar Ruşayfah Jordan 81 C3
Ar Rustāq Oman 84 E6
Ar Rutbah Iraq 87 F4
Ar Ruwaydah Saudi Arabia 84 B5
Ar Ruwaydah Saudi Arabia 84 B6
Ar Ruwayḩah Syria 81 C2
Års Denmark 41 F8
Ars Iran 84 D2
Arseno Lake Canada 116 H1
Arsen'yev Rus. Fed. 70 D3
Arsk Rus. Fed. 38 K4
Arta Greece 55 I5
Artem Rus. Fed. 70 D4
Artemisa Cuba 129 D8
Artemivs'k Ukr. 39 H6
Artemovsk Ukr. see Artemivs'k
Artenay France 52 E2
Artesia AZ U.S.A. 125 I5
Artesia NM U.S.A. 123 G6
Arthur Canada 130 E2
Arthur NE U.S.A. 126 C3
Arthur TN U.S.A. 130 D5
Arthur, Lake U.S.A. 130 E3
Arthur's Pass National Park N.Z. 109 C6
Arthur's Town Bahamas 129 F7
Arti Rus. Fed. 37 R4
Artigas research station Antarctica 148 A2
Artigas Uruguay 140 E4
Art'ik Armenia 87 F2
Artillery Lake Canada 117 I2
Artisia Botswana 97 H3
Artois reg. France 48 B4
Artois, Collines d' hills France 48 B4
Artos Dağı mt. Turkey 87 F3
Artova Turkey 86 E2
Artsakh aut. reg. Azer. see Dağlıq Qarabağ
Artsiz Ukr. see Artsyz
Artsyz Ukr. 55 M2
Artur de Paiva Angola see Kuvango
Artux China 76 E4
Artvin Turkey 87 F2
Artyk Turkm. 84 E2
Aru, Kepulauan is Indon. 104 F1
Arua Uganda 94 D3
Aruanã Brazil 141 A1

▶Aruba terr. West Indies 133 K6
Self-governing Netherlands Territory.
north america 9, 112–113

Arumã Brazil 138 F4
Arunachal Pradesh state India 79 H4
Arundel U.K. 45 G8
Arun Gol r. China 70 B3
Arun He r. China see Arun Gol
Arun Qi China see Naji
Aruppukkottai India 80 C4
Arusha Tanz. 94 D4
Aruwimi r. Dem. Rep. Congo 94 C3
Arvada U.S.A. 122 G5
Arvagh Rep. of Ireland 47 E4
Arvayheer Mongolia 76 J2
Arviat Canada 117 M2
Arvidsjaur Sweden 40 K4
Arvika Sweden 41 H7
Arvonia U.S.A. 131 F5
Arwā' Saudi Arabia 84 B6
Arwād i. Syria 81 B2
Arwala Indon. 104 D1
Arxan China 69 L3
Aryanah Tunisia see L'Ariana
Arys' Kazakh. 76 C3
Arzamas Rus. Fed. 39 I5
Arzanah i. U.A.E. 84 D5
Arzberg Germany 49 M4
Arzew Alg. 53 F6
Arzgir Rus. Fed. 87 G1
Arzila Morocco see Asilah
Aš Czech Rep. 49 M4
Asaba Nigeria 92 D4
Asad, Buḩayrat al resr Syria 81 D1
Asadābād Afgh. 85 H3
Asadābād Iran 84 C3
Asahi-dake vol. Japan 70 F4
Asahikawa Japan 70 F4
'Asal Egypt 81 A5
Āsalē l. Eth. 94 E2
Asālem Iran 84 C2
'Asalūyeh Iran 84 D5
Asan-man b. S. Korea 71 B5
Asansol India 79 F5
Āsayita Eth. 94 E2
Asbach Germany 49 H4
Asbestos Mountains S. Africa 96 F5
Asbury Park U.S.A. 131 H3
Ascalon Israel see Ashqelon
Ascea Italy 54 F4
Ascensión Bol. 138 F7
Ascensión Mex. 123 G7
Ascension atoll Micronesia see Pohnpei

▶Ascension i. S. Atlantic Ocean 144 H6
Dependency of St Helena.

Aschaffenburg Germany 49 J5
Ascheberg Germany 49 H3
Aschersleben Germany 49 L3
Ascoli Piceno Italy 54 E3
Asculum Italy see Ascoli Piceno
Asculum Picenum Italy see Ascoli Piceno
Ascutney U.S.A. 131 I2
Āseb Eritrea see Assab
Åseda Sweden 41 I8
Åsele Sweden 40 J4
Asenovgrad Bulg. 55 K3
Aşfar, Jabal al mt. Jordan 81 C3
Aşfar, Tall al hill Syria 81 C3
Aşgabat Turkm. see Ashgabat
Asha Rus. Fed. 37 R5
Ashburn U.S.A. 129 D6
Ashburton watercourse Australia 104 A5
Ashburton N.Z. 109 C6
Ashburton Range hills Australia 104 F4
Ashdod Israel 81 B4
Ashdown U.S.A. 127 E5
Asheboro U.S.A. 128 E5
Asher U.S.A. 127 D5
Ashern Canada 117 L5
Asheville U.S.A. 128 D5
Asheweig r. Canada 118 D3
Ashford Australia 108 E2
Ashford U.K. 45 H7
Ash Fork U.S.A. 125 G4

▶Ashgabat Turkm. 84 E2
Capital of Turkmenistan.

Ashibetsu Japan 70 F4
Ashikaga Japan 71 E5
Ashington U.K. 44 F3
Ashizuri-misaki pt Japan 71 D6
Ashkelon Israel see Ashqelon
Ashkhabad Turkm. see Ashgabat
Ashkum U.S.A. 130 B3
Ashkun reg. Afgh. 85 H3
Ashland AL U.S.A. 129 C5
Ashland ME U.S.A. 128 G2
Ashland NH U.S.A. 131 J2
Ashland OH U.S.A. 130 D3
Ashland OR U.S.A. 122 C4
Ashland VA U.S.A. 131 G5
Ashland WI U.S.A. 126 F2
Ashland City U.S.A. 130 B5
Ashley Australia 108 D2
Ashley MI U.S.A. 130 C2
Ashley ND U.S.A. 126 D2

▶Ashmore and Cartier Islands terr. Australia 104 C3
Australian External Territory.

Ashmore Reef Australia 104 C3
Ashmore Reefs Australia 106 D1
Ashmyany Belarus 41 N9
Ashqelon Israel 81 B4
Ash Shabakah Iraq 87 F5
Ash Shaddādah Syria 87 F3
Ash Shallūfah Egypt 81 A4
Ash Sham Syria see Damascus
Ash Shanāfīyah Iraq 87 G5
Ash Shaqīq well Saudi Arabia 87 F5
Ash Sharawrah Saudi Arabia 82 G6
Ash Shāriqah U.A.E. see Sharjah
Ash Sharqāṭ Iraq 87 F4
Ash Shaṭrah Iraq 87 G5
Ash Shaṭṭ Egypt 81 A5
Ash Shawbak Jordan 81 B4
Ash Shaybānī well Saudi Arabia 87 F5
Ash Shaykh Ibrāhīm Syria 81 D2
Ash Shiblīyāt hill Saudi Arabia 81 C5
Ash Shiḩr Yemen 82 G7
Ash Shu'aybah Saudi Arabia 87 F6
Ash Shu'bah Saudi Arabia 82 F4
Ash Shurayf Saudi Arabia see Khaybar
Ashta India 78 D5
Ashtabula U.S.A. 130 E3
Ashtarak Armenia 87 G2
Ashti Maharashtra India 78 D5
Ashti Maharashtra India 80 B2
Ashti Maharashtra India 80 C2
Āshtiān Iran 84 C3
Ashton S. Africa 96 E7
Ashton U.S.A. 122 F3
Ashton-under-Lyne U.K. 44 E5
Ashuanipi r. Canada 119 I3
Ashuanipi Lake Canada 119 I3
Ashur Iraq see Ash Sharqāṭ
Ashville U.S.A. 129 C5
Ashwaubenon U.S.A. 130 A1
Asi r. Asia 86 E3 see 'Āṣī, Nahr al
'Āṣī r. Lebanon/Syria see Orontes
'Āṣī, Nahr al r. Asia 86 E3
also known as Asi or Orontes
Āsīā Bak Iran 84 C3
Asifabad India 80 C2
Asika India 80 E2
Asilah Morocco 53 C6
Asinara, Golfo dell' b. Sardinia Italy 54 C4
Asino Rus. Fed. 60 J4
Asipovichy Belarus 39 F5
Asīr Iran 84 D5
'Asīr reg. Saudi Arabia 82 F5
Asisium Italy see Assisi
Askale Jammu and Kashmir 78 C2
Aşkale Turkey 87 F3
Asker Norway 41 G7
Askersund Sweden 41 I7
Askim Norway 41 G7
Askino Rus. Fed. 37 R4
Askival hill U.K. 46 C4
Asl Egypt see 'Asal
Aslanköy r. Turkey 81 B1
Asmar reg. Afgh. 85 H3

▶Asmara Eritrea 82 E6
Capital of Eritrea.

Āsmera Eritrea see Asmara
Åsnen l. Sweden 41 I8
Aso-Kuju National Park Japan 71 C6
Asonli India 72 B2
Asop India 78 C4
Asori Indon. 65 J7
Āsosa Eth. 94 D2
Asotin U.S.A. 122 D3
Aspang-Markt Austria 43 P7
Aspatria U.K. 44 D4
Aspen U.S.A. 122 G5
Asperg Germany 49 J6
Aspermont U.S.A. 127 C5
Aspiring, Mount N.Z. 109 B7
Aspro, Cape Cyprus 81 A2
Aspromonte, Parco Nazionale dell' nat. park Italy 54 F5
Aspron, Cape Cyprus see Aspro, Cape
Aspur India 85 I6
Asquith Canada 117 J4
As Sa'an Syria 81 C2
Assab Eritrea 82 F7
As Sabsab well Saudi Arabia 84 C5
Assad, Lake resr Syria see Asad, Buḩayrat al
Aş Şadr U.A.E. 84 D5
Aş Şafā lava field Syria 81 C3
Aş Şafāqis Tunisia see Sfax
Aş Şaff Egypt 86 C5
Aş Şafīrah Syria 81 C2
Aş Şaḩrā' al Gharbīyah des. Egypt see Western Desert
Aş Şaḩrā' ash Sharqīyah des. Egypt see Eastern Desert
Assake-Audan, Vpadina depr. Kazakh./Uzbek. 87 J2
'Assal, Lac l. Djibouti see Assal, Lake

▶Assal, Lake Djibouti 82 F7
Lowest point in Africa.
africa 88–89

Aş Şāliḩīyah Syria 87 F4
As Sallūm Egypt 86 B5
As Salmān Iraq 87 G5
As Salt Jordan 81 B3
Assam state India 79 G4
Assamakka Niger 92 D3
As Samāwah Iraq 87 G5
As Samrā' Jordan 81 C3
Aş Şanām reg. Saudi Arabia 82 H5
As Sarīr reg. Libya 93 F2
Assateague Island U.S.A. 131 H4
As Sawādah reg. Saudi Arabia 84 B6
Assayeta Eth. see Āsayita
As Sayh Saudi Arabia 84 B6
Assen Neth. 48 G1
Assenede Belgium 48 D3
Assesse Belgium 48 F4
As Sidrah Libya 93 E1
As Sīfah Oman 84 E6
Assigny, Lac l. Canada 119 I3
As Sikak Saudi Arabia 84 C5
Assiniboia Canada 117 J5
Assiniboine r. Canada 117 L5
Assiniboine, Mount Canada 114 G4
Assis Brazil 141 A3
Assisi Italy 54 E3
Aßlar Germany 49 I4
Aş Şubayḩīyah Kuwait 84 B4
Aş Şufayrī well Saudi Arabia 84 B4
As Sukhnah Syria 81 D2
As Sulaymānīyah Iraq 87 G4
As Sulaymī Saudi Arabia 82 F4
Aş Şulb reg. Saudi Arabia 84 C5
Aş Şummān plat. Saudi Arabia 84 B5
Aş Şummān plat. Saudi Arabia 84 C6
As Sūq Saudi Arabia 82 F5
As Sūrīyah country Asia see Syria
Aş Şuwar Syria 87 F4

As Suwaydā' Syria 81 C3
As Suways Egypt see Suez
As Suways governorate Egypt 81 A4
Assynt, Loch l. U.K. 46 D2
Astakida i. Greece 55 L7
Astakos Greece 55 I5
Astalu Island Pak. see Astola Island
▶Astana Kazakh. 76 D1
Capital of Kazakhstan.
Astaneh Iran 84 C2
Astara Azer. 87 H3
Āstārā Iran 82 G2
Asterabad Iran see Gorgān
Asti Italy 54 C2
Astillero Peru 138 E6
Astin Tag mts China see Altun Shan
Astipálaia i. Greece see Astypalaia
Astola Island Pak. 85 F5
Astor r. Pak. 85 I3
Astorga Spain 53 C2
Astoria U.S.A. 122 C3
Åstorp Sweden 41 H8
Astrabad Iran see Gorgān
Astrakhan' Rus. Fed. 39 K7
Astrakhan' Bazar Azer. see Cälilabad
Astravyets Belarus 41 N9
Astrida Rwanda see Butare
Asturias aut. comm. Spain 53 C2
Asturias, Principado de aut. comm. Spain see Asturias
Asturica Augusta Spain see Astorga
Astypalaia i. Greece 55 L6
Asuncion i. N. Mariana Is 65 L3
▶Asunción Para. 140 E3
Capital of Paraguay.
Aswad Oman 84 E5
Aswān Egypt see Aswân
Aswân Egypt 82 D5
Asyūṭ Egypt see Asyûṭ
Asyûṭ Egypt 86 C6
Ata i. Tonga 103 I4
Atacama, Desierto de des. Chile see Atacama Desert
Atacama, Salar de salt flat Chile 140 C2
▶Atacama Desert Chile 140 C3
Driest place in the world.
Atafu atoll Tokelau 103 I2
Atafu i. Tokelau 146 I6
'Aṭā'iṭah, Jabal al mt. Jordan 81 B4
Atakent Turkey 81 B1
Atakpamé Togo 92 D4
Atalándi Greece see Atalanti
Atalanti Greece 55 J5
Atalaya Peru 138 D6
Ataléia Brazil 141 C2
Atambua Indon. 104 D2
Ataniya Turkey see Adana
'Ataq Yemen 82 G7
Atâr Mauritania 92 B2
Atari Pak. 85 I4
Atascadero U.S.A. 124 C4
Atasu Kazakh. 76 D2
Ataúro, Ilha de i. East Timor 104 D2
Atáviros mt. Greece see Attavyros
Atayurt Turkey 81 A1
Atbara Sudan 82 D6
Atbara r. Sudan 82 D6
Atbasar Kazakh. 76 C1
Atchison U.S.A. 126 E4
Atebubu Ghana 92 C4
Ateransk Kazakh. see Atyrau
Āteshān Iran 84 D3
Āteshkhāneh, Kūh-e hill Afgh. 85 F3
Atessa Italy 54 F3
Ath Belgium 48 D4
Athabasca r. Canada 117 I3
Athabasca, Lake Canada 117 I3
Athalia U.S.A. 130 D4
'Athāmīn, Birkat al well Iraq 84 A4
Atharan Hazari Pak. 85 I4
Athboy Rep. of Ireland 47 F4
Athenae Greece see Athens
Athenry Rep. of Ireland 47 D4
Athens Canada 131 H1
▶Athens Greece 55 J6
Capital of Greece.
Athens AL U.S.A. 129 C5
Athens GA U.S.A. 129 D5
Athens MI U.S.A. 130 C2
Athens OH U.S.A. 130 D4
Athens PA U.S.A. 131 G3
Athens TN U.S.A. 128 C5
Athens TX U.S.A. 127 E5
Atherstone U.K. 45 F6
Atherton Australia 106 D3
Athies France 48 C5
Athina Greece see Athens
Athinai Greece see Athens
Athleague Rep. of Ireland 47 D4
Athlone Rep. of Ireland 47 E4
Athnā', Wādī al watercourse Jordan 81 D3
Athni India 80 B2
Athol N.Z. 109 B7
Athol U.S.A. 131 I2
Atholl, Forest of reg. U.K. 46 E4
Athos mt. Greece 55 K4
Ath Thamad Egypt 81 B5
Ath Thāyat mt. Saudi Arabia 81 C5
Ath Thumāmī well Saudi Arabia 84 B5
Athy Rep. of Ireland 47 F5
Ati Chad 93 E3
Aṭīābād Iran 84 E3
Atico Peru 138 D7
Atikameg Canada 116 H4
Atikameg r. Canada 118 E3
Atik Lake Canada 117 M4
Atikokan Canada 115 I5
Atikonak Lake Canada 119 I3
Atka Rus. Fed. 61 Q3
Atka Island U.S.A. 114 A4
Atkarsk Rus. Fed. 39 J6
Atkri Indon. 65 I7
▶Atlanta GA U.S.A. 129 C5
State capital of Georgia.
Atlanta IN U.S.A. 130 B3
Atlanta MI U.S.A. 130 C1
Atlantic IA U.S.A. 126 E3
Atlantic NC U.S.A. 129 E5
Atlantic City U.S.A. 131 H4
Atlantic-Indian-Antarctic Basin sea feature S. Atlantic Ocean 144 H10
Atlantic-Indian Ridge sea feature Southern Ocean 144 H9
▶Atlantic Ocean 144
2nd largest ocean in the world.
Atlantic Peak U.S.A. 122 F4
Atlantis S. Africa 96 D7
Atlas Méditerranéen mts Alg. see Atlas Tellien
Atlas Mountains Africa 50 C5
Atlas Saharien mts Alg. 50 E5
Atlas Tellien mts Alg. 53 H6
Atlin Lake Canada 116 C3
Atmakur India 80 C3
Atmore U.S.A. 129 C6
Atnur India 80 C2
Atocha Bol. 138 E8
Atoka U.S.A. 127 D5
Atouat mt. Laos 66 D3
Atouila, Erg des. Mali 92 C2
Atqan China see Aqqan
Atrak r. Iran/Turkm. see Atrek
Atrak, Rūd-e r. Iran/Turkm. 84 D2
Atrato r. Col. 138 C2
Atrek r. Iran/Turkm. 84 D2
also known as Atrak, alt. Etrek
Atropatene country Asia see Azerbaijan
Atsonupuri vol. Rus. Fed. 70 G3
Aṭ Ṭafīlah Jordan 81 B4
Aṭ Ṭā'if Saudi Arabia 82 F5
Attalea Turkey see Antalya
Attalia Turkey see Antalya
At Tamīmī Libya 86 A4
Attapu Laos 66 D4
Attavyros mt. Greece 55 L6
Attawapiskat Canada 118 E3
Attawapiskat r. Canada 118 E3
Attawapiskat Lake Canada 118 D3
Aṭ Ṭawīl mts Saudi Arabia 87 E5
At Taysīyah plat. Saudi Arabia 87 F5
Attendorn Germany 49 H3
Attersee l. Austria 43 N7
Attica IN U.S.A. 130 B3
Attica NY U.S.A. 131 F2
Attica OH U.S.A. 130 D3
Attigny France 48 E5
Attikamagen Lake Canada 119 I3
Attila Line Cyprus 81 A2
Attleborough U.K. 45 I6
Attopeu Laos see Attapu
Attu Greenland 115 M3
Aṭ Ṭubayq reg. Saudi Arabia 81 C5
▶Attu Island U.S.A. 61 S4
Most westerly point of North America.
At Tūnisīyah country Africa see Tunisia
Aṭ Ṭūr Egypt 86 D5
Attur India 80 C4
Aṭ Ṭuwayyah well Saudi Arabia 87 F6
Atuk Mountain hill U.S.A. 114 A3
Åtvidaberg Sweden 41 I7
Atwater U.S.A. 124 C3
Atwood U.S.A. 126 C4
Atwood Lake U.S.A. 130 E3
Atyashevo Rus. Fed. 39 J5
Atyrau Kazakh. 74 E2
Atyraū admin. div. Kazakh. see Atyrauskaya Oblast'
Atyrau Oblast admin. div. Kazakh. see Atyrauskaya Oblast'
Atyrauskaya Oblast' admin. div. Kazakh. 37 Q6
Aua Island P.N.G. 65 K7
Aub Germany 49 K5
Aubagne France 52 G5
Aubange Belgium 48 F5
Aubenas France 52 G4
Aubergenville France 48 B6
Auboué France 48 F5
Aubrey Cliffs mts U.S.A. 125 G4
Aubry Lake Canada 114 F3
Auburn r. Australia 107 E5
Auburn Canada 130 E2
Auburn AL U.S.A. 129 C5
Auburn CA U.S.A. 124 C2
Auburn IN U.S.A. 130 C3
Auburn KY U.S.A. 130 B5
Auburn ME U.S.A. 131 J1
Auburn NE U.S.A. 126 E3
Auburn NY U.S.A. 131 G2
Auburn Range hills Australia 106 E5
Aubusson France 52 F4
Auch France 52 E5
Auche Myanmar 66 B1
Auchterarder U.K. 46 F4
▶Auckland N.Z. 109 E3
5th most populous city in Oceania.
Auckland Islands N.Z. 103 G7
Auden Canada 118 D4
Audenarde Belgium see Oudenaarde
Audo mts Eth. 94 E3
Audo Range mts Eth. see Audo
Audruicq France 48 C4
Audubon U.S.A. 126 E3
Aue Germany 49 M4
Auerbach Germany 49 M4
Auerbach in der Oberpfalz Germany 49 L5
Auersberg mt. Germany 49 M4
Augathella Australia 107 D5
Augher U.K. 47 E3
Aughnacloy U.K. 47 F3
Aughrim Rep. of Ireland 47 F5
Augrabies S. Africa 96 E5
Augrabies Falls S. Africa 96 E5
Augrabies Falls National Park S. Africa 96 E5
Au Gres U.S.A. 130 D1
Augsburg Germany 43 M6
Augusta Australia 105 A8
Augusta Sicily Italy 54 F6
Augusta AR U.S.A. 127 F5
Augusta GA U.S.A. 129 D5
Augusta KY U.S.A. 130 C4
▶Augusta ME U.S.A. 131 K1
State capital of Maine.
Augusta MT U.S.A. 122 E3
Augusta Auscorum France see Auch
Augusta Taurinorum Italy see Turin
Augusta Treverorum Germany see Trier
Augusta Vindelicorum Germany see Augsburg
Augusto de Lima Brazil 141 B2
Augustus, Mount Australia 105 B6
Auke Bay U.S.A. 116 C3
Aukštaitijos nacionalinis parkas nat. park Lith. 41 O9
Aulavik National Park Canada 114 G2
Auld, Lake salt flat Australia 104 C5
Auliye Ata Kazakh. see Taraz
Aulnoye-Aymeries France 48 D4
Aulon Albania see Vlorë
Ault France 48 B4
Aumale Alg. see Sour el Ghozlane
Aumale France 48 B5
Aundh India 80 B2
Aundhi India 80 D1
Aunglan Myanmar see Myede
Auob watercourse Namibia/S. Africa 96 E4
Aupaluk Canada 119 H2
Aur i. Malaysia 67 D7
Aura Fin. 41 M6
Auraiya India 78 D4
Aurangabad Bihar India 79 F4
Aurangabad Maharashtra India 80 B2
Aure r. France 45 F9
Aurich Germany 49 H1
Aurigny i. Channel Is see Alderney
Aurilândia Brazil 141 A2
Aurillac France 52 F4
Aurora CO U.S.A. 122 G5
Aurora IL U.S.A. 130 A3
Aurora MO U.S.A. 127 E4
Aurora NE U.S.A. 126 D3
Aurora UT U.S.A. 125 H2
Aurora Island Vanuatu see Maéwo
Aurukun Australia 106 C2
Aus Namibia 96 C4
Au Sable U.S.A. 130 D1
Au Sable Point U.S.A. 130 D1
Auskerry i. U.K. 46 G1
Austin IN U.S.A. 130 C4
Austin MN U.S.A. 126 E3
Austin NV U.S.A. 124 E2
▶Austin TX U.S.A. 127 D6
State capital of Texas.
Austin, Lake salt flat Australia 105 B6
Austintown U.S.A. 130 E3
Austral Downs Australia 106 B4
Australes, Îles is Fr. Polynesia see Tubuai Islands
▶Australia country Oceania 102 C4
Largest country in Oceania. Most populous country in Oceania.
oceania 8, 100–101
Australian - Antarctic Basin sea feature Southern Ocean 146 C9
Australian Antarctic Territory reg. Antarctica 148 G2
Australian Capital Territory admin. div. Australia 108 D5
▶Austria country Europe 43 N7
europe 5, 34–35
Austvågøy i. Norway 40 I2
Autazes Brazil 139 G4
Autesiodorum France see Auxerre
Authie r. France 48 B4
Autti Fin. 40 O3
Auvergne reg. France 52 F4
Auvergne, Monts d' mts France 52 F4
Auxerre France 52 F3
Auxi-le-Château France 48 C4
Auxonne France 52 G3
Auyuittuq National Park Canada 115 L3
Auzangate, Nevado mt. Peru 138 D6
Ava MO U.S.A. 127 E4
Ava NY U.S.A. 131 H2
Avallon France 52 F3
Avalon U.S.A. 124 D5
Avalon Peninsula Canada 119 L5
Avān Iran 87 G3
Avarau atoll Cook Is see Palmerston
Avaré Brazil 141 A3
Avaricum France see Bourges
▶Avarua Cook Is 147 J7
Capital of the Cook Islands, on Rarotonga island.
Avawam U.S.A. 130 D5
Avaz Iran 85 F3
Aveiro Port. 53 B3
Aveiro, Ria de est. Port. 53 B3
Āvej Iran 84 C3
Avellino Italy 54 F4
Avenal U.S.A. 124 C3
Avenhorn Neth. 48 E2
Avenio France see Avignon
Aversa Italy 54 F4
Avesnes-sur-Helpe France 48 D4
Avesta Sweden 41 J6
Aveyron r. France 52 E4
Avezzano Italy 54 E3
Aviemore U.K. 46 F3
Avignon France 52 G5
Ávila Spain 53 D3
Avilés Spain 53 D2
Avion France 48 C4
Avis U.S.A. 131 G3
Avlama Dağı mt. Turkey 81 A1
Avlama Dağı mt. Turkey 81 A1
Avlona Albania see Vlorë
Avnyugskiy Rus. Fed. 38 J3
Avoca Australia 108 A6
Avoca r. Australia 108 A5
Avoca Rep. of Ireland 47 F5
Avoca IA U.S.A. 126 E3
Avoca NY U.S.A. 131 G2
Avola Sicily Italy 54 F6
Avon r. England U.K. 45 E6
Avon r. England U.K. 45 E7
Avon r. England U.K. 45 F8
Avon r. Scotland U.K. 46 F3
Avon U.S.A. 131 G2
Avondale U.S.A. 125 G5
Avonmore r. Rep. of Ireland 47 F5
Avonmore U.S.A. 130 F3
Avonmouth U.K. 45 E7
Avranches France 52 D2
Avre r. France 48 C5
Avsuyu Turkey 81 C1
Avuavu Solomon Is 103 G2
Avveel Fin. see Ivalo
Avvil Fin. see Ivalo
A'waj r. Syria 81 B3
Awakino N.Z. 109 E4
Awālī Bahrain 84 C5
Awanui N.Z. 109 D2
Āwarē Eth. 94 E3
'Awāriḍ, Wādī al watercourse Syria 81 D2
Awarua Point N.Z. 109 B7
Āwash Eth. 94 E3
Āwash r. Eth. 94 E2
Awa-shima i. Japan 71 E5
Āwash National Park Eth. 94 D3
Awasib Mountains Namibia 96 B3
Awat China 76 F3
Awatere r. N.Z. 109 E5
Awbārī Libya 92 E2
Awbeg r. Rep. of Ireland 47 D5
'Awdah well Saudi Arabia 84 C6
'Awdah, Hawr al imp. l. Iraq 87 G5
Aw Dheegle Somalia 93 H4
Awe, Loch l. U.K. 46 D4
Aweil Sudan 93 F4
Awka Nigeria 92 D4
Awserd W. Sahara 92 B2
Axe r. England U.K. 45 D8
Axe r. England U.K. 45 E7
Axedale Australia 108 B6
Axel Heiberg Glacier Antarctica 148 I1
Axel Heiberg Island Canada 115 I2
Axim Ghana 92 C4
Axminster U.K. 45 E8
Axum Eth. see Āksum
Ay France 48 E5
Ayachi, Jbel mt. Morocco 50 D5
Ayacucho Arg. 140 E5
Ayacucho Peru 138 D6
Ayadaw Myanmar 66 A2
Ayagoz Kazakh. 76 F2
Ayaguz Kazakh. see Ayagoz
Ayakkum Hu salt l. China 79 G1
Ayaköz Kazakh. see Ayagoz
Ayan Rus. Fed. 61 O4
Ayancık Turkey 86 D2
Ayang N. Korea 71 B5
Ayaş Turkey 86 D2
Aybak Afgh. 85 H2
Aybas Kazakh. 39 K7
Aydar r. Ukr. 39 H6
Aydarkul', Ozero l. Uzbek. 76 C3
Aydın Turkey 55 L6
Aydıncık Turkey 81 A1
Aydın Dağları mts Turkey 55 L5
Āyelu Terara vol. Eth. 82 F7
Ayer U.S.A. 131 J2
Ayers Rock hill Australia see Uluṟu
Ayeyarwady r. Myanmar see Irrawaddy
Ayila Ri'gyü mts China 78 D2
Áyios Dhimítrios Greece see Agios Dimitrios
Áyios Evstrátios i. Greece see Agios Efstratios
Áyios Nikólaos Greece see Agios Nikolaos
Áyios Yeóryios i. Greece see Agios Georgios
Aylesbury N.Z. 109 D6
Aylesbury U.K. 45 G7
Aylett U.S.A. 131 G5
Ayllón Spain 53 E3
Aylmer Ont. Canada 130 E2
Aylmer Que. Canada 131 H1
Aylmer Lake Canada 117 I1
'Ayn al 'Abd well Saudi Arabia 84 C4
'Ayn al Baidā' Saudi Arabia 81 C4
'Ayn al Bayḍā' well Syria 81 C2
'Ayn al Ghazalah well Libya 86 A4
'Ayn al Maqfī spring Egypt 86 C6
'Ayn Dāllah spring Egypt 86 B6
Ayní Tajik. 85 H2
'Ayn 'Īsá Syria 81 D1
'Ayn Tabaghbugh spring Egypt 86 B5
'Ayn Tumayrah spring Egypt 86 B5
'Ayn Zaytūn Egypt 86 B5
Ayod Sudan 82 D8
Ayon, Ostrov i. Rus. Fed. 61 R3
'Ayoûn el 'Atroûs Mauritania 92 C3
Ayr Australia 106 D3
Ayr Canada 130 E2
Ayr U.K. 46 E5
Ayr r. U.K. 46 E5
Ayr, Point of U.K. 44 D5
Ayrancı Turkey 86 D3
Ayre, Point of Isle of Man 44 C4
Aytos Bulg. 55 L3
Ayuthia Thai. see Ayutthaya
Ayutthaya Thai. 67 C4
Ayvacık Turkey 55 L5
Ayvalı Turkey 86 E3
Ayvalık Turkey 55 L5
Azak Rus. Fed. see Azov
Azalia U.S.A. 130 C4
Azamgarh India 79 E4
Azaouād reg. Mali 92 C3
Azaouagh, Vallée de watercourse Mali/Niger 92 D3
Azaran Iran see Hashtrud
Azärbaycan country Asia see Azerbaijan
Azärbayjan country Asia see Azerbaijan
Azare Nigeria 92 E3
A'zāz Syria 81 C1
Azbine mts Niger see L'Aïr, Massif de
Azdavay Turkey 86 D2
▶Azerbaijan country Asia 87 G2
asia 6, 58–59
Azerbaydzhanskaya S.S.R. country Asia see Azerbaijan
Azhikal India 80 B4
Aziscohos Lake U.S.A. 131 J1
'Azīzābād Iran 84 E4
Aziziye Turkey see Pınarbaşı
Azogues Ecuador 138 C4
▶Azores terr. N. Atlantic Ocean 144 G3
Autonomous region of Portugal.
europe 5, 34–35
Azores-Biscay Rise sea feature N. Atlantic Ocean 144 G3
Azotus Israel see Ashdod
Azov Rus. Fed. 39 H7
Azov, Sea of Rus. Fed./Ukr. 39 H7
Azovs'ke More sea Rus. Fed./Ukr. see Azov, Sea of
Azovskoye More sea Rus. Fed./Ukr. see Azov, Sea of
Azraq, Bahr el r. Sudan 82 D6 see Blue Nile
Azraq ash Shīshān Jordan 81 C4
Azrou Morocco 50 C5
Aztec U.S.A. 125 I3
Azuaga Spain 53 D4
Azuero, Península de pen. Panama 133 H7
Azul, Cordillera mts Peru 138 C5
Azuma-san vol. Japan 71 F5
'Azza Gaza see Gaza
Azzaba Alg. 54 B6
Az Zahrān Saudi Arabia see Dhahran
Az Zaqāziq Egypt 86 C5
Az Zarbah Syria 81 C1
Az Zarqā' Jordan 81 C3
Az Zawr, Ra's pt Saudi Arabia 87 H6
Azzeffāl hills Mauritania/W. Sahara 92 B2
Az Zubayr Iraq 87 G5
Az Zuqur i. Yemen 82 F7

B

Baa Indon. 104 C2
Baabda Lebanon 81 B3
Ba'albek Lebanon 81 C2
Ba'al Hazor mt. West Bank 81 B4
Baan Baa Australia 108 D3
Baardheere Somalia 94 E3
Bab India 78 D4
Bābā, Kūh-e mts Afgh. 85 H3
Baba Burnu pt Turkey 55 L5
Babadağ mt. Azer. 87 H2
Babadag Romania 55 M2
Babadaykhan Turkm. 85 F2
Babadurmaz Turkm. 84 E2
Babaeski Turkey 55 L4
Babahoyo Ecuador 138 C4
Babai India 78 D5
Babai r. Nepal 79 E3
Bābā Kalān Iran 84 C4
Bāb al Mandab strait Africa/Asia 82 F7
Babanusa Sudan 82 C7
Babao Qinghai China see Qilian
Babao Yunnan China 72 E4
Babar i. Indon. 104 E1
Babar, Kepulauan is Indon. 104 E1
Babati Tanz. 95 D4
Babayevo Rus. Fed. 38 G4
Babayurt Rus. Fed. 87 G2
B'abdâ Lebanon see Baabda
Bab el Mandeb, Straits of Africa/Asia see Bāb al Mandab
Babi, Pulau i. Indon. 67 B7
Babian Jiang r. China 72 D4
Babine r. Canada 116 E4
Babine Lake Canada 116 E4
Babine Range mts Canada 116 E4
Bābol Iran 84 D2
Bābol Sar Iran 84 D2
Babongo Cameroon 93 E4
Baboon Point S. Africa 96 D7
Baboua Cent. Afr. Rep. 94 B3
Babruysk Belarus 39 F5
Babstovo Rus. Fed. 70 D2
Babu China see Hezhou
Babuhri India 78 B4
Babusar Pass Pak. 85 I3
Babuyan i. Phil. 65 G3
Babuyan Channel Phil. 65 G3
Babuyan Islands Phil. 65 G3
Bacaadweyn Somalia 94 E3
Bacabal Brazil 139 J4
Bacan i. Indon. 65 H7
Bacanora Mex. 123 F7
Bacău Romania 55 L1
Baccaro Point Canada 119 I6
Băc Giang Vietnam 66 D2
Bacha China 70 D2
Bach Ice Shelf Antarctica 148 L2
Bach Long Vi, Đao i. Vietnam 66 D2
Bachu China 76 E4
Bachuan China see Tongliang
Back r. Australia 106 C3
Back r. Canada 117 M1
Bačka Palanka Serb. and Mont. 55 H2
Backbone Mountain U.S.A. 130 F4
Backbone Ranges mts Canada 116 D2
Backe Sweden 40 J5
Backstairs Passage Australia 107 B7
Bắc Lạc Vietnam 66 D2
Băc Liêu Vietnam 67 D5
Băc Ninh Vietnam 66 D2
Bacoachi Mex. 123 F7
Bacoachi watercourse Mex. 123 F7
Bacobampo Mex. 123 F8
Bacolod Phil. 65 G4
Băc Quang Vietnam 66 D2
Bacqueville, Lac l. Canada 118 G2
Bacqueville-en-Caux France 45 H9
Bacubirito Mex. 123 G8
Bād Iran 84 D3
Bada China see Xilin
Bada mt. Eth. 94 D3
Bada i. Myanmar 67 B5
Bad Abbach Germany 49 M6
Badagara India 80 B4
Badain Jaran Shamo des. China 76 J3
Badajoz Spain 53 C4
Badami India 80 B3
Badampaharh India 79 F5
Badanah Saudi Arabia 87 F5
Badanjilin Shamo des. China see Badain Jaran Shamo
Badaojiang China see Baishan
Badarpur India 79 H4
Badaun India see Budaun
Bad Axe U.S.A. 130 D2
Bad Bergzabern Germany 49 H5
Bad Berleburg Germany 49 I3
Bad Bevensen Germany 49 K1
Bad Blankenburg Germany 49 L4
Bad Camberg Germany 49 I4
Badderen Norway 40 M2
Bad Driburg Germany 49 J3
Bad Düben Germany 49 M3
Bad Dürkheim Germany 49 I5
Bad Dürrenberg Germany 49 M3
Bademli Turkey see Aladağ
Bademli Geçidi pass Turkey 86 C3
Bad Ems Germany 49 H4
Baden Austria 43 P6
Baden Switz. 52 I3
Baden-Baden Germany 49 I6
Baden-Württemberg land Germany 49 I6
Bad Essen Germany 49 I2
Bad Grund (Harz) Germany 49 K3
Bad Harzburg Germany 49 K3
Bad Hersfeld Germany 49 J4
Bad Hofgastein Austria 43 N7
Bad Homburg vor der Höhe Germany 49 I4
Badia Polesine Italy 54 D2
Badin Pak. 85 H5
Bad Ischl Austria 43 N7
Bādiyat ash Shām des. Asia see Syrian Desert
Badkhyzskiy Zapovednik nature res. Turkm. 85 F3
Bad Kissingen Germany 49 K4
Bad Königsdorff Poland see Jastrzębie-Zdrój
Bad Kösen Germany 49 L3
Bad Kreuznach Germany 49 H5
Bad Laasphe Germany 49 I4
Badlands reg. ND U.S.A. 126 C2
Badlands reg. SD U.S.A. 126 C3
Badlands National Park U.S.A. 126 C3
Bad Langensalza Germany 49 K3
Bad Lauterberg im Harz Germany 49 K3
Bad Liebenwerda Germany 49 N3
Bad Lippspringe Germany 49 I3
Bad Marienberg (Westerwald) Germany 49 H4
Bad Mergentheim Germany 49 J5
Bad Nauheim Germany 49 I4
Badnawar India 78 C5
Badnera India 80 C1
Bad Neuenahr-Ahrweiler Germany 48 H4
Bad Neustadt an der Saale Germany 49 K4
Badnor India 78 C4
Badong China 73 F2
Ba Đông Vietnam 67 D5
Badou Togo 92 D4
Bad Pyrmont Germany 49 J3
Badrah Iraq 87 G4
Bad Reichenhall Germany 43 N7
Badr Ḥunayn Saudi Arabia 82 E5
Bad Sachsa Germany 49 K3
Bad Salzdetfurth Germany 49 K2
Bad Salzuflen Germany 49 I2
Bad Salzungen Germany 49 K4
Bad Schwalbach Germany 49 I4
Bad Schwartau Germany 43 M4
Bad Segeberg Germany 43 M4
Badu Island Australia 106 C1
Badulla Sri Lanka 80 D5
Bad Vilbel Germany 49 I4
Bad Wilsnack Germany 49 L2
Bad Windsheim Germany 49 K5
Badzhal Rus. Fed. 70 D2
Badzhal'skiy Khrebet mts Rus. Fed. 70 D2
Bad Zwischenahn Germany 49 I1
Bae Colwyn U.K. see Colwyn Bay
Baesweiler Germany 48 G4
Baeza Spain 53 E5
Bafatá Guinea-Bissau 92 B3
Baffa Pak. 85 I3
Baffin Bay sea Canada/Greenland 115 L2
▶Baffin Island Canada 115 L3
2nd largest island in North America and 5th in the world.
world 12–13
Bafia Cameroon 92 E4
Bafilo Togo 92 D4
Bafing r. Africa 92 B3
Bafoulabé Mali 92 B3
Bafoussam Cameroon 92 E4
Bāfq Iran 84 D4
Bafra Turkey 86 D2
Bafra Burnu pt Turkey 86 D2
Bāft Iran 84 E4
Bafwaboli Dem. Rep. Congo 94 C3
Bafwasende Dem. Rep. Congo 94 C3
Bagaha India 79 F4
Bagalkot India 80 B2
Bagalkote India see Bagalkot
Bagamoyo Tanz. 95 D4
Bagan China 72 C1
Bagan Datoh Malaysia see Bagan Datuk
Bagan Datuk Malaysia 67 C7
Bagansiapiapi Indon. 67 C7
Bagata Dem. Rep. Congo 94 B4
Bagdad U.S.A. 125 G4
Bagdarin Rus. Fed. 69 K2
Bagé Brazil 140 F4
Bagerhat Bangl. 79 G5
Bageshwar India 78 D3
Baggs U.S.A. 122 G4
Baggy Point U.K. 45 C7
Bagh India 78 C5
Bàgh' a' Chaisteil U.K. see Castlebay
Baghak Pak. 85 G4
Baghbaghū Iran 85 F2
▶Baghdād Iraq 87 G4
Capital of Iraq.
Bāgh-e Malek Iran 84 C4
Bagherhat Bangl. see Bagerhat
Bāghīn Iran 84 E4
Baghlān Afgh. 85 H2
Baghrān Afgh. 85 G3
Bağırsak r. Turkey 81 C1
Bağırsak Deresi r. Syria/Turkey see Sājūr, Nahr
Bagley U.S.A. 126 E2
Baglung Nepal 79 E3
Bagnères-de-Luchon France 52 E5
Bago Myanmar see Pegu
Bago Phil. 65 G4
Bagong China see Sansui
Bagor India 85 I5
Bagrationovsk Rus. Fed. 41 L9
Bagrax China see Bohu
Bagrax Hu l. China see Bosten Hu
Baguio Phil. 65 G3
Bagur, Cabo c. Spain see Begur, Cap de
Bagzane, Monts mts Niger 92 D3
Bahādorābād-e Bālā Iran 84 E4
Bahalda India 79 F5
Bahāmabād Iran see Rafsanjān
▶Bahamas, The country West Indies 129 E7
north america 9, 112–113
Bahara Pak. 85 G5
Baharampur India 79 G4
Bahardipur Pak. 85 H5
Bahariya Oasis oasis Egypt see Bahrīyah, Wāḥāt al
Bahau Malaysia 67 C7
Bahawalnagar Pak. 85 I4
Bahawalpur Pak. 85 H4
Bahçe Adana Turkey 81 B1
Bahçe Osmaniye Turkey 86 E3
Baher Dar Eth. see Bahir Dar
Baheri India 78 D3
Bahia Brazil see Salvador
Bahia state Brazil 141 C1
Bahía Asunción Mex. 123 E8
Bahía Blanca Arg. 140 D5
Bahía Kino Mex. 123 F7
Bahía Laura Arg. 140 C7
Bahía Negra Para. 140 E2
Bahía Tortugas Mex. 123 E8
Bahir Dar Eth. 94 D2
Bahl India 78 C3
Bahlā Oman 84 E6
Bahomonte Indon. 65 G7
Bahraich India 79 E4
▶Bahrain country Asia 84 C5
asia 6, 58–59
Bahrain, Gulf of Asia 84 C5
Bahrām Beyg Iran 84 C2

Bahrāmjerd Iran 84 E4
Bahrīyah, Wāḥāt al oasis Egypt 86 C6
Bahuaja-Sonene, Parque Nacional nat. park Peru 138 E6
Baia Mare Romania 55 J1
Baiazeh Iran 84 D3
Baicang China 79 G3
Bai Canh, Hon i. Vietnam 67 D5
Baicheng Henan China see Xiping
Baicheng Jilin China 70 A3
Baicheng Xinjiang China 76 F3
Baidoa Somalia see Baydhabo
Baidoi Co l. China 79 F2
Baidu China 73 H3
Baie-aux-Feuilles Canada see Tasiujaq
Baie-Comeau Canada 119 H4
Baie-du-Poste Canada see Mistissini
Baie-St-Paul Canada 119 H5
Baie-Trinite Canada 119 I4
Baie Verte Canada 119 K4
Baiguan China see Shangyu
Baiguo Hubei China 73 G2
Baiguo Hunan China 73 G3
Baihanchang China 72 C3
Baihar India 78 E5
Baihe Jilin China 70 C4
Baihe Shaanxi China 73 F1
Baiji Iraq see Bayjī
▶Baikal, Lake Rus. Fed. 68 J2
Deepest lake in the world and in Asia. 3rd largest lake in Asia.
Baikunthpur India 79 E5
Baile Átha Cliath Rep. of Ireland see Dublin
Baile Átha Luain Rep. of Ireland see Athlone
Baile Mhartainn U.K. 46 B3
Băileşti Romania 55 J2
Bailey Range hills Australia 105 C7
Bailianhe Shuiku resr China 73 G2
Bailieborough Rep. of Ireland 47 F4
Bailleul France 48 C4
Baillie r. Canada 117 J1
Bailong China see Hadapu
Bailong Jiang r. China 72 E1
Baima Qinghai China 72 D1
Baima Xizang China see Baxoi
Baima Jian mt. China 73 H2
Baimuru P.N.G. 65 K8
Bain r. U.K. 44 G5
Bainang China 79 G3
Bainbridge GA U.S.A. 129 C6
Bainbridge IN U.S.A. 130 B4
Bainbridge NY U.S.A. 131 H2
Bainduru India 80 B3
Baingoin China 79 G3
Baini China see Yuqing
Baiona Spain 53 B2
Baiqên China 72 D1
Baiquan China 70 B3
Bā'ir Jordan 81 C4
Bā'ir, Wādī watercourse Jordan/Saudi Arabia 81 C4
Bairab Co l. China 79 E2
Bairat India 78 D4
Baird U.S.A. 127 D5
Baird Mountains U.S.A. 114 C3
▶Bairiki Kiribati 146 H5
Capital of Kiribati, on Tarawa atoll.
Bairin Youqi China see Daban
Bairnsdale Australia 108 C6
Baisha Chongqing China 72 E2
Baisha Hainan China 73 F5
Baisha Sichuan China 73 F2
Baishan Guangxi China see Mashan
Baishan Jilin China 70 B4
Baishan Jilin China see Baishanzhen
Baishanzhen China 70 B4
Baishui Shaanxi China 73 F1
Baishui Sichuan China 72 E1
Baishui Jiang r. China 72 E1
Baisogala Lith. 41 M9
Baitadi Nepal 78 E3
Baitang China 72 C1
Bai Thượng Vietnam 66 D3
Baixi China see Yibin
Baiyashi China see Dong'an
Baiyin China 68 I5
Baiyü China 72 C2
Baiyuda Desert Sudan 82 D6
Baja Hungary 54 H1
Baja, Punta pt Mex. 123 E7
Baja California pen. Mex. 123 E7
Baja California state Mex. 123 E7
Baja California Norte state Mex. see Baja California
Baja California Sur state Mex. 123 E8
Bajan Mex. 127 C7
Bajau i. Indon. 67 D7
Bajaur reg. Pak. 85 H3
Bajawa Indon. 104 C2
Baj Baj India 79 G5
Bājgīrān Iran 84 E2
Bājil Yemen 82 F7
Bajo Caracoles Arg. 140 B7
Bajoga Nigeria 92 E3
Bajoi China 72 D2
Bajrakot India 79 F5
Bakala Cent. Afr. Rep. 93 F4
Bakanas Kazakh. 76 E3
Bakar Pak. 85 H5
Bakel Senegal 92 B3
Baker CA U.S.A. 124 E4
Baker ID U.S.A. 122 E3
Baker LA U.S.A. 127 F6
Baker MT U.S.A. 122 G3
Baker NV U.S.A. 125 F2
Baker OR U.S.A. 122 D3
Baker WV U.S.A. 131 F4
Baker, Mount vol. U.S.A. 122 C2
Baker Butte mt. U.S.A. 125 H4
▶Baker Island terr. N. Pacific Ocean 103 I1
United States Unincorporated Territory.
Baker Island U.S.A. 116 C4
Baker Lake salt flat Australia 105 D6
Baker Lake Canada 117 M1
Baker Lake l. Canada 117 M1
Baker's Dozen Islands Canada 118 F2
Bakersfield U.S.A. 124 D4
Bakersville U.S.A. 128 D4
Bå Kêv Cambodia 67 D4
Bakhardok Turkm. 84 E2
Bākharz mts Iran 85 F3
Bakhasar India 78 B4
Bakhirevo Rus. Fed. 70 C2
Bakhmach Ukr. 39 G6
Bakhma Dam Iraq see Bēkma, Sadd
Bakhmut Ukr. see Artemivs'k
Bākhtarān Iran see Kermānshāh
Bakhtegan, Daryācheh-ye l. Iran 84 D4
Bakhtiari Country reg. Iran 84 C3
Bakı Azer. see Baku
Bakırköy Turkey 55 M4
Bakkejord Norway 40 K2
Baklan India 78 C2
Bako Eth. 94 D3
Bakongan Indon. 67 B7
Bakouma Cent. Afr. Rep. 94 C3
Baksan Rus. Fed. 87 F2
▶Baku Azer. 87 H2
Capital of Azerbaijan.
Baku Dem. Rep. Congo 94 D3
Bakutis Coast Antarctica 148 J2
Baky Azer. see Baku
Balâ Turkey 86 D3
Bala U.K. 45 D6
Bala, Cerros de mts Bol. 138 E6
Balabac i. Phil. 64 F5
Balabac Strait Malaysia/Phil. 64 F5
Baladeh Māzandarān Iran 84 C2
Baladeh Māzandarān Iran 84 C2
Baladek Rus. Fed. 70 D1
Balaghat India 78 E5
Balaghat Range hills India 80 B2
Bālā Ḥowẓ Iran 84 E4
Balaka Malawi 95 D5
Balakän Azer. 87 G2
Balakhna Rus. Fed. 38 I4
Balakhta Rus. Fed. 68 G1
Balaklava Australia 107 B7
Balaklava Ukr. 86 D1
Balakleya Ukr. see Balakliya
Balakliya Ukr. 39 H6
Balakovo Rus. Fed. 39 J5
Bala Lake U.K. see Tegid, Llyn
Balaman India 78 E4
Balan India 78 B4
Balanda Rus. Fed. see Kalininsk
Balanda r. Rus. Fed. 39 J6
Balan Dağı hill Turkey 55 M6
Balanga Phil. 65 G4
Balangir India see Bolangir
Balaözen r. Kazakh./Rus. Fed. see Malyy Uzen'
Balarampur India see Balrampur
Balashov Rus. Fed. 39 I6
Balasore India see Baleshwar
Balaton, Lake Hungary 54 G1
Balatonboglár Hungary 54 G1
Balatonfüred Hungary 54 G1
Balbina Brazil 139 G4
Balbina, Represa de resr Brazil 139 G4
Balbriggan Rep. of Ireland 47 F4
Balchik Bulg. 55 M3
Balclutha N.Z. 109 B8
Balcones Escarpment U.S.A. 127 C6
Bald Knob U.S.A. 130 E5
Bald Mountain U.S.A. 125 F3
Baldock Lake Canada 117 L3
Baldwin Canada 130 F1
Baldwin FL U.S.A. 129 D6
Baldwin MI U.S.A. 130 C2
Baldwin PA U.S.A. 130 F3
Baldy Mount Canada 122 D2
Baldy Mountain hill Canada 117 K5
Baldy Peak U.S.A. 125 I5
Bale Indon. 64 C7
Bâle Switz. see Basel
Baléa Mali 92 B3
Baleares is Spain see Balearic Islands
Baleares, Islas is Spain see Balearic Islands
Baleares Insulae is Spain see Balearic Islands
Balearic Islands is Spain 53 G4
Balears is Spain see Balearic Islands
Balears, Illes is Spain see Balearic Islands
Baleia, Ponta da pt Brazil 141 D2
Bale Mountains National Park Eth. 94 D3
Baler Phil. 65 G3
Baleshwar India 79 F5
Balestrand Norway 41 E6
Baléyara Niger 92 D3
Balezino Rus. Fed. 37 Q4
Balfe's Creek Australia 106 D4
Balfour Downs Australia 104 C5
Balgo Australia 104 D5
Balguntay China 76 G3
Bali India 78 C4
Bali i. Indon. 104 A2
Bali, Laut sea Indon. 104 A1
Balia India see Ballia
Baliapal India 79 F5
Balige Indon. 67 B7
Baliguda India 80 D1
Balıkesir Turkey 55 L5
Balīkh r. Syria/Turkey 81 D2
Balikpapan Indon. 64 F7
Balimila Reservoir India 80 D2
Balimo P.N.G. 65 K8
Balin China 70 A2
Baling Malaysia 67 C6
Balingen Germany 43 L6
Balintore U.K. 46 F3
Bali Sea Indon. see Bali, Laut
Balk Neth. 48 F2
Balkan Mountains Bulg./Serb. and Mont. 55 J3
Balkassar Pak. 85 I3
Balkhash Kazakh. 76 D2
▶Balkhash, Lake Kazakh. 76 D2
4th largest lake in Asia.
Balkhash, Ozero l. Kazakh. see Balkhash, Lake
Balkuduk Kazakh. 39 J7
Ballachulish U.K. 46 D4
Balladonia Australia 105 C8
Balladoran Australia 108 D3
Ballaghaderreen Rep. of Ireland 47 D4
Ballan Australia 108 B6
Ballangen Norway 40 J2
Ballantine U.S.A. 122 F3
Ballantrae U.K. 46 E5
Ballarat Australia 108 A6
Ballard, Lake salt flat Australia 105 C7
Ballarpur India 80 C2
Ballater U.K. 46 F3
Ballé Mali 92 C3
Ballena, Punta pt Chile 140 B3
Balleny Islands Antarctica 148 H2
Ballia India 79 F4
Ballina Australia 108 F2
Ballina Rep. of Ireland 47 C3
Ballinafad Rep. of Ireland 47 D3
Ballinalack Rep. of Ireland 47 E4
Ballinamore Rep. of Ireland 47 E3
Ballinasloe Rep. of Ireland 47 D4
Ballindine Rep. of Ireland 47 D4
Ballinger U.S.A. 127 D6
Ballinluig U.K. 46 F4
Ballinrobe Rep. of Ireland 47 C4
Ballon d'Alsace mt. France 43 K7
Ballston Spa U.S.A. 131 I2
Ballybay Rep. of Ireland 47 F3
Ballybrack Rep. of Ireland 47 B6
Ballybunnion Rep. of Ireland 47 C5
Ballycanew Rep. of Ireland 47 F5
Ballycastle Rep. of Ireland 47 C3
Ballycastle U.K. 47 F2
Ballyclare U.K. 47 G3
Ballyconnell Rep. of Ireland 47 E3
Ballygar Rep. of Ireland 47 D4
Ballygawley U.K. 47 E3
Ballygorman Rep. of Ireland 47 E2
Ballyhaunis Rep. of Ireland 47 D4
Ballyheigue Rep. of Ireland 47 C5
Ballykelly U.K. 47 E2
Ballylynan Rep. of Ireland 47 E5
Ballymacmague Rep. of Ireland 47 E5
Ballymahon Rep. of Ireland 47 E4
Ballymena U.K. 47 F3
Ballymoney U.K. 47 F2
Ballymote Rep. of Ireland 47 D3
Ballynahinch U.K. 47 G3
Ballyshannon Rep. of Ireland 47 D3
Ballyteige Bay Rep. of Ireland 47 F5
Ballyvaughan Rep. of Ireland 47 C4
Ballyward U.K. 47 F3
Balmartin U.K. see Baile Mhartainn
Balmer India see Barmer
Balmertown Canada 117 M5
Balmorhea U.S.A. 127 C6
Balochistan prov. Pak. 85 G4
Balombo Angola 95 B5
Balonne r. Australia 108 D2
Balotra India 78 C4
Balqash Kazakh. see Balkhash
Balqash Köli l. Kazakh. see Balkhash, Lake
Balrampur India 79 E4
Balranald Australia 108 A5
Balş Romania 55 K2
Balsam Lake Canada 131 F1
Balsas Brazil 139 I5
Balta Ukr. 39 F7
Baltasound U.K. 46 [inset]
Baltay Rus. Fed. 39 J5
Bălţi Moldova 39 E7
Baltic U.S.A. 130 E3
Baltic Sea g. Europe 41 J9
Balṭīm Egypt see Balṭīm
Balṭīm Egypt 86 C5
Baltimore S. Africa 97 I2
Baltimore MD U.S.A. 131 G4
Baltimore OH U.S.A. 130 D4
Baltinglass Rep. of Ireland 47 F5
Baltistan reg. Jammu and Kashmir 78 C2
Baltiysk Rus. Fed. 41 K9
Balu India 72 B3
Baluarte, Arroyo watercourse U.S.A. 127 D7
Baluch Ab well Iran 84 E4
Balumundam Indon. 67 B7
Balurghat India 79 G4
Balve Germany 49 H3
Balvi Latvia 41 O8
Balya Turkey 55 L5
Balykchy Kyrg. 76 E3
Balykshi Kazakh. 74 E2
Balyqshy Kazakh. see Balykshi
Bam Iran 84 E4
Bām Iran 84 E2
Bama China 72 E3
▶Bamako Mali 92 C3
Capital of Mali.
Bamba Mali 92 C3
Bambari Cent. Afr. Rep. 94 C3
Bambel Indon. 67 B7
Bamberg Germany 49 K5
Bamberg U.S.A. 129 D5
Bambili Dem. Rep. Congo 94 C3
Bambio Cent. Afr. Rep. 94 B3
Bamboesberg mts S. Africa 97 H6
Bamboo Creek Australia 104 C5
Bambouti Cent. Afr. Rep. 94 C3
Bambuí Brazil 141 B3
Bamda China 72 C2
Bamenda Cameroon 92 E4
Bāmīān Afgh. 85 G3
Bamiantong China see Muling
Bamingui Cent. Afr. Rep. 94 C3
Bamingui-Bangoran, Parc National du nat. park Cent. Afr. Rep. 94 B3
Bâmnak Cambodia 67 D4
Bamnet Narong Thai. 66 C4
Bamor India 78 D4
Bamori India 80 C1
Bam Posht reg. Iran 85 F5
Bam Posht, Kūh-e mts Iran 85 F5
Bampton U.K. 45 D8
Bampūr Iran 85 F5
Bampūr watercourse Iran 85 E5
Bamrūd Iran 85 F3
Bam Tso l. China 79 G3
Bamyili Australia 104 F3
Banaba i. Kiribati 103 G2
Banabuiu, Açude resr Brazil 139 K5
Bañados del Izozog swamp Bol. 138 F7
Banagher Rep. of Ireland 47 E4
Banalia Dem. Rep. Congo 94 C3
Banamana, Lagoa l. Moz. 97 K2
Banamba Mali 92 C3
Banámichi Mex. 123 F7
Banana Australia 106 E5
Bananal, Ilha do i. Brazil 139 H6
Bananga India 67 A6
Banapur India 80 E2
Banas r. India 78 D4
Banaz Turkey 55 M5
Ban Ban Laos 66 C3
Banbar China 72 B2
Ban Bo Laos 66 C3
Banbridge U.K. 47 F3
Ban Bua Chum Thai. 66 C4
Ban Bua Yai Thai. 66 C4
Ban Bungxai Laos 66 D4
Banbury U.K. 45 F6
Ban Cang Vietnam 66 C2
Banc d'Arguin, Parc National du nat. park Mauritania 92 B2
Ban Channabot Thai. 66 C3
Banchory U.K. 46 G3
Bancroft Canada 131 G1
Bancroft Zambia see Chililabombwe
Banda Dem. Rep. Congo 94 C3
Banda India 78 E4
Banda, Kepulauan is Indon. 65 H7
Banda, Laut sea Indon. 65 H8
Banda Aceh Indon. 67 A6
Banda Banda, Mount Australia 108 F3
Banda Daud Shah Pak. 85 H3
Bandahara, Gunung mt. Indon. 67 B7
Bandama r. Côte d'Ivoire 92 C4
Bandān Kūh mts Iran 85 F4
Bandar India see Machilipatnam
Bandar Moz. 95 D5
Bandar Abbas Iran see Bandar-e 'Abbās
Bandarban Bangl. 79 H5
Bandar-e 'Abbās Iran 84 E5
Bandar-e Anzalī Iran 84 C2
Bandar-e Deylam Iran 84 C4
Bandar-e Emām Khomeynī Iran 84 C4
Bandar-e Lengeh Iran 84 D5
Bandar-e Ma'shur Iran 84 C4
Bandar-e Nakhīlū Iran 84 D5
Bandar-e Pahlavī Iran see Bandar-e Anzalī
Bandar-e Shāh Iran see Bandar-e Torkeman
Bandar-e Shāhpūr Iran see Bandar-e Emām Khomeynī
Bandar-e Shīū' Iran 84 D5
Bandar-e Torkeman Iran 84 D2
Bandar Labuan Malaysia see Labuan
Bandar Lampung Indon. 64 D8
Bandarpunch mt. India 78 D3
▶Bandar Seri Begawan Brunei 64 E6
Capital of Brunei.
Banda Sea sea Indon. see Banda, Laut
Band-e Amīr l. Afgh. 85 G3
Band-e Amīr, Daryā-ye r. Afgh. 85 G2
Band-e Bābā mts Afgh. 85 F3
Bandeira Brazil 141 C1
Bandeirante Brazil 141 A1
Bandeiras, Pico de mt. Brazil 141 C3
Bandelierkop S. Africa 97 I2
Banderas Mex. 127 B6
Banderas, Bahía de b. Mex. 132 C4
Band-e Sar Qom Iran 84 D3
Band-e Torkestān mts Afgh. 85 F3
Bandhi Pak. 85 H5
Bandhogarh India 78 E5
Bandi r. India 78 C4
Bandiagara Mali 92 C3
Bandikui India 78 D4
Bandipur National Park India 80 C4
Bandırma Turkey 55 L4
Bandjarmasin Indon. see Banjarmasin
Bandon Rep. of Ireland 47 D6
Bandon r. Rep. of Ireland 47 D6
Ban Don Thai. see Surat Thani
Bandon U.S.A. 122 B4
Band Qīr Iran 84 C4
Bandra India 80 B2
Bandundu Dem. Rep. Congo 94 B4
Bandung Indon. 64 D8
Bandya Australia 105 C6
Bāneh Iran 84 B3
Banera India 78 C4
Banes Cuba 133 I4
Banff Canada 116 H5
Banff U.K. 46 G3
Banff National Park Canada 116 G5
Banfora Burkina 92 C3
Banga Dem. Rep. Congo 95 C4
Bangalore India 80 C3
Bangalow Australia 108 F2
Bangaon India 79 G5
Bangar Brunei 64 F6
Bangassou Cent. Afr. Rep. 94 C3
Bangdag Co salt l. China 79 E2
Banggai Indon. 65 G7
Banggai, Kepulauan is Indon. 65 G7
Banggi i. Malaysia 64 F5
Banghāzī Libya see Benghazi
Banghiang, Xé r. Laos 66 D3
Bangka i. Indon. 64 D7
Bangka, Selat sea chan. Indon. 64 D7
Bangkalan Indon. 64 E8
Bangkaru i. Indon. 67 B7
Bangko Indon. 64 C7
▶Bangkok Thai. 67 C4
Capital of Thailand.
Bangkok, Bight of b. Thai. 67 C4
Bangkor China 79 F3
Bangla state India see West Bengal
▶Bangladesh country Asia 79 G4
asia 6, 58–59
Bangma Shan mts China 72 C4
Bang Mun Nak Thai. 66 C3
Bangolo Côte d'Ivoire 92 C4
Bangong Co salt l. China/Jammu and Kashmir 78 D2
Bangor Northern Ireland U.K. 47 G3
Bangor Wales U.K. 44 C5
Bangor ME U.S.A. 128 G2
Bangor MI U.S.A. 130 B2
Bangor PA U.S.A. 131 H3
Bangor Erris Rep. of Ireland 47 C3
Bangs, Mount U.S.A. 125 G3
Bang Saphan Yai Thai. 67 B5
Bangsund Norway 40 G4
Bangued Phil. 65 G3
▶Bangui Cent. Afr. Rep. 94 B3
Capital of Central African Republic.
Bangweulu, Lake Zambia 95 C5
Banhā Egypt 86 C5
Banhine, Parque Nacional de nat. park Moz. 97 K2
Ban Hin Heup Laos 66 C3
Ban Houayxay Laos 66 C2
Ban Houei Sai Laos see Ban Houayxay
Ban Huai Khon Thai. 66 C3
Ban Huai Yang Thai. 67 B5
Bani, Jbel ridge Morocco 50 C6
Bania Cent. Afr. Rep. 94 B3
Bani-Bangou Niger 92 D3
Banifing r. Mali 92 C3
Banī Forūr, Jazīreh-ye i. Iran 84 D5
Banihal Pass and Tunnel Jammu and Kashmir 78 C2
Banister r. U.S.A. 130 F5
Banī Suwayf Egypt 86 C5
Banī Walīd Libya 93 E1
Banī Wuṭayfah well Saudi Arabia 84 C5
Bāniyās Al Qunayṭirah Syria 81 B3
Bāniyās Ṭarṭūs Syria 81 B2
Bani Yas reg. U.A.E. 84 D6
Banja Luka Bos.-Herz. 54 G2
Banjarmasin Indon. 64 E7
Banjes, Liqeni i resr Albania 55 I4
▶Banjul Gambia 92 B3
Capital of The Gambia.
Banka India 79 F4
Banka Banka Australia 104 F4
Bankapur India 80 B3
Bankass Mali 92 C3
Ban Kengkabao Laos 66 D3
Ban Khao Yoi Thai. 67 B4
Ban Khok Kloi Thai. 67 B5
Bankilaré Niger 92 D3
Banks Island B.C. Canada 116 D4
Banks Island N.W.T. Canada 114 F2
Banks Islands Vanuatu 103 G3
Banks Lake Canada 117 M2
Banks Lake U.S.A. 122 D3
Banks Peninsula N.Z. 109 D6
Banks Strait Australia 107 [inset]
Bankura India 79 F5
Ban Lamduan Thai. 67 C4
Banlan China 73 F3
Ban Mae La Luang Thai. 66 B3
Banmaw Myanmar see Bhamo
Banmo Myanmar see Bhamo
Bann r. Rep. of Ireland 47 F5
Bann r. U.K. 47 F2
Ban Nakham Laos 66 D3
Bannerman Town Bahamas 129 E7
Banning U.S.A. 124 E5
Banningville Dem. Rep. Congo see Bandundu
Ban Noi Myanmar 66 B3
Ban Nong Kung Thai. 66 D3
Bannu Pak. 85 H3
Bano India 79 F5
Bañolas Spain see Banyoles
Ban Phai Thai. 66 C3
Ban Phôn Laos see Ban Phon
Ban Phon Laos 66 D4
Banqiao Yunnan China 72 C3
Banqiao Yunnan China 72 E3
Bansi Bihar India 79 F4
Bansi Rajasthan India 78 C4
Bansi Uttar Pradesh India 78 D4
Bansi Uttar Pradesh India 79 E4
Bansihari India 79 G4
Banská Bystrica Slovakia 43 Q6
Banspani India 79 F5
Bansur India 78 D4
Ban Sut Ta Thai. 66 B3
Ban Suwan Wari Thai. 66 D4
Banswara India 78 C5
Banteer Rep. of Ireland 47 D5
Ban Tha Song Yang Thai. 66 B3
Banthat mts Cambodia/Thai. see Cardamom Range
Ban Tha Tum Thai. 66 C4
Ban Tôp Laos 66 D3
Bantry Rep. of Ireland 47 C6
Bantry Bay Rep. of Ireland 47 C6
Bantval India 80 B3
Ban Wang Chao Thai. 66 B3
Ban Woen Laos 66 C3
Ban Xepian Laos 66 D4
Banyak, Pulau-pulau is Indon. 67 B7
Ban Yang Yong Thai. 67 B4
Banyo Cameroon 92 E4
Banyoles Spain 53 H2
Banyuwangi Indon. 104 A2
Banzare Coast Antarctica 148 G2
Banzare Seamount sea feature Indian Ocean 145 N9
Banzart Tunisia see Bizerte
Banzkow Germany 49 L1
Banzyville Dem. Rep. Congo see Mobayi-Mbongo
Bao'an China see Shenzhen
Baochang China 69 L4
Baocheng China 72 E1
Baoding China 69 L5
Baofeng China 73 G1
Bao Ha Vietnam 66 D2
Baohe China see Weixi
Baoji Shaanxi China 72 E1
Baoji Shaanxi China 72 E1
Baokang Hubei China 73 F2
Baokang Nei Mongol China 70 A3
Baolin China 70 C3
Bao Lôc Vietnam 67 D5
Baoqing China 70 D3
Baoro Cent. Afr. Rep. 94 B3
Baoshan China 72 C3
Baotou China 69 K4
Baotou Shan mt. China/N. Korea 70 C4
Baoulé r. Mali 92 C3
Baoxing China 72 D2
Baoying China 73 H1
Baoyou China see Ledong
Bap India 78 C4
Bapatla India 80 D3
Bapaume France 48 C4
Baptiste Lake Canada 131 F1
Bapu China see Meigu
Baq'ā' oasis Saudi Arabia 87 F6
Baqbaq Egypt see Buqbuq
Baqên Xizang China 72 B1
Baqên Xizang China 72 B2
Baqiu China 73 G3
Ba'qūbah Iraq 87 G4
Bar Serb. and Mont. 55 H3
Bara Sudan 82 D7
Baraawe Somalia 94 E3
Bara Banki India see Barabanki
Barabanki India 78 E4
Baraboo U.S.A. 126 F3
Baracaju r. Brazil 141 A1
Baracaldo Spain see Barakaldo
Baracoa Cuba 133 J4
Baradá, Nahr r. Syria 81 C3
Baradine Australia 108 D3
Baradine r. Australia 108 D3
Baragarh India see Bargarh
Barahona Dom. Rep. 133 J5
Barail Range mts India 79 H4
Baraka watercourse Eritrea/Sudan 93 G3
Barakaldo Spain 53 E2
Baraki Barak Afgh. 85 H3
Baralaba Australia 106 E5
Bara Lacha Pass India 78 D2
Baralzon Lake Canada 117 L3
Baram India 79 F5
Baram r. Malaysia 64 E6
Baramati India 80 B2
Baramula India see Baramulla
Baramulla India 78 C2
Baran India 78 D4
Baran r. Pak. 85 H5
Bārān, Kūh-e mts Iran 85 F3
Baranavichy Belarus 41 O10
Barang, Dasht-i des. Afgh. 85 F3
Baranikha Rus. Fed. 61 R3
Baranīs Egypt 82 E5
Baranīs Egypt see Baranīs
Barannda India 78 E4
Baranof Island U.S.A. 116 C3
Baranovichi Belarus see Baranavichy
Baranowicze Belarus see Baranavichy
Baraouéli Mali 92 C3
Baraque de Fraiture hill Belgium 48 F4
Barasat India 79 G5
Barat Daya, Kepulauan is Indon. 104 D1
Baraut India 78 D3
Barbacena Brazil 141 C3
▶Barbados country West Indies 133 M6
north america 9, 112–113
Barbar, Gebel el mt. Egypt see Barbar, Jabal
Barbar, Jabal mt. Egypt 81 A5
Barbara Lake Canada 118 D4
Barbastro Spain 53 G2
Barbate de Franco Spain 53 D5
Barberton S. Africa 97 J3
Barberton U.S.A. 130 E3
Barbezieux-St-Hilaire France 52 D4
Barbour Bay Canada 117 M2
Barbourville U.S.A. 130 D5
Barboza Phil. 65 G4
Barbuda i. Antigua and Barbuda 133 L5
Barby (Elbe) Germany 49 L3
Barcaldine Australia 106 D4
Barce Libya see Al Marj
Barcelona Spain 53 H3
Barcelona Venez. 138 F1
Barcelonnette France 52 H4
Barcelos Brazil 138 F4
Barchfeld Germany 49 K4
Barcino Spain see Barcelona
Barclay de Tolly atoll Fr. Polynesia see Raroia
Barclayville Liberia 92 C4
Barcoo watercourse Australia 106 C5
Barcoo Creek watercourse Australia see Cooper Creek
Barcoo National Park Australia see Welford National Park
Barcs Hungary 54 G2
Bärdä Azer. 87 G2
Bárðarbunga mt. Iceland 40 [inset]
Bardaskan Iran 84 E3
Bardawīl, Khabrat al salt pan Saudi Arabia 81 D4
Bardawīl, Sabkhat al lag. Egypt 81 A4
Barddhaman India 79 F5
Bardejov Slovakia 39 D6
Bardera Somalia see Baardheere
Bardhaman India see Barddhaman
Bar Đôn Vietnam 67 D4
Bardsey Island U.K. 45 C6
Bardsīr Iran 84 E4
Barðsneshorn pt Iceland 36 D2
Bardstown U.S.A. 130 C5
Barduli Italy see Barletta
Bardwell U.S.A. 127 F4
Bareilly India 78 D3
Barellan Australia 108 C5
Barentin France 45 H9
Barentsburg Svalbard 60 C2
Barents Sea Arctic Ocean 38 I1
Barentu Eritrea 82 E6
Barfleur, Pointe de pt France 45 F9
Bārgāh Iran 84 E5
Bargarh India 79 E5
Barghamad Iran 84 E2
Bargrennan U.K. 46 E5
Bargteheide Germany 49 K1
Barguna Bangl. 79 G5
Barhaj India 79 E4
Barham Australia 108 B5
Bari Italy 54 G4
Bari Doab lowland Pak. 85 I4
Barika Alg. 50 F4
Barinas Venez. 138 D2
Baripada India 79 F5
Bariri Brazil 141 A3
Bari Sadri India 78 C4
Barisal Bangl. 79 G5
Barisan, Pegunungan mts Indon. 64 C7
Barito r. Indon. 64 E7
Barium Italy see Bari
Barkal Bangl. 79 H5
Barkam China 72 D2
Barkan, Ra's-e pt Iran 84 C4
Barkava Latvia 41 O8
Bark Lake Canada 131 G1
Barkly East S. Africa 97 H6
Barkly Homestead Australia 106 A3
Barkly-Oos S. Africa see Barkly East
Barkly Tableland reg. Australia 106 A3
Barkly-Wes S. Africa see Barkly West
Barkly West S. Africa 96 G5
Barkol China 76 H3
Barla Turkey 55 N5
Bârlad Romania 55 L1
Bar-le-Duc France 48 F6
Barlee, Lake salt flat Australia 105 B7
Barlee Range hills Australia 105 A5
Barletta Italy 54 G4
Barlow Canada 116 B2
Barlow Lake Canada 117 K2
Barmah Forest Australia 108 B5
Barmedman Australia 108 C5
Barmen-Elberfeld Germany see Wuppertal
Barmer India 78 B4
Barm Fīrūz, Kūh-e mt. Iran 84 C4
Barmouth U.K. 45 C6
Barnala India 78 C3
Barnard Castle U.K. 44 F4
Barnato Australia 108 B3
Barnaul Rus. Fed. 68 E2
Barnegat Bay U.S.A. 131 H4
Barnes Icecap Canada 115 K2
Barnesville GA U.S.A. 129 D5
Barnesville MN U.S.A. 126 D2
Barneveld Neth. 48 F2
Barneville-Carteret France 45 F9
Barneys Lake imp. l. Australia 108 B4
Barney Top mt. U.S.A. 125 H3
Barnsley U.K. 44 F5
Barnstable U.S.A. 131 J3
Barnstaple U.K. 45 C7
Barnstaple Bay U.K. see Bideford Bay
Barnstorf Germany 49 I2
Baro Nigeria 92 D4
Baroda Gujarat India see Vadodara
Baroda Madhya Pradesh India 78 D4

Baroghil Pass Afgh. 85 I2
Barong China 72 C2
Barons Range hills Australia 105 D6
Barpathar India 72 B3
Barpeta India 79 G4
Bar Pla Soi Thai. see Chon Buri
Barques, Point Aux U.S.A. 130 D1
Barquisimeto Venez. 138 E1
Barra Brazil 139 J6
Barra i. U.K. 46 B4
Barra, Ponta da pt Moz. 97 L2
Barra, Sound of sea chan. U.K. 46 B3
Barraba Australia 108 E3
Barra Bonita Brazil 141 A3
Barracão do Barreto Brazil 139 G5
Barra do Bugres Brazil 139 G7
Barra do Corda Brazil 139 I5
Barra do Cuieté Brazil 141 C2
Barra do Garças Brazil 139 H7
Barra do Piraí Brazil 141 C3
Barra do São Manuel Brazil 139 G5
Barra do Turvo Brazil 141 A4
Barra Falsa, Ponta da pt Moz. 97 L2
Barraigh i. U.K. see Barra
Barra Mansa Brazil 141 B3
Barrana Pak. 85 I4
Barranca Peru 138 C4
Barranqueras Arg. 140 E3
Barranquilla Col. 138 D1
Barre MA U.S.A. 131 I2
Barre VT U.S.A. 131 I1
Barre des Ecrins mt. France 52 H4
Barreiras Brazil 139 J6
Barreirinha Brazil 139 G4
Barreirinhas Brazil 139 J4
Barreiro Port. 53 B4
Barreiros Brazil 139 K5
Barren Island India 67 A4
Barren Island Kiribati see Starbuck Island
Barren River Lake U.S.A. 130 B5
Barretos Brazil 141 A3
Barrett, Mount hill Australia 104 D4
Barrhead Canada 116 H4
Barrhead U.K. 46 E5
Barrie Canada 130 F1
Barrier Bay Antarctica 148 E2
Barrière Canada 116 F5
Barrier Range hills Australia 107 C6
Barrington Canada 119 I6
Barrington, Mount Australia 108 E4
Barrington Tops National Park Australia 108 E4
Barringun Australia 108 B2
Barro Alto Brazil 141 A1
Barrocão Brazil 141 C2
Barron U.S.A. 126 F2
Barrow r. Rep. of Ireland 47 F5
Barrow U.S.A. 114 C2
Barrow, Point U.S.A. 114 C2
Barrow Creek Australia 104 F5
Barrow-in-Furness U.K. 44 D4
Barrow Island Australia 104 A5
Barrow Range hills Australia 105 D6
Barrow Strait Canada 115 I2
Barr Smith Range hills Australia 105 C6
Barry U.K. 45 D7
Barrydale S. Africa 96 E7
Barry Mountains Australia 108 C6
Barrys Bay Canada 131 G1
Barryville U.S.A. 131 H3
Barsa-Kel'mes, Shor salt marsh Uzbek. 87 J2
Barsalpur India 78 C3
Barshatas Kazakh. 76 E2
Barshi India see Barsi
Barsi India 80 B2
Barsinghausen Germany 49 J2
Barstow U.S.A. 124 E4
Barsur India 80 D2
Bar-sur-Aube France 52 G2
Bartang Tajik. 85 H2
Barth Germany 43 N3
Bartica Guyana 139 G2
Bartın Turkey 86 D2
Bartle Frere, Mount Australia 106 D3
Bartlett U.S.A. 126 D3
Bartlett Reservoir U.S.A. 125 H5
Barton U.S.A. 131 I1
Barton-upon-Humber U.K. 44 G5
Bartoszyce Poland 43 R3
Bartow U.S.A. 129 D7
Barú, Volcán vol. Panama 133 H7
Barung i. Indon. 64 E8
Barunga Australia see Bamyili
Barun-Torey, Ozero l. Rus. Fed. 69 L2
Barus Indon. 67 B7
Baruunturuun Mongolia 76 H2
Baruun-Urt Mongolia 69 K3
Baruva India 80 E2
Barwani India 78 C5
Barwéli Mali see Baraouéli
Barwon r. Australia 108 C3
Barygaza India see Bharuch
Barysaw Belarus 41 P9
Barysh Rus. Fed. 39 J5
Basaga Turkm. 85 G2
Basăk, Tônlé r. Cambodia 67 D5
Basalt r. Australia 106 D3
Basalt Island Hong Kong China 73 [inset]
Basankusu Dem. Rep. Congo 94 B3
Basar India 80 C2
Basarabi Romania 55 M2
Basargechar Armenia see Vardenis
Bascuñán, Cabo c. Chile 140 B3
Basel Switz. 52 H3
Bashākerd, Kūhhā-ye mts Iran 84 E5
Bashanta Rus. Fed. see Gorodovikovsk
Bashaw Canada 116 H4
Bashee r. S. Africa 97 I7
Bāshī Iran 84 C4
Bashi Channel Phil./Taiwan 65 G2
Bashmakovo Rus. Fed. 39 I5
Bāsht Iran 84 C4
Bashtanka Ukr. 39 G7
Basi Punjab India 78 D3
Basi Rajasthan India 78 D4
Basia India 79 F5
Basilan i. Phil. 65 G5
Basildon U.K. 45 H7
Basile, Pico mt. Equat. Guinea 92 D4
Basin U.S.A. 122 F3
Basingstoke U.K. 45 F7
Basin Lake Canada 117 J4
Basirhat India 79 G5
Basīţ, Ra's al pt Syria 81 B2
Başkale Turkey 87 G3
Baskatong, Réservoir resr Canada 118 G5
Baskerville, Cape Australia 104 C4
Başkomutan Tarıhı Milli Parkı nat. park Turkey 55 N5
Başköy Turkey 81 A1
Baskunchak, Ozero l. Rus. Fed. 39 J6
Basle Switz. see Basel
Basmat India 80 C2
Basoko Dem. Rep. Congo 94 C3
Basra Iraq 87 G5
Bassano Canada 117 H5
Bassano del Grappa Italy 54 D2
Bassar Togo 92 D4
Bassas da India reef Indian Ocean 95 D6
Bassas de Pedro Padua Bank sea feature India 80 B3
Bassein Myanmar 66 A3
Bassein r. Myanmar 66 A3
Basse-Normandie admin. reg. France 45 F9
Bassenthwaite Lake U.K. 44 D4
Basse Santa Su Gambia 92 B3
▶Basse-Terre Guadeloupe 133 L5
Capital of Guadeloupe.
▶Basseterre St Kitts and Nevis 133 L5
Capital of St Kitts and Nevis.
Bassett NE U.S.A. 126 D3
Bassett VA U.S.A. 130 F5
Bassikounou Mauritania 92 C3
Bass Rock i. U.K. 46 G4
Bass Strait Australia 107 D8
Bassum Germany 49 I2
Basswood Lake Canada 118 C4
Båstad Sweden 41 H8
Bastānābād Iran 84 B2
Bastheim Germany 49 K4
Basti India 79 E4
Bastia Corsica France 52 I5
Bastioes r. Brazil 139 K5
Bastogne Belgium 48 F4
Bastrop LA U.S.A. 127 F5
Bastrop TX U.S.A. 127 D6
Basul r. Pak. 85 G5
Basuo China see Dongfang
Basutoland country Africa see Lesotho
Başyayla Turkey 81 A1
Bata Equat. Guinea 92 D4
Batabanó, Golfo de b. Cuba 133 H4
Batagay Rus. Fed. 61 O3
Batala India 78 C3
Batalha Port. 53 B4
Batam i. Indon. 67 D7
Batamay Rus. Fed. 61 N3
Batamshinskiy Kazakh. 76 A1
Batamshy Kazakh. see Batamshinskiy
Batan Jiangsu China 73 I1
Batan Qinghai China 72 D1
Batan i. Phil. 65 G2
Batang China 72 C2
Batangafo Cent. Afr. Rep. 94 B3
Batangas Phil. 65 G4
Batangtoru Indon. 67 B7
Batan Islands Phil. 65 G2
Batavia Indon. see Jakarta
Batavia NY U.S.A. 131 F2
Batavia OH U.S.A. 130 C4
Bataysk Rus. Fed. 39 H7
Batchawana Mountain hill Canada 118 D5
Bătdâmbâng Cambodia 67 C4
Bateemeucica, Gunung mt. Indon. 67 A6
Batéké, Plateaux Congo 94 B4
Batemans Bay Australia 108 E5
Bates Range hills Australia 105 C6
Batesville AR U.S.A. 127 F5
Batesville IN U.S.A. 130 C4
Batesville MS U.S.A. 127 F5
Batetskiy Rus. Fed. 38 F4
Bath N.B. Canada 119 I5
Bath Ont. Canada 131 G1
Bath U.K. 45 E7
Bath ME U.S.A. 131 K2
Bath NY U.S.A. 131 G2
Bath PA U.S.A. 131 H3
Batha watercourse Chad 93 E3
Bathgate U.K. 46 F5
Bathinda India 78 C3
Bathurst Australia 108 D4
Bathurst Canada 119 I5
Bathurst Gambia see Banjul
Bathurst S. Africa 97 H7
Bathurst, Cape Canada 114 F2
Bathurst, Lake Australia 108 D5
Bathurst Inlet Canada 114 H3
Bathurst Inlet inlet Canada 114 H3
Bathurst Island Australia 104 E2
Bathurst Island Canada 115 I2
Batié Burkina 92 C4
Batı Menteşe Dağları mts Turkey 55 L6
Batı Toroslar mts Turkey 55 N6
Batken Kyrg. 76 D4
Batkes Indon. 104 E1
Bāţlāq-e Gavkhūnī marsh Iran 84 D3
Batley U.K. 44 F5
Batlow Australia 108 D5
Batman Turkey 87 F3
Batna Alg. 50 F4
Batok, Bukit hill Sing. 67 [inset]
▶Baton Rouge U.S.A. 127 F6
State capital of Louisiana.
Batopilas Mex. 123 G8
Batouri Cameroon 93 E4
Batrā' tourist site Jordan see Petra
Batrā', Jabal al mt. Jordan 81 B5
Batroûn Lebanon 81 B2
Båtsfjord Norway 40 P1
Battambang Cambodia see Bătdâmbâng
Batticaloa Sri Lanka 80 D5
Batti Malv i. India 67 A5
Battipaglia Italy 54 F4
Battle r. Canada 117 I4
Battle Creek U.S.A. 130 C2
Battleford Canada 117 I4
Battle Mountain U.S.A. 124 E1
Battle Mountain mt. U.S.A. 124 E1
Battura Glacier Jammu and Kashmir 78 C1
Batu mt. Eth. 94 D3
Batu, Pulau-pulau is Indon. 64 B7
Batudaka i. Indon. 65 G7
Batu Gajah Malaysia 67 C6
Batumi Georgia see Bat'umi
Bat'umi Georgia 87 F2
Batu Pahat Malaysia 67 C7
Batu Putih, Gunung mt. Malaysia 67 C6
Baturaja Indon. 64 C7
Baturité Brazil 139 K4
Batyrevo Rus. Fed. 39 J5
Batys Qazaqstan admin. div. Kazakh. see Zapadnyy Kazakhstan
Bau Sarawak Malaysia 64 E6
Baubau Indon. 65 G8
Baucau East Timor 104 D2
Bauchi Nigeria 92 D3
Bauda India see Boudh
Baudette U.S.A. 126 E1
Baudh India see Boudh
Baugé France 52 D3
Bauhinia Australia 106 E5
Baukau East Timor see Baucau
Bauld, Cape Canada 119 L4
Baume-les-Dames France 52 H3
Baunach r. Germany 49 K5
Baundal India 78 C2
Baura Bangl. 79 G4
Bauru Brazil 141 A3
Bausendorf Germany 48 G4
Bauska Latvia 41 N8
Bautino Kazakh. 87 H1
Bautzen Germany 43 O5
Bavaria land Germany see Bayern
Bavaria reg. Germany 49 L6
Bavda India 80 B2
Baviaanskloofberge mts S. Africa 96 F7
Bavispe r. Mex. 123 F7
Bavla India 78 C5
Bavly Rus. Fed. 37 Q5
Baw Myanmar 66 A2
Bawal India 78 D3
Baw Baw National Park Australia 108 C6
Bawdeswell U.K. 45 I6
Bawdwin Myanmar 66 B2
Bawean i. Indon. 64 E8
Bawinkel Germany 49 H2
Bawlake Myanmar 66 B3
Bawolung China 72 D2
Baxi China 72 D1
Baxley U.S.A. 129 D6
Baxoi China 72 C2
Baxter Mountain U.S.A. 125 J2
Bay China see Baicheng
Bayamo Cuba 133 I4
Bayan Heilong. China 70 B3
Bayan Qinghai China 72 C1
Bayan Mongolia 69 K3
Bayana India 78 D4
Bayanaul Kazakh. 76 E1
Bayanbulag Mongolia 76 I2
Bayanbulak China 76 F3
Bayanday Rus. Fed. 68 J2
Bayan Gol China see Dengkou
Bayan Har Shan mts China 72 B1
Bayan Har Shankou pass China 72 C1
Bayanhongor Mongolia 76 J2
Bayan Hot China 68 J5
Bayan Mod China 68 I4
Bayan Obo China 69 J4
Bayan-Ovoo Mongolia 76 H3
Bayan Ul Hot China 69 L4
Bayard U.S.A. 125 I5
Bayasgalant Mongolia 69 K3
Bayat Turkey 55 N5
Bayāz Iran 84 E4
Baybay Phil. 65 G4
Bayboro U.S.A. 129 E5
Bayburt Turkey 87 F2
Bay City MI U.S.A. 130 D2
Bay City TX U.S.A. 127 D6
Baydaratskaya Guba Rus. Fed. 60 H3
Baydhabo Somalia 94 E3
Bayerischer Wald mts Germany 49 M5
Bayerischer Wald nat. park Germany 49 M5
Bayern land Germany 49 L6
Bayer Wald, Nationalpark nat. park Germany 43 N6
Bayeux France 45 G9
Bayfield Canada 130 E2
Bayındır Turkey 55 L5
Bay Islands is Hond. see La Bahía, Islas de
Bayizhen China 72 B2
Bayjī Iraq 87 F4
Baykal, Ozero l. Rus. Fed. see Baikal, Lake
Baykal-Amur Magistral Rus. Fed. 70 C1
Baykal Range mts Rus. Fed. see Baykal'skiy Khrebet
Baykal'skiy Khrebet mts Rus. Fed. 69 J2
Baykan Turkey 87 F3
Bay-Khaak Rus. Fed. 76 H1
Baykibashevo Rus. Fed. 37 R4
Baykonur Kazakh. see Baykonyr
Baykonyr Kazakh. 76 B2
Baymak Rus. Fed. 60 G4
Bay Minette U.S.A. 129 C6
Baynūna'h reg. U.A.E. 84 D6
Bayombong Phil. 65 G3
Bayona Spain see Baiona
Bayonne France 52 D5
Bayonne U.S.A. 131 H3
Bay Port U.S.A. 130 D2
Bayqongyr Kazakh. see Baykonyr
Bayram-Ali Turkm. see Bayramaly
Bayramaly Turkm. 85 F2
Bayramiç Turkey 55 L5
Bayreuth Germany 49 L5
Bayrūt Lebanon see Beirut
Bays, Lake of Canada 130 F1
Bayshore U.S.A. 130 C1
Bay Shore U.S.A. 131 I3
Bay Springs U.S.A. 127 F6
Bayston Hill U.K. 45 E6
Baysun Uzbek. 85 G2
Bayt Lahm West Bank see Bethlehem
Baytown U.S.A. 127 E6
Bay View N.Z. 109 F4
Bayy al Kabīr, Wādī watercourse Libya 93 E1
Baza Spain 53 E5
Baza, Sierra de mts Spain 53 E5
Bazardüzü Dağı mt. Azer./Rus. Fed. see Bazardyuzyu, Gora
Bazardyuzyu, Gora mt. Azer./Rus. Fed. 87 G2
Bāzār-e Māsāl Iran 84 C2
Bazarnyy Karabulak Rus. Fed. 39 J5
Bazaruto, Ilha do i. Moz. 95 D6
Bazdar Pak. 85 G5
Bazhong China 72 E2
Bazhou China see Bazhong
Bazin r. Canada 118 G5
Bazmān Iran 85 F5
Bazmān, Kūh-e mt. Iran 85 F4
Bcharré Lebanon 81 C2
Be r. Vietnam 67 D5
Beach U.S.A. 126 C2
Beachy Head hd U.K. 45 H8
Beacon U.S.A. 131 I3
Beacon Bay S. Africa 97 H7
Beaconsfield U.K. 45 G7
Beagle, Canal sea chan. Arg. 140 C8
Beagle Bank reef Australia 104 C3
Beagle Bay Australia 104 C4
Beagle Gulf Australia 104 E3
Bealanana Madag. 95 E5
Béal an Átha Rep. of Ireland see Ballina
Béal Átha na Sluaighe Rep. of Ireland see Ballinasloe
Beale, Lake India 80 B2
Beaminster U.K. 45 E8
Bear r. U.S.A. 122 E4
Bearalváhki Norway see Berlevåg
Bear Cove Point Canada 117 O2
Beardmore Canada 118 D4
Beardmore Glacier Antarctica 148 H1
Beardmore Reservoir Australia 108 D1
Bear Island Arctic Ocean see Bjørnøya
Bear Island Canada 118 E3
Bear Island Rep. of Ireland 47 C6
Bear Lake l. Canada 118 A3
Bear Lake U.S.A. 130 B1
Bear Lake l. U.S.A. 122 F4
Bearma r. India 78 D4
Bear Mountain U.S.A. 126 C3
Bearnaraigh i. U.K. see Berneray
Bear Paw Mountain U.S.A. 122 F2
Bearpaw Mountains U.S.A. 122 F2
Bearskin Lake Canada 117 N4
Beas Dam India 78 C3
Beata, Cabo c. Dom. Rep. 133 J5
Beatrice U.S.A. 126 D3
Beatrice, Cape Australia 106 B2
Beatton r. Canada 116 F3
Beatton River Canada 116 F3
Beatty U.S.A. 124 E3
Beattyville Canada 118 F4
Beattyville U.S.A. 130 D5
Beaucaire France 52 G5
Beauchene Island Falkland Is 140 E8
Beaufort Australia 108 A6
Beaufort NC U.S.A. 129 E5
Beaufort SC U.S.A. 129 D5
Beaufort Island Hong Kong China 73 [inset]
Beaufort Sea Canada/U.S.A. 114 D2
Beaufort West S. Africa 96 F7
Beaulieu r. Canada 117 H2
Beauly U.K. 46 E3
Beauly r. U.K. 46 E3
Beaumaris U.K. 44 C5
Beaumont Belgium 48 E4
Beaumont N.Z. 109 B7
Beaumont MS U.S.A. 127 F6
Beaumont TX U.S.A. 127 E6
Beaune France 52 G3
Beaupréau France 52 D3
Beauquesne France 48 C4
Beauraing Belgium 48 E4
Beauséjour Canada 117 L5
Beauvais France 48 C5
Beauval France 48 C4
Beaver r. Alberta/Saskatchewan Canada 117 J4
Beaver r. Ont. Canada 118 D3
Beaver r. Y.T. Canada 116 E3
Beaver OK U.S.A. 127 C4
Beaver PA U.S.A. 130 E3
Beaver UT U.S.A. 125 G2
Beaver r. U.S.A. 125 G2
Beaver Creek Canada 149 A2
Beavercreek U.S.A. 130 C4
Beaver Creek r. MT U.S.A. 126 B1
Beaver Creek r. ND U.S.A. 126 C2
Beaver Dam KY U.S.A. 130 B5
Beaver Dam WI U.S.A. 126 F3
Beaver Falls U.S.A. 130 E3
Beaverhead Mountains U.S.A. 122 E3
Beaverhill Lake Alta Canada 117 H4
Beaver Hill Lake Canada 117 M4
Beaverhill Lake N.W.T. Canada 117 J2
Beaver Island U.S.A. 128 C2
Beaverlodge Canada 116 G4
Beaverton Canada 130 F1
Beaverton MI U.S.A. 130 C2
Beaverton OR U.S.A. 122 C3
Beawar India 78 C4
Beazley Arg. 140 C4
Bebedouro Brazil 141 A3
Bebington U.K. 44 D5
Bebra Germany 49 J4
Bêca China 72 C2
Bécard, Lac l. Canada 119 G1
Beccles U.K. 45 I6
Bečej Serb. and Mont. 55 I2
Becerreá Spain 53 C2
Béchar Alg. 50 D5
Bechhofen Germany 49 K5
Bechuanaland country Africa see Botswana
Beckley U.S.A. 130 E5
Beckum Germany 49 I3
Becky Peak U.S.A. 125 F2
Bečov nad Teplou Czech Rep. 49 M4
Bedale U.K. 44 F4
Bedburg Germany 48 G4
Bedelē Eth. 94 D3
Bederkesa Germany 49 I1
Bedford N.S. Canada 119 J5
Bedford Que. Canada 131 I1
Bedford E. Cape S. Africa 97 H7
Bedford Kwazulu-Natal S. Africa 97 J5
Bedford U.K. 45 G6
Bedford IN U.S.A. 130 B4
Bedford KY U.S.A. 130 C4
Bedford PA U.S.A. 131 F3
Bedford VA U.S.A. 130 F5
Bedford, Cape Australia 106 D2
Bedford Downs Australia 104 D4
Bedgerebong Australia 108 C4
Bedi India 78 B5
Bedla India 78 C4
Bedlington U.K. 44 F3
Bedok Sing. 67 [inset]
Bedok Jetty Sing. 67 [inset]
Bedok Reservoir Sing. 67 [inset]
Bedou China 73 F3
Bedourie Australia 106 B5
Bedum Neth. 48 G1
Bedworth U.K. 45 F6
Beechworth Australia 108 C6
Beechy Canada 117 J5
Beecroft Peninsula Australia 108 E5
Beed India see Bid
Beelitz Germany 49 M2
Beenleigh Australia 108 F1
Beernem Belgium 48 D3
Beersheba Israel 81 B4
Be'ér Sheva' Israel see Beersheba
Be'ér Sheva' watercourse Israel 81 B4
Beervlei Dam S. Africa 96 F7
Beerwah Australia 108 F1
Beetaloo Australia 104 F4
Beethoven Peninsula Antarctica 148 L2
Beeville U.S.A. 127 D6
Befori Dem. Rep. Congo 94 C3
Beg, Lough l. U.K. 47 F3
Bega Australia 108 D6
Begari r. Pak. 85 H4
Begicheva, Ostrov i. Rus. Fed. see Bol'shoy Begichev, Ostrov
Begur, Cap de c. Spain 53 H3
Begusarai India 79 F4
Béhague, Pointe pt Fr. Guiana 139 H3
Behbehān Iran 84 C4
Behrendt Mountains Antarctica 148 L2
Behrūsī Iran 84 D4
Behshahr Iran 84 D2
Behsūd Afgh. 85 G3
Bei'an China 70 B2
Bei'ao China see Dongtou
Beibei China 72 E2
Beichuan China 72 E2
Beida Libya see Al Bayḍā'
Beigang Taiwan see Peikang
Beiguan China see Anyang
Beihai China 73 F4
Bei Hulsan Hu salt l. China 79 H1
▶Beijing China 69 L5
Capital of China.
Beijing municipality China 69 L4
Beik Myanmar see Mergui
Beilen Neth. 48 G2
Beiliu China 73 F4
Beilngries Germany 49 L5
Beiluheyan China 72 B1
Beinn an Oir hill U.K. 46 D5
Beinn an Tuirc hill U.K. 46 D5
Beinn Bheigeir hill U.K. 46 C5
Beinn Bhreac hill U.K. 46 D4
Beinn Dearg mt. U.K. 46 E3
Beinn Heasgarnich mt. U.K. 46 E4
Beinn Mholach hill U.K. 46 C2
Beinn Mhòr hill U.K. 46 B3
Beinn na Faoghlia i. U.K. see Benbecula
Beipan Jiang r. China 72 E3
Beipiao China 69 M4
Beira Moz. 95 D5
▶Beirut Lebanon 81 B3
Capital of Lebanon.
Bei Shan mts China 76 I3
Beitbridge Zimbabwe 95 C6
Beith U.K. 46 E5
Beit Jālā West Bank 81 B4
Beja Port. 53 C4
Béja Tunisia 54 C6
Bejaïa Alg. 53 I5
Béjar Spain 53 D3
Beji r. Pak. 76 C6
Bekaa valley Lebanon see El Béqaa
Bekdash Turkm. 87 I2
Békés Hungary 55 I1
Békéscsaba Hungary 55 I1
Bekily Madag. 95 E6
Bekkai Japan 70 G4
Bēkma, Sadd dam Iraq 87 G3
Bekovo Rus. Fed. 39 I5
Bekwai Ghana 92 C4
Bela India 79 E4
Bela Pak. 85 G5
Belab r. Pak. 85 H4
Bela-Bela S. Africa 97 I3
Bélabo Cameroon 92 E4
Bela Crkva Serb. and Mont. 55 I2
Bel Air U.S.A. 131 G4
Belalcázar Spain 53 D4
Bělá nad Radbuzou Czech Rep. 49 M5
Belapur India 80 B2
Belaraboon Australia 108 B4
▶Belarus country Europe 39 E5
europe 5, 34–35
Belau country N. Pacific Ocean see Palau
Bela Vista Brazil 140 E2
Bela Vista Moz. 97 K4
Bela Vista de Goiás Brazil 141 A2
Belawan Indon. 67 B7
Belaya r. Rus. Fed. 61 S3
also known as Bila
Belaya Glina Rus. Fed. 39 I7
Belaya Kalitva Rus. Fed. 39 I6
Belaya Kholunitsa Rus. Fed. 38 K4
Belaya Tserkva Ukr. see Bila Tserkva
Belbédji Niger 92 D3
Bełchatów Poland 43 Q5
Belcher U.S.A. 130 D5
Belcher Islands Canada 118 F2
Belchiragh Afgh. 85 G3
Belcoo U.K. 47 E3
Belden U.S.A. 124 C1
Belding U.S.A. 130 C2
Beleapani reef India see Cherbaniani Reef
Belebey Rus. Fed. 37 Q5
Beledweyne Somalia 94 E3
Belém Brazil 139 I4
Belém Novo Brazil 141 A5
Belén Arg. 140 C3
Belen Antalya Turkey 81 A1
Belen Hatay Turkey 81 C1
Belen U.S.A. 123 G6
Belep, Îles is New Caledonia 103 G3
Belev Rus. Fed. 39 H5
Belfast S. Africa 97 J3
▶Belfast U.K. 47 G3
Capital of Northern Ireland.
Belfast U.S.A. 128 G2
Belfast Lough inlet U.K. 47 G3
Bēlfodiyo Eth. 94 D2
Belford U.K. 44 F3
Belfort France 52 H3
Belgaum India 80 B3
Belgern Germany 49 N3
Belgian Congo country Africa see Congo, Democratic Republic of
België country Europe see Belgium
Belgique country Europe see Belgium
▶Belgium country Europe 48 E4
europe 5, 34–35
Belgorod Rus. Fed. 39 H6
Belgorod-Dnestrovskyy Ukr. see Bilhorod-Dnistrovs'kyy
Belgrade ME U.S.A. 131 K1
Belgrade MT U.S.A. 122 F3
▶Belgrade Serb. and Mont. 55 I2
Capital of Serbia and Montenegro.
Belgrano II research station Antarctica 148 A1
Belice r. Sicily Italy 54 E6
Belinskiy Rus. Fed. 39 I5
Belinyu Indon. 64 D7
Belitung i. Indon. 64 D7
Belize Angola 95 B4
▶Belize Belize 132 G5
Former capital of Belize.
▶Belize country Central America 132 G5
north america 9, 112–113
Beljak Austria see Villach
Belkina, Mys pt Rus. Fed. 70 E3
Bel'kovskiy, Ostrov i. Rus. Fed. 61 O2
Bell Australia 108 E1
Bell r. Australia 108 D4
Bell r. Canada 118 F4
Bella Bella Canada 116 D4
Bellac France 52 E3
Bella Coola Canada 116 E4
Bellaire U.S.A. 130 C1
Bellary India 80 C3
Bellata Australia 108 D2
Bella Unión Uruguay 140 E4
Bella Vista U.S.A. 124 B1
Bellbrook Australia 108 F3
Bell Cay reef Australia 106 E4
Belledonne mts France 52 G4
Bellefontaine U.S.A. 130 D3
Bellefonte U.S.A. 131 G3
Belle Fourche U.S.A. 126 C2
Belle Fourche r. U.S.A. 126 C2
Belle Glade U.S.A. 129 D7
Belle-Île i. France 52 C3
Belle Isle i. Canada 119 L4
Belle Isle, Strait of Canada 119 K4
Belleville Canada 131 G1
Belleville IL U.S.A. 126 F4
Belleville KS U.S.A. 126 D4
Bellevue IA U.S.A. 126 F3
Bellevue MI U.S.A. 130 C2
Bellevue OH U.S.A. 130 D3
Bellevue WA U.S.A. 122 C3
Bellin Canada see Kangirsuk
Bellingham U.K. 44 E3
Bellingham U.S.A. 122 C2
Bellingshausen research station Antarctica 148 A2
Bellingshausen Sea Antarctica 148 L2
Bellinzona Switz. 52 I3
Bellows Falls U.S.A. 131 I2
Bellpat Pak. 85 H4
Belluno Italy 54 E1
Belluru India 80 C3
Bell Ville Arg. 140 D4
Bellville S. Africa 96 D7
Belm Germany 49 I2
Belmont Australia 108 E4
Belmont U.K. 46 [inset]
Belmont U.S.A. 131 F2
Belmonte Brazil 141 D1
▶Belmopan Belize 132 G5
Capital of Belize.
Belmore, Mount hill Australia 108 F2
Belmullet Rep. of Ireland 47 C3
Belo Madag. 95 E6
Belo Campo Brazil 141 C1
Belœil Belgium 48 D4
Belogorsk Rus. Fed. 70 C2
Belogorsk Ukr. see Bilohirs'k
Beloha Madag. 95 E6
Belo Horizonte Brazil 141 C2
Beloit KS U.S.A. 126 D4
Beloit WI U.S.A. 126 F3
Belokurikha Rus. Fed. 76 F1
Belo Monte Brazil 139 H4
Belomorsk Rus. Fed. 38 G2
Belonia India 79 G5
Belorechensk Rus. Fed. 87 E1
Belorechenskaya Rus. Fed. see Belorechensk
Belören Turkey 86 D3
Beloretsk Rus. Fed. 60 G4
Belorussia country Europe see Belarus
Belorusskaya S.S.R. country Europe see Belarus
Belostok Poland see Białystok
Belot, Lac l. Canada 114 F3
Belo Tsiribihina Madag. 95 E5
Belovo Rus. Fed. 68 F2
Beloyarskiy Rus. Fed. 37 T3
Beloye, Ozero l. Rus. Fed. 38 H3
Beloye More sea Rus. Fed. see White Sea
Belozersk Rus. Fed. 38 H3
Belpre U.S.A. 130 E4
Beltana Australia 107 B6
Belted Range mts U.S.A. 124 E3
Belton U.S.A. 127 D6
Bel'ts' Moldova see Bălţi
Bel'tsy Moldova see Bălţi
Belukha, Gora mt. Kazakh./Rus. Fed. 76 G2
Belush'ye Rus. Fed. 38 J2
Belvidere IL U.S.A. 126 F3
Belvidere NJ U.S.A. 131 H3
Belyando r. Australia 106 D4
Belyayevka Ukr. see Bilyayivka
Belyy Rus. Fed. 38 G5
Belyy, Ostrov i. Rus. Fed. 60 I2
Belzig Germany 49 M2
Belzoni U.S.A. 127 F5
Bemaraha, Plateau du Madag. 95 E5
Bembe Angola 95 B4
Bemidji U.S.A. 126 E2
Béna Burkina 92 C3
Bena Dibele Dem. Rep. Congo 94 C4
Ben Alder mt. U.K. 46 E4
Benalla Australia 108 B6
Benares India see Varanasi
Ben Arous Tunisia 54 D6
Benavente Spain 53 D2
Ben Avon mt. U.K. 46 F3
Benbane Head hd U.K. 47 F2
Benbecula i. U.K. 46 B3
Ben Boyd National Park Australia 108 E6

Benburb U.K. 47 F3
Bên Cat Vietnam 67 D5
Bencha China 73 I1
Ben Chonzie hill U.K. 46 F4
Ben Cleuch hill U.K. 46 F4
Ben Cruachan mt. U.K. 46 D4
Bend U.S.A. 122 C3
Bendearg mt. S. Africa 97 H6
Bender Moldova see Tighina
Bender-Bayla Somalia 94 F3
Bendery Moldova see Tighina
Bendigo Australia 108 B6
Bendoc Australia 108 D6
Bene Moz. 95 D5
Benedict, Mount hill Canada 119 K3
Benenitra Madag. 95 E6
Benešov Czech Rep. 43 O6
Bénestroff France 48 G6
Benevento Italy 54 F4
Beneventum Italy see Benevento
Benezette U.S.A. 131 F3
Beng, Nam r. Laos 66 C3
Bengal, Bay of sea Indian Ocean 77 G8
Bengamisa Dem. Rep. Congo 94 C3
Bengbu China 73 H1
Benghazi Libya 93 F1
Bengkalis Indon. 67 C7
Bengkalis i. Indon. 67 C7
Bengkulu Indon. 64 C7
Bengtsfors Sweden 41 H7
Benguela Angola 95 B5
Benha Egypt see Banhā
Ben Hiant hill U.K. 46 C4
Ben Hope hill U.K. 46 E2
Ben Horn hill U.K. 46 E2
Beni r. Bol. 138 E6
Beni Dem. Rep. Congo 94 C3
Beni Nepal 79 E3
Beni-Abbès Alg. 50 D5
Beniah Lake Canada 117 H2
Benidorm Spain 53 F4
Beni Mellal Morocco 50 C5
Benin country Africa 92 D4
africa 7, 90–91
Benin, Bight of g. Africa 92 D4
Benin City Nigeria 92 D4
Beni-Saf Alg. 53 F6
Beni Snassen, Monts des mts Morocco 53 E6
Beni Suef Egypt see Banī Suwayf
Benito, Islas is Mex. 123 E7
Benito Juárez Arg. 140 E5
Benito Juárez Mex. 125 F5
Benjamim Constant Brazil 138 E4
Benjamin U.S.A. 127 D5
Benjamín Hill Mex. 123 F7
Benjina Indon. 65 I8
Benkelman U.S.A. 126 C3
Ben Klibreck hill U.K. 46 E2
Ben Lavin Nature Reserve S. Africa 97 I2
Ben Lawers mt. U.K. 46 E4
Ben Lomond mt. Australia 108 E3
Ben Lomond hill U.K. 46 E4
Ben Lomond National Park Australia 107 [inset]
Ben Macdui mt. U.K. 46 F3
Benmara Australia 106 B3
Ben More hill U.K. 46 C4
Ben More mt. U.K. 46 E4
Benmore, Lake N.Z. 109 C7
Ben More Assynt hill U.K. 46 E2
Bennetta, Ostrov i. Rus. Fed. 61 P2
Bennett Island Rus. Fed. see Bennetta, Ostrov
Bennett Lake Canada 116 C3
Bennettsville U.S.A. 129 E5
Ben Nevis mt. U.K. 46 D4
Bennington NH U.S.A. 131 J2
Bennington VT U.S.A. 131 I2
Benoni S. Africa 97 I4
Ben Rinnes hill U.K. 46 F3
Bensheim Germany 49 I5
Benson AZ U.S.A. 125 H6
Benson MN U.S.A. 126 E2
Benta Seberang Malaysia 67 C6
Benteng Indon. 65 G8
Bentinck Island Myanmar 67 B5
Bentiu Sudan 82 C8
Bent Jbaïl Lebanon 81 B3
Bentley U.K. 44 F5
Bento Gonçalves Brazil 141 A5
Benton AR U.S.A. 127 E5
Benton CA U.S.A. 124 D3
Benton IL U.S.A. 126 F4
Benton KY U.S.A. 127 F4
Benton LA U.S.A. 127 E5
Benton MO U.S.A. 127 F4
Benton PA U.S.A. 131 G3
Bentong Malaysia see Bentung
Benton Harbor U.S.A. 130 B2
Bentonville U.S.A. 127 E4
Bên Tre Vietnam 67 D5
Bentuang Karimun National Park Indon. 64 E6
Bentung Malaysia 67 C7
Benue r. Nigeria 92 D4
Benum, Gunung mt. Malaysia 67 C7
Ben Vorlich hill U.K. 46 E4
Benwee Head hd Rep. of Ireland 47 C3
Benwood U.S.A. 130 E3
Ben Wyvis mt. U.K. 46 E3
Benxi Liaoning China 70 A4
Benxi Liaoning China 70 B4
Beograd Serb. and Mont. see Belgrade
Béoumi Côte d'Ivoire 92 C4
Beppu Japan 71 C6
Béqaa valley Lebanon see El Béqaa
Berach r. India 78 C4
Beraketa Madag. 95 E6
Bérard, Lac l. Canada 119 H2
Berasia India 78 D5
Berat Albania 55 H4
Beravina Madag. 95 E5
Berbak National Park Indon. 64 C7
Berber Sudan 82 D6
Berbera Somalia 94 E2
Berbérati Cent. Afr. Rep. 94 B3
Berchtesgaden, Nationalpark nat. park Germany 43 N7
Berck France 48 B4
Berdichev Ukr. see Berdychiv
Berdigestyakh Rus. Fed. 61 N3
Berdyans'k Ukr. 39 H7
Berdychiv Ukr. 39 F6
Berea KY U.S.A. 130 C5
Berea OH U.S.A. 130 E3
Beregovo Ukr. see Berehove
Beregovoy Rus. Fed. 70 B1
Berehove Ukr. 39 D6
Bereina P.N.G. 65 L8
Bereket Turkm. see Gazandzhyk
Berekum Ghana 92 C4
Berenice Egypt see Baranīs
Berenice Libya see Benghazi
Berens r. Canada 117 L4
Berens Island Canada 117 L4
Berens River Canada 117 L4
Beresford U.S.A. 126 D3
Bereza Belarus see Byaroza
Berezino Belarus see Byerazino
Berezivka Ukr. 39 F7
Berezne Ukr. 39 E6
Bereznik Rus. Fed. 38 I3
Berezniki Rus. Fed. 37 R4
Berezov Rus. Fed. see Berezovo
Berezovka Rus. Fed. 70 B2
Berezovka Ukr. see Berezivka
Berezovo Rus. Fed. 37 T3
Berezovyy Rus. Fed. 70 D2
Berga Germany 49 L3
Berga Spain 53 G2
Bergama Turkey 55 L5
Bergamo Italy 54 C2
Bergby Sweden 41 J6
Bergen Mecklenburg-Vorpommern Germany 43 N3
Bergen Niedersachsen Germany 49 J2
Bergen Norway 41 D6
Bergen U.S.A. 131 G2
Bergen op Zoom Neth. 48 E3
Bergerac France 52 E4
Bergères-lès-Vertus France 48 E6
Bergheim (Erft) Germany 48 G4
Bergisches Land reg. Germany 49 H4
Bergisch Gladbach Germany 48 H4
Bergland Namibia 96 C2
Bergomum Italy see Bergamo
Bergoo U.S.A. 130 E4
Bergsjö Sweden 41 J6
Bergsviken Sweden 40 L4
Bergtheim Germany 49 K5
Bergues France 48 C4
Bergum Neth. 48 G1
Bergville S. Africa 97 I5
Berhampur India see Baharampur
Beringa, Ostrov i. Rus. Fed. 61 R4
Beringen Belgium 48 F3
Beringovskiy Rus. Fed. 61 S3
Bering Sea N. Pacific Ocean 61 S4
Bering Strait Rus. Fed./U.S.A. 61 U3
Berīs, Ra's pt Iran 85 F5
Berislav Ukr. see Beryslav
Berkåk Norway 40 G5
Berkane Morocco 53 E6
Berkel r. Neth. 48 G2
Berkeley U.S.A. 124 B3
Berkeley Springs U.S.A. 131 F4
Berkhout Neth. 48 F2
Berkner Island Antarctica 148 A1
Berkovitsa Bulg. 55 J3
Berkshire Downs hills U.K. 45 F7
Berkshire Hills U.S.A. 131 I2
Berland r. Canada 116 G4
Berlare Belgium 48 E3
Berlevåg Norway 40 P1

Berlin Germany 49 N2
Capital of Germany.

Berlin land Germany 49 N2
Berlin MD U.S.A. 131 H4
Berlin NH U.S.A. 131 J1
Berlin PA U.S.A. 131 F4
Berlin Lake U.S.A. 130 E3
Bermagui Australia 108 E6
Bermejo r. Arg./Bol. 140 E3
Bermejo Bol. 138 F8
Bermen, Lac l. Canada 119 H3

Bermuda terr. N. Atlantic Ocean 133 L2
United Kingdom Overseas Territory.
north america 9, 112–113

Bermuda Rise sea feature N. Atlantic Ocean 144 D4

Bern Switz. 52 H3
Capital of Switzerland.

Bernalillo U.S.A. 123 G6
Bernardino de Campos Brazil 141 A3
Bernardo O'Higgins, Parque Nacional nat. park Chile 140 B7
Bernasconi Arg. 140 D5
Bernau Germany 49 N2
Bernburg (Saale) Germany 49 L3
Berne Germany 49 I1
Berne Switz. see Bern
Berne U.S.A. 130 C3
Berner Alpen mts Switz. 52 H3
Berneray i. Scotland U.K. 46 B3
Berneray i. Scotland U.K. 46 B4
Bernier Island Australia 105 A6
Bernina Pass Switz. 52 J3
Bernkastel-Kues Germany 48 H5
Beroea Greece see Veroia
Beroea Syria see Aleppo
Beroroha Madag. 95 E6
Beroun Czech Rep. 43 O6
Berounka r. Czech Rep. 43 O6
Berovina Madag. see Beravina
Berri Australia 107 C7
Berriane Alg. 50 E5
Berridale Australia 108 D6
Berriedale U.K. 46 F2
Berrigan Australia 108 B5
Berrima Australia 108 E5
Berrouaghia Alg. 53 H5
Berry Australia 108 E5
Berry U.S.A. 130 C4
Berryessa, Lake U.S.A. 124 B2
Berry Head hd U.K. 45 D8
Berry Islands Bahamas 129 E7
Berryville U.S.A. 131 G4
Berseba Namibia 96 C4
Bersenbrück Germany 49 H2
Bertam Malaysia 67 C6
Berté, Lac l. Canada 119 H4
Berthoud Pass U.S.A. 122 G5
Bertolínia Brazil 139 J5
Bertoua Cameroon 92 E4
Bertraghboy Bay Rep. of Ireland 47 C4
Beru atoll Kiribati 103 H2
Beruri Brazil 138 F4
Beruwala Sri Lanka 80 C5
Berwick Australia 108 B7
Berwick U.S.A. 131 G3
Berwick-upon-Tweed U.K. 44 E3
Berwyn hills U.K. 45 D6
Beryslav Ukr. 55 O1
Berytus Lebanon see Beirut
Besalampy Madag. 95 E5
Besançon France 52 H3
Besar, Gunung mt. Malaysia 67 C7
Besbay Kazakh. 76 A2
Beserah Malaysia 67 C7
Beshkent Uzbek. 85 G2
Beshneh Iran 84 D4
Besikama Indon. 104 D2
Besitang Indon. 67 B6
Beskra Alg. see Biskra
Beslan Rus. Fed. 87 G2
Besnard Lake Canada 117 J4
Besni Turkey 86 E3
Besor watercourse Israel 81 B4
Beşparmak Dağları mts Cyprus see Pentadaktylos Range
Bessbrook U.K. 47 F3
Bessemer U.S.A. 129 C5
Besshoky, Gora hill Kazakh. 87 I1
Besskorbnaya Rus. Fed. 39 I7
Bessonovka Rus. Fed. 39 J5
Betanzos Spain 53 B2
Bethal S. Africa 97 I4
Bethanie Namibia 96 C4
Bethany U.S.A. 126 E3
Bethel U.S.A. 119 H5
Bethel Park U.S.A. 130 E3
Bethesda U.K. 44 C5
Bethesda MD U.S.A. 131 G4
Bethesda OH U.S.A. 130 E3
Bethlehem S. Africa 97 I5
Bethlehem U.S.A. 131 H3
Bethlehem West Bank 81 B4
Bethulie S. Africa 97 G6
Béthune France 48 C4
Beti Pak. 85 H4
Betim Brazil 141 B2
Bet Lehem West Bank see Bethlehem
Betma India 78 C5
Betong Thai. 67 C6
Betoota Australia 106 C5
Betpak-Dala plain Kazakh. 76 D2
Betroka Madag. 95 E6
Bet She'an Israel 81 B3
Betsiamites Canada 119 H4
Betsiamites r. Canada 119 H4
Bettiah India 79 F4
Bettyhill U.K. 46 E2
Bettystown Rep. of Ireland 47 F4
Betul India 78 D5
Betwa r. India 78 D4
Betws-y-coed U.K. 45 D5
Betzdorf Germany 49 H4
Beulah Australia 107 C7
Beulah MI U.S.A. 130 B1
Beulah ND U.S.A. 126 C2
Beult r. U.K. 45 H7
Beuthen Poland see Bytom
Bever r. Germany 49 H2
Beverley U.K. 44 G5
Beverly MA U.S.A. 131 J2
Beverly OH U.S.A. 130 E4
Beverly Hills U.S.A. 124 D4
Beverly Lake Canada 117 K1
Beverstedt Germany 49 I1
Beverungen Germany 49 J3
Beverwijk Neth. 48 E2
Bewani P.N.G. 65 K7
Bexbach Germany 49 H5
Bexhill U.K. 45 H8
Bexley, Cape Canada 114 G3
Beyānlū Iran 84 B3
Beyce Turkey see Orhaneli
Bey Dağları mts Turkey 55 N6
Beykoz Turkey 55 M4
Beyla Guinea 92 C4
Beylagan Azer. see Beyläqan
Beyläqan Azer. 87 G3
Beyneu Kazakh. 74 E2
Beypazarı Turkey 55 N4
Beypınarı Turkey 86 E3
Beypore India 80 B4
Beyrouth Lebanon see Beirut
Beyşehir Turkey 86 C3
Beyşehir Gölü l. Turkey 86 C3
Beytonovo Rus. Fed. 70 B1
Beytüşşebap Turkey 87 F3
Bezameh Iran 84 E3
Bezbozhnik Rus. Fed. 38 K4
Bezhanitsy Rus. Fed. 38 F4
Bezhetsk Rus. Fed. 38 H4
Béziers France 52 F5
Bezmein Turkm. see Byuzmeyin
Bezwada India see Vijayawada
Bhabha India see Bhabhua
Bhabhar India 78 B4
Bhabhua India 79 E4
Bhabua India see Bhabhua
Bhachau India 78 B5
Bhachbhar India 78 B4
Bhadgaon Nepal see Bhaktapur
Bhadohi India 79 E4
Bhadra India 78 C3
Bhadrachalam Road Station India see Kottagudem
Bhadrak India 79 F5
Bhadrakh India see Bhadrak
Bhadravati India 80 B3
Bhag Pak. 85 G4
Bhagalpur India 79 F4
Bhainsa India 80 C2
Bhainsdehi India 78 D5
Bhairab Bazar Bangl. 79 G4
Bhairi Hol mt. Pak. 85 G5
Bhaktapur Nepal 79 F4
Bhalki India 80 C2
Bhamo Myanmar 66 B1
Bhamragarh India 80 D2
Bhandara India 78 D5
Bhanjanagar India 80 E2
Bhanrer Range hills India 78 D5
Bhaptiahi India 79 F4
Bharat country Asia see India
Bharatpur India 78 D4
Bhareli r. India 79 H4
Bharuch India 78 C5
Bhatapara India 79 E5
Bhatarsaigh i. U.K. see Vatersay
Bhatghar Lake India 80 B2
Bhatinda India see Bathinda
Bhatnair India see Hanumangarh
Bhatpara India 79 G5
Bhaunagar India see Bhavnagar
Bhavani r. India 80 C4
Bhavani Sagar l. India 80 C4
Bhavnagar India 78 C5
Bhawana Pak. 85 I4
Bhawanipatna India 80 D2
Bhearnaraigh, Eilean i. U.K. see Berneray
Bheemavaram India see Bhimavaram
Bhekuzulu S. Africa 97 J4
Bhera Pak. 85 I3
Bhikhna Thori Nepal 79 F4
Bhilai India 78 E5
Bhildi India 78 C4
Bhilwara India 78 C4
Bhima r. India 80 C2
Bhimar India 78 B4
Bhimavaram India 80 D2
Bhimlath India 78 E5
Bhind India 78 D4
Bhinga India 79 E4
Bhiwandi India 80 B2
Bhiwani India 78 D3
Bhogaipur India 78 D4
Bhojpur Nepal 79 F4
Bhola Bangl. 79 G5
Bhongweni S. Africa 97 I6
Bhopal India 78 D5
Bhopalpatnam India 80 D2
Bhrigukaccha India see Bharuch
Bhuban India 80 E1
Bhubaneshwar India 80 E1
Bhubaneswar India see Bhubaneshwar
Bhuj India 78 B5
Bhumiphol Dam Thai. 66 B3
Bhusawal India 78 C5
Bhutan country Asia 79 G4
asia 6, 58–59
Bhuttewala India 78 B4
Bia r. Ghana 92 C4
Bia, Phou mt. Laos 66 C3
Biabān mts Iran 84 E5
Biafo Glacier Jammu and Kashmir 78 C2
Biafra, Bight of g. Africa see Benin, Bight of
Biak Indon. 65 J7
Biak i. Indon. 65 J7
Biała Podlaska Poland 39 D5
Białogard Poland 43 O4
Białystok Poland 39 D5
Bianco, Monte mt. France/Italy see Blanc, Mont
Biandangang Kou r. mouth China 73 I1
Bianzhao China 70 A3
Bianzhuang China see Cangshan
Biaora India 78 D5
Biarritz France 52 D5
Bi'ār Tabrāk well Saudi Arabia 84 B5
Bibai Japan 70 F4
Bibbenluke Australia 108 D6
Bibbiena Italy 54 D3
Bibby Island Canada 117 M2
Biberach an der Riß Germany 43 L6
Bibile Sri Lanka 80 D5
Biblis Germany 49 I5
Biblos Lebanon see Jbail
Bicas Brazil 141 C3
Biçer Turkey 55 N5
Bicester U.K. 45 F7
Bichabhera India 78 C4
Bicheng China see Bishan
Bichevaya Rus. Fed. 70 D3
Bichi r. Rus. Fed. 70 E1
Bickerton Island Australia 106 B2
Bickleigh U.K. 45 D8
Bicknell U.S.A. 130 B4
Bicuari, Parque Nacional do nat. park Angola 95 B5
Bid India 80 B2
Bida Nigeria 92 D4
Bidar India 80 C2
Biddeford U.S.A. 131 J2
Biddinghuizen Neth. 48 F2
Bidean nam Bian mt. U.K. 46 D4
Bideford U.K. 45 C7
Bideford Bay U.K. 45 C7
Bidokht Iran 84 E3
Bidzhan Rus. Fed. 70 C3
Bié Angola see Kuito
Biedenkopf Germany 49 I4
Biel Switz. 52 H3
Bielawa Poland 43 P5
Bielefeld Germany 49 I2
Bielitz Poland see Bielsko-Biała
Biella Italy 54 C2
Bielsko-Biała Poland 43 Q6
Bielstein hill Germany 49 J3
Bienenbüttel Germany 49 K1
Biên Hoa Vietnam 67 D5
Bienne Switz. see Biel
Bienville, Lac l. Canada 119 G3
Bié Plateau Angola 95 B5
Bierbank Australia 108 B1
Biesiesvlei S. Africa 97 G4
Bietigheim-Bissingen Germany 49 J6
Bièvre Belgium 48 F5
Bifoun Gabon 94 B4
Big r. Canada 119 K3
Biga Turkey 55 L4
Bigadiç Turkey 55 M5
Biga Yarımadası pen. Turkey 55 L5
Big Baldy Mountain U.S.A. 122 F3
Big Bar Creek Canada 116 F5
Big Bear Lake U.S.A. 124 E4
Big Belt Mountains U.S.A. 122 F3
Big Bend Swaziland 97 J4
Big Bend National Park U.S.A. 127 C6
Bigbury-on-Sea U.K. 45 D8
Big Canyon watercourse U.S.A. 127 C6
Biger Nuur salt l. Mongolia 76 I2
Big Falls U.S.A. 126 E1
Big Fork r. U.S.A. 126 E1
Biggar Canada 117 J4
Biggar U.K. 46 F5
Biggar, Lac l. Canada 118 G4
Bigge Island Australia 104 D3
Biggenden Australia 107 F5
Bigger, Mount Canada 116 B3
Biggesee l. Germany 49 H3
Biggleswade U.K. 45 G6
Biggs CA U.S.A. 124 C2
Biggs OR U.S.A. 122 C3
Big Hole r. U.S.A. 122 E3
Bighorn r. U.S.A. 122 G3
Bighorn Mountains U.S.A. 122 G3
Big Island Nunavut Canada 115 K3
Big Island N.W.T. Canada 116 G2
Big Island Ont. Canada 117 M5
Big Kalzas Lake Canada 116 C2
Big Lake l. Canada 117 H1
Big Lake U.S.A. 127 C6
Bignona Senegal 92 B3
Big Pine U.S.A. 124 D3
Big Pine Peak U.S.A. 124 D4
Big Raccoon r. U.S.A. 130 B4
Big Rapids U.S.A. 130 C2
Big River Canada 117 J4
Big Sable Point U.S.A. 130 B1
Big Salmon r. Canada 116 C2
Big Sand Lake Canada 117 L3
Big Sandy r. U.S.A. 122 F4
Big Sandy Lake Canada 117 J4
Big Smokey Valley U.S.A. 124 E2
Big South Fork National River and Recreation Area park U.S.A. 130 C5
Big Spring U.S.A. 127 C5
Big Stone Canada 117 I5
Big Stone Gap U.S.A. 130 D5
Bigstone Lake Canada 117 M4
Big Timber U.S.A. 122 F3
Big Trout Lake Canada 117 N4
Big Trout Lake l. Canada 117 N4
Big Valley Canada 117 H4
Big Water U.S.A. 125 H3
Bihać Bos.-Herz. 54 F2
Bihar state India 79 F4
Bihariganj India 79 F4
Bihar Sharif India 79 F4
Bihor, Vârful mt. Romania 55 J1
Bihoro Japan 70 G4
Bijagós, Arquipélago dos is Guinea-Bissau 92 B3
Bijaipur India 78 D4
Bijapur India 80 B2
Bījār Iran 84 B3
Bijbehara Jammu and Kashmir 78 C2
Bijeljina Bos.-Herz. 55 H2
Bijelo Polje Serb. and Mont. 55 H3
Bijeraghogarh India 78 E5
Bijiang China see Zhiziluo
Bijie China 72 E3
Bijji India 80 D2
Bijnor India 78 D3
Bijnore India see Bijnor
Bijnot Pak. 85 H4
Bijrān well Saudi Arabia 84 C5
Bijrān, Khashm hill Saudi Arabia 84 C5
Bikampur India 78 C4
Bikaner India 78 C3
Bīkhūyeh Iran 84 D5
Bikin Rus. Fed. 70 D3
Bikin r. Rus. Fed. 70 D3
Bikini atoll Marshall Is 146 H5
Bikori Sudan 82 D7
Bikoro Dem. Rep. Congo 94 B4
Bikou China 72 E1
Bikramganj India 79 F4
Bilād Banī Bū 'Alī Oman 83 I5
Bilaigarh India 80 D1
Bilara India 78 C4
Bilaspur Chhattisgarh India 79 E5
Bilaspur Himachal Pradesh India 78 D3
Biläsuvar Azer. 87 H3
Bila Tserkva Ukr. 39 F6
Bilauktaung Range mts Myanmar/Thai. 67 B4
Bilbao Spain 53 E2
Bilbays Egypt 86 C5
Bilbeis Egypt see Bilbays
Bilbo Spain see Bilbao
Bilecik Turkey 55 M4
Biłgoraj Poland 39 D6
Bilharamulo Tanz. 94 D4
Bilhaur India 78 E4
Bilhorod-Dnistrovs'kyy Ukr. 55 N1
Bili Dem. Rep. Congo 94 C3
Bilibino Rus. Fed. 61 R3
Bilin Myanmar 66 B3
Bill U.S.A. 122 G4
Billabalong Australia 105 A6
Billabong Creek r. Australia see Moulamein Creek
Billericay U.K. 45 H7
Billiluna Australia 104 D4
Billingham U.K. 44 F4
Billings U.S.A. 122 F3
Billiton i. Indon. see Belitung
Bill of Portland hd U.K. 45 E8
Bill Williams r. U.S.A. 125 F4
Bill Williams Mountain U.S.A. 125 G4
Bilma Niger 92 E3
Bilo r. Rus. Fed. see Belaya
Biloela Australia 106 E5
Bilohirs'k Ukr. 86 D1
Bilohir"ya Ukr. 39 E6
Biloku Guyana 139 G3
Biloli India 80 C2
Bilovods'k Ukr. 39 H6
Biloxi U.S.A. 127 F6
Bilpa Morea Claypan salt flat Australia 106 B5
Bilston U.K. 46 F5
Biltine Chad 93 F3
Bilto Norway 40 L2
Bilugyun Island Myanmar 66 B3
Bilyayivka Ukr. 55 N1
Bilzen Belgium 48 F4
Bima Indon. 104 B2
Bimberi, Mount Australia 108 D5
Bimini Islands Bahamas 129 E7
Bimlipatam India 80 D2
Bināb Iran 84 C2
Bina-Etawa India 78 D4
Binaija, Gunung mt. Indon. 63 E8
Bīnālūd, Kūh-e mts Iran 84 E2
Binboğa Daği mt. Turkey 86 E3
Bincheng China see Binzhou
Binchuan China 72 D3
Bindebango Australia 108 C1
Bindle Australia 108 D1
Bindu Dem. Rep. Congo 95 B4
Bindura Zimbabwe 95 D5
Binefar Spain 53 G3
Binga Zimbabwe 95 C5
Binga, Monte mt. Moz. 95 D5
Bingara Australia 108 E2
Bingaram i. India 80 B4
Bing Bong Australia 106 B2
Bingen am Rhein Germany 49 H5
Bingham U.S.A. 131 K1
Binghamton U.S.A. 131 H2
Bingmei China see Congjiang
Bingöl Turkey 87 F3
Bingol Dağı mt. Turkey 87 F3
Bingxi China see Yushan
Bingzhongluo China 72 C2
Binh Gia Vietnam 66 D2
Binika India 79 E5
Binjai Indon. 67 B7
Bin Mürkhan well U.A.E. 84 D5
Binnaway Australia 108 D3
Binpur India 79 F5
Bintan i. Indon. 67 D7
Bint Jbeil Lebanon see Bent Jbaïl
Bintulu Sarawak Malaysia 64 E6
Binxian Heilong. China 70 B3
Binxian Shaanxi China 73 F1
Binya Australia 108 C5
Binyang China 73 F4
Bin-Yauri Nigeria 92 D3
Binzhou Guangxi China see Binyang
Binzhou Heilong. China see Binxian
Binzhou Shandong China 69 L5
Bioco i. Equat. Guinea 92 D4
Biograd na Moru Croatia 54 F3
Bioko i. Equat. Guinea see Bioco
Biokovo mts Croatia 54 G3
Biquinhas Brazil 141 B2
Bir India see Bid
Bira Rus. Fed. 70 D2
Bi'r Abū Jady oasis Syria 81 D1
Birag, Kūh-e mts Iran 85 F5
Birāk Libya 93 E2
Birakan Rus. Fed. 70 C2
Bi'r al 'Abd Egypt 81 A4
Bi'r al Ḥalbā well Syria 81 D2
Bi'r al Jifjāfah well Egypt 81 A4
Bi'r al Khamsah well Egypt 86 B5
Bi'r al Māliḥah well Egypt 81 A5
Bi'r al Mulūsi Iraq 87 F4
Bi'r al Munbaṭiḥ well Syria 81 D2
Bi'r al Qaṭrānī well Egypt 86 B5
Bi'r al Ubbayiḍ well Egypt 86 B6
Birandozero Rus. Fed. 38 H3
Bi'r an Nuṣf well Egypt see Bi'r an Nuṣṣ
Bi'r an Nuṣṣ well Egypt 86 B5
Bir Anzarane W. Sahara 92 B2
Birao Cent. Afr. Rep. 94 C2
Bi'r ar Rābiyah well Egypt 86 B5
Biratnagar Nepal 79 F4
Bi'r aṭ Ṭarfāwī well Libya 86 B5
Bi'r Başīrī well Syria 81 C2
Bi'r Bayḍā' well Egypt 81 B4
Bi'r Baylī well Egypt 86 B5
Bîr Beïda well Egypt see Bi'r Bayḍā'
Bi'r Buṭaymān Syria 87 E3
Birch r. Canada 117 H3
Birch Hills Canada 117 J4
Birch Island Canada 116 G5
Birch Lake N.W.T. Canada 116 G2
Birch Lake Ont. Canada 117 M5
Birch Lake Sask. Canada 117 I4
Birch Mountains Canada 116 H3
Birch River U.S.A. 130 E4
Birch Run U.S.A. 130 D2
Bircot Eth. 94 E3
Birdaard Neth. 48 F1
Bîr Dignâsh well Egypt see Bi'r Diqnāsh
Bi'r Diqnāsh well Egypt 86 B5
Bird Island N. Mariana Is see Farallon de Medinilla
Birdseye U.S.A. 125 H2
Birdsville Australia 107 B5
Birecik Turkey 86 E3
Bîr el 'Abd Egypt see Bi'r al 'Abd
Bir el Arbi well Alg. 53 I6
Bîr el Istabl well Egypt see Bi'r Iṣṭabl
Bîr el Khamsa well Egypt see Bi'r al Khamsah
Bîr el Nuṣṣ well Egypt see Bi'r an Nuṣṣ
Bîr el Obeiyid well Egypt see Bi'r al Ubbayiḍ
Bîr el Qaṭrâni well Egypt see Bi'r al Qaṭrānī
Bîr el Râbia well Egypt see Bi'r ar Rābiyah
Birendranagar Nepal see Surkhet
Bir en Natrûn well Sudan 82 C6
Bireun Indon. 67 B6
Bi'r Fāḍil well Saudi Arabia 84 C6
Bi'r Fajr well Saudi Arabia 86 E5
Bi'r Fu'ād well Egypt 86 B5
Bîr Gifgâfa well Egypt see Bi'r al Jifjāfah
Bi'r Ḥajal well Syria 81 D2
Birhan mt. Eth. 94 D2
Bi'r Ḥasanah well Egypt 81 A4
Bi'r Ḥayzān well Saudi Arabia 86 E6
Bi'r Ibn Hirmās Saudi Arabia see Al Bi'r
Bir Ibn Juhayyim Saudi Arabia 84 C6
Birigüi Brazil 141 A3
Bīrīn Syria 81 C2
Bi'r Iṣṭabl well Egypt 86 B5
Bīrjand Iran 84 E3
Bi'r Jubnī well Libya 86 B5
Birkât Hamad well Iraq 87 G5
Birkenfeld Germany 49 H5
Birkenhead U.K. 44 D5
Birkirkara Malta 54 F7
Birksgate Range hills Australia 105 E6
Bîrlad Romania see Bârlad
Bi'r Laḥfān well Egypt 81 A4
Birlik Kazakh. see Brlik
Birmal reg. Afgh. 85 H3
Birmingham U.K. 45 F6
Birmingham U.S.A. 129 C5
Bîr Mogreïn Mauritania 92 B2
Bi'r Muḥaymid al Wazwaz well Syria 81 D2
Bi'r Nāḥid oasis Egypt 86 C5
Birnin-Gwari Nigeria 92 D3
Birnin-Kebbi Nigeria 92 D3
Birnin Konni Niger 92 D3
Birobidzhan Rus. Fed. 70 D2
Bi'r Qaṣīr as Sirr well Egypt 86 B5
Birr Rep. of Ireland 47 E4
Bi'r Rawḍ Sālim well Egypt 81 A4
Birrie r. Australia 108 C2
Birrindudu Australia 104 E4
Bîr Rôd Sâlim well Egypt see Bi'r Rawḍ Sālim
Birsay U.K. 46 F1
Bi'r Shalatayn Egypt 82 E5
Bîr Shalatein Egypt see Bi'r Shalatayn
Birsk Rus. Fed. 37 R4
Birstall U.K. 45 F6
Birstein Germany 49 J4
Bi'r Ṭalḥah well Saudi Arabia 84 B6
Birthday Mountain hill Australia 106 C2
Birtle Canada 117 K5
Biru China 72 B2
Birur India 80 B3
Bi'r Usaylīlah well Saudi Arabia 84 B6
Biruxiong China see Biru
Biržai Lith. 41 N8
Bisa India 66 A1
Bisa i. Indon. 65 H7
Bisalpur India 78 D3
Bisau India 78 C3
Bisbee U.S.A. 123 F7
Biscay, Bay of sea France/Spain 52 B4
Biscay Abyssal Plain sea feature N. Atlantic Ocean 144 H3
Biscayne National Park U.S.A. 129 D7
Biscoe Islands Antarctica 148 L2
Biscotasi Lake Canada 118 E5
Biscotasing Canada 118 E5
Bisezhai China 72 D4
Bishan China 72 E2
Bishbek Kyrg. see Bishkek
Bishenpur India see Bishnupur

Bishkek Kyrg. 76 D3
Capital of Kyrgyzstan.

Bishnath India 72 B3
Bishnupur Manipur India 79 H4
Bishnupur W. Bengal India 79 F5
Bisho S. Africa 97 H7
Bishop U.S.A. 124 D3
Bishop Auckland U.K. 44 F4
Bishop Lake Canada 116 G1
Bishop's Stortford U.K. 45 H7
Bishopville U.S.A. 129 D5

Bishrī, Jabal hills Syria 81 D2
Bishui Heilong. China 70 A1
Bishui Henan China see Biyang
Biskra Alg. 50 F5
Bislig Phil. 65 H5
▶Bismarck U.S.A. 126 C2
State capital of North Dakota.
Bismarck Archipelago is P.N.G. 65 L7
Bismarck Range mts P.N.G. 65 K7
Bismarck Sea P.N.G. 65 L7
Bismark (Altmark) Germany 49 L2
Bismil Turkey 87 F3
Bismo Norway 40 F6
Bison U.S.A. 126 C2
Bispgården Sweden 40 J5
Bispingen Germany 49 K1
Bissa, Djebel mt. Alg. 53 G5
Bissamcuttak India 80 D2
▶Bissau Guinea-Bissau 92 B3
Capital of Guinea-Bissau.
Bissaula Nigeria 92 E4
Bissett Canada 117 M5
Bistcho Lake Canada 116 G3
Bistrița Romania 55 K1
Bistrița r. Romania 55 L1
Bitburg Germany 48 G5
Bitche France 49 H5
Bithur India 78 E4
Bithynia reg. Turkey 55 M4
Bitkine Chad 93 E3
Bitlis Turkey 87 F3
Bitola Macedonia 55 I4
Bitolj Macedonia see Bitola
Bitonto Italy 54 G4
Bitrān, Jabal hill Saudi Arabia 84 B6
Bitra Par reef India 80 B4
Bitter Creek r. U.S.A. 125 I2
Bitterfeld Germany 49 M3
Bitterfontein S. Africa 96 D6
Bitter Lakes Egypt 86 D5
Bitterroot r. U.S.A. 122 E3
Bitterroot Range mts U.S.A. 122 E3
Bitterwater U.S.A. 124 C3
Bittkau Germany 49 L2
Bitung Indon. 65 H6
Biu Nigeria 92 E3
Biwa-ko l. Japan 71 D6
Biwmaris U.K. see Beaumaris
Biyang China 73 G1
Bīye K'obē Eth. 94 E2
Biysk Rus. Fed. 68 F2
Bizana S. Africa 97 I6
Bizerta Tunisia see Bizerte
Bizerte Tunisia 54 C6
Bīzhanābād Iran 84 E5
▶Bjargtangar hd Iceland 40 [inset]
Most westerly point of Europe.
Bjästa Sweden 40 K5
Bjelovar Croatia 54 G2
Bjerkvik Norway 40 J2
Bjerringbro Denmark 41 F8
Bjørgan Norway 40 G5
Björkliden Sweden 40 K2
Björklinge Sweden 41 J6
Bjorli Norway 40 F5
Björna Sweden 40 K5
Björneborg Fin. see Pori
▶Bjørnøya i. Arctic Ocean 60 C2
Part of Norway.
Bjurholm Sweden 40 K5
Bla Mali 92 C3
Black r. Man. Canada 117 L5
Black r. Ont. Canada 118 E4
Black r. AR U.S.A. 127 F5
Black r. AR U.S.A. 127 F5
Black r. AZ U.S.A. 125 H5
Black r. Vietnam 66 D2
Blackadder Water r. U.K. 46 G5
Blackall Australia 106 D5
Blackbear r. Canada 117 N4
Black Birch Lake Canada 117 J3
Black Bourton U.K. 45 F7
Blackbull Australia 106 C3
Blackburn U.K. 44 E5
Blackbutt Australia 108 F1
Black Butte mt. U.S.A. 124 B2
Black Butte Lake U.S.A. 124 B2
Black Canyon gorge U.S.A. 125 F4
Black Canyon of the Gunnison National Park U.S.A. 125 J2
Black Combe hill U.K. 44 D4
Black Creek watercourse U.S.A. 125 I4
Black Donald Lake Canada 131 G1
Blackdown Tableland National Park Australia 106 E4
Blackduck U.S.A. 126 E2
Blackfalds Canada 116 H4
Blackfoot U.S.A. 122 E4
Black Foot r. U.S.A. 122 E3
Black Forest mts Germany 43 L7
Black Hill hill U.K. 44 F5
Black Hills SD U.S.A. 120 G3
Black Hills SD U.S.A. 122 G3
Black Island Canada 117 L5
Black Lake Canada 117 J3
Black Lake l. Canada 117 J3
Black Lake l. U.S.A. 130 C1
Black Mesa mt. U.S.A. 125 I5
Black Mesa ridge U.S.A. 125 H3
Black Mountain Pak. 85 I3
Black Mountain hill U.K. 45 D7
Black Mountain AK U.S.A. 114 B3
Black Mountain CA U.S.A. 124 E4
Black Mountain KY U.S.A. 130 D5
Black Mountain NM U.S.A. 125 I5
Black Mountains hills U.K. 45 D7
Black Mountains U.S.A. 125 F4
Black Nossob watercourse Namibia 96 D2
Black Pagoda India see Konarka
Blackpool U.K. 44 D5
Black Range mts U.S.A. 125 I5
Black River MI U.S.A. 130 D1
Black River NY U.S.A. 131 H1
Black River Falls U.S.A. 126 F2
Black Rock hill Jordan see 'Unāb, Jabal al
Black Rock Desert U.S.A. 122 D4
Blacksburg U.S.A. 130 E5
Black Sea Asia/Europe 39 H8
Blacks Fork r. U.S.A. 122 F4
Blackshear U.S.A. 129 D6
Blacksod Bay Rep. of Ireland 47 B3
Black Springs U.S.A. 124 D2
Blackstairs Mountains hills Rep. of Ireland 47 F5
Blackstone U.S.A. 131 F5
Black Sugarloaf mt. Australia 108 E3
Black Tickle Canada 119 L3
Blackville Australia 108 E3
Blackwater Australia 106 E4
Blackwater Rep. of Ireland 47 F5
Blackwater r. Rep. of Ireland 47 E5
Blackwater r. Rep. of Ireland/U.K. 47 F3
Blackwater watercourse U.S.A. 127 C5
Blackwater Lake Canada 116 F2
Blackwater Reservoir U.K. 46 E4
Blackwood r. Australia 105 A8
Blackwood National Park Australia 106 D4
Bladensburg National Park Australia 106 C4
Blaenavon U.K. 45 D7
Blagodarnyy Rus. Fed. 87 F1
Blagoevgrad Bulg. 55 J3
Blagoveshchensk Amurskaya Oblast' Rus. Fed. 70 B2
Blagoveshchensk Respublika Bashkortostan Rus. Fed. 37 R4
Blaikiston, Mount Canada 116 H5
Blaine Lake Canada 117 J4
Blair U.S.A. 126 D3
Blair Athol Australia 106 D4
Blair Atholl U.K. 46 F4
Blairgowrie U.K. 46 F4
Blairsden U.S.A. 124 C2
Blairsville U.S.A. 129 D5
Blakang Mati, Pulau i. Sing. see Sentosa
Blakely U.S.A. 129 C6
Blakeney U.K. 45 I6
▶Blanc, Mont mt. France/Italy 52 H4
5th highest mountain in Europe.
Blanca, Bahía b. Arg. 140 D5
Blanca, Sierra mt. U.S.A. 123 G6
Blanca Peak U.S.A. 123 G5
Blanche, Lake salt flat S.A. Australia 107 B6
Blanche, Lake salt flat W.A. Australia 104 C5
Blanchester U.S.A. 130 D4
Blanc Nez, Cap c. France 48 B4
Blanco r. Bol. 138 F6
Blanco U.S.A. 125 J3
Blanco, Cape U.S.A. 122 B4
Blanc-Sablon Canada 119 K4
Bland r. Australia 108 C4
Bland U.S.A. 130 E5
Blanda r. Iceland 40 [inset]
Blandford Forum U.K. 45 E8
Blanding U.S.A. 125 I3
Blanes Spain 53 H3
Blangah, Telok Sing. 67 [inset]
Blangkejeren Indon. 67 B7
Blangpidie Indon. 67 B7
Blankenberge Belgium 48 D3
Blankenheim Germany 48 G4
Blanquilla, Isla i. Venez. 138 F1
Blansko Czech Rep. 43 P6
Blantyre Malawi 95 D5
Blarney Rep. of Ireland 47 D6
Blaufelden Germany 49 J5
Blåviksjön Sweden 40 K4
Blaye France 52 D4
Blayney Australia 108 D4
Blaze, Point Australia 104 E3
Bleckede Germany 49 K1
Bleilochtalsperre resr Germany 49 L4
Blenheim Canada 130 E2
Blenheim N.Z. 109 D5
Blenheim Palace tourist site U.K. 45 F7
Blerick Neth. 48 G3
Blessington Lakes Rep. of Ireland 47 F4
Bletchley U.K. 45 G6
Blida Alg. 53 H5
Blies r. Germany 49 H5
Bligh Water b. Fiji 103 H3
Blind River Canada 118 E5
Bliss U.S.A. 122 E4
Blissfield U.S.A. 130 D3
Blitta Togo 92 D4
Blocher U.S.A. 130 C4
Block Island U.S.A. 131 J3
Block Island Sound sea chan. U.S.A. 131 J3
Bloemfontein S. Africa 97 H5
Bloemhof S. Africa 97 G4
Bloemhof Dam S. Africa 97 G4
Bloemhof Dam Nature Reserve S. Africa 97 G4
Blomberg Germany 49 J3
Blönduós Iceland 40 [inset]
Blongas Indon. 104 B2
Bloods Range mts Australia 105 E6
Bloodsworth Island U.S.A. 131 G4
Bloodvein r. Canada 117 L5
Bloody Foreland pt Rep. of Ireland 47 D2
Bloomer U.S.A. 126 F2
Bloomfield Canada 131 G2
Bloomfield IA U.S.A. 126 E3
Bloomfield IN U.S.A. 130 B4
Bloomfield MO U.S.A. 127 F4
Bloomfield NM U.S.A. 125 J3
Blooming Prairie U.S.A. 126 E3
Bloomington IL U.S.A. 126 F3
Bloomington IN U.S.A. 130 B4
Bloomington MN U.S.A. 126 E2
Bloomsburg U.S.A. 131 G3
Blossburg U.S.A. 131 G3
Blosseville Kyst coastal area Greenland 115 P3
Blouberg S. Africa 97 I2
Blouberg Nature Reserve S. Africa 97 I2
Blountstown U.S.A. 129 C6
Blountville U.S.A. 130 D5
Bloxham U.K. 45 F6
Blue r. Canada 116 D3
Blue watercourse U.S.A. 125 I5
Blue Bell Knoll mt. U.S.A. 125 H2
Blueberry r. Canada 116 F3
Blue Diamond U.S.A. 125 F3
Blue Earth U.S.A. 126 E3
Bluefield VA U.S.A. 128 D4
Bluefield WV U.S.A. 130 E5
Bluefields Nicaragua 133 H6
Blue Hills Turks and Caicos Is 129 F8
Blue Knob hill U.S.A. 131 F3
Blue Mesa Reservoir U.S.A. 125 J2
Blue Mountain hill Canada 119 K4
Blue Mountain India 79 H5
Blue Mountain Lake U.S.A. 131 H2
Blue Mountain Pass Lesotho 97 H5
Blue Mountains Australia 108 D4
Blue Mountains U.S.A. 122 D3
Blue Mountains National Park Australia 108 E4
Blue Nile r. Eth./Sudan 82 D6
also known as Ābay Wenz (Ethiopia), Bahr el Azraq (Sudan)
Bluenose Lake Canada 114 G3
Blue Ridge GA U.S.A. 129 C5
Blue Ridge VA U.S.A. 130 F5
Blue Ridge mts U.S.A. 130 E5
Blue Stack hill Rep. of Ireland 47 D3
Blue Stack Mts hills Rep. of Ireland 47 D3
Bluestone Lake U.S.A. 130 E5
Bluewater U.S.A. 125 J4
Bluff N.Z. 109 B8
Bluff U.S.A. 125 I3
Bluffdale U.S.A. 125 H1
Bluff Island Hong Kong China 73 [inset]
Bluff Knoll mt. Australia 105 B8
Bluffton IN U.S.A. 130 C3
Bluffton OH U.S.A. 130 D3
Blumenau Brazil 141 A4
Blustry Mountain Canada 122 C2
Blyde River Canyon Nature Reserve S. Africa 97 J3
Blyth Canada 130 E2
Blyth England U.K. 44 F3
Blyth England U.K. 44 F5
Blythe U.S.A. 125 F5
Blytheville U.S.A. 127 F5
Bø Norway 41 F7
Bo Sierra Leone 92 B4
Boa Esperança Brazil 141 B3
Bo'ai Henan China 73 G1
Bo'ai Yunnan China 72 E4
Boali Cent. Afr. Rep. 94 B3
Boalsert Neth. see Bolsward
Boane Moz. 97 K4
Boa Nova Brazil 141 C1
Boardman U.S.A. 130 E3
Boatlaname Botswana 97 G2
Boa Viagem Brazil 139 K5
Boa Vista Brazil 138 F3
Boa Vista i. Cape Verde 92 [inset]
Bobadah Australia 108 C4
Bobai China 73 F4
Bobaomby, Tanjona c. Madag. 95 E5
Bobbili India 80 D2
Bobcaygeon Canada 131 F1
Bobo-Dioulasso Burkina 92 C3
Bobotov Kuk mt. Serb. and Mont. see Durmitor
Bobriki Rus. Fed. see Novomoskovsk
Bobrinets Ukr. see Bobrynets'
Bobrov Rus. Fed. 39 I6
Bobrovitsa Ukr. see Bobrovytsya
Bobrovytsya Ukr. 39 F6
Bobruysk Belarus see Babruysk
Bobrynets' Ukr. 39 G6
Bobs Lake Canada 131 G1
Bobuk Sudan 82 D7
Bobures Venez. 138 D2
Boby mt. Madag. 95 E6
Boca de Macareo Venez. 138 F2
Boca do Acre Brazil 138 E5
Boca do Jari Brazil 139 H4
Bocaiúva Brazil 141 C2
Bocaranga Cent. Afr. Rep. 94 B3
Boca Raton U.S.A. 129 D7
Bocas del Toro Panama 133 H7
Bochnia Poland 43 R6
Bocholt Germany 48 G3
Bochum Germany 49 H3
Bochum S. Africa 97 I2
Bockenem Germany 49 K2
Bocoio Angola 95 B5
Bocoyna Mex. 123 G8
Boda Cent. Afr. Rep. 94 B3
Bodalla Australia 108 E6
Bodallin Australia 105 B7
Bodaybo Rus. Fed. 61 M4
Boddam U.K. 46 H3
Bode r. Germany 49 L3
Bodega Head hd U.S.A. 124 B2
Bodélé reg. Chad 93 E3
Boden Sweden 40 L4
Bodenham U.K. 45 E6
Bodensee l. Germany/Switz. see Constance, Lake
Bodenteich Germany 49 K2
Bodenwerder Germany 49 J3
Bodie U.S.A. 124 D2
Bodinayakkanur India 80 C4
Bodmin U.K. 45 C8
Bodmin Moor moorland U.K. 45 C8
Bodø Norway 40 I3
Bodoquena Brazil 139 G7
Bodoquena, Serra da hills Brazil 140 E2
Bodrum Turkey 55 L6
Bodträskfors Sweden 40 L3
Boechout Belgium 48 E3
Boende Dem. Rep. Congo 93 F5
Boerne U.S.A. 127 D6
Boeuf r. U.S.A. 127 F6
Boffa Guinea 92 B3
Bogalay Myanmar see Bogale
Bogale Myanmar 66 A3
Bogale r. Myanmar 66 A4
Bogalusa U.S.A. 127 F6
Bogan r. Australia 108 C2
Bogandé Burkina 92 C3
Bogan Gate Australia 108 C4
Bogani Nani Wartabone National Park Indon. 65 G6
Boğazlıyan Turkey 86 D3
Bogcang Zangbo r. China 79 F3
Bogda Shan mts China 76 G3
Boggabilla Australia 108 E2
Boggabri Australia 108 E3
Boggeragh Mts hills Rep. of Ireland 47 C5
Boghar Alg. 53 H6
Boghari Alg. see Ksar el Boukhari
Bognor Regis U.K. 45 G8
Bogodukhov Ukr. see Bohodukhiv
Bog of Allen reg. Rep. of Ireland 47 E4
Bogong, Mount Australia 108 C6
Bogopol' Rus. Fed. 70 D3
Bogor Indon. 64 D8
Bogoroditsk Rus. Fed. 39 H5
Bogorodsk Rus. Fed. 38 I4
Bogorodskoye Khabarovskiy Kray Rus. Fed. 70 F1
Bogorodskoye Kirovskaya Oblast' Rus. Fed. 38 K4
▶Bogotá Col. 138 D3
Capital of Colombia and 5th most populous city in South America.
Bogotol Rus. Fed. 60 J4
Bogoyavlenskoye Rus. Fed. see Pervomayskiy
Bogra Bangl. 79 G4
Boguchany Rus. Fed. 61 K4
Boguchar Rus. Fed. 39 I6
Bogué Mauritania 92 B3
Bo Hai g. China 69 L5
Bohain-en-Vermandois France 48 D5
Bohai Wan b. China 62 D4
Bohemia reg. Czech Rep. 43 N6
Bohemian Forest mts Germany see Böhmer Wald
Böhlen Germany 49 M3
Bohlokong S. Africa 97 I5
Böhme r. Germany 49 J2
Böhmer Wald mts Germany 49 M5
Bohmte Germany 49 I2
Bohodukhiv Ukr. 39 G6
Bohol i. Phil. 65 G5
Bohol Sea Phil. 65 G5
Böhöt Mongolia 69 J3
Bohu China 76 G3
Boiaçu Brazil 138 F4
Boichoko S. Africa 96 F5
Boigu Island Australia 65 K8
Boikhutso S. Africa 97 H4
Boileau, Cape Australia 104 C4
Boim Brazil 139 G4
Boipeba, Ilha i. Brazil 141 D1
Bois r. Brazil 141 A2
Bois Blanc Island U.S.A. 128 C2
▶Boise U.S.A. 122 D4
State capital of Idaho.
Boise City U.S.A. 127 C4
Boissevain Canada 117 K5
Boitumelong S. Africa 97 G4
Boizenburg Germany 49 K1
Bojd Iran 84 E3
Bojnūrd Iran 84 E2
Bokaak atoll Marshall Is see Taongi
Bokajan India 79 H4
Bokaro India 79 F5
Bokaro Reservoir India 79 F5
Bokatola Dem. Rep. Congo 94 B4
Boké Guinea 92 B3
Bokele Dem. Rep. Congo 94 C4
Bokhara r. Australia 108 C2
Bo Kheo Cambodia see Bâ Kêv
Boknafjorden sea chan. Norway 41 D7
Bokoko Dem. Rep. Congo 94 C3
Bokoro Chad 93 E3
Bokovskaya Rus. Fed. 39 I6
Bokspits S. Africa 96 E4
Boktor Rus. Fed. 70 E2
Bokurdak Turkm. see Bakhardok
Bol Chad 93 E3
Bolaiti Dem. Rep. Congo 93 F5
Bolama Guinea-Bissau 92 B3
Bolangir India 80 D1
Bolan Pass Pak. 85 G4
Bolbec France 52 E2
Bole China 76 F3
Bole Ghana 92 C4
Boleko Dem. Rep. Congo 94 B4
Bolen Rus. Fed. 70 D2
Bolgar Rus. Fed. 39 K5
Bolgatanga Ghana 92 C3
Bolgrad Ukr. see Bolhrad
Bolhrad Ukr. 55 M2
Boli China 70 C3
Bolia Dem. Rep. Congo 94 B4
Boliden Sweden 40 L4
Bolingbrook U.S.A. 130 A3
Bolintin-Vale Romania 55 K2
Bolivar Peru 138 C5
Bolivar NY U.S.A. 131 F2
Bolivar TN U.S.A. 127 F5
Bolívar, Pico mt. Venez. 138 D2
Bolivia Cuba 129 E8
▶Bolivia country S. America 138 E7
5th largest country in South America.
south america 9, 136–137
Bolkhov Rus. Fed. 39 H5
Bollène France 52 G4
Bollnäs Sweden 41 J6
Bollon Australia 108 C2
Bollstabruk Sweden 40 J5
Bolmen l. Sweden 41 H8
Bolobo Dem. Rep. Congo 94 B4
Bologna Italy 54 D2
Bolognesi Peru 138 D5
Bologoye Rus. Fed. 38 G4
Bolokanang S. Africa 97 G5
Bolomba Dem. Rep. Congo 94 B3
Bolon' Rus. Fed. see Achan
Bolovens, Phouphieng plat. Laos 66 D4
Bolpur India 79 F5
Bolsena, Lago di l. Italy 54 D3
Bol'shakovo Rus. Fed. 41 L9
Bol'shaya Chernigovka Rus. Fed. 37 Q5
Bol'shaya Glushitsa Rus. Fed. 39 K5
Bol'shaya Imandra, Ozero l. Rus. Fed. 40 R3
Bol'shaya Martinovka Rus. Fed. 39 I7
Bol'shaya Tsarevshchina Rus. Fed. see Volzhskiy
Bol'shenarymskoye Kazakh. 76 F2
Bol'shevik, Ostrov i. Rus. Fed. 61 L2
Bol'shezemel'skaya Tundra lowland Rus. Fed. 38 L2
Bol'shiye Barsuki, Peski des. Kazakh. 76 A2
Bol'shiye Chirki Rus. Fed. 38 J3
Bol'shiye Kozly Rus. Fed. 38 H2
Bol'shoy Aluy r. Rus. Fed. 61 Q3
Bol'shoy Begichev, Ostrov i. Rus. Fed. 149 E2
Bol'shoye Murashkino Rus. Fed. 38 J5
Bol'shoy Irgiz r. Rus. Fed. 39 J6
Bol'shoy Kamen' Rus. Fed. 70 D4
Bol'shoy Kavkaz mts Asia/Europe see Caucasus
Bol'shoy Kundysh r. Rus. Fed. 38 J4
Bol'shoy Lyakhovskiy, Ostrov i. Rus. Fed. 61 P2
Bol'shoy Tokmak Kyrg. see Tokmok
Bol'shoy Tokmak Ukr. see Tokmak
Bolsward Neth. 48 F1
Bolton Canada 130 F2
Bolton U.K. 44 E5
Bolu Turkey 55 N4
Boluntay China 79 H1
Boluo China 73 G4
Bolus Head hd Rep. of Ireland 47 B6
Bolvadin Turkey 55 N5
Bolzano Italy 54 D1
Boma Dem. Rep. Congo 95 B4
Bomaderry Australia 108 E5
Bombala Australia 108 D6
Bombay India see Mumbai
Bombay Beach U.S.A. 125 F5
Bomberai, Semenanjung pen. Indon. 65 I7
Bomboma Dem. Rep. Congo 94 B3
Bom Comércio Brazil 138 E5
Bomdila India 79 H4
Bomi China 72 B2
Bomili Dem. Rep. Congo 94 C3
Bom Jardim Brazil 141 D1
Bom Jardim de Goiás Brazil 141 A2
Bom Jesus Brazil 141 A5
Bom Jesus da Gurgueia, Serra do hills Brazil 139 J5
Bom Jesus da Lapa Brazil 141 C1
Bom Jesus do Norte Brazil 141 C3
Bømlo i. Norway 41 D7
Bomokandi r. Dem. Rep. Congo 94 C3
Bom Retiro Brazil 141 A4
Bom Sucesso Brazil 141 B3
Bon, Cap c. Tunisia 54 D6
Bon, Ko i. Thai. 67 B5
Bona Alg. see Annaba
Bona, Mount U.S.A. 116 A2
Bonāb Iran 84 B2
Bon Air U.S.A. 131 G5
Bonaire i. Neth. Antilles 133 K6
Bonanza Peak U.S.A. 122 C2
Bonaparte Archipelago is Australia 104 D3
Bonaparte Lake Canada 116 F5
Bonar Bridge U.K. 46 E3
Bonavista Canada 119 L4
Bonavista Bay Canada 119 L4
Bonchester Bridge U.K. 46 G5
Bondo Dem. Rep. Congo 94 C3
Bondokodi Indon. 64 F8
Bondoukou Côte d'Ivoire 92 C4
Bonduel U.S.A. 130 A1
Bondyuzhskiy Rus. Fed. see Mendeleyevsk
Bône Alg. see Annaba
Bone, Teluk b. Indon. 65 G8
Bönen Germany 49 H3
Bonerate, Kepulauan is Indon. 104 C1
Bo'ness U.K. 46 F4
▶Bonete, Cerro mt. Arg. 140 C3
3rd highest mountain in South America.
Bonga Eth. 94 D3
Bongaigaon India 79 G4
Bongandanga Dem. Rep. Congo 94 C3
Bongani S. Africa 96 F5
Bongao Phil. 64 F5
Bongba China 78 E2
Bong Co l. China 79 G3
Bongo, Massif des mts Cent. Afr. Rep. 94 C3
Bongo, Serra do mts Angola 95 B4
Bongolava mts Madag. 95 E5
Bongor Chad 93 E3
Bông Sơn Vietnam 67 E4
Bonham U.S.A. 127 D5
Bonheiden Belgium 48 E3
Boni Mali 92 C3
Bonifacio Corsica France 52 I6
Bonifacio, Bocche di strait France/Italy see Bonifacio, Strait of
Bonifacio, Bouches de strait France/Italy see Bonifacio, Strait of
Bonifacio, Strait of France/Italy 52 I6
▶Bonin Islands Japan 71 F8
Part of Japan.
▶Bonn Germany 48 H4
Former capital of Germany.
Bonna Germany see Bonn
Bonnåsjøen Norway 40 I3
Bonners Ferry U.S.A. 122 D2
Bonnet, Lac du resr Canada 117 M5
Bonneville France 52 H3
Bonneville Salt Flats U.S.A. 125 G1
Bonnières-sur-Seine France 48 B5
Bonnie Rock Australia 105 B7
Bonnieville U.S.A. 130 C5
Bonnyrigg U.K. 46 F5
Bonnyville Canada 117 I4
Bonobono Phil. 64 F5
Bonom Mhai mt. Vietnam 67 D5
Bononia Italy see Bologna
Bonorva Sardinia Italy 54 C4
Bonshaw Australia 108 E2
Bontebok National Park S. Africa 96 E8
Bonthe Sierra Leone 92 B4
Bontoc Phil. 73 I5
Bontosunggu Indon. 64 F8
Bontrug S. Africa 97 G7
Bonvouloir Islands P.N.G. 106 E1
Bonwapitse Botswana 97 H2
Boo, Kepulauan is Indon. 65 H7
Book Cliffs ridge U.S.A. 125 I2
Booker U.S.A. 127 C4
Boolba Australia 108 D2
Booligal Australia 108 B4
Boomer U.S.A. 130 E4
Boomi Australia 108 D2
Boon U.S.A. 130 C1
Boonah Australia 108 F1
Boone CO U.S.A. 123 G5
Boone IA U.S.A. 126 E3
Boone NC U.S.A. 128 D4
Boone Lake U.S.A. 130 D5
Boones Mill U.S.A. 130 F5
Booneville AR U.S.A. 127 E5
Booneville KY U.S.A. 130 D5
Booneville MS U.S.A. 127 F5
Böön Tsagaan Nuur salt l. Mongolia 76 I2
Boonville CA U.S.A. 124 B2
Boonville IN U.S.A. 130 B4
Boonville MO U.S.A. 126 E4
Boonville NY U.S.A. 131 H2
Boorabin National Park Australia 105 C7
Boorama Somalia 94 E3
Booroorban Australia 108 B5
Boorowa Australia 108 D5
Boort Australia 108 A6
Boothby, Cape Antarctica 148 D2
Boothia, Gulf of Canada 115 J3
Boothia Peninsula Canada 115 I2
Bootle U.K. 44 E5
Booué Gabon 94 B4
Boppard Germany 49 H4
Boqê China 79 G3
Boqueirão, Serra do hills Brazil 139 J6
Bor Czech Rep. 49 M5
Bor Rus. Fed. 38 J4
Bor Sudan 93 G4
Bor Turkey 86 D3
Bor Serb. and Mont. 55 J2
Boraha, Nosy i. Madag. 95 F5
Borah Peak U.S.A. 122 E3
Borai India 80 D1
Borakalalo Nature Reserve S. Africa 97 H3
Boran Kazakh. see Buran
Boraphet, Bung l. Thai. 66 C4
Boraphet, Nong l. Thai. see Boraphet, Bung
Borås Sweden 41 H8
Borasambar India 80 D1
Borāzjān Iran 84 C4
Borba Brazil 139 G4
Borba China 72 C1
Borborema, Planalto da plat. Brazil 139 K5
Borchen Germany 49 I3
Borçka Turkey 87 F2
Bor Dağı mt. Turkey 55 M6
Bordeaux France 52 D4
Borden Island Canada 115 G2
Borden Peninsula Canada 115 J2
Border Ranges National Park Australia 108 F2
Borðeyri Iceland 40 [inset]
Bordj Bou Arréridj Alg. 53 I5
Bordj Bounaama Alg. 53 G6
Bordj Flye Ste-Marie Alg. 92 C2
Bordj Messaouda Alg. 50 F5
Bordj Mokhtar Alg. 92 D2
Bordj Omar Driss Alg. see Bordj Omer Driss
Bordj Omer Driss Alg. 92 D2
Boreas Abyssal Plain sea feature Arctic Ocean 149 H1
Borel r. Canada 119 H2
Borgå Fin. see Porvoo
Borgarfjörður Iceland 40 [inset]
Borgarnes Iceland 40 [inset]
Børgefjell Nasjonalpark nat. park Norway 40 H4
Borger U.S.A. 127 C5
Borgholm Sweden 41 J8
Borgne, Lake b. U.S.A. 127 F6
Borgo San Lorenzo Italy 54 D3
Bori India 80 C1
Bori r. India 78 C5
Borikhan Laos 66 C3
Borislav Ukr. see Boryslav
Borisoglebsk Rus. Fed. 39 I6
Borisov Belarus see Barysaw
Borisovka Rus. Fed. 39 H6
Borispol' Ukr. see Boryspil'
Bo River Post Sudan 93 F4
Borja Peru 138 C4
Borken Germany 48 G3
Borkenes Norway 40 J2
Borkovskaya Rus. Fed. 38 K2
Borkum Germany 48 G1
Borkum i. Germany 48 G1
Borlänge Sweden 41 I6
Borlaug Norway 41 E6
Borlu Turkey 55 M5
Borna Germany 49 M3
Born-Berge hill Germany 49 K3
Borndiep sea chan. Neth. 48 F1
Borne Neth. 48 G2
▶Borneo i. Asia 64 E6
Largest island in Asia and 3rd in the world.
asia 56–57
world 12–13
Bornholm county Denmark 149 H3
Bornholm i. Denmark 41 I9
Bornova Turkey 55 L5
Borodino Rus. Fed. 60 J3
Borodinskoye Rus. Fed. 41 P6
Borogontsy Rus. Fed. 61 O3
Borohoro Shan mts China 76 F3
Borok-Sulezhskiy Rus. Fed. 38 H4
Boromo Burkina 92 C3
Boron U.S.A. 124 E4
Borondi India 80 D2
Boroughbridge U.K. 44 F4
Borovichi Rus. Fed. 38 G4
Borovoy Kirovskaya Oblast' Rus. Fed. 38 K4
Borovoy Respublika Kareliya Rus. Fed. 40 R4
Borovoy Respublika Komi Rus. Fed. 38 L3
Borpeta India see Barpeta
Borrisokane Rep. of Ireland 47 D5
Borroloola Australia 106 B3
Børsa Norway 40 G5
Borșa Romania 39 E7
Borshchiv Ukr. 39 E6
Borshchovochnyy Khrebet mts Rus. Fed. 69 J3
Bortala China see Bole
Borton U.S.A. 130 B4
Borūjen Iran 84 C4
Borūjerd Iran 84 C3
Borun Iran 84 E3
Borve U.K. 46 C3
Boryslav Ukr. 39 D6
Boryspil' Ukr. 39 F6
Borzna Ukr. 39 G6
Borzya Rus. Fed. 69 L2
Bosanska Dubica Bos.-Herz. 54 G2
Bosanska Gradiška Bos.-Herz. 54 G2
Bosanska Krupa Bos.-Herz. 54 G2
Bosanski Novi Bos.-Herz. 54 G2
Bosansko Grahovo Bos.-Herz. 54 G2
Boscawen Island Tonga see Niuatoputapu
Bose China 72 E4
Boshof S. Africa 97 G5
Boshruyeh Iran 84 E3
Bosna i Hercegovina country Europe see Bosnia-Herzegovina
Bosna Saray Bos.-Herz. see Sarajevo
▶Bosnia-Herzegovina country Europe 54 G2
europe 5, 34–35
Bosobogolo Pan salt pan Botswana 96 F3
Bosobolo Dem. Rep. Congo 94 B3
Bōsō-hantō pen. Japan 71 F6
Bosporus strait Turkey 55 M4
Bossaga Turkm. see Basaga
Bossangoa Cent. Afr. Rep. 94 B3
Bossembélé Cent. Afr. Rep. 94 B3
Bossier City U.S.A. 127 E5
Bossiesvlei Namibia 96 C3
Bossut, Cape Australia 104 C4
Bostan China 79 F1
Bostān Iran 84 B4
Bostan Pak. 85 G4
Bostāneh, Ra's-e pt Iran 84 D5
Bosten Hu l. China 76 G3
Boston U.K. 45 G6

▶Boston U.S.A. 131 J2
State capital of Massachusetts.
Boston Mountains U.S.A. 127 E5
Boston Spa U.K. 44 F5
Boswell U.S.A. 130 B3
Botad India 78 B5
Botany Bay Australia 108 E4
Botev mt. Bulg. 55 K3
Botevgrad Bulg. 55 J3
Bothaville S. Africa 97 H4
Bothnia, Gulf of Fin./Sweden 41 K6
Bothwell Canada 130 E2
Botkins U.S.A. 130 C3
Botlikh Rus. Fed. 87 G2
Botoşani Romania 39 E7
Botou China 69 L5
Bô Trach Vietnam 66 D3
Botshabelo S. Africa 97 H5
▶Botswana country Africa 95 C6
africa 7, 90–91
Botte Donato, Monte mt. Italy 54 G5
Bottenviken g. Fin./Sweden see Bothnia, Gulf of
Bottesford U.K. 44 G5
Bottrop Germany 48 G3
Botucatu Brazil 141 A3
Botuporã Brazil 141 C1
Botwood Canada 119 L4
Bouaflé Côte d'Ivoire 92 C4
Bouaké Côte d'Ivoire 92 C4
Bouar Cent. Afr. Rep. 94 B3
Bouârfa Morocco 50 D5
Bouba Ndjida, Parc National de nat. park Cameroon 93 E4
Bouca Cent. Afr. Rep. 94 B3
Boucaut Bay Australia 104 F3
Bouchain France 48 D4
Bouctouche Canada 119 I5
Boudh India 80 E1
Bougaa Alg. 53 I5
Bougainville, Cape Australia 104 D3
Bougainville Island P.N.G. 102 F2
Bougainville Reef Australia 106 D2
Boughessa Mali 92 D3
Bougie Alg. see Bejaïa
Bougouni Mali 92 C3
Bougtob Alg. 50 E5
Bouillon Belgium 48 F5
Bouira Alg. 53 H5
Bou Izakarn Morocco 92 C2
Boujdour W. Sahara 92 B2
Boulder Australia 105 C7
Boulder CO U.S.A. 122 G4
Boulder MT U.S.A. 122 E3
Boulder UT U.S.A. 125 H3
Boulder Canyon gorge U.S.A. 125 F3
Boulder City U.S.A. 125 F4
Boulevard U.S.A. 124 E5
Boulia Australia 106 B4
Boulogne France see Boulogne-sur-Mer
Boulogne-Billancourt France 48 C6
Boulogne-sur-Mer France 48 B4
Boumerdes Alg. 53 H5
Bouna Côte d'Ivoire 92 C4
Bou Naceur, Jbel mt. Morocco 50 D5
Boû Nâga Mauritania 92 B3
Boundary Mountains U.S.A. 131 J1
Boundary Peak U.S.A. 124 D3
Boundiali Côte d'Ivoire 92 C4
Boundji Congo 94 B4
Boun Nua Laos 66 C2
Bountiful U.S.A. 125 H1
Bounty Islands N.Z. 103 H6
Bounty Trough sea feature S. Pacific Ocean 146 H9
Bourail New Caledonia 103 G4
Bourbon reg. France see Bourbonnais
Bourbon terr. Indian Ocean see Réunion
Bourbon U.S.A. 130 B3
Bourbonnais reg. France 52 F3
Bourem Mali 92 C3
Bouressa Mali see Boughessa
Bourg-Achard France 45 H9
Bourganeuf France 52 E4
Bourg-en-Bresse France 52 G3
Bourges France 52 F3
Bourget Canada 131 H1
Bourgogne reg. France see Burgundy
Bourgogne, Canal de France 52 G3
Bourke Australia 108 B3
Bourne U.K. 45 G6
Bournemouth U.K. 45 F8
Bourtoutou Chad 93 F3
Bou Saâda Alg. 53 I6
Bou Salem Tunisia 54 C6
Bouse U.S.A. 125 F5
Bouse Wash watercourse U.S.A. 125 F4
Boussu Belgium 48 D4
Boutilimit Mauritania 92 B3
Bouvet Island terr. S. Atlantic Ocean see Bouvetøya
▶Bouvetøya terr. S. Atlantic Ocean 144 I9
Dependency of Norway.
Bouy France 48 E5
Bova Marina Italy 54 F6
Bovenden Germany 49 J3
Bow r. Alta Canada 117 I5
Bowa China see Muli
Bowbells U.S.A. 126 C1
Bowden U.S.A. 130 F4
Bowditch atoll Tokelau see Fakaofo
Bowen Australia 106 E4
Bowen, Mount Australia 108 D6
Bowenville Australia 108 E1
Bowers Ridge sea feature Bering Sea 146 H2
Bowie Australia 106 D4
Bowie AZ U.S.A. 125 I5
Bowie TX U.S.A. 127 D5
Bow Island Canada 117 I5
Bowkan Iran 84 B2
Bowling Green KY U.S.A. 130 B5
Bowling Green MO U.S.A. 126 F4
Bowling Green OH U.S.A. 130 D3
Bowling Green VA U.S.A. 131 G4
Bowling Green Bay National Park Australia 106 D3
Bowman U.S.A. 126 C2
Bowman, Mount Canada 122 C2
Bowman Island Antarctica 148 F2
Bowman Peninsula Antarctica 148 L2
Bowmore U.K. 46 C5
Bowo China see Bomi
Bowral Australia 108 E5
Bowser Lake Canada 116 D3
Boxberg Germany 49 J5
Box Elder U.S.A. 126 C2
Box Elder r. U.S.A. 126 C2
Boxtel Neth. 48 F3
Boyabat Turkey 86 D2
Boyana tourist site Bulg. 55 J3
Boyang China 73 H2
Boyd r. Australia 108 F2
Boyd Lagoon salt flat Australia 105 D6
Boyd Lake Canada 117 K2
Boydton U.S.A. 131 F5
Boyers U.S.A. 130 F3
Boykins U.S.A. 131 G5
Boyle Canada 117 H4
Boyle Rep. of Ireland 47 D4
Boyne r. Rep. of Ireland 47 F4
Boyne City U.S.A. 130 C1
Boysen Reservoir U.S.A. 122 F4
Boysun Uzbek. see Baysun
Boyuibe Bol. 138 F8
Böyük Qafqaz mts Asia/Europe see Caucasus
▶Bozcaada i. Turkey 55 L5
Most westerly point of Asia.
Bozdağ mt. Turkey 55 L5
Bozdağ mt. Turkey 81 C1
Boz Dağları mts Turkey 55 L5
Bozdoğan Turkey 55 M6
Bozeat U.K. 45 G6
Bozeman U.S.A. 122 F3
Bozen Italy see Bolzano
Bozhou China 73 G1
Bozoum Cent. Afr. Rep. 94 B3
Bozova Turkey 86 E3
Bozqūsh, Kūh-e mts Iran 84 B2
Bozüyük Turkey 55 N5
Bozyazı Turkey 81 A1
Bra Italy 54 B2
Brač i. Croatia 54 G3
Bracadale U.K. 46 C3
Bracadale, Loch b. U.K. 46 C3
Bracara Port. see Braga
Bracciano, Lago di l. Italy 54 E3
Bracebridge Canada 130 F1
Brachet, Lac au l. Canada 119 H4
Bräcke Sweden 40 I5
Brackenheim Germany 49 J5
Brackettville U.S.A. 127 C6
Bracknell U.K. 45 G7
Bradano r. Italy 54 G4
Bradenton U.S.A. 129 D7
Bradford Canada 130 F1
Bradford U.K. 44 F5
Bradford OH U.S.A. 130 C3
Bradford PA U.S.A. 131 F3
Bradley U.S.A. 130 B3
Brady U.S.A. 127 D6
Brady Glacier U.S.A. 116 B3
Brae U.K. 46 [inset]
Braemar U.K. 46 F3
Braga Port. 53 B3
Bragado Arg. 140 D5
Bragança Brazil 139 I4
Bragança Port. 53 C3
Bragança Paulista Brazil 141 B3
Brahin Belarus 39 F6
Brahlstorf Germany 49 K1
Brahmanbaria Bangl. 79 G5
Brahmapur India 80 E2
Brahmaputra r. Asia 79 H4
also known as Dihang (India) or Jamuna (Bangladesh) or Siang (India) or Yarlung Zangbo (China)
Brahmaur India 78 D2
Brăila Romania 55 L2
Braine France 48 D5
Braine-le-Comte Belgium 48 E4
Brainerd U.S.A. 126 E2
Braintree U.K. 45 H7
Braithwaite Point Australia 104 F2
Brak r. S. Africa 97 I2
Brake (Unterweser) Germany 49 I1
Brakel Belgium 48 D4
Brakel Germany 49 J3
Brakwater Namibia 96 C2
Bramfield Australia 105 F8
Bramming Denmark 41 F9
Brämön i. Sweden 40 J5
Brampton Canada 130 F2
Brampton England U.K. 44 E4
Brampton England U.K. 45 I6
Bramsche Germany 49 I2
Bramwell Australia 106 C2
Brancaster U.K. 45 H6
Branch Canada 119 L5
Branco r. Brazil 138 F4
Brandberg mt. Namibia 95 B6
Brandbu Norway 41 G6
Brande Denmark 41 F9
Brandenburg Germany 49 M2
Brandenburg land Germany 49 N2
Brandenburg U.S.A. 130 B5
Brandfort S. Africa 97 H5
Brandis Germany 49 N3
Brandon Canada 117 L5
Brandon U.K. 45 H6
Brandon MS U.S.A. 127 F5
Brandon VT U.S.A. 131 I2
Brandon Head hd Rep. of Ireland 47 B5
Brandon Mountain hill Rep. of Ireland 47 B5
Brandvlei S. Africa 96 E6
Braniewo Poland 43 Q3
Bransfield Strait Antarctica 148 L2
Branson U.S.A. 127 C4
Brantford Canada 130 E2
Branxton Australia 108 E4
Bras d'Or Lake Canada 119 J5
Brasil country S. America see Brazil
Brasil, Planalto do plat. Brazil 139 J7
Brasileia Brazil 138 E6
▶Brasília Brazil 141 B1
Capital of Brazil.
Brasília de Minas Brazil 141 B2
Braslav Belarus see Braslaw
Braslaw Belarus 41 O9
Braşov Romania 55 K2
Brassey, Mount Australia 105 F5
Brassey Range hills Australia 105 C6
Brasstown Bald mt. U.S.A. 129 D5
▶Bratislava Slovakia 43 P6
Capital of Slovakia.
Bratsk Rus. Fed. 68 I1
Bratskoye Vodokhranilishche resr Rus. Fed. 68 I1
Brattleboro U.S.A. 131 I2
Braunau am Inn Austria 43 N6
Braunfels Germany 49 I4
Braunlage Germany 49 K3
Braunsbedra Germany 49 L3
Braunschweig Germany 49 K2
Brava i. Cape Verde 92 [inset]
Brave U.S.A. 130 E4
Bråviken inlet Sweden 41 J7
Bravo, Cerro mt. Bol. 138 F7
Bravo del Norte, Río r. Mex./U.S.A. 123 G7 see Rio Grande
Brawley U.S.A. 125 F5
Bray Rep. of Ireland 47 F4
Bray Island Canada 115 K3
Brazeau r. Canada 116 H4
Brazeau, Mount Canada 116 G4
▶Brazil country S. America 139 G5
Largest country in South America and 5th in the world. Most populous country in South America and 5th in the world.
south america 9, 136–137
Brazil U.S.A. 130 B4
Brazil Basin sea feature S. Atlantic Ocean 144 G7
Brazos r. U.S.A. 127 E6
▶Brazzaville Congo 95 B4
Capital of Congo.
Brčko Bos.-Herz. 54 H2
Bré Rep. of Ireland see Bray
Breadalbane Australia 106 B4
Breaksea Sound inlet N.Z. 109 A7
Bream Bay N.Z. 109 E2
Brechfa U.K. 45 C7
Brechin U.K. 46 G4
Brecht Belgium 48 E3
Breckenridge MI U.S.A. 130 C2
Breckenridge MN U.S.A. 126 D2
Breckenridge TX U.S.A. 127 D5
Břeclav Czech Rep. 43 P6
Brecon U.K. 45 D7
Brecon Beacons reg. U.K. 45 D7
Brecon Beacons National Park U.K. 45 D7
Breda Neth. 48 E3
Bredasdorp S. Africa 96 E8
Bredbo Australia 108 D5
Breddin Germany 49 M2
Bredevoort Neth. 48 G3
Bredviken Sweden 40 I3
Bree Belgium 48 F3
Breed U.S.A. 130 A1
Bregenz Austria 43 L7
Breiðafjörður b. Iceland 40 [inset]
Breiðdalsvík Iceland 40 [inset]
Breidenbach Germany 49 I4
Breien U.S.A. 126 C2
Breitenfelde Germany 49 K1
Breitengüßbach Germany 49 K5
Breiter Luzinsee l. Germany 49 N1
Breivikbotn Norway 40 M1
Breizh reg. France see Brittany
Brejo Velho Brazil 141 C1
Brekstad Norway 40 F5
Bremen Germany 49 I1
Bremen land Germany 49 I1
Bremen IN U.S.A. 130 B3
Bremen OH U.S.A. 130 D4
Bremer Bay Australia 105 B8
Bremerhaven Germany 49 I1
Bremer Range hills Australia 105 C8
Bremersdorp Swaziland see Manzini
Bremervörde Germany 49 J1
Bremm Germany 48 H4
Brenham U.S.A. 127 D6
Brenna Norway 40 H4
Brennero, Passo di pass Austria/Italy see Brenner Pass
Brennerpaß pass Austria/Italy see Brenner Pass
Brenner Pass Austria/Italy 54 D1
Brentwood U.K. 45 H7
Brescia Italy 54 D2
Breslau Poland see Wrocław
Bresle r. France 48 B4
Brésolles, Lac l. Canada 119 H3
Bressanone Italy 54 D1
Bressay i. U.K. 46 [inset]
Bressuire France 52 D3
Brest Belarus 41 M10
Brest France 52 B2
Brest-Litovsk Belarus see Brest
Bretagne reg. France see Brittany
Breteuil France 48 C5
Brétigny-sur-Orge France 48 C6
Breton Canada 116 H4
Breton Sound b. U.S.A. 127 F6
Brett, Cape N.Z. 109 E2
Bretten Germany 49 I5
Bretton U.K. 44 E5
Breueh, Pulau i. Indon. 67 A6
Brevard U.S.A. 129 D5
Breves Brazil 139 H4
Brewarrina Australia 108 C2
Brewer U.S.A. 128 G2
Brewster NE U.S.A. 126 D3
Brewster OH U.S.A. 130 E3
Brewster, Kap c. Greenland see Kangikajik
Brewster, Lake imp. l. Australia 108 B4
Brewton U.S.A. 129 C6
Breyten S. Africa 97 I4
Breytovo Rus. Fed. 38 H4
Brezhnev Rus. Fed. see Naberezhnyye Chelny
Brezno Slovakia 43 Q6
Brezovo Polje hill Croatia 54 G2
Bria Cent. Afr. Rep. 94 C3
Briançon France 52 H4
Brian Head mt. U.S.A. 125 G3
Bribbaree Australia 108 C5
Bribie Island Australia 108 F1
Briceni Moldova 39 E6
Brichany Moldova see Briceni
Brichen' Moldova see Briceni
Bridgend U.K. 45 D7
Bridge of Orchy U.K. 46 E4
Bridgeport CA U.S.A. 124 D2
Bridgeport CT U.S.A. 131 I3
Bridgeport IL U.S.A. 130 B4
Bridgeport NE U.S.A. 126 C3
Bridger Peak U.S.A. 122 G4
Bridgeton U.S.A. 131 H4
Bridgetown Australia 105 B8
▶Bridgetown Barbados 133 M6
Capital of Barbados.
Bridgetown Canada 119 I5
Bridgeville U.S.A. 131 H4
Bridgewater Canada 119 I5
Bridgewater U.S.A. 131 H2
Bridgnorth U.K. 45 E6
Bridgton U.S.A. 131 J1
Bridgwater U.K. 45 D7
Bridgwater Bay U.K. 45 D7
Bridlington U.K. 44 G4
Bridlington Bay U.K. 44 G4
Bridport Australia 107 [inset]
Bridport U.K. 45 E8
Brie reg. France 52 F2
Brie-Comte-Robert France 48 C6
Brieg Poland see Brzeg
Briery Knob mt. U.S.A. 130 E4
Brig Switz. 52 H3
Brigg U.K. 44 G5
Brigham City U.S.A. 122 E4
Brightlingsea U.K. 45 I7
Brighton Canada 131 G1
Brighton U.K. 45 G8
Brighton CO U.S.A. 122 G5
Brighton MI U.S.A. 130 D2
Brighton NY U.S.A. 131 G2
Brighton WV U.S.A. 130 D4
Brignoles France 52 H5
Brikama Gambia 92 B3
Brillion U.S.A. 130 A1
Brilon Germany 49 I3
Brindisi Italy 54 G4
Brinkley U.S.A. 127 F5
Brion, Île i. Canada 119 J5
Brioude France 52 F4
Brisay Canada 119 H3
▶Brisbane Australia 108 F1
State capital of Queensland and 3rd most populous city in Oceania.
Brisbane Ranges National Park Australia 108 B6
Bristol U.K. 45 E7
Bristol CT U.S.A. 131 I3
Bristol FL U.S.A. 129 C6
Bristol NH U.S.A. 131 J2
Bristol RI U.S.A. 131 J3
Bristol TN U.S.A. 130 D5
Bristol VT U.S.A. 131 I1
Bristol Bay U.S.A. 114 B4
Bristol Channel est. U.K. 45 C7
Bristol Lake U.S.A. 125 F4
Britannia Island New Caledonia see Maré
British Antarctic Territory reg. Antarctica 148 L2
British Columbia prov. Canada 116 F5
British Empire Range mts Canada 115 J1
British Guiana country S. America see Guyana
British Honduras country Central America see Belize
▶British Indian Ocean Territory terr. Indian Ocean 145 M6
United Kingdom Overseas Territory.
British Solomon Islands country S. Pacific Ocean see Solomon Islands
Brito Godins Angola see Kiwaba N'zogi
Brits S. Africa 97 H3
Britstown S. Africa 96 F6
Brittany reg. France 52 C2
Britton U.S.A. 126 D2
Brive-la-Gaillarde France 52 E4
Briviesca Spain 53 E2
Brixham U.K. 45 D8
Brixia Italy see Brescia
Brlik Kazakh. 76 D3
Brno Czech Rep. 43 P6
Broach India see Bharuch
Broad r. U.S.A. 129 D5
Broadalbin U.S.A. 131 H2
Broad Arrow Australia 105 C7
Broadback r. Canada 118 F4
Broad Bay U.K. see Tuath, Loch a'
Broadford Australia 108 B6
Broadford Rep. of Ireland 47 D5
Broadford U.K. 46 D3
Broad Law hill U.K. 46 F5
Broadmere Australia 106 A3
Broad Peak China/Jammu and Kashmir 85 J3
Broad Sound sea chan. Australia 106 E4
Broadstairs U.K. 45 I7
Broadus U.S.A. 122 G3
Broadview Canada 117 K5
Broadway U.S.A. 131 F4
Broadwood N.Z. 109 D2
Brochet Canada 117 K3
Brochet, Lac l. Canada 117 K3
Brocken mt. Germany 49 K3
Brockman, Mount Australia 104 B5
Brockport NY U.S.A. 131 G2
Brockport PA U.S.A. 131 F3
Brockton U.S.A. 131 J2
Brockville Canada 131 H1
Brockway U.S.A. 131 F3
Brodeur Peninsula Canada 115 J2
Brodhead U.S.A. 130 C5
Brodick U.K. 46 D5
Brodnica Poland 43 Q4
Brody Ukr. 39 E6
Broken Arrow U.S.A. 127 E4
Broken Bay Australia 108 E4
Broken Bow NE U.S.A. 126 D3
Broken Bow OK U.S.A. 127 E5
Brokenhead r. Canada 117 L5
Broken Hill Australia 107 C6
Broken Hill Zambia see Kabwe
Broken Plateau sea feature Indian Ocean 145 O8
Brokopondo Suriname 139 G2
Brokopondo Stuwmeer resr Suriname see Professor van Blommestein Meer
Bromberg Poland see Bydgoszcz
Brome Germany 49 K2
Bromsgrove U.K. 45 E6
Brønderslev Denmark 41 F8
Brønnøysund Norway 40 H4
Bronson FL U.S.A. 129 D6
Bronson MI U.S.A. 130 C3
Brooke U.K. 45 I6
Brookfield U.S.A. 130 A2
Brookhaven U.S.A. 127 F6
Brookings OR U.S.A. 122 B4
Brookings SD U.S.A. 126 D2
Brookline U.S.A. 131 J2
Brooklyn U.S.A. 130 C2
Brooklyn Park U.S.A. 126 E2
Brookneal U.S.A. 131 F5
Brooks Canada 117 I5
Brooks Brook Canada 116 C2
Brooks Range mts U.S.A. 114 D3
Brookston U.S.A. 130 B3
Brooksville FL U.S.A. 129 D6
Brooksville KY U.S.A. 130 C4
Brookton Australia 105 B8
Brookville IN U.S.A. 130 C4
Brookville PA U.S.A. 130 F3
Brookville Lake U.S.A. 130 C4
Broom, Loch inlet U.K. 46 D3
Broome Australia 104 C4
Brora U.K. 46 F2
Brora r. U.K. 46 F2
Brösarp Sweden 41 I9
Brosna r. Rep. of Ireland 47 E4
Brosville U.S.A. 130 F5
Brothers is India 67 A5
Brough U.K. 44 E4
Brough Ness pt U.K. 46 G2
Broughshane U.K. 47 F3
Broughton Island Canada see Qikiqtarjuaq
Broughton Islands Australia 108 F4
Brovary Ukr. 39 F6
Brovinia Australia 107 E5
Brovst Denmark 41 F8
Brown City U.S.A. 130 D2
Brown Deer U.S.A. 130 B2
Browne Range hills Australia 105 D6
Brownfield U.S.A. 127 C5
Browning U.S.A. 122 E2
Brown Mountain U.S.A. 124 E4
Brownstown U.S.A. 130 B4
Brownsville KY U.S.A. 130 B5
Brownsville PA U.S.A. 130 F3
Brownsville TN U.S.A. 127 F5
Brownsville TX U.S.A. 127 D7
Brownwood U.S.A. 127 D6
Browse Island Australia 104 C3
Bruay-la-Bussière France 48 C4
Bruce Peninsula Canada 130 E1
Bruce Peninsula National Park Canada 130 E1
Bruce Rock Australia 105 B7
Bruchsal Germany 49 I5
Brück Germany 49 M2
Bruck an der Mur Austria 43 O7
Brue r. U.K. 45 E7
Bruges Belgium see Brugge
Brugge Belgium 48 D3
Brühl Baden-Württemberg Germany 49 I5
Brühl Nordrhein-Westfalen Germany 48 G4
Bruin KY U.S.A. 130 D4
Bruin PA U.S.A. 130 F3
Bruin Point mt. U.S.A. 125 H2
Bruint India 79 I3
Brūk, Wādī el watercourse Egypt see Burūk, Wādī al
Brukkaros Namibia 96 D3
Brûlé Canada 116 G4
Brûlé, Lac l. Canada 119 J3
Brûly Belgium 48 E5
Brumado Brazil 141 C1
Brumath France 49 H6
Brumunddal Norway 41 G6
Brunau Germany 49 L2
Brundisium Italy see Brindisi
Bruneau U.S.A. 122 E4
▶Brunei country Asia 64 E6
asia 6, 58–59
Brunei Brunei see Bandar Seri Begawan
Brunette Downs Australia 106 A3
Brunflo Sweden 40 I5
Brunico Italy 54 D1
Brünn Czech Rep. see Brno
Brunner, Lake N.Z. 109 C6
Bruno Canada 117 J4
Brunswick Germany see Braunschweig
Brunswick GA U.S.A. 129 D6
Brunswick MD U.S.A. 131 G4
Brunswick ME U.S.A. 131 K2
Brunswick, Península de pen. Chile 140 B8
Brunswick Bay Australia 104 D3
Brunswick Lake Canada 118 E4
Bruntál Czech Rep. 43 P6
Brunt Ice Shelf Antarctica 148 B2
Bruntville S. Africa 97 J5
Bruny Island Australia 107 [inset]
Brusa Turkey see Bursa
Brusenets Rus. Fed. 38 I3
Brushton U.S.A. 131 H1
Brusque Brazil 141 A4
Brussel Belgium see Brussels
▶Brussels Belgium 48 E4
Capital of Belgium.
Bruthen Australia 108 C6
Bruxelles Belgium see Brussels
Bruzual Venez. 138 E2
Bryan OH U.S.A. 130 C3
Bryan TX U.S.A. 127 D6
Bryan, Mount hill Australia 107 B7
Bryan Coast Antarctica 148 L2
Bryansk Rus. Fed. 39 G5
Bryanskoye Rus. Fed. 87 G1
Bryant Pond U.S.A. 131 J1
Bryantsburg U.S.A. 130 C4
Bryce Canyon National Park U.S.A. 125 G3
Bryce Mountain U.S.A. 125 I5
Brynbuga U.K. see Usk
Bryne Norway 41 D7
Bryukhovetskaya Rus. Fed. 39 H7
Brzeg Poland 43 P5
Brześć nad Bugiem Belarus see Brest
Bua r. Malawi 95 D5
Bu'aale Somalia 94 E3
Buala Solomon Is 103 F2
Bu'ayj well Saudi Arabia 84 C5
Būbīyān Island Kuwait 84 C4
Bucak Turkey 55 N6
Bucaramanga Col. 138 D2
Buccaneer Archipelago is Australia 104 C4
Buchanan Liberia 92 B4
Buchanan MI U.S.A. 130 B3
Buchanan VA U.S.A. 130 F5
Buchanan, Lake salt flat Australia 106 D4
Buchan Gulf Canada 115 K2
▶Bucharest Romania 55 L2
Capital of Romania.
Büchen Germany 49 K1
Buchen (Odenwald) Germany 49 J5
Buchholz Germany 49 M1
Bucholz in der Nordheide Germany 49 J1
Buchon, Point U.S.A. 124 C4
Buchy France 48 B5
Bucin, Pasul pass Romania 55 K1
Buckambool Mountain hill Australia 108 B3
Bückeburg Germany 49 J2
Bücken Germany 49 J2
Buckeye U.S.A. 125 G5
Buckhannon U.S.A. 130 E4
Buckhaven U.K. 46 F4
Buckhorn Lake Canada 131 F1
Buckie U.K. 46 G3
Buckingham U.K. 45 G6
Buckingham U.S.A. 131 F5
Buckingham Bay Australia 63 F9
Buckland Tableland reg. Australia 106 E5
Buckleboo Australia 105 G8
Buckle Island Antarctica 148 H2
Buckley watercourse Australia 106 B4
Buckley Bay Antarctica 148 G2
Bucklin U.S.A. 126 D4
Buckskin Mountains U.S.A. 125 G4
Bucks Mountain U.S.A. 124 C2
Bucksport U.S.A. 119 H5
Bückwitz Germany 49 M2
Bucureşti Romania see Bucharest
Bucyrus U.S.A. 130 D3
Buda-Kashalyova Belarus 39 F5
Budalin Myanmar 66 A2
▶Budapest Hungary 55 H1
Capital of Hungary.
Budaun India 78 D3
Budawang National Park Australia 108 E5
Budda Australia 108 B3
Budd Coast Antarctica 148 F2
Buddusò Sardinia Italy 54 C4
Bude U.K. 45 C8
Bude U.S.A. 127 F6
Budennovsk Rus. Fed. 87 G1
Buderim Australia 108 F1
Būding Iran 84 E5
Büdingen Germany 49 J4
Budīyah, Jabal hills Egypt 81 A5
Budongquan China 79 H2
Budoni Sardinia Italy 54 C4
Budū', Sabkhat al salt pan Saudi Arabia 84 C6
Budweis Czech Rep. see České Budějovice
Buenaventura Col. 138 C3
Buena Vista i. N. Mariana Is see Tinian
Buena Vista CO U.S.A. 122 G5
Buena Vista VA U.S.A. 130 F5
Buendia, Embalse de resr Spain 53 E3
▶Buenos Aires Arg. 140 E4
Capital of Argentina. 2nd most populous city in South America.
Buenos Aires, Lago l. Arg./Chile 140 B7
Buerarema Brazil 141 D1
Buet r. Canada 119 H1
Búfalo Mex. 127 B7
Buffalo r. Canada 116 H2
Buffalo KY U.S.A. 130 C5
Buffalo MO U.S.A. 126 E4
Buffalo NY U.S.A. 131 F2
Buffalo OK U.S.A. 127 D4
Buffalo SD U.S.A. 126 C2
Buffalo TX U.S.A. 127 D6
Buffalo WY U.S.A. 122 G3
Buffalo Head Hills Canada 116 G3
Buffalo Head Prairie Canada 116 G3
Buffalo Hump mt. U.S.A. 122 E3
Buffalo Lake Alta Canada 117 H4
Buffalo Lake N.W.T. Canada 116 H2
Buffalo Narrows Canada 117 I4
Buffels watercourse S. Africa 96 C5
Buffels Drift S. Africa 97 H2
Buftea Romania 55 K2
Bug r. Poland 43 S5
Buga Col. 138 C3
Bugaldie Australia 108 D3
Bugdayli Turkm. 84 D2
Buggenhout Belgium 48 E3
Bugojno Bos.-Herz. 54 G2
Bugrino Rus. Fed. 38 K1
Bugsuk i. Phil. 64 F5
Bugt China 70 A2
Bugul'ma Rus. Fed. 37 Q5
Bügür China see Luntai
Buguruslan Rus. Fed. 37 Q5
Būhābād Iran 84 D4
Buhera Zimbabwe 95 D5
Bühl Germany 49 I6
Buhuşi Romania 55 L1
Buick Canada 116 F3
Builth Wells U.K. 45 D6
Bui National Park Ghana 92 C4
Buinsk Rus. Fed. 39 K5
Bu'in Zahrā Iran 84 C3
Buir Nur l. Mongolia 69 L3
Buitepos Namibia 96 D2
Bujanovac Serb. and Mont. 55 I3
▶Bujumbura Burundi 94 C4
Capital of Burundi.
Bukachacha Rus. Fed. 69 L2
Buka Daban mt. China 79 G1
Buka Island P.N.G. 102 F2
Būkand Iran 84 D4
Bukavu Dem. Rep. Congo 94 C4
Bukhara Uzbek. 85 G2
Bukhoro Uzbek. see Bukhara
Bukit Baka - Bukit Raya National Park Indon. 64 E7
Bukit Timah Sing. 67 [inset]
Bukittinggi Indon. 64 C7
Bukkapatnam India 80 C3
Bukoba Tanz. 94 D4
Bükreş Romania see Bucharest
Būl, Kūh-e mt. Iran 84 D4
Bula P.N.G. 65 K8
Bülach Switz. 52 I3
Bulan i. Indon. 67 C7
Bulancak Turkey 86 E2
Bulandshahr India 78 D3
Bulanık Turkey 87 F3
Bulava Rus. Fed. 70 F2
Bulawayo Zimbabwe 95 C6
Buldan Turkey 55 M5
Buldana India see Buldhana
Buldhana India 80 C1
Buleda reg. Pak. 85 F5
Bulembu Swaziland 97 J3
Bulgan Bulgan Mongolia 76 J2
Bulgan Hovd Mongolia see Bürenhayrhan
Bulgar Rus. Fed. see Bolgar
▶Bulgaria country Europe 55 K3
europe 5, 34–35
Bŭlgariya country Europe see Bulgaria

Bulkley Ranges *mts* Canada **116** D4
Bullawarra, Lake *salt flat* Australia **108** A1
Bullen *r.* Canada **117** K1
Buller *r.* N.Z. **109** C5
Buller, Mount Australia **108** C6
Bulleringa National Park Australia **106** C3
Bullfinch Australia **105** B7
Bullhead City U.S.A. **125** F4
Bulli Australia **108** E5
Bullion Mountains U.S.A. **124** E4
Bullo *r.* Australia **104** E3
Bulloo Downs Australia **107** C6
Bulloo Lake *salt flat* Australia **107** C6
Büllsport Namibia **96** C3
Bully Choop Mountain U.S.A. **124** B1
Bulman Australia **104** F3
Bulman Gorge Australia **104** F3
Bulmer Lake Canada **116** F2
Buloh, Pulau *i.* Sing. **67** [inset]
Buloke, Lake *dry lake* Australia **108** A6
Bulolo P.N.G. **65** L8
Bulsar India *see* **Valsad**
Bultfontein S. Africa **97** H5
Bulukumba Indon. **65** G8
Bulun Rus. Fed. **61** N2
Bulungu Dem. Rep. Congo **95** C4
Bulungur Uzbek. **85** G2
Bumba Dem. Rep. Congo **94** C3
Būmbah Libya **86** A4
Bumbah, Khalīj *b.* Libya **86** A4
Bumhkang Myanmar **66** B1
Bumpha Bum *mt.* Myanmar **66** B1
Buna Dem. Rep. Congo **94** B4
Buna Kenya **94** D3
Bunayyān *well* Saudi Arabia **84** C6
Bunazi Tanz. **94** D4
Bunbeg Rep. of Ireland **47** D2
Bunbury Australia **105** A8
Bunclody Rep. of Ireland **47** F5
Buncrana Rep. of Ireland **47** E2
Bunda Tanz. **94** D4
Bundaberg Australia **106** F5
Bundaleer Australia **108** C2
Bundarra Australia **108** E3
Bundi India **78** C4
Bundjalung National Park Australia **108** F2
Bundoran Rep. of Ireland **47** D3
Bunduqiya Sudan **93** G4
Buner *reg.* Pak. **85** I3
Bungalaut, Selat *sea chan.* Indon. **64** B7
Bungay U.K. **45** I6
Bungendore Australia **108** D5
Bunger Hills Antarctica **148** F2
Bungle Bungle National Park Australia *see* **Purnululu National Park**
Bungo-suidō *sea chan.* Japan **71** D6
Bunguran, Kepulauan *is* Indon. *see* **Natuna, Kepulauan**
Bunguran, Pulau *i.* Indon. *see* **Natuna Besar**
Bunia Dem. Rep. Congo **94** D3
Bunianga Dem. Rep. Congo **94** C4
Buningonia *well* Australia **105** C7
Bunji Jammu and Kashmir **78** C2
Bunker Group *atolls* Australia **106** F4
Bunkeya Dem. Rep. Congo **95** C5
Bunnell U.S.A. **129** D6
Bünsum China **79** E3
Bunya Mountains National Park Australia **108** E1
Bünyan Turkey **86** D3
Bunyu *i.* Indon. **64** F6
Buôn Mê Thuôt Vietnam **67** E4
Buorkhaya, Guba *b.* Rus. Fed. **61** O2
Bup *r.* China **79** F3
Buqayq Saudi Arabia *see* **Abqaiq**
Buqbuq Egypt **86** B5
Bura Kenya **94** D4
Buraan Somalia **94** E2
Buram Sudan **93** F3
Buran Kazakh. **76** G2
Buranhaém Brazil **141** C2
Buranhaém *r.* Brazil **141** D2
Burao Somalia **94** E3
Burāq Syria **81** C3
Buray *r.* India **78** C5
Buraydah Saudi Arabia **82** F4
Burbach Germany **49** I4
Burbank U.S.A. **124** D4
Burcher Australia **108** C4
Burdaard Neth. *see* **Birdaard**
Burdalyk Turkm. **85** G2
Burdigala France *see* **Bordeaux**
Burdur Turkey **55** N6
Burdur Gölü *l.* Turkey **55** N6
Burdwan India *see* **Barddhaman**
Burē Eth. **94** D2
Bure *r.* U.K. **45** I6
Bureå Sweden **40** L4
Bureinskiy Khrebet *mts* Rus. Fed. **70** D2
Bürenhayrhan Mongolia **76** H2
Bureya *r.* Rus. Fed. **70** C2
Bureya Range *mts* Rus. Fed. *see* **Bureinskiy Khrebet**
Bureyinskiy Zapovednik *nature res.* Rus. Fed. **70** D2
Burford Canada **130** E2
Burgas Bulg. **55** L3
Burgaw U.S.A. **129** E5
Burg bei Magdeburg Germany **49** L2
Burgbernheim Germany **49** K5
Burgdorf Germany **49** K2
Burgeo Canada **119** K5
Burgersdorp S. Africa **97** H6
Burgersfort S. Africa **97** J3
Burges, Mount *hill* Australia **105** C7
Burgess Hill U.K. **45** G8
Burghaun Germany **49** J4
Burghausen Germany **43** N6
Burghead U.K. **46** F3
Burgh-Haamstede Neth. **48** D3
Burgio, Serra di *hill Sicily* Italy **54** F6
Burglengenfeld Germany **49** M5
Burgos Mex. **127** D7
Burgos Spain **53** E2
Burgstädt Germany **49** M4
Burgsvik Sweden **41** K8
Burgum Neth. *see* **Bergum**
Burgundy *reg.* France **52** G3
Burhan Budai Shan *mts* China **76** H4
Burhaniye Turkey **55** L5
Burhanpur India **78** D5
Burhar-Dhanpuri India **79** E5
Buri Brazil **141** A3
Burias *i.* Phil. **65** G4
Burin Canada **119** L5
Burin Peninsula Canada **119** L5
Buriram Thai. **66** C4
Buritama Brazil **141** A3
Buriti Alegre Brazil **141** A2
Buriti Bravo Brazil **139** J5
Buritirama Brazil **139** J6
Buritis Brazil **141** B1
Burj Pak. **85** G4
Burke U.S.A. **126** D3
Burke Island Antarctica **148** K2
Burke Pass N.Z. *see* **Burkes Pass**
Burkes Pass N.Z. **109** C7
Burkesville U.S.A. **130** C5
Burketown Australia **106** B3
Burkeville U.S.A. **131** F5
▶**Burkina** *country* Africa **92** C3
africa **7, 90–91**
Burkina Faso *country* Africa *see* **Burkina**
Burk's Falls Canada **118** F5
Burley U.S.A. **122** E4
Burlington Canada **130** F2
Burlington *CO* U.S.A. **126** C4
Burlington *IA* U.S.A. **126** F3
Burlington *KS* U.S.A. **126** E4
Burlington *KY* U.S.A. **130** C4
Burlington *VT* U.S.A. **131** I1
Burlington *WI* U.S.A. **130** A2
Burmantovo Rus. Fed. **37** S3
Burnaby Canada **116** F5
Burnet U.S.A. **127** D6
Burney U.S.A. **124** C1
Burney, Monte *vol.* Chile **140** B8
Burnham U.S.A. **131** G3
Burnie Australia **107** [inset]
Burniston U.K. **44** G4
Burnley U.K. **44** E5
Burns U.S.A. **122** D4
Burnside *r.* Canada **114** H3
Burnside U.S.A. **130** C5
Burnside, Lake *salt flat* Australia **105** C6
Burns Junction U.S.A. **122** D4
Burns Lake Canada **116** E4
Burntisland U.K. **46** F4
Burnt Lake Canada *see* **Brûlé, Lac**
Burntwood *r.* Canada **117** L4
Burog Co *l.* China **79** F2
Buron *r.* Canada **119** H2
Burovoy Uzbek. **85** F1
Burqin China **76** G2
Burqu' Jordan **81** D3
Burra Australia **107** B7
Burravoe U.K. **46** [inset]
Burrel Albania **55** I4
Burrel U.S.A. **124** D3
Burren *reg.* Rep. of Ireland **47** C4
Burrendong Reservoir Australia **108** D4
Burren Junction Australia **108** D3
Burrewarra Point Australia **108** E5
Burrinjuck Australia **108** D5
Burrinjuck Reservoir Australia **108** D5
Burro, Serranías del *mts* Mex. **127** C6
Burr Oak Reservoir U.S.A. **130** D4
Burro Creek *watercourse* U.S.A. **125** G4
Burro Peak U.S.A. **125** I5
Burrowa Pine Mountain National Park Australia **108** C6
Burrow Head *hd* U.K. **46** E6
Burrows U.S.A. **130** B3
Burrundie Australia **104** E3
Bursa Turkey **55** M4
Būr Safāga Egypt *see* **Būr Safājah**
Būr Safājah Egypt **82** D4
Būr Sa'īd Egypt *see* **Port Said**
Būr Sa'īd Egypt *see* **Port Said**
Būr Sa'īd *governorate* Egypt *see* **Būr Sa'īd**
Būr Sa'īd *governorate* Egypt **81** A4
Bursinskoye Vodokhranilishche *resr* Rus. Fed. **70** C2
Bürstadt Germany **49** I5
Būr Sudan Sudan *see* **Port Sudan**
Burt Lake U.S.A. **128** C2
Burton U.S.A. **130** D2
Burton, Lac *l.* Canada **118** F3
Burtonport Rep. of Ireland **47** D3
Burton upon Trent U.K. **45** F6
Burträsk Sweden **40** L4
Burt Well Australia **105** F5
Buru *i.* Indon. **65** H7
Burūk, Wādī al *watercourse* Egypt **81** A4
Burullus, Baḥra el *lag.* Egypt *see* **Burullus, Lake**
Burullus, Buḥayrat al *lag.* Egypt *see* **Burullus, Lake**
Burullus, Lake *lag.* Egypt **86** C5
Burultokay China *see* **Fuhai**
Burūn, Ra's *pt* Egypt **81** A4
▶**Burundi** *country* Africa **94** C4
africa **7, 90–91**
Burunniy Rus. Fed. *see* **Tsagan Aman**
Bururi Burundi **94** C4
Burwash Landing Canada **116** B2
Burwick U.K. **46** G2
Buryn' Ukr. **39** G6
Bury St Edmunds U.K. **45** H6
Burzil Pass Jammu and Kashmir **78** C2
Busan S. Korea *see* **Pusan**
Busanga Dem. Rep. Congo **94** C4
Busby U.S.A. **122** G3
Buseire Syria *see* **Al Buşayrah**
Bush *r.* U.K. **47** F2
Būshehr Iran **84** C4
Bushêngcaka China **79** E2
Bushenyi Uganda **94** D4
Bushire Iran *see* **Būshehr**
Bushmills U.K. **47** F2
Bushnell U.S.A. **129** D6
Businga Dem. Rep. Congo **94** C3
Buṣrá ash Shām Syria **81** C3
Busse Rus. Fed. **70** B2
Busselton Australia **105** A8
Bussum Neth. **48** F2
Bustillos, Lago *l.* Mex. **123** G7
Busto Arsizio Italy **54** C2
Buta Dem. Rep. Congo **94** C3
Butare Rwanda **94** C4
Butaritari *atoll* Kiribati **146** H5
Bute Australia **107** B7
Bute *i.* U.K. **46** D5
Butedale Canada **116** D4
Butha Buthe Lesotho **97** I5
Butha Qi China *see* **Zalantun**
Buthidaung Myanmar **66** A2
Butler *AL* U.S.A. **127** F5
Butler *GA* U.S.A. **129** C5
Butler *IN* U.S.A. **130** C3
Butler *KY* U.S.A. **130** C4
Butler *MO* U.S.A. **126** E4
Butler *PA* U.S.A. **130** F3
Butlers Bridge Rep. of Ireland **47** E3
Buton *i.* Indon. **65** G7
Bütow Germany **49** M1
Butte *MT* U.S.A. **122** E3
Butte *NE* U.S.A. **126** D3
Buttelstedt Germany **49** L3
Butterworth Malaysia **67** C6
Butterworth S. Africa **97** I7
Buttes, Sierra *mt.* U.S.A. **124** C2
Buttevant Rep. of Ireland **47** D5
Butt of Lewis *hd* U.K. **46** C2
Button Bay Canada **117** M3
Butuan Phil. **65** H5
Butuo China **72** D3
Buturlinovka Rus. Fed. **39** I6
Butwal Nepal **79** E4
Butzbach Germany **49** I4
Buulobarde Somalia **94** E3
Buur Gaabo Somalia **94** E4
Buurhabaka Somalia **94** E3
Buxar India **79** F4
Buxtehude Germany **49** J1
Buxton U.K. **44** F5
Buy Rus. Fed. **38** I4
Buyant Mongolia **76** I2
Buynaksk Rus. Fed. **87** G2
Büyükçekmece Turkey **86** C2
Büyük Egri Dağ *mt.* Turkey **81** A1
Büyükmenderes *r.* Turkey **55** L6
Buzancy France **48** E5
Buzău Romania **55** L2
Buzdyak Rus. Fed. **37** Q5
Búzi Moz. **95** D5
Büzmeyin Turkm. *see* **Byuzmeyin**
Buzuluk Rus. Fed. **37** Q5
Buzuluk *r.* Rus. Fed. **39** I6
Buzzards Bay U.S.A. **131** J3
Byakar Bhutan *see* **Jakar**
Byala Bulg. **55** K3
Byala Slatina Bulg. **55** J3
Byalynichy Belarus **39** F5
Byarezina *r.* Belarus **39** F5
Byaroza Belarus **41** N10
Byblos *tourist site* Lebanon **81** B2
Bydgoszcz Poland **43** Q4
Byelorussia *country* Europe *see* **Belarus**
Byerazino Belarus **39** F5
Byers U.S.A. **122** G5
Byeshankovichy Belarus **39** F5
Byesville U.S.A. **130** E4
Bygland Norway **41** E7
Bykhaw Belarus **39** F5
Bykhov Belarus *see* **Bykhaw**
Bykle Norway **41** E7
Bykovo Rus. Fed. **39** J6
Bylas U.S.A. **125** H5
Bylot Island Canada **115** K2
Byramgore Reef India **80** A4
Byrd Glacier Antarctica **148** H1
Byrdstown U.S.A. **130** C5
Byrkjelo Norway **41** E6
Byrock Australia **108** C3
Byron U.S.A. **131** J1
Byron, Cape Australia **108** F2
Byron Bay Australia **108** F2
Byron Island Kiribati *see* **Nikunau**
Byrranga, Gory *mts* Rus. Fed. **61** K2
Byske Sweden **40** L4
Byssa Rus. Fed. **70** C1
Byssa *r.* Rus. Fed. **70** C1
Bytom Poland **43** Q5
Bytów Poland **43** P3
Byurgyutli Turkm. **84** D2
Byuzmeyin Turkm. **84** E2
Byzantium Turkey *see* **İstanbul**

C

Ca, Sông *r.* Vietnam **66** D3
Caacupé Para. **140** E3
Caatinga Brazil **141** B2
Caazapá Para. **140** E3
Cabaiguán Cuba **129** E8
Caballas Peru **138** C6
Caballococha Peru **138** D4
Cabanaconde Peru **138** D7
Cabanatuan Phil. **65** G3
Cabano Canada **119** H5
Cabdul Qaadir Somalia **94** E2
Cabeceira Rio Manso Brazil **139** G7
Cabeceiras Brazil **141** B1
Cabeza del Buey Spain **53** D4
Cabezas Bol. **138** F7
Cabimas Venez. **138** D1
Cabinda Angola **95** B4
Cabinda *prov.* Angola **95** B5
Cabinet Inlet Antarctica **148** L2
Cabinet Mountains U.S.A. **122** E2
Cabistra Turkey *see* **Ereğli**
Cabo Frio Brazil **141** C3
Cabo Frio, Ilha do *i.* Brazil **141** C3
Cabonga, Réservoir *resr* Canada **118** F5
Cabool U.S.A. **127** E4
Caboolture Australia **108** F1
Cabo Orange, Parque Nacional de *nat. park* Brazil **139** H3
Cabo Pantoja Peru **138** C4
Cabora Bassa, Lake *resr* Moz. **95** D5
Cabo Raso Arg. **140** C6
Caborca Mex. **123** E7
Cabot Head *hd* Canada **130** E1
Cabot Strait Canada **119** J5
Cabourg France **45** G9
Cabo Verde *country* N. Atlantic Ocean *see* **Cape Verde**
Cabo Verde, Ilhas do *is* N. Atlantic Ocean **92** [inset]
Cabo Yubi Morocco *see* **Tarfaya**
Cabral, Serra do *mts* Brazil **141** B2
Cābrayıl Azer. **87** G3
Cabrera *i.* Spain **53** H4
Cabri Canada **117** I5
Cabullona Mex. **123** F7
Caçador Brazil **141** A4
Çacagoin China *see* **Qagca**
Čačak Serb. and Mont. **55** I3
Caccia, Capo *c. Sardinia* Italy **54** C4
Cacequi Brazil **140** F3
Cáceres Brazil **139** G7
Cáceres Spain **53** C4
Cache Creek Canada **116** F5
Cache Peak U.S.A. **122** E4
Cacheu Guinea-Bissau **92** B3
Cachi, Nevados de *mts* Arg. **140** C2
Cachimbo, Serra do *hills* Brazil **139** H5
Cachoeira Brazil **141** D1
Cachoeira Alta Brazil **141** A2
Cachoeira de Goiás Brazil **141** A2
Cachoeira do Arari Brazil **139** I4
Cachoeiro de Itapemirim Brazil **141** C3
Cacine Guinea-Bissau **92** B3
Caciporé, Cabo *c.* Brazil **139** H3
Cacolo Angola **95** B5
Cacongo Angola **95** B4
Cactus U.S.A. **127** C4
Caçu Brazil **141** A2
Caculé Brazil **141** C1
Čadca Slovakia **43** Q6
Cadereyta Mex. **127** C7
Cadibarrawirracanna, Lake *salt flat* Australia **107** A6
Cadillac Canada **117** J5
Cadillac U.S.A. **130** C1
Cadiz Phil. **65** G4
Cádiz Spain **53** C5
Cadiz *IN* U.S.A. **130** C4
Cadiz *KY* U.S.A. **128** C4
Cadiz *OH* U.S.A. **130** E3
Cádiz, Golfo de *g.* Spain **53** C5
Cadiz Lake U.S.A. **125** F4
Cadomin Canada **116** G4
Cadotte *r.* Canada **116** G3
Cadotte Lake Canada **116** G3
Caen France **52** D2
Caerdydd U.K. *see* **Cardiff**
Caerffili U.K. *see* **Caerphilly**
Caerfyrddin U.K. *see* **Carmarthen**
Caergybi U.K. *see* **Holyhead**
Caernarfon U.K. **45** C5
Caernarfon Bay U.K. **45** C5
Caernarvon U.K. *see* **Caernarfon**
Caerphilly U.K. **45** D7
Caesaraugusta Spain *see* **Zaragoza**
Caesarea Alg. *see* **Cherchell**
Caesarea Cappadociae Turkey *see* **Kayseri**
Caesarea Philippi Syria *see* **Bāniyās**
Caesarodunum France *see* **Tours**
Caesaromagus U.K. *see* **Chelmsford**
Caetité Brazil **141** C1
Cafayate Arg. **140** C3
Cafelândia Brazil **141** A3
Caffa Ukr. *see* **Feodosiya**
Cagayan de Oro Phil. **65** G5
Cagles Mill Lake U.S.A. **130** B4
Cagli Italy **54** E3
Cagliari *Sardinia* Italy **54** C5
Cagliari, Golfo di *b. Sardinia* Italy **54** C5
Cahama Angola **95** B5
Caha Mts *hills* Rep. of Ireland **47** C6
Cahermore Rep. of Ireland **47** B6
Cahersiveen Rep. of Ireland **47** B6
Cahir Rep. of Ireland **47** E5
Cahirciveen Rep. of Ireland *see* **Cahersiveen**
Cahora Bassa, Lago de *resr* Moz. *see* **Cabora Bassa, Lake**
Cahore Point Rep. of Ireland **47** F5
Cahors France **52** E4
Cahuapanas Peru **138** C5
Cahul Moldova **55** M2
Caia Moz. **95** D5
Caiabis, Serra dos *hills* Brazil **139** G6
Caianda Angola **95** C5
Caiapó *r.* Brazil **141** A1
Caiapó, Serra do *mts* Brazil **141** A2
Caiapônia Brazil **141** A2
Caibarién Cuba **129** E8
Cai Bâu, Đao *i.* Vietnam **66** D2
Caicara Venez. **138** E2
Caicos Islands Turks and Caicos Is **133** J4
Caicos Passage Bahamas/Turks and Caicos Is **129** F8
Caidian China **73** G2
Caiguna Australia **105** D8
Caimodorro *mt.* Spain **53** F3
Cainnyigoin China **72** D1
Cains Store U.S.A. **130** C5
Caipe Arg. **140** C2
Caird Coast Antarctica **148** B1
Cairngorm Mountains U.K. **46** F3
Cairnryan U.K. **46** D6
Cairns Australia **106** D3
Cairnsmore of Carsphairn *hill* U.K. **46** E5
▶**Cairo** Egypt **86** C5
Capital of Egypt and most populous city in Africa.
Cairo U.S.A. **129** C6
Caisleán an Bharraigh Rep. of Ireland *see* **Castlebar**
Caiundo Angola **95** B5
Caiwarro Australia **108** B2
Caiyuanzhen China *see* **Shengsi**
Caizi Hu *l.* China **73** H2
Cajamarca Peru **138** C5
Cajati Brazil **141** A4
Cajuru Brazil **141** B3
Çaka'lho China *see* **Yanjing**
Čakovec Croatia **54** G1
Çal *Denizli* Turkey **55** M5
Çal *Hakkâri* Turkey *see* **Çukurca**
Cala S. Africa **97** H6
Calabar Nigeria **92** D4
Calabogie Canada **131** G1
Calabria, Parco Nazionale della *nat. park* Italy **54** G5
Calafat Romania **55** J3
Calagua Mex. **123** F8
Calagurris Spain *see* **Calahorra**
Calahorra Spain **53** F2
Calai Angola **95** B5
Calais France **48** B4
Calais U.S.A. **119** I5
Calalasteo, Sierra de *mts* Arg. **140** C3
Calama Brazil **138** F5
Calama Chile **140** C2
Calamajué Mex. **123** E7
Calamar Col. **138** D1
Calamian Group *is* Phil. **64** F4
Calamocha Spain **53** F3
Calandula Angola **95** B4
Calang Indon. **67** A6
Calanscio Sand Sea *des.* Libya **82** B3
Calapan Phil. **65** G4
Călărași Romania **55** L2
Calatayud Spain **53** F3
Calayan *i.* Phil. **65** G3
Calbayog Phil. **65** G4
Calbe (Saale) Germany **49** L3
Calçoene Brazil **139** H3
Calcutta India *see* **Kolkata**
Caldas da Rainha Port. **53** B4
Caldas Novas Brazil **139** I7
Calden Germany **49** J3
Calder *r.* Canada **116** G1
Caldera Chile **140** B3
Caldervale Australia **106** D5
Caldew *r.* U.K. **44** E4
Caldwell *ID* U.S.A. **122** D4
Caldwell *KS* U.S.A. **127** D4
Caldwell *OH* U.S.A. **130** E4
Caldwell *TX* U.S.A. **127** D6
Caledon *r.* Lesotho/S. Africa **97** H6
Caledon S. Africa **96** D8
Caledon Bay Australia **106** B2
Caledonia Canada **130** F2
Caledonia *admin. div.* U.K. *see* **Scotland**
Caledonia U.S.A. **131** G2
Caleta el Cobre Chile **140** B2
Calexico U.S.A. **125** F5
Calf of Man *i.* Isle of Man **44** C4
Calgary Canada **116** H5
Calhoun U.S.A. **130** B5
Cali Col. **138** C3
Calicut India **80** B4
Caliente U.S.A. **125** F3
California U.S.A. **130** F3
California *state* U.S.A. **123** C4
California, Golfo de *g.* Mex. *see* **California, Gulf of**
California, Gulf of Mex. **123** E7
California Aqueduct *canal* U.S.A. **124** C3
Cälilabad Azer. **87** H3
Calingasta Arg. **140** C4
Calipatria U.S.A. **125** F5
Calistoga U.S.A. **124** B2
Calkiní Mex. **132** F4
Callabonna, Lake *salt flat* Australia **107** C6
Callabonna Creek *watercourse* Australia **107** C6
Callaghan, Mount U.S.A. **124** E2
Callan Rep. of Ireland **47** E5
Callan *r.* U.K. **47** F3
Callander Canada **118** F5
Callander U.K. **46** E4
Callang Phil. **73** I5
Callao Peru **138** C6
Callao U.S.A. **125** G2
Callicoon U.S.A. **131** H3
Calling Lake Canada **116** H4
Callington U.K. **45** C8
Calliope Australia **106** E5
Callipolis Turkey *see* **Gallipoli**
Calmar U.S.A. **126** F3
Caloosahatchee *r.* U.S.A. **129** D7
Caloundra Australia **108** F1
Caltagirone *Sicily* Italy **54** F6
Caltanissetta *Sicily* Italy **54** F6
Calucinga Angola **95** B5
Calulo Angola **95** B4
Calunga Angola **95** B5
Caluquembe Angola **95** B5
Caluula Somalia **94** F2
Caluula, Raas *pt* Somalia **94** F2
Calvert Hills Australia **106** B3
Calvert Island Canada **116** D5
Calvi *Corsica* France **52** I5
Calvià Spain **53** H4
Calvinia S. Africa **96** D6
Calvo, Monte *mt.* Italy **54** F4
Cam *r.* U.K. **45** H6
Camaçari Brazil **141** D1
Camache Reservoir U.S.A. **124** C2
Camachigama *r.* Canada **118** F5
Camacho Mex. **127** C7
Camacuio Angola **95** B5
Camacupa Angola **95** B5
Camagüey Cuba **133** I4
Camagüey, Archipiélago de *is* Cuba **133** I4
Camah, Gunung *mt.* Malaysia **67** C6
Camamu Brazil **141** D1
Camana Peru **138** D7
Camanongue Angola **95** C5
Camapuã Brazil **139** H7
Camaquã Brazil **140** F4
Çamardı Turkey **86** D3
Çamargo Bol. **138** E8
Camargue *reg.* France **52** G5
Camarillo U.S.A. **124** D4
Camarones Arg. **140** C6
Camarones, Bahía *b.* Arg. **140** C6
Camas *r.* U.S.A. **122** E4
Ca Mau Vietnam **67** D5
Cambay India *see* **Khambhat**
Cambay, Gulf of India *see* **Khambhat, Gulf of**
Camberley U.K. **45** G7
▶**Cambodia** *country* Asia **67** D4
asia **6, 58–59**
Camboriú Brazil **141** A4
Camborne U.K. **45** B8
Cambrai France **48** D4
Cambria *admin. div.* U.K. *see* **Wales**
Cambrian Mountains *hills* U.K. **45** D6
Cambridge Canada **130** E2
Cambridge N.Z. **109** E3
Cambridge U.K. **45** H6
Cambridge *MA* U.S.A. **131** J2
Cambridge *MD* U.S.A. **131** G4
Cambridge *MN* U.S.A. **126** E2
Cambridge *NY* U.S.A. **131** I2
Cambridge *OH* U.S.A. **130** E3
Cambridge Bay Canada **115** H3
Cambridge City U.S.A. **130** C4
Cambridge Springs U.S.A. **130** E3
Cambrien, Lac *l.* Canada **119** H2
Cambulo Angola **95** C4
Cambundi-Catembo Angola **95** B5
Cambuquira Brazil **141** B3
Cam Co *l.* China **79** E2
Camden *AL* U.S.A. **129** C5
Camden *AR* U.S.A. **127** E5
Camden *NJ* U.S.A. **131** H4
Camden *NY* U.S.A. **131** H2
Camden *SC* U.S.A. **129** D5
Camdenton U.S.A. **126** E4
Cameia Angola **95** C5
Cameia, Parque Nacional da *nat. park* Angola **95** C5
Cameron *AZ* U.S.A. **125** H4
Cameron *LA* U.S.A. **127** E6
Cameron *MO* U.S.A. **126** E4
Cameron *TX* U.S.A. **127** D6
Cameron Highlands *mts* Malaysia **67** C6
Cameron Hills Canada **116** G3
Cameron Island Canada **115** H2
Cameron Park U.S.A. **124** C2
▶**Cameroon** *country* Africa **92** E4
africa **7, 90–91**
Cameroon, Mount *vol.* Cameroon *see* **Cameroun, Mont**
Cameroun *country* Africa *see* **Cameroon**
Cameroun, Mont *vol.* Cameroon **92** D4
Cametá Brazil **139** I4
Camiña Chile **138** E7
Camiri Bol. **138** F8
Camisea Peru **138** D6
Camocim Brazil **139** J4
Camooweal Australia **106** B3
Camooweal Caves National Park Australia **106** B4
Camorta *i.* India **77** H10
Campana Mex. **127** C7
Campana, Isla *i.* Chile **140** A7
Campania Island Canada **116** D4
Campbell S. Africa **96** F5
Campbell, Cape N.Z. **109** E5
Campbell, Mount *hill* Australia **104** E5
Campbellford Canada **131** G1
Campbell Hill *hill* U.S.A. **130** D3
Campbell Island N.Z. **146** H9
Campbell Lake Canada **117** J2
Campbell Plateau *sea feature* S. Pacific Ocean **146** H9
Campbell Range *hills* Australia **104** D3
Campbell River Canada **116** E5
Campbellsville U.S.A. **130** C5
Campbellton Canada **119** I5
Campbelltown Australia **108** E5
Campbeltown U.K. **46** D5
Campeche Mex. **132** F5
Campeche, Bahía de *g.* Mex. **132** F5
Camperdown Australia **108** A7
Câmpina Romania **55** K2
Campina Grande Brazil **139** K5
Campinas Brazil **141** B3
Campina Verde Brazil **141** A2
Campo Cameroon **92** D4
Campobasso Italy **54** F4
Campo Belo Brazil **141** B3
Campo Belo do Sul Brazil **141** A4
Campo de Diauarum Brazil **139** H6
Campo Florido Brazil **141** A2
Campo Gallo Arg. **140** D3
Campo Grande Brazil **140** F2
Campo Largo Brazil **141** A4
Campo Maior Brazil **139** J4
Campo Maior Port. **53** C4
Campo Mourão Brazil **140** F2
Campos Brazil **141** C3
Campos Altos Brazil **141** B2
Campos Novos Brazil **141** A4
Campos Sales Brazil **139** J5
Campton U.S.A. **130** D5
Câmpulung Romania **55** K2
Câmpulung Moldovenesc Romania **55** K1
Camp Verde U.S.A. **125** H4
Cam Ranh Vietnam **67** E5
Camrose Canada **117** H4
Camrose U.K. **45** B7
Camsell Lake Canada **117** I2
Camsell Portage Canada **117** I3
Camsell Range *mts* Canada **116** F2
Camulodunum U.K. *see* **Colchester**
Çan Turkey **55** L4
Canaan *r.* Canada **119** I5
Canaan U.S.A. **131** I2
Canaan Peak U.S.A. **125** H3
Canabrava Brazil **141** B2
Canacona India **80** B3
▶**Canada** *country* N. America **114** H4
Largest country in North America and 2nd in the world. 3rd most populous country in North America.
north america **9, 112–113**
Canada Basin *sea feature* Arctic Ocean **149** A1
Canadian U.S.A. **127** C5
Canadian *r.* U.S.A. **127** E5
Canadian Abyssal Plain *sea feature* Arctic Ocean **149** A1
Cañadon Grande, Sierra *mts* Arg. **140** C7
Canaima, Parque Nacional *nat. park* Venez. **138** F2
Çanakkale Turkey **55** L4
Çanakkale Boğazı *strait* Turkey *see* **Dardanelles**
Canalejas Arg. **140** C5
Cañamares Spain **53** E3
Canandaigua U.S.A. **131** G2
Cananea Mex. **123** F7
Cananéia Brazil **141** B4
Canápolis Brazil **141** A2
Cañar Ecuador **138** C4
Canarias *terr.* N. Atlantic Ocean *see* **Canary Islands**
Canárias, Ilha das *i.* Brazil **139** J4
Canarias, Islas *terr.* N. Atlantic Ocean *see* **Canary Islands**
▶**Canary Islands** *terr.* N. Atlantic Ocean **92** B2
Autonomous Community of Spain.
africa **7, 90–91**
Canaseraga U.S.A. **131** G2
Canastota U.S.A. **131** H2
Canastra, Serra da *mts* Brazil **141** B2
Canastra, Serra da *mts* Brazil **141** A1
Canatiba Brazil **141** C1
Canatlán Mex. **127** B7
Canaveral, Cape U.S.A. **129** D6
Cañaveras Spain **53** E3
Canavieiras Brazil **141** D1
Canbelego Australia **108** C3
▶**Canberra** Australia **108** D5
Capital of Australia.
Cancún Mex. **133** G4
Çandar Turkey *see* **Kastamonu**
Çandarlı Turkey **55** L5
Candela Mex. **127** C7
Candela *r.* Mex. **127** C7
Candelaria Mex. **123** G7
Candia Greece *see* **Iraklion**
Cândido de Abreu Brazil **141** A4
Çandır Turkey **86** D2
Candle Lake Canada **117** J4
Candlewood, Lake U.S.A. **131** I3
Cando U.S.A. **126** D1
Candon Phil. **73** I5
Cane *r.* Australia **104** A5
Canea Greece *see* **Chania**
Canela Brazil **141** A5
Canelones Uruguay **140** E4
Cane Valley U.S.A. **130** C5
Cangallo Peru **138** D6
Cangamba Angola **95** B5
Cangandala, Parque Nacional de *nat. park* Angola **95** B4
Cangbu *r.* China *see* **Brahmaputra**
Cango Caves S. Africa **96** F7
Cangola Angola **95** B4
Cangshan China **73** H1

Canguaretama Brazil 139 K5
Canguçu Brazil 140 F4
Canguçu, Serra do hills Brazil 140 F4
Cangwu China 73 F4
Cangzhou China 69 L5
Caniapiscau Canada 119 H3
Caniapiscau r. Canada 119 H2
Caniapiscau, Lac l. Canada 119 H3
Caniçado Moz. see Guija
Canicattì Sicily Italy 54 E6
Canim Lake Canada 116 F5
Canindé Brazil 139 K4
Canisteo U.S.A. 131 G2
Canisteo r. U.S.A. 131 G2
Canisteo Peninsula Antarctica 148 K2
Cañitas de Felipe Pescador Mex. 127 C8
Çankırı Turkey 86 D2
Canna Australia 105 A7
Canna i. U.K. 46 C3
Cannanore India 80 B4
Cannanore Islands India 80 B4
Cannelton U.S.A. 130 B5
Cannes France 52 H5
Cannock U.K. 45 E6
Cannon Beach U.S.A. 122 C3
Cann River Australia 108 D6
Canoas Brazil 141 A5
Canoas, Rio das r. Brazil 141 A4
Canoeiros Brazil 141 B2
Canoe Lake Canada 117 I4
Canoe Lake l. Canada 117 I4
Canoinhas Brazil 141 A4
Canon City U.S.A. 123 G5
Cañon Largo watercourse U.S.A. 125 J3
Canoona Australia 106 E4
Canora Canada 117 K5
Canowindra Australia 108 D4
Canso Canada 119 J5
Canso, Cape Canada 119 J5
Cantabrian Mountains Spain see Cantábrica, Cordillera
Cantábrica, Cordillera mts Spain 53 D2
Cantábrico, Mar sea Spain 53 C2
Canterbury U.K. 45 I7
Canterbury Bight b. N.Z. 109 C7
Canterbury Plains N.Z. 109 C6
Cần Thơ Vietnam 67 D5
Cantil U.S.A. 124 E4
Canton GA U.S.A. 129 C5
Canton IL U.S.A. 126 F3
Canton MO U.S.A. 126 F3
Canton MS U.S.A. 127 F5
Canton NY U.S.A. 131 H1
Canton OH U.S.A. 130 E3
Canton PA U.S.A. 131 G3
Canton SD U.S.A. 126 D3
Canton TX U.S.A. 127 E5
Canton Island atoll Kiribati see Kanton
Cantuaria U.K. see Canterbury
Canunda National Park Australia 107 C8
Canutama Brazil 138 F5
Canutillo Mex. 127 B7
Canvey Island U.K. 45 H7
Canwood Canada 117 J4
Cany-Barville France 45 H9
Canyon Canada 116 B2
Canyon U.S.A. 127 C5
Canyon City U.S.A. 122 D3
Canyondam U.S.A. 124 C1
Canyon de Chelly National Monument nat. park U.S.A. 125 I3
Canyon Ferry Lake U.S.A. 122 F3
Canyon Lake U.S.A. 125 H5
Canyonlands National Park U.S.A. 125 I2
Canyon Ranges mts Canada 116 E2
Canyons of the Ancients National Monument nat. park U.S.A. 125 I3
Canyonville U.S.A. 122 C4
Cao Băng Vietnam 66 D2
Caocheng China see Caoxian
Caohai China see Weining
Caohe China see Qichun
Caohu China 76 F3
Caojiahe China see Qichun
Caojian China 72 C3
Cao Nguyên Đắc Lắc plat. Vietnam 67 E4
Caoshi China 70 B4
Caoxian China 73 G1
Caozhou China see Heze
Capac U.S.A. 130 D2
Çapakçur Turkey see Bingöl
Capanaparo r. Venez. 138 E2
Capanema Brazil 139 I4
Capão Bonito Brazil 141 A4
Caparaó, Serra do mts Brazil 141 C3
Cap-aux-Meules Canada 119 J5
Cap-de-la-Madeleine Canada 119 G5
Cape r. Australia 106 D4
Cape Arid National Park Australia 105 C8
Cape Barren Island Australia 107 [inset]
Cape Basin sea feature S. Atlantic Ocean 144 I8
Cape Breton Highlands National Park Canada 119 J5
Cape Breton Island Canada 119 J5
Cape Charles Canada 119 L3
Cape Charles U.S.A. 131 G5
Cape Coast Ghana 92 C4
Cape Coast Castle Ghana see Cape Coast
Cape Cod Bay U.S.A. 131 J3
Cape Cod National Seashore nature res. U.S.A. 131 K3
Cape Coral U.S.A. 129 D7
Cape Crawford Australia 106 A3
Cape Dorset Canada 115 K3
Cape Fanshaw U.S.A. 116 C3
Cape Fear r. U.S.A. 129 E5
Cape George Canada 119 J5
Cape Girardeau U.S.A. 127 F4
Cape Johnson Depth sea feature N. Pacific Ocean 146 E5
Cape Juby Morocco see Tarfaya
Cape Krusenstern National Monument nat. park U.S.A. 114 B3
Capel Australia 105 A8
Cape Le Grand National Park Australia 105 C8
Capelinha Brazil 141 C2
Capella Australia 106 E4
Capelle aan de IJssel Neth. 48 E3
Capelongo Angola see Kuvango
Cape May U.S.A. 131 H4
Cape May Court House U.S.A. 131 H4
Cape May Point U.S.A. 131 H4
Cape Melville National Park Australia 106 D2
Capenda-Camulemba Angola 95 B4
Cape of Good Hope Nature Reserve S. Africa 96 D8
Cape Palmerston National Park Australia 106 E4
Cape Range National Park Australia 104 A5
Cape St George Canada 119 K4

► Cape Town S. Africa 96 D7
Legislative capital of South Africa.

Cape Tribulation National Park Australia 106 D2
Cape Upstart National Park Australia 106 D3
► Cape Verde country N. Atlantic Ocean 92 [inset]
africa 7, 90–91
Cape Verde Basin sea feature N. Atlantic Ocean 144 F5
Cape Verde Plateau sea feature N. Atlantic Ocean 144 F4
Cape Vincent U.S.A. 131 G1
Cape York Peninsula Australia 106 C2
Cap-Haïtien Haiti 133 J5
Capim r. Brazil 139 I4
Capitán Arturo Prat research station Antarctica 148 A2

► Capitol Hill N. Mariana Is 65 L3
Capital of the Northern Mariana Islands, on Saipan.

Capitol Reef National Park U.S.A. 125 H2
Capivara, Represa resr Brazil 141 A3
Čapljina Bos.-Herz. 54 G3
Cappoquin Rep. of Ireland 47 E5
Capraia, Isola di i. Italy 54 C3
Caprara, Punta pt Sardinia Italy 54 C4
Capri, Isola di i. Italy 54 F4
Capricorn Channel Australia 106 E4
Capricorn Group atolls Australia 106 F4
Caprivi Strip reg. Namibia 95 C5
Cap Rock Escarpment U.S.A. 127 C5
Capsa Tunisia see Gafsa
Captain Cook HI U.S.A. 123 [inset]
Captina r. U.S.A. 130 E4
Capuava Brazil 141 B4
Caquetá r. Col. 138 E4
Caracal Romania 55 K2

► Caracas Venez. 138 E1
Capital of Venezuela.

Caraguatatuba Brazil 141 B3
Caraí Brazil 141 C2
Carajás Brazil 139 H5
Carajás, Serra dos hills Brazil 139 H5
Carales Sardinia Italy see Cagliari
Caralis Sardinia Italy see Cagliari
Carandaí Brazil 141 C3
Caransebeş Romania 55 J2
Caraquet Canada 119 I5
Caratasca, Laguna de lag. Hond. 133 H5
Caratinga Brazil 141 C2
Carauari Brazil 138 E4
Caravaca de la Cruz Spain 53 F4
Caravelas Brazil 141 D2
Carberry Canada 117 L5
Carbó Mex. 123 F7
Carbonara, Capo c. Sardinia Italy 54 C5
Carbondale CO U.S.A. 125 J2
Carbondale PA U.S.A. 131 H3
Carboneras Mex. 127 D7
Carbonia Sardinia Italy 54 C5
Carbonita Brazil 141 C2
Carcaixent Spain 53 F4
Carcajou Canada 116 G3
Carcajou r. Canada 116 D1
Carcar Phil. 65 G4
Carcassonne France 52 F5
Cardamomes, Chaîne des mts Cambodia/Thai. see Cardamom Range
Cardamom Hills India 80 C4
Cardamom Range mts Cambodia/Thai. 67 C4
Cárdenas Cuba 133 H4
Cárdenas Mex. 132 E4
Cardenyabba watercourse Australia 108 A2
Çardi Turkey see Harmancık
Cardiel, Lago l. Arg. 140 B7

► Cardiff U.K. 45 D7
Capital of Wales.

Cardiff U.S.A. 131 G4
Cardigan U.K. 45 C6
Cardigan Bay U.K. 45 C6
Cardinal Lake Canada 116 G3
Cardington U.S.A. 130 D3
Cardón, Cerro hill Mex. 123 E8
Cardoso Brazil 141 A3
Cardoso, Ilha do i. Brazil 141 B4
Cardston Canada 116 H5
Careen Lake Canada 117 I3
Carei Romania 55 J1
Carentan France 52 D2
Carey U.S.A. 130 D3
Carey, Lake salt flat Australia 105 C7
Carey Lake Canada 117 K2
Cargados Carajos Islands Mauritius 145 L7
Carhaix-Plouguer France 52 C2
Cariacica Brazil 141 C3
Cariamanga Ecuador 138 C4
Caribbean Sea N. Atlantic Ocean 133 H5
Cariboo Mountains Canada 116 F4
Caribou r. Man. Canada 117 M3
Caribou r. N.W.T. Canada 116 E2
Caribou U.S.A. 128 G2
Caribou Lake Canada 115 J4
Caribou Mountains Canada 116 H3
Carichic Mex. 123 G8
Carignan France 48 F5
Carinda Australia 108 C3
Cariñena Spain 53 F3
Carinhanha r. Brazil 141 C1
Carlabhagh U.K. see Carloway
Carleton U.S.A. 130 D2
Carleton, Mount hill Canada 119 I5
Carletonville S. Africa 97 H4
Carlin U.S.A. 124 E1
Carlingford Lough inlet Rep. of Ireland/U.K. 47 F3
Carlinville U.S.A. 126 F4
Carlisle U.K. 44 E4
Carlisle IN U.S.A. 130 B4
Carlisle KY U.S.A. 130 C4
Carlisle NY U.S.A. 131 H2
Carlisle PA U.S.A. 131 G3
Carlisle Lakes salt flat Australia 105 D7
Carlit, Pic mt. France 52 E5
Carlos Chagas Brazil 141 C2
Carlow Rep. of Ireland 47 F5
Carloway U.K. 46 C2
Carlsbad Czech Rep. see Karlovy Vary
Carlsbad CA U.S.A. 124 E5
Carlsbad NM U.S.A. 123 G6
Carlsbad Caverns National Park U.S.A. 123 G6
Carlsberg Ridge sea feature Indian Ocean 145 L5
Carlson Inlet Antarctica 148 L1
Carlton U.S.A. 126 E2
Carlton Hill Australia 104 E3
Carluke U.K. 46 F5
Carlyle Canada 117 K5
Carmacks Canada 116 B2
Carmagnola Italy 54 B2
Carman Canada 117 L5
Carmana Iran see Kermān
Carmarthen U.K. 45 C7
Carmarthen Bay U.K. 45 C7
Carmaux France 52 F4
Carmel IN U.S.A. 130 B4
Carmel NY U.S.A. 131 I3
Carmel, Mount hill Israel 81 B3
Carmel Head hd U.K. 44 C5
Carmel Valley U.S.A. 124 C3
Carmen r. Mex. 127 B6
Carmen U.S.A. 123 F7
Carmen, Isla i. Mex. 123 F8
Carmen de Patagones Arg. 140 D6
Carmi U.S.A. 126 F4
Carmichael U.S.A. 124 C2
Carmo da Cachoeira Brazil 141 B3
Carmo do Paranaíba Brazil 141 B2
Carmona Angola see Uíge
Carmona Spain 53 D5
Carnac France 52 C3
Carnamah Australia 105 A7
Carnarvon Australia 105 A6
Carnarvon S. Africa 96 F6
Carnarvon National Park Australia 106 D5
Carnarvon Range hills Australia 105 C6
Carnarvon Range mts Australia 106 E5
Carn Dearg hill U.K. 46 E3
Carndonagh Rep. of Ireland 47 E2
Carnegie Australia 105 C6
Carnegie, Lake salt flat Australia 105 C6
Carn Eighe mt. U.K. 46 D3
Carnes Australia 105 F7
Carney Island Antarctica 148 J2
Carnforth U.K. 44 E4
Carn Glas-choire hill U.K. 46 F3
Car Nicobar i. India 67 A5
Carnlough U.K. 47 G3
Carn nan Gabhar mt. U.K. 46 F4
Carn Odhar hill U.K. 46 E3
Carnot Cent. Afr. Rep. 94 B3
Carnoustie U.K. 46 G4
Carnsore Point Rep. of Ireland 47 F5
Carnwath U.K. 46 F5
Caro U.S.A. 130 D2
Carola Cay reef Australia 106 F3
Carol City U.S.A. 129 D7
Carolina Brazil 139 I5
Carolina S. Africa 97 J4
Carolina Beach U.S.A. 129 E5
Caroline Canada 116 H4
Caroline Island atoll Kiribati 147 J6
Caroline Islands N. Pacific Ocean 65 K5
Caroline Peak N.Z. 109 A7
Caroline Range hills Australia 104 D4
Caroní r. Venez. 138 F2
Carp Canada 131 G1
Carpathian Mountains Europe 39 C6
Carpații mts Europe see Carpathian Mountains
Carpații Meridionali mts Romania see Transylvanian Alps
Carpații Occidentali mts Romania 55 J2
Carpentaria, Gulf of Australia 106 B2
Carpentras France 52 G4
Carpi Italy 54 D2
Carpinteria U.S.A. 124 D4
Carpio U.S.A. 126 C1
Carra, Lough l. Rep. of Ireland 47 C4
Carraig na Siuire Rep. of Ireland see Carrick-on-Suir
Carrantuohill mt. Rep. of Ireland 47 C6
Carrara Italy 54 D2
Carrasco, Parque Nacional nat. park Bol. 138 F7
Carrathool Australia 108 B5
Carrhae Turkey see Harran
Carrickfergus U.K. 47 G3
Carrickmacross Rep. of Ireland 47 F4
Carrick-on-Shannon Rep. of Ireland 47 D4
Carrick-on-Suir Rep. of Ireland 47 E5
Carrigallen Rep. of Ireland 47 E4
Carrigtwohill Rep. of Ireland 47 D6
Carrillo Mex. 127 C7
Carrington U.S.A. 126 D2
Carrizal Mex. 123 G7
Carrizal Bajo Chile 140 B3
Carrizo U.S.A. 125 H4
Carrizo Creek r. U.S.A. 127 C4
Carrizo Springs U.S.A. 127 D6
Carrizo Wash watercourse U.S.A. 125 I4
Carrizozo U.S.A. 123 G6
Carroll U.S.A. 126 E3
Carrollton AL U.S.A. 127 F5
Carrollton GA U.S.A. 129 C5
Carrollton IL U.S.A. 126 F4
Carrollton KY U.S.A. 130 C4
Carrollton MO U.S.A. 126 E4
Carrollton OH U.S.A. 130 E3
Carrolltown U.S.A. 131 F3
Carron r. U.K. 46 E3
Carrot r. Canada 117 K4
Carrothers U.S.A. 130 D3
Carrot River Canada 117 K4
Carrowmore Lake Rep. of Ireland 47 C3
Carrsville U.S.A. 131 G5
Carruthers Lake Canada 117 K2
Carruthersville U.S.A. 127 F4
Carry Falls Reservoir U.S.A. 131 H1
Çarşamba Turkey 86 E2
Carson r. U.S.A. 124 D2
Carson City MI U.S.A. 130 C2

► Carson City NV U.S.A. 124 D2
State capital of Nevada.

Carson Escarpment Australia 104 D3
Carson Lake U.S.A. 124 D2
Carson Sink l. U.S.A. 124 D2
Carstensz Pyramid mt. Indon. see Jaya, Puncak
Carstensz-top mt. Indon. see Jaya, Puncak
Carswell Lake Canada 117 I3
Cartagena Col. 138 C1
Cartagena Spain 53 F5
Carteret Group is P.N.G. see Kilinailau Islands
Carteret Island Solomon Is see Malaita
Cartersville U.S.A. 129 C5
Carthage tourist site Tunisia 54 D6
Carthage MO U.S.A. 127 E4
Carthage NC U.S.A. 129 E5
Carthage NY U.S.A. 131 H2
Carthage TX U.S.A. 127 E5
Carthago tourist site Tunisia see Carthage
Carthago Nova Spain see Cartagena
Cartier Island Australia 104 C3
Cartmel U.K. 44 E4
Cartwright Man. Canada 117 L5
Cartwright Nfld. and Lab. Canada 119 K3
Caruarú Brazil 139 K5
Carúpano Venez. 138 F1
Carver U.S.A. 130 D5
Carvin France 48 C4
Cary U.S.A. 128 E5
Caryapundy Swamp Australia 107 C6
Casablanca Morocco 50 C5
Casa Branca Brazil 141 B3
Casa de Piedra, Embalse resr Arg. 140 C5
Casa Grande U.S.A. 125 H5
Casale Monferrato Italy 54 C2
Casalmaggiore Italy 54 D2
Casas Grandes Mex. 123 G7
Casca Brazil 141 A5
Cascada de Bassaseachic, Parque Nacional nat. park Mex. 123 F7
Cascade Australia 105 C8
Cascade r. N.Z. 109 B7
Cascade ID U.S.A. 122 D3
Cascade MT U.S.A. 122 F3
Cascade Point N.Z. 109 B7
Cascade Range mts Canada/U.S.A. 122 C4
Cascade Reservoir U.S.A. 122 D3
Cascais Port. 53 B4
Cascavel Brazil 140 F2
Casco Bay U.S.A. 131 K2
Caserta Italy 54 F4
Casey research station Antarctica 148 F2
Casey Bay Antarctica 148 D2
Caseyr, Raas c. Somalia see Gwardafuy, Gees
Cashel Rep. of Ireland 47 E5
Cashmere Australia 108 D1
Casino Australia 108 F2
Casiquiare, Canal r. Venez. 138 E3
Casita Mex. 123 F7
Casnewydd U.K. see Newport
Caspe Spain 53 F3
Casper U.S.A. 122 G4
Caspian Lowland Kazakh./Rus. Fed. 74 D2

► Caspian Sea l. Asia/Europe 87 H1
Largest lake in the world and in Asia/Europe. Lowest point in Europe.
asia 56–57
europe 32–33
world 12–13

Cass U.S.A. 130 F4
Cass r. U.S.A. 130 D2
Cassacatiza Moz. 95 D5
Cassadaga U.S.A. 130 F2
Cassaigne Alg. see Sidi Ali
Cassamba Angola 95 C5
Cass City U.S.A. 130 D2
Cassel France 48 C4
Casselman Canada 131 H1
Cássia Brazil 141 B3
Cassiar Mountains Canada 116 D2
Cassilândia Brazil 141 A2
Cassilis Australia 108 D4
Cassino Italy 54 E4
Cassley r. U.K. 46 E3
Cassongue Angola 95 B5
Cassopolis U.S.A. 130 B3
Cassville U.S.A. 127 E4
Castanhal Brazil 139 I4
Castanho Brazil 138 F5
Castaños Mex. 127 C7
Castelfranco Veneto Italy 54 D2
Castell-nedd U.K. see Neath
Castell Newydd Emlyn U.K. see Newcastle Emlyn
Castelló de la Plana Spain 53 F4
Castellón Spain see Castelló de la Plana
Castellón de la Plana Spain see Castelló de la Plana
Castelo Branco Port. 53 C4
Castelo de Vide Port. 53 C4
Casteltermini Sicily Italy 54 E6
Castelvetrano Sicily Italy 54 E6
Castiglione della Pescaia Italy 54 D3
Castignon, Lac l. Canada 119 H2
Castilla y León reg. Spain 52 B6
Castlebar Rep. of Ireland 47 C4
Castlebay U.K. 46 B4
Castlebellingham Rep. of Ireland 47 F4
Castleblayney Rep. of Ireland 47 F3
Castlebridge Rep. of Ireland 47 F5
Castle Carrock U.K. 44 E4
Castle Cary U.K. 45 E7
Castle Dale U.S.A. 125 H2
Castlederg U.K. 47 E3
Castledermot Rep. of Ireland 47 F5
Castle Dome Mountains U.S.A. 125 F5
Castle Donington U.K. 45 F6
Castle Douglas U.K. 46 F6
Castleford U.K. 44 F5
Castlegar Canada 116 G5
Castlegregory Rep. of Ireland 47 B5
Castle Island Bahamas 129 F8
Castleisland Rep. of Ireland 47 C5
Castlemaine Australia 108 B6
Castlemaine Rep. of Ireland 47 C5
Castlemartyr Rep. of Ireland 47 D6
Castle Mountain Alta Canada 116 H5
Castle Mountain Y.T. Canada 116 C1
Castle Mountain U.S.A. 124 C4
Castle Peak hill Hong Kong China 73 [inset]
Castle Peak Bay Hong Kong China 73 [inset]
Castlepoint N.Z. 109 F5
Castlepollard Rep. of Ireland 47 E4
Castlerea Rep. of Ireland 47 D4
Castlereagh r. Australia 108 C3
Castle Rock U.S.A. 122 G5
Castletown Isle of Man 44 C4
Castletown Rep. of Ireland 47 E5
Castor Canada 117 I4
Castor r. U.S.A. 127 F4
Castor, Rivière du r. Canada 118 F3
Castra Regina Germany see Regensburg
Castres France 52 F5
Castricum Neth. 48 E2

► Castries St Lucia 133 L6
Capital of St Lucia.

Castro Brazil 141 A4
Castro Chile 140 B6
Castro Alves Brazil 141 D1
Castro Verde Port. 53 B5
Castroville U.S.A. 124 C3
Çat Turkey 87 F3
Catacaos Peru 138 B5
Cataguases Brazil 141 C3
Catahoula Lake U.S.A. 127 E6
Çatak Turkey 87 F3
Catalão Brazil 141 B2
Çatalca Yarımadası pen. Turkey 55 M4
Catalina U.S.A. 125 H5
Catalonia aut. comm. Spain see Cataluña
Cataluña aut. comm. Spain 53 G3
Catalunya aut. comm. Spain see Cataluña
Catamarca Arg. 140 C3
Catana Sicily Italy see Catania
Catanduanes i. Phil. 65 G4
Catanduva Brazil 141 A3
Catania Sicily Italy 54 F6
Catanzaro Italy 54 G5
Cataract Creek watercourse U.S.A. 125 G3
Catarina U.S.A. 127 D6
Catarino Rodriguez Mex. 127 C7
Catarman Phil. 65 G4
Catastrophe, Cape Australia 107 A7
Catawba r. U.S.A. 129 D5
Cataxa Moz. 95 D5
Cat Ba, Đao i. Vietnam 66 D2
Catbalogan Phil. 65 G4
Catembe Moz. 97 K4
Catengue Angola 95 B5
Catete Angola 95 B4
Cathcart Australia 108 D6
Cathcart S. Africa 97 H7
Cathedral Peak S. Africa 97 I5
Cathedral Rock National Park Australia 108 F3
Catherdaniel Rep. of Ireland 47 B6
Catherine, Mount U.S.A. 125 G2
Catheys Valley U.S.A. 124 C3
Cathlamet U.S.A. 122 C3
Catió Guinea-Bissau 92 B3
Catisimiña Venez. 138 F3
Cat Island Bahamas 129 F7
Cat Lake Canada 117 N5
Catlettsburg U.S.A. 130 D4
Catoche, Cabo c. Mex. 129 C8
Cato Island and Bank reef Australia 106 F4
Catriló Arg. 140 D5
Cats, Mont des hill France 48 C4
Catskill U.S.A. 131 I2
Catskill Mountains U.S.A. 131 H2
Catuane Moz. 97 K4
Cauayan Phil. 65 G5
Caubvick, Mount Canada 119 J2
Cauca r. Col. 133 J7
Caucaia Brazil 139 K4
Caucasia Col. 138 C2
Caucasus mts Asia/Europe 87 F2
Cauchon Lake Canada 117 L4
Caudry France 48 D4
Caulonia Italy 54 G5
Caungula Angola 95 B4
Cauquenes Chile 140 B5
Causapscal Canada 119 I4
Cavagliá Italy 54 C2
Cavalcante, Serra do hills Brazil 141 B1
Cavalier U.S.A. 126 D1
Cavan Rep. of Ireland 47 E4
Çavdır Turkey 55 M6
Cave City U.S.A. 130 C5
Cave Creek U.S.A. 125 H5
Caveira r. Brazil 141 C1
Cavern Island Myanmar 67 B5
Cave Run Lake U.S.A. 130 D4
Caviana, Ilha i. Brazil 139 H3
Cawdor U.K. 46 F3
Cawnpore India see Kanpur
Cawston U.K. 45 I6
Caxias Brazil 139 J4
Caxias do Sul Brazil 141 A5
Caxito Angola 95 B4
Çay Turkey 55 N5
Cayambe, Volcán vol. Ecuador 138 C3
Çaybaşı Turkey see Çayeli
Çaycuma Turkey 55 O4
Çayeli Turkey 87 F2

► Cayenne Fr. Guiana 139 H3
Capital of French Guiana.

Cayeux-sur-Mer France 48 B4
Çayırhan Turkey 55 N4
Cayman Brac i. Cayman Is 133 I5

► Cayman Islands terr. West Indies 133 H5
United Kingdom Overseas Territory.
north america 9, 112–113

Cayman Trench sea feature Caribbean Sea 144 C4
Caynabo Somalia 94 E3
Cay Sal i. Bahamas 129 D8
Cay Sal Bank sea feature Bahamas 129 D8
Cay Santa Domingo i. Bahamas 129 F8
Cayucos U.S.A. 124 C4
Cayuga Canada 130 F2
Cayuga Lake U.S.A. 131 G2
Cay Verde i. Bahamas 129 F8
Cazê China 79 F3
Cazenovia U.S.A. 131 H2
Cazombo Angola 95 C5
Ceadâr-Lunga Moldova see Ciadîr-Lunga
Ceanannus Mór Rep. of Ireland see Kells
Ceann a Deas na Hearadh pen. U.K. see South Harris
Ceará Brazil see Fortaleza
Ceara Abyssal Plain sea feature S. Atlantic Ocean 144 F6
Ceatharlach Rep. of Ireland see Carlow
Ceballos Mex. 127 B7
Cebu Phil. 65 G4
Cebu i. Phil. 65 G4
Cecil Plains Australia 108 E1
Cecil Rhodes, Mount hill Australia 105 C6
Cecina Italy 54 D3
Cedar r. ND U.S.A. 126 C2
Cedar r. NE U.S.A. 126 D3
Cedar City U.S.A. 125 G3
Cedaredge U.S.A. 125 J2
Cedar Falls U.S.A. 126 E3
Cedar Grove U.S.A. 130 B2
Cedar Hill NM U.S.A. 125 J3
Cedar Hill TN U.S.A. 130 B5
Cedar Island U.S.A. 131 H5
Cedar Lake Canada 117 K4
Cedar Point U.S.A. 130 D3
Cedar Rapids U.S.A. 126 F3
Cedar Run U.S.A. 131 H4
Cedar Springs U.S.A. 130 C2
Cedartown U.S.A. 129 C5
Cedarville S. Africa 97 I6
Cedros Mex. 123 F8
Cedros, Cerro mt. Mex. 123 E7
Cedros, Isla i. Mex. 123 E7
Ceduna Australia 105 F8
Ceeldheere Somalia 94 E3
Ceerigaabo Somalia 94 E2
Cefalù Sicily Italy 54 F5
Cegléd Hungary 55 H1
Cêgnê China 72 B1
Ceheng China 72 E3
Çekerek Turkey 86 D2
Celaya Mex. 132 D4
Celbridge Rep. of Ireland 47 F4

► Celebes i. Indon. 65 G7
4th largest island in Asia.

Celebes Basin sea feature Pacific Ocean 146 E5
Celebes Sea Indon./Phil. 65 G6
Celestún Mex. 132 F4
Celina OH U.S.A. 130 C3
Celina TN U.S.A. 130 C5
Celje Slovenia 54 F1
Celle Germany 49 K2
Celovec Austria see Klagenfurt
Celtic Sea Rep. of Ireland/U.K. 42 D5
Celtic Shelf sea feature N. Atlantic Ocean 144 H2
Cenderawasih, Teluk b. Indon. 65 J7
Centane S. Africa see Kentani
Centenary Zimbabwe 95 D5
Center NE U.S.A. 126 D3
Center TX U.S.A. 127 E6
Centereach U.S.A. 131 I3
Center Point U.S.A. 129 C5
Centerville AL U.S.A. 129 C5
Centerville IA U.S.A. 126 E3
Centerville MO U.S.A. 127 F4
Centerville TX U.S.A. 127 E6
Centerville WV U.S.A. 130 E4
Centrafricaine, République country Africa see Central African Republic
Central admin. dist. Botswana 97 H2
Central U.S.A. 125 I5
Central, Cordillera mts Col. 138 C3
Central, Cordillera mts Peru 138 C6
Central African Empire country Africa see Central African Republic
► Central African Republic country Africa 94 B3
africa 7, 90–91
Central Brahui Range mts Pak. 85 G4
Central Butte Canada 122 G2
Central City U.S.A. 126 D3
Centralia IL U.S.A. 126 F4
Centralia WA U.S.A. 122 C3
Central Kalahari Game Reserve nature res. Botswana 96 F2
Central Kara Rise sea feature Arctic Ocean 149 F1
Central Makran Range mts Pak. 85 G5
Central Mount Stuart hill Australia 104 F5
Central Pacific Basin sea feature Pacific Ocean 146 H5
Central Provinces state India see Madhya Pradesh
Central Range mts P.N.G. 65 K7
Central Russian Upland hills Rus. Fed. 39 H5
Central Siberian Plateau Rus. Fed. 61 M3
Central Square U.S.A. 131 G2
Centre U.S.A. 129 C5
Centreville U.S.A. 131 G4
Cenxi China 73 F4
Cenyang China see Hengfeng
Ceos i. Greece see Kea
Cephaloedium Sicily Italy see Cefalù
Cephalonia i. Greece 55 I5
Ceram i. Indon. see Seram
Ceram Sea Indon. see Seram, Laut
Cerbat Mountains U.S.A. 125 F4
Čerchov mt. Czech Rep. 49 M5
Ceres Arg. 140 D3
Ceres Brazil 141 A1
Ceres S. Africa 96 D7
Ceres U.S.A. 124 C3
Céret France 52 F5
Cerezo de Abajo Spain 53 E3
Cerignola Italy 54 F4
Cerigo i. Greece see Kythira
Cêringgolêb China see Dongco
Çerkeş Turkey 86 D2
Çerkeşli Turkey 55 M4
Çermik Turkey 87 E3
Cernăuți Ukr. see Chernivtsi

Cernavodă Romania 55 M2
Cerralvo, Isla i. Mex. 132 C4
Cërrik Albania 55 H4
Cerritos Mex. 132 D4
Cerro Azul Brazil 141 A4
Cerro de Pasco Peru 138 C6
Cerros Colorados, Embalse resr Arg. 140 C5
Cervantes, Cerro mt. Arg. 140 B8
Cervati, Monte mt. Italy 54 F4
Cervione Corsica France 52 I5
Cervo Spain 53 C2
Cesena Italy 54 E2
Cēsis Latvia 41 N8
Česká Republika country Europe see Czech Republic
České Budějovice Czech Rep. 43 O6
Českomoravská Vysočina hills Czech Rep. 43 O6
Český Krumlov Czech Rep. 43 O6
Český Les mts Czech Rep./Germany 49 M5
Çeşme Turkey 55 L5
Cessnock Australia 108 E4
Cetatea Albă Ukr. see Bilhorod-Dnistrovs'kyy
Cetinje Serb. and Mont. 54 H3
Cetraro Italy 54 F5

▶Ceuta N. Africa 53 D6
Spanish Territory.

Ceva-i-Ra reef Fiji 103 H4
Cévennes mts France 52 F5
Cévennes, Parc National des nat. park France 52 F4
Cevizli Turkey 81 C1
Cevizlik Turkey see Maçka
Ceyhan Turkey 86 D3
Ceyhan r. Turkey 81 B1
Ceyhan Boğazı r. mouth Turkey 81 B1
Ceylanpınar Turkey 87 F3
Ceylon country Asia see Sri Lanka
Chaacha Turkm. 85 F2
Chābahār Iran 85 F5
Chabrol i. New Caledonia see Lifou
Chabug China 79 E2
Chabyêr Caka salt l. China 79 F3
Chachapoyas Peru 138 C5
Chäche Turkm. see Chaacha
Chachoengsao Thai. 67 C4
Chachran Pak. 85 H4
Chachro Pak. 85 H5
Chaco r. U.S.A. 125 I3
Chaco Boreal reg. Para. 140 E2
Chaco Culture National Historical Park nat. park U.S.A. 125 J3
Chaco Mesa plat. U.S.A. 125 J4

▶Chad country Africa 93 E3
5th largest country in Africa.
africa 7, 90–91

Chad, Lake Africa 93 E3
Chadaasan Mongolia 68 I3
Chadan Rus. Fed. 76 H1
Chadibe Botswana 97 H2
Chadileo r. Arg. 140 C5
Chadron U.S.A. 126 C3
Chadyr-Lunga Moldova see Ciadîr-Lunga
Chae Hom Thai. 66 B3
Chaeryŏng N. Korea 71 B5
Chae Son National Park Thai. 66 B3
Chagai Pak. 85 G4
Chagai Hills Afgh./Pak. 85 F4
Chagdo Kangri mt. China 79 F2
Chaghā Khūr mt. Iran 84 C4
Chaghcharān Afgh. 85 G3
Chagny France 52 G3
Chagoda Rus. Fed. 38 G4
Chagos Archipelago is B.I.O.T. 145 M6
Chagos-Laccadive Ridge sea feature Indian Ocean 145 M6
Chagos Trench sea feature Indian Ocean 145 M6
Chagoyan Rus. Fed. 70 C1
Chagrayskoye Plato plat. Kazakh. see Shagyray, Plato
Chagyl Turkm. 87 I2
Chāh Ākhvor Iran 85 E3
Chāh 'Ali Akbar Iran 84 E3
Chahbounia Alg. 53 H6
Chahchaheh Turkm. 85 F2
Chāh-e Āb Afgh. 85 H2
Chāh-e Bāgh well Iran 84 D4
Chāh-e Bāzargānī Iran 84 D4
Chāh-e Dow Chāhī Iran 84 D4
Chāh-e Gonbad well Iran 84 D3
Chāh-e Kavīr well Iran 84 E3
Chāh-e Khorāsān well Iran 84 D3
Chāh-e Khoshāb Iran 84 E3
Chāh-e Malek well Iran 84 D3
Chāh-e Malek Mīrzā well Iran 84 D4
Chāh-e Mūjān well Iran 84 D3
Chāh-e Qeyşar well Iran 84 D4
Chāh-e Qobād well Iran 84 D3
Chāh-e Rāh Iran 84 D4
Chāh-e Raḩmān well Iran 85 E4
Chāh-e Shūr well Iran 84 D3
Chāh-e Tūnī well Iran 84 E3
Chāh Kūh Iran 84 D4
Chāh Lak Iran 84 E5
Chāh Pās well Iran 84 D3
Chah Sandan Pak. 85 F4
Chaibasa India 79 F5
Chaigneau, Lac l. Canada 119 I3
Chainat Thai. 66 C4
Chainjoin Co l. China 79 F2
Chai Prakan Thai. 66 B3
Chaitén Chile 140 B6
Chai Wan Hong Kong China 73 [inset]
Chaiya Thai. 67 B5
Chaiyaphum Thai. 66 C4
Chajarí Arg. 140 E4
Chakai India 79 F4
Chak Amru Pak. 85 I3
Chakar r. Pak. 85 H4
Chakaria Bangl. 79 H5
Chakdarra Pak. 85 I3
Chakku Pak. 85 G5
Chakmaktin Lake Afgh. 85 I2
Chakonipau, Lac l. Canada 119 H2
Chakoria Bangl. see Chakaria
Ch'ak'vi Georgia 87 F2
Chala Peru 138 D7
Chalap Dalan mts Afgh. 85 G3
Chalatenango El Salvador 132 G6
Chaláua Moz. 95 D5
Chalaxung China 72 C1
Chalcedon Turkey see Kadıköy
Chalengkou China 76 H4
Chaleur Bay inlet Canada 119 I4
Chaleurs, Baie des inlet Canada see Chaleur Bay
Chali China 72 C2
Chaling China 73 G3
Chalisgaon India 80 B1
Chalki i. Greece 55 L6
Chalkida Greece 55 J5
Challakere India 80 C3
Challans France 52 D3
Challapata Bol. 138 E7

▶Challenger Deep sea feature N. Pacific Ocean 146 F5
Deepest point in the world (Mariana Trench).

Challenger Fracture Zone sea feature S. Pacific Ocean 146 M8
Challis U.S.A. 122 E3
Chalmette U.S.A. 127 F6
Châlons-en-Champagne France 48 E6
Châlons-sur-Marne France see Châlons-en-Champagne
Chalon-sur-Saône France 52 G3
Chālūs Iran 84 C2
Cham Germany 49 M5
Cham, Kūh-e hill Iran 84 C3
Chamaico Arg. 140 D5
Chamais Bay Namibia 96 B4
Chaman Pak. 74 F3
Chaman Bid Iran 84 E2
Chamao, Khao mt. Thai. 67 C4
Chamba India 78 D2
Chamba Tanz. 95 D5
Chambal r. India 78 D4
Chambas Cuba 129 E8
Chambeaux, Lac l. Canada 119 H3
Chamberlain r. Australia 104 D4
Chamberlain Canada 117 J5
Chamberlain U.S.A. 126 D3
Chamberlain Lake U.S.A. 128 G2
Chambers U.S.A. 125 I4
Chambersburg U.S.A. 131 G4
Chambers Island U.S.A. 130 B1
Chambéry France 52 G4
Chambeshi r. Zambia 95 C5
Chambi, Jebel mt. Tunisia 54 C7
Chamdo China see Qamdo
Chamechaude mt. France 52 G4
Chamiss Bay Canada 116 E5
Chamoli India see Gopeshwar
Chamonix-Mont_Blanc France 52 H4
Champa India 79 E5
Champagne-Ardenne admin. reg. France 48 E6
Champagne Castle mt. S. Africa 97 I5
Champagne Humide reg. France 52 G2
Champagne Pouilleuse reg. France 52 F2
Champagnole France 52 G3
Champagny Islands Australia 104 D3
Champaign U.S.A. 126 F3
Champasak Laos 66 D4
Champdoré, Lac l. Canada 119 I3
Champhai India 79 H5
Champion Canada 116 H5
Champlain U.S.A. 131 G4
Champlain, Lake Canada/U.S.A. 131 I1
Champotón Mex. 132 F5
Chamrajnagar India 80 C4
Chamzinka Rus. Fed. 39 J5
Chana Thai. 67 C6
Chanak Turkey see Çanakkale
Chañaral Chile 140 B3
Chanārān Iran 84 E2
Chanda India see Chandrapur
Chandalar r. U.S.A. 114 D3
Chandausi India 78 D3
Chandbali India 79 F5
Chandeleur Islands U.S.A. 127 F6
Chanderi India 78 D4
Chandigarh India 78 D3
Chandil India 79 F5
Chandler Canada 119 I4
Chandler AZ U.S.A. 125 H5
Chandler IN U.S.A. 130 B4
Chandler OK U.S.A. 127 D5
Chandod India 78 C5
Chandos Lake Canada 131 G1
Chandpur Bangl. 79 G5
Chandpur India 78 D3
Chandragiri India 80 C3
Chandrapur India 80 C2
Chandvad India 80 B1
Chandyr r. Turkm. 84 D2
Chandyr Uzbek. 85 G2
Chang, Ko i. Thai. 67 C4
Chang'an China 73 F1
Changane r. Moz. 97 K3
Changbai China 70 C4
Changbai Shan mts China/N. Korea 70 B4
Chang Cheng research station Antarctica see Great Wall
Changcheng China 73 F5
Changchow Fujian China see Zhangzhou
Changchow Jiangsu China see Changzhou
Changchun China 70 B4
Changchunling China 70 B3
Changde China 73 F2
Changgang China 73 G3
Changge China 73 G1
Changgi-ap pt S. Korea 71 C5
Changgo China 79 F3
Chang Hu l. China 73 G2
Changhua Taiwan 73 I3
Changhŭng S. Korea 71 B6
Changhwa Taiwan see Changhua
Changi Sing. 67 [inset]
Changji China 76 G3
Changjiang China 73 F5
Chang Jiang r. China 73 I2 see Yangtze
Changjiang Kou China see Mouth of the Yangtze
Changjin-ho resr N. Korea 71 B4
Changkiang China see Zhanjiang
Changlang India 79 H4
Changleng China see Xinjian
Changling China 70 A3
Changlung Jammu and Kashmir 83 M3
Changma China 76 I4
Changning Jiangxi China see Xunwu
Changning Sichuan China 72 E2
Changnyŏn N. Korea 71 B5
Ch'ang-pai Shan mts China/N. Korea see Changbai Shan
Changpu China see Suining
Changp'yŏng S. Korea 71 C5
Changsan-got pt N. Korea 71 B5
Changsha China 73 G2
Changshan China 73 H2
Changshi China 72 E3
Changshoujie China 73 G2
Changshu China 73 I2
Changtai China 73 H3
Changteh China see Changde
Changting Fujian China 73 H3
Changting Heilong. China 70 C3
Ch'angwŏn S. Korea 71 C6
Changxing China 73 H2
Changyang China 73 F2
Changyŏn N. Korea 71 B5
Changyuan China 73 G1
Changzhi China 69 K5
Changzhou China 73 H2
Chañi, Nevado de mt. Arg. 140 C2
Chania Greece 55 K7
Chanion, Kolpos b. Greece 55 J7
Chankou China 72 E1
Channahon U.S.A. 130 A3
Channapatna India 80 C3
Channel Islands English Chan. 45 E9
Channel Islands U.S.A. 124 D5
Channel Islands National Park U.S.A. 124 D4
Channel-Port-aux-Basques Canada 119 K5
Channel Rock i. Bahamas 129 E8
Channel Tunnel France/U.K. 45 I7
Channing U.S.A. 127 C5
Chantada Spain 53 C2
Chanthaburi Thai. 67 C4
Chantilly France 48 C5
Chanumla India 67 A5
Chanute U.S.A. 126 E4
Chanuwala Pak. 85 I3
Chany, Ozero salt l. Rus. Fed. 60 I4
Chaohu China 73 H2
Chao Hu l. China 73 H2
Chaor He r. China see Qulin Gol
Chaouèn Morocco 53 D6
Chaowula Shan mt. China 72 C1
Chaoyang Guangdong China 73 H4
Chaoyang Heilong. China see Jiayin
Chaoyang Liaoning China 69 M4
Chaoyangcun China 70 B2
Chaozhong China 70 A2
Chaozhou China 73 H4
Chapada Diamantina, Parque Nacional nat. park Brazil 141 C1
Chapada dos Veadeiros, Parque Nacional da nat. park Brazil 141 B1
Chapais Canada 118 G4
Chapak Guzar Afgh. 85 G2
Chapala, Laguna de l. Mex. 132 D4
Chapayev Kazakh. 74 E1
Chapayevo Kazakh. see Chapayev
Chapayevsk Rus. Fed. 39 K5
Chapecó Brazil 140 F3
Chapecó r. Brazil 140 F3
Chapel-en-le-Frith U.K. 44 F5
Chapelle-lez-Herlaimont Belgium 48 E4
Chapeltown U.K. 44 F5
Chapleau Canada 118 E5
Chaplin Canada 117 J5
Chaplin Lake Canada 117 J5
Chaplygin Rus. Fed. 39 H5
Chapman, Mount Canada 116 G5
Chapmanville U.S.A. 130 D5
Chappell U.S.A. 126 C3
Chappell Islands Australia 107 [inset]
Chapra Bihar India see Chhapra
Chapra Jharkhand India see Chatra
Chapri Pass Afgh. 85 G3
Charagua Bol. 138 F7
Charay Mex. 123 F8
Charcas Mex. 132 D4
Charcot Island Antarctica 148 L2
Chard Canada 117 I4
Chard U.K. 45 E8
Chardara Kazakh. see Shardara
Chardara, Step' plain Kazakh. 76 C3
Chardon U.S.A. 130 E3
Chardzhev Turkm. see Turkmenabat
Chardzhou Turkm. see Turkmenabat
Charef Alg. 53 H6
Charef, Oued watercourse Morocco 50 D5
Charente r. France 52 D4
Chari r. Cameroon/Chad 93 E3
Chārī Iran 84 E4
Chārīkār Afgh. 85 H3
Chariton U.S.A. 126 E3
Chärjew Turkm. see Turkmenabat
Charkayuvom Rus. Fed. 38 L2
Chār Kent Afgh. 85 G2
Charkhlik China see Ruoqiang
Charleroi Belgium 48 E4
Charles, Cape U.S.A. 131 H5
Charlesbourg Canada 119 H5
Charles City IA U.S.A. 126 E3
Charles City VA U.S.A. 131 G5
Charles de Gaulle airport France 48 C5
Charles Hill Botswana 96 E2
Charles Island Galápagos Ecuador see Santa María, Isla
Charles Lake Canada 117 I3
Charles Point Australia 104 E3
Charleston N.Z. 109 C5
Charleston IL U.S.A. 126 F4
Charleston MO U.S.A. 127 F4
Charleston SC U.S.A. 129 E5

▶Charleston WV U.S.A. 130 E4
State capital of West Virginia.

Charleston Peak U.S.A. 125 F3
Charlestown Rep. of Ireland 47 D4
Charlestown IN U.S.A. 130 C4
Charlestown NH U.S.A. 131 I2
Charlestown RI U.S.A. 131 J3
Charles Town U.S.A. 131 G4
Charleville Australia 107 D5
Charleville Rep. of Ireland see Rathluirc
Charleville-Mézières France 48 E5
Charlevoix U.S.A. 130 C1
Charlie Lake Canada 116 F3
Charlotte MI U.S.A. 130 C2
Charlotte NC U.S.A. 129 D5
Charlotte TN U.S.A. 130 B5

▶Charlotte Amalie Virgin Is (U.S.A.) 133 L5
Capital of the U.S. Virgin Islands.

Charlotte Harbor b. U.S.A. 129 D7
Charlotte Lake Canada 116 E4
Charlottesville U.S.A. 131 F4

▶Charlottetown Canada 119 J5
Provincial capital of Prince Edward Island.

Charlton Australia 108 A6
Charlton Island Canada 118 F3
Charron Lake Canada 117 M4
Charsadda Pak. 85 H3
Charshanga Turkm. 85 G2
Charshangngy Turkm. see Charshanga
Charters Towers Australia 106 D4
Chartres France 52 E2
Chas India 79 F5
Chase Canada 116 G5
Chase U.S.A. 130 C2
Chase City U.S.A. 131 F5
Chashmeh Nūrī Iran 84 E3
Chashmeh-ye Ab-e Garm spring Iran 84 E3
Chashmeh-ye Garm Ab spring Iran 84 E3
Chashmeh-ye Magu well Iran 84 E3
Chashmeh-ye Mūkīk spring Iran 84 E3
Chashmeh-ye Palasi Iran 84 D3
Chashmeh-ye Safid spring Iran 84 E3
Chashmeh-ye Shotoran well Iran 84 D3
Chashniki Belarus 39 F5
Chaska U.S.A. 126 E2
Chaslands Mistake c. N.Z. 109 B8
Chasŏng N. Korea 70 B4
Chasseral mt. Switz. 43 K7
Chassiron, Pointe de pt France 52 D3
Chastab, Kūh-e mts Iran 84 D3
Chāt Iran 84 D2
Chatanika U.S.A. 114 D3
Châteaubriant France 52 D3
Château-du-Loir France 52 E3
Châteaudun France 52 E2
Chateaugay U.S.A. 131 H1
Châteauguay Canada 131 I1
Châteauguay r. Canada 119 H2
Châteauguay, Lac l. Canada 119 H2
Châteaulin France 52 B2
Châteaumeillant France 52 F3
Châteauneuf-en-Thymerais France 48 B6
Châteauneuf-sur-Loire France 52 F3
Chateau Pond l. Canada 119 K3
Châteauroux France 52 E3
Château-Salins France 48 G6
Château-Thierry France 48 D5
Chateh Canada 116 G3
Châtelet Belgium 48 E4
Châtellerault France 52 E3
Chatfield U.S.A. 118 B6
Chatham Canada 130 D2
Chatham U.K. 45 H7
Chatham MA U.S.A. 131 K3
Chatham NY U.S.A. 131 I2
Chatham PA U.S.A. 131 H4
Chatham VA U.S.A. 130 F5
Chatham, Isla i. Chile 140 B8
Chatham Island Galápagos Ecuador see San Cristóbal, Isla
Chatham Island N.Z. 103 I6
Chatham Island Samoa see Savai'i
Chatham Islands N.Z. 103 I6
Chatham Rise sea feature S. Pacific Ocean 146 I8
Chatham Strait U.S.A. 116 C3
Châtillon-sur-Seine France 52 G3
Chatkal Range mts Kyrg./Uzbek. 76 D3
Chatom U.S.A. 127 F6
Chatra India 79 F4
Chatra Nepal 79 F4
Chatsworth Canada 130 E1
Chatsworth U.S.A. 131 H4
Chattagam Bangl. see Chittagong
Chattanooga U.S.A. 129 C5
Chattarpur India see Chhatarpur
Chatteris U.K. 45 H6
Chattisgarh state India see Chhattisgarh
Chatturat Thai. 66 C4
Chatyr-Tash Kyrg. 76 E3
Châu Đốc Vietnam 67 D5
Chauhtan India 78 B4
Chauk Myanmar 66 A2
Chaumont France 52 G2
Chauncey U.S.A. 130 D4
Chaungzon Myanmar 66 B3
Chaunskaya Guba b. Rus. Fed. 61 R3
Chauny France 48 D5
Chau Phu Vietnam see Châu Đốc
Chausy Belarus see Chavusy
Chautauqua, Lake U.S.A. 130 F2
Chauter Pak. 85 G4
Chauvin Canada 117 I4
Chavakachcheri Sri Lanka 80 D4
Chaves Port. 53 C3
Chavigny, Lac l. Canada 118 G2
Chavusy Belarus 39 F5
Chawal r. Pak. 85 G4
Chây r. Vietnam 66 D2
Chayatyn, Khrebet ridge Rus. Fed. 70 E1
Chayevo Rus. Fed. 38 H4
Chaykovskiy Rus. Fed. 37 Q4
Chazhegovo Rus. Fed. 38 L3
Chazy U.S.A. 131 I1
Cheadle U.K. 45 F6
Cheaha Mountain hill U.S.A. 129 C5
Cheat r. U.S.A. 130 F4
Cheatham Lake U.S.A. 130 B5
Cheb Czech Rep. 49 M4
Chebba Tunisia 54 D7
Cheboksarskoye Vodokhranilishche resr Rus. Fed. 38 J5
Cheboksary Rus. Fed. 38 J4
Cheboygan U.S.A. 128 C2
Chechen', Ostrov i. Rus. Fed. 87 G2
Chech'ŏn S. Korea 71 C5
Chedabucto Bay Canada 119 J5
Cheddar U.K. 45 E7
Cheduba Myanmar 66 A3
Cheduba Island Myanmar 66 A3
Chée r. France 48 E6
Cheektowaga U.S.A. 131 F2
Cheepie Australia 108 B1
Cheetham, Cape Antarctica 148 H2
Chefoo China see Yantai
Chefornak U.S.A. 114 B3
Chefu Moz. 97 K2
Chegdomyn Rus. Fed. 70 D2
Chegga Mauritania 92 C2
Chegutu Zimbabwe 95 D5
Chehalis U.S.A. 122 C3
Chehar Burj Iran 84 E2
Chehardeh Iran 84 E3
Chehel Chashmeh, Kūh-e hill Iran 84 B3
Chehel Dokhtarān, Kūh-e mt. Iran 85 F4
Chehell'āyeh Iran 84 E4
Cheju S. Korea 71 B6
Cheju-do i. S. Korea 71 B6
Cheju-haehyŏp sea chan. S. Korea 71 B6
Chek Chue Hong Kong China see Stanley
Chekhov Moskovskaya Oblast' Rus. Fed. 39 H5
Chekhov Sakhalinskaya Oblast' Rus. Fed. 70 F3
Chekiang prov. China see Zhejiang
Chekichler Turkm. see Chekishlyar
Chekishlyar Turkm. 84 D2
Chek Lap Kok reg. Hong Kong China 73 [inset]
Chek Mun Hoi Hap Hong Kong China see Tolo Channel
Chekunda Rus. Fed. 70 D2
Chela, Serra da mts Angola 95 B5
Chelan, Lake U.S.A. 122 C2
Cheleken Turkm. 84 D2
Chélif, Oued r. Alg. 53 G5
Cheline Moz. 97 L2
Chelkar Kazakh. see Shalkar
Chełm Poland 39 D6
Chelmer r. U.K. 45 H7
Chełmno Poland 43 Q4
Chelmsford U.K. 45 H7
Chelsea MI U.S.A. 130 C2
Chelsea VT U.S.A. 131 I2
Cheltenham U.K. 45 E7
Chelva Spain 53 F4
Chelyabinsk Rus. Fed. 60 H4
Chelyuskin Rus. Fed. 149 E1
Chemba Moz. 95 D5
Chêm Co l. China 78 D2
Chemenibit Turkm. 85 F3
Chemnitz Germany 49 M4
Chemulpo S. Korea see Inch'ŏn
Chenab r. India/Pak. 78 B3
Chenachane, Oued watercourse Alg. 92 C2
Chendir r. Turkm. see Chandyr
Cheney U.S.A. 122 D3
Cheney Reservoir U.S.A. 126 D4
Chengalpattu India 80 D3
Chengbu China 73 F3
Chengchow China see Zhengzhou
Chengde China 69 L4
Chengdu China 72 E2
Chengele India 72 C2
Chenggong China 72 D3
Chenghai China 73 H4
Cheng Hai l. China 72 D3
Chengjiang China see Taihe
Chengmai China 73 F5
Chengtu China see Chengdu
Chengwu China 73 G1
Chengxian China 72 E1
Chengxiang Chongqing China see Wuxi
Chengxiang Jiangxi China see Quannan
Chengzhong China see Ningming
Cheniu Shan i. China 73 H1
Chenkaladi Sri Lanka 80 D5
Chennai India 80 D3
Chenqian Shan i. China 73 I2
Chenqing China 70 B2
Chenqingqiao China see Chenqing
Chenstokhov Poland see Częstochowa
Chentejn Nuruu mts Mongolia 69 J3
Chenxi China 73 F3
Chenyang China see Chenxi
Chenying China see Wannian
Chenzhou China 73 G3
Cheo Reo Vietnam 67 E4
Chepén Peru 138 C5
Chepes Arg. 140 C4
Chepo Panama 133 I7
Chepstow U.K. 45 E7
Cheptsa r. Rus. Fed. 38 K4
Chequamegon Bay U.S.A. 126 F2
Cher r. France 52 E3
Chera state India see Kerala
Cheraw U.S.A. 129 E5
Cherbaniani Reef India 80 A3
Cherbourg France 52 D2
Cherchell Alg. 53 H5
Cherchen China see Qiemo
Cherdakly Rus. Fed. 39 K5
Cherdyn' Rus. Fed. 37 R3
Chereapani reef India see Byramgore Reef
Cheremkhovo Rus. Fed. 68 I2
Cheremshany Rus. Fed. 70 D3
Cheremukhovka Rus. Fed. 38 K4
Cherepanovo Rus. Fed. 68 E2
Cherepovets Rus. Fed. 38 H4
Cherevkovo Rus. Fed. 38 J3
Chergui, Chott ech imp. l. Alg. 50 D5
Chéria Alg. 54 B7
Cheriton U.S.A. 131 H5
Cheriyam atoll India 80 B4
Cherkassy Ukr. see Cherkasy
Cherkasy Ukr. 39 G6
Cherkessk Rus. Fed. 87 F1
Cherla India 80 D2
Chernaya Rus. Fed. 38 M1
Chernaya r. Rus. Fed. 38 M1
Chernigov Ukr. see Chernihiv
Chernigovka Rus. Fed. 70 D3
Chernihiv Ukr. 39 F6
Cherninivka Ukr. 39 H7
Chernivtsi Ukr. 39 E6
Chernobyl' Ukr. see Chornobyl'
Chernogorsk Rus. Fed. 68 G2
Chernovtsy Ukr. see Chernivtsi
Chernoye More sea Asia/Europe see Black Sea
Chernushka Rus. Fed. 37 R4
Chernyakhiv Ukr. 39 F6
Chernyakhovsk Rus. Fed. 41 L9
Chernyanka Rus. Fed. 39 H6
Chernyayeve Rus. Fed. 70 B1
Chernyshevsk Rus. Fed. 69 L2
Chernyshevskiy Rus. Fed. 61 M3
Chernyshkovskiy Rus. Fed. 39 I6
Chernyye Zemli reg. Rus. Fed. 39 J7
Chernyy Irtysh r. China/Kazakh. see Ertix He
Chernyy Porog Rus. Fed. 38 G3
Chernyy Yar Rus. Fed. 39 J6
Cherokee U.S.A. 126 E3
Cherokee Sound Bahamas 129 E7

▶Cherrapunji India 79 G4
Highest recorded annual rainfall in the world.

Cherry Creek r. U.S.A. 126 C2
Cherry Creek Mountains U.S.A. 125 F1
Cherry Hill U.S.A. 131 H4
Cherry Island Solomon Is 103 G3
Cherry Lake U.S.A. 124 D2
Cherskiy Rus. Fed. 149 C2
Cherskiy Range mts Rus. Fed. see Cherskogo, Khrebet
Cherskogo, Khrebet mts Rus. Fed. 61 P3
Cherskogo, Khrebet mts Rus. Fed. 69 K2
Chertkov Ukr. see Chortkiv
Chertkovo Rus. Fed. 39 I6
Cherven Bryag Bulg. 55 K3
Chervonoarmeyskoye Ukr. see Vil'nyans'k
Chervonoarmiys'k Donets'ka Oblast' Ukr. see Krasnoarmiys'k
Chervonoarmiys'k Rivnens'ka Oblast' Ukr. see Radyvyliv
Chervonograd Ukr. see Chervonohrad
Chervonohrad Ukr. 39 E6
Chervyen' Belarus 39 F5
Cherwell r. U.K. 45 F7
Cherykaw Belarus 39 F5
Chesapeake U.S.A. 131 G5
Chesapeake Bay U.S.A. 131 G4
Chesham U.K. 45 G7
Cheshire Plain U.K. 44 E5
Cheshme 2-y Turkm. 85 F2
Cheshskaya Guba b. Rus. Fed. 38 J2
Cheshtebe Tajik. 85 I2
Cheshunt U.K. 45 G7
Chesnokovka Rus. Fed. see Novoaltaysk
Chester Canada 119 I5
Chester U.K. 44 E5
Chester CA U.S.A. 124 C1
Chester IL U.S.A. 126 F4
Chester MT U.S.A. 122 F2
Chester OH U.S.A. 130 E4
Chester SC U.S.A. 129 D5
Chester r. U.S.A. 131 G4
Chesterfield U.K. 44 F5
Chesterfield U.S.A. 131 G5
Chesterfield, Îles is New Caledonia 103 F3
Chesterfield Inlet Canada 117 N2
Chesterfield Inlet inlet Canada 117 M2
Chester-le-Street U.K. 44 F4
Chestertown MD U.S.A. 131 G4
Chestertown NY U.S.A. 131 I2
Chesterville Canada 131 H1
Chestnut Ridge U.S.A. 130 F3
Chesuncook Lake U.S.A. 128 G2
Chetaïbi Alg. 54 B6
Chéticamp Canada 119 J5
Chetlat i. India 80 B4
Chetumal Mex. 132 G5
Chetwynd Canada 116 F4
Cheung Chau Hong Kong China 73 [inset]
Chevelon Creek r. U.S.A. 125 H4
Cheviot N.Z. 109 D6
Cheviot Hills U.K. 44 E3
Cheviot Range hills Australia 106 C5
Chevreulx r. Canada 118 G3
Cheyenne OK U.S.A. 127 D5

▶Cheyenne WY U.S.A. 122 G4
State capital of Wyoming.

Cheyenne r. U.S.A. 126 C2
Cheyenne Wells U.S.A. 126 C4
Cheyne Bay Australia 105 B8
Cheyur India 80 D3
Chezacut Canada 116 E4
Chhapra India 79 F4
Chhata India 78 D4
Chhatak Bangl. 79 G4
Chhatarpur Jharkhand India 79 F4
Chhatarpur Madhya Pradesh India 78 D4
Chhatr Pak. 85 H4
Chhatrapur India 80 E2
Chhattisgarh state India 79 E5
Chhay Arêng, Stœng r. Cambodia 67 C5
Chhindwara India 78 D5
Chhitkul India 78 D3
Chhukha Bhutan 79 G4
Chi, Lam r. Thai. 67 C4
Chi, Mae Nam r. Thai. 66 D4
Chiai Taiwan 73 I4
Chiamboni Somalia 94 E4
Chiange Angola 95 B5
Chiang Kham Thai. 66 C3
Chiang Khan Thai. 66 C3
Chiang Mai Thai. 66 B3
Chiang Rai Thai. 66 B3
Chiang Saen Thai. 66 C2
Chiari Italy 54 C2
Chiautla Mex. 132 E5
Chiavenno Italy 54 C1
Chiayi Taiwan see Chiai
Chiba Japan 71 F6
Chibi China 73 G2
Chibia Angola 95 B5
Chibizovka Rus. Fed. see Zherdevka
Chiboma Moz. 95 D6
Chibougamau Canada 118 G4
Chibougamau, Lac l. Canada 118 G4
Chibu-Sangaku National Park Japan 71 E5
Chibuto Moz. 97 K3
Chibuzhang Hu l. China 79 G2
Chicacole India see Srikakulam

▶Chicago U.S.A. 130 B3
4th most populous city in North America.

Chic-Chocs, Monts mts Canada 119 I4
Chichagof U.S.A. 116 B3
Chichagof Island U.S.A. 116 C3
Chichak r. Pak. 85 G5
Chichaoua Morocco 50 C5
Chichatka Rus. Fed. 70 A1
Chicheng China see Pengxi
Chichester U.K. 45 G8
Chichester Range mts Australia 104 B5
Chichgarh India 80 D1
Chichibu Japan 71 E6
Chichibu-Tama National Park Japan 71 E6
Chichijima-rettō is Japan 71 F8
Chickasha U.S.A. 127 D5
Chiclana de la Frontera Spain 53 C5
Chiclayo Peru 138 C5
Chico r. Arg. 140 C6

Cochrane r. Canada 117 K3
Cockburn Australia 107 C7
Cockburnspath U.K. 46 G5
Cockburn Town Bahamas 129 F7
Cockburn Town Turks and Caicos Is see Grand Turk
Cockermouth U.K. 44 D4
Cocklebiddy Australia 105 D8
Cockscomb mt. S. Africa 96 G7
Coco r. Hond./Nicaragua 133 H6
Coco, Cayo i. Cuba 129 E8
Coco, Isla de i. N. Pacific Ocean 133 G7
Cocobeach Gabon 94 A3
Coco Channel India 67 A4
Cocomórachic Mex. 123 G7
Coconino Plateau U.S.A. 125 G4
Cocopara National Park Australia 108 C5
Cocos Brazil 141 B1
Cocos Basin sea feature Indian Ocean 145 O5
▶Cocos Islands terr. Indian Ocean 64 B9
Australian External Territory.
asia 6
Cocos Ridge sea feature N. Pacific Ocean 147 O5
Cocuy, Sierra Nevada del mt. Col. 138 D2
Cod, Cape U.S.A. 131 J3
Codajás Brazil 138 F4
Coderre Canada 117 J5
Codfish Island N.Z. 109 A8
Codigoro Italy 54 E2
Cod Island Canada 119 J2
Codlea Romania 55 K2
Codó Brazil 139 J4
Codsall U.K. 45 E6
Cod's Head hd Rep. of Ireland 47 B6
Cody U.S.A. 122 F3
Coeburn U.S.A. 130 D5
Coen Australia 106 C2
Coesfeld Germany 49 H3
Coeur d'Alene U.S.A. 122 D3
Coeur d'Alene Lake U.S.A. 122 D3
Coevorden Neth. 48 G2
Coffee Bay S. Africa 97 I6
Coffeyville U.S.A. 127 E4
Coffin Bay Australia 107 A7
Coffin Bay National Park Australia 107 A7
Coffs Harbour Australia 108 F3
Cofimvaba S. Africa 97 H7
Cognac France 52 D4
Cogo Equat. Guinea 92 D4
Coguno Moz. 97 L3
Cohoes U.S.A. 131 I2
Cohuna Australia 108 B5
Coiba, Isla de i. Panama 133 H7
Coigeach, Rubha pt U.K. 46 D2
Coihaique Chile 140 B7
Coimbatore India 80 C4
Coimbra Port. 53 B3
Coipasa, Salar de salt flat Bol. 138 E7
Coire Switz. see Chur
Colac Australia 108 A7
Colair Lake India see Kolleru Lake
Colatina Brazil 141 C2
Colbitz Germany 49 L2
Colborne Canada 131 G2
Colby U.S.A. 126 C4
Colchester U.K. 45 H7
Colchester U.S.A. 131 I3
Cold Bay U.S.A. 114 B4
Coldingham U.K. 46 G5
Colditz Germany 49 M3
Cold Lake Canada 117 I4
Cold Lake l. Canada 117 I4
Coldspring U.S.A. 127 E6
Coldstream Canada 116 G5
Coldstream U.K. 46 G5
Coldwater Canada 130 F1
Coldwater KS U.S.A. 127 D4
Coldwater MI U.S.A. 130 C3
Coldwater r. U.S.A. 127 F5
Coleambally Australia 108 B5
Colebrook U.S.A. 131 J1
Coleman r. Australia 106 C2
Coleman U.S.A. 127 D6
Çölemerik Turkey see Hakkâri
Colenso S. Africa 97 I5
Cole Peninsula Antarctica 148 L2
Coleraine Australia 107 C8
Coleraine U.K. 47 F2
Coles, Punta de pt Peru 138 D7
Coles Bay Australia 107 [inset]
Colesberg S. Africa 97 G6
Coleville Canada 117 I5
Colfax CA U.S.A. 124 C2
Colfax LA U.S.A. 127 E6
Colfax WA U.S.A. 122 D3
Colhué Huapí, Lago l. Arg. 140 C7
Coligny S. Africa 97 H4
Colima Mex. 132 D5
Colima, Nevado de vol. Mex. 132 D5
Coll i. U.K. 46 C4
Collado Villalba Spain 53 E3
Collarenebri Australia 108 D2
College Station U.S.A. 127 D6
Collerina Australia 108 C2
Collie N.S.W. Australia 108 D3
Collie W.A. Australia 105 B8
Collier Bay Australia 104 D4
Collier Range National Park Australia 105 B6
Collingwood Canada 130 E1
Collingwood N.Z. 109 D5
Collins U.S.A. 127 F6
Collins Glacier Antarctica 148 E2
Collinson Peninsula Canada 115 H2
Collipulli Chile 140 B5
Collmberg hill Germany 49 N3
Collooney Rep. of Ireland 47 D3
Colmar France 52 H2
Colmenar Viejo Spain 53 E3
Colmonell U.K. 46 E5
Colne r. U.K. 45 H7
Cologne Germany 48 G4
Coloma U.S.A. 130 B2
Colomb-Béchar Alg. see Béchar
Colômbia Brazil 141 A3
Colombia Mex. 127 D7
▶Colombia country S. America 138 D3
2nd most populous and 4th largest country in South America.
south america 9, 136–137
Colombian Basin sea feature S. Atlantic Ocean 144 C5
▶Colombo Sri Lanka 80 C5
Former capital of Sri Lanka.
Colomiers France 52 E5
Colón Buenos Aires Arg. 140 D4
Colón Entre Ríos Arg. 140 E4
Colón Cuba 129 D8
Colón Panama 133 I7
Colon U.S.A. 130 C3
Colón, Archipiélago de is Ecuador see Galapagos Islands
Colona Australia 105 F7
Colonelganj India 79 E4
Colonel Hill Bahamas 129 F8
Colonet, Cabo c. Mex. 123 D7
Colônia r. Brazil 141 D1
Colonia Micronesia 65 J5
Colonia Agrippina Germany see Cologne
Colonia Díaz Mex. 123 F7
Colonia Julia Fenestris Italy see Fano
Colonia Las Heras Arg. 140 C7
Colonial Heights U.S.A. 131 G5
Colonna, Capo c. Italy 54 G5
Colonsay i. U.K. 46 C4
Colorado r. Arg. 140 D5
Colorado r. Mex./U.S.A. 123 E7
Colorado r. U.S.A. 127 D6
Colorado state U.S.A. 122 G5
Colorado City AZ U.S.A. 125 G3
Colorado City TX U.S.A. 127 C5
Colorado Desert U.S.A. 124 E5
Colorado National Monument nat. park U.S.A. 125 I2
Colorado Plateau U.S.A. 125 I3
Colorado River Aqueduct canal U.S.A. 125 F4
Colorado Springs U.S.A. 122 G5
Colossae Turkey see Honaz
Colotlán Mex. 132 D4
Cölpin Germany 49 N1
Colquiri Bol. 138 E7
Colquitt U.S.A. 129 C6
Colson U.S.A. 130 D5
Colsterworth U.K. 45 G6
Colstrip U.S.A. 122 G3
Coltishall U.K. 45 I6
Colton CA U.S.A. 124 E4
Colton NY U.S.A. 131 H1
Colton UT U.S.A. 125 H2
Columbia KY U.S.A. 130 C5
Columbia LA U.S.A. 127 E5
Columbia MD U.S.A. 131 G4
Columbia MO U.S.A. 126 E4
Columbia MS U.S.A. 127 F6
Columbia NC U.S.A. 128 E5
Columbia PA U.S.A. 131 G3
▶Columbia SC U.S.A. 129 D5
State capital of South Carolina.
Columbia TN U.S.A. 128 C5
Columbia r. U.S.A. 122 C3
Columbia, District of admin. dist. U.S.A. 131 G4
Columbia, Mount Canada 116 G4
Columbia, Sierra mts Mex. 123 E7
Columbia City U.S.A. 130 C3
Columbia Lake Canada 116 H5
Columbia Mountains Canada 116 F4
Columbia Plateau U.S.A. 122 D3
Columbine, Cape S. Africa 96 C7
Columbus GA U.S.A. 129 C5
Columbus IN U.S.A. 130 C4
Columbus MS U.S.A. 127 F5
Columbus MT U.S.A. 122 F3
Columbus NC U.S.A. 129 D5
Columbus NE U.S.A. 126 D3
Columbus NM U.S.A. 123 G7
▶Columbus OH U.S.A. 130 D4
State capital of Ohio.
Columbus TX U.S.A. 127 D6
Columbus Grove U.S.A. 130 C3
Columbus Salt Marsh U.S.A. 124 D2
Colusa U.S.A. 124 B2
Colville N.Z. 109 E3
Colville U.S.A. 122 D2
Colville r. U.S.A. 114 C2
Colville Channel N.Z. 109 E3
Colville Lake Canada 114 F3
Colwyn Bay U.K. 44 D5
Comacchio Italy 54 E2
Comacchio, Valli di lag. Italy 54 E2
Comai China 79 G3
Comalcalco Mex. 132 F5
Comanche U.S.A. 127 D6
Comandante Ferraz research station Antarctica 148 A2
Comandante Salas Arg. 140 C4
Comănești Romania 55 L1
Combahee r. U.S.A. 129 D5
Combarbalá Chile 140 B4
Comber U.K. 47 G3
Combermere Bay Myanmar 66 A3
Combles France 48 C4
Combol i. Indon. 67 C7
Combomune Moz. 97 K2
Comboyne Australia 108 F3
Comencho, Lac l. Canada 118 G4
Comendador Dom. Rep. see Elías Piña
Comendador Gomes Brazil 141 A2
Comeragh Mountains hills Rep. of Ireland 47 E5
Comercinho Brazil 141 C2
Cometela Moz. 97 L1
Comfort U.S.A. 127 D6
Comilla Bangl. 79 G5
Comines Belgium 48 C4
Comino, Capo c. Sardinia Italy 54 C4
Comitán de Domínguez Mex. 132 F5
Commack U.S.A. 131 I3
Commentry France 52 F3
Committee Bay Canada 115 J3
Commonwealth Territory admin. div. Australia see Jervis Bay Territory
Como Italy 54 C2
Como, Lago di Italy see Como, Lake
Como, Lake Italy 54 C2
Como Chamling l. China 79 G3
Comodoro Rivadavia Arg. 140 C7
Comores country Africa see Comoros
Comorin, Cape India 80 C4
Comoro Islands country Africa see Comoros
▶Comoros country Africa 95 E5
africa 7, 90–91
Compiègne France 48 C5
Comprida, Ilha i. Brazil 141 B4
Comrat Moldova 55 M1
Comrie U.K. 46 F4
Comstock U.S.A. 127 C6
Cona China 79 G4
▶Conakry Guinea 92 B4
Capital of Guinea.
Cona Niyeo Arg. 140 C6
Conceição r. Brazil 141 B2
Conceição da Barra Brazil 141 D2
Conceição do Araguaia Brazil 139 I5
Conceição do Mato Dentro Brazil 141 C2
Concepción Chile 140 B5
Concepción Mex. 127 C7
Concepción r. Mex. 123 E7
Concepción Para. 140 E2
Concepción, Punta pt Mex. 123 F8
Concepción de la Vega Dom. Rep. see La Vega
Conception, Point U.S.A. 124 C4
Conception Island Bahamas 129 F8
Conchas U.S.A. 123 G6
Conchas Lake U.S.A. 123 G6
Concho U.S.A. 125 I4
Conchos r. Nuevo León/Tamaulipas Mex. 127 D7
Conchos r. Mex. 127 B6
Concord CA U.S.A. 124 B3
Concord NC U.S.A. 129 D5
▶Concord NH U.S.A. 131 J2
State capital of New Hampshire.
Concord VT U.S.A. 131 J1
Concordia Arg. 140 E4
Concordia Mex. 127 B8
Concordia Peru 138 D4
Concordia S. Africa 96 C5
Concordia KS U.S.A. 126 D4
Concordia KY U.S.A. 130 B4
Concord Peak Afgh. 85 I2
Con Cuông Vietnam 66 D3
Condamine Australia 108 E1
Condamine r. Australia 108 D1
Côn Đao Vietnam 67 D5
Condeúba Brazil 141 C1
Condobolin Australia 108 C4
Condom France 52 E5
Condon U.S.A. 122 C3
Condor, Cordillera del mts Ecuador/Peru 138 C4
Condroz reg. Belgium 48 E4
Conecuh r. U.S.A. 129 C6
Conegliano Italy 54 E2
Conejos Mex. 127 C7
Conejos U.S.A. 123 G5
Conemaugh r. U.S.A. 130 F3
Conestogo Lake Canada 130 E2
Conesus Lake U.S.A. 131 G2
Conflict Group is P.N.G. 106 E1
Confoederatio Helvetica country Europe see Switzerland
Confusion Range mts U.S.A. 125 G2
Congdü China see Nyalam
Conghua China 73 G4
Congjiang China 73 F3
Congleton U.K. 44 E5
▶Congo country Africa 94 B4
africa 7, 90–91
▶Congo r. Congo/Dem. Rep. Congo 94 B4
2nd longest river and largest drainage basin in Africa.
formerly known as Zaire
africa 88–89
Congo (Brazzaville) country Africa see Congo
Congo (Kinshasa) country Africa see Congo, Democratic Republic of
▶Congo, Democratic Republic of country Africa 94 C4
3rd largest and 4th most populous country in Africa.
africa 7, 90–91
Congo, Republic of country Africa see Congo
Congo Basin Dem. Rep. Congo 94 C4
Congo Cone sea feature S. Atlantic Ocean 144 I6
Congo Free State country Africa see Congo, Democratic Republic of
Congonhas Brazil 141 C3
Congress U.S.A. 125 G4
Conimbla National Park Australia 108 D4
Coningsby U.K. 45 G5
Coniston Canada 118 E5
Coniston U.K. 44 D4
Conjuboy Australia 106 D3
Conklin Canada 117 I4
Conn r. Canada 118 F3
Conn, Lough l. Rep. of Ireland 47 C3
Connacht reg. Rep. of Ireland see Connaught
Connaught reg. Rep. of Ireland 47 C4
Conneaut U.S.A. 130 E3
Connecticut state U.S.A. 131 I3
Connemara reg. Rep. of Ireland 47 C4
Connemara National Park Rep. of Ireland 47 C4
Connersville U.S.A. 130 C4
Connolly, Mount Canada 116 C2
Connors Range hills Australia 106 E4
Conoble Australia 108 B4
Conquista Brazil 141 B2
Conrad U.S.A. 122 F2
Conrad Rise sea feature Southern Ocean 145 K9
Conroe U.S.A. 127 E6
Conselheiro Lafaiete Brazil 141 C3
Consett U.K. 44 F4
Consolación del Sur Cuba 129 D8
Côn Sơn i. Vietnam 67 D5
Consort Canada 117 I4
Constance Germany see Konstanz
Constance, Lake Germany/Switz. 43 L7
Constância dos Baetas Brazil 138 F5
Constanța Romania 55 M2
Constantia tourist site Cyprus see Salamis
Constantia Germany see Konstanz
Constantina Spain 53 D5
Constantine Alg. 50 F4
Constantine, Cape U.S.A. 114 C4
Constantinople Turkey see İstanbul
Constitución de 1857, Parque Nacional nat. park Mex. 125 F5
Consul Canada 117 I5
Contact U.S.A. 122 E4
Contagalo Brazil 141 C3
Contamana Peru 138 C5
Contas r. Brazil 141 D1
Contoy, Isla i. Mex. 129 C8
Contria Brazil 141 B2
Contwoyto Lake Canada 117 I1
Convención Col. 138 D2
Convent U.S.A. 127 F6
Conway U.K. see Conwy
Conway AR U.S.A. 127 E5
Conway ND U.S.A. 126 D1
Conway NH U.S.A. 131 J2
Conway SC U.S.A. 129 E5
Conway, Cape Australia 106 E4
Conway, Lake salt flat Australia 107 A6
Conway National Park Australia 106 E4
Conway Reef Fiji see Ceva-i-Ra
Conwy U.K. 44 D5
Conwy r. U.K. 45 D5
Coober Pedy Australia 105 F7
Cooch Behar India see Koch Bihar
Coochbehar India see Koch Bihar
Cook Australia 105 E7
Cook, Cape Canada 116 E5
Cook, Grand Récif de reef New Caledonia 103 G3
Cook, Mount N.Z. see Aoraki
Cookes Peak U.S.A. 123 G6
Cookeville U.S.A. 128 C4
Cookhouse S. Africa 97 G7
Cook Ice Shelf Antarctica 148 H2
Cook Inlet sea chan. U.S.A. 114 C3
▶Cook Islands terr. S. Pacific Ocean 146 J7
Self-governing New Zealand Territory.
oceania 8, 100–101
Cooksburg U.S.A. 131 H2
Cooks Passage Australia 106 D2
Cookstown U.K. 47 F3
Cook Strait N.Z. 109 E5
Cooktown Australia 106 D2
Coolabah Australia 108 C3
Cooladdi Australia 108 B1
Coolah Australia 108 D3
Coolamon Australia 108 C5
Coolgardie Australia 105 C7
Coolibah Australia 104 E3
Coolidge U.S.A. 125 H5
Cooloola National Park Australia 107 F5
Coolum Beach Australia 107 F5
Cooma Australia 108 D6
Coombah Australia 107 C7
Coonabarabran Australia 108 D3
Coonamble Australia 108 D3
Coondambo Australia 107 A6
Coondapoor India see Kundapura
Coongoola Australia 108 B1
Coon Rapids U.S.A. 126 E2
Cooper Creek watercourse Australia 107 B6
Cooper Mountain Canada 116 G5
Coopernook Australia 108 F3
Cooper's Town Bahamas 129 E7
Cooperstown ND U.S.A. 126 D2
Cooperstown NY U.S.A. 131 H2
Coopracambra National Park Australia 108 D6
Coorabie Australia 105 F7
Coorong National Park Australia 107 B8
Coorow Australia 105 B7
Coosa r. U.S.A. 129 C5
Coos Bay U.S.A. 122 B4
Coos Bay b. U.S.A. 122 B4
Cootamundra Australia 108 D5
Cootehill Rep. of Ireland 47 E3
Cooyar Australia 108 E1
Copala Mex. 132 E5
Cope U.S.A. 126 C4
Copemish U.S.A. 130 C1
▶Copenhagen Denmark 41 H9
Capital of Denmark.
Copenhagen U.S.A. 131 H2
Copertino Italy 54 H4
Copeton Reservoir Australia 108 E2
Cö Pi, Phou mt. Laos/Vietnam 66 D3
Copiapó Chile 140 B3
Copley Australia 107 B6
Copparo Italy 54 D2
Copper Cliff Canada 118 E5
Copper Harbor U.S.A. 128 C2
Coppermine Canada see Kugluktuk
Coppermine r. Canada 116 H1
Coppermine Point Canada 118 D5
Copperton S. Africa 96 F5
Copp Lake Canada 116 H2
Coqên Xizang China 79 F3
Coqên Xizang China see Maindong
Coquilhatville Dem. Rep. Congo see Mbandaka
Coquille i. Micronesia see Pikelot
Coquille U.S.A. 122 B4
Coquimbo Chile 140 B3
Coquitlam Canada 116 F5
Corabia Romania 55 K3
Coração de Jesus Brazil 141 B2
Coracesium Turkey see Alanya
Coraki Australia 108 F2
Coral Bay Australia 105 A5
Coral Harbour Canada 115 J3
Coral Sea S. Pacific Ocean 102 F3
Coral Sea Basin S. Pacific Ocean 146 G6
▶Coral Sea Islands Territory terr. Australia 102 F3
Australian External Territory.
Corangamite, Lake Australia 108 A7
Corat Azer. 87 H2
Corbeny France 48 D5
Corbett Inlet Canada 117 M2
Corbett National Park India 78 D3
Corbie France 48 C5
Corbin U.S.A. 130 C5
Corby U.K. 45 G6
Corcaigh Rep. of Ireland see Cork
Corcoran U.S.A. 124 D3
Corcovado, Golfo de sea chan. Chile 140 B6
Corcyra i. Greece see Corfu
Cordele U.S.A. 129 D6
Cordelia U.S.A. 124 B2
Cordell U.S.A. 127 D5
Cordilheiras, Serra das hills Brazil 139 I5
Cordillera Azul, Parque Nacional nat. park Peru 138 C5
Cordillera de los Picachos, Parque Nacional nat. park Col. 138 D3
Cordillo Downs Australia 107 C5
Cordisburgo Brazil 141 B2
Córdoba Arg. 140 D4
Córdoba Durango Mex. 127 C7
Córdoba Veracruz Mex. 132 E5
Córdoba Spain 53 D5
Córdoba, Sierras de mts Arg. 140 D4
Cordova Spain see Córdoba
Cordova U.S.A. 114 D3
Corduba Spain see Córdoba
Corfu i. Greece 55 H5
Coria Spain 53 C4
Coribe Brazil 141 B1
Coricudgy mt. Australia 108 E4
Corigliano Calabro Italy 54 G5
Coringa Islands Australia 106 E3
Corinium U.K. see Cirencester
Corinth Greece 55 J6
Corinth KY U.S.A. 130 C4
Corinth MS U.S.A. 127 F5
Corinth NY U.S.A. 131 I2
Corinth, Gulf of sea chan. Greece 55 J5
Corinthus Greece see Corinth
Corinto Brazil 141 B2
Cork Rep. of Ireland 47 D6
Corleone Sicily Italy 54 E6
Çorlu Turkey 55 L4
Cormeilles France 45 H9
Cornelia S. Africa 97 I4
Cornélio Procópio Brazil 141 A3
Cornélios Brazil 141 A5
Cornell U.S.A. 126 F2
Corner Brook Canada 119 K4
Corner Inlet b. Australia 108 C7
Corner Seamounts sea feature N. Atlantic Ocean 144 E3
Corneto Italy see Tarquinia
Cornillet, Mont hill France 48 E5
Corning AR U.S.A. 127 F4
Corning CA U.S.A. 124 B2
Corning NY U.S.A. 131 G2
Cornish watercourse Australia 106 D4
Corn Islands is Nicaragua see Maíz, Islas del
Corno, Monte mt. Italy 54 E3
Corno di Campo mt. Italy/Switz. 52 J3
Cornwall Canada 131 H1
Cornwallis Island Canada 115 I2
Cornwall Island Canada 115 I2
Coro Venez. 138 E1
Coroaci Brazil 141 C2
Coroatá Brazil 139 J4
Corofin Rep. of Ireland 47 C5
Coromandel Brazil 141 B2
Coromandel Coast India 80 D4
Coromandel Peninsula N.Z. 109 E3
Coromandel Range hills N.Z. 109 E3
Corona CA U.S.A. 124 E5
Corona NM U.S.A. 123 G6
Coronado U.S.A. 124 E5
Coronado, Bahía de b. Costa Rica 133 H7
Coronation Canada 117 I4
Coronation Gulf Canada 114 G3
Coronation Island S. Atlantic Ocean 148 A2
Coronda Arg. 140 D4
Coronel Fabriciano Brazil 141 C2
Coronel Oviedo Para. 140 E3
Coronel Pringles Arg. 140 D5
Coronel Suárez Arg. 140 D5
Çorovodë Albania 55 I4
Corowa Australia 108 C5
Corpus Christi U.S.A. 127 D7
Corque Bol. 138 E7
Corral de Cantos mt. Spain 53 D4
Corrales Mex. 127 B7
Corralilla Cuba 129 D8
Corrandibby Range hills Australia 105 A6
Corrente Brazil 139 I6
Corrente r. Bahia Brazil 141 C1
Corrente r. Minas Gerais Brazil 141 A2
Correntes Brazil 139 H7
Correntina Brazil 141 B1
Correntina r. Brazil see Éguas
Corrib, Lough l. Rep. of Ireland 47 C4
Corrientes Arg. 140 E3
Corrientes, Cabo c. Col. 138 C2
Corrientes, Cabo c. Cuba 129 C8
Corrientes, Cabo c. Mex. 132 C4
Corrigin Australia 105 B8
Corris U.K. 45 D6
Corry U.S.A. 130 F3
Corse i. France see Corsica
Corse, Cap c. Corsica France 52 I5
Corsham U.K. 45 E7
Corsica i. France 52 I5
Corsicana U.S.A. 127 D5
Corte Corsica France 52 I5
Cortegana Spain 53 C5
Cortes, Sea of g. Mex. see California, Gulf of
Cortez U.S.A. 125 I3
Cortina d'Ampezzo Italy 54 E1
Cortland U.S.A. 131 G2
Corton U.K. 45 I6
Cortona Italy 54 D3
Coruche Port. 53 B4
Çoruh Turkey see Artvin
Çoruh r. Turkey 87 F2
Çorum Turkey 86 D2
Corumbá Brazil 139 G7
Corumbá r. Brazil 141 A2
Corumbá de Goiás Brazil 141 A1
Corumbaíba Brazil 141 A2
Corumbaú, Ponta pt Brazil 141 D2
Corunna Spain see A Coruña
Corunna U.S.A. 130 C2
Corvallis U.S.A. 122 C3
Corwen U.K. 45 D6
Corydon IA U.S.A. 126 E3
Corydon IN U.S.A. 130 B4
Coryville U.S.A. 131 F3
Cos i. Greece see Kos
Cosentia Italy see Cosenza
Cosenza Italy 54 G5
Coshocton U.S.A. 130 E3
Cosne-Cours-sur-Loire France 52 F3
Costa Blanca coastal area Spain 53 F4
Costa Brava coastal area Spain 53 H3
Costa de la Luz coastal area Spain 53 C5
Costa del Sol coastal area Spain 53 D5
Costa de Miskitos coastal area Nicaragua see Costa de Mosquitos
Costa de Mosquitos coastal area Nicaragua 133 H6
Costa Marques Brazil 138 F6
Costa Rica Brazil 139 H7
▶Costa Rica country Central America 133 H6
north america 9, 112–113
Costa Rica Mex. 132 C4
Costa Verde coastal area Spain 53 C2
Costermansville Dem. Rep. Congo see Bukavu
Costești Romania 55 K2
Costigan Lake Canada 117 J3
Coswig Germany 49 M3
Cotabato Phil. 65 G5
Cotagaita Bol. 138 E8
Cotahuasi Peru 138 D7
Cote, Mount U.S.A. 116 D3
Coteau des Prairies slope U.S.A. 126 D2
Coteau du Missouri slope ND U.S.A. 126 C1
Coteau du Missouri slope SD U.S.A. 126 C2
Côte d'Azur coastal area France 52 H5
▶Côte d'Ivoire country Africa 92 C4
africa 7, 90–91
Côte Française de Somalis country Africa see Djibouti
Cotentin pen. France 45 F9
Côtes de Meuse ridge France 48 E5
Cothi r. U.K. 45 C7
Cotiaeum Turkey see Kütahya
Cotiella mt. Spain 53 G2
Cotonou Benin 92 D4
Cotopaxi, Volcán vol. Ecuador 138 C4
Cotswold Hills U.K. 45 E7
Cottage Grove U.S.A. 122 C4
Cottbus Germany 43 O5
Cottenham U.K. 45 H6
Cottian Alps mts France/Italy 52 H4
Cottica Suriname 139 H3
Cottiennes, Alpes mts France/Italy see Cottian Alps
Cottonwood AZ U.S.A. 125 G4
Cottonwood CA U.S.A. 124 B1
Cottonwood r. U.S.A. 126 D4
Cottonwood Falls U.S.A. 126 D4
Cotulla U.S.A. 127 D6
Coudersport U.S.A. 131 F3
Couëdic, Cape de Australia 107 B8
Coulee City U.S.A. 122 D3
Coulee Dam U.S.A. 122 D3
Coulman Island Antarctica 148 H2
Coulogne France 48 B4
Coulommiers France 48 D6
Coulonge r. Canada 118 F5
Coulterville U.S.A. 124 C3
Council U.S.A. 122 D3
Council Bluffs U.S.A. 126 E3
Council Grove U.S.A. 126 D4
Councillor Island Australia 107 [inset]
Counselor U.S.A. 125 J3
Coupeville U.S.A. 122 C2
Courageous Lake Canada 117 I1
Courland Lagoon b. Lith./Rus. Fed. 41 L9
Courtenay Canada 116 E5
Courtland U.S.A. 131 G5
Courtmacsherry Rep. of Ireland 47 D6
Courtmacsherry Bay Rep. of Ireland 47 D6
Courtown Rep. of Ireland 47 F5
Courtrai Belgium see Kortrijk
Coushatta U.S.A. 127 E5
Coutances France 52 D2
Coutts Canada 117 I5
Couture, Lac l. Canada 118 G2
Couvin Belgium 48 E4
Cove Fort U.S.A. 125 G2
Cove Island Canada 130 E1
Cove Mountains hills U.S.A. 131 F4
Coventry U.K. 45 F6
Covered Wells U.S.A. 125 G5
Covesville U.S.A. 131 F5
Covilhã Port. 53 C3
Covington GA U.S.A. 129 D5
Covington IN U.S.A. 130 B3
Covington KY U.S.A. 130 C4
Covington LA U.S.A. 127 F6
Covington MI U.S.A. 126 F2
Covington TN U.S.A. 127 F5
Covington VA U.S.A. 130 E5
Cowal, Lake dry lake Australia 108 C4
Cowan, Lake salt flat Australia 105 C7
Cowansville Canada 131 I1
Cowargarzê China 72 C1
Cowcowing Lakes salt flat Australia 105 B7
Cowdenbeath U.K. 46 F4
Cowell Australia 107 B7
Cowes U.K. 45 F8
Cowichan Lake Canada 116 E5
Cowley Australia 108 B1
Cowper Point Canada 115 G2
Cowra Australia 108 D4
Cox r. Australia 106 A2
Coxá r. Brazil 141 B1
Coxen Hole Hond. see Roatán
Coxilha de Santana hills Brazil/Uruguay 140 E4
Coxilha Grande hills Brazil 140 F3
Coxim Brazil 139 H7
Cox's Bazar Bangl. 79 G5
Coyame Mex. 127 B6
Coyhaique Chile see Coihaique
Coyote Lake U.S.A. 124 E4
Coyote Peak hill U.S.A. 125 F5
Cozhê China 79 F2
Cozie, Alpi mts France/Italy see Cottian Alps
Cozumel Mex. 133 G4
Cozumel, Isla de i. Mex. 133 G4
Craboon Australia 108 D4
Cracovia Poland see Kraków
Cracow Australia 106 E5
Cracow Poland see Kraków
Cradle Mountain Lake St Clair National Park Australia 107 [inset]
Cradock S. Africa 97 G7
Craig U.K. 46 D3
Craig AK U.S.A. 116 C4
Craig CO U.S.A. 125 J1
Craigavon U.K. 47 F3
Craigieburn Australia 108 B6
Craig Island Taiwan see Mienhua Yü
Craignure U.K. 46 D4
Craigsville U.S.A. 130 E4

Crail U.K. 46 G4
Crailsheim Germany 49 K5
Craiova Romania 55 J2
Cramlington U.K. 44 F3
Cranberry Lake U.S.A. 131 H1
Cranberry Portage Canada 117 K4
Cranborne Chase for. U.K. 45 E8
Cranbourne Australia 108 B7
Cranbrook Canada 116 H5
Crandon U.S.A. 126 F2
Crane Lake Canada 117 I5
Cranston KY U.S.A. 130 D4
Cranston RI U.S.A. 131 J3
Cranz Rus. Fed. see Zelenogradsk
Crary Ice Rise Antarctica 148 I1
Crary Mountains Antarctica 148 J1
Crater Lake National Park U.S.A. 122 C4
Crater Peak U.S.A. 124 C1
Craters of the Moon National Monument nat. park U.S.A. 122 E4
Crateús Brazil 139 J5
Crato Brazil 139 K5
Crawford CO U.S.A. 125 J2
Crawford NE U.S.A. 126 C3
Crawfordsville U.S.A. 130 B3
Crawfordville FL U.S.A. 129 C6
Crawfordville GA U.S.A. 129 D5
Crawley U.K. 45 G7
Crazy Mountains U.S.A. 122 F3
Creag Meagaidh mt. U.K. 46 E4
Crécy-en-Ponthieu France 48 B4
Credenhill U.K. 45 E6
Crediton U.K. 45 D8
Cree r. Canada 117 J3
Creel Mex. 123 G8
Cree Lake Canada 117 J3
Creemore Canada 130 E1
Creighton Canada 117 K4
Creil France 48 C5
Creil Neth. 48 F2
Crema Italy 54 C2
Cremlingen Germany 49 K2
Cremona Canada 116 H5
Cremona Italy 54 D2
Crépy-en-Valois France 48 C5
Cres i. Croatia 54 F2
Crescent U.S.A. 122 C4
Crescent City CA U.S.A. 122 B4
Crescent City FL U.S.A. 129 D6
Crescent Group is Paracel Is 64 E3
Crescent Head Australia 108 F3
Crescent Junction U.S.A. 125 I2
Crescent Valley U.S.A. 124 E1
Cressy Australia 108 A7
Crest Hill hill Hong Kong China 73 [inset]
Crestline U.S.A. 130 D3
Creston Canada 116 G5
Creston IA U.S.A. 126 E3
Creston WY U.S.A. 122 G4
Crestview U.S.A. 129 C6
Creswick Australia 108 A6
Creta i. Greece see Crete
Crete i. Greece 55 K7
Crete U.S.A. 126 D3
Creus, Cap de c. Spain 53 H2
Creuse r. France 52 E3
Creußen Germany 49 L5
Creutzwald France 48 G5
Creuzburg Germany 49 K3
Crevasse Valley Glacier Antarctica 148 J1
Crewe U.K. 45 E5
Crewe U.S.A. 131 F5
Crewkerne U.K. 45 E8
Crianlarich U.K. 46 E4
Criccieth U.K. 45 C6
Criciúma Brazil 141 A5
Crieff U.K. 46 F4
Criffel hill U.K. 46 F6
Criffell hill U.K. see Criffel
Crikvenica Croatia 54 F2
Crillon, Mount U.S.A. 116 B3
Crimea pen. Ukr. 86 D1
Crimmitschau Germany 49 M4
Crimond U.K. 46 H3
Crisfield U.S.A. 131 H5
Cristalândia Brazil 139 I6
Cristalina Brazil 141 B2
Cristalino r. Brazil see Mariembero
Cristóbal Colón, Pico mt. Col. 138 D1
Crixás Brazil 141 A1
Crixás Açu r. Brazil 141 A1
Crixás Mirim r. Brazil 141 A1
Crna Gora aut. rep. Serb. and Mont. 54 H3
Crni Vrh mt. Serb. and Mont. 55 J2
Crnomelj Slovenia 54 F2
Croagh Patrick hill Rep. of Ireland 47 C4
Croajingolong National Park Australia 108 D6
▶Croatia country Europe 54 G2
europe 5, 34–35
Crocker, Banjaran mts Malaysia 64 E6
Crockett U.S.A. 127 E6
Crofton KY U.S.A. 130 B5
Crofton NE U.S.A. 126 D3
Croghan U.S.A. 131 H2
Croisilles France 48 C4
Croker, Cape Canada 130 E1
Croker Island Australia 104 F2
Cromarty U.K. 46 E3
Cromarty Firth est. U.K. 46 E3
Cromer U.K. 45 I6
Crook U.K. 44 F4
Crooked Harbour b. Hong Kong China 73 [inset]
Crooked Island Bahamas 129 F8
Crooked Island Hong Kong China 73 [inset]
Crooked Island Passage Bahamas 129 F8
Crookston U.S.A. 126 D2
Crooksville U.S.A. 130 D4
Crookwell Australia 108 D5
Croom Rep. of Ireland 47 D5
Croppa Creek Australia 108 E2
Crosby U.K. 44 D5
Crosby MN U.S.A. 126 E2
Crosby ND U.S.A. 126 C1
Crosbyton U.S.A. 127 C5
Cross Bay Canada 117 M2
Cross City U.S.A. 129 D6
Cross Fell hill U.K. 44 E4
Crossfield Canada 116 H5
Crossgar U.K. 47 G3
Crosshaven Rep. of Ireland 47 D6
Cross Inn U.K. 45 C6
Cross Lake Canada 117 L4
Cross Lake l. Canada 117 L4
Cross Lake l. U.S.A. 131 G2
Crossmaglen U.K. 47 F3
Crossman Peak U.S.A. 125 F4
Crossville U.S.A. 128 C5
Crotch Lake Canada 131 G1
Croton Italy see Crotone
Crotone Italy 54 G5
Crouch r. U.K. 45 H7
Crow r. Canada 116 E3
Crow Agency U.S.A. 122 G3
Crowal watercourse Australia 108 C3
Crowborough U.K. 45 H7
Crowdy Bay National Park Australia 108 F3
Crowell U.S.A. 127 D5
Crowland U.K. 45 G6
Crowley U.S.A. 127 E6
Crowley, Lake U.S.A. 124 D3
Crown Point IN U.S.A. 130 B3
Crownpoint U.S.A. 125 I4
Crown Point NY U.S.A. 131 I2
Crown Prince Olav Coast Antarctica 148 D2
Crown Princess Martha Coast Antarctica 148 B1
Crows Nest Australia 108 F1
Crowsnest Pass Canada 116 H5
Crowsnest Pass pass Canada 116 H5
Crow Wing r. U.S.A. 126 E2
Croydon Australia 106 C3
Crozet U.S.A. 131 F4
Crozet, Îles is Indian Ocean 145 L9
Crozet Basin sea feature Indian Ocean 145 M8
Crozet Plateau sea feature Indian Ocean 145 K8
Crozon France 52 B2
Cruces Cuba 129 D8
Cruden Bay U.K. 46 H3
Cruillas Mex. 127 D7
Crum U.S.A. 130 D5
Crumlin U.K. 47 F3
Crusheen Rep. of Ireland 47 D5
Cruz Alta Brazil 140 F3
Cruz del Eje Arg. 140 D4
Cruzeiro Brazil 141 B3
Cruzeiro do Sul Brazil 138 D5
Cry Lake Canada 116 D3
Crysdale, Mount Canada 116 F4
Crystal U.S.A. 125 I3
Crystal City Canada 117 L5
Crystal City U.S.A. 127 D6
Crystal Falls U.S.A. 126 F2
Crystal Lake U.S.A. 130 A2
Crystal River U.S.A. 129 D6
Csongrád Hungary 55 I1
Cua Lon r. Vietnam 67 D5
Cuamba Moz. 95 D5
Cuando r. Angola/Zambia 95 C5
Cuangar Angola 95 B5
Cuango Angola 95 B4
Cuanza r. Angola 95 B4
Cuatro Ciénegas Mex. 127 C7
Cuauhtémoc Mex. 123 G7
Cuba NM U.S.A. 123 G5
Cuba NY U.S.A. 131 F2

▶Cuba country West Indies 133 H4
5th largest island and 5th most populous country in North America.
north america 9, 112–113

Cubal Angola 95 B5
Cubango r. Angola/Namibia 95 C5
Cubatão Brazil 141 B3
Cub Hills Canada 117 J4
Çubuk Turkey 86 D2
Cucapa, Sierra mts Mex. 125 F5
Cuchi Angola 95 B5
Cuchilla Grande hills Uruguay 140 E4
Cucuí Brazil 138 E3
Cucurpe Mex. 123 F7
Cúcuta Col. 138 D2
Cudal Australia 108 D4
Cuddalore India 80 C4
Cuddapah India 80 C3
Cuddeback Lake U.S.A. 124 E4
Cue Australia 105 B6
Cuéllar Spain 53 D3
Cuemba Angola 95 B5
Cuenca Ecuador 138 C4
Cuenca Spain 53 E3
Cuenca, Serranía de mts Spain 53 E3
Cuencamé Mex. 127 C7
Cuernavaca Mex. 132 E5
Cuero U.S.A. 127 D6
Cuervos Mex. 125 F5
Cugir Romania 55 J2
Cuiabá Amazonas Brazil 139 G5
Cuiabá Mato Grosso Brazil 139 G7
Cuiabá r. Brazil 139 G7
Cuihua China see Daguan
Cuijiang China see Ninghua
Cuijk Neth. 48 F3
Cuilcagh hill Rep. of Ireland/U.K. 47 E3
Cuillin Hills U.K. 46 C3
Cuillin Sound sea chan. U.K. 46 C3
Cuilo Angola 95 B4
Cuiluan China 70 C3
Cuité r. Brazil 141 C2
Cuito r. Angola 95 C5
Cuito Cuanavale Angola 95 B5
Cukai Malaysia 67 C6
Çukurca Turkey 84 A2
Çukurova plat. Turkey 81 B1
Cu Lao Cham i. Vietnam 66 E4
Cu Lao Re i. Vietnam 66 E4
Cu Lao Thu i. Vietnam 67 E5
Cu Lao Xanh i. Vietnam 67 E4
Culcairn Australia 108 C5
Culfa Azer. 87 G3
Culgoa r. Australia 108 C2
Culiacán Mex. 132 C4
Culiacán Rosales Mex. see Culiacán
Culion Phil. 65 F4
Culion i. Phil. 64 F4
Cullen U.K. 46 G3
Cullen Point Australia 106 C1
Cullera Spain 53 F4
Cullivoe U.K. 46 [inset]
Cullman U.S.A. 129 C5
Cullybackey U.K. 47 F3
Cul Mòr hill U.K. 46 D2
Culpeper U.S.A. 131 G4
Culuene r. Brazil 139 H6
Culver, Point Australia 105 D8
Culverden N.Z. 109 D6
Cumaná Venez. 138 F1
Cumari Brazil 141 A2
Cumbal, Nevado de vol. Col. 138 C3
Cumberland KY U.S.A. 130 D5
Cumberland MD U.S.A. 131 F4
Cumberland VA U.S.A. 131 F5
Cumberland r. U.S.A. 128 C4
Cumberland, Lake U.S.A. 130 C5
Cumberland Lake Canada 117 K4
Cumberland Mountains U.S.A. 130 D5
Cumberland Peninsula Canada 115 L3
Cumberland Plateau U.S.A. 128 C5
Cumberland Point U.S.A. 126 F2
Cumberland Sound sea chan. Canada 115 L3
Cumbernauld U.K. 46 F5
Cumbres de Majalca, Parque Nacional nat. park Mex. 123 G7
Cumbres de Monterey, Parque Nacional nat. park Mex. 127 C7
Cumbum India 80 C3
Cumlosen Germany 49 L1
Cummings U.S.A. 124 B2
Cummins Australia 107 A7
Cummins Range hills Australia 104 D4
Cumnock Australia 108 D4
Cumnock U.K. 46 E5
Çumra Turkey 86 D3
Cumuruxatiba Brazil 141 D2
Cunagua Cuba see Bolivia
Cunderdin Australia 105 B7
Cunene r. Angola 95 B5
also known as Kunene
Cuneo Italy 54 B2
Cung Son Vietnam 67 E4
Cunnamulla Australia 108 B2
Cunningsburgh U.K. 46 [inset]
Cupar U.K. 46 F4
Cupica, Golfo de b. Col. 138 C2
Curaçá Brazil 139 K5
Curaçá r. Brazil 138 D4
Curaçao i. Neth. Antilles 133 K6
Curaray r. Ecuador 138 D4
Curdlawidny Lagoon salt flat Australia 107 B6
Curia Switz. see Chur
Curicó Chile 140 B4
Curitiba Brazil 141 A4
Curitibanos Brazil 141 A4
Curlewis Australia 108 E3
Curnamona Australia 107 B6
Currabubula Australia 108 E3
Currais Novos Brazil 139 K5
Curran U.S.A. 130 D1
Currane, Lough l. Rep. of Ireland 47 B6
Currant U.S.A. 125 F2
Curranyalpa Australia 108 B3
Currawilla Australia 106 C5
Currawinya National Park Australia 108 B2
Currie Australia 102 E5
Currie U.S.A. 125 F1
Currituck U.S.A. 131 G5
Currockbilly, Mount Australia 108 E5
Curtis Channel Australia 106 F5
Curtis Island Australia 106 E4
Curtis Island N.Z. 103 I5
Curuá r. Brazil 139 H5
Curup Indon. 64 C7
Curupira, Serra mts Brazil/Venez. 138 F3
Cururupu Brazil 139 J4
Curvelo Brazil 141 B2
Curwood, Mount hill U.S.A. 126 F2
Cusco Peru 138 D6
Cushendall U.K. 47 F2
Cushendun U.K. 47 F2
Cushing U.S.A. 127 D4
Cusseta U.S.A. 129 C5
Custer MT U.S.A. 122 G3
Custer SD U.S.A. 126 C3
Cut Bank U.S.A. 122 E2
Cuthbert U.S.A. 129 C6
Cuthbertson Falls Australia 104 F3
Cut Knife Canada 117 I4
Cutler Ridge U.S.A. 129 D7
Cuttaburra Creek r. Australia 108 B2
Cuttack India 80 E1
Cuvelai Angola 95 B5
Cuxhaven Germany 43 L4
Cuya Chile 138 D7
Cuyahoga Falls U.S.A. 130 E3
Cuyama U.S.A. 124 D4
Cuyama r. U.S.A. 124 C4
Cuyo Islands Phil. 65 G4
Cuyuni r. Guyana 139 G2
Cuzco Peru see Cusco
Cwmbran U.K. 45 D7
Cyangugu Rwanda 94 C4
Cyclades is Greece 55 K6
Cydonia Greece see Chania
Cygnet U.S.A. 130 D3
Cymru admin. div. U.K. see Wales
Cynthiana U.S.A. 130 C4
Cypress Hills Canada 117 I5
▶Cyprus country Asia 81 A2
asia 6, 58–59
Cyrenaica reg. Libya 93 F2
Cythera i. Greece see Kythira
Czar Canada 117 I4
Czechia country Europe see Czech Republic

▶Czechoslovakia
Divided in 1993 into the Czech Republic and Slovakia.

▶Czech Republic country Europe 43 O6
europe 5, 34–35
Czernowitz Ukr. see Chernivtsi
Czersk Poland 43 P4
Częstochowa Poland 43 Q5

D

Đa, Sông r. Vietnam see Black
Da'an China 70 B3
Dabāb, Jabal aḍ mt. Jordan 81 B4
Dabakala Côte d'Ivoire 92 C4
Daban China 69 L4
Dabao China 72 D2
Daba Shan mts China 73 F1
Dabba China see Daocheng
Dabein Myanmar 66 B3
Dabhoi India 78 C5
Dab'i, Wādī aḍ watercourse Jordan 81 C4
Dabie Shan mts China 73 G2
Dablana India 78 C4
Dabola Guinea 92 B3
Dabqig China 69 J5
Dąbrowa Górnicza Poland 43 Q5
Dabsan Hu salt l. China 79 H1
Dabs Nur l. China 70 A3
Dabu Guangdong China 73 H3
Dabu Guangxi China see Liucheng
Dabusu Pao l. China see Dabs Nur
Dacca Bangl. see Dhaka
Dachau Germany 43 M6
Dachuan China see Dazhou
Dacre Canada 131 G1
Daday Turkey 86 D2
Dade City U.S.A. 129 D6
Dadeville U.S.A. 129 C5
Dādkān Iran 85 F5
Dadong China see Donggang
Dadra India see Achalpur
Dadu Pak. 85 G5
Daegu S. Korea see Taegu
Daejŏn S. Korea see Taejŏn
Daet Phil. 65 G4
Dafang China 72 E3
Dafeng China 73 I1
Dafengman China 70 B4
Dafla Hills India 79 H4
Dafoe Canada 117 J5
Dafoe r. Canada 117 M4
Dagana Senegal 92 B3
Dagcagoin China see Zoigê
Dagcanglhamo China 72 D1
Daghmar Oman 84 E6
Dağlıq Qarabağ aut. reg. Azer. 87 G3
Daglung China 79 G3
Dagö i. Estonia see Hiiumaa
Dagon Myanmar see Rangoon
Daguan China 72 D3
Daguokui Shan hill China 70 C3
Dagupan Phil. 65 G3
Dagxoi Sichuan China see Yidun
Dagxoi Sichuan China see Sowa
Dagzê China 79 G3
Dagzê Co salt l. China 79 F3
Dahadinni r. Canada 116 E2
Dahalach, Isole is Eritrea see Dahlak Archipelago
Dahana des. Saudi Arabia see Ad Dahnā'
Dahe China see Ziyuan
Daheiding Shan mt. China 70 C3
Dahei Shan mts China 70 B4
Daheng China 73 H3
Dahezhen China 70 D3
Da Hinggan Ling mts China 70 A2
Dahlak Archipelago is Eritrea 82 F6
Dahlak Marine National Park Eritrea 82 F6
Daḥl al Furayy well Saudi Arabia 84 B5
Dahlem Germany 48 G4
Dahlenburg Germany 49 K1
Dahm, Ramlat des. Saudi Arabia/Yemen 82 G6
Dahmani Tunisia 54 C7
Dahme Germany 49 N3
Dahn Germany 49 H5
Dahnā' plain Saudi Arabia 84 B5
Dahod India 78 C5
Dahomey country Africa see Benin
Dahongliutan Aksai Chin 78 D2
Dahra Senegal see Dara
Dähre Germany 49 K2
Dahūk Iraq 87 F3
Dai i. Indon. 104 E1
Daik Indon. 64 C7
Daik-u Myanmar 66 B3
Dailekh Nepal 79 E3
Dailly U.K. 46 E5
Daimiel Spain 53 E4
Dainkog China 72 C1
Dainkognubma China 72 C1
Daintree National Park Australia 106 D3
Dairen China see Dalian
Dai-sen vol. Japan 71 D6
Daisetsu-zan National Park Japan 70 F4
Daishan China 73 I2
Daiyun Shan mts China 73 H3
Dajarra Australia 106 B4
Dajin Chuan r. China 72 D2
Da Juh China 79 H1

▶Dakar Senegal 92 B3
Capital of Senegal.

Dākhilah, Wāḥāt ad oasis Egypt 82 C4
Dakhla W. Sahara see Ad Dakhla
Dakhla Oasis oasis Egypt see Dākhilah, Wāḥāt ad
Dak Kon Vietnam 66 D4
Dakoank India 67 A6
Dakol'ka r. Belarus 39 F5
Dakor India 78 C5
Dakoro Niger 92 D3
Dakota City IA U.S.A. 126 E3
Dakota City NE U.S.A. 126 D3
Đakovica Serb. and Mont. 55 I3
Đakovo Croatia 54 H2
Daktuy Rus. Fed. 70 B1
Dala Angola 95 C5
Dalaba Guinea 92 B3
Dalai China see Da'an
Dalain Hob China 76 J3
Dālakī Iran 84 C4
Dalälven r. Sweden 41 J6
Dalaman Turkey 55 M6
Dalandzadgad Mongolia 68 I4
Dalap-Uliga-Darrit Marshall Is see Delap-Uliga-Djarrit
Đa Lat Vietnam 67 E5
Dalatando Angola see N'dalatando
Dalaud India 78 C5
Dalauda India 78 C5
Dalbandin Pak. 85 G4
Dalbeattie U.K. 46 F6
Dalbeg Australia 106 D4
Dalby Australia 108 E1
Dalby Isle of Man 44 C4
Dale Hordaland Norway 41 D6
Dale Sogn og Fjordane Norway 41 D6
Dale City U.S.A. 131 G4
Dale Hollow Lake U.S.A. 130 C5
Dalen Neth. 48 G2
Dalet Myanmar 66 A3
Daletme Myanmar 66 A2
Dalfors Sweden 41 I6
Dalgān Iran 84 E5
Dalgety Australia 108 D6
Dalgety r. Australia 105 A6
Dalhart U.S.A. 127 C4
Dalhousie Canada 119 I4
Dalhousie, Cape Canada 114 F2
Dali Shaanxi China 73 F1
Dali Yunnan China 72 D3
Dalian China 69 M5
Daliang China see Shunde
Daliang Shan mts China 72 D2
Daliji China 73 H1
Dalin China 70 A4
Dalizi China 70 B4
Dalkeith U.K. 46 F5
Dallas OR U.S.A. 122 C3
Dallas TX U.S.A. 127 D5
Dalles City U.S.A. see The Dalles
Dall Island U.S.A. 116 C4
Dalmā i. U.A.E. 84 D5
Dalmacija reg. Bos.-Herz./Croatia see Dalmatia
Dalman India 78 E4
Dalmas, Lac l. Canada 119 H3
Dalmatia reg. Bos.-Herz./Croatia 74 A2
Dalmellington U.K. 46 E5
Dalmeny Canada 117 J4
Dalmi India 79 F5
Dal'negorsk Rus. Fed. 70 D3
Dal'nerechensk Rus. Fed. 70 D3
Dal'niye Zelentsy Rus. Fed. 38 H1
Dalny China see Dalian
Daloa Côte d'Ivoire 92 C4

▶Dalol Eth. 82 F7
Highest recorded annual mean temperature in the world.

Daloloia Group is P.N.G. 106 E1
Dalou Shan mts China 72 E3
Dalqān well Saudi Arabia 84 B5
Dalry U.K. 46 E5
Dalrymple U.K. 46 E5
Dalrymple, Lake Australia 106 D4
Daltenganj India 79 F4
Dalton Canada 118 D4
Dalton S. Africa 97 J5
Dalton GA U.S.A. 129 C5
Dalton MA U.S.A. 131 I2
Dalton PA U.S.A. 131 H3
Daltonganj India see Daltenganj
Dalton-in-Furness U.K. 44 D4
Daludalu Indon. 67 C7
Daluo China 72 D4
Daly r. Australia 104 E3
Daly City U.S.A. 124 B3
Daly River Australia 104 E3
Daly Waters Australia 104 F4
Damagaram Takaya Niger 92 D3
Daman India 80 B1
Daman and Diu union terr. India 80 A1
Damanhûr Egypt see Damanhūr
Damanhūr Egypt 86 C5
Damant Lake Canada 117 J2
Damão India see Daman
Damar i. Indon. 104 E1
Damara Cent. Afr. Rep. 94 B3
Damaraland reg. Namibia 95 B6
Damas Syria see Damascus

▶Damascus Syria 81 C3
Capital of Syria.

Damascus U.S.A. 130 E5
Damaturu Nigeria 92 E3
Damāvand Iran 84 D3
Damāvand, Qolleh-ye mt. Iran 84 D3
Dambulla Sri Lanka 80 D5
Damdy Kazakh. 76 B1
Damghan Iran 84 D2
Damianópolis Brazil 141 B1
Damietta Egypt see Dumyāṭ
Daming Shan mt. China 73 F4
Dāmīyā Jordan 81 B3
Damjong China 72 B1
Damlasu Turkey 81 D1
Dammam Saudi Arabia 82 H4
Damme Belgium 48 D3
Damme Germany 49 I2
Damoh India 78 D5
Damour Lebanon 81 B3
Dampar, Tasik l. Malaysia 67 C7
Dampier Archipelago is Australia 104 B5
Dampier Island P.N.G. see Karkar Island
Dampier Land reg. Australia 104 C4
Dampier Strait P.N.G. 65 L8
Dampir, Selat sea chan. Indon. 65 I7
Damqoq Zangbo r. China see Maquan He
Dam Qu r. China 72 B1
Dâmrei, Chuŏr Phnum mts Cambodia 67 D5
Damroh India 72 B2
Damwâld Neth. see Damwoude
Damwoude Neth. 48 G1
Damxoi China see Comai
Damxung China 79 G3
Dānā Jordan 81 B4
Dana Nepal 79 E3
Danakil reg. Africa see Denakil
Danané Côte d'Ivoire 92 C4
Đa Năng Vietnam 66 E3
Đa Nang, Vinh b. Vietnam 66 E3
Danao Phil. 65 G4
Danata Turkm. 84 D2
Danba China 72 D2
Danbury CT U.S.A. 131 I3
Danbury NC U.S.A. 128 D4
Danby U.S.A. 131 I2
Danby Lake U.S.A. 125 F4
Dandaragan Australia 105 A7
Dande Eth. 94 D3
Dandel'dhura Nepal 78 E3
Dandeli India 80 B3
Dandong China 71 B4
Dandot Pak. 85 I3
Dandridge U.S.A. 128 D4
Dane r. U.K. 44 E5
Daneborg Greenland 149 I2
Danese U.S.A. 130 E5
Danfeng China see Shizong
Dangan Liedao i. China 73 G4
Dangara Tajik. see Danghara
Dangbizhen Rus. Fed. 70 C3
Dangchang China 72 E1
Dangchengwan China see Subei
Danger Islands atoll Cook Is see Pukapuka
Danger Point S. Africa 96 D8
Danghara Tajik. 85 H2
Danghe Nanshan mts China 76 H4
Dang La pass China see Tanggula Shankou
Dangla Shan mts China see Tanggula Shan
Dangqên China 79 G3
Dângrêk, Chuŏr Phnum mts Cambodia/Thai. see Phanom Dong Rak, Thiu Khao
Dangriga Belize 132 G5
Dangshan China 73 H1
Dangtu China 73 H2
Daniel's Harbour Canada 119 K4
Daniëlskuil S. Africa 96 F5
Danilov Rus. Fed. 38 I4
Danilovka Rus. Fed. 39 J6
Danilovskaya Vozvyshennost' hills Rus. Fed. 38 H4
Danjiang China see Leishan
Danjiangkou China 73 F1
Danjiangkou Shuiku resr China 73 F1
Danjo-guntō is Japan 71 C6
Dank Oman 84 E6
Dankhar India 78 D2
Dankov Rus. Fed. 39 H5
Danlí Hond. 133 G6
Danmark country Europe see Denmark
Dannebrog Ø i. Greenland see Qillak
Dannenberg (Elbe) Germany 49 L1
Dannenwalde Germany 49 N1
Dannevirke N.Z. 109 F5
Dannhauser S. Africa 97 J5
Dano Burkina 92 C3
Danshui Taiwan see Tanshui
Dansville U.S.A. 131 G2
Danta India 78 C4
Dantan India 79 F5
Dantevada India see Dantewara
Dantewada India see Dantewara
Dantewara India 80 D2
Dantu China 73 H1

▶Danube r. Europe 43 P6
2nd longest river in Europe. Also spelt Donau (Austria/Germany) or Duna (Hungary) or Dunaj (Slovakia) or Dunărea (Romania) or Dunav (Bulgaria/Croatia/Serbia and Montenegro) or Dunay (Ukraine).

Danube Delta Romania/Ukr. 55 M2
Danubyu Myanmar 66 A3
Danville IL U.S.A. 130 B3
Danville IN U.S.A. 130 B4
Danville KY U.S.A. 130 C5
Danville OH U.S.A. 130 D3
Danville PA U.S.A. 131 G3
Danville VA U.S.A. 130 F5
Danville VT U.S.A. 131 I1
Danxian China see Danzhou
Danzhai China 72 E3
Danzhou Guangxi China 73 F3
Danzhou Hainan China 73 F5
Danzig Poland see Gdańsk
Danzig, Gulf of Poland/Rus. Fed. see Gdańsk, Gulf of
Daocheng China 72 D2
Daokou China see Huaxian
Dao Tay Sa is S. China Sea see Paracel Islands
Daoud Alg. see Aïn Beïda
Daoukro Côte d'Ivoire 92 C4
Daozhen China 72 E2
Dapaong Togo 92 D3
Dapeng Wan b. Hong Kong China see Mirs Bay
Daphabum mt. India 79 I4
Daporijo India 79 H4
Dapu China see Liucheng
Da Qaidam Zhen China 76 I4
Daqiao China 72 D3
Daqing China 70 B3
Daqiu China 73 H3
Dāq Mashī Iran 84 E3
Daqq-e Patargān salt flat Iran 85 F3
Daqq-e Tundi, Dasht-e imp. l. Afgh. 85 F3
Daqu Shan i. China 73 I2
Dara Senegal 92 B3
Dar'ā Syria 81 C3
Dâra, Gebel mt. Egypt see Dārah, Jabal
Dārāb Iran 84 D4
Darāgāh Iran 84 D4
Dārah, Jabal mt. Egypt 86 D6
Daraj Libya 92 E1
Dārākūyeh Iran 84 D4
Dārān Iran 84 C3
Đa Răng, Sông r. Vietnam 67 E4
Daraut-Korgon Kyrg. 85 I2
Darazo Nigeria 92 E3
Darband, Kūh-e mt. Iran 84 E4
Darband-e Hajjī Boland Turkm. 85 F2
Darbhanga India 79 F4
Darcang China 72 C1
Dardanelle U.S.A. 127 E5
Dardanelles strait Turkey 55 L4
Dardania prov. Serb. and Mont. see Kosovo
Dardesheim Germany 49 K3
Dardo China see Kangding
Dar el Beida Morocco see Casablanca
Darende Turkey 86 E3

▶Dar es Salaam Tanz. 95 D4
Former capital of Tanzania.

Darfo Boario Terme Italy 54 D2
Dargai Pak. 85 H3
Darganata Turkm. 85 F1
Dargaville N.Z. 109 D2
Dargo Australia 108 C6
Dargo Zangbo r. China 79 F3
Darhan Mongolia 68 J3
Darien U.S.A. 129 D6
Darién, Golfo del g. Col. 138 C2
Darién, Parque Nacional de nat. park Panama 133 I7
Dariga Pak. 85 G5
Darjeeling India see Darjiling
Darjiling India 79 G4
Darkhazīneh Iran 84 C4
Darlag China 72 C1

▶Darling r. Australia 108 B3
2nd longest river in Oceania. Part of the longest (Murray-Darling).

Darling Downs hills Australia 108 D1
Darling Range hills Australia 105 A8
Darlington U.K. 44 F4
Darlington U.S.A. 126 F3
Darlington Point Australia 108 C5
Darlot, Lake salt flat Australia 105 C6
Darłowo Poland 43 P3
Darma Pass China/India 78 E3
Darmstadt Germany 49 I5
Darnah Libya 86 A4
Darnall S. Africa 97 J5
Darnick Australia 108 A4
Darnley, Cape Antarctica 148 E2
Daroca Spain 53 F3
Daroot-Korgon Kyrg. see Daraut-Korgon
Darovskoy Rus. Fed. 38 J4
Darr watercourse Australia 106 C4
Darreh Bīd Iran 84 E3
Darreh-ye Bāhābād Iran 84 D4
Darreh-ye Shahr Iran 84 B3
Darsi India 80 C3
Dart r. U.K. 45 D8
Dartang China see Baqên
Dartford U.K. 45 H7
Dartmoor Australia 107 C8
Dartmoor hills U.K. 45 C8
Dartmoor National Park U.K. 45 D8
Dartmouth Canada 119 J5

Dartmouth U.K. 45 D8
Dartmouth, Lake salt flat Australia 107 D5
Dartmouth Reservoir Australia 108 C6
Darton U.K. 44 F5
Daru P.N.G. 65 K8
Daru Sierra Leone 92 B4
Daruba Indon. 65 H6
Darvaza Turkm. 84 E1
Darvoz, Qatorkŭhi mts Tajik. 85 H2
Darwazgai Afgh. 85 G4
Darwen U.K. 44 E5
Darweshan Afgh. 85 G4
▶Darwin Australia 104 E3
Capital of Northern Territory.
Darwin, Monte mt. Chile 140 C8
Daryācheh-ye Orūmīyeh salt l. Iran see Urmia, Lake
Dar'yalyktakyr, Ravnina plain Kazakh. 76 B2
Dar"yoi Amu r. Asia see Amudar'ya
Dārzīn Iran 84 E4
Dās i. U.A.E. 84 D5
Dasada India 78 B5
Dashennongjia mt. China see Shennong Ding
Dashhowuz Turkm. see Dashoguz
Dashkesan Azer. see Daşkäsän
Dashkhovuz Turkm. see Dashoguz
Dashköpri Turkm. see Tashkepri
Dashoguz Turkm. 83 I1
Dasht Iran 84 E2
Dashtiari Iran 85 F5
Daska Pak. 85 I3
Daşkäsän Azer. 87 G2
Daşoguz Turkm. see Dashoguz
Dasongshu China 72 E3
Daspar mt. Pak. 85 I2
Dassel Germany 49 J3
Dastgardān Iran 84 E3
Datadian Indon. 64 F6
Datça Turkey 55 L6
Date Japan 70 F4
Date Creek watercourse U.S.A. 125 G4
Dateland U.S.A. 125 G5
Datha India 78 C5
Datia India 78 D4
Datian China 73 H3
Datian Ding mt. China 73 F4
Datil U.S.A. 125 J4
Datong Anhui China 73 H2
Datong Heilong. China 70 B3
Datong Shanxi China 69 K4
Datong He r. China 68 I5
Dattapur India 80 C1
Datu, Tanjung c. Indon./Malaysia 67 E7
Daudkandi Bangl. 79 G5
Daugava r. Latvia 41 N8
Daugavpils Latvia 41 O9
Daulatabad India 80 B2
Daulatabad Iran see Malāyer
Daulatpur Bangl. 79 G5
Daun Germany 48 G4
Daungyu r. Myanmar 66 A2
Dauphin Canada 117 K5
Dauphiné reg. France 52 G4
Dauphiné, Alpes du mts France 52 G4
Dauphin Lake Canada 117 L5
Daurie Creek r. Australia 105 A6
Dausa India 78 D4
Dâu Tiêng, Hô resr Vietnam 67 D5
Dava U.K. 46 F3
Däväçi Azer. 87 H2
Davanagere India see Davangere
Davangere India 80 B3
Davao Phil. 65 H5
Davao Gulf Phil. 65 H5
Dāvarī Iran 84 E5
Dāvarzan Iran 84 E2
Davel S. Africa 97 I4
Davenport IA U.S.A. 126 F3
Davenport WA U.S.A. 122 D3
Davenport Downs Australia 106 C5
Davenport Range hills Australia 104 F5
Daventry U.K. 45 F6
Daveyton S. Africa 97 I4
David Panama 133 H7
David City U.S.A. 126 D3
Davidson Canada 117 J5
Davidson, Mount hill Australia 104 E5
Davis research station Antarctica 148 E2
Davis r. Australia 104 C5
Davis i. Myanmar see Than Kyun
Davis CA U.S.A. 124 C2
Davis WV U.S.A. 130 F4
Davis, Mount hill U.S.A. 130 F4
Davis Bay Antarctica 148 G2
Davis Dam U.S.A. 125 F4
Davis Inlet Canada 119 J3
Davis Sea Antarctica 148 F2
Davis Strait Canada/Greenland 115 M3
Davlekanovo Rus. Fed. 37 Q5
Davos Switz. 52 I3
Davy Lake Canada 117 I3
Dawa Co l. China 79 F3
Dawa Wenz r. Eth. 94 E3
Dawaxung China 79 F3
Dawê China 72 D2
Dawei Myanmar see Tavoy
Dawei r. mouth Myanmar see Tavoy
Dawera i. Indon. 104 E1
Dawna Range mts Myanmar/Thai. 66 B3
Dawna Taungdan mts Myanmar/Thai. see Dawna Range
Dawo China see Maqên
Dawqah Oman 83 H6
Dawson r. Australia 106 E4
Dawson Canada 116 B1
Dawson GA U.S.A. 129 C6
Dawson ND U.S.A. 126 D2
Dawson, Mount Canada 116 G5
Dawson Bay Canada 117 K4
Dawson Creek Canada 116 F4
Dawson Inlet Canada 117 M2
Dawson Range mts Canada 116 A2
Dawsons Landing Canada 116 E5
Dawu Hubei China 73 G2
Dawu Qinghai China see Maqên
Dawu Taiwan see Tawu
Dawukou China see Shizuishan
Dawu Shan hill China 73 G2
Dax France 52 D5
Daxian China see Dazhou
Daxiang Ling mts China 72 D2
Daxin China 72 E4
Daxing Yunnan China see Lüchun
Daxing Yunnan China see Ninglang
Daxing'an Ling mts China see Da Hinggan Ling
Da Xueshan mts China 72 D2
Dayan China see Lijiang
Dayangshu China 70 B2
Dayao China 72 D3
Dayao Shan mts China 73 F4
Daye China 73 G2
Daying China 72 E2
Daying Jiang r. China 72 C3
Dayishan China see Guanyun
Daylesford Australia 108 B6
Daylight Pass U.S.A. 124 E3
Dayong China see Zhangjiajie
Dayr Abū Sa'īd Jordan 81 B3
Dayr az Zawr Syria 87 F4
Dayr Ḥāfir Syria 81 C1
Daysland Canada 117 H4
Dayton OH U.S.A. 130 C4
Dayton TN U.S.A. 128 C5
Dayton VA U.S.A. 131 F4
Dayton WA U.S.A. 122 D3
Daytona Beach U.S.A. 129 D6
Dayu Ling mts China 73 G3
Da Yunhe canal China 73 H1
Dayyīna i. U.A.E. 84 D5
Dazhongji China see Dafeng
Dazhou China 72 E2
Dazhou Dao i. China 73 F5
Dazhu China 72 E2
Dazu China 72 E2
Dazu Rock Carvings tourist site China 72 E2
De Aar S. Africa 96 G6
Dead r. Rep. of Ireland 47 D5
Deadman Lake U.S.A. 124 E4
Deadman's Cay Bahamas 129 F8
Dead Mountains U.S.A. 125 F4
▶Dead Sea salt l. Asia 81 B4
Lowest point in the world and in Asia.
asia 56–57
Deadwood U.S.A. 126 C2
Deakin Australia 105 E7
Deal U.K. 45 I7
Dealesville S. Africa 97 G5
De'an China 73 G2
Dean, Forest of U.K. 45 E7
Deán Funes Arg. 140 D4
Deanuvuotna inlet Norway see Tanafjorden
Dearborn U.S.A. 130 D2
Dearne r. U.K. 44 F5
Deary U.S.A. 122 D3
Dease r. Canada 116 D3
Dease Lake Canada 116 D3
Dease Lake l. Canada 116 D3
Dease Strait Canada 114 H3
▶Death Valley depr. U.S.A. 124 E3
Lowest point in the Americas.
north america 110–111
Death Valley Junction U.S.A. 124 E3
Death Valley National Park U.S.A. 124 E3
Deauville France 52 E2
Deaver U.S.A. 122 F3
De Baai S. Africa see Port Elizabeth
Debao China 72 E4
Debar Macedonia 55 I4
Debden Canada 117 J4
Debenham U.K. 45 I6
De Beque U.S.A. 125 I2
De Biesbosch, Nationaal Park nat. park Neth. 48 E3
Débo, Lac l. Mali 92 C3
Deborah East, Lake salt flat Australia 105 B7
Deborah West, Lake salt flat Australia 105 B7
Debrecen Hungary 55 I1
Debre Markos Eth. 82 E7
Debre Tabor Eth. 82 E7
Debre Zeyit Eth. 94 D3
Decatur AL U.S.A. 129 C5
Decatur GA U.S.A. 129 C5
Decatur IL U.S.A. 126 F4
Decatur IN U.S.A. 130 C3
Decatur MI U.S.A. 130 C2
Decatur MS U.S.A. 127 F5
Decatur TX U.S.A. 127 D5
▶Deccan plat. India 80 C2
Plateau making up most of southern and central India.
Deception Bay Australia 108 F1
Dechang China 72 D3
Děčín Czech Rep. 43 O5
Decker U.S.A. 122 G3
Decorah U.S.A. 126 F3
Dedap i. Indon. see Penasi, Pulau
Dedaye Myanmar 66 A3
Deddington U.K. 45 F7
Dedeğöl Dağları mts Turkey 55 N6
Dedeleben Germany 49 K2
Dedelstorf Germany 49 K2
Dedemsvaart Neth. 48 G2
Dedo de Deus mt. Brazil 141 B4
Dédougou Burkina 92 C3
Dedovichi Rus. Fed. 38 F4
Dedu China see Wudalianchi
Dee r. Rep. of Ireland 47 F4
Dee est. U.K. 44 D5
Dee r. England/Wales U.K. 45 D5
Dee r. Scotland U.K. 46 G3
Deel r. Rep. of Ireland 47 D5
Deel r. Rep. of Ireland 47 F4
Deep Bay Hong Kong China 73 [inset]
Deep Creek Lake U.S.A. 130 F4
Deep Creek Range mts U.S.A. 125 G2
Deep River Canada 118 F5
Deepwater Australia 108 E2
Deeri Somalia 94 E3
Deering U.S.A. 114 B3
Deering, Mount Australia 105 E6
Deer Island U.S.A. 114 B4
Deer Lake Canada 117 M4
Deer Lake l. Canada 117 M4
Deer Lodge U.S.A. 122 E3
Deesa India see Disa
Deeth U.S.A. 122 E4
Defeng China see Liping
Defensores del Chaco, Parque Nacional nat. park Para. 140 D2
Defiance U.S.A. 130 C3
Defiance Plateau U.S.A. 125 I4
Degana India 78 C4
Degeh Bur Eth. 94 E3
Degema Nigeria 92 D4
Deggendorf Germany 49 M6
Degh r. Pak. 85 I4
De Grey r. Australia 104 B5
De Groote Peel, Nationaal Park nat. park Neth. 48 F3
Degtevo Rus. Fed. 39 I6
De Haan Belgium 48 D3
Dehak Iran 85 F4
De Hamert, Nationaal Park nat. park Neth. 48 G3
Deh Bīd Iran 84 D4
Deh-Dasht Iran 84 C4
Dehej India 78 C5
Deheq Iran 84 C3
Dehestān Iran 84 D4
Deh Golān Iran 84 B3
Dehgon Afgh. 85 F3
Dehi Afgh. 85 G3
Dehkūyeh Iran 84 D5
Dehlorān Iran 84 B3
De Hoge Veluwe, Nationaal Park nat. park Neth. 48 F2
De Hoop Nature Reserve S. Africa 96 E8
Dehqonobod Uzbek. see Dekhkanabad
Dehra Dun India 78 D3
Dehradun India see Dehra Dun
Dehri India 79 F4
Deh Shū Afgh. 85 F4
Deim Zubeir Sudan 93 F4
Deinze Belgium 48 D4
Deir-ez-Zor Syria see Dayr az Zawr
Dej Romania 55 J1
Deji China see Rinbung
Dejiang China 73 F2
De Jouwer Neth. see Joure
De Kalb IL U.S.A. 126 F3
De Kalb MS U.S.A. 127 F5
De Kalb TX U.S.A. 127 E5
De Kalb Junction U.S.A. 131 H1
De-Kastri Rus. Fed. 70 F2
Dekemhare Eritrea 82 E6
Dekhkanabad Uzbek. 85 G2
Dekina Nigeria 92 D4
Dékoa Cent. Afr. Rep. 94 B3
De Koog Neth. 48 E1
De Kooy Neth. 48 E2
Delaki Indon. 104 D2
Delamar Lake U.S.A. 125 F3
De Land U.S.A. 129 D6
Delano U.S.A. 124 D4
Delano Peak U.S.A. 125 G2
▶Delap-Uliga-Djarrit Marshall Is 146 H5
Capital of the Marshall Islands, on Majuro atoll.
Delārām Afgh. 85 F3
Delareyville S. Africa 97 G4
Delaronde Lake Canada 117 J4
Delavan U.S.A. 118 C6
Delaware U.S.A. 130 D3
Delaware r. U.S.A. 131 H4
Delaware state U.S.A. 131 H4
Delaware, East Branch r. U.S.A. 131 H3
Delaware Bay U.S.A. 131 H4
Delaware Lake U.S.A. 130 D3
Delaware Water Gap National Recreational Area park U.S.A. 131 H3
Delay r. Canada 119 H2
Delbarton U.S.A. 130 D5
Delbrück Germany 49 I3
Delburne Canada 116 H4
Delegate Australia 108 D6
De Lemmer Neth. see Lemmer
Delémont Switz. 52 H3
Delevan CA U.S.A. 124 B2
Delevan NY U.S.A. 131 F2
Delfinópolis Brazil 141 B3
Delft Neth. 48 E2
Delfzijl Neth. 48 G1
Delgada, Point U.S.A. 124 A1
Delgado, Cabo c. Moz. 95 E5
Delhi Canada 130 E2
Delhi China 76 I4
Delhi India 78 D3
Delhi CO U.S.A. 123 G5
Delhi LA U.S.A. 127 F5
Delhi NY U.S.A. 131 H2
Delice Turkey 86 D3
Delice r. Turkey 86 D2
Delījān Iran 84 C3
Déline Canada 116 F1
Delingha China see Delhi
Delisle Canada 117 J5
Delitzsch Germany 49 M3
Delligsen Germany 49 J3
Dell Rapids U.S.A. 126 D3
Dellys Alg. 53 H5
Del Mar U.S.A. 124 E5
Delmenhorst Germany 49 I1
Delnice Croatia 54 F2
Del Norte U.S.A. 123 G5
Delong China see Ande
De-Longa, Ostrova is Rus. Fed. 61 Q2
De Long Islands Rus. Fed. see De-Longa, Ostrova
De Long Mountains U.S.A. 114 B3
De Long Strait Rus. Fed. see Longa, Proliv
Deloraine Canada 117 K5
Delphi U.S.A. 130 B3
Delphos U.S.A. 130 C3
Delportshoop S. Africa 96 G5
Delray Beach U.S.A. 129 D7
Delrey U.S.A. 130 A3
Del Rio Mex. 123 F7
Del Rio U.S.A. 127 C6
Delsbo Sweden 41 J6
Delta CO U.S.A. 125 I2
Delta OH U.S.A. 130 C3
Delta UT U.S.A. 125 G2
Delta Downs Australia 106 C3
Delta Junction U.S.A. 114 D3
Deltona U.S.A. 129 D6
Delungra Australia 108 E2
Delvin Rep. of Ireland 47 E4
Delvinë Albania 55 I5
Delwara India 78 C4
Demavend mt. Iran see Damāvand, Qolleh-ye
Demba Dem. Rep. Congo 95 C4
Dembī Dolo Eth. 82 D8
Demerara Guyana see Georgetown
Demerara Abyssal Plain sea feature S. Atlantic Ocean 144 E5
Demidov Rus. Fed. 39 F5
Deming U.S.A. 123 G6
Demirci Turkey 55 M5
Demirköy Turkey 55 L4
Demirtaş Turkey 81 A1
Demmin Germany 43 N4
Demopolis U.S.A. 129 C5
Demotte U.S.A. 130 B3
Dempo, Gunung vol. Indon. 64 C7
Dêmqog Jammu and Kashmir 78 D2
Demta Indon. 65 K7
Dem'yanovo Rus. Fed. 38 J3
De Naawte S. Africa 96 E6
Denakil reg. Africa 94 E2
Denali mt. U.S.A. see McKinley, Mount
Denali National Park and Preserve U.S.A. 114 C3
Denan Eth. 94 E3
Denau Uzbek. 85 G2
Denbigh Canada 131 G1
Denbigh U.K. 44 D5
Den Bosch Neth. see 's-Hertogenbosch
Den Burg Neth. 48 E1
Den Chai Thai. 66 C3
Dendâra Mauritania 92 C3
Dendermonde Belgium 48 E3
Dendi mt. Eth. 94 D3
Dendre r. Belgium 48 E3
Dendron S. Africa 97 I2
Denezhkin Kamen', Gora mt. Rus. Fed. 37 R3
Dêngka China see Têwo
Dêngkagoin China see Têwo
Dengkou China 68 J4
Dêngqên China 72 B2
Dengta China 73 G4
Dengxian China see Dengzhou
Dengzhou China 73 G1
Den Haag Neth. see The Hague
Denham Australia 105 A6
Denham r. Australia 104 E3
Den Ham Neth. 48 G2
Denham Range mts Australia 106 E4
Den Helder Neth. 48 E2
Denholm Canada 117 I4
Denia Spain 53 G4
Denial Bay Australia 107 A7
Deniliquin Australia 108 B5
Denio U.S.A. 122 D4
Denison IA U.S.A. 126 E3
Denison TX U.S.A. 127 D5
Denison, Cape Antarctica 148 G2
Denison Plains Australia 104 E4
Deniyaya Sri Lanka 80 D5
Denizli Turkey 55 M6
Denman Australia 108 E4
Denman Glacier Antarctica 148 F2
Denmark Australia 102 B5
▶Denmark country Europe 41 G8
europe 5, 34–35
Denmark U.S.A. 130 B1
Denmark Strait Greenland/Iceland 36 A2
Dennis, Lake salt flat Australia 104 E5
Dennison IL U.S.A. 130 B4
Dennison OH U.S.A. 130 E3
Denny U.K. 46 F4
Denow Uzbek. see Denau
Denpasar Indon. 104 A2
Denton MD U.S.A. 131 H4
Denton TX U.S.A. 127 D5
D'Entrecasteaux, Point Australia 105 A8
D'Entrecasteaux, Récifs reef New Caledonia 103 G3
D'Entrecasteaux Islands P.N.G. 102 F2
D'Entrecasteaux National Park Australia 105 A8
▶Denver CO U.S.A. 122 G5
State capital of Colorado.
Denver PA U.S.A. 131 G3
Denys r. Canada 118 F3
Deo India 79 F4
Deoband India 78 D3
Deogarh Jharkhand India see Deoghar
Deogarh Orissa India 79 F5
Deogarh Rajasthan India 78 C4
Deogarh Uttar Pradesh India 78 D4
Deogarh mt. India 79 E5
Deoghar India 79 F4
Deolali India 80 B2
Deoli India 79 F5
Deori Chhattisgarh India 80 D1
Deori Madhya Pradesh India 78 D5
Deoria India 79 E4
Deosai, Plains of Jammu and Kashmir 78 C2
Deosil India 79 E5
De Panne Belgium 48 C3
De Pere U.S.A. 130 A1
Deposit U.S.A. 131 H2
Depsang Point hill Aksai Chin 78 D2
Deputatskiy Rus. Fed. 61 O3
Dêqên Xizang China 79 G3
Dêqên Xizang China 79 G3
Dêqên Xizang China see Dagzê
De Queen U.S.A. 127 E5
Dera Ghazi Khan Pak. 85 H4
Dera Ismail Khan Pak. 85 H4
Derajat reg. Pak. 85 H4
Derawar Fort Pak. 85 H4
Derbent Rus. Fed. 87 H2
Derbesiye Turkey see Şenyurt
Derbur China 70 A2
Derby Australia 104 C4
Derby U.K. 45 F6
Derby CT U.S.A. 131 I3
Derby KS U.S.A. 127 D4
Derby NY U.S.A. 131 F2
Derg r. Rep. of Ireland/U.K. 47 E3
Derg, Lough l. Rep. of Ireland 47 D5
Dergachi Rus. Fed. 39 K6
Dergachi Ukr. see Derhachi
Derhachi Ukr. 39 H6
De Ridder U.S.A. 127 E6
Derik Turkey 87 F3
Derm Namibia 96 D2
Derna Libya see Darnah
Dernberg, Cape Namibia 96 B4
Dêrong China 72 C2
Derravaragh, Lough l. Rep. of Ireland 47 E4
Derry U.K. see Londonderry
Derry U.S.A. 131 J2
Derryveagh Mts hills Rep. of Ireland 47 D3
Dêrub China see Rutög
Derudeb Sudan 82 E6
De Rust S. Africa 96 F7
Derventa Bos.-Herz. 54 G2
Derwent r. England U.K. 44 F6
Derwent r. England U.K. 44 G5
Derwent Water l. U.K. 44 D4
Derweze Turkm. see Darvaza
Derzhavinsk Kazakh. 76 C1
Derzhavinskiy Kazakh. see Derzhavinsk
Desaguadero r. Arg. 140 C4
Désappointement, Îles du is Fr. Polynesia 147 K6
Desatoya Mountains U.S.A. 124 E2
Deschambault Lake Canada 117 K4
Deschutes r. U.S.A. 122 C3
Desē Eth. 94 D2
Deseado Arg. 140 C7
Deseado r. Arg. 140 C7
Desengaño, Punta pt Arg. 140 C7
Deseret U.S.A. 125 G2
Deseret Peak U.S.A. 125 G1
Deseronto Canada 131 G1
Desert Canal Pak. 85 H4
Desert Center U.S.A. 125 F5
Desert Lake U.S.A. 125 F3
Desert View U.S.A. 125 H3
Deshler U.S.A. 130 D3
De Smet U.S.A. 126 D2
▶Des Moines IA U.S.A. 126 E3
State capital of Iowa.
Des Moines NM U.S.A. 127 C4
Des Moines r. U.S.A. 126 F3
Desna r. Rus. Fed./Ukr. 39 F6
Desnogorsk Rus. Fed. 39 G5
Desolación, Isla i. Chile 140 B8
Des Plaines U.S.A. 130 B2
Dessau Germany 49 M3
Dessye Eth. see Desē
Destelbergen Belgium 48 D3
Destruction Bay Canada 149 A2
Desvres France 48 B4
Detah Canada 116 H2
Dete Zimbabwe 95 C5
Detmold Germany 49 I3
Detrital Wash watercourse U.S.A. 125 F3
Detroit U.S.A. 130 D2
Detroit Lakes U.S.A. 126 E2
Dett Zimbabwe see Dete
Deua National Park Australia 108 D5
Deuben Germany 49 M3
Deurne Neth. 48 F3
Deutschland country Europe see Germany
Deutschlandsberg Austria 43 O7
Deutzen Germany 49 M3
Deva Romania 55 J2
Deva U.K. see Chester
Devana U.K. see Aberdeen
Devangere India see Davangere
Devanhalli India 80 C3
Deve Bair pass Bulg./Macedonia see Velbŭzhdki Prokhod
Develi Turkey 86 D3
Deventer Neth. 48 G2
Deveron r. U.K. 46 G3
Devét Skal hill Czech Rep. 43 P6
Devgarh India 80 B2
Devghar India see Deoghar
Devikot India 78 B4
Devil's Bridge U.K. 45 D6
Devil's Gate pass U.S.A. 124 D2
Devil's Lake U.S.A. 126 D1
Devil's Paw mt. U.S.A. 116 C3
Devil's Peak U.S.A. 124 D3
Devil's Point Bahamas 129 F7
Devine U.S.A. 127 D6
Devizes U.K. 45 F7
Devli India 78 C4
Devnya Bulg. 55 L3
Devon r. U.K. 46 F4
Devon Island Canada 115 I2
Devonport Australia 107 [inset]
Devrek Turkey 55 N4
Devrukh India 80 B2
Dewa, Tanjung pt Indon. 67 A7
Dewangiri Bhutan 79 G4
Dewas India 78 D5
De Weerribben, Nationaal Park nat. park Neth. 48 G2
Dewetsdorp S. Africa 97 H5
De Witt AR U.S.A. 127 F5
De Witt IA U.S.A. 126 F3
Dewsbury U.K. 44 F5
Dexing China 73 H2
Dexter ME U.S.A. 131 K1
Dexter MI U.S.A. 130 D2
Dexter MO U.S.A. 127 F4
Dexter NM U.S.A. 123 G6
Dexter NY U.S.A. 131 G1
Deyang China 72 E2
Dey-Dey Lake salt flat Australia 105 E7
Deyhuk Iran 84 E3
Deyong, Tanjung pt Indon. 65 J8
Dêyü Co l. China 79 F2
Deyyer Iran 84 C5
Dez r. Iran 82 G3
Dezadeash Lake Canada 116 B2
Dezfūl Iran 84 C3
▶Dezhneva, Mys c. Rus. Fed. 61 T3
Most easterly point of Asia.
Dezhou Shandong China 69 L5
Dezhou Sichuan China see Dechang
Dezh Shāhpūr Iran see Marīvān
Dhabarau India 79 E4
Dhahab, Wādī adh r. Syria 81 B3
Dhāhiriya West Bank 81 B4
Dhahran Saudi Arabia 84 C5
▶Dhaka Bangl. 79 G5
Capital of Bangladesh and 5th most populous city in Asia.
Dhalbhum reg. India 79 F5
Dhalgaon India 80 B2
Dhamār Yemen 82 F7
Dhamoni India 78 D4
Dhamtari India 80 D1
Dhana Pak. 85 H5
Dhana Sar Pak. 85 H4
Dhanbad India 79 F5
Dhanera India 78 C4
Dhang Range mts Nepal 79 E3
Dhankuta Nepal 79 F4
Dhansia India 78 C3
Dhar India 78 C5
Dhar Adrar hills Mauritania 92 B3
Dharampur India 80 B1
Dharan Bazar Nepal 79 F4
Dharashiv India see Osmanabad
Dhari India 78 B5
Dharmapuri India 80 C3
Dharmavaram India 80 C3
Dharmsala Himachal Pradesh India see Dharmshala
Dharmsala Orissa India 79 F5
Dharmshala India 78 D2
Dharnaoda India 78 D4
Dhar Oualâta hills Mauritania 92 C3
Dhar Tîchît hills Mauritania 92 C3
Dharug National Park Australia 108 E4
Dharur India 80 C2
Dharwad India 80 B3
Dharwar India see Dharwad
Dharwas India 78 D2
Dhasan r. India 78 D4
Dhāt al Ḥājj Saudi Arabia 86 E5
Dhaulagiri mt. Nepal 79 E3
Dhaulpur India see Dholpur
Dhaura India 78 D4
Dhaurahra India 78 E4
Dhawlagiri mt. Nepal see Dhaulagiri
Dhebar Lake India see Jaisamand Lake
Dhekelia Sovereign Base Area military base Cyprus 81 A2
Dhemaji India 79 H4
Dhenkanal India 80 E1
Dhībān Jordan 81 B4
Dhidhimótikhon Greece see Didymoteicho
Dhing India 79 H4
Dhirwāh, Wādī adh watercourse Jordan 81 C4
Dhodhekánisos is Greece see Dodecanese
Dhola India 78 B5
Dholera India 78 C5
Dholpur India 78 D4
Dhomokós Greece see Domokos
Dhone India 80 C3
Dhoraji India 78 B5
Dhori India 78 B5
Dhrangadhra India 78 B5
Dhubāb Yemen 82 F7
Dhubri India 79 G4
Dhuburi India see Dhubri
Dhudial Pak. 85 I3
Dhule India 80 B1
Dhulia India see Dhule
Dhulian India 79 F4
Dhulian Pak. 85 I3
Dhuma India 78 D5
Dhund r. India 78 D4
Dhurwai India 78 D4
Dhuusa Marreeb Somalia 94 E3
Dia i. Greece 55 K7
Diablo, Mount U.S.A. 124 C3
Diablo, Picacho del mt. Mex. 123 E7
Diablo Range mts U.S.A. 124 C3
Diagbe Dem. Rep. Congo 94 C3
Diamante Arg. 140 D4
Diamantina watercourse Australia 106 B5
Diamantina Brazil 141 C2
Diamantina, Chapada plat. Brazil 141 C1
Diamantina Deep sea feature Indian Ocean 145 O8
Diamantina Gates National Park Australia 106 C4
Diamantino Brazil 139 G6
Diamond Islets Australia 106 E3
Diamond Peak U.S.A. 125 F2
Dianbai China 73 F4
Diancang Shan mt. China 72 D3
Dian Chi l. China 72 D3
Diandioumé Mali 92 C3
Diane Bank sea feature Australia 106 E2
Dianjiang China 72 E2
Dianópolis Brazil 139 I6
Dianyang China see Shidian
Diaobingshan China see Tiefa
Diaoling China 70 C3
Diapaga Burkina 92 D3
Diarizos r. Cyprus 81 A2
Diavolo, Mount hill India 67 A4
Diaz Point Namibia 96 B4
Dibaya Dem. Rep. Congo 95 C4
Dibella well Niger 92 E3
Dibeng S. Africa 96 F4
Dibete Botswana 97 H2
Dibrugarh India 79 H4
Dibse Syria see Dibsī
Dibsī Syria 81 D2
Dickens U.S.A. 127 C5
Dickinson U.S.A. 126 C2
Dicle r. Turkey 87 F3 see Tigris
Dīdēsa Wenz r. Eth. 94 D3
Didiéni Mali 92 C3
Didsbury Canada 116 H5
Didwana India 78 C4
Didymoteicho Greece 55 L4
Die France 52 G4
Dieblich Germany 49 H4
Diébougou Burkina 92 C3
Dieburg Germany 49 I5
Diedenhofen France see Thionville
Diefenbaker, Lake Canada 117 I5
Diego de Almagro, Isla i. Chile 140 A8
Diégo Suarez Madag. see Antsirañana
Diekirch Lux. 48 G5
Diéma Mali 92 C3
Diemel r. Germany 49 J3
Điên Biên Vietnam see Điên Biên Ph
Điên Biên Phu Vietnam 66 C2
Diên Châu Vietnam 66 D3
Diên Khanh Vietnam 67 E4
Diepholz Germany 49 I2
Dieppe France 48 B5
Dierks U.S.A. 127 E5
Di'er Songhua Jiang r. China 70 B3
Diessen Neth. 48 F3
Diest Belgium 48 F4
Dietikon Switz. 52 I3
Diez Germany 49 I4
Diffa Niger 92 E3
Digby Canada 119 I5
Diggi India 78 C4
Diglur India 80 C2
Digne France see Digne-les-Bains
Digne-les-Bains France 52 H4
Digoin France 52 F3
Digos Phil. 65 H5
Digras India 80 C1
Digri Pak. 85 H5
Digul r. Indon. 65 K8
Digya National Park Ghana 92 C4
Dihang r. India 79 H4 see Brahmaputra
Dihōk Iraq see Dahūk
Dihourse, Lac l. Canada 119 I2
Diinsoor Somalia 94 E3
Dijon France 52 G3
Dik Chad 93 E4
Diken India 78 C4
Dikhil Djibouti 82 F7
Dikili Turkey 55 L5
Diklosmta mt. Rus. Fed. 39 J8
Diksal India 80 B2
Diksmuide Belgium 48 C3
Dikson Rus. Fed. 60 J2
Dīla Eth. 94 D3

Dilaram Iran 84 E4
Dili East Timor 104 D2
Capital of East Timor.
Di Linh Vietnam 67 E5
Dillenburg Germany 49 I4
Dilley U.S.A. 127 D6
Dillingen (Saar) Germany 48 G5
Dillingen an der Donau Germany 43 M6
Dillingham U.S.A. 114 C4
Dillon r. Canada 117 I4
Dillon MT U.S.A. 122 E3
Dillon SC U.S.A. 129 E5
Dillwyn U.S.A. 131 F5
Dilolo Dem. Rep. Congo 95 C5
Dilsen Belgium 48 F3
Dimapur India 79 H4
Dimashq Syria see Damascus
Dimbokro Côte d'Ivoire 92 C4
Dimboola Australia 107 C8
Dimitrov Ukr. see Dymytrov
Dimitrovgrad Bulg. 55 K3
Dimitrovgrad Rus. Fed. 39 K5
Dimitrovo Bulg. see Pernik
Dimmitt U.S.A. 127 C5
Dīmona Israel 81 B4
Dimpho Pan salt pan Botswana 96 E3
Dinagat i. Phil. 65 H4
Dinajpur Bangl. 79 G4
Dinan France 52 C2
Dinant Belgium 48 E4
Dinapur India 79 F4
Dinar Turkey 55 N5
Dīnār, Kūh-e mt. Iran 84 C4
Dinara Planina mts Bos.-Herz./Croatia see Dinaric Alps
Dinaric Alps mts Bos.-Herz./Croatia 54 G2
Dinbych U.K. see Denbigh
Dinbych-y-pysgod U.K. see Tenby
Dinder National Park Sudan 93 G3
Dindi r. India 80 C2
Dindigul India 80 C4
Dindima Nigeria 92 E3
Dindiza Moz. 97 K2
Dindori India 78 E5
Dingcheng China see Dingyuan
Dingelstädt Germany 49 K3
Dingla Nepal 79 F4
Dingle Rep. of Ireland 47 B5
Dingle Bay Rep. of Ireland 47 B5
Dingnan China 73 G3
Dingo Australia 106 E4
Dingolfing Germany 49 M6
Dingping China see Linshui
Dingtao China 73 G1
Dinguiraye Guinea 92 B3
Dingwall U.K. 46 E3
Dingxi China 72 E1
Dingyuan China 73 H1
Dinh Lâp Vietnam 66 D2
Dinkelsbühl Germany 49 K5
Dinngyê China 79 F3
Dinokwe Botswana 97 H2
Dinosaur U.S.A. 125 I1
Dinosaur National Monument nat. park U.S.A. 125 I1
Dinslaken Germany 48 G3
Dinwiddie U.S.A. 131 G5
Dioïla Mali 92 C3
Dionísio Cerqueira Brazil 140 F3
Diorama Brazil 141 A2
Dioscurias Georgia see Sokhumi
Diouloulou Senegal 92 B3
Diourbel Senegal 92 B3
Diphu India 79 H4
Dipkarpaz Cyprus see Rizokarpason
Diplo Pak. 85 H5
Dipolog Phil. 65 G5
Dipperu National Park Australia 106 E4
Dipu China see Anji
Dir reg. Pak. 85 I3
Dirang India 79 H4
Diré Mali 92 C3
Direction, Cape Australia 106 C2
Dirē Dawa Eth. 94 E3
Dirico Angola 95 C5
Dirk Hartog Island Australia 105 A6
Dirranbandi Australia 108 D2
Ḑirs Saudi Arabia 94 E2
Dirschau Poland see Tczew
Dirty Devil r. U.S.A. 125 H3
Disa India 78 C4
Disang r. India 79 H4
Disappointment, Cape S. Georgia 140 I8
Disappointment, Cape U.S.A. 122 B3
Disappointment Islands Fr. Polynesia see Désappointement, Îles du
Disappointment, Lake salt flat Australia 105 C5
Disappointment Lake Canada 119 J3
Disaster Bay Australia 108 D6
Discovery Bay Australia 107 C8
Disko i. Greenland see Qeqertarsuaq
Disko Bugt b. Greenland see Qeqertarsuup Tunua
Dispur India 79 G4
Disputanta U.S.A. 131 G5
Disraëli Canada 119 H5
Diss U.K. 45 I6
Distrito Federal admin. dist. Brazil 141 B1
Disūq Egypt 86 C5
Ditloung S. Africa 96 F5
Dittaino r. Sicily Italy 54 F6
Diu India 80 A1
Dīvān Darreh Iran 84 B3
Divehi country Indian Ocean see Maldives
Divi, Point India 80 D3
Divichi Azer. see Däväçi
Divide Mountain U.S.A. 116 A2
Divinópolis Brazil 141 B3
Divnoye Rus. Fed. 39 I7
Divo Côte d'Ivoire 92 C4
Divriği Turkey 86 E3
Diwana Pak. 85 G5
Diwaniyah Iraq see Ad Dīwānīyah
Dixfield U.S.A. 131 J1
Dixon CA U.S.A. 124 C2
Dixon IL U.S.A. 126 F3
Dixon KY U.S.A. 130 B5
Dixon MT U.S.A. 122 E3
Dixon Entrance sea chan. Canada/U.S.A. 116 C4
Dixonville Canada 116 G3
Dixville Canada 131 J1
Diyadin Turkey 87 F3
Diyarbakır Turkey 87 F3
Diz Pak. 85 F5
Diz Chah Iran 84 D3
Dize Turkey see Yüksekova
Dizney U.S.A. 130 D5
Djado Niger 92 E2
Djado, Plateau du Niger 92 E2
Djaja, Puntjak mt. Indon. see Jaya, Puncak
Djakarta Indon. see Jakarta
Djakovica Serb. and Mont. see Đakovica
Djakovo Croatia see Đakovo
Djambala Congo 94 B4
Djanet Alg. 92 D2
Djarrit-Uliga-Dalap Marshall Is see Delap-Uliga-Djarrit
Djelfa Alg. 53 H6
Djéma Cent. Afr. Rep. 94 C3
Djenné Mali 92 C3
Djerdap nat. park Serb. and Mont. 55 J2
Djibo Burkina 92 C3
Djibouti country Africa 82 F7
africa 7, 90–91
Djibouti Djibouti 82 F7
Capital of Djibouti.
Djidjelli Alg. see Jijel
Djougou Benin 92 D4
Djoum Cameroon 92 E4
Djourab, Erg du des. Chad 93 E3
Djúpivogur Iceland 40 [inset]
Djurås Sweden 41 I6
Djurdjura National Park Alg. 53 I5
Dmitriya Lapteva, Proliv sea chan. Rus. Fed. 61 P2
Dmitriyev-L'govskiy Rus. Fed. 39 G5
Dmitriyevsk Ukr. see Makiyivka
Dmitrov Rus. Fed. 38 H4
Dmytriyevs'k Ukr. see Makiyivka
Dnepr r. Rus. Fed. 39 F5 see Dnieper
Dneprodzerzhinsk Ukr. see Dniprodzerzhyns'k
Dnepropetrovsk Ukr. see Dnipropetrovs'k
Dnieper r. Europe 39 G7
3rd longest river in Europe. Also spelt Dnepr (Rus. Fed.) or Dnipro (Ukraine) or Dnyapro (Belarus).
Dniester r. Ukr. 39 F6
also spelt Dnister (Ukraine) or Nistru (Moldova)
Dnipro r. Ukr. 39 G7 see Dnieper
Dniprodzerzhyns'k Ukr. 39 G6
Dnipropetrovs'k Ukr. 39 G6
Dnister r. Ukr. 39 F6 see Dniester
Dno Rus. Fed. 38 F4
Dnyapro r. Belarus 39 F6 see Dnieper
Doāb Afgh. 85 G3
Doaba Pak. 85 H3
Doba Chad 93 E4
Doba China see Toiba
Dobele Latvia 41 M8
Döbeln Germany 49 N3
Doberai, Jazirah pen. Indon. 65 I7
Doberai Peninsula Indon. see Doberai, Jazirah
Dobo Indon. 65 I8
Doboj Bos.-Herz. 54 H2
Do Borjī Iran 84 D4
Döbraberg hill Germany 49 L4
Dobrich Bulg. 55 L3
Dobrinka Rus. Fed. 39 I5
Dobroye Rus. Fed. 39 H5
Dobrudja reg. Romania see Dobruja
Dobruja reg. Romania 55 L3
Dobrush Belarus 39 F5
Dobryanka Rus. Fed. 37 R4
Dobzha China 79 G3
Doce r. Brazil 141 D2
Dochart r. U.K. 46 E4
Do China Qala Afgh. 85 H4
Docking U.K. 45 H6
Doctor Hicks Range hills Australia 105 D7
Doctor Pedro P. Peña Para. 140 D2
Doda India 78 C2
Doda Betta mt. India 80 C4
Dod Ballapur India 80 C3
Dodecanese is Greece 55 L7
Dodekanisos is Greece see Dodecanese
Dodge City U.S.A. 126 C4
Dodgeville U.S.A. 126 F3
Dodman Point U.K. 45 C8
Dodoma Tanz. 95 D4
Capital of Tanzania.
Dodsonville U.S.A. 130 D4
Doetinchem Neth. 48 G3
Dog r. Canada 118 C4
Dogai Coring salt l. China 79 G2
Dogaicoring Qangco salt l. China 79 G2
Doğanşehir Turkey 86 E3
Dogên Co l. Xizang China see Bam Tso
Dogên Co l. Xizang China 79 G3
Doghārūn Iran 85 F3
Dog Island Canada 119 J2
Dog Lake Man. Canada 117 L5
Dog Lake Ont. Canada 118 C4
Dog Lake Ont. Canada 118 D4
Dōgo i. Japan 71 D5
Dogondoutchi Niger 92 D3
Dog Rocks is Bahamas 129 E7
Doğubeyazıt Turkey 87 G3
Doğu Menteşe Dağları mts Turkey 55 M6
Dogxung Zangbo r. China 79 F3
Do'gyaling China 79 G3
Doha Qatar 84 C5
Capital of Qatar.
Dohad India see Dahod
Dohazari Bangl. 79 H5
Dohrighat India 79 E4
Doi i. Fiji 103 I4
Doi Inthanon National Park Thai. 66 B3
Doi Luang National Park Thai. 66 B3
Doire U.K. see Londonderry
Doi Saket Thai. 66 B3
Dois Irmãos, Serra dos hills Brazil 139 J5
Dok-dō i. N. Pacific Ocean see Liancourt Rocks
Dokhara, Dunes de des. Alg. 50 F5
Dokka Norway 41 G6
Dokkum Neth. 48 F1
Dokri Pak. 85 H5
Dokshukino Rus. Fed. see Nartkala
Dokshytsy Belarus 41 O9
Dokuchayeva, Mys c. Rus. Fed. 70 G3
Dokuchayevka Kazakh. see Karamendy
Dokuchayevs'k Ukr. 39 H7
Dolak, Pulau i. Indon. 65 J8
Dolbenmaen U.K. 45 C6
Dol-de-Bretagne France 52 D2
Dole France 52 G3
Dolgellau U.K. 45 D6
Dolgen Germany 49 N1
Dolgiy, Ostrov i. Rus. Fed. 38 L1
Dolgorukovo Rus. Fed. 39 H5
Dolina Ukr. see Dolyna
Dolinsk Rus. Fed. 70 F3
Dolisie Congo see Loubomo
Dolleman Island Antarctica 148 L2
Dollnstein Germany 49 L6
Dolomites mts Italy 54 D2
Dolomiti mts Italy see Dolomites
Dolomiti Bellunesi, Parco Nazionale delle nat. park Italy 54 D1
Dolomitiche, Alpi mts Italy see Dolomites
Dolonnur China see Duolun
Dolo Odo Eth. 94 E3
Dolores Arg. 140 E5
Dolores Uruguay 140 E4
Dolores U.S.A. 125 I3
Dolphin and Union Strait Canada 114 G3
Dolphin Head hd Namibia 96 B3
Đô Lương Vietnam 66 D3
Dolyna Ukr. 39 D6
Domaniç Turkey 55 M5
Domar China 76 F5
Domartang China see Banbar
Domažlice Czech Rep. 49 M5
Domba China 72 B1
Dom Bākh Iran 84 B3
Dombås Norway 40 F5
Dombóvár Hungary 54 H1
Dombrau Poland see Dąbrowa Górnicza
Dombrovitsa Ukr. see Dubrovytsya
Dombrowa Poland see Dąbrowa Górnicza
Domda China see Qingshuihe
Dome Argus ice feature Antarctica 148 E1
Dome Charlie ice feature Antarctica 148 F2
Dome Creek Canada 116 F4
Dome Rock Mountains U.S.A. 125 F5
Domeyko Chile 140 B3
Domfront France 52 D2
Dominica country West Indies 133 L5
north america 9, 112–113
Dominicana, República country West Indies see Dominican Republic
Dominican Republic country West Indies 133 J5
north america 9, 112–113
Dominion, Cape Canada 115 K3
Dominique i. Fr. Polynesia see Hiva Oa
Dömitz Germany 49 L1
Dom Joaquim Brazil 141 C2
Dommel r. Neth. 48 F3
Domo Eth. 94 E3
Domokos Greece 55 J5
Dompu Indon. 104 B2
Domula China see Duomula
Domuyo, Volcán vol. Arg. 140 B5
Domville, Mount hill Australia 108 E2
Don Mex. 123 F8
Don r. Rus. Fed. 39 H7
5th longest river in Europe.
Don r. U.K. 46 G3
Don, Xé r. Laos 66 D4
Donaghadee U.K. 47 G3
Donaghmore U.K. 47 F3
Donald Australia 108 A6
Donaldsonville U.S.A. 127 F6
Donalsonville U.S.A. 129 C6
Doñana, Parque Nacional de nat. park Spain 53 C5
Donau r. Austria/Germany 43 P6 see Danube
Donauwörth Germany 49 K6
Don Benito Spain 53 D4
Doncaster U.K. 44 F5
Dondo Angola 95 B4
Dondo Moz. 95 D5
Dondra Head hd Sri Lanka 80 D5
Donegal Rep. of Ireland 47 D3
Donegal Bay Rep. of Ireland 47 D3
Donets'k Ukr. 39 H7
Donetsko-Amrovsiyevka Ukr. see Amvrosiyivka
Donets'kyy Kryazh hills Rus. Fed./Ukr. 39 H6
Donga r. Cameroon/Nigeria 92 D4
Dong'an China 73 F3
Dongane, Lagoa lag. Moz. 97 L3
Dongara Australia 105 A7
Dongbo China see Mêdog
Dongchuan Yunnan China see Yao'an
Dongchuan Yunnan China 72 D3
Dongco China 79 F2
Dong Co l. China 79 F2
Dongfang China 73 F5
Dongfanghong China 70 D3
Donggang China 71 B5
Donggi Conag l. China 72 C1
Donggou China see Donggang
Donggu China 73 G3
Dongguan China 73 G4
Dong Hai sea N. Pacific Ocean see East China Sea
Đông Hơi Vietnam 66 D3
Donghuang China see Xishui
Dongjiang Shuiku resr China 73 G3
Dongjug China 72 B2
Dongkou China 73 F3
Donglan China 72 E3
Dongliao He r. China 70 A4
Dongmen China see Luocheng
Dongminzhutun China 70 A3
Dongning China 70 C3
Dongo Angola 95 B5
Dongo Dem. Rep. Congo 94 B3
Dongola Sudan 82 D6
Dongou Congo 94 B3
Dong Phraya Yen esc. Thai. 66 C4
Dongping Guangdong China 73 G4
Dongping Hunan China see Anhua
Dongpo China see Meishan
Dongqiao China 79 G3
Dongshan Fujian China 73 H4
Dongshan Jiangsu China 73 I2
Dongshan Jiangxi China see Shangyou
Dongshao China 73 G3
Dongsha Qundao is China 64 F2
Dongsheng Nei Mongol China 69 K5
Dongsheng Sichuan China see Shuangliu
Dongshuan China see Tangdan
Dongtai China 73 I1
Dongting Hu l. China 73 G2
Dongtou China 73 I3
Đông Triều Vietnam 66 D2
Dong Ujimqin Qi China see Uliastai
Đông Văn Vietnam 66 D2
Dongxiang China 73 H2
Dongxi Liandao i. China 73 H1
Dongxing Guangxi China 72 E4
Dongxing Heilong. China 70 B3
Dongyang China 73 I2
Dongying China 69 L5
Dongzhi China 73 H2
Donkerbroek Neth. 48 G1
Donnacona Canada 119 H5
Donnellys Crossing N.Z. 109 D2
Donner Pass U.S.A. 124 C2
Donnersberg hill Germany 49 H5
Donostia - San Sebastián Spain 53 F2
Donoussa i. Greece 55 K6
Donskoye Rus. Fed. 39 I7
Donyztau, Sor dry lake Kazakh. 76 A2
Dooagh Rep. of Ireland 47 B4
Doomadgee Australia 106 B3
Doon r. U.K. 46 E5
Doon, Loch l. U.K. 46 E5
Doonbeg r. Rep. of Ireland 47 C5
Doorn Neth. 48 F2
Door Peninsula U.S.A. 130 B1
Doorwerth Neth. 48 F3
Dooxo Nugaaleed valley Somalia 94 E3
Doqêmo China 72 B2
Do Qu r. China 72 D2
Dor watercourse Afgh. 85 F4
Dora U.S.A. 127 C5
Dora, Lake salt flat Australia 104 C5
Dorado Mex. 127 B7
Dorah Pass Pak. 85 H2
Doran Lake Canada 117 I2
Dorbiljin China see Emin
Dorbod China see Taikang
Dorbod Qi China see Ulan Hua
Dorchester U.K. 45 E8
Dordabis Namibia 96 C2
Dordogne r. France 52 D4
Dordrecht Neth. 48 E3
Dordrecht S. Africa 97 H6
Doreenville Namibia 96 D2
Doré Lake Canada 117 J4
Doré Lake l. Canada 117 J4
Dores do Indaiá Brazil 141 B2
Dori r. Afgh. 85 G4
Dori Burkina 92 C3
Doring r. S. Africa 96 D6
do Rio Manso, Represa resr Brazil 139 G6
Dorisvale Australia 104 E3
Dorking U.K. 45 G7
Dormagen Germany 48 G3
Dormans France 48 D5
Dormidontovka Rus. Fed. 70 D3
Dornoch U.K. 46 E3
Dornoch Firth est. U.K. 46 E3
Dornum Germany 49 H1
Doro Mali 92 C3
Dorogobuzh Rus. Fed. 39 G5
Dorogorskoye Rus. Fed. 38 J2
Dorohoi Romania 39 E7
Döröö Nuur salt l. Mongolia 76 H2
Dorostol Bulg. see Silistra
Dorotea Sweden 40 J4
Dorpat Estonia see Tartu
Dorre Island Australia 105 A6
Dorrigo Australia 108 F3
Dorris U.S.A. 122 C4
Dorsale Camerounaise slope Cameroon/Nigeria 92 E4
Dorset Canada 131 F1
Dorsoidong Co l. China 79 G2
Dortmund Germany 49 H3
Dörtyol Turkey 81 C1
Dorum Germany 49 I1
Doruma Dem. Rep. Congo 94 C3
Dorüneh, Kūh-e mts Iran 84 E3
Dorval airport Canada 118 G5
Dörverden Germany 49 J2
Dorylaeum Turkey see Eskişehir
Dos Bahías, Cabo c. Arg. 140 C6
Dos de Mayo Peru 138 C5
Doshakh, Koh-i- mt. Afgh. see Do Shākh, Kūh-e
Do Shākh, Kūh-e mt. Afgh. 85 F3
Đo Son Vietnam 66 D2
Dos Palos U.S.A. 124 C3
Dosse r. Germany 49 M2
Dosso Niger 92 D3
Dothan U.S.A. 129 C6
Dotsero U.S.A. 125 J2
Douai France 48 D4
Douala Cameroon 92 D4
Douarnenez France 52 B2
Double Headed Shot Cays is Bahamas 129 D8
Double Island Hong Kong China 73 [inset]
Double Island Point Australia 107 F5
Double Mountain Fork r. U.S.A. 127 C5
Double Peak U.S.A. 124 D4
Double Point Australia 106 D3
Double Springs U.S.A. 129 C5
Doubs r. France/Switz. 52 G3
Doubtful Sound inlet N.Z. 109 A7
Doubtless Bay N.Z. 109 D2
Douentza Mali 92 C3
Dougga tourist site Tunisia 54 C6
Douglas Isle of Man 44 C4
Capital of the Isle of Man.
Douglas S. Africa 96 F5
Douglas U.K. 46 F5
Douglas AZ U.S.A. 123 F7
Douglas GA U.S.A. 129 D6
Douglas WY U.S.A. 122 G4
Douglas Reef i. Japan see Okino-Tori-shima
Douglasville U.S.A. 129 C5
Douhudi China see Gong'an
Doulatpur Bangl. see Daulatpur
Douliu Taiwan see Touliu
Doullens France 48 C4
Douna Mali 92 C3
Doune U.K. 46 E4
Doupovské Hory mts Czech Rep. 49 N4
Dourada, Serra hills Brazil 141 A2
Dourada, Serra mts Brazil 141 A1
Dourados Brazil 140 F2
Douro r. Port. 53 B3
also known as Duero (Spain)
Doushi China see Gong'an
Doushui Shuiku resr China 73 G3
Douve r. France 45 F9
Douzy France 48 F5
Dove r. U.K. 45 F6
Dove Brook Canada 119 K3
Dove Creek U.S.A. 125 I3
Dover U.K. 45 I7
Dover DE U.S.A. 131 H4
State capital of Delaware.
Dover NH U.S.A. 131 J2
Dover NJ U.S.A. 131 H3
Dover OH U.S.A. 130 E3
Dover TN U.S.A. 128 C4
Dover, Strait of France/U.K. 52 E1
Dover-Foxcroft U.S.A. 131 K1
Dovey r. U.K. see Dyfi
Dovrefjell Nasjonalpark nat. park Norway 40 F5
Dowagiac U.S.A. 130 B3
Dowi, Tanjung pt Indon. 67 B7
Dowlaiswaram India 80 D2
Dowlatābād Afgh. 85 F3
Dowlatābād Fārs Iran 84 C4
Dowlatābād Fārs Iran 84 D4
Dowlatābād Khorāsān Iran 84 E2
Dowlatābād Khorāsān Iran 85 F2
Dowl at Yār Afgh. 85 G3
Downieville U.S.A. 124 C2
Downpatrick U.K. 47 G3
Downsville U.S.A. 131 H2
Dow Rūd Iran 84 C3
Doyle U.S.A. 124 C1
Doylestown U.S.A. 131 H3
Dozdān r. Iran 84 E5
Dōzen is Japan 71 D5
Dozois, Réservoir resr Canada 118 F5
Dozulé France 45 G9
Dracena Brazil 141 A3
Drachten Neth. 48 G1
Drăgănești-Olt Romania 55 K2
Drăgășani Romania 55 K2
Dragonera, Isla i. Spain see Sa Dragonera
Dragoon U.S.A. 125 H5
Dragsfjärd Fin. 41 M6
Draguignan France 52 H5
Drahichyn Belarus 41 N10
Drake Australia 108 F2
Drake U.S.A. 126 C2
Drakensberg mts S. Africa 97 I3
Drake Passage S. Atlantic Ocean 144 D9
Drakes Bay U.S.A. 124 B3
Drama Greece 55 K4
Drammen Norway 41 G7
Drang, Prêk r. Cambodia 67 D4
Drangedal Norway 41 F7
Dransfeld Germany 49 J3
Draper, Mount U.S.A. 116 B3
Draperstown U.K. 47 F3
Drapsaca Afgh. see Kunduz
Dras Jammu and Kashmir 78 C2
Drasan Pak. 85 I2
Drau r. Austria see Drava
Drava r. Europe 54 H2
also known as Drau (Austria), Drave or Drava (Slovenia and Croatia), Dráva (Hungary)
Dráva r. Hungary see Drava
Drave r. Slovenia/Croatia see Drava
Drayton Valley Canada 116 H4
Drazinda Pak. 85 H4
Dréan Alg. 54 B6
Dreistelzberge hill Germany 49 J4
Drentse Hoofdvaart canal Neth. 48 G2
Drepano, Akra pt Greece 55 J5
Dresden Canada 130 D2
Dresden Germany 43 N5
Dreux France 48 B6
Drevsjø Norway 41 H6
Drewryville U.S.A. 131 G5
Dri China 72 C2
Driffield U.K. 44 G4
Driftwood U.S.A. 131 F3
Driggs U.S.A. 122 F4
Drillham Australia 108 E1
Drimoleague Rep. of Ireland 47 C6
Drina r. Bos.-Herz./Serb. and Mont. 55 H2
Driscoll Island Antarctica 148 J1
Drissa Belarus see Vyerkhnyadzvinsk
Drniš Croatia 54 G3
Drobeta - Turnu Severin Romania 55 J2
Drochtersen Germany 49 J1
Drogheda Rep. of Ireland 47 F4
Drogichin Belarus see Drahichyn
Drogobych Ukr. see Drohobych
Drohobych Ukr. 39 D6
Droichead Átha Rep. of Ireland see Drogheda
Droichead Nua Rep. of Ireland see Newbridge
Droitwich U.K. see Droitwich Spa
Droitwich Spa U.K. 45 E6
Dromedary, Cape Australia 108 E6
Dromod Rep. of Ireland 47 E4
Dromore Northern Ireland U.K. 47 E3
Dromore Northern Ireland U.K. 47 F3
Dronfield U.K. 44 F5
Dronning Louise Land reg. Greenland 149 I1
Dronning Maud Land reg. Antarctica see Queen Maud Land
Dronten Neth. 48 F2
Druk-Yul country Asia see Bhutan
Drumheller Canada 117 H5
Drummond atoll Kiribati see Tabiteuea
Drummond U.S.A. 122 E3
Drummond, Lake U.S.A. 131 G5
Drummond Island Kiribati see McKean
Drummond Range hills Australia 106 D5
Drummondville Canada 119 G5
Drummore U.K. 46 E6
Drury Lake Canada 116 C2
Druskieniki Lith. see Druskininkai
Druskininkai Lith. 41 N10
Druzhina Rus. Fed. 61 P3
Druzhnaya Gorka Rus. Fed. 41 Q7
Dry r. Australia 104 F3
Dryanovo Bulg. 55 K3
Dryberry Lake Canada 117 M5
Dryden Canada 117 M5
Dryden U.S.A. 131 G2
Dry Fork r. U.S.A. 122 G4
Drygalski Ice Tongue Antarctica 148 H1
Drygalski Island Antarctica 148 F2
Dry Lake U.S.A. 125 F3
Dry Lake l. U.S.A. 126 D1
Drymen U.K. 46 E4
Dry Ridge U.S.A. 130 C4
Drysdale r. Australia 104 D3
Drysdale River National Park Australia 104 D3
Dry Tortugas is U.S.A. 129 D7
Du'an China 73 F4
Duaringa Australia 106 E4
Duarte, Pico mt. Dom. Rep. 133 J5
Duartina Brazil 141 A3
Ḑubā Saudi Arabia 82 E4
Dubai U.A.E. 84 D5
Dubakella Mountain U.S.A. 124 B1
Dubawnt r. Canada 117 L2
Dubawnt Lake Canada 117 K2
Dubayy U.A.E. see Dubai
Dubbo Australia 108 D4
Dublin Rep. of Ireland 47 F4
Capital of the Republic of Ireland.
Dublin U.S.A. 129 D5
Dubna Rus. Fed. 38 H4
Dubno Ukr. 39 E6
Dubois ID U.S.A. 122 E3
Dubois IN U.S.A. 130 B4
Du Bois U.S.A. 131 F3
Dubovka Rus. Fed. 39 J6
Dubovskoye Rus. Fed. 39 I7
Dübrar Pass Azer. 87 H2
Dubréka Guinea 92 B4
Dubris U.K. see Dover
Dubrovnik Croatia 54 H3
Dubrovytsya Ukr. 39 E6
Dubuque U.S.A. 126 F3
Dubysa r. Lith. 41 M9
Duc de Gloucester, Îles du is Fr. Polynesia 147 K7
Duchang China 73 H2
Ducheng China see Yunan
Duchesne U.S.A. 125 H1
Duchesne r. U.S.A. 125 I1
Duchess Australia 106 B4
Duchess Canada 117 I5
Ducie Island atoll Pitcairn Is 147 L7
Duck Bay Canada 117 K4
Duck Creek r. Australia 104 B5
Duck Lake Canada 117 J4
Duckwater Peak U.S.A. 125 F2
Đưc Trong Vietnam 67 E5
Dudelange Lux. 48 G5
Duderstadt Germany 49 K3
Dudhi India 79 E4
Dudhwa India 78 E3
Dudinka Rus. Fed. 60 J3
Dudley U.K. 45 E6
Dudleyville U.S.A. 125 H5
Dudna r. India 80 C2
Dudu India 78 C4
Duékoué Côte d'Ivoire 92 C4
Duen, Bukit vol. Indon. 64 C7
Duero r. Spain 53 C3
also known as Douro (Portugal)
Duffel Belgium 48 E3
Dufferin, Cape Canada 118 F2
Duffer Peak U.S.A. 122 D4
Duff Islands Solomon Is 103 G2
Duffreboy, Lac l. Canada 119 H2
Dufftown U.K. 46 F3
Dufourspitze mt. Italy/Switz. 54 B2
Dufrost, Pointe pt Canada 118 F1
Dugi Otok i. Croatia 54 F2
Dugi Rat Croatia 54 G3
Du He r. China 73 F1
Duida-Marahuaca, Parque Nacional nat. park Venez. 138 E3
Duisburg Germany 48 G3
Duiwelskloof S. Africa 97 J2
Dujiangyan China 72 D2
Dukān Dam Iraq 87 G4
Dukathole S. Africa 97 H6
Duke Island U.S.A. 116 D4
Duke of Clarence atoll Tokelau see Nukunonu
Duke of Gloucester Islands Fr. Polynesia see Duc de Gloucester, Îles du
Duke of York atoll Tokelau see Atafu
Duk Fadiat Sudan 93 G4
Dukhovnitskoye Rus. Fed. 39 K5
Duki Pak. 85 H4
Duki Rus. Fed. 70 D2
Duki r. Rus. Fed. 70 D2
Dukou China see Panzhihua
Dūkštas Lith. 41 O9
Dulac U.S.A. 127 F6
Dulan China 76 I4
Dulce r. Arg. 140 D4
Dulce U.S.A. 123 G5
Dul'durga Rus. Fed. 69 K2
Dulhunty r. Australia 106 C1
Dulishi Hu salt l. China 79 E2
Duliu Jiang r. China 73 F3
Dullewala Pak. 85 H4
Dullstroom S. Africa 97 J3
Dülmen Germany 49 H3
Dulmera India 78 C3
Dulovo Bulg. 55 L3
Duluth U.S.A. 126 E2
Dulverton U.K. 45 D7
Dūmā Syria 81 C3
Dumaguete Phil. 65 G5
Dumai Indon. 67 C7
Dumaran i. Phil. 64 G4
Dumaresq r. Australia 108 E2
Dumas U.S.A. 127 C5
Ḑumayr Syria 81 C3
Ḑumayr, Jabal mts Syria 81 C3
Dumbakh Iran see Dom Bākh
Dumbarton U.K. 46 E5
Dumbe S. Africa 97 J4
Ďumbier mt. Slovakia 43 Q6
Dumchele Jammu and Kashmir 78 D2
Dumdum i. Indon. 67 D7
Dumfries U.K. 46 F5
Dumka India 79 F4
Dumont d'Urville research station Antarctica 148 G2
Dumont d'Urville Sea Antarctica 148 G2
Dümpelfeld Germany 48 G4
Dumyāṭ Egypt 86 C5
Dumyāṭ Egypt see Dumyāṭ
Duna r. Hungary 54 H2 see Danube
Dünaburg Latvia see Daugavpils
Dunaj r. Slovakia see Danube
Dunajská Streda Slovakia 43 P7
Dunakeszi Hungary 55 H1
Dunany Point Rep. of Ireland 47 F4

Eliase Indon. **104** E2
Elías Piña Dom. Rep. **133** J5
Elichpur India *see* **Achalpur**
Elida U.S.A. **130** C3
Elie U.K. **46** G4
Elila *r.* Dem. Rep. Congo **94** C4
Elim U.S.A. **114** B3
Elimberrum France *see* **Auch**
Eling China *see* **Yinjiang**
Elingampangu Dem. Rep. Congo **94** C4
Eliot, Mount Canada **119** J2
Élisabethville Dem. Rep. Congo *see* **Lubumbashi**
Eliseu Martins Brazil **139** J5
El Iskandarîya Egypt *see* **Alexandria**
Elista Rus. Fed. **39** J7
Elizabeth *NJ* U.S.A. **131** H3
Elizabeth *WV* U.S.A. **130** E4
Elizabeth, Mount *hill* Australia **104** D4
Elizabeth Bay Namibia **96** B4
Elizabeth City U.S.A. **128** E4
Elizabeth Island Pitcairn Is *see* **Henderson Island**
Elizabeth Point Namibia **96** B4
Elizabethton U.S.A. **128** D4
Elizabethtown *IL* U.S.A. **126** F4
Elizabethtown *KY* U.S.A. **130** C5
Elizabethtown *NC* U.S.A. **129** E5
Elizabethtown *NY* U.S.A. **131** I1
El Jadida Morocco **50** C5
El Jaralito Mex. **127** B7
El Jem Tunisia **54** D7
Elk *r.* Canada **116** H5
Ełk Poland **43** S4
Elk *r.* U.S.A. **131** H4
El Kaa Lebanon *see* **Qaa**
El Kab Sudan **82** D6
Elkader U.S.A. **126** F3
El Kala Alg. **54** C6
Elk City U.S.A. **127** D5
Elkedra Australia **106** A4
Elkedra *watercourse* Australia **106** B4
El Kef Tunisia *see* **Le Kef**
El Kelaâ des Srarhna Morocco **50** C5
Elkford Canada **116** H5
Elk Grove U.S.A. **124** C2
El Khalil West Bank *see* **Hebron**
El Khandaq Sudan **82** D6
El Khârga Egypt *see* **Al Khārijah**
El Kharrûba Egypt *see* **Al Kharrūbah**
Elkhart *IN* U.S.A. **130** C3
Elkhart *KS* U.S.A. **127** C4
El Khartûm Sudan *see* **Khartoum**
El Khenachich *esc.* Mali *see* **El Khnâchîch**
El Khnâchîch *esc.* Mali **92** C2
Elkhorn U.S.A. **126** F3
Elkhorn City U.S.A. **130** D5
Elkhovo Bulg. **55** L3
Elki Turkey *see* **Beytüşşebap**
Elkin U.S.A. **128** D4
Elkins U.S.A. **130** F4
Elk Island National Park Canada **117** H4
Elk Lake Canada **118** E5
Elk Lake *l.* U.S.A. **130** C1
Elkland U.S.A. **131** G3
Elk Mountain U.S.A. **122** G4
Elk Mountains U.S.A. **125** J2
Elko Canada **116** H5
Elko U.S.A. **125** F1
Elk Point Canada **117** I4
Elk Point U.S.A. **126** D3
Elk Springs U.S.A. **125** I1
Elkton *MD* U.S.A. **131** H4
Elkton *VA* U.S.A. **131** F4
El Kûbri Egypt *see* **Al Kūbrī**
El Kuntilla Egypt *see* **Al Kuntillah**
Elkview U.S.A. **130** E4
Ellas *country* Europe *see* **Greece**
Ellaville U.S.A. **129** C5
Ell Bay Canada **117** O1
Ellef Ringnes Island Canada **115** H2
Ellen, Mount U.S.A. **125** H2
Ellenburg Depot U.S.A. **131** I1
Ellendale U.S.A. **126** D2
Ellensburg U.S.A. **122** C3
Ellenville U.S.A. **131** H3
El León, Cerro *mt.* Mex. **127** B7
Ellesmere, Lake N.Z. **109** D6

▶**Ellesmere Island** Canada **115** J2
4th largest island in North America.

Ellesmere Island National Park Reserve Canada *see* **Quttinirpaaq National Park**
Ellesmere Port U.K. **44** E5
Ellettsville U.S.A. **130** B4
Ellice *r.* Canada **117** K1
Ellice Island *atoll* Tuvalu *see* **Funafuti**
Ellice Islands *country* S. Pacific Ocean *see* **Tuvalu**
Ellicott City U.S.A. **131** G4
Ellijay U.S.A. **129** C5
Ellingen Germany **49** K5
Elliot Australia **104** F4
Elliot S. Africa **97** H6
Elliot, Mount Australia **106** D3
Elliotdale S. Africa **97** I6
Elliot Knob *mt.* U.S.A. **130** F4
Elliot Lake Canada **118** E5
Ellisras S. Africa **97** H2
Elliston U.S.A. **130** E5
Ellon U.K. **46** G3
Ellora Caves *tourist site* India **80** B1
Ellsworth *KS* U.S.A. **126** D4
Ellsworth *ME* U.S.A. **128** G2
Ellsworth *NE* U.S.A. **126** C3
Ellsworth *WI* U.S.A. **126** E2
Ellsworth Land *reg.* Antarctica **148** K1
Ellsworth Mountains Antarctica **148** L1
Ellwangen (Jagst) Germany **49** K6
El Maghreb *country* Africa *see* **Morocco**
Elmakuz Dağı *mt.* Turkey **81** A1
Elmalı Turkey **55** M6
El Malpais National Monument *nat. park* U.S.A. **125** J4
El Manşûra Egypt *see* **Al Manşūrah**
El Maţarîya Egypt *see* **Al Maţarīyah**
El Mazâr Egypt *see* **Al Mazār**
El Meghaïer Alg. **50** F5
El Milia Alg. **50** F4
El Minya Egypt *see* **Al Minyā**
Elmira *Ont.* Canada **130** E2
Elmira *P.E.I.* Canada **119** J5
Elmira *MI* U.S.A. **130** C1
Elmira *NY* U.S.A. **131** G2
El Mirage U.S.A. **125** G5
El Moral Spain **53** E5
Elmore Australia **108** B6
El Mreyyé *reg.* Mauritania **92** C3
Elmshorn Germany **49** J1
El Muglad Sudan **82** C7
Elmvale Canada **130** F1
Elnesvågen Norway **40** E5
El Nevado, Cerro *mt.* Col. **138** D3
El Oasis Mex. **125** F5
El Obeid Sudan **82** D7
El Odaiya Sudan **82** C7
El Oro Mex. **127** C7
Elorza Venez. **138** E2
El Oued Alg. **50** F5
Eloy U.S.A. **125** H5
El Palmito Mex. **127** B7
El Paso *IL* U.S.A. **126** F3
El Paso *KS* U.S.A. *see* **Derby**
El Paso *TX* U.S.A. **123** G7
Elphin U.K. **46** D2
Elphinstone *i.* Myanmar *see* **Thayawthadangyi Kyun**
El Portal U.S.A. **124** D3
El Porvenir Mex. **127** B6
El Porvenir Panama **133** I7
El Prat de Llobregat Spain **53** H3
El Progreso Hond. **132** G5
El Puerto de Santa María Spain **53** C5
El Qâhira Egypt *see* **Cairo**
El Qasimiye *r.* Lebanon **81** B3
El Quds Israel/West Bank *see* **Jerusalem**
El Quşeima Egypt *see* **Al Quşaymah**
El Quşeir Egypt *see* **Al Quşayr**
El Qûşîya Egypt *see* **Al Qūşīyah**
El Regocijo Mex. **127** B8
El Reno U.S.A. **127** D5
Elrose Canada **117** I5
Elsa Canada **116** C2
El Şaff Egypt *see* **Aş Şaff**
El Sahuaro Mex. **123** E7
El Salado Mex. **127** C7
El Salto Mex. **127** B8

▶**El Salvador** *country* Central America **132** G6
north america 9, 112–113

El Salvador Chile **140** C3
El Salvador Mex. **127** C7
Elsass *reg.* France *see* **Alsace**
El Sauz Mex. **123** G7
Else *r.* Germany **49** I2
El Sellûm Egypt *see* **As Sallūm**
Elsen Nur *l.* China **79** H2
Elsey Australia **104** F3
El Shallûfa Egypt *see* **Ash Shallūfah**
El Sharana Australia **104** F3
El Shatt Egypt *see* **Ash Shaţţ**
Elsie U.S.A. **130** C2
Elsinore Denmark *see* **Helsingør**
Elsinore *CA* U.S.A. **124** E5
Elsinore *UT* U.S.A. **125** G2
Elsinore Lake U.S.A. **124** E5
El Sueco Mex. **123** G7
El Suweis Egypt *see* **Suez**
El Suweis *governorate* Egypt *see* **As Suways**
El Tama, Parque Nacional *nat. park* Venez. **138** D2
El Tarf Alg. **54** C6
El Teleno *mt.* Spain **53** C2
El Temascal Mex. **127** D7
El Ter *r.* Spain **53** H2
El Thamad Egypt *see* **Ath Thamad**
El Tigre Venez. **138** F2
Eltmann Germany **49** K5
El'ton Rus. Fed. **39** J6
El'ton, Ozero *l.* Rus. Fed. **39** J6
El Tren Mex. **123** E7
El Tuparro, Parque Nacional *nat. park* Col. **138** E2
El Ţûr Egypt *see* **Aţ Ţūr**
El Turbio Chile **140** B8
El Uqşur Egypt *see* **Luxor**
Eluru India **80** D2
Elva Estonia **41** O7
Elvanfoot U.K. **46** F5
Elvas Port. **53** C4
Elverum Norway **41** G6
Elvira Brazil **138** D5
El Wak Kenya **94** E3
El Wâţya *well* Egypt *see* **Al Wāţiyah**
Elwood *IN* U.S.A. **130** C3
Elwood *NE* U.S.A. **126** D3
El Wuz Sudan **82** D7
Elx Spain *see* **Elche-Elx**
Elxleben Germany **49** K3
Ely U.K. **45** H6
Ely *MN* U.S.A. **126** F2
Ely *NV* U.S.A. **125** F2
Elyria U.S.A. **130** D3
Elz Germany **49** I4
El Zagâzîg Egypt *see* **Az Zaqāzīq**
Elze Germany **49** J2
Émaé *i.* Vanuatu **103** G3
Emāmrūd Iran **84** D2
Emām Şaḩēb Afgh. **85** H2
Emām Taqī Iran **84** E2
Emån *r.* Sweden **41** J8
Emas, Parque Nacional das *nat. park* Brazil **139** H7
Emba Kazakh. **76** A2
Emba *r.* Kazakh. **76** A2
Embalenhle S. Africa **97** I4
Embarcación Arg. **140** D2
Embarras Portage Canada **117** I3
Embi Kazakh. *see* **Emba**
Embira *r.* Brazil *see* **Envira**
Emborcação, Represa de *resr* Brazil **141** B2
Embrun Canada **131** H1
Embu Kenya **94** D4
Emden Germany **49** H1
Emden Deep *sea feature* N. Pacific Ocean *see* **Cape Johnson Depth**
Emei China *see* **Emeishan**
Emeishan China **72** D2
Emei Shan *mt.* China **72** D2
Emerald Australia **106** E4
Emeril Canada **119** I3
Emerita Augusta Spain *see* **Mérida**
Emerson Canada **117** L5
Emerson U.S.A. **130** D4
Emery U.S.A. **125** H2
Emesa Syria *see* **Homs**
Emet Turkey **55** M5
eMgwenya S. Africa **97** J3
Emigrant Pass U.S.A. **124** E1
Emigrant Valley U.S.A. **125** F3
eMijindini S. Africa **97** J3
Emi Koussi *mt.* Chad **93** E3
Emile *r.* Canada **116** G2
Emiliano Zapata Mex. **132** F5
Emin China **76** F2
Emine, Nos *pt* Bulg. **55** L3
Eminence U.S.A. **130** C4
Eminska Planina *hills* Bulg. **55** L3
Emirdağ Turkey **55** N5
Emir Dağı *mt.* Turkey **55** N5
Emir Dağları *mts* Turkey **55** N5
Emmaboda Sweden **41** I8
Emmaste Estonia **41** M7
Emmaville Australia **108** E2
Emmeloord Neth. **48** F2
Emmelshausen Germany **49** H4
Emmen Neth. **48** G2
Emmen Switz. **52** I3
Emmerich Germany **48** G3
Emmet Australia **106** D5
Emmetsburg U.S.A. **126** E3
Emmett U.S.A. **122** D4
Emmiganuru India **80** C3
Emo Canada **117** M5
Emona Slovenia *see* **Ljubljana**
Emory Peak U.S.A. **127** C6
Empalme Mex. **123** F8
Empangeni S. Africa **97** J5
Emperor Seamount Chain *sea feature* N. Pacific Ocean **146** H2
Emperor Trough *sea feature* N. Pacific Ocean **146** H2
Empingham Reservoir U.K. *see* **Rutland Water**
Emplawas Indon. **104** E2
Empoli Italy **54** D3
Emporia *KS* U.S.A. **126** D4
Emporia *VA* U.S.A. **131** G5
Emporium U.S.A. **131** F3
Empress Canada **117** I5
Empty Quarter *des.* Saudi Arabia *see* **Rub' al Khālī**
Ems *r.* Germany **49** H1
Emsdale Canada **130** F1
Emsdetten Germany **49** H2
Ems-Jade-Kanal *canal* Germany **49** H1
Emzinoni S. Africa **97** I4
Enafors Sweden **40** H5
Encantadas, Serra das *hills* Brazil **140** F4
Encarnación Para. **140** E3
Enchi Ghana **92** C4
Encinal U.S.A. **127** D6
Encinitas U.S.A. **124** E5
Encino U.S.A. **123** G6
Encruzilhada Brazil **141** C1
Endako Canada **116** E4
Endau-Rompin *nat. park* Malaysia **67** C7
Ende Indon. **104** C2
Endeavour Strait Australia **106** C1
Endeh Indon. *see* **Ende**
Enderby Canada **116** G5
Enderby *atoll* Micronesia *see* **Puluwat**
Enderby Land *reg.* Antarctica **148** D2
Endicott U.S.A. **131** G2
Endicott Mountains U.S.A. **114** C3
EnenKio *terr.* N. Pacific Ocean *see* **Wake Island**
Energodar Ukr. *see* **Enerhodar**
Enerhodar Ukr. **39** G7
Enewetak *atoll* Marshall Is **146** G5
Enez Turkey **55** L4
Enfe Lebanon **81** B2
Enfião, Ponta do *pt* Angola **95** B5
Enfidaville Tunisia **54** D6
Enfield U.S.A. **128** E4
Engan Norway **40** F5
Engaru Japan **70** F3
Engcobo S. Africa **97** H6
En Gedi Israel **81** B4
Engelhard U.S.A. **128** F5
Engel's Rus. Fed. **39** J6
Engelschmangat *sea chan.* Neth. **48** E1
Enggano *i.* Indon. **64** C8
Enghien Belgium **48** E4
England *admin. div.* U.K. **45** E6
Englee Canada **119** L4
Englehart Canada **118** F5
Englewood *FL* U.S.A. **129** D7
Englewood *OH* U.S.A. **130** C4
English U.S.A. **130** B4
English *r.* Canada **117** M5
English Bazar India *see* **Ingraj Bazar**
English Channel France/U.K. **45** F9
English Coast Antarctica **148** L2
Engozero Rus. Fed. **38** G2
Enhlalakahle S. Africa **97** J5
Enid U.S.A. **127** D4
Eniwa Japan **70** F4
Eniwetok *atoll* Marshall Is *see* **Enewetak**
Enjiang China *see* **Yongfeng**
Enkeldoorn Zimbabwe *see* **Chivhu**
Enkhuizen Neth. **48** F2
Enköping Sweden **41** J7
Enna *Sicily* Italy **54** F6
Ennadai Lake Canada **117** K2
En Nahud Sudan **82** C7
Ennedi, Massif *mts* Chad **93** F3
Ennell, Lough *l.* Rep. of Ireland **47** E4
Enngonia Australia **108** B2
Enning U.S.A. **126** C2
Ennis Rep. of Ireland **47** D5
Ennis *MT* U.S.A. **122** F3
Ennis *TX* U.S.A. **127** D5
Enniscorthy Rep. of Ireland **47** F5
Enniskillen U.K. **47** E3
Ennistymon Rep. of Ireland **47** C5
Enn Nâqoûra Lebanon **81** B3
Enns *r.* Austria **43** O6
Eno Fin. **40** Q5
Enoch U.S.A. **125** G3
Enontekiö Fin. **40** M2
Enosburg Falls U.S.A. **131** I1
Enosville U.S.A. **130** B4
Enping China **73** G4
Ens Neth. **48** F2
Ensay Australia **108** C6
Enschede Neth. **48** G2
Ense Germany **49** I3
Ensenada Mex. **123** D7
Enshi China **73** F2
Ensley U.S.A. **129** C6
Entebbe Uganda **94** D3
Enterprise Canada **116** G2
Enterprise *AL* U.S.A. **129** C6
Enterprise *OR* U.S.A. **122** D3
Enterprise *UT* U.S.A. **125** G3
Entre Rios Bol. **138** F8
Entre Rios Brazil **139** H5
Entre Rios de Minas Brazil **141** B3
Entroncamento Port. **53** B4
Enugu Nigeria **92** D4
Enurmino Rus. Fed. **61** T3
Envira Brazil **138** D5
Envira *r.* Brazil **138** D5
Enyamba Dem. Rep. Congo **94** C4
Eochaill Rep. of Ireland *see* **Youghal**
Epe Neth. **48** F2
Epéna Congo **94** B3
Épernay France **48** D5
Ephraim U.S.A. **125** H2
Ephrata U.S.A. **131** G3
Epi *i.* Vanuatu **103** G3
Epidamnus Albania *see* **Durrës**
Épinal France **52** H2
Episkopi Bay Cyprus **81** A2
Episkopis, Kolpos *b.* Cyprus *see* **Episkopi Bay**
ePitoli S. Africa *see* **Pretoria**
Epomeo, Monte *hill* Italy **54** E4
Epping U.K. **45** H7
Epping Forest National Park Australia **106** D4
Eppstein Germany **49** I4
Eppynt, Mynydd *hills* U.K. **45** D6
Epsom U.K. **45** G7
Epte *r.* France **48** B5
Eqlīd Iran **84** D4

▶**Equatorial Guinea** *country* Africa **92** D4
africa 7, 90–91

Équerdreville-Hainneville France **45** F9
Erac Creek *watercourse* Australia **108** B1
Erandol India **80** B1
Erawadi *r.* Myanmar *see* **Irrawaddy**
Erawan National Park Thai. **67** B4
Erbaa Turkey **86** E2
Erbendorf Germany **49** M5
Erbeskopf *hill* Germany **48** H5
Ercan *airport* Cyprus **81** A2
Erciş Turkey **87** F3
Erciyes Dağı *mt.* Turkey **86** D3
Érd Hungary **54** H1
Erdaobaihe China *see* **Baihe**
Erdaogou China **72** B1
Erdao Jiang *r.* China **70** B4
Erdek Turkey **55** L4
Erdemli Turkey **81** B1
Erdenet Mongolia **76** J2
Erdi *reg.* Chad **93** F3
Erdniyevskiy Rus. Fed. **39** J7
Erebus, Mount *vol.* Antarctica **148** H1
Erechim Brazil **140** F3
Ereentsav Mongolia **69** L3
Ereğli *Konya* Turkey **86** D3
Ereğli *Zonguldak* Turkey **55** N4
Erego Moz. *see* **Errego**
Erei, Monti *mts Sicily* Italy **54** F6
Erementaŭ Kazakh. *see* **Yereymentau**
Erenhot China **69** K4
Erepucu, Lago de *l.* Brazil **139** G4
Erevan Armenia *see* **Yerevan**
Erfurt Germany **49** L4
Erfurt *airport* Germany **49** K4
Ergani Turkey **87** E3
'Erg Chech *des.* Alg./Mali **92** C2
Ergel Mongolia **69** J4
Ergene *r.* Turkey **55** L4
Ērgļi Latvia **41** N8
Ergu China **70** C3
Ergun China **69** M2
Ergun He *r.* China/Rus. Fed. *see* **Argun'**
Ergun Youqi China *see* **Ergun**
Ergun Zuoqi China *see* **Genhe**
Er Hai *l.* China **72** D3
Erhulai China **70** B4
Eriboll, Loch *inlet* U.K. **46** E2
Ericht *r.* U.K. **46** F4
Ericht, Loch *l.* U.K. **46** E4
Erickson Canada **117** L5
Erie *KS* U.S.A. **127** E4
Erie *PA* U.S.A. **130** E2
Erie, Lake Canada/U.S.A. **130** E2
'Erîgât *des.* Mali **92** C3
Erik Eriksenstretet *sea chan.* Svalbard **60** D2
Eriksdale Canada **117** L5
Erimo-misaki *c.* Japan **70** F4
Erin Canada **130** E2
Erinpura Road India **78** C4
Eriskay *i.* U.K. **46** B3

▶**Eritrea** *country* Africa **82** E6
africa 7, 90–91

Erlangen Germany **49** L5
Erlangping China **73** F1
Erldunda Australia **105** F6
Erlistoun *watercourse* Australia **105** C6
Erlong Shan *mt.* China **70** C4
Erlongshan Shuiku *resr* China **70** B4
Ermak Kazakh. *see* **Aksu**
Ermelo Neth. **48** F2
Ermelo S. Africa **97** I4
Ermenek Turkey **81** A1
Ermenek *r.* Turkey **81** A1
Ermont Egypt *see* **Armant**
Ermoupoli Greece **55** K6
Ernakulam India **80** C4
Erne *r.* Rep. of Ireland/U.K. **47** D3
Ernest Giles Range *hills* Australia **105** C6
Erode India **80** C4
Eromanga Australia **107** C5
Erongo *admin. reg.* Namibia **96** B1
Erp Neth. **48** F3
Erqu China *see* **Zhouzhi**
Errabiddy Hills Australia **105** A6
Er Rachidia Morocco **50** D5
Er Raoui *des.* Alg. **50** D6
Errego Moz. **95** D5
Er Remla Tunisia **54** D7
Er Renk Sudan **82** D7
Errigal *hill* Rep. of Ireland **47** D2
Errinundra National Park Australia **108** D6
Erris Head *hd* Rep. of Ireland **47** B3
Errol U.S.A. **131** J1
Erromango *i.* Vanuatu **103** G3
Erronan *i.* Vanuatu *see* **Futuna**
Erseka Albania *see* **Ersekë**
Ersekë Albania **55** I4
Erskine U.S.A. **126** D2
Ersmark Sweden **40** L5
Ertai China **76** H2
Ertil' Rus. Fed. **39** I6
Ertis *r.* Kazakh./Rus. Fed. *see* **Irtysh**
Ertix He *r.* China/Kazakh. **76** G2
Ērtra *country* Africa *see* **Eritrea**
Eruh Turkey **87** F3
Erwin U.S.A. **128** D4
Erwitte Germany **49** I3
Erxleben *Sachsen-Anhalt* Germany **49** L2
Erxleben *Sachsen-Anhalt* Germany **49** L2
Eryuan China **72** C3
Erzerum Turkey *see* **Erzurum**
Erzgebirge *mts* Czech Rep./Germany **49** N4
Erzhan China **70** B2
Erzin Turkey **81** C1
Erzincan Turkey **87** E3
Erzurum Turkey **87** F3
Esa-ala P.N.G. **106** E1
Esan-misaki *pt* Japan **70** F4
Esashi Japan **70** F3
Esbjerg Denmark **41** F9
Esbo Fin. *see* **Espoo**
Escalante U.S.A. **125** H3
Escalante *r.* U.S.A. **125** H3
Escalante Desert U.S.A. **125** G3
Escalón Mex. **127** B7
Escambia *r.* U.S.A. **129** C6
Escanaba U.S.A. **128** C2
Escárcega Mex. **132** F5
Escatrón Spain **53** F3
Escaut *r.* Belgium **48** D4
Esch Neth. **48** F3
Eschede Germany **49** K2
Eschscholtz *atoll* Marshall Is *see* **Bikini**
Esch-sur-Alzette Lux. **48** F5
Eschwege Germany **49** K3
Eschweiler Germany **48** G4
Escondido *r.* Mex. **127** C6
Escondido U.S.A. **124** E5
Escudilla *mt.* U.S.A. **125** I5
Escuinapa Mex. **132** C4
Escuintla Guat. **132** F6
Eséka Cameroon **92** E4
Eşen Turkey **55** M6
Esenguly Turkm. **84** D2
Esens Germany **49** H1
Eşfahān Iran **84** C3
Esfarayen, Reshteh-ye *mts* Iran **84** E2
Esfideh Iran **85** E3
Eshan China **72** D3
Eshāqābād Iran **84** E3
Eshkamesh Afgh. **85** H2
Eshkanān Iran **84** D5
Eshowe S. Africa **97** J5
Esikhawini S. Africa **97** K5
Esil Kazakh. *see* **Yesil'**
Esil *r.* Kazakh./Rus. Fed. *see* **Ishim**
Esk Australia **108** F1
Esk *r.* Australia **107** [inset]
Esk *r.* U.K. **44** D4
Eskdalemuir U.K. **46** F5
Esker Canada **119** I3
Eskifjörður Iceland **40** [inset]
Eski Gediz Turkey **55** M5
Eskilstuna Sweden **41** J7
Eskimo Lakes Canada **114** E3
Eskimo Point Canada *see* **Arviat**
Eski Mosul Iraq **87** F3
Eskipazar Turkey **86** D2
Eskişehir Turkey **55** N5
Eski-Yakkabag Uzbek. **85** G2
Esla *r.* Spain **53** C3
Eslāmābād-e Gharb Iran **84** B3
Esler Dağı *mt.* Turkey **55** M6
Eslohe (Sauerland) Germany **49** I3
Eslöv Sweden **41** H9
Esmā'īlī-ye Soflá Iran **84** E4
Eşme Turkey **55** M5
Esmeraldas Ecuador **138** C3
Esmont U.S.A. **131** F5
Esnagami Lake Canada **118** D4
Esnes France **48** D4
Espakeh Iran **85** F5
Espalion France **52** F4
España *country* Europe *see* **Spain**
Espanola Canada **118** E5
Espanola U.S.A. **127** B4
Espelkamp Germany **49** I2
Esperance Australia **105** C8
Esperance Bay Australia **105** C8
Esperanza *research station* Antarctica **148** A2
Esperanza Arg. **140** B8
Esperanza Mex. **123** F8
Espichel, Cabo *c.* Port. **53** B4
Espigão, Serra do *mts* Brazil **141** A4
Espigüete *mt.* Spain **53** D2
Espinazo Mex. **127** C7
Espinhaço, Serra do *mts* Brazil **141** C2
Espinosa Brazil **141** C1
Espírito Santo Brazil *see* **Vila Velha**
Espírito Santo *state* Brazil **141** C2
Espíritu Santo *i.* Vanuatu **103** G3
Espíritu Santo, Isla *i.* Mex. **120** E7
Espoo Fin. **41** N6
Espuña *mt.* Spain **53** F5
Esqueda Mex. **123** F7
Esquel Arg. **140** B6
Esquimalt Canada **116** F5
Essaouira Morocco **92** C1
Es Semara W. Sahara **92** B2
Essen Belgium **48** E3

▶**Essen** Germany **48** H3
5th most populous city in Europe.

Essen (Oldenburg) Germany **49** H2
Essequibo *r.* Guyana **139** G2
Essex Canada **130** D2
Essex *CA* U.S.A. **125** F4
Essex *MD* U.S.A. **131** G4
Essex *NY* U.S.A. **131** I1
Essexville U.S.A. **130** D2
Esslingen am Neckar Germany **49** J6
Esso Rus. Fed. **61** Q4
Essoyla Rus. Fed. **38** G3
Eşţahbān Iran **84** D4
Estância Brazil **139** K6
Estancia U.S.A. **123** G6
Estand, Kūh-e *mt.* Iran **85** F4
Estats, Pic d' *mt.* France/Spain **52** E5
Estcourt S. Africa **97** I5
Este *r.* Germany **49** J1
Estelí Nicaragua **133** G6
Estella Spain **53** E2
Estepa Spain **53** D5
Estepona Spain **53** D5
Esteras de Medinaceli Spain **53** E3
Esterhazy Canada **117** K5
Estero Bay U.S.A. **124** C4
Esteros Para. **140** D2
Estevan Canada **117** K5
Estevan Group *is* Canada **116** D4
Estherville U.S.A. **126** E3
Estill U.S.A. **129** D5
Eston Canada **117** I5

▶**Estonia** *country* Europe **41** N7
europe 5, 34–35

Estonskaya S.S.R. *country* Europe *see* **Estonia**
Estrées-St-Denis France **48** C5
Estrela Brazil **141** A5
Estrela, Serra da *mts* Port. **53** C3
Estrela do Sul Brazil **141** B2
Estrella *mt.* Spain **53** E4
Estrella, Punta *pt* Mex. **123** E7
Estremoz Port. **53** C4
Estrondo, Serra *hills* Brazil **139** I5
Etadunna Australia **107** B6
Etah India **78** D4
Étain France **48** F5
Etamamiou Canada **119** K4
Étampes France **52** F2
Étaples France **48** B4
Etawah *Rajasthan* India **78** D4
Etawah *Uttar Pradesh* India **78** D4
eThandakukhanya S. Africa **97** J4
Ethelbert Canada **117** K5
Ethel Creek Australia **105** C5
E'Thembini S. Africa **96** F5

▶**Ethiopia** *country* Africa **94** D3
3rd most populous country in Africa.
africa 7, 90–91

Etimesğut Turkey **86** D3
Etive, Loch *inlet* U.K. **46** D4
Etna, Mount *vol. Sicily* Italy **54** F6
Etne Norway **41** D7
Etobicoke Canada **130** F2
Etolin Strait U.S.A. **114** B3
Etorofu-tō *i.* Rus. Fed. *see* **Iturup, Ostrov**
Etosha National Park Namibia **95** B5
Etosha Pan *salt pan* Namibia **95** B5
Etoumbi Congo **94** B3
Etrek *r.* Iran/Turkm. *see* **Atrek**
Étrépagny France **48** B5
Étretat France **45** H9
Ettelbruck Lux. **48** G5
Etten-Leur Neth. **48** E3
Ettlingen Germany **49** I6
Ettrick Water *r.* U.K. **46** F5
Euabalong Australia **108** C4
Euboea *i.* Greece *see* **Evvoia**
Eucla Australia **105** E7
Euclid U.S.A. **130** E3
Euclides da Cunha Brazil **139** K6
Eucumbene, Lake Australia **108** D6
Eudistes, Lac des *l.* Canada **119** I4
Eudora U.S.A. **127** F5
Eudunda Australia **107** B7
Eufaula *AL* U.S.A. **129** C6
Eufaula *OK* U.S.A. **127** E5
Eufaula Lake *resr* U.S.A. **127** E5
Eugene U.S.A. **122** C3
Eugenia, Punta *pt* Mex. **123** E8
Eugowra Australia **108** D4
Eulo Australia **108** B2
Eumungerie Australia **108** D3
Eungella Australia **106** E4
Eungella National Park Australia **106** E4
Eunice *LA* U.S.A. **127** E6
Eunice *NM* U.S.A. **127** C5
Eupen Belgium **48** G4

▶**Euphrates** *r.* Asia **87** G5
Longest river in western Asia. Also known as Al Furāt (Iraq/Syria) or Fırat (Turkey).

Eura Fin. **41** M6
Eure *r.* France **48** B5
Eureka *CA* U.S.A. **122** B4
Eureka *KS* U.S.A. **126** D4
Eureka *MT* U.S.A. **122** E2
Eureka *NV* U.S.A. **125** F2
Eureka *OH* U.S.A. **130** D4
Eureka *SD* U.S.A. **126** D2
Eureka *UT* U.S.A. **125** G2
Eureka Sound *sea chan.* Canada **115** J2
Eureka Springs U.S.A. **127** E4
Eureka Valley U.S.A. **124** E3
Euriowie Australia **107** C6
Euroa Australia **108** B6
Eurombah Australia **107** E5
Eurombah Creek *r.* Australia **107** E5
Europa, Île *i.* Indian Ocean **95** E6
Europa, Punta de *pt* Gibraltar *see* **Europa Point**
Europa Point Gibraltar **53** D5
Euskirchen Germany **48** G4
Eutaw U.S.A. **129** C5
Eutsuk Lake Canada **116** E4
Eutzsch Germany **49** M3
Eva Downs Australia **104** F4
Evans, Lac *l.* Canada **118** F4
Evans, Mount U.S.A. **122** G5
Evansburg Canada **116** H4
Evans City U.S.A. **130** E3
Evans Head Australia **108** F2
Evans Head *hd* Australia **108** F2
Evans Ice Stream Antarctica **148** L1
Evans Strait Canada **117** P2
Evanston *IL* U.S.A. **130** B2
Evanston *WY* U.S.A. **122** F4
Evansville Canada **118** E5
Evansville *IN* U.S.A. **130** B5
Evansville *WY* U.S.A. **122** G4
Evant U.S.A. **127** D6
Eva Perón Arg. *see* **La Plata**
Evart U.S.A. **130** C2
Evaton S. Africa **97** H4
Evaz Iran **84** D5
Evening Shade U.S.A. **127** F4
Evensk Rus. Fed. **61** Q3
Everard, Cape Australia **108** D6
Everard, Lake *salt flat* Australia **107** A6
Everard, Mount Australia **105** F5
Everard Range *hills* Australia **105** F6
Everdingen Neth. **48** F3
Everek Turkey *see* **Develi**

▶**Everest, Mount** China/Nepal **79** F4
Highest mountain in the world and in Asia.
asia 56–57
world 12–13

Everett *PA* U.S.A. **131** F3
Everett *WA* U.S.A. **122** C3
Evergem Belgium **48** D3
Everglades *swamp* U.S.A. **129** D7
Everglades National Park U.S.A. **129** D7
Evergreen U.S.A. **129** C6
Evesham Australia **106** C4
Evesham U.K. **45** F6
Evesham, Vale of *valley* U.K. **45** F6
Evijärvi Fin. **40** M5
Evje Norway **41** E7
Évora Port. **53** C4
Evoron, Ozero *l.* Rus. Fed. **70** E2
Évreux France **48** B5
Evros *r.* Bulgaria *see* **Maritsa**
Evros *r.* Turkey *see* **Meriç**
Evrotas *r.* Greece **55** J6
Évry France **48** C6
Evrychou Cyprus **81** A2
Evrykhou Cyprus *see* **Evrychou**
Evvoia *i.* Greece **55** K5
Ewan Australia **106** D3
Ewaso Ngiro *r.* Kenya **94** E3

Forillon, Parc National de nat. park Canada 119 I4
Forked River U.S.A. 131 H4
Forks U.S.A. 122 B3
Fork Union U.S.A. 131 F5
Forlì Italy 54 E2
Forman U.S.A. 126 D2
Formby U.K. 44 D5
Formentera i. Spain 53 G4
Formentor, Cap de c. Spain 53 H4
Formerie France 48 B5
Former Yugoslav Republic of Macedonia country Europe see Macedonia
Formiga Brazil 141 B3
Formosa Arg. 140 E3
Formosa country Asia see Taiwan
Formosa Brazil 141 B1
Formosa, Serra hills Brazil 139 G6
Formosa Bay Kenya see Ungwana Bay
Formosa Strait China/Taiwan see Taiwan Strait
Formoso r. Bahia Brazil 141 B1
Formoso r. Tocantins Brazil 141 A1
Fornos Moz. 97 L2
Forres U.K. 46 F3
Forrest Vic. Australia 108 A7
Forrest W.A. Australia 105 E7
Forrestal Range mts Antarctica 148 A1
Forrest City U.S.A. 127 F5
Forrest Lake Canada 117 I3
Forrest Lakes salt flat Australia 105 E7
Fors Sweden 40 J5
Forsayth Australia 106 C3
Forsnäs Sweden 40 M3
Forssa Fin. 41 M6
Forster Australia 108 F4
Forsyth GA U.S.A. 129 D5
Forsyth MT U.S.A. 122 G3
Forsyth Range hills Australia 106 C4
Fort Abbas Pak. 85 I4
Fort Albany Canada 118 E3
Fortaleza Brazil 139 K4
Fort Amsterdam U.S.A. see New York
Fort Archambault Chad see Sarh
Fort Ashby U.S.A. 131 F4
Fort Assiniboine Canada 116 H4
Fort Augustus U.K. 46 E3
Fort Beaufort S. Africa 97 H7
Fort Benton U.S.A. 122 F3
Fort Brabant Canada see Tuktoyaktuk
Fort Bragg U.S.A. 124 B2
Fort Branch U.S.A. 130 B4
Fort Carillon U.S.A. see Ticonderoga
Fort Charlet Alg. see Djanet
Fort Chimo Canada see Kuujjuaq
Fort Chipewyan Canada 117 I3
Fort Collins U.S.A. 122 G4
Fort-Coulonge Canada 118 F5
Fort Crampel Cent. Afr. Rep. see Kaga Bandoro
Fort-Dauphin Madag. see Tôlañaro
Fort Davis U.S.A. 127 C6
▶Fort-de-France Martinique 133 L6
Capital of Martinique.
Fort de Kock Indon. see Bukittinggi
Fort de Polignac Alg. see Illizi
Fort Dodge U.S.A. 126 E3
Fort Duchesne U.S.A. 125 I1
Fort Edward U.S.A. 131 I2
Fortescue r. Australia 104 B5
Forte Veneza Brazil 139 H5
Fort Flatters Alg. see Bordj Omer Driss
Fort Foureau Cameroon see Kousséri
Fort Franklin Canada see Déline
Fort Gardel Alg. see Zaouatallaz
Fort Gay U.S.A. 130 D4
Fort George Canada see Chisasibi
Fort Good Hope Canada 114 F3
Fort Gouraud Mauritania see Fdérik
Forth r. U.K. 46 F4
Forth, Firth of est. U.K. 46 F4
Fort Hertz Myanmar see Putao
Fortification Range mts U.S.A. 125 F2
Fortín General Mendoza Para. 140 D2
Fortín Leonida Escobar Para. 140 D2
Fortín Madrejón Para. 140 E2
Fortín Pilcomayo Arg. 140 D2
Fortín Ravelo Bol. 138 F7
Fortín Sargento Primero Leyes Arg. 140 E2
Fortín Suárez Arana Bol. 138 F7
Fortín Teniente Juan Echauri López Para. 140 D2
Fort Jameson Zambia see Chipata
Fort Johnston Malawi see Mangochi
Fort Kent U.S.A. 128 G2
Fort Lamy Chad see Ndjamena
Fort Laperrine Alg. see Tamanrasset
Fort Laramie U.S.A. 122 G4
Fort Lauderdale U.S.A. 129 D7
Fort Liard Canada 116 F2
Fort Mackay Canada 117 I3
Fort Macleod Canada 116 H5
Fort Madison U.S.A. 126 F3
Fort Manning Malawi see Mchinji
Fort McMurray Canada 117 I3
Fort McPherson Canada 114 E3
Fort Meyers Beach U.S.A. 129 D7
Fort Morgan U.S.A. 126 C3
Fort Munro Pak. 85 H4
Fort Myers U.S.A. 129 D7
Fort Nelson Canada 116 F3
Fort Nelson r. Canada 116 F3
Fort Norman Canada see Tulita
Fort Orange U.S.A. see Albany
Fort Payne U.S.A. 129 C5
Fort Peck U.S.A. 122 G2
Fort Peck Reservoir U.S.A. 122 G3
Fort Pierce U.S.A. 129 D7
Fort Portal Uganda 94 D3
Fort Providence Canada 116 G2
Fort Randall U.S.A. see Cold Bay
Fort Resolution Canada 116 H2
Fortrose N.Z. 109 B8
Fortrose U.K. 46 E3
Fort Rosebery Zambia see Mansa
Fort Rousset Congo see Owando
Fort Rupert Canada see Waskaganish
Fort Sandeman Pak. see Zhob
Fort Saskatchewan Canada 116 H4
Fort Scott U.S.A. 126 E4
Fort Severn Canada 118 D2
Fort-Shevchenko Kazakh. 74 E2
Fort Simpson Canada 116 F2
Fort Smith Canada 117 H2
Fort Smith U.S.A. 127 E5
Fort St James Canada 116 E4
Fort St John Canada 116 F3
Fort Stockton U.S.A. 127 C6
Fort Sumner U.S.A. 123 G6
Fort Supply U.S.A. 127 D4
Fort Thomas U.S.A. 125 I5
Fort Trinquet Mauritania see Bîr Mogreïn
Fortuna U.S.A. 126 C1
Fortune Bay Canada 119 L5
Fort Valley U.S.A. 129 D5
Fort Vermilion Canada 116 G3
Fort Victoria Zimbabwe see Masvingo
Fort Ware Canada see Ware
Fort Wayne U.S.A. 130 C3
Fort William U.K. 46 D4
Fort Worth U.S.A. 127 D5
Fort Yates U.S.A. 126 C2
Fort Yukon U.S.A. 114 D3
Forum Iulii France see Fréjus
Forūr, Jazīreh-ye i. Iran 84 D5
Forvik Norway 40 H4
Foshan China 73 G4
Fo Shek Chau Hong Kong China see Basalt Island
Fossano Italy 54 B2
Fossil U.S.A. 122 C3
Fossil Downs Australia 104 D4
Foster Australia 108 C7
Foster U.S.A. 130 C4
Foster, Mount Canada/U.S.A. 116 C3
Foster Lakes Canada 117 J3
Fostoria U.S.A. 130 D3
Fotadrevo Madag. 95 E6
Fotherby U.K. 44 G5
Fotokol Cameroon 93 E3
Fotuna i. Vanuatu see Futuna
Fougères France 52 D2
Foula i. U.K. 46 [inset]
Foul Island Myanmar 66 A3
Foulness Point U.K. 45 H7
Foul Point Sri Lanka 80 D4
Foumban Cameroon 92 E4
Foundation Ice Stream glacier Antarctica 148 L1
Fount U.S.A. 130 D5
Fountains Abbey (NT) tourist site U.K. 44 F4
Fourches, Mont des hill France 52 G2
Four Corners U.S.A. 124 E4
Fouriesburg S. Africa 97 I5
Fourmies France 48 E4
Fournier, Lac l. Canada 119 I4
Fournoi i. Greece 55 L6
Fourpeaked Mountain U.S.A. 114 C4
Fouta Djallon reg. Guinea 92 B3
Foveaux Strait N.Z. 109 A8
Fowey r. U.K. 45 C8
Fowler CO U.S.A. 123 G5
Fowler IN U.S.A. 130 B3
Fowler Ice Rise Antarctica 148 L1
Fowlers Bay Australia 102 D5
Fowlers Bay b. Australia 105 F8
Fowlerville U.S.A. 130 C2
Fox r. B.C. Canada 116 E3
Fox r. Man. Canada 117 M3
Fox r. U.S.A. 126 F3
Fox Creek Canada 116 G4
Fox Creek U.S.A. 130 C5
Foxdale Isle of Man 44 C4
Foxe Basin g. Canada 115 K3
Foxe Channel Canada 115 J3
Foxe Peninsula Canada 115 K3
Fox Glacier N.Z. 109 C6
Fox Islands U.S.A. 114 B4
Fox Lake Canada 116 H3
Fox Mountain Canada 116 C2
Fox Valley Canada 117 I5
Foyers U.K. 46 E3
Foyle r. Rep. of Ireland/U.K. 47 E3
Foyle, Lough b. Rep. of Ireland/U.K. 47 E2
Foynes Rep. of Ireland 47 C5
Foz de Areia, Represa de resr Brazil 141 A4
Foz do Cunene Angola 95 B5
Foz do Iguaçu Brazil 140 F3
Fraga Spain 53 G3
Frakes, Mount Antarctica 148 K1
Framingham U.S.A. 131 J2
Framnes Mountains Antarctica 148 E2
Franca Brazil 141 B3
Français, Récif des reef New Caledonia 103 G3
Francavilla Fontana Italy 54 G4
▶France country Europe 52 F3
3rd largest and 4th most populous country in Europe.
europe 5, 34–35
Frances Australia 107 C8
Frances Lake Canada 116 D2
Frances Lake l. Canada 116 D2
Franceville Gabon 94 B4
Francis Canada 117 K5
Francis atoll Kiribati see Beru
Francis, Lake U.S.A. 131 J1
Francisco de Orellana Ecuador see Puerto Francisco de Orellana
Francisco I. Madero Coahuila Mex. 127 C7
Francisco I. Madero Durango Mex. 127 B7
Francisco Zarco Mex. 124 E5
Francistown Botswana 95 C6
Francois Canada 119 K5
François Lake Canada 116 E4
Francois Peron National Park Australia 105 A6
Francs Peak U.S.A. 122 F4
Franeker Neth. 48 F1
Frankenberg Germany 49 N4
Frankenberg (Eder) Germany 49 I3
Frankenhöhe hills Germany 43 M6
Frankenmuth U.S.A. 130 D2
Frankenthal (Pfalz) Germany 49 I5
Frankenwald mts Germany 49 L4
Frankford Canada 131 G1
Frankfort IN U.S.A. 130 B3
▶Frankfort KY U.S.A. 130 C4
State capital of Kentucky.
Frankfort MI U.S.A. 130 B1
Frankfort OH U.S.A. 130 D4
Frankfurt Germany see Frankfurt am Main
Frankfurt am Main Germany 49 I4
Frankfurt an der Oder Germany 43 O4
Frank Hann National Park Australia 105 C8
Frankin Lake U.S.A. 125 F1
Fränkische Alb hills Germany 49 K6
Fränkische Schweiz reg. Germany 49 L5
Frankland, Cape Australia 107 [inset]
Franklin AZ U.S.A. 125 I5
Franklin GA U.S.A. 129 C5
Franklin IN U.S.A. 130 B4
Franklin KY U.S.A. 130 B5
Franklin LA U.S.A. 127 F6
Franklin MA U.S.A. 131 J2
Franklin NC U.S.A. 129 D5
Franklin NE U.S.A. 126 D3
Franklin NH U.S.A. 131 J2
Franklin PA U.S.A. 130 F3
Franklin TN U.S.A. 128 C5
Franklin TX U.S.A. 127 D6
Franklin VA U.S.A. 131 G5
Franklin WV U.S.A. 130 F4
Franklin Bay Canada 149 A2
Franklin D. Roosevelt Lake resr U.S.A. 122 D2
Franklin Furnace U.S.A. 130 D4
Franklin-Gordon National Park Australia 107 [inset]
Franklin Island Antarctica 148 H1
Franklin Mountains Canada 116 F2
Franklin Strait Canada 115 I2
Franklinton U.S.A. 127 F6
Franklinville U.S.A. 131 F2
Frankston Australia 108 B7
Fränsta Sweden 40 J5
Frantsa-Iosifa, Zemlya is Rus. Fed. 60 G2
Franz Canada 118 D4
Franz Josef Glacier N.Z. 109 C6
Frasca, Capo della c. Sardinia Italy 54 C5
Frascati Italy 54 E4
Fraser r. Australia 104 C4
Fraser r. B.C. Canada 116 F5
Fraser r. Nfld. and Lab. Canada 119 J2
Fraser, Mount hill Australia 105 B6
Fraserburg S. Africa 96 E6
Fraserburgh U.K. 46 G3
Fraserdale Canada 118 E4
Fraser Island Australia 106 F5
Fraser Island National Park Australia 106 F5
Fraser Lake Canada 116 E4
Fraser National Park Australia 108 B6
Fraser Plateau Canada 116 E4
Fraser Range hills Australia 105 C8
Frauenfeld Switz. 52 I3
Fray Bentos Uruguay 140 E4
Frazeysburg U.S.A. 130 D3
Frechen Germany 48 G4
Freckleton U.K. 44 E5
Frederic U.S.A. 130 C1
Frederica U.S.A. 131 H4
Fredericia Denmark 41 F9
Frederick MD U.S.A. 131 G4
Frederick OK U.S.A. 127 D5
Frederick Reef Australia 106 F4
Fredericksburg TX U.S.A. 127 D6
Fredericksburg VA U.S.A. 131 G4
Fredericktown U.S.A. 126 F4
▶Fredericton Canada 119 I5
Provincial capital of New Brunswick.
Frederikshåb Greenland see Paamiut
Frederikshavn Denmark 41 G8
Frederiksværk Denmark 41 H9
Fredonia AZ U.S.A. 125 G3
Fredonia KS U.S.A. 127 E4
Fredonia NY U.S.A. 130 F2
Fredonia WI U.S.A. 130 B2
Fredrika Sweden 40 K4
Fredrikshamn Fin. see Hamina
Fredrikstad Norway 41 G7
Freedonyer Peak U.S.A. 124 C1
Freehold U.S.A. 131 H3
Freeland U.S.A. 131 H3
Freeling Heights hill Australia 107 B6
Freel Peak U.S.A. 124 D2
Freels, Cape Canada 119 L4
Freeman U.S.A. 126 D3
Freeman, Lake U.S.A. 130 B3
Freeport FL U.S.A. 129 C6
Freeport IL U.S.A. 126 F3
Freeport TX U.S.A. 127 E6
Freeport City Bahamas 129 E7
Freer U.S.A. 127 D7
Freesoil U.S.A. 130 B1
Free State prov. S. Africa 97 H5
▶Freetown Sierra Leone 92 B4
Capital of Sierra Leone.
Fregenal de la Sierra Spain 53 C4
Fregon Australia 105 F6
Fréhel, Cap c. France 52 C2
Freiberg Germany 49 N4
Freiburg Switz. see Fribourg
Freiburg im Breisgau Germany 43 K6
Freisen Germany 49 H5
Freising Germany 43 M6
Freistadt Austria 43 O6
Fréjus France 52 H5
Fremantle Australia 105 A8
Fremont CA U.S.A. 124 C3
Fremont IN U.S.A. 130 C3
Fremont MI U.S.A. 130 C2
Fremont NE U.S.A. 126 D3
Fremont OH U.S.A. 130 D3
Fremont r. U.S.A. 125 H2
Fremont Junction U.S.A. 125 H2
Frenchburg U.S.A. 130 D5
French Cay i. Turks and Caicos Is 129 F8
French Congo country Africa see Congo
▶French Guiana terr. S. America 139 H3
French Overseas Department.
south america 9, 136–137
French Guinea country Africa see Guinea
French Island Australia 108 B7
French Lick U.S.A. 130 B4
Frenchman r. U.S.A. 122 G2
Frenchman Lake CA U.S.A. 124 C2
Frenchman Lake NV U.S.A. 125 F3
Frenchpark Rep. of Ireland 47 D4
French Pass N.Z. 109 D5
▶French Polynesia terr. S. Pacific Ocean 147 K7
French Overseas Territory.
oceania 8, 100–101
French Somaliland country Africa see Djibouti
▶French Southern and Antarctic Lands terr. Indian Ocean 145 M8
French Overseas Territory.
French Sudan country Africa see Mali
French Territory of the Afars and Issas country Africa see Djibouti
Frenda Alg. 53 G6
Frentsjer Neth. see Franeker
Freren Germany 49 H2
Fresco r. Brazil 139 H5
Freshford Rep. of Ireland 47 E5
Fresnillo Mex. 132 D4
Fresno U.S.A. 124 D3
Fresno r. U.S.A. 124 C3
Fresno Reservoir U.S.A. 122 F2
Fressel, Lac l. Canada 118 G3
Freu, Cap des c. Spain 53 H4
Freudenberg Germany 49 H4
Freudenstadt Germany 43 L6
Frévent France 48 C4
Frew watercourse Australia 106 A4
Frewena Australia 106 A3
Freycinet Estuary inlet Australia 105 A6
Freycinet Peninsula Australia 107 [inset]
Freyenstein Germany 49 M1
Freyming-Merlebach France 48 G5
Fria Guinea 92 B3
Fria, Cape Namibia 95 B5
Friant U.S.A. 124 D3
Frias Arg. 140 C3
Fribourg Switz. 52 H3
Friday Harbor U.S.A. 122 C2
Friedeburg Germany 49 H1
Friedens U.S.A. 131 F3
Friedland Rus. Fed. see Pravdinsk
Friedrichshafen Germany 43 L7
Friedrichskanal canal Germany 49 L2
Friend U.S.A. 126 D3
Friendly Islands country S. Pacific Ocean see Tonga
Friendship U.S.A. 126 F3
Friesack Germany 49 M2
Friese Wad tidal flat Neth. 48 F1
Friesoythe Germany 49 H1
Frinton-on-Sea U.K. 45 I7
Frio r. U.S.A. 127 D6
Frio watercourse U.S.A. 127 C5
Frisco Mountain U.S.A. 125 G2
Frissell, Mount hill U.S.A. 131 I2
Fritzlar Germany 49 J3
Frjentsjer Neth. see Franeker
Frobisher Bay Canada see Iqaluit
Frobisher Bay b. Canada 115 L3
Frobisher Lake Canada 117 I3
Frohavet b. Norway 40 F5
Frohburg Germany 49 M3
Froissy France 48 C5
Frolovo Rus. Fed. 39 I6
Frome watercourse Australia 107 B6
Frome U.K. 45 E7
Frome r. U.K. 45 E8
Frome, Lake salt flat Australia 107 B6
Frome Downs Australia 107 B6
Fröndenberg Germany 49 H3
Frontera Coahuila Mex. 127 C7
Frontera Tabasco Mex. 132 F5
Fronteras Mex. 123 F7
Front Royal U.S.A. 131 F4
Frosinone Italy 54 E4
Frostburg U.S.A. 131 F4
Frøya i. Norway 40 F5
Fruges France 48 C4
Fruita U.S.A. 125 I2
Fruitland U.S.A. 125 H1
Fruitvale U.S.A. 125 I2
Frunze Kyrg. see Bishkek
Frusino Italy see Frosinone
Fruska Gora nat. park Serb. and Mont. 55 H2
Frýdek-Místek Czech Rep. 43 Q6
Fu'an China 73 H3
Fucheng Anhui China see Fengyang
Fucheng Shaanxi China see Fuxian
Fuchuan China 73 F3
Fuchun Jiang r. China 73 I2
Fude China 73 H3
Fuding China 73 I3
Fudul reg. Saudi Arabia 84 B6
Fuenlabrada Spain 53 E3
Fuerte r. Mex. 123 F8
Fuerte Olimpo Para. 140 E2
Fuerteventura i. Canary Is 92 B2
Fufeng China 72 E1
Fuga i. Phil. 65 G3
Fugong China 72 C3
Fugou China 73 G1
Fuhai China 76 G2
Fuḩaymī Iraq 87 F4
Fujairah U.A.E. 84 E5
Fujeira U.A.E. see Fujairah
Fuji Japan 71 E6
Fujian prov. China 73 H3
Fuji-Hakone-Izu National Park Japan 71 E6
Fujin China 70 C3
Fujinomiya Japan 71 E6
Fuji-san vol. Japan 71 E6
Fujiyoshida Japan 71 E6
Fûka Egypt see Fūkah
Fūkah Egypt 86 B5
Fukien prov. China see Fujian
Fukuchiyama Japan 71 D6
Fukue-jima i. Japan 71 C6
Fukui Japan 71 E5
Fukuoka Japan 71 C6
Fukushima Japan 71 F5
Fukuyama Japan 71 D6
Fûl, Gebel hill Egypt see Fūl, Jabal
Fūl, Jabal hill Egypt 81 A5
Fulchhari Bangl. 79 G4
Fulda Germany 49 J4
Fulda r. Germany 49 J3
Fulham U.K. 45 G7
Fuli China see Jixian
Fuliji China 73 H1
Fuling China 72 E2
Fulitun China see Jixian
Fullerton CA U.S.A. 124 E5
Fullerton NE U.S.A. 126 D3
Fullerton, Cape Canada 117 N2
Fulton IN U.S.A. 130 B3
Fulton MO U.S.A. 126 F4
Fulton MS U.S.A. 127 F5
Fulton NY U.S.A. 131 G2
Fumane Moz. 97 K3
Fumay France 48 E5
Fumin China 72 D3
Funabashi Japan 71 E6
Funafuti atoll Tuvalu 103 H2
Funan China 73 G1
▶Funchal Madeira 92 B1
Capital of Madeira.
Fundão Brazil 141 C2
Fundão Port. 53 C3
Fundi Italy see Fondi
Fundición Mex. 123 F8
Fundy, Bay of g. Canada 119 I5
Fundy National Park Canada 119 I5
Fünen i. Denmark see Fyn
Funeral Peak U.S.A. 124 E3
Fünfkirchen Hungary see Pécs
Fung Wong Shan hill Hong Kong China see Lantau Peak
Funhalouro Moz. 97 L2
Funing Jiangsu China 73 H1
Funing Yunnan China 72 E4
Funiu Shan mts China 73 F1
Funtua Nigeria 92 D3
Funzie U.K. 46 [inset]
Fuqing China 73 H3
Fürgun, Kūh-e mt. Iran 84 E5
Furmanov Rus. Fed. 38 I4
Furmanovka Kazakh. see Moyynkum
Furmanovo Kazakh. see Zhalpaktal
Furnas, Represa resr Brazil 141 B3
Furneaux Group is Australia 107 [inset]
Furnes Belgium see Veurne
Furong China see Wan'an
Fürstenau Germany 49 H2
Fürstenberg Germany 49 N1
Fürstenwalde Germany 43 O4
Fürth Germany 49 K5
Furth im Wald Germany 49 M5
Furukawa Japan 71 F5
Fury and Hecla Strait Canada 115 J3
Fusan S. Korea see Pusan
Fushun China 70 A4
Fushuncheng China see Shuncheng
Fusong China 70 B4
Fu Tau Pun Chau i. Hong Kong China 73 [inset]
Futuna i. Vanuatu 103 H3
Futuna Islands Wallis and Futuna Is see Hoorn, Îles de
Fuxian Liaoning China see Wafangdian
Fuxian Shaanxi China 69 J5
Fuxian Hu l. China 72 D3
Fuxin China 69 M4
Fuxing China see Wangmo
Fuxinzhen China see Fuxin
Fuyang Anhui China 73 G1
Fuyang Guangxi China see Fuchuan
Fuyang Zhejiang China 73 H2
Fuying Dao i. China 73 I3
Fuyu Anhui China see Susong
Fuyu Heilong. China 70 B3
Fuyu Jilin China 70 B3
Fuyu Jilin China see Songyuan
Fuyuan Heilong. China 70 D2
Fuyuan Yunnan China 72 E3
Fuyun China 76 G2
Fuzhou Fujian China 73 H3
Fuzhou Jiangxi China 73 H3
Füzuli Azer. 87 G3
Fyn i. Denmark 41 G9
Fyne, Loch inlet U.K. 46 D5

↓ G

Gaaf Atoll Maldives see Huvadhu Atoll
Gaâfour Tunisia 54 C6
Gaalkacyo Somalia 94 E3
Gabakly Turkm. see Kabakly
Gabasumdo China see Tongde
Gabbs U.S.A. 124 E2
Gabbs Valley Range mts U.S.A. 124 D2
Gabd Pak. 85 F5
Gabela Angola 95 B5
Gaberones Botswana see Gaborone
Gabès Tunisia 50 G5
Gabès, Golfe de g. Tunisia 50 G5
Gabo Island Australia 108 D6
▶Gabon country Africa 94 B4
africa 7, 90–91
▶Gaborone Botswana 97 G3
Capital of Botswana.
Gābrīk Iran 84 E5
Gabrovo Bulg. 55 K3
Gabú Guinea-Bissau 92 B3
Gadag India 80 B3
Gadaisu P.N.G. 106 E1
Gadchiroli India 80 D1
Gäddede Sweden 40 I4
Gadê China 72 C1
Gades Spain see Cádiz
Gadhap Pak. 85 G5
Gadhka India 85 H6
Gadhra India 78 B5
Gadra Pak. 85 H5
Gadsden U.S.A. 129 C5
Gadwal India 80 C2
Gadyach Ukr. see Hadyach
Gæi'dnuvuop'pi Norway 40 M2
Gaer U.K. 45 D7
Găești Romania 55 K2
Gaeta Italy 54 E4
Gaeta, Golfo di g. Italy 54 E4
Gaferut i. Micronesia 65 L5
Gaffney U.S.A. 129 D5
Gafsa Tunisia 54 C7
Gagarin Rus. Fed. 39 G5
Gagnoa Côte d'Ivoire 92 C4
Gagnon Canada 119 H4
Gago Coutinho Angola see Lumbala N'guimbo
Gagra Georgia 39 I8
Gaiab watercourse Namibia 96 D5
Gaibanda Bangl. see Gaibandha
Gaibandha Bangl. 79 G4
Gaifi, Wâdi el watercourse Egypt see Jayfī, Wādī al
Gail U.S.A. 127 C5
Gaildorf Germany 49 J6
Gaillac France 52 E5
Gaillimh Rep. of Ireland see Galway
Gaillon France 48 B5
Gaindainqoinkor China see Lhünzhub
Gainesboro U.S.A. 130 C5
Gainesville FL U.S.A. 129 D6
Gainesville GA U.S.A. 129 D5
Gainesville MO U.S.A. 127 E4
Gainesville TX U.S.A. 127 D5
Gainsborough U.K. 44 G5
Gairdner, Lake salt flat Australia 107 A6
Gairloch U.K. 46 D3
Gair Loch b. U.K. 46 D3
Gajah Hutan, Bukit hill Malaysia/Thai. 67 C6
Gajipur India see Ghazipur
Gajol India 79 G4
Gakarosa mt. S. Africa 96 F4
Gala China 79 G3
Galaasiya Uzbek. 85 G2
Gala Co l. China 79 G3
Galâla el Baharîya, Gebel el plat. Egypt see Jalālah al Baḩrīyah, Jabal
Galana r. Kenya 94 E4
Galanta Slovakia 43 P6
Galaosiyo Uzbek. see Galaasiya
▶Galapagos Islands is Ecuador 147 O6
Part of Ecuador. Most westerly point of South America.
Galapagos Rise sea feature Pacific Ocean 147 N6
Galashiels U.K. 46 G5
Galați Romania 55 M2
Galatina Italy 54 H4
Gala Water r. U.K. 46 G5
Galax U.S.A. 130 E5
Galaymor Turkm. see Kala-I-Mor
Galbally Rep. of Ireland 47 D5
Galdhøpiggen mt. Norway 41 F6
Galeana Chihuahua Mex. 123 G7
Galeana Nuevo León Mex. 127 C7
Galena AK U.S.A. 114 C3
Galena IL U.S.A. 126 F3
Galena MD U.S.A. 131 H4
Galena MO U.S.A. 127 E4
Galera, Punta pt Chile 140 B6
Galesburg IL U.S.A. 126 F3
Galesburg MI U.S.A. 130 C2
Galeshewe S. Africa 96 G5
Galeton U.S.A. 131 G3
Galey r. Rep. of Ireland 47 C5
Galheirão r. Brazil 141 B1
Galiano Island Canada 116 F5
Galich Rus. Fed. 38 I4
Galichskaya Vozvyshennost' hills Rus. Fed. 38 I4
Galicia aut. comm. Spain 53 C2
Galičica nat. park Macedonia 55 I4
Galilee, Lake salt flat Australia 106 D4
Galilee, Sea of l. Israel 81 B3
Galion U.S.A. 130 D3
Galiuro Mountains U.S.A. 125 H5
Galizia aut. comm. Spain see Galicia
Gallabat Sudan 82 E7
Gallatin MO U.S.A. 126 E4
Gallatin TN U.S.A. 130 B5
Galle Sri Lanka 80 D5
Gallego Rise sea feature Pacific Ocean 147 M6
Gallegos r. Arg. 140 C8
Gallia country Europe see France
▶Gallinas, Punta pt Col. 138 D1
Most northerly point of South America.
Gallipoli Italy 54 H4
Gallipoli Turkey 55 L4
Gallipolis U.S.A. 130 D4
Gällivare Sweden 40 L3
Gällö Sweden 40 I5
Gallo Island U.S.A. 131 G2
Gallo Mountains U.S.A. 125 I4
Gallup U.S.A. 125 I4
Gallyaaral Uzbek. 85 G1
Galmisdale U.K. 46 C4
Galong Australia 108 D5
Galoya Sri Lanka 80 D4
Gal Oya National Park Sri Lanka 80 D5
Galston U.K. 46 E5
Galt U.S.A. 124 C2
Galtat Zemmour W. Sahara 92 B2
Galtee Mountains hills Rep. of Ireland 47 D5
Galtymore hill Rep. of Ireland 42 C4
Galūgāh, Kūh-e mts Iran 84 D4
Galveston IN U.S.A. 130 B3
Galveston TX U.S.A. 127 E6
Galveston Bay U.S.A. 127 E6
Galwa Nepal 79 E3
Galway Rep. of Ireland 47 C4
Galway Bay Rep. of Ireland 47 C4
Gâm r. Vietnam 66 D2
Gamalakhe S. Africa 97 J6
Gamba China 79 G3
Gamba Gabon 94 A4
Gambēla Eth. 94 D3
Gambēla National Park Eth. 94 D3
Gambell U.S.A. 114 A3
Gambella Eth. see Gambēla
▶Gambia, The country Africa 92 B3
africa 7, 90–91
Gambier, Îles is Fr. Polynesia 147 L7
Gambier Islands Australia 107 B7
Gambier Islands Fr. Polynesia see Gambier, Îles
Gambo Canada 119 L4
Gamboma Congo 94 B4
Gamboola Australia 106 C3
Gamboula Cent. Afr. Rep. 94 B3
Gamda China see Zamtang
Gamlakarleby Fin. see Kokkola
Gamleby Sweden 41 J8
Gammelstaden Sweden 40 M4
Gammon Ranges National Park Australia 107 B6
Gamova, Mys pt Rus. Fed. 70 C4
Gamshadzai Kūh mts Iran 85 F4
Gamtog China 72 C2
Gamud mt. Eth. 94 D3
Gana China 72 D1
Ganado U.S.A. 125 I4
Gananoque Canada 131 G1
Ganāveh Iran 84 C4
Gäncä Azer. 87 G2
Gancheng China 73 F5
Ganda Angola 95 B5
Gandaingoin China 79 G3
Gandajika Dem. Rep. Congo 95 C4
Gandak Dam Nepal 79 E4
Gandari Mountain Pak. 85 H4
Gandava Pak. 85 G4
Gander Canada 119 L4
Ganderkesee Germany 49 I1
Gandesa Spain 53 G3
Gandhidham India 78 B5
Gandhinagar India 78 C5
Gandhi Sagar resr India 78 C4
Gandía Spain 53 F4
Gandzha Azer. see Gäncä
Ganga r. Bangl./India 79 G5 see Ganges

Ganga Cone sea feature Indian Ocean see Ganges Cone
Gangán Arg. 140 C6
Ganganagar India 78 C3
Gangapur India 78 D4
Ganga Sera India 78 B4
Gangaw Myanmar 66 A2
Gangawati India 80 C3
Gangaw Range mts Myanmar 66 B2
Gangca China 76 J4
Gangdisê Shan mts China 79 E3
Ganges r. Bangl./India 79 G5 also known as Ganga
Ganges France 52 F5
Ganges, Mouths of the Bangl./India 79 G5
Ganges Cone sea feature Indian Ocean 145 N4
Gangouyi China 68 J5
Gangra Turkey see Çankırı
Gangtok India 79 G4
Gangu China 72 E1
Gani Indon. 65 H7
Gan Jiang r. China 73 H2
Ganjig China 69 M4
Ganluo China 72 D2
Ganmain Australia 108 C5
Gannan China 70 A3
Gannat France 52 F3
Gannett Peak U.S.A. 122 F4
Ganq China 76 H4
Ganshui China 72 E2
Gansu prov. China 72 D1
Gantheaume Point Australia 104 C4
Gantsevichi Belarus see Hantsavichy
Ganxian China 73 G3
Ganye Nigeria 92 E4
Ganyu China 73 H1
Ganyushkino Kazakh. 37 P6
Ganzhou China 73 G3
Ganzi Sudan 93 G4
Gao Mali 92 C3
Gaocheng China see Litang
Gaocun China see Mayang
Gaohe China see Huaining
Gaohebu China see Huaining
Gaoleshan China see Xianfeng
Gaoliangjian China see Hongze
Gaomutang China 73 F3
Gaoping China 73 G1
Gaotai China 76 I4
Gaoting China see Daishan
Gaotingzhen China see Daishan
Gaoua Burkina 92 C3
Gaoual Guinea 92 B3
Gaoxiong Taiwan see Kaohsiung
Gaoyao China see Zhaoqing
Gaoyou China 73 H1
Gaoyou Hu l. China 73 H1
Gap France 52 H4
Gap Carbon hd Alg. 53 F6
Gapuwiyak Australia 106 A2
Gaqoi China 79 E3
Gar China 78 E2
Gar Pak. 85 F5
Gar' r. Rus. Fed. 70 C1
Gara, Lough l. Rep. of Ireland 47 D4
Garabekevyul Turkm. 85 G2
Garabekewül Turkm. see Garabekevyul
Garabil Belentligi hills Turkm. see Karabil', Vozvyshennost'
Garabogaz Aylagy b. Turkm. see Kara-Bogaz-Gol, Zaliv
Garabogazköl Aylagy b. Turkm. see Kara-Bogaz-Gol, Zaliv
Garabogazköl Bogazy sea chan. Turkm. see Kara-Bogaz-Gol, Proliv
Garägheh Iran 85 F4
Garagum des. Turkm. see Kara Kumy
Garagum des. Turkm. see Karakum Desert
Garagum Kanaly canal Turkm. see Karakumskiy Kanal
Garah Australia 108 D2
Garalo Mali 92 C3
Garamätnyyaz Turkm. see Karamet-Niyaz
Garamba r. Dem. Rep. Congo 94 C3
Garanhuns Brazil 139 K5
Ga-Rankuwa S. Africa 97 H3
Garapuava Brazil 141 B2
Gårasavvon Sweden see Karesuando
Garautha India 78 D4
Garba China see Jiulong
Garbahaarey Somalia 94 E3
Garba Tula Kenya 94 D3
Garberville U.S.A. 124 B1
Garbo China see Lhozhag
Garbsen Germany 49 J2
Garça Brazil 141 A3
Garco China 79 G2
Garda, Lago di Italy see Garda, Lake
Garda, Lake Italy 54 D2
Garde, Cap de c. Alg. 54 B6
Gardelegen Germany 49 L2
Garden City U.S.A. 126 C4
Garden Hill Canada 117 M4
Garden Mountain U.S.A. 130 E5
Gardeyz Afgh. see Gardēz
Gardēz Afgh. 85 H3
Gardinas Belarus see Hrodna
Gardiner U.S.A. 131 K1
Gardiner, Mount Australia 104 F5
Gardiner Range hills Australia 104 E4
Gardiners Island U.S.A. 131 I3
Gardīz Afgh. see Gardēz
Gardner atoll Micronesia see Faraulep
Gardner U.S.A. 131 J2
Gardner Inlet Antarctica 148 L1
Gardner Island atoll Kiribati see Nikumaroro
Gardner Pinnacles is U.S.A. 146 I4
Gáregasnjárga Fin. see Karigasniemi
Garelochhead U.K. 46 E4
Garet El Djenoun mt. Alg. 92 D2
Gargano, Parco Nazionale del nat. park Italy 54 F4
Gargantua, Cape Canada 118 D5
Gargunsa China see Gar
Gargždai Lith. 41 L9
Garhchiroli India see Gadchiroli
Garhi Madhya Pradesh India 80 C1
Garhi Rajasthan India 78 C5
Garhi Ikhtiar Khan Pak. 85 H4
Garhi Khairo Pak. 85 G4
Garhwa India 79 E4
Gari Rus. Fed. 37 S4
Gariau Indon. 65 I7
Garibaldi, Mount Canada 116 F5
Gariep Dam resr S. Africa 97 G6
Garies S. Africa 96 C6
Garigliano r. Italy 54 E4
Garissa Kenya 94 D4
Garkalne Latvia 41 N8
Garkung Caka l. China 79 F2
Garland U.S.A. 127 D5
Garm Tajik. see Gharm
Garm Āb Iran 85 E3
Garmab Iran 84 E3
Garmī Iran 84 C2
Garmsar Iran 84 D3
Garmsel reg. Afgh. 85 F4
Garner IA U.S.A. 126 E3
Garner KY U.S.A. 130 D5
Garnett U.S.A. 126 E4
Garnpung Lake imp. l. Australia 108 A4
Garo Hills India 79 G4
Garonne r. France 52 D4
Garoowe Somalia 94 E3
Garopaba Brazil 141 A5
Garoua Cameroon 92 E4
Garoua Boulai Cameroon 93 E4
Garqêntang China see Sog
Garré Arg. 140 D5
Garrett U.S.A. 130 C3
Garrison U.S.A. 126 E2
Garruk Pak. 85 G4
Garry r. U.K. 46 E3
Garrychyrla Turkm. see imeni Kerbabayeva
Garry Lake Canada 117 K1
Garrynahine U.K. 46 C2
Garsen Kenya 94 E4
Garshy Turkm. see Karshi
Garsila Sudan 93 F3
Gartar China see Qianning
Garth U.K. 45 D6
Gartog China see Markam
Gartok China see Garyarsa
Gartow Germany 49 L1
Garub Namibia 96 C4
Garvagh U.K. 47 F3
Garve U.K. 46 E3
Garwa India see Garhwa
Garwha India see Garhwa
Gar Xincun China 78 E2
Gary IN U.S.A. 130 B3
Gary WV U.S.A. 130 E5
Garyarsa China 78 E3
Garyi China 72 C2
Garyū-zan mt. Japan 71 D6
Garza García Mex. 127 C7
Garzê China 72 C2
Gasan-Kuli Turkm. see Esenguly
Gasan-Kuliyskiy Zapovednik nature res. Turkm. 84 D2
Gas City U.S.A. 130 C3
Gascogne reg. France see Gascony
Gascogne, Golfe de g. France see Gascony, Gulf of
Gascony reg. France 52 D5
Gascony, Gulf of France 52 C5
Gascoyne r. Australia 105 A6
Gascoyne Junction Australia 105 A6
Gasherbrum I mt. China/Jammu and Kashmir 78 D2
Gashua Nigeria 92 E3
Gask Iran 85 E3
Gaspar Cuba 129 E8
Gaspar, Selat sea chan. Indon. 64 D7
Gaspé Canada 119 I4
Gaspé, Cap c. Canada 119 I4
Gaspé, Péninsule de pen. Canada 119 I4
Gassan vol. Japan 71 F5
Gassaway U.S.A. 130 E4
Gasselte Neth. 48 G2
Gasteiz Spain see Vitoria-Gasteiz
Gastello Rus. Fed. 70 F2
Gaston U.S.A. 131 G5
Gaston, Lake U.S.A. 131 G5
Gastonia U.S.A. 129 D5
Gata, Cabo de c. Spain 53 E5
Gata, Cape Cyprus 81 A2
Gata, Sierra de mts Spain 53 C3
Gataga r. Canada 116 E3
Gatas, Akra c. Cyprus see Gata, Cape
Gatchina Rus. Fed. 41 Q7
Gate City U.S.A. 130 D5
Gatehouse of Fleet U.K. 46 E6
Gatentiri Indon. 65 K8
Gateshead U.K. 44 F4
Gates of the Arctic National Park and Preserve U.S.A. 114 C3
Gatesville U.S.A. 127 D6
Gateway U.S.A. 125 I2
Gatineau Canada 131 H1
Gatineau r. Canada 118 G5
Gatong China see Jomda
Gatooma Zimbabwe see Kadoma
Gatton Australia 108 F1
Gatvand Iran 84 C3
Gatyana S. Africa see Willowvale
Gau i. Fiji 103 H3
Gauer Lake Canada 117 L3
Gauhati India see Guwahati
Gaujas nacionālais parks nat. park Latvia 41 N8
Gaul country Europe see France
Gaula r. Norway 40 G5
Gaume reg. Belgium 48 F5
Gaurama Brazil 141 A4
Gauribidanur India 80 C3
Gauteng prov. S. Africa 97 I4
Gavarr Armenia see Kamo
Gāvbandī Iran 84 D5
Gāvbūs, Kūh-e mts Iran 84 D5

▶Gavdos i. Greece 55 K7
Most southerly point of Europe.

Gavião r. Brazil 141 C1
Gavīleh Iran 84 B3
Gav Khūnī Iran 84 D3
Gävle Sweden 41 J6
Gavrilovka Vtoraya Rus. Fed. 39 I5
Gavrilov-Yam Rus. Fed. 38 H4
Gawachab Namibia 96 C4
Gawai Myanmar 72 C3
Gawan India 79 F4
Gawilgarh Hills India 78 D5
Gawler Australia 107 B7
Gawler Ranges hills Australia 107 A7
Gaxun Nur salt l. China 76 J3
Gaya India 79 F4
Gaya Niger 92 D3
Gaya He r. China 70 C4
Gayéri Burkina 92 D3
Gaylord U.S.A. 130 C1
Gayndah Australia 107 E5
Gayny Rus. Fed. 38 L3
Gaysin Ukr. see Haysyn
Gayutino Rus. Fed. 38 H4
Gaz Iran 84 C3

▶Gaza terr. Asia 81 B4
Semi-autonomous region.
asia 6

▶Gaza Gaza 81 B4
Capital of Gaza.

Gaza prov. Moz. 97 K2
Gazan Pak. 85 G4
Gazandzhyk Turkm. 84 D2
Gazanjyk Turkm. see Gazandzhyk
Gaza Strip terr. Asia see Gaza
Gaziantep Turkey 86 E3
Gaziantep prov. Turkey 81 C1
Gazibenli Turkey see Yahyalı
Gazīk Iran 85 F3
Gazimağusa Cyprus see Famagusta
Gazimurskiy Khrebet mts Rus. Fed. 69 L2
Gazimurskiy Zavod Rus. Fed. 69 L2
Gazipaşa Turkey 81 A1
Gazli Uzbek. 85 F1
Gaz Māhū Iran 84 E5
Gbarnga Liberia 92 C4
Gboko Nigeria 92 D4
Gcuwa S. Africa see Butterworth
Gdańsk Poland 43 Q3
Gdańsk, Gulf of Poland/Rus. Fed. 43 Q3
Gdańska, Zatoka g. Poland/Rus. Fed. see Gdańsk, Gulf of
Gdingen Poland see Gdynia
Gdov Rus. Fed. 41 O7
Gdynia Poland 43 Q3
Gearhart Mountain U.S.A. 122 C4
Gearraidh na h-Aibhne U.K. see Garrynahine
Gebe i. Indon. 65 H6
Gebesee Germany 49 K3
Geçitkale Cyprus see Lefkonikon
Gedaref Sudan 82 E7
Gedern Germany 49 J4
Gedinne Belgium 48 E5
Gediz r. Turkey 55 L5
Gedney Drove End U.K. 45 H6
Gedong, Tanjong pt Sing. 67 [inset]
Gedser Denmark 41 G9
Geel Belgium 48 F3
Geelong Australia 108 B7
Geelvink Channel Australia 105 A7
Geel Vloer salt pan S. Africa 96 E5
Gees Gwardafuy c. Somalia see Gwardafuy, Gees
Geeste Germany 49 H2
Geesthacht Germany 49 K1
Ge Hu l. China 73 H2
Geidam Nigeria 92 E3
Geiersberg hill Germany 49 J5
Geikie r. Canada 117 K3
Geilenkirchen Germany 48 G4
Geilo Norway 41 F6
Geiranger Norway 40 E5
Geislingen an der Steige Germany 49 J6
Geisûm, Gezâ'ir is Egypt see Qaysūm, Juzur
Geita Tanz. 94 D4
Geithain Germany 49 M3
Gejiu China 72 D4
Gekdepe Turkm. 84 E2
Gela Sicily Italy 54 F6
Gêladaindong mt. China 79 G2
Geladī Eth. 94 E3
Gelang, Tanjung pt Malaysia 67 C7
Geldern Germany 48 G3
Gelendzhik Rus. Fed. 86 E1
Gelephu Bhutan 79 G4
Gelibolu Turkey see Gallipoli
Gelidonya Burnu pt Turkey see Yardımcı Burnu
Gelincik Dağı mt. Turkey 55 N5
Gelmord Iran 84 E3
Gelnhausen Germany 49 J4
Gelsenkirchen Germany 48 H3
Gemas Malaysia 67 C7
Gemena Dem. Rep. Congo 94 B3
Geminokağı Cyprus see Karavostasi
Gemlik Turkey 55 M4
Gemona del Friuli Italy 54 E1
Gemsa Egypt see Jamsah
Gemsbok National Park Botswana 96 E3
Gemsbokplein well S. Africa 96 E4
Genalē Wenz r. Eth. 94 E3
Genappe Belgium 48 E4
General Acha Arg. 140 D5
General Alvear Arg. 140 C5
General Belgrano II research station Antarctica see Belgrano II
General Bernardo O'Higgins research station Antarctica 148 A2
General Bravo Mex. 127 D7

▶General Carrera, Lago l. Arg./Chile 140 B7
Deepest lake in South America.

General Conesa Arg. 140 D6
General Freire Angola see Muxaluando
General Juan Madariaga Arg. 140 E5
General La Madrid Arg. 140 D5
General Machado Angola see Camacupa
General Pico Arg. 140 D5
General Pinedo Arg. 140 D3
General Roca Arg. 140 C5
General Salgado Brazil 141 A3
General San Martín research station Antarctica see San Martín
General Santos Phil. 65 H5
General Simón Bolívar Mex. 127 C7
General Trías Mex. 123 G7
General Villegas Arg. 140 D5
Genesee U.S.A. 131 G3
Geneseo U.S.A. 131 G2
Geneva S. Africa 97 H4
Geneva Switz. 52 H3
Geneva AL U.S.A. 129 C6
Geneva IL U.S.A. 130 A3
Geneva NE U.S.A. 126 D3
Geneva NY U.S.A. 131 G2
Geneva OH U.S.A. 130 E3
Geneva, Lake France/Switz. 52 H3
Genève Switz. see Geneva
Genf Switz. see Geneva
Gengda China see Gana
Gengma China 72 C4
Gengxuan China see Gengma
Genhe China 70 A2
Genichesk Ukr. see Heniches'k
Genji India 78 C5
Genk Belgium 48 F4
Gennep Neth. 48 F3
Genoa Australia 108 D6
Genoa Italy 54 C2
Genoa, Gulf of Italy 54 C2
Genova Italy see Genoa
Genova, Golfo di Italy see Genoa, Gulf of
Gent Belgium see Ghent
Genthin Germany 49 M2
Gentioux, Plateau de France 52 F4
Genua Italy see Genoa
Geographe Bay Australia 105 A8
Geographical Society Ø i. Greenland 115 P2
Geok-Tepe Turkm. see Gekdepe
Georga, Zemlya i. Rus. Fed. 60 F1
George r. Canada 119 I2
George S. Africa 96 F7
George, Lake Australia 108 D5
George, Lake FL U.S.A. 129 D6
George, Lake NY U.S.A. 131 I2
George Land i. Rus. Fed. see Georga, Zemlya
Georges Mills U.S.A. 131 I2
George Sound inlet N.Z. 109 A7
Georgetown Australia 106 C3

▶George Town Cayman Is 133 H5
Capital of the Cayman Islands.

Georgetown Gambia 92 B3

▶Georgetown Guyana 139 G2
Capital of Guyana.

George Town Malaysia 67 C6
Georgetown DE U.S.A. 131 H4
Georgetown GA U.S.A. 129 C6
Georgetown IL U.S.A. 130 B4
Georgetown KY U.S.A. 130 C4
Georgetown OH U.S.A. 130 D4
Georgetown SC U.S.A. 129 E5
Georgetown TX U.S.A. 127 D6
George VI Sound sea chan. Antarctica 148 L2
George V Land reg. Antarctica 148 G2
George West U.S.A. 127 D6
▶Georgia country Asia 87 F2
asia 6, 58–59
Georgia state U.S.A. 129 D5
Georgia, Strait of Canada 116 E5
Georgiana U.S.A. 127 G6
Georgian Bay Canada 130 E1
Georgian Bay Islands National Park Canada 130 F1
Georgienne, Baie b. Canada see Georgian Bay
Georgina watercourse Australia 106 B5
Georgiu-Dezh Rus. Fed. see Liski
Georgiyevka Vostochnyy Kazakhstan Kazakh. 76 F2
Georgiyevka Zhambylskaya Oblast' Kazakh. see Korday
Georgiyevsk Rus. Fed. 87 F1
Georgiyevskoye Rus. Fed. 38 J4
Georg von Neumayer research station Antarctica see Neumayer
Gera Germany 49 M4
Geraardsbergen Belgium 48 D4
Geral, Serra mts Brazil 141 A4
Geral de Goiás, Serra hills Brazil 141 B1
Geraldine N.Z. 109 C7
Geral do Paraná, Serra hills Brazil 141 B1
Geraldton Australia 105 A7
Gerar watercourse Israel 81 B4
Gerber U.S.A. 124 B1
Gercüş Turkey 87 F3
Gerede Turkey 86 D2
Gereshk Afgh. 85 G4
Gerik Malaysia 67 C6
Gerlach U.S.A. 124 D1
Gerlachovský štít mt. Slovakia 43 R6
Germaine, Lac l. Canada 119 I3
Germania country Europe see Germany
Germanicea Turkey see Kahramanmaraş
Germansen Landing Canada 116 E4
German South-West Africa country Africa see Namibia
Germantown OH U.S.A. 130 C4
Germantown WI U.S.A. 130 A2

▶Germany country Europe 43 L5
2nd most populous country in Europe.
europe 5, 34–35

Germersheim Germany 49 I5
Gernsheim Germany 49 I5
Gerolstein Germany 48 G4
Gerolzhofen Germany 49 K5
Gerona Spain see Girona
Gerrit Denys is P.N.G. see Lihir Group
Gers r. France 52 E4
Gersfeld (Rhön) Germany 49 J4
Gersoppa India 80 B3
Gerstungen Germany 49 K4
Gerwisch Germany 49 L2
Géryville Alg. see El Bayadh
Gêrzê China 79 F2
Gerze Turkey 86 D2
Gescher Germany 48 H3
Gesoriacum France see Boulogne-sur-Mer
Gessie U.S.A. 130 B3
Gete r. Belgium 48 F4
Gettysburg PA U.S.A. 131 G4
Gettysburg SD U.S.A. 126 D2
Gettysburg National Military Park nat. park U.S.A. 131 G4
Getz Ice Shelf Antarctica 148 J2
Geumpang Indon. 67 B6
Geureudong, Gunung vol. Indon. 67 B6
Geurie Australia 108 D4
Gevaş Turkey 87 F3
Gevgelija Macedonia 55 J4
Gexto Spain see Algorta
Gey Iran see Nīkshahr
Geyikli Turkey 55 L5
Geysdorp S. Africa 97 G4
Geyserville U.S.A. 124 B2
Geyve Turkey 55 N4
Gezīr Iran 84 D5
Ghaap Plateau S. Africa 96 F4
Ghāb, Wādī al r. Syria 81 C2
Ghabāghib Syria 81 C3
Ghabeish Sudan 82 C7
Ghadaf, Wādī al watercourse Jordan 81 C4
Ghadamés Libya see Ghadāmis
Ghadāmis Libya 92 D1
Ghaem Shahr Iran 84 D2
Ghaghara r. India 79 F4
Ghaibi Dero Pak. 85 G5
Ghalend Iran 85 F4
Ghalkarteniz, Solonchak salt marsh Kazakh. 76 B2
Ghallaorol Uzbek. see Gallyaaral
▶Ghana country Africa 92 C4
africa 7, 90–91
Ghanādah, Rās pt U.A.E. 84 D5
Ghantila India 78 B5
Ghanwā Saudi Arabia 82 G4
Ghanzi Botswana 95 C6
Ghanzi admin. dist. Botswana 96 F2
Ghap'an Armenia see Kapan
Ghardaïa Alg. 50 E5
Gharghoda India 80 D1
Ghārib, Gebel mt. Egypt see Ghārib, Jabal
Ghārib, Jabal mt. Egypt 86 D5
Gharm Tajik. 85 H2
Gharq Ābād Iran 84 C3
Gharwa India see Garhwa
Gharyān Libya 93 E1
Ghāt Libya 92 E2
Ghatgan India 79 F5
Ghatol India 78 C5
Ghawdex i. Malta see Gozo
Ghazal, Bahr el watercourse Chad 93 E3
Ghazaouet Alg. 53 F6
Ghaziabad India 78 D3
Ghazi Ghat Pak. 85 H4
Ghazipur India 79 E4
Ghazna Afgh. see Ghaznī
Ghaznī Afgh. 85 H3
Ghaznī r. Afgh. 85 G3
Ghazoor Afgh. 85 G3
Ghazzah Gaza see Gaza
Ghebar Gumbad Iran 84 E3
Ghent Belgium 48 D3
Gheorghe Gheorghiu-Dej Romania see Onești
Gheorgheni Romania 55 K1
Gherla Romania 55 J1
Ghijduwon Uzbek. see Gizhduvan
Ghilzai reg. Afgh. 85 G4
Ghīnah, Wādī al watercourse Saudi Arabia 81 D4
Ghisonaccia Corsica France 52 I5
Ghorak Afgh. 85 G3
Ghost Lake Canada 116 H2
Ghotaru India 78 B4
Ghotki Pak. 85 H5
Ghuari r. India 79 F4
Ghudamis Libya see Ghadāmis
Ghurayfah hill Saudi Arabia 81 C4
Ghūrī Iran 84 D4
Ghurian Afgh. 85 F3
Ghurrab, Jabal hill Saudi Arabia 84 B5
Ghuzor Uzbek. see Guzar
Ghyvelde France 48 C3
Gia Đinh Vietnam 67 D5
Giaginskaya Rus. Fed. 87 F1
Gialias r. Cyprus 81 A2
Gia Nghia Vietnam 67 D4
Giannitsa Greece 55 J4
Giant's Castle mt. S. Africa 97 I5
Giant's Causeway lava field U.K. 47 F2
Gianysada i. Greece 55 L7
Gia Rai Vietnam 67 D5
Giarre Sicily Italy 54 F6
Gibb r. Australia 104 D3
Gibbonsville U.S.A. 122 E3
Gibeon Namibia 96 C3
Gibraltar terr. Europe 53 D5

▶Gibraltar Gibraltar 144 H3
United Kingdom Overseas Territory.
europe 5, 34–35

Gibraltar, Strait of Morocco/Spain 53 C6
Gibraltar Range National Park Australia 108 F2
Gibson Australia 105 C8
Gibson City U.S.A. 130 A3
Gibson Desert Australia 105 C6
Gichgeniyn Nuruu mts Mongolia 76 H2
Gidar Pak. 85 G4
Giddalur India 80 C3
Giddi, Gebel el hill Egypt see Jiddī, Jabal al
Giddings U.S.A. 127 D6
Gīdolē Eth. 93 G4
Gien France 52 F3
Gießen Germany 49 I4
Gīfan Iran 84 E2
Gifford r. Canada 115 J2
Gifhorn Germany 49 K2
Gift Lake Canada 116 H4
Gifu Japan 71 E6
Giganta, Cerro mt. Mex. 123 F8
Gigha i. U.K. 46 D5
Gīgīga Eth. see Jijiga
Gijón Spain see Gijón-Xixón
Gijón-Xixón Spain 53 D2
Gila r. U.S.A. 125 F5
Gila Bend U.S.A. 125 G5
Gila Bend Mountains U.S.A. 125 G5
Gīlān-e Gharb Iran 84 B3
Gilbert r. Australia 106 C3
Gilbert AZ U.S.A. 125 H5
Gilbert WV U.S.A. 130 E5
Gilbert Islands Kiribati 146 H5
Gilbert Islands country Pacific Ocean see Kiribati
Gilbert Peak U.S.A. 125 H1
Gilbert Ridge sea feature Pacific Ocean 146 H6
Gilbert River Australia 106 C3
Gilbués Brazil 139 I5
Gil Chashmeh Iran 84 E3
Gilé Moz. 95 D5
Giles Creek r. Australia 104 E4
Gilford Island Canada 116 E5
Gilgai Australia 108 E2
Gilgandra Australia 108 D3
Gil Gil Creek r. Australia 108 D2
Gilgit Jammu and Kashmir 78 C2
Gilgit r. Jammu and Kashmir 83 L2
Gilgunnia Australia 108 C4
Gilındire Turkey see Aydıncık
Gillam Canada 117 M3
Gillen, Lake salt flat Australia 105 D6
Gilles, Lake salt flat Australia 107 B7
Gillett U.S.A. 131 G3
Gillette U.S.A. 122 G3
Gilliat Australia 106 C4
Gillingham England U.K. 45 E7
Gillingham England U.K. 45 H7
Gilling West U.K. 44 F4
Gilman U.S.A. 130 B3
Gilmer U.S.A. 127 E5
Gilmour Island Canada 118 F2
Gilroy U.S.A. 124 C3
Gīmbī Eth. 94 D3
Gimhae S. Korea see Kimhae
Gimli Canada 117 L5
Gimol'skoye, Ozero l. Rus. Fed. 38 G3
Ginebra, Laguna l. Bol. 138 E6
Gineifa Egypt see Junayfah
Gin Gin Australia 106 E5
Gingin Australia 105 A7
Gīnīr Eth. 94 E3
Ginosa Italy 54 G4
Ginzo de Limia Spain see Xinzo de Limia
Gioia del Colle Italy 54 G4
Gipouloux r. Canada 118 G3
Gippsland reg. Australia 108 B7
Girā, Wādī watercourse Egypt see Jirā', Wādī
Gīrān Rīg mt. Iran 84 E4
Girard U.S.A. 130 E2
Girardin, Lac l. Canada 119 I2
Girdab Iran 84 E3
Giresun Turkey 86 E2
Girgenti Sicily Italy see Agrigento
Giridh India see Giridih
Giridih India 79 F4
Girilambone Australia 108 C3
Girna r. India 78 C5
Gir National Park India 78 B5
Girne Cyprus see Kyrenia
Girón Ecuador 138 C4
Giron Sweden see Kiruna
Girona Spain 53 H3
Gironde est. France 52 D4
Girot Pak. 85 I3
Girral Australia 108 C4
Girraween National Park Australia 108 E2
Girvan U.K. 46 E5
Girvas Rus. Fed. 38 G3
Gisborne N.Z. 109 G4
Giscome Canada 116 F4
Gislaved Sweden 41 H8
Gisors France 48 B5
Gissar Tajik. see Hisor
Gissar Range mts Tajik./Uzbek. 85 G2
Gissarskiy Khrebet mts Tajik./Uzbek. see Gissar Range
Gitarama Rwanda 94 C4
Gitega Burundi 94 C4
Giuba r. Somalia see Jubba
Giulianova Italy 54 E3
Giurgiu Romania 55 K3
Giuvala, Pasul pass Romania 55 K2
Givar Iran 84 E2
Givet France 48 E4
Givors France 52 G4
Givry-en-Argonne France 48 E6
Giyani S. Africa 97 J2
Giza Egypt 86 C5
Gizhduvan Uzbek. 85 G1
Gizhiga Rus. Fed. 61 R3
Gjakovë Serb. and Mont. see Đakovica
Gjilan Serb. and Mont. see Gnjilane
Gjirokastër Albania 55 I4
Gjirokastra Albania see Gjirokastër
Gjoa Haven Canada 115 I3
Gjøra Norway 40 F5
Gjøvik Norway 41 G6
Glace Bay Canada 119 K5
Glacier Bay National Park and Preserve U.S.A. 116 B3
Glacier National Park Canada 116 G5
Glacier National Park U.S.A. 122 E2
Glacier Peak vol. U.S.A. 122 C2
Gladstad Norway 40 G4
Gladstone Australia 106 E4
Gladstone Canada 117 L5
Gladwin U.S.A. 130 C2
Gladys U.S.A. 130 F5
Gladys Lake Canada 116 C3
Glamis U.K. 46 F4
Glamis U.S.A. 125 F5
Glamoč Bos.-Herz. 54 G2
Glan r. Germany 49 H5
Glandorf Germany 49 I2
Glanton U.K. 44 F3
Glasgow U.K. 46 E5
Glasgow KY U.S.A. 130 C5
Glasgow MT U.S.A. 122 G2
Glasgow VA U.S.A. 130 F5
Glaslyn Canada 117 I4
Glass, Loch l. U.K. 46 E3
Glass Mountain U.S.A. 124 D3
Glastonbury U.K. 45 E7
Glauchau Germany 49 M4
Glazov Rus. Fed. 38 L4
Gleiwitz Poland see Gliwice
Glen U.S.A. 131 J1
Glen Allen U.S.A. 131 G5
Glen Alpine Dam S. Africa 97 I2
Glenamaddy Rep. of Ireland 47 D4
Glenamoy r. Rep. of Ireland 47 C3
Glen Arbor U.S.A. 130 C1
Glenbawn Reservoir Australia 108 E4
Glenboro Canada 117 L5
Glen Canyon gorge U.S.A. 125 H3
Glen Canyon Dam U.S.A. 125 H3
Glencoe Canada 130 E2
Glencoe S. Africa 97 J5
Glencoe U.S.A. 126 E2
Glendale AZ U.S.A. 125 G5
Glendale CA U.S.A. 124 D4
Glendale UT U.S.A. 125 G3
Glendale Lake U.S.A. 131 F3
Glen Davis Australia 108 E4
Glenden Australia 106 E4
Glendive U.S.A. 122 G3
Glendon Canada 117 I4
Glendo Reservoir U.S.A. 122 G4
Glenfield U.S.A. 131 H2
Glengavlen Rep. of Ireland 47 E3
Glengyle Australia 106 B5
Glen Innes Australia 108 E2
Glenluce U.K. 46 E6
Glen Lyon U.S.A. 131 G3
Glenlyon Peak Canada 116 C2
Glen More valley U.K. 46 E3
Glenmorgan Australia 108 D1
Glenn U.S.A. 124 B2
Glennallen U.S.A. 114 D3
Glennie U.S.A. 130 D1
Glenns Ferry U.S.A. 122 E4
Glenora Canada 116 D3
Glenore Australia 106 C3
Glenormiston Australia 106 B4
Glenreagh Australia 108 F3
Glen Rose U.S.A. 127 D5
Glenrothes U.K. 46 F4
Glens Falls U.S.A. 131 I2
Glen Shee valley U.K. 46 F4
Glenties Rep. of Ireland 47 D3
Glenveagh National Park Rep. of Ireland 47 E2
Glenville U.S.A. 130 E4

Glenwood AR U.S.A. 127 E5
Glenwood IA U.S.A. 126 E3
Glenwood MN U.S.A. 126 E2
Glenwood NM U.S.A. 125 I5
Glenwood Springs U.S.A. 125 J2
Glevum U.K. see Gloucester
Glinde Germany 49 K1
Glittertinden mt. Norway 41 F6
Gliwice Poland 43 Q5
Globe U.S.A. 125 H5
Glogau Poland see Głogów
Głogów Poland 43 P5
Glomfjord Norway 40 H3
Glomma r. Norway 40 G7
Glommersträsk Sweden 40 K4
Glorieuses, Îles is Indian Ocean 95 E5
Glorioso Islands Indian Ocean see Glorieuses, Îles
Gloster U.S.A. 127 F6
Gloucester Australia 108 E3
Gloucester U.K. 45 E7
Gloucester MA U.S.A. 131 J2
Gloucester VA U.S.A. 131 G5
Gloversville U.S.A. 131 H2
Glovertown Canada 119 L4
Glöwen Germany 49 M2
Glubinnoye Rus. Fed. 70 D3
Glubokiy Krasnoyarskiy Kray Rus. Fed. 68 H2
Glubokiy Rostovskaya Oblast' Rus. Fed. 39 I6
Glubokoye Belarus see Hlybokaye
Glubokoye Kazakh. 76 F1
Gluggarnir hill Faroe Is 40 [inset]
Glukhov Ukr. see Hlukhiv
Glusburn U.K. 44 F5
Glynebwy U.K. see Ebbw Vale
Gmelinka Rus. Fed. 39 J6
Gmünd Austria 43 O6
Gmunden Austria 43 N7
Gnarp Sweden 41 J5
Gnarrenburg Germany 49 J1
Gnesen Poland see Gniezno
Gniezno Poland 43 P4
Gnjilane Serb. and Mont. 55 I3
Gnowangerup Australia 105 B8
Gnows Nest Range hills Australia 105 B7
Goa India 80 B3
Goa state India 80 B3
Goageb Namibia 96 C4
Goalen Head hd Australia 108 E6
Goalpara India 79 G4
Goat Fell hill U.K. 46 D5
Goba Eth. 94 E3
Gobabis Namibia 96 D2
Gobannium U.K. see Abergavenny
Gobas Namibia 96 D4
Gobi des. China/Mongolia 68 J4
Gobindpur India 79 F5
Gobles U.S.A. 130 C2
Gobō Japan 71 D6
Goch Germany 48 G3
Gochas Namibia 96 D3
Go Công Vietnam 67 D5
Godalming U.K. 45 G7
Godavari r. India 80 D2
Godavari, Cape India 80 D2
Godda India 79 F4
Godē Eth. 94 E3
Godere Eth. 94 E3
Goderich Canada 130 E2
Goderville France 45 H9
Godhavn Greenland see Qeqertarsuaq
Godhra India 78 C5
Godia Creek b. India 85 H6
Gods r. Canada 117 M3
Gods Lake Canada 117 M4
God's Mercy, Bay of Canada 117 O2
Godthåb Greenland see Nuuk
Godwin-Austen, Mount China/Jammu and Kashmir see K2
Goedereede Neth. 48 D3
Goedgegun Swaziland see Nhlangano
Goegap Nature Reserve S. Africa 96 D5
Goélands, Lac aux l. Canada 119 J3
Goes Neth. 48 D3
Gogama Canada 118 E5
Gogebic Range hills U.S.A. 126 F2
Gogra r. India see Ghaghara
Goiana Brazil 139 L5
Goiandira Brazil 141 A2
Goianésia Brazil 141 A1
Goiânia Brazil 141 A2
Goiás Brazil 141 A1
Goiás state Brazil 141 A2
Goinsargoin China 72 C2
Goio-Erê Brazil 140 F2
Gojra Pak. 85 I4
Gokak India 80 B2
Gokarn India 80 B3
Gök Çay r. Turkey 81 A1
Gökçeada i. Turkey 55 K4
Gökdepe Turkm. see Gëkdepe
Gökdere r. Turkey 81 A1
Goklenkuy, Solonchak salt l. Turkm. 84 E1
Gökova Körfezi b. Turkey 55 L6
Gokprosh Hills Pak. 85 F5
Göksun Turkey 86 E3
Goksu Parkı Turkey 81 A1
Gokteik Myanmar 66 B2
Gokwe Zimbabwe 95 C5
Gol Norway 41 F6
Golaghat India 79 H4
Gölbaf Iran 84 E4
Gölbaşı Turkey 86 E3
Golconda U.S.A. 124 E1
Gölcük Turkey 55 M4
Gold U.S.A. 131 G3
Gołdap Poland 43 S3
Gold Beach U.S.A. 122 B4
Goldberg Germany 49 M1
Gold Coast country Africa see Ghana
Gold Coast Australia 108 F2
Golden U.S.A. 122 G5
Golden Bay N.Z. 109 D5
Goldendale U.S.A. 122 C3
Goldene Aue reg. Germany 49 K3
Golden Gate Highlands National Park S. Africa 97 I5
Golden Hinde mt. Canada 116 E5
Golden Lake Canada 131 G1
Golden Prairie Canada 117 I5
Goldenstedt Germany 49 I2
Goldfield U.S.A. 124 E3
Goldsand Lake Canada 117 K3
Goldsboro U.S.A. 129 E5
Goldstone Lake U.S.A. 124 E4
Goldsworthy Australia 104 B5
Goldthwaite U.S.A. 127 D6
Goldvein U.S.A. 131 G4
Göle Turkey 87 F2
Golestān Afgh. 85 F3
Goleta U.S.A. 124 D4
Golets-Davydov, Gora mt. Rus. Fed. 69 J2
Golfo di Orosei Gennargentu e Asinara, Parco Nazionale del nat. park Sardinia Italy 54 C4
Gölgeli Dağları mts Turkey 55 M6
Goliad U.S.A. 127 D6
Golingka China see Gongbo'gyamda
Gölköy Turkey 86 E2
Gollel Swaziland see Lavumisa
Golm Germany 49 M2
Golmberg hill Germany 49 N2
Golmud China 76 H4
Golovnino Rus. Fed. 70 G4
Golpāyegān Iran 84 C3
Gölpazarı Turkey 55 N4
Golspie U.K. 46 F3
Gol Vardeh Iran 85 F3
Golyama Syutkya mt. Bulg. 55 K4
Golyam Persenk mt. Bulg. 55 K4
Golyshi Rus. Fed. see Vetluzhskiy
Golzow Germany 49 M2
Goma Dem. Rep. Congo 94 C4
Gomang Co salt l. China 79 G3
Gomati r. India 83 N4
Gombak, Bukit hill Sing. 67 [inset]
Gombe Nigeria 92 E3
Gombe r. Tanz. 95 D4
Gombi Nigeria 92 E3
Gombroon Iran see Bandar-e 'Abbās
Gomel' Belarus see Homyel'
Gómez Palacio Mex. 127 C7
Gomīshān Iran 84 D2
Gommern Germany 49 L2
Gomo Co salt l. China 79 F2
Gonābād Iran 84 E2
Gonaïves Haiti 133 J5
Gonarezhou National Park Zimbabwe 95 D6
Gonbad-e Kavus Iran 84 D2
Gonda India 79 E4
Gondal India 78 B5
Gondar Eth. see Gonder
Gonder Eth. 94 D2
Gondia India 78 E5
Gondiya India see Gondia
Gönen Turkey 55 L4
Gonfreville-l'Orcher France 45 H9
Gong'an China 73 G2
Gongbalou China see Gamba
Gongbo'gyamda China 72 B2
Gongchang China see Longxi
Gongcheng China 73 F3
Gongga Shan mt. China 72 D2
Gonghe Qinghai China 76 J4
Gonghe Yunnan China see Mouding
Gongjiang China see Yudu
Gongogi r. Brazil 141 D1
Gongolgon Australia 108 C3
Gongpoquan China 76 I3
Gongquan China see Gongxian
Gongtang China see Damxung
Gongwang Shan mts China 72 D3
Gongxian China 72 E2
Gonjo China 72 C2
Gonjog China see Coqên
Gonzales CA U.S.A. 124 C3
Gonzales TX U.S.A. 127 D6
Gonzha Rus. Fed. 70 B1
Goochland U.S.A. 131 G5
Goodenough, Cape Antarctica 148 G2
Goodenough Island P.N.G. 102 F2
Gooderham Canada 131 F1
Good Hope, Cape of S. Africa 96 D8
Good Hope Mountain Canada 122 B2
Gooding U.S.A. 122 E4
Goodland IN U.S.A. 130 B3
Goodland KS U.S.A. 126 C4
Goodlettsville U.S.A. 130 B5
Goodooga Australia 108 C2
Goodspeed Nunataks Antarctica 148 E2
Goole U.K. 44 G5
Goolgowi Australia 108 B5
Goolma Australia 108 D4
Gooloogong Australia 108 D4
Goomalling Australia 105 B7
Goombalie Australia 108 B2
Goondiwindi Australia 108 E2
Goongarrie, Lake salt flat Australia 105 C7
Goongarrie National Park Australia 105 C7
Goonyella Australia 106 D4
Goorly, Lake salt flat Australia 105 B7
Goose Bay Canada see Happy Valley - Goose Bay
Goose Creek U.S.A. 129 D5
Goose Lake U.S.A. 122 C4
Gooty India 80 C3
Gopalganj Bangl. 79 G5
Gopalganj India 79 F4
Gopeshwar India 78 D3
Göppingen Germany 49 J6
Gorakhpur India 79 E4
Goražde Bos.-Herz. 54 H3
Gorbernador U.S.A. 125 J3
Gorczański Park Narodowy nat. park Poland 43 R6
Gorda, Punta pt U.S.A. 124 A1
Gördes Turkey 55 M5
Gordil Cent. Afr. Rep. 94 C3
Gordon r. Canada 117 O1
Gordon U.K. 46 G5
Gordon U.S.A. 126 C3
Gordon, Lake Australia 107 [inset]
Gordon Downs Australia 104 E4
Gordon Lake Canada 117 I3
Gordon Lake U.S.A. 131 F4
Gordonsville U.S.A. 131 F4
Goré Chad 93 E4
Gorē Eth. 94 D3
Gore N.Z. 109 B8
Gore U.S.A. 131 F4
Gorebridge U.K. 46 F5
Gore Point U.S.A. 114 C4
Gorey Rep. of Ireland 47 F5
Gorg Iran 85 E4
Gorgān Iran 84 D2
Gorgan Bay Iran 84 D2
Gorge Range hills Australia 104 B5
Gorgona, Isla i. Col. 138 C3
Gorham U.S.A. 131 J1
Gori Georgia 82 F1
Gorinchem Neth. 48 E3
Goris Armenia 87 G3
Gorizia Italy 54 E2
Gorki Belarus see Horki
Gor'kiy Rus. Fed. see Nizhniy Novgorod
Gor'kovskoye Vodokhranilishche resr Rus. Fed. 38 I4
Gorlice Poland 39 D6
Görlitz Germany 43 O5
Gorlovka Ukr. see Horlivka
Gorna Dzhumaya Bulg. see Blagoevgrad
Gorna Oryakhovitsa Bulg. 55 K3
Gornji Milanovac Serb. and Mont. 55 I2
Gornji Vakuf Bos.-Herz. 54 G3
Gorno-Altaysk Rus. Fed. 76 G1
Gornotrakiyska Nizina lowland Bulg. 55 K3
Gornozavodsk Permskaya Oblast' Rus. Fed. 37 R4
Gornozavodsk Sakhalinskaya Oblast' Rus. Fed. 70 F3
Gornyak Rus. Fed. 76 F1
Gornye Klyuchi Rus. Fed. 70 D3
Gornyy Rus. Fed. 39 K6
Goro i. Fiji see Koro
Gorodenka Ukr. see Horodenka
Gorodets Rus. Fed. 38 I4
Gorodishche Penzenskaya Oblast' Rus. Fed. 39 J5
Gorodishche Volgogradskaya Oblast' Rus. Fed. 39 J6
Gorodok Belarus see Haradok
Gorodok Rus. Fed. see Zakamensk
Gorodok Khmel'nyts'ka Oblast' Ukr. see Horodok
Gorodok L'vivs'ka Oblast' Ukr. see Horodok
Gorodovikovsk Rus. Fed. 39 I7
Goroka P.N.G. 65 L8
Gorokhovets Rus. Fed. 38 I4
Gorom Gorom Burkina 92 C3
Gorong, Kepulauan is Indon. 65 I7
Gorongosa mt. Moz. 95 D5
Gorongosa, Parque Nacional de nat. park Moz. 95 D5
Gorontalo Indon. 65 G6
Gorshechnoye Rus. Fed. 39 H6
Gort Rep. of Ireland 47 D4
Gortahork Rep. of Ireland 47 D2
Gorutuba r. Brazil 141 C1
Gorveh Iran 84 E4
Goryachiy Klyuch Rus. Fed. 87 E1
Görzke Germany 49 M2
Gorzów Wielkopolski Poland 43 O4
Gosainthan mt. China see Xixabangma Feng
Gosforth U.K. 44 F3
Goshen CA U.S.A. 124 D3
Goshen IN U.S.A. 130 C3
Goshen NH U.S.A. 131 I2
Goshen NY U.S.A. 131 H3
Goshen VA U.S.A. 130 F5
Goshoba Turkm. see Koshoba
Goslar Germany 49 K3
Gospić Croatia 54 F2
Gosport U.K. 45 F8
Gossi Mali 92 C3
Gostivar Macedonia 55 I4
Gosu China 72 C1
Göteborg Sweden see Gothenburg
Götene Sweden 41 H7
Gotenhafen Poland see Gdynia
Gotha Germany 49 K4
Gothenburg Sweden 41 G8
Gothenburg U.S.A. 126 C3
Gotland i. Sweden 41 K8
Gotō-rettō is Japan 71 C6
Gotse Delchev Bulg. 55 J4
Gotska Sandön i. Sweden 41 K7
Gōtsu Japan 71 D6
Göttingen Germany 49 J3
Gott Peak Canada 116 F5
Gottwaldow Czech Rep. see Zlín
Gouda Neth. 48 E2
Goudiri Senegal 92 B3
Goudoumaria Niger 92 E3
Goûgaram Niger 92 D3

▶Gough Island S. Atlantic Ocean 144 H8
Dependency of St Helena.

Gouin, Réservoir resr Canada 118 G4
Goulburn Australia 108 D5
Goulburn r. N.S.W. Australia 108 E4
Goulburn r. Vic. Australia 108 B6
Goulburn Islands Australia 104 F2
Goulburn River National Park Australia 108 E4
Gould Coast Antarctica 148 J1
Goulou atoll Micronesia see Ngulu
Goundam Mali 92 C3
Goundi Chad 93 E4
Goupil, Lac l. Canada 119 H3
Gouraya Alg. 53 G5
Gourcy Burkina 92 C3
Gourdon France 52 E4
Gouré Niger 92 E3
Gouripur Bangl. 79 G4
Gourits r. S. Africa 96 E8
Gourma-Rharous Mali 92 C3
Gournay-en-Bray France 48 B5
Goussainville France 48 C5
Gouverneur U.S.A. 131 H1
Governador Valadares Brazil 141 C2
Governor's Harbour Bahamas 129 E7
Govĭ Altayn Nuruu mts Mongolia 76 I3
Govind Ballash Pant Sagar resr India 79 E4
Gowal Pak. 85 H4
Gowanda U.S.A. 131 F2
Gowan Range hills Australia 106 D5
Gowārān Afgh. 85 G4
Gowd-e Mokh l. Iran 84 D4
Gowd-e Zereh plain Afgh. 85 F4
Gowmal Kalay Afgh. 85 H3
Gowna, Lough l. Rep. of Ireland 47 E4
Goya Arg. 140 E3
Göyçay Azer. 87 G2
Goyder watercourse Australia 105 F6
Goymatdag hills Turkm. see Koymatdag, Gory
Göynük Turkey 55 N4
Goyoum Cameroon 92 E4
Gozareh Afgh. 85 F3
Goz-Beïda Chad 93 F3
Gozha Co salt l. China 78 E2
Gözkaya Turkey 81 C1
Gozo i. Malta 54 F6
Graaf-Reinet S. Africa 96 G7
Grabfeld plain Germany 49 K4
Grabo Côte d'Ivoire 92 C4
Grabouw S. Africa 96 D8
Grabow Germany 49 L1
Gračac Croatia 54 F2
Gracefield Canada 118 F5
Gracey U.S.A. 130 B5
Gradaús, Serra dos hills Brazil 139 H5
Gradiška Bos.-Herz. see Bosanska Gradiška
Grady U.S.A. 127 C5
Gräfenhainichen Germany 49 M3
Grafenwöhr Germany 49 L5
Grafton Australia 108 F2
Grafton ND U.S.A. 126 D1
Grafton WI U.S.A. 130 B2
Grafton WV U.S.A. 130 E4
Grafton, Cape Australia 106 D3
Grafton, Mount U.S.A. 125 F2
Grafton Passage Australia 106 D3
Graham NC U.S.A. 128 E4
Graham TX U.S.A. 127 D5
Graham, Mount U.S.A. 125 I5
Graham Bell Island Rus. Fed. see Greem-Bell, Ostrov
Graham Island B.C. Canada 116 C4
Graham Island Nunavut Canada 115 I2
Graham Land reg. Antarctica 148 L2
Grahamstown S. Africa 97 H7
Grahovo Bos.-Herz. see Bosansko Grahovo
Graigue Rep. of Ireland 47 F5
Grajaú Brazil 139 I5
Grajaú r. Brazil 139 J4
Grammont Belgium see Geraardsbergen
Grammos mt. Greece 55 I4
Grampian Mountains U.K. 46 E4
Grampians National Park Australia 107 C8
Granada Nicaragua 133 G6
Granada Spain 53 E5
Granada U.S.A. 126 C4
Granard Rep. of Ireland 47 E4
Granbury U.S.A. 127 D5
Granby Canada 119 G5
Gran Canaria i. Canary Is 92 B2
Gran Chaco reg. Arg./Para. 140 D3
Grand r. MO U.S.A. 130 B2
Grand r. SD U.S.A. 126 C2
Grand Atlas mts Morocco see Haut Atlas
Grand Bahama i. Bahamas 129 E7
Grand Ballon mt. France 43 K7
Grand Bank Canada 119 L5
Grand Banks of Newfoundland sea feature N. Atlantic Ocean 144 E3
Grand-Bassam Côte d'Ivoire 92 C4
Grand Bay Canada 119 I5
Grand Bend Canada 130 E2
Grand Blanc U.S.A. 130 D2
Grand Canal Rep. of Ireland 47 E4
Grand Canary i. Canary Is see Gran Canaria
Grand Canyon U.S.A. 125 G3
Grand Canyon gorge U.S.A. 125 G3
Grand Canyon National Park U.S.A. 125 G3
Grand Canyon - Parashant National Monument nat. park U.S.A. 125 G3
Grand Cayman i. Cayman Is 133 H5
Grande r. Bahia Brazil 141 B1
Grande r. São Paulo Brazil 141 A3
Grande r. Nicaragua 133 H6
Grande, Bahía b. Arg. 140 C8
Grande, Ilha i. Brazil 141 B3
Grande Cache Canada 116 G4
Grande Comore i. Comoros see Njazidja
Grande Prairie Canada 116 G4
Grand Erg de Bilma des. Niger 92 E3
Grand Erg Occidental des. Alg. 50 D5
Grand Erg Oriental des. Alg. 50 F6
Grande-Rivière Canada 119 I4
Grandes, Salinas salt marsh Arg. 140 C4
Grande-Vallée Canada 119 I4
Grand Falls N.B. Canada 119 I5
Grand Falls Nfld. and Lab. Canada 119 L4
Grand Forks Canada 116 G5
Grand Forks U.S.A. 126 D2
Grand Gorge U.S.A. 131 H2
Grand Haven U.S.A. 130 B2
Grandin, Lac l. Canada 116 G1
Grandioznyy, Pik mt. Rus. Fed. 68 H2
Grand Island U.S.A. 126 D3
Grand Isle U.S.A. 127 F6
Grand Junction U.S.A. 125 I2
Grand Lac Germain l. Canada 119 I4
Grand-Lahou Côte d'Ivoire 92 C4
Grand Lake N.B. Canada 119 I5
Grand Lake Nfld. and Lab. Canada 119 J3
Grand Lake Nfld. and Lab. Canada 119 K4
Grand Lake LA U.S.A. 127 E6
Grand Lake MI U.S.A. 130 D1
Grand Lake St Marys U.S.A. 130 C3
Grand Ledge U.S.A. 130 C2
Grand Manan Island Canada 119 I5
Grand Marais MI U.S.A. 128 C2
Grand Marais MN U.S.A. 126 F2
Grand-Mère Canada 119 G5
Grand Mesa U.S.A. 125 J2
Grândola Port. 53 B4
Grand Passage New Caledonia 103 G3
Grand Rapids Canada 117 L4
Grand Rapids MI U.S.A. 130 C2
Grand Rapids MN U.S.A. 126 E2
Grand-Sault Canada see Grand Falls
Grand St-Bernard, Col du pass Italy/Switz. see Great St Bernard Pass
Grand Teton mt. U.S.A. 122 F4
Grand Teton National Park U.S.A. 122 F4
Grand Traverse Bay U.S.A. 130 C1

▶Grand Turk Turks and Caicos Is 133 J4
Capital of the Turks and Caicos Islands.

Grandville U.S.A. 130 C2
Grandvilliers France 48 B5
Grand Wash Cliffs mts U.S.A. 125 F4
Grange Rep. of Ireland 47 E6
Grängesberg Sweden 41 I6
Grangeville U.S.A. 122 D3
Granisle Canada 116 E4
Granite Falls U.S.A. 126 E2
Granite Mountain U.S.A. 124 E1
Granite Mountains CA U.S.A. 125 F4
Granite Mountains CA U.S.A. 125 F5
Granite Peak MT U.S.A. 122 F3
Granite Peak UT U.S.A. 125 G1
Granite Range mts AK U.S.A. 116 A3
Granite Range mts NV U.S.A. 124 D1
Granitola, Capo c. Sicily Italy 54 E6
Granja Brazil 139 J4
Gran Laguna Salada l. Arg. 140 C6
Gränna Sweden 41 I7
Gran Paradiso mt. Italy 54 B2
Gran Paradiso, Parco Nazionale del nat. park Italy 54 B2
Gran Pilastro mt. Austria/Italy 43 M7
Gran San Bernardo, Colle del pass Italy/Switz. see Great St Bernard Pass
Gran Sasso e Monti della Laga, Parco Nazionale del nat. park Italy 54 E3
Granschütz Germany 49 M3
Gransee Germany 49 N1
Grant U.S.A. 126 C3
Grant, Mount U.S.A. 124 E2
Grantham U.K. 45 G6
Grant Island Antarctica 148 J2
Grant Lake Canada 116 G1
Grantown-on-Spey U.K. 46 F3
Grant Range mts U.S.A. 125 F2
Grants U.S.A. 125 J4
Grants Pass U.S.A. 122 C4
Grantsville UT U.S.A. 125 G1
Grantsville WV U.S.A. 130 E4
Granville Canada 116 B2
Granville France 52 D2
Granville AZ U.S.A. 125 I5
Granville NY U.S.A. 131 I2
Granville TN U.S.A. 130 C5
Granville Lake Canada 117 K3
Grão Mogol Brazil 141 C2
Grapevine Mountains U.S.A. 124 E3
Gras, Lac de l. Canada 117 I1
Graskop S. Africa 97 J3
Grasplatz Namibia 96 B4
Grass r. Canada 117 L3
Grass r. U.S.A. 131 H1
Grasse France 52 H5
Grassflat U.S.A. 131 F3
Grassington U.K. 44 F4
Grasslands National Park Canada 117 J5
Grassrange U.S.A. 122 F3
Grass Valley U.S.A. 124 C2
Grassy Butte U.S.A. 126 C2
Grästorp Sweden 41 H7
Gratz U.S.A. 130 C4
Graudenz Poland see Grudziądz
Graus Spain 53 G2
Gravatai Brazil 141 A5
Grave, Pointe de pt France 52 D4
Gravelbourg Canada 117 J5
Gravel Hill Lake Canada 117 K2
Gravelines France 48 C4
Gravelotte S. Africa 97 J2
Gravenhurst Canada 130 F1
Grave Peak U.S.A. 122 E3
Gravesend Australia 108 E2
Gravesend U.K. 45 H7
Gravina in Puglia Italy 54 G4
Grawn U.S.A. 130 C1
Gray France 52 G3
Gray GA U.S.A. 129 D5
Gray KY U.S.A. 130 C5
Gray ME U.S.A. 131 J2
Grayback Mountain U.S.A. 122 C4
Gray Lake Canada 117 I2
Grayling r. Canada 116 E3
Grayling U.S.A. 130 C1
Grays U.K. 45 H7
Grays Harbor inlet U.S.A. 122 B3
Grays Lake U.S.A. 122 F4
Grayson U.S.A. 130 D4
Graz Austria 43 O7
Greasy Lake Canada 116 F2
Great Abaco i. Bahamas 129 E7
Great Australian Bight g. Australia 105 E8
Great Baddow U.K. 45 H7
Great Bahama Bank sea feature Bahamas 129 E7
Great Barrier Island N.Z. 109 E3
Great Barrier Reef Australia 106 D1
Great Barrier Reef Marine Park (Cairns Section) Australia 106 D3
Great Barrier Reef Marine Park (Capricorn Section) Australia 106 E4
Great Barrier Reef Marine Park (Central Section) Australia 106 E3
Great Barrier Reef Marine Park (Far North Section) Australia 106 D2
Great Barrington U.S.A. 131 I2
Great Basalt Wall National Park Australia 106 D3
Great Basin U.S.A. 124 E2
Great Basin National Park U.S.A. 125 F2
Great Bear r. Canada 116 E1

▶Great Bear Lake Canada 116 G1
4th largest lake in North America.

Great Belt sea chan. Denmark 41 G9
Great Bend U.S.A. 126 D4
Great Bitter Lake Egypt 81 A4
Great Blasket Island Rep. of Ireland 47 B5

▶Great Britain i. U.K. 42 G4
Largest island in Europe.
europe 32–33

Great Clifton U.K. 44 D4
Great Coco Island Cocos Is 64 A4
Great Cumbrae i. U.K. 46 E5
Great Dismal Swamp National Wildlife Refuge nature res. U.S.A. 131 G5
Great Dividing Range mts Australia 108 B6
Great Eastern Erg des. Alg. see Grand Erg Oriental
Greater Antarctica reg. Antarctica see East Antarctica
Greater Antilles is Caribbean Sea 133 H4
Greater Khingan Mountains China see Da Hinggan Ling
Greater St Lucia Wetland Park nature res. S. Africa 97 K4
Greater Tunb i. The Gulf 84 D5
Great Exuma i. Bahamas 129 F8
Great Falls U.S.A. 122 F3
Great Fish r. S. Africa 97 H7
Great Fish Point S. Africa 97 H7
Great Fish River Reserve Complex nature res. S. Africa 97 H7
Great Gandak r. India 79 F4
Great Ganges atoll Cook Is see Manihiki
Great Guana Cay i. Bahamas 129 E7
Great Inagua i. Bahamas 133 J4
Great Karoo plat. S. Africa 96 F7
Great Kei r. S. Africa 97 I7
Great Lake Australia 107 [inset]
Great Malvern U.K. 45 E6
Great Meteor Tablemount sea feature N. Atlantic Ocean 144 G4
Great Namaqualand reg. Namibia 96 C4
Great Nicobar i. India 67 A6
Great Ormes Head hd U.K. 44 D5
Great Ouse r. U.K. 45 H6
Great Oyster Bay Australia 107 [inset]
Great Palm Islands Australia 106 D3
Great Plain of the Koukdjuak Canada 115 K3
Great Plains U.S.A. 126 C3
Great Point U.S.A. 131 J3
Great Rift Valley Africa 94 D4
Great Ruaha r. Tanz. 95 D4
Great Sacandaga Lake U.S.A. 131 H2
Great Salt Lake U.S.A. 125 G1
Great Salt Lake Desert U.S.A. 125 G1
Great Sand Hills Canada 117 I5
Great Sand Sea des. Egypt/Libya 86 B5
Great Sandy Desert Australia 104 C5
Great Sandy Island Australia see Fraser Island
Great Sea Reef Fiji 103 H3

▶Great Slave Lake Canada 116 H2
Deepest and 5th largest lake in North America.

Great Smoky Mountains U.S.A. 129 C5
Great Smoky Mountains National Park U.S.A. 128 D5
Great Snow Mountain Canada 116 E3
Great St Bernard Pass Italy/Switz. 54 B2
Greatstone-on-Sea U.K. 45 H8
Great Stour r. U.K. 45 I7
Great Torrington U.K. 45 C8
Great Victoria Desert Australia 105 E7
Great Wall research station Antarctica 148 A2
Great Wall tourist site China 69 L4
Great Waltham U.K. 45 H7
Great Western Erg des. Alg. see Grand Erg Occidental
Great West Torres Islands Myanmar 67 B5
Great Whernside hill U.K. 44 F4
Great Yarmouth U.K. 45 I6
Grebenkovskiy Ukr. see Hrebinka
Grebyonka Ukr. see Hrebinka
Greco, Cape Cyprus see Greko, Cape
Gredos, Sierra de mts Spain 53 D3
▶Greece country Europe 55 I5
europe 5, 34–35
Greece U.S.A. 131 G2
Greeley U.S.A. 122 G4
Greely Center U.S.A. 126 D3
Greem-Bell, Ostrov i. Rus. Fed. 60 H1
Green r. KY U.S.A. 130 B5
Green r. WY U.S.A. 125 I2
Green Bay U.S.A. 130 A1
Green Bay b. U.S.A. 130 B1
Greenbrier U.S.A. 130 B5
Greenbrier r. U.S.A. 130 E5
Green Cape Australia 108 E6
Greencastle Bahamas 129 E7
Greencastle U.K. 47 F3
Greencastle U.S.A. 130 B4
Green Cove Springs U.S.A. 129 D6
Greene ME U.S.A. 131 J1
Greene NY U.S.A. 131 H2
Greeneville U.S.A. 128 D4
Greenfield CA U.S.A. 124 C3
Greenfield IN U.S.A. 130 C4
Greenfield MA U.S.A. 131 I2
Greenfield OH U.S.A. 130 D4
Green Head hd Australia 105 A7
Greenhill Island Australia 104 F2
Green Island Taiwan see Lü Tao
Green Lake Canada 117 J4

▶Greenland terr. N. America 115 N3
Self-governing Danish Territory.
Largest island in the world and in North America.
north america 9, 110–111, 112–113
world 12–13

Greenland Basin sea feature Arctic Ocean 149 I2
Greenland Fracture Zone sea feature Arctic Ocean 149 I1
Greenland Sea Greenland/Svalbard 60 A2
Greenlaw U.K. 46 G5
Green Mountains U.S.A. 131 I1
Greenock U.K. 46 E5
Greenore Rep. of Ireland 47 F3
Greenport U.S.A. 131 I3
Green River P.N.G. 65 K7
Green River UT U.S.A. 125 H2
Green River WY U.S.A. 122 F4
Green River Lake U.S.A. 130 C5
Greensboro U.S.A. 129 D5
Greensburg IN U.S.A. 130 C4
Greensburg KS U.S.A. 126 D4
Greensburg KY U.S.A. 130 C5
Greensburg LA U.S.A. 127 F6
Greensburg PA U.S.A. 130 F3
Greens Peak U.S.A. 125 I4
Greenstone Point U.K. 46 D3
Green Swamp U.S.A. 129 E5
Greentown U.S.A. 130 C3
Greenup IL U.S.A. 126 F4
Greenup KY U.S.A. 130 D4
Green Valley Canada 131 H1
Greenville Canada 116 D4
Greenville Liberia 92 C4
Greenville AL U.S.A. 129 C6
Greenville IL U.S.A. 126 F4
Greenville KY U.S.A. 130 B5
Greenville ME U.S.A. 128 G2
Greenville MI U.S.A. 130 C2
Greenville MS U.S.A. 127 F5
Greenville NC U.S.A. 128 E5

Greenville NH U.S.A. 131 J2
Greenville OH U.S.A. 130 C3
Greenville PA U.S.A. 130 E3
Greenville SC U.S.A. 129 D5
Greenville TX U.S.A. 127 D5
Greenwich atoll Micronesia see Kapingamarangi
Greenwich CT U.S.A. 131 I3
Greenwich OH U.S.A. 130 D3
Greenwood AR U.S.A. 127 E5
Greenwood IN U.S.A. 130 B4
Greenwood MS U.S.A. 127 F5
Greenwood SC U.S.A. 129 D5
Gregory r. Australia 106 B3
Gregory, Lake salt flat S.A. Australia 107 B6
Gregory, Lake salt flat W.A. Australia 104 D5
Gregory, Lake salt flat W.A. Australia 105 B6
Gregory Downs Australia 106 B3
Gregory National Park Australia 104 E4
Gregory Range hills Qld Australia 106 C3
Gregory Range hills W.A. Australia 104 C5
Greifswald Germany 43 N3
Greiz Germany 49 M4
Greko, Cape Cyprus 81 B2
Gremikha Rus. Fed. 149 G2
Gremyachinsk Rus. Fed. 37 R4
Grenå Denmark 41 G8
Grenaa Denmark see Grenå
Grenada U.S.A. 127 F5
▶Grenada country West Indies 133 L6
north america 9, 112–113
Grenade France 52 E5
Grenen spit Denmark 41 G8
Grenfell Australia 108 D4
Grenfell Canada 117 K5
Grenoble France 52 G4
Grense-Jakobselv Norway 40 Q2
Grenville, Cape Australia 106 C1
Grenville Island Fiji see Rotuma
Greshak Pak. 85 G5
Gresham U.S.A. 122 C3
Gressåmoen Nasjonalpark nat. park Norway 40 H4
Greta r. U.K. 44 E4
Gretna U.K. 46 F6
Gretna LA U.S.A. 127 F6
Gretna VA U.S.A. 130 F5
Greußen Germany 49 K3
Grevelingen sea chan. Neth. 48 D3
Greven Germany 49 H2
Grevena Greece 55 I4
Grevenbicht Neth. 48 F3
Grevenbroich Germany 48 G3
Grevenmacher Lux. 48 G5
Grevesmühlen Germany 43 M4
Grey, Cape Australia 106 B2
Greybull U.S.A. 122 F3
Greybull r. U.S.A. 122 F3
Grey Hunter Peak Canada 116 C2
Grey Islands Canada 119 L4
Greylock, Mount U.S.A. 131 I2
Greymouth N.Z. 109 C6
Grey Range hills Australia 108 A2
Grey's Plains Australia 105 A6
Greytown S. Africa 97 J5
Grez-Doiceau Belgium 48 E4
Gribanovskiy Rus. Fed. 39 I6
Gridley U.S.A. 124 C2
Griffin U.S.A. 129 C5
Griffith Australia 108 C5
Grigan i. N. Mariana Is see Agrihan
Grik Malaysia see Gerik
Grim, Cape Australia 107 [inset]
Grimari Cent. Afr. Rep. 94 C3
Grimma Germany 49 M3
Grimmen Germany 43 N3
Grimnitzsee l. Germany 49 N2
Grimsby U.K. 44 G5
Grímsey i. Iceland 40 [inset]
Grimshaw Canada 116 G3
Grímsstaðir Iceland 40 [inset]
Grimstad Norway 41 F7
Grindavík Iceland 40 [inset]
Grindsted Denmark 41 F9
Grind Stone City U.S.A. 130 D1
Grindul Chituc spit Romania 55 M2
Grinnell Peninsula Canada 115 I2
Griqualand East reg. S. Africa 97 I6
Griqualand West reg. S. Africa 96 F5
Griquatown S. Africa 96 F5
Grise Fiord Canada 115 J2
Grishino Ukr. see Krasnoarmiys'k
Gris Nez, Cap c. France 48 B4
Gritley U.K. 46 G2
Grizzly Bear Mountain hill Canada 116 F1
Grmeč mts Bos.-Herz. 54 G2
Grobbendonk Belgium 48 E3
Groblersdal S. Africa 97 I3
Groblershoop S. Africa 96 F5
Grodekovo Rus. Fed. 70 C3
Grodno Belarus see Hrodna
Groen watercourse S. Africa 96 F6
Groen watercourse S. Africa 96 C6
Groix, Île de i. France 52 C3
Grombalia Tunisia 54 D6
Gronau (Westfalen) Germany 48 H2
Grong Norway 40 H4
Groningen Neth. 48 G1
Groninger Wad tidal flat Neth. 48 G1
Grønland terr. N. America see Greenland
Groom Lake U.S.A. 125 F3
Groot-Aar Pan salt pan S. Africa 96 E4
Groot Berg r. S. Africa 96 D7
Groot Brakrivier S. Africa 96 F8
Grootdraaidam dam S. Africa 97 I4
Grootdrink S. Africa 96 E5
Groote Eylandt i. Australia 106 B2
Grootfontein Namibia 95 B5
Groot Karas Berg plat. Namibia 96 D4
Groot Letaba r. S. Africa 97 J2
Groot Marico S. Africa 97 H3
Groot Swartberge mts S. Africa 96 E7
Grootvloer salt pan S. Africa 96 E5
Groot Winterberg mt. S. Africa 97 H7
Gros Morne National Park Canada 119 K4
Gross Barmen Namibia 96 C2
Große Aue r. Germany 49 J2
Große Laaber r. Germany 49 M6
Großengottern Germany 49 K3
Großenkneten Germany 49 I2
Großenlüder Germany 49 J4
Großer Arber mt. Germany 49 N5
Großer Beerberg hill Germany 49 K4
Großer Eyberg hill Germany 49 H5
Großer Gleichberg hill Germany 49 K4
Großer Kornberg hill Germany 49 M4
Großer Osser mt. Czech Rep./Germany 49 N5
Großer Rachel mt. Germany 43 N6
Grosser Speikkogel mt. Austria 43 O7
Grosseto Italy 54 D3
Grossevichi Rus. Fed. 70 E3
Groß-Gerau Germany 49 I5
Großglockner mt. Austria 43 N7
Groß Oesingen Germany 49 K2
Großrudestedt Germany 49 L3
Groß Schönebeck Germany 49 N2
Gross Ums Namibia 96 D2
Großvenediger mt. Austria 43 N7
Gros Ventre Range mts U.S.A. 122 F4
Groswater Bay Canada 119 K3
Groton U.S.A. 126 D2
Grottoes U.S.A. 131 F4
Grou Neth. see Grouw
Groundhog r. Canada 118 E4
Grouw Neth. 48 F1
Grove U.S.A. 127 E4
Grove City U.S.A. 130 D4
Grove Hill U.S.A. 129 C6
Grove Mountains Antarctica 148 E2
Grover Beach U.S.A. 124 C4
Grovertown U.S.A. 130 B3
Groveton NH U.S.A. 131 J1
Groveton TX U.S.A. 127 E6
Growler Mountains U.S.A. 125 G5
Groznyy Rus. Fed. 87 G2
Grubišno Polje Croatia 54 G2
Grudovo Bulg. see Sredets
Grudziądz Poland 43 Q4
Grünau Namibia 96 D4
Grünberg Poland see Zielona Góra
Grundarfjörður Iceland 40 [inset]
Grundy U.S.A. 130 D5
Gruñidora Mex. 127 C7
Grünstadt Germany 49 I5
Gruver U.S.A. 127 C4
Gruzinskaya S.S.R. country Asia see Georgia
Gryazi Rus. Fed. 39 H5
Gryazovets Rus. Fed. 38 I4
Gryfice Poland 43 O4
Gryfino Poland 43 O4
Gryfów Śląski Poland 43 O5
Gryllefjord Norway 40 J2
Grytviken S. Georgia 140 I8
Gua India 79 F5
Guacanayabo, Golfo de b. Cuba 133 I4
Guachochi Mex. 123 G8
Guadajoz r. Spain 53 D5
Guadalajara Mex. 132 D4
Guadalajara Spain 53 E3
Guadalcanal i. Solomon Is 103 G2
Guadalete r. Spain 53 C5
Guadalope r. Spain 53 F3
Guadalquivir r. Spain 53 C5
Guadalupe Mex. 127 C7
Guadalupe i. Mex. 123 D7
Guadalupe watercourse Mex. 124 E5
Guadalupe U.S.A. 124 C4
Guadalupe, Sierra de mts Spain 53 D4
Guadalupe Aguilera Mex. 127 B7
Guadalupe Bravos Mex. 123 G7
Guadalupe Mountains National Park U.S.A. 123 G7
Guadalupe Peak U.S.A. 123 G7
Guadalupe Victoria Baja California Mex. 125 F5
Guadalupe Victoria Durango Mex. 127 B7
Guadarrama, Sierra de mts Spain 53 D3
▶Guadeloupe terr. West Indies 133 L5
French Overseas Department.
north america 9, 112–113
Guadeloupe Passage Caribbean Sea 133 L5
Guadiana r. Port./Spain 53 C5
Guadix Spain 53 E5
Guafo, Isla i. Chile 140 B6
Guaíba Brazil 141 A5
Guaiçuí Brazil 141 B2
Guaíra Brazil 140 F2
Guajaba, Cayo i. Cuba 129 E8
Guaje, Llano de plain Mex. 127 C7
Gualala U.S.A. 124 B2
Gualeguay Arg. 140 E4
Gualeguaychu Arg. 140 E4
Gualicho, Salina salt flat Arg. 140 C6
▶Guam terr. N. Pacific Ocean 65 K4
United States Unincorporated Territory.
oceania 8, 100–101
Guamblin, Isla i. Chile 140 A6
Guampí, Sierra de mts Venez. 138 E2
Guamúchil Mex. 123 F8
Guanabacoa Cuba 129 D8
Guanacevi Mex. 127 B7
Guanahacabibes, Península de pen. Cuba 129 C8
Guanajay Cuba 129 D8
Guanajuato Mex. 132 D4
Guanambi Brazil 141 C1
Guanare Venez. 138 E2
Guandu China 73 G3
Guane Cuba 133 H4
Guang'an China 72 E2
Guangchang China 73 H3
Guangdong prov. China 73 [inset]
Guanghai China 73 G4
Guanghan China 72 E2
Guanghua China see Laohekou
Guangming China see Xide
Guangming Ding mt. China 73 H2
Guangnan China 72 E3
Guangshan China 73 G2
Guangxi aut. reg. China see Guangxi Zhuangzu Zizhiqu
Guangxi Zhuangzu Zizhiqu aut. reg. China 72 F4
Guangyuan China 72 E1
Guangze China 73 H3
Guangzhou China 73 G4
Guanhães Brazil 141 C2
Guanhe Kou r. mouth China 73 H1
Guanipa r. Venez. 138 F2
Guanling China 72 E3
Guanmian Shan mts China 73 F2
Guannan China 73 H1
Guanpo China 73 F1
Guanshui China 70 B4
Guansuo China see Guanling
Guantánamo Cuba 133 I4
Guanxian China see Dujiangyan
Guanyang China 73 F3
Guanyinqiao China 72 D2
Guanyun China 73 H1
Guapé Brazil 141 B3
Guapí Col. 138 C3
Guaporé r. Bol./Brazil 138 E6
Guaporé Brazil 141 A5
Guaqui Bol. 138 E7
Guará r. Brazil 141 B1
Guarabira Brazil 139 K5
Guaranda Ecuador 138 C4
Guarapari Brazil 141 C3
Guarapuava Brazil 141 A4
Guararapes Brazil 141 A3
Guaratinguetá Brazil 141 B3
Guaratuba Brazil 141 A4
Guaratuba, Baía de b. Brazil 141 A4
Guarda Port. 53 C3
Guardafui, Cape Somalia see Gwardafuy, Gees
Guardiagrele Italy 54 F3
Guardo Spain 53 D2
Guárico, del Embalse resr Venez. 138 E2
Guarujá Brazil 141 B3
Guasave Mex. 123 F8
Guasdualito Venez. 138 D2
▶Guatemala country Central America 132 F5
4th most populous country in Central and North America.
north america 9, 112–113
Guatemala Guat. see Guatemala City
▶Guatemala City Guat. 132 F6
Capital of Guatemala.
Guaviare r. Col. 138 E3
Guaxupé Brazil 141 B3
Guayaquil Ecuador 138 C4
Guayaquil, Golfo de g. Ecuador 138 B4
Guaymas Mex. 123 F8
Guba Eth. 94 D2
Gubakha Rus. Fed. 37 R4
Gubbi India 80 C3
Gubio Nigeria 92 E3
Gubkin Rus. Fed. 39 H6
Gucheng China 73 F1
Gudari India 80 D2
Gudbrandsdalen valley Norway 41 F6
Gudermes Rus. Fed. 87 G2
Gudivada India 80 D2
Gudiyattam India 80 C3
Gudur Andhra Pradesh India 80 C3
Gudur Andhra Pradesh India 80 C3
Gudvangen Norway 41 E6
Gudzhal r. Rus. Fed. 70 D2
Guè, Rivière du r. Canada 119 H2
Guecho Spain see Algorta
Guéckédou Guinea 92 B4
Guelma Alg. 54 B6
Guelmine Morocco 92 B2
Guelph Canada 130 E2
Guémez Mex. 127 D8
Guénange France 48 G5
Guerara Alg. 50 E5
Guérard, Lac l. Canada 119 I2
Guercif Morocco 50 D5
Guéret France 52 E3
▶Guernsey terr. Channel Is 45 E9
United Kingdom Crown Dependency.
europe 5, 34–35
Guernsey U.S.A. 122 G4
Guérou Mauritania 92 B3
Guerrah Et-Tarf salt pan Alg. 54 B7
Guerrero Negro Mex. 123 E8
Guers, Lac l. Canada 119 I2
Gueugnon France 52 G3
Gufeng China see Pingnan
Gufu China see Xingshan
Gugē mt. Eth. 94 D3
Gügerd, Küh-e mts Iran 84 D3
Guguan i. N. Mariana Is 65 L3
Guhakolak, Tanjung pt Indon. 64 D8
Guhe China 73 H2
Güh Küh mt. Iran 84 E5
Guhuai China see Pingyu
Guiana Basin sea feature N. Atlantic Ocean 144 E5
Guiana Highlands mts S. America 138 E2
Guichi China see Chizhou
Guidan-Roumji Niger 92 D3
Guider Cameroon 93 E4
Guiding China 72 E3
Guidong China 73 G3
Guidonia-Montecelio Italy 54 E4
Guigang China 73 F4
Guiglo Côte d'Ivoire 92 C4
Guignicourt France 48 D5
Guija Moz. 97 K3
Guiji Shan mts China 73 I2
Guildford U.K. 45 G7
Guilford U.S.A. 128 G2
Guilherme Capelo Angola see Cacongo
Guilin China 73 F3
Guillaume-Delisle, Lac l. Canada 118 F2
Guimarães Brazil 139 J4
Guimarães Port. 53 B3
Guinan China 72 D1
▶Guinea country Africa 92 B3
africa 7, 90–91
Guinea, Gulf of Africa 92 D4
Guinea Basin sea feature N. Atlantic Ocean 144 H5
▶Guinea-Bissau country Africa 92 B3
africa 7, 90–91
Guinea-Conakry country Africa see Guinea
Guinea Ecuatorial country Africa see Equatorial Guinea
Guiné-Bissau country Africa see Guinea-Bissau
Guinée country Africa see Guinea
Güines Cuba 133 H4
Guînes France 48 B4
Guines, Lac l. Canada 119 J3
Guingamp France 52 C2
Guipavas France 52 B2
Guiping China 73 F4
Güira de Melena Cuba 129 D8
Guiratinga Brazil 139 H7
Guiscard France 48 D5
Guise France 48 D5
Guishan China see Xinping
Guishun China 72 E3
Guixi Chongqing China see Dianjiang
Guixi Jiangxi China 73 H2
Guiyang Guizhou China 72 E3
Guiyang Hunan China 73 G3
Guizhou prov. China 72 E3
Guizi China 73 F4
Gujarat state India 78 C5
Gujar Khan Pak. 85 I3
Gujerat state India see Gujarat
Gujranwala Pak. 85 I3
Gujrat Pak. 85 I3
Gukovo Rus. Fed. 39 H6
Gulabgarh Jammu and Kashmir 78 D2
Gulbarga India 80 C2
Gulbene Latvia 41 O8
Gul'cha Kyrg. see Gülchö
Gülchö Kyrg. 76 D3
Gülcihan Turkey 81 B1
Gülek Boğazı pass Turkey 86 D3
Gulfport U.S.A. 127 F6
Gulian China 70 A1
Gulin China 72 E3
Gulistan Uzbek. 76 C3
Guliston Uzbek. see Gulistan
Gülitz Germany 49 L1
Guliya Shan mt. China 70 A2
Gulja China see Yining
Gul Kach Pak. 85 H4
Gul'kevichi Rus. Fed. 87 F1
Gull Lake Canada 117 I5
Gullrock Lake Canada 117 M5
Gullträsk Sweden 40 L3
Güllük Körfezi b. Turkey 55 L6
Gülnar Turkey 81 A1
Gulū China see Xincai
Gulu Uganda 94 D3
Guluwuru Island Australia 106 B1
Gulyayevskiye Koshki, Ostrova is Rus. Fed. 38 L1
Guma China see Pishan
Gumal r. Pak. 85 H4
Gumare Botswana 95 C5
Gumbaz Pak. 85 H4
Gumbinnen Rus. Fed. see Gusev
Gumdag Turkm. 84 D2
Gumel Nigeria 92 D3
Gümgüm Turkey see Varto
Gumla India 79 F5
Gummersbach Germany 49 H3
Gümüşhacıköy Turkey 86 D2
Gümüşhane Turkey 87 E2
Guna India 78 D4
Gunan China see Qijiang
Guna Terara mt. Eth. 82 E7
Gunbar Australia 108 B5
Gunbower Australia 108 B5
Güncang China 72 B2
Gund r. Tajik. see Gunt
Gundagai Australia 108 D5
Gundelsheim Germany 49 J5
Güney Turkey 55 M5
Güneydoğu Toroslar plat. Turkey 86 F3
Gunglilap Myanmar 66 B1
Gungu Dem. Rep. Congo 95 B4
Gunib Rus. Fed. 87 G2
Gunisao r. Canada 117 L4
Gunisao Lake Canada 117 L4
Gunnaur India 78 D3
Gunnbjørn Fjeld nunatak Greenland 115 P3
Gunnedah Australia 108 E3
Gunning Australia 108 D5
Gunnison U.S.A. 123 G5
Gunnison r. U.S.A. 125 I2
Güns Hungary see Kőszeg
Gunt r. Tajik. 85 H2
Guntakal India 80 C3
Güntersberge Germany 49 K3
Guntur India 80 D2
Gunung Gading National Park Malaysia 67 E7
Gunung Leuser National Park Indon. 67 B7
Gunung Lorentz National Park Indon. 65 J7
Gunung Niyut Reserve nature res. Indon. 67 E7
Gunung Palung National Park Indon. 64 E7
Gunungsitoli Indon. 67 B7
Günyüzü Turkey 86 C3
Gunza Angola see Porto Amboim
Günzburg Germany 43 M6
Gunzenhausen Germany 49 K5
Guo He r. China 73 H1
Guovdageaidnu Norway see Kautokeino
Guozhen China see Baoji
Gupis Jammu and Kashmir 78 C1
Gurbantünggüt Shamo des. China 76 G3
Gurdaspur India 78 C2
Gurdon U.S.A. 127 E5
Gurdzhaani Georgia see Gurjaani
Güre Turkey 55 M5
Gurgan Iran see Gorgān
Gurgaon India 78 D3
Gurgei, Jebel mt. Sudan 93 F3
Gurha India 78 B4
Guri, Embalse de resr Venez. 138 F2
Gurig National Park Australia 104 F2
Gurinhatã Brazil 141 A2
Gurjaani Georgia 87 G2
Gur Khar Iran 85 E4
Guro Moz. 95 D5
Guru China 79 G3
Gürün Turkey 86 E3
Gurupá Brazil 139 H4
Gurupi Brazil 139 I6
Gurupi r. Brazil 139 I4
Gurupi, Serra do hills Brazil 139 I4
Guru Sikhar mt. India 78 C4
Guruzala India 80 C2
Gur'yev Kazakh. see Atyrau
Gur'yevsk Rus. Fed. 41 L9
Gur'yevskaya Oblast' admin. div. Kazakh. see Atyrauskaya Oblast'
Gurz Afgh. 85 G3
Gusau Nigeria 92 D3
Güsen Germany 49 L2
Gusev Rus. Fed. 41 M9
Gushan China 71 A5
Gushgy Turkm. 85 F3
Gushi China 73 G1
Gusino Rus. Fed. 39 F5
Gusinoozersk Rus. Fed. 61 L4
Gus'-Khrustal'nyy Rus. Fed. 38 I5
Guspini Sardinia Italy 54 C5
Gustav Holm, Kap c. Greenland see Tasiilap Karra
Gustavo Sotelo Mex. 123 E7
Güsten Germany 49 L3
Gustine U.S.A. 124 C3
Güstrow Germany 43 N4
Güterfelde Germany 49 N2
Gütersloh Germany 49 I3
Guthrie AZ U.S.A. 125 I5
Guthrie KY U.S.A. 130 B5
Guthrie OK U.S.A. 127 D5
Guthrie TX U.S.A. 127 C5
Gutian Fujian China 73 H3
Gutian Fujian China 73 H3
Gutian Shuiku resr China 73 H3
Guting China see Yutai
Gutsuo China 79 F3
Guwahati India 79 G4
Guwēr Iraq 87 F3
Guwlumayak Turkm. see Kuuli-Mayak
Guxhagen Germany 49 J3
Guxian China 73 G3
▶Guyana country S. America 139 G2
south america 9, 136–137
Guyane Française terr. S. America see French Guiana
Guyang Hunan China see Guzhang
Guyang Nei Mongol China 69 K4
Guyenne reg. France 52 D4
Guy Fawkes River National Park Australia 108 F3
Guyi China see Sanjiang
Guymon U.S.A. 127 C4
Guyra Australia 108 E3
Guysborough Canada 119 J5
Guyuan Hebei China 69 L4
Guyuan Ningxia China 68 J5
Guzar Uzbek. 85 G2
Güzeloluk Turkey 81 B1
Güzelyurt Cyprus see Morfou
Guzhang China 73 F2
Guzhen China 73 H1
Guzhou China see Rongjiang
Guzmán Mex. 123 G7
Guzmán, Lago de l. Mex. 123 G7
Gvardeysk Rus. Fed. 41 L9
Gvasyugi Rus. Fed. 70 E3
Gwa Myanmar 66 A3
Gwabegar Australia 108 D3
Gwadar West Bay Pak. 85 F5
Gwaii Haanas National Park Reserve Canada 116 D4
Gwalior India 78 D4
Gwanda Zimbabwe 95 C6
Gwane Dem. Rep. Congo 94 C3
Gwardafuy, Gees c. Somalia 94 F2
Gwash Pak. 85 G4
Gwatar Bay Pak. 85 F5
Gwedaukkon Myanmar 66 A1
Gweebarra Bay Rep. of Ireland 47 D3
Gweedore Rep. of Ireland 47 D2
Gwelo Zimbabwe see Gweru
Gweru Zimbabwe 95 C5
Gweta Botswana 95 C6
Gwinner U.S.A. 126 D2
Gwoza Nigeria 92 E3
Gwydir r. Australia 108 D2
Gyablung China 72 B2
Gyaca China 72 B2
Gyagartang China 72 D1
Gya'gya China see Saga
Gyaijêpozhanggê China see Zhidoi
Gyai Qu r. China 72 B2
Gyairong China 72 C1
Gyaisi China see Jiulong
Gyali i. Greece 55 L6
Gyamotang China see Dêngqên
Gyamug China 78 E2
Gyandzha Azer. see Gäncä
Gyangkar China see Dinngyê
Gyangnyi Caka salt l. China 79 F2
Gyangrang China 79 F3
Gyangtse China see Gyangzê
Gyangzê China 79 G3
Gyaring China 72 C1
Gyaring Co l. China 79 G3
Gyaring Hu l. China 72 C1
Gyarishing India 72 B2
Gyaros i. Greece 55 K6
Gyarubtang China 72 B2
Gydan, Khrebet mts Rus. Fed. see Kolymskiy, Khrebet
Gydan Peninsula Rus. Fed. 60 I2
Gydanskiy Poluostrov pen. Rus. Fed. see Gydan Peninsula
Gyêgu China see Yushu
Gyêmdong China 72 B2
Gyigang China see Zayü
Gyimda China 72 B2
Gyirong Xizang China 79 F3
Gyirong Xizang China 79 F3
Gyiza China 72 B1
Gyldenløve Fjord inlet Greenland see Umiiviip Kangertiva
Gympie Australia 107 F5
Gyobingauk Myanmar 66 A3
Gyöngyös Hungary 43 Q7
Győr Hungary 54 G1
Gypsum Point Canada 116 H2
Gypsumville Canada 117 L5
Gyrfalcon Islands Canada 119 H2
Gytheio Greece 55 J6
Gyula Hungary 55 I1
Gyulafehérvár Romania see Alba Iulia
Gyümai China see Darlag
Gyumri Armenia 87 F2
Gyzylarbat Turkm. 84 E2
Gyzylbaydak Turkm. see Krasnoye Znamya
Gyzyletrek Turkm. 84 D2
Gzhatsk Rus. Fed. see Gagarin

H

Ha Bhutan 79 G4
Haa-Alif Atoll Maldives see Ihavandhippolhu Atoll
Ha'apai Group is Tonga 103 I3
Haapajärvi Fin. 40 N5
Haapavesi Fin. 40 N4
Haapsalu Estonia 41 M7
Ha 'Arava watercourse Israel/Jordan see 'Arabah, Wādī al
Ha'Arava, Naḥal watercourse Israel/Jordan see Jayb, Wādī al
Haarlem Neth. 48 E2
Haarlem S. Africa 96 F7
Haarstrang ridge Germany 49 H3
Hab r. Pak. 85 G5
Habahe China 76 G2
Habana Cuba see Havana
Habarane Sri Lanka 80 D4
Habarōn well Saudi Arabia 84 C6
Habaswein Kenya 94 D3
Habay Canada 116 G3
Habbān Yemen 82 G7
Ḥabbānīyah, Hawr al l. Iraq 87 F4
Hab Chauki Pak. 85 G5
Habiganj Bangl. 79 G4
Habra India 79 G5
Hachijō-jima i. Japan 71 E6
Hachinohe Japan 70 F4
Hachita U.S.A. 125 I6
Hacıköy Turkey see Çekerek
Hack, Mount Australia 107 B6
Hackberry U.S.A. 125 G4
Hackensack U.S.A. 131 H3
Ha Côi Vietnam 66 D2
Hacufera Moz. 95 D6
Hadabat al Budū plain Saudi Arabia 84 C6
Haḍabat al Jilf al Kabīr plat. Egypt see Jilf al Kabīr, Haḍabat al
Hadagalli India 80 B3
Hada Mountains Afgh. 85 G4
Hadapu China 72 E1
Hadayang China 70 B2
Ḥadd, Ra's al pt Oman 85 E6
Haddington U.K. 46 G5
Haddummati Atoll Maldives see Hadhdhunmathi Atoll
Haddunmahti Atoll Maldives see Hadhdhunmathi Atoll
Hadejia Nigeria 92 E3
Ḥadera Israel 81 B3
Ḥadera r. Israel 81 B3
Haderslev Denmark 41 F9
Hadhdhunmathi Atoll Maldives 77 D11
Hadhramaut reg. Yemen see Ḥaḍramawt
Hādī, Jabal al mts Jordan 81 C4
Hadım Turkey 86 D3
Hadleigh U.K. 45 H6
Hadong S. Korea 71 B6
Ḥadraj, Wādī watercourse Saudi Arabia 81 C4
Ḥaḍramawt reg. Yemen 94 E2
Hadranum Sicily Italy see Adrano
Hadrian's Wall tourist site U.K. 44 E3
Hadrumetum Tunisia see Sousse
Hadsund Denmark 41 G8
Hadyach Ukr. 39 G6
Haeju N. Korea 71 B5
Haeju-man b. N. Korea 71 B5
Haenam S. Korea 71 B6
Haenertsburg S. Africa 97 I2
Ha'erbin China see Harbin
Ḥafar al 'Atk well Saudi Arabia 84 B5
Ḥafar al Bāṭin Saudi Arabia 82 G4
Hafford Canada 117 J4
Hafik Turkey 86 E3
Ḥafirah, Qā' al salt pan Jordan 81 C4
Hafirat Nasah Saudi Arabia 84 B5
Hafizabad Pak. 85 I3
Haflong India 79 H4
Hafnarfjörður Iceland 40 [inset]
Hafren r. U.K. see Severn
Haft Gel Iran 84 C4
Hafursfjörður b. Iceland 40 [inset]
Haga Myanmar see Haka
Hagar Nish Plateau Eritrea 82 E6
▶Hagåtña Guam 65 K4
Capital of Guam.
Hagelberg hill Germany 49 M2
Hagen Germany 49 H3
Hagenow Germany 49 L1
Hagerhill U.S.A. 130 D5
Hagerstown U.S.A. 131 G4
Hagfors Sweden 41 H6
Haggin, Mount U.S.A. 122 E3
Hagi Japan 71 C6
Ha Giang Vietnam 66 D2
Ha Giao, Sông r. Vietnam 67 E4
Hagley U.K. 45 E6
Hag's Head hd Rep. of Ireland 47 C5
Hague U.S.A. 131 I2
Haguenau France 49 H6
Hahajima-rettō is Japan 71 F8
Hai Tanz. 93 G5
Hai'an China 73 F4
Haib watercourse Namibia 96 C5
Haibowan China see Wuhai
Haicheng Guangdong China see Haifeng
Haicheng Liaoning China 69 M4
Hai Dương Vietnam 66 D2
Haifa Israel 81 B3
Haifa, Bay of Israel 81 B3
Haifeng China 73 G4
Haig Australia 105 D7
Haiger Germany 49 I4
Haikakan country Asia see Armenia
Haikang China see Leizhou
Haikou China 73 F5
Ḥā'il Saudi Arabia 87 F6
Ḥā'il, Wādī watercourse Saudi Arabia 87 F6
Hailar China 69 L3
Hailey U.S.A. 122 E4
Haileybury Canada 118 F5
Hailin China 70 C3
Hailong China see Meihekou
Hailsham U.K. 45 H8
Hailun China 70 B3
Hailuoto Fin. 40 N4
Hainan i. China 73 F5
Hainan prov. China 73 F5
Hai-nang Myanmar 66 B2
Hainan Strait China 73 F5
Hainaut reg. France 48 D4
Haines U.S.A. 116 C3
Haines Junction Canada 116 B2
Haines Road Canada/U.S.A. 116 B2
Hainichen Germany 49 N4
Hainleite ridge Germany 49 K3
Hai Phong Vietnam 66 D2
Haiphong Vietnam see Hai Phong
Haiqing China 70 D3
Haitan Dao i. China 73 H3
▶Haiti country West Indies 133 J5
north america 9, 112–113
Haitou China 73 F5
Haiwee Reservoir U.S.A. 124 E3
Haiya Sudan 82 E6
Haiyan Qinghai China 68 I5
Haiyan Zhejiang China 73 I2
Haiyang China see Xiuning
Haiyang Dao i. China 71 A5
Haiyou China see Sanmen
Haizhou Wan b. China 73 H1
Hāj Ali Qoli, Kavīr-e salt l. Iran 84 D3
Hajdúböszörmény Hungary 55 I1
Hajeb El Ayoun Tunisia 54 C7
Ḥajhir mt. Yemen 83 H7
Haji Pak. 85 G4
Hajipur India 79 F4
Hajir reg. Saudi Arabia 84 C5
Ḥajjah Yemen 82 F6
Ḥājjīābād Fārs Iran 84 D4

Ingonish Canada 119 J5
Ingraj Bazar India 79 G4
Ingram U.S.A. 130 F5
Ingray Lake Canada 116 G1
Ingrid Christensen Coast Antarctica 148 E2
Ingwavuma S. Africa 97 K4
Ingwavuma r. S. Africa/Swaziland see Ngwavuma
Ingwiller France 49 H6
Inhaca Moz. 97 K3
Inhaca, Península pen. Moz. 97 K4
Inhambane Moz. 97 L2
Inhambane prov. Moz. 97 L2
Inhaminga Moz. 95 D5
Inharrime Moz. 97 L3
Inhassoro Moz. 95 D6
Inhaúmas Brazil 141 B1
Inhobim Brazil 141 C1
Inhumas Brazil 141 A2
Inis Rep. of Ireland see Ennis
Inis Córthaidh Rep. of Ireland see Enniscorthy
Inishark i. Rep. of Ireland 47 B4
Inishbofin i. Rep. of Ireland 47 B4
Inisheer i. Rep. of Ireland 47 C4
Inishkea North i. Rep. of Ireland 47 B3
Inishkea South i. Rep. of Ireland 47 B3
Inishmaan i. Rep. of Ireland 47 C4
Inishmore i. Rep. of Ireland 47 C4
Inishmurray i. Rep. of Ireland 47 D3
Inishowen pen. Rep. of Ireland 47 E2
Inishowen Head hd Rep. of Ireland 47 F2
Inishtrahull i. Rep. of Ireland 47 E2
Inishturk i. Rep. of Ireland 47 B4
Injune Australia 107 E5
Inkerman Australia 106 C3
Inklin Canada 116 C3
Inklin r. Canada 116 C3
Inkylap Turkm. 85 F2
Inland Kaikoura Range mts N.Z. 109 D6
Inland Sea Japan see Seto-naikai
Inlet U.S.A. 131 H2
Inn r. Europe 43 M7
Innaanganeq c. Greenland 115 L2
Innamincka Australia 107 C5
Innamincka Regional Reserve nature res. Australia 107 C5
Inndyr Norway 40 I3
Inner Sound sea chan. U.K. 46 D3
Innes National Park Australia 107 B7
Innisfail Australia 106 D3
Innisfail Canada 116 H4
Innokent'yevka Rus. Fed. 70 C2
Innoko r. U.S.A. 114 C3
Innsbruck Austria 43 M7
Innuksuak r. Canada 118 F2
Inny r. Rep. of Ireland 47 E4
Inocência Brazil 141 A2
Inongo Dem. Rep. Congo 94 B4
İnönü Turkey 55 N5
Inoucdjouac Canada see Inukjuak
Inowrocław Poland 43 Q4
In Salah Alg. 92 D2
Insch U.K. 46 G3

▶Inscription, Cape Austr. 106 B3
Most westerly point of Oceania.

Insein Myanmar 66 B3
Insterburg Rus. Fed. see Chernyakhovsk
Inta Rus. Fed. 37 S2
Interamna Italy see Teramo
Interlaken Switz. 52 H3
International Falls U.S.A. 126 E1
Interview Island India 67 A4
Intracoastal Waterway canal U.S.A. 127 E6
Intutu Peru 138 D4
Inubō-zaki pt Japan 71 F6
Inukjuak Canada 118 F2
Inuvik Canada 114 E3
Inveraray U.K. 46 D4
Inverbervie U.K. 46 G4
Invercargill N.Z. 109 B8
Inverell Australia 108 E2
Invergordon U.K. 46 E3
Inverkeithing U.K. 46 F4
Inverleigh Australia 106 C3
Invermay Canada 117 K5
Inverness Canada 119 J5
Inverness U.K. 46 E3
Inverness CA U.S.A. 124 B2
Inverness FL U.S.A. 129 D6
Inverurie U.K. 46 G3
Investigator Channel Myanmar 67 B4
Investigator Group is Australia 105 F8
Investigator Ridge sea feature Indian Ocean 145 O6
Investigator Strait Australia 107 B7
Inwood U.S.A. 131 F4
Inya Rus. Fed. 76 G1
Inyanga Zimbabwe see Nyanga
Inyangani mt. Zimbabwe 95 D5
Inyokern U.S.A. 124 E4
Inyo Mountains U.S.A. 124 D3
Inyonga Tanz. 95 D4
Inza Rus. Fed. 39 J5
Inzhavino Rus. Fed. 39 I5
Ioannina Greece 55 I5
Iokanga r. Rus. Fed. 38 H2
Iola U.S.A. 126 E4
Iolgo, Khrebet mts Rus. Fed. 76 G1
Iolotan' Turkm. see Yeloten
Iona Canada 119 J5
Iona i. U.K. 46 C4
Iona, Parque Nacional do nat. park Angola 95 B5
Ione U.S.A. 124 E2
Iongo Angola 95 B4
Ionia U.S.A. 130 C2
Ionian Islands Greece 55 H5
Ionian Sea Greece/Italy 54 H5
Ionioi Nisoi is Greece see Ionian Islands
Ios i. Greece 55 K6
Iowa state U.S.A. 126 E3
Iowa City U.S.A. 126 F3
Iowa Falls U.S.A. 126 E3
Ipameri Brazil 141 A2
Ipanema Brazil 141 C2
Iparía Peru 138 D5
Ipatinga Brazil 141 C2
Ipatovo Rus. Fed. 39 I7
Ipelegeng S. Africa 97 G4
Ipiales Col. 138 C3
Ipiaú Brazil 141 D1
Ipirá Brazil 141 D1
Ipiranga Brazil 141 A4
iPitoli S. Africa see Pretoria
Ipixuna r. Brazil 138 F5
Ipoh Malaysia 67 C6
Iporá Brazil 141 A2
Ippy Cent. Afr. Rep. 94 C3
İpsala Turkey 55 L4
Ipswich Australia 108 F1
Ipswich U.K. 45 I6
Ipswich U.S.A. 126 D2
Ipu Brazil 139 J4

▶Iqaluit Canada 115 L3
Territorial capital of Nunavut.

Iquique Chile 140 B2
Iquiri r. Brazil see Ituxi
Iquitos Peru 138 D4
Īrafshān reg. Iran 85 F5
Irai Brazil 140 F3
Irakleio Greece see Iraklion
Iraklion Greece 55 K7
Iramaia Brazil 141 C1
▶Iran country Asia 84 D3
asia 6, 58–59
Iran, Pegunungan mts Indon. 64 E6
Īrānshahr Iran 85 F5
Irapuato Mex. 132 D4
▶Iraq country Asia 87 F4
asia 6, 58–59
Irara Brazil 141 D1
Irati Brazil 141 A4
Irayel' Rus. Fed. 38 L2
Irazú, Volcán vol. Costa Rica 133 H7
Irbid Jordan 81 B3
Irbil Iraq see Arbīl
Irbit Rus. Fed. 60 H4
Irecê Brazil 139 J6

▶Ireland i. Rep. of Ireland/U.K. 47
4th largest island in Europe.

▶Ireland, Republic of country Europe 47 E4
europe 5, 34–35
Irema Dem. Rep. Congo 94 C4
Irgiz Kazakh. 76 B2
Irgiz r. Kazakh. 76 B2
Iri S. Korea see Iksan
Irian, Teluk b. Indon. see Cenderawasih, Teluk
Iriba Chad 93 F3
Īrī Dāgh mt. Iran 84 B2
Iriga Phil. 65 G4
Irîgui reg. Mali/Mauritania 92 C3
Iringa Tanz. 95 D4
Iriri r. Brazil 139 H4
Irish Free State country Europe see Ireland, Republic of
Irish Sea Rep. of Ireland/U.K. 47 G4
Irituia Brazil 139 I4
'Irj well Saudi Arabia 84 C5
Irkutsk Rus. Fed. 68 I2
Irma Canada 117 I4
Irmak Turkey 86 D3
Irminger Basin sea feature N. Atlantic Ocean 144 F2
Iron Baron Australia 107 B7
Irondequoit U.S.A. 131 G2
Iron Mountain U.S.A. 126 F2
Iron Mountain mt. U.S.A. 125 G3
Iron Range National Park Australia 106 C2
Iron River U.S.A. 126 F2
Ironton MO U.S.A. 126 F4
Ironton OH U.S.A. 130 D4
Ironwood Forest National Monument nat. park U.S.A. 125 H5
Iroquois r. U.S.A. 130 B3
Iroquois Falls Canada 118 E4
Irosin Phil. 65 G4
Irpen' Ukr. see Irpin'
Irpin' Ukr. 39 F6
'Irq al Ḥarūrī des. Saudi Arabia 84 B5
Irq al Maẓhūr des. Saudi Arabia 84 A5
'Irq Banbān des. Saudi Arabia 84 B5
'Irq Jahām des. Saudi Arabia 84 B5
Irrawaddy r. Myanmar 66 A4
Irrawaddy, Mouths of the Myanmar 66 A4
Irshad Pass Afgh./Jammu and Kashmir 85 I2
Irta Rus. Fed. 38 K3
Irthing r. U.K. 44 E4

▶Irtysh r. Kazakh./Rus. Fed. 76 E1
5th longest river in Asia. Part of the 2nd longest river in Asia (Ob'-Irtysh).

Irún Spain 53 F2
Iruña Spain see Pamplona
Iruñea Spain see Pamplona
Irvine U.K. 46 E5
Irvine CA U.S.A. 124 E5
Irvine KY U.S.A. 130 D5
Irvine Glacier Antarctica 148 L2
Irving U.S.A. 127 D5
Irvington U.S.A. 130 B5
Irwin r. Australia 105 A7
Irwinton U.S.A. 129 D5
Isa Nigeria 92 D3
Isaac r. Australia 106 E4
Isabel U.S.A. 126 C2
Isabela Phil. 65 G5
Isabela, Isla i. Galápagos Ecuador 138 [inset]
Isabelia, Cordillera mts Nicaragua 133 G6
Isabella Lake U.S.A. 124 D4
Isachsen, Cape Canada 115 H2
Ísafjarðardjúp est. Iceland 40 [inset]
Ísafjörður Iceland 40 [inset]
Isa Khel Pak. 85 H3
Isar r. Germany 49 M6
Isbister U.K. 46 [inset]
Ischia, Isola d' i. Italy 54 E4
Ise Japan 71 E6
Isère r. France 52 G4
Isère, Pointe pt Fr. Guiana 139 H2
Iserlohn Germany 49 H3
Isernhagen Germany 49 J2
Isernia Italy 54 F4
Ise-shima National Park Japan 71 E6
Ise-wan b. Japan 71 E6
Iseyin Nigeria 92 D4
Isfahan Iran see Eşfahān
Isfana Kyrg. 85 H2
Isheyevka Rus. Fed. 39 K5
Ishigaki Japan 69 M8
Ishikari-wan b. Japan 70 F4
Ishim r. Kazakh./Rus. Fed. 76 D1
Ishinomaki Japan 71 F5
Ishinomaki-wan b. Japan 69 Q5
Ishioka Japan 71 F5
Ishkoshim Tajik. 85 H2
Ishpeming U.S.A. 128 C2
Ishtikhon Uzbek. see Ishtykhan
Ishtragh Afgh. 85 H2
Ishtykhan Uzbek. 85 G2
Ishurdi Bangl. 79 G4
Ishwardi Bangl. see Ishurdi
Isiboro Sécure, Parque Nacional nat. park Bol. 138 E7
Isigny-sur-Mer France 45 F9
Işıklar Dağı mts Turkey 55 L4
Işıklı Turkey 55 M5
Isil'kul' Rus. Fed. 60 I4
Isipingo S. Africa 97 J5
Isiro Dem. Rep. Congo 94 C3
Isisford Australia 106 D5
Iskateley Rus. Fed. 38 L2
İskenderun Turkey 81 C1
İskenderun Körfezi b. Turkey 81 B1
İskilip Turkey 86 D2
Iskitim Rus. Fed. 60 J4
Iskŭr r. Bulg. 55 K3
Iskushuban Somalia 94 F2
Isla r. Scotland U.K. 46 F4
Isla r. Scotland U.K. 46 G3
Isla Gorge National Park Australia 106 E5
İslahiye Turkey 86 E3
Islamabad India see Anantnag

▶Islamabad Pak. 85 I3
Capital of Pakistan.

Islamgarh Pak. 85 H5
Islamkot Pak. 85 H5
Island r. Canada 116 F2
Ísland country Europe see Iceland
Island U.S.A. 130 B5
Island Falls U.S.A. 128 G2
Island Lagoon salt flat Australia 107 B6
Island Lake Canada 117 M4
Island Lake l. Canada 117 M4
Island Magee pen. U.K. 47 G3
Island Pond U.S.A. 131 J1
Islands, Bay of N.Z. 109 E2
Islay i. U.K. 46 C5

▶Isle of Man terr. Irish Sea 44 C4
United Kingdom Crown Dependency.
europe 5

Isle of Wight U.S.A. 131 G5
Isle Royale National Park U.S.A. 126 F2
Ismail Ukr. see Izmayil
Ismâ'ïlîya Egypt see Al Ismā'īlīyah
Ismâ'ïlîya governorate Egypt see Ismā'īlīyah
Ismā'īlīyah governorate Egypt 81 A4
Ismailly Azer. see İsmayıllı
İsmayıllı Azer. 87 H2
Isojoki Fin. 40 L5
Isoka Zambia 95 D5
Isokylä Fin. 40 O3
Isokyrö Fin. 40 M5
Isola di Capo Rizzuto Italy 54 G5
Ispahan Iran see Eşfahān
Isparta Turkey 55 N6
Isperikh Bulg. 55 L3
Ispikan Pak. 85 F5
İspir Turkey 87 F2
Ispisar Tajik. see Khŭjand
Isplinji Pak. 85 G4
▶Israel country Asia 81 B4
asia 6, 58–59
Israelite Bay Australia 105 C8
Isra'īl country Asia see Israel
Isselburg Germany 48 G3
Issia Côte d'Ivoire 92 C4
Issoire France 52 F4
Issyk-Kul' Kyrg. see Balykchy
Issyk-Kul', Ozero salt l. Kyrg. see Ysyk-Köl
Istalif Afgh. 85 H3

▶İstanbul Turkey 55 M4
2nd most populous city in Europe.

İstanbul Boğazı strait Turkey see Bosporus
Īstgāh-e Eznā Iran 84 C3
Istiaia Greece 55 J5
Istik r. Tajik. 85 I2
Istra pen. Croatia see Istria
Istres France 52 G5
Istria pen. Croatia 54 E2
Iswardi Bangl. see Ishurdi
Itabapoana r. Brazil 141 C3
Itaberá Brazil 141 A3
Itaberaba Brazil 141 C1
Itaberaí Brazil 141 A2
Itabira Brazil 141 C2
Itabirito Brazil 141 C3
Itabuna Brazil 141 D1
Itacajá Brazil 139 I5
Itacarambi Brazil 141 B1
Itacoatiara Brazil 139 G4
Itaetê Brazil 141 C1
Itagmatana Iran see Hamadān
Itaguaçu Brazil 141 C2
Itaí Brazil 141 A3
Itaiópolis Brazil 141 A4
Itäisen Suomenlahden kansallispuisto nat. park Fin. 41 O6
Itaituba Brazil 139 G4
Itajaí Brazil 141 A4
Itajubá Brazil 141 B3
Itajuipe Brazil 141 D1
Italia country Europe see Italy
Italia, Laguna l. Bol. 138 F6

▶Italy country Europe 54 E3
5th most populous country in Europe.
europe 5, 34–35

Itamarandiba Brazil 141 C2
Itambé Brazil 141 C1
Itambé, Pico de mt. Brazil 141 C2
It Amelân i. Neth. see Ameland
Itampolo Madag. 95 E6
Itanagar India 79 H4
Itanguari r. Brazil 141 B1
Itanhaém Brazil 141 B4
Itanhém Brazil 141 C2
Itanhém r. Brazil 141 D2
Itaobim Brazil 141 C2
Itapaci Brazil 141 A1
Itapajipe Brazil 141 A2
Itapebi Brazil 141 D1
Itapecerica Brazil 141 B3
Itapemirim Brazil 141 C3
Itaperuna Brazil 141 C3
Itapetinga Brazil 141 C1
Itapetininga Brazil 141 A3
Itapeva Brazil 141 A3
Itapeva, Lago l. Brazil 141 A5
Itapicuru Brazil 139 J6
Itapicuru, Serra de hills Brazil 139 I5
Itapicuru Mirim Brazil 139 J4
Itapipoca Brazil 139 K4
Itapira Brazil 141 B3
Itaporanga Brazil 141 A3
Itapuã Brazil 141 A5
Itaqui Brazil 140 E3
Itararé Brazil 141 A4
Itarsi India 78 D5
Itarumã Brazil 141 A2
Itatiba Brazil 141 B3
Itatuba Brazil 138 F5
Itaúna Brazil 141 B3
Itaúnas Brazil 141 D2
Itbayat i. Phil. 65 G2
Itchen Lake Canada 117 H1
Itea Greece 55 J5
Ithaca MI U.S.A. 130 C2
Ithaca NY U.S.A. 131 G2
It Hearrenfean Neth. see Heerenveen
iThekweni S. Africa see Durban
Ith Hils ridge Germany 49 J2
Ithrah Saudi Arabia 81 C4
Itihusa-yama mt. Japan 71 C6
Itilleq Greenland 115 M3
Itimbiri r. Dem. Rep. Congo 94 C3
Itinga Brazil 141 C2
Itiquira Brazil 139 H7
Itiruçu Brazil 141 C1
Itiúba, Serra de hills Brazil 139 K6
Itō Japan 71 E6
iTswane S. Africa see Pretoria
Ittiri Sardinia Italy 54 C4
Ittoqqortoormiit Greenland 115 P2
Itu Brazil 141 B3
Itu Abu Island Spratly Is 64 E4
Ituaçu Brazil 141 C1
Ituberá Brazil 141 D1
Ituí r. Brazil 138 D4
Ituiutaba Brazil 141 A2
Itumbiara Brazil 141 A2
Itumbiara, Barragem resr Brazil 141 A2
Ituni Guyana 139 G2
Itupiranga Brazil 139 I5
Ituporanga Brazil 141 A4
Iturama Brazil 141 A2
Iturbide Mex. 127 D7
Ituri r. Dem. Rep. Congo 94 C3
Iturup, Ostrov i. Rus. Fed. 70 G3
Itutinga Brazil 141 B3
Ituxi r. Brazil 138 F5
Ītyop'ia country Africa see Ethiopia
Itz r. Germany 49 K5
Itzehoe Germany 43 L4
Iuka U.S.A. 127 F5
Iul'tin Rus. Fed. 61 T3
Ivalo Fin. 40 O2
Ivalojoki r. Fin. 40 O2
Ivanava Belarus 41 N10
Ivanhoe Australia 108 B4
Ivanhoe U.S.A. 126 D2
Ivanhoe Lake Canada 117 J2
Ivankiv Ukr. 39 F6
Ivankovtsy Rus. Fed. 70 D2
Ivano-Frankivs'k Ukr. 39 E6
Ivano-Frankovsk Ukr. see Ivano-Frankivs'k
Ivanovka Rus. Fed. 70 B2
Ivanovo Belarus see Ivanava
Ivanovo tourist site Bulg. 55 K3
Ivanovo Rus. Fed. 38 I4
Ivanteyevka Rus. Fed. 39 K5
Ivantsevichi Belarus see Ivatsevichy
Ivatsevichy Belarus 41 N10
Ivaylovgrad Bulg. 55 L4
Ivdel' Rus. Fed. 37 S3
Ivittuut Greenland 115 N3
Iviza i. Spain see Ibiza
Ivory Coast country Africa see Côte d'Ivoire
Ivrea Italy 54 B2
İvrindi Turkey 55 L5
Ivris Ugheltekhili pass Georgia 87 G2
Ivry-la-Bataille France 48 B6
Ivugivik Canada see Ivujivik
Ivujivik Canada 115 K3
Ivyanyets Belarus 41 O10
Ivydale U.S.A. 130 E4
Iwaki Japan 71 F5
Iwaki-san vol. Japan 70 F4
Iwakuni Japan 71 D6
Iwamizawa Japan 70 F4
Iwo Nigeria 92 D4
Iwye Belarus 41 N10
Ixelles Belgium 48 E4
Ixiamas Bol. 138 E6
Ixmiquilpán Mex. 132 E4
Ixopo S. Africa 97 J6
Ixtlán Mex. 132 D4
Ixworth U.K. 45 H6
İyirmi Altı Bakı Komissarı Azer. see 26 Bakı Komissarı
Izabal, Lago de l. Guat. 132 G5
Izberbash Rus. Fed. 87 G2
Izegem Belgium 48 D4
Īzeh Iran 84 C4
Izgal Pak. 85 I3
Izhevsk Rus. Fed. 37 Q4
Izhma Respublika Komi Rus. Fed. 38 L2
Izhma Respublika Komi Rus. Fed. see Sosnogorsk
Izhma r. Rus. Fed. 38 L2
Izmail Ukr. see Izmayil
Izmayil Ukr. 55 M2
İzmir Turkey 55 L5
İzmir Körfezi g. Turkey 55 L5
İzmit Turkey see Kocaeli
İzmit Körfezi b. Turkey 55 M4
Izozog Bol. 138 F7
Izra' Syria 81 C3
Iztochni Rodopi mts Bulg. 55 K4
Izu-hantō pen. Japan 71 E6
Izuhara Japan 71 C6
Izumo Japan 71 D6

▶Izu-Ogasawara Trench sea feature N. Pacific Ocean 146 F3
5th deepest trench in the world.

Izu-shotō is Japan 71 E6
Izyaslav Ukr. 39 E6
Iz"yayu Rus. Fed. 38 M2
Izyum Ukr. 39 H6

↓ J

Jabal Dab Saudi Arabia 84 C6
Jabalón r. Spain 53 D4
Jabalpur India 78 D5
Jabbūl, Sabkhat al salt flat Syria 81 C2
Jabir reg. Oman 84 E6
Jabiru Australia 104 F3
Jablah Syria 81 B2
Jablanica Bos.-Herz. 54 G3
Jaboatão Brazil 139 L5
Jaboticabal Brazil 141 A3
Jabung, Tanjung pt Indon. 64 C7
Jacaraci Brazil 141 C1
Jacareacanga Brazil 139 G5
Jacareí Brazil 141 B3
Jacarézinho Brazil 141 A3
Jáchymov Czech Rep. 49 M4
Jacinto Brazil 141 C2
Jack r. Australia 106 D2
Jack Lake Canada 131 F1
Jackman U.S.A. 128 G2
Jacksboro U.S.A. 127 D5
Jackson Australia 108 D1
Jackson AL U.S.A. 129 C6
Jackson CA U.S.A. 124 C2
Jackson GA U.S.A. 129 D5
Jackson KY U.S.A. 130 D5
Jackson MI U.S.A. 130 C2
Jackson MN U.S.A. 126 E3

▶Jackson MS U.S.A. 127 F5
State capital of Mississippi.

Jackson NC U.S.A. 128 E4
Jackson OH U.S.A. 130 D4
Jackson TN U.S.A. 127 F4
Jackson WY U.S.A. 122 F4
Jackson, Mount Antarctica 148 L2
Jackson Head hd N.Z. 109 B6
Jacksonville AR U.S.A. 127 E5
Jacksonville FL U.S.A. 129 D6
Jacksonville IL U.S.A. 126 F4
Jacksonville NC U.S.A. 129 E5
Jacksonville OH U.S.A. 130 D4
Jacksonville TX U.S.A. 127 E6
Jacksonville Beach U.S.A. 129 D6
Jack Wade U.S.A. 114 D3
Jacmel Haiti 133 J5
Jacobabad Pak. 85 H4
Jacobina Brazil 139 J6
Jacob Lake U.S.A. 125 G3
Jacobsdal S. Africa 96 G5
Jacques-Cartier, Détroit de sea chan. Canada 119 I4
Jacques Cartier, Mont mt. Canada 119 I4
Jacques Cartier Passage Canada see Jacques-Cartier, Détroit de
Jacuí Brazil 141 B3
Jacuípe r. Brazil 139 K6
Jacunda Brazil 139 I4
Jaddangi India 80 D2
Jaddi, Ras pt Pak. 85 F5
Jadebusen b. Germany 49 I1
J. A. D. Jensen Nunatakker nunataks Greenland 115 N3
Jadotville Dem. Rep. Congo see Likasi
Jādū Libya 92 E1
Jaén Spain 53 E5
Ja'farābād Iran 84 E2
Jaffa, Cape Australia 107 B8
Jaffna Sri Lanka 80 C4
Jafr, Qa' al imp. l. Jordan 81 C4
Jagadhri India 78 D3
Jagalur India 80 C3
Jagatsinghapur India see Jagatsinghpur
Jagatsinghpur India 79 F5
Jagdalpur India 80 D2
Jagdaqi China 70 B2
Jagersfontein S. Africa 97 G5
Jaggang China 78 D2
Jaggayyapeta India 80 D2
Jaghin Iran 84 E5
Jagok Tso salt l. China see Urru Co
Jagsamka China see Luding
Jagst r. Germany 49 J5
Jagtial India 80 C2
Jaguariaíva Brazil 141 A4
Jaguaripe Brazil 141 D1
Jagüey Grande Cuba 129 D8
Jahanabad India see Jehanabad
Jahmah well Iraq 87 G5
Jahrom Iran 84 D4
Jaicós Brazil 139 J5
Jaigarh India 80 B2
Jailolo Gilolo i. Indon. see Halmahera
Jaintapur Bangl. see Jaintiapur
Jaintiapur Bangl. 79 H4
Jaipur India 78 C4
Jaipurhat Bangl. see Joypurhat
Jais India 79 E4
Jaisalmer India 78 B4
Jaisamand Lake India 78 C4
Jaitaran India 78 C4
Jaitgarh hill India 80 C1
Jajapur India see Jajpur
Jajarkot Nepal 83 N4
Jajce Bos.-Herz. 54 G2
Jajnagar state India see Orissa
Jajpur India 79 F5
Jakar Bhutan 79 G4

▶Jakarta Indon. 64 D8
Capital of Indonesia.

Jakes Corner Canada 116 C2
Jakhan India 78 B5
Jakin mt. Afgh. 85 G4
Jakkī Kowr Iran 85 F5
Jäkkvik Sweden 40 J3
Jakliat India 78 C3
Jakobshavn Greenland see Ilulissat
Jakobstad Fin. 40 M5
Jal U.S.A. 127 C5
Jalaid China see Inder
Jalājil Saudi Arabia 84 B5
Jalālābād Afgh. 85 H3
Jalal-Abad Kyrg. 76 D3
Jalālah al Baḥrīyah, Jabal plat. Egypt 86 C5
Jalāmid, Ḥazm al ridge Saudi Arabia 87 E5
Jalandhar India 78 C3
Jalapa Mex. 132 E5
Jalapa Enríquez Mex. see Jalapa
Jalapur Pirwala Pak. 85 H4
Jalasjärvi Fin. 40 M5
Jalaun India 78 D4
Jalawlā' Iraq 87 G4
Jaldak Afgh. 85 G4
Jaldrug India 80 C2
Jales Brazil 141 A3
Jalesar India 78 D4
Jalgaon India 78 C5
Jalībah Iraq 87 G5
Jalingo Nigeria 92 E4
Jallābī Iran 84 E5
Jalna India 80 B2
Jālo Iran 85 F5
Jalón r. Spain 53 F3
Jalor India see Jalore
Jalore India 78 C4
Jalpa Mex. 132 D4
Jalpaiguri India 79 G4
Jālū Libya 93 F2
Jalūlā Iraq see Jalawlā'
Jām reg. Iran 85 F3
▶Jamaica country West Indies 133 I5
north america 9, 112–113
Jamaica Channel Haiti/Jamaica 133 I5
Jamalpur Bangl. 79 G4
Jamalpur India 79 F4
Jamanxim r. Brazil 139 G4
Jambi Indon. 64 C7
Jambin Australia 106 E5
Jambo India 78 C4
Jambuair, Tanjung pt Indon. 67 B6
Jamda India 79 F5
Jamekunte India 80 C2
James r. N. Dakota/S. Dakota U.S.A. 126 D3
James r. VA U.S.A. 131 G5
James, Baie b. Canada see James Bay
Jamesabad Pak. 85 H5
James Bay Canada 118 E3
Jamesburg U.S.A. 131 H3
James Island Galápagos Ecuador see San Salvador, Isla
Jameson Land reg. Greenland 115 P2
James Peak N.Z. 109 B7
James Ranges mts Australia 105 F6
James Ross Island Antarctica 148 A2
James Ross Strait Canada 115 I3
Jamestown Australia 107 B7
Jamestown Canada see Wawa
Jamestown S. Africa 97 H6

▶Jamestown St Helena 144 H7
Capital of St Helena and Dependencies.

Jamestown ND U.S.A. 126 D2
Jamestown NY U.S.A. 130 F2
Jamestown TN U.S.A. 130 C5
Jamkhed India 80 B2
Jammu India 78 C2

▶Jammu and Kashmir terr. Asia 78 D2
Disputed territory (India/Pakistan).
asia 6, 58–59

Jamnagar India 78 B5
Jampur Pak. 85 H4
Jamrud Pak. 85 H3
Jämsä Fin. 41 N6
Jamsah Egypt 86 D6
Jämsänkoski Fin. 40 N6
Jamshedpur India 79 F5
Jamtari Nigeria 92 E4
Jamui India 79 F4
Jamuna r. Bangl. see Raimangal
Jamuna r. India see Yamuna
Janā i. Saudi Arabia 84 C5
Janāb, Wādī al watercourse Jordan 81 C4
Janakpur India 79 E5
Janaúba Brazil 141 C1
Jand Pak. 85 I3
Jandaia Brazil 141 A2
Jandaq Iran 84 D3
Jandola Pak. 85 H3
Jandowae Australia 108 E1
Janesville CA U.S.A. 124 C1
Janesville WI U.S.A. 126 F3
Jangada Brazil 141 A4
Jangal Iran 84 E3
Jangamo Moz. 97 L3
Jangaon India 80 C2
Jangipur India 79 G4
Jangnga Turkm. see Dzhanga
Jangngai Ri mts China 79 F2
Jänickendorf Germany 49 N2
Jani Khel Pak. 85 H3

▶Jan Mayen terr. Arctic Ocean 149 I2
Part of Norway.

Jan Mayen Fracture Zone sea feature Arctic Ocean 149 I2
Janos Mex. 123 F7
Jans Bay Canada 117 I4
Jansenville S. Africa 96 G7
Januária Brazil 141 B1
Janūb Sīnā' governorate Egypt 81 A5
Janûb Sînâ' governorate Egypt see Janūb Sīnā'
Janzar mt. Pak. 85 F5
Jaodar Pak. 85 F5
▶Japan country Asia 71 D5
asia 6, 58–59
Japan, Sea of N. Pacific Ocean 71 D5
Japan Alps National Park Japan see Chibu-Sangaku National Park
Japan Trench sea feature N. Pacific Ocean 146 F3
Japiim Brazil 138 D5
Japurá r. Brazil 138 F4
Japvo Mount India 79 H4
Jarābulus Syria 81 D1
Jaraguá Brazil 141 A1
Jaraguá, Serra mts Brazil 141 A4
Jaraguá do Sul Brazil 141 A4
Jarash Jordan 81 B3
Jarboesville U.S.A. see Lexington Park
Jardine River National Park Australia 106 C1
Jardinésia Brazil 141 A2
Jardinópolis Brazil 141 B3
Jargalang China 70 A4
Jargalant Bayanhongor Mongolia 76 I2
Jargalant Dornod Mongolia 69 L3
Jargalant Hovd Mongolia see Hovd
Jari r. Brazil 139 H4
Järna Sweden 41 J7
Jarocin Poland 43 P5
Jarosław Poland 39 D6
Järpen Sweden 40 H5
Jarqŭrghon Uzbek. see Dzharkurgan
Jarrettsville U.S.A. 131 G4
Jarú Brazil 138 F6
Jarud China see Lubei
Järvakandi Estonia 41 N7
Järvenpää Fin. 41 N6

Karluk U.S.A. 114 C4
Karlyuk Turkm. 85 G2
Karmala India 80 B2
Karmel, Har hill Israel see Carmel, Mount
Karmona Spain see Córdoba
Karmøy i. Norway 41 D7
Karmpur Pak. 85 I4
Karnabchul', Step' plain Uzbek. 85 G2
Karnafuli Reservoir Bangl. 79 H5
Karnal India 78 D3
Karnataka state India 80 B3
Karnavati India see Ahmadabad
Karnes City U.S.A. 127 D6
Karnobat Bulg. 55 L3
Karodi Pak. 85 G5
Karoi Zimbabwe 95 C5
Karokpi Myanmar 66 B4
Karo La pass China 79 G3
Karong India 79 H4
Karonga Malawi 95 D4
Karonie Australia 105 C7
Karoo National Park S. Africa 96 F7
Karoo Nature Reserve S. Africa 96 G7
Karoonda Australia 107 B7
Karora Eritrea 82 E6
Káros i. Greece see Keros
Karossa Indon. 64 F7
Karossa, Tanjung pt Indon. 104 B2
Karow Germany 49 M1
Karpasia pen. Cyprus 81 B2
Karpas Peninsula Cyprus see Karpasia
Karpathos i. Greece 55 L7
Karpathou, Steno sea chan. Greece 55 L6
Karpaty mts Europe see Carpathian Mountains
Karpenisi Greece 55 I5
Karpilovka Belarus see Aktsyabrski
Karpinsk Rus. Fed. 37 S4
Karpogory Rus. Fed. 38 J2
Karpuz r. Turkey 81 A1
Karratha Australia 104 B5
Karroo plat. S. Africa see Great Karoo
Karrychirla Turkm. see imeni Kerbabayeva
Kars Turkey 87 F2
Kärsämäki Fin. 40 N5
Kārsava Latvia 41 O8
Karshi Turkm. 87 I2
Karshi Uzbek. 85 G2
Karshinskaya Step' plain Uzbek. 85 G2
Karskiye Vorota, Proliv strait Rus. Fed. 60 G3
Karskoye More sea Rus. Fed. see Kara Sea
Karstädt Germany 49 L1
Karstula Fin. 40 N5
Karsu Turkey 81 C1
Karsun Rus. Fed. 39 J5
Kartal Turkey 55 M4
Kartaly Rus. Fed. 60 H4
Kartayel' Rus. Fed. 38 L2
Karttula Fin. 40 O5
Karumba Australia 106 C3
Karumbhar Island India 78 B5
Karun, Kūh-e hill Iran 84 C4
Kārūn, Rūd-e r. Iran 84 C4
Karuni Indon. 104 B2
Karur India 80 C4
Karvia Fin. 40 M5
Karviná Czech Rep. 43 Q6
Karwar India 80 B3
Karyagino Azer. see Füzuli
Karymskoye Rus. Fed. 69 K2
Karynzharyk, Peski des. Kazakh. 87 I2
Karystos Greece 55 K5
Kaş Turkey 55 M6
Kasa India 80 B2
Kasaba Turkey see Turgutlu
Kasabonika Canada 118 C3
Kasabonika Lake Canada 118 C3
Kasaï r. Dem. Rep. Congo 94 B4 also known as Kwa
Kasaï, Plateau du Dem. Rep. Congo 95 C4
Kasaji Dem. Rep. Congo 95 C5
Kasama Zambia 95 D5
Kasan Uzbek. 85 G2
Kasane Botswana 95 C5
Kasaragod India 80 B3
Kasargod India see Kasaragod
Kasargode India see Kasaragod
Kasatkino Rus. Fed. 70 C2
Kasba Lake Canada 117 K2
Kasba Tadla Morocco 50 C5
Kasenga Dem. Rep. Congo 95 C5
Kasengu Dem. Rep. Congo 95 C4
Kasese Dem. Rep. Congo 94 C4
Kasese Uganda 94 D3
Kasevo Rus. Fed. see Neftekamsk
Kasganj India 78 D4
Kasha China see Gonjo
Kashabowie Canada 118 C4
Kāshān Iran 84 C3
Kashary Rus. Fed. 39 I6
Kashechewan Canada 118 E3
Kashgar China see Kashi
Kashi China 76 E4
Kashihara Japan 71 D6
Kashima-nada b. Japan 71 F5
Kashin Rus. Fed. 38 H4
Kashipur India 78 D3
Kashira Rus. Fed. 39 H5
Kashiwazaki Japan 71 E5
Kashkarantsy Rus. Fed. 38 H2
Kashku'iyeh Iran 84 D4
Kāshmar Iran 84 E3
Kashmir terr. Asia see Jammu and Kashmir
Kashmir, Vale of reg. India 78 C2
Kashyukulu Dem. Rep. Congo 95 C4
Kasi India see Varanasi
Kasigar Afgh. 85 H3
Kasimov Rus. Fed. 39 I5
Kaskattama r. Canada 117 N3
Kaskinen Fin. 40 L5
Kas Klong i. Cambodia see Kŏng, Kaôh
Kaskö Fin. see Kaskinen
Kaslo Canada 116 G5
Kasmere Lake Canada 117 K3
Kasongo Dem. Rep. Congo 95 C4
Kasongo-Lunda Dem. Rep. Congo 95 B4
Kasos i. Greece 55 L7
Kaspīy Mangy Oypaty lowland Kazakh./Rus. Fed. see Caspian Lowland
Kaspiysk Rus. Fed. 87 G2
Kaspiyskiy Rus. Fed. see Lagan'
Kaspiyskoye More l. Asia/Europe see Caspian Sea
Kassa Slovakia see Košice
Kassala Sudan 82 E6
Kassandras, Akra pt Greece 55 J5
Kassandras, Kolpos b. Greece 55 J4
Kassel Germany 49 J3
Kasserine Tunisia 54 C7
Kastag Pak. 85 F5
Kastamonu Turkey 86 D2
Kastellaun Germany 49 H4
Kastelli Greece 55 J7
Kastéllion Greece see Kastelli
Kastellorizon i. Greece see Megisti
Kasterlee Belgium 48 E3
Kastoria Greece 55 I4
Kastornoye Rus. Fed. 39 H6
Kastsyukovichy Belarus 39 G5
Kasulu Tanz. 95 D4
Kasumkent Rus. Fed. 87 H2
Kasungu Malawi 95 D5
Kasungu National Park Malawi 95 D5
Kasur Pak. 85 I4
Katâdtlit Nunât terr. N. America see Greenland
Katahdin, Mount U.S.A. 128 G2
Kataklik Jammu and Kashmir 78 D2
Katako-Kombe Dem. Rep. Congo 94 C4
Katakwi Uganda 94 D3
Katana India 78 C5
Katangi India 78 D5
Katanning Australia 105 B8
Katavi National Park Tanz. 95 D4
Katawaz reg. Afgh. 85 G3
Katchall i. India 67 A6
Katea Dem. Rep. Congo 95 C4
Katerini Greece 55 J4
Katesh Tanz. 95 D4
Kate's Needle mt. Canada/U.S.A. 116 C3
Katete Zambia 95 D5
Katherîna, Gebel mt. Egypt see Kātrīnā, Jabal
Katherine Australia 104 F3
Katherine Gorge National Park Australia see Nitmiluk National Park
Kathi India 85 I6
Kathiawar pen. India 78 B5
Kathihar India see Katihar
Kathiraveli Sri Lanka 80 D4
Kathiwara India 78 C5
Kathleen Falls Australia 104 E3
Kathlehong S. Africa 97 I4

▶Kathmandu Nepal 79 F4
Capital of Nepal.

Kathu S. Africa 96 F4
Kathua India 78 C2
Kati Mali 92 C3
Katihar India 79 F4
Kati-Kati S. Africa 97 H7
Katima Mulilo Namibia 95 C5
Katimik Lake Canada 117 L4
Katiola Côte d'Ivoire 92 C4
Kā Tiritiri o te Moana mts N.Z. see Southern Alps
Katkop Hills S. Africa 96 E6
Katmai National Park and Preserve U.S.A. 114 C4
Katmandu Nepal see Kathmandu
Kato Achaïa Greece 55 I5
Kat O Chau Hong Kong China see Crooked Island
Kat O Hoi b. Hong Kong China see Crooked Harbour
Katoomba Australia 108 E4
Katowice Poland 43 Q5
Katoya India 79 G5
Katrancık Dağı mts Turkey 55 M6
Kātrīnā, Jabal mt. Egypt 86 D5
Katrine, Loch l. U.K. 46 E4
Katrineholm Sweden 41 J7
Katse Dam Lesotho 97 I5
Katsina Nigeria 92 D3
Katsina-Ala Nigeria 92 D4
Katsuura Japan 71 F6
Kattaktoc, Cap c. Canada 119 I2
Kattakurgan Uzbek. 85 G2
Kattamudda Well Australia 104 D5
Kattaqŭrghon Uzbek. see Kattakurgan
Kattasang Hills Afgh. 85 G3
Kattegat strait Denmark/Sweden 41 G8
Kattowitz Poland see Katowice
Katumbar India 78 D4
Katunino Rus. Fed. 38 J4
Katuri Pak. 85 H4
Katwa India see Katoya
Katwijk aan Zee Neth. 48 E2
Katzenbuckel hill Germany 49 J5
Kauai i. U.S.A. 123 [inset]
Kauai Channel U.S.A. 123 [inset]
Kaub Germany 49 H4
Kaufungen Germany 49 J3
Kauhajoki Fin. 40 M5
Kauhava Fin. 40 M5
Kaukauna U.S.A. 130 A1
Kaukkwè Hills Myanmar 66 B1
Kaukonen Fin. 40 N3
Kaula i. HI U.S.A. 123 [inset]
Kaulakahi Channel HI U.S.A. 123 [inset]
Kaumajet Mountains Canada 119 J2
Kaunakakai HI U.S.A. 123 [inset]
Kaunas Lith. 41 M9
Kaunata Latvia 41 O8
Kaundy, Vpadina depr. Kazakh. 87 I2
Kaunia Bangl. 79 G4
Kaura-Namoda Nigeria 92 D3
Kau Sai Chau i. Hong Kong China 73 [inset]
Kaustinen Fin. 40 M5
Kautokeino Norway 40 M2
Kau-ye Kyun i. Myanmar 67 B5
Kavadarci Macedonia 55 J4
Kavak Turkey 86 E2
Kavaklıdere Turkey 55 M6
Kavala Greece 55 K4
Kavalas, Kolpos b. Greece 55 K4
Kavalerovo Rus. Fed. 70 D3
Kavali India 80 D3
Kavār Iran 84 D4
Kavaratti India 80 B4
Kavaratti atoll India 80 B4
Kavarna Bulg. 55 M3
Kavendou, Mont mt. Guinea 92 B3
Kaveri r. India 80 C4
Kavīr Iran 84 C3
Kavīr salt flat Iran 84 D3
Kavīr, Dasht-e des. Iran 84 D3
Kavīr Kūshk well Iran 84 E3
Kavkasioni mts Asia/Europe see Caucasus
Kawa Myanmar 66 B3
Kawagama Lake Canada 131 F1
Kawagoe Japan 71 E6
Kawaguchi Japan 71 E6
Kawaihae HI U.S.A. 123 [inset]
Kawaikini, Mount HI U.S.A. 123 [inset]
Kawakawa N.Z. 109 E2
Kawambwa Zambia 95 C4
Kawana Zambia 95 C5
Kawardha India 78 E5
Kawartha Lakes Canada 131 F1
Kawasaki Japan 71 E6
Kawau Island N.Z. 109 E3
Kawawachikamach Canada 119 I3
Kawdut Myanmar 66 B4
Kawerau N.Z. 109 F4
Kawhia N.Z. 109 E4
Kawhia Harbour N.Z. 109 E4
Kawich Peak U.S.A. 124 E3
Kawich Range mts U.S.A. 124 E3
Kawinaw Lake Canada 117 L4
Kaw Lake U.S.A. 127 D4
Kawlin Myanmar 66 A2
Kawm Umbū Egypt 82 D5
Kawngmeum Myanmar 66 B2
Kawthaung Myanmar 67 B5
Kaxgar China see Kashi
Kaxgar He r. China 76 E4
Kax He r. China 76 F3
Kaxtax Shan mts China 79 E1
Kaya Burkina 92 C3
Kayadibi Turkey 86 E3
Kayan r. Indon. 64 F6
Kayankulam India 80 C4
Kayar India 80 C2
Kaycee U.S.A. 122 G4
Kaydak, Sor dry lake Kazakh. 87 I1
Kaydanovo Belarus see Dzyarzhynsk
Kayembe-Mukulu Dem. Rep. Congo 95 C4
Kayenta U.S.A. 125 H3
Kayes Mali 92 B3
Kaymaz Turkey 55 N5
Kaynar Kazakh. 76 E2
Kaynar Turkey 86 E3
Kayseri Turkey 86 D3
Kayuyu Dem. Rep. Congo 94 C4
Kayyngdy Kyrg. 76 D3
Kazach'ye Rus. Fed. 61 O2
Kazakh Azer. see Qazax
Kazakhskaya S.S.R. country Asia see Kazakhstan
Kazakhskiy Melkosopochnik plain Kazakh. 76 D1
Kazakhskiy Zaliv b. Kazakh. 87 I2

▶Kazakhstan country Asia 74 F2
4th largest country in Asia.
asia 6, 58–59

Kazakhstan Kazakh. see Aksay
Kazakstan country Asia see Kazakhstan
Kazan r. Canada 117 M2
Kazan' Rus. Fed. 38 K5
Kazandzhik Turkm. see Gazandzhyk
Kazanka r. Rus. Fed. 38 K5
Kazanlı Turkey 81 B1
Kazanlŭk Bulg. 55 K3
Kazan-rettō is Japan see Volcano Islands
Kazatin Ukr. see Kozyatyn

▶Kazbek mt. Georgia/Rus. Fed. 39 J8
4th highest mountain in Europe.

Kaz Dağı mts Turkey 55 L5
Kāzerūn Iran 84 C4
Kazhim Rus. Fed. 38 K3
Kazidi Tajik. see Qozideh
Kazi Magomed Azer. see Qazımämmäd
Kazincbarcika Hungary 39 D6
Kaziranga National Park India 79 H4
Kazret'i Georgia 87 G2
Kaztalovka Kazakh. 37 P6
Kazy Turkm. 84 E2
Kazym r. Rus. Fed. 37 T3
Kazymskiy Mys Rus. Fed. 37 T3
Kea i. Greece 55 K6
Keady U.K. 47 F3
Keams Canyon U.S.A. 125 H4
Kéamu i. Vanuatu see Anatom
Kearney U.S.A. 126 D3
Kearny U.S.A. 125 H5
Keban Turkey 86 E3
Keban Barajı resr Turkey 86 E3
Kébémèr Senegal 92 B3
Kebili Tunisia 50 F5
Kebīr, Nahr al r. Lebanon/Syria 81 B2
Kebkabiya Sudan 93 F3
Kebnekaise mt. Sweden 40 K3
Kebock Head hd U.K. 46 C2
K'ebrī Dehar Eth. 94 E3
Kech reg. Pak. 85 F5
Kechika r. Canada 116 E3
Keçiborlu Turkey 55 N6
Kecskemét Hungary 55 H1
K'eda Georgia 87 F2
Kėdainiai Lith. 41 M9
Kedairu Passage Fiji see Kadavu Passage
Kedgwick Canada 119 I5
Kedian China 73 G2
Kedong China 70 B3
Kedva r. Rus. Fed. 38 L2
Kędzierzyn-Koźle Poland 43 Q5
Keele r. Canada 116 E1
Keele Peak Canada 116 D2
Keeler U.S.A. 124 E3
Keeley Lake Canada 117 I4
Keeling Islands terr. Indian Ocean see Cocos Islands
Keen, Mount hill U.K. 46 G4
Keene CA U.S.A. 124 D4
Keene KY U.S.A. 130 C5
Keene NH U.S.A. 131 I2
Keene OH U.S.A. 130 E3
Keepit, Lake resr Australia 108 E3
Keep River National Park Australia 104 E3
Keerbergen Belgium 48 E3
Keer-weer, Cape Australia 106 C2
Keetmanshoop Namibia 96 C4
Keewatin Canada 117 M5
Kefallinia i. Greece see Cephalonia
Kefallonia i. Greece see Cephalonia
Kefamenanu Indon. 104 D2
Kefe Ukr. see Feodosiya
Keffi Nigeria 92 D4
Keflavík Iceland 40 [inset]
Kegalla Sri Lanka 80 D5
Kegen Kazakh. 76 E3
Keglo, Baie de b. Canada 119 I2
Keg River Canada 116 G3
Kegul'ta Rus. Fed. 39 J7
Kehra Estonia 41 N7
Kehsi Mansam Myanmar 66 B2
Keighley U.K. 44 F5
Keila Estonia 41 N7
Keimoes S. Africa 96 E5
Keitele Fin. 40 O5
Keitele l. Fin. 40 O5
Keith Australia 107 C8
Keith U.K. 46 G3
Keith Arm b. Canada 116 F1
Kejimkujik National Park Canada 119 I5
Kekaha HI U.S.A. 123 [inset]
Kékes mt. Hungary 43 R7
Kekri India 78 C4
K'elafo Eth. 94 E3
Kelai i. Maldives 80 B5
Kelang Malaysia 67 C7
Kelberg Germany 48 G4
Kelheim Germany 49 L6
Kelibia Tunisia 54 D6
Kelifskiy Uzboy marsh Turkm. 85 F2
Kelīrī Iran 84 E5
Kelkheim (Taunus) Germany 49 I4
Kelkit Turkey 87 E2
Kelkit r. Turkey 86 E2
Kéllé Congo 94 B4
Keller Lake Canada 116 F2
Kellett, Cape Canada 114 F2
Kelleys Island U.S.A. 130 D3
Kelliher Canada 117 K5
Kelloselkä Fin. 40 P3
Kells Rep. of Ireland 47 F4
Kells r. U.K. 47 F3
Kelly U.S.A. 130 B5
Kelly Lake Canada 116 E1
Kelly Range hills Australia 105 C6
Kelmė Lith. 41 M9
Kelmis Belgium 48 G4
Kelo Chad 93 E4
Kelowna Canada 116 G5
Kelp Head hd Canada 116 E5
Kelseyville U.S.A. 124 B2
Kelso U.K. 46 G5
Kelso CA U.S.A. 125 F4
Kelso WA U.S.A. 122 C3
Keluang Malaysia 67 C7
Kelvington Canada 117 K4
Kem' Rus. Fed. 38 G2
Kem' r. Rus. Fed. 38 G2
Ke Macina Mali see Massina
Kemah Turkey 86 E3
Kemaliye Turkey 86 E3
Kemalpaşa Turkey 55 L5
Kemano Canada 116 E4
Kembé Cent. Afr. Rep. 94 C3
Kemeneshát hills Hungary 54 G1
Kemer Antalya Turkey 55 N6
Kemer Muğla Turkey 55 M6
Kemer Barajı resr Turkey 55 M6
Kemerovo Rus. Fed. 60 J4
Kemi Fin. 40 N4
Kemijärvi Fin. 40 O3
Kemijärvi l. Fin. 40 O3
Kemijoki r. Fin. 40 N4
Kemiö Fin. see Kimito
Kemir Turkm. 84 D2
Kemmerer U.S.A. 122 F4
Kemnath Germany 49 L5
Kemnay U.K. 46 G3
Kemp Coast reg. Antarctica see Kemp Land
Kempele Fin. 40 N4
Kempen Germany 48 G3
Kempisch Kanaal canal Belgium 48 F3
Kemp Land reg. Antarctica 148 D2
Kemp Peninsula Antarctica 148 A2
Kemp's Bay Bahamas 129 E7
Kempsey Australia 108 F3
Kempt, Lac l. Canada 118 G5
Kempten (Allgäu) Germany 43 M7
Kempton U.S.A. 130 B3
Kempton Park S. Africa 97 I4
Kemptville Canada 131 H1
Kemujan i. Indon. 64 E8
Ken r. India 78 E4
Kenai U.S.A. 114 C3
Kenai Fiords National Park U.S.A. 114 C4
Kenai Mountains U.S.A. 114 C4
Kenamu r. Canada 119 K3
Kenansville U.S.A. 129 E5
Kenâyis, Râs el pt Egypt see Ḥikmah, Ra's al
Kenbridge U.S.A. 131 F5
Kendal U.K. 44 E4
Kendall Australia 108 F3
Kendall, Cape Canada 115 J3
Kendallville U.S.A. 130 C3
Kendari Indon. 65 G7
Kendawangan Indon. 64 E7
Kendégué Chad 93 E3
Kendrapara India 79 F5
Kendraparha India see Kendrapara
Kendrick Peak U.S.A. 125 H4
Kendujhar India see Keonjhar
Kendujhargarh India see Keonjhar
Kendyrli-Kayasanskoye, Plato plat. Kazakh. 87 I2
Kendyrlisor, Solonchak salt l. Kazakh. 87 I2
Kenebri Australia 108 D3
Kenedy U.S.A. 127 D6
Kenema Sierra Leone 92 B4
Keneurgench Turkm. 83 I1
Kenge Dem. Rep. Congo 95 B4
Keng Lap Myanmar 66 C2
Kengtung Myanmar 66 B2
Kenhardt S. Africa 96 E5
Kéniéba Mali 92 B3
Kénitra Morocco 50 C5
Kenmare Rep. of Ireland 47 C6
Kenmare U.S.A. 126 C1
Kenmare River inlet Rep. of Ireland 47 B6
Kenmore U.S.A. 131 F2
Kenn Germany 48 G5
Kenna U.S.A. 127 C5
Kennebec U.S.A. 126 D3
Kennebec r. U.S.A. 128 G2
Kennebunkport U.S.A. 131 J2
Kennedy, Cape U.S.A. see Canaveral, Cape
Kennedy Range National Park Australia 105 A6
Kennedy Town Hong Kong China 73 [inset]
Kenner U.S.A. 127 F6
Kennet r. U.K. 45 G7
Kenneth Range hills Australia 105 B5
Kennett U.S.A. 127 F4
Kennewick U.S.A. 122 D3
Kenn Reef Australia 106 F4
Kenogami r. Canada 118 D4
Keno Hill Canada 116 C2
Kenora Canada 117 M5
Kenosha U.S.A. 130 B2
Kenozero, Ozero l. Rus. Fed. 38 H3
Kent r. U.K. 44 E4
Kent OH U.S.A. 130 E3
Kent TX U.S.A. 127 B6
Kent VA U.S.A. 130 E5
Kent WA U.S.A. 122 C3
Kentani S. Africa 97 I7
Kent Group is Australia 107 [inset]
Kentland U.S.A. 130 B3
Kenton U.S.A. 130 D3
Kent Peninsula Canada 114 H3
Kentucky state U.S.A. 130 C5
Kentucky Lake U.S.A. 127 F4
▶Kenya country Africa 94 D3
africa 7, 90–91

▶Kenya, Mount Kenya 94 D4
2nd highest mountain in Africa.

Kenyir, Tasik resr Malaysia 67 C6
Keokuk U.S.A. 126 F3
Keoladao National Park India 78 D4
Keonjhar India 79 F5
Keonjhargarh India see Keonjhar
Keosauqua U.S.A. 126 F3
Keowee, Lake resr U.S.A. 129 D5
Kepina r. Rus. Fed. 38 I2
Keppel Bay Australia 106 E4
Kepsut Turkey 55 M5
Kera India 79 F5
Kerāh Iran 84 E4
Kerala state India 80 B4
Kerang Australia 108 A5
Kerava Fin. 41 N6
Kerba Alg. 53 G5
Kerbela Iraq see Karbalā'
Kerben Kyrg. 76 D3
Kerbi r. Rus. Fed. 70 E1
Kerbodot, Lac l. Canada 119 I3
Kerch Ukr. 86 E1
Kerchem'ya Rus. Fed. 38 L3
Kerema P.N.G. 65 L8
Keremeos Canada 116 G5
Kerempe Burun pt Turkey 86 D2
Keren Eritrea 82 E6
Kerewan Gambia 92 B3
Kergeli Turkm. 84 E2
Kerguélen, Îles is Indian Ocean 145 M9
Kerguelen Islands Indian Ocean see Kerguélen, Îles
Kerguelen Plateau sea feature Indian Ocean 145 M9
Kericho Kenya 94 D4
Kerikeri N.Z. 109 D2
Kerimäki Fin. 40 P6
Kerinci, Gunung vol. Indon. 64 C7
Kerinci Seblat National Park Indon. 64 C7
Kerintji vol. Indon. see Kerinci, Gunung
Keriya He watercourse China 68 E5
Keriya Shankou pass China 79 E2
Kerken Germany 48 G3
Kerkenah, Îles is Tunisia 54 D7
Kerki Turkm. 85 G2
Kerkichi Turkm. 85 G2
Kerkinitis, Limni l. Greece 55 J4
Kérkira i. Greece see Corfu
Kerkouane tourist site Tunisia 54 D6
Kerkyra Greece 55 H5
Kerkyra i. Greece see Corfu
Kerma Sudan 82 D6
Kermadec Islands S. Pacific Ocean 103 I5

▶Kermadec Trench sea feature S. Pacific Ocean 146 I8
4th deepest trench in the world.

Kermān Iran 84 E4
Kerman U.S.A. 124 C3
Kermān Desert Iran 84 E4
Kermānshāh Iran 84 B3
Kermānshāhān Iran 84 D4
Kermine Uzbek. see Navoi
Kermit U.S.A. 127 C6
Kern r. U.S.A. 124 D4
Kernertut, Cap c. Canada 119 I2
Keros i. Greece 55 K6
Keros Rus. Fed. 38 L3
Kérouané Guinea 92 C4
Kerpen Germany 48 G4
Kerr, Cape Antarctica 148 H1
Kerrobert Canada 117 I5
Kerrville U.S.A. 127 D6
Kerry Head hd Rep. of Ireland 47 C5
Kerteminde Denmark 41 G9
Kerulen r. China/Mongolia see Herlen Gol
Kerur India 80 B2
Keryneia Cyprus see Kyrenia
Kerzaz Alg. 92 C2
Kerzhenets r. Rus. Fed. 38 J4
Kesagami Lake Canada 118 E4
Kesälahti Fin. 40 P6
Keşan Turkey 55 L4
Keşap Turkey 39 H8
Kesariya India 79 F4
Kesennuma Japan 71 F5
Keshan China 70 B2
Keshem Afgh. 85 H2
Keshena U.S.A. 130 A1
Keshendeh-ye Bala Afgh. 85 G2
Keshod India 78 B5
Keshvar Iran 84 C3
Keskin Turkey 86 D3
Keskozero Rus. Fed. 38 G3
Kesova Gora Rus. Fed. 38 H4
Kessel Neth. 48 G3
Kestell S. Africa 97 I5
Kesten'ga Rus. Fed. 40 Q4
Kestilä Fin. 40 O4
Keswick Canada 130 F1
Keswick U.K. 44 D4
Keszthely Hungary 54 G1
Ketapang Indon. 64 E7
Ketchikan U.S.A. 116 D4
Keti Bandar Pak. 85 G5
Ketmen', Khrebet mts China/Kazakh. 76 F3
Kettering U.K. 45 G6
Kettering U.S.A. 130 C4
Kettle r. Canada 116 G5
Kettle Creek r. U.S.A. 131 G3
Kettle Falls U.S.A. 122 D2
Kettleman City U.S.A. 124 D3
Kettle River Range mts U.S.A. 122 D2
Keuka U.S.A. 131 G2
Keuka Lake U.S.A. 131 G2
Keumgang, Mount N. Korea see Kumgang-san
Keumsang, Mount N. Korea see Kumgang-san
Keuruu Fin. 40 N5
Kew Turks and Caicos Is 129 F8
Kewanee U.S.A. 126 F3
Kewaunee U.S.A. 130 B1
Keweenaw Bay U.S.A. 126 F2
Keweenaw Peninsula U.S.A. 126 F2
Keweenaw Point U.S.A. 128 C2
Key, Lough l. Rep. of Ireland 47 D3
Keyala Sudan 93 G4
Keyano Canada 119 G3
Keya Paha r. U.S.A. 126 D3
Key Harbour Canada 118 E5
Keyihe China 70 A2
Key Largo U.S.A. 129 D7
Keymir Turkm. see Kemir
Keynsham U.K. 45 E7
Keyser U.S.A. 131 F4
Keystone Lake U.S.A. 127 D4
Keystone Peak U.S.A. 125 H6
Keysville U.S.A. 131 F5
Keytesville U.S.A. 126 E4
Keyvy, Vozvyshennost' hills Rus. Fed. 38 H2
Key West U.S.A. 129 D7
Kez Rus. Fed. 37 Q4
Kezi Zimbabwe 95 C6
Kgalagadi admin. dist. Botswana 96 E3
Kgalazadi admin. dist. Botswana see Kgalagadi
Kgatlen admin. dist. Botswana see Kgatleng
Kgatleng admin. dist. Botswana 97 H3
Kgomofatshe Pan salt pan Botswana 96 E2
Kgoro Pan salt pan Botswana 96 G3
Kgotsong S. Africa 97 H4
Khabab Syria 81 C3
Khabar Iran 84 D4
Khabarikha Rus. Fed. 38 L2
Khabarovsk Rus. Fed. 70 D2
Khabarovskiy Kray admin. div. Rus. Fed. 70 D2
Khabarovsk Kray admin. div. Rus. Fed. see Khabarovskiy Kray
Khabary Rus. Fed. 68 D2
Khabis Iran see Shahdād
Khabody Pass Afgh. 85 F3
Khachmas Azer. see Xaçmaz
Khadar, Jabal mt. Oman 84 E6
Khadro Pak. 85 H5
Khafs Banbān well Saudi Arabia 84 B5
Khagaria India 79 F4
Khagrachari Bangl. 79 G5
Khagrachhari Bangl. see Khagrachari
Khairgarh Pak. 85 H4
Khairpur Punjab Pak. 85 I4
Khairpur Sindh Pak. 85 H5
Khāiz, Kūh-e mt. Iran 84 C4
Khaja Du Koh hill Afgh. 85 G2
Khajuha India 78 E4
Khāk-e Jabbar Afgh. 85 H3
Khakhea Botswana 96 F3
Khakīr Afgh. 85 G3
Khak-rēz Afgh. 85 G4
Khakriz reg. Afgh. 85 G4
Khalach Turkm. 85 G2
Khalajestan reg. Iran 84 C3
Khalatse Jammu and Kashmir 78 D2
Khalifat mt. Pak. 85 G4
Khalīj Surt g. Libya see Sirte, Gulf of
Khalilabad India 79 E4
Khalīlī Iran 84 D5
Khalkabad Turkm. 85 F1
Khalkhāl Iran 84 C2
Khálki i. Greece see Chalki
Khalkis Greece see Chalkida
Khallikot India 80 E2
Khalturin Rus. Fed. see Orlov
Khamar-Daban, Khrebet mts Rus. Fed. 68 I2
Khamaria India 80 D1
Khambhat India 78 C5
Khambhat, Gulf of India 80 A2
Khamgaon India 80 C1
Khamir Yemen 82 F6
Khamis Mushayț Saudi Arabia 82 F6
Khamkkeut Laos 66 D3
Khamma well Saudi Arabia 84 B5
Khammam India 80 D2
Khammouan Laos see Muang Khammouan
Khamra Rus. Fed. 61 M3
Khamseh reg. Iran 84 C3
Khan Afgh. 85 H3
Khan, Nam r. Laos 66 C3
Khānābād Afgh. 85 H2
Khān al Baghdādī Iraq 87 F4
Khān al Mashāhidah Iraq 87 G4
Khān al Muşallā Iraq 87 G4
Khanapur India 80 B2
Khān ar Raḥbah Iraq 87 G5
Khanasur Pass Iran/Turkey 87 G3
Khanbalik China see Beijing
Khānch Iran 84 B2
Khandu India 85 I6
Khandwa India 78 D5
Khandyga Rus. Fed. 61 O3
Khanewal Pak. 85 H4
Khanh Dương Vietnam 67 E4
Khan Hung Vietnam see Soc Trăng
Khaniá Greece see Chania
Khānī Yek Iran 84 D4
Khanka, Lake China/Rus. Fed. 70 D3
Khanka, Ozero l. China/Rus. Fed. see Khanka, Lake
Khankendi Azer. see Xankändi
Khanna India 78 D3
Khannā, Qā' salt pan Jordan 81 C3
Khanpur Pak. 85 H4
Khān Ruḥābah Iraq see Khān ar Raḥbah
Khansar Pak. 85 H4
Khān Shaykhūn Syria 81 C2
Khantayskoye, Ozero l. Rus. Fed. 60 K3
Khanthabouli Laos see Savannakhét
Khanty-Mansiysk Rus. Fed. 60 H3
Khān Yūnis Gaza 81 B4
Khanzi admin. dist. Botswana see Ghanzi
Khao Ang Rua Nai Wildlife Reserve nature res. Thai. 67 C4
Khao Banthat Wildlife Reserve nature res. Thai. 67 B6
Khao Chum Thong Thai. 67 B5
Khaoen Si Nakarin National Park Thai. 67 B4
Khao Laem National Park Thai. 66 B4
Khao Laem Reservoir Thai. 66 B4
Khao Luang National Park Thai. 67 B5

Khao Pu-Khao Ya National Park Thai. 67 B6
Khao Soi Dao Wildlife Reserve nature res. Thai. 67 C4
Khao Sok National Park Thai. 67 B5
Khao Yai National Park Thai. 67 C4
Khapalu Jammu and Kashmir 76 E4
Khaptad National Park Nepal 78 E3
Kharabali Rus. Fed. 39 J7
Kharagpur Bihar India 79 F4
Kharagpur W. Bengal India 79 F5
Khārān r. Iran 83 I4
Kharari India see Abu Road
Kharda India 80 B2
Khardi India 78 C6
Khardong La pass Jammu and Kashmir see Khardung La
Khardung La pass Jammu and Kashmir 78 D2
Kharez Ilias Afgh. 85 F3
Kharfiyah Iraq 87 G5
Kharga Egypt see Al Khārijah
Kharga r. Rus. Fed. 70 D1
Khârga, El Wâhât el oasis Egypt see Khārijah, Wāḥāt al
Kharga Oasis Egypt see Khārijah, Wāḥāt al
Khārg Islands Iran 84 C4
Khargon India 78 C5
Khari r. Rajasthan India 78 C4
Khari r. Rajasthan India 78 C4
Kharian Pak. 85 I3
Khariar India 80 D1
Khārijah, Wāḥāt al oasis Egypt 82 D5
Kharīm, Gebel hill Egypt see Kharīm, Jabal
Kharīm, Jabal hill Egypt 81 A4
Kharkhara r. India 78 E5
Kharkiv Ukr. 39 H6
Khar'kov Ukr. see Kharkiv
Khār Kūh mt. Iran 84 D4
Kharlovka Rus. Fed. 38 H1
Kharlu Rus. Fed. 40 Q6
Kharmanli Bulg. 55 K4
Kharoti reg. Afgh. 85 H3
Kharovsk Rus. Fed. 38 I4
Kharsia India 79 E5

▶Khartoum Sudan 82 D6
Capital of Sudan.

Kharwar reg. Afgh. 85 H3
Khasardag, Gora mt. Turkm. 84 E2
Khasav'yurt Rus. Fed. 87 G2
Khash Afgh. 85 F4
Khāsh Iran 85 F4
Khash Desert Afgh. 85 F4
Khashgort Rus. Fed. 37 T2
Khashm el Girba Sudan 82 E7
Khashm Ṣana' Saudi Arabia 86 E6
Khash Rūd r. Afgh. 85 F4
Khashuri Georgia 87 F2
Khasi Hills India 79 G4
Khaskovo Bulg. 55 K4
Khatanga Rus. Fed. 61 L2
Khatanga, Gulf of Rus. Fed. see Khatangskiy Zaliv
Khatangskiy Zaliv b. Rus. Fed. 61 L2
Khatayakha Rus. Fed. 38 M2
Khatinza Pass Pak. 85 H2
Khatmat al Malāha Oman 84 E5
Khatyrka Rus. Fed. 61 S3
Khavda India 78 B5
Khawak Pass Afgh. 85 H3
Khayamnandi S. Africa 97 G6
Khaybar Saudi Arabia 82 E4
Khayelitsha S. Africa 96 D8
Khayrān, Ra's al pt Oman 84 E6
Khê Bo Vietnam 66 D3
Khedrī Iran 84 E3
Khefa Israel see Haifa
Khehuene, Ponta pt Moz. 97 L2
Khemis Miliana Alg. 53 H5
Khemmarat Thai. 66 D3
Khenchela Alg. 54 B7
Khenifra Morocco 50 C5
Kherāmeh Iran 84 D4
Kherrata Alg. 53 I5
Kherreh Iran 84 D5
Khersan r. Iran 84 C4
Kherson Ukr. 55 O1
Kheta r. Rus. Fed. 61 L2
Kheyrābād Iran 84 D4
Khezerābād Iran 84 D2
Khiching India 79 F5
Khilok Rus. Fed. 69 K2
Khilok r. Rus. Fed. 69 J2
Khinganskiy Zapovednik nature res. Rus. Fed. 70 C2
Khinsar Pak. 85 H5
Khíos i. Greece see Chios
Khirbat Isrīyah Syria 81 C2
Khitai Pass Aksai Chin 78 D2
Khīyāv Iran 84 B2
Khiytola Rus. Fed. 41 P6
Khlevnoye Rus. Fed. 39 H5
Khlong, Mae r. Thai. 67 C4
Khlong Saeng Wildlife Reserve nature res. Thai. 67 B5
Khlong Wang Chao National Park Thai. 66 B3
Khlung Thai. 67 C4
Khmel'nik Ukr. see Khmil'nyk
Khmel'nitskiy Ukr. see Khmel'nyts'kyy
Khmel'nyts'kyy Ukr. 39 E6
Khmer Republic country Asia see Cambodia
Khmil'nyk Ukr. 39 E6
Khoai, Hon i. Vietnam 67 D5
Khobda Kazakh. 76 A1
Khobi Georgia 87 F2
Khodā Āfarid spring Iran 84 E3
Khodzha-Kala Turkm. 84 E2
Khodzhambaz Turkm. 85 G2
Khodzhaolen Turkm. 84 E2
Khodzhapir'yakh, Gora mt. Uzbek. 85 G2
Khodzhent Tajik. see Khŭjand
Khodzheyli Uzbek. 76 A3
Khojand Tajik. see Khŭjand
Khokhowe Pan salt pan Botswana 96 E3
Khokhropar Pak. 85 H5
Khoksar India 78 D2
Kholm Afgh. 85 G2
Kholm Poland see Chełm
Kholm Rus. Fed. 38 F4
Kholmsk Rus. Fed. 70 F3
Kholon Israel see Ḥolon
Khomas admin. reg. Namibia 96 C2
Khomas Highland hills Namibia 96 B2
Khomeyn Iran 84 C3
Khomeynīshahr Iran 84 C3
Khong, Mae Nam r. Laos/Thai. 66 D4 see Mekong
Khonj Iran 84 D5
Khonj, Kūh-e mts Iran 84 D5
Khon Kaen Thai. 66 C3
Khon Kriel Cambodia see Phumĭ Kon Kriel
Khonsa India 79 H4
Khonuu Rus. Fed. 61 P3
Khoper r. Rus. Fed. 39 I6
Khor Rus. Fed. 70 D3
Khor r. Rus. Fed. 70 D3
Khorat Plateau Thai. 66 C3
Khorda India see Khurda
Khordha India see Khurda
Khoreyver Rus. Fed. 38 M2
Khorinsk Rus. Fed. 69 J2
Khorixas Namibia 95 B6
Khormūj, Kūh-e mt. Iran 84 C4
Khorog Tajik. see Khorugh
Khorol Rus. Fed. 70 D3
Khorol Ukr. 39 G6
Khoroslū Dāgh hills Iran 84 B2
Khorramābād Iran 84 C3
Khorramshahr Iran 84 C4
Khorugh Tajik. 85 H2
Khosheutovo Rus. Fed. 39 J7
Khosūyeh Iran 84 D4
Khotan China see Hotan
Khouribga Morocco 50 C5
Khovaling Tajik. 85 H2
Khowrjān Iran 84 D4
Khowrnag, Kūh-e mt. Iran 84 D3
Khowst reg. Afgh./Pak. 85 H3
Khreum Myanmar 66 A2
Khroma r. Rus. Fed. 61 P2
Khromtau Kazakh. 76 A1
Khrushchev Ukr. see Svitlovods'k
Khrysokhou Bay Cyprus see Chrysochou Bay
Khrystynivka Ukr. 39 F6
Khuar Pak. 85 I3
Khudumelapye Botswana 96 G2
Khudzhand Tajik. see Khŭjand
Khufaysah, Khashm al hill Saudi Arabia 84 B6
Khugiana Afgh. see Pirzada
Khuis Botswana 96 E4
Khŭjand Tajik. 76 C3
Khŭjayli Uzbek. see Khodzheyli
Khu Khan Thai. 67 D4
Khulays Saudi Arabia 82 E5
Khulkhuta Rus. Fed. 39 J7
Khulm r. Afgh. 85 G2
Khulna Bangl. 79 G5
Khulo Georgia 87 F2
Khuma S. Africa 97 H4
Khŭm Batheay Cambodia 67 D5
Khunayzīr, Jabal al mts Syria 81 C2
Khūnīk Bālā Iran 84 E3
Khūnīnshahr Iran see Khorramshahr
Khunjerab Pass China/Jammu and Kashmir 78 C1
Khunsar Iran 84 C3
Khun Yuam Thai. 66 B3
Khūr Iran 84 E3
Khūran sea chan. Iran 84 D5
Khurays Saudi Arabia 82 G4
Khurd, Koh-i- mt. Afgh. 85 G3
Khurda India 80 E1
Khurdha India see Khurda
Khurja India 78 D3
Khurmalik Afgh. 85 F3
Khurmuli Rus. Fed. 70 E2
Khūrrāb Iran 84 D4
Khurz Iran 84 D3
Khushab Pak. 85 I3
Khushalgarh Pak. 85 H3
Khushshah, Wādī al watercourse Jordan/Saudi Arabia 81 C5
Khust Ukr. 39 D6
Khutse Game Reserve nature res. Botswana 96 G2
Khutsong S. Africa 97 H4
Khutu r. Rus. Fed. 70 E2
Khuzdar Pak. 85 G5
Khvāf Iran 85 F3
Khvāf reg. Iran 85 F3
Khvājeh Iran 84 B2
Khvalynsk Rus. Fed. 39 K5
Khvodrān Iran 84 D4
Khvord Nārvan Iran 84 E3
Khvormūj Iran 84 C4
Khvoy Iran 84 B2
Khvoynaya Rus. Fed. 38 G4
Khwaja Amran mt. Pak. 85 G4
Khwaja Muhammad Range mts Afgh. 85 H2
Khyber Pass Afgh./Pak. 85 H3
Kiama Australia 108 E5
Kiamichi r. U.S.A. 127 E5
Kiangsi prov. China see Jiangxi
Kiangsu prov. China see Jiangsu
Kiantajärvi l. Fin. 40 P4
Kīāseh Iran 84 D2
Kiatassuaq i. Greenland 115 M2
Kibaha Tanz. 95 D4
Kibali r. Dem. Rep. Congo 94 C3
Kibangou Congo 94 B4
Kibaya Tanz. 95 D4
Kiboga Uganda 94 D3
Kibombo Dem. Rep. Congo 94 C4
Kibondo Tanz. 94 D4
Kibre Mengist Eth. 93 G4
Kibris country Asia see Cyprus
Kibungo Rwanda 94 D4
Kičevo Macedonia 55 I4
Kichmengskiy Gorodok Rus. Fed. 38 J4
Kiçik Qafqaz mts Asia see Lesser Caucasus
Kicking Horse Pass Canada 116 G5
Kidal Mali 92 D3
Kidderminster U.K. 45 E6
Kidepo Valley National Park Uganda 94 D3
Kidira Senegal 92 B3
Kidmang Jammu and Kashmir 78 D2
Kidnappers, Cape N.Z. 109 F4
Kidsgrove U.K. 45 E5
Kiel Germany 43 M3
Kiel U.S.A. 130 A2
Kiel Canal Germany 43 L3
Kielce Poland 43 R5
Kielder Water resr U.K. 44 E3
Kieler Bucht b. Germany 43 M3
Kienge Dem. Rep. Congo 95 C5
Kierspe Germany 49 H3

▶Kiev Ukr. 39 F6
Capital of Ukraine.

Kiffa Mauritania 92 B3
Kifisia Greece 55 J5
Kifrī Iraq 87 G4

▶Kigali Rwanda 94 D4
Capital of Rwanda.

Kiği Turkey 87 F3
Kiglapait Mountains Canada 119 J2
Kigoma Tanz. 95 C4
Kihlanki Fin. 40 M3
Kihniö Fin. 40 M5
Kiholo HI U.S.A. 123 [inset]
Kiiminki Fin. 40 N4
Kii-sanchi mts Japan 71 D6
Kii-suidō sea chan. Japan 71 D6
Kikerino Rus. Fed. 41 P7
Kikinda Serb. and Mont. 55 I2
Kikki Pak. 85 F5
Kikládhes is Greece see Cyclades
Kiknur Rus. Fed. 38 J4
Kikonai Japan 70 F4
Kikori P.N.G. 65 K8
Kikori r. P.N.G. 65 K8
Kikwit Dem. Rep. Congo 95 B4
Kilafors Sweden 41 J6
Kilar India 78 D2
Kilauea HI U.S.A. 123 [inset]
Kilauea Crater HI U.S.A. 123 [inset]
Kilchu N. Korea 70 C4
Kilcoole Rep. of Ireland 47 F4
Kilcormac Rep. of Ireland 47 E4
Kilcoy Australia 108 F1
Kildare Rep. of Ireland 47 F4
Kil'dinstroy Rus. Fed. 40 R2
Kilemary Rus. Fed. 38 J4
Kilembe Dem. Rep. Congo 95 B4
Kilfinan U.K. 46 D5
Kilgore U.S.A. 127 E5
Kilham U.K. 44 E3
Kilia Ukr. see Kiliya
Kılıç Dağı mt. Syria/Turkey see Aqra', Jabal al
Kilifi Kenya 94 D4
Kilik Pass China/Jammu and Kashmir 78 C1

▶Kilimanjaro vol. Tanz. 94 D4
Highest mountain in Africa.
africa 88–89

Kilimanjaro National Park Tanz. 94 D4
Kilinailau Islands P.N.G. 102 F2
Kilindoni Tanz. 95 D4
Kilingi-Nõmme Estonia 41 N7
Kilis Turkey 81 C1
Kilis prov. Turkey 81 C1
Kiliya Ukr. 55 M2
Kilkee Rep. of Ireland 47 C5
Kilkeel U.K. 47 G3
Kilkenny Rep. of Ireland 47 E5
Kilkhampton U.K. 45 C8
Kilkis Greece 55 J4
Killala Rep. of Ireland 47 C3
Killala Bay Rep. of Ireland 47 C3
Killaloe Rep. of Ireland 47 D5
Killam Canada 117 I4
Killarney N.T. Australia 104 E4
Killarney Qld Australia 108 F2
Killarney Canada 118 E5
Killarney Rep. of Ireland 47 C5
Killarney National Park Rep. of Ireland 47 C6
Killary Harbour b. Rep. of Ireland 47 C4
Killbuck U.S.A. 130 E3
Killeen U.S.A. 127 D6
Killenaule Rep. of Ireland 47 E5
Killimor Rep. of Ireland 47 D4
Killin U.K. 46 E4
Killinchy U.K. 47 G3
Killini mt. Greece see Kyllini
Killinick Rep. of Ireland 47 F5
Killorglin Rep. of Ireland 47 C5
Killurin Rep. of Ireland 47 F5
Killybegs Rep. of Ireland 47 D3
Kilmacrenan Rep. of Ireland 47 E2
Kilmaine Rep. of Ireland 47 C4
Kilmallock Rep. of Ireland 47 D5
Kilmaluag U.K. 46 C3
Kilmarnock U.K. 46 E5
Kilmelford U.K. 46 D4
Kil'mez' Rus. Fed. 38 K4
Kil'mez' r. Rus. Fed. 38 K4
Kilmona Rep. of Ireland 47 D6
Kilmore Australia 108 B6
Kilmore Quay Rep. of Ireland 47 F5
Kilosa Tanz. 95 D4
Kilpisjärvi Fin. 40 L2
Kilrea U.K. 47 F3
Kilrush Rep. of Ireland 47 C5
Kilsyth U.K. 46 E5
Kiltan atoll India 80 B4
Kiltullagh Rep. of Ireland 47 D4
Kilwa Masoko Tanz. 95 D4
Kilwinning U.K. 46 E5
Kim U.S.A. 127 C4
Kimba Australia 105 G8
Kimba Congo 94 B4
Kimball U.S.A. 126 C3
Kimball, Mount U.S.A. 114 D3
Kimbe P.N.G. 102 F2
Kimberley S. Africa 96 G5
Kimberley Plateau Australia 104 D4
Kimberley Range hills Australia 105 B6
Kimch'aek N. Korea 71 C4
Kimch'ŏn S. Korea 71 C5
Kimhae S. Korea 71 C6
Kimhandu mt. Tanz. 95 D4
Kimi Greece see Kymi
Kimito Fin. 41 M6
Kimmirut Canada 115 L3
Kimolos i. Greece 55 K6
Kimovsk Rus. Fed. 39 H5
Kimpese Dem. Rep. Congo 95 B4
Kimpoku-san mt. Japan see Kinpoku-san
Kimry Rus. Fed. 38 H4
Kimsquit Canada 116 E4
Kimvula Dem. Rep. Congo 95 B4
Kinabalu, Gunung mt. Sabah Malaysia 64 F5
Kinango Kenya 95 D4
Kinaskan Lake Canada 116 D3
Kinbasket Lake Canada 116 G4
Kinbrace U.K. 46 F2
Kincaid Canada 117 J5
Kincardine Canada 130 E1
Kincardine U.K. 46 F4
Kinchega National Park Australia 107 C7
Kincolith Canada 116 D4
Kinda Dem. Rep. Congo 95 C4
Kindat Myanmar 66 A2
Kinde U.S.A. 130 D2
Kinder Scout hill U.K. 44 F5
Kindersley Canada 117 I5
Kindia Guinea 92 B3
Kindu Dem. Rep. Congo 94 C4
Kinel' Rus. Fed. 39 K5
Kineshma Rus. Fed. 38 I4
Kingaroy Australia 108 E1
King Christian Island Canada 115 H2
King City U.S.A. 124 C3
King Edward VII Land pen. Antarctica see Edward VII Peninsula
Kingfield U.S.A. 131 J1
Kingfisher U.S.A. 127 D5
King George U.S.A. 131 G4
King George, Mount Canada 122 E2
King George Island Antarctica 148 A2
King George Islands Canada 118 F2
King George Islands Fr. Polynesia see Roi Georges, Îles du
King Hill hill Australia 104 C5
Kingisepp Rus. Fed. 41 P7
King Island Australia 107 [inset]
King Island Canada 116 E4
King Island Myanmar see Kadan Kyun
Kingisseppa Estonia see Kuressaare
Kinglake National Park Australia 108 B6
King Leopold and Queen Astrid Coast Antarctica 148 E2
King Leopold Range National Park Australia 104 D4
King Leopold Ranges hills Australia 104 D4
Kingman U.S.A. 125 F4

▶Kingman Reef terr. N. Pacific Ocean 146 J5
United States Unincorporated Territory.

King Mountain Canada 116 D3
King Mountain hill U.S.A. 127 C6
Kingoonya Australia 107 A6
King Peak Antarctica 148 L1
King Peninsula Antarctica 148 K2
Kingri Pak. 85 H4
Kings r. Rep. of Ireland 47 E5
Kings r. CA U.S.A. 124 C3
Kings r. NV U.S.A. 122 D4
King Salmon U.S.A. 114 C4
Kingsbridge U.K. 45 D8
Kingsburg U.S.A. 124 D3
Kings Canyon National Park U.S.A. 124 D3
Kingscliff Australia 108 F2
Kingscote Australia 107 B7
Kingscourt Rep. of Ireland 47 F4
King Sejong research station Antarctica 148 A2
King's Lynn U.K. 45 H6
Kingsmill Group is Kiribati 103 H2
Kingsnorth U.K. 45 H7
King Sound b. Australia 104 C4
Kings Peak U.S.A. 125 H1
Kingsport U.S.A. 128 D4
Kingston Australia 107 [inset]
Kingston Canada 131 G1

▶Kingston Jamaica 133 I5
Capital of Jamaica.

▶Kingston Norfolk I. 103 G4
Capital of Norfolk Island.

Kingston MO U.S.A. 126 E4
Kingston NY U.S.A. 131 H3
Kingston OH U.S.A. 130 D4
Kingston PA U.S.A. 131 H3
Kingston Peak U.S.A. 125 F4
Kingston South East Australia 107 B8
Kingston upon Hull U.K. 44 G5

▶Kingstown St Vincent 133 L6
Capital of St Vincent.

Kingstree U.S.A. 129 E5
Kingsville U.S.A. 127 D7
Kingswood U.K. 45 E7
Kington U.K. 45 D6
Kingungi Dem. Rep. Congo 95 B4
Kingurutik r. Canada 119 J2
Kingussie U.K. 46 E3
King William U.S.A. 131 G5
King William Island Canada 115 I3
King William's Town S. Africa 97 H7
Kingwood TX U.S.A. 127 E6
Kingwood WV U.S.A. 130 F4
Kinloch N.Z. 109 B7
Kinloss U.K. 46 F3
Kinmen Taiwan see Chinmen
Kinmen i. Taiwan see Chinmen Tao
Kinmount Canada 131 F1
Kinna Sweden 41 H8
Kinnegad Rep. of Ireland 47 E4
Kinneret, Yam l. Israel see Galilee, Sea of
Kinniyai Sri Lanka 80 D4
Kinnula Fin. 40 N5
Kinoje r. Canada 118 E3
Kinoosao Canada 117 K3
Kinpoku-san mt. Japan 71 E5
Kinross U.K. 46 F4
Kinsale Rep. of Ireland 47 D6
Kinsale U.S.A. 131 G4

▶Kinshasa Dem. Rep. Congo 95 B4
Capital of the Democratic Republic of Congo and 3rd most populous city in Africa.

Kinsley U.S.A. 126 D4
Kinsman U.S.A. 130 E3
Kinston U.S.A. 129 E5
Kintore U.K. 46 G3
Kintyre pen. U.K. 46 D5
Kinu Myanmar 66 A2
Kinushseo r. Canada 118 E3
Kinyeti mt. Sudan 93 G4
Kinzig r. Germany 49 I4
Kiowa CO U.S.A. 122 G5
Kiowa KS U.S.A. 127 D4
Kipahigan Lake Canada 117 K4
Kiparissia Greece see Kyparissia
Kipawa, Lac l. Canada 118 F5
Kipling Canada 117 K5
Kipling Station Canada see Kipling
Kipnuk U.S.A. 114 B4
Kiptopeke U.S.A. 131 H5
Kipungo Angola see Quipungo
Kipushi Dem. Rep. Congo 95 C5
Kirakira Solomon Is 103 G3
Kirandul India 80 D2
Kirchdorf Germany 49 I2
Kirchheim-Bolanden Germany 49 I5
Kirchheim unter Teck Germany 49 J6
Kircubbin U.K. 47 G3
Kirdimi Chad 93 E3
Kirenga r. Rus. Fed. 69 J1
Kirensk Rus. Fed. 61 L4
Kireyevsk Rus. Fed. 39 H5
Kirghizia country Asia see Kyrgyzstan
Kirghiz Range mts Kazakh./Kyrg. 76 D3
Kirgizskaya S.S.R. country Asia see Kyrgyzstan
Kirgizskiy Khrebet mts Kazakh./Kyrg. see Kirghiz Range
Kirgizstan country Asia see Kyrgyzstan
Kiri Dem. Rep. Congo 94 B4
Kiribati country Pacific Ocean 146 I6
Kırıkhan Turkey 81 C1
Kırıkkale Turkey 86 D3
Kirillov Rus. Fed. 38 H4
Kirillovo Rus. Fed. 70 F3
Kirin China see Jilin
Kirin prov. China see Jilin
Kirinda Sri Lanka 80 D5
Kirinyaga mt. Kenya see Kenya, Mount
Kirishi Rus. Fed. 38 G4
Kirishima-Yaku National Park Japan 71 C7
Kirishima-yama vol. Japan 71 C7
Kiritimati atoll Kiribati 147 J5
Kiriwina Islands P.N.G. see Trobriand Islands
Kırkağaç Turkey 55 L5
Kirk Bulāg Dāgi mt. Iran 84 B2
Kirkby U.K. 44 E5
Kirkby in Ashfield U.K. 45 F5
Kirkby Lonsdale U.K. 44 E4
Kirkby Stephen U.K. 44 E4
Kirkcaldy U.K. 46 F4
Kirkcolm U.K. 46 D6
Kirkcudbright U.K. 46 E6
Kirkenær Norway 41 H6
Kirkenes Norway 40 Q2
Kirkfield Canada 131 F1
Kirkintilloch U.K. 46 E5
Kirkkonummi Fin. 41 N6
Kirkland U.S.A. 125 G4
Kirkland Lake Canada 118 E4
Kırklareli Turkey 55 L4
Kirklin U.S.A. 130 B3
Kirk Michael Isle of Man 44 C4
Kirkoswald U.K. 44 E4
Kirkpatrick, Mount Antarctica 148 H1
Kirksville U.S.A. 126 E3
Kirkūk Iraq 87 G4
Kirkwall U.K. 46 G2
Kirkwood S. Africa 97 G7
Kirman Iran see Kermān
Kirn Germany 49 H5
Kirov Kaluzhskaya Oblast' Rus. Fed. 39 G5
Kirov Kirovskaya Oblast' Rus. Fed. 38 K4
Kirova, Zaliv b. Azer. see Qızılağac Körfäzi
Kirovabad Azer. see Gäncä
Kirovabad Tajik. see Panj
Kirovakan Armenia see Vanadzor
Kirovo Ukr. see Kirovohrad
Kirovo-Chepetsk Rus. Fed. 38 K4
Kirovo-Chepetskiy Rus. Fed. see Kirovo-Chepetsk
Kirovograd Ukr. see Kirovohrad
Kirovohrad Ukr. 39 G6
Kirovsk Leningradskaya Oblast' Rus. Fed. 38 F4
Kirovsk Murmanskaya Oblast' Rus. Fed. 40 R3
Kirovsk Turkm. see Babadaykhan
Kirovs'ke Ukr. 86 D1
Kirovskiy Rus. Fed. 70 D3
Kirovskoye Ukr. see Kirovs'ke
Kırpaşa pen. Cyprus see Karpasia
Kirpili Turkm. 84 E2
Kirriemuir U.K. 46 F4
Kirs Rus. Fed. 38 L4
Kirsanov Rus. Fed. 39 I5
Kırşehir Turkey 86 D3
Kirthar National Park Pak. 85 G5
Kirthar Range mts Pak. 85 G5
Kirtland U.S.A. 125 I3
Kirtorf Germany 49 J4
Kiruna Sweden 40 L3
Kirundu Dem. Rep. Congo 94 C4
Kirwan Escarpment Antarctica 148 B2
Kiryū Japan 71 E5
Kisa Sweden 41 I8
Kisama, Parque Nacional de nat. park Angola see Quiçama, Parque Nacional do
Kisandji Dem. Rep. Congo 95 B4
Kisangani Dem. Rep. Congo 94 C3
Kisantu Dem. Rep. Congo 95 B4
Kisar i. Indon. 104 D2
Kisaran Indon. 67 B7
Kiselevsk Rus. Fed. 68 F2
Kisel'ovka Rus. Fed. 70 E2
Kishanganj India 79 F4
Kishangarh Madhya Pradesh India 78 D4
Kishangarh Rajasthan India 78 B4
Kishangarh Rajasthan India 78 C4
Kishangarh Rajasthan India 78 D4
Kishi Nigeria 92 D4
Kishinev Moldova see Chişinău
Kishkenekol' Kazakh. 75 G1
Kishoreganj Bangl. 79 G4
Kishorganj Bangl. see Kishoreganj
Kisi Nigeria see Kishi
Kisii Kenya 94 D4
Kiska Island U.S.A. 61 S4
Kiskittogisu Lake Canada 117 L4
Kiskitto Lake Canada 117 L4
Kiskunfélegyháza Hungary 55 H1
Kiskunhalas Hungary 55 H1
Kiskunsági nat. park Hungary 55 H1
Kislovodsk Rus. Fed. 87 F2
Kismaayo Somalia 94 E4
Kismayu Somalia see Kismaayo
Kisoro Uganda 93 F5
Kispiox Canada 116 E4
Kispiox r. Canada 116 E4
Kisseraing Island Myanmar see Kanmaw Kyun
Kissidougou Guinea 92 B4
Kissimmee U.S.A. 129 D6
Kissimmee, Lake U.S.A. 129 D7
Kississing Lake Canada 117 K4
Kistendey Rus. Fed. 39 I5
Kistigan Lake Canada 117 M4
Kistna r. India see Krishna
Kisumu Kenya 94 D4
Kisykkamys Kazakh. see Dzhangala
Kita Mali 92 C3
Kitab Uzbek. 85 G2
Kita-Daitō-jima i. Japan 69 O7
Kitaibaraki Japan 71 F5
Kita-Iō-jima vol. Japan 65 K1
Kitakami Japan 71 F5
Kita-Kyūshū Japan 71 C6
Kitale Kenya 94 D3
Kitami Japan 70 F4
Kit Carson U.S.A. 126 C4
Kitchener Canada 130 E2
Kitchigama r. Canada 118 F4
Kitee Fin. 40 Q5
Kitgum Uganda 94 D3
Kithira i. Greece see Kythira
Kithnos i. Greece see Kythnos
Kiti, Cape Cyprus see Kition, Cape
Kitimat Canada 116 D4
Kitinen r. Fin. 40 O3
Kition, Cape Cyprus 81 A2
Kitiou, Akra c. Cyprus see Kition, Cape
Kitkatla Canada 116 D4
Kitob Uzbek. see Kitab
Kitsault Canada 116 D4
Kittanning U.S.A. 130 F3
Kittatinny Mountains hills U.S.A. 131 H3
Kittery U.S.A. 131 J2
Kittilä Fin. 40 N3
Kittur India 80 B3
Kitty Hawk U.S.A. 128 F4
Kitui Kenya 94 D4
Kitwanga Canada 116 D4
Kitwe Zambia 95 C5
Kitzbüheler Alpen mts Austria 43 N7
Kitzingen Germany 49 K5
Kitzscher Germany 49 M3
Kiu Lom Reservoir Thai. 66 B3
Kiunga P.N.G. 65 K8
Kiuruvesi Fin. 40 O5
Kivalina U.S.A. 114 B3
Kivijärvi Fin. 40 N5
Kiviõli Estonia 41 O7
Kivu, Lake Dem. Rep. Congo/Rwanda 94 C4
Kiwaba N'zogi Angola 95 B4
Kiwai Island P.N.G. 65 K8
Kiyev Ukr. see Kiev
Kiyevskoye Vodokhranilishche resr Ukr. see Kyyivs'ke Vodoskhovyshche
Kıyıköy Turkey 55 M4
Kizel Rus. Fed. 37 R4
Kizema Rus. Fed. 38 J3
Kızılcadağ Turkey 55 M6
Kızılca Dağ mt. Turkey 86 C3
Kızılcahamam Turkey 86 D2
Kızıldağ mt. Turkey 81 A1
Kızıldağ mt. Turkey 81 B1
Kızıl Dağı mt. Turkey 86 E3
Kızılırmak Turkey 86 D2
Kızılırmak r. Turkey 86 D2
Kızıltepe Turkey 87 F3
Kizil"yurt Rus. Fed. 87 G2
Kızkalesi Turkey 81 B1
Kizlyar Rus. Fed. 87 G2
Kizlyarskiy Zaliv b. Rus. Fed. 87 G1
Kizner Rus. Fed. 38 K4
Kizyl-Arbat Turkm. see Gyzylarbat
Kizyl-Atrek Turkm. see Gyzyletrek
Kjøllefjord Norway 40 O1
Kjøpsvik Norway 40 J2
Kladno Czech Rep. 43 O5
Klagenfurt Austria 43 O7
Klagetoh U.S.A. 125 I4
Klaipėda Lith. 41 L9
Klaksvík Faroe Is 40 [inset]
Klamath U.S.A. 122 B4
Klamath r. U.S.A. 114 F5
Klamath Falls U.S.A. 122 C4
Klamath Mountains U.S.A. 122 C4
Klarälven r. Sweden 41 H7
Klatovy Czech Rep. 43 N6
Klawer S. Africa 96 D6
Klazienaveen Neth. 48 G2
Kleides Islands Cyprus 81 B2
Kleinbegin S. Africa 96 E5
Klein Karas Namibia 96 D4
Klein Nama Land reg. S. Africa see Namaqualand
Klein Roggeveldberge mts S. Africa 96 E7
Kleinsee S. Africa 96 C5
Klemtu Canada 116 D4
Klerksdorp S. Africa 97 H4
Kletnya Rus. Fed. 39 G5
Kletsk Belarus see Klyetsk
Kletskaya Rus. Fed. 39 I6
Kletskiy Rus. Fed. see Kletskaya
Kleve Germany 48 G3
Klidhes Islands Cyprus see Kleides Islands
Klimkovka Rus. Fed. 38 K4
Klimovo Rus. Fed. 39 G5
Klin Rus. Fed. 38 H4
Klingenberg am Main Germany 49 J5
Klingenthal Germany 49 M4
Klingkang, Banjaran mts Indon./Malaysia 64 E6
Klink Germany 49 M1
Klínovec mt. Czech Rep. 49 N4
Klintehamn Sweden 41 K8
Klintsy Rus. Fed. 39 G5
Ključ Bos.-Herz. 54 G2
Kłodzko Poland 43 P5
Klondike r. Canada 116 B1
Klondike Gold Rush National Historical Park nat. park U.S.A. 116 C3
Kloosterhaar Neth. 48 G2
Klosterneuburg Austria 43 P6
Klötze (Altmark) Germany 49 L2
Kluane Lake Canada 116 B2
Kluane National Park Canada 116 B2
Kluang Malaysia see Keluang
Kluczbork Poland 43 Q5
Klukhori Rus. Fed. see Karachayevsk
Klukwan U.S.A. 116 C3
Klupro Pak. 85 H5
Klyetsk Belarus 41 O10
Klyuchevskaya, Sopka vol. Rus. Fed. 61 R4
Klyuchi Rus. Fed. 70 B2
Knåda Sweden 41 I6
Knaresborough U.K. 44 F4
Knee Lake Man. Canada 117 M4
Knee Lake Sask. Canada 117 J4
Knetzgau Germany 49 K5
Knife r. U.S.A. 126 C2
Knight Inlet Canada 116 E5
Knighton U.K. 45 D6
Knights Landing U.S.A. 124 C2
Knightstown U.S.A. 130 C4
Knin Croatia 54 G2
Knittelfeld Austria 43 O7
Knjaževac Serb. and Mont. 55 J3

Knob Lake Canada see Schefferville
Knob Lick U.S.A. 130 C5
Knob Peak hill Australia 104 E3
Knock Rep. of Ireland 47 D4
Knockaboy hill Rep. of Ireland 47 C6
Knockalongy hill Rep. of Ireland 47 D3
Knockalough Rep. of Ireland 47 C5
Knockanaffrin hill Rep. of Ireland 47 E5
Knock Hill hill U.K. 46 G3
Knockmealdown Mts hills Rep. of Ireland 47 D5
Knocknaskagh hill Rep. of Ireland 47 D5
Knokke-Heist Belgium 48 D3
Knorrendorf Germany 49 N1
Knowle U.K. 45 F6
Knowlton Canada 131 I1
Knox IN U.S.A. 130 B3
Knox PA U.S.A. 130 F3
Knox, Cape Canada 116 C4
Knox Coast Antarctica 148 F2
Knoxville GA U.S.A. 129 D5
Knoxville TN U.S.A. 128 D5
Knud Rasmussen Land reg. Greenland 115 L2
Knysna S. Africa 96 F8
Ko, Gora mt. Rus. Fed. 70 E3
Koartac Canada see Quaqtaq
Koba Indon. 64 D7
Kobbfoss Norway 40 P2
Kōbe Japan 71 D6
København Denmark see Copenhagen
Kobenni Mauritania 92 C3
Koblenz Germany 49 H4
Koboldo Rus. Fed. 70 D1
Kobrin Belarus see Kobryn
Kobroör i. Indon. 65 I8
Kobryn Belarus 41 N10
Kobuk Valley National Park U.S.A. 114 C3
K'obulet'i Georgia 87 F2
Kocaeli Turkey 55 M4
Kocaeli Yarımadası pen. Turkey 55 M4
Kočani Macedonia 55 J4
Koçasu r. Turkey 55 M4
Kočevje Slovenia 54 F2
Koch Bihar India 79 G4
Kocher r. Germany 49 J5
Kochevo Rus. Fed. 37 Q4
Kochi India see Cochin
Kōchi Japan 71 D6
Koçhisar Turkey see Kızıltepe
Koch Island Canada 115 K3
Kochkor Kyrg. 76 E3
Kochkorka Kyrg. see Kochkor
Kochkurovo Rus. Fed. 39 J5
Kochubeyevskoye Rus. Fed. 87 F1
Kod India 80 B3
Kodala India 80 E2
Kodarma India 79 F4
Koderma India see Kodarma
Kodiak U.S.A. 114 C4
Kodiak Island U.S.A. 114 C4
Kodibeleng Botswana 97 H2
Kodino Rus. Fed. 38 H3
Kodiyakkarai India 80 C4
Kodok Sudan 82 D8
Kodyma Ukr. 39 F6
Kodzhaele mt. Bulg./Greece 55 K4
Koedoesberg mts S. Africa 96 E7
Koegrabie S. Africa 96 E5
Koekenaap S. Africa 96 D6
Koersel Belgium 48 F3
Koës Namibia 96 D3
Kofa Mountains U.S.A. 125 G5
Koffiefontein S. Africa 96 G5
Koforidua Ghana 92 C4
Kōfu Japan 71 E6
Kogaluc r. Canada 118 F2
Kogaluc, Baie de b. Canada 118 F2
Kogaluk r. Canada 119 J2
Kogan Australia 108 E1
Køge Denmark 41 H9
Kogon r. Guinea 92 B3
Kogon Uzbek. see Kagan
Kohan Pak. 85 G5
Kohat Pak. 85 H3
Kohestānāt Afgh. 85 G3
Kohila Estonia 41 N7
Kohima India 79 H4
Kohistan reg. Afgh. 85 H3
Kohistan reg. Pak. 85 I3
Kohler Range mts Antarctica 148 K2
Kohlu Pak. 85 H4
Kohsan Afgh. 85 F3
Kohtla-Järve Estonia 41 O7
Kohŭng S. Korea 71 B6
Koidern Mountain Canada 116 A2
Koidu Sierra Leone see Sefadu
Koihoa India 67 A5
Koilkonda India 80 C2
Koin N. Korea 71 B4
Koin r. Rus. Fed. 38 K3
Koi Sanjaq Iraq 87 G3
Kŏje-do i. S. Korea 71 C6
Kojonup Australia 105 B8
Kokand Uzbek. 76 D3
Kökar Fin. 41 L7
Kokchetav Kazakh. see Kokshetau
Kokemäenjoki r. Fin. 41 L6
Kokerboom Namibia 96 D5
Ko Kha Thai. 66 B3
Kokkilai Sri Lanka 80 D4
Kokkola Fin. 40 M5
Koko Nigeria 92 D3
Kokomo U.S.A. 130 B3
Kokong Botswana 96 F3
Kokos i. Indon. 67 A7
Kokosi S. Africa 97 H4
Kokpekti Kazakh. 76 F2
Koksan N. Korea 71 B5
Kokshaal-Tau, Khrebet mts China/Kyrg. see Kakshaal-Too
Koksharka Rus. Fed. 38 J4
Kokshetau Kazakh. 75 F1
Koksoak r. Canada 119 H2
Kokstad S. Africa 97 I6
Koktal Kazakh. 76 E3
Kokterek Kazakh. 39 K6
Koktokay China see Fuyun
Kola i. Indon. 65 I8
Kola Rus. Fed. 40 R2
Kolachi r. Pak. 85 G5
Kolahoi mt. Jammu and Kashmir 78 C2
Kolaka Indon. 65 G7
Ko Lanta Thai. 67 B6
Kola Peninsula Rus. Fed. 38 H2
Kolar Chhattisgarh India 80 D2
Kolar Karnataka India 80 C3
Kolaras India 78 D4
Kolar Gold Fields India 80 C3
Kolari Fin. 40 M3
Kolarovgrad Bulg. see Shumen
Kolasib India 79 H4
Kolayat India 78 C4
Kolberg Poland see Kołobrzeg
Kol'chugino Rus. Fed. 38 H4
Kolda Senegal 92 B3
Kolding Denmark 41 F9
Kole Kasaï-Oriental Dem. Rep. Congo 94 C4
Kole Orientale Dem. Rep. Congo 94 C3
Koléa Alg. 53 H5
Kolekole mt. HI U.S.A. 123 [inset]
Koler Sweden 40 L4
Kolguyev, Ostrov i. Rus. Fed. 38 K1
Kolhan reg. India 79 F5
Kolhapur India 80 B2
Kolhumadulu Atoll Maldives 77 D11
Kolikata India see Kolkata
Kõljala Estonia 41 M7
Kolkasrags pt Latvia 41 M8
▶Kolkata India 79 G5
3rd most populous city in Asia.
Kolkhozabad Khatlon Tajik. see Vose
Kolkhozabad Khatlon Tajik. see Kolkhozobod
Kolkhozobod Tajik. 85 H2
Kollam India see Quilon
Kolleru Lake India 80 D2
Kollum Neth. 48 G1
Kolmanskop Namibia 96 B4
Köln Germany see Cologne
Köln-Bonn airport Germany 49 H4
Kołobrzeg Poland 43 O3
Kologriv Rus. Fed. 38 J4
Kolokani Mali 92 C3
Kolombangara i. Solomon Is 103 F2
Kolomea Ukr. see Kolomyya
Kolomna Rus. Fed. 39 H5
Kołomyja Ukr. see Kolomyya
Kolomyya Ukr. 39 E6
Kolondiéba Mali 92 C3
Kolonedale Indon. 65 G7
Koloni Cyprus 81 A2
Kolonkwane Botswana 96 E4
Kolozsvár Romania see Cluj-Napoca
Kolpashevo Rus. Fed. 60 J4
Kol'skiy Poluostrov pen. Rus. Fed. see Kola Peninsula
Kölük Turkey see Kâhta
Koluli Eritrea 82 F7
Kolumadulu Atoll Maldives see Kolhumadulu Atoll
Kolva r. Rus. Fed. 38 M2
Kolvan India 80 B2
Kolvereid Norway 40 G4
Kolvik Norway 40 N1
Kolvitskoye, Ozero l. Rus. Fed. 40 R3
Kolwa reg. Pak. 85 G5
Kolwezi Dem. Rep. Congo 95 C5
Kolyma r. Rus. Fed. 61 R3
Kolyma Lowland Rus. Fed. see Kolymskaya Nizmennost'
Kolyma Range mts Rus. Fed. see Kolymskiy, Khrebet
Kolymskaya Nizmennost' lowland Rus. Fed. 61 Q3
Kolymskiy, Khrebet mts Rus. Fed. 61 R3
Kolyshley Rus. Fed. 39 J5
Kom mt. Bulg. 55 J3
Komadugu-gana watercourse Nigeria 92 E3
Komaggas S. Africa 96 C5
Komaio P.N.G. 65 K8
Komaki Japan 71 E6
Komandnaya, Gora mt. Rus. Fed. 70 E2
Komandorskiye Ostrova is Rus. Fed. 61 R4
Komárno Slovakia 43 Q7
Komati r. Swaziland 97 J3
Komatipoort S. Africa 97 J3
Komatsu Japan 71 E5
Komba i. Indon. 104 C1
Komga S. Africa 97 H7
Komintern Ukr. see Marhanets'
Kominternivs'ke Ukr. 55 N1
Komiža Croatia 54 G3
Komló Hungary 54 H1
Kommunarsk Ukr. see Alchevs'k
Komodo National Park Indon. 104 B2
Kôm Ombo Egypt see Kawm Umbū
Komono Congo 94 B4
Komoran i. Indon. 65 J8
Komotini Greece 55 K4
Kompong Cham Cambodia see Kâmpóng Cham
Kompong Chhnang Cambodia see Kâmpóng Chhnăng
Kompong Kleang Cambodia see Kâmpóng Khleăng
Kompong Som Cambodia see Sihanoukville
Kompong Speu Cambodia see Kâmpóng Spœ
Kompong Thom Cambodia see Kâmpóng Thum
Komrat Moldova see Comrat
Komsberg mts S. Africa 96 E7
Komsomol Kazakh. see Karabalyk
Komsomolabad Tajik. see Komsomolobod
Komsomolets Kazakh. see Karabalyk
Komsomolets, Ostrov i. Rus. Fed. 60 K1
Komsomolobod Tajik. 85 H2
Komsomol's'k Ukr. 39 G6
Komsomol'skiy Chukotskiy Avtonomnyy Okrug Rus. Fed. 149 C2
Komsomol'skiy Khanty-Mansiyskiy Avtonomnyy Okrug Rus. Fed. see Yugorsk
Komsomol'skiy Respublika Kalmykiya-Khalm'g-Tangch Rus. Fed. 39 J7
Komsomol'sk-na-Amure Rus. Fed. 70 E2
Komsomol'skoye Kazakh. 76 B1
Komsomol'skoye Rus. Fed. 39 J6
Kömürlü Turkey 87 F2
Kon India 79 E4
Konacık Turkey 81 B1
Konada India 80 D2
Konarak India see Konarka
Konarka India 79 F6
Konch India 78 D4
Kondagaon India 80 D2
Kondinin Australia 105 B8
Kondinskoye Rus. Fed. see Oktyabr'skoye
Kondoa Tanz. 95 D4
Kondol' Rus. Fed. 39 J5
Kondopoga Rus. Fed. 38 G3
Kondoz Afgh. see Kunduz
Kondrovo Rus. Fed. 39 G5
Köneürgenç Turkm. see Keneurgench
Kong Cameroon 92 E4
Kông, Kaôh i. Cambodia 67 C5
Kông, Tônlé r. Cambodia 67 D4
Kong, Xé r. Laos 66 D4
Kong Christian IX Land reg. Greenland 115 O3
Kong Christian X Land reg. Greenland 115 P2
Kongelab atoll Marshall Is see Rongelap
Kong Frederik IX Land reg. Greenland 115 M3
Kong Frederik VI Kyst coastal area Greenland 115 N3
Kongolo Dem. Rep. Congo 95 C4
Kongor Sudan 93 G4
Kong Oscars Fjord inlet Greenland 115 P2
Kongoussi Burkina 92 C3
Kongsberg Norway 41 F7
Kongsvinger Norway 41 H6
Kongur Shan mt. China 76 E4
Königsberg Rus. Fed. see Kaliningrad
Königsee Germany 49 L4
Königswinter Germany 49 H4
Königs Wusterhausen Germany 49 N2
Konimekh Uzbek. see Kanimekh
Konin Poland 43 Q4
Konjic Bos.-Herz. 54 G3
Konkiep watercourse Namibia 96 C5
Könnern Germany 49 L3
Konnevesi Fin. 40 O5
Konosha Rus. Fed. 38 I3
Konotop Ukr. 39 G6
Konpara India 79 E5
Kon Plong Vietnam 67 E4
Konqi He r. China 76 G3
Konso Eth. 94 D3
Konstantinograd Ukr. see Krasnohrad
Konstantinovka Rus. Fed. 70 B2
Konstantinovka Ukr. see Kostyantynivka
Konstantinovy Lázně Czech Rep. 49 M5
Konstanz Germany 43 L7
Kontha Myanmar 66 B2
Kontiolahti Fin. 40 P5
Konttila Fin. 40 O4
Kon Tum Vietnam 67 D4
Kontum, Plateau du Vietnam 67 E4
Könugard Ukr. see Kiev
Konushin, Mys pt Rus. Fed. 38 I2
Konya Turkey 86 D3
Konz Germany 48 G5
Konzhakovskiy Kamen', Gora mt. Rus. Fed. 37 R4
Koocanusa, Lake resr Canada/U.S.A. 116 H5
Kooch Bihar India see Koch Bihar
Kookynie Australia 105 C7
Koolyanobbing Australia 105 B7
Koondrook Australia 108 B5
Koorawatha Australia 108 D5
Koordarrie Australia 104 A5
Kootenay r. Canada 116 G5
Kootenay Lake Canada 116 G5
Kootenay National Park Canada 116 G5
Kootjieskolk S. Africa 96 E6
Kópasker Iceland 40 [inset]
Kopbirlik Kazakh. 76 E2
Koper Slovenia 54 E2
Kopet Dag mts Iran/Turkm. 84 E2
Kopet-Dag, Khrebet mts Iran/Turkm. see Kopet Dag
Köpetdag Gershi mts Iran/Turkm. see Kopet Dag
Köping Sweden 41 J7
Köpmanholmen Sweden 40 K5
Kopong Botswana 97 G3
Koppal India 80 C3
Koppang Norway 41 G6
Kopparberg Sweden 41 I7
Koppeh Dāgh mts Iran/Turkm. see Kopet Dag
Köppel hill Germany 49 H4
Koppi r. Rus. Fed. 70 F2
Koppies S. Africa 97 H4
Koppieskraal Pan salt pan S. Africa 96 E4
Koprivnica Croatia 54 G1
Köprülü Turkey 81 A1
Köprülü Kanyon Milli Parkı nat. park Turkey 55 N6
Kopyl' Belarus see Kapyl'
Kora India 78 E4
Korablino Rus. Fed. 39 I5
K'orahē Eth. 94 E3
Korak Pak. 85 G5
Koramlik China 79 F1
Korangal India 80 C2
Korangi Pak. 85 G5
Korān va Monjan Afgh. 85 H2
Koraput India 80 D2
Korat Thai. see Nakhon Ratchasima
Koratla India 80 C2
Korba India 79 E5
Korbach Germany 49 I3
Korçë Albania 55 I4
Korčula Croatia 54 G3
Korčula i. Croatia 54 G3
Korčulanski Kanal sea chan. Croatia 54 G3
Korday Kazakh. 76 D3
Kord Kūy Iran 84 D2
Kords reg. Iran 85 F5
▶Korea, North country Asia 71 B5
asia 6, 58–59
▶Korea, South country Asia 71 B5
asia 6, 58–59
Korea Bay g. China/N. Korea 71 B5
Korea Strait Japan/S. Korea 71 C6
Koregaon India 80 B2
Korenovsk Rus. Fed. 87 E1
Korenovskaya Rus. Fed. see Korenovsk
Korepino Rus. Fed. 37 R3
Korets' Ukr. 39 E6
Körfez Turkey 55 M4
Korff Ice Rise Antarctica 148 L1
Korfovskiy Rus. Fed. 70 D2
Korgalzhyn Kazakh. 76 D1
Korgen Norway 40 H3
Korhogo Côte d'Ivoire 92 C4
Koribundu Sierra Leone 92 B4
Kori Creek inlet India 78 B5
Korinthiakos Kolpos sea chan. Greece see Corinth, Gulf of
Korinthos Greece see Corinth
Kőris-hegy hill Hungary 54 G1
Koritnik mt. Albania 55 I3
Koritsa Albania see Korçë
Kōriyama Japan 71 F5
Korkuteli Turkey 55 N6
Korla China 76 G3
Kormakitis, Cape Cyprus 81 A2
Körmend Hungary 54 G1
Kornat nat. park Croatia 54 F3
Korneyevka Rus. Fed. 39 K6
Koro Côte d'Ivoire 92 C4
Koro i. Fiji 103 H3
Koro Mali 92 C3
Koroc r. Canada 119 I2
Köroğlu Dağları mts Turkey 55 O4
Köroğlu Tepesi mt. Turkey 86 D2
Korogwe Tanz. 95 D4
Korong Vale Australia 108 A6
Koronia, Limni l. Greece 55 J4
▶Koror Palau 65 I5
Capital of Palau.
Koro Sea b. Fiji 103 H3
Korosten' Ukr. 39 F6
Korostyshiv Ukr. 39 F6
Koro Toro Chad 93 E3
Korpilahti Fin. 40 N5
Korpo Fin. 41 L6
Korppoo Fin. see Korpo
Korsakov Rus. Fed. 70 F3
Korsnäs Fin. 40 L5
Korsør Denmark 41 G9
Korsun'-Shevchenkivs'kyy Ukr. 39 F6
Korsun'-Shevchenkovskiy Ukr. see Korsun'-Shevchenkivs'kyy
Korsze Poland 43 R3
Kortesjärvi Fin. 40 M5
Korti Sudan 82 D6
Kortkeros Rus. Fed. 38 K3
Kortrijk Belgium 48 D4
Korvala Fin. 40 O3
Koryakskaya, Sopka vol. Rus. Fed. 61 Q4
Koryakskiy Khrebet mts Rus. Fed. 61 S3
Koryazhma Rus. Fed. 38 J3
Koryŏng S. Korea 71 C6
Kos i. Greece 55 L6
Kosa Rus. Fed. 37 Q4
Kosam India 78 E4
Kosan N. Korea 71 B5
Kościan Poland 43 P4
Kosciusko, Mount Australia see Kosciuszko, Mount
Kosciuszko, Mount Australia 108 D6
Kosciuszko National Park Australia 108 D6
Köse Turkey 87 E2
Köseçobanlı Turkey 81 A1
Kosgi India 80 C2
Kosh-Agach Rus. Fed. 76 G2
Koshikijima-rettō is Japan 71 C7
Koshk Afgh. 85 F3
Koshk-e Kohneh Afgh. 85 F3
Koshki Rus. Fed. 39 K5
Koshoba Turkm. 87 I2
Koshrabad Uzbek. 85 G1
Kosi Bay S. Africa 97 K4
Košice Slovakia 39 D6
Kosigi India 80 C3
Koskullskulle Sweden 40 L3
Köslin Poland see Koszalin
Kosma r. Rus. Fed. 38 K2
Koson Uzbek. see Kasan
Kosŏng N. Korea 71 C5
Kosova prov. Serb. and Mont. see Kosovo
Kosovo prov. Serb. and Mont. 55 I3
Kosovo-Metohija prov. Serb. and Mont. see Kosovo
Kosovska Mitrovica Serb. and Mont. 55 I3
Kosrae atoll Micronesia 146 G5
Kosrap China 85 J2
Kösseine hill Germany 49 L5
Kosta-Khetagurovo Rus. Fed. see Nazran'
Kostanay Kazakh. 74 F1
Kostenets Bulg. 55 J3
Kosti Sudan 82 D7
Kostinbrod Bulg. 55 J3
Kostino Rus. Fed. 60 J3
Kostomuksha Rus. Fed. 40 Q4
Kostopil' Ukr. 39 E6
Kostopol' Ukr. see Kostopil'
Kostroma Rus. Fed. 38 I4
Kostrzyn Poland 43 O4
Kostyantynivka Ukr. 39 H6
Kostyukovichi Belarus see Kastsyukovichy
Kos'yu Rus. Fed. 37 R2
Koszalin Poland 43 P3
Kőszeg Hungary 54 G1
Kota Andhra Pradesh India 80 D3
Kota Chhattisgarh India 79 E5
Kota Rajasthan India 78 C4
Kota Baharu Malaysia see Kota Bharu
Kotabaru Aceh Indon. 67 B7
Kotabaru Kalimantan Selatan Indon. 64 F7
Kota Bharu Malaysia 67 C6
Kotabumi Indon. 64 C7
Kot Addu Pak. 85 H4
Kota Kinabalu Sabah Malaysia 64 F5
Kotamobagu Indon. 65 G6
Kotaneelee Range mts Canada 116 E2
Kotaparh India 80 D2
Kotapinang Indon. 67 C7
Kotatengah Indon. 67 C7
Kota Tinggi Malaysia 67 C7
Kotcho r. Canada 116 F3
Kotcho Lake Canada 116 F3
Kot Diji Pak. 85 H5
Kotel'nich Rus. Fed. 38 K4
Kotel'nikovo Rus. Fed. 39 I7
Kotel'nyy, Ostrov i. Rus. Fed. 61 O2
Kotgar India 80 D2
Kotgarh India 78 D3
Kothagudem India see Kottagudem
Köthen (Anhalt) Germany 49 L3
Kotido Uganda 93 G4
Kotikovo Rus. Fed. 70 D3
Kot Imamgarh Pak. 85 H5
Kotka Fin. 41 O6
Kot Kapura India 78 C3
Kotkino Rus. Fed. 38 K2
Kotlas Rus. Fed. 38 J3
Kotli Pak. 85 I3
Kotlik U.S.A. 114 B3
Kötlutangi pt Iceland 40 [inset]
Kotly Rus. Fed. 41 P7
Kotorkoshi Nigeria 92 D3
Kotovo Rus. Fed. 39 J6
Kotovsk Rus. Fed. 39 I5
Kotra India 78 C4
Kotra Pak. 85 G4
Kotri r. India 80 D2
Kot Sarae Pak. 85 G6
Kottagudem India 80 D2
Kottarakara India 80 C4
Kottayam India 80 C4
Kotte Sri Lanka see Sri Jayewardenepura Kotte
Kotto r. Cent. Afr. Rep. 94 C3
Kotturu India 80 C3
Kotuy r. Rus. Fed. 61 L2
Kotzebue U.S.A. 114 B3
Kotzebue Sound sea chan. U.S.A. 114 B3
Kötzting Germany 49 M5
Kouango Cent. Afr. Rep. 94 C3
Koubia Guinea 92 B3
Kouchibouguac National Park Canada 119 I5
Koudougou Burkina 92 C3
Kouebokkeveld mts S. Africa 96 D7
Koufey Niger 92 E3
Koufonisi i. Greece 55 L7
Kougaberge mts S. Africa 96 F7
Koukourou r. Cent. Afr. Rep. 94 B3
Koulen Cambodia see Kulen
Koulikoro Mali 92 C3
Koumac New Caledonia 103 G4
Koumpentoum Senegal 92 B3
Koundâra Guinea 92 B3
Kountze U.S.A. 127 E6
Koupéla Burkina 92 C3
Kourou Fr. Guiana 139 H2
Kouroussa Guinea 92 C3
Kousséri Cameroon 93 E3
Koutiala Mali 92 C3
Kouvola Fin. 41 O6
Kovallberget Sweden 40 J4
Kovdor Rus. Fed. 40 Q3
Kovdozero, Ozero l. Rus. Fed. 40 R3
Kovel' Ukr. 39 E6
Kovernino Rus. Fed. 38 I4
Kovilpatti India 80 C4
Kovno Lith. see Kaunas
Kovriga, Gora hill Rus. Fed. 38 K2
Kovrov Rus. Fed. 38 I4
Kovylkino Rus. Fed. 39 I5
Kovzhskoye, Ozero l. Rus. Fed. 38 H3
Kowanyama Australia 106 C2
Kowloon Hong Kong China 73 [inset]
Kowloon Peak hill Hong Kong China 73 [inset]
Kowloon Peninsula Hong Kong China 73 [inset]
Kowŏn N. Korea 71 B5
Kōyama-misaki pt Japan 71 C6
Köyceğiz Turkey 55 M6
Koygorodok Rus. Fed. 38 K3
Koymatdag, Gory hills Turkm. 84 D1
Koyna Reservoir India 80 B2
Köytendag Turkm. see Charshanga
Koyuk U.S.A. 114 B3
Koyukuk r. U.S.A. 114 C3
Koyulhisar Turkey 86 E2
Kozağacı Turkey see Günyüzü
Kō-zaki pt Japan 71 C6
Kozan Turkey 86 D3
Kozani Greece 55 I4
Kozara mts Bos.-Herz. 54 G2
Kozara nat. park Bos.-Herz. 54 G2
Kozarska Dubica Bos.-Herz. see Bosanska Dubica
Kozelets' Ukr. 39 F6
Kozel'sk Rus. Fed. 39 G5
Kozhikode India see Calicut
Kozhva Rus. Fed. 38 M2
Kozlu Turkey 55 N4
Koz'modem'yansk Rus. Fed. 38 J4
Kožuf mts Greece/Macedonia 55 J4
Kōzu-shima i. Japan 71 E6
Kozyatyn Ukr. 39 F6
Kpalimé Togo 92 D4
Kpandae Ghana 92 C4
Kpungan Pass India/Myanmar 66 B1
Kra, Isthmus of Thai. 67 B5
Krabi Thai. 67 B5
Kra Buri Thai. 67 B5
Krâchéh Cambodia 67 D4
Kraddsele Sweden 40 J4
Kragerø Norway 41 F7
Kraggenburg Neth. 48 F2
Kragujevac Serb. and Mont. 55 I2
Krakatau vol. Indon. 64 D8
Krakau Poland see Kraków
Kraków Poland 43 Q5
Krakower See l. Germany 49 M1
Krâlănh Cambodia 67 C4
Kralendijk Neth. Antilles 133 K6
Kramators'k Ukr. 39 H6
Kramfors Sweden 40 J5
Krammer est. Neth. 48 E3
Kranidi Greece 55 J6
Kranj Slovenia 54 F1
Kranji Reservoir Sing. 67 [inset]
Kranskop S. Africa 97 J5
Krasavino Rus. Fed. 38 J3
Krasilov Ukr. see Krasyliv
Krasino Rus. Fed. 60 G2
Kraskino Rus. Fed. 70 C4
Krāslava Latvia 41 O9
Kraslice Czech Rep. 49 M4
Krasnaya Gorbatka Rus. Fed. 38 I5
Krasnaya Zarya Rus. Fed. 39 H5
Krasnoarmeysk Rus. Fed. 39 J6
Krasnoarmeysk Ukr. see Krasnoarmiys'k
Krasnoarmiys'k Ukr. 39 H6
Krasnoborsk Rus. Fed. 38 J3
Krasnodar Rus. Fed. 86 E1
Krasnodar Kray admin. div. Rus. Fed. see Krasnodarskiy Kray
Krasnodarskiy Kray admin. div. Rus. Fed. 86 E1
Krasnodon Ukr. 39 H6
Krasnogorodskoye Rus. Fed. 41 P8
Krasnogorsk Rus. Fed. 70 F2
Krasnogorskoye Rus. Fed. 38 L4
Krasnograd Ukr. see Krasnohrad
Krasnogvardeysk Uzbek. see Bulungur
Krasnogvardeyskoye Rus. Fed. 39 I7
Krasnohrad Ukr. 39 G6
Krasnohvardiys'ke Ukr. 39 G7
Krasnokamsk Rus. Fed. 37 R4
Krasnoperekops'k Ukr. 39 G7
Krasnopol'ye Rus. Fed. 70 F2
Krasnorechenskiy Rus. Fed. 70 D3
Krasnoslobodsk Rus. Fed. 39 I5
Krasnotur'insk Rus. Fed. 37 S4
Krasnoufimsk Rus. Fed. 37 R4
Krasnovishersk Rus. Fed. 37 R3
Krasnovodsk Turkm. see Turkmenbashi
Krasnovodsk, Mys pt Turkm. 84 D2
Krasnovodskiy Gosudarstvenny Zapovednik nature res. Turkm. 84 D2
Krasnovodskiy Zaliv b. Turkm. 84 D2
Krasnovodskoye Plato plat. Turkm. 87 I2
Krasnowodsk Aylagy b. Turkm. see Krasnovodskiy Zaliv
Krasnoyarovo Rus. Fed. 70 C2
Krasnoyarsk Rus. Fed. 60 K4
Krasnoyarskoye Vodokhranilishche resr Rus. Fed. 68 G2
Krasnoye Lipetskaya Oblast' Rus. Fed. 39 H5
Krasnoye Respublika Kalmykiya - Khalm'g-Tangch Rus. Fed. see Ulan Erge
Krasnoye Znamya Turkm. 85 F2
Krasnoznamenskiy Kazakh. see Yegindykol'
Krasnoznamenskoye Kazakh. see Yegindykol'
Krasnyy Rus. Fed. 39 F5
Krasnyy Chikoy Rus. Fed. 69 J2
Krasnyye Baki Rus. Fed. 38 J4
Krasnyy Kamyshanik Rus. Fed. see Komsomol'skiy
Krasnyy Kholm Rus. Fed. 38 H4
Krasnyy Kut Rus. Fed. 39 J6
Krasnyy Luch Ukr. 39 H6
Krasnyy Lyman Ukr. 39 H6
Krasnyy Yar Rus. Fed. 39 K7
Krasyliv Ukr. 39 E6
Kratie Cambodia see Krâchéh
Kratke Range mts P.N.G. 65 L8
Kraulshavn Greenland see Nuussuaq
Krâvanh, Chuŏr Phnum mts Cambodia/Thai. see Cardamom Range
Kraynovka Rus. Fed. 87 G2
Krefeld Germany 48 G3
Kremenchug Ukr. see Kremenchuk
Kremenchugskoye Vodokhranilishche resr Ukr. see Kremenchuts'ka Vodoskhovyshche
Kremenchuk Ukr. 39 G6
Kremenchuts'ka Vodoskhovyshche resr Ukr. 39 G6
Křemešník hill Czech Rep. 43 O6
Kremges Ukr. see Svitlovods'k
Kremmidi, Akra pt Greece 55 J6
Krems Austria see Krems an der Donau
Krems an der Donau Austria 43 O6
Kresta, Zaliv g. Rus. Fed. 61 T3
Kresttsy Rus. Fed. 38 G4
Kretinga Lith. 41 L9
Kreuzau Germany 48 G4
Kreuztal Germany 49 H4
Kreva Belarus 41 O9
Kribi Cameroon 92 D4
Krichev Belarus see Krychaw
Kriel S. Africa 97 I4
Krikellos Greece 55 I5
Kril'on, Mys c. Rus. Fed. 70 F3
Krishna India 80 C2
Krishna r. India 80 D2
Krishnanagar India 79 G5
Krishnaraja Sagara l. India 80 C3
Kristiania Norway see Oslo
Kristiansand Norway 41 E7
Kristianstad Sweden 41 I8
Kristiansund Norway 40 E5
Kristiinankaupunki Fin. see Kristinestad
Kristinehamn Sweden 41 I7
Kristinestad Fin. 40 L5
Kristinopol' Ukr. see Chervonohrad
Kriti i. Greece see Crete
Krivoy Rog Ukr. see Kryvyy Rih
Križevci Croatia 54 G1
Krk i. Croatia 54 F2
Krkonošský narodní park nat. park Czech Rep./Poland 43 O5
Krokom Sweden 40 I5
Krokstadøra Norway 40 F5
Krokstranda Norway 40 I3
Krolevets' Ukr. 39 G6
Kronach Germany 49 L4
Krŏng Kaôh Kŏng Cambodia 67 C5
Kronoby Fin. 40 M5
Kronprins Christian Land reg. Greenland 149 I1
Kronprins Frederik Bjerge nunataks Greenland 115 O3
Kronshtadt Rus. Fed. 41 P7
Kronstadt Romania see Braşov
Kronstadt Rus. Fed. see Kronshtadt
Kronwa Myanmar 66 B4
Kroonstad S. Africa 97 H4
Kropotkin Rus. Fed. 87 F1
Kropstädt Germany 49 M3
Krosno Poland 39 D6
Krotoszyn Poland 43 P5
Kruger National Park S. Africa 97 J2
Kruglikovo Rus. Fed. 70 D2
Kruglyakov Rus. Fed. see Oktyabr'skiy
Krui Indon. 64 C8
Kruisfontein S. Africa 96 G8
Kruja Albania see Krujë
Krujë Albania 55 H4
Krumovgrad Bulg. 55 K4
Krungkao Thai. see Ayutthaya
Krung Thep Thai. see Bangkok
Krupa Bos.-Herz. see Bosanska Krupa
Krupa na Uni Bos.-Herz. see Bosanska Krupa
Krupki Belarus 39 F5
Krusenstern, Cape U.S.A. 114 B3
Kruševac Serb. and Mont. 55 I3
Krušné Hory mts Czech Rep. 49 M4
Kruzof Island U.S.A. 116 C3
Krychaw Belarus 39 F5
Krylov Seamount sea feature N. Atlantic Ocean 144 G4
Krym' pen. Ukr. see Crimea
Krymsk Rus. Fed. 86 E1
Krymskaya Rus. Fed. see Krymsk
Kryms'kyy Pivostriv pen. Ukr. see Crimea
Krystynopol Ukr. see Chervonohrad
Krytiko Pelagos sea Greece 55 K6
Kryvyy Rih Ukr. 39 G7
Ksabi Alg. 50 D6
Ksar Chellala Alg. 53 H6
Ksar el Boukhari Alg. 53 H6
Ksar el Kebir Morocco 53 D6
Ksar-es-Souk Morocco see Er Rachidia
Ksenofontova Rus. Fed. 37 R3
Kshirpai India 79 F5
Ksour Essaf Tunisia 54 D7
Kstovo Rus. Fed. 38 J4
Kū', Jabal al hill Saudi Arabia 82 G4
Kuah Malaysia 67 B6
Kuaidamao China see Tonghua
Kuala Belait Brunei 64 E6
Kuala Dungun Malaysia see Dungun
Kuala Kangsar Malaysia 67 C6

Kualakapuas Indon. 64 E7
Kuala Kerai Malaysia 67 C6
Kuala Lipis Malaysia 67 C6
▶Kuala Lumpur Malaysia 67 C7
National capital of Malaysia.
Kuala Nerang Malaysia 67 C6
Kuala Pilah Malaysia 67 C7
Kuala Rompin Malaysia 67 C7
Kuala Selangor Malaysia 67 C7
Kualasimpang Indon. 67 B6
Kuala Terengganu Malaysia 67 C6
Kualatungal Indon. 64 C7
Kuamut Sabah Malaysia 64 F5
Kuandian China 70 B4
Kuantan Malaysia 67 C7
Kuba Azer. see Quba
Kuban' r. Rus. Fed. 39 H7
Kubār Syria 87 E4
Kubaybāt Syria 81 C2
Kubaysah Iraq 87 F4
Kubenskoye, Ozero l. Rus. Fed. 38 H4
Kubrat Bulg. 55 L3
Kubuang Indon. 64 F6
Kuchaman Road India 85 I5
Kuchema Rus. Fed. 38 I2
Kuching Sarawak Malaysia 64 E6
Kucing Sarawak Malaysia see Kuching
Kuçovë Albania 55 H4
Kuda India 78 B5
Kudal India 80 B3
Kudap Indon. 67 C7
Kudat Sabah Malaysia 64 F5
Kudligi India 80 C3
Kudremukh mt. India 80 B3
Kudus Indon. 64 E8
Kudymkar Rus. Fed. 37 Q4
Kueishan Tao i. Taiwan 73 I3
Kufstein Austria 43 N7
Kugaaruk Canada 115 J3
Kugesi Rus. Fed. 38 J4
Kugka Lhai China 79 G3
Kugluktuk Canada 114 G3
Kugmallit Bay Canada 149 A2
Kūh, Ra's-al- pt Iran 84 E5
Kūhak Iran 85 F5
Kuhanbokano mt. China 79 E3
Kuhbier Germany 49 M1
Kūhdasht Iran 84 B3
Kūhīn Iran 84 C2
Kūhīrī Iran 85 F5
Kuhmo Fin. 40 P4
Kuhmoinen Fin. 41 N6
Kūhpāyeh mt. Iran 84 E4
Kūhrān, Kūh-e mt. Iran 84 E5
Kühren Germany 49 M3
Kui Buri Thai. 67 B4
Kuis Namibia 96 C3
Kuiseb watercourse Namibia 96 B2
Kuitan China 73 G4
Kuito Angola 95 B5
Kuitun China see Kuytun
Kuiu Island U.S.A. 116 C3
Kuivaniemi Fin. 40 N4
Kujang N. Korea 71 B5
Kuji Japan 71 F4
Kujū-san vol. Japan 71 C6
Kukālār, Kūh-e hill Iran 84 C4
Kukan Rus. Fed. 70 D2
Kukës Albania 55 I3
Kukesi Albania see Kukës
Kukmor Rus. Fed. 38 K4
Kukshi India 78 C5
Kukunuru India 80 D2
Kukurtli Turkm. 84 E2
Kūl r. Iran 84 D5
Kula Turkey 55 M5
Kulaisila India 79 F5
Kula Kangri mt. China/Bhutan 79 G3
Kulandy Kazakh. 76 A2
Kulaneh reg. Pak. 85 F5
Kular Rus. Fed. 61 O2
Kuldīga Latvia 41 L8
Kuldja China see Yining
Kul'dur Rus. Fed. 70 C2
Kule Botswana 96 E2
Kulebaki Rus. Fed. 39 I5
Kulen Cambodia 67 D4
Kulgera Australia 105 F6
Kulikovo Rus. Fed. 38 J3
Kulim Malaysia 67 C6
Kulin Australia 105 B8
Kulja Australia 105 B7
Kulkyne watercourse Australia 108 B3
Kullu India 78 D3
Kulmbach Germany 49 L4
Kŭlob Tajik. 85 H2
Kuloy Rus. Fed. 38 I3
Kuloy r. Rus. Fed. 38 I2
Kulp Turkey 87 F3
Kul'sary Kazakh. 74 E2
Külsheim Germany 49 J5
Kulu India see Kullu
Kulu Turkey 86 D3
Kulunda Rus. Fed. 68 D2
Kulundinskaya Step' plain Kazakh./Rus. Fed. 68 D2
Kulundinskoye, Ozero salt l. Rus. Fed. 68 D2
Kulusuk Greenland 115 O3
Kulwin Australia 107 C7
Kulyab Tajik. see Kŭlob
Kuma r. Rus. Fed. 39 J7
Kumagaya Japan 71 E5
Kumai, Teluk b. Indon. 64 E7
Kumalar Dağı mts Turkey 55 N5
Kumamoto Japan 71 C6
Kumano Japan 71 E6
Kumanovo Macedonia 55 I3
Kumara Rus. Fed. 70 B2
Kumasi Ghana 92 C4
Kumayri Armenia see Gyumri
Kumba Cameroon 92 D4
Kumbakonam India 80 C4
Kumbe Indon. 65 K8
Kümbet Turkey 55 N5
Kumbharli Ghat mt. India 80 B2
Kumbla India 80 B3
Kumchuru Botswana 96 F2
Kum-Dag Turkm. see Gumdag
Kumdah Saudi Arabia 82 G5
Kumel well Iran 84 D3
Kumeny Rus. Fed. 38 K4
Kumertau Rus. Fed. 60 G4
Kumgang-san mt. N. Korea 71 C5
Kumguri India 79 G4
Kumhwa S. Korea 71 B5
Kumi S. Korea 71 C5
Kumi Uganda 93 G4
Kumkurgan Uzbek. 85 G2
Kumla Sweden 41 I7
Kumlu Turkey 81 C1
Kummersdorf-Alexanderdorf Germany 49 N2
Kumo Nigeria 92 E3
Kŭmŏ-do i. S. Korea 71 B6
Kumon Range mts Myanmar 66 B1
Kumphawapi Thai. 66 C3
Kums Namibia 96 D5
Kumta India 80 B3
Kumu Dem. Rep. Congo 94 C3
Kumukh Rus. Fed. 87 G2
Kumul China see Hami
Kumund India 80 D1
Kumylzhenskaya Rus. Fed. see Kumylzhenskiy
Kumylzhenskiy Rus. Fed. 39 I6
Kun r. Myanmar 66 B3
Kunar r. Afgh. 85 H3
Kunashir, Ostrov i. Rus. Fed. 70 G3
Kunashirskiy Proliv sea chan. Japan/Rus. Fed. see Nemuro-kaikyō
Kunchaung Myanmar 66 B2
Kunchuk Tso salt l. China 79 E2
Kunda Estonia 41 O7
Kunda India 79 E4
Kundapura India 80 B3
Kundelungu, Parc National de nat. park Dem. Rep. Congo 95 C5
Kundelungu Ouest, Parc National de nat. park Dem. Rep. Congo 95 C5
Kundia India 78 C4
Kundur i. Indon. 64 C6
Kunduz Afgh. 85 H2
Kunene r. Angola see Cunene
Kuneneng admin. dist. Botswana see Kweneng
Künes China see Xinyuan
Kungälv Sweden 41 G8
Kunghit Island Canada 116 D4
Kungrad Uzbek. 76 A3
Kungsbacka Sweden 41 H8
Kungshamn Sweden 41 G7
Kungu Dem. Rep. Congo 94 B3
Kungur mt. China see Kongur Shan
Kungur Rus. Fed. 37 R4
Kunhing Myanmar 66 B2
Kuni r. India 80 C2
Kūnīch Iran 84 E5
Kunié i. New Caledonia see Pins, Île des
Kunigai India 80 C3
Kunimi-dake mt. Japan 71 C6
Kunlavav India 78 B5
Kunlong Myanmar 66 B2
Kunlun Shan mts China 78 D1
Kunlun Shankou pass China 79 H2
Kunming China 72 D3
Kunsan S. Korea 71 B6
Kunshan China 73 I2
Kununurra Australia 104 E3
Kunwak r. Canada 117 L2
Kun'ya Rus. Fed. 38 F4
Kunyang Yunnan China see Jinning
Kunyang Zhejiang China see Pingyang
Kunya-Urgench Turkm. see Keneurgench
Künzelsau Germany 49 J5
Künzels-Berg hill Germany 49 L3
Kuocang Shan mts China 73 I2
Kuohijärvi l. Fin. 41 N6
Kuolayarvi Rus. Fed. 40 P3
Kuopio Fin. 40 O5
Kuortane Fin. 40 M5
Kupa r. Croatia/Slovenia 54 G2
Kupang Indon. 104 C2
Kupari India 79 F5
Kupiškis Lith. 41 N9
Kupreanof Island U.S.A. 116 C3
Kupwara India 78 C2
Kup"yans'k Ukr. 39 H6
Kuqa China 76 F3
Kür r. Georgia 87 G2
also known as Kur (Russian Federation), Kura
Kur r. Rus. Fed. 70 D2
also known as Kür (Georgia), Kura
Kuragino Rus. Fed. 68 G2
Kurakh Rus. Fed. 39 J8
Kurama Range mts Asia 83 K1
Kuraminskiy Khrebet mts Asia see Kurama Range
Kūrān Dap Iran 85 E5
Kurashiki Japan 71 D6
Kurasia India 79 E5
Kurayn i. Saudi Arabia 84 C5
Kurayoshi Japan 71 D6
Kurchatov Rus. Fed. 39 G6
Kurchum Kazakh. 76 F2
Kürdämir Azer. 87 H2
Kŭrdzhali Bulg. 55 K4
Kure Japan 71 D6
Küre Turkey 86 D2
Kure Atoll U.S.A. 146 I4
Kuressaare Estonia 41 M7
Kurgal'dzhino Kazakh. see Korgalzhyn
Kurgal'dzhinskiy Kazakh. see Korgalzhyn
Kurgan Rus. Fed. 60 H4
Kurganinsk Rus. Fed. 87 F1
Kurgannaya Rus. Fed. see Kurganinsk
Kurgantyube Tajik. see Qŭrghonteppa
Kuri Afgh. 85 H2
Kuri India 78 B4
Kuria Muria Islands Oman see Ḥalāniyāt, Juzur al
Kuridala Australia 106 C4
Kurigram Bangl. 79 G4
Kurikka Fin. 40 M5
Kuril Basin sea feature Sea of Okhotsk 146 F2
Kuril Islands Rus. Fed. 70 H3
Kurilovka Rus. Fed. 39 K6
Kuril'sk Rus. Fed. 70 G3
Kuril'skiye Ostrova is Rus. Fed. see Kuril Islands
Kuril Trench sea feature N. Pacific Ocean 146 F3
Kurkino Rus. Fed. 39 H5
Kurmashkino Kazakh. see Kurchum
Kurmuk Sudan 82 D7
Kurnool India 80 C3
Kuroiso Japan 71 F5
Kurort Schmalkalden Germany 49 K4
Kurovskiy Rus. Fed. 70 B1
Kurow N.Z. 109 C7
Kurram Pak. 85 H3
Kurri Kurri Australia 108 E4
Kursavka Rus. Fed. 87 F1
Kürshim Kazakh. see Kurchum
Kurshskiy Zaliv b. Lith./Rus. Fed. see Courland Lagoon
Kuršių marios b. Lith./Rus. Fed. see Courland Lagoon
Kursk Rus. Fed. 39 H6
Kurskaya Rus. Fed. 87 G1
Kurskiy Zaliv b. Lith./Rus. Fed. see Courland Lagoon
Kurşunlu Turkey 86 D2
Kurtalan Turkey 87 F3
Kurtoğlu Burnu pt Turkey 55 M6
Kurtpınar Turkey 81 B1
Kurucaşile Turkey 86 D2
Kuruçay Turkey 86 E3
Kurukshetra India 78 D3
Kuruktag mts China 76 G3
Kuruman S. Africa 96 F4
Kuruman watercourse S. Africa 96 E4
Kurume Japan 71 C6
Kurumkan Rus. Fed. 69 K2
Kurunegala Sri Lanka 80 D5
Kurupam India 80 D2
Kurush, Jebel hills Sudan 82 D5
Kur'ya Rus. Fed. 37 R3
Kuryk Kazakh. 87 H2
Kuşadası Turkey 55 L6
Kuşadası Körfezi b. Turkey 55 L6
Kusaie atoll Micronesia see Kosrae
Kusary Azer. see Qusar
Kuşcenneti nature res. Turkey 81 B1
Kuschke Nature Reserve S. Africa 97 I3
Kusel Germany 49 H5
Kuş Gölü l. Turkey 55 L4
Kushalgarh India 78 C5
Kushchevskaya Rus. Fed. 39 H7
Kushimoto Japan 71 D6
Kushiro Japan 70 G4
Kushka Turkm. see Gushgy
Kushkopola Rus. Fed. 38 J3
Kushmurun Kazakh. 74 F1
Kushtagi India 80 C3
Kushtia Bangl. 79 G5
Kushtih Iran 85 E4
Kuskan Turkey 81 A1
Kuskokwim r. U.S.A. 114 B3
Kuskokwim Bay U.S.A. 114 B4
Kuskokwim Mountains U.S.A. 114 C3
Kuşluyan Turkey see Gölköy
Kusŏng N. Korea 71 B5
Kustanay Kazakh. see Kostanay
Küstence Romania see Constanța
Küstenkanal canal Germany 49 H1
Kustia Bangl. see Kushtia
Kut Iran 84 C4
Kut, Ko i. Thai. 67 C5
Kūt 'Abdollāh Iran 84 C4
Kutacane Indon. 67 B7
Kütahya Turkey 55 M5
K'ut'aisi Georgia 87 F2
Kut-al-Imara Iraq see Al Kūt
Kutan Rus. Fed. 87 G1
Kutanibong Indon. 67 B7
Kutaraja Indon. see Banda Aceh
Kutayfat Ţurayf vol. Saudi Arabia 81 D4
Kutch, Gulf of India see Kachchh, Gulf of
Kutch, Rann of marsh India see Kachchh, Rann of
Kutchan Japan 70 F4
Kutina Croatia 54 G2
Kutjevo Croatia 54 G2
Kutkai Myanmar 66 B2
Kutno Poland 43 Q4
Kutru India 80 D2
Kutu Dem. Rep. Congo 94 B4
Kutubdia Island Bangl. 79 G5
Kutum Sudan 93 F3
Kutztown U.S.A. 131 H3
Kuujjua r. Canada 114 G2
Kuujjuaq Canada 119 H2
Kuujjuarapik Canada 118 F3
Kuuli-Mayak Turkm. 84 D1
Kuusamo Fin. 40 P4
Kuusankoski Fin. 41 O6
Kuvango Angola 95 B5
Kuvshinovo Rus. Fed. 38 G4
▶Kuwait country Asia 84 B4
asia 6, 58–59
▶Kuwait Kuwait 84 B4
Capital of Kuwait.
Kuwajleen atoll Marshall Is see Kwajalein
Kuybyshev Novosibirskaya Oblast' Rus. Fed. 60 I4
Kuybyshev Respublika Tatarstan Rus. Fed. see Bolgar
Kuybyshev Samarskaya Oblast' Rus. Fed. see Samara
Kuybysheve Ukr. 39 H7
Kuybyshevka-Vostochnaya Rus. Fed. see Belogorsk
Kuybyshevskoye Vodokhranilishche resr Rus. Fed. 39 K5
Kuyeda Rus. Fed. 37 R4
Kuygan Kazakh. 76 D2
Kuytun China 76 F3
Kuytun Rus. Fed. 68 I2
Kuyucak Turkey 55 M6
Kuzino Rus. Fed. 37 R4
Kuznechnoye Rus. Fed. 41 P6
Kuznetsk Rus. Fed. 39 J5
Kuznetsovo Rus. Fed. 70 E3
Kuznetsovs'k Ukr. 39 E6
Kuzovatovo Rus. Fed. 39 J5
Kvænangen sea chan. Norway 40 L1
Kvaløya i. Norway 40 K2
Kvalsund Norway 40 M1
Kvarnerić sea chan. Croatia 54 F2
Kvitøya ice feature Svalbard 60 E2
Kwa r. Dem. Rep. Congo see Kasaï
Kwabhaca S. Africa see Mount Frere
Kwadelen atoll Marshall Is see Kwajalein
Kwajalein atoll Marshall Is 146 H5
Kwale Nigeria 92 D4
KwaMashu S. Africa 97 J5
KwaMhlanga S. Africa 97 I3
Kwa Mtoro Tanz. 95 D4
Kwangch'ŏn S. Korea 71 B5
Kwangchow China see Guangzhou
Kwangju S. Korea 71 B6
Kwangsi Chuang Autonomous Region aut. reg. China see Guangxi Zhuangzu Zizhiqu
Kwangtung prov. China see Guangdong
Kwanmo-bong mt. N. Korea 70 C4
Kwanobuhle S. Africa 97 G7
KwaNojoli S. Africa 97 G7
Kwanonqubela S. Africa 97 H7
Kwanonzame S. Africa 96 G6
Kwanza r. Angola see Cuanza
Kwatinidubu S. Africa 97 H7
KwaZamokhule S. Africa 97 I4
Kwazamukucinga S. Africa 96 G7
Kwazamuxolo S. Africa 96 G6
KwaZanele S. Africa 97 I4
Kwazulu-Natal prov. S. Africa 97 J5
Kweichow prov. China see Guizhou
Kweiyang China see Guiyang
Kwekwe Zimbabwe 95 C5
Kweneng admin. dist. Botswana 96 G2
Kwenge r. Dem. Rep. Congo 95 B4
Kwetabohigan r. Canada 118 E4
Kwezi-Naledi S. Africa 97 H6
Kwidzyn Poland 43 Q4
Kwikila P.N.G. 65 L8
Kwilu r. Angola/Dem. Rep. Congo 95 B4
Kwo Chau Kwan To is Hong Kong China see Ninepin Group
Kwoka mt. Indon. 65 I7
Kyabra Australia 107 C5
Kyabram Australia 108 B6
Kyadet Myanmar 66 A2
Kyaikkami Myanmar 66 B3
Kyaiklat Myanmar 66 A3
Kyaikto Myanmar 66 B3
Kyakhta Rus. Fed. 68 J2
Kyalite Australia 108 A5
Kyancutta Australia 105 F8
Kyangin Myanmar 66 B3
Kyangngoin China 72 B2
Kyaukhnyat Myanmar 66 B3
Kyaukkyi Myanmar 66 B3
Kyaukme Myanmar 66 B2
Kyaukpadaung Myanmar 66 A2
Kyaukpyu Myanmar 66 A3
Kyaukse Myanmar 66 B2
Kyauktaw Myanmar 66 A2
Kyaunggon Myanmar 66 A3
Kybartai Lith. 41 M9
Kyebogyi Myanmar 66 B3
Kyêbxang Co l. China 79 G2
Kyeikdon Myanmar 66 B3
Kyeikywa Myanmar 66 B3
Kyeintali Myanmar 66 A3
Kyela Tanz. 95 D4
Kyelang India 78 D2
Kyidaunggan Myanmar 66 B3
Kyiv Ukr. see Kiev
Kyklades is Greece see Cyclades
Kyle Canada 117 I5
Kyle of Lochalsh U.K. 46 D3
Kyll r. Germany 48 G5
Kyllini mt. Greece 55 J6
Kymi Greece 55 K5
Kymis, Akra pt Greece 55 K5
Kyneton Australia 108 B6
Kynuna Australia 106 C4
Kyoga, Lake Uganda 94 D3
Kyōga-misaki pt Japan 71 D6
Kyogle Australia 108 F2
Kyong Myanmar 66 B2
Kyŏngju S. Korea 71 C6
Kyonpyaw Myanmar 66 A3
Kyōto Japan 71 D6
Kyparissia Greece 55 I6
Kypros country Asia see Cyprus
Kypshak, Ozero salt l. Kazakh. 75 F1
Kyra Rus. Fed. 69 K3
Kyra Panagia i. Greece 55 K5
Kyrenia Cyprus 81 A2
Kyrenia Mountains Cyprus see Pentadaktylos Range
Kyrgyz Ala-Too mts Kazakh./Kyrg. see Kirghiz Range
▶Kyrgyzstan country Asia 76 D3
asia 6, 58–59
Kyritz Germany 49 M2
Kyrksæterøra Norway 40 F5
Kyrta Rus. Fed. 37 R3
Kyssa Rus. Fed. 38 J2
Kytalyktakh Rus. Fed. 61 O3
Kythira i. Greece 55 J6
Kythnos i. Greece 55 K6
Kyunglung China 78 E3
Kyunhla Myanmar 66 A2
Kyun Pila i. Myanmar 67 B5
Kyuquot Canada 116 E5
Kyurdamir Azer. see Kürdämir
Kyūshū i. Japan 71 C7
Kyushu-Palau Ridge sea feature N. Pacific Ocean 146 F4
Kyustendil Bulg. 55 J3
Kywebwe Myanmar 66 B3
Kywong Australia 108 C5
Kyyev Ukr. see Kiev
Kyyiv Ukr. see Kiev
Kyyivs'ke Vodoskhovyshche resr Ukr. 39 F6
Kyyjärvi Fin. 40 N5
Kyzyl Rus. Fed. 76 H1
Kyzyl-Art, Pereval pass Kyrg./Tajik. see Kyzylart Pass
Kyzylart Pass Kyrg./Tajik. 85 I2
Kyzyl-Burun Azer. see Siyäzän
Kyzyl-Kiya Kyrg. see Kyzyl-Kyya
Kyzylkum, Peski des. Kazakh./Uzbek. see Kyzylkum Desert
Kyzylkum Desert Kazakh./Uzbek. 76 B3
Kyzyl-Kyya Kyrg. 76 D3
Kyzyl-Mazhalyk Rus. Fed. 76 H1
Kyzylorda Kazakh. 76 C3
Kyzylrabot Tajik. see Qizilrabot
Kyzylsay Kazakh. 87 I2
Kyzylysor Kazakh. 87 H1
Kyzylzhar Kazakh. 76 C2
Kzyl-Dzhar Kazakh. see Kyzylzhar
Kzyl-Orda Kazakh. see Kyzylorda
Kzyltu Kazakh. see Kishkenekol'

L

Laagri Estonia 41 N7
Laam Atoll Maldives see Hadhdhunmathi Atoll
La Angostura, Presa de resr Mex. 127 F5
Laanila Fin. 40 O2
Laascaanood Somalia 94 E3
La Ascensión, Bahía de b. Mex. 133 G5
Laasgoray Somalia 94 E2
▶Laâyoune W. Sahara 92 B2
Capital of Western Sahara.
La Babia Mex. 127 C6
La Bahía, Islas de is Hond. 133 G5
La Baie Canada 119 H4
La Baleine, Grande Rivière de r. Canada 118 F3
La Baleine, Petite Rivière de r. Canada 118 F3
La Baleine, Rivière à r. Canada 119 I2
La Banda Arg. 140 D3
La Barge U.S.A. 122 F4
Labasa Fiji 103 H3
La Baule-Escoublac France 52 C3
Labazhskoye Rus. Fed. 38 L2
Labe r. Czech Rep. see Elbe
Labé Guinea 92 B3
La Belle U.S.A. 129 D7
La Bénoué, Parc National de nat. park Cameroon 93 E4
Laberge, Lake Canada 116 C2
Labian, Tanjung pt Malaysia 64 F5
La Biche, Lac l. Canada 117 H4
Labinsk Rus. Fed. 87 F1
Labis Malaysia 67 C7
La Boquilla Mex. 127 B7
La Boucle du Baoulé, Parc National de nat. park Mali 92 C3
Labouheyre France 52 D4
Laboulaye Arg. 140 D4
Labrador reg. Canada 119 J3
Labrador City Canada 119 I3
Labrador Sea Canada/Greenland 115 M3
Labrang China see Xiahe
Lábrea Brazil 138 F5
Labuan Malaysia 64 F5
Labudalin China see Ergun
Labuhanbilik Indon. 67 C7
Labuhanruku Indon. 67 B7
Labuna Indon. 65 H7
Labutta Myanmar 66 A3
Labyrinth, Lake salt flat Australia 107 A6
Labytnangi Rus. Fed. 60 H3
Laç Albania 55 H4
La Cabrera, Sierra de mts Spain 53 C2
La Cadena Mex. 127 B7
Lac Allard Canada 119 J4
La Calle Alg. see El Kala
La Cañiza Spain see A Cañiza
La Capelle France 48 D5
La Carlota Arg. 140 D4
La Carolina Spain 53 E4
Lăcăuți, Vârful mt. Romania 55 L2
Laccadive, Minicoy and Amindivi Islands union terr. India see Lakshadweep
Laccadive Islands India 80 B4
Lac du Bonnet Canada 117 L5
Lacedaemon Greece see Sparti
La Ceiba Hond. 133 G5
Lacepede Bay Australia 107 B8
Lacepede Islands Australia 104 C4
Lacha, Ozero l. Rus. Fed. 38 H3
Lachendorf Germany 49 K2
Lachine U.S.A. 130 D1
▶Lachlan r. Australia 108 A5
5th longest river in Oceania.
La Chorrera Panama 133 I7
Lachute Canada 118 G5
Laçın Azer. 87 G3
La Ciotat France 52 G5
Lac La Biche Canada 117 I4
Lac la Martre Canada see Wha Ti
Lacolle Canada 131 I1
La Colorada Sonora Mex. 123 F7
La Colorada Zacatecas Mex. 127 C8
Lacombe Canada 116 H4
La Comoé, Parc National de nat. park Côte d'Ivoire 92 C4
Laconi Sardinia Italy 54 C5
Laconia U.S.A. 131 J2
La Corey Canada 117 I4
La Coruña Spain see A Coruña
La Corvette, Lac de l. Canada 118 G3
La Coubre, Pointe de pt France 52 D4
La Crete Canada 116 G3
La Crosse KS U.S.A. 126 D4
La Crosse VA U.S.A. 131 F5
La Crosse WI U.S.A. 126 F3
La Cruz Mex. 132 C4
Lac Thiên Vietnam 67 E4
La Cuesta Mex. 127 C6
La Culebra, Sierra de mts Spain 53 C3
La Cygne U.S.A. 126 E4
Ladainha Brazil 141 C2
Ladakh reg. Jammu and Kashmir 78 D2
Ladakh Range mts India 78 D2
Ladang, Ko i. Thai. 67 B6
La Demajagua Cuba 129 D8
La Demanda, Sierra de mts Spain 53 E2
La Déroute, Passage de strait Channel Is/France 45 E9
Ladik Turkey 86 D2
Lādīz Iran 85 F4
Ladnun India 78 C4
▶Ladoga, Lake Rus. Fed. 41 Q6
2nd largest lake in Europe.
Ladong China 73 F3
Ladozhskoye Ozero l. Rus. Fed. see Ladoga, Lake
Ladrones terr. N. Pacific Ocean see Northern Mariana Islands
Ladu mt. India 79 H4
Ladue r. Canada/U.S.A. 116 A2
Ladva-Vetka Rus. Fed. 38 G3
Ladybank U.K. 46 F4
Ladybrand S. Africa 97 H5
Lady Frere S. Africa 97 H6
Lady Grey S. Africa 97 H6
Ladysmith S. Africa 97 I5
Ladysmith U.S.A. 126 F2
Ladzhanurges Georgia see Lajanurpekhi
Lae P.N.G. 65 L8
Laem Ngop Thai. 67 C4
Lærdalsøyri Norway 41 E6
La Esmeralda Bol. 138 F8
Læsø i. Denmark 41 G8
Lafayette Alg. see Bougaa
Lafayette AL U.S.A. 129 C5
Lafayette IN U.S.A. 130 B3
Lafayette LA U.S.A. 127 E6
Lafayette TN U.S.A. 130 B5
Lafé Cuba 129 C8
La Fère France 48 D5
Laferte r. Canada 116 G2
La Ferté-Gaucher France 48 D6
La-Ferté-Milon France 48 D5
La Ferté-sous-Jouarre France 48 D6
Lafia Nigeria 92 D4
Lafiagi Nigeria 92 D4
Laflamme r. Canada 118 F4
Lafleche Canada 117 J5
La Flèche France 52 D3
La Follette U.S.A. 130 C5
La Forest, Lac l. Canada 119 H3
Laforge Canada 119 G3
Laforge r. Canada 119 G3
La Frégate, Lac de l. Canada 118 G3
Lāft Iran 84 D5
Laful India 67 A6
La Galissonnière, Lac l. Canada 119 J4
▶La Galite i. Tunisia 54 C6
Most northerly point of Africa.
La Galite, Canal de sea chan. Tunisia 54 C6
La Gallega Mex. 127 B7
Lagan' Rus. Fed. 39 J7
Lagan r. U.K. 47 G3
La Garamba, Parc National de nat. park Dem. Rep. Congo 94 C3
Lagarto Brazil 139 K6
Lage Germany 49 I3
Lågen r. Norway 41 G7
Lage Vaart canal Neth. 48 F2
Lagg U.K. 46 D5
Laggan U.K. 46 E3
Lagh Bor watercourse Kenya/Somalia 94 E3
Laghouat Alg. 50 E5
Lagkor Co salt l. China 79 F2
La Gloria Mex. 127 D7
Lago Agrio Ecuador see Nueva Loja
Lagoa Santa Brazil 141 C2
Lagoa Vermelha Brazil 141 A5
Lagodekhi Georgia 87 G2
Lagolândia Brazil 141 A1
La Gomera i. Canary Is 92 B2
La Gonâve, Île de i. Haiti 133 J5
Lagong i. Indon. 67 E7
▶Lagos Nigeria 92 D4
Former capital of Nigeria. 2nd most populous city in Africa.
Lagos Port. 53 B5
Lagosa Tanz. 95 C4
La Grande r. Canada 118 F3
La Grande U.S.A. 122 D3
La Grande 2, Réservoir resr Canada 118 F3
La Grande 3, Réservoir resr Canada 118 G3
La Grande 4, Réservoir resr Que. Canada 119 G3
Lagrange Australia 104 C4
La Grange CA U.S.A. 124 C3
La Grange GA U.S.A. 129 C5
Lagrange U.S.A. 130 C3
La Grange KY U.S.A. 128 C4
La Grange TX U.S.A. 127 D6
La Gran Sabana plat. Venez. 138 F2
La Grita Venez. 138 D2
La Guajira, Península de pen. Col. 138 D1
Laguna Brazil 141 A5
Laguna Dam U.S.A. 125 F5
Laguna Mountains U.S.A. 124 E5
Lagunas Chile 140 C2
Laguna San Rafael, Parque Nacional nat. park Chile 140 B7
Laha China 70 B2
La Habana Cuba see Havana
La Habra U.S.A. 124 E5
Lahad Datu Sabah Malaysia 64 F5
La Hague, Cap de c. France 52 D2
Laharpur India 78 E4
Lahat Indon. 64 C7
Lahe Myanmar 66 A1
Lahemaa rahvuspark nat. park Estonia 41 N7
La Hève, Cap de c. France 45 H9
Lahewa Indon. 67 B7
Laḥij Yemen 82 F7
Lāhījān Iran 84 C2
Lahn r. Germany 49 H4
Lahnstein Germany 49 H4
Laholm Sweden 41 H8
Lahontan Reservoir U.S.A. 124 D2
Lahore Pak. 85 I4
Lahri Pak. 85 H4
Lahti Fin. 41 N6
Laï Chad 93 E4
Lai'an China 73 H1
Laibach Slovenia see Ljubljana
Laibin China 73 F4
Laidley Australia 108 F1
Laifeng China 73 F2
L'Aigle France 52 E2
Laihia Fin. 40 M5
Lai-hka Myanmar 66 B2
Lai-Hsak Myanmar 66 B2
Laimakuri India 79 H4
Laingsburg S. Africa 96 E7
Laingsburg U.S.A. 130 C2
Lainioälven r. Sweden 40 M3
Lair U.S.A. 130 C4
L'Aïr, Massif de mts Niger 92 D3
Lairg U.K. 46 E2
La Isabela Cuba 129 D8
Laishevo Rus. Fed. 38 K5
Laitila Fin. 41 L6
Laives Italy 54 D1
Laiwu China 69 L5
Laiwui Indon. 65 H7
Laiyang China 69 M5
Laizhou China 69 L5
Laizhou Wan b. China 69 L5
Lajamanu Australia 104 E4
Lajanurpekhi Georgia 87 F2
Lajeado Brazil 141 A5
Lajes Rio Grande do Norte Brazil 139 K5
Lajes Santa Catarina Brazil 141 A4
La Junta Mex. 123 G7
La Junta U.S.A. 126 C4
La Juventud, Isla de i. Cuba 133 H4
Lakadiya India 78 B5
La Kagera, Parc National de nat. park Rwanda see Akagera National Park
L'Akagera, Parc National de nat. park Rwanda see Akagera National Park
Lake U.S.A. 130 D5
Lake Andes U.S.A. 126 D3
Lakeba i. Fiji 103 I3
Lake Bardawil Reserve nature res. Egypt 81 A4
Lake Bolac Australia 108 A6
Lake Butler U.S.A. 129 D6
Lake Cargelligo Australia 108 C4
Lake Cathie Australia 108 F3
Lake Charles U.S.A. 127 E6
Lake City CO U.S.A. 125 J3

Lake City FL U.S.A. 129 D6
Lake City MI U.S.A. 130 C1
Lake Clark National Park and Preserve U.S.A. 114 C3
Lake Clear U.S.A. 131 H1
Lake District National Park U.K. 44 D4
Lake Eyre National Park Australia 107 B6
Lakefield Australia 106 D2
Lakefield Canada 131 F1
Lakefield National Park Australia 106 D2
Lake Forest U.S.A. 130 B2
Lake Gairdner National Park Australia 107 B7
Lake Geneva U.S.A. 126 F3
Lake George MI U.S.A. 130 C2
Lake George NY U.S.A. 131 I2
Lake Grace Australia 105 B8
Lake Harbour Canada see Kimmirut
Lake Havasu City U.S.A. 125 F4
Lakehurst U.S.A. 131 H3
Lake Isabella U.S.A. 124 D4
Lake Jackson U.S.A. 127 E6
Lake King Australia 105 B8
Lake Kopiago P.N.G. 65 K8
Lakeland FL U.S.A. 129 D7
Lakeland GA U.S.A. 129 D6
Lake Louise Canada 116 G5
Lakemba i. Fiji see Lakeba
Lake Mills U.S.A. 126 E3
Lake Nash Australia 106 B4
Lake Odessa U.S.A. 130 C2
Lake Paringa N.Z. 109 B6
Lake Placid FL U.S.A. 129 D7
Lake Placid NY U.S.A. 131 I1
Lake Pleasant U.S.A. 131 H2
Lakeport CA U.S.A. 124 B2
Lakeport MI U.S.A. 130 D2
Lake Providence U.S.A. 127 F5
Lake Range mts U.S.A. 124 D1
Lake River Canada 118 E3
Lakes Entrance Australia 108 D6
Lakeside AZ U.S.A. 125 I4
Lakeside VA U.S.A. 131 G5
Lake Tabourie Australia 108 E5
Lake Tekapo N.Z. 109 C7
Lake Torrens National Park Australia 107 B6
Lakeview MI U.S.A. 130 C2
Lakeview OH U.S.A. 130 D3
Lakeview OR U.S.A. 122 C4
Lake Village U.S.A. 127 F5
Lake Wales U.S.A. 129 D7
Lakewood CO U.S.A. 122 G5
Lakewood NJ U.S.A. 131 H3
Lakewood NY U.S.A. 130 F2
Lakewood OH U.S.A. 130 E3
Lake Worth U.S.A. 129 D7
Lakha India 78 B4
Lakhdenpokh'ya Rus. Fed. 40 Q6
Lakhimpur Assam India see North Lakhimpur
Lakhimpur Uttar Pradesh India 78 E4
Lakhisarai India 79 F4
Lakhish r. Israel 81 B4
Lakhnadon India 78 D5
Lakhpat India 78 B5
Lakhtar India 78 B5
Lakin U.S.A. 126 C4
Lakitusaki r. Canada 118 E3
Lakki Pak. 85 H3
Lakonikos Kolpos b. Greece 55 J6
Lakor i. Indon. 104 E2
Lakota Côte d'Ivoire 92 C4
Lakota U.S.A. 126 D1
Laksefjorden sea chan. Norway 40 O1
Lakselv Norway 40 N1
Lakshadweep is India see Laccadive Islands
Lakshadweep union terr. India 80 B4
Lakshettipet India 80 C2
Lakshmipur Bangl. 79 G5
Laksmipur Bangl. see Lakshmipur
Lalaghat India 79 H4
La Laguna, Picacho de mt. Mex. 132 B4
Lalbara India 80 D1
Lāleh Zār, Kūh-e mt. Iran 84 E4
Lalganj India 79 F4
Lālī Iran 84 C3
La Ligua Chile 140 B4
Laliki Indon. 104 D1
Lalin China 70 B3
Lalín Spain 53 B2
La Línea de la Concepción Spain 53 D5
Lalin He r. China 70 B3
Lalitpur India 78 D4
Lalitpur Nepal see Patan
Lalmanirhat Bangl. see Lalmonirhat
Lalmonirhat Bangl. 79 G4
La Loche Canada 117 I3
La Loche, Lac l. Canada 117 I3
La Louvière Belgium 48 E4
Lal'sk Rus. Fed. 38 J3
Lalung La pass China 79 F3
Lama Bangl. 79 H5
La Macarena, Parque Nacional nat. park Col. 138 D3
La Maddalena Sardinia Italy 54 C4
La Madeleine, Îles de is Canada 119 J5
La Madeleine, Monts de mts France 52 F3
Lamadian China 70 B3
Lamadianzi China see Lamadian
La Maiko, Parc National de nat. park Dem. Rep. Congo 94 C4
La Malbaie Canada 119 H5
La Mancha Mex. 127 C7
La Mancha reg. Spain 53 E4
La Manche strait France/U.K. see English Channel
La Máquina Mex. 127 B6
Lamar CO U.S.A. 126 C4
Lamar MO U.S.A. 127 E4
Lamard Iran 84 D5
La Margeride, Monts de mts France 52 F4
La Marmora, Punta mt. Sardinia Italy 54 C5
La Marne au Rhin, Canal de France 48 G6
La Marque U.S.A. 127 E6
La Martre, Lac l. Canada 116 G2
Lamas r. Turkey 81 B1
La Mauricie, Parc National de nat. park Canada 119 G5
Lambaréné Gabon 94 B4
Lambasa Fiji see Labasa
Lambayeque Peru 138 C5
Lambay Island Rep. of Ireland 47 G4
Lambert atoll Marshall Is see Ailinglapalap
▶Lambert Glacier Antarctica 148 E2
Largest series of glaciers in the world.
Lambert's Bay S. Africa 96 D7
Lambeth Canada 130 E2
Lambi India 78 C3
Lambourn Downs hills U.K. 45 F7
Lame Indon. 67 B7
La Medjerda, Monts de mts Alg. 54 B6
Lamego Port. 53 C3
Lamèque, Île i. Canada 119 I5
La Merced Arg. 140 C3
La Merced Peru 138 C6
Lameroo Australia 107 C7
La Mesa U.S.A. 124 E5
Lamesa U.S.A. 127 C5
Lamia Greece 55 J5
Lamington National Park Australia 108 F2
La Misión Mex. 124 E5
Lamma Island Hong Kong China 73 [inset]
Lammerlaw Range mts N.Z. 109 B7
Lammermuir Hills U.K. 46 G5
Lammhult Sweden 41 I8
Lammi Fin. 41 N6
Lamont CA U.S.A. 124 D4
Lamont WY U.S.A. 122 G4
La Montagne d'Ambre, Parc National de nat. park Madag. 95 E5
La Montaña de Covadonga, Parque Nacional de nat. park Spain see Los Picos de Europa, Parque Nacional de
La Mora Mex. 127 C7
La Morita Chihuahua Mex. 127 B6
La Morita Coahuila Mex. 127 C6
Lamotrek atoll Micronesia 65 L5
La Moure U.S.A. 126 D2
Lampang Thai. 66 B3
Lam Pao Reservoir Thai. 66 C3
Lampasas U.S.A. 127 D6
Lampazos Mex. 127 C7
Lampedusa, Isola di i. Sicily Italy 54 E7
Lampeter U.K. 45 C6
Lamphun Thai. 66 B3
Lampsacus Turkey see Lâpseki
Lam Tin Hong Kong China 73 [inset]
Lamu Kenya 94 E4
Lamu Myanmar 66 A3
Lanai i. HI U.S.A. 123 [inset]
Lanai City HI U.S.A. 123 [inset]
La Nao, Cabo de c. Spain 53 G4
Lanao, Lake Phil. 65 G5
Lanark Canada 131 G1
Lanark U.K. 46 F5
Lanbi Kyun i. Myanmar 67 B5
Lancang China 72 C4
Lancang Jiang r. Xizang/Yunnan China see Mekong
Lancaster Canada 131 H1
Lancaster U.K. 44 E4
Lancaster CA U.S.A. 124 D4
Lancaster KY U.S.A. 130 C5
Lancaster MO U.S.A. 126 E3
Lancaster NH U.S.A. 131 J1
Lancaster OH U.S.A. 130 D4
Lancaster PA U.S.A. 131 G3
Lancaster SC U.S.A. 129 D5
Lancaster VA U.S.A. 131 G5
Lancaster WI U.S.A. 126 F3
Lancaster Canal U.K. 44 E5
Lancaster Sound strait Canada 115 J2
Lanchow China see Lanzhou
Landana Angola see Cacongo
Landau an der Isar Germany 49 M6
Landau in der Pfalz Germany 49 I5
Landeck Austria 43 M7
Lander watercourse Australia 104 E5
Lander U.S.A. 122 F4
Landesbergen Germany 49 J2
Landfall Island India 67 A4
Landhi Pak. 85 G5
Landis Canada 117 I4
Landor Australia 105 B6
Landsberg Poland see Gorzów Wielkopolski
Landsberg am Lech Germany 43 M6
Land's End pt U.K. 45 B8
Landshut Germany 49 M6
Landskrona Sweden 41 H9
Landstuhl Germany 49 H5
Land Wursten reg. Germany 49 I1
Lanesborough Rep. of Ireland 47 E4
La'nga Co l. China 78 E3
Langao China 73 F1
Langar Afgh. 85 H3
Langberg mts S. Africa 96 F5
Langdon U.S.A. 126 D1
Langeac France 52 F4
Langeberg mts S. Africa 96 D7
Langeland i. Denmark 41 G9
Längelmäki Fin. 41 N6
Langelsheim Germany 49 K3
Langen Germany 49 I1
Langenburg Canada 117 K5
Langenhagen Germany 49 J2
Langenhahn Germany 49 H4
Langenlonsheim Germany 49 H5
Langenthal Switz. 52 H3
Langenweddingen Germany 49 L2
Langeoog Germany 49 H1
Langesund Norway 41 F7
Langfang China 69 L5
Langgapayung Indon. 67 B7
Langgar China 72 B2
Langgöns Germany 49 I4
Langjan Nature Reserve S. Africa 97 I2
Langjökull ice cap Iceland 40 [inset]
Langka Indon. 67 B6
Langkawi i. Malaysia 67 B6
Lang Kha Toek, Khao mt. Thai. 67 B5
Langklip S. Africa 96 E5
Langley Canada 116 F5
Langley U.S.A. 130 D5
Langlo Crossing Australia 107 D5
Langmusi China see Dagcanglhamo
Langong, Xé r. Laos 66 D3
Langøya i. Norway 40 I2
Langphu mt. China 79 F3
Langport U.K. 45 E7
Langqên Zangbo r. China 78 D3
Langqi China 73 H3
Langres France 52 G3
Langres, Plateau de France 52 G3
Langru China 78 D1
Langsa Indon. 67 B6
Langsa, Teluk b. Indon. 67 B6
Långsele Sweden 40 J5
Lang Son Vietnam 66 D2
Langtang National Park Nepal 79 F3
Langtao Myanmar 66 B1
Langting India 79 H4
Langtoft U.K. 44 G4
Langtry U.S.A. 127 C6
Languan China see Lantian
Languedoc reg. France 52 E5
Långvattnet Sweden 40 L4
Langwedel Germany 49 J2
Langxi China 73 H2
Langzhong China 72 E2
Lanigan Canada 117 J5
Lanín, Parque Nacional nat. park Arg. 140 B5
Lanín, Volcán vol. Arg./Chile 140 B5
Lanji India 78 E5
Lanka country Asia see Sri Lanka
Länkäran Azer. 87 H3
Lannion France 52 C2
Lanping China 72 C3
Lansån Sweden 40 M3
L'Anse U.S.A. 126 F2
Lanshan China 73 G3
▶Lansing U.S.A. 130 C2
State capital of Michigan.
Lanta, Ko i. Thai. 67 B6
Lantau Island Hong Kong China 73 [inset]
Lantau Peak hill Hong Kong China 73 [inset]
Lantian China 73 F1
Lanxi Heilong. China 70 B3
Lanxi Zhejiang China 73 H2
Lan Yü i. Taiwan 73 I4
Lanzarote i. Canary Is 92 B2
Lanzhou China 68 I5
Lanzijing China 70 A3
Laoag Phil. 65 G3
Laoang Phil. 65 H4
Laobie Shan mts China 72 C4
Laobukou China 73 F3
Lao Cai Vietnam 66 C2
Laodicea Syria see Latakia
Laodicea Turkey see Denizli
Laodicea ad Lycum Turkey see Denizli
Laodicea ad Mare Syria see Latakia
Laohekou China 73 F1
Laohupo China see Logpung
Laojie China see Yongping
Laojunmiao China see Yumen
La Okapi, Parc National de nat. park Dem. Rep. Congo 94 C3
Lao Ling mts China 70 B4
Laon France 48 D5
La Oroya Peru 138 C6
▶Laos country Asia 66 C3
asia 6, 58–59
Laotougou China 70 C4
Laotuding Shan hill China 70 B4
Laowohi pass Jammu and Kashmir see Khardung La
Laoye Ling mts Heilongjiang/Jilin China 70 B4
Laoye Ling mts Heilongjiang/Jilin China 70 C4
Lapa Brazil 141 A4
La Palma i. Canary Is 92 B2
La Palma Panama 133 I7
La Palma U.S.A. 125 H5
La Palma del Condado Spain 53 C5
La Panza Range mts U.S.A. 124 C4
La Paragua Venez. 138 F2
La Parilla Mex. 127 B8
La Paya, Parque Nacional nat. park Col. 138 D3
La Paz Arg. 140 E4
▶La Paz Bol. 138 E7
Official capital of Bolivia.
La Paz Hond. 132 G6
La Paz Mex. 132 B4
La Pedrera Col. 138 E4
Lapeer U.S.A. 130 D2
La Pendjari, Parc National de nat. park Benin 92 D3
La Perla Mex. 127 B6
La Pérouse Strait Japan/Rus. Fed. 70 F3
La Pesca Mex. 127 D8
Lapinlahti Fin. 40 O5
Lapithos Cyprus 81 A2
Lap Lae Thai. 66 C3
La Plant U.S.A. 126 C2
La Plata Arg. 140 E4
La Plata MD U.S.A. 131 G4
La Plata MO U.S.A. 126 E3
La Plata, Isla i. Ecuador 138 B4
La Plata, Río de sea chan. Arg./Uruguay 140 E4
La Plonge, Lac l. Canada 117 J4
Lapmežciems Latvia 41 M8
Lapominka Rus. Fed. 38 I2
La Porte U.S.A. 130 B3
Laporte U.S.A. 131 G3
Laporte, Mount Canada 116 E2
La Potherie, Lac l. Canada 119 G2
La Poza Grande Mex. 123 E8
Lappajärvi Fin. 40 M5
Lappajärvi l. Fin. 40 M5
Lappeenranta Fin. 41 P6
Lappersdorf Germany 49 M5
Lappi Fin. 41 L6
Lappland reg. Europe 40 K3
La Pryor U.S.A. 127 D6
Lâpseki Turkey 55 L4
Laptevo Rus. Fed. see Yasnogorsk
Laptev Sea Rus. Fed. 61 N2
Lapua Fin. 40 M5
Lapurdum France see Bayonne
La Purísima Mex. 123 E8
Laqiya Arbain well Sudan 82 C5
La Quiaca Arg. 140 C2
L'Aquila Italy 54 E3
La Quinta U.S.A. 124 E5
Lār Iran 84 D5
Larache Morocco 53 C6
Lārak i. Iran 84 E5
Laramie U.S.A. 122 G4
Laramie r. U.S.A. 122 G4
Laramie Mountains U.S.A. 122 G4
Laranda Turkey see Karaman
Laranjal Paulista Brazil 141 B3
Laranjeiras do Sul Brazil 140 F3
Laranjinha r. Brazil 141 A3
Larantuka Indon. 104 C2
Larat Indon. 104 E1
Larat i. Indon. 104 E1
Larba Alg. 53 H5
Lärbro Sweden 41 K8
L'Archipélago de Mingan, Réserve du Parc National de nat. park Canada 119 J4
L'Ardenne, Plateau de plat. Belgium see Ardennes
Laredo Spain 53 E2
Laredo U.S.A. 127 D7
La Reina Adelaida, Archipiélago de is Chile 140 B8
Largeau Chad see Faya
Largo U.S.A. 129 D7
Largs U.K. 46 E5
Lārī Iran 84 B2
L'Ariana Tunisia 54 D6
Larimore U.S.A. 126 D2
La Rioja Arg. 140 C3
La Rioja aut. comm. Spain 53 E2
Larisa Greece 55 J5
Larissa Greece see Larisa
Laristan reg. Iran 84 E5
Larkana Pak. 85 H5
Lark Harbour Canada 119 K4
Lar Koh mt. Afgh. 85 F3
Lark Passage Australia 106 D2
L'Arli, Parc National de nat. park Burkina 92 D3
Larnaca Cyprus 81 A2
Larnaca Bay Cyprus 81 A2
Larnaka Cyprus see Larnaca
Larnakos, Kolpos b. Cyprus see Larnaca Bay
Larne U.K. 47 G3
Larned U.S.A. 126 D4
La Robe Noire, Lac de l. Canada 119 J4
La Robla Spain 53 D2
La Roche-en-Ardenne Belgium 48 F4
La Rochelle France 52 D3
La Roche-sur-Yon France 52 D3
La Roda Spain 53 E4
La Romana Dom. Rep. 133 K5
La Ronge Canada 117 J4
La Ronge, Lac l. Canada 117 J4
La Rosa Mex. 127 C7
La Rosita Mex. 127 C6
Larrey Point Australia 104 B4
Larrimah Australia 104 F3
Lars Christensen Coast Antarctica 148 E2
Larsen Ice Shelf Antarctica 148 L2
Larsmo Fin. see Luoto
Larvik Norway 41 G7
Las Adjuntas, Presa de resr Mex. 127 D8
La Sal U.S.A. 125 I2
La Salle Canada 131 I1
La Salle U.S.A. 118 C6
La Salonga Nord, Parc National de nat. park Dem. Rep. Congo 94 C4
La Sambre à l'Oise, Canal de France 48 D5
Las Animas U.S.A. 126 C4
Las Anod Somalia see Laascaanood
La Sarre Canada 118 F4
Las Avispas Mex. 123 F7
La Savonnière, Lac l. Canada 119 G3
La Scie Canada 119 L4
Las Cruces CA U.S.A. 124 C4
Las Cruces NM U.S.A. 123 G6
La Selle, Pic mt. Haiti 133 J5
La Semois, Vallée de valley Belgium/France 48 E5
La Serena Chile 140 B3
Las Esperanças Mex. 127 C7
Las Flores Arg. 140 E5
Las Guacamatas, Cerro mt. Mex. 123 F7
Lāshār r. Iran 85 F5
Lashburn Canada 117 I4
Las Heras Arg. 140 C4
Lashio Myanmar 66 B2
Lashkar India 78 D4
Lashkar Gāh Afgh. 85 G4
Las Juntas Chile 140 C3
Las Lomitas Arg. 140 D2
Las Marismas marsh Spain 53 C5
Las Martinetas Arg. 140 C7
Las Mesteñas Mex. 127 B6
Las Minas, Cerro de mt. Hond. 132 G6
Las Nopaleras, Cerro mt. Mex. 127 C7
La Société, Archipel de is Fr. Polynesia see Society Islands
La Somme, Canal de France 48 C5
Las Palmas watercourse Mex. 124 E5
▶Las Palmas de Gran Canaria Canary Is 92 B2
Joint capital of the Canary Islands.
Las Petas Bol. 139 G7
La Spezia Italy 54 C2
Las Piedras, Río de r. Peru 138 E6
Las Plumas Arg. 140 C6
Laspur Pak. 85 I2
Lassance Brazil 141 B2
Lassen Peak vol. U.S.A. 124 C1
Lassen Volcanic National Park U.S.A. 124 C1
Las Tablas Panama 133 H7
Las Tablas de Daimiel, Parque Nacional de nat. park Spain 53 E4
Last Chance U.S.A. 126 C4
Las Termas Arg. 140 D3
Last Mountain Lake Canada 117 J5
Las Tórtolas, Cerro mt. Chile 140 C3
Lastoursville Gabon 94 B4
Lastovo i. Croatia 54 G3
Las Tres Vírgenes, Volcán vol. Mex. 123 E8
Lastrup Germany 49 H2
Las Tunas Cuba 133 I4
Las Varas Chihuahua Mex. 123 G7
Las Varas Nayarit Mex. 132 C4
Las Varillas Arg. 140 D4
Las Vegas NM U.S.A. 123 G6
Las Vegas NV U.S.A. 125 F3
Las Viajas, Isla de i. Peru 138 C6
Las Villuercas mt. Spain 53 D4
La Tabatière Canada 119 K4
Latacunga Ecuador 138 C4
Latady Island Antarctica 148 L2
Latakia Syria 81 B2
La Teste France 52 D4
Latham Australia 105 B7
Lathen Germany 49 H2
Latheron U.K. 46 F2
Lathi India 78 B4
Latho Jammu and Kashmir 78 D2
Lathrop U.S.A. 124 C3
Latina Italy 54 E4
La Tortuga, Isla i. Venez. 138 E1
Latrobe U.S.A. 130 F3
Latrun West Bank 81 B4
Lattaquié Syria see Latakia
Lattrop Neth. 48 G2
La Tuque Canada 119 G5
Latur India 80 C2
▶Latvia country Europe 41 N8
europe 5, 34–35
Latvija country Europe see Latvia
Latviyskaya S.S.R. country Europe see Latvia
Lauca, Parque Nacional nat. park Chile 138 E7
Lauchhammer Germany 43 N5
Lauder U.K. 46 G5
Laudio Spain see Llodio
Lauenbrück Germany 49 J1
Lauenburg (Elbe) Germany 49 K1
Lauf an der Pegnitz Germany 49 L5
Laufen Switz. 52 H3
Lauge Koch Kyst reg. Greenland 115 L2
Laughlen, Mount Australia 105 F5
Laughlin Peak U.S.A. 123 G5
Lauka Estonia 41 M7
Launceston Australia 107 [inset]
Launceston U.K. 45 C8
Laune r. Rep. of Ireland 47 C5
Launggyaung Myanmar 66 B1
Launglon Myanmar 67 B4
Launglon Bok Islands Myanmar 67 B4
La Unión Bol. 138 F7
Laura Australia 106 D2
Laurel DE U.S.A. 131 H4
Laurel MS U.S.A. 127 F6
Laurel MT U.S.A. 122 F3
Laureldale U.S.A. 131 H3
Laurel Hill hills U.S.A. 130 F4
Laurencekirk U.K. 46 G4
Laurieton Australia 108 F3
Laurinburg U.S.A. 129 E5
Lauru i. Solomon Is see Choiseul
Lausanne Switz. 52 H3
Laut i. Indon. 64 F7
Laut i. Indon. 67 E6
Lautem East Timor 104 D2
Lautersbach (Hessen) Germany 49 J4
Laut Kecil, Kepulauan is Indon. 64 F8
Lautoka Fiji 103 H3
Lauvuskylä Fin. 40 P5
Lauwersmeer l. Neth. 48 G1
Lava Beds National Monument nat. park U.S.A. 122 C4
Laval Canada 118 G5
Laval France 52 D2
La Vanoise, Massif de mts France 52 H4
La Vanoise, Parc National de nat. park France 52 H4
Lavapié, Punta pt Chile 140 B5
Lāvar Iran 84 C4
Laveaga Peak U.S.A. 124 C3
La Vega Dom. Rep. 133 J5
Laverne U.S.A. 127 D4
Laverton Australia 105 C7
La Víbora Mex. 127 C7
La Vila Joiosa Spain see Villajoyosa - La Vila Joiosa
La Viña Peru 138 C5
Lavongal i. P.N.G. see New Hanover
Lavras Brazil 141 B3
Lavumisa Swaziland 97 J4
Lavushi-Manda National Park Zambia 95 D5
Lawa India 78 C4
Lawa Myanmar 66 B1
Lawa Pak. 85 H3
Lawashi r. Canada 118 E3
Law Dome ice feature Antarctica 148 F2
Lawit, Gunung mt. Malaysia 67 C6
Lawksawk Myanmar 66 B2
Lawn Hill National Park Australia 106 B3
La Woëvre, Plaine de plain France 48 F5
Lawra Ghana 92 C3
Lawrence IN U.S.A. 130 B4
Lawrence KS U.S.A. 126 E4
Lawrence MA U.S.A. 131 J2
Lawrenceburg IN U.S.A. 130 C4
Lawrenceburg KY U.S.A. 130 C4
Lawrenceburg TN U.S.A. 128 C5
Lawrenceville GA U.S.A. 129 D5
Lawrenceville IL U.S.A. 130 B4
Lawrenceville VA U.S.A. 131 G5
Lawrence Wells, Mount hill Australia 105 C6
Lawton U.S.A. 127 D5
Lawz, Jabal al mt. Saudi Arabia 86 D5
Laxå Sweden 41 I7
Laxey Isle of Man 44 C4
Lax Kw'alaams Canada 116 D4
Laxo U.K. 46 [inset]
Laya r. Rus. Fed. 38 M2
Laydennyy, Mys c. Rus. Fed. 38 J1
Laylá Saudi Arabia 82 G5
Layla salt pan Saudi Arabia 81 D4
Laysan Island U.S.A. 146 I4
Laytonville U.S.A. 124 B2
Laza Myanmar 66 B1
Lazarev Rus. Fed. 70 F1
Lazarevac Serb. and Mont. 55 I2
Lázaro Cárdenas Mex. 132 D5
Lazcano Uruguay 140 F4
Lazdijai Lith. 41 M9
Lazikou China 72 D1
Lazo Primorskiy Kray Rus. Fed. 70 D4
Lazo Respublika Sakha (Yakutiya) Rus. Fed. 61 O3
Lead U.S.A. 126 C2
Leader Water r. U.K. 46 G5
Leadville Australia 108 D4
Leaf r. U.S.A. 127 F6
Leaf Bay Canada see Tasiujaq
Leaf Rapids Canada 117 K3
Leakey U.S.A. 127 D6
Leaksville U.S.A. see Eden
Leamington Canada 130 D2
Leamington Spa, Royal U.K. 45 F6
Leane, Lough l. Rep. of Ireland 47 C5
Leap Rep. of Ireland 47 C6
Leatherhead U.K. 45 G7
L'Eau Claire, Lac à l. Canada 118 G2
L'Eau Claire, Rivière à r. Canada 118 G2
L'Eau d'Heure l. Belgium 48 E4
Leavenworth IN U.S.A. 130 B4
Leavenworth KS U.S.A. 126 E4
Leavenworth WA U.S.A. 122 C3
Leavitt Peak U.S.A. 124 D2
Lebach Germany 48 G5
▶Lebanon country Asia 81 B2
asia 6, 58–59
Lebanon IN U.S.A. 130 B3
Lebanon KY U.S.A. 130 C5
Lebanon MO U.S.A. 126 E4
Lebanon NH U.S.A. 131 I2
Lebanon OH U.S.A. 130 C4
Lebanon OR U.S.A. 122 C3
Lebanon PA U.S.A. 131 G3
Lebanon TN U.S.A. 128 C4
Lebanon VA U.S.A. 130 D5
Lebanon Junction U.S.A. 130 C5
Lebanon Mountains Lebanon see Liban, Jebel
Lebbeke Belgium 48 E3
Lebec U.S.A. 124 D4
Lebedyan' Rus. Fed. 39 H5
Lebel-sur-Quévillon Canada 118 F4
Le Blanc France 52 E3
Lębork Poland 43 P3
Lebowakgomo S. Africa 97 I3
Lebrija Spain 53 C5
Łebsko, Jezioro lag. Poland 43 P3
Lebu Chile 140 B5
Lebyazh'ye Kazakh. see Akku
Lebyazh'ye Rus. Fed. 38 K4
Le Caire Egypt see Cairo
Le Cateau-Cambrésis France 48 D4
Le Catelet France 48 D4
Lecce Italy 54 H4
Lecco Italy 54 C2
Lech r. Austria/Germany 43 M7
Lechaina Greece 55 I6
Lechang China 73 G3
Le Chasseron mt. Switz. 52 H3
Le Chesne France 48 E5
Lechtaler Alpen mts Austria 43 M7
Leck Germany 43 L3
Lecompte U.S.A. 127 E6
Le Creusot France 52 G3
Le Crotoy France 48 B4
Lectoure France 52 E5
Ledang, Gunung mt. Malaysia 67 C7
Ledbury U.K. 45 E6
Ledesma Spain 53 D3
Ledmore U.K. 46 E2
Ledmozero Rus. Fed. 40 R4
Ledong Hainan China 66 E3
Ledong Hainan China 73 F5
Le Dorat France 52 E3
Leduc Canada 116 H4
Lee r. Rep. of Ireland 47 D6
Lee IN U.S.A. 130 B3
Lee MA U.S.A. 131 I2
Leech Lake U.S.A. 126 E2
Leeds U.K. 44 F5
Leedstown U.K. 45 B8
Leek Neth. 48 G1
Leek U.K. 45 E5
Leende Neth. 48 F3
Leer (Ostfriesland) Germany 49 H1
Leesburg FL U.S.A. 129 D6
Leesburg GA U.S.A. 129 C6
Leesburg OH U.S.A. 130 D4
Leesburg VA U.S.A. 131 G4
Leese Germany 49 J2
Lee Steere Range hills Australia 105 C6
Leesville U.S.A. 127 E6
Leesville Lake OH U.S.A. 130 E3
Leesville Lake VA U.S.A. 130 F5
Leeton Australia 108 C5
Leeu-Gamka S. Africa 96 E7
Leeuwarden Neth. 48 F1
Leeuwin, Cape Australia 105 A8
Leeuwin-Naturaliste National Park Australia 105 A8
Lee Vining U.S.A. 124 D3
Leeward Islands Caribbean Sea 133 L5
Lefka Cyprus 81 A2
Lefkada Greece 55 I5
Lefkada i. Greece 55 I5
Lefkás Greece see Lefkada
Lefke Cyprus see Lefka
Lefkimmi Greece 55 I5
Lefkoniko Cyprus see Lefkonikon
Lefkonikon Cyprus 81 A2
Lefkoşa Cyprus see Nicosia
Lefkosia Cyprus see Nicosia
Lefroy r. Canada 119 H2
Lefroy, Lake salt flat Australia 105 C7
Legarde r. Canada 118 D4
Legaspi Phil. 65 G4
Legden Germany 48 H2
Legges Tor mt. Australia 107 [inset]
Leghorn Italy see Livorno
Legnago Italy 54 D2
Legnica Poland 43 P5
Le Grand U.S.A. 124 C3
Legune Australia 104 E3
Leh India 78 D2
Le Havre France 52 E2
Lehi U.S.A. 125 H1
Lehighton U.S.A. 131 H3
Lehmo Fin. 40 P5
Lehre Germany 49 K2
Lehrte Germany 49 J2
Lehtimäki Fin. 40 M5
Lehututu Botswana 96 E2
Leiah Pak. 85 H4
Leibnitz Austria 43 O7
Leicester U.K. 45 F6
Leichhardt r. Australia 102 B3
Leichhardt Falls Australia 106 B3
Leichhardt Range mts Australia 106 D4
Leiden Neth. 48 E2
Leie r. Belgium 48 D3
Leigh N.Z. 109 E3
Leigh U.K. 44 E5
Leighton Buzzard U.K. 45 G7
Leiktho Myanmar 66 B3
Leimen Germany 49 I5
Leine r. Germany 49 J2
Leinefelde Germany 49 K3
Leinster Australia 105 C6
Leinster reg. Rep. of Ireland 47 F4
Leinster, Mount hill Rep. of Ireland 47 F5
Leipsic U.S.A. 130 D3
Leipsoi i. Greece 55 L6
Leipzig Germany 49 M3
Leipzig-Halle airport Germany 49 M3
Leiranger Norway 40 I3
Leiria Port. 53 B4
Leirvik Norway 41 D7
Leishan China 73 F3
Leisler, Mount hill Australia 105 E5
Leisnig Germany 49 M3
Leitchfield U.S.A. 130 B5
Leith Hill hill U.K. 45 G7
Leiva, Cerro mt. Col. 138 D3
Leixlip Rep. of Ireland 47 F4
Leiyang China 73 G3
Leizhou China 73 F4
Leizhou Bandao pen. China 73 F4

Leizhou Wan *b.* China **73** F4
Lek *r.* Neth. **48** E3
Leka Norway **40** G4
Lékana Congo **94** B4
Le Kef Tunisia **54** C6
Lekhainá Greece *see* **Lechaina**
Lekitobi Indon. **65** G7
Lekkersing S. Africa **96** C5
Lékoni Gabon **94** B4
Leksand Sweden **41** I6
Leksozero, Ozero *l.* Rus. Fed. **40** Q5
Lelai, Tanjung *pt* Indon. **65** H6
Leland U.S.A. **130** C1
Leli China *see* **Tianlin**
Lélouma Guinea **92** B3
Lelystad Neth. **48** F2
Le Maire, Estrecho de *sea chan.* Arg. **140** C9
Léman, Lac *l.* France/Switz. *see* **Geneva, Lake**
Le Mans France **52** E2
Le Mars U.S.A. **126** D3
Lemberg France **49** H5
Lemberg Ukr. *see* **L'viv**
Lembruch Germany **49** I2
Lemdiyya Alg. *see* **Médéa**
Leme Brazil **141** B3
Lemele Neth. **48** G2
Lemesos Cyprus *see* **Limassol**
Lemgo Germany **49** I2
Lemhi Range *mts* U.S.A. **122** E3
Lemi Fin. **41** O6
Lemieux Islands Canada **115** L3
Lemmenjoen kansallispuisto *nat. park* Fin. **40** N2
Lemmer Neth. **48** F2
Lemmon U.S.A. **126** C2
Lemmon, Mount U.S.A. **125** H5
Lemnos *i.* Greece *see* **Limnos**
Lemoncove U.S.A. **124** D3
Lemoore U.S.A. **124** D3
Le Moyne, Lac *l.* Canada **119** H2
Lemro *r.* Myanmar **66** A2
Lemtybozh Rus. Fed. **37** R3
Le Murge *hills* Italy **54** G4
Lemvig Denmark **41** F8
Lem'yu *r.* Rus. Fed. **38** M3
Lena *r.* Rus. Fed. **68** J1
Lena U.S.A. **130** A1
Lena, Mount U.S.A. **125** I1
Lenadoon Point Rep. of Ireland **47** C3
Lenchung Tso *salt l.* China **79** E2
Lencóis Brazil **141** C1
Lençóis Maranhenses, Parque Nacional dos *nat. park* Brazil **139** J4
Lendeh Iran **84** C4
Lendery Rus. Fed. **40** Q5
Le Neubourg France **45** H9
Lengerich Germany **49** H2
Lenglong Ling *mts* China **68** I5
Lengshuijiang China **73** F3
Lengshuitan China **73** F3
Lenham U.K. **45** H7
Lenhovda Sweden **41** I8
Lenin Tajik. **85** H2
Lenin, Qullai *mt.* Kyrg./Tajik. *see* **Lenin Peak**
Lenina, Pik *mt.* Kyrg./Tajik. *see* **Lenin Peak**
Leninabad Tajik. *see* **Khŭjand**
Leninakan Armenia *see* **Gyumri**
Lenin Atyndagy Choku *mt.* Kyrg./Tajik. *see* **Lenin Peak**
Lenine Ukr. **86** D1
Leningrad Rus. Fed. *see* **St Petersburg**
Leningrad Tajik. **85** H2
Leningrad Oblast *admin. div.* Rus. Fed. *see* **Leningradskaya Oblast'**
Leningradskaya Rus. Fed. **39** H7
Leningradskaya Oblast' *admin. div.* Rus. Fed. **41** R7
Leningradskiy Rus. Fed. **61** S3
Leningradskiy Tajik. *see* **Leningrad**
Lenino Ukr. *see* **Lenine**
Leninobod Tajik. *see* **Khŭjand**
Lenin Peak Kyrg./Tajik. **85** I2
Leninsk Kazakh. *see* **Baykonyr**
Leninsk Rus. Fed. **39** J6
Leninskiy Rus. Fed. **39** H5
Leninsk-Kuznetskiy Rus. Fed. **60** J4
Leninskoye Kazakh. **39** K6
Leninskoye *Kirovskaya Oblast'* Rus. Fed. **38** J4
Leninskoye *Yevreyskaya Avtonomnaya Oblast'* Rus. Fed. **70** D3
Lenkoran' Azer. *see* **Länkäran**
Lenne *r.* Germany **49** H3
Lennoxville Canada **131** J1
Lenoir U.S.A. **128** D5
Lenore U.S.A. **130** D5
Lenore Lake Canada **117** J4
Lenox U.S.A. **131** I2
Lens France **48** C4
Lensk Rus. Fed. **61** M3
Lenti Hungary **54** G1
Lentini *Sicily* Italy **54** F6
Lenya Myanmar **67** B5
Lenzen Germany **49** L1
Léo Burkina **92** C3
Leoben Austria **43** O7
Leodhais, Eilean *i.* U.K. *see* **Lewis, Isle of**
Leominster U.K. **45** E6
Leominster U.S.A. **131** J2
León Mex. **132** D4
León Nicaragua **133** G6
León Spain **53** D2
Leon *r.* U.S.A. **127** D6
Leonardtown U.S.A. **131** G4
Leonardville Namibia **96** D2
Leongatha Australia **108** B7
Leonidi Greece **55** J6
Leonidovo Rus. Fed. **70** F2
Leonora Australia **105** C7
Leopold U.S.A. **130** E4
Leopold and Astrid Coast Antarctica *see* **King Leopold and Queen Astrid Coast**
Léopold II, Lac *l.* Dem. Rep. Congo *see* **Mai-Ndombe, Lac**
Leopoldina Brazil **141** C3
Leopoldo de Bulhões Brazil **141** A2
Léopoldville Dem. Rep. Congo *see* **Kinshasa**
Leoti U.S.A. **126** C4
Leoville Canada **117** J4
Lepalale S. Africa *see* **Ellisras**
Lepaya Latvia *see* **Liepāja**
Lepel' Belarus *see* **Lyepyel'**
Lepellé *r.* Canada **119** H1
Lephalala *r.* S. Africa **97** H2
Lephepe Botswana **97** G2
Lephoi S. Africa **97** G6
Leping China **73** H2
Lepontine, Alpi *mts* Italy/Switz. **54** C1
Leppävirta Fin. **40** O5
Lepreau, Point Canada **119** I5
Lepsa Kazakh. *see* **Lepsy**
Lepsy Kazakh. **76** E2
Le Puy France *see* **Le Puy-en-Velay**
Le Puy-en-Velay France **52** F4
Le Quesnoy France **48** D4
Lerala Botswana **97** H2
Leratswana S. Africa **97** H5
Léré Mali **92** C3
Lereh Indon. **65** J7
Leribe Lesotho *see* **Hlotse**
Lérida Col. **138** D4
Lérida Spain *see* **Lleida**
Lerik Azer. **87** H3
Lerma Spain **53** E2
Lermontov Rus. Fed. **87** F1
Lermontovka Rus. Fed. **70** D3
Lermontovskiy Rus. Fed. *see* **Lermontov**
Leros *i.* Greece **55** L6
Le Roy U.S.A. **131** G2
Le Roy, Lac *l.* Canada **118** G2
Lerum Sweden **41** H8
Lerwick U.K. **46** [inset]
Les Amirantes *is* Seychelles *see* **Amirante Islands**
Lesbos *i.* Greece **55** K5
Les Cayes Haiti **133** J5
Le Seu d'Urgell Spain **53** G2
Leshan China **72** D2
Leshukonskoye Rus. Fed. **38** J2
Lesi *watercourse* Sudan **93** F4
Leskhimstroy Ukr. *see* **Syeverodonets'k**
Leskovac Serb. and Mont. **55** I3
Leslie U.S.A. **130** C2
Lesneven France **52** B2
Lesnoy *Kirovskaya Oblast'* Rus. Fed. **38** L4
Lesnoy *Murmanskaya Oblast'* Rus. Fed. *see* **Umba**
Lesnoye Rus. Fed. **38** G4
Lesogorsk Rus. Fed. **70** F2
Lesopil'noye Rus. Fed. **70** D3
Lesosibirsk Rus. Fed. **60** K4
▶**Lesotho** *country* Africa **97** I5
africa 7, 90–91
Lesozavodsk Rus. Fed. **70** D3
L'Espérance Rock *i.* Kermadec Is **103** I5
Les Pieux France **45** F9
Les Sables-d'Olonne France **52** D3
Lesse *r.* Belgium **48** E4
Lesser Antarctica *reg.* Antarctica *see* **West Antarctica**
Lesser Antilles *is* Caribbean Sea **133** K6
Lesser Caucasus *mts* Asia **87** F2
Lesser Himalaya *mts* India/Nepal **78** D3
Lesser Khingan Mountains China *see* **Xiao Hinggan Ling**
Lesser Slave Lake Canada **116** H4
Lesser Tunb *i.* The Gulf **84** D5
Lessines Belgium **48** D4
L'Est, Canal de France **48** G6
L'Est, Île de *i.* Canada **119** J5
L'Est, Pointe de *pt* Canada **119** J4
Lester U.S.A. **130** E5
Lestijärvi Fin. **40** N5
Les Vans France **52** G4
Lesvos *i.* Greece *see* **Lesbos**
Leszno Poland **43** P5
Letaba S. Africa **97** J2
Letchworth U.K. **45** G7
Le Télégraphe *hill* France **52** G3
Leteri India **78** D4
Letha Range *mts* Myanmar **66** A2
Lethbridge *Alta* Canada **117** H5
Lethbridge *Nfld. and Lab.* Canada **119** L4
Leti *i.* Indon. **104** D2
Leti, Kepulauan *is* Indon. **104** D2
Leticia Col. **138** E4
Letlhakeng Botswana **97** G3
Letnerechenskiy Rus. Fed. **38** G2
Letniy Navolok Rus. Fed. **38** H2
Le Touquet-Paris-Plage France **48** B4
Letpadan Myanmar **66** A3
Le Tréport France **48** B4
Letsitele S. Africa **97** J2
Letsopa S. Africa **97** G4
Letterkenny Rep. of Ireland **47** E3
Letung Indon. **67** D7
Lëtzebuerg *country* Europe *see* **Luxembourg**
Letzlingen Germany **49** L2
Léua Angola **95** C5
Leucas Greece *see* **Lefkada**
Leucate, Étang de *l.* France **52** F5
Leuchars U.K. **46** G4
Leukas Greece *see* **Lefkada**
Leung Shuen Wan Chau *i. Hong Kong* China *see* **High Island**
Leunovo Rus. Fed. **38** I2
Leupp U.S.A. **125** H4
Leupung Indon. **67** A6
Leura Australia **106** E4
Leusden Neth. **48** F2
Leuser, Gunung *mt.* Indon. **67** B7
Leutershausen Germany **49** K5
Leuven Belgium **48** E4
Levadeia Greece **55** J5
Levan U.S.A. **125** H2
Levanger Norway **40** G5
Levante, Riviera di *coastal area* Italy **54** C2
Levanto Italy **54** C2
Levashi Rus. Fed. **87** G2
Levelland U.S.A. **127** C5
Leven *England* U.K. **44** G5
Leven *Scotland* U.K. **46** G4
Leven, Loch *l.* U.K. **46** F4
Lévêque, Cape Australia **104** C4
Leverkusen Germany **48** G3
Lévézou *mts* France **52** F4
Levice Slovakia **43** Q6
Levin N.Z. **109** E5
Lévis Canada **119** H5
Levitha *i.* Greece **55** L6
Levittown *NY* U.S.A. **131** I3
Levittown *PA* U.S.A. **131** H3
Levkás *i.* Greece *see* **Lefkada**
Levkímmi Greece *see* **Lefkimmi**
Levskigrad Bulg. *see* **Karlovo**
Lev Tolstoy Rus. Fed. **39** H5
Lévy, Cap *c.* France **45** F9
Lewe Myanmar **66** B3
Lewerberg *mt.* S. Africa **96** C5
Lewes U.K. **45** H8
Lewes U.S.A. **131** H4
Lewis *CO* U.S.A. **125** I3
Lewis *IN* U.S.A. **130** B4
Lewis *KS* U.S.A. **126** D4
Lewis, Isle of *i.* U.K. **46** C2
Lewis, Lake *salt flat* Australia **104** F5
Lewisburg *KY* U.S.A. **130** B5
Lewisburg *PA* U.S.A. **131** G3
Lewisburg *WV* U.S.A. **130** E5
Lewis Cass, Mount Canada/U.S.A. **116** D3
Lewis Hills *hill* Canada **119** K4
Lewis Pass N.Z. **109** D6
Lewis Range *hills* Australia **104** E5
Lewis Range *mts* U.S.A. **122** E2
Lewis Smith, Lake U.S.A. **129** C5
Lewiston *ID* U.S.A. **122** D3
Lewiston *ME* U.S.A. **131** J1
Lewistown *IL* U.S.A. **126** F3
Lewistown *MT* U.S.A. **122** F3
Lewistown *PA* U.S.A. **131** G3
Lewisville U.S.A. **127** E5
Lexington *KY* U.S.A. **130** C4
Lexington *MI* U.S.A. **130** D2
Lexington *NC* U.S.A. **128** D5
Lexington *NE* U.S.A. **126** D3
Lexington *TN* U.S.A. **127** F5
Lexington *VA* U.S.A. **130** F5
Lexington Park U.S.A. **131** G4
Leyden Neth. *see* **Leiden**
Leye China **72** E3
Leyla Dāgh *mt.* Iran **84** B2
Leyte *i.* Phil. **65** G4
Lezha Albania *see* **Lezhë**
Lezhë Albania **55** H4
Lezhi China **72** E2
Lezhu China **73** G4
L'gov Rus. Fed. **39** G6
Lhagoi Kangri *mt.* China **79** F3
Lhari China **72** B2
Lharigarbo China *see* **Amdo**
Lhasa China **79** G3
Lhasoi China **72** B2
Lhatog China **72** C2
Lhaviyani Atoll Maldives *see* **Faadhippolhu Atoll**
Lhazê *Xizang* China **72** B2
Lhazê *Xizang* China **79** F3
Lhazhong China **79** F3
Lhokkruet Indon. **67** A6
Lhokseumawe Indon. **67** B6
Lhoksukon Indon. **67** B6
Lhomar China **79** G3
Lhorong China **72** B2

▶**Lhotse** *mt.* China/Nepal **79** F4
4th highest mountain in the world and in Asia.
world 12–13

Lhozhag China **79** G3
Lhuentse Bhutan **79** G4
Lhünzê China **72** B2
Lhünzhub China **79** G3
Liancheng China *see* **Guangnan**
Liancourt France **48** C5
Liancourt Rocks *i.* N. Pacific Ocean **71** C5
Liandu China *see* **Lishui**
Liangdang China **72** E1
Liangdaohe China **79** G3
Lianghe *Chongqing* China **73** F2
Lianghe *Yunnan* China **72** C3
Lianghekou *Chongqing* China *see* **Lianghe**
Lianghekou *Gansu* China **72** E1
Lianghekou *Sichuan* China **72** D2
Liangping China **72** E2
Liangshan China *see* **Liangping**
Liang Shan *mt.* Myanmar **66** B1
Liangshi China *see* **Shaodong**
Liangtian China **73** F4
Liangyuan China *see* **Shangqiu**
Liangzhou China *see* **Wuwei**
Liangzi Hu *l.* China **73** G2
Lianhe China *see* **Qianjiang**
Lianhua China **73** G3
Lianhua Shan *mts* China **73** G4
Lianjiang *Fujian* China **73** H3
Lianjiang *Jiangxi* China *see* **Xingguo**
Liannan China **73** G3
Lianping China **73** G3
Lianran China *see* **Anning**
Lianshan *Guangdong* China **73** G3
Lianshan *Liaoning* China **69** M4
Lianshui China **73** H1
Liant, Cape *i.* Thai. *see* **Samae San, Ko**
Liantang China *see* **Nanchang**
Lianxian China *see* **Lianzhou**
Lianyin China **70** A1
Lianyungang China **73** H1
Lianzhou *Guangdong* China **73** G3
Lianzhou *Guangxi* China *see* **Hepu**
Liaocheng China **69** L5
Liaodong Bandao *pen.* China **69** M4
Liaodong Wan *b.* China **69** M4
Liaogao China *see* **Songtao**
Liao He *r.* China **70** A4
Liaoning *prov.* China **70** A4
Liaoyang China **70** A4
Liaoyuan China **70** B4
Liaozhong China **70** A4
Liapades Greece **55** H5
Liard *r.* Canada **116** F2
Liard Highway Canada **116** F2
Liard Plateau Canada **116** E2
Liard River Canada **116** E3
Liari Pak. **85** G5
Liathach *mt.* U.K. **46** D3
Liban *country* Asia *see* **Lebanon**
Liban, Jebel *mts* Lebanon **81** C2
Libau Latvia *see* **Liepāja**
Libby U.S.A. **122** E2
Libenge Dem. Rep. Congo **94** B3
Liberal U.S.A. **127** C4
Liberdade Brazil **141** B3
Liberec Czech Rep. **43** O5
▶**Liberia** *country* Africa **92** C4
africa 7, 90–91
Liberia Costa Rica **133** G6
Liberty *IN* U.S.A. **130** C4
Liberty *KY* U.S.A. **130** C5
Liberty *ME* U.S.A. **131** K1
Liberty *MO* U.S.A. **126** E4
Liberty *MS* U.S.A. **127** F6
Liberty *NY* U.S.A. **131** H3
Liberty *TX* U.S.A. **127** E6
Liberty Lake U.S.A. **131** G4
Libin Belgium **48** F5
Libnī, Gebel *hill* Egypt *see* **Libnī, Jabal**
Libnī, Jabal *hill* Egypt **81** A4
Libo China **72** E3
Libobo, Tanjung *pt* Indon. **65** H7
Libode S. Africa **97** I6
Libong, Ko *i.* Thai. **67** B6
Libourne France **52** D4
Libral Well Australia **104** D5
Libre, Sierra *mts* Mex. **123** F7

▶**Libreville** Gabon **94** A3
Capital of Gabon.

▶**Libya** *country* Africa **93** E2
4th largest country in Africa.
africa 7, 90–91

Libyan Desert Egypt/Libya **82** C5
Libyan Plateau Egypt **86** B5
Licantén Chile **140** B4
Licata *Sicily* Italy **54** E6
Lice Turkey **87** F3
Lich Germany **49** I4
Lichas *pen.* Greece **55** J5
Licheng *Guangxi* China *see* **Lipu**
Licheng *Jiangsu* China *see* **Jinhu**
Lichfield U.K. **45** F6
Lichinga Moz. **95** D5
Lichte Germany **49** L4
Lichtenau Germany **49** I3
Lichtenburg S. Africa **97** H4
Lichtenfels Germany **49** L4
Lichtenvoorde Neth. **48** G3
Lichuan *Hubei* China **73** F2
Lichuan *Jiangxi* China **73** H3
Lida Belarus **41** N10
Liddel Water *r.* U.K. **46** G5
Lidfontein Namibia **96** D3
Lidköping Sweden **41** H7
Lidsjöberg Sweden **40** I4
Liebenau Germany **49** J2
Liebenburg Germany **49** K2
Liebenwalde Germany **49** N2
Liebig, Mount Australia **105** E5
▶**Liechtenstein** *country* Europe **52** I3
europe 5, 34–35
Liège Belgium **48** F4
Liegnitz Poland *see* **Legnica**
Lieksa Fin. **40** Q5
Lielupe *r.* Latvia **41** N8
Lielvārde Latvia **41** N8
Lienart Dem. Rep. Congo **94** C3
Lienchung *i.* Taiwan *see* **Matsu Tao**
Lienz Austria **43** N7
Liepāja Latvia **41** L8
Liepaya Latvia *see* **Liepāja**
Lier Belgium **48** E3
Lierre Belgium *see* **Lier**
Lieshout Neth. **48** F3
Lietuva *country* Europe *see* **Lithuania**
Liévin France **48** C4
Lièvre *r.* Canada **118** G5
Liezen Austria **43** O7
Liffey *r.* Rep. of Ireland **47** F4
Lifford Rep. of Ireland **47** E3
Lifi Mahuida *mt.* Arg. **140** C6
Lifou *i.* New Caledonia **103** G4
Lifu *i.* New Caledonia *see* **Lifou**
Līgatne Latvia **41** N8
Lightning Ridge Australia **108** C2
Ligny-en-Barrois France **48** F6
Ligonha *r.* Moz. **95** D5
Ligonier U.S.A. **130** C3
Ligui Mex. **123** F8
Ligure, Mar *sea* France/Italy *see* **Ligurian Sea**
Ligurian Sea France/Italy **54** C3
Ligurienne, Mer *sea* France/Italy *see* **Ligurian Sea**
Ligurta U.S.A. **125** F5
Lihir Group *is* P.N.G. **102** F2
Lihou Reef and Cays Australia **106** E3
Liivi laht *b.* Estonia/Latvia *see* **Riga, Gulf of**
Lijiang *Yunnan* China **72** D3
Lijiang *Yunnan* China *see* **Yuanjiang**
Lijiazhai China **73** G2
Lika *reg.* Croatia **54** F2
Likasi Dem. Rep. Congo **95** C5
Likati Dem. Rep. Congo **94** C3
Likely Canada **116** F4
Likhachevo Ukr. *see* **Pervomays'kyy**
Likhachyovo Ukr. *see* **Pervomays'kyy**
Likhapani India **79** H4
Likhás *pen.* Greece *see* **Lichas**
Likhoslavl' Rus. Fed. **38** G4
Liku Indon. **64** D6
Likupa Rus. Fed. **38** I4
L'Île-Rousse *Corsica* France **52** I5
Lilienthal Germany **49** I1
Liling China **73** G3
Lilla Pak. **85** I3
Lilla Edet Sweden **41** H7
Lille Belgium **48** E3
Lille France **48** D4
Lille (Lesquin) *airport* France **48** D4
Lille Bælt *sea chan.* Denmark *see* **Little Belt**
Lillebonne France **45** H9
Lillehammer Norway **41** G6
Lillers France **48** C4
Lillesand Norway **41** F7
Lillestrøm Norway **41** G7
Lilley U.S.A. **130** C2
Lillholmsjö Sweden **40** I5
Lillian, Point *hill* Australia **105** D6
Lillington U.S.A. **129** E5
Lillooet Canada **116** F5
Lillooet *r.* Canada **116** F5
Lillooet Range *mts* Canada **116** F5

▶**Lilongwe** Malawi **95** D5
Capital of Malawi.

Lilydale Australia **107** B7

▶**Lima** Peru **138** C6
Capital of Peru and 4th most populous city in South America.

Lima *MT* U.S.A. **122** E3
Lima *NY* U.S.A. **131** G2
Lima *OH* U.S.A. **130** C3
Lima Duarte Brazil **141** C3
Lima Islands China *see* **Wanshan Qundao**
Liman Rus. Fed. **39** J7
Limar Indon. **104** D1
Limassol Cyprus **81** A2
Limavady U.K. **47** F2
Limay *r.* Arg. **140** C5
Limbaži Latvia **41** N8
Limbunya Australia **104** E4
Limburg an der Lahn Germany **49** I4
Lim Chu Kang *hill* Sing. **67** [inset]
Lime Acres S. Africa **96** F5
Limeira Brazil **141** B3
Limerick Rep. of Ireland **47** D5
Limestone Point Canada **117** L4
Limingen Norway **40** H4
Limingen *l.* Norway **40** H4
Limington U.S.A. **131** J2
Liminka Fin. **40** N4
Limmen Bight *b.* Australia **106** B2
Limnos *i.* Greece **55** K5
Limoeiro Brazil **139** K5
Limoges Canada **131** H1
Limoges France **52** E4
Limón Costa Rica *see* **Puerto Limón**
Limon U.S.A. **126** C4
Limonlu Turkey **81** B1
Limonum France *see* **Poitiers**
Limousin *reg.* France **52** E4
Limoux France **52** F5
Limpopo *prov.* S. Africa **97** I2
Limpopo *r.* S. Africa/Zimbabwe **97** K3
Limu China **73** F3
Linah *well* Saudi Arabia **87** F5
Linakhamari Rus. Fed. **40** Q2
Lin'an China *see* **Jianshui**
Linares Chile **140** B5
Linares Mex. **127** D7
Linares Spain **53** E4
Lincang China **72** D4
Lincheng *Hainan* China *see* **Lingao**
Lincheng *Hunan* China *see* **Huitong**
Linchuan China *see* **Fuzhou**
Linck Nunataks *nunataks* Antarctica **148** K1
Lincoln Arg. **140** D4
Lincoln U.K. **44** G5
Lincoln *CA* U.S.A. **124** C2
Lincoln *IL* U.S.A. **126** F3
Lincoln *MI* U.S.A. **130** D1

▶**Lincoln** *NE* U.S.A. **126** D3
State capital of Nebraska.

Lincoln City *IN* U.S.A. **130** B4
Lincoln City *OR* U.S.A. **122** B3
Lincoln Island Paracel Is **64** E3
Lincoln National Park Australia **107** A7
Lincoln Sea Canada/Greenland **149** J1
Lincolnshire Wolds *hills* U.K. **44** G5
Lincolnton U.S.A. **129** D5
Linda, Serra *hills* Brazil **141** C1
Linda Creek *watercourse* Australia **106** B4
Lindau Germany **49** M2
Lindau (Bodensee) Germany **43** L7
Lindeman Group *is* Australia **106** E4
Linden Canada **116** H5
Linden Germany **49** I4
Linden Guyana **139** G2
Linden *AL* U.S.A. **129** C5
Linden *MI* U.S.A. **130** D2
Linden *TN* U.S.A. **128** C5
Linden *TX* U.S.A. **127** E5
Linden Grove U.S.A. **126** E2
Lindern (Oldenburg) Germany **49** H2
Lindesnes *c.* Norway **41** E7
Líndhos Greece *see* **Lindos**
Lindi *r.* Dem. Rep. Congo **94** C3
Lindi Tanz. **95** D4
Lindian China **70** B3
Lindisfarne *i.* U.K. *see* **Holy Island**
Lindley S. Africa **97** H4
Lindos Greece **51** J4
Lindos, Akra *pt* Greece **55** M6
Lindsay Canada **131** F1
Lindsay *CA* U.S.A. **124** D3
Lindsay *MT* U.S.A. **122** G3
Lindsborg U.S.A. **126** D4
Lindside U.S.A. **130** E5
Lindum U.K. *see* **Lincoln**
Line Islands Kiribati **147** J5
Linesville U.S.A. **130** E3
Linfen China **69** K5
Lingampet India **80** C2
Linganamakki Reservoir India **80** B3
Lingao China **73** F5
Lingayen Phil. **65** G3
Lingbi China **73** H1
Lingcheng *Anhui* China *see* **Lingbi**
Lingcheng *Guangxi* China *see* **Lingshan**
Lingcheng *Hainan* China *see* **Lingshui**
Lingchuan *Guangxi* China **73** F3
Lingchuan *Shanxi* China **73** G1
Lingelethu S. Africa **97** H7
Lingen (Ems) Germany **49** H2
Lingga, Kepulauan *is* Indon. **64** D7
Lingle U.S.A. **122** G4
Lingomo Dem. Rep. Congo **94** C3
Lingshan China **73** F4
Lingshui China **73** F5
Lingshui Wan *b.* China **73** F5
Lingsugur India **80** C2
Lingtai China **72** E1
Linguère Senegal **92** B3
Lingui China **73** F3
Lingxi China *see* **Yongshun**
Lingxian China *see* **Yanling**
Lingxiang China **73** G2
Lingyang China *see* **Cili**
Lingyun China **72** E3
Lingzi Thang Plains *reg.* Aksai Chin **78** D2
Linhai China **73** I2
Linhares Brazil **141** C2
Linh Cam Vietnam **66** D3
Linhe China **69** J4
Linhpa Myanmar **66** A1
Linjiang China **70** B4
Linjin China **73** F1
Linköping Sweden **41** I7
Linkou China **70** C3
Linli China **73** F2
Linlithgow U.K. **46** F5
Linn *MO* U.S.A. **126** F4
Linn *TX* U.S.A. **127** D7
Linn, Mount U.S.A. **124** B1
Linnansaaren kansallispuisto *nat. park* Fin. **40** P5
Linnhe, Loch *inlet* U.K. **46** D4
Linnich Germany **48** G4
Linosa, Isola di *i. Sicily* Italy **54** E7
Linpo Myanmar **66** B2
Linquan China **73** G1
Linru China *see* **Ruzhou**
Linruzhen China **73** G1
Lins Brazil **141** A3
Linshu China **73** H1
Linshui China **72** E2
Lintan China **72** D1
Lintao China **72** D1
Linton *IN* U.S.A. **130** B4
Linton *ND* U.S.A. **126** C2
Linwu China **73** G3
Linxi China **69** L4
Linxia China **72** D1
Linxiang China **73** G2
Linyi *Shandong* China **69** L5
Linyi *Shandong* China **73** H1
Linying China **73** G1
Linz Austria **43** O6
Lion, Golfe du *g.* France **52** F5
Lions, Gulf of France *see* **Lion, Golfe du**
Lions Bay Canada **116** F5
Lioua Chad **93** E3
Lipari *Sicily* Italy **54** F5
Lipari, Isole *is* Italy **54** F5
Lipetsk Rus. Fed. **39** H5
Lipin Bor Rus. Fed. **38** H3
Liping China **73** F3
Lipova Romania **55** I1
Lipovtsy Rus. Fed. **70** C3
Lippe *r.* Germany **49** G3
Lippstadt Germany **49** I3
Lipsoi *i.* Greece *see* **Leipsoi**
Lipti Lekh *pass* Nepal **78** E3
Liptrap, Cape Australia **108** B7
Lipu China **73** F3
Lira Uganda **94** D3
Liranga Congo **94** B4
Lircay Peru **138** D6
Lisala Dem. Rep. Congo **94** C3
L'Isalo, Massif de *mts* Madag. **95** E6
L'Isalo, Parc National de *nat. park* Madag. **95** E6
Lisbellaw U.K. **47** E3
Lisboa Port. *see* **Lisbon**

▶**Lisbon** Port. **53** B4
Capital of Portugal.

Lisbon *ME* U.S.A. **131** J1
Lisbon *NH* U.S.A. **131** J1
Lisbon *OH* U.S.A. **130** E3
Lisburn U.K. **47** F3
Liscannor Bay Rep. of Ireland **47** C5
Lisdoonvarna Rep. of Ireland **47** C4
Lishan Taiwan **73** I3
Lishe Jiang *r.* China **72** D3
Lishi *Jiangxi* China *see* **Dingnan**
Lishi *Shanxi* China **69** K5
Lishu China **70** B4
Lishui China **73** H2
Li Shui *r.* China **73** F2
Lisichansk Ukr. *see* **Lysychans'k**
Lisieux France **52** E2
Liskeard U.K. **45** C8
Liski Rus. Fed. **39** H6
Liskot India **78** D3
L'Isle-Adam France **48** C5
Lismore Australia **108** F2
Lismore Rep. of Ireland **47** E5
Lisnarrick U.K. **47** E3
Lisnaskea U.K. **47** E3
Liss *mt.* Saudi Arabia **81** D4
Lissa Poland *see* **Leszno**
Lister, Mount Antarctica **148** H1
Listowel Canada **130** E2
Listowel Rep. of Ireland **47** C5
Lit Sweden **40** I5
Litang *Guangxi* China **73** F4
Litang *Sichuan* China **72** D2
Līṭānī, Nahr el *r.* Lebanon **81** B3
Litchfield *CA* U.S.A. **124** C1
Litchfield *CT* U.S.A. **131** I3
Litchfield *IL* U.S.A. **126** F4
Litchfield *MI* U.S.A. **130** C2
Litchfield *MN* U.S.A. **126** E2
Lit-et-Mixe France **52** D4
Lithgow Australia **108** E4
Lithino, Akra *pt* Greece **55** K7
▶**Lithuania** *country* Europe **41** M9
europe 5, 34–35
Lititz U.S.A. **131** G3
Litoměřice Czech Rep. **43** O5
Litovko Rus. Fed. **70** D2
Litovskaya S.S.R. *country* Europe *see* **Lithuania**
Little *r.* U.S.A. **127** E6
Little Abaco *i.* Bahamas **129** E7
Little Abitibi *r.* Canada **118** E4
Little Abitibi Lake Canada **118** E4
Little Andaman *i.* India **67** A5
Little Bahama Bank *sea feature* Bahamas **129** E7
Little Barrier *i.* N.Z. **109** E3
Little Belt *sea chan.* Denmark **41** F9
Little Belt Mountains U.S.A. **122** F3
Little Bitter Lake Egypt **81** A4
Little Cayman *i.* Cayman Is **133** H5
Little Churchill *r.* Canada **117** M3
Little Chute U.S.A. **130** A1
Little Coco Island Cocos Is **67** A4
Little Colorado *r.* U.S.A. **125** H3
Little Creek Peak U.S.A. **125** G3
Little Current Canada **118** E5
Little Current *r.* Canada **118** D4
Little Desert National Park Australia **107** C8
Little Egg Harbor *inlet* U.S.A. **131** H4
Little Exuma *i.* Bahamas **129** F8
Little Falls U.S.A. **126** E2
Littlefield *AZ* U.S.A. **125** G3
Littlefield *TX* U.S.A. **127** C5
Little Fork *r.* U.S.A. **126** E1
Little Grand Rapids Canada **117** M4
Littlehampton U.K. **45** G8
Little Inagua Island Bahamas **129** F8
Little Karas Berg *plat.* Namibia **96** D4
Little Karoo *plat.* S. Africa **96** E7
Little Lake U.S.A. **124** E4
Little Mecatina *r. Nfld. and Lab./Que.* Canada *see* **Petit Mécatina**
Little Mecatina Island Canada *see* **Petit Mécatina, Île du**
Little Minch *sea chan.* U.K. **46** B3
Little Missouri *r.* U.S.A. **126** C2
Little Namaqualand *reg.* S. Africa *see* **Namaqualand**
Little Nicobar *i.* India **67** A6
Little Ouse *r.* U.K. **45** H6
Little Pamir *mts* Asia **85** I2
Little Rancheria *r.* Canada **116** D2
Little Rann *marsh* India **78** B5
Little Red River Canada **116** H3

▶**Little Rock** U.S.A. **127** E5
State capital of Arkansas.

Littlerock U.S.A. **124** E4
Little Sable Point U.S.A. **130** B2
Little Salmon Lake Canada **116** C2
Little Salt Lake U.S.A. **125** G3
Little Sandy Desert Australia **105** B5
Little San Salvador *i.* Bahamas **129** F7
Little Smoky Canada **116** G4
Little Tibet *reg.* Jammu and Kashmir *see* **Ladakh**
Littleton U.S.A. **122** G5
Little Valley U.S.A. **131** F2
Little Wind *r.* U.S.A. **122** F4

itunde Moz. 95 D5
iu'an China see Lu'an
iuba China 72 E1
iucheng China 73 F3
iuchiu Yü i. Taiwan 73 I4
iuchong He r. China 72 E3
iuchow China see Liuzhou
iuhe China 70 B4
iuheng Dao i. China 73 I2
iujiachang China 73 F2
iujiaxia Shuiku resr China 72 D1
iukesong China 70 B3
iulin China see Jonê
iupan Shan mts China 72 E1
iupanshui China see Lupanshui
iuquan China 73 H1
iuwa Plain National Park Zambia 95 C5
iuyang China 73 G2
iuzhan China 70 B2
iuzhou China 73 F3
īvāni Latvia 41 O8
ive Oak U.S.A. 129 D6
iveringa Australia 102 C3
ivermore CA U.S.A. 124 C3
ivermore KY U.S.A. 130 B5
ivermore, Mount U.S.A. 127 B6
ivermore Falls U.S.A. 131 J1
iverpool Australia 108 E4
iverpool Canada 119 I5
iverpool U.K. 44 E5
iverpool Bay Canada 114 E3
iverpool Plains Australia 108 E3
iverpool Range mts Australia 108 D3
ivia U.S.A. 130 B5
ivingston U.K. 46 F5
ivingston AL U.S.A. 127 F5
ivingston KY U.S.A. 130 C5
ivingston MT U.S.A. 122 F3
ivingston TN U.S.A. 130 C5
ivingston TX U.S.A. 127 E6
ivingston, Lake U.S.A. 127 E6
ivingstone Zambia 95 C5
ivingston Island Antarctica 148 L2
ivingston Manor U.S.A. 131 H3
ivno Bos.-Herz. 54 G3
ivny Rus. Fed. 39 H5
ivojoki r. Fin. 40 O4
ivonia MI U.S.A. 130 D2
ivonia NY U.S.A. 131 G2
ivorno Italy 54 D3
ivramento do Brumado Brazil 141 C1
iwā Oman 84 E5
iwā', Wādī al watercourse Syria 81 C3
iwale Tanz. 95 D4
ixian Gansu China 72 E1
ixian Sichuan China 72 D2
ixus Morocco see Larache
iyang China see Hexian
iyuan China see Sangzhi
izard U.K. 45 B9
izarda Brazil 139 I5
izard Point U.K. 45 B9
izarra Spain see Estella
izemores U.S.A. 130 E4
iziping China 72 D2
izy-sur-Ourcq France 48 D5
jouwert Neth. see Leeuwarden

Ljubljana Slovenia 54 F1
Capital of Slovenia.

jugarn Sweden 41 K8
jungan r. Sweden 40 J5
jungaverk Sweden 40 J5
jungby Sweden 41 H8
jusdal Sweden 41 J6
jusnan r. Sweden 41 J6
jusne Sweden 41 J6
aima, Volcán vol. Chile 140 B5
anandras U.K. see Presteigne
anbadarn Fawr U.K. 45 C6
anbedr Pont Steffan U.K. see Lampeter
anbister U.K. 45 D6
andeilo U.K. 45 D7
andissilio U.K. 45 C7
andovery U.K. 45 D7
andrindod Wells U.K. 45 D6
andudno U.K. 44 D5
andysul U.K. 45 C6
anegwad U.K. 45 C7
anelli U.K. 45 C7
anfair Caereinion U.K. 45 D6
anfair-ym-Muallt U.K. see Builth Wells
angefni U.K. 44 C5
angollen U.K. 45 D6
angurig U.K. 45 D6
anllyfni U.K. 45 C5
annerch-y-medd U.K. 44 C5
annor U.K. 45 C6
ano Mex. 123 F7
ano U.S.A. 127 D6
ano r. U.S.A. 127 D6
ano Estacado plain U.S.A. 127 C5
anos plain Col./Venez. 138 E2
anquihue, Lago l. Chile 140 B6
anrhystud U.K. 45 C6
antrisant U.K. 45 D7
anuwchllyn U.K. 45 D6
anwnog U.K. 45 D6
anymddyfri U.K. see Llandovery
ay U.K. 45 D5
eida Spain 53 G3
erena Spain 53 C4
iria Spain 53 F4
odio Spain 53 E2
oyd George, Mount Canada 116 E3
oyd Lake Canada 117 I3
oydminster Canada 117 I4
uchmayor Spain see Llucmajor
ucmajor Spain 53 H4
ullaillaco, Volcán vol. Chile 140 C2
o r. China/Vietnam 66 D2
a r. Chile 140 B2
a U.S.A. 125 H2
ban' r. Rus. Fed. 38 K4
batejo mt. Spain 53 D5
batse Botswana 97 G3
baye r. Cent. Afr. Rep. 94 B3
bejün Germany 49 L3
benberg hill Germany 49 M3
beria Arg. 140 E5
bito Angola 95 B5
bos Arg. 140 E5
bos, Cabo c. Mex. 123 E7
bos, Isla i. Mex. 123 F8
bos de Tierra, Isla i. Peru 138 B5
burg Germany 49 M2
c Binh Vietnam 66 D2
chaline U.K. 46 D4
Lo Chau Hong Kong China see Beaufort Island
Loch Baghasdail U.K. see Lochboisdale
Lochboisdale U.K. 46 B3
Lochcarron U.K. 46 D3
Lochearnhead U.K. 46 E4
Lochem Neth. 48 G2
Lochern National Park Australia 106 C5
Loches France 52 E3
Loch Garman Rep. of Ireland see Wexford
Lochgelly U.K. 46 F4
Lochgilphead U.K. 46 D4
Lochinver U.K. 46 D2
Loch Lomond and The Trossachs National Park U.K. 46 E4
Lochmaddy U.K. 46 B3
Lochnagar mt. U.K. 46 F4
Loch nam Madadh U.K. see Lochmaddy
Loch Raven Reservoir U.S.A. 131 G4
Lochy, Loch l. U.K. 46 E4
Lock Australia 107 A7
Lockerbie U.K. 46 F5
Lockhart Australia 108 C5
Lockhart U.S.A. 127 D6
Lock Haven U.S.A. 131 G3
Löcknitz r. Germany 49 L1
Lockport U.S.A. 131 F2
Lôc Ninh Vietnam 67 D5
Lod Israel 81 B4
Loddon r. Australia 108 A5
Lodève France 52 F5
Lodeynoye Pole Rus. Fed. 38 G3
Lodge, Mount Canada/U.S.A. 116 B3
Lodhikheda India 78 D5
Lodhran Pak. 85 H4
Lodi Italy 54 C2
Lodi CA U.S.A. 124 C2
Lodi OH U.S.A. 130 D3
Lødingen Norway 40 I2
Lodja Dem. Rep. Congo 94 C4
Lodomeria Rus. Fed. see Vladimir
Lodrani India 78 B5
Lodwar Kenya 94 D3
Łódź Poland 43 Q5
Loei Thai. 66 C3
Loeriesfontein S. Africa 96 D6
Lofoten is Norway 40 H2
Lofusa Sudan 93 G4
Log Rus. Fed. 39 I6
Loga Niger 92 D3
Logan IA U.S.A. 126 E3
Logan OH U.S.A. 130 D4
Logan UT U.S.A. 122 F4
Logan WV U.S.A. 130 E5

Logan, Mount Canada 116 A2
2nd highest mountain in North America.

Logan, Mount U.S.A. 122 C2
Logan Creek r. Australia 106 D4
Logan Lake Canada 116 F5
Logan Mountains Canada 116 D2
Logansport IN U.S.A. 130 B3
Logansport LA U.S.A. 127 E6
Logatec Slovenia 54 F2
Logpung China 72 D1
Logroño Spain 53 E2
Logtak Lake India 79 H4
Lohardaga India 79 F5
Loharu India 78 C3
Lohatlha S. Africa 96 F5
Lohawat India 78 C4
Lohfelden Germany 49 J3
Lohil r. China/India see Zayü Qu
Lohiniva Fin. 40 N3
Lohjanjärvi l. Fin. 41 M6
Löhne Germany 49 I2
Lohne (Oldenburg) Germany 49 I2
Lohtaja Fin. 40 M4
Loi, Nam r. Myanmar 66 C2
Loikaw Myanmar 66 B3
Loi Lan mt. Myanmar/Thai. 66 B3
Loi-lem Myanmar 66 B2
Loi Lun Myanmar 66 B2
Loimaa Fin. 41 M6
Loipyet Hills Myanmar 66 B1
Loire r. France 52 C3
Loi Sang mt. Myanmar 66 B2
L'Oise à l'Aisne, Canal de France 48 D5
Loi Song mt. Myanmar 66 B2
Loja Ecuador 138 C4
Loja Spain 53 D5
Lokan tekojärvi l. Fin. 40 O3
Lokchim r. Rus. Fed. 38 K3
Lokeren Belgium 48 E3
Lokgwabe Botswana 96 E3
Lokichar Kenya 74 C6
Lokichokio Kenya 94 D3
Lokilalaki, Gunung mt. Indon. 65 G7
Løkken Denmark 41 F8
Løkken Norway 40 F5
Loknya Rus. Fed. 38 F4
Lokoja Nigeria 92 D4
Lokolama Dem. Rep. Congo 94 B4
Lokossa Benin 92 D4
Lokot' Rus. Fed. 39 G5
Lol Sudan 93 F4
Lola Guinea 92 C4
Lola, Mount U.S.A. 124 C2
Loleta U.S.A. 124 A1
Lolland i. Denmark 41 G9
Lollondo Tanz. 94 D4
Lolo U.S.A. 122 E3
Loloda Indon. 65 H6
Lolo Pass U.S.A. 122 E3
Lolowau Indon. 67 B7
Lolwane S. Africa 96 F4
Lom Bulg. 55 J3
Lom Norway 41 F6
Loma U.S.A. 125 I2
Lomami r. Dem. Rep. Congo 94 C3
Lomar Pass Afgh. 85 G3
Lomas, Bahía de b. Chile 140 C8
Lomas de Zamora Arg. 140 E4
Lombarda, Serra hills Brazil 139 H3
Lomblen i. Indon. 104 C2
Lombok Indon. 104 B2
Lombok i. Indon. 104 B2
Lombok, Selat sea chan. Indon. 104 A2

Lomé Togo 92 D4
Capital of Togo.

Lomela Dem. Rep. Congo 94 C4
Lomela r. Dem. Rep. Congo 93 F5
Lomira U.S.A. 130 A2
Lomme France 48 C4
Lommel Belgium 48 F3
Lomond Canada 119 K4
Lomond, Loch l. U.K. 46 E4
Lomonosov Rus. Fed. 41 P7
Lomonosov Ridge sea feature Arctic Ocean 149 B1
Lomovoye Rus. Fed. 38 I2
Lomphat Cambodia see Lumphăt
Lompoc U.S.A. 124 C4
Lom Sak Thai. 66 C3
Łomża Poland 43 S4
Lon, Hon i. Vietnam 67 E4
Lonar India 80 C2
Londa Bangl. 79 G5
Londa India 80 B3
Londinières France 48 B5
Londinium U.K. see London
Londoko Rus. Fed. 70 D2
London Canada 130 E2

London U.K. 45 G7
Capital of the United Kingdom and of England. 4th most populous city in Europe.

London KY U.S.A. 130 C5
London OH U.S.A. 130 D4
Londonderry U.K. 47 E3
Londonderry OH U.S.A. 130 D4
Londonderry VT U.S.A. 131 I2
Londonderry, Cape Australia 104 D3
Londrina Brazil 141 A3
Lone Pine U.S.A. 124 D3
Long Thai. 66 B3
Longa Angola 95 B5
Longa, Proliv sea chan. Rus. Fed. 61 S2
Long'an China 72 E4
Long Ashton U.K. 45 E7
Long Bay U.S.A. 129 E5
Longbeach N.Z. 109 C7
Long Beach U.S.A. 124 D5
Longbo China see Shuangpai
Long Branch U.S.A. 131 I3
Longchang China 72 E2
Longcheng Anhui China see Xiaoxian
Longcheng Guangdong China see Longmen
Longcheng Yunnan China see Chenggong
Longchuan China see Nanhua
Longchuan Jiang r. China 72 C4
Long Creek r. Canada 117 K5
Long Creek U.S.A. 122 D3
Long Eaton U.K. 45 F6
Longford Rep. of Ireland 47 E4
Longgang Chongqing China see Dazu
Longgang Guangdong China 73 G4
Longhoughton U.K. 44 F3
Longhui China 73 F3
Longhurst, Mount Antarctica 148 H1
Long Island Bahamas 129 F8
Long Island N.S. Canada 119 I5
Long Island Nunavut Canada 118 F3
Long Island India 67 A4
Long Island P.N.G. 65 L8
Long Island U.S.A. 131 I3
Long Island Sound sea chan. U.S.A. 131 I3
Longjiang China 70 A3
Longjin China see Qingliu
Longju China 72 B2
Longlac Canada 118 D4
Long Lake l. Canada 118 D4
Long Lake U.S.A. 131 H2
Long Lake l. ME U.S.A. 128 G2
Long Lake l. MI U.S.A. 130 D1
Long Lake l. ND U.S.A. 126 C2
Long Lake l. NY U.S.A. 131 H1
Longli China 72 E3
Longlin China 72 E3
Longling China 72 C3
Longmeadow U.S.A. 131 I2
Long Melford U.K. 45 H6
Longmen Guangdong China 73 G4
Longmen Heilong. China 70 B2
Longmen Shan hill China 73 F1
Longmen Shan mts China 72 E1
Longming China 72 E4
Longmont U.S.A. 122 G4
Longnan China 73 G3
Long Phu Vietnam 67 D5
Longping China see Luodian
Long Point Ont. Canada 130 E2
Long Point Man. Canada 117 L4
Long Point Ont. Canada 130 E2
Long Point N.Z. 109 B8
Long Point Bay Canada 130 E2
Long Prairie U.S.A. 126 E2
Long Preston U.K. 44 E4
Longquan Guizhou China see Fenggang
Longquan Guizhou China see Danzhai
Longquan Hunan China see Xintian
Longquan Xi r. China 73 I2
Long Range Mountains Nfld. and Lab. Canada 119 K4
Long Range Mountains Nfld. and Lab. Canada 119 K5
Longreach Australia 106 D4
Longriba China 72 D1
Longshan Guizhou China see Longli
Longshan Hunan China 73 F2
Longshan Yunnan China see Longling
Long Shan mts China 72 E1
Longsheng China 73 F3
Longs Peak U.S.A. 122 G4
Long Stratton U.K. 45 I6
Longtom Lake Canada 116 G1
Longtown U.K. 44 E3
Longue-Pointe Canada 119 I4
Longueuil Canada 118 G5
Longuyon France 48 F5
Longvale U.S.A. 124 B2
Longview TX U.S.A. 127 E5
Longview WA U.S.A. 122 C3
Longwangmiao China 70 D3
Longwei Co l. China 79 G2
Longxi China 72 E1
Longxian Guangdong China see Wengyuan
Longxian Shaanxi China 72 E1
Longxingchang China see Wuyuan
Longxi Shan mt. China 73 H3
Longxu China see Cangwu
Long Xuyên Vietnam 67 D5
Longyan China 73 H3

Longyearbyen Svalbard 60 C2
Capital of Svalbard.

Longzhen China 70 B2
Longzhou China 72 E4
Longzhouping China see Changyang
Löningen Germany 49 H2
Lonoke U.S.A. 127 F5
Lönsboda Sweden 41 I8
Lons-le-Saunier France 52 G3
Lonton Myanmar 66 B1
Looc Phil. 65 G4
Loochoo Islands Japan see Ryukyu Islands
Loogootee U.S.A. 130 B4
Lookout, Cape Canada 118 E3
Lookout, Cape U.S.A. 129 E5
Lookout, Point Australia 108 F1
Lookout, Point U.S.A. 130 D1
Lookout Mountain U.S.A. 125 I4
Lookout Point Australia 105 B8
Loolmalasin vol. crater Tanz. 94 D4
Loon Canada 118 C4
Loon r. Canada 116 H3
Loongana Australia 105 D7
Loon Lake Canada 117 I4
Loop Head hd Rep. of Ireland 47 C5
Lop China 78 E1
Lopasnya Rus. Fed. see Chekhov
Lopatina, Gora mt. Rus. Fed. 70 F2
Lop Buri Thai. 66 C4
Lopez Phil. 65 G4
Lopez, Cap c. Gabon 94 A4
Lop Nur salt flat China 76 H3
Lopphavet b. Norway 40 L1
Loptyuga Rus. Fed. 38 K3
Lora Pak. 85 G5
Lora r. Venez. 138 D2
Lora del Río Spain 53 D5
Lorain U.S.A. 130 D3
Loralai Pak. 85 H4
Loralai r. Pak. 85 H4
Loramie, Lake U.S.A. 130 C3
Lorca Spain 53 F5
Lorch Germany 49 H4
Lordegān Iran 84 C4
Lord Howe Atoll Solomon Is see Ontong Java Atoll
Lord Howe Island Australia 103 F5
Lord Howe Rise sea feature S. Pacific Ocean 146 G7
Lord Loughborough Island Myanmar 67 B5
Lordsburg U.S.A. 125 I5
Lore East Timor 104 D2
Lore Lindu National Park Indon. 64 G7
Lorena Brazil 141 B3
Lorengau P.N.G. 65 L7
Loreto Brazil 139 I5
Loreto Mex. 123 F8
Lorient France 52 C3
Lorillard r. Canada 117 N1
Loring U.S.A. 122 G2
Lorn, Firth of est. U.K. 46 D4
Lorne Australia 106 D5
Lorne watercourse Australia 106 B3
Lorrain, Plateau France 49 G6
Lorraine Australia 106 B3
Lorraine admin. reg. France 48 G6
Lorraine reg. France 48 F5
Lorsch Germany 49 I5
Lorup Germany 49 H2
Losal India 78 C4
Los Alamítos, Sierra de mt. Mex. 127 C7
Los Alamos CA U.S.A. 124 C4
Los Alamos NM U.S.A. 123 G6
Los Alerces, Parque Nacional nat. park Arg. 140 B6
Los Ángeles Chile 140 B5

Los Angeles U.S.A. 124 D4
3rd most populous city in North America.

Los Angeles Aqueduct canal U.S.A. 124 D4
Los Arabos Cuba 129 D8
Los Banos U.S.A. 124 C3
Los Blancos Arg. 140 D2
Los Caballos Mesteños, Llano de plain Mex. 127 B6
Los Canarreos, Archipiélago de is Cuba 133 H4
Los Cerritos watercourse Mex. 123 F8
Los Chonos, Archipiélago de is Chile 140 A6
Los Coronados, Islas is Mex. 124 E5
Los Desventurados, Islas de is S. Pacific Ocean 147 O7
Los Estados, Isla de i. Arg. 140 D8
Los Gigantes, Llanos de plain Mex. 127 B6
Los Glaciares, Parque Nacional nat. park Arg. 140 B8
Losheim Germany 48 G5
Los Hoyos Mex. 123 F7
Lošinj i. Croatia 54 F2
Los Jardines de la Reina, Archipiélago de is Cuba 133 I4
Los Juríes Arg. 140 D3
Los Katios, Parque Nacional nat. park Col. 133 I7
Loskop Dam S. Africa 97 I3
Los Lunas U.S.A. 123 G6
Los Menucos Arg. 140 C6
Los Mexicanos, Lago de l. Mex. 123 G7
Los Mochis Mex. 123 F8
Los Molinos U.S.A. 124 B1
Los Mosquitos, Golfo de b. Panama 133 H7
Losombo Dem. Rep. Congo 94 B3
Los Palacios Cuba 129 D8
Los Picos de Europa, Parque Nacional de nat. park Spain 53 D2
Los Remedios r. Mex. 127 B7
Los Roques, Islas is Venez. 138 E1
Losser Neth. 48 G2
Lossie r. U.K. 46 F3
Lossiemouth U.K. 46 F3
Lößnitz Germany 49 M4
Lost Creek KY U.S.A. 130 D5
Lost Creek WV U.S.A. 130 E4
Los Teques Venez. 138 E1
Los Testigos is Venez. 138 F1
Lost Hills U.S.A. 124 D4
Lost Trail Pass U.S.A. 122 E3
Lostwithiel U.K. 45 C8
Los Vidrios Mex. 125 G6
Los Vilos Chile 140 B4
Lot r. France 52 E4
Lota Chile 140 B5
Lotfābād Turkm. 84 E2
Lothringen reg. France see Lorraine
Lotikipi Plain Kenya/Sudan 94 D3
Loto Dem. Rep. Congo 94 C4
Lotsane r. Botswana 97 I2
Lot's Wife i. Japan see Sōfu-gan
Lotta r. Fin./Rus. Fed. 40 Q2
also known as Lutto
Lotte Germany 49 H2
Louang Namtha Laos 66 C2
Louangphrabang Laos 66 C3
Loubomo Congo 95 B4
Loudéac France 52 C2
Loudi China 73 F3
L'Ouest, Pointe de pt Canada 119 I4
Louga Senegal 92 B3
Loughborough U.K. 45 F6
Lougheed Island Canada 115 H2
Loughor r. U.K. 45 C7
Loughrea Rep. of Ireland 47 D4
Loughton U.K. 45 H7
Louhans France 52 G3
Louisa KY U.S.A. 130 D4
Louisa VA U.S.A. 131 G4
Louisbourg Canada 119 K5
Louisburg Canada see Louisbourg
Louisburgh Rep. of Ireland 47 C4
Louise Falls Canada 116 G2
Louis-Gentil Morocco see Youssoufia
Louisiade Archipelago is P.N.G. 106 F1
Louisiana U.S.A. 126 F4
Louisiana state U.S.A. 127 F6
Louis Trichardt S. Africa 97 I2
Louisville GA U.S.A. 129 D5
Louisville IL U.S.A. 126 F4
Louisville KY U.S.A. 130 C4
Louisville MS U.S.A. 127 F5
Louisville Ridge sea feature S. Pacific Ocean 146 I8
Louis-XIV, Pointe pt Canada 118 F3
Loukhi Rus. Fed. 40 R3
Loukoléla Congo 94 B4
Loukouo Congo 93 E5
Loulé Port. 53 B5
Loum Cameroon 92 D4
Louny Czech Rep. 43 N5
Loup r. U.S.A. 126 D3
Loups-Marins, Lacs des lakes Canada 118 G2
Loups-Marins, Petit lac des l. Canada 119 G2
L'Our, Vallée de valley Germany/Lux. 48 G5
Lourdes Canada 119 K4
Lourdes France 52 D5
Lourenço Marques Moz. see Maputo
Lousã Port. 53 B3
Loushan China 70 C3
Loushanguan China see Tongzi
Louth Australia 108 B3
Louth U.K. 44 G5
Loutra Aidipsou Greece 55 J5
Louvain Belgium see Leuven
Louviers France 48 B5
Louwater-Suid Namibia 96 C2
Louwsburg S. Africa 97 J4
Lövånger Sweden 40 L4
Lovat' r. Rus. Fed. 38 F4
Lovech Bulg. 55 K3
Lovell U.S.A. 131 J1
Lovelock U.S.A. 124 D1
Lovendegem Belgium 48 D3
Lovers' Leap mt. U.S.A. 130 E5
Loviisa Fin. 41 O6
Lovington U.S.A. 127 C5
Lovozero Rus. Fed. 38 G1
Lóvua Angola 95 C4
Lóvua Angola 95 C5
Low, Cape Canada 115 J3
Lowa Dem. Rep. Congo 94 C4
Lowa r. Dem. Rep. Congo 94 C4
Lowarai Pass Pak. 85 H3
Lowell IN U.S.A. 130 B3
Lowell MA U.S.A. 131 J2
Lower Arrow Lake Canada 116 G5
Lower California pen. Mex. see Baja California
Lower Glenelg National Park Australia 107 C8
Lower Granite Gorge U.S.A. 125 G4
Lower Hutt N.Z. 109 E5
Lower Laberge Canada 116 C2
Lower Lake U.S.A. 124 B2
Lower Lough Erne l. U.K. 47 E3
Lower Post Canada 116 D3
Lower Red Lake U.S.A. 126 E2
Lower Saxony land Germany see Niedersachsen
Lower Tunguska r. Rus. Fed. see Nizhnyaya Tunguska
Lower Zambezi National Park Zambia 95 C5
Lowestoft U.K. 45 I6
Łowicz Poland 43 Q4
Low Island Kiribati see Starbuck Island
Lowkhi Afgh. 85 F4
Lowther Hills U.K. 46 F5
Lowville U.S.A. 131 H2
Loxstedt Germany 49 I1
Loxton Australia 107 C7
Loyal, Loch l. U.K. 46 E2
Loyalsock Creek r. U.S.A. 131 G3
Loyalton U.S.A. 124 C2
Loyalty Islands New Caledonia see Loyauté, Îles
Loyang China see Luoyang
Loyauté, Îles is New Caledonia 103 G4
Loyev Belarus see Loyew
Loyew Belarus 39 F6
Lozère, Mont mt. France 52 F4
Loznica Serb. and Mont. 55 H2
Lozova Ukr. 39 H6
Lozovaya Ukr. see Lozova
Lua r. Dem. Rep. Congo 94 B3
Luacano Angola 95 C5
Lu'an China 73 H2
Luân Châu Vietnam 66 C2
Luanchuan China 73 F1

Luanda Angola 95 B4
Capital of Angola.

Luang, Khao mt. Thai. 67 B5
Luang, Thale lag. Thai. 67 C6
Luang Namtha Laos see Louang Namtha
Luang Phrabang, Thiu Khao mts Laos/Thai. 66 C3
Luang Prabang Laos see Louangphrabang
Luanhaizi China 72 B1
Luanshya Zambia 95 C5
Luanza Dem. Rep. Congo 95 C4
Luao Angola see Luau
Luarca Spain 53 C2
Luashi Dem. Rep. Congo 95 C5
Luau Angola 95 C5
Luba Equat. Guinea 92 D4
Lubaczów Poland 39 D6
Lubalo Angola 95 B4
Lubānas ezers l. Latvia 41 O8
Lubang Islands Phil. 64 F4
Lubango Angola 95 B5
Lubao Dem. Rep. Congo 95 C4
Lubartów Poland 39 D6
Lübbecke Germany 49 I2
Lubbeskolk salt pan S. Africa 96 D5
Lubbock U.S.A. 127 C5
Lübbow Germany 49 L2
Lübeck Germany 43 M4
Lubeck U.S.A. 130 E4
Lubefu Dem. Rep. Congo 95 C4
Lubei China 69 M4
Lüben Poland see Lubin
Lubersac France 52 E4
Lubin Poland 43 P5
Lublin Poland 39 D6
Lubnān country Asia see Lebanon
Lubnān, Jabal mts Lebanon see Liban, Jebel
Lubny Ukr. 39 G6
Lubok Antu Sarawak Malaysia 64 E6
Lübtheen Germany 49 L1
Lubudi Dem. Rep. Congo 95 C4
Lubukkinggau Indon. 64 C7
Lubukpakam Indon. 67 B7
Lubuksikaping Indon. 64 C6
Lubumbashi Dem. Rep. Congo 95 C5
Lubutu Dem. Rep. Congo 94 C4
Lübz Germany 49 M1
Lucala Angola 95 B4
Lucan Canada 130 E2
Lucan Rep. of Ireland 47 F4
Lucania, Mount Canada 116 A2
Lucapa Angola 95 C4
Lucas U.S.A. 130 B5
Lucasville U.S.A. 130 D4
Lucca Italy 54 D3
Luce Bay U.K. 46 E6
Lucedale U.S.A. 127 F6
Lucélia Brazil 141 A3
Lucena Phil. 65 G4
Lucena Spain 53 D5
Lučenec Slovakia 43 Q6
Lucera Italy 54 F4
Lucerne Switz. 52 I3
Lucerne Valley U.S.A. 124 E4
Lucero Mex. 123 G7
Luchegorsk Rus. Fed. 70 D3
Lucheng Guangxi China see Luchuan
Lucheng Sichuan China see Kangding
Luchuan China 73 F4
Lüchun China 72 D4
Lucipara, Kepulauan is Indon. 65 H8
Łuck Ukr. see Luts'k
Luckeesarai India see Lakhisarai
Luckenwalde Germany 49 N2
Luckhoff S. Africa 96 G5
Lucknow Canada 130 E2
Lucknow India 78 E4
Lücongpo China 73 F2
Lucrecia, Cabo c. Cuba 133 I4
Lucusse Angola 95 C5
Lucy Creek Australia 106 B4
Lüda China see Dalian
Lüdenscheid Germany 49 H3
Lüderitz Namibia 96 B4
Ludewa Tanz. 95 D5
Ludhiana India 78 C3
Ludian China 72 D3
Luding China 72 D2
Ludington U.S.A. 130 B2
Ludlow U.K. 45 E6
Ludlow U.S.A. 124 E4
Ludogorie reg. Bulg. 55 L3
Ludowici U.S.A. 129 D6
Ludvika Sweden 41 I6
Ludwigsburg Germany 49 J6
Ludwigsfelde Germany 49 N2
Ludwigshafen am Rhein Germany 49 I5
Ludwigslust Germany 49 L1
Ludza Latvia 41 O8
Luebo Dem. Rep. Congo 95 C4
Luena Angola 95 B5
Luena Flats plain Zambia 95 C5
Lüeyang China 72 E1
Lufeng Guangdong China 73 G4
Lufeng Yunnan China 72 D3
Lufkin U.S.A. 127 E6
Lufu China see Shilin
Luga Rus. Fed. 41 P7
Luga r. Rus. Fed. 41 P7
Lugano Switz. 52 I3
Lugansk Ukr. see Luhans'k
Lugau Germany 49 M4
Lügde Germany 49 J3
Lugdunum France see Lyon
Lugg r. U.K. 45 E6
Luggudontsen mt. China 79 G3
Lugo Italy 54 D2
Lugo Spain 53 C2
Lugoj Romania 55 I2
Luhans'k Ukr. 39 H6
Luhe China 73 H1
Luhe r. Germany 49 K1
Luḥfī, Wādī watercourse Jordan 81 C3
Luhit r. China/India see Zayü Qu
Luhit r. India 79 H4
Luhua China see Heishui
Luhuo China 72 D2
Luhyny Ukr. 39 F6
Luia Angola 95 C4
Luiana Angola 95 C5
Luichow Peninsula China see Leizhou Bandao
Luik Belgium see Liège
Luimneach Rep. of Ireland see Limerick
Luiro r. Fin. 40 O3
Luis Echeverría Álvarez Mex. 124 E5
Luitpold Coast Antarctica 148 A1
Luiza Dem. Rep. Congo 95 C4
Lujiang China 73 H2
Lüjing China 72 E1
Lukackek Rus. Fed. 70 D1
Lukapa Angola see Lucapa
Lukavac Bos.-Herz. 54 H2
Lukenga, Lac l. Dem. Rep. Congo 95 C4
Lukenie r. Dem. Rep. Congo 94 B4
Lukh r. Rus. Fed. 38 I4
Lukhovitsy Rus. Fed. 39 H5
Luk Keng Hong Kong China 73 [inset]
Lukou China see Zhuzhou
Lukovit Bulg. 55 K3
Łuków Poland 39 D6
Lukoyanov Rus. Fed. 39 J5
Lukusuzi National Park Zambia 95 D5
Luleå Sweden 40 M4
Luleälven r. Sweden 40 M4
Lüleburgaz Turkey 55 L4
Luliang China 72 D3
Lüliang Shan mts China 69 K5

Lulimba Dem. Rep. Congo **95** C4
Luling U.S.A. **127** D6
Lulonga *r.* Dem. Rep. Congo **94** B3
Luluabourg Dem. Rep. Congo *see* Kananga
Lülung China **79** F3
Lumachomo China **79** F3
Lumajang Indon. **64** E8
Lumajangdong Co *salt l.* China **78** E2
Lumbala *Moxico* Angola *see* Lumbala Kaquengue
Lumbala *Moxico* Angola *see* Lumbala N'guimbo
Lumbala Kaquengue Angola **95** C5
Lumbala N'guimbo Angola **95** C5
Lumberton U.S.A. **129** E5
Lumbini Nepal **79** E4
Lumbis Indon. **64** F6
Lumbrales Spain **53** C3
Lumezzane Italy **54** D2
Lumi P.N.G. **65** K7
Lumphăt Cambodia **67** D4
Lumpkin U.S.A. **129** C5
Lumsden Canada **117** J5
Lumsden N.Z. **109** B7
Lumut Malaysia **67** C6
Lumut, Tanjung *pt* Indon. **64** D7
Luna U.S.A. **125** I5
Lunan China *see* Shilin
Lunan Bay U.K. **46** G4
Lunan Lake Canada **117** M1
Lunan Shan *mts* China **72** D3
Luna Pier U.S.A. **130** D3
Lund Pak. **85** H5
Lund Sweden **41** H9
Lund *NV* U.S.A. **125** F2
Lund *UT* U.S.A. **125** G2
Lundar Canada **117** L5
Lundy Island U.K. **45** C7
Lune *r.* Germany **49** I1
Lune *r.* U.K. **44** E4
Lüneburg Germany **49** K1
Lüneburger Heide *reg.* Germany **49** K1
Lünen Germany **49** H3
Lunenburg U.S.A. **131** F5
Lunéville France **52** H2
Lunga *r.* Zambia **95** C5
Lungdo China **79** E2
Lunggar China **79** E3
Lung Kwu Chau *i. Hong Kong* China **73** [inset]
Lungleh India *see* Lunglei
Lunglei India **79** H5
Lungmari *mt.* China **79** F3
Lungmu Co *salt l.* China **78** E2
Lungnaquilla Mountain *hill* Rep. of Ireland **47** F5
Lungwebungu *r.* Zambia **95** C5
Lunh Nepal **79** E3
Luni India **78** C4
Luni *r.* India **78** B4
Luni *r.* Pak. **85** H4
Luninets Belarus *see* Luninyets
Luning U.S.A. **124** D2
Luninyets Belarus **41** O10
Lunkaransar India **78** C3
Lunkha India **78** C3
Lünne Germany **49** H2
Lunsar Sierra Leone **92** B4
Lunsklip S. Africa **97** I3
Luntai China **76** F3
Luobei China **70** C3
Luobuzhuang China **76** G4
Luocheng *Fujian* China *see* Hui'an
Luocheng *Guangxi* China **73** F3
Luodian China **72** E3
Luoding China **73** F4
Luodou Sha *i.* China **73** F4
Luohe China **73** G1
Luo He *r.* China **73** G1
Luonan China **73** F1
Luoning China **73** F1
Luoping China **72** E3
Luotian China **73** G2
Luoto Fin. **40** M5
Luoxiao Shan *mts* China **73** G3
Luoxiong China *see* Luoping
Luoyang *Guangdong* China *see* Boluo
Luoyang *Henan* China **73** G1
Luoyang *Zhejiang* China *see* Taishun
Luoyuan China **73** H3
Luozigou China **70** C4
Lupane Zimbabwe **95** C5
Lupanshui China **72** E3
L'Upemba, Parc National de *nat. park* Dem. Rep. Congo **95** C4
Lupeni Romania **55** J2
Lupilichi Moz. **95** D5
Lupton U.S.A. **125** I4
Luqiao China *see* Luding
Luqu China **72** D1
Lu Qu *r.* China *see* Tao He
Luquan China **66** C1
Luray U.S.A. **131** F4
Luremo Angola **95** B4
Lurgan U.K. **47** F3
Luring China *see* Oma
Lúrio Moz. **95** E5
Lurio *r.* Moz. **95** E5

▶**Lusaka** Zambia **95** C5
Capital of Zambia.

Lusambo Dem. Rep. Congo **95** C4
Lusancay Islands and Reefs P.N.G. **102** F2
Lusangi Dem. Rep. Congo **95** C4
Luseland Canada **117** I4
Lush, Mount *hill* Australia **104** D4
Lushi China **73** F1
Lushnja Albania *see* Lushnjë
Lushnjë Albania **55** H4
Lushui China **72** C3
Lushuihe China **70** B4
Lüsi China **73** I1
Lusikisiki S. Africa **97** I6
Lusk U.S.A. **122** G4
Luso Angola *see* Luena
Lussvale Australia **108** C1
Lut, Bahrat *salt l.* Asia *see* Dead Sea
Lut, Dasht-e *des.* Iran **84** E4
Lü Tao *i.* Taiwan **73** I4
Lutetia France *see* Paris
Lūt-e Zangī Aḥmad *des.* Iran **84** E4
Luther U.S.A. **130** C1
Luther Lake Canada **130** E2
Lutherstadt Wittenberg Germany **49** M3
Luton U.K. **45** G7
Łutselk'e Canada **117** I2
Luts'k Ukr. **39** E6
Lutselgeest Neth. **48** F2
Luttenberg Neth. **48** G2
Lutto *r.* Fin./Rus. Fed. *see* Lotta
Lutz U.S.A. **129** D6

Lützelbach Germany **49** J5
Lützow-Holm Bay Antarctica **148** D2
Lutzputs S. Africa **96** E5
Lutzville S. Africa **96** D6
Luumäki Fin. **41** O6
Luuq Somalia **94** E3
Luverne *AL* U.S.A. **129** C6
Luverne *MN* U.S.A. **126** D3
Luvuei Angola **95** C5
Luvuvhu *r.* S. Africa **97** J2
Luwero Uganda **94** D3
Luwingu Zambia **95** C5
Luwuk Indon. **65** G7
▶**Luxembourg** *country* Europe **48** G5
europe 5, 34–35

▶**Luxembourg** Lux. **48** G5
Capital of Luxembourg.

Luxembourg *country* Europe *see* Luxembourg
Luxeuil-les-Bains France **52** H3
Luxi *Hunan* China **73** F2
Luxi *Yunnan* China **72** C3
Luxi *Yunnan* China **72** D3
Luxolweni S. Africa **97** G6
Luxor Egypt **82** D4
Luyi China **73** G1
Luyksgestel Neth. **48** F3
Luza Rus. Fed. **38** J3
Luza *r.* Rus. Fed. **38** J3
Luza *r.* Rus. Fed. **38** M2
Luzern Switz. *see* Lucerne
Luzhai China **73** F3
Luzhang China *see* Lushui
Luzhi China **72** E3
Luzhou China **72** E2
Luziânia Brazil **141** B2
Luzon *i.* Phil. **65** G3
Luzon Strait Phil. **65** G2
Luzy France **52** F3
L'viv Ukr. **39** E6
L'vov Ukr. *see* L'viv
Lwów Ukr. *see* L'viv
Lyady Rus. Fed. **41** P7
Lyakhavichy Belarus **41** O10
Lyakhovichi Belarus *see* Lyakhavichy
Lyallpur Pak. *see* Faisalabad
Lyamtsa Rus. Fed. **38** H2
Lycia *reg.* Turkey **55** M6
Lyck Poland *see* Ełk
Lycksele Sweden **40** K4
Lycopolis Egypt *see* Asyūṭ
Lydd U.K. **45** H8
Lydda Israel *see* Lod
Lyddan Island Antarctica **148** B2
Lydenburg S. Africa **97** J3
Lydia *reg.* Turkey **55** L5
Lydney U.K. **45** E7
Lyel'chytsy Belarus **39** F6
Lyell, Mount U.S.A. **124** D3
Lyell Brown, Mount *hill* Australia **105** E5
Lyell Island Canada **116** D4
Lyepyel' Belarus **41** P9
Lykens U.S.A. **131** G3
Lyman U.S.A. **122** F4
Lyme Bay U.K. **45** E8
Lyme Regis U.K. **45** E8
Lymington U.K. **45** F8
Lynchburg *OH* U.S.A. **130** D4
Lynchburg *TN* U.S.A. **128** C5
Lynchburg *VA* U.S.A. **130** F5
Lynchville U.S.A. **131** J1
Lyndhurst *N.S.W.* Australia **108** D4
Lyndhurst *Qld* Australia **106** D3
Lyndhurst *S.A.* Australia **107** B6
Lyndon Australia **105** A5
Lyndon *r.* Australia **105** A5
Lyndonville U.S.A. **131** I1
Lyne *r.* U.K. **44** D4
Lyness U.K. **46** F2
Lyngdal Norway **41** E7
Lynn U.K. *see* King's Lynn
Lynn *IN* U.S.A. **130** C3
Lynn *MA* U.S.A. **131** J2
Lynndyl U.S.A. **125** G2
Lynn Lake Canada **117** K3
Lynton U.K. **45** D7
Lynx Lake Canada **117** J2
Lyon France **52** G4
Lyon *r.* U.K. **46** F4
Lyon Mountain U.S.A. **131** I1
Lyons Australia **105** F7
Lyons France *see* Lyon
Lyons *GA* U.S.A. **129** D5
Lyons *NY* U.S.A. **131** G2
Lyons Falls U.S.A. **131** H2
Lyozna Belarus **39** F5
Lyra Reef P.N.G. **102** F2
Lys *r.* France **48** D4
Lysekil Sweden **41** G7
Lyskovo Rus. Fed. **38** J4
Lys'va Rus. Fed. **37** R4
Lysychans'k Ukr. **39** H6
Lysyye Gory Rus. Fed. **39** J6
Lytham St Anne's U.K. **44** D5
Lytton Canada **116** F5
Lyuban' Belarus **41** P10
Lyubertsy Rus. Fed. **37** N4
Lyubeshiv Ukr. **39** E6
Lyubim Rus. Fed. **38** I4
Lyubytino Rus. Fed. **38** G4
Lyudinovo Rus. Fed. **39** G5
Lyunda *r.* Rus. Fed. **38** J4
Lyzha *r.* Rus. Fed. **38** M2

↓ M

Ma *r.* Myanmar **66** B2
Ma, Nam *r.* Laos **66** C2
Ma'agan Israel **81** B3
Maale Maldives *see* Male
Maale Atholhu *atoll* Maldives *see* Male Atoll
Maalhosmadulu Atholhu Uthuruburi *atoll* Maldives *see* North Maalhosmadulu Atoll
Maalhosmadulu Atoll Maldives **80** B5
Ma'ān Jordan **81** B4
Maan Turkey *see* Nusratiye
Maaninka Fin. **40** O5
Maaninkavaara Fin. **40** P3
Ma'anshan China **73** H2
Maardu Estonia **41** N7
Maarianhamina Fin. *see* Mariehamn
Ma'arrat an Nu'mān Syria **81** C2
Maarssen Neth. **48** F2
Maas *r.* Neth. **48** E3
also known as Meuse (Belgium/France)
Maaseik Belgium **48** F3
Maasin Phil. **65** G4

Maasmechelen Belgium **48** F4
Maas-Schwalm-Nette *nat. park* Germany/Neth. **48** F3
Maastricht Neth. **48** F4
Maaza Plateau Egypt **86** C6
Maba *Guangdong* China *see* Qujiang
Maba *Jiangsu* China **73** H1
Mabai China *see* Maguan
Mabalane Moz. **97** K2
Mabana Dem. Rep. Congo **94** C3
Mabaruma Guyana **138** G2
Mabein Myanmar **66** B2
Mabel Creek Australia **105** F7
Mabel Downs Australia **104** D4
Mabella Canada **118** C4
Mabel Lake Canada **116** G5
Maberly Canada **131** G1
Mabian China **72** D2
Mablethorpe U.K. **44** H5
Mabopane S. Africa **97** I3
Mabote Moz. **97** L2
Mabou Canada **119** J5
Mabrak, Jabal *mt.* Jordan **81** B4
Mabuasehube Game Reserve *nature res.* Botswana **96** F3
Mabule Botswana **96** G3
Mabutsane Botswana **96** F3
Macá, Monte *mt.* Chile **140** B7
Macadam Plains Australia **105** B6
Macaé Brazil **141** C3
Macajuba Brazil **141** C1
Macaloge Moz. **95** D5
MacAlpine Lake Canada **115** H3
Macamic Canada **118** F4
Macandze Moz. **97** K2
Macao China *see* Macau
Macao *aut. reg.* China *see* Macau
Macapá Brazil **139** H3
Macará Ecuador **138** C4
Macarani Brazil **141** C1
Macas Ecuador **138** C4
Macassar Indon. *see* Makassar
Macau Brazil **139** K5
Macau China **73** G4
Macau *aut. reg.* China **73** G4
Macaúba Brazil **139** H6
Macauley Island N.Z. **103** I5
Macau Special Administrative Region *aut. reg.* China *see* Macau
Maccaretane Moz. **97** K3
Macclenny U.S.A. **129** D6
Macclesfield U.K. **44** E5
Macdiarmid Canada **118** C4
Macdonald, Lake *salt flat* Australia **105** E5
Macdonald Range *hills* Australia **104** D3
Macdonnell Ranges *mts* Australia **105** E5
MacDowell Lake Canada **117** M4
Macduff U.K. **46** G3
Macedo de Cavaleiros Port. **53** C3
Macedon *mt.* Australia **108** B6
Macedon *country* Europe *see* Macedonia
▶**Macedonia** *country* Europe **55** I4
europe 5, 34–35
Maceió Brazil **139** K5
Macenta Guinea **92** C4
Macerata Italy **54** E3
Macfarlane, Lake *salt flat* Australia **107** B7
Macgillycuddy's Reeks *mts* Rep. of Ireland **47** C6
Machachi Ecuador **138** C4
Machaila Moz. **97** K2
Machakos Kenya **94** D4
Machala Ecuador **138** C4
Machali China *see* Madoi
Machanga Moz. **95** D6
Machar Marshes Sudan **82** D8
Machattie, Lake *salt flat* Australia **106** B5
Machatuine Moz. **97** K3
Machault France **48** E5
Machaze Moz. *see* Chitobe
Macheng China **73** G2
Macherla India **80** C2
Machhagan India **79** F5
Machias *ME* U.S.A. **128** H2
Machias *NY* U.S.A. **131** F2
Machilipatnam India **80** D2
Machiques Venez. **138** D1
Mach Kowr Iran **85** F5
Machrihanish U.K. **46** D5
Machu Picchu *tourist site* Peru **138** D6
Machynlleth U.K. **45** D6
Macia Moz. **97** K3
Macias Nguema *i.* Equat. Guinea *see* Bioco
Măcin Romania **55** M2
Macintyre *r.* Australia **108** E2
Macintyre Brook *r.* Australia **108** E2
Mack U.S.A. **125** I2
Maçka Turkey **87** E2
Mackay Australia **106** E4
MacKay *r.* Canada **117** I3
Mackay U.S.A. **122** E3
Mackay, Lake *salt flat* Australia **104** E5
MacKay Lake Canada **117** I2
Mackenzie *r.* Australia **106** E4
Mackenzie Canada **116** F4
Mackenzie *r.* Canada **116** F2
Mackenzie Guyana *see* Linden
Mackenzie *atoll* Micronesia *see* Ulithi
Mackenzie Bay Antarctica **148** E2
Mackenzie Bay Canada **114** E3
Mackenzie Highway Canada **116** G2
Mackenzie King Island Canada **115** G2
Mackenzie Mountains Canada **116** C1

▶**Mackenzie-Peace-Finlay** *r.* Canada **114** E3
2nd longest river in North America.

Mackillop, Lake *salt flat* Australia *see* Yamma Yamma, Lake
Mackintosh Range *hills* Australia **105** D6
Macklin Canada **117** I4
Macksville Australia **108** F3
Maclean Australia **108** F2
Maclear S. Africa **97** I6
MacLeod Canada *see* Fort Macleod
MacLeod, Lake *imp. l.* Australia **105** A6
Macmillan *r.* Canada **116** C2
Macmillan Pass Canada **116** D2
Macomb U.S.A. **126** F3
Macomer *Sardinia* Italy **54** C4
Mâcon France **52** G3
Macon *GA* U.S.A. **129** D5

Macon *MO* U.S.A. **126** E4
Macon *MS* U.S.A. **127** F5
Macon *OH* U.S.A. **130** D4
Macondo Angola **95** C5
Macoun Lake Canada **117** K3
Macpherson Robertson Land *reg.* Antarctica *see* Mac. Robertson Land
Macpherson's Strait India **67** A5
Macquarie *r.* Australia **108** C3
Macquarie, Lake *b.* Australia **108** E4

▶**Macquarie Island** S. Pacific Ocean **146** G9
Part of Australia. Most southerly point of Oceania.

Macquarie Marshes Australia **108** C3
Macquarie Mountain Australia **108** D4
Macquarie Ridge *sea feature* S. Pacific Ocean **146** G9
MacRitchie Reservoir Sing. **67** [inset]
Mac. Robertson Land *reg.* Antarctica **148** E2
Macroom Rep. of Ireland **47** D6
Macumba Australia **107** A5
Macumba *watercourse* Australia **107** B5
Macuzari, Presa *resr* Mex. **123** F8
Mādabā Jordan **81** B4
Madadeni S. Africa **97** J4

▶**Madagascar** *country* Africa **95** E6
Largest island in Africa and 4th in the world.
africa 7, 88–89, 90–91
world 12–13

Madagascar Basin *sea feature* Indian Ocean **145** L7
Madagascar Ridge *sea feature* Indian Ocean **145** K8
Madagasikara *country* Africa *see* Madagascar
Madakasira India **80** C3
Madama Niger **93** E2
Madan Bulg. **55** K4
Madanapalle India **80** C3
Madang P.N.G. **65** L8
Madaoua Niger **92** D3
Madaripur Bangl. **79** G5
Madau Turkm. **84** D2
Madaw Turkm. *see* Madau
Madawaska Canada **131** G1
Madawaska *r.* Canada **131** G1
Madaya Myanmar **66** B2
Madded India **80** D2

▶**Madeira** *r.* Brazil **138** G4
4th longest river in South America.

▶**Madeira** *terr.* N. Atlantic Ocean **92** B1
Autonomous Region of Portugal.
africa 7, 90–91

Madeira, Arquipélago da *terr.* N. Atlantic Ocean *see* Madeira
Maden Turkey **87** E3
Madera Mex. **123** F7
Madera U.S.A. **124** C3
Madgaon India **80** B3
Madha India **80** B2
Madhavpur India **78** B5
Madhepura India **79** F4
Madhipura India *see* Madhepura
Madhubani India **79** F4
Madhya Pradesh *state* India **78** D5
Madibogo S. Africa **97** G4
Madidi *r.* Bol. **138** E6
Madikeri India **80** B3
Madikwe Game Reserve *nature res.* S. Africa **97** H3
Madill U.S.A. **127** D5
Madīnat ath Thawrah Syria **81** D2
Madingo-Kayes Congo **95** B4
Madingou Congo **95** B4
Madison *FL* U.S.A. **129** D6
Madison *GA* U.S.A. **129** D5
Madison *IN* U.S.A. **130** C4
Madison *ME* U.S.A. **131** K1
Madison *NE* U.S.A. **126** D3
Madison *SD* U.S.A. **126** D2
Madison *VA* U.S.A. **131** F4

▶**Madison** *WI* U.S.A. **126** F3
State capital of Wisconsin.

Madison *WV* U.S.A. **130** E4
Madison *r.* U.S.A. **122** F3
Madison Heights U.S.A. **130** F5
Madisonville *KY* U.S.A. **130** B5
Madisonville *TX* U.S.A. **127** E6
Madiun Indon. **64** E8
Madley, Mount *hill* Australia **105** C6
Madoc Canada **131** G1
Mado Gashi Kenya **94** D3
Madoi China **72** C1
Madona Latvia **41** O8
Madpura India **78** B4
Madra Dağı *mts* Turkey **55** L5
Madrakah Saudi Arabia **82** E5
Madrakah, Ra's *c.* Oman **83** I6
Madras India *see* Chennai
Madras *state* India *see* Tamil Nadu
Madras U.S.A. **122** C3
Madre, Laguna *lag.* Mex. **127** D7
Madre, Laguna *lag.* U.S.A. **127** D7
Madre de Dios *r.* Peru **138** E6
Madre de Dios, Isla *i.* Chile **140** A8
Madre del Sur, Sierra *mts* Mex. **132** D5
Madre Mountain U.S.A. **125** J4
Madre Occidental, Sierra *mts* Mex. **123** F7
Madre Oriental, Sierra *mts* Mex. **127** C7

▶**Madrid** Spain **53** E3
Capital of Spain.

Madridejos Spain **53** E4
Madruga Cuba **129** D8
Madugula India **80** D2
Madura *i.* Indon. **64** E8
Madura, Selat *sea chan.* Indon. **64** E8
Madurai India **80** C4
Madurantakam India **80** C3
Madvār, Kūh-e *mt.* Iran **84** D4
Madvezh'ya *vol.* Rus. Fed. **70** H3
Madwas India **79** E4
Maé *i.* Vanuatu *see* Émaé
Maebashi Japan **71** E5

Mae Hong Son Thai. **66** B3
Mae Ping National Park Thai. **66** B3
Mae Ramat Thai. **66** B3
Mae Sai Thai. **66** B2
Mae Sariang Thai. **66** B3
Mae Sot Thai. **66** B3
Mae Suai Thai. **66** B3
Mae Tuen Wildlife Reserve *nature res.* Thai. **66** B3
Maevatanana Madag. **95** E5
Maéwo *i.* Vanuatu **103** G3
Mae Wong National Park Thai. **66** B4
Mae Yom National Park Thai. **66** C3
Mafeking Canada **117** K4
Mafeking S. Africa *see* Mafikeng
Mafeteng Lesotho **97** H5
Maffra Australia **108** C6
Mafia Island Tanz. **95** D4
Mafikeng S. Africa **97** G3
Mafinga Tanz. **95** D4
Mafra Brazil **141** A4
Mafraq Jordan *see* Al Mafraq
Magabeni S. Africa **97** J6
Magadan Rus. Fed. **61** Q4
Magadi Kenya **94** D4
Magaiza Moz. **97** K2
Magallanes Chile *see* Punta Arenas
Magallanes, Estrecho de Chile *see* Magellan, Strait of
Magangue Col. **138** D2
Mağara Dağı *mt.* Turkey **81** A1
Magaramkent Rus. Fed. **87** H2
Magaria Niger **92** D3
Magarida P.N.G. **106** E1
Magas Rus. Fed. **87** G2
Magazine Mountain *hill* U.S.A. **127** E5
Magdagachi Rus. Fed. **70** B1
Magdalena Bol. **138** F6
Magdalena *r.* Col. **138** D1
Magdalena *Baja California Sur* Mex. **123** E8
Magdalena *Sonora* Mex. **123** F7
Magdalena *r.* Mex. **123** F7
Magdalena, Bahía *b.* Mex. **132** B4
Magdalena, Isla *i.* Chile **140** B6
Magdeburg Germany **49** L2
Magdelaine Cays *atoll* Australia **106** E3
Magellan, Strait of Chile **140** B8
Magellan Seamounts *sea feature* N. Pacific Ocean **146** F4
Magenta, Lake *salt flat* Australia **105** B8
Magerøya *i.* Norway **40** N1
Maggiorasca, Monte *mt.* Italy **54** C2
Maggiore, Lago Italy *see* Maggiore, Lake
Maggiore, Lake Italy **54** C2
Maghāgha Egypt *see* Maghāghah
Maghāghah Egypt **86** C5
Maghama Mauritania **92** B3
Maghâra, Gebel *hill* Egypt *see* Maghārah, Jabal
Maghārah, Jabal *hill* Egypt **81** A4
Maghera U.K. **47** F3
Magherafelt U.K. **47** F3
Maghnia Alg. **53** F6
Maghor Afgh. **85** F3
Maghull U.K. **44** E5
Magilligan Point U.K. **47** F2
Magma U.S.A. **125** H5
Magna Grande *mt. Sicily* Italy **54** F6
Magnetic Island Australia **106** D3
Magnetic Passage Australia **106** D3
Magnetity Rus. Fed. **40** R2
Magnitogorsk Rus. Fed. **60** G4
Magnolia *AR* U.S.A. **127** E5
Magnolia *MS* U.S.A. **127** F6
Magny-en-Vexin France **48** B5
Mago Rus. Fed. **70** F1
Màgoé Moz. **95** D5
Magog Canada **131** I1
Mago National Park Eth. **94** D3
Magosa Cyprus *see* Famagusta
Magpie *r.* Canada **119** I4
Magpie, Lac *l.* Canada **119** I4
Magṭa' Laḥjar Mauritania **92** B3
Magu Tanz. **94** D4
Magu, Khrebet *mts* Rus. Fed. **70** E1
Maguan China **72** E4
Magude Moz. **97** K3
Magueyal Mex. **127** C7
Magura Bangl. **79** G5
Maguse Lake Canada **117** M2
Magway Myanmar *see* Magwe
Magwe Myanmar **66** A2
Magyar Köztársaság *country* Europe *see* Hungary
Magyichaung Myanmar **66** A2
Mahābād Iran **84** B2
Mahabharat Range *mts* Nepal **79** F4
Mahaboobnagar India *see* Mahbubnagar
Mahad India **80** B2
Mahadeo Hills India **78** D5
Mahaffey U.S.A. **131** F3
Mahajan India **78** C3
Mahajanga Madag. **95** E5
Mahakam *r.* Indon. **64** F7
Mahalapye Botswana **97** H2
Mahale Mountains National Park Tanz. **95** C4
Mahalevona Madag. **95** E5
Mahallāt Iran **84** C3
Māhān Iran **84** E4
Mahanadi *r.* India **80** E1
Mahanoro Madag. **95** E5
Maha Oya Sri Lanka **80** D5
Maharashtra *state* India **80** B2
Maha Sarakham Thai. **66** C3
Mahasham, Wādi el *watercourse* Egypt *see* Muhashsham, Wādī al
Mahaxai Laos **66** D3
Mahbubabad India **80** D2
Mahbubnagar India **80** C2
Mahd adh Dhahab Saudi Arabia **82** F5
Mahdia Alg. **53** G6
Mahdia Guyana **139** G2
Mahdia Tunisia **54** D7
Mahe China **72** E1
Mahé *i.* Seychelles **145** L6
Mahendragiri *mt.* India **80** E2
Mahenge Tanz. **95** D4
Mahesana India **78** C5
Mahi *r.* India **78** C5
Mahia Peninsula N.Z. **109** F4
Mahilyow Belarus **39** F5
Mahim India **80** B2
Mah Jan Iran **84** D4
Mahlabatini S. Africa **97** J5
Mahlsdorf Germany **49** L2
Mahmudabad Iran **84** D2
Maḥmūd-e 'Erāqī Afgh. *see* Maḥmūd-e Rāqī
Maḥmūd-e Rāqī Afgh. **85** H3

Mahnomen U.S.A. **126** D2
Maho Sri Lanka **80** D5
Mahoba India **78** D4
Maholi India **78** E4
Mahón Spain **53** I4
Mahony Lake Canada **116** E1
Mahrauni India **78** D4
Mahrès Tunisia **54** D7
Māhrūd Iran **85** F3
Mahsana India *see* Mahesana
Mahudaung *mts* Myanmar **66** A2
Mahukona *HI* U.S.A. **123** [inset]
Mahur India **80** C2
Mahuva India **78** B5
Mahwa India **78** D4
Mahya Dağı *mt.* Turkey **55** L4
Mai *i.* Vanuatu *see* Émaé
Maiaia Moz. *see* Nacala
Maibang India **66** A1
Maicao Col. **138** D1
Maicasagi *r.* Canada **118** F4
Maicasagi, Lac *l.* Canada **118** F4
Maichen China **73** F4
Maidenhead U.K. **45** G7
Maidstone Canada **117** I4
Maidstone U.K. **45** H7
Maiduguri Nigeria **92** E3
Maiella, Parco Nazionale della *nat. park* Italy **54** F3
Mai Gudo *mt.* Eth. **94** D3
Maigue *r.* Rep. of Ireland **47** D5
Maihar India **78** E4
Maiji Shan *mt.* China **72** E1
Maikala Range *hills* India **78** E5
Maiko *r.* Dem. Rep. Congo **94** C3
Mailan Hill *mt.* India **79** E5
Mailly-le-Camp France **48** E6
Mailsi Pak. **85** I4
Main *r.* Germany **49** I4
Main *r.* U.K. **47** F3
Main Brook Canada **119** L4
Mainburg Germany **49** L6
Main Channel *lake channel* Canada **130** E1
Maindargi India **80** C2
Mai-Ndombe, Lac *l.* Dem. Rep. Congo **94** B4
Main-Donau-Kanal *canal* Germany **49** K5
Maindong China **79** F3
Main Duck Island Canada **131** G2
Maine *state* U.S.A. **131** K1
Maine, Gulf of Canada/U.S.A. **131** K2
Mainé Hanari, Cerro *hill* Col. **138** D4
Maïné-Soroa Niger **92** E3
Maingkaing Myanmar **66** A1
Maingkwan Myanmar **66** B1
Maingy Island Myanmar **67** B4
Mainhardt Germany **49** J5
Mainkung China **72** C2
Mainland *i. Scotland* U.K. **46** F1
Mainland *i. Scotland* U.K. **46** [inset]
Mainleus Germany **49** L4
Mainoru Australia **104** F3
Mainpat *reg.* India **79** E5
Mainpuri India **78** D4
Main Range National Park Australia **108** F2
Maintenon France **48** B6
Maintirano Madag. **95** E5
Mainz Germany **49** I4
Maio *i.* Cape Verde **92** [inset]
Maipú Arg. **140** E5
Maiskhal Island Bangl. **79** G5
Maisons-Laffitte France **48** C6
Maitengwe Botswana **95** C6
Maitland *N.S.W.* Australia **108** E4
Maitland *S.A.* Australia **107** B7
Maitland *r.* Australia **104** B5
Maitri *research station* Antarctica **148** C2
Maiwo *i.* Vanuatu *see* Maéwo
Maiyu, Mount *hill* Australia **104** E4
Maíz, Islas del *is* Nicaragua **133** H6
Maizar Pak. **85** H3
Maizuru Japan **71** D6
Maja Jezercë *mt.* Albania **55** H3
Majene Indon. **64** F7
Majestic U.S.A. **130** D5
Majḥūd *well* Saudi Arabia **84** C6
Majī Eth. **94** D3
Majiang *Guangxi* China **73** F4
Majiang *Guizhou* China **72** E3
Majiazi China **70** B2
Majōl *country* N. Pacific Ocean *see* Marshall Islands
Major, Puig *mt.* Spain **53** H4
Majorca *i.* Spain **53** H4
Mājro *atoll* Marshall Is *see* Majuro
Majunga Madag. *see* Mahajanga
Majuro *atoll* Marshall Is **146** H5
Majwemasweu S. Africa **97** H5
Makabana Congo **94** B4
Makale Indon. **65** F7

▶**Makalu** *mt.* China/Nepal **79** F4
5th highest mountain in the world and in Asia.
world 12–13

Makalu Barun National Park Nepal **79** F4
Makanchi Kazakh. **76** F2
Makanpur India **78** E4
Makari Mountain National Park Tanz. *see* Mahale Mountains National Park
Makarov Rus. Fed. **70** F2
Makarov Basin *sea feature* Arctic Ocean **149** B1
Makarska Croatia **54** G3
Makarwal Pak. **85** H3
Makar'ye Rus. Fed. **38** K4
Makar'yev Rus. Fed. **38** I4
Makasar, Selat *strait* Indon. *see* Makassar, Selat
Makassar Indon. **64** F8
Makassar, Selat *strait* Indon. **64** F7
Makassar Strait Indon. *see* Makassar, Selat
Makat Kazakh. **74** E2
Makatini Flats *lowland* S. Africa **97** K4
Makedonija *country* Europe *see* Macedonia
Makeni Sierra Leone **92** B4
Makete Tanz. **95** D4
Makeyevka Ukr. *see* Makiyivka
Makgadikgadi *depr.* Botswana **95** C6
Makgadikgadi Pans National Park Botswana **95** C6
Makhachkala Rus. Fed. **87** G2
Makhad Pak. **85** H3
Makhado S. Africa *see* Louis Trichardt
Makhāzin, Kathīb al *des.* Egypt **81** A4

Makhâzin, Kathîb el des. Egypt see Makhâzin, Kathîb al
Makhazine, Barrage El dam Morocco 53 D6
Makhmūr Iraq 87 F4
Makhtal India 80 C2
Makin atoll Kiribati see Butaritari
Makindu Kenya 94 D4
Makinsk Kazakh. 75 G1
Makira i. Solomon Is see San Cristobal
Makiyivka Ukr. 39 H6
Makkah Saudi Arabia see Mecca
Makkovik Canada 119 K3
Makkovik, Cape Canada 119 K3
Makkum Neth. 48 F1
Makó Hungary 55 I1
Makokou Gabon 94 B3
Makopong Botswana 96 F3
Makotipoko Congo 93 E5
Makran reg. Iran/Pak. 85 F5
Makrana India 78 C4
Makran Coast Range mts Pak. 85 F5
Makri India 80 D2
Maksatikha Rus. Fed. 38 G4
Maksi India 78 D5
Maksimovka Rus. Fed. 70 E3
Maksotag Iran 85 F4
Maksudangarh India 78 D5
Mākū Iran 84 B2
Makunguwiro Tanz. 95 D5
Makurdi Nigeria 92 D4
Makwassie S. Africa 97 G4
Mal India 79 G4
Mala Rep. of Ireland see Mallow
Mala i. Solomon Is see Malaita
Malå Sweden 40 K4
Mala, Punta pt Panama 133 H7
Malabar Coast India 80 B3

▶Malabo Equat. Guinea 92 D4
Capital of Equatorial Guinea.

Malaca Spain see Málaga
Malacca Malaysia see Melaka
Malacca, Strait of Indon./Malaysia 67 B6
Malad City U.S.A. 122 E4
Maladzyechna Belarus 41 O9
Malá Fatra nat. park Slovakia 43 Q6
Málaga Spain 53 D5
Malaga U.S.A. 127 B5
Malagasy Republic country Africa see Madagascar
Malaita i. Solomon Is 103 G2
Malakal Sudan 82 D8
Malakanagiri India see Malkangiri
Malakheti Nepal 78 E3
Malakula i. Vanuatu 103 G3
Malan, Ras pt Pak. 85 G5
Malang Indon. 64 E8
Malangana Nepal see Malangwa
Malange Angola see Malanje
Malangwa Nepal 79 F4
Malanje Angola 95 B4
Malappuram India 80 C4
Mälaren l. Sweden 41 J7
Malargüe Arg. 140 C5
Malartic Canada 118 F4
Malaspina Glacier U.S.A. 116 A3
Malatya Turkey 86 E3
Malavalli India 80 C3
▶Malawi country Africa 95 D5
africa 7, 90–91
Malawi, Lake Africa see Nyasa, Lake
Malawi National Park Zambia see Nyika National Park
Malaya pen. Malaysia see Peninsular Malaysia
Malaya Pera Rus. Fed. 38 L2
Malaya Vishera Rus. Fed. 38 G4
Malaybalay Phil. 65 H5
Malāyer Iran 84 C3
Malay Peninsula Asia 67 B4
Malay Reef Australia 106 E3
▶Malaysia country Asia 64 D5
asia 6, 58–59
Malaysia, Semenanjung pen. Malaysia see Peninsular Malaysia
Malazgirt Turkey 87 F3
Malbon Australia 106 C4
Malbork Poland 43 Q3
Malborn Germany 48 G5
Malchin Germany 43 N4
Malcolm Australia 105 C7
Malcolm, Point Australia 105 C8
Malcolm Island Myanmar 67 B5
Maldegem Belgium 48 D3
Malden U.S.A. 127 F4
Malden Island Kiribati 147 J6
▶Maldives country Indian Ocean 77 D10
asia 6, 58–59
Maldon Australia 108 B6
Maldon U.K. 45 H7
Maldonado Uruguay 140 F4

▶Male Maldives 77 D11
Capital of the Maldives.

Maleas, Akra pt Greece 55 J6
Male Atoll Maldives 77 D11
Malebogo S. Africa 97 G5
Malegaon Maharashtra India 80 B1
Malegaon Maharashtra India 80 C2
Malé Karpaty hills Slovakia 43 P6
Malek Siāh, Kūh-e mt. Afgh. 85 F4
Malele Dem. Rep. Congo 95 B4
Maler Kotla India 78 C3
Maleševske Planine mts Bulg./Macedonia 55 J4
Malgobek Rus. Fed. 87 G2
Malgomaj l. Sweden 40 J4
Malḩa, Naqb mt. Egypt see Māliḩah, Naqb
Malhada Brazil 141 C1
Malheur r. U.S.A. 122 D3
Malheur Lake U.S.A. 122 D4
▶Mali country Africa 92 C3
africa 7, 90–91
Mali Dem. Rep. Congo 94 C4
Mali Guinea 92 B3
Maliana East Timor 104 D2
Malianjing China 76 I3
Māliḩah, Naqb mt. Egypt 81 A5
Malik Naro mt. Pak. 85 F4
Mali Kyun i. Myanmar 67 B4
Malili Indon. 65 G7
Malin Ukr. see Malyn
Malindi Kenya 94 E4
Malines Belgium see Mechelen
Malin Head hd Rep. of Ireland 47 E2
Malin More Rep. of Ireland 47 D3
Malipo China 72 E4
Mali Raginac mt. Croatia 54 F2
Malita Phil. 65 H5
Malka r. Rus. Fed. 87 G2
Malkangiri India 80 D2
Malkapur India 80 B2
Malkara Turkey 55 L4
Mal'kavichy Belarus 41 O10
Malko Tŭrnovo Bulg. 55 L4
Mallacoota Australia 108 D6
Mallacoota Inlet b. Australia 108 D6
Mallaig U.K. 46 D4
Mallani reg. India 85 H5
Mallawī Egypt 86 C6
Mallee Cliffs National Park Australia 107 C7
Mallery Lake Canada 117 L1
Mallét Brazil 141 A4
Mallorca i. Spain see Majorca
Mallow Rep. of Ireland 47 D5
Mallowa Well Australia 104 D5
Mallwyd U.K. 45 D6
Malm Norway 40 G4
Malmberget Sweden 40 L3
Malmédy Belgium 48 G4
Malmesbury S. Africa 96 D7
Malmesbury U.K. 45 E7
Malmö Sweden 41 H9
Malmyzh Rus. Fed. 38 K4
Maloca Brazil 139 G3
Malone U.S.A. 131 H1
Malonje mt. Tanz. 95 D4
Maloshuyka Rus. Fed. 38 H3
Malosmadulu Atoll Maldives see Maalhosmadulu Atoll
Måløy Norway 40 D6
Maloyaroslavets Rus. Fed. 39 H5
Malozemel'skaya Tundra lowland Rus. Fed. 38 K2
Malpelo, Isla de i. N. Pacific Ocean 133 H8
Malprabha r. India 80 C2
▶Malta country Europe 54 F7
europe 5, 34–35
Malta Latvia 41 O8
Malta ID U.S.A. 122 E4
Malta MT U.S.A. 122 G2
Malta Channel Italy/Malta 54 F6
Maltahöhe Namibia 96 C3
Maltby U.K. 44 F5
Maltby le Marsh U.K. 44 H5
Malton U.K. 44 G4
Malukken is Indon. see Moluccas
Maluku is Indon. see Moluccas
Maluku, Laut sea Indon. 65 H6
Ma'lūlā, Jabal mts Syria 81 C3
Malung Sweden 41 H6
Maluti Mountains Lesotho 97 I5
Malu'u Solomon Is 103 G2
Malvan India 80 B2
Malvasia Greece see Monemvasia
Malvern U.K. see Great Malvern
Malvern U.S.A. 127 E5
Malvérnia Moz. see Chicualacuala
Malvinas, Islas terr. S. Atlantic Ocean see Falkland Islands
Malyn Ukr. 39 F6
Malyy Anyuy r. Rus. Fed. 61 R3
Malyye Derbety Rus. Fed. 39 J7
Malyy Kavkaz mts Asia see Lesser Caucasus
Malyy Lyakhovskiy, Ostrov i. Rus. Fed. 61 P2
Malyy Uzen' r. Kazakh./Rus. Fed. 39 K6
Mama r. Rus. Fed. 61 P3
Mamadysh Rus. Fed. 38 K5
Mamafubedu S. Africa 97 I4
Mamatān Nāvar l. Afgh. 85 G4
Mamba China 72 B4
Mambai Brazil 141 B1
Mambasa Dem. Rep. Congo 94 C3
Mamburao Phil. 65 G4
Mamelodi S. Africa 97 I3
Mamfe Cameroon 92 D4
Mamison Pass Georgia/Rus. Fed. 87 F2
Mamit India 79 H5
Mammoth U.S.A. 125 H5
Mammoth Cave National Park U.S.A. 130 B5
Mammoth Reservoir U.S.A. 124 D3
Mamonas Brazil 141 C1
Mamoré r. Bol./Brazil 138 E6
Mamou Guinea 92 B3
Mampikony Madag. 95 E5
Mampong Ghana 92 C4
Mamuju Indon. 64 F7
Mamuno Botswana 96 E2
Man Côte d'Ivoire 92 C4
Man India 80 B2
Man r. India 80 B2
Man U.S.A. 130 E5

▶Man, Isle of terr. Irish Sea 44 C4
United Kingdom Crown Dependency.
europe 5

Manacapuru Brazil 138 F4
Manacor Spain 53 H4
Manado Indon. 65 G6

▶Managua Nicaragua 133 G6
Capital of Nicaragua.

Manakara Madag. 95 E6
Manakau mt. N.Z. 109 D6
Manākhah Yemen 82 F6

▶Manama Bahrain 84 C5
Capital of Bahrain.

Manamadurai India 80 C4
Mana Maroka National Park S. Africa 97 H5
Manamelkudi India 80 C4
Manam Island P.N.G. 65 L7
Mananara Avaratra Madag. 95 E5
Manangoora Australia 106 B3
Mananjary Madag. 95 E6
Manantali, Lac de l. Mali 92 B3
Manantenina Madag. 95 E6
Mana Pass China/India 78 D3
Mana Pools National Park Zimbabwe 95 C5

▶Manapouri, Lake N.Z. 109 A7
Deepest lake in Oceania.

Manasa India 78 C4
Manas He r. China 76 G2
Manas Hu l. China 76 G2
Manāşīr reg. U.A.E. 84 D6
Manaslu mt. Nepal 79 F3
Manassas U.S.A. 131 G4
Manastir Macedonia see Bitola
Manas Wildlife Sanctuary nature res. Bhutan 79 G4
Man-aung Myanmar see Cheduba
Man-aung Kyun i. Myanmar see Cheduba Island
Manaus Brazil 138 F4
Manavgat Turkey 86 C3
Manbazar India 79 F5
Manbij Syria 81 C1
Manby U.K. 44 H5
Mancelona U.S.A. 130 C1
Manchar India 80 B2
Manchester U.K. 44 E5
Manchester CT U.S.A. 131 I3
Manchester IA U.S.A. 126 F3
Manchester KY U.S.A. 130 D5
Manchester MD U.S.A. 131 G4
Manchester MI U.S.A. 130 C2
Manchester NH U.S.A. 131 J2
Manchester OH U.S.A. 130 D4
Manchester TN U.S.A. 128 C5
Manchester VT U.S.A. 131 I2
Mancılık Turkey 86 E3
Mand Pak. 85 F5
Mand, Rūd-e r. Iran 84 C4
Manda Tanz. 95 D4
Manda, Jebel mt. Sudan 93 F4
Manda, Parc National de nat. park Chad 93 E4
Mandabe Madag. 95 E6
Mandai Sing. 67 [inset]
Mandal Afgh. 85 F3
Mandal Norway 41 E7

▶Mandala, Puncak mt. Indon. 65 K7
3rd highest mountain in Oceania.

Mandalay Myanmar 66 B2
Mandale Myanmar see Mandalay
Mandalgovĭ Mongolia 68 J3
Mandalī Iraq 87 G4
Mandalt China 69 K4
Mandan U.S.A. 126 C2
Mandas Sardinia Italy 54 C5
Mandasa India 80 E2
Mandasor India see Mandsaur
Mandav Hills India 78 B5
Mandera Kenya 94 E3
Manderfield U.S.A. 125 G2
Manderscheid Germany 48 G4
Mandeville Jamaica 133 I5
Mandeville N.Z. 109 B7
Mandha India 78 B4
Mandhoúdhíon Greece see Mantoudi
Mandi India 78 D3
Mandiana Guinea 92 C3
Mandi Burewala Pak. 85 I4
Mandié Moz. 95 D5
Mandini S. Africa 97 J5
Mandira Dam India 79 F5
Mandla India 78 E5
Mandleshwar India 78 C5
Mandrael India 78 D4
Mandritsara Madag. 95 E5
Mandsaur India 78 C4
Mandurah Australia 105 A8
Manduria Italy 54 G4
Mandvi India 78 B5
Mandya India 80 C3
Manerbio Italy 54 D2
Manevychi Ukr. 39 E6
Manfalūţ Egypt 86 C6
Manfredonia Italy 54 F4
Manfredonia, Golfo di g. Italy 54 G4
Manga Brazil 141 C1
Manga Burkina 92 C3
Mangabeiras, Serra das hills Brazil 139 I6
Mangai Dem. Rep. Congo 94 B4
Mangaia i. Cook Is 147 J7
Mangakino N.Z. 109 E4
Mangalagiri India 80 D2
Mangaldai India 66 A1
Mangaldoi India see Mangaldai
Mangalia Romania 55 M3
Mangalmé Chad 93 E3
Mangalore India 80 B3
Mangaon India 80 B2
Mangareva Islands Fr. Polynesia see Gambier, Îles
Mangaung Free State S. Africa 97 H5
Mangaung Free State S. Africa see Bloemfontein
Mangawan India 79 E4
Ma'ngê China see Luqu
Mangea i. Cook Is see Mangaia
Mangghyshlaq Kazakh. see Mangystau
Mangghystaū Kazakh. see Mangystau
Mangghystaū admin. div. Kazakh. see Mangistauskaya Oblast'
Mangghyt Uzbek. see Mangit
Manghit Uzbek. see Mangit
Mangin Range mts Myanmar see Mingin Range
Mangistau Kazakh. see Mangystau
Mangistauskaya Oblast' admin. div. Kazakh. 87 I2
Mangit Uzbek. 76 B3
Mangla Bangl. see Mongla
Mangla China see Guinan
Mangla Pak. 85 I3
Manglaqiongtuo China see Guinan
Mangnai China 76 H4
Mangnai Zhen China 76 H4
Mangochi Malawi 95 D5
Mangoky r. Madag. 95 E6
Mangole i. Indon. 65 H7
Mangoli India 80 B2
Mangotsfield U.K. 45 E7
Mangqystaū Shyghanaghy b. Kazakh. see Mangyshlakskiy Zaliv
Mangra China see Guinan
Mangral India 78 B5
Mangrul India 80 C1
Mangshi China see Luxi
Mangualde Port. 53 C3
Manguéni, Plateau du Niger 92 E2
Mangui China 70 A2
Mangula Zimbabwe see Mhangura
Mangum U.S.A. 127 D5
Mangyshlak Kazakh. see Mangystau
Mangyshlak, Poluostrov pen. Kazakh. 87 H1
Mangyshlak Oblast admin. div. Kazakh. see Mangistauskaya Oblast'
Mangyshlakskaya Oblast' admin. div. Kazakh. see Mangistauskaya Oblast'
Mangyshlakskiy Zaliv b. Kazakh. 87 H1
Mangystau Kazakh. 87 H2
Manhā Brazil 141 B1
Manhattan U.S.A. 126 D4
Manhica Moz. 97 K3
Manhoca Moz. 97 K4
Manhuaçu Brazil 141 C3
Manhuaçu r. Brazil 141 C2
Mani China 79 F2
Mania r. Madag. 95 E5
Maniago Italy 54 E1
Manicouagan Canada 119 H4
Manicouagan r. Canada 119 H4
Manicouagan, Réservoir resr Canada 119 H4
Manic Trois, Réservoir resr Canada 119 H4
Manīfah Saudi Arabia 84 C5
Maniganggo China 72 C2
Manigotagan Canada 117 L5
Manihiki atoll Cook Is 146 J6
Maniitsoq Greenland 115 M3
Manikchhari Bangl. 79 H5
Manikgarh India see Rajura

▶Manila Phil. 65 G4
Capital of the Philippines.

Manila U.S.A. 122 F4
Manildra Australia 108 D4
Manilla Australia 108 E3
Maningrida Australia 104 F3
Manipur India see Imphal
Manipur state India 79 H4
Manisa Turkey 55 L5
Manistee U.S.A. 130 B1
Manistee r. U.S.A. 130 B1
Manistique U.S.A. 128 C2
Manitoba prov. Canada 117 L4
Manitoba, Lake Canada 117 L5
Manito Lake Canada 117 I4
Manitou Canada 117 L5
Manitou, Lake U.S.A. 130 B3
Manitou Beach U.S.A. 131 G2
Manitou Falls Canada 117 M5
Manitou Islands U.S.A. 130 B1
Manitoulin Island Canada 118 E5
Manitouwadge Canada 118 D4
Manitowoc U.S.A. 130 B1
Maniwaki Canada 118 G5
Manizales Col. 138 C2
Manja Madag. 95 E6
Manjarabad India 80 B3
Manjeri India 80 C4
Manjhand Pak. 85 H5
Manjhi India 79 F4
Manjra r. India 80 C2
Man Kabat Myanmar 66 B1
Mankaiana Swaziland see Mankayane
Mankato KS U.S.A. 126 D4
Mankato MN U.S.A. 126 E2
Mankayane Swaziland 97 J4
Mankera Pak. 85 H4
Mankono Côte d'Ivoire 92 C4
Mankota Canada 117 J5
Manley Hot Springs U.S.A. 114 C3
Manmad India 80 B1
Mann r. Australia 104 F3
Mann, Mount Australia 105 E6
Manna Indon. 64 C7
Man Na Myanmar 66 B2
Mannahill Australia 107 B7
Mannar Sri Lanka 80 C4
Mannar, Gulf of India/Sri Lanka 80 C4
Manneru r. India 80 D3
Mannessier, Lac l. Canada 119 H3
Mannheim Germany 49 I5
Mannicolo Islands Solomon Is see Vanikoro Islands
Manning r. Australia 108 F3
Manning Canada 116 G3
Manning U.S.A. 129 D5
Mannington U.S.A. 130 E4
Manningtree U.K. 45 I7
Mann Ranges mts Australia 105 E6
Mannsville KY U.S.A. 130 C5
Mannsville NY U.S.A. 131 G2
Mannu, Capo c. Sardinia Italy 54 C4
Mannville Canada 117 I4
Man-of-War Rocks is U.S.A. see Gardner Pinnacles
Manoharpur India 78 D4
Manohar Thana India 78 D4
Manokotak U.S.A. 114 C4
Manokwari Indon. 65 I7
Manoron Myanmar 67 B5
Manosque France 52 G5
Manouane r. Canada 119 H4
Manouane, Lac l. Canada 119 H4
Man Pan Myanmar 66 B2
Manp'o N. Korea 70 B4
Manra i. Kiribati 103 I2
Manresa Spain 53 G3
Mansa Gujarat India 78 C5
Mansa Punjab India 78 C3
Mansa Zambia 95 C5
Mansa Konko Gambia 92 B3
Man Sam Myanmar 66 B2
Mansehra Pak. 83 L3
Mansel Island Canada 115 K3
Mansfield Australia 108 C6
Mansfield U.K. 45 F5
Mansfield LA U.S.A. 127 E5
Mansfield OH U.S.A. 130 D3
Mansfield PA U.S.A. 131 G3
Mansfield, Mount U.S.A. 131 I1
Man Si Myanmar 66 B1
Mansi Myanmar 66 A1
Manso r. Brazil see Mortes, Rio das
Manta Ecuador 138 B4
Mantaro r. Peru 138 D6
Manteca U.S.A. 124 C3
Mantena Brazil 141 C2
Manteo U.S.A. 128 F5
Mantes-la-Jolie France 48 B6
Mantiqueira, Serra da mts Brazil 141 B3
Manton U.S.A. 130 C1
Mantoudi Greece 55 J5
Mantova Italy see Mantua
Mäntsälä Fin. 41 N6
Mänttä Fin. 40 N5
Mantua Cuba 129 C8
Mantua Italy 54 D2
Mantuan Downs Australia 106 D5
Manturovo Rus. Fed. 38 J4
Mäntyharju Fin. 41 O6
Mäntyjärvi Fin. 40 O3
Manú Peru 138 D6
Manu, Parque Nacional nat. park Peru 138 D6
Manuae atoll Fr. Polynesia 147 J7
Manua Islands American Samoa 103 I3
Manuel Ribas Brazil 141 A4
Manuel Vitorino Brazil 141 C1
Manuelzinho Brazil 139 H5
Manui i. Indon. 65 G7
Manukau N.Z. 109 E3
Manukau Harbour N.Z. 109 E3
Manunda watercourse Australia 107 B7
Manusela National Park Indon. 65 H7
Manus Island P.N.G. 65 L7
Manvi India 80 C3
Many U.S.A. 127 E6
Manyana Botswana 97 G3
Manyas Turkey 55 L4
Manyas Gölü l. Turkey see Kuş Gölü
Manych-Gudilo, Ozero l. Rus. Fed. 39 I7
Many Island Lake Canada 117 I5
Manyoni Tanz. 95 D4
Manzai Pak. 85 H3
Manzanares Spain 53 E4
Manzanillo Cuba 133 I4
Manzanillo Mex. 132 D5
Manzhouli China 69 L3
Manzini Swaziland 97 J4
Mao Chad 93 E3
Maó Spain see Mahón
Maoba Guizhou China 72 E3
Maoba Hubei China 73 F2
Maocifan China 73 G2
Mao'ergai China 72 D1
Maoke, Pegunungan mts Indon. 65 J7
Maokeng S. Africa 97 H4
Maokui Shan mt. China 70 A4
Maolin China 70 A4
Maoming China 73 F4
Ma On Shan hill Hong Kong China 73 [inset]
Maopi T'ou c. Taiwan 73 I4
Maopora i. Indon. 104 D1
Maotou Shan mt. China 72 D3
Mapai Moz. 97 J2
Mapam Yumco l. China 79 E3
Mapanza Zambia 95 C5
Maphodi S. Africa 97 G6
Mapimí Mex. 127 C7
Mapimí, Bolsón de des. Mex. 127 B7
Mapin i. Phil. 64 F5
Mapinhane Moz. 97 L2
Mapiri Bol. 138 E7
Maple r. MI U.S.A. 130 C2
Maple r. ND U.S.A. 126 D2
Maple Creek Canada 117 I5
Maple Heights U.S.A. 130 E3
Maple Peak U.S.A. 125 I5
Mapmakers Seamounts sea feature N. Pacific Ocean 146 H4
Mapoon Australia 106 C1
Mapor i. Indon. 67 D7
Mapoteng Lesotho 97 H5
Maprik P.N.G. 65 K7
Mapuera r. Brazil 139 G4
Mapulanguene Moz. 97 K3

▶Maputo Moz. 97 K3
Capital of Mozambique.

Maputo prov. Moz. 97 K3
Maputo r. Moz./S. Africa 97 K4
Maputo, Baía de b. Moz. 97 K4
Maputsoe Lesotho 97 H5
Maqanshy Kazakh. see Makanchi
Maqar an Na'am well Iraq 87 F5
Maqat Kazakh. see Makat
Maqên China 72 D1
Maqên Kangri mt. China 72 C1
Maqnā Saudi Arabia 86 D5
Maqteïr reg. Mauritania 92 B2
Maqu China 72 D1
Ma Qu r. China see Yellow River
Maquan He r. China 79 F3
Maquela do Zombo Angola 95 B4
Maquinchao Arg. 140 C6
Mar r. Pak. 85 G5
Mar, Serra do mts Rio de Janeiro/São Paulo Brazil 141 B3
Mar, Serra do mts Rio Grande do Sul/Santa Catarina Brazil 141 A5
Mara r. Canada 117 I1
Mara India 79 E5
Mara S. Africa 97 I2
Maraã Brazil 138 E4
Maraba Brazil 139 I5
Maraboon, Lake resr Australia 106 E4
Maracá, Ilha de i. Brazil 139 H3
Maracaibo Venez. 138 D1
Maracaibo, Lago de Venez. see Maracaibo, Lake
Maracaibo, Lake Venez. 138 D2
Maracaju Brazil 140 E2
Maracaju, Serra de hills Brazil 140 E2
Maracanda Uzbek. see Samarkand
Maracás Brazil 141 C1
Maracás, Chapada de hills Brazil 141 C1
Maracay Venez. 138 E1
Marādah Libya 93 E2
Maradi Niger 92 D3
Marāgheh Iran 84 B2
Marahuaca, Cerro mt. Venez. 138 E3
Marajó, Baía de est. Brazil 139 I4
Marajó, Ilha de i. Brazil 139 H4
Marakele National Park S. Africa 97 H3
Maralal Kenya 94 D3
Maralbashi China see Bachu
Maralinga Australia 105 E7
Maralwexi China see Bachu
Maramasike i. Solomon Is 103 G2
Maramba Zambia see Livingstone
Marambio research station Antarctica 148 A2
Maran Malaysia 67 C7
Maran mt. Pak. 85 G4
Marana U.S.A. 125 H5
Marand Iran 84 B2
Marandellas Zimbabwe see Marondera
Marang Malaysia 67 C6
Marang Myanmar 67 B5
Maranhão r. Brazil 141 A1
Maranoa r. Australia 108 D1
Marañón r. Peru 138 D4
Marão Moz. 97 L3
Marão mt. Port. 53 C3
Mara Rosa Brazil 141 A1
Maraş Turkey see Kahramanmaraş
Marathon Canada 118 D4
Marathon FL U.S.A. 129 D7
Marathon NY U.S.A. 131 G2
Marathon TX U.S.A. 127 C6
Maratua i. Indon. 64 F6
Maraú Brazil 141 D1
Maravillas Creek watercourse U.S.A. 127 C6
Märäzä Azer. 87 H2
Marbella Spain 53 D5
Marble Bar Australia 104 B5
Marble Canyon U.S.A. 125 H3
Marble Canyon gorge U.S.A. 125 H3
Marble Hall S. Africa 97 I3
Marble Hill U.S.A. 127 F4
Marble Island Canada 117 N2
Marbul Pass Jammu and Kashmir 78 C2
Marburg S. Africa 97 J6
Marburg Slovenia see Maribor
Marburg an der Lahn Germany 49 I4
Marca, Ponta do pt Angola 95 B5
Marcali Hungary 54 G1
Marcelino Ramos Brazil 141 A4
March U.K. 45 H6
Marche reg. France 52 E3
Marche-en-Famenne Belgium 48 F4
Marchena Spain 53 D5
Marchinbar Island Australia 106 B1
Mar Chiquita, Lago l. Arg. 140 D4
Marchtrenk Austria 43 O6
Marco U.S.A. 129 D7
Marcoing France 48 D4
Marcona Peru 138 C7
Marcopeet Islands Canada 118 F2
Marcus Baker, Mount U.S.A. 114 D3
Marcy, Mount U.S.A. 131 I1
Mardan Pak. 85 I3
Mar del Plata Arg. 140 E5
Mardīān Afgh. 85 G2
Mardin Turkey 87 F3
Maré i. New Caledonia 103 G4
Maree, Loch l. U.K. 46 D3
Mareh Iran 85 E5
Marengo IA U.S.A. 126 E3
Marengo IN U.S.A. 130 B4
Marevo Rus. Fed. 38 G4
Marfa U.S.A. 127 B6
Marganets Ukr. see Marhanets'
Margao India see Madgaon
Margaret r. Australia 104 D4
Margaret watercourse Australia 107 B6
Margaret, Mount hill Australia 104 B5
Margaret Lake Alta Canada 116 H3
Margaret Lake N.W.T. Canada 116 G1
Margaret River Australia 105 A8
Margaretville U.S.A. 131 H2
Margarita, Isla de i. Venez. 138 F1
Margaritovo Rus. Fed. 70 D4
Margate U.K. 45 I7
Margherita, Lake Eth. see Abaya, Lake

▶Margherita Peak Dem. Rep. Congo/Uganda 94 C3
3rd highest mountain in Africa.

Marghilon Uzbek. see Margilan
Margilan Uzbek. 76 D3
Mārgo, Dasht-i des. Afgh. see Mārgow, Dasht-e
Margog Caka l. China 79 F2
Mārgow, Dasht-e des. Afgh. 85 F4
Margraten Neth. 48 F4
Marguerite Canada 116 F4
Marguerite, Pic mt. Dem. Rep. Congo/Uganda see Margherita Peak
Marguerite Bay Antarctica 148 L2
Margyang China 79 G3
Marhaj Khalīl Iraq 87 G4
Marhanets' Ukr. 39 G7
Marhoum Alg. 50 D5
Mari Myanmar 66 B1
Maria atoll Fr. Polynesia 147 J7
María Elena Chile 140 C2
Maria Island Australia 106 A2
Maria Island Myanmar 67 B5
Maria Island National Park Australia 107 [inset]
Mariala National Park Australia 107 D5
Mariana Brazil 141 C3
Marianao Cuba 129 D8
Mariana Ridge sea feature N. Pacific Ocean 146 F4

▶Mariana Trench sea feature N. Pacific Ocean 146 F5
Deepest trench in the world.

Mariani India 79 H4
Mariánica, Cordillera mts Spain see Morena, Sierra
Marian Lake Canada 116 G2
Marianna AR U.S.A. 127 F5
Marianna FL U.S.A. 129 C6
Mariano Machado Angola see Ganda
Mariánské Lázně Czech Rep. 49 M5
Marias r. U.S.A. 122 F3
Marías, Islas is Mex. 132 C4

▶Mariato, Punta pt Panama 133 H7
Most southerly point of North America.

Maria van Diemen, Cape N.Z. 109 D2
Ma'rib Yemen 82 G6
Maribor Slovenia 54 F1
Marica r. Bulg. see Maritsa
Maricopa AZ U.S.A. 125 G5
Maricopa CA U.S.A. 124 D4
Maricopa Mountains U.S.A. 125 G5
Maridi Sudan 93 F4
Marie Byrd Land reg. Antarctica 148 J1
Marie-Galante i. Guadeloupe 133 L5
Mariehamn Fin. 41 K6
Mariembero r. Brazil 141 A1
Marienbad Czech Rep. see Mariánské Lázně
Marienberg Germany 49 N4
Marienburg Poland see Malbork
Marienhafe Germany 49 H1
Mariental Namibia 96 C3
Marienwerder Poland see Kwidzyn
Mariestad Sweden 41 H7
Mariet r. Canada 118 F2
Marietta GA U.S.A. 129 C5
Marietta OH U.S.A. 130 E4
Marietta OK U.S.A. 127 D5
Marignane France 52 G5
Marii, Mys pt Rus. Fed. 62 G2
Mariinsk Rus. Fed. 60 J4
Mariinskiy Posad Rus. Fed. 38 J4
Marijampolė Lith. 41 M9
Marília Brazil 141 A3
Marillana Australia 104 B5
Marimba Angola 95 B4
Marín Spain 53 B2
Marina U.S.A. 124 C3
Marina di Gioiosa Ionica Italy 54 G5
Mar'ina Gorka Belarus see Mar"ina Horka
Mar"ina Horka Belarus 41 P10
Marinduque i. Phil. 65 G4
Marinette U.S.A. 130 B1
Maringá Brazil 141 A3
Maringa r. Dem. Rep. Congo 94 B3

Maringo U.S.A. 130 D3
Marinha Grande Port. 53 B4
Marion AL U.S.A. 129 C5
Marion AR U.S.A. 127 F5
Marion IL U.S.A. 126 F4
Marion IN U.S.A. 130 C3
Marion KS U.S.A. 126 D4
Marion MI U.S.A. 130 C1
Marion NY U.S.A. 131 G2
Marion OH U.S.A. 130 D3
Marion SC U.S.A. 129 E5
Marion VA U.S.A. 130 E5
Marion, Lake U.S.A. 129 D5
Marion Reef Australia 106 F3
Maripa Venez. 138 E2
Mariposa U.S.A. 124 D3
Marisa Indon. 65 G6
Mariscal Estigarribia Para. 140 D2
Maritime Alps mts France/Italy 52 H4
Maritime Kray admin. div. Rus. Fed. see Primorskiy Kray
Maritimes, Alpes mts France/Italy see Maritime Alps
Maritsa r. Bulg. 55 L4
also known as Evros (Greece), Marica (Bulgaria), Meriç (Turkey)
Marittime, Alpi mts France/Italy see Maritime Alps
Mariupol' Ukr. 39 H7
Mariusa nat. park Venez. 138 F2
Marīvān Iran 84 B3
Marjan Afgh. see Wazi Khwa
Marjayoûn Lebanon 81 B3
Marka Somalia 94 E3
Markala Mali 92 C3
Markam China 72 C2
Markaryd Sweden 41 H8
Markdale Canada 130 E1
Marken S. Africa 97 I2
Markermeer l. Neth. 48 F2
Market Deeping U.K. 45 G6
Market Drayton U.K. 45 E6
Market Harborough U.K. 45 G6
Markethill U.K. 47 F3
Market Weighton U.K. 44 G5
Markha r. Rus. Fed. 61 M3
Markham Canada 130 F2
Markit China 76 E4
Markkleeberg Germany 49 M3
Markleeville U.S.A. 124 D2
Marklohe Germany 49 J2
Markog Qu r. China 72 D1
Markounda Cent. Afr. Rep. 94 B3
Markovo Rus. Fed. 61 S3
Markranstädt Germany 49 M3
Marks Rus. Fed. 39 J6
Marks U.S.A. 127 F5
Marksville U.S.A. 127 E6
Marktheidenfeld Germany 49 J5
Marktredwitz Germany 49 M4
Marl Germany 48 H3
Marla Australia 105 F6
Marlborough Downs hills U.K. 45 F7
Marle France 48 D5
Marlette U.S.A. 130 D2
Marlin U.S.A. 127 D6
Marlinton U.S.A. 130 E4
Marlo Australia 108 D6
Marmagao India 80 B3
Marmande France 52 E4
Marmara, Sea of g. Turkey 55 M4
Marmara Denizi g. Turkey see Marmara, Sea of
Marmara Gölü l. Turkey 55 M5
Marmarica reg. Libya 86 B5
Marmaris Turkey 55 M6
Marmarth U.S.A. 126 C2
Marmet U.S.A. 130 E4
Marmion, Lake salt l. Australia 105 C7
Marmion Lake Canada 117 N5
Marmolada mt. Italy 54 D1
Marne r. France 48 C6
Marne-la-Vallée France 48 C6
Marnitz Germany 49 L1
Maroantsetra Madag. 95 E5
Maroc country Africa see Morocco
Marol Jammu and Kashmir 78 D2
Marol Pak. 85 I4
Maroldsweisach Germany 49 K4
Maromokotro mt. Madag. 95 E5
Marondera Zimbabwe 95 D5
Maroochydore Australia 108 F1
Maroonah Australia 105 A5
Maroon Peak U.S.A. 122 G5
Marosvás>01a>rhely Romania see Târgu Mureş
Maroua Cameroon 93 E3
Marovoay Madag. 95 E5
Marqādah Syria 87 F4
Mar Qu r. China see Markog Qu
Marquard S. Africa 97 H5
Marquesas Islands Fr. Polynesia 147 K6
Marquesas Keys is U.S.A. 129 D7
Marquês de Valença Brazil 141 C3
Marquette U.S.A. 128 C2
Marquez U.S.A. 127 D6
Marquion France 48 D4
Marquise France 48 B4
Marquises, Îles is Fr. Polynesia see Marquesas Islands
Marra Australia 108 A3
Marra r. Australia 108 C3
Marra, Jebel mt. Sudan 93 F3
Marracuene Moz. 97 K3
Marrakech Morocco 50 C5
Marrakesh Morocco see Marrakech
Marrangua, Lagoa l. Moz. 97 L3
Marra Plateau Sudan 93 F3
Marrar Australia 108 C5
Marrawah Australia 107 [inset]
Marree Australia 107 B6
Marrowbone U.S.A. 130 C5
Marruecos country Africa see Morocco
Marrupa Moz. 95 D5
Marryat Australia 105 F6
Marsá al 'Alam Egypt 82 D4
Marsa 'Alam Egypt see Marsá al 'Alam
Marsa al Burayqah Libya 93 E1
Marsabit Kenya 94 D3
Marsala Sicily Italy 54 E6
Marsá Maṭrūḥ Egypt 86 B5
Marsberg Germany 49 I3
Marsciano Italy 54 E3
Marsden Australia 108 C4
Marsden Canada 117 I4
Marsdiep sea chan. Neth. 48 E2
Marseille France 52 G5
Marseilles France see Marseille
Marsfjället mt. Sweden 40 I4
Marshall watercourse Australia 106 B4
Marshall AR U.S.A. 127 E5
Marshall IL U.S.A. 130 B4
Marshall MI U.S.A. 130 C2
Marshall MN U.S.A. 126 E2
Marshall MO U.S.A. 126 E4
Marshall TX U.S.A. 127 E5
▶Marshall Islands country N. Pacific Ocean 146 H5
oceania 8, 100–101
Marshalltown U.S.A. 126 E3
Marshfield MO U.S.A. 127 E4
Marshfield WI U.S.A. 126 F2
Marsh Harbour Bahamas 129 E7
Mars Hill U.S.A. 128 H2
Marsh Island U.S.A. 127 F6
Marsh Peak U.S.A. 125 I1
Marsh Point Canada 117 M3
Marsing U.S.A. 122 D4
Märsta Sweden 41 J7
Marsyaty Rus. Fed. 37 S3
Martaban Myanmar 66 B3
Martaban, Gulf of Myanmar 66 B3
Martapura Indon. 64 E7
Marten River Canada 118 F5
Marte R. Gómez, Presa resr Mex. 127 D7
Martha's Vineyard i. U.S.A. 131 J3
Martigny Switz. 52 H3
Martim Vaz, Ilhas is S. Atlantic Ocean see Martin Vas, Ilhas
Martin r. Canada 116 F2
Martin Slovakia 43 Q6
Martin MI U.S.A. 130 C2
Martin SD U.S.A. 126 C3
Martinez Lake U.S.A. 125 F5
Martinho Campos Brazil 141 B2
▶Martinique terr. West Indies 133 L6
French Overseas Department.
north america 9, 112–113
Martinique Passage Dominica/Martinique 133 L5
Martin Peninsula Antarctica 148 K2
Martinsburg U.S.A. 131 G4
Martins Ferry U.S.A. 130 E3
Martinsville IL U.S.A. 130 B4
Martinsville IN U.S.A. 130 B4
Martinsville VA U.S.A. 130 F5
▶Martin Vas, Ilhas is S. Atlantic Ocean 144 G7
Most easterly point of South America.
Martin Vaz Islands S. Atlantic Ocean see Martin Vas, Ilhas
Martök Kazakh. see Martuk
Marton N.Z. 109 E5
Martorell Spain 53 G3
Martos Spain 53 E5
Martuk Kazakh. 74 E1
Martuni Armenia 87 G2
Maruf Afgh. 85 G4
Maruim Brazil 139 K6
Marukhis Ugheltekhili pass Georgia/Rus. Fed. 87 F2
Marulan Australia 108 D5
Marusthali reg. India 85 H5
Marvast Iran 84 D4
Marv Dasht Iran 84 D4
Marvejols France 52 F4
Marvine, Mount U.S.A. 125 H2
Marwayne Canada 117 I4
Mary r. Australia 104 E3
Mary Turkm. 85 F2
Maryborough Qld Australia 107 F5
Maryborough Vic. Australia 108 A6
Marydale S. Africa 96 F5
Mary Frances Lake Canada 117 J2
Mary Lake Canada 117 K2
Maryland state U.S.A. 131 G4
Maryport U.K. 44 D4
Mary's Harbour Canada 119 L3
Marysvale U.S.A. 125 G2
Marysville CA U.S.A. 124 C2
Marysville KS U.S.A. 126 D4
Marysville OH U.S.A. 130 D3
Maryvale N.T. Australia 105 F6
Maryvale Qld Australia 106 D3
Maryville MO U.S.A. 126 E3
Maryville TN U.S.A. 128 D5
Marzagão Brazil 141 A2
Marzahna Germany 49 M2
Masada tourist site Israel 81 B4
Masāhūn, Kūh-e mt. Iran 84 D4
Masai Steppe plain Tanz. 95 D4
Masaka Uganda 94 D4
Masakhane S. Africa 97 H6
Masalembu Besar i. Indon. 64 E8
Masallı Azer. 87 H3
Masan S. Korea 71 C6
Masasi Tanz. 95 D5
Masavi Bol. 138 F7
Masbate Phil. 65 G4
Masbate i. Phil. 65 G4
Mascara Alg. 53 G6
Mascarene Basin sea feature Indian Ocean 145 L7
Mascarene Plain sea feature Indian Ocean 145 L7
Mascarene Ridge sea feature Indian Ocean 145 L6
Mascote Brazil 141 D1
Masein Myanmar 66 A2
Masela Indon. 104 E2
Masela i. Indon. 104 E2
▶Maseru Lesotho 97 H5
Capital of Lesotho.
Mashai Lesotho 97 I5
Mashan China 73 F4
Masherbrum mt. Jammu and Kashmir 78 D2
Mashhad Iran 85 E2
Mashket r. Pak. 85 F5
Mashki Chah Pak. 85 F4
Masi Norway 40 M2
Masiáca Mex. 123 F8
Masibambane S. Africa 97 H6
Masīlah, Wādī al watercourse Yemen 82 H6
Masilo S. Africa 97 H5
Masi-Manimba Dem. Rep. Congo 95 B4
Masindi Uganda 94 D3
Masinyusane S. Africa 96 F6
Masira, Gulf of Oman see Maṣīrah, Khalīj
Maṣīrah, Jazīrat i. Oman 83 I5
Maṣīrah, Khalīj b. Oman 83 I6
Masira Island Oman see Maṣīrah, Jazīrat
Masjed Soleymān Iran 84 C4
Mask, Lough l. Rep. of Ireland 47 C4
Maskūtān Iran 85 E5
Maslovo Rus. Fed. 37 S3
Masoala, Tanjona c. Madag. 95 F5
Mason MI U.S.A. 130 C2
Mason OH U.S.A. 130 C4
Mason TX U.S.A. 127 D6
Mason, Lake salt flat Australia 105 B6
Mason Bay N.Z. 109 A8
Mason City U.S.A. 126 E3
Masontown U.S.A. 130 F4
Masqaṭ Oman see Muscat
Masqaṭ reg. Oman see Muscat
'Masrūg well Oman 84 D6
Massa Italy 54 D2
Massachusetts state U.S.A. 131 I2
Massachusetts Bay U.S.A. 131 J2
Massadona U.S.A. 125 I1
Massafra Italy 54 G4
Massakory Chad 93 E3
Massa Marittimo Italy 54 D3
Massangena Moz. 95 D6
Massango Angola 95 B4
Massawa Eritrea 82 E6
Massawippi, Lac l. Canada 131 I1
Massena U.S.A. 131 H1
Massenya Chad 93 E3
Masset Canada 116 C4
Massieville U.S.A. 130 D4
Massif Central mts France 52 F4
Massilia France see Marseille
Massillon U.S.A. 130 E3
Massina Mali 92 C3
Massinga Moz. 97 L2
Massingir Moz. 97 K2
Massingir, Barragem de resr Moz. 97 K2
Masson Island Antarctica 148 F2
Mastchoh Tajik. 85 H2
Masterton N.Z. 109 E5
Masticho, Akra pt Greece 55 L5
Mastung Pak. 74 F4
Mastūrah Saudi Arabia 82 E5
Masty Belarus 41 N10
Masuda Japan 71 C6
Masuku Gabon see Franceville
Masulipatam India see Machilipatnam
Masulipatnam India see Machilipatnam
Masuna i. American Samoa see Tutuila
Masvingo Zimbabwe 95 D6
Masvingo prov. Zimbabwe 97 J1
Maswa Tanz. 94 D4
Maswaar i. Indon. 65 I7
Maṣyāf Syria 81 C2
Mat, Hon i. Vietnam 66 D3
Mat, Nam r. Laos 66 D3
Mata Myanmar 66 B1
Matabeleland South prov. Zimbabwe 97 I1
Matachewan Canada 118 E5
Matadi Dem. Rep. Congo 95 B4
Matador U.S.A. 127 C5
Matagalpa Nicaragua 133 G6
Matagami Canada 118 F4
Matagami, Lac l. Canada 118 F4
Matagorda Island U.S.A. 127 D6
Matak i. Indon. 67 D7
Matakana Island N.Z. 109 F3
Matala Angola 95 B5
Maṭālī', Jabal hill Saudi Arabia 87 F6
Matam Senegal 92 B3
Matamey Niger 92 D3
Matamoros U.S.A. 131 H3
Matamoros Coahuila Mex. 127 C7
Matamoros Tamaulipas Mex. 127 D7
Matandu r. Tanz. 95 D4
Matane Canada 119 I4
Matanzas Cuba 133 H4
Matapan, Cape pt Greece see Tainaro, Akra
Matapédia, Lac l. Canada 119 I4
Maṭār well Saudi Arabia 84 B5
Matara Sri Lanka 80 D5
Mataram Indon. 104 B2
Matarani Peru 138 D7
Mataranka Australia 104 F3
Mataripe Brazil 141 D1
Mataró Spain 53 H3
Matasiri i. Indon. 64 F7
Matatiele S. Africa 97 I6
Matatila Dam India 78 D4
Mataura N.Z. 109 B8
▶Matā'utu Wallis and Futuna Is 103 I3
Capital of Wallis and Futuna.
Mata-Utu Wallis and Futuna Is see Matā'utu
Matawai N.Z. 109 F4
Matay Kazakh. 76 E2
Matcha Tajik. see Mastchoh
Mategua Bol. 138 F6
Matehuala Mex. 127 C8
Matemanga Tanz. 95 D5
Matera Italy 54 G4
Mateur Tunisia 54 C6
Mathaji India 78 B4
Matheson Canada 118 E4
Mathews U.S.A. 131 G5
Mathis U.S.A. 127 D6
Mathoura Australia 108 B5
Mathura India 78 D4
Mati Phil. 65 H5
Matiali India 79 G4
Matias Cardoso Brazil 141 C1
Matías Romero Mex. 132 E5
Matimekosh Canada 119 I3
Matin India 79 E5
Matinenda Lake Canada 118 E5
Matizi China 72 D1
Matla r. India 79 G5
Matlabas r. S. Africa 97 H2
Matli Pak. 85 H5
Matlock U.K. 45 F5
Mato, Cerro mt. Venez. 138 E2
Matobo Hills Zimbabwe 95 C6
Mato Grosso Brazil 138 G7
Mato Grosso state Brazil 141 A1
Mato Grosso, Planalto do plat. Brazil 139 H7
Matopo Hills Zimbabwe see Matobo Hills
Matos Costa Brazil 141 A4
Matosinhos Port. 53 B3
Mato Verde Brazil 141 C1
Maṭraḥ Oman 84 E6
Matroosberg mt. S. Africa 96 D7
Matsesta Rus. Fed. 87 E2
Matsue Japan 71 D6
Matsumoto Japan 71 E5
Matsu Tao i. Taiwan 73 I3
Matsuyama Japan 71 D6
Mattagami r. Canada 118 E4
Mattamuskeet, Lake U.S.A. 128 E5
Mattawa Canada 118 F5
Matterhorn mt. Italy/Switz. 54 B2
Matterhorn mt. U.S.A. 122 E4
Matthew Town Bahamas 133 J4
Maṭṭī, Sabkhat salt pan Saudi Arabia 84 D6
Mattoon U.S.A. 126 F4
Matturai Sri Lanka see Matara
Matuku i. Fiji 103 H3
Matumbo Angola 95 B5
Maturín Venez. 138 F2
Matusadona National Park Zimbabwe 95 C5
Matwabeng S. Africa 97 H5
Maty Island P.N.G. see Wuvulu Island
Mau India see Maunath Bhanjan
Maúa Moz. 95 D5
Maubeuge France 48 D4
Maubin Myanmar 66 A3
Ma-ubin Myanmar 66 B1
Maubourguet France 52 E5
Mauchline U.K. 46 E5
Maudaha India 78 E4
Maude Australia 107 D7
Maud Seamount sea feature S. Atlantic Ocean 144 I10
Mau-é-ele Moz. see Marão
Maués Brazil 139 G4
Maughold Head hd Isle of Man 44 C4
Maug Islands N. Mariana Is 65 L2
Maui i. HI U.S.A. 123 [inset]
Maukkadaw Myanmar 66 A2
Maulbronn Germany 49 I6
Maule r. Chile 140 B5
Maulvi Bazar Bangl. see Moulvibazar
Maumee U.S.A. 130 D3
Maumee Bay U.S.A. 130 D3
Maumere Indon. 104 C2
Maumturk Mts hills Rep. of Ireland 47 C4
Maun Botswana 95 C5
Mauna Kea vol. HI U.S.A. 123 [inset]
Mauna Loa vol. HI U.S.A. 123 [inset]
Maunath Bhanjan India 79 E4
Maunatlala Botswana 97 H2
Maungaturoto N.Z. 109 E3
Maungdaw Myanmar 66 A2
Maungmagan Islands Myanmar 67 B4
Maurepas, Lake U.S.A. 127 F6
Mauriac France 52 F4
Maurice country Indian Ocean see Mauritius
Maurice, Lake salt flat Australia 105 E7
Maurik Neth. 48 F3
▶Mauritania country Africa 92 B3
africa 7, 90–91
Mauritanie country Africa see Mauritania
▶Mauritius country Indian Ocean 145 L7
africa 7, 90–91
Maurs France 52 F4
Mauston U.S.A. 126 F3
Mava Dem. Rep. Congo 94 C3
Mavago Moz. 95 D5
Mavan, Kūh-e hill Iran 84 E3
Mavanza Moz. 97 L2
Mavinga Angola 95 C5
Mavrovo nat. park Macedonia 55 I4
Mavume Moz. 97 L2
Mavuya S. Africa 97 H6
Ma Wan i. Hong Kong China 73 [inset]
Māwān, Khashm hill Saudi Arabia 84 B6
Mawana India 78 D3
Mawanga Dem. Rep. Congo 95 B4
Ma Wang Dui tourist site China 73 G2
Mawei China 73 H3
Mawjib, Wādī al r. Jordan 81 B4
Mawkmai Myanmar 66 B2
Mawlaik Myanmar 66 A2
Mawlamyaing Myanmar see Moulmein
Mawlamyine Myanmar see Moulmein
Mawqaq Saudi Arabia 87 F6
Mawson research station Antarctica 148 E2
Mawson Coast Antarctica 148 E2
Mawson Escarpment Antarctica 148 E2
Mawson Peninsula Antarctica 148 H2
Maw Taung mt. Myanmar 67 B5
Mawza Yemen 82 F7
Maxán Arg. 140 C3
Maxhamish Lake Canada 116 F3
Maxia, Punta mt. Sardinia Italy 54 C5
Maxixe Moz. 97 L2
Maxmo Fin. 40 M5
May, Isle of i. U.K. 46 G4
Maya r. Rus. Fed. 61 O3
Mayaguana i. Bahamas 129 F8
Mayaguana Passage Bahamas 129 F8
Mayagüez Puerto Rico 133 K5
Mayahi Niger 92 D3
Mayakovskiy, Qullai mt. Tajik. 85 H2
Mayakovskogo, Pik mt. Tajik. see Mayakovskiy, Qullai
Mayama Congo 94 B4
Maya Mountains Belize/Guat. 132 G5
Mayan China see Mayanhe
Mayang China 73 F3
Mayanhe China 72 E1
Mayar hill U.K. 46 F4
Maybeury U.S.A. 130 E5
Maybole U.K. 46 E5
Maych'ew Eth. 94 D2
Maydān Shahr Afgh. see Meydān Shahr
Maydh Somalia 82 G7
Maydos Turkey see Eceabat
Mayen Germany 49 H4
Mayenne France 52 D2
Mayenne r. France 52 D3
Mayer U.S.A. 125 G4
Mayêr Kangri mt. China 79 F2
Mayersville U.S.A. 127 F5
Mayerthorpe Canada 116 H4
Mayfield N.Z. 109 C6
Mayi He r. China 70 C3
Maykop Rus. Fed. 87 F1
Maymyo Myanmar 66 B2
Mayna Respublika Khakasiya Rus. Fed. 60 K4
Mayna Ul'yanovskaya Oblast' Rus. Fed. 39 J5
Mayni India 80 B2
Maynooth Canada 131 G1
Mayo Canada 116 C2
Mayo U.S.A. 129 D6
Mayo Alim Cameroon 92 E4
Mayoko Congo 94 B4
Mayo Lake Canada 116 C2
Mayo Landing Canada see Mayo
Mayor, Puig mt. Spain see Major, Puig
Mayor Island N.Z. 109 F3
Mayor Pablo Lagerenza Para. 140 D1
▶Mayotte terr. Africa 95 E5
French Territorial Collectivity.
africa 7, 90–91
Mayskiy Amurskaya Oblast' Rus. Fed. 70 C1
Mayskiy Kabardino-Balkarskaya Respublika Rus. Fed. 87 G2
Mays Landing U.S.A. 131 H4
Mayson Lake Canada 117 J3
Maysville U.S.A. 130 D4
Mayumba Gabon 94 B4
Mayum La pass China 79 E3
Mayuram India 80 C4
Mayville MI U.S.A. 130 D2
Mayville ND U.S.A. 126 D2
Mayville NY U.S.A. 130 F2
Mayville WI U.S.A. 130 A2
Mazabuka Zambia 95 C5
Mazaca Turkey see Kayseri
Mazagan Morocco see El Jadida
Mazar China 78 D1
Mazar, Koh-i- mt. Afgh. 85 G3
Mazara, Val di valley Sicily Italy 54 E6
Mazara del Vallo Sicily Italy 54 E6
Mazār-e Sharīf Afgh. 85 G2
Mazārī' reg. U.A.E. 84 D6
Mazatán Mex. 123 F7
Mazatlán Mex. 132 C4
Mazatzal Peak U.S.A. 125 H4
Mazdaj Iran 87 H4
Mažeikiai Lith. 41 M8
Mazīm Oman 84 E6
Mazocahui Mex. 123 F7
Mazocruz Peru 138 E7
Mazomora Tanz. 95 D4
Mazu Dao i. Taiwan see Matsu Tao
Mazunga Zimbabwe 95 C6
Mazyr Belarus 39 F5
Mazzouna Tunisia 54 C7
▶Mbabane Swaziland 97 J4
Capital of Swaziland.
Mbahiakro Côte d'Ivoire 92 C4
Mbaïki Cent. Afr. Rep. 94 B3
Mbakaou, Lac de l. Cameroon 92 E4
Mbala Zambia 95 D4
Mbale Uganda 94 D3
Mbalmayo Cameroon 92 E4
Mbam r. Cameroon 92 E4
Mbandaka Dem. Rep. Congo 94 B4
M'banza Congo Angola 95 B4
Mbarara Uganda 93 G5
Mbari r. Cent. Afr. Rep. 94 C3
Mbaswana S. Africa 97 K4
Mbemkuru r. Tanz. 95 D4
Mbeya Tanz. 95 D4
Mbinga Tanz. 95 D5
Mbini Equat. Guinea 92 D4
Mbizi Zimbabwe 95 D6
Mboki Cent. Afr. Rep. 94 C3
Mbomo Congo 94 B3
Mbouda Cameroon 92 E4
Mbour Senegal 92 B3
Mbout Mauritania 92 B3
Mbozi Tanz. 95 D4
Mbrès Cent. Afr. Rep. 94 B3
Mbuji-Mayi Dem. Rep. Congo 95 C4
Mbulu Tanz. 94 D4
Mburucuyá Arg. 140 E3
McAdam Canada 119 I5
McAlester U.S.A. 127 E5
McAlister mt. Australia 108 D5
McAllen U.S.A. 127 D7
McArthur r. Australia 106 B2
McArthur U.S.A. 130 D4
McArthur Mills Canada 131 G1
McBain U.S.A. 130 C1
McBride Canada 116 F4
McCall U.S.A. 122 D3
McCamey U.S.A. 127 C6
McCammon U.S.A. 122 E4
McCauley Island Canada 116 D4
McClintock, Mount Antarctica 148 H1
McClintock Channel Canada 115 H2
McClintock Range hills Australia 104 D4
McClure, Lake U.S.A. 124 C3
McClure Strait Canada 114 G2
McClusky U.S.A. 126 C2
McComb U.S.A. 127 F6
McConaughy, Lake U.S.A. 126 C3
McConnellsburg U.S.A. 131 G4
McConnelsville U.S.A. 130 E4
McCook U.S.A. 126 C3
McCormick U.S.A. 129 D5
McCrea r. Canada 116 H2
McCreary Canada 117 L5
McDame Canada 116 D3
McDermitt U.S.A. 122 D4
McDonald Islands Indian Ocean 145 M9
McDonald Peak U.S.A. 122 E3
McDonough U.S.A. 129 C5
McDougall's Bay S. Africa 96 C5
McDowell Peak U.S.A. 125 H5
McFarland U.S.A. 124 D4
McGill U.S.A. 125 F2
McGivney Canada 119 I5
McGrath AK U.S.A. 114 C3
McGrath MN U.S.A. 126 E2
McGraw U.S.A. 131 G2
McGregor r. Canada 116 F4
McGregor S. Africa 96 D7
McGregor, Lake Canada 116 H5
McGregor Range hills Australia 107 C5
McGuire, Mount U.S.A. 122 E3
Mchinga Tanz. 95 D4
Mchinji Malawi 95 D5
McIlwraith Range hills Australia 106 C2
McInnes Lake Canada 117 M4
McIntosh U.S.A. 126 C2
McKay Range hills Australia 104 C5
McKean i. Kiribati 103 I2
McKee U.S.A. 130 C5
McKenzie r. U.S.A. 122 C3
McKinlay r. Australia 106 C4
▶McKinley, Mount U.S.A. 114 C3
Highest mountain in North America.
north america 110–111
McKinney U.S.A. 127 D5
McKittrick U.S.A. 124 D4
McLaughlin U.S.A. 126 C2
McLeansboro U.S.A. 126 F4
McLennan Canada 116 G4
McLeod r. Canada 116 H4
McLeod Bay Canada 117 I2
McLeod Lake Canada 116 F4
McLoughlin, Mount U.S.A. 122 C4
McMillan, Lake U.S.A. 127 B5
McMinnville OR U.S.A. 122 C3
McMinnville TN U.S.A. 128 C5
McMurdo research station Antarctica 148 H1
McMurdo Sound b. Antarctica 148 H1
McNary U.S.A. 125 I4
McNaughton Lake Canada see Kinbasket Lake
McPherson U.S.A. 126 D4
McQuesten r. Canada 116 B2
McRae U.S.A. 129 D5
McTavish Arm b. Canada 116 G1
McVeytown U.S.A. 131 G3
McVicar Arm b. Canada 116 F1
Mdantsane S. Africa 97 H7
M'Daourouch Alg. 54 B6
Mê, Hon i. Vietnam 66 D3
Mead, Lake resr U.S.A. 125 F3
Meade U.S.A. 127 C4
Meade r. U.S.A. 114 C2
Meadow Australia 105 A6
Meadow SD U.S.A. 126 C2
Meadow UT U.S.A. 125 G2
Meadow Lake Canada 117 I4
Meadville MS U.S.A. 127 F6
Meadville PA U.S.A. 130 E3
Meaford Canada 130 E1
Meaken-dake vol. Japan 70 G4
Mealhada Port. 53 B3
Mealy Mountains Canada 119 K3
Meandarra Australia 108 D1
Meander River Canada 116 G3
Meaux France 48 C6
Mecca Saudi Arabia 82 E5
Mecca CA U.S.A. 124 E5
Mecca OH U.S.A. 130 E3
Mechanic Falls U.S.A. 131 J1
Mechanicsville U.S.A. 131 G5
Mechelen Belgium 48 E3
Mechelen Neth. 48 F4
Mecherchar i. Palau see Eil Malk
Mecheria Alg. 50 D5
Mechernich Germany 48 G4
Mecitözü Turkey 86 D2
Meckenheim Germany 48 H4
Mecklenburger Bucht b. Germany 43 M3
Mecklenburg-Vorpommern land Germany 49 M1
Mecklenburg - West Pomerania land Germany see Mecklenburg-Vorpommern
Meda r. Australia 104 C4
Meda Port. 53 C3
Medak India 80 C2
Medan Indon. 67 B7
Medanosa, Punta pt Arg. 140 C7
Médanos de Coro, Parque Nacional nat. park Venez. 138 E1
Medawachchiya Sri Lanka 80 D4
Médéa Alg. 53 H5
Medebach Germany 49 I3
Medellín Col. 138 C2
Meden r. U.K. 44 G5
Medenine Tunisia 50 G5
Mederdra Mauritania 92 B3
Medford NY U.S.A. 131 I3
Medford OK U.S.A. 127 D4
Medford OR U.S.A. 122 C4
Medford WI U.S.A. 126 F2
Medgidia Romania 55 M2
Media U.S.A. 131 H4
Mediaş Romania 55 K1
Medicine Bow r. U.S.A. 122 G4
Medicine Bow Mountains U.S.A. 122 G4
Medicine Bow Peak U.S.A. 122 G4
Medicine Hat Canada 117 I5
Medicine Lake U.S.A. 122 G2
Medicine Lodge U.S.A. 127 D4
Medina Brazil 141 C2
Medina Saudi Arabia 82 E5
Medina ND U.S.A. 126 D2
Medina NY U.S.A. 131 F2
Medina OH U.S.A. 130 E3
Medinaceli Spain 53 E3
Medina del Campo Spain 53 D3
Medina de Rioseco Spain 53 D3
Medina Lake U.S.A. 127 D6
Medinipur India 79 F5
Mediolanum Italy see Milan
Mediterranean Sea 50 K5
Mednyy, Ostrov i. Rus. Fed. 146 H2
Médoc reg. France 52 D4
Mêdog China 72 B2
Medora U.S.A. 126 C2
Medstead Canada 117 I4
Meduro atoll Marshall Is see Majuro
Medvedevo Rus. Fed. 38 J4
Medveditsa r. Rus. Fed. 39 I6
Medvednica mts Croatia 54 F2
Medvezh'i, Ostrova is Rus. Fed. 61 R2
Medvezh'ya, Gora mt. Rus. Fed. 70 E3
Medvezh'yegorsk Rus. Fed. 38 G3
Medway r. U.K. 45 H7
Meekatharra Australia 105 B6
Meeker CO U.S.A. 125 J1
Meeker OH U.S.A. 130 D3
Meelpaeg Reservoir Canada 119 K4
Meemu Atoll Maldives see Mulaku Atoll
Meerane Germany 49 M4
Meerlo Neth. 48 G3
Meerut India 78 D3
Mega Escarpment Eth./Kenya 94 D3
Megalopoli Greece 55 J6
Megamo Indon. 65 I7
Mégantic, Lac l. Canada 119 H5
Megara Greece 55 J5
Megezez mt. Eth. 94 D3
▶Meghalaya state India 79 G4
Highest mean annual rainfall in the world.
Meghasani mt. India 79 F5
Meghri Armenia 87 G3
Megin Turkm. 84 E2
Megisti i. Greece 55 M6
Megri Armenia see Meghri
Mehamn Norway 40 O1
Mehar Pak. 85 G5
Meharry, Mount Australia 105 B5
Mehbubnagar India see Mahbubnagar
Mehdia Tunisia see Mahdia
Meherpur Bangl. 79 G5
Meherrin U.S.A. 131 F5

Meherrin r. U.S.A. 131 G5
Mehlville U.S.A. 126 F4
Mehrakān salt marsh Iran 84 D5
Mehrān Hormozgan Iran 84 D5
Mehrān Īlām Iran 84 B3
Mehren Germany 48 G4
Mehriz Iran 84 D4
Mehsana India see Mahesana
Mehtar Lām Afgh. 85 H3
Meia Ponte r. Brazil 141 A2
Meicheng China see Minqing
Meiganga Cameroon 93 E4
Meighen Island Canada 115 I2
Meigu China 72 D2
Meihekou China 70 B4
Meikeng China 73 G3
Meikle r. Canada 116 G3
Meikle Says Law hill U.K. 46 G5
Meiktila Myanmar 66 A2
Meilin China see Ganxian
Meilleur r. Canada 116 E2
Meilu China 73 F4
Meine Germany 49 K2
Meinersen Germany 49 K2
Meiningen Germany 49 K4
Meishan Anhui China see Jinzhai
Meishan Sichuan China 72 D2
Meishan Shuiku resr China 73 G2
Meißen Germany 43 N5
Meister r. Canada 116 D2
Meitan China 72 E3
Meixi China 70 C3
Meixian China see Meizhou
Meixing China see Xiaojin
Meizhou China 73 H3
Mej r. India 78 D4
Mejicana mt. Arg. 140 C3
Mejillones Chile 140 B2
Mékambo Gabon 94 B3
Mek'elē Eth. 94 D2
Mekelle Eth. see Mek'elē
Mékhé Senegal 92 B3
Mekhtar Pak. 85 H4
Meknassy Tunisia 54 C7
Meknès Morocco 50 C5
Mekong r. Xizang/Yunnan China 72 C2
Mekong r. Laos/Thai. 66 D4
also known as Mae Nam Khong (Laos/Thailand)
Mekong, Mouths of the Vietnam 67 D5
Mekoryuk U.S.A. 114 B3
Melaka Malaysia 67 C7
Melanau, Gunung hill Indon. 67 E7
Melanesia is Pacific Ocean 146 G6
Melanesian Basin sea feature Pacific Ocean 146 G5
▶Melbourne Australia 108 B6
State capital of Victoria. 2nd most populous city in Oceania.
Melbourne U.S.A. 129 D6
Melby U.K. 46 [inset]
Meldorf Germany 43 L3
Melekess Rus. Fed. see Dimitrovgrad
Melenki Rus. Fed. 39 I5
Melet Turkey see Mesudiye
Mélèzes, Rivière aux r. Canada 119 H2
Melfa U.S.A. 131 H5
Melfi Chad 93 E3
Melfi Italy 54 F4
Melfort Canada 117 J4
Melhus Norway 40 G5
Meliadine Lake Canada 117 M2
Melide Spain 53 C2
▶Melilla N. Africa 53 E6
Spanish Territory.
Melimoyu, Monte mt. Chile 140 B6
Meliskerke Neth. 48 D3
Melita Canada 117 K5
Melitene Turkey see Malatya
Melitopol' Ukr. 39 G7
Melk Austria 43 O6
Melka Guba Eth. 94 D3
Melksham U.K. 45 E7
Mellakoski Fin. 40 N3
Mellansel Sweden 40 K5
Melle Germany 49 I2
Mellerud Sweden 41 H7
Mellette U.S.A. 126 D2
Mellid Spain see Melide
Mellilia N. Africa see Melilla
Mellor Glacier Antarctica 148 E2
Mellrichstadt Germany 49 K4
Mellum i. Germany 49 I1
Melmoth S. Africa 97 J5
Mel'nichoye Rus. Fed. 70 D3
Melo Uruguay 140 F4
Meloco Moz. 95 D5
Melolo Indon. 104 C2
Melozitna r. U.S.A. 114 C3
Melrhir, Chott salt l. Alg. 50 F5
Melrose Australia 105 C6
Melrose U.K. 46 G5
Melrose U.S.A. 126 E2
Melsungen Germany 49 J3
Melton Australia 108 B6
Melton Mowbray U.K. 45 G6
Melun France 52 F2
Melville Canada 117 K5
Melville, Cape Australia 106 D2
Melville, Lake Canada 119 K3
Melville Bugt b. Greenland see Qimusseriarsuaq
Melville Island Australia 104 E2
Melville Island Canada 115 H2
Melville Peninsula Canada 115 J3
Melvin U.S.A. 130 A3
Melvin, Lough l. Rep. of Ireland/U.K. 47 D3
Mēmar Co salt l. China 79 E2
Memba Moz. 95 E5
Memberamo r. Indon. 65 J7
Memel Lith. see Klaipėda
Memel S. Africa 97 I4
Memmelsdorf Germany 49 K5
Memmingen Germany 43 M7
Mempawah Indon. 64 D6
Memphis tourist site Egypt 86 C5
Memphis MI U.S.A. 130 D2
Memphis TN U.S.A. 127 F5
Memphis TX U.S.A. 127 C5
Memphrémagog, Lac l. Canada 131 I1
Mena Ukr. 39 G6
Mena U.S.A. 127 E5
Menado Indon. see Manado
Ménaka Mali 92 D3
Menard U.S.A. 127 D6
Menasha U.S.A. 130 A1
Mendanha Brazil 141 C2
Mendarik i. Indon. 67 D7
Mende France 52 F4
Mendefera Eritrea 82 E7
Mendeleyev Ridge sea feature Arctic Ocean 149 B1
Mendeleyevsk Rus. Fed. 38 L5
Mendenhall U.S.A. 127 F6
Mendenhall, Cape U.S.A. 114 B4
Mendenhall Glacier U.S.A. 116 C3
Méndez Mex. 127 D7
Mendī Eth. 94 D3
Mendi P.N.G. 65 K8
Mendip Hills U.K. 45 E7
Mendocino U.S.A. 124 B2
Mendocino, Cape U.S.A. 124 A1
Mendocino, Lake U.S.A. 124 B2
Mendooran Australia 108 D3
Mendota CA U.S.A. 124 C3
Mendota IL U.S.A. 126 F3
Mendoza Arg. 140 C4
Menemen Turkey 55 L5
Ménerville Alg. see Thenia
Mengban China 72 D4
Mengcheng China 73 H1
Menghai China 72 D4
Mengjin China 73 G1
Mengla China 72 D4
Menglang China see Lancang
Menglie China see Jiangcheng
Mengyang China see Mingshan
Mengzi China 72 D4
Menihek Canada 119 I3
Menihek Lakes Canada 119 I3
Menindee Australia 107 C7
Menindee Lake Australia 107 C7
Ménistouc, Lac l. Canada 119 I3
Menkere Rus. Fed. 61 N3
Mennecy France 48 C6
Menominee U.S.A. 130 B1
Menomonee Falls U.S.A. 130 A2
Menomonie U.S.A. 126 F2
Menongue Angola 95 B5
Menorca i. Spain see Minorca
Mentawai, Kepulauan is Indon. 64 B7
Mentawai, Selat sea chan. Indon. 64 C7
Menteroda Germany 49 K3
Mentmore U.S.A. 125 I4
Menton France 52 H5
Mentone U.S.A. 127 C6
Menuf Egypt see Minūf
Menzel Bourguiba Tunisia 54 C6
Menzelet Barajı resr Turkey 86 E3
Menzelinsk Rus. Fed. 37 Q4
Menzel Temime Tunisia 54 D6
Menzies Australia 105 C7
Menzies, Mount Antarctica 148 E2
Meobbaai b. Namibia 96 B3
Meoqui Mex. 127 B6
Meppel Neth. 48 G2
Meppen Germany 49 H2
Mepuze Moz. 97 K2
Meqheleng S. Africa 97 H5
Mequon U.S.A. 130 B2
Merak Indon. 64 D8
Meråker Norway 40 G5
Merano Italy 54 D1
Meratswe r. Botswana 96 G2
Merauke Indon. 65 K8
Merca Somalia see Marka
Mercantour, Parc National du nat. park France 52 H4
Merced U.S.A. 124 C3
Merced r. U.S.A. 124 C3
Mercedes Arg. 140 E3
Mercedes Uruguay 140 E4
Mercer ME U.S.A. 131 K1
Mercer PA U.S.A. 130 E3
Mercer WI U.S.A. 126 F2
Mercês Brazil 141 C3
Mercury Islands N.Z. 109 E3
Mercy, Cape Canada 115 L3
Merdenik Turkey see Göle
Mere Belgium 48 D4
Mere U.K. 45 E7
Meredith U.S.A. 131 J2
Meredith, Lake U.S.A. 127 C5
Merefa Ukr. 39 H6
Merga Oasis Sudan 82 C6
Mergui Myanmar 67 B4
Mergui Archipelago is Myanmar 67 B5
Meriç r. Turkey 55 L4
also known as Evros (Greece), Marica, Maritsa (Bulgaria)
Mérida Mex. 132 G4
Mérida Spain 53 C4
Mérida Venez. 138 D2
Mérida, Cordillera de mts Venez. 138 D2
Meriden U.S.A. 131 I3
Meridian MS U.S.A. 127 F5
Meridian TX U.S.A. 127 D6
Mérignac France 52 D4
Merijärvi Fin. 40 N4
Merikarvia Fin. 41 L6
Merimbula Australia 108 D6
Merín, Laguna l. Brazil/Uruguay see Mirim, Lagoa
Meringur Australia 107 C7
Merir i. Palau 65 I6
Merjayoun Lebanon see Marjayoûn
Merkel U.S.A. 127 C5
Merluna Australia 106 C2
Mermaid Reef Australia 104 B4
Meron, Har mt. Israel 81 B3
Merowe Sudan 82 D6
Mērqung Co l. China 79 F3
Merredin Australia 105 B7
Merrick hill U.K. 46 E5
Merrickville Canada 131 H1
Merrill MI U.S.A. 130 C2
Merrill WI U.S.A. 126 F2
Merrill, Mount Canada 116 E2
Merrillville U.S.A. 130 B3
Merriman U.S.A. 126 C3
Merritt Canada 116 F5
Merritt Island U.S.A. 129 D6
Merriwa Australia 108 E4
Merrygoen Australia 108 D3
Mersa Fatma Eritrea 82 F7
Mersa Maṭrûḥ Egypt see Marsá Maṭrūḥ
Mersch Lux. 48 G5
Merseburg (Saale) Germany 49 L3
Mersey est. U.K. 44 E5
Mersin Turkey see İçel
Mersing Malaysia 67 C7
Mērsrags Latvia 41 M8
Merta India 78 C4
Merthyr Tydfil U.K. 45 D7
Mértola Port. 53 C5
Mertz Glacier Antarctica 148 G2
Mertz Glacier Tongue Antarctica 148 G2
Mertzon U.S.A. 127 C6
Méru France 48 C5
▶Meru vol. Tanz. 94 D4
4th highest mountain in Africa.
Merui Pak. 85 F4
Merv Turkm. see Mary
Merweville S. Africa 96 E7
Merzifon Turkey 86 D2
Merzig Germany 48 G5
Merz Peninsula Antarctica 148 L2
Mesa AZ U.S.A. 125 H5
Mesa NM U.S.A. 123 G6
Mesabi Range hills U.S.A. 126 E2
Mesagne Italy 54 G4
Mesa Negra mt. U.S.A. 125 J4
Mesara, Ormos b. Greece 55 K7
Mesa Verde National Park U.S.A. 125 I3
Meschede Germany 49 I3
Mese Myanmar 66 B3
Meselefors Sweden 40 J4
Mesgouez Lake Canada 118 G4
Meshed Iran see Mashhad
Meshkān Iran 84 E2
Meshra'er Req Sudan 82 C8
Mesick U.S.A. 130 C1
Mesimeri Greece 55 J4
Mesolongi Greece 55 I5
Mesolóngion Greece see Mesolongi
Mesquita Brazil 141 C2
Mesquite NV U.S.A. 125 F3
Mesquite TX U.S.A. 127 D5
Mesquite Lake U.S.A. 125 F4
Messaad Alg. 50 E5
Messana Sicily Italy see Messina
Messina Sicily Italy 54 F5
Messina S. Africa 97 J2
Messina, Strait of Italy 54 F5
Messina, Stretta di Italy see Messina, Strait of
Messini Greece 55 J6
Messiniakos Kolpos b. Greece 55 J6
Mesta r. Bulg. 55 K4
Mesta r. Greece see Nestos
Mestghanem Alg. see Mostaganem
Mestlin Germany 49 L1
Meston, Akra pt Greece 55 K5
Mestre Italy 54 E2
Mesudiye Turkey 86 E2
Meta r. Col./Venez. 138 E2
Métabetchouan Canada 119 H4
Meta Incognita Peninsula Canada 115 L3
Metairie U.S.A. 127 F6
Metallifere, Colline mts Italy 54 D3
Metán Arg. 140 C3
Meteghan Canada 119 I5
Meteor Depth sea feature S. Atlantic Ocean 144 G9
Methoni Greece 55 I6
Methuen U.S.A. 131 J2
Methven U.K. 46 F4
Metionga Lake Canada 118 C4
Metković Croatia 54 G3
Metlaoui Tunisia 50 F5
Metoro Moz. 95 D5
Metro Indon. 64 D8
Metropolis U.S.A. 127 F4
Metsada tourist site Israel see Masada
Metter U.S.A. 129 D5
Mettet Belgium 48 E4
Mettingen Germany 49 H2
Mettler U.S.A. 124 D4
Mettur India 80 C4
Metu Eth. 94 D3
Metz France 48 G5
Metz U.S.A. 130 C3
Meulaboh Indon. 67 B6
Meureudu Indon. 67 B6
Meuse r. Belgium/France 48 F3
also known as Maas (Netherlands)
Meuselwitz Germany 49 M3
Mevagissey U.K. 45 C8
Mēwa China 72 D1
Mexia U.S.A. 127 D6
Mexiana, Ilha i. Brazil 139 I3
Mexicali Mex. 125 F5
Mexican Hat U.S.A. 125 I3
Mexican Water U.S.A. 125 I3
▶Mexico country Central America 132 D4
2nd most populous and 3rd largest country in Central and North America.
north america 9, 112–113
México Mex. see Mexico City
Mexico ME U.S.A. 131 J1
Mexico MO U.S.A. 126 F4
Mexico NY U.S.A. 131 G2
Mexico, Gulf of Mex./U.S.A. 121 H6
▶Mexico City Mex. 132 E5
Capital of Mexico. Most populous city in North America and 2nd in the world.
Meybod Iran 84 D3
Meydanī, Ra's-e pt Iran 84 E5
Meydān Shahr Afgh. 85 H3
Meyenburg Germany 49 M1
Meyersdale U.S.A. 130 F4
Meymaneh Afgh. 85 G3
Meymeh Iran 84 C3
Meynypil'gyno Rus. Fed. 149 C2
Mezada tourist site Israel see Masada
Mezdra Bulg. 55 J3
Mezen' Rus. Fed. 38 J2
Mezen' r. Rus. Fed. 38 J2
Mézenc, Mont mt. France 52 G4
Mezenskaya Guba b. Rus. Fed. 38 I2
Mezhdurechensk Kemerovskaya Oblast' Rus. Fed. 68 F2
Mezhdurechensk Respublika Komi Rus. Fed. 38 K3
Mezhdurechnye Rus. Fed. see Shali
Mezhdusharskiy, Ostrov i. Rus. Fed. 60 G2
Mezitli Turkey 81 B1
Mezőtúr Hungary 55 I1
Mežvidi Latvia 41 O8
Mhàil, Rubh' a' pt U.K. 46 C5
Mhangura Zimbabwe 95 D5
Mhlume Swaziland 97 J4
Mhow India 78 C5
Mi r. Myanmar 79 H5
Miahuatlán Mex. 132 E5
Miajadas Spain 53 D4
Miaméré Cent. Afr. Rep. 94 B3
Miami AZ U.S.A. 125 H5
Miami FL U.S.A. 129 D7
Miami OK U.S.A. 127 E4
Miami Beach U.S.A. 129 D7
Miancaowan China 72 C1
Miāndehī Iran 84 E3
Miandowāb Iran 84 B2
Miandrivazo Madag. 95 E5
Mīāneh Iran 84 B2
Miang, Phu mt. Thai. 66 C3
Miani India 85 I4
Miani Hor b. Pak. 85 G5
Mianjoi Afgh. 85 G3
Mianning China 72 D2
Mianwali Pak. 85 H3
Mianxian China 72 E1
Mianyang Hubei China see Xiantao
Mianyang Shaanxi China see Mianxian
Mianyang Sichuan China 72 E2
Mianzhu China 72 E2
Miaoli Taiwan 73 I3
Miarinarivo Madag. 95 E5
Miarritze France see Biarritz
Miass Rus. Fed. 60 H4
Mica Creek Canada 116 G4
Mica Mountain U.S.A. 125 H5
Micang Shan mts China 72 E1
Michalovce Slovakia 39 D6
Michel Canada 117 I4
Michelau in Oberfranken Germany 49 L4
Michelson, Mount U.S.A. 114 D3
Michelstadt Germany 49 J5
Michendorf Germany 49 N2
Micheng China see Midu
Michigan state U.S.A. 130 C2
▶Michigan, Lake U.S.A. 130 B2
3rd largest lake in North America and 5th in the world.
world 12–13
Michigan City U.S.A. 130 B3
Michinberi India 80 D2
Michipicoten Bay Canada 118 D5
Michipicoten Island Canada 118 D5
Michipicoten River Canada 118 D5
Michurin Bulg. see Tsarevo
Michurinsk Rus. Fed. 39 I5
Micronesia country N. Pacific Ocean see Micronesia, Federated States of
Micronesia is Pacific Ocean 146 F5
▶Micronesia, Federated States of country N. Pacific Ocean 146 G5
oceania 8, 100–101
Midai i. Indon. 67 D7
Mid-Atlantic Ridge sea feature Atlantic Ocean 144 E4
Mid-Atlantic Ridge sea feature Atlantic Ocean 144 G8
Middelburg Neth. 48 D3
Middelburg E. Cape S. Africa 97 G6
Middelburg Mpumalanga S. Africa 97 I3
Middelfart Denmark 41 F9
Middelharnis Neth. 48 E3
Middelwit S. Africa 97 H3
Middle Alkali Lake U.S.A. 122 C4
Middle America Trench sea feature N. Pacific Ocean 147 N5
Middle Andaman i. India 67 A4
Middle Atlas mts Morocco see Moyen Atlas
Middle Bay Canada 119 K4
Middlebourne U.S.A. 130 E4
Middleburg U.S.A. 131 G3
Middleburgh U.S.A. 131 H2
Middlebury IN U.S.A. 130 C3
Middlebury VT U.S.A. 131 I1
Middle Caicos i. Turks and Caicos Is 129 G8
Middle Concho r. U.S.A. 127 C6
Middle Congo country Africa see Congo
Middle Island Thai. see Tasai, Ko
Middle Loup r. U.S.A. 126 D3
Middlemarch N.Z. 109 C7
Middlemount Australia 106 E4
Middle River U.S.A. 131 G4
Middlesbrough U.K. 44 F4
Middle Strait India see Andaman Strait
Middleton Australia 106 C4
Middleton Canada 119 I5
Middleton Island atoll American Samoa see Rose Island
Middletown CA U.S.A. 124 B2
Middletown CT U.S.A. 131 I3
Middletown NY U.S.A. 131 H3
Middletown VA U.S.A. 131 F4
Midelt Morocco 50 D5
Midhurst U.K. 45 G8
Midi, Canal du France 52 F5
Mid-Indian Basin sea feature Indian Ocean 145 N6
Mid-Indian Ridge sea feature Indian Ocean 145 M7
Midland Canada 131 F1
Midland CA U.S.A. 125 F5
Midland IN U.S.A. 130 B4
Midland MI U.S.A. 130 C2
Midland SD U.S.A. 126 C2
Midland TX U.S.A. 127 C5
Midleton Rep. of Ireland 47 D6
Midnapore India see Medinipur
Midnapur India see Medinipur
Midongy Atsimo Madag. 95 E6
Mid-Pacific Mountains sea feature N. Pacific Ocean 146 G4
Midu China 72 D3
Miðvágur Faroe Is 40 [inset]
Midway Oman see Thamarīt
▶Midway Islands terr. N. Pacific Ocean 146 I4
United States Unincorporated Territory.
Midway Well Australia 105 C5
Midwest U.S.A. 122 G4
Midwest City U.S.A. 127 D5
Midwoud Neth. 48 F2
Midyat Turkey 87 F3
Midye Turkey see Kıyıköy
Mid Yell U.K. 46 [inset]
Midzhur mt. Bulg./Serb. and Mont. 86 A2
Miehikkälä Fin. 41 O6
Miekojärvi l. Fin. 40 N3
Mielec Poland 39 D6
Mienhua Yü i. Taiwan 73 I3
Mieraslompolo Fin. 40 O2
Mierašluoppal Fin. see Mieraslompolo
Miercurea-Ciuc Romania 55 K1
Mieres Spain 53 D2
Mieres del Camín Spain see Mieres
Mī'ēso Eth. 94 E3
Mieste Germany 49 L2
Mifflinburg U.S.A. 131 G3
Mifflintown U.S.A. 131 G3
Migang Shan mt. China 72 E1
Migdol S. Africa 97 G4
Miging India 72 B2
Miguel Auza Mex. 127 C7
Miguel Hidalgo, Presa resr Mex. 123 F8
Mihalıççık Turkey 55 N5
Mihara Japan 71 D6
Mihintale Sri Lanka 80 D4
Mihmandar Turkey 81 B1
Mijares r. Spain see Millárs
Mijdrecht Neth. 48 E2
Mikhaylov Rus. Fed. 39 H5
Mikhaylovgrad Bulg. see Montana
Mikhaylovka Amurskaya Oblast' Rus. Fed. 70 C2
Mikhaylovka Primorskiy Kray Rus. Fed. 70 D4
Mikhaylovka Tul'skaya Oblast' Rus. Fed. see Kimovsk
Mikhaylovka Volgogradskaya Oblast' Rus. Fed. 39 I6
Mikhaylovskiy Rus. Fed. 76 E1
Mikhaylovskoye Rus. Fed. see Shpakovskoye
Mikhaytov Island Antarctica 148 E2
Mikhrot Timna Israel 81 B5
Mikir Hills India 79 H4
Mikkeli Fin. 41 O6
Mikkelin mlk Fin. 41 O6
Mikkwa r. Canada 116 H3
Mikonos i. Greece see Mykonos
Mikoyan Armenia see Yeghegnadzor
Mikulkin, Mys c. Rus. Fed. 38 J2
Mikumi National Park Tanz. 95 D4
Mikun' Rus. Fed. 38 K3
Mikuni-sanmyaku mts Japan 71 E5
Mikura-jima i. Japan 71 E6
Milaca U.S.A. 126 E2
Miladhunmadulu Atoll Maldives 80 B5
Miladummadulu Atoll Maldives see Miladhunmadulu Atoll
Milan Italy 54 C2
Milan MI U.S.A. 130 D2
Milan MO U.S.A. 126 E3
Milan OH U.S.A. 130 D3
Milange Moz. 95 D5
Milano Italy see Milan
Milas Turkey 55 L6
Milazzo Sicily Italy 54 F5
Milazzo, Capo di c. Sicily Italy 54 F5
Milbank U.S.A. 126 D2
Milbridge U.S.A. 128 H2
Milde r. Germany 49 L2
Mildenhall U.K. 45 H6
Mildura Australia 107 C7
Mile China 72 D3
Mileiz, Wâdi el watercourse Egypt see Mulayz, Wādī al
Miles Australia 108 E1
Miles City U.S.A. 122 G3
Milestone Rep. of Ireland 47 D5
Miletto, Monte mt. Italy 54 F4
Mileura Australia 105 B6
Milford Rep. of Ireland 47 E2
Milford DE U.S.A. 131 H4
Milford IL U.S.A. 130 B3
Milford MA U.S.A. 131 J2
Milford MI U.S.A. 130 D2
Milford NE U.S.A. 126 D3
Milford NH U.S.A. 131 J2
Milford PA U.S.A. 131 H3
Milford UT U.S.A. 125 G2
Milford VA U.S.A. 131 G4
Milford Haven U.K. 45 B7
Milford Sound N.Z. 109 A7
Milford Sound inlet N.Z. 109 A7
Milgarra Australia 106 C3
Milḥ, Baḥr al l. Iraq see Razāzah, Buḥayrat ar
Miliana Alg. 53 H5
Milid Turkey see Malatya
Milikapiti Australia 104 E2
Miling Australia 105 B7
Milk r. U.S.A. 122 G2
Milk, Wadi el watercourse Sudan 82 D6
Mil'kovo Rus. Fed. 61 Q4
Millaa Millaa Australia 106 D3
Millárs r. Spain 53 F4
Millau France 52 F4
Millbrook Canada 131 F1
Mill Creek r. U.S.A. 124 B1
Milledgeville U.S.A. 129 D5
Mille Lacs lakes U.S.A. 126 E2
Mille Lacs, Lac des l. Canada 115 I5
Millen U.S.A. 129 D5
Millennium Island atoll Kiribati see Caroline Island
Miller U.S.A. 126 D2
Miller Lake Canada 130 E1
Millerovo Rus. Fed. 39 I6
Millersburg OH U.S.A. 130 E3
Millersburg PA U.S.A. 131 G3
Millers Creek U.S.A. 130 D5
Millersville U.S.A. 131 G4
Millerton Lake U.S.A. 124 D3
Millet Canada 116 H4
Milleur Point U.K. 46 D5
Mill Hall U.S.A. 131 G3
Millicent Australia 107 C8
Millington MI U.S.A. 130 D2
Millington TN U.S.A. 127 F5
Millinocket U.S.A. 128 G2
Mill Island Canada 115 K3
Millmerran Australia 108 E1
Millom U.K. 44 D4
Millport U.K. 46 E5
Millsboro U.S.A. 131 H4
Mills Creek watercourse Australia 106 C4
Mills Lake Canada 116 G2
Millstone KY U.S.A. 130 D5
Millstone WV U.S.A. 130 E4
Millstream-Chichester National Park Australia 104 B5
Millthorpe Australia 108 D4
Milltown Canada 119 I5
Milltown U.S.A. 122 E3
Milltown Malbay Rep. of Ireland 47 C5
Millungera Australia 106 C3
Millville U.S.A. 131 H4
Millwood U.S.A. 130 B5
Millwood Lake U.S.A. 127 E5
Milly Milly Australia 105 B6
Milne Land i. Greenland see Ilimananngip Nunaa
Milner U.S.A. 125 I1
Milo r. Guinea 92 C3
Milogradovo Rus. Fed. 70 D4
Milolii HI U.S.A. 123 [inset]
Milos i. Greece 55 K6
Milparinka Australia 107 C6
Milpitas U.S.A. 124 C3
Milroy U.S.A. 131 G3
Milton N.Z. 109 B8
Milton DE U.S.A. 131 H4
Milton NH U.S.A. 131 J2
Milton WV U.S.A. 130 D4
Milton Keynes U.K. 45 G6
Miluo China 73 G2
Milverton Canada 130 E2
Milwaukee U.S.A. 130 B2
▶Milwaukee Deep sea feature Caribbean Sea 144 D4
Deepest point in the Atlantic Ocean (Puerto Rico Trench).
Mimbres watercourse U.S.A. 125 J5
Mimili Australia 105 F6
Mimisal India 80 C4
Mimizan France 52 D4
Mimongo Gabon 94 B4
Mimosa Rocks National Park Australia 108 E6
Mina Mex. 127 C7
Mina U.S.A. 124 D2
Mīnāb Iran 84 E5
Minaçu Brazil 141 A1
Minahasa, Semenanjung pen. Indon. 65 G6
Minahassa Peninsula Indon. see Minahasa, Semenanjung
Minaker Canada see Prophet River
Minakh Syria 81 C1
Minaki Canada 117 M5
Minamia Australia 104 F3
Minami-Daitō-jima i. Japan 69 O7
Minami-Iō-jima vol. Japan 65 K2
Min'an China see Longshan
Minaret of Jam tourist site Afgh. 85 G3
Minas Indon. 67 C7
Minas Uruguay 140 E4
Minas de Matahambre Cuba 129 D8
Minas Gerais state Brazil 141 B2
Minas Novas Brazil 141 C2
Minatitlán Mex. 132 F5
Minbu Myanmar 66 A2
Minbya Myanmar 66 A2
Minchinmávida vol. Chile 140 B6
Mindanao i. Phil. 65 H5
Mindanao Trench sea feature N. Pacific Ocean see Philippine Trench
Mindelo Cape Verde 92 [inset]
Minden Canada 131 F1
Minden Germany 49 I2
Minden LA U.S.A. 127 E5
Minden NE U.S.A. 120 H3
Minden NV U.S.A. 124 D2
Mindon Myanmar 66 A3
Mindoro i. Phil. 65 G4
Mindoro Strait Phil. 65 F4
Mindouli Congo 94 B4
Mine Head hd Rep. of Ireland 47 E6
Minehead U.K. 45 D7
Mineola U.S.A. 131 I3
Mineral U.S.A. 131 G4
Mineral'nyye Vody Rus. Fed. 87 F1
Mineral Wells U.S.A. 127 D5
Mineralwells U.S.A. 130 E4
Minersville PA U.S.A. 131 G3
Minersville UT U.S.A. 125 G2
Minerva U.S.A. 130 E3
Minerva Reefs Fiji 103 I4
Minfeng China 79 E1
Minga Dem. Rep. Congo 95 C5
Mingäçevir Azer. 87 G2
Mingäçevir Su Anbarı resr Azer. 87 G2
Mingala Cent. Afr. Rep. 94 C3
Mingan, Îles de is Canada 119 J4
Mingan Archipelago National Park Reserve Canada see L'Archipélago de Mingan, Réserve du Parc National de
Mingbulak Uzbek. 76 B3
Mingechaur Azer. see Mingäçevir
Mingechaurskoye Vodokhranilishche resr Azer. see Mingäçevir Su Anbarı
Mingenew Australia 105 A7
Mingfeng China see Yuan'an
Minggang China 73 G1
Mingguang China 73 H1
Mingin Range mts Myanmar 66 A2
Minglanilla Spain 53 F4
Mingoyo Tanz. 95 D5
Mingshan China 72 D2
Mingshui Gansu China 76 I3
Mingshui Heilong. China 70 B3
Mingteke China 78 C1
Mingulay i. U.K. 46 B4
Mingxi China 73 H3
Mingzhou China see Suide
Minhe China see Jinxian
Minhla Magwe Myanmar 66 A3
Minhla Pegu Myanmar 66 A3
Minho r. Port./Spain see Miño
Minicoy atoll India 80 B4
Minigwal, Lake salt flat Australia 105 C7
Minilya Australia 105 A5
Minilya r. Australia 105 A5
Minipi Lake Canada 119 J3
Miniss Lake Canada 117 N5
Minitonas Canada 117 K4
Minjian China see Mabian
Min Jiang r. Sichuan China 72 E2
Min Jiang r. China 73 H3
Minna Nigeria 92 D4
Minna Bluff pt Antarctica 148 H1
Minne Sweden 40 I5
Minneapolis KS U.S.A. 126 D4
Minneapolis MN U.S.A. 126 E2
Minnedosa Canada 117 L5
Minnehaha Springs U.S.A. 130 F4
Minneola U.S.A. 127 C4
Minnesota r. U.S.A. 126 E2
Minnesota state U.S.A. 126 E2
Minnewaukan U.S.A. 126 D1
Minnitaki Lake Canada 117 N5
Miño r. Port./Spain 53 B3
also known as Minho
Minorca i. Spain 53 H3
Minot U.S.A. 126 C1
Minqār, Ghadīr imp. l. Syria 81 C3
Minqing China 73 H3
Minquan China 73 G1
Min Shan mts China 72 D1
Minsin Myanmar 66 A1
▶Minsk Belarus 41 O10
Capital of Belarus.
Mińsk Mazowiecki Poland 43 R4
Minsterley U.K. 45 E6
Mintaka Pass China/Jammu and Kashmir 78 C1
Minto, Lac l. Canada 118 G2
Minto, Mount Antarctica 148 H2

Minto Inlet Canada 114 G2
Minton Canada 117 J5
Mīnudasht Iran 84 D2
Minūf Egypt 86 C5
Minusinsk Rus. Fed. 68 G2
Minvoul Gabon 94 B3
Minxian China 72 E1
Minya Konka *mt.* China *see* Gongga Shan
Minywa Myanmar 66 A2
Minzong India 79 I4
Mio U.S.A. 130 C1
Miquelon Canada 118 F4
Miquelon *i.* St Pierre and Miquelon 119 K5
Mirabad Afgh. 85 F4
Mirabel *airport* Canada 118 G5
Mirabela Brazil 141 B2
Mirador, Parque Nacional de *nat. park* Brazil 139 I5
Mīrah, Wādī al *watercourse* Iraq/Saudi Arabia 87 F4
Miraí Brazil 141 C3
Miraj India 80 B2
Miramar Arg. 140 E5
Miramichi Canada 119 I5
Miramichi Bay Canada 119 I5
Mirampelou, Kolpos *b.* Greece 55 K7
Miranda Brazil 140 E2
Miranda Moz. *see* Macaloge
Miranda U.S.A. 124 B1
Miranda, Lake *salt flat* Australia 105 C6
Miranda de Ebro Spain 53 E2
Mirandela Port. 53 C3
Mirandola Italy 54 D2
Mirante Brazil 141 C1
Mirante, Serra do *hills* Brazil 141 A3
Mirassol Brazil 141 A3
Mir-Bashir Azer. *see* Tärtär
Mirbāţ Oman 83 H6
Mirboo North Australia 108 C7
Mirepoix France 52 E5
Mirgarh Pak. 85 I4
Mirgorod Ukr. *see* Myrhorod
Miri *Sarawak* Malaysia 64 E6
Miri *mt.* Pak. 85 F4
Mirialguda India 80 C2
Miri Hills India 79 H4
Mirim, Lagoa *l.* Brazil/Uruguay 140 F4
Mirim, Lagoa do *l.* Brazil 141 A5
Mirintu *watercourse* Australia 108 A2
Mirjan India 80 B3
Mirny *research station* Antarctica 148 F2
Mirnyy *Arkhangel'skaya Oblast'* Rus. Fed. 38 I3
Mirnyy *Respublika Sakha (Yakutiya)* Rus. Fed. 61 M3
Mirond Lake Canada 117 K4
Mironovka Ukr. *see* Myronivka
Mirow Germany 49 M1
Mirpur Khas Pak. 85 H5
Mirpur Sakro Pak. 85 G5
Mirs Bay *Hong Kong* China 73 [inset]
Mirtoan Sea Greece *see* Mirtoö Pelagos
Mirtoö Pelagos *sea* Greece 55 J6
Miryalaguda India *see* Mirialguda
Miryang S. Korea 71 C6
Mirzachirla Turkm. *see* Murzechirla
Mirzachul Uzbek. *see* Gulistan
Mirzapur India 79 E4
Mirzawal India 78 C3
Misaw Lake Canada 117 K3
Miscou Island Canada 119 I5
Misehkow *r.* Canada 118 C4
Mīsh, Kūh-e *hill* Iran 84 E3
Misha India 67 A6
Mishāsh al Ashāwī *well* Saudi Arabia 84 C5
Mishāsh aẓ Ẓuayyinī *well* Saudi Arabia 84 C5
Mishawaka U.S.A. 130 B3
Mishicot U.S.A. 130 B1
Mi-shima *i.* Japan 71 C6
Mishmi Hills India 79 H3
Mishvan' Rus. Fed. 38 L2
Misima Island P.N.G. 106 F1
Misis Dağ *hills* Turkey 81 B1
Miskin Oman 84 E6
Miskitos, Cayos *is* Nicaragua 133 H6
Miskolc Hungary 39 D6
Mismā, Tall al *hill* Jordan 81 C3
Misoöl *i.* Indon. 65 I7
Misquah Hills U.S.A. 126 F2
Misr *country* Africa *see* Egypt
Misraç Turkey *see* Kurtalan
Mişrātah Libya 93 E1
Missinaibi *r.* Canada 118 E4
Mission Beach Australia 106 D3
Mission Viejo U.S.A. 124 E5
Missisa *r.* Canada 118 D3
Missisa Lake Canada 118 D3
Missisicabi *r.* Canada 118 F4
Mississauga Canada 130 F2
Mississinewa Lake U.S.A. 130 C3

▶Mississippi *r.* U.S.A. 127 F6
4th longest river in North America. Part of the longest (Mississippi-Missouri).

Mississippi *state* U.S.A. 127 F5
Mississippi Delta U.S.A. 127 F6
Mississippi Lake Canada 131 G1

▶Mississippi-Missouri *r.* U.S.A. 121 I4
Longest river and largest drainage basin in North America and 4th longest river in the world.
north america 110–111
world 12–13

Mississippi Sound *sea chan.* U.S.A. 127 F6
Missolonghi Greece *see* Mesolongi
Missoula U.S.A. 122 E3

▶Missouri *r.* U.S.A. 126 F4
3rd longest river in North America. Part of the longest (Mississippi-Missouri).

Missouri *state* U.S.A. 126 E4
Mistanipisipou *r.* Canada 119 J4
Mistassibi *r.* Canada 115 K5
Mistassini Canada 119 G4
Mistassini *r.* Canada 119 G4
Mistassini, Lac *l.* Canada 118 G4
Mistastin Lake Canada 119 J3
Mistelbach Austria 43 P6
Mistinibi, Lac *l.* Canada 119 J2
Mistissini Canada 118 G4
Misty Fiords National Monument Wilderness *nat. park* U.S.A. 116 D4
Misumba Dem. Rep. Congo 95 C4
Misuratah Libya *see* Mişrātah
Mitchell Australia 107 D5
Mitchell *r. N.S.W.* Australia 108 F2
Mitchell *r. Qld* Australia 106 C2
Mitchell *r. Vic.* Australia 108 C6
Mitchell Canada 130 E2
Mitchell *IN* U.S.A. 130 B4
Mitchell *OR* U.S.A. 122 C3
Mitchell *SD* U.S.A. 126 D3
Mitchell, Lake Australia 106 D3
Mitchell, Mount U.S.A. 128 D5
Mitchell and Alice Rivers National Park Australia 106 C2
Mitchell Island Cook Is *see* Nassau
Mitchell Island *atoll* Tuvalu *see* Nukulaelae
Mitchell Point Australia 104 E2
Mitchelstown Rep. of Ireland 47 D5
Mīt Ghamr Egypt *see* Mīt Ghamr
Mīt Ghamr Egypt 86 C5
Mithi Pak. 85 H5
Mithrau Pak. 85 H5
Mitilíni Greece *see* Mytilini
Mitkof Island U.S.A. 116 C3
Mito Japan 71 F5
Mitole Tanz. 95 D4
Mitre *mt.* N.Z. 109 E5
Mitre Island Solomon Is 103 H3
Mitrofanovka Rus. Fed. 39 H6
Mitrovica Serb. and Mont. *see* Kosovska Mitrovica
Mitrovicë Serb. and Mont. *see* Kosovska Mitrovica
Mitsinjo Madag. 95 E5
Mits'iwa Eritrea *see* Massawa
Mitta Mitta Australia 108 C6
Mittellandkanal *canal* Germany 49 I2
Mitterteich Germany 49 M5
Mittimatalik Canada *see* Pond Inlet
Mittweida Germany 49 M4
Mitú Col. 138 D3
Mitumba, Chaîne des *mts* Dem. Rep. Congo 95 C5
Mitzic Gabon 94 B3
Miughalaigh *i.* U.K. *see* Mingulay
Miura Japan 71 E6
Mixian China *see* Xinmi
Miyake-jima *i.* Japan 71 E6
Miyako Japan 71 F5
Miyakonojō Japan 71 C7
Miyang China *see* Mile
Miyani India 78 B5
Miyazaki Japan 71 C7
Miyazu Japan 71 D6
Miyi China 72 D3
Miyoshi Japan 71 D6
Mīzāni Afgh. 85 G3
Mīzan Teferī Eth. 94 D3
Mizdah Libya 93 E1
Mizen Head *hd* Rep. of Ireland 47 C6
Mizhhir"ya Ukr. 39 D6
Mizo Hills *state* India *see* Mizoram
Mizoram *state* India 79 H5
Mizpe Ramon Israel 81 B4
Mizusawa Japan 71 F5
Mjölby Sweden 41 I7
Mkata Tanz. 95 D4
Mkushi Zambia 95 C5
Mladá Boleslav Czech Rep. 43 O5
Mladenovac Serb. and Mont. 55 I2
Mława Poland 43 R4
Mlilwane Nature Reserve Swaziland 97 J4
Mljet *i.* Croatia 54 G3
Mlungisi S. Africa 97 H6
Mmabatho S. Africa 97 G3
Mmamabula Botswana 97 H2
Mmathethe Botswana 97 G3
Mo Norway 41 D6
Moa *i.* Indon. 104 E2
Moab *reg.* Jordan 81 B4
Moab U.S.A. 125 I2
Moa Island Australia 106 C1
Moala *i.* Fiji 103 H3
Mo'alla Iran 84 D3
Moamba Moz. 97 K3
Moanda Gabon 94 B4
Moapa U.S.A. 125 F3
Moate Rep. of Ireland 47 E4
Mobārakeh Iran 84 C3
Mobayembongo Dem. Rep. Congo *see* Mobayi-Mbongo
Mobayi-Mbongo Dem. Rep. Congo 94 C3
Moberly U.S.A. 126 E4
Moberly Lake Canada 116 F4
Mobha India 78 C5
Mobile *AL* U.S.A. 127 F6
Mobile *AZ* U.S.A. 125 G5
Mobile Bay U.S.A. 127 F6
Moble *watercourse* Australia 108 B1
Mobridge U.S.A. 126 C2
Mobutu, Lake Dem. Rep. Congo/Uganda *see* Albert, Lake
Mobutu Sese Seko, Lake Dem. Rep. Congo/Uganda *see* Albert, Lake
Moca Geçidi *pass* Turkey 81 A1
Moçambique *country* Africa *see* Mozambique
Moçambique Moz. 95 E5
Moçâmedes Angola *see* Namibe
Môc Châu Vietnam 66 D2
Mocha Yemen 82 F7
Mocha, Isla *i.* Chile 140 B5
Mochirma, Parque Nacional *nat. park* Venez. 138 F1
Mochudi Botswana 97 H3
Mochudi *admin. dist.* Botswana *see* Kgatleng
Mocimboa da Praia Moz. 95 E5
Möckern Germany 49 L2
Möckmühl Germany 49 J5
Mockträsk Sweden 40 L4
Mocoa Col. 138 C3
Mococa Brazil 141 B3
Mocoduene Moz. 97 L2
Mocorito Mex. 123 G8
Moctezuma *Chihuahua* Mex. 123 G7
Moctezuma *San Luis Potosí* Mex. 132 D4
Moctezuma *Sonora* Mex. 123 F7
Mocuba Moz. 95 D5
Mocun China 73 G4
Modan Indon. 65 I7
Modane France 52 H4
Modder *r.* S. Africa 97 G5
Modena Italy 54 D2
Modena U.S.A. 125 G3
Modesto U.S.A. 124 C3
Modesto Lake U.S.A. 124 C3
Modot Mongolia 69 J3
Modung China 72 C2
Moe Australia 108 C7
Moel Sych *hill* U.K. 45 D6
Moelv Norway 41 G6
Moen Norway 40 K2
Moenjodaro *tourist site* Pak. 85 H5
Moenkopi U.S.A. 125 H3
Moenkopi Wash *r.* U.S.A. 125 H4
Moeraki Point N.Z. 109 C7
Moero, Lake Dem. Rep. Congo/Zambia *see* Mweru, Lake
Moers Germany 48 G3
Moffat U.K. 46 F5
Moga India 78 C3

▶Mogadishu Somalia 94 E3
Capital of Somalia.

Mogador Morocco *see* Essaouira
Mogadore Reservoir U.S.A. 130 E3
Moganyaka S. Africa 97 I3
Mogaung Myanmar 66 B1
Mogdy Rus. Fed. 70 D2
Mögelin Germany 49 M2
Mogilev Belarus *see* Mahilyow
Mogilev Podol'skiy Ukr. *see* Mohyliv Podil's'kyy
Mogi-Mirim Brazil 141 B3
Mogiquiçaba Brazil 141 D2
Mogocha Rus. Fed. 69 L2
Mogod *mts* Tunisia 54 C6
Mogoditshane Botswana 97 G3
Mogollon Mountains U.S.A. 125 I5
Mogollon Plateau U.S.A. 125 H4
Mogontiacum Germany *see* Mainz
Mogroum Chad 93 E3
Moguqi China 70 A3
Mogwadi S. Africa *see* Dendron
Mogwase S. Africa 97 H3
Mogzon Rus. Fed. 69 K2
Mohács Hungary 54 H2
Mohaka *r.* N.Z. 109 F4
Mohala India 80 D1
Mohale Dam Lesotho 97 I5
Mohale's Hoek Lesotho 97 H6
Mohall U.S.A. 126 C1
Mohammad Iran 84 E3
Mohammadia Alg. 53 G6
Mohan *r.* India/Nepal 78 E3
Mohana India 78 D4
Mohave, Lake U.S.A. 125 F4
Mohawk *r.* U.S.A. 131 I2
Mohawk Mountains U.S.A. 125 G5
Moher, Cliffs of Rep. of Ireland 47 C5
Mohill Rep. of Ireland 47 E4
Möhne *r.* Germany 49 H3
Möhnetalsperre *resr* Germany 49 I3
Mohon Peak U.S.A. 125 G4
Mohoro Tanz. 95 D4
Mohyliv Podil's'kyy Ukr. 39 E6
Moi Norway 41 E7
Moijabana Botswana 97 H2
Moincêr China 78 E3
Moinda China 79 G3
Moine Moz. 97 K3
Moineşti Romania 55 L1
Mointy Kazakh. *see* Moyynty
Mo i Rana Norway 40 I3
Moirang India 72 B3
Mõisaküla Estonia 41 N7
Moisie Canada 119 I4
Moisie *r.* Canada 119 I4
Moissac France 52 E4
Mojave U.S.A. 124 D4
Mojave *r.* U.S.A. 124 E4
Mojave Desert U.S.A. 124 E4
Mojiang China 72 D4
Moji das Cruzes Brazil 141 B3
Mojos, Llanos de *plain* Bol. 138 E6
Moju *r.* Brazil 139 I4
Mokama India 79 F4
Mokau N.Z. 109 E4
Mokau *r.* N.Z. 109 E4
Mokelumne *r.* U.S.A. 124 C2
Mokelumne Aqueduct *canal* U.S.A. 124 C2
Mokhoabong Pass Lesotho 97 I5
Mokhotlong Lesotho 97 I5
Mokhtārān Iran 84 E3
Moknine Tunisia 54 D7
Mokohinau Islands N.Z. 109 E2
Mokokchung India 79 H4
Mokolo Cameroon 93 E3
Mokolo *r.* S. Africa 97 H2
Mokp'o S. Korea 71 B6
Mokrous Rus. Fed. 39 J6
Moksha *r.* Rus. Fed. 39 I5
Mokshan Rus. Fed. 39 J5
Möksy Fin. 40 N5
Mōktama Myanmar *see* Martaban
Mōktama, Gulf of Myanmar *see* Martaban, Gulf of
Mokundurra India *see* Mukandwara
Mokwa Nigeria 92 D4
Molatón *mt.* Spain 53 F4
Moldavia *country* Europe *see* Moldova
Moldavskaya S.S.R. *country* Europe *see* Moldova
Molde Norway 40 E5
Moldjord Norway 40 I3
▶Moldova *country* Europe 39 F7
europe 5, 34–35
Moldoveanu, Vârful *mt.* Romania 55 K2
Moldovei de Sud, Cîmpia *plain* Moldova 55 M1
Molega Lake Canada 119 I5
Molen *r.* S. Africa 97 I4
Mole National Park Ghana 92 C4
Molepolole Botswana 97 G3
Molėtai Lith. 41 N9
Molfetta Italy 54 G4
Molière Alg. *see* Bordj Bounaama
Molihong Shan *mt.* China *see* Morihong Shan
Molina de Aragón Spain 53 F3
Moline U.S.A. 127 D4
Molkom Sweden 41 H7
Mollagara Turkm. *see* Mollakara
Mollakara Turkm. 84 D2
Mol Len *mt.* India 79 H4
Möllenbeck Germany 49 N1
Mollendo Peru 138 D7
Mölln Germany 49 K1
Mölnlycke Sweden 41 H8
Molochnyy Rus. Fed. 40 R2
Molodechno Belarus *see* Maladzyechna
Molodezhnaya *research station* Antarctica 148 D2
Molokai *i. HI* U.S.A. 123 [inset]
Moloma *r.* Rus. Fed. 38 K4
Molong Australia 108 D4
Molopo *watercourse* Botswana/S. Africa 96 E5
Molotov Rus. Fed. *see* Perm'
Molotovsk Kyrg. *see* Kayyngdy
Molotovsk *Arkhangel'skaya Oblast'* Rus. Fed. *see* Severodvinsk
Molotovsk *Kirovskaya Oblast'* Rus. Fed. *see* Nolinsk
Moloundou Cameroon 93 E4
Molson Lake Canada 117 L4
Molu *i.* Indon. 65 I8
Moluccas *is* Indon. 65 H7
Molucca Sea *sea* Indon. *see* Maluku, Laut
Moma Moz. 95 D5
Momba Australia 108 A3
Mombaça Brazil 139 K5
Mombasa Kenya 94 D4
Mombetsu *Hokkaidō* Japan *see* Monbetsu
Mombetsu *Hokkaidō* Japan *see* Monbetsu
Mombi New India 79 H4
Mombum Indon. 65 J8
Momchilgrad Bulg. 55 K4
Momence U.S.A. 130 B3
Momi, Ra's *pt* Yemen 83 H7
Mompós Col. 138 D2
Møn *i.* Denmark 41 H9
Mon India 79 H4
Mona *terr.* Irish Sea *see* Isle of Man
Mona U.S.A. 125 H2
Monaca U.S.A. 130 E3
Monach, Sound of *sea chan.* U.K. 46 B3
Monach Islands U.K. 46 B3
▶Monaco *country* Europe 52 H5
europe 5, 34–35
Monaco Basin *sea feature* N. Atlantic Ocean 144 G4
Monadhliath Mountains U.K. 46 E3
Monaghan Rep. of Ireland 47 F3
Monahans U.S.A. 127 C6
Mona Passage Dom. Rep./Puerto Rico 133 K5
Monapo Moz. 95 E5
Monar, Loch *l.* U.K. 46 D3
Monarch Mountain Canada 116 E5
Monarch Pass U.S.A. 123 G5
Mona Reservoir U.S.A. 125 H2
Monashee Mountains Canada 116 G5
Monastir Macedonia *see* Bitola
Monastir Tunisia 54 D7
Monastyrishche Ukr. *see* Monastyryshche
Monastyryshche Ukr. 39 F6
Monbetsu *Hokkaidō* Japan 70 F3
Monbetsu *Hokkaidō* Japan 70 F4
Moncalieri Italy 54 B2
Monchegorsk Rus. Fed. 40 R3
Mönchengladbach Germany 48 G3
Monchique Port. 53 B5
Moncks Corner U.S.A. 129 D5
Monclova Mex. 127 C7
Moncouche, Lac *l.* Canada 119 H4
Moncton Canada 119 I5
Mondego *r.* Port. 53 B3
Mondlo S. Africa 97 J4
Mondo Chad 93 E3
Mondovì Italy 54 B2
Mondragone Italy 54 E4
Mondy Rus. Fed. 68 I2
Monemvasia Greece 55 J6
Monessen U.S.A. 130 F3
Moneta U.S.A. 122 G4
Moneygall Rep. of Ireland 47 E5
Moneymore U.K. 47 F3
Monfalcone Italy 54 E2
Monfalut Egypt *see* Manfalūţ
Monforte Spain 53 C2
Monga Dem. Rep. Congo 94 C3
Mongala *r.* Dem. Rep. Congo 94 B3
Mongar Bhutan 79 G4
Mongbwalu Dem. Rep. Congo 94 D3
Mông Cai Vietnam 66 D2
Mongers Lake *salt flat* Australia 105 B7
Mong Hang Myanmar 66 B2
Mong Hkan Myanmar 66 C2
Mong Hpayak Myanmar 66 B2
Mong Hsat Myanmar 66 B2
Mong Hsawk Myanmar 66 B2
Mong Hsu Myanmar 66 B2
Monghyr India *see* Munger
Mong Kung Myanmar 66 B2
Mong Kyawt Myanmar 66 B3
Mongla Bangl. 79 G5
Mong Lin Myanmar 66 C2
Mong Loi Myanmar 66 C2
Mong Long Myanmar 66 B2
Mong Nai Myanmar 66 B2
Mong Nawng Myanmar 66 B2
Mongo Chad 93 E3
▶Mongolia *country* Asia 68 I3
asia 6, 58–59
Mongol Uls *country* Asia *see* Mongolia
Mongonu Nigeria 92 E3
Mongora Pak. 85 I3
Mongour *hill* U.K. 46 G4
Mong Pan Myanmar 66 B2
Mong Ping Myanmar 66 B2
Mong Pu Myanmar 66 B2
Mong Pu-awn Myanmar 66 B2
Mong Si Myanmar 66 B2
Mongu Zambia 95 C5
Mong Un Myanmar 66 C2
Mong Yai Myanmar 66 B2
Mong Yang Myanmar 66 C2
Mong Yawn Myanmar 66 B2
Mong Yawng Myanmar 66 C2
Mönh Hayrhan Uul *mt.* Mongolia 76 H2
Moniaive U.K. 46 F5
Monitor Mountain U.S.A. 124 E2
Monitor Range *mts* U.S.A. 124 E2
Monivea Rep. of Ireland 47 D4
Monkey Bay Malawi 95 D5
Monkira Australia 106 C5
Monkton Canada 130 E2
Monmouth U.K. 45 E7
Monmouth U.S.A. 126 F3
Monmouth Mountain Canada 116 F5
Monnow *r.* U.K. 45 E7
Mono, Punta del *pt* Nicaragua 133 H6
Mono Lake U.S.A. 124 D2
Monolithos Greece 55 L6
Monomoy Point U.S.A. 131 J3
Monon U.S.A. 130 B3
Monopoli Italy 54 G4
Monreal del Campo Spain 53 F3
Monreale *Sicily* Italy 54 E5
Monroe *IN* U.S.A. 130 C3
Monroe *LA* U.S.A. 127 E5
Monroe *MI* U.S.A. 130 D3
Monroe *NC* U.S.A. 129 D5
Monroe *WI* U.S.A. 126 F3
Monroe Center U.S.A. 126 F2
Monroe Lake U.S.A. 130 B4
Monroeton U.S.A. 131 G3

▶Monrovia Liberia 92 B4
Capital of Liberia.

Mons Belgium 48 D4
Monschau Germany 48 G4
Monselice Italy 54 D2
Montabaur Germany 49 H4
Montagu S. Africa 96 E7
Montague Canada 119 J5
Montague *MI* U.S.A. 130 B2
Montague *TX* U.S.A. 127 D5
Montague Range *hills* Australia 105 B6
Montalto *mt.* Italy 54 F5
Montalto Uffugo Italy 54 G5
Montana Bulg. 55 J3
Montana *state* U.S.A. 122 F3
Montargis France 52 F3
Montauban France 52 E4
Montauk U.S.A. 131 J3
Montauk Point U.S.A. 131 J3
Mont-aux-Sources *mt.* Lesotho 97 I5
Montbard France 52 G3
Montblanc Spain 53 G3
Montblanch Spain *see* Montblanc
Montbrison France 52 G4
Montceau-les-Mines France 52 G3
Montcornet France 48 E5
Mont-de-Marsan France 52 D5
Montdidier France 48 C5
Monte Alegre Brazil 139 H4
Monte Alegre de Goiás Brazil 141 B1
Monte Alegre de Minas Brazil 141 A2
Monte Azul Brazil 141 C1
Monte Azul Paulista Brazil 141 A3
Montebello Canada 118 G5
Montebello Islands Australia 104 A5
Montebelluna Italy 54 E2
Monte-Carlo Monaco 52 H5
Monte Christo S. Africa 97 H2
Monte Cristi Dom. Rep. 133 J5
Monte Dourado Brazil 139 H4
Monte Falterona, Campigna e delle Foreste Casentinesi, Parco Nazionale del *nat. park* Italy 54 D3
Montego Bay Jamaica 133 I5
Montélimar France 52 G4
Monte Lindo *r.* Para. 140 E2
Montello U.S.A. 126 F3
Montemorelos Mex. 127 D7
Montemor-o-Novo Port. 53 B4
Montenegro *aut. rep.* Serb. and Mont. *see* Crna Gora
Montepulciano Italy 54 D3
Monte Quemado Arg. 140 D3
Montereau-faut-Yonne France 52 F2
Monterey Mex. *see* Monterrey
Monterey *CA* U.S.A. 124 C3
Monterey *VA* U.S.A. 130 F4
Monterey Bay U.S.A. 124 B3
Montería Col. 138 C2
Monteros Arg. 140 C3
Monterrey *Baja California* Mex. 125 F5
Monterrey *Nuevo León* Mex. 127 C7
Montervary *hd* Rep. of Ireland 47 C6
Montesano U.S.A. 122 C3
Montesano sulla Marcellana Italy 54 F4
Monte Santo Brazil 139 K6
Monte Santu, Capo di *c. Sardinia* Italy 54 C4
Montes Claros Brazil 141 C2
Montesilvano Italy 54 F3
Montevarchi Italy 54 D3

▶Montevideo Uruguay 140 E4
Capital of Uruguay.

Montevideo U.S.A. 126 E2
Montezuma U.S.A. 126 E3
Montezuma Creek U.S.A. 125 I3
Montezuma Peak U.S.A. 124 E3
Montfort Neth. 48 F3
Montgomery U.K. 45 D6

▶Montgomery *AL* U.S.A. 129 C5
State capital of Alabama.

Montgomery *WV* U.S.A. 130 E4
Montgomery Islands Australia 104 C3
Monthey Switz. 52 H3
Monticello *AR* U.S.A. 127 F5
Monticello *FL* U.S.A. 129 D6
Monticello *IN* U.S.A. 130 B3
Monticello *KY* U.S.A. 130 C5
Monticello *MO* U.S.A. 126 F3
Monticello *NY* U.S.A. 131 H3
Monticello *UT* U.S.A. 125 I3
Montignac France 52 E4
Montignies-le-Tilleul Belgium 48 E4
Montigny-lès-Metz France 48 G5
Montilla Spain 53 D5
Monti Sibillini, Parco Nazionale dei *nat. park* Italy 54 E3
Montividiu Brazil 141 A2
Montivilliers France 45 H9
Mont-Joli Canada 119 H4
Mont-Laurier Canada 118 G5
Montluçon France 52 F3
Montmagny Canada 119 H5
Montmédy France 48 F5
Montmirail France 48 D6
Montmorillon France 52 E3
Montmort-Lucy France 48 D6
Monto Australia 106 E5
Montour Falls U.S.A. 131 G2
Montoursville U.S.A. 131 G3
Montpelier *ID* U.S.A. 122 F4

▶Montpelier *VT* U.S.A. 131 I1
State capital of Vermont.

Montpellier France 52 F5
Montréal Canada 118 G5
Montreal *r. Ont.* Canada 118 D5
Montreal *r. Ont.* Canada 118 F5
Montreal Lake Canada 117 J4
Montreal Lake *l.* Canada 117 J4
Montreal River Canada 118 D5
Montreuil France 48 B4
Montreux Switz. 52 H3
Montrose *well* S. Africa 96 E4
Montrose U.K. 46 G4
Montrose *CO* U.S.A. 125 J2
Montrose *PA* U.S.A. 131 H3
Montross U.S.A. 131 G4
Monts, Pointe des *pt* Canada 119 I4

▶Montserrat *terr.* West Indies 133 L5
United Kingdom Overseas Territory.
north america 9, 112–113

Mont-St-Aignan France 45 I9
Montviel, Lac *l.* Canada 119 H3
Monument Valley *reg.* U.S.A. 125 H3
Monywa Myanmar 66 A2
Monza Italy 54 C2
Monze, Cape *pt* Pak. *see* Muari, Ras
Monzón Spain 53 G3
Mooi *r.* S. Africa 97 J5
Mooifontein Namibia 96 C4
Mookane Botswana 97 H2
Mookgopong S. Africa *see* Naboomspruit
Moolawatana Australia 107 B6
Moomba Australia 107 C6
Moomin Creek *r.* Australia 108 D2
Moonaree Australia 107 A6
Moonbi Range *mts* Australia 108 E3
Moonda Lake *salt flat* Australia 107 C5
Moonie Australia 108 E1
Moonie *r.* Australia 108 D2
Moora Australia 105 B7
Mooraberree Australia 106 C5
Moorcroft U.S.A. 122 G3
Moore *r.* Australia 105 A7
Moore U.S.A. 122 F3
Moore, Lake *salt flat* Australia 105 B7
Moore Embayment *b.* Antarctica 148 H1
Moorefield U.S.A. 131 F4
Moore Haven U.S.A. 129 D7
Moore Reef Australia 106 E3
Moore Reservoir U.S.A. 131 J1
Moore River National Park Australia 105 A7
Moores Island Bahamas 129 E7
Moorfoot Hills U.K. 46 F5
Moorhead U.S.A. 126 D2
Moorman U.S.A. 130 B5
Moornanyah Lake *imp. l.* Australia 108 A4
Mooroopna Australia 108 B6
Moorreesburg S. Africa 96 D7
Moorrinya National Park Australia 106 D4
Moose *r.* Canada 118 E4
Moose Factory Canada 118 E4
Moosehead Lake U.S.A. 128 G2
Moose Jaw Canada 117 J5
Moose Jaw *r.* Canada 117 J5
Moose Lake U.S.A. 126 E2
Mooselookmeguntic Lake U.S.A. 131 J1
Moose Mountain Creek *r.* Canada 117 K5
Moosilauke, Mount U.S.A. 131 J1
Moosomin Canada 117 K5
Moosonee Canada 118 E4
Mootwingee National Park Australia 107 C6
Mopane S. Africa 97 I2
Mopeia Moz. 95 D5
Mopipi Botswana 95 C6
Mopti Mali 92 C3
Moqor Afgh. 85 G3
Moquegua Peru 138 D7
Mora Cameroon 93 E3
Mora Spain 53 E4
Mora Sweden 41 I6
Mora *MN* U.S.A. 126 E2
Mora *NM* U.S.A. 123 G6
Mora *r.* U.S.A. 123 G6
Moradabad India 78 D3
Morada Nova Brazil 139 K5
Moraine Lake Canada 117 J1
Moraleda, Canal *sea chan.* Chile 140 B6
Moram India 80 C2
Moramanga Madag. 95 E5
Moran U.S.A. 122 F4
Moranbah Australia 106 E4
Morang Nepal *see* Biratnagar
Morar, Loch *l.* U.K. 46 D4
Morari, Tso *l.* Jammu and Kashmir 78 D2
Moratuwa Sri Lanka 80 C5
Moravia *reg.* Czech Rep. 43 P6
Moravia U.S.A. 131 G2
Morawa Australia 105 A7
Moray Firth *b.* U.K. 46 E3
Moray Range *hills* Australia 104 E3
Morbach Germany 48 H5
Morbeng S. Africa *see* Soekmekaar
Morbi India 78 B5
Morcenx France 52 D4
Morcillo Mex. 127 B7
Mordaga China 69 M2
Mor Dağı *mt.* Turkey 87 G3
Morden Canada 117 L5
Mordovo Rus. Fed. 39 I5
Moreau *r.* U.S.A. 126 C2
Moreau, South Fork *r.* U.S.A. 126 C2
Morecambe U.K. 44 E4
Morecambe Bay U.K. 44 D4
Moree Australia 108 D2
Morehead P.N.G. 65 K8
Morehead U.S.A. 130 D4
Morehead City U.S.A. 133 I2
Moreland U.S.A. 130 C5
More Laptevykh *sea* Rus. Fed. *see* Laptev Sea
Morelia Mex. 132 D5
Morella Australia 106 C4
Morella Spain 53 F3
Morelos Mex. 123 G8
Morena India 78 D4
Morena, Sierra *mts* Spain 53 C5
Morenci *AZ* U.S.A. 125 I5
Morenci *MI* U.S.A. 130 C3
Moreni Romania 55 K2
Moreno Mex. 123 F7
Moreno Valley U.S.A. 124 E5
Moresby, Mount Canada 116 C4
Moresby Island Canada 116 C4
Moreswe Pan *salt pan* Botswana 96 G2
Moreton Bay Australia 108 F1
Moreton-in-Marsh U.K. 45 F7
Moreton Island Australia 108 F1
Moreton Island National Park Australia 108 F1
Moreuil France 48 C5
Morez France 52 H3
Morfou Cyprus 81 A2
Morfou Bay Cyprus 81 A2
Morgan U.S.A. 122 F4

Morgan City U.S.A. **127** F6
Morgan Hill U.S.A. **124** C3
Morganton U.S.A. **128** D5
Morgantown *KY* U.S.A. **130** B5
Morgantown *WV* U.S.A. **130** F4
Morgenzon S. Africa **97** I4
Morges Switz. **52** H3
Morhar *r.* India **79** F4
Mori China **76** H3
Mori Japan **70** F4
Moriah, Mount U.S.A. **125** F2
Moriarty's Range *hills* Australia **108** B2
Morice Lake Canada **116** E4
Morichal Col. **138** D3
Morihong Shan *mt.* China **70** B4
Morija Lesotho **97** H5
Morin Dawa China *see* **Nirji**
Moringen Germany **49** J3
Morioka Japan **71** F5
Moris Mex. **123** F7
Morisset Australia **108** E4
Moriyoshi-zan *vol.* Japan **71** F5
Morjärv Sweden **40** M3
Morjen *r.* Pak. **85** F4
Morki Rus. Fed. **38** K4
Morlaix France **52** C2
Morley U.K. **44** F5
Mormam Flat Dam U.S.A. **125** H5
Mormant France **48** C6
Mormon Lake U.S.A. **125** H4
Mormugao India *see* **Marmagao**
Morne Diablotins *vol.* Dominica **133** L5
Morney *watercourse* Australia **106** C5
Mornington, Isla *i.* Chile **140** A7
Mornington Abyssal Plain *sea feature* S. Atlantic Ocean **144** C9
Mornington Island Australia **106** B3
Mornington Peninsula National Park Australia **108** B7
Moro Pak. **85** G5
Moro U.S.A. **122** C3
Morobe P.N.G. **65** L8
▶**Morocco** *country* Africa **92** C1
africa **7, 90–91**
Morocco U.S.A. **130** B3
Morococala *mt.* Bol. **138** E7
Morogoro Tanz. **95** D4
Moro Gulf Phil. **65** G5
Morojaneng S. Africa **97** H5
Morokweng S. Africa **96** F4
Morombe Madag. **95** E6
Morón Cuba **129** E8
Mörön Mongolia **76** J2
Morondava Madag. **95** E6
Morón de la Frontera Spain **53** D5

▶**Moroni** Comoros **95** E5
Capital of the Comoros.

Moroni U.S.A. **125** H2
Moron Us He *r.* China *see* **Tongtian He**
Morotai *i.* Indon. **65** H6
Moroto Uganda **94** D3
Morozovsk Rus. Fed. **39** I6
Morpeth Canada **130** E2
Morpeth U.K. **44** F3
Morphou Cyprus *see* **Morfou**
Morrill U.S.A. **130** C5
Morrilton U.S.A. **127** E5
Morrin Canada **117** H5
Morrinhos Brazil **141** A2
Morris Canada **117** L5
Morris *IL* U.S.A. **126** F3
Morris *MN* U.S.A. **126** E2
Morris *PA* U.S.A. **131** G3

▶**Morris Jesup, Kap** *c.* Greenland **149** I1
Most northerly point of North America.

Morrison U.S.A. **126** F3
Morristown *AZ* U.S.A. **125** G5
Morristown *NJ* U.S.A. **131** H3
Morristown *NY* U.S.A. **131** H1
Morristown *TN* U.S.A. **128** D4
Morrisville U.S.A. **131** H2
Morro Brazil **141** B2
Morro Bay U.S.A. **124** C4
Morro d'Anta Brazil **141** D2
Morro do Chapéu Brazil **139** J6
Morro Grande *hill* Brazil **139** H4
Morrosquillo, Golfo de *b.* Col. **138** C2
Morrumbene Moz. **97** L2
Morschen Germany **49** J3
Morse Canada **117** J5
Morse U.S.A. **127** C4
Morse, Cape Antarctica **148** G2
Morse Reservoir U.S.A. **130** B3
Morshanka Rus. Fed. **39** I5
Morshansk Rus. Fed. *see* **Morshanka**
Morsott Alg. **54** C7
Mort *watercourse* Australia **106** C4
Mortagne-au-Perche France **52** E2
Mortagne-sur-Sèvre France **52** D3
Mortara Italy **54** C2
Mortehoe U.K. **45** C7
Morteros Arg. **140** D4
Mortes, Rio das *r.* Brazil **141** A1
Mortimer's Bahamas **129** F8
Mortlake Australia **108** A7
Mortlock Islands Micronesia **146** G5
Mortlock Islands P.N.G. *see* **Tauu Islands**
Morton U.K. **45** G6
Morton *TX* U.S.A. **127** C5
Morton *WA* U.S.A. **122** C3
Morton National Park Australia **108** E5
Morundah Australia **108** C5
Morupule Botswana **97** H2
Moruroa *atoll* Fr. Polynesia *see* **Mururoa**
Moruya Australia **108** E5
Morven Australia **107** D5
Morven *hill* U.K. **46** F2
Morvern *reg.* U.K. **46** D4
Morvi India *see* **Morbi**
Morwara India **78** B4
Morwell Australia **108** C7
Morzhovets, Ostrov *i.* Rus. Fed. **38** I2
Mosbach Germany **49** J5
Mosborough U.K. **44** F5
Mosby U.S.A. **122** G3

▶**Moscow** Rus. Fed. **38** H5
Capital of the Russian Federation and 3rd most populous city in Europe.

Moscow *ID* U.S.A. **122** D3
Moscow *PA* U.S.A. **131** H3
Moscow University Ice Shelf Antarctica **148** G2
Mosel *r.* Germany **49** H4
Moselebe *watercourse* Botswana **96** F3
Moselle *r.* France **48** G5
Möser Germany **49** L2
Moses, Mount U.S.A. **124** E1
Moses Lake U.S.A. **122** D3
Mosgiel N.Z. **109** C7
Moshaweng *watercourse* S. Africa **96** F4
Moshchnyy, Ostrov *i.* Rus. Fed. **41** O7
Moshi Tanz. **94** D4
Mosh'yuga Rus. Fed. **38** L2
Mosi-oa-Tunya *waterfall* Zambia/Zimbabwe *see* **Victoria Falls**
Mosjøen Norway **40** H4
Moskal'vo Rus. Fed. **70** F1
Moskenesøy *i.* Norway **40** H3
Moskva Rus. Fed. *see* **Moscow**
Moskva Tajik. **85** H2
Mosonmagyaróvár Hungary **43** P7
Mosquera Col. **138** C3
Mosquero U.S.A. **123** G6
Mosquito *r.* Brazil **141** C1
Mosquito Creek Lake U.S.A. **130** E3
Mosquito Lake Canada **117** K2
Moss Norway **41** G7
Mossâmedes Angola *see* **Namibe**
Mossat U.K. **46** G3
Mossburn N.Z. **109** B7
Mosselbaai S. Africa *see* **Mossel Bay**
Mossel Bay S. Africa **96** F8
Mossel Bay *b.* S. Africa **96** F8
Mossgiel Australia **108** B4
Mossman Australia **106** D3
Mossoró Brazil **139** K5
Moss Vale Australia **108** E5
Mossy *r.* Canada **117** K4
Most Czech Rep. **43** N5
Mostaganem Alg. **53** G6
Mostar Bos.-Herz. **54** G3
Mostoos Hills Canada **117** I4
Mostovskoy Rus. Fed. **87** F1
Mosty Belarus *see* **Masty**
Mosul Iraq **87** F3
Møsvatnet *l.* Norway **41** F7
Motala Sweden **41** I7
Motaze Moz. **97** K3
Motetema S. Africa **97** I3
Moth India **78** D4
Motherwell U.K. **46** F5
Motian Ling *hill* China **70** A4
Motihari India **79** F4
Motilla del Palancar Spain **53** F4
Motiti Island N.Z. **109** F3
Motokwe Botswana **96** F3
Motril Spain **53** E5
Motru Romania **55** J2
Mott U.S.A. **126** C2
Motu Ihupuku *i.* N.Z. *see* **Campbell Island**
Motul Mex. **132** G4
Mouaskar Alg. *see* **Mascara**
Mouding China **72** D3
Moudjéria Mauritania **92** B3
Moudros Greece **55** K5
Mouhijärvi Fin. **41** M6
Mouila Gabon **94** B4
Moulamein Australia **108** B5
Moulamein Creek *r.* Australia **108** A5
Moulavibazar Bangl. *see* **Moulvibazar**
Mould Bay Canada **114** G2
Moulèngui Binza Gabon **94** B4
Moulins France **52** F3
Moulmein Myanmar **66** B3
Moulouya, Oued *r.* Morocco **50** D4
Moultrie U.S.A. **129** D6
Moultrie, Lake U.S.A. **129** E5
Moulvibazar Bangl. **79** G4
Mound City *KS* U.S.A. **126** E4
Mound City *SD* U.S.A. **126** C2
Moundou Chad **93** E4
Moundsville U.S.A. **130** E4
Moŭng Roessei Cambodia **67** C4
Mount Abu India **78** C4
Mountain *r.* Canada **116** D1
Mountainair U.S.A. **123** G6
Mountain Brook U.S.A. **129** C5
Mountain City U.S.A. **130** E5
Mountain Home *AR* U.S.A. **127** E4
Mountain Home *ID* U.S.A. **122** E4
Mountain Home *UT* U.S.A. **125** H1
Mountain Lake Park U.S.A. **130** F4
Mountain View U.S.A. **127** E5
Mountain Zebra National Park S. Africa **97** G7
Mount Airy U.S.A. **130** E5
Mount Aspiring National Park N.Z. **109** B7
Mount Assiniboine Provincial Park Canada **116** H5
Mount Ayliff S. Africa **97** I6
Mount Ayr U.S.A. **126** E3
Mount Bellew Rep. of Ireland **47** D4
Mount Buffalo National Park Australia **108** C6
Mount Carmel U.S.A. **130** B4
Mount Carmel Junction U.S.A. **125** G3
Mount Cook National Park N.Z. **109** C6
Mount Coolon Australia **106** D4
Mount Darwin Zimbabwe **95** D5
Mount Denison Australia **104** F5
Mount Desert Island U.S.A. **128** G2
Mount Dutton Australia **107** A5
Mount Eba Australia **107** A6
Mount Elgon National Park Uganda **94** D3
Mount Fletcher S. Africa **97** I6
Mount Forest Canada **130** E2
Mount Frankland National Park Australia **105** B8
Mount Frere S. Africa **97** I6
Mount Gambier Australia **107** C8
Mount Gilead U.S.A. **130** D3
Mount Hagen P.N.G. **65** K8
Mount Holly U.S.A. **131** H4
Mount Hope Australia **108** B4
Mount Hope U.S.A. **130** E5
Mount Howitt Australia **107** C5
Mount Isa Australia **106** B4
Mount Jackson U.S.A. **131** F4
Mount Jewett U.S.A. **131** F3
Mount Joy U.S.A. **131** G3
Mount Kaputar National Park Australia **108** E3
Mount Keith Australia **105** C6
Mount Lofty Range *mts* Australia **107** B7
Mount Magnet Australia **105** B7
Mount Manara Australia **108** A4
Mount McKinley National Park U.S.A. *see* **Denali National Park and Preserve**
Mount Meadows Reservoir U.S.A. **124** C1
Mountmellick Rep. of Ireland **47** E4
Mount Moorosi Lesotho **97** H6
Mount Morgan Australia **106** E4
Mount Morris *MI* U.S.A. **130** D2
Mount Morris *NY* U.S.A. **131** G2
Mount Murchison Australia **108** A3
Mount Nebo U.S.A. **130** E4
Mount Olivet U.S.A. **130** C4
Mount Pearl Canada **119** L5
Mount Pleasant Canada **119** I5
Mount Pleasant *IA* U.S.A. **126** F3
Mount Pleasant *MI* U.S.A. **130** C2
Mount Pleasant *TX* U.S.A. **127** E5
Mount Pleasant *UT* U.S.A. **125** H2
Mount Rainier National Park U.S.A. **122** C3
Mount Remarkable National Park Australia **107** B7
Mount Revelstoke National Park Canada **116** G5
Mount Robson Provincial Park Canada **116** G4
Mount Rogers National Recreation Area *park* U.S.A. **130** E5
Mount Sanford Australia **104** E4
Mount's Bay U.K. **45** B8
Mount Shasta U.S.A. **122** C4
Mountsorrel U.K. **45** F6
Mount Sterling U.S.A. **130** D4
Mount St Helens National Volcanic Monument *nat. park* U.S.A. **122** C3
Mount Swan Australia **106** A4
Mount Union U.S.A. **131** G3
Mount Vernon Australia **105** B6
Mount Vernon *IL* U.S.A. **126** F4
Mount Vernon *IN* U.S.A. **128** C4
Mount Vernon *KY* U.S.A. **130** C5
Mount Vernon *MO* U.S.A. **127** E4
Mount Vernon *OH* U.S.A. **130** D3
Mount Vernon *TX* U.S.A. **127** E5
Mount Vernon *WA* U.S.A. **122** C2
Mount William National Park Australia **107** [inset]
Mount Willoughby Australia **105** F6
Moura Australia **106** E5
Moura Brazil **138** F4
Moura Port. **53** C4
Mourdi, Dépression du *depr.* Chad **93** F3
Mourdiah Mali **92** C3
Mourne *r.* U.K. **47** E3
Mourne Mountains *hills* U.K. **47** F3
Mousa *i.* U.K. **46** [inset]
Mouscron Belgium **48** D4
Mousgougou Chad **94** B2
Moussafoyo Chad **93** E4
Moussoro Chad **93** E3
Moutamba Congo **94** B4
Mouth of the Yangtze China **73** I2
Moutong Indon. **65** G6
Mouy France **48** C5
Mouydir, Monts du *plat.* Alg. **92** D2
Mouzon France **48** F5
Movas Mex. **123** F7
Mowbullan, Mount Australia **108** E1
Moxey Town Bahamas **129** E7
Moy *r.* Rep. of Ireland **47** C3
Moyale Eth. **94** D3
Moyen Atlas *mts* Morocco **50** C5
Moyen Congo *country* Africa *see* **Congo**
Moyeni Lesotho **97** H6
Moynalyk Rus. Fed. **76** I1
Moynaq Uzbek. *see* **Muynak**
Moyo *i.* Indon. **104** B2
Moyobamba Peru **138** C5
Moyock U.S.A. **131** G5
Moyola *r.* U.K. **47** F3
Moyu China **78** D1
Moyynkum Kazakh. **76** D3
Moyynkum, Peski *des.* Kazakh. **76** C3
Moyynty Kazakh. **76** D2
▶**Mozambique** *country* Africa **95** D6
africa **7, 90–91**
Mozambique Channel Africa **95** E6
Mozambique Ridge *sea feature* Indian Ocean **145** K7
Mozdok Rus. Fed. **87** G2
Mozdūrān Iran **85** F2
Mozhaysk Rus. Fed. **39** H5
Mozhga Rus. Fed. **38** L4
Mozhnābād Iran **85** F3
Mozo Myanmar **72** B4
Mozyr' Belarus *see* **Mazyr**
Mpaathutlwa Pan *salt pan* Botswana **96** E3
Mpanda Tanz. **95** D4
Mpen India **79** I4
Mpika Zambia **95** D5
Mpolweni S. Africa **97** J5
Mporokoso Zambia **95** D4
Mpulungu Zambia **95** D4
Mpumalanga *prov.* S. Africa **97** I4
Mpunde *mt.* Tanz. **95** D4
Mpwapwa Tanz. **95** D4
Mqanduli S. Africa **97** I6
Mqinvartsveri *mt.* Georgia/Rus. Fed. *see* **Kazbek**
Mrewa Zimbabwe *see* **Murehwa**
Mrkonjić-Grad Bos.-Herz. **54** G2
M'Saken Tunisia **54** D7
Mshinskaya Rus. Fed. **41** P7
M'Sila Alg. **53** I6
Msta *r.* Rus. Fed. **38** F4
Mstislavl' Belarus *see* **Mstsislaw**
Mstsislaw Belarus **39** F5
Mtelo Kenya **94** D3
Mtoko Zimbabwe *see* **Mutoko**
Mtorwi Tanz. **95** D4
Mtsensk Rus. Fed. **39** H5
Mts'ire Kavkasioni Asia *see* **Lesser Caucasus**
Mtubatuba S. Africa **97** K5
Mtunzini S. Africa **97** J5
Mtwara Tanz. **95** E5
Mu *r.* Myanmar **66** A2
Mu'āb, Jibāl *reg.* Jordan *see* **Moab**
Muanda Dem. Rep. Congo **95** B4
Muang Ham Laos **66** D2
Muang Hiam Laos **66** C2
Muang Hinboun Laos **66** D3
Muang Hôngsa Laos **66** C3
Muang Khammouan Laos **66** D3
Muang Khi Laos **66** C3
Muang Không Laos **67** D4
Muang Khoua Laos **66** C2
Muang Lamam Laos *see* **Ban Phon**
Muang Mok Laos **66** D3
Muang Ngoy Laos **66** C2
Muang Ou Nua Laos **66** C2
Muang Pakbeng Laos **66** C3
Muang Paktha Laos **66** C2
Muang Pakxan Laos *see* **Muang Xaignabouri**
Muang Phalan Laos **64** D3
Muang Phin Laos **66** D3
Muang Phôn-Hông Laos **66** C3
Muang Sam Sip Thai. **66** D4
Muang Sing Laos **66** C2
Muang Soum Laos **66** C3
Muang Souy Laos **66** C3
Muang Thadua Laos **66** C3
Muang Thai *country* Asia *see* **Thailand**
Muang Va Laos **66** C2
Muang Vangviang Laos **66** C3
Muang Xaignabouri Laos **66** C3
Muang Xaignabouri Laos **66** C3
Muang Xay Laos **66** C2
Muang Xon Laos **66** C2
Muar Malaysia **67** C7
Muarabungo Indon. **64** C7
Muarateweh Indon. **64** E7
Muari, Ras *pt* Pak. **85** G5
Mu'ayqil, Khashm al *hill* Saudi Arabia **84** C5
Mubarek Uzbek. **85** G2
Mubarraz *well* Saudi Arabia **87** F5
Mubende Uganda **94** D3
Mubi Nigeria **92** E3
Muborak Uzbek. *see* **Mubarek**
Mubur *i.* Indon. **67** D7
Mucajaí, Serra do *mts* Brazil **138** F3
Mucalic *r.* Canada **119** I2
Muccan Australia **104** C5
Much Germany **49** H4
Muchinga Escarpment Zambia **95** D5
Muchuan China **72** D2
Muck *i.* U.K. **46** C4
Mucojo Moz. **95** E5
Muconda Angola **95** C5
Mucubela Moz. **95** D5
Mucugê Brazil **141** C1
Mucur Turkey **86** D3
Mucuri Brazil **141** D2
Mucuri *r.* Brazil **141** D2
Mudabidri India **80** B3
Mudan China *see* **Heze**
Mudanjiang China **70** C3
Mudan Jiang *r.* China **70** C3
Mudan Ling *mts* China **70** B4
Mudanya Turkey **55** M4
Muḍaybī Oman **84** E6
Mudaysīsāt, Jabal al *hill* Jordan **81** C4
Muddus nationalpark *nat. park* Sweden **40** K3
Muddy *r.* U.S.A. **125** F3
Muddy Gap Pass U.S.A. **122** G4
Muddy Peak U.S.A. **125** F3
Mūd-e Dahanāb Iran **84** E3
Mudersbach Germany **49** H4
Mudgal India **80** C3
Mudgee Australia **108** D4
Mudhol India **80** B2
Mudigere India **80** B3
Mudjatik *r.* Canada **117** J3
Mud Lake U.S.A. **124** E3
Mudraya *country* Africa *see* **Egypt**
Mudurnu Turkey **55** N4
Mud'yuga Rus. Fed. **38** H3
Mueda Moz. **95** D5
Mueller Range *hills* Australia **104** D4
Muertos Cays *is* Bahamas **129** D7
Muftyuga Rus. Fed. **38** J2
Mufulira Zambia **95** C5
Mufumbwe Zambia **95** C5
Mufu Shan *mts* China **73** G2
Muğan Düzü *lowland* Azer. **87** H3
Mugarripug China **79** F2
Mughalbhin Pak. *see* **Jati**
Mughal Kot Pak. **85** H4
Mughal Sarai India **79** E4
Mūghār Iran **84** D3
Mughayrā' Saudi Arabia **81** C5
Mughayrā' well Saudi Arabia **84** B5
Muğla Turkey **55** M6
Mugodzhary, Gory *mts* Kazakh. **76** A2
Mugxung China **72** B1
Mūḥ, Sabkhat *imp. l.* Syria **81** D2
Muhammad Ashraf Pak. **85** H5
Muhammad Qol Sudan **82** E5
Muhammarah Iran *see* **Khorramshahr**
Muhashsham, Wādī al *watercourse* Egypt **81** B4
Muḥaysh, Wādī al *watercourse* Jordan **81** C5
Muhaysin Syria **81** D1
Mühlanger Germany **49** M3
Mühlberg Germany **49** N3
Mühlhausen (Thüringen) Germany **49** K3
Mühlig-Hofmann Mountains Antarctica **148** C2
Muhos Fin. **40** N4
Muḥradah Syria **81** C2
Muhri Pak. **85** G4
Mui Bai Bung *c.* Vietnam *see* **Mui Ca Mau**
Mui Ba Lang An *pt* Vietnam **66** E4
Mui Ca Mau *c.* Vietnam **67** D5
Mui Dinh *hd* Vietnam **67** E5
Mui Độc *pt* Vietnam **66** D3
Muié Angola **95** C5
Mui Kê *pt* Vietnam **67** E5
Mui Nây *pt* Vietnam **67** E4
Muineachán Rep. of Ireland *see* **Monaghan**
Muine Bheag Rep. of Ireland **47** F5
Muir U.S.A. **130** C2
Muirkirk U.K. **46** E5
Muir of Ord U.K. **46** E3
Mui Ron *hd* Vietnam **66** D3
Muite Moz. **95** D5
Muji China **78** D1
Muju S. Korea **71** B5
Mukacheve Ukr. **39** D6
Mukachevo Ukr. *see* **Mukacheve**
Mukah *Sarawak* Malaysia **64** E6
Mukalla Yemen **82** G7
Mukandwara India **78** D4
Mukdahan Thai. **66** D3
Mukden China *see* **Shenyang**
Muketei *r.* Canada **118** D3
Mukhen Rus. Fed. **70** E2
Mukhino Rus. Fed. **70** B1
Mukhtuya Rus. Fed. *see* **Lensk**
Mukinbudin Australia **105** B7
Mu Ko Chang Marine National Park Thai. **67** C5
Mukojima-rettō *is* Japan **71** F8
Mukry Turkm. **85** G2
Muktsar India **78** C3
Mukutawa *r.* Canada **117** L4
Mukwonago U.S.A. **130** A2
Mula *r.* India **80** B2
Mulakatholhu *atoll* Maldives *see* **Mulaku Atoll**
Mulaku Atoll Maldives **77** D11
Mulan China **70** C3
Mulanje, Mount Malawi **95** D5
Mulapula, Lake *salt flat* Australia **107** B6
Mulatos Mex. **123** F7
Mulayḥ Saudi Arabia **84** B5
Mulayḥah, Jabal *hill* U.A.E. **84** D5
Mulayz, Wādī al *watercourse* Egypt **81** A4
Mulchatna *r.* U.S.A. **114** C3
Mulde *r.* Germany **49** M3
Mule Creek *NM* U.S.A. **125** I5
Mule Creek *WY* U.S.A. **122** G4
Mulegé Mex. **123** E8
Mules *i.* Indon. **104** C2
Muleshoe U.S.A. **127** C5
Mulga Park Australia **105** E6
Mulgathing Australia **105** F7
Mulhacén *mt.* Spain **53** E5
Mülhausen France *see* **Mulhouse**
Mülheim an der Ruhr Germany **48** G3
Mulhouse France **52** H3
Muli China **72** D3
Muli Rus. Fed. *see* **Vysokogorniy**
Mulia Indon. **65** J7
Muling *Heilong.* China **70** C3
Muling *Heilong.* China **70** C3
Muling He *r.* China **70** D3
Mull *i.* U.K. **46** D4
Mull, Sound of *sea chan.* U.K. **46** C4
Mullaghcleevaun *hill* Rep. of Ireland **47** F4
Mullaittivu Sri Lanka **80** D4
Mullaley Australia **108** D3
Mullengudgery Australia **108** C3
Mullens U.S.A. **130** E5
Muller *watercourse* Australia **104** F5
Muller, Pegunungan *mts* Indon. **64** E6
Mullett Lake U.S.A. **130** C1
Mullewa Australia **105** A7
Mullica *r.* U.S.A. **131** H4
Mullingar Rep. of Ireland **47** E4
Mullion Creek Australia **108** D4
Mull of Galloway *c.* U.K. **46** E6
Mull of Kintyre *hd* U.K. **46** D5
Mull of Oa *hd* U.K. **46** C5
Mullumbimby Australia **108** F2
Mulobezi Zambia **95** C5
Mulshi Lake India **80** B2
Multai India **78** D5
Multan Pak. **85** H4
Multia Fin. **40** N5
Multien *reg.* France **48** C6
Mulug India **80** C2

▶**Mumbai** India **80** B2
2nd most populous city in Asia and 5th in the world.

Mumbil Australia **108** D4
Mumbwa Zambia **95** C5
Muminabad Tajik. *see* **Leningrad**
Mŭ'minobod Tajik. *see* **Leningrad**
Mun, Mae Nam *r.* Thai. **66** D4
Muna *i.* Indon. **65** G8
Muna Mex. **132** G4
Muna *r.* Rus. Fed. **61** N3
Munabao Pak. **85** H5
Munaðarnes Iceland **40** [inset]
Münchberg Germany **49** L4
München Germany *see* **Munich**
München-Gladbach Germany *see* **Mönchengladbach**
Münchhausen Germany **49** I4
Muncho Lake Canada **116** E3
Muncie U.S.A. **130** C3
Muncoonie West, Lake *salt flat* Australia **106** B5
Muncy U.S.A. **131** G3
Munda Pak. **85** H4
Mundel Lake Sri Lanka **80** C5
Mundesley U.K. **45** I6
Mundford U.K. **45** H6
Mundiwindi Australia **105** C5
Mundra India **78** B5
Mundrabilla Australia **102** C5
Munds Park U.S.A. **125** H4
Mundubbera Australia **107** E5
Mundwa India **78** C4
Munfordville U.S.A. **130** C5
Mungallala Australia **107** D5
Mungana Australia **106** D3
Mungári Moz. **95** D5
Mungbere Dem. Rep. Congo **94** C3
Mungeli India **79** E5
Munger India **79** F4
Mu Nggava *i.* Solomon Is *see* **Rennell**
Mungindi Australia **108** D2
Mungla Bangl. *see* **Mongla**
Mungo Angola **95** B5
Mungo, Lake Australia **108** A4
Mungo National Park Australia **108** A4
Munich Germany **43** M6
Munising U.S.A. **128** C2
Munjpur India **78** B5
Munkács Ukr. *see* **Mukacheve**
Munkedal Sweden **41** G7
Munkelva Norway **40** P2
Munkfors Sweden **41** H7
Munkhafaḍ al Qaṭṭārah *depr.* Egypt *see* **Qattara Depression**
Munku-Sardyk, Gora *mt.* Mongolia/Rus. Fed. **68** I2
Münnerstadt Germany **49** K4
Munnik S. Africa **97** I2
Munroe Lake Canada **117** L3
Munsan S. Korea **71** B5
Münster *Hessen* Germany **49** I5
Münster *Niedersachsen* Germany **49** K2
Münster *Nordrhein-Westfalen* Germany **49** H3
Munster *reg.* Rep. of Ireland **47** D5
Münsterland *reg.* Germany **49** H3
Muntadgin Australia **105** B7
Munyal-Par *sea feature* India *see* **Bassas de Pedro Padua Bank**
Munzur Vadisi Milli Parkı *nat. park* Turkey **51** L4
Muojärvi *l.* Fin. **40** P4
Mương Lam Vietnam **66** D3
Mương Nhie Vietnam **66** C2
Muong Sai Laos *see* **Muang Xay**
Muonio Fin. **40** M3
Muonioälven *r.* Fin./Sweden **40** M3
Muonionjoki *r.* Fin./Sweden *see* **Muonioälven**
Mupa, Parque Nacional da *nat. park* Angola **95** B5
Muping China *see* **Baoxing**
Muqaynimah *well* Saudi Arabia **84** C6
Muqdisho Somalia *see* **Mogadishu**
Muquem Brazil **141** A1
Muqui Brazil **141** C3
Mur *r.* Austria **43** P7
also known as Mura (Croatia/Slovenia)
Mura *r.* Croatia/Slovenia *see* **Mur**
Murai, Tanjong *pt* Sing. **67** [inset]
Murai Reservoir Sing. **67** [inset]
Murakami Japan **71** E5
Murallón, Cerro *mt.* Chile **140** B7
Muramvya Burundi **94** C4
Murashi Rus. Fed. **38** K4
Murat *r.* Turkey **87** E3
Muratlı Turkey **55** L4
Muraysah, Ra's al *pt* Libya **86** B5
Murchison *watercourse* Australia **105** A6
Murchison, Mount Antarctica **148** H2
Murchison, Mount *hill* Australia **105** B6
Murchison Falls National Park Uganda **94** D3
Murcia Spain **53** F5
Murcia *aut. comm.* Spain **53** F5
Murdo U.S.A. **126** C3
Murehwa Zimbabwe **95** D5
Mureșul *r.* Romania **55** I1
Muret France **52** E5
Murewa Zimbabwe *see* **Murehwa**
Murfreesboro *AR* U.S.A. **127** E5
Murfreesboro *TN* U.S.A. **128** C5
Murg *r.* Germany **49** I6
Murgab Tajik. *see* **Murghob**
Murgab Turkm. *see* **Murgap**
Murgab *r.* Turkm. *see* **Murgap**
Murgap Turkm. **85** F2
Murgap *r.* Turkm. **83** J2
Murghab *r.* Afgh. **85** F3
Murghab *reg.* Afgh. **85** F3
Murgha Kibzai Pak. **85** H4
Murghob Tajik. **85** I2
Murgh Pass Afgh. **85** H3
Murgon Australia **107** E5
Murgoo Australia **105** B6
Muri India **79** F5
Muriaé Brazil **141** C3
Murid Pak. **85** G4
Muriege Angola **95** C4
Müritz *l.* Germany **49** M1
Müritz, Nationalpark *nat. park* Germany **49** N1
Murmansk Rus. Fed. **40** R2
Murmanskaya Oblast' *admin. div.* Rus. Fed. **40** S2
Murmanskiy Bereg *coastal area* Rus. Fed. **38** G1
Murmansk Oblast *admin. div.* Rus. Fed. *see* **Murmanskaya Oblast'**
Muro, Capo di *c. Corsica* France **52** I6
Murom Rus. Fed. **38** I5
Muroran Japan **70** F4
Muros Spain **53** B2
Muroto Japan **71** D6
Muroto-zaki *pt* Japan **71** D6
Murphy *ID* U.S.A. **122** D4
Murphy *NC* U.S.A. **129** D5
Murphysboro U.S.A. **126** F4
Murrah *reg.* Saudi Arabia **84** C6
Murrah al Kubrá, Al Buḥayrah al *l.* Egypt *see* **Great Bitter Lake**
Murrah aṣ Ṣughrá, Al Buḥayrah al *l.* Egypt *see* **Little Bitter Lake**
Murra Murra Australia **108** C2
Murrat el Kubra, Buheirat *l.* Egypt *see* **Great Bitter Lake**
Murrat el Sughra, Buheirat *l.* Egypt *see* **Little Bitter Lake**

▶**Murray** *r. S.A.* Australia **107** B7
3rd longest river in Oceania. Part of the longest (Murray-Darling).

Murray *r. W.A.* Australia **105** A8
Murray *KY* U.S.A. **127** F4
Murray *UT* U.S.A. **125** H1
Murray, Lake P.N.G. **65** K8
Murray, Lake U.S.A. **129** D5
Murray, Mount Canada **116** D2
Murray Bridge Australia **107** B7

▶**Murray-Darling** *r.* Austr. **102** E5
Longest river and largest drainage basin in Oceania.
oceania **98–99**

Murray Downs Australia **104** F5
Murray Range *hills* Australia **105** E6
Murraysburg S. Africa **96** F6
Murray Sunset National Park Australia **107** C7
Murrhardt Germany **49** J6
Murrieta U.S.A. **124** E5
Murringo Australia **108** D5
Murrisk *reg.* Rep. of Ireland **47** C4
Murroogh Rep. of Ireland **47** C4

▶**Murrumbidgee** *r.* Australia **108** A5
4th longest river in Oceania.

Murrumburrah Australia **108** D5
Murrurundi Australia **108** E3
Mursan India **78** D4
Murshidabad India **79** G4
Murska Sobota Slovenia **54** G1
Mūrt Iran **85** F5
Murtoa Australia **107** C8
Murua *i.* P.N.G. *see* **Woodlark Island**
Murud India **80** B2
Murud, Gunung *mt.* Indon. **64** F6
Murunkan Sri Lanka **80** D4
Murupara N.Z. **109** F4
Mururoa *atoll* Fr. Polynesia **147** K7
Murviedro Spain *see* **Sagunto**
Murwara India **78** E5
Murwillumbah Australia **108** F2
Murzechirla Turkm. **85** F2
Murzūq Libya **93** E2
Mürzzuschlag Austria **43** O7
Muş Turkey **87** F3
Mūsā, Khowr-e *b.* Iran **84** C4
Musa Khel Bazar Pak. **85** H4
Musala *mt.* Bulg. **55** J3
Musala *i.* Indon. **67** B7
Musan N. Korea **70** C4
Musandam Peninsula Oman/U.A.E. **84** E5
Mūsá Qal'eh, Rūd-e *r.* Afgh. **85** G3
Musay'īd Qatar *see* **Umm Sa'id**

▶**Muscat** Oman **84** E6
Capital of Oman.

Muscat *reg.* Oman **84** E5
Muscat and Oman *country* Asia *see* **Oman**
Muscatine U.S.A. **126** F3

Musgrave Australia 106 C2
Musgrave Harbour Canada 119 L4
Musgrave Ranges mts Australia 105 E6
Mushāsh al Kabid well Jordan 81 C5
Mushayyish, Wādī al watercourse Jordan 81 C4
Mushie Dem. Rep. Congo 94 B4
Mushkaf Pak. 85 G4
Music Mountain U.S.A. 125 G4
Musinia Peak U.S.A. 125 H2
Muskeg r. Canada 116 F2
Muskeget Channel U.S.A. 131 J3
Muskegon MI U.S.A. 128 C3
Muskegon MI U.S.A. 130 B2
Muskegon r. U.S.A. 130 B2
Muskegon Heights U.S.A. 130 B2
Muskeg River Canada 116 G4
Muskogee U.S.A. 127 E5
Muskoka, Lake Canada 130 F1
Muskrat Dam Lake Canada 117 N4
Musmar Sudan 82 E6
Musoma Tanz. 94 D4
Musquanousse, Lac l. Canada 119 J4
Musquaro, Lac l. Canada 119 J4
Mussau Island P.N.G. 65 L7
Musselburgh U.K. 46 F5
Musselkanaal Neth. 48 H2
Musselshell r. U.S.A. 122 G3
Mussende Angola 95 B5
Mustafakemalpaşa Turkey 55 M4
Mustjala Estonia 41 M7
Mustvee Estonia 41 O7
Musu-dan pt N. Korea 70 C4
Muswellbrook Australia 108 E4
Muṭ Egypt 82 C4
Mut Turkey 81 A1
Mutá, Ponta do pt Brazil 141 D1
Mutare Zimbabwe 95 D5
Mutayr reg. Saudi Arabia 84 B5
Mutina Italy see Modena
Muting Indon. 65 K8
Mutis Col. 138 C2
Mutnyy Materik Rus. Fed. 38 L2
Mutoko Zimbabwe 95 D5
Mutsamudu Comoros 95 E5
Mutsu Japan 70 F4
Muttaburra Australia 106 D4
Muttonbird Islands N.Z. 109 A8
Mutton Island Rep. of Ireland 47 C5
Muttukuru India 80 D3
Muttupet India 80 C4
Mutum Brazil 141 C2
Mutunópolis Brazil 141 A1
Mutur Sri Lanka 80 D4
Mutusjärvi r. Fin. 40 O2
Muurola Fin. 40 N3
Mu Us Shamo des. China 69 J5
Muxaluando Angola 95 B4
Muxi China see Muchuan
Muxima Angola 95 B4
Muyezerskiy Rus. Fed. 40 R5
Muyinga Burundi 94 D4
Muynak Uzbek. 76 A3
Mŭynoq Uzbek. see Muynak
Muyumba Dem. Rep. Congo 95 C4
Muyunkum, Peski des. Kazakh. see Moyynkum, Peski
Muyuping China 73 F2
Muzaffarabad Pak. 85 I3
Muzaffargarh Pak. 85 H4
Muzaffarnagar India 78 D3
Muzaffarpur India 79 F4
Muzamane Moz. 97 K2
Muzhi Rus. Fed. 37 S2
Mūzīn Iran 85 F5
Muzon, Cape U.S.A. 116 C4
Múzquiz Mex. 127 C7
Muztag mt. China 78 E2
Muz Tag mt. China 79 F1
Muztagata mt. China 85 I2
Muztor Kyrg. see Toktogul
Mvadi Gabon 94 B3
Mvolo Sudan 93 F4
Mvuma Zimbabwe 95 D5
Mwanza Malawi 95 D5
Mwanza Tanz. 94 D4
Mweelrea hill Rep. of Ireland 47 C4
Mweka Dem. Rep. Congo 95 C4
Mwene-Ditu Dem. Rep. Congo 95 C4
Mwenezi Zimbabwe 95 D6
Mwenga Dem. Rep. Congo 94 C4
Mweru, Lake Dem. Rep. Congo/Zambia 95 C4
Mweru Wantipa National Park Zambia 95 C4
Mwimba Dem. Rep. Congo 95 C4
Mwinilunga Zambia 95 C5
Myadaung Myanmar 66 B2
Myadzyel Belarus 41 O9
Myajlar India 78 B4
Myall Lakes National Park Australia 108 F4
Myanaung Myanmar 66 A3
▶Myanmar country Asia 66 A2
asia 6, 58–59
Myauk-U Myanmar see Myohaung
Myaungmya Myanmar 66 A3
Myawadi Thai. 66 B3
Mybster U.K. 46 F2
Myebon Myanmar 66 A2
Myede Myanmar 66 A3
Myeik Myanmar see Mergui
Myingyan Myanmar 66 A2
Myinkyado Myanmar 66 B2
Myinmoletkat mt. Myanmar 67 B4
Myitkyina Myanmar 66 B1
Myitson Myanmar 66 B2
Myitta Myanmar 67 B4
Myittha Myanmar 66 B2
Mykolayiv Ukr. 55 O1
Mykonos i. Greece 55 K6
Myla Rus. Fed. 38 K2
Myla r. Rus. Fed. 38 K2
Mylae Sicily Italy see Milazzo
Mylasa Turkey see Milas
Mymensing Bangl. see Mymensingh
Mymensingh Bangl. 79 G4
Mynämäki Fin. 41 M6
Myohaung Myanmar 66 A2
Myŏnggan N. Korea 70 C4
Myory Belarus 41 O9
Mýrdalsjökull ice cap Iceland 40 [inset]
Myre Norway 40 I2
Myrheden Sweden 40 L4
Myrhorod Ukr. 39 G6
Myrnam Canada 117 I4
Myronivka Ukr. 39 F6
Myrtle Beach U.S.A. 129 E5
Myrtleford Australia 108 C6
Myrtle Point U.S.A. 122 B4
Mys Articheskiy c. Rus. Fed. 149 E1
Mysia reg. Turkey 55 L5
Mys Lazareva Rus. Fed. see Lazarev
Myślibórz Poland 43 O4
My Son Sanctuary tourist site Vietnam 66 E4
Mysore India 80 C3
Mysore state India see Karnataka
Mys Shmidta Rus. Fed. 61 T3
Mysy Rus. Fed. 38 L3
My Tho Vietnam 67 D5
Mytilene i. Greece see Lesbos
Mytilini Greece 55 L5
Mytilini Strait Greece/Turkey 55 L5
Mytishchi Rus. Fed. 38 H5
Myton U.S.A. 125 H1
Myyeldino Rus. Fed. 38 L3
Mzamomhle S. Africa 97 H6
Mže r. Czech Rep. 49 M5
Mzimba Malawi 95 D5
Mzuzu Malawi 95 D5

↓ N

Naab r. Germany 49 M5
Naalehu HI U.S.A. 123 [inset]
Naantali Fin. 41 M6
Naas Rep. of Ireland 47 F4
Naba Myanmar 66 B1
Nababeep S. Africa 96 C5
Nababganj Bangl. see Nawabganj
Nabadwip India see Navadwip
Nabarangapur India 80 D2
Nabarangpur India see Nabarangapur
Nabari Japan 71 E6
Nabatîyé et Tahta Lebanon 81 B3
Nabatiyet et Tahta Lebanon see Nabatîyé et Tahta
Nabberu, Lake salt flat Australia 105 C6
Nabburg Germany 49 M5
Naberera Tanz. 95 D4
Naberezhnyye Chelny Rus. Fed. 37 Q4
Nabesna U.S.A. 116 A2
Nabeul Tunisia 54 D6
Nabha India 78 D3
Nabil'skiy Zaliv lag. Rus. Fed. 70 F2
Nabire Indon. 65 J7
Nabi Younés, Ras en pt Lebanon 81 B3
Nāblus West Bank 81 B3
Naboomspruit S. Africa 97 I3
Nabq Reserve nature res. Egypt 86 D5
Nābulus West Bank see Nāblus
Nacala Moz. 95 E5
Nachalovo Rus. Fed. 39 K7
Nachicapau, Lac l. Canada 119 I2
Nachingwea Tanz. 95 D5
Nachna India 78 B4
Nachuge India 67 A5
Nacimiento Reservoir U.S.A. 124 C4
Naco U.S.A. 123 F7
Nacogdoches U.S.A. 127 E6
Nada China see Danzhou
Nadaleen r. Canada 116 C2
Nådendal Fin. see Naantali
Nadezhdinskoye Rus. Fed. 70 D2
Nadiad India 78 C5
Nadol India 78 C4
Nador Morocco 53 E6
Nadqān, Qalamat well Saudi Arabia 84 C6
Nadūshan Iran 84 D3
Nadvirna Ukr. 39 E6
Nadvoitsy Rus. Fed. 38 G3
Nadvornaya Ukr. see Nadvirna
Nadym Rus. Fed. 60 I3
Næstved Denmark 41 G9
Nafarroa aut. comm. Spain see Navarra
Nafas, Ra's an mt. Egypt 81 B5
Nafḥa, Har hill Israel 81 B4
Nafpaktos Greece 55 I5
Nafplio Greece 55 J6
Naftalan Azer. 87 G2
Naft-e Safid Iran 84 C4
Naft-e Shāh Iran see Naft Shahr
Naft Shahr Iran 84 B3
Nafūd ad Daḥl des. Saudi Arabia 84 B6
Nafūd al Ghuwayṭah des. Saudi Arabia 81 D5
Nafūd al Jur'ā des. Saudi Arabia 84 B5
Nafūd as Sirr des. Saudi Arabia 84 B5
Nafūd as Surrah des. Saudi Arabia 84 A6
Nafūd Qunayfidhah des. Saudi Arabia 84 B5
Nafūsah, Jabal hills Libya 92 E1
Nafy Saudi Arabia 82 F4
Nag, Co l. China 79 G2
Naga Phil. 65 G4
Nagagami r. Canada 118 D4
Nagagami Lake Canada 118 D4
Nagahama Japan 71 D6
Naga Hills India 79 H4
Naga Hills state India see Nagaland
Nagaland state India 79 H4
Nagamangala India 80 C3
Nagambie Australia 108 B6
Nagano Japan 71 E5
Nagaoka Japan 71 E5
Nagaon India 79 H4
Nagapatam India see Nagapattinam
Nagapattinam India 80 C4
Nagar Himachal Pradesh India 83 M3
Nagar Karnataka India 80 B3
Nagaram India 80 D2
Nagari Hills India 80 C3
Nagarjuna Sagar Reservoir India 80 C2
Nagar Parkar Pak. 85 H5
Nagasaki Japan 71 C6
Nagato Japan 71 C6
Nagaur India 78 C4
Nagbhir India 80 C1
Nagda India 78 C5
Nageezi U.S.A. 125 J3
Nagercoil India 80 C4
Nagha Kalat Pak. 85 G5
Nag' Ḥammādī Egypt see Naj' Ḥammādī
Nagina India 78 D3
Nagold r. Germany 49 I6
Nagong Chu r. China see Parlung Zangbo
Nagorno-Karabakh aut. reg. Azer. see Dağlıq Qarabağ
Nagornyy Karabakh aut. reg. Azer. see Dağlıq Qarabağ
Nagorsk Rus. Fed. 38 K4
Nagoya Japan 71 E6
Nagpur India 78 D5
Nagqu China 72 B2
Nag Qu r. China 72 B2
Nagurskoye Rus. Fed. 60 F1
Nagyatád Hungary 54 G1
Nagybecskerek Serb. and Mont. see Zrenjanin
Nagyenyed Romania see Aiud
Nagykanizsa Hungary 54 G1
Nagyvárad Romania see Oradea
Naha Japan 69 N7
Nahan India 78 D3
Nahanni Butte Canada 116 F2
Nahanni National Park Canada 116 E2
Nahanni Range mts Canada 116 F2
Naharāyim Jordan 81 B3
Nahariyya Israel 81 B3
Nahāvand Iran 84 C3
Nahr Dijlah r. Iraq/Syria 87 G5 see Tigris
Nahuel Huapi, Parque Nacional nat. park Arg. 140 B6
Nahunta U.S.A. 129 D6
Naica Mex. 127 B7
Nai Ga Myanmar 72 C3
Naij Tal China 79 H2
Naikliu Indon. 104 C2
Nain Canada 119 J2
Nā'īn Iran 84 D3
Nainital India 78 D3
Naini Tal India see Nainital
Nairn U.K. 46 F3
Nairn r. U.K. 46 F3

▶Nairobi Kenya 94 D4
Capital of Kenya.

Naissus Serb. and Mont. see Niš
Naivasha Kenya 94 D4
Najafābād Iran 84 C3
Na'jān Saudi Arabia 84 B5
Najd reg. Saudi Arabia 82 F4
Nájera Spain 53 E2
Naj' Ḥammādī Egypt 82 D4
Naji China 70 A2
Najibabad India 78 D3
Najin N. Korea 70 C4
Najitun China see Naji
Najrān Saudi Arabia 82 F6
Nakadōri-shima i. Japan 71 C6
Na Kae Thai. 66 D3
Nakambé r. Burkina/Ghana see White Volta
Nakanbe r. Burkina/Ghana see White Volta
Nakanno Rus. Fed. 61 L3
Nakano-shima i. Japan 71 D5
Nakasongola Uganda 93 G4
Nakatsu Japan 71 C6
Nakatsugawa Japan 71 E6
Nakfa Eritrea 82 E6
Nakhichevan' Azer. see Naxçıvan
Nakhl Egypt 81 A5
Nakhodka Rus. Fed. 70 D4
Nakhola India 79 H4
Nakhon Nayok Thai. 67 C4
Nakhon Pathom Thai. 67 C4
Nakhon Phanom Thai. 66 D3
Nakhon Ratchasima Thai. 66 C4
Nakhon Sawan Thai. 66 C4
Nakhon Si Thammarat Thai. 67 B5
Nakhtarana India 78 B5
Nakina Canada 118 D4
Nakina r. Canada 116 C3
Naknek U.S.A. 114 C4
Nakonde Zambia 95 D4
Nakskov Denmark 41 G9
Naktong-gang r. S. Korea 71 C6
Nakuru Kenya 94 D4
Nakusp Canada 116 G5
Nal Pak. 85 G5
Nal r. Pak. 85 G5
Na-lang Myanmar 66 B2
Nalázi Moz. 97 K3
Nalbari India 79 G4
Nal'chik Rus. Fed. 87 F2
Naldurg India 80 C2
Nalgonda India 80 C2
Naliya India 78 B5
Nallamala Hills India 80 C3
Nallıhan Turkey 55 N4
Nālūt Libya 92 E1
Namaacha Moz. 97 K3
Namacurra Moz. 95 D5
Namadgi National Park Australia 108 D5
Namahadi S. Africa 97 I4
Namak, Daryācheh-ye salt flat Iran 84 C3
Namak, Kavīr-e salt flat Iran 84 E3
Namakkal India 80 C4
Namakwaland reg. Namibia see Great Namaqualand
Namakzar-e Shadad salt flat Iran 84 E4
Namaland reg. Namibia see Great Namaqualand
Namangan Uzbek. 76 D3
Namaqualand reg. Namibia see Great Namaqualand
Namaqualand reg. S. Africa 96 C5
Namaqua National Park S. Africa 96 C6
Namas Indon. 65 K8
Namatanai P.N.G. 102 F2
Nambour Australia 108 F1
Nambucca Heads Australia 108 F3
Nambung National Park Australia 105 A7
Năm Căn Vietnam 67 D5
Namcha Barwa mt. China see Namjagbarwa Feng
Namche Bazar Nepal 79 F4
Nam Co salt l. China 79 G3
Namdalen valley Norway 40 H4
Namdalseid Norway 40 G4
Nam Đinh Vietnam 66 D2
Namen Belgium see Namur
Nam-gang r. N. Korea 71 B5
Namhae-do i. S. Korea 71 B6
Namhsan Myanmar 66 B2
Namib Desert Namibia 96 B3
Namibe Angola 95 B5
▶Namibia country Africa 95 B6
africa 7, 90–91
Namibia Abyssal Plain sea feature N. Atlantic Ocean 144 I8
Namib-Naukluft Game Park nature res. Namibia 96 B3
Namie Japan 71 F5
Namīn Iran 87 H3
Namjagbarwa Feng mt. China 72 B2
Namlan Myanmar 66 B2
Namlang r. Myanmar 66 B2
Nam Loi r. Myanmar see Nanlei He
Nam Nao National Park Thai. 66 C3
Nam Ngum Reservoir Laos 66 C3
Namoi r. Australia 108 D3
Namonuito atoll Micronesia 65 L5
Nampa mt. Nepal 78 E3
Nampa U.S.A. 122 D4
Nampala Mali 92 C3
Nam Phong Thai. 66 C3
Namp'o N. Korea 71 B5
Nampula Moz. 95 D5
Namsai Myanmar 66 B1
Namsang Myanmar 66 B2
Namsen r. Norway 40 G4
Nam She Tsim hill Hong Kong China see Sharp Peak
Namsos Norway 40 G4
Namti Myanmar 66 B1
Namtok Myanmar 66 B3
Namtok Chattakan National Park Thai. 66 C3
Namton Myanmar 66 B2
Namtsy Rus. Fed. 61 N3
Namtu Myanmar 66 B2
Namu Canada 116 E5
Namuli, Monte mt. Moz. 95 D5
Namuno Moz. 95 D5
Namur Belgium 48 E4
Namutoni Namibia 95 B5
Namwŏn S. Korea 71 B6
Namya Ra Myanmar 66 B1
Namyit Island S. China Sea 64 E4
Nan Thai. 66 C3
Nana Bakassa Cent. Afr. Rep. 94 B3
Nanaimo Canada 116 F5
Nanam N. Korea 70 C4
Nan'an China 73 H3
Nanango Australia 108 F1
Nananib Plateau Namibia 96 C3
Nanao Japan 71 E5
Nanatsu-shima i. Japan 71 E5
Nanbai China see Zunyi
Nanbin China see Shizhu
Nanbu China 72 E2
Nancha China 70 C3
Nanchang Jiangxi China 73 G2
Nanchang Jiangxi China 73 G2
Nanchong China 72 E2
Nanchuan China 72 E2
Nancowry i. India 67 A6
Nancun China 73 G1
Nancy France 48 G6
Nancy (Essey) airport France 48 G6
Nanda Devi mt. India 78 E3
Nanda Kot mt. India 78 E3
Nandan China 72 E3
Nandapur India 80 D2
Nanded India 80 C2
Nander India see Nanded
Nandewar Range mts Australia 108 E3
Nandod India 80 B1
Nandurbar India 78 C5
Nandyal India 80 C3
Nanfeng Guangdong China 73 F4
Nanfeng Jiangxi China 73 H3
Nang China 72 B2
Nanga Eboko Cameroon 92 E4
Nanga Parbat mt. Jammu and Kashmir 78 C2
Nangar National Park Australia 108 D4
Nangatayap Indon. 64 E7
Nangin Myanmar 67 B5
Nangnim-sanmaek mts N. Korea 71 B4
Nangqên China 72 C1
Nangulangwa Tanz. 95 D4
Nanguneri India 80 C4
Nanhua China 72 D3
Nanhui China 73 I2
Nanjian China 72 D3
Nanjiang China 72 E1
Nanjing China 73 H1
Nanji Shan i. China 73 I3
Nanka Jiang r. China 72 C4
Nankang China 73 G3
Nanking China see Nanjing
Nankova Angola 95 B5
Nanlei He r. China 72 C4
also known as Nam Loi (Myanmar)
Nanling China 73 H2
Nan Ling mts China 73 F3
Nanliu Jiang r. China 73 F4
Nanlong China see Nanbu
Nannilam India 80 C4
Nannine Australia 105 B6
Nanning China 73 F4
Nannup Australia 105 A8
Na Noi Thai. 66 C3
Nanortalik Greenland 115 N3
Nanouki atoll Kiribati see Nonouti
Nanouti atoll Kiribati see Nonouti
Nanpan Jiang r. China 72 E3
Nanping China 73 H3
Nanpu China see Pucheng
Nanri Dao i. China 73 H3
Nansei-shotō is Japan see Ryukyu Islands
Nansen Basin sea feature Arctic Ocean 149 H1
Nansen Sound sea chan. Canada 115 I1
Nan-sha Ch'ün-tao is S. China Sea see Spratly Islands
Nanshan Island S. China Sea 64 F4
Nansha Qundao is S. China Sea see Spratly Islands
Nansio Tanz. 94 D4
Nantes France 52 D3
Nantes à Brest, Canal de France 52 C3
Nanteuil-le-Haudouin France 48 C5
Nanthi Kadal lag. Sri Lanka 80 D4
Nanticoke Canada 130 E2
Nanticoke U.S.A. 131 H4
Nantong China 73 I2
Nantou China 73 [inset]
Nant'ou Taiwan 73 I4
Nantucket U.S.A. 131 J3
Nantucket Island U.S.A. 131 K3
Nantucket Sound g. U.S.A. 131 J3
Nantwich U.K. 45 E5
Nanumaga i. Tuvalu see Nanumanga
Nanumanga i. Tuvalu 103 H2
Nanumea atoll Tuvalu 103 H2
Nanuque Brazil 141 C2
Nanusa, Kepulauan is Indon. 65 H6
Nanxi China 72 E2
Nanxian China 73 G2
Nanxiong China 73 G3
Nanyang China 73 G1
Nanyuki Kenya 94 D4
Nanzhang China 73 F2
Nanzhao China see Zhao'an
Nanzhou China see Nanxian
Naococane, Lac l. Canada 119 H3
Naoero country S. Pacific Ocean see Nauru
Naogaon Bangl. 79 G4
Naokot Pak. 85 H5
Naoli He r. China 70 D3
Naomid, Dasht-e des. Afgh./Iran 85 F3
Naoshera Jammu and Kashmir 78 C2
Napa U.S.A. 124 B2
Napaktulik Lake Canada 117 H1
Napanee Canada 131 G1
Napasoq Greenland 115 M3
Naperville U.S.A. 130 A3
Napier N.Z. 109 F4
Napier Range hills Australia 104 D4
Napierville Canada 131 I1
Naples Italy 54 F4
Naples FL U.S.A. 129 D7
Naples ME U.S.A. 131 J2
Naples TX U.S.A. 127 E5
Naples UT U.S.A. 125 I1
Napo China 72 E4
Napoleon IN U.S.A. 130 C4
Napoleon ND U.S.A. 126 D2
Napoleon OH U.S.A. 130 C3
Napoli Italy see Naples
Naqadeh Iran 84 B2
Nara India 78 B5
Nara Japan 71 D6
Nara Mali 92 C3
Narach Belarus 41 O9
Naracoorte Australia 107 C8
Naradhan Australia 108 C4
Narainpur India 80 D2
Naralua India 79 F4
Naranjal Ecuador 138 C4
Naranjo Mex. 123 F8
Narasapur India 80 D2
Narasaraopet India 80 D2
Narasinghapur India 80 E1
Narathiwat Thai. 67 C6
Nara Visa U.S.A. 127 C5
Narayanganj Bangl. 79 G5
Narayanganj India 78 E5
Narayangarh India 78 C4
Narbada r. India see Narmada
Narberth U.K. 45 C7
Narbo France see Narbonne
Narbonne France 52 F5
Narborough Island Galápagos Ecuador see Fernandina, Isla
Narcea r. Spain 53 C2
Narcondam Island India 67 A4
Nardò Italy 54 H4
Narechi r. Pak. 85 H4
Narembeen Australia 105 B8
Nares Abyssal Plain sea feature S. Atlantic Ocean 144 D4
Nares Deep sea feature N. Atlantic Ocean 144 D4
Nares Strait Canada/Greenland 115 K2
Naretha Australia 105 D7
Narew r. Poland 43 R4
Narib Namibia 96 C3
Narikel Jinjira i. Bangl. see St Martin's Island
Narimanov Rus. Fed. 39 J7
Narimskiy Khrebet mts Kazakh. see Narymskiy Khrebet
Narin Afgh. 85 H2
Narin reg. Afgh. 85 H2
Narince Turkey 86 E3
Narin Gol watercourse China 79 H1
Narizon, Punta pt Mex. 123 F8
Narkher India 78 D5
Narmada r. India 78 C5
Narman Turkey 87 F2
Narnaul India 78 D3
Narni Italy 54 E3
Narnia Italy see Narni
Narodnaya, Gora mt. Rus. Fed. 37 S3
Naro-Fominsk Rus. Fed. 39 H5
Narok Kenya 94 D4
Narooma Australia 108 E6
Narovchat Rus. Fed. 39 I5
Narowlya Belarus 39 F6
Närpes Fin. 40 L5
Narrabri Australia 108 D3
Narragansett Bay U.S.A. 131 J3
Narran r. Australia 108 C2
Narrandera Australia 108 C5
Narran Lake Australia 108 C2
Narrogin Australia 105 B8
Narromine Australia 108 D4
Narrows U.S.A. 130 E5
Narrowsburg U.S.A. 131 H3
Narsapur India 80 C2
Narsaq Greenland 115 N3
Narshingdi Bangl. see Narsingdi
Narsimhapur India see Narsinghpur
Narsingdi Bangl. 79 G5
Narsinghpur India 78 D5
Narsipatnam India 80 D2
Nartkala Rus. Fed. 87 F2
Naruto Japan 71 D6
Narva Estonia 41 P7
Narva Bay Estonia/Rus. Fed. 41 O7
Narva laht b. Estonia/Rus. Fed. see Narva Bay
Narva Reservoir resr Estonia/Rus. Fed. see Narvskoye Vodokhranilishche
Narva veehoidla resr Estonia/Rus. Fed. see Narvskoye Vodokhranilishche
Narvik Norway 40 J2
Narvskiy Zaliv b. Estonia/Rus. Fed. see Narva Bay
Narvskoye Vodokhranilishche resr Estonia/Rus. Fed. 41 P7
Narwana India 78 D3
Nar'yan-Mar Rus. Fed. 38 L2
Narymskiy Khrebet mts Kazakh. 76 F2
Naryn Kyrg. 76 E3
Näsåker Sweden 40 J5
Nashik India 80 B1
Nashua U.S.A. 131 J2
Nashville AR U.S.A. 127 E5
Nashville GA U.S.A. 129 D6
Nashville IN U.S.A. 130 B4
Nashville NC U.S.A. 128 E5
Nashville OH U.S.A. 130 D3

▶Nashville TN U.S.A. 128 C4
State capital of Tennessee.

Naṣīb Syria 81 C3
Näsijärvi l. Fin. 41 M6
Nasik India see Nashik
Nasir Pak. 85 H4
Nasir Sudan 82 D8
Nasirabad Bangl. see Mymensingh
Nasirabad India 78 C4
Naskaupi r. Canada 119 J3
Naṣr Egypt 86 C5
Nasratabad Iran see Zābol
Naṣrīān-e Pā'īn Iran 84 B3
Nass r. Canada 116 D4
Nassau r. Australia 106 C2

▶Nassau Bahamas 129 E7
Capital of The Bahamas.

Nassau i. Cook Is 103 J3
Nassau U.S.A. 131 I2
Nassawadox U.S.A. 131 H5
Nasser, Lake resr Egypt 82 D5
Nässjö Sweden 41 I8
Nassuttooq inlet Greenland 115 M3
Nastapoca r. Canada 118 F2
Nastapoka Islands Canada 118 F2
Nasugbu Phil. 65 G4
Nasva Rus. Fed. 38 F4
Nata Botswana 95 C6
Natal Brazil 139 K5
Natal Indon. 64 B6
Natal prov. S. Africa see Kwazulu-Natal
Natal Basin sea feature Indian Ocean 145 K8
Natal Drakensberg Park nat. park S. Africa 97 I5
Naṭanz Iran 84 C3
Natashquan Canada 119 J4
Natashquan r. Canada 119 J4
Natchez U.S.A. 127 F6
Natchitoches U.S.A. 127 E6
Nathalia Australia 108 B6
Nathia Gali Pak. 85 I3
Nati, Punta pt Spain 53 H3
Natillas Mex. 127 C7
National City U.S.A. 124 E5
National West Coast Tourist Recreation Area park Namibia 96 B2
Natitingou Benin 92 D3
Natividad, Isla i. Mex. 123 E8
Natividade Brazil 139 I6
Natkyizin Myanmar 66 B4
Natla r. Canada 116 D2
Natmauk Myanmar 66 A2
Nator Bangl. see Natore
Nátora Mex. 123 F7
Natore Bangl. 79 G4
Natori Japan 71 F5
Natron, Lake salt l. Tanz. 94 D4
Nattai National Park Australia 108 E5
Nattalin Myanmar 66 A3
Nattaung mt. Myanmar 66 B3
Na'tū Iran 85 F3
Natuna, Kepulauan is Indon. 67 D6
Natuna Besar i. Indon. 67 E6
Natural Bridges National Monument nat. park U.S.A. 125 H3
Naturaliste, Cape Australia 105 A8
Naturaliste Plateau sea feature Indian Ocean 145 P8
Naturita U.S.A. 125 I2
Nauchas Namibia 96 C2
Nau Co l. China 79 E2
Nauen Germany 49 M2
Naufragados, Ponta dos pt Brazil 141 A4
Naujoji Akmenė Lith. 41 M8
Naukh India 78 C4
Naumburg (Hessen) Germany 49 J3
Naumburg (Saale) Germany 49 L3
Naunglon Myanmar 66 B3
Naungpale Myanmar 66 B3
Naupada India 80 E2
Na'ūr Jordan 81 B4
Nauroz Kalat Pak. 85 G4
Naurskaya Rus. Fed. 87 G2
Nauru i. Nauru 103 G2
▶Nauru country S. Pacific Ocean 103 G2
oceania 8, 100–101
Naustdal Norway 41 D6
Nauta Peru 138 D4
Nautaca Uzbek. see Karshi
Naute Dam Namibia 96 C4
Nauzad Afgh. 85 G3
Nava Mex. 127 C6
Navadwip India 79 G5
Navahrudak Belarus 41 N10
Navajo Lake U.S.A. 125 J3
Navajo Mountain U.S.A. 125 H3
Navalmoral de la Mata Spain 53 D4
Navalvillar de Pela Spain 53 D4
Navan Rep. of Ireland 47 F4
Navangar India see Jamnagar
Navapolatsk Belarus 41 P9
Nāvar, Dasht-e depr. Afgh. 85 G3
Navarin, Mys c. Rus. Fed. 61 S3
Navarra aut. comm. Spain 53 F2
Navarra, Comunidad Foral de aut. comm. Spain see Navarra
Navarre Australia 108 A6
Navarre aut. comm. Spain see Navarra
Navarro r. U.S.A. 124 B2
Navashino Rus. Fed. 38 I5
Navasota U.S.A. 127 D6

▶Navassa Island terr. West Indies 133 I5
United States Unincorporated Territory.

Naver r. U.K. 46 E2
Näverede Sweden 40 I5
Navlakhi India 78 B5
Navlya Rus. Fed. 39 G5
Năvodari Romania 55 M2
Navoi Uzbek. 85 G1
Navoiy Uzbek. see Navoi
Navojoa Mex. 123 F8
Navolato Mex. 132 C4
Návpaktos Greece see Nafpaktos
Návplion Greece see Nafplio
Navşar Turkey see Şemdinli
Navsari India 80 B1
Nawá Syria 81 C3
Nawabganj Bangl. 79 G4
Nawabshah Pak. 85 H5
Nawada India 79 F4
Nāwah Afgh. 85 G3
Nawalgarh India 78 C4
Nawanshahr India 78 D3
Nawan Shehar India see Nawanshahr
Nawar, Dasht-i depr. Afgh. see Nāvar, Dasht-e
Nawarangpur India see Nabarangapur
Nawngcho Myanmar see Nawnghkio
Nawnghkio Myanmar 66 B2
Nawng Hpa Myanmar 66 B2
Nawngleng Myanmar 66 B2
Nawoiy Uzbek. see Navoi
Naxçıvan Azer. 87 G3
Naxos i. Greece 55 K6
Nayagarh India 80 E1
Nayak Afgh. 85 G3
Nayar Mex. 132 D4
Nāy Band, Kūh-e mt. Iran 84 E3

Nayong China 72 E3
Nayoro Japan 70 F3
Nazaré Brazil 141 D1
Nazareno Mex. 127 C7
Nazareth Israel 81 B3
Nazário Brazil 141 A2
Nazas Mex. 127 B7
Nazas r. Mex. 127 B7
Nazca Peru 138 D6
Nazca Ridge sea feature S. Pacific Ocean 147 O7
Nāzīl Iran 85 F4
Nazilli Turkey 55 M6
Nazimabad Pak. 85 G5
Nazımiye Turkey 87 E3
Nazir Hat Bangl. 79 G5
Nazko Canada 116 F4
Nazran' Rus. Fed. 87 G2
Nazrēt Eth. 94 D3
Nazwá Oman 84 E6
Ncojane Botswana 96 E2
N'dalatando Angola 95 B4
Ndélé Cent. Afr. Rep. 94 C3
Ndendé Gabon 94 B4
Ndende i. Solomon Is see Ndeni
Ndeni i. Solomon Is 103 G3

▶Ndjamena Chad 93 E3
Capital of Chad.

N'Djamena Chad see Ndjamena
Ndjouani i. Comoros see Nzwani
Ndoi i. Fiji see Doi
Ndola Zambia 95 C5
Nduke i. Solomon Is see Kolombangara
Ndwedwe S. Africa 97 J5
Ne, Hon i. Vietnam 66 D3
Neabul Creek r. Australia 108 C1
Neagh, Lough l. U.K. 47 F3
Neah Bay U.S.A. 122 B2
Neale, Lake salt flat Australia 105 E6
Nea Liosia Greece 55 J5
Neapoli Greece 55 J6
Neapolis Italy see Naples
Nea Roda Greece 55 J4
Neath U.K. 45 D7
Neath r. U.K. 45 D7
Nebbi Uganda 94 D3
Nebine Creek r. Australia 108 C2
Nebitdag Turkm. 84 D2
Neblina, Pico da mt. Brazil 138 E3
Nebo Australia 106 E4
Nebo, Mount U.S.A. 125 H2
Nebolchi Rus. Fed. 38 G4
Nebraska state U.S.A. 126 C3
Nebraska City U.S.A. 126 E3
Nebrodi, Monti mts Sicily Italy 54 F6
Neches r. U.S.A. 127 E6
Nechisar National Park Eth. 94 D3
Nechranice, Vodní nádrž resr Czech Rep. 49 N4
Neckar r. Germany 49 I5
Neckarsulm Germany 49 J5
Necker Island U.S.A. 146 J4
Necochea Arg. 140 E5
Nederland country Europe see Netherlands
Nederlandse Antillen terr. West Indies see Netherlands Antilles
Neder Rijn r. Neth. 48 F3
Nedlouc, Lac l. Canada 119 G2
Nedluk Lake Canada see Nedlouc, Lac
Nêdong China 79 G3
Nedre Soppero Sweden 40 L2
Nédroma Alg. 53 F6
Needle Mountain U.S.A. 122 F3
Needles U.S.A. 125 F4
Neemach India see Neemuch
Neemuch India 78 C4
Neenah U.S.A. 130 A1
Neepawa Canada 117 L5
Neergaard Lake Canada 115 J2
Neerijnen Neth. 48 F3
Neerpelt Belgium 48 F3
Neftçala Azer. 87 H3
Neftechala Azer. see 26 Bakı Komissarı
Neftechala Azer. see Neftçala
Neftegorsk Sakhalinskaya Oblast' Rus. Fed. 70 F1
Neftegorsk Samarskaya Oblast' Rus. Fed. 39 K5
Neftekamsk Rus. Fed. 37 Q4
Neftekumsk Rus. Fed. 87 G1
Nefteyugansk Rus. Fed. 60 I3
Neftezavodsk Turkm. see Seydi
Neftezawodsk Turkm. see Seydi
Nefyn U.K. 45 C6
Nefza Tunisia 54 C6
Negage Angola 95 B4
Negār Iran 84 E4
Negara Indon. 104 A2
Negēlē Eth. 94 D3
Negev des. Israel 81 B4
Negomane Moz. 95 D5
Negombo Sri Lanka 80 C5
Negotino Macedonia 55 J4
Negra, Cordillera mts Peru 138 C5
Negra, Punta pt Peru 138 B5
Negra, Serra mts Brazil 141 C2
Negrais, Cape Myanmar 66 A4
Négrine Alg. 54 B7
Negro r. Arg. 140 D6
Negro r. Brazil 139 G7
Negro r. Brazil 141 A4
Negro r. S. America 138 G4
Negro, Cabo c. Morocco 53 D6
Negroponte i. Greece see Evvoia
Negros i. Phil. 65 G5
Negru Vodă, Podișul plat. Romania 55 M3
Nehbandān Iran 85 F4
Nehe China 70 B2
Neijiang China 72 E2
Neilburg Canada 117 I4
Neimenggu aut. reg. China see Nei Mongol Zizhiqu
Nei Mongol Zizhiqu aut. reg. China 70 A2
Neinstedt Germany 49 L3
Neiva Col. 138 C3
Neixiang China 73 F1
Nejanilini Lake Canada 117 L3
Nejd reg. Saudi Arabia see Najd
Neka Iran 84 D2
Nek'emtē Eth. 94 D3
Nekrasovskoye Rus. Fed. 38 I4
Neksø Denmark 41 I9
Nelang India 78 D3
Nelia Australia 106 C4
Nelidovo Rus. Fed. 38 G4
Neligh U.S.A. 126 D3
Nel'kan Rus. Fed. 61 P3
Nellore India 80 C3
Nelluz watercourse Turkey 81 D1
Nel'ma Rus. Fed. 70 E3
Nelson Canada 116 G5
Nelson r. Canada 117 M3
Nelson N.Z. 109 D5
Nelson U.K. 44 E5
Nelson U.S.A. 125 G4
Nelson, Cape Australia 107 C8
Nelson, Cape P.N.G. 65 L8
Nelson, Estrecho strait Chile 140 A8
Nelson Bay Australia 108 F4
Nelson Forks Canada 116 F3
Nelsonia U.S.A. 131 H5
Nelson Lakes National Park N.Z. 109 D6
Nelson Reservoir U.S.A. 122 G2
Nelspruit S. Africa 97 J3
Néma Mauritania 92 C3
Nema Rus. Fed. 38 K4
Neman r. Belarus/Lith. see Nyoman
Neman Rus. Fed. 41 M9
Nemausus France see Nîmes
Nemawar India 78 D5
Nemed Rus. Fed. 38 L3
Nementcha, Monts des mts Alg. 54 B7
Nemetocenna France see Arras
Nemetskiy, Mys c. Rus. Fed. 40 Q2
Nemirov Ukr. see Nemyriv
Némiscau r. Canada 118 F4
Némiscau, Lac l. Canada 118 F4
Nemor He r. China 70 B2
Nemours Alg. see Ghazaouet
Nemours France 52 F2
Nemrut Dağı mt. Turkey 87 F3
Nemunas r. Lith. see Nyoman
Nemuro Japan 70 G4
Nemuro-kaikyō sea chan. Japan/Rus. Fed. 70 G4
Nemyriv Ukr. 39 F6
Nenagh Rep. of Ireland 47 D5
Nenana U.S.A. 114 D3
Nene r. U.K. 45 H6
Nenjiang China 70 B2
Nen Jiang r. China 70 B3
Neosho U.S.A. 127 E4
▶Nepal country Asia 79 E3
asia 6, 58–59
Nepalganj Nepal 79 E3
Nepean Canada 131 H1
Nepean, Point Australia 108 B7
Nephi U.S.A. 125 H2
Nephin hill Rep. of Ireland 47 C3
Nephin Beg Range hills Rep. of Ireland 47 C3
Nepisiguit r. Canada 119 I5
Nepoko r. Dem. Rep. Congo 94 C3
Nérac France 52 E4
Nerang Australia 108 F1
Nera Tso l. China 79 H3
Nerchinsk Rus. Fed. 69 L2
Nerekhta Rus. Fed. 38 I4
Néret, Lac l. Canada 119 H3
Neretva r. Bos.-Herz./Croatia 54 G3
Nêri Pünco l. China 79 G3
Neriquinha Angola 95 C5
Neris r. Lith. 41 M9 also known as Viliya (Belarus/Lithuania)
Nerl' r. Rus. Fed. 38 H4
Nerópolis Brazil 141 A2
Neryungri Rus. Fed. 61 N4
Nes Neth. 48 F1
Nes Norway 41 F6
Nes' Rus. Fed. 38 J2
Nesbyen Norway 41 F6
Neskaupstaður Iceland 40 [inset]
Nesle France 48 C5
Nesna Norway 40 H3
Nesri India 80 B2
Ness r. U.K. 46 E3
Ness, Loch l. U.K. 46 E3
Ness City U.S.A. 126 D4
Nesse r. Germany 49 K4
Nesselrode, Mount Canada/U.S.A. 116 C3
Nestor Falls Canada 117 M5
Nestos r. Greece 55 K4 also known as Mesta
Nesvizh Belarus see Nyasvizh
Netanya Israel 81 B3
▶Netherlands country Europe 48 F2
europe 5, 34–35

▶Netherlands Antilles terr. West Indies 133 K6
Self-governing Netherlands Territory.
north america 9, 112–113

Netphen Germany 49 I4
Netrakona Bangl. 79 G4
Netrokona Bangl. see Netrakona
Nettilling Lake Canada 115 K3
Neubrandenburg Germany 49 N1
Neuburg an der Donau Germany 49 L6
Neuchâtel Switz. 52 H3
Neuchâtel, Lac de l. Switz. 52 H3
Neuendettelsau Germany 49 K5
Neuenhaus Germany 48 G2
Neuenkirchen Germany 49 J1
Neuenkirchen (Oldenburg) Germany 49 I2
Neufchâteau Belgium 48 F5
Neufchâteau France 52 G2
Neufchâtel-en-Bray France 48 B5
Neufchâtel-Hardelot France 48 B4
Neuharlingersiel Germany 49 H1
Neuhausen Rus. Fed. see Gur'yevsk
Neuhof Germany 49 J4
Neu Kaliß Germany 49 L1
Neukirchen Hessen Germany 49 J4
Neukirchen Sachsen Germany 49 M4
Neukuhren Rus. Fed. see Pionerskiy
Neumarkt in der Oberpfalz Germany 49 L5
Neumayer research station Antarctica 148 B2
Neumünster Germany 43 L3
Neunburg vorm Wald Germany 49 M5
Neunkirchen Austria 43 P7
Neunkirchen Germany 49 H5
Neuquén Arg. 140 C5
Neuruppin Germany 49 M2
Neu Sandez Poland see Nowy Sącz
Neuse r. U.S.A. 129 E5
Neusiedler See l. Austria/Hungary 43 P7
Neusiedler See Seewinkel, Nationalpark nat. park Austria 43 P7
Neuss Germany 48 G3
Neustadt (Wied) Germany 49 H4
Neustadt am Rübenberge Germany 49 J2
Neustadt an der Aisch Germany 49 K5
Neustadt an der Hardt Germany see Neustadt an der Weinstraße
Neustadt an der Waldnaab Germany 49 M5
Neustadt an der Weinstraße Germany 49 I5
Neustadt bei Coburg Germany 49 L4
Neustadt-Glewe Germany 49 L1
Neustrelitz Germany 49 N1
Neutraubling Germany 49 M6
Neuville-lès-Dieppe France 48 B5
Neuwied Germany 49 H4
Neu Wulmstorf Germany 49 J1
Nevada IA U.S.A. 126 E3
Nevada MO U.S.A. 126 E4
Nevada state U.S.A. 122 D5
Nevada, Sierra mts Spain 53 E5
Nevada, Sierra mts U.S.A. 124 C1
Nevada City U.S.A. 124 C2
Nevado, Cerro mt. Arg. 140 C5
Nevado, Sierra del mts Arg. 140 C5
Nevasa India 80 B2
Nevatim Israel 81 B4
Nevdubstroy Rus. Fed. see Kirovsk
Nevel' Rus. Fed. 38 F4
Nevel'sk Rus. Fed. 70 F3
Never Rus. Fed. 70 B1
Nevers France 52 F3
Nevertire Australia 108 C3
Nevesinje Bos.-Herz. 54 H3
Nevinnomyssk Rus. Fed. 87 F1
Nevşehir Turkey 86 D3
Nevskoye Rus. Fed. 70 D3
New r. CA U.S.A. 125 F5
New r. WV U.S.A. 130 E5
Newala Tanz. 95 D5
New Albany IN U.S.A. 130 C4
New Albany MS U.S.A. 127 F5
New Amsterdam Guyana 139 G2
New Amsterdam U.S.A. see New York
New Angledool Australia 108 C2
Newark DE U.S.A. 131 H4
Newark NJ U.S.A. 131 H3
Newark NY U.S.A. 131 G2
Newark OH U.S.A. 130 D3
Newark airport U.S.A. 128 F3
Newark Lake U.S.A. 125 F2
Newark-on-Trent U.K. 45 G5
New Bedford U.S.A. 131 J3
Newberg U.S.A. 122 C3
New Berlin U.S.A. 131 H2
New Bern U.S.A. 129 E5
Newberry IN U.S.A. 130 B4
Newberry MI U.S.A. 128 C2
Newberry SC U.S.A. 129 D5
Newberry National Volcanic Monument nat. park U.S.A. 122 C4
Newberry Springs U.S.A. 124 E4
New Bethlehem U.S.A. 130 F3
Newbiggin-by-the-Sea U.K. 44 F3
New Bight Bahamas 129 F7
New Bloomfield U.S.A. 131 G3
Newboro Canada 131 G1
New Boston OH U.S.A. 130 D4
New Boston TX U.S.A. 127 E5
New Braunfels U.S.A. 127 D6
Newbridge Rep. of Ireland 47 F4
New Britain i. P.N.G. 65 L8
New Britain U.S.A. 131 I3
New Britain Trench sea feature S. Pacific Ocean 146 G6
New Brunswick prov. Canada 119 I5
New Brunswick U.S.A. 131 H3
New Buffalo U.S.A. 130 B3
Newburgh Canada 131 G1
Newburgh U.K. 46 G3
Newburgh U.S.A. 131 H3
Newbury U.K. 45 F7
Newburyport U.S.A. 131 J2
Newby Bridge U.K. 44 E4

▶New Caledonia terr. S. Pacific Ocean 103 G4
French Overseas Territory.
oceania 8, 100–101

New Caledonia Trough sea feature Tasman Sea 146 G7
New Carlisle Canada 119 I4
Newcastle Australia 108 E4
Newcastle Canada 131 F2
Newcastle Rep. of Ireland 47 F4
Newcastle S. Africa 97 I4
Newcastle U.K. 47 G3
New Castle CO U.S.A. 125 J2
New Castle IN U.S.A. 130 C4
New Castle KY U.S.A. 130 C4
New Castle PA U.S.A. 130 E3
Newcastle UT U.S.A. 125 G3
New Castle VA U.S.A. 130 E5
Newcastle WY U.S.A. 122 G4
Newcastle Emlyn U.K. 45 C6
Newcastle-under-Lyme U.K. 45 E5
Newcastle upon Tyne U.K. 44 F4
Newcastle Waters Australia 104 F4
Newcastle West Rep. of Ireland 47 C5
Newchwang China see Yingkou
New City U.S.A. 131 I3
Newcomb U.S.A. 125 I3
New Concord U.S.A. 130 E4
New Cumberland U.S.A. 130 E3
New Cumnock U.K. 46 E5
New Deer U.K. 46 G3

▶New Delhi India 78 D3
Capital of India.

New Don Pedro Reservoir U.S.A. 124 C3
Newell U.S.A. 126 C2
Newell, Lake salt flat Australia 105 D6
Newell, Lake Canada 117 I5
New England National Park Australia 108 F3
New England Range mts Australia 108 E3
New England Seamounts sea feature N. Atlantic Ocean 144 E3
Newenham, Cape U.S.A. 114 B4
Newent U.K. 45 E7
New Era U.S.A. 130 B2
Newfane NY U.S.A. 131 F2
Newfane VT U.S.A. 131 I2
Newfoundland i. Canada 119 K4
Newfoundland prov. Canada see Newfoundland and Labrador
Newfoundland and Labrador prov. Canada 119 K3
Newfoundland Evaporation Basin salt l. U.S.A. 125 G1
New Galloway U.K. 46 E5
New Georgia i. Solomon Is 103 F2
New Georgia Islands Solomon Is 103 F2
New Georgia Sound sea chan. Solomon Is 103 F2
New Glasgow Canada 119 J5

▶New Guinea i. Indon./P.N.G. 65 K8
Largest island in Oceania and 2nd in the world.
oceania 98–99
world 12–13

New Halfa Sudan 82 E6
New Hampshire state U.S.A. 131 J1
New Hampton U.S.A. 126 E3
New Hanover i. P.N.G. 102 F2
New Haven CT U.S.A. 131 I3
New Haven IN U.S.A. 130 C3
New Haven WV U.S.A. 130 E4
New Hebrides country S. Pacific Ocean see Vanuatu
New Hebrides Trench sea feature S. Pacific Ocean 146 H7
New Holstein U.S.A. 130 A2
New Iberia U.S.A. 127 F6
Newington S. Africa 97 J3
Newinn Rep. of Ireland 47 E5
New Ireland i. P.N.G. 102 F2
New Jersey state U.S.A. 131 H4
New Kensington U.S.A. 130 F3
New Kent U.S.A. 131 G5
Newkirk U.S.A. 127 D4
New Lanark U.K. 46 F5
Newland Range hills Australia 105 C7
New Lexington U.S.A. 130 D4
New Liskeard Canada 118 F5
New London CT U.S.A. 131 I3
New London MO U.S.A. 126 F4
New Madrid U.S.A. 127 F4
Newman Australia 105 B5
Newman U.S.A. 124 C3
Newmarket Canada 130 F1
Newmarket Rep. of Ireland 47 C5
Newmarket U.K. 45 H6
New Market U.S.A. 131 F4
Newmarket-on-Fergus Rep. of Ireland 47 D5
New Martinsville U.S.A. 130 E4
New Meadows U.S.A. 122 D3
New Mexico state U.S.A. 123 G6
New Miami U.S.A. 130 C4
New Milford U.S.A. 131 H3
Newnan U.S.A. 129 C5
New Orleans U.S.A. 127 F6
New Paris IN U.S.A. 130 C3
New Paris OH U.S.A. 130 C4
New Philadelphia U.S.A. 130 E3
New Pitsligo U.K. 46 G3
New Plymouth N.Z. 109 E4
Newport Mayo Rep. of Ireland 47 C4
Newport Tipperary Rep. of Ireland 47 D5
Newport England U.K. 45 E6
Newport England U.K. 45 F8
Newport Wales U.K. 45 D7
Newport AR U.S.A. 127 F5
Newport IN U.S.A. 130 B4
Newport KY U.S.A. 130 C4
Newport MI U.S.A. 130 D3
Newport NH U.S.A. 131 I2
Newport NJ U.S.A. 131 H4
Newport OR U.S.A. 122 B3
Newport RI U.S.A. 131 J3
Newport VT U.S.A. 131 I1
Newport WA U.S.A. 122 D2
Newport Beach U.S.A. 124 E5
Newport News U.S.A. 131 G5
Newport Pagnell U.K. 45 G6
New Port Richey U.S.A. 129 D6
New Providence i. Bahamas 129 E7
Newquay U.K. 45 B8
New Roads U.S.A. 127 F6
New Rochelle U.S.A. 131 I3
New Rockford U.S.A. 126 D2
New Romney U.K. 45 H8
New Ross Rep. of Ireland 47 F5
Newry Australia 104 E4
Newry U.K. 47 F3
New Siberia Islands Rus. Fed. 61 P2
New Smyrna Beach U.S.A. 129 D6
New South Wales state Australia 108 C4
New Stanton U.S.A. 130 F3
Newton U.K. 44 E5
Newton GA U.S.A. 129 C6
Newton IA U.S.A. 126 E3
Newton IL U.S.A. 126 F4
Newton KS U.S.A. 126 D4
Newton MA U.S.A. 131 J2
Newton MS U.S.A. 127 F5
Newton NC U.S.A. 128 D5
Newton NJ U.S.A. 131 H3
Newton TX U.S.A. 127 E6
Newton Abbot U.K. 45 D8
Newton Mearns U.K. 46 E5
Newton Stewart U.K. 46 E6
Newtown Rep. of Ireland 47 D5
Newtown England U.K. 45 E6
Newtown Wales U.K. 45 D6
Newtown U.S.A. 130 C4
New Town U.S.A. 126 C1
Newtownabbey U.K. 47 G3
Newtownards U.K. 47 G3
Newtownbarry Rep. of Ireland see Bunclody
Newtownbutler U.K. 47 E3
Newtownmountkennedy Rep. of Ireland 47 F4
Newtown St Boswells U.K. 46 G5
Newtownstewart U.K. 47 E3
New Ulm U.S.A. 126 E2
Newville U.S.A. 131 G3
New World Island Canada 119 L4

▶New York U.S.A. 131 I3
2nd most populous city in North America and 4th in the world.

New York state U.S.A. 131 H2

▶New Zealand country Oceania 109 D5
3rd largest and 3rd most populous country in Oceania.
oceania 8, 100–101

Neya Rus. Fed. 38 I4
Ney Bīd Iran 84 E4
Neyrīz Iran 84 D4
Neyshābūr Iran 84 E2
Nezhin Ukr. see Nizhyn
Nezperce U.S.A. 122 D3
Ngabé Congo 94 B4
Nga Chong, Khao mt. Myanmar/Thai. 66 B4
Ngagahtawng Myanmar 72 C3
Ngagau mt. Tanz. 95 D4
Ngalu Indon. 104 C2
Ngamring China 79 F3
Ngangla Ringco salt l. China 79 E3
Nganglong Kangri mt. China 78 E2
Nganglong Kangri mts China 78 E2
Ngangzê Co salt l. China 79 F3
Ngangzê Shan mts China 79 F3
Ngaoundal Cameroon 92 E4
Ngaoundéré Cameroon 93 E4
Ngape Myanmar 66 A2
Ngaputaw Myanmar 66 A3
Ngarrab China see Gyaca
Ngathainggyaung Myanmar 66 A3
Ngau i. Fiji see Gau
Ngawa China see Aba
Ngeaur i. Palau see Angaur
Ngeruangel i. Palau 65 I5
Ngga Pulu mt. Indon. see Jaya, Puncak
Ngiap r. Laos 66 C3
Ngilmina Indon. 104 D2
Ngiva Angola see Ondjiva
Ngo Congo 94 B4
Ngoako Ramalepe S. Africa see Duiwelskloof
Ngoc Linh mt. Vietnam 66 D4
Ngoin, Co salt l. China 79 G3
Ngoko r. Cameroon/Congo 93 E4
Ngola Shankou pass China 72 C1
Ngom Qu r. China see Ji Qu
Ngong Shuen Chau pen. Hong Kong China see Stonecutters' Island
Ngoqumaima China 79 F2
Ngoring China 72 C1
Ngoring Hu l. China 72 C1
Ngourti Niger 92 E3
Nguigmi Niger 92 E3
Nguiu Australia 104 E2
Ngükang China 72 B2
Ngukurr Australia 104 F3
Ngulu atoll Micronesia 65 J5
Ngunza Angola see Sumbe
Ngunza-Kabolu Angola see Sumbe
Nguru Nigeria 92 E3
Nguyên Binh Vietnam 66 D2
Ngwaketse admin. dist. Botswana see Southern
Ngwane country Africa see Swaziland
Ngwathe S. Africa 97 H4
Ngwavuma r. S. Africa/Swaziland 97 K4
Ngwelezana S. Africa 97 J5
Nhachengue Moz. 97 L2
Nhamalabué Moz. 95 D5
Nha Trang Vietnam 67 E4
Nhecolândia Brazil 139 G7
Nhill Australia 107 C8
Nhlangano Swaziland 97 J4
Nho Quan Vietnam 66 D2
Nhow i. Fiji see Gau
Nhulunbuy Australia 106 B2
Niacam Canada 117 J4
Niafounké Mali 92 C3
Niagara U.S.A. 128 C2
Niagara Falls Canada 130 F2
Niagara Falls U.S.A. 130 F2
Niagara-on-the-Lake Canada 130 F2
Niagzu Aksai Chin 78 D2
Niah Sarawak Malaysia 64 E6
Niakaramandougou Côte d'Ivoire 92 C4

▶Niamey Niger 92 D3
Capital of Niger.

Niām Kand Iran 84 E5
Niampak Indon. 65 H6
Niangara Dem. Rep. Congo 94 C3
Niangay, Lac l. Mali 92 C3
Nianzishan China 70 A3
Nias i. Indon. 67 B7
Niassa, Lago l. Africa see Nyasa, Lake
Niaur i. Palau see Angaur
Niāzābād Iran 85 F3
Nibil Well Australia 104 D5
Nica Latvia 41 L8

▶Nicaragua country Central America 133 G6
4th largest country in Central and North America.
north america 9, 116–117

Nicaragua, Lago de Nicaragua see Nicaragua, Lake
Nicaragua, Lake Nicaragua 133 G6
Nicastro Italy 54 G5
Nice France 52 H5
Nice U.S.A. 124 B2
Nicephorium Syria see Ar Raqqah
Niceville U.S.A. 129 C6
Nichicun, Lac l. Canada 119 H3
Nicholas Channel Bahamas/Cuba 129 D8
Nicholasville U.S.A. 130 C5
Nichols U.S.A. 130 A1
Nicholson r. Australia 106 B3
Nicholson Lake Canada 117 K2
Nicholson Range hills Australia 105 B6
Nicholville U.S.A. 131 H1
Nicobar Islands India 67 A5
Nicolaus U.S.A. 124 C2

▶Nicosia Cyprus 81 A2
Capital of Cyprus.

Nicoya, Península de pen. Costa Rica 133 G7
Nida Lith. 41 L9
Nidagunda India 80 C2
Nidd r. U.K. 44 F4
Nidda Germany 49 J4
Nidder r. Germany 49 I4
Nidzica Poland 43 R4
Niebüll Germany 43 L3
Nied r. France 48 G5
Niederanven Lux. 48 G5
Niederaula Germany 49 J4
Niedere Tauern mts Austria 43 N7
Niedersachsen land Germany 49 I2
Niedersächsisches Wattenmeer, Nationalpark nat. park Germany 48 G1
Niefang Equat. Guinea 92 E4
Niellé Côte d'Ivoire 92 C3
Nienburg (Weser) Germany 49 J2
Niers r. Germany 48 F3
Nierstein Germany 49 I5
Nieuwe-Niedorp Neth. 48 E2
Nieuwerkerk aan de IJssel Neth. 48 E3
Nieuw Nickerie Suriname 139 G2
Nieuwolda Neth. 48 G1
Nieuwoudtville S. Africa 96 D6
Nieuwpoort Belgium 48 C3
Nieuw-Vossemeer Neth. 48 E3
Niğde Turkey 86 D3

▶Niger country Africa 92 D3
africa 7, 90–91

▶Niger r. Africa 92 D4
3rd longest river in Africa.

Niger, Mouths of the Nigeria 92 D4
Niger Cone sea feature S. Atlantic Ocean 144 I5

▶Nigeria country Africa 92 D4
Most populous country in Africa.
africa 7, 90–91

Nighthawk Lake Canada 118 E4
Nigrita Greece 55 J4
Nihing Pak. 85 G4
Nihon country Asia see Japan
Niigata Japan 71 E5
Niihama Japan 71 D6
Niihau i. HI U.S.A. 123 [inset]
Nii-jima i. Japan 71 E6
Niimi Japan 71 D6
Niitsu Japan 71 E5
Nijil, Wādī watercourse Jordan 81 B4
Nijkerk Neth. 48 F2
Nijmegen Neth. 48 F3
Nijverdal Neth. 48 G2
Nikel' Rus. Fed. 40 Q2
Nikki Benin 92 D4
Nikkō National Park Japan 71 E5
Nikolayev Ukr. see Mykolayiv
Nikolayevka Rus. Fed. 39 J5
Nikolayevsk Rus. Fed. 39 J6
Nikolayevskiy Rus. Fed. see Nikolayevsk
Nikolayevsk-na-Amure Rus. Fed. 70 F1
Nikol'sk Rus. Fed. 38 J4
Nikol'skiy Kazakh. see Satpayev
Nikol'skoye Kamchatskaya Oblast' Rus. Fed. 61 R4
Nikol'skoye Vologod. Oblast' Rus. Fed. see Sheksna
Nikopol' Ukr. 39 G7
Niksar Turkey 86 E2
Nīkshahr Iran 85 F5
Nikšić Serb. and Mont. 54 H3
Nīkū Jahān Iran 85 F5
Nikumaroro atoll Kiribati 103 I2
Nikunau i. Kiribati 103 H2
Nīl, Bahr el r. Africa see Nile
Nilagiri India 79 F5
Niland U.S.A. 125 F5
Nilande Atoll Maldives see Nilandhoo Atoll
Nilandhe Atoll Maldives see Nilandhoo Atoll
Nilandhoo Atoll Maldives 77 D11
Nilang India see Nelang
Nilanga India 80 C2
Nilaveli Sri Lanka 80 D4

▶Nile r. Africa 86 C5
Longest river in the world and in Africa.
africa 88–89
world 12–13

Niles MI U.S.A. 130 B3
Niles OH U.S.A. 130 E3
Nilgiri Hills India 80 C4
Nil Pass Afgh. 85 G3
Nilphamari Bangl. 79 G4
Nilsiä Fin. 40 P5
Nimach India see Neemuch
Niman r. Rus. Fed. 70 D2
Nimba, Monts mts Africa see Nimba Mountains
Nimbal India 80 B2
Nimba Mountains Africa 92 C4
Nimberra Well Australia 105 C5
Nimelen r. Rus. Fed. 70 E1
Nîmes France 52 G5
Nimmitabel Australia 107 E8
Nimrod Glacier Antarctica 148 H1
Nimu Jammu and Kashmir 78 D2
Nimule Sudan 93 G4
Nimwegen Neth. see Nijmegen
Nindigully Australia 108 D2
Nine Degree Channel India 80 B4
Nine Islands P.N.G. see Kilinailau Islands
Ninepin Group is Hong Kong China 73 [inset]
Ninetyeast Ridge sea feature Indian Ocean 145 N8
Ninety Mile Beach Australia 108 C7
Ninety Mile Beach N.Z. 109 D2
Nineveh U.S.A. 131 H2
Ning'an China 70 C3
Ningbo China 73 I2
Ningde China 73 H3
Ning'er China see Pu'er
Ningguo China 73 H2
Ninghai China 73 I2
Ningxia Hui Autonomous Region aut. reg. China see Ningxia Huizu Zizhiqu
Ninghua China 73 H3
Ninging India 79 H3
Ningjiang China see Songyuan
Ningjing Shan mts China 72 C2
Ninglang China 72 D3
Ningming China 72 E4
Ningnan China 72 D3
Ningqiang China 72 E1
Ningwu China 69 K5
Ningxia aut. reg. China see Ningxia Huizu Zizhiqu
Ningxia Huizu Zizhiqu aut. reg. China 72 E1
Ningxian China 69 J5
Ningxiang China 73 G2
Ningzhou China see Huaning
Ninh Binh Vietnam 66 D2
Ninh Hoa Vietnam 67 E4
Ninigo Group atolls P.N.G. 65 K7
Ninnis Glacier Antarctica 148 G2
Ninnis Glacier Tongue Antarctica 148 H2
Ninohe Japan 71 F4
Niobrara r. U.S.A. 126 D3
Niokolo Koba, Parc National du nat. park Senegal 92 B3
Niono Mali 92 C3
Nioro Mali 92 C3
Niort France 52 D3
Nipani India 80 B2
Nipawin Canada 117 J4
Niphad India 80 B1
Nipigon Canada 115 J5
Nipigon, Lake Canada 115 J5
Nipishish Lake Canada 119 J3

Nipissing, Lake Canada 118 F5
Nippon country Asia see Japan
Nippon Hai sea N. Pacific Ocean see Japan, Sea of
Nipton U.S.A. 125 F4
Niquelândia Brazil 141 A1
Nīr Ardabīl Iran 84 B2
Nīr Yazd Iran 84 D4
Nira r. India 80 B2
Nirji China 70 B2
Nirmal India 80 C2
Nirmali India 79 F4
Nirmal Range hills India 80 C2
Niš Serb. and Mont. 55 I3
Nisa Port. 53 C4
Nisarpur India 80 B1
Niscemi Sicily Italy 54 F6
Nīshāpūr Iran see Neyshābūr
Nishino-shima vol. Japan 71 F8
Nishi-Sonogi-hantō pen. Japan 71 C6
Nisibis Turkey see Nusaybin
Nisiros i. Greece see Nisyros
Niskibi r. Canada 117 N3
Nisling r. Canada 116 B2
Nispen Neth. 48 E3
Nissan r. Sweden 41 H8
Nistru r. Moldova 55 N1 see Dniester
Nisutlin r. Canada 116 C2
Nisyros i. Greece 55 L6
Niṭā Saudi Arabia 84 C5
Nitchequon Canada 119 H3
Nitendi i. Solomon Is see Ndeni
Niterói Brazil 141 C3
Nith r. U.K. 46 F5
Nitibe East Timor 104 D2
Niti Pass China/India 78 D3
Niti Shankou pass China/India see Niti Pass
Nitmiluk National Park Australia 104 F3
Nitra Slovakia 43 Q6
Nitro U.S.A. 130 E4
Niuafo'ou i. Tonga 103 I3
Niuatoputopu i. Tonga 103 I3

▶Niue terr. S. Pacific Ocean 103 J3
Self-governing New Zealand Overseas Territory.
oceania 8, 100–101

Niujing China see Binchuan
Niulakita i. Tuvalu 103 H3
Niutao i. Tuvalu 103 H2
Niutoushan China 73 H2
Nivala Fin. 40 N5
Nive watercourse Australia 106 D5
Nivelles Belgium 48 E4
Niwai India 78 C4
Niwas India 78 E5
Nixia China see Sêrxü
Nixon U.S.A. 124 D2
Niya China see Minfeng
Niya He r. China 79 E1
Nizamabad India 80 C2
Nizam Sagar l. India 80 C2
Nizh Aydere Turkm. 84 E2
Nizhnedevitsk Rus. Fed. 39 H6
Nizhnekamsk Rus. Fed. 38 K5
Nizhnekamskoye Vodokhranilishche resr Rus. Fed. 37 Q4
Nizhnekolymsk Rus. Fed. 61 R3
Nizhnetambovskoye Rus. Fed. 70 E2
Nizhneudinsk Rus. Fed. 68 H2
Nizhnevartovsk Rus. Fed. 60 I3
Nizhnevolzhsk Rus. Fed. see Narimanov
Nizhneyansk Rus. Fed. 61 O2
Nizhniy Baskunchak Rus. Fed. 39 J6
Nizhniye Kresty Rus. Fed. see Cherskiy
Nizhniy Lomov Rus. Fed. 39 I5
Nizhniy Novgorod Rus. Fed. 38 I4
Nizhniy Odes Rus. Fed. 38 L3
Nizhniy Pyandzh Tajik. see Panji Poyon
Nizhniy Tagil Rus. Fed. 37 R4
Nizhnyaya Mola Rus. Fed. 38 J2
Nizhnyaya Omra Rus. Fed. 38 L3
Nizhnyaya Pirenga, Ozero l. Rus. Fed. 40 R3
Nizhnyaya Tunguska r. Rus. Fed. 60 J3
Nizhnyaya Tura Rus. Fed. 37 R4
Nizhyn Ukr. 39 F6
Nizina r. U.S.A. 116 A2
Nizina Mazowiecka reg. Poland 43 R4
Nizip Turkey 81 C1
Nízke Tatry nat. park Slovakia 43 Q6
Nizwá Oman see Nazwá
Nizza France see Nice
Njallavarri mt. Norway 40 L2
Njavve Sweden 40 K3
Njazidja i. Comoros 95 E5
Njombe Tanz. 95 D4
Njurundabommen Sweden 40 J5
Nkambe Cameroon 92 E4
Nkandla S. Africa 97 J5
Nkawkaw Ghana 92 C4
Nkhata Bay Malawi 95 D5
Nkhotakota Malawi 95 D5
Nkondwe Tanz. 95 D4
Nkongsamba Cameroon 92 D4
Nkululeko S. Africa 97 H6
Nkwenkwezi S. Africa 97 H7
Noakhali Bangl. 79 G5
Noatak r. U.S.A. 114 B3
Nobber Rep. of Ireland 47 F4
Nobeoka Japan 71 C6
Noblesville U.S.A. 130 B3
Noboribetsu Japan 70 F4
Noccundra Australia 107 C5
Nockatunga Australia 107 C5
Nocona U.S.A. 127 D5
Noel Kempff Mercado, Parque Nacional nat. park Bol. 138 F6
Noelville Canada 118 E5
Nogales Mex. 123 F7
Nogales U.S.A. 123 F7
Nōgata Japan 71 C6
Nogent-le-Rotrou France 52 E2
Nogent-sur-Oise France 48 C5
Noginsk Rus. Fed. 38 H5
Nogliki Rus. Fed. 70 F2
Nogoa r. Australia 106 E4
Nohar India 78 C3
Noheji Japan 70 F4
Nohfelden Germany 48 H5
Noida India 78 D3
Noirmoutier, Île de i. France 52 C3
Noirmoutier-en-l'Île France 52 C3
Noisseville France 48 G5
Nokhowch, Kūh-e mt. Iran 85 F5
Nōkis Uzbek. see Nukus
Nok Kundi Pak. 85 F4
Nokomis Canada 117 J5
Nokomis Lake Canada 117 K3
Nokou Chad 93 E3
Nokrek Peak India 79 G4
Nola Cent. Afr. Rep. 94 B3
Nolin River Lake U.S.A. 130 B5
Nolinsk Rus. Fed. 38 K4
No Mans Land i. U.S.A. 131 J3
Nome U.S.A. 114 B3
Nomgon Mongolia 68 J4
Nomhon China 76 I4
Nomoi Islands Micronesia see Mortlock Islands
Nomonde S. Africa 97 H6
Nomzha Rus. Fed. 38 I4
Nonacho Lake Canada 117 I2
Nondweni S. Africa 97 J5
Nong'an China 70 B3
Nông Hèt Laos 66 D3
Nonghui China see Guang'an
Nong Khai Thai. 66 C3
Nongoma S. Africa 97 J4
Nongstoin India 79 G4
Nonidas Namibia 96 B2
Nonni r. China see Nen Jiang
Nonning Australia 107 B7
Nonnweiler Germany 48 G5
Nonoava Mex. 123 G8
Nonouti atoll Kiribati 103 H2
Nonthaburi Thai. 67 C4
Nonzwakazi S. Africa 96 G6
Noolyeanna Lake salt flat Australia 107 B5
Noondie, Lake salt flat Australia 105 B7
Noonkanbah Australia 104 D4
Noonthorangee Range hills Australia 107 C6
Noorama Creek watercourse Australia 108 B1
Noordbeveland i. Neth. 48 D3
Noorderhaaks i. Neth. 48 E2
Noordoost Polder Neth. 48 F2
Noordwijk-Binnen Neth. 48 E2
Nootka Island Canada 116 E5
Nora r. Rus. Fed. 70 C2
Norak Tajik. 85 H2
Norak, Obanbori resr Tajik. 85 H2
Norala Phil. 65 G5
Noranda Canada 118 F4
Nor-Bayazet Armenia see Kamo
Norberg Sweden 41 I6
Nord Greenland see Station Nord
Nord, Canal du France 48 D4
Nordaustlandet i. Svalbard 60 D2
Nordegg Canada 116 G4
Norden Germany 49 H1
Nordenshel'da, Arkhipelag is Rus. Fed. 60 K2
Nordenskjold Archipelago is Rus. Fed. see Nordenshel'da, Arkhipelag
Norderney Germany 49 H1
Norderstedt Germany 49 K1
Nordfjordeid Norway 40 D6
Nordfold Norway 40 I3
Nordfriesische Inseln Germany see North Frisian Islands
Nordhausen Germany 49 K3
Nordholz Germany 49 I1
Nordhorn Germany 48 H2
Nordkapp c. Norway see North Cape
Nordkjosbotn Norway 40 K2
Nordkynhalvøya i. Norway 40 O1
Nordli Norway 40 H4
Nördlingen Germany 49 K6
Nordmaling Sweden 40 K5
Nord- og Østgrønland, Nationalparken i nat. park Greenland 115 O2

▶Nordøstrundingen c. Greenland 149 I1
Most easterly point of North America.

Nord-Ostsee-Kanal Germany see Kiel Canal
Norðoyar i. Faroe Is 36 E3
Nord - Pas-de-Calais admin. reg. France 48 C4
Nordpfälzer Bergland reg. Germany 49 H5
Nordre Strømfjord inlet Greenland see Nassuttooq
Nordrhein-Westfalen land Germany 49 H3
Nordvik Rus. Fed. 61 M2
Nore r. Rep. of Ireland 47 F5
Nore, Pic de mt. France 52 F5
Noreg country Europe see Norway
Norfolk NE U.S.A. 126 D3
Norfolk NY U.S.A. 131 H1
Norfolk VA U.S.A. 131 G5

▶Norfolk Island terr. S. Pacific Ocean 103 G4
Australian External Territory.
oceania 8, 100–101

Norfolk Island Ridge sea feature Tasman Sea 146 H7
Norfork Lake U.S.A. 127 E4
Norg Neth. 48 G1
Norge country Europe see Norway
Norheimsund Norway 41 E6
Noril'sk Rus. Fed. 60 J3
Norkyung China see Bainang
Norland Canada 131 F1
Norma Co l. China 79 G2
Norman U.S.A. 127 D5
Norman, Lake resr U.S.A. 128 D5
Normanby Island P.N.G. 106 E1
Normandes, Îles is English Chan. see Channel Islands
Normandia Brazil 139 G3
Normandie reg. France see Normandy
Normandie, Collines de hills France 52 D2
Normandy reg. France 52 D2
Normanton Australia 106 C3
Norquay Canada 117 K5
Ñorquinco Arg. 140 B6
Norra Kvarken strait Fin./Sweden 40 L5
Norra Storfjället mts Sweden 40 I4
Norrent-Fontes France 48 C4
Norris Lake U.S.A. 130 D5
Norristown U.S.A. 131 H3
Norrköping Sweden 41 J7
Norrtälje Sweden 41 K7
Norseman Australia 105 C8
Norsjö Sweden 40 K4
Norsk Rus. Fed. 70 C1
Norsup Vanuatu 103 G3
Norte, Punta pt Arg. 140 E5
Norte, Serra do hills Brazil 139 G6
Nortelândia Brazil 139 G6
Nörten-Hardenberg Germany 49 J3
North, Cape Antarctica 148 H2
North, Cape Canada 119 J5
Northallerton U.K. 44 F4
Northam Australia 105 B7
Northampton Australia 102 B4
Northampton U.K. 45 G6
Northampton MA U.S.A. 131 I2
Northampton PA U.S.A. 131 H3
North Andaman i. India 67 A4
North Anna r. U.S.A. 131 G5
North Arm b. Canada 116 H2
North Atlantic Ocean Atlantic Ocean 121 O4
North Augusta U.S.A. 129 D5
North Aulatsivik Island Canada 119 J2
North Australian Basin sea feature Indian Ocean 145 P6
North Baltimore U.S.A. 130 D3
North Battleford Canada 117 I4
North Bay Canada 118 F5
North Belcher Islands Canada 118 F2
North Berwick U.K. 46 G4
North Berwick U.S.A. 131 J2
North Bourke Australia 108 B3
North Branch U.S.A. 126 E2
North Caicos i. Turks and Caicos Is 129 G8
North Canton U.S.A. 130 E3
North Cape Canada 119 I5
North Cape Norway 40 N1
North Cape N.Z. 109 D2
North Cape U.S.A. 114 A4
North Caribou Lake Canada 117 N4
North Carolina state U.S.A. 128 E4
North Cascades National Park U.S.A. 122 C2
North Channel lake channel Canada 118 E5
North Channel U.K. 47 G2
North Charleston U.S.A. 129 E5
North Chicago U.S.A. 130 B2
Northcliffe Glacier Antarctica 148 F2
North Collins U.S.A. 131 F2
North Concho r. U.S.A. 127 C6
North Conway U.S.A. 131 J1
North Dakota state U.S.A. 126 C2
North Downs hills U.K. 45 G7
North East U.S.A. 130 F2
Northeast Foreland c. Greenland see Nordøstrundingen
North-East Frontier Agency state India see Arunachal Pradesh
Northeast Pacific Basin sea feature N. Pacific Ocean 147 J4
Northeast Point Bahamas 129 F8
Northeast Providence Channel Bahamas 129 E7
North Edwards U.S.A. 124 E4
Northeim Germany 49 J3
Northern prov. S. Africa see Limpopo
Northern Areas admin. div. Pak. 85 I2
Northern Cape prov. S. Africa 96 D5
Northern Donets r. Rus. Fed./Ukr. see Severskiy Donets
Northern Dvina r. Rus. Fed. see Severnaya Dvina
Northern Indian Lake Canada 117 L3
Northern Ireland prov. U.K. 47 F3
Northern Lau Group is Fiji 103 I3
Northern Light Lake Canada 118 C4

▶Northern Mariana Islands terr. N. Pacific Ocean 65 K3
United States Commonwealth.
oceania 8, 100–101

Northern Rhodesia country Africa see Zambia
Northern Sporades is Greece see Voreioi Sporades
Northern Territory admin. div. Australia 102 D3
Northern Transvaal prov. S. Africa see Limpopo
North Esk r. U.K. 46 G4
Northfield MN U.S.A. 126 E2
Northfield VT U.S.A. 131 I1
North Foreland c. U.K. 45 I7
North Fork U.S.A. 124 D3
North Fork Pass Canada 114 E3
North French r. Canada 118 E4
North Frisian Islands Germany 43 L3
North Geomagnetic Pole (2000) Arctic Ocean 115 K2
North Grimston U.K. 44 G4
North Haven U.S.A. 131 I3
North Head hd N.Z. 109 E3
North Henik Lake Canada 117 L2
North Hero U.S.A. 131 I1
North Horr Kenya 94 D3
North Island India 80 B4

▶North Island N.Z. 109 D4
3rd largest island in Oceania.

North Jadito Canyon gorge U.S.A. 125 H4
North Judson U.S.A. 130 B3
North Kingsville U.S.A. 130 E3
North Knife r. Canada 117 M3
North Knife Lake Canada 117 L3
▶North Korea country Asia 71 B5
asia 6, 58–59
North Lakhimpur India 79 H4
North Las Vegas U.S.A. 125 F3
North Little Rock U.S.A. 127 E5
North Loup r. U.S.A. 126 D3
North Luangwa National Park Zambia 95 D5
North Maalhosmadulu Atoll Maldives 80 B5
North Magnetic Pole Canada 149 L1
North Malosmadulu Atoll Maldives see North Maalhosmadulu Atoll
North Mam Peak U.S.A. 125 J2
North Muskegon U.S.A. 130 B2
North Palisade mt. U.S.A. 124 D3
North Perry U.S.A. 130 E3
North Platte U.S.A. 126 C3
North Platte r. U.S.A. 126 C3
North Pole Arctic Ocean 149 I1
North Port U.S.A. 129 D7
North Reef Island India 67 A4
North Rhine - Westphalia land Germany see Nordrhein-Westfalen
North Rim U.S.A. 125 G3
North Rona i. U.K. see Rona
North Ronaldsay i. U.K. 46 G1
North Ronaldsay Firth sea chan. U.K. 46 G1
North Saskatchewan r. Canada 117 J4
North Schell Peak U.S.A. 125 F2
North Sea Europe 42 H2
North Seal r. Canada 117 L3
North Sentinel Island India 67 A5
North Shields U.K. 44 F3
North Shoal Lake Canada 117 L5
North Shoshone Peak U.S.A. 124 E2
North Siberian Lowland Rus. Fed. 60 L2
North Siberian Lowland Rus. Fed. 149 E2
North Simlipal National Park India 79 F5
North Sinai governorate Egypt see Shamāl Sīnā'
North Slope plain U.S.A. 114 D3
North Somercotes U.K. 44 H5
North Spirit Lake Canada 117 M4
North Stradbroke Island Australia 108 F1
North Sunderland U.K. 44 F3
North Syracuse U.S.A. 131 G2
North Taranaki Bight b. N.Z. 109 E4
North Terre Haute U.S.A. 130 B4
Northton U.K. 46 B3
North Tonawanda U.S.A. 131 F2
North Trap reef N.Z. 109 A8
North Troy U.S.A. 131 I1
North Tyne r. U.K. 44 E4
North Uist i. U.K. 46 B3
Northumberland National Park U.K. 44 E3
Northumberland Strait Canada 119 I5
North Vancouver Canada 116 F5
North Vernon U.S.A. 130 C4
Northville U.S.A. 131 H2
North Wabasca Lake Canada 116 H3
North Walsham U.K. 45 I6
Northway Junction U.S.A. 116 A2
North West prov. S. Africa 96 G4
Northwest Atlantic Mid-Ocean Channel N. Atlantic Ocean 144 E1
North West Cape Australia 104 A5
North West Frontier prov. Pak. 85 H3
North West Nelson Forest Park nat. park N.Z. see Kahurangi National Park
Northwest Pacific Basin sea feature N. Pacific Ocean 146 G3
Northwest Providence Channel Bahamas 129 E7
North West River Canada 119 K3
Northwest Territories admin. div. Canada 116 J2
Northwich U.K. 44 E5
North Wildwood U.S.A. 131 H4
North Windham U.S.A. 131 J2
Northwind Ridge sea feature Arctic Ocean 149 B1
Northwood U.S.A. 131 J2
North York Canada 130 F2
North York Moors moorland U.K. 44 G4
North York Moors National Park U.K. 44 G4
Norton U.K. 44 G4
Norton KS U.S.A. 126 D4
Norton VA U.S.A. 130 D5
Norton VT U.S.A. 131 J1
Norton de Matos Angola see Balombo
Norton Shores U.S.A. 130 B2
Norton Sound sea chan. U.S.A. 114 B3
Nortonville U.S.A. 130 B5
Norvegia, Cape Antarctica 148 B2
Norwalk CT U.S.A. 131 I3
Norwalk OH U.S.A. 130 D3
▶Norway country Europe 40 E6
europe 5, 34–35
Norway U.S.A. 131 J1
Norway House Canada 117 L4
Norwegian Basin sea feature N. Atlantic Ocean 144 H1
Norwegian Bay Canada 115 I2
Norwegian Sea N. Atlantic Ocean 149 H2
Norwich Canada 130 E2
Norwich U.K. 45 I6
Norwich CT U.S.A. 131 I3
Norwich NY U.S.A. 131 H2
Norwood CO U.S.A. 125 I2
Norwood NY U.S.A. 131 H1
Norwood OH U.S.A. 130 C4
Nose Lake Canada 117 I1
Noshiro Japan 71 F4
Nosop watercourse Africa 96 D2
also known as Nossob
Nosovaya Rus. Fed. 38 L1
Noṣratābād Iran 85 E4
Noss, Isle of i. U.K. 46 [inset]
Nossebro Sweden 41 H7
Nossen Germany 49 N3
Nossob watercourse Africa 96 D2
also known as Nosop
Notakwanon r. Canada 119 J2
Notch Peak U.S.A. 125 G2
Noteć r. Poland 43 O4
Notikewin r. Canada 116 G3
Noto, Golfo di g. Sicily Italy 54 F6
Notodden Norway 41 F7
Noto-hantō pen. Japan 71 E5
Notre Dame, Monts mts Canada 119 H5
Notre Dame Bay Canada 119 L4
Notre-Dame-de-Koartac Canada see Quaqtaq
Nottawasaga Bay Canada 130 E1
Nottaway r. Canada 118 F4
Nottingham U.K. 45 F6
Nottingham Island Canada 115 K3
Nottoway r. U.S.A. 131 G5
Nottuln Germany 49 H3
Notukeu Creek r. Canada 117 J5
Nouabalé-Ndoki, Parc National nat. park Congo 94 B3
Nouâdhibou Mauritania 92 B2
Nouâdhibou, Râs c. Mauritania 92 B2

▶Nouakchott Mauritania 92 B3
Capital of Mauritania.

Nouâmghâr Mauritania 92 B3
Nouei Vietnam 66 D4

▶Nouméa New Caledonia 103 G4
Capital of New Caledonia.

Nouna Burkina 92 C3
Noupoort S. Africa 96 G6
Nousu Fin. 40 P3
Nouveau-Brunswick prov. Canada see New Brunswick
Nouveau-Comptoir Canada see Wemindji
Nouvelle Calédonie i. S. Pacific Ocean 103 G4
Nouvelle Calédonie terr. S. Pacific Ocean see New Caledonia
Nouvelle-France, Cap de c. Canada 115 K3
Nouvelles Hébrides country S. Pacific Ocean see Vanuatu
Nova América Brazil 141 A1
Nova Chaves Angola see Muconda
Nova Freixa Moz. see Cuamba
Nova Friburgo Brazil 141 C3
Nova Gaia Angola see Cambundi-Catembo
Nova Goa India see Panaji
Nova Gradiška Croatia 54 G2
Nova Iguaçu Brazil 141 C3
Nova Kakhovka Ukr. 55 O1
Nova Lima Brazil 141 C2
Nova Lisboa Angola see Huambo
Novalukoml' Belarus 39 F5
Nova Mambone Moz. 95 D6
Nova Nabúri Moz. 95 D5
Nova Odesa Ukr. 39 F7
Nova Paraiso Brazil 138 F3
Nova Pilão Arcado Brazil 139 J5
Nova Ponte Brazil 141 B2
Nova Ponte, Represa resr Brazil 141 B2
Novara Italy 54 C2
Nova Roma Brazil 141 B1
Nova Scotia prov. Canada 119 I6
Nova Sento Sé Brazil 139 J5
Novato U.S.A. 124 B2
Nova Trento Brazil 141 A4
Nova Venécia Brazil 141 C2
Nova Xavantino Brazil 139 H6
Novaya Kakhovka Ukr. see Nova Kakhovka
Novaya Kazanka Kazakh. 37 P6
Novaya Ladoga Rus. Fed. 38 G3
Novaya Lyalya Rus. Fed. 37 S4
Novaya Odessa Ukr. see Nova Odesa
Novaya Sibir', Ostrov i. Rus. Fed. 61 P2
Novaya Ussura Rus. Fed. 70 E2

▶Novaya Zemlya is Rus. Fed. 60 G2
3rd largest island in Europe.

Nova Zagora Bulg. 55 L3
Novelda Spain 53 F4
Nové Zámky Slovakia 43 Q7
Novgorod Rus. Fed. see Velikiy Novgorod
Novgorod-Severskiy Ukr. see Novhorod-Sivers'kyy
Novgorod-Volynskiy Ukr. see Novohrad-Volyns'kyy
Novhorod-Sivers'kyy Ukr. 39 G6
Novi Grad Bos.-Herz. see Bosanski Novi
Novi Iskŭr Bulg. 55 J3
Novikovo Rus. Fed. 70 F3
Novi Kritsim Bulg. see Stamboliyski
Novi Ligure Italy 54 C2
Novi Pazar Bulg. 55 L3
Novi Pazar Serb. and Mont. 55 I3
Novi Sad Serb. and Mont. 55 H2
Novo Acre Brazil 141 C1
Novoalekseyevka Kazakh. see Khobda
Novoaltaysk Rus. Fed. 68 E2
Novoanninskiy Rus. Fed. 39 I6
Novo Aripuanã Brazil 138 F5
Novoazovs'k Ukr. 39 H7
Novocheboksarsk Rus. Fed. 38 J4
Novocherkassk Rus. Fed. 39 I7
Novo Cruzeiro Brazil 141 C2
Novodugino Rus. Fed. 38 G5
Novodvinsk Rus. Fed. 38 I2
Novoekonomicheskoye Ukr. see Dymytrov
Novogeorgiyevka Rus. Fed. 70 B2
Novogrudok Belarus see Navahrudak
Novo Hamburgo Brazil 141 A5
Novohradské Hory mts Czech Rep. 43 O6
Novohrad-Volyns'kyy Ukr. 39 E6
Novokhopersk Rus. Fed. 39 I6
Novokiyevskiy Uval Rus. Fed. 70 C2
Novokubansk Rus. Fed. 87 F1
Novokubanskiy Rus. Fed. see Novokubansk
Novokuybyshevsk Rus. Fed. 39 K5
Novokuznetsk Rus. Fed. 68 F2
Novolazarevskaya research station Antarctica 148 C2
Novolukoml' Belarus see Novalukoml'
Novo Mesto Slovenia 54 F2
Novomikhaylovskiy Rus. Fed. 86 E1
Novomoskovsk Rus. Fed. 39 H5
Novomoskovs'k Ukr. 39 G6
Novonikolayevsk Rus. Fed. see Novosibirsk
Novonikolayevskiy Rus. Fed. 39 I6
Novooleksiyivka Ukr. 39 G7
Novopashiyskiy Rus. Fed. see Gornozavodsk
Novopokrovka Rus. Fed. 70 D3
Novopokrovskaya Rus. Fed. 39 I7
Novopolotsk Belarus see Navapolatsk
Novopskov Ukr. 39 H6
Novo Redondo Angola see Sumbe
Novorossiyka Rus. Fed. 70 C1
Novorossiysk Rus. Fed. 86 E1
Novorybnaya Rus. Fed. 61 L2
Novorzhev Rus. Fed. 38 F4
Novoselovo Rus. Fed. 68 G1
Novoselskoye Rus. Fed. see Achkhoy-Martan
Novosel'ye Rus. Fed. 41 P7
Novosergiyevka Rus. Fed. 37 Q5
Novoshakhtinsk Rus. Fed. 39 H7
Novosheshminsk Rus. Fed. 38 K5
Novosibirsk Rus. Fed. 60 J4
Novosibirskiye Ostrova is Rus. Fed. see New Siberia Islands
Novosil' Rus. Fed. 39 H5
Novosokol'niki Rus. Fed. 38 F4
Novospasskoye Rus. Fed. 39 J5
Novotroyits'ke Ukr. 39 G7
Novoukrainka Ukr. see Novoukrayinka
Novoukrayinka Ukr. 39 F6
Novouzensk Rus. Fed. 39 K6
Novovolyns'k Ukr. 39 E6
Novovoronezh Rus. Fed. 39 H6
Novovoronezhskiy Rus. Fed. see Novovoronezh
Novo-Voskresenovka Rus. Fed. 70 B1
Novozybkov Rus. Fed. 39 F5
Nový Jičín Czech Rep. 43 P6
Novyy Afon Georgia see Akhali Ap'oni
Novyy Bor Rus. Fed. 38 L2
Novyy Donbass Ukr. see Dymytrov
Novyye Petushki Rus. Fed. see Petushki
Novyy Kholmogory Rus. Fed. see Archangel
Novyy Margelan Uzbek. see Fergana
Novyy Nekouz Rus. Fed. 38 H4
Novyy Oskol Rus. Fed. 39 H6
Novyy Port Rus. Fed. 60 I3
Novyy Urengoy Rus. Fed. 60 I3
Novyy Urgal Rus. Fed. 70 D2
Novyy Uzen' Kazakh. see Zhanaozen
Novyy Zay Rus. Fed. 38 L5
Now Iran 84 D4
Nowabganj Bangl. see Nawabganj
Nowata U.S.A. 127 E4
Nowdī Iran 84 C2
Nowgong India see Nagaon
Now Kharegan Iran 84 D2
Nowleye Lake Canada 117 K2
Nowogard Poland 43 O4
Noworadomsk Poland see Radomsko
Nowra Australia 108 E5
Nowrangapur India see Nabarangapur
Nowshera Pak. 85 I3
Nowyak Lake Canada 117 L2
Nowy Sącz Poland 43 R6
Nowy Targ Poland 43 R6
Noxen U.S.A. 131 G3
Noy, Xé r. Laos 66 D3
Noyabr'sk Rus. Fed. 60 I3
Noyes Island U.S.A. 116 C4
Noyon France 48 C5
Nozizwe S. Africa 97 G6
Nqamakwe S. Africa 97 H7
Nqutu S. Africa 97 J5
Nsanje Malawi 95 D5
Nsombo Zambia 95 C5
Nsukka Nigeria 92 D4
Nsumbu National Park Zambia see Sumbu National Park
Ntambu Zambia 95 C5
Ntha S. Africa 97 H4
Ntoum Gabon 94 A3
Ntungamo Uganda 94 D4
Nuanetsi Zimbabwe see Mwenezi
Nu'aym reg. Oman 84 D6
Nuba Mountains Sudan 82 D7
Nubian Desert Sudan 82 D5
Nudo Coropuna mt. Peru 138 D7
Nueces r. U.S.A. 127 D7
Nueltin Lake Canada 117 L2
Nueva Ciudad Guerrero Mex. 127 D7
Nueva Gerona Cuba 133 H4
Nueva Harberton Arg. 140 C8
Nueva Imperial Chile 140 B5
Nueva Loja Ecuador 138 C3
Nueva Rosita Mex. 127 C7
Nueva San Salvador El Salvador 132 G6
Nueva Villa de Padilla Mex. 127 D7
Nueve de Julio Arg. see 9 de Julio
Nuevitas Cuba 133 I4
Nuevo, Golfo g. Arg. 140 D6
Nuevo Casas Grandes Mex. 123 G7
Nuevo Ideal Mex. 127 B7
Nuevo Laredo Mex. 127 D7
Nuevo León Mex. 125 F5
Nuevo León state Mex. 127 D7
Nuevo Rocafuerte Ecuador 138 C4
Nugaal watercourse Somalia 94 E3
Nugget Point N.Z. 109 B8
Nugur India 80 D2
Nuguria Islands P.N.G. 102 F2
Nuh, Ras pt Pak. 85 F5
Nuhaka N.Z. 109 F4
Nui atoll Tuvalu 103 H2
Nui Con Voi r. Vietnam see Red River
Nuiqsut U.S.A. 114 C2
Nui Ti On mt. Vietnam 66 D4
Nujiang China 72 C2
Nu Jiang r. China/Myanmar see Salween
Nu Jiang r. China/Myanmar see Salween
Nukey Bluff hill Australia 107 A7
Nukha Azer. see Şäki

▶Nuku'alofa Tonga 103 I4
Capital of Tonga.

Nukufetau atoll Tuvalu 103 H2
Nukuhiva i. Fr. Polynesia see Nuku Hiva
Nuku Hiva i. Fr. Polynesia 147 K6
Nukuhu P.N.G. 65 L8
Nukulaelae atoll Tuvalu 103 H2
Nukulailai atoll Tuvalu see Nukulaelae
Nukumanu Islands P.N.G. 103 F2
Nukunau i. Kiribati see Nikunau
Nukunono atoll Tokelau 103 I2
Nukunonu atoll Tokelau see Nukunono
Nukus Uzbek. 76 A3
Nulato U.S.A. 114 C3
Nullagine Australia 104 C5
Nullarbor Australia 105 E7
Nullarbor National Park Australia 105 E7
Nullarbor Plain Australia 105 E7
Nullarbor Regional Reserve park Australia 105 E7
Nuluarniavik, Lac l. Canada 118 F2
Nulu'erhu Shan mts China 69 L4
Num i. Indon. 65 J7
Numalla, Lake salt flat Australia 108 B2
Numan Nigeria 94 B3
Numanuma P.N.G. 106 E1
Numazu Japan 71 E6
Numbulwar Australia 106 A2
Numedal valley Norway 41 F6
Numfoor i. Indon. 65 I7
Numin He r. China 70 B3
Numurkah Australia 108 B6
Nunaksaluk Island Canada 119 J3
Nunakuluut i. Greenland 115 N3
Nunap Isua c. Greenland see Farewell, Cape
Nunarsuit i. Greenland see Nunakuluut
Nunavik reg. Canada 118 G1

Nunavut admin. div. Canada 117 L2
Nunda U.S.A. 131 G2
Nundle Australia 108 E3
Nuneaton U.K. 45 F6
Nungba India 79 H4
Nungesser Lake Canada 117 M5
Nungnain Sum China 69 L3
Nunivak Island U.S.A. 114 B4
Nunkapasi India 80 E1
Nunkun mt. Jammu and Kashmir 78 D2
Nunligran Rus. Fed. 61 T3
Nuñomoral Spain 53 C3
Nunspeet Neth. 48 F2
Nuojiang China see Tongjiang
Nuoro Sardinia Italy 54 C4
Nupani i. Solomon Is 103 G3
Nuqrah Saudi Arabia 82 F4
Nur r. Iran 84 D2
Nūrābād Iran 84 C4
Nurakita i. Tuvalu see Niulakita
Nurata Uzbek. 76 C3
Nur Dağları mts Turkey 81 B1
Nurek Tajik. see Norak
Nurek Reservoir Tajik. see Norak, Obanbori
Nurekskoye Vodokhranilishche resr Tajik. see Norak, Obanbori
Nuremberg Germany 49 L5
Nuri Mex. 123 F7
Nuristan reg. Afgh. 85 H3
Nurla Jammu and Kashmir 78 D2
Nurlat Rus. Fed. 39 K5
Nurmes Fin. 40 P5
Nurmo Fin. 40 M5
Nürnberg Germany see Nuremberg
Nurota Uzbek. see Nurata
Nurri, Mount hill Australia 108 C3
Nusawulan Indon. 65 I7
Nusaybin Turkey 87 F3
Nu Shan mts China 72 C3
Nushki Pak. 85 G4
Nusratiye Turkey 81 D1
Nutak Canada 119 J2
Nutarawit Lake Canada 117 L2
Nutrioso U.S.A. 125 I5
Nuttal Pak. 85 H4
Nutwood Downs Australia 104 F3
Nutzotin Mountains U.S.A. 116 A2
▶Nuuk Greenland 115 M3
Capital of Greenland.
Nuupas Fin. 40 O3
Nuussuaq Greenland 115 M2
Nuussuaq pen. Greenland 115 M2
Nuwaybi' al Muzayyinah Egypt 86 D5
Nuweiba el Muzeina Egypt see Nuwaybi' al Muzayyinah
Nuwerus S. Africa 96 D6
Nuweveldberge mts S. Africa 96 E7
Nuyts, Point Australia 105 B8
Nuyts Archipelago is Australia 105 F8
Nuzvid India 80 D2
Nwanedi Nature Reserve S. Africa 97 J2
Nxai Pan National Park Botswana 95 C5
Nyagan' Rus. Fed. 37 T3
Nyagquka China see Yajiang
Nyagrong China see Xinlong
Nyahururu Kenya 94 D3
Nyah West Australia 108 A5
Nyainqêntanglha Feng mt. China 79 G3
Nyainqêntanglha Shan mts China 79 G3
Nyainrong China 72 B1
Nyainronglung China see Nyainrong
Nyåker Sweden 40 K5
Nyakh Rus. Fed. see Nyagan'
Nyaksimvol' Rus. Fed. 37 S3
Nyala Sudan 93 F3
Nyalam China 79 F3
Nyalikungu Tanz. see Maswa
Nyamandhlovu Zimbabwe 95 C5
Nyamtumbo Tanz. 95 D5
Nyande Zimbabwe see Masvingo
Nyandoma Rus. Fed. 38 I3
Nyandomskiy Vozvyshennost' hills Rus. Fed. 38 H3
Nyanga Congo 94 B4
Nyanga Zimbabwe 95 D5
Nyangbo China 72 B2
Nyarling r. Canada 116 H2
▶Nyasa, Lake Africa 95 D4
3rd largest lake in Africa.
Nyasaland country Africa see Malawi
Nyashabozh Rus. Fed. 38 L2
Nyasvizh Belarus 41 O10
Nyaungdon Myanmar see Yandoon
Nyaunglebin Myanmar 66 B3
Nyborg Denmark 41 G9
Nyborg Norway 40 P1
Nybro Sweden 41 I8
Nyeboe Land reg. Greenland 115 M1
Nyêmo China 79 G3
Nyenchen Tanglha Range mts China see Nyainqêntanglha Shan
Nyeri Kenya 94 D4
Nyi, Co l. China 79 F2
Nyika National Park Zambia 95 D5
Nyima China 79 F3
Nyimba Zambia 95 D5
Nyingchi China 72 B2
Nyinma China see Maqu
Nyíregyháza Hungary 39 D7
Nyiru, Mount Kenya 94 D3
Nykarleby Fin. 40 M5
Nykøbing Denmark 41 G9
Nykøbing Sjælland Denmark 41 G9
Nyköping Sweden 41 J7
Nyland Sweden 40 J5
Nylstroom S. Africa 97 I3
Nylsvley nature res. S. Africa 97 I3
Nymagee Australia 108 C4
Nymboida National Park Australia 108 F2
Nynäshamn Sweden 41 J7
Nyngan Australia 108 C3
Nyogzê China 79 E3
Nyoman r. Belarus/Lith. 41 M10 also known as Neman or Nemunas
Nyon Switz. 52 H3
Nyons France 52 G4
Nýřany Czech Rep. 49 N5
Nyrob Rus. Fed. 37 R3
Nysa Poland 43 P5
Nysh Rus. Fed. 70 F2
Nyssa U.S.A. 122 D4
Nystad Fin. see Uusikaupunki
Nytva Rus. Fed. 37 R4
Nyuksenitsa Rus. Fed. 38 J3
Nyunzu Dem. Rep. Congo 95 C4
Nyurba Rus. Fed. 61 M3
Nyyskiy Zaliv lag. Rus. Fed. 70 F1
Nzambi Congo 94 B4
Nzega Tanz. 95 D4
Nzérékoré Guinea 92 C4
N'zeto Angola 95 B4
Nzwani i. Comoros 95 E5

O

Oahe, Lake U.S.A. 126 C2
Oahu i. HI U.S.A. 123 [inset]
Oaitupu i. Tuvalu see Vaitupu
Oak Bluffs U.S.A. 131 J3
Oak City U.S.A. 125 G2
Oak Creek U.S.A. 125 J1
Oakdale U.S.A. 127 E6
Oakes U.S.A. 126 D2
Oakey Australia 108 E1
Oak Grove KY U.S.A. 130 B5
Oak Grove LA U.S.A. 127 F5
Oak Grove MI U.S.A. 130 C1
Oakham U.K. 45 G6
Oak Harbor U.S.A. 130 D3
Oak Hill OH U.S.A. 130 D4
Oak Hill WV U.S.A. 130 E5
Oakhurst U.S.A. 124 D3
Oak Lake Canada 117 K5
Oakland CA U.S.A. 124 B3
Oakland MD U.S.A. 130 F4
Oakland ME U.S.A. 131 K1
Oakland NE U.S.A. 126 D3
Oakland OR U.S.A. 122 C4
Oakland airport U.S.A. 124 B3
Oakland City U.S.A. 130 B4
Oaklands Australia 108 C5
Oak Lawn U.S.A. 130 B3
Oakley U.S.A. 126 C4
Oakover r. Australia 104 C5
Oak Park IL U.S.A. 130 B3
Oak Park MI U.S.A. 130 C2
Oak Park Reservoir U.S.A. 125 I1
Oakridge U.S.A. 122 C4
Oak Ridge U.S.A. 128 C4
Oakvale Australia 107 C7
Oak View U.S.A. 124 D4
Oakville Canada 130 F2
Oakwood OH U.S.A. 130 C3
Oakwood TN U.S.A. 130 B5
Oamaru N.Z. 109 C7
Oaro N.Z. 109 D6
Oasis CA U.S.A. 124 E3
Oasis NV U.S.A. 122 E4
Oates Coast reg. Antarctica see Oates Land
Oates Land reg. Antarctica 148 H2
Oaxaca Mex. 132 E5
Oaxaca de Juárez Mex. see Oaxaca
Ob' r. Rus. Fed. 68 E2
Ob, Gulf of sea chan. Rus. Fed. see Obskaya Guba
Oba Canada 118 D4
Oba i. Vanuatu see Aoba
Obala Cameroon 92 E4
Obama Japan 71 D6
Oban U.K. 46 D4
O Barco Spain 53 C2
Obbia Somalia see Hobyo
Obdorsk Rus. Fed. see Salekhard
Óbecse Serb. and Mont. see Bečej
Obed Canada 116 G4
Oberaula Germany 49 J4
Oberdorla Germany 49 K3
Oberhausen Germany 48 G3
Oberlin KS U.S.A. 126 C4
Oberlin LA U.S.A. 127 E6
Oberlin OH U.S.A. 130 D3
Obermoschel Germany 49 H5
Oberon Australia 108 D4
Oberpfälzer Wald mts Germany 49 M5
Obersinn Germany 49 J4
Oberthulba Germany 49 J4
Obertshausen Germany 49 I4
Oberwälder Land reg. Germany 49 J3
Obi i. Indon. 65 H7
Óbidos Brazil 139 G4
Obihiro Japan 70 F4
Obil'noye Rus. Fed. 39 J7
▶Ob'-Irtysh r. Rus. Fed. 60 H3
2nd longest river and largest drainage basin in Asia and 5th longest river in the world.
asia 56–57
world 12–13
Obluch'ye Rus. Fed. 70 C2
Obninsk Rus. Fed. 39 H5
Obo Cent. Afr. Rep. 94 C3
Obock Djibouti 82 F7
Ŏbŏk N. Korea 70 C4
Obokote Dem. Rep. Congo 94 C4
Obo Liang China 76 H4
Obouya Congo 94 B4
Oboyan' Rus. Fed. 39 H6
Obozerskiy Rus. Fed. 38 I3
Obregón, Presa resr Mex. 123 F8
Obrenovac Serb. and Mont. 55 I2
Obruk Turkey 86 D3
Observatory Hill hill Australia 105 F7
Obshchiy Syrt hills Rus. Fed. 37 Q5
Obskaya Guba sea chan. Rus. Fed. 60 I3
Obuasi Ghana 92 C4
Ob"yachevo Rus. Fed. 38 K3
Ocala U.S.A. 129 D6
Ocampo Mex. 127 C7
Ocaña Col. 138 D2
Ocaña Spain 53 E4
Occidental, Cordillera mts Chile 138 E7
Occidental, Cordillera mts Col. 138 C3
Occidental, Cordillera mts Peru 138 D7
Oceana U.S.A. 130 E5
Ocean Cay i. Bahamas 129 E7
Ocean City MD U.S.A. 131 H4
Ocean City NJ U.S.A. 131 H4
Ocean Falls Canada 116 E4
Ocean Island Kiribati see Banaba
Ocean Island atoll U.S.A. see Kure Atoll
Oceanside U.S.A. 124 E5
Ocean Springs U.S.A. 127 F6
Ochakiv Ukr. 55 N1
Och'amch'ire Georgia 87 F2
Ocher Rus. Fed. 37 Q4
Ochiishi-misaki pt Japan 70 G4
Ochil Hills U.K. 46 F4
Ochrida, Lake Albania/Macedonia see Ohrid, Lake
Ochsenfurt Germany 49 K5
Ochtrup Germany 49 H2
Ocilla U.S.A. 129 D6
Ockelbo Sweden 41 J6
Ocolaşul Mare, Vârful mt. Romania 55 K1
Oconomowoc U.S.A. 130 A2
Oconto U.S.A. 130 B1
Octeville-sur-Mer France 45 H9
October Revolution Island Rus. Fed. see Oktyabr'skoy Revolyutsii, Ostrov
Ocussi enclave East Timor 104 D2
Ocussi-Ambeno enclave East Timor see Ocussi
Oda, Jebel mt. Sudan 82 E5
Ódáðahraun lava field Iceland 40 [inset]
Ŏdaejin N. Korea 70 C4
Odae-san National Park S. Korea 71 C5
Ōdate Japan 71 F4
Odawara Japan 71 E6
Odda Norway 41 E6
Odei r. Canada 117 L3
Odell U.S.A. 130 B3
Odem U.S.A. 127 D7
Odemira Port. 53 B5
Ödemiş Turkey 55 L5
Ödenburg Hungary see Sopron
Odense Denmark 41 G9
Odenwald reg. Germany 49 I5
Oder r. Germany 49 J3 also known as Odra (Poland)
Oderbucht b. Germany 43 O3
Oder-Havel-Kanal canal Germany 49 N2
Odesa Ukr. 55 N1
Ödeshog Sweden 41 I7
Odessa Ukr. see Odesa
Odessa TX U.S.A. 127 C6
Odessa WA U.S.A. 122 D3
Odessus Bulg. see Varna
Odiel r. Spain 53 C5
Odienné Côte d'Ivoire 92 C4
Odintsovo Rus. Fed. 38 H5
Ŏdôngk Cambodia 67 D5
Odra r. Germany/Pol. 43 Q6 also known as Oder (Germany)
Odzala, Parc National d' nat. park Congo 94 B3
Oea Libya see Tripoli
Oé-Cusse enclave East Timor see Ocussi
Oecussi enclave East Timor see Ocussi
Oeiras Brazil 139 J5
Oekussi enclave East Timor see Ocussi
Oelsnitz Germany 49 M4
Oenkerk Neth. 48 F1
Oenpelli Australia 104 F3
Oesel i. Estonia see Hiiumaa
Oeufs, Lac des l. Canada 119 G3
Of Turkey 87 F2
O'Fallon r. U.S.A. 122 G3
Ofanto r. Italy 54 G4
Ofaqim Israel 81 B4
Offa Nigeria 92 D4
Offenbach am Main Germany 49 I4
Offenburg Germany 43 K6
Oga Japan 71 E5
Ogadēn reg. Eth. 94 E3
Oga-hantō pen. Japan 71 E5
Ōgaki Japan 71 E6
Ogallala U.S.A. 126 C3
Ogasawara-shotō is Japan see Bonin Islands
Ogbomosho Nigeria 92 D4
Ogbomoso Nigeria see Ogbomosho
Ogden IA U.S.A. 126 E3
Ogden UT U.S.A. 122 F4
Ogden, Mount Canada 116 C3
Ogdensburg U.S.A. 131 H1
Ogidaki Canada 118 D5
Ogilvie r. Canada 114 E3
Ogilvie Mountains Canada 114 D3
Oglethorpe, Mount U.S.A. 129 C5
Oglio r. Italy 54 D2
Oglongi Rus. Fed. 70 E1
Ogmore Australia 106 E4
Ogoamas, Gunung mt. Indon. 65 G6
Ogodzha Rus. Fed. 70 D1
Ogoja Nigeria 92 D4
Ogoki r. Canada 118 D4
Ogoki Lake Canada 126 G1
Ogoki Reservoir Canada 118 C4
Ogoron Rus. Fed. 70 C1
Ogosta r. Bulg. 55 J3
Ogre Latvia 41 N8
Ogulin Croatia 54 F2
Ogurchinskiy, Ostrov i. Turkm. 84 D2
Ogurjaly Adasy i. Turkm. see Ogurchinskiy, Ostrov
Oğuzeli Turkey 81 C1
Ohai N.Z. 109 A7
Ohakune N.Z. 109 E4
Ohanet Alg. 92 D2
Ōhata Japan 70 F4
Ohcejohka Fin. see Utsjoki
O'Higgins, Lago l. Chile 140 B7
Ohio r. U.S.A. 130 A5
Ohio state U.S.A. 130 D3
Ohm r. Germany 49 I4
Ohrdruf Germany 49 K4
Ohře r. Czech Rep. 49 N4
Ohre r. Germany 49 L2
Ohrid Macedonia 55 I4
Ohrid, Lake Albania/Macedonia 55 I4
Ohridsko Ezero l. Albania/Macedonia see Ohrid, Lake
Ohrigstad S. Africa 97 J3
Öhringen Germany 49 J5
Ohrit, Liqeni i l. Albania/Macedonia see Ohrid, Lake
Ohura N.Z. 109 E4
Oiapoque r. Brazil/Fr. Guiana 139 H3
Oich r. U.K. 46 E3
Oiga China 72 B2
Oignies France 48 C4
Oil City U.S.A. 130 F3
Oise r. France 48 C6
Ōita Japan 71 C6
Oiti mt. Greece 55 J5
Ojai U.S.A. 124 D4
Ojalava i. Samoa see Upolu
Ojinaga Mex. 127 B6
Ojiya Japan 71 E5
Ojo Caliente U.S.A. 123 G5
Ojo de Laguna Mex. 123 G7
▶Ojos del Salado, Nevado mt. Arg./Chile 140 C3
2nd highest mountain in South America.
Oka r. Rus. Fed. 39 I4
Oka r. Rus. Fed. 68 I1
Okahandja Namibia 96 C1
Okahukura N.Z. 109 E4
Okakarara Namibia 95 B6
Okak Islands Canada 119 J2
Okanagan Lake Canada 116 G5
Okanda Sri Lanka 80 D5
Okano r. Gabon 94 B4
Okanogan U.S.A. 122 D2
Okanogan r. U.S.A. 122 D2
Okara Pak. 85 I4
Okarem Turkm. 84 D2
Okataina vol. N.Z. see Tarawera, Mount
Okaukuejo Namibia 95 B5
Okavango r. Africa 95 C5
▶Okavango Delta swamp Botswana 95 C5
Largest oasis in the world.
Okavango Swamps Botswana see Okavango Delta
Okaya Japan 71 E5
Okayama Japan 71 D6
Okazaki Japan 71 E6
Okeechobee U.S.A. 129 D7
Okeechobee, Lake U.S.A. 129 D7
Okeene U.S.A. 127 D4
Okefenokee Swamp U.S.A. 129 D6
Okehampton U.K. 45 C8
Okemah U.S.A. 127 D5
Oker r. Germany 49 K2
Okha India 78 B5
Okha Rus. Fed. 70 F1
Okha Rann marsh India 78 B5
Okhotsk Rus. Fed. 61 P4
Okhotsk, Sea of Japan/Rus. Fed. 70 G3
Okhotskoye More sea Japan/Rus. Fed. see Okhotsk, Sea of
Okhtyrka Ukr. 39 G6
Okinawa i. Japan 71 B8
Okinawa-guntō is Japan see Okinawa-shotō
Okinawa-shotō is Japan 71 B8
Okino-Daitō-jima i. Japan 69 O8
Okino-Tori-shima i. Japan 69 P8
Oki-shotō is Japan 69 O5
Oki-shotō is Japan 71 D5
Okkan Myanmar 66 A3
Oklahoma state U.S.A. 127 D5
▶Oklahoma City U.S.A. 127 D5
State capital of Oklahoma.
Okmulgee U.S.A. 127 D5
Okolona KY U.S.A. 130 C4
Okolona MS U.S.A. 127 F5
Okondja Gabon 94 B4
Okovskiy Les for. Rus. Fed. 38 G5
Okoyo Congo 94 B4
Øksfjord Norway 40 M1
Oktemberyan Armenia see Hoktemberyan
Oktwin Myanmar 66 B3
Oktyabr' Kazakh. see Kandyagash
Oktyabr'sk Kazakh. see Kandyagash
Oktyabr'skiy Belarus see Aktsyabrski
Oktyabr'skiy Amurskaya Oblast' Rus. Fed. 70 C1
Oktyabr'skiy Arkhangel'skaya Oblast' Rus. Fed. 38 I3
Oktyabr'skiy Kamchatskaya Oblast' Rus. Fed. 61 Q4
Oktyabr'skiy Respublika Bashkortostan Rus. Fed. 37 Q5
Oktyabr'skiy Volgogradskaya Oblast' Rus. Fed. 39 I7
Oktyabr'skoye Rus. Fed. 37 T3
Oktyabr'skoy Revolyutsii, Ostrov i. Rus. Fed. 61 K2
Okulovka Rus. Fed. 38 G4
Okushiri-tō i. Japan 70 E4
Okusi enclave East Timor see Ocussi
Okuta Nigeria 92 D4
Okwa watercourse Botswana 96 G1
Ólafsvík Iceland 40 [inset]
Olakkur India 80 C3
Olancha U.S.A. 124 D3
Olancha Peak U.S.A. 124 D3
Öland i. Sweden 41 J8
Olary Australia 107 C7
Olathe CO U.S.A. 125 J2
Olathe KS U.S.A. 126 E4
Olavarría Arg. 140 D5
Oława Poland 43 P5
Olbernhau Germany 49 N4
Olbia Sardinia Italy 54 C4
Old Bahama Channel Bahamas/Cuba 129 E8
Old Bastar India 80 D2
Oldcastle Rep. of Ireland 47 E4
Old Cork Australia 106 C4
Old Crow Canada 114 E3
Oldeboorn Neth. 48 F1
Oldenburg Germany 49 I1
Oldenburg in Holstein Germany 43 M3
Oldenzaal Neth. 48 G2
Olderdalen Norway 40 L2
Old Forge U.S.A. 131 H2
Old Gidgee Australia 105 B6
Oldham U.K. 44 E5
Old Harbor U.S.A. 114 C4
Old Head of Kinsale hd Rep. of Ireland 47 D6
Oldman r. Canada 116 I5
Oldmeldrum U.K. 46 G3
Old Perlican Canada 119 L5
Old River U.S.A. 124 D4
Olds Canada 116 H5
Old Speck Mountain U.S.A. 131 J1
Old Station U.S.A. 124 C1
Old Wives Lake Canada 117 J5
Olean U.S.A. 131 F2
Olecko Poland 43 S3
Olekma r. Rus. Fed. 61 N3
Olekminsk Rus. Fed. 61 N3
Olekminskiy-Stanovik mts Rus. Fed. 69 M2
Oleksandrivs'k Ukr. see Zaporizhzhya
Oleksandriya Ukr. 39 G6
Ølen Norway 41 D7
Olenegorsk Rus. Fed. 40 R2
Olenek Rus. Fed. 61 M3
Olenek r. Rus. Fed. 61 M2
Olenek Bay Rus. Fed. see Olenekskiy Zaliv
Olenekskiy Zaliv b. Rus. Fed. 61 N2
Olenino Rus. Fed. 38 G4
Olenitsa Rus. Fed. 38 G2
Olenivs'ki Kar"yery Ukr. see Dokuchayevs'k
Olenya Rus. Fed. see Olenegorsk
Oleshky Ukr. see Tsyurupyns'k
Olevs'k Ukr. 39 E6
Ol'ga Rus. Fed. 70 D4
Olga, Lac l. Canada 118 F4
Olga, Mount Australia 105 E6
Ol'ginsk Rus. Fed. 70 D1
Olginskoye Rus. Fed. see Kochubeyevskoye
Ölgiy Mongolia 76 G2
Olhão Port. 53 C5
Olia Chain mts Australia 105 E6
Olifants r. Moz./S. Africa 97 J3 also known as Elefantes
Olifants watercourse Namibia 96 D3
Olifants S. Africa 97 J2
Olifants r. W. Cape S. Africa 96 D6
Olifants r. W. Cape S. Africa 96 E7
Olifantshoek S. Africa 96 F4
Olifantsrivierberge mts S. Africa 96 D7
Olimarao atoll Micronesia 65 L5
Olimbos hill Cyprus see Olympos
Olimbos mt. Greece see Olympus, Mount
Olimpos Beydağları Milli Parkı nat. park Turkey 55 N6
Olinda Brazil 139 L5
Olinga Moz. 95 D5
Olio Australia 106 C4
Oliphants Drift S. Africa 97 H3
Olisipo Port. see Lisbon
Oliva Spain 53 F4
Oliva, Cordillera de mts Arg./Chile 140 C3
Olivares, Cerro de mt. Arg./Chile 140 C4
Olive Hill U.S.A. 130 D4
Olivehurst U.S.A. 124 C2
Oliveira dos Brejinhos Brazil 141 C1
Olivença Moz. see Lupilichi
Olivenza Spain 53 C4
Oliver Lake Canada 117 K3
Olivet MI U.S.A. 130 C2
Olivet SD U.S.A. 126 D3
Olivia U.S.A. 126 E2
Ol'khovka Rus. Fed. 39 J6
Ollagüe Chile 140 C2
Ollombo Congo 94 B4
Olmaliq Uzbek. see Almalyk
Olmos Peru 138 C5
Olmütz Czech Rep. see Olomouc
Olney U.K. 45 G6
Olney IL U.S.A. 126 F4
Olney MD U.S.A. 131 G4
Olney TX U.S.A. 127 D5
Olofström Sweden 41 I8
Olomane r. Canada 119 J4
Olomouc Czech Rep. 43 P6
Olonets Rus. Fed. 38 G3
Olongapo Phil. 65 G4
Oloron-Ste-Marie France 52 D5
Olosenga atoll American Samoa see Swains Island
Olot Spain 53 H2
Olot Uzbek. see Alat
Olovyannaya Rus. Fed. 69 L2
Oloy, Qatorkŭhi mts Asia see Alai Range
Olpe Germany 49 H3
Olsztyn Poland 43 R4
Olt r. Romania 55 K3
Olten Switz. 52 H3
Olteniţa Romania 55 L2
Oltu Turkey 87 F2
Oluan Pi c. Taiwan 73 I4
Ol'viopol' Ukr. see Pervomays'k
Olymbos hill Cyprus see Olympos
▶Olympia U.S.A. 122 C3
State capital of Washington.
Olympic National Park U.S.A. 122 C3
Olympos hill Cyprus 81 A2
Olympos Greece see Olympus, Mount
Olympos nat. park Greece 55 J4
Olympus, Mount Greece 55 J4
Olympus, Mount U.S.A. 122 C3
Olyutorskiy Rus. Fed. 61 R3
Olyutorskiy, Mys c. Rus. Fed. 61 S4
Olyutorskiy Zaliv b. Rus. Fed. 61 R4
Olzheras Rus. Fed. see Mezhdurechensk
Oma China 79 E2
Oma r. Rus. Fed. 38 J2
Omagh U.K. 47 E3
Omaha U.S.A. 126 E3
Omaheke admin. reg. Namibia 96 D2
Omal'skiy Khrebet mts Rus. Fed. 70 E1
▶Oman country Asia 83 I6
asia 6, 58–59
Oman, Gulf of Asia 84 E5
Omarkot Pak. 85 H4
Omaruru Namibia 95 B6
Omate Peru 138 D7
Omaweneno Botswana 96 F3
Omba i. Vanuatu see Aoba
Ombai, Selat sea chan. East Timor/Indon. 104 D2
Ombalantu Namibia see Uutapi
Omboué Gabon 94 A4
Ombu China 79 F3
Omdraaisvlei S. Africa 96 F6
Omdurman Sudan 82 D6
Omeo Australia 108 C6
Omer U.S.A. 130 D1
Ometepec Mex. 132 E5
Omgoy Wildlife Reserve nature res. Thai. 66 B3
Om Hajēr Eritrea 82 E7
Omīdīyeh Iran 84 C4
Omineca Mountains Canada 116 E3
Omitara Namibia 96 C2
Ōmiya Japan 71 E6
Ommaney, Cape U.S.A. 116 C3
Ommen Neth. 48 G2
Omolon Rus. Fed. 61 R3
Omo National Park Eth. 94 D3
Omsk Rus. Fed. 60 I4
Omsukchan Rus. Fed. 61 Q3
Ōmū Japan 70 F3
O-mu Myanmar 66 B2
Omu, Vârful mt. Romania 55 K2
Ōmura Japan 71 C6
Omutninsk Rus. Fed. 38 L4
Onaman Lake Canada 118 D4
Onamia U.S.A. 126 E2
Onancock U.S.A. 131 H5
Onangué, Lac l. Gabon 94 B4
Onaping Lake Canada 118 E5
Onatchiway, Lac l. Canada 119 H4
Onavas Mex. 123 F7
Onawa U.S.A. 126 D3
Onaway U.S.A. 130 C1
Onbingwin Myanmar 67 B4
Oncativo Arg. 140 D4
Onchan Isle of Man 44 C4
Oncócua Angola 95 B5
Öncül Turkey 81 D1
Ondal India see Andal
Ondangwa Namibia 95 B5
Onderstedorings S. Africa 96 E6
Ondjiva Angola 95 B5
Ondo Nigeria 92 D4
Öndörhaan Mongolia 69 K3
Ondozero Rus. Fed. 38 G3
One Botswana 96 E2
One and a Half Degree Channel Maldives 77 D11
Onega Rus. Fed. 38 H3
Onega r. Rus. Fed. 38 H3
Onega, Lake Rus. Fed. 37 N3
▶Onega, Lake Rus. Fed. 38 G3
3rd largest lake in Europe.
Onega Bay g. Rus. Fed. see Onezhskaya Guba
One Hundred and Fifty Mile House Canada see 150 Mile House
One Hundred Mile House Canada see 100 Mile House
Oneida NY U.S.A. 131 H2
Oneida TN U.S.A. 130 C5
Oneida Lake U.S.A. 131 H2
O'Neill U.S.A. 126 D3
Onekama U.S.A. 130 B1
Onekotan, Ostrov i. Rus. Fed. 61 Q5
Oneonta AL U.S.A. 129 C5
Oneonta NY U.S.A. 131 H2
Oneşti Romania 55 L1
Onezhskaya Guba g. Rus. Fed. 38 G2
Onezhskoye Ozero l. Rus. Fed. see Onega, Lake
Onezhskoye Ozero l. Rus. Fed. see Onega, Lake
Ong r. India 80 D1
Onga Gabon 94 B4
Ongers watercourse S. Africa 96 F5
Ongi Mongolia 68 I3
Ongiyn Gol r. Mongolia 76 J3
Ongjin N. Korea 71 B5
Ongole India 80 D3
Onida U.S.A. 126 C2
Onilahy r. Madag. 95 E6
Onistagane, Lac l. Canada 119 H4
Onitsha Nigeria 92 D4
Onjati Mountain Namibia 96 C2
Onjiva Angola see Ondjiva
Ono-i-Lau i. Fiji 103 I4
Onomichi Japan 71 D6
Onon atoll Micronesia see Namonuito
Onor, Gora mt. Rus. Fed. 70 F2
Onotoa atoll Kiribati 103 H2
Onseepkans S. Africa 96 D5
Onslow Australia 104 A5
Onslow Bay U.S.A. 129 E5
Onstwedde Neth. 48 H1
Ontake-san vol. Japan 71 E6
Ontario prov. Canada 130 E1
Ontario U.S.A. 124 E4
Ontario, Lake Canada/U.S.A. 131 G2
Ontong Java Atoll Solomon Is 103 F2
Onutu atoll Kiribati see Onotoa
Onverwacht Suriname 139 G2
Onyx U.S.A. 124 D4
Oodnadatta Australia 107 A5
Oodweyne Somalia 94 E3
Ooldea Australia 105 E7
Ooldea Range hills Australia 105 E7
Oologah Lake resr U.S.A. 127 E4
Ooratippra r. Australia 106 B4
Oos-Londen S. Africa see East London
Oostburg Neth. 48 D3
Oostende Belgium see Ostend
Oostendorp Neth. 48 F2
Oosterhout Neth. 48 E3
Oosterschelde est. Neth. 48 D3
Oosterwolde Neth. 48 G2
Oostvleteren Belgium 48 C4
Oost-Vlieland Neth. 48 F1
Ootacamund India see Udagamandalam
Ootsa Lake Canada 116 E4
Ootsa Lake l. Canada 116 E4
Opal Mex. 127 C7
Opala Dem. Rep. Congo 94 C4
Oparino Rus. Fed. 38 K4
Oparo i. Fr. Polynesia see Rapa
Opasatika r. Canada 118 E4
Opasatika Lake Canada 118 E4
Opasquia Canada 117 M4
Opataca, Lac l. Canada 118 G4
Opava Czech Rep. 43 P6
Opel hill Germany 49 H5
Opelika U.S.A. 129 C5
Opelousas U.S.A. 127 E6
Opeongo Lake Canada 118 F5
Opheim U.S.A. 122 G2
Opienge Dem. Rep. Congo 94 C3
Opinaca r. Canada 118 F3
Opinaca, Réservoir resr Canada 118 F3
Opinnagau r. Canada 118 E3
Opiscotéo, Lac l. Canada 119 H3
Op Luang National Park Thai. 66 B3
Opmeer Neth. 48 E2
Opochka Rus. Fed. 41 P8
Opocopa, Lac l. Canada 119 I3
Opodepe Mex. 132 B3
Opole Poland 43 P5
Oporto Port. 53 B3
Opotiki N.Z. 109 F4
Opp U.S.A. 129 C6
Oppdal Norway 40 F5
Oppeln Poland see Opole
Opportunity U.S.A. 122 D3
Opunake N.Z. 109 D4
Opuwo Namibia 95 B5
Oqsu r. Tajik. 85 I2
Oracle U.S.A. 125 H5
Oradea Romania 55 I1
Orahovac Serb. and Mont. 55 I3
Orai India 78 D4
Oraibi U.S.A. 125 H4
Oraibi Wash watercourse U.S.A. 125 H4
Oral Kazakh. see Ural'sk
Oran Alg. 53 F6
Orán Arg. 140 D2
O Rang Cambodia 67 D4
Orang India 79 H4
Ŏrang N. Korea 70 C4
Orange Australia 108 D4
Orange France 52 G4
Orange r. Namibia/S. Africa 96 C5
Orange CA U.S.A. 124 E5
Orange MA U.S.A. 131 I2
Orange TX U.S.A. 127 E6

Orange VA U.S.A. 131 F4
Orange, Cabo c. Brazil 139 H3
Orangeburg U.S.A. 129 D5
Orange City U.S.A. 126 D3
Orange Cone sea feature
S. Atlantic Ocean 144 I8
Orange Free State prov. S. Africa see
Free State
Orangeville Canada 130 E2
Orange Walk Belize 132 G5
Oranienburg Germany 49 N2
Oranje r. Namibia/S. Africa see
Orange
Oranje Gebergte hills Suriname
139 G3
Oranjemund Namibia 96 C5

▶Oranjestad Aruba 133 J6
Capital of Aruba.

Oranmore Rep. of Ireland 47 D4
Orapa Botswana 95 C6
Orăştie Romania 55 J2
Oraşul Stalin Romania see Braşov
Oravais Fin. 40 M5
Orba Co l. China 78 E2
Orbetello Italy 54 D3
Orbost Australia 108 D6
Orcadas research station
S. Atlantic Ocean 148 A2
Orchard City U.S.A. 125 J2
Orchha India 78 D4
Orchila, Isla i. Venez. 138 E1
Orchy r. U.K. 46 D4
Orcutt U.S.A. 124 C4
Ord r. Australia 104 E3
Ord U.S.A. 126 D3
Ord, Mount hill Australia 104 D4
Ördenes Spain see Ordes
Orderville U.S.A. 125 G3
Ordes Spain 53 B2
Ordesa - Monte Perdido, Parque
Nacional nat. park Spain 53 G2
Ord Mountain U.S.A. 124 E4
Ord River Dam Australia 104 E4
Ordu Hatay Turkey see Yayladağı
Ordu Ordu Turkey 86 E2
Ordubad Azer. 87 G3
Ordway U.S.A. 126 C4
Ordzhonikidze Rus. Fed. see
Vladikavkaz
Ore Nigeria 92 D4
Oreana U.S.A. 124 D1
Örebro Sweden 41 I7
Oregon IL U.S.A. 126 F3
Oregon OH U.S.A. 130 D3
Oregon state U.S.A. 122 C4
Oregon City U.S.A. 122 C3
Orekhov Ukr. see Orikhiv
Orekhovo-Zuyevo Rus. Fed. 38 H5
Orel Rus. Fed. 39 H5
Orel, Gora mt. Rus. Fed. 70 E1
Orel', Ozero l. Rus. Fed. 70 E1
Orem U.S.A. 125 H1
Ore Mountains Czech Rep./Germany
see Erzgebirge
Orenburg Rus. Fed. 60 G4
Orense Spain see Ourense
Oreor Palau see Koror
Orepuki N.Z. 109 A8
Öresund strait Denmark/Sweden
41 H9
Oretana, Cordillera mts Spain see
Toledo, Montes de
Orewa N.Z. 109 E3
Oreye Belgium 48 F4
Orfanou, Kolpos b. Greece 55 J4
Orford Australia 107 [inset]
Orford U.K. 45 I6
Orford Ness hd U.K. 45 I6
Organabo Fr. Guiana 139 H2
Organ Pipe Cactus National
Monument nat. park U.S.A. 125 G5
Orge r. France 48 C6
Orgūn Afgh. 85 H3
Orhaneli Turkey 55 M5
Orhangazi Turkey 55 M4
Orhon Gol r. Mongolia 76 J2
Orichi Rus. Fed. 38 K4
Oriental, Cordillera mts Bol. 138 E7
Oriental, Cordillera mts Col. 138 D2
Oriental, Cordillera mts Peru
138 E6
Orihuela Spain 53 F4
Orikhiv Ukr. 39 G7
Orillia Canada 130 F1
Orimattila Fin. 41 N6
Orin U.S.A. 122 G4
Orinoco r. Col./Venez. 138 F2
Orinoco Delta Venez. 138 F2
Orissa state India 80 E1
Orissaare Estonia 41 M7
Oristano Sardinia Italy 54 C5
Orivesi Fin. 41 N6
Orivesi l. Fin. 40 P5
Oriximiná Brazil 139 G4
Orizaba Mex. 132 E5

▶Orizaba, Pico de vol. Mex. 132 E5
3rd highest mountain in North
America.

Orizona Brazil 141 A2
Orkanger Norway 40 F5
Örkelljunga Sweden 41 H8
Orkla r. Norway 40 F5
Orkney S. Africa 97 H4
Orkney is U.K. 46 F1
Orla U.S.A. 127 C6
Orland U.S.A. 124 B2
Orlândia Brazil 141 B3
Orlando U.S.A. 129 D6
Orland Park U.S.A. 130 B3
Orleaes Brazil 141 A5
Orléans France 52 E3
Orleans IN U.S.A. 130 B4
Orleans VT U.S.A. 131 I1
Orléans, Île d' i. Canada 119 H5
Orléansville Alg. see Ech Chélif
Orlik Rus. Fed. 68 H2
Orlov Rus. Fed. 38 K4
Orlov Gay Rus. Fed. 39 K6
Orlovskiy Rus. Fed. 39 I7
Orly airport France 48 C6
Ormara Pak. 85 G5
Ormara, Ras hd Pak. 85 G5
Ormiston Canada 117 J5
Ormoc Phil. 65 G4
Ormskirk U.K. 44 E5
Ormstown Canada 131 I1
Ornach Pak. 85 G5
Ornain r. France 48 E6
Orne r. France 52 D2
Ørnes Norway 40 H3
Örnsköldsvik Sweden 40 K5
Orobie, Alpi mts Italy 54 C1
Orobo, Serra do hills Brazil 141 C1
Orodara Burkina 92 C3
Orofino U.S.A. 122 D3
Oro Grande U.S.A. 124 E4
Orogrande U.S.A. 123 G6
Orol Dengizi salt l. Kazakh./Uzbek.
see Aral Sea
Oromocto Canada 119 I5
Oromocto Lake Canada 119 I5
Oron Israel 81 B4
Orona atoll Kiribati 103 I2
Orono U.S.A. 128 G2
Orontes r. Asia 86 E3 see
'Āṣī, Nahr al
Orontes r. Lebanon/Syria 81 C2
Oroqen Zizhiqi China see Alihe
Oroquieta Phil. 65 G5
Orós, Açude resr Brazil 139 K5
Orosei, Golfo di b. Sardinia Italy
54 C4
Orosháza Hungary 55 I1
Oroville U.S.A. 124 C2
Oroville, Lake U.S.A. 124 C2
Orqohan China 70 A2
Orr U.S.A. 126 E1
Orsa Sweden 41 I6
Orsha Belarus 39 F5
Orshanka Rus. Fed. 38 J4
Orsk Rus. Fed. 60 G4
Ørsta Norway 40 E5
Orta Toroslar plat. Turkey 81 A1
Ortegal, Cabo c. Spain 53 C2
Orthez France 52 D5
Ortigueira Spain 53 C2
Ortiz Mex. 123 F7
Ortles mt. Italy 54 D1
Orton U.K. 44 E4
Ortona Italy 54 F3
Ortonville U.S.A. 126 D2
Ortospana Afgh. see Kābul
Orulgan, Khrebet mts Rus. Fed.
61 N3
Orumbo Namibia 96 C2
Orūmīyeh Iran see Urmia
Oruro Bol. 138 E7
Orūzgān Afgh. 85 G3
Orvieto Italy 54 E3
Orville Coast Antarctica 148 L1
Orwell OH U.S.A. 130 E3
Orwell VT U.S.A. 131 I2
Oryol Rus. Fed. see Orel
Os Norway 40 G5
Osa Rus. Fed. 37 R4
Osa, Península de pen. Costa Rica
133 H7
Osage IA U.S.A. 126 E3
Osage WV U.S.A. 130 E4
Osage WY U.S.A. 122 G3
Ōsaka Japan 71 D6
Osakarovka Kazakh. 76 D1
Osawatomie U.S.A. 126 E4
Osborne U.S.A. 126 D4
Osby Sweden 41 H8
Osceola IA U.S.A. 126 E3
Osceola MO U.S.A. 126 E4
Osceola NE U.S.A. 126 D3
Oschatz Germany 49 N3
Oschersleben (Bode) Germany
49 L2
Oschiri Sardinia Italy 54 C4
Ösel i. Estonia see Hiiumaa
Osetr r. Rus. Fed. 39 H5
Ōse-zaki pt Japan 71 C6
Osgoode Canada 131 H1
Osgood Mountains U.S.A. 122 D4
Osh Kyrg. 76 D3
Oshakati Namibia 95 B5
Oshawa Canada 131 F2
Oshika-hantō pen. Japan 71 F5
Ō-shima i. Japan 70 E4
Ō-shima i. Japan 71 E6
Oshkosh NE U.S.A. 126 C3
Oshkosh WI U.S.A. 130 A1
Oshmyany Belarus see Ashmyany
Oshnovīyeh Iran 84 B2
Oshogbo Nigeria 92 D4
Oshtorān Kūh mt. Iran 84 C3
Oshwe Dem. Rep. Congo 94 B4
Osijek Croatia 54 H2
Osilinka r. Canada 116 E3
Osimo Italy 54 E3
Osipenko Ukr. see Berdyans'k
Osipovichi Belarus see Asipovichy
Osiyan India 78 C4
Osizweni S. Africa 97 J4
Osječenica mts Bos.-Herz. 54 G2
Ösjön l. Sweden 40 I5
Oskaloosa U.S.A. 126 E3
Oskarshamn Sweden 41 J8
Öskemen Kazakh. see
Ust'-Kamenogorsk

▶Oslo Norway 41 G7
Capital of Norway.

Oslofjorden sea chan. Norway
41 G7
Osmanabad India 80 C2
Osmancık Turkey 86 D2
Osmaneli Turkey 55 M4
Osmaniye Turkey 86 E3
Osmannagar India 80 C2
Os'mino Rus. Fed. 41 P7
Osnabrück Germany 49 I2
Osnaburg atoll Fr. Polynesia see
Mururoa
Osogbo Nigeria see Oshogbo
Osogovska Planina mts
Bulg./Macedonia 55 J3
Osogovske Planine mts
Bulg./Macedonia see
Osogovska Planina
Osogovski Planini mts
Bulg./Macedonia see
Osogovska Planina
Osorno Chile 140 B6
Osorno Spain 53 D2
Osoyoos Canada 116 G5
Osøyri Norway 41 D6
Osprey Reef Australia 106 D2
Oss Neth. 48 F3
Ossa, Mount Australia 107 [inset]
Osseo U.S.A. 118 C5
Ossineke U.S.A. 130 D1
Ossining U.S.A. 131 I3
Ossipee U.S.A. 131 J2
Ossipee Lake U.S.A. 131 J2
Oßmannstedt Germany 49 L3
Ossokmanuan Lake Canada 119 I3
Ossora Rus. Fed. 61 R4
Ostashkov Rus. Fed. 38 G4
Ostbevern Germany 49 H2
Oste r. Germany 49 J1
Ostend Belgium 48 C3
Ostende Belgium see Ostend
Osterburg (Altmark) Germany 49 L2
Österbymo Sweden 41 I8
Österdalälven l. Sweden 41 H6
Østerdalen valley Norway 41 G5
Osterfeld Germany 49 L3
Osterholz-Scharmbeck Germany
49 I1
Osterode am Harz Germany 49 K3
Österreich country Europe see
Austria
Östersund Sweden 40 I5
Osterwieck Germany 49 K3
Ostfriesische Inseln Germany see
East Frisian Islands
Ostfriesland reg. Germany 49 H1
Östhammar Sweden 41 K6
Ostrava Czech Rep. 43 Q6
Ostróda Poland 43 Q4
Ostrogozhsk Rus. Fed. 39 H6
Ostrov Czech Rep. 49 M4
Ostrov Rus. Fed. 41 P8
Ostrovets Poland see
Ostrowiec Świętokrzyski
Ostrovskoye Rus. Fed. 38 I4
Ostrov Vrangelya i. Rus. Fed. see
Wrangel Island
Ostrów Poland see
Ostrów Wielkopolski
Ostrowiec Poland see
Ostrowiec Świętokrzyski
Ostrowiec Świętokrzyski Poland
39 D6
Ostrów Mazowiecka Poland 43 R4
Ostrowo Poland see
Ostrów Wielkopolski
Ostrów Wielkopolski Poland 43 P5
O'Sullivan Lake Canada 118 D4
Osŭm r. Bulg. 55 K3
Ōsumi-shotō is Japan 71 C7
Osuna Spain 53 D5
Oswego KS U.S.A. 127 E4
Oswego NY U.S.A. 131 G2
Oswestry U.K. 45 D6
Otago Peninsula N.Z. 109 C7
Otahiti i. Fr. Polynesia see Tahiti
Otaki N.Z. 109 E5
Otanmäki Fin. 40 O4
Otaru Japan 70 F4
Otavi Namibia 95 B5
Ōtawara Japan 71 F5
Otdia atoll Marshall Is see Wotje
Otelnuc, Lac l. Canada 119 H2
Otematata N.Z. 109 C7
Otepää Estonia 41 O7
Otgon Tenger Uul mt. Mongolia
76 I2
Otinapa Mex. 127 B7
Otira N.Z. 109 C6
Otis U.S.A. 126 C3
Otish, Monts hills Canada 119 H4
Otjinene Namibia 95 B6
Otjiwarongo Namibia 95 B6
Otjozondjupa admin. reg. Namibia
96 C1
Otley U.K. 44 F5
Otorohanga N.Z. 109 E4
Otoskwin r. Canada 117 N5
Otpan, Gora hill Kazakh. 87 H1
Otpor Rus. Fed. see Zabaykal'sk
Otradnoye Rus. Fed. see Otradnyy
Otradnyy Rus. Fed. 39 K5
Otranto Italy 54 H4
Otranto, Strait of Albania/Italy
54 H4
Otrogovo Rus. Fed. see Stepnoye
Otrozhnyy Rus. Fed. 61 S3
Otsego Lake U.S.A. 131 H2
Ōtsu Japan 71 D6
Otta Norway 41 F6

▶Ottawa Canada 131 H1
Capital of Canada.

Ottawa r. Canada 118 G5
also known as Rivière des Outaouais
Ottawa IL U.S.A. 126 F3
Ottawa KS U.S.A. 126 E4
Ottawa OH U.S.A. 130 C3
Ottawa Islands Canada 118 E2
Otter r. U.K. 45 D8
Otterbein U.S.A. 130 B3
Otterburn U.K. 44 E3
Otter Rapids Canada 118 E4
Ottersberg Germany 49 J1
Ottignies Belgium 48 E4
Ottumwa U.S.A. 126 E3
Ottweiler Germany 49 H5
Otukpo Nigeria 92 D4
Oturkpo Nigeria see Otukpo
Otuzco Peru 138 C5
Otway, Cape Australia 108 A7
Otway National Park Australia
108 A7
Ouachita r. U.S.A. 127 F6
Ouachita, Lake U.S.A. 127 E5
Ouachita Mountains
Arkansas/Oklahoma U.S.A. 121 I5
Ouachita Mountains
Arkansas/Oklahoma U.S.A. 127 E5
Ouadda Cent. Afr. Rep. 94 C3
Ouaddaï reg. Chad 93 F3

▶Ouagadougou Burkina 92 C3
Capital of Burkina.

Ouahigouya Burkina 92 C3
Ouahran Alg. see Oran
Ouaka r. Cent. Afr. Rep. 94 B3
Oualâta Mauritania 92 C3
Ouallam Niger 92 D3
Ouanda-Djailé Cent. Afr. Rep.
94 C3
Ouando Cent. Afr. Rep. 94 C3
Ouango Cent. Afr. Rep. 94 C3
Ouara r. Cent. Afr. Rep. 94 C3
Ouarâne reg. Mauritania 92 C2
Ouargaye Burkina 92 D3
Ouargla Alg. 50 F5
Ouarogou Burkina see Ouargaye
Ouarzazate Morocco 50 C5
Oubangui r. Cent. Afr. Rep./
Dem. Rep. Congo see Ubangi
Oubergpas pass S. Africa 96 G7
Oudenaarde Belgium 48 D4
Oudtshoorn S. Africa 96 F7
Oud-Turnhout Belgium 48 E3
Oued Tlélat Alg. 53 F6
Oued Zem Morocco 50 C5
Oued Zénati Alg. 54 B6
Ouessant, Île d' i. France 52 B2
Ouesso Congo 94 B3
Ouezzane Morocco 53 D6
Oughter, Lough l. Rep. of Ireland
47 E3
Ouguati Namibia 96 B1
Ouistreham France 45 G9
Oujda Morocco 53 F6
Oujeft Mauritania 92 B3
Oulainen Fin. 40 N4
Oulangan kansallispuisto nat. park
Fin. 40 P3
Ouled Djellal Alg. 53 I6
Ouled Farès Alg. 53 G5
Ouled Naïl, Monts des mts Alg.
53 H6
Oulu Fin. 40 N4
Oulujärvi l. Fin. 40 O4
Oulujoki r. Fin. 40 N4
Oulunsalo Fin. 40 N4
Oulx Italy 54 B2
Oum-Chalouba Chad 93 F3
Oum el Bouaghi Alg. 54 B7
Oum-Hadjer Chad 93 E3
Ounasjoki r. Fin. 40 N3
Oundle U.K. 45 G6
Oungre Canada 117 K5
Ounianga Kébir Chad 93 F3
Oupeye Belgium 48 F4
Our r. Lux. 48 G5
Ouray CO U.S.A. 125 J2
Ouray UT U.S.A. 125 I1
Ourcq r. France 48 D5
Ourense Spain 53 C2
Ouricuri Brazil 139 J5
Ourinhos Brazil 141 A3
Ouro r. Brazil 141 A1
Ouro Preto Brazil 141 C3
Ourthe r. Belgium 48 F4
Ous Rus. Fed. 37 S3
Ouse r. England U.K. 44 G5
Ouse r. England U.K. 45 H8
Outaouais, Rivière des r. Canada
118 G5 see Ottawa
Outardes r. Canada 119 H4
Outardes Quatre, Réservoir resr
Canada 119 H4
Outer Hebrides is U.K. 46 B3
Outer Mongolia country Asia see
Mongolia
Outer Santa Barbara Channel
U.S.A. 124 D5
Outjo Namibia 95 B6
Outlook Canada 117 J5
Outokumpu Fin. 40 P5
Out Skerries is U.K. 46 [inset]
Ouvéa atoll New Caledonia 103 G4
Ouyanghai Shuiku resr China 73 G3
Ouyen Australia 107 C7
Ouzel r. U.K. 45 G6
Ovace, Punta d' mt. Corsica France
52 I6
Ovacık Turkey 81 A1
Ovada Italy 54 C2
Ovalle Chile 140 B4
Ovamboland reg. Namibia 95 B5
Ovan Gabon 94 B3
Ovar Port. 53 B3
Overath Germany 49 H4
Överkalix Sweden 40 M3
Overlander Roadhouse Australia
105 A6
Overland Park U.S.A. 126 E4
Overton U.S.A. 125 F3
Övertorneå Sweden 40 M3
Överum Sweden 41 J8
Overveen Neth. 48 E2
Ovid CO U.S.A. 126 C3
Ovid NY U.S.A. 131 G2
Oviedo Spain 53 D2
Ovoot Mongolia 69 K3
Øvre Anarjokka Nasjonalpark
nat. park Norway 40 N2
Øvre Dividal Nasjonalpark nat. park
Norway 40 K2
Øvre Rendal Norway 41 G6
Ovruch Ukr. 39 F6
Ovsyanka Rus. Fed. 70 B1
Owando Congo 94 B4
Owa Rafa i. Solomon Is see
Santa Ana
Owasco Lake U.S.A. 131 G2
Owase Japan 71 E6
Owatonna U.S.A. 126 E2
Owbeh Afgh. 85 F3
Owego U.S.A. 131 G2
Owel, Lough l. Rep. of Ireland 47 E4
Owen Island Myanmar 67 B5
Owenmore r. Rep. of Ireland 47 C3
Owenmore r. Rep. of Ireland 47 D3
Owenreagh r. U.K. 47 E3
Owen River N.Z. 109 D5
Owens r. U.S.A. 124 E3
Owensboro U.S.A. 130 B5
Owen Sound Canada 130 E1
Owen Sound inlet Canada 130 E1
Owen Stanley Range mts P.N.G.
65 L8
Owenton U.S.A. 130 C4
Owerri Nigeria 92 D4
Owikeno Lake Canada 116 E5
Owingsville U.S.A. 130 D4
Owl r. Canada 117 M3
Owl Creek Mountains U.S.A. 122 F4
Owo Nigeria 92 D4
Owosso U.S.A. 130 C2
Owyhee U.S.A. 122 D4
Owyhee r. U.S.A. 122 D4
Owyhee Mountains U.S.A. 122 D4
Öxarfjörður b. Iceland 40 [inset]
Oxbow Canada 117 K5
Ox Creek r. U.S.A. 126 C1
Oxelösund Sweden 41 J7
Oxford N.Z. 109 D6
Oxford U.K. 45 F7
Oxford IN U.S.A. 130 B3
Oxford MA U.S.A. 131 J2
Oxford MD U.S.A. 131 G4
Oxford MS U.S.A. 127 F5
Oxford NC U.S.A. 128 E4
Oxford NY U.S.A. 131 H2
Oxford OH U.S.A. 130 C4
Oxford House Canada 117 M4
Oxford Lake Canada 117 M4
Oxley Australia 108 B5
Oxleys Peak Australia 108 E3
Oxley Wild Rivers National Park
Australia 108 F3
Ox Mountains hills Rep. of Ireland
see Slieve Gamph
Oxnard U.S.A. 124 D4
Oxtongue Lake Canada 131 F1
Oxus r. Asia see Amudar'ya
Øya Norway 40 H3
Oyama Japan 71 E5
Oyem Gabon 94 B3
Oyen Canada 117 I5
Oygon Mongolia 76 I2
Oykel r. U.K. 46 E3
Oyo Nigeria 92 D4
Oyonnax France 52 G3
Oyster Rocks is India 80 B3
Oyten Germany 49 J1
Oytograk China 79 E1
Oyukludağı mt. Turkey 81 A1
Özalp Turkey 87 G3
Ozamiz Phil. 65 G5
Ozark AL U.S.A. 129 C6
Ozark AR U.S.A. 127 E5
Ozark MO U.S.A. 127 E4
Ozark Plateau U.S.A. 127 E4
Ozarks, Lake of the U.S.A. 126 E4
O'zbekiston country Asia see
Uzbekistan
Özen Kazakh. see Kyzylsay
Ozernovskiy Rus. Fed. 61 Q4
Ozernyy Rus. Fed. 39 G5
Ozerpakh Rus. Fed. 70 F1
Ozersk Rus. Fed. 41 M9
Ozerskiy Rus. Fed. 70 F3
Ozery Rus. Fed. 39 H5
Ozeryane Rus. Fed. 70 C2
Ozieri Sardinia Italy 54 C4
Ozinki Rus. Fed. 39 K6
Oznachennoye Rus. Fed. see
Sayanogorsk
Ozona U.S.A. 127 C6
Ozuki Japan 71 C6

↓ P

Paamiut Greenland 115 N3
Pa-an Myanmar 66 B3
Paanopa i. Kiribati see Banaba
Paarl S. Africa 96 D7
Paatsjoki r. Europe see Patsoyoki
Paballelo S. Africa 96 E5
P'abal-li N. Korea 70 C4
Pabbay i. U.K. 46 B3
Pabianice Poland 43 Q5
Pabianitz Poland see Pabianice
Pabna Bangl. 79 G4
Pabradė Lith. 41 N9
Pab Range mts Pak. 85 G5
Pacaás Novos, Parque Nacional
nat. park Brazil 138 F6
Pacaraimã, Serra mts S. America see
Pakaraima Mountains
Pacasmayo Peru 138 C5
Pachagarh Bangl. see Panchagarh
Pacheco Chihuahua Mex. 123 F7
Pacheco Zacatecas Mex. 127 C7
Pachikha Rus. Fed. 38 J3
Pachino Sicily Italy 54 F6
Pachmarhi India 78 D5
Pachor India 78 D5
Pachora India 80 B1
Pachpadra India 78 C4
Pachuca Mex. 132 E4
Pachuca de Soto Mex. see Pachuca
Pacific-Antarctic Ridge sea feature
S. Pacific Ocean 147 J9
Pacific Grove U.S.A. 124 C3

▶Pacific Ocean 146–147
Largest ocean in the world.

Pacific Rim National Park Canada
116 E5
Pacitan Indon. 64 E8
Packsaddle Australia 107 C6
Pacoval Brazil 139 H4
Pacuí r. Brazil 141 B2
Paczków Poland 43 P5
Padali Rus. Fed. see Amursk
Padampur India 78 C3
Padang Indon. 64 C7
Padang i. Indon. 67 C7
Padang Endau Malaysia 67 C7
Padangpanjang Indon. 64 C7
Padangsidimpuan Indon. 67 B7
Padany Rus. Fed. 38 G3
Padatha, Kūh-e mt. Iran 84 C3
Padaung Myanmar 66 A3
Padcaya Bol. 138 F8
Padderborn-Lippstadt airport
Germany 49 I3
Paden City U.S.A. 130 E4
Paderborn Germany 49 I3
Padeşu, Vârful mt. Romania 55 J2
Padibyu Myanmar 66 B2
Padilla Bol. 138 F7
Padjelanta nationalpark nat. park
Sweden 40 J3
Padova Italy see Padua
Padrão, Ponta pt Angola 95 B4
Padrauna India 79 F4
Padre Island U.S.A. 127 D7
Padstow U.K. 45 C8
Padsvillye Belarus 41 O9
Padua India 80 D2
Padua Italy 54 D2
Paducah KY U.S.A. 127 F4
Paducah TX U.S.A. 127 C5
Padum Jammu and Kashmir 78 D2
Paegam N. Korea 70 C4
Paektu-san mt. China/N. Korea see
Baotou Shan
Paengnyŏng-do i. S. Korea 71 B5
Pafos Cyprus see Paphos
Pafuri Moz. 97 J2
Pag Croatia 54 F2
Pag i. Croatia 54 F2
Paga Indon. 104 C2
Pagadian Phil. 65 G5
Pagai Selatan i. Indon. 64 C7
Pagalu i. Equat. Guinea see Annobón
Pagan i. N. Mariana Is 65 L3
Pagasitikos Kolpos b. Greece 55 J5
Pagatan Indon. 64 F7
Page U.S.A. 125 H3
Paget, Mount S. Georgia 140 I8
Paget Cay reef Australia 106 F3
Pagon i. N. Mariana Is see Pagan
Pagosa Springs U.S.A. 123 G5
Pagqên China see Gadê
Pagwa River Canada 118 D4
Pagwi P.N.G. 65 K7
Pahala HI U.S.A. 123 [inset]
Pahang r. Malaysia 67 C7
Pahlgam Jammu and Kashmir 78 C2
Pahoa HI U.S.A. 123 [inset]
Pahokee U.S.A. 129 D7
Pahra Kariz Afgh. 85 F3
Pahranagat Range mts U.S.A.
125 F3
Pahrump U.S.A. 125 F3
Pahuj r. India 78 D4
Pahute Mesa plat. U.S.A. 124 E3
Pai Thai. 66 B3
Paicines U.S.A. 124 C3
Paide Estonia 41 N7
Paignton U.K. 45 D8
Päijänne l. Fin. 41 N6
Paikü Co l. China 79 F3
Pailin Cambodia 67 C4
Pailolo Channel HI U.S.A. 123 [inset]
Paimio Fin. 41 M6
Painel Brazil 141 A4
Painesville U.S.A. 130 E3
Pains Brazil 141 B3
Painted Desert U.S.A. 125 H3
Painted Rock Dam U.S.A. 125 G5
Paint Hills Canada see Wemindji
Paint Rock U.S.A. 127 D6
Paintsville U.S.A. 130 D5
Paisley U.K. 46 E5
Paita Peru 138 B5
Paitou China 73 I2
Paiva Couceiro Angola see Quipungo
Paizhou China 73 G2
Pajala Sweden 40 M3
Paka Malaysia 67 C6
Pakala India 80 C3
Pakanbaru Indon. see Pekanbaru
Pakangyi Myanmar 66 A2
Pakaraima Mountains Guyana
138 G3
Pakaraima Mountains S. America
138 F3
Pakaur India 79 F4
Pakesley Canada 118 E5
Pakhachi Rus. Fed. 61 R3
Pakhoi China see Beihai
Paki Nigeria 92 D3

▶Pakistan country Asia 85 H4
4th most populous country in Asia.
asia 6, 58–59

Pakkat Indon. 67 B7
Paknampho Thai. see Nakhon Sawan
Pakokku Myanmar 66 A2
Pakowki Lake imp. l. Canada 117 I5
Pakpattan Pak. 85 I4
Pak Phanang Thai. 67 C5
Pak Phayun Thai. 67 C6
Pakruojis Lith. 41 M9
Paks Hungary 54 H1
Pakse Laos see Pakxé
Pak Tam Chung Hong Kong China
73 [inset]
Pak Thong Chai Thai. 66 C4
Pakur India see Pakaur
Pakxé Laos 66 D4
Pakxeng Laos 66 C2
Pala Chad 93 E4
Pala Myanmar 67 B4
Palaestinia reg. Asia see Palestine
Palaiochora Greece 55 J7
Palaiseau France 48 C6
Palakkad India see Palghat
Palakkat India see Palghat
Palamakoloi Botswana 96 F2
Palamau India see Palamu
Palamós Spain 53 H3
Palamu India 79 F5
Palana Rus. Fed. 61 Q4
Palandur India 80 D1
Palangān, Kūh-e mts Iran 85 F4
Palangkaraya Indon. 64 E7
Palani India 80 C4
Palanpur India 78 C4
Palantak Pak. 85 G5
Palapye Botswana 97 H2
Palatka Rus. Fed. 61 Q3
Palatka U.S.A. 129 D6
▶Palau country N. Pacific Ocean
65 I5
asia 6, 58–59
Palau Islands Palau 65 I5
Palauk Myanmar 67 B4
Palaw Myanmar 67 B4
Palawan i. Phil. 64 F5
Palawan Passage strait Phil. 64 F5
Palawan Trough sea feature
N. Pacific Ocean 146 D5
Palayankottai India 80 C4
Palchal Lake India 80 D2
Paldiski Estonia 41 N7
Palekh Rus. Fed. 38 I4
Palembang Indon. 64 C7
Palena Chile 140 B6
Palencia Spain 53 D2
Palermo Sicily Italy 54 E5
Palestine reg. Asia 81 B3
Palestine U.S.A. 127 E6
Paletwa Myanmar 66 A2
Palezgir Pak. 85 H4
Palghat India 80 C4
Palgrave, Mount hill Australia
105 A5
Palhoca Brazil 141 A4
Pali Chhattisgarh India 80 D1
Pali Maharashtra India 80 B2
Pali Rajasthan India 78 C4

▶Palikir Micronesia 146 G5
Capital of Micronesia.

Palinuro, Capo c. Italy 54 F4
Paliouri, Akra pt Greece 55 J5
Palisade U.S.A. 125 I2
Paliseul Belgium 48 F5
Palitana India 78 B5
Palivere Estonia 41 M7
Palk Bay Sri Lanka 80 C4
Palkino Rus. Fed. 41 P8
Palkonda Range mts India 80 C3
Palk Strait India/Sri Lanka 80 C4
Palla Bianca mt. Austria/Italy see
Weißkugel
Pallamallawa Australia 108 E2
Pallas Green Rep. of Ireland 47 D5
Pallas ja Ounastunturin kansal-
lispuisto nat. park Fin. 40 M2
Pallasovka Rus. Fed. 39 J6
Pallavaram India 80 D3
Palliser, Cape N.Z. 109 E5
Palliser, Îles is Fr. Polynesia 147 K7
Palliser Bay N.Z. 109 E5
Pallu India 78 C3
Palma r. Brazil 141 B1
Palma del Río Spain 53 D5
Palma de Mallorca Spain 53 H4
Palmaner India 80 C3
Palmares Brazil 139 K5
Palmares do Sul Brazil 141 A5
Palmas Brazil 141 A4
Palmas, Cape Liberia 92 C4
Palm Bay U.S.A. 129 D7
Palmdale U.S.A. 124 D4
Palmeira Brazil 141 A4
Palmeira das Missões Brazil 140 F3
Palmeira dos Índios Brazil 139 K5
Palmeirais Brazil 139 J5
Palmeiras Brazil 141 C1
Palmeirinhas, Ponta das pt Angola
95 B4
Palmer research station Antarctica
148 L2
Palmer r. Australia 106 C3
Palmer watercourse Australia 105 F6
Palmer U.S.A. 114 D3
Palmer Land reg. Antarctica 148 L2
Palmerston N.T. Australia 104 E3
Palmerston N.T. Australia see Darwin
Palmerston Canada 130 E2
Palmerston atoll Cook Is 103 J3
Palmerston N.Z. 109 C7
Palmerston North N.Z. 109 E5
Palmerton U.S.A. 131 H3
Palmerville Australia 106 D2
Palmetto Point Bahamas 129 E7
Palmi Italy 54 F5

Palmira Col. 138 C3
Palmira Cuba 129 D8
Palm Springs U.S.A. 124 E5
Palmyra Syria see Tadmur
Palmyra MO U.S.A. 126 F4
Palmyra PA U.S.A. 131 G3
Palmyra VA U.S.A. 131 F5

▶Palmyra Atoll terr. N. Pacific Ocean 146 J5
United States Unincorporated Territory.

Palmyras Point India 79 F5
Palni Hills India 80 C4
Palo Alto U.S.A. 124 B3
Palo Blanco Mex. 127 C7
Palo Chino watercourse Mex. 123 E7
Palo Duro watercourse U.S.A. 127 C5
Paloich Sudan 82 D7
Palojärvi Fin. 40 M2
Palojoensuu Fin. 40 M2
Palomaa Fin. 40 O2
Palomar Mountain U.S.A. 124 E5
Paloncha India 80 D2
Palo Pinto U.S.A. 127 D5
Palopo Indon. 65 G7
Palos, Cabo de c. Spain 53 F5
Palo Verde U.S.A. 125 F5
Paltamo Fin. 40 O4
Palu Indon. 64 F7
Palu i. Indon. 104 C2
Palu Turkey 87 E3
Pal'vart Turkm. 85 G2
Palwal India 78 D3
Palwancha India see Paloncha
Palyeskaya Nizina marsh Belarus/Ukr. see Pripet Marshes
Pambarra Moz. 97 L1
Pambula Australia 108 D6
Pamidi India 80 C3
Pamiers France 52 E5
Pamir mts Asia 85 I2
Pamlico Sound sea chan. U.S.A. 129 E5
Pamouscachiou, Lac l. Canada 119 H4
Pampa U.S.A. 127 C5
Pampa de Infierno Arg. 140 D3
Pampas reg. Arg. 140 D5
Pampeluna Spain see Pamplona
Pamphylia reg. Turkey 55 N6
Pamplin U.S.A. 131 F5
Pamplona Col. 138 D2
Pamplona Spain 53 F2
Pampow Germany 49 L1
Pamukova Turkey 55 N4
Pamzal Jammu and Kashmir 78 D2
Pana U.S.A. 126 F4
Panaca U.S.A. 125 F3
Panache, Lake Canada 118 E5
Panagyurishte Bulg. 55 K3
Panaitan i. Indon. 64 D8
Panaji India 80 B3
▶Panama country Central America 133 H7
north america 9, 112–113

▶Panama i. Indon. 104 C2
Most southerly point of Asia.

Panamá Panama see Panama City
Panamá, Golfo de Panama see Panama, Gulf of
Panama, Gulf of Panama 133 I7
Panama, Isthmus of Panama 133 I7
Panamá, Istmo de Panama see Panama, Isthmus of
Panama Canal Panama 133 I7

▶Panama City Panama 133 I7
Capital of Panama.

Panama City U.S.A. 129 C6
Panamint Range mts U.S.A. 124 E3
Panamint Valley U.S.A. 124 E3
Panao Peru 138 C5
Panarea, Isola i. Italy 54 F5
Panarik Indon. 67 E7
Panay i. Phil. 65 G4
Panayarvi Natsional'nyy Park nat. park Rus. Fed. 40 Q3
Pancake Range mts U.S.A. 125 F2
Pančevo Serb. and Mont. 55 I2
Panchagarh Bangl. 79 G4
Pancsova Serb. and Mont. see Pančevo
Panda Moz. 97 L3
Pandan, Selat strait Sing. 67 [inset]
Pandan Reservoir Sing. 67 [inset]
Pandeiros r. Brazil 141 B1
Pandharpur India 80 B2
Pandy U.K. 45 E7
Paneas Syria see Bāniyās
Panevėžys Lith. 41 N9
Panfilov Kazakh. see Zharkent
Pang, Nam r. Myanmar 66 B2
Panghsang Myanmar 66 B2
Pangi Range mts Pak. 85 I3
Pangkalanbuun Indon. 64 E7
Pangkalansusu Indon. 67 B6
Pangkalpinang Indon. 64 D7
Pangkalsiang, Tanjung pt Indon. 65 G7
Panglang Myanmar 66 B1
Pangman Canada 117 J5
Pangnirtung Canada 115 L3
Pangody Rus. Fed. 60 I3
Pangong Tso salt l. China/Jammu and Kashmir see Bangong Co
Pang Sida National Park Thai. 67 C4
Pang Sua, Sungai r. Sing. 67 [inset]
Pangtara Myanmar 72 C4
Pangu He r. China 70 B1
Panguitch U.S.A. 125 G3
Panhandle U.S.A. 127 C5
Panipat India 78 D3
Panir Pak. 85 G4
Panj Tajik. 85 H2
Panjāb Afgh. 85 G3
Panjakent Tajik. 85 G2
Panjang i. Indon. 67 E7
Panjang, Bukit Sing. 67 [inset]
Panjgur Pak. 85 G5
Panjim India see Panaji
Panji Poyon Tajik. 85 H2
Panjnad r. Pak. 85 H4
Panjshir reg. Afgh. 85 H3
Pankakoski Fin. 40 Q5
Panlian China see Miyi
Panna India 78 E4
Panna reg. India 78 D4
Pannawonica Australia 104 B5
Pano Lefkara Cyprus 81 A2
Panorama Brazil 141 A3
Panormus Sicily Italy see Palermo
Panshi China 70 B4
Panshui China see Pu'an

▶Pantanal marsh Brazil 139 G7
Largest area of wetlands in the world.

Pantanal Matogrossense, Parque Nacional do nat. park Brazil 139 G7
Pantano U.S.A. 125 H6
Pantar i. Indon. 104 D2
Pantelaria Sicily Italy see Pantelleria
Pantelleria Sicily Italy 54 D6
Pantelleria, Isola di i. Sicily Italy 54 E6
Pantha Myanmar 66 A2
Panther r. U.S.A. 130 B5
Panth Piploda India 78 C5
Panticapaeum Ukr. see Kerch
Pantonlabu Indon. 67 B6
Pánuco Sinaloa Mex. 127 B8
Pánuco Veracruz Mex. 132 E4
Panwari India 78 D4
Panxian China 72 E3
Panyu China 73 G4
Panzhihua China 72 D3
Panzi Dem. Rep. Congo 95 B4
Paola Italy 54 G5
Paola U.S.A. 126 E4
Paoli U.S.A. 130 B4
Paoua Cent. Afr. Rep. 94 B3
Paôy Pêt Cambodia 67 C4
Pápa Hungary 54 G1
Papa, Monte del mt. Italy 54 F4
Papagni r. India 80 C3
Papaikou HI U.S.A. 123 [inset]
Papakura N.Z. 109 E3
Papanasam India 80 C4
Papantla Mex. 132 E4
Paparoa National Park N.Z. 109 C6
Papa Stour i. U.K. 46 [inset]
Papa Westray i. U.K. 46 G1
Papay i. U.K. see Papa Westray

▶Papeete Fr. Polynesia 147 K7
Capital of French Polynesia.

Papenburg Germany 49 H1
Paphos Cyprus 81 A2
Paphus Cyprus see Paphos
Papillion U.S.A. 126 D3
Papoose Lake U.S.A. 125 F3
Pappenheim Germany 49 K6
Papua, Gulf of P.N.G. 65 K8

▶Papua New Guinea country Oceania 102 E2
2nd largest and 2nd most populous country in Oceania.
oceania 8, 100–101

Papun Myanmar 66 B3
Pa Qal'eh Iran 84 D4
Par U.K. 45 C8
Pará r. Brazil 141 B2
Pará, Rio do r. Brazil 139 I4
Paraburdoo Australia 105 B5
Paracatu Brazil 141 B2
Paracatu r. Brazil 141 B2
Paracel Islands S. China Sea 64 E3
Parachilna Australia 107 B6
Parachute U.S.A. 125 I2
Paraćin Serb. and Mont. 55 I3
Paracuru Brazil 139 K4
Pará de Minas Brazil 141 B2
Paradis Canada 118 F4
Paradise r. Canada 119 K3
Paradise U.S.A. 124 C2
Paradise Hill Canada 117 I4
Paradise Peak U.S.A. 124 E2
Paradise River Canada 119 K3
Paradwip India 79 F5
Paraetonium Egypt see Marsá Maṭrūḥ
Paragominas Brazil 139 I4
Paragould U.S.A. 127 F4
Paragua i. Phil. see Palawan
Paraguaçu Paulista Brazil 141 A3
Paraguay r. Arg./Para. 140 E3
▶Paraguay country S. America 140 E2
south america 9, 136–137
Paraíba do Sul r. Brazil 141 C3
Parainen Fin. see Pargas
Paraíso do Norte Brazil 139 I6
Paraisópolis Brazil 141 B3
Parak Iran 84 D5
Parakou Benin 92 D4
Paralakhemundi India 80 E2
Paralkot India 80 D2
Paramagudi India see Paramakkudi
Paramakkudi India 80 C4

▶Paramaribo Suriname 139 G2
Capital of Suriname.

Paramillo, Parque Nacional nat. park Col. 138 C2
Paramirim Brazil 141 C1
Paramo Frontino mt. Col. 138 C2
Paramus U.S.A. 131 H3
Paramushir, Ostrov i. Rus. Fed. 61 Q4
Paran watercourse Israel 81 B4
Paraná Arg. 140 D4
Paranã Brazil 141 B1
Paranã r. Brazil 141 A1
Paraná state Brazil 141 A4

▶Paraná r. S. America 140 E4
Part of the Río de la Plata - Paraná, 2nd longest river in South America.

Paraná, Serra do hills Brazil 141 B1
Paranaguá Brazil 141 A4
Paranaíba Brazil 141 A2
Paranaíba r. Brazil 141 A3
Paranapiacaba, Serra mts Brazil 141 A4
Paranavaí Brazil 140 F2
Parangi Aru r. Sri Lanka 80 D4
Parang Pass India 78 D2
Parângul Mare, Vârful mt. Romania 55 J2
Paranthan Sri Lanka 80 D4
Paraopeba Brazil 141 B2
Pārāpāra Iraq 87 G4
Paraparaumu N.Z. 109 E5
Paras Mex. 127 D7
Paras Pak. 85 I3
Paraspori, Akra pt Greece 55 L7
Parateca Brazil 141 C1
Paratinga Brazil 141 C1
Parāū, Kūh-e mt. Iraq 87 G4
Paraúna Brazil 141 A2
Parbhani India 80 C2
Parchim Germany 49 L1
Parding China 79 G2
Pardo r. Bahia Brazil 141 D1
Pardo r. Mato Grosso do Sul Brazil 140 F2
Pardo r. São Paulo Brazil 141 A3
Pardoo Australia 104 B5
Pardubice Czech Rep. 43 O5
Parece Vela i. Japan see Okino-Tori-shima
Parecis, Serra dos hills Brazil 138 F6
Pareh Iran 84 B2
Parenda India 80 B2
Parent Canada 118 G5
Parent, Lac l. Canada 118 F4
Pareora N.Z. 109 C7
Parepare Indon. 64 F7
Parga Greece 55 I5
Pargas Fin. 41 M6
Parghelia Italy 54 F5
Pargi India 80 C2
Paria, Gulf of Trin. and Tob./Venez. 133 L6
Paria, Península de pen. Venez. 138 F1
Paria Plateau U.S.A. 125 G3
Parikkala Fin. 41 P6
Parikud Islands India 80 E2
Parima, Serra mts Brazil 138 F3
Parima-Tapirapecó, Parque Nacional nat. park Venez. 138 F3
Parintins Brazil 139 G4
Paris Canada 130 E2

▶Paris France 48 C6
Capital of France and most populous city in Europe.

Paris IL U.S.A. 130 B4
Paris KY U.S.A. 130 C4
Paris MO U.S.A. 126 E4
Paris TN U.S.A. 127 F4
Paris TX U.S.A. 127 E5
Paris Crossing U.S.A. 130 C4
Parit Buntar Malaysia 67 C6
Pārīz Iran 84 D4
Pārk Iran 85 F5
Park U.K. 47 E3
Parkano Fin. 41 M5
Park City U.S.A. 130 B5
Parke Lake Canada 119 K3
Parker AZ U.S.A. 125 F4
Parker CO U.S.A. 122 G5
Parker Dam U.S.A. 125 F4
Parker Lake Canada 117 M2
Parker Range hills Australia 105 B8
Parkersburg U.S.A. 130 E4
Parkers Lake U.S.A. 130 C5
Parkes Australia 108 D4
Park Falls U.S.A. 126 F2
Park Forest U.S.A. 130 B3
Parkhar Tajik. see Farkhor
Parkhill Canada 130 E2
Park Rapids U.S.A. 126 E2
Parkutta Jammu and Kashmir 78 D2
Park Valley U.S.A. 122 E4
Parla Kimedi India see Paralakhemundi
Parlakimidi India see Paralakhemundi
Parli Vaijnath India 80 C2
Parlung Zangbo r. China 72 B2
Parma Italy 54 D2
Parma ID U.S.A. 122 D4
Parma OH U.S.A. 130 E3
Parnaíba Brazil 139 J4
Parnaíba r. Brazil 139 J4
Parnassos mt. Greece 55 J5
Parnassus N.Z. 109 D6
Parner India 80 B2
Parnon mts Greece 55 J6
Pärnu Estonia 41 N7
Pärnu-Jaagupi Estonia 41 N7
Paro Bhutan 79 G4
Parona Turkey see Fındık
Paroo watercourse Australia 108 A3
Paroo Channel watercourse Australia 108 A3
Paropamisus mts Afgh. 85 F3
Paros Greece 55 K6
Paros i. Greece 55 K6
Parowan U.S.A. 125 G3
Parral Chile 140 B5
Parramatta Australia 108 E4
Parramore Island U.S.A. 131 H5
Parras Mex. 127 C7
Parrett r. U.K. 45 D7
Parry, Cape Canada 149 A2
Parry, Kap c. Greenland see Kangaarsussuaq
Parry, Lac l. Canada 118 G2
Parry Bay Canada 115 J3
Parry Channel Canada 115 G2
Parry Islands Canada 115 G2
Parry Range hills Australia 104 A5
Parry Sound Canada 130 E1
Parsnip Peak U.S.A. 125 F2
Parsons KS U.S.A. 127 E4
Parsons WV U.S.A. 130 F4
Parsons Range hills Australia 104 F3
Partabgarh India 80 B2
Partabpur India 79 E5
Partenstein Germany 49 J4
Parthenay France 52 D3
Partizansk Rus. Fed. 70 D4
Partney U.K. 44 H5
Partridge r. Canada 118 E4
Partry Rep. of Ireland 47 C4
Partry Mts hills Rep. of Ireland 47 C4
Paru r. Brazil 139 H4
Pārūd Iran 85 F5
Paryang China 79 E3
Parys S. Africa 97 H4
Pasa Dağı mt. Turkey 86 D3
Pasadena CA U.S.A. 124 D4
Pasadena TX U.S.A. 127 E6
Pasado, Cabo c. Ecuador 138 B4
Pa Sang Thai. 66 B3
Pasawng Myanmar 66 B3
Pascagama r. Canada 118 G4
Pascagoula U.S.A. 127 F6
Pascagoula r. U.S.A. 127 F6
Paşcani Romania 55 L1
Pasco U.S.A. 122 D3
Pascoal, Monte hill Brazil 141 D2
Pascua, Isla de i. S. Pacific Ocean see Easter Island
Pas de Calais strait France/U.K. see Dover, Strait of
Pasewalk Germany 43 O4
Pasfield Lake Canada 117 J3
Pasha Rus. Fed. 38 G3
Pashih Haihsia sea chan. Phil./Taiwan see Bashi Channel
Pashkovo Rus. Fed. 70 C2
Pashkovskiy Rus. Fed. 39 H7
Pashtun Zarghun Afgh. 85 F3
Pashū'īyeh Iran 84 E4
Pasi Ga Myanmar 66 B1
Pasighat India 79 H3
Pasinler Turkey 87 F3
Pasir Gudang Malaysia 67 [inset]
Pasir Mas Malaysia 67 C6
Pasir Putih Malaysia 67 C6
Paskūh Iran 85 F5
Pasni Pak. 145 M4
Paso de los Toros Uruguay 140 E4
Paso de San Antonio Mex. 127 C6
Pasok Myanmar 66 A2
Paso Robles U.S.A. 124 C4
Pasquia Hills Canada 117 K4
Passaic U.S.A. 131 H3
Passa Tempo Brazil 141 B3
Passau Germany 43 N6
Passo del San Gottardo Switz. see St Gotthard Pass
Passo Fundo Brazil 140 F3
Passos Brazil 141 B3
Passur r. Bangl. see Pusur
Passuri Nadi r. Bangl. see Pusur
Pastavy Belarus 41 O9
Pastaza r. Peru 138 C4
Pasto Col. 138 C3
Pastora Peak U.S.A. 125 I3
Pastos Bons Brazil 139 J5
Pasu Jammu and Kashmir 78 C1
Pasur Turkey see Kulp
Pasvalys Lith. 41 N8
Pasvikelva r. Europe see Patsoyoki
Patache, Punta pt Chile 140 B2
Patagonia reg. Arg. 140 B8
Pataliputra India see Patna
Patan Gujarat India see Somnath
Patan Gujarat India 78 C5
Patan Maharashtra India 80 B2
Patan Nepal 79 F4
Patan Pak. 85 I3
Patandar, Koh-i- mt. Pak. 85 G5
Patavium Italy see Padua
Patea N.Z. 109 E4
Patea inlet N.Z. see Doubtful Sound
Pate Island Kenya 94 E4
Pateley Bridge U.K. 44 F4
Patensie S. Africa 96 G7
Patera India 78 D4
Paterson Australia 108 E4
Paterson r. Australia 108 C2
Paterson U.S.A. 131 H3
Paterson Range hills Australia 104 C5
Pathanamthitta India 80 C4
Pathankot India 78 C2
Pathari India 78 D5
Pathein Myanmar see Bassein
Pathfinder Reservoir U.S.A. 122 G4
Pathiu Thai. 67 B5
Pathum Thani Thai. 67 C4
Patía r. Col. 138 C3
Patiala India 78 D3
Patkai Bum mts India/Myanmar 79 H4
Patkaklik China 79 F1
Patmos i. Greece 55 L6
Patna India 79 F4
Patnagarh India 79 E5
Patnos Turkey 87 F3
Pato Branco Brazil 140 F3
Patoda India 80 B2
Patoka r. U.S.A. 130 B4
Patoka Lake U.S.A. 130 B4
Patos Albania 55 H4
Patos Brazil 139 K5
Patos, Lagoa dos l. Brazil 140 F4
Patos de Minas Brazil 141 B2
Patquía Arg. 140 C4
Patra Greece see Patras
Patrae Greece see Patras
Pátrai Greece see Patras
Patras Greece 55 I5
Patreksfjörður Iceland 40 [inset]
Patricio Lynch, Isla i. Chile 140 A7
Patrick Creek watercourse Australia 106 D4
Patrimônio Brazil 141 A2
Patrocínio Brazil 141 B2
Patrū Iran 85 E3
Patsoyoki r. Europe 40 Q2
Pattadakal tourist site India 80 B2
Pattani Thai. 67 C6
Pattaya Thai. 67 C4
Pattensen Germany 49 J2
Patterson CA U.S.A. 124 C3
Patterson LA U.S.A. 127 F6
Patterson, Mount Canada 116 C1
Patti India 79 E4
Pattijoki Fin. 40 N4
Pättikkä Fin. 40 L2
Patton U.S.A. 131 F3
Pattullo, Mount Canada 116 D3
Patu Brazil 139 K5
Patuakhali Bangl. 79 G5
Patuanak Canada 117 J4
Patuca, Punta pt Hond. 133 H5
Patur India 80 C1
Patuxent r. U.S.A. 131 G4
Patuxent Range mts Antarctica 148 L1
Patvinsuon kansallispuisto nat. park Fin. 40 Q5
Pau France 52 D5
Pauhunri mt. China/India 79 G4
Pauillac France 52 D4
Pauini Brazil 138 E5
Pauiní r. Brazil 138 E5
Pauk Myanmar 66 A2
Paukkaung Myanmar 66 A3
Paulatuk Canada 149 A2
Paulden U.S.A. 125 G4
Paulding U.S.A. 130 C3
Paulicéia Brazil 141 A3
Paulis Dem. Rep. Congo see Isiro
Paul Island Canada 119 J2
Paulo Afonso Brazil 139 K5
Paulo de Faria Brazil 141 A3
Paulpietersburg S. Africa 97 J4
Paul Roux S. Africa 97 H5
Pauls Valley U.S.A. 127 D5
Paumotu, Îles is Fr. Polynesia see Tuamotu Islands
Paung Myanmar 66 B3
Paungbyin Myanmar 66 A1
Paungde Myanmar 66 A3
Pauni India 80 C1
Pauri India 78 D3
Pavagada India 80 C3
Pavão Brazil 141 C2
Pāveh Iran 84 B3
Pavia Italy 54 C2
Pāvilosta Latvia 41 L8
Pavino Rus. Fed. 38 J4
Pavlikeni Bulg. 55 K3
Pavlodar Kazakh. 76 E1
Pavlof Volcano U.S.A. 114 B4
Pavlograd Ukr. see Pavlohrad
Pavlohrad Ukr. 39 G6
Pavlovka Rus. Fed. 39 J5
Pavlovo Rus. Fed. 38 I5
Pavlovsk Altayskiy Kray Rus. Fed. 68 E2
Pavlovsk Voronezhskaya Oblast' Rus. Fed. 39 I6
Pavlovskaya Rus. Fed. 39 H7
Pawahku Myanmar 66 B1
Pawai India 78 E4
Pawnee U.S.A. 127 D4
Pawnee r. U.S.A. 126 D4
Pawnee City U.S.A. 126 D3
Paw Paw MI U.S.A. 130 C2
Paw Paw WV U.S.A. 131 F4
Pawtucket U.S.A. 131 J3
Pawut Myanmar 67 B4
Paxson U.S.A. 114 D3
Paxton U.S.A. 130 A3
Payakumbuh Indon. 64 C7
Paya Lebar Sing. 67 [inset]
Payette U.S.A. 122 D3
Pay-Khoy, Khrebet hills Rus. Fed. 60 H3
Payne Canada see Kangirsuk
Payne, Lac l. Canada 118 G2
Paynes Creek U.S.A. 124 C1
Payne's Find Australia 105 B7
Paynesville U.S.A. 126 E2
Paysandú Uruguay 140 E4
Pays de Bray reg. France 48 B5
Payshanba Uzbek. 85 G1
Payson U.S.A. 125 H4
Pazar Turkey 87 F2
Pazarcık Turkey 86 E3
Pazardzhik Bulg. 55 K3
Pazin Croatia 54 E2
Pe Myanmar 67 B4
Peabody KS U.S.A. 126 D4
Peabody MA U.S.A. 131 J2
Peace r. Canada 116 I3
Peace Point Canada 117 H3
Peace River Canada 116 G3
Peach Creek U.S.A. 130 E5
Peach Springs U.S.A. 125 G4
Peacock Hills Canada 117 I1
Peak Charles hill Australia 105 C8
Peak Charles National Park Australia 105 C8
Peak District National Park U.K. 44 F5
Peake watercourse Australia 107 B6
Peaked Mountain hill U.S.A. 128 G2
Peak Hill N.S.W. Australia 108 D4
Peak Hill W.A. Australia 105 B6
Peale, Mount U.S.A. 125 I2
Peanut U.S.A. 124 B1
Pearce U.S.A. 125 I6
Pearce Point Australia 104 E3
Pearisburg U.S.A. 130 E5
Pearl r. U.S.A. 127 F6
Pearl Harbor inlet HI U.S.A. 123 [inset]
Pearsall U.S.A. 127 D6
Pearson U.S.A. 129 D6
Pearston S. Africa 97 G7
Peary Channel Canada 115 I2
Peary Land reg. Greenland 149 J1
Pease r. U.S.A. 127 D5
Peawanuck Canada 118 D3
Pebane Moz. 95 D5
Pebas Peru 138 D4
Peć Serb. and Mont. 55 I3
Peçanha Brazil 141 C2
Peças, Ilha das i. Brazil 141 A4
Pechenga Rus. Fed. 40 Q2
Pechora Rus. Fed. 38 M2
Pechora r. Rus. Fed. 38 L1
Pechora Sea Rus. Fed. see Pechorskoye More
Pechorskaya Guba b. Rus. Fed. 38 L1
Pechorskoye More sea Rus. Fed. 149 G2
Pechory Rus. Fed. 41 O8
Peck U.S.A. 130 D2
Pecos U.S.A. 127 C6
Pecos r. U.S.A. 127 C6
Pécs Hungary 54 H1
Pedda Vagu r. India 80 C2
Pedder, Lake Australia 107 [inset]
Peddie S. Africa 97 H7
Pedernales Dom. Rep. 133 J5
Pedersöre Fin. 40 M5
Pediaios r. Cyprus 81 A2
Pediva Angola 95 B5
Pedra Azul Brazil 141 C1
Pedra Preta, Serra da mts Brazil 141 A1
Pedras de Maria da Cruz Brazil 141 B1
Pedregulho Brazil 141 B3
Pedreiras Brazil 139 J4
Pedriceña Mex. 127 C7
Pedro, Point Sri Lanka 80 D4
Pedro Betancourt Cuba 129 D8
Pedro II, Ilha reg. Brazil/Venez. 138 E3
Pedro Juan Caballero Para. 140 E2
Peebles U.K. 46 F5
Peebles U.S.A. 130 D4
Pee Dee r. U.S.A. 129 E5
Peekskill U.S.A. 131 I3
Peel r. Australia 108 E3
Peel r. Canada 114 E3
Peel Isle of Man 44 C4
Peer Belgium 48 F3
Peera Peera Poolanna Lake salt flat Australia 107 B5
Peerless Lake Canada 116 H3
Peerless Lake l. Canada 116 H3
Peers Canada 116 G4
Peery Lake salt flat Australia 108 A3
Pegasus Bay N.Z. 109 D6
Pegnitz Germany 49 L5
Pegu Myanmar 66 B3
Pegu Yoma mts Myanmar 66 A3
Pegysh Rus. Fed. 38 K3
Pehuajó Arg. 140 D5
Peikang Taiwan 73 I4
Peine Chile 140 C2
Peine Germany 49 K2
Peint India 80 B1
Peipsi järv l. Estonia/Rus. Fed. see Peipus, Lake
Peipus, Lake Estonia/Rus. Fed. 41 O7
Peiraias Greece see Piraeus
Pei Shan mts China see Bei Shan
Peißen Germany 49 L3
Peixe Brazil 139 I6
Peixe r. Brazil 141 A1
Peixian Jiangsu China see Pizhou
Peixian Jiangsu China 73 H1
Peixoto de Azevedo Brazil 139 H6
Pejë Serb. and Mont. see Peć
Pèk Laos see Xiangkhoang
Peka Lesotho 97 H5
Pekan Malaysia 67 C7
Pekanbaru Indon. 64 C6
Pekin U.S.A. 126 F3
Peking China see Beijing
Pekinga Benin 92 D3
Pelabohan Klang Malaysia see Pelabuhan Kelang
Pelabuhan Kelang Malaysia 67 C7
Pelagie, Isole is Sicily Italy 54 E7
Pelaihari Indon. 64 E7
Peleaga, Vârful mt. Romania 55 J2
Pelee Island Canada 130 D3
Pelee Point Canada 130 D3
Peles Rus. Fed. 38 K3
Pélican, Lac du l. Canada 119 G2
Pelican Lake Canada 117 K4
Pelican Lake U.S.A. 126 E1
Pelican Narrows Canada 117 K4
Pelkosenniemi Fin. 40 O3
Pella S. Africa 96 D5
Pellatt Lake Canada 117 I1
Pelleluhu Islands P.N.G. 65 K7
Pello Fin. 40 M3
Pelly r. Canada 116 C2
Pelly Crossing Canada 116 B2
Pelly Lake Canada 117 K1
Pelly Mountains Canada 116 C2
Peloponnese admin. reg. Greece 55 J6
Pelopónnesos admin. reg. Greece see Peloponnese
Peloponnisos admin. reg. Greece see Peloponnese
Pelotas Brazil 140 F4
Pelotas, Rio das r. Brazil 141 A4
Pelusium tourist site Egypt 81 A4
Pelusium, Bay of Egypt see Ţīnah, Khalīj aţ
Pemangkat Indon. 67 E7
Pematangsiantar Indon. 67 B7
Pemba Moz. 95 E5
Pemba Island Tanz. 95 D4
Pemberton Canada 116 F5
Pembina r. Canada 116 H4
Pembina r. U.S.A. 126 D1
Pembine U.S.A. 128 C2
Pembre Indon. 65 J8
Pembroke Canada 118 F5
Pembroke U.K. 45 C7
Pembroke U.S.A. 129 D5
Pembrokeshire Coast National Park U.K. 45 B7
Pen India 80 B2
Peña Cerredo mt. Spain see Torrecerredo
Peñalara mt. Spain 53 E3
Penamar Brazil 141 C1
Peña Nevada, Cerro mt. Mex. 132 E4
Penang Malaysia see George Town
Penang i. Malaysia see Pinang
Penápolis Brazil 141 A3
Peñaranda de Bracamonte Spain 53 D3
Penarie Australia 108 A5
Penarlâg U.K. see Hawarden
Peñarroya mt. Spain 53 F3
Peñarroya-Pueblonuevo Spain 53 D4
Penarth U.K. 45 D7
Peñas, Cabo de c. Spain 53 D2
Penas, Golfo de g. Chile 140 A7
Penasi, Pulau i. Indon. 67 A6
Peña Ubiña mt. Spain 53 D2
Pench National Park India 78 D5
Pender U.S.A. 126 D3
Pendle Hill hill U.K. 44 E5
Pendleton U.S.A. 122 D3
Pendleton Bay Canada 116 E4
Pend Oreille r. U.S.A. 122 D2
Pend Oreille Lake U.S.A. 122 D2
Pendra India 79 E5
Penduv India 80 B2
Pendzhikent Tajik. see Panjakent
Penebangan i. Indon. 64 D7
Peneda Gerês, Parque Nacional da nat. park Port. 53 B3
Penetanguishene Canada 130 F1
Penfro U.K. see Pembroke
Peng'an China 72 E2
Penganga r. India 80 C2
Peng Chau i. Hong Kong China 73 [inset]
P'engchia Yü i. Taiwan 73 I3
Penge Dem. Rep. Congo 95 C4
Penge S. Africa 97 J3
P'enghu Ch'üntao is Taiwan 73 H4
P'enghu Liehtao is Taiwan see P'enghu Ch'üntao
P'enghu Tao i. Taiwan 73 H4
Peng Kang hill Sing. 67 [inset]
Penglaizhen China see Daying
Pengshan China 72 D2
Pengshui China 73 F2
Pengwa Myanmar 66 A2
Pengxi China 72 E2
Penha Brazil 141 A4
Penhoek Pass S. Africa 97 H6
Penhook U.S.A. 130 F5
Peniche Port. 53 B4
Penicuik U.K. 46 F5
Penig Germany 49 M4
Peninga Rus. Fed. 40 R5
Peninsular Malaysia Malaysia 67 D6
Penitente, Serra do hills Brazil 139 I5
Penn U.S.A. see Penn Hills
Pennell Coast Antarctica 148 H2
Penn Hills U.S.A. 130 F3
Pennine, Alpi mts Italy/Switz. 54 B2
Pennine Alps mts Italy/Switz. see Pennine, Alpi
Pennines hills U.K. 44 E4
Pennington Gap U.S.A. 130 D5
Pennsburg U.S.A. 131 H3
Penns Grove U.S.A. 131 H4
Pennsville U.S.A. 131 H4
Pennsylvania state U.S.A. 130 F3
Pennville U.S.A. 130 C3
Penn Yan U.S.A. 131 G2
Penny Icecap Canada 115 L3
Penny Point Antarctica 148 H1
Penola Australia 107 C8
Peñón Blanco Mex. 127 B7
Penong Australia 105 F7
Penonomé Panama 133 H7
Penrhyn atoll Cook Is 147 J6
Penrhyn Basin sea feature S. Pacific Ocean 147 J6
Penrith Australia 108 E4
Penrith U.K. 44 E4
Pensacola U.S.A. 129 C6
Pensacola Mountains Antarctica 148 L1
Pensi La pass Jammu and Kashmir 78 D2

Plasencia Spain 53 C3
Plaster City U.S.A. 125 F5
Plaster Rock Canada 119 I5
Plastun Rus. Fed. 70 E3
Platani r. Sicily Italy 54 E6
Platberg mt. S. Africa 97 I5
▶Plateau Antarctica
Lowest recorded annual mean temperature in the world.
world 16–17
Plateau of Tibet China 79 F2
Platina U.S.A. 124 B1
Platinum U.S.A. 149 B3
Plato Col. 138 D2
Platte r. U.S.A. 126 E3
Platte City U.S.A. 126 E4
Plattling Germany 49 M6
Plattsburgh U.S.A. 131 I1
Plattsmouth U.S.A. 126 E3
Plau Germany 49 M1
Plauen Germany 49 M4
Plauer See l. Germany 49 M1
Plavsk Rus. Fed. 39 H5
Playa Noriega, Lago l. Mex. 123 F7
Playas Ecuador 138 B4
Playas Lake U.S.A. 125 I6
Plây Cu Vietnam 67 E4
Pleasant, Lake U.S.A. 125 G5
Pleasant Bay U.S.A. 131 K3
Pleasant Grove U.S.A. 125 H1
Pleasant Hill Lake U.S.A. 130 D3
Pleasanton U.S.A. 127 D6
Pleasant Point N.Z. 109 C7
Pleasantville U.S.A. 131 H4
Pleasure Ridge Park U.S.A. 130 C4
Pleaux France 52 F4
Pledger Lake Canada 118 E4
Plei Doch Vietnam 67 D4
Pleinfeld Germany 49 K5
Pleiße r. Germany 49 M3
Plenty watercourse Australia 106 B5
Plenty, Bay of g. N.Z. 109 F3
Plentywood U.S.A. 122 G2
Plesetsk Rus. Fed. 38 I3
Pleshchentsy Belarus see Plyeshchanitsy
Pletipi, Lac l. Canada 119 H4
Plettenberg Germany 49 H3
Plettenberg Bay S. Africa 96 F8
Pleven Bulg. 55 K3
Plevna Bulg. see Pleven
Pljevlja Serb. and Mont. 55 H3
Płock Poland 43 Q4
Pločno mt. Bos.-Herz. 54 G3
Plodovoye Rus. Fed. 38 F3
Ploemeur France 52 C3
Ploești Romania see Ploiești
Ploiești Romania 55 L2
Plomb du Cantal mt. France 52 F4
Ploskoye Rus. Fed. see Stanovoye
Płoty Poland 43 O4
Ploudalmézeau France 52 B2
Plouzané France 52 B2
Plovdiv Bulg. 55 K3
Plover Cove Reservoir Hong Kong China 73 [inset]
Plozk Poland see Płock
Plum U.S.A. 130 F3
Plumridge Lakes salt flat Australia 105 D7
Plungė Lith. 41 L9
Plutarco Elías Calles, Presa resr Mex. 123 F7
Pluto, Lac l. Canada 119 H3
Plyeshchanitsy Belarus 41 O9
Ply Huey Wati, Khao mt. Myanmar/Thai. 66 B3
▶Plymouth Montserrat 133 L5
Capital of Montserrat, largely abandoned in 1997 owing to volcanic activity.
Plymouth U.K. 45 C8
Plymouth CA U.S.A. 124 C2
Plymouth IN U.S.A. 130 B3
Plymouth MA U.S.A. 131 J3
Plymouth NC U.S.A. 128 E5
Plymouth NH U.S.A. 131 J2
Plymouth WI U.S.A. 130 B2
Plymouth Bay U.S.A. 131 J3
Plynlimon hill U.K. 45 D6
Plyussa Rus. Fed. 41 P7
Plzeň Czech Rep. 43 N6
Pô Burkina 92 C3
Po r. Italy 54 E2
Pô, Parc National de nat. park Burkina 92 C3
Pobeda Peak China/Kyrg. 76 F3
Pobedy, Pik mt. China/Kyrg. see Pobeda Peak
Pocahontas U.S.A. 127 F4
Pocatello U.S.A. 122 E4
Pochala Sudan 93 G4
Pochayiv Ukr. 39 E6
Pochep Rus. Fed. 39 G5
Pochinki Rus. Fed. 39 J5
Pochinok Rus. Fed. 39 G5
Pochutla Mex. 132 E5
Pocking Germany 43 N6
Pocklington U.K. 44 G5
Poções Brazil 141 C1
Pocomoke City U.S.A. 131 H4
Pocomoke Sound b. U.S.A. 131 H5
Poconé Brazil 139 G7
Pocono Mountains hills U.S.A. 131 H3
Pocono Summit U.S.A. 131 H3
Poços de Caldas Brazil 141 B3
Podanur India 80 C4
Poddor'ye Rus. Fed. 38 F4
Podgorenskiy Rus. Fed. 39 H6
Podgorica Serb. and Mont. 55 H3
Podgornoye Rus. Fed. 60 J4
Podile India 80 C3
Podișul Transilvaniei plat. Romania see Transylvanian Basin
Podkamennaya Tunguska r. Rus. Fed. 61 K3
Podocarpus, Parque Nacional nat. park Ecuador 138 C4
Podol'sk Rus. Fed. 39 H5
Podporozh'ye Rus. Fed. 38 G3
Podujevë Serb. and Mont. see Podujevo
Podujevo Serb. and Mont. 55 I3
Podz' Rus. Fed. 38 K3
Poelela, Lagoa l. Moz. 97 L3
Poeppel Corner salt flat Australia 107 B5
Poetovio Slovenia see Ptuj
Pofadder S. Africa 96 D5
Pogar Rus. Fed. 39 G5
Poggibonsi Italy 54 D3
Poggio di Montieri mt. Italy 54 D3
Pogradec Albania 55 I4
Pogranichnik Afgh. 85 F3
Po Hai g. China see Bo Hai
P'ohang S. Korea 71 C5
Pohnpei atoll Micronesia 146 G5
Pohri India 78 D4
Poi India 79 H4
Poiana Mare Romania 55 J3
Poinsett, Cape Antarctica 148 F2
Point Arena U.S.A. 124 B2
Point au Fer Island U.S.A. 127 F6
Pointe a la Hache U.S.A. 127 F6
Pointe-à-Pitre Guadeloupe 133 L5
Pointe-Noire Congo 95 B4
Point Hope U.S.A. 114 B3
Point Lake Canada 116 H1
Point of Rocks U.S.A. 122 F4
Point Pelee National Park Canada 130 D3
Point Pleasant NJ U.S.A. 131 H3
Point Pleasant WV U.S.A. 130 D4
Poitiers France 52 E3
Poitou reg. France 52 E3
Poix-de-Picardie France 48 B5
Pojuca r. Brazil 141 D1
Pokaran India 78 B4
Pokataroo Australia 108 D2
Pokcha Rus. Fed. 37 R3
Pokhara Nepal 79 E3
Pokhvistnevo Rus. Fed. 37 Q5
Pok Liu Chau i. Hong Kong China see Lamma Island
Poko Dem. Rep. Congo 94 C3
Pokosnoye Rus. Fed. 68 I1
Pokran Pak. 85 G5
P'ok'r Kovkas mts Asia see Lesser Caucasus
Pokrovka Chitinskaya Oblast' Rus. Fed. 70 A1
Pokrovka Primorskiy Kray Rus. Fed. 70 C4
Pokrovsk Respublika Sakha (Yakutiya) Rus. Fed. 61 N3
Pokrovsk Saratovskaya Oblast' Rus. Fed. see Engel's
Pokrovskoye Rus. Fed. 39 H7
Pokshen'ga r. Rus. Fed. 38 J3
Pol India 78 C5
Pola Croatia see Pula
Polacca Wash watercourse U.S.A. 125 H4
Pola de Lena Spain 53 D2
Pola de Siero Spain 53 D2
▶Poland country Europe 36 J5
europe 5, 34–35
Poland NY U.S.A. 131 H2
Poland OH U.S.A. 130 E3
Polar Plateau Antarctica 148 A1
Polatlı Turkey 86 D3
Polatsk Belarus 41 P9
Polavaram India 80 D2
Polcirkeln Sweden 40 L3
Pol-e Fāsā Iran 84 D4
Pole-Khatum Iran 85 F2
Pol-e Khomrī Afgh. 85 H3
Pol-e Safīd Iran 84 D2
Polessk Rus. Fed. 41 L9
Poles'ye marsh Belarus/Ukr. see Pripet Marshes
Polgahawela Sri Lanka 80 D5
Poli Cyprus see Polis
Políaigos i. Greece see Polyaigos
Police Poland 43 O4
Policoro Italy 54 G4
Poligny France 52 G3
Polikastron Greece see Polykastro
Polillo Islands Phil. 65 G3
Polis Cyprus 81 A2
Polis'ke Ukr. 39 F6
Polis'kyy Zapovidnyk nature res. Ukr. 39 F6
Politovo Rus. Fed. 38 K2
Políyiros Greece see Polygyros
Polkowice Poland 43 P5
Pollachi India 80 C4
Pollard Islands U.S.A. see Gardner Pinnacles
Polle Germany 49 J3
Pollino, Monte mt. Italy 54 G5
Pollino, Parco Nazionale del nat. park Italy 54 G5
Pollock Pines U.S.A. 124 C2
Pollock Reef Australia 105 C8
Polmak Norway 40 O1
Polnovat Rus. Fed. 37 T3
Polo Fin. 40 P4
Poloat atoll Micronesia see Puluwat
Pologi Ukr. see Polohy
Polohy Ukr. 39 H7
Polonne Ukr. 39 E6
Polonnoye Ukr. see Polonne
Polotsk Belarus see Polatsk
Polperro U.K. 45 C8
Polska country Europe see Poland
Polson U.S.A. 122 E3
Polta r. Rus. Fed. 38 I2
Poltava Ukr. 39 G6
Poltoratsk Turkm. see Ashgabat
Põltsamaa Estonia 41 N7
Polunochnoye Rus. Fed. 37 S3
Põlva Estonia 41 O7
Polvadera U.S.A. 123 G6
Polvijärvi Fin. 40 P5
Polyaigos i. Greece 55 K6
Polyanovgrad Bulg. see Karnobat
Polyarnyy Chukotskiy Avtonomnyy Okrug Rus. Fed. 61 S3
Polyarnyy Murmanskaya Oblast' Rus. Fed. 40 R2
Polyarnyye Zori Rus. Fed. 40 R3
Polyarnyy Ural mts Rus. Fed. 37 S2
Polygyros Greece 55 J4
Polykastro Greece 55 J4
Polynesia is Pacific Ocean 146 I6
Polynésie Française terr. S. Pacific Ocean see French Polynesia
Pom Indon. 65 J7
Pomarkku Fin. 41 M6
Pombal Pará Brazil 139 H4
Pombal Paraíba Brazil 139 K5
Pombal Port. 53 B4
Pomene Moz. 97 L2
Pomeroy S. Africa 97 J5
Pomeroy U.K. 47 F3
Pomeroy OH U.S.A. 130 D4
Pomeroy WA U.S.A. 122 D3
Pomezia Italy 54 E4
Pomfret S. Africa 96 F3
Pomona Namibia 96 B4
Pomona U.S.A. 124 E4
Pomorie Bulg. 55 L3
Pomorska, Zatoka b. Poland 43 O3
Pomorskie, Pojezierze reg. Poland 43 O4
Pomorskiy Bereg coastal area Rus. Fed. 38 G2
Pomorskiy Proliv sea chan. Rus. Fed. 38 K1
Pomos Point Cyprus 81 A2
Pomo Tso l. China see Puma Yumco
Pomou, Akra pt Cyprus see Pomos Point
Pomozdino Rus. Fed. 38 L3
Pompain China 72 B2
Pompano Beach U.S.A. 129 D7
Pompei Italy 54 F4
Pompéia Brazil 141 A3
Pompey France 48 G6
Pompeyevka Rus. Fed. 70 C2
Ponape atoll Micronesia see Pohnpei
Ponask Lake Canada 117 M4
Ponazyrevo Rus. Fed. 38 J4
Ponca City U.S.A. 127 D4
Ponce Puerto Rico 133 K5
Ponce de Leon Bay U.S.A. 129 D7
Poncheville, Lac l. Canada 118 F4
Pondicherry India 80 C4
Pondicherry union terr. India 80 C4
Pondichéry India see Pondicherry
Pond Inlet Canada 149 K2
Ponds Bay Canada see Pond Inlet
Ponente, Riviera di coastal area Italy 54 B3
Poneto U.S.A. 130 C3
Ponferrada Spain 53 C2
Pongara, Pointe pt Gabon 94 A3
Pongaroa N.Z. 109 F5
Pongo watercourse Sudan 93 F4
Pongola r. S. Africa 97 K4
Pongolapoort Dam l. S. Africa 97 J4
Ponnagyun Myanmar 66 A2
Ponnaivar r. India 80 C4
Ponnampet India 80 B3
Ponnani India 80 B4
Ponnyadaung Range mts Myanmar 66 A2
Pono Indon. 65 I8
Ponoka Canada 116 H4
Ponoy r. Rus. Fed. 38 I2
Pons r. Canada 119 H2
▶Ponta Delgada Arquipélago dos Açores 144 G3
Capital of the Azores.
Ponta Grossa Brazil 141 A4
Pontal Brazil 141 A3
Pontalina Brazil 141 A2
Pont-à-Mousson France 48 G6
Ponta Porã Brazil 140 E2
Pontarfynach U.K. see Devil's Bridge
Pont-Audemer France 45 H9
Pontault-Combault France 48 C6
Pontax r. Canada 118 F4
Pontchartrain, Lake U.S.A. 127 F6
Pont-de-Loup Belgium 48 E4
Ponte Alta do Norte Brazil 139 I6
Ponte de Sor Port. 53 B4
Ponte Firme Brazil 141 B2
Pontefract U.K. 44 F5
Ponteix Canada 117 J5
Ponteland U.K. 44 F3
Ponte Nova Brazil 141 C3
Pontes-e-Lacerda Brazil 139 G7
Pontevedra Spain 53 B2
Ponthierville Dem. Rep. Congo see Ubundu
Pontiac IL U.S.A. 126 F3
Pontiac MI U.S.A. 130 D2
Pontiae is Italy see Ponziane, Isole
Pontianak Indon. 64 D7
Pontine Islands is Italy see Ponziane, Isole
Pont-l'Abbé France 52 B3
Pontoise France 48 C5
Ponton watercourse Australia 105 C7
Ponton Canada 117 L4
Pontotoc U.S.A. 127 F5
Pont-Ste-Maxence France 48 C5
Pontypool U.K. 45 D7
Pontypridd U.K. 45 D7
Ponza, Isola di i. Italy 54 E4
Ponziane, Isole is Italy 54 E4
Poochera Australia 105 F8
Poole U.K. 45 F8
Poole U.S.A. 130 B5
Poolowanna Lake salt flat Australia 107 B5
Poona India see Pune
Pooncarie Australia 107 C7
Poonch India see Punch
Poopelloe, Lake salt l. Australia 108 B3
Poopó, Lago de l. Bol. 138 E7
Poor Knights Islands N.Z. 109 E2
Popayán Col. 138 C3
Poperinge Belgium 48 C4
Popigay r. Rus. Fed. 61 L2
Popiltah Australia 107 C7
Popilta Lake imp. l. Australia 107 C7
Poplar r. Canada 117 L4
Poplar U.S.A. 122 G2
Poplar Bluff U.S.A. 127 F4
Poplar Camp U.S.A. 130 E5
Poplarville U.S.A. 127 F6
▶Popocatépetl, Volcán vol. Mex. 132 E5
5th highest mountain in North America.
Popokabaka Dem. Rep. Congo 95 B4
Popondetta P.N.G. 65 L8
Popovichskaya Rus. Fed. see Kalininskaya
Popovo Bulg. 55 L3
Popovo Polje plain Bos.-Herz. 54 G3
Poppberg hill Germany 49 L5
Poppenberg hill Germany 49 K3
Poprad Slovakia 43 R6
Poquoson U.S.A. 131 G5
Porali r. Pak. 85 G5
Porangahau N.Z. 109 F5
Porangatu Brazil 141 A1
Porbandar India 78 B5
Porcher Island Canada 116 D4
Porcos r. Brazil 141 B1
Porcupine, Cape Canada 119 K3
Porcupine Abyssal Plain sea feature N. Atlantic Ocean 144 G2
Porcupine Gorge National Park Australia 106 D4
Porcupine Hills Canada 117 K4
Porcupine Mountains U.S.A. 126 F2
Poreč Croatia 54 E2
Porecatu Brazil 141 A3
Poretskoye Rus. Fed. 39 J5
Pori Fin. 41 L6
Porirua N.Z. 109 E5
Porkhov Rus. Fed. 41 P8
Porlamar Venez. 138 F1
Pormpuraaw Australia 106 C2
Pornic France 52 C3
Poronaysk Rus. Fed. 70 F2
Porong China see Baingoin
Poros Greece 55 J6
Porosozero Rus. Fed. 38 G3
Porpoise Bay Antarctica 148 G2
Porsangen sea chan. Norway 40 N1
Porsangerhalvøya pen. Norway 40 N1
Porsgrunn Norway 41 F7
Porsuk r. Turkey 55 N5
Portadown U.K. 47 F3
Portaferry U.K. 47 G3
Portage MI U.S.A. 130 C2
Portage PA U.S.A. 131 F3
Portage WI U.S.A. 126 F3
Portage Lakes U.S.A. 130 E3
Portage la Prairie Canada 117 L5
Portal U.S.A. 126 C1
Port Alberni Canada 116 E5
Port Albert Australia 108 C7
Portalegre Port. 53 C4
Portales U.S.A. 127 C5
Port-Alfred Canada see La Baie
Port Alfred S. Africa 97 H7
Port Alice Canada 116 E5
Port Allegany U.S.A. 131 F3
Port Allen U.S.A. 127 F6
Port Alma Australia 106 E4
Port Angeles U.S.A. 122 C2
Port Antonio Jamaica 133 I5
Portarlington Rep. of Ireland 47 E4
Port Arthur Australia 107 [inset]
Port Arthur U.S.A. 127 E6
Port Askaig U.K. 46 C5
Port Augusta Australia 107 B7
▶Port-au-Prince Haiti 133 J5
Capital of Haiti.
Port Austin U.S.A. 130 D1
Port aux Choix Canada 119 K4
Portavogie U.K. 47 G3
Port Beaufort S. Africa 96 E8
Port Blair India 67 A5
Port Bolster Canada 130 F1
Portbou Spain 53 H2
Port Burwell Canada 130 E2
Port Campbell Australia 108 A7
Port Campbell National Park Australia 108 A7
Port Carling Canada 130 F1
Port-Cartier Canada 119 I4
Port Chalmers N.Z. 109 C7
Port Charlotte U.S.A. 129 D7
Port Clements Canada 116 C4
Port Clinton U.S.A. 130 D3
Port Credit Canada 130 F2
Port-de-Paix Haiti 133 J5
Port Dickson Malaysia 67 C7
Port Douglas Australia 106 D3
Port Edward Canada 116 D4
Port Edward S. Africa 97 J6
Porteira Brazil 139 G4
Porteirinha Brazil 141 C1
Portel Brazil 139 H4
Port Elgin Canada 130 E1
Port Elizabeth S. Africa 97 G7
Port Ellen U.K. 46 C5
Port Erin Isle of Man 44 C4
Porter Lake N.W.T. Canada 117 J2
Porter Lake Sask. Canada 117 J3
Porter Landing Canada 116 D3
Porterville S. Africa 96 D7
Porterville U.S.A. 124 D3
Port Étienne Mauritania see Nouâdhibou
Port Everglades U.S.A. see Fort Lauderdale
Port Fitzroy N.Z. 109 E3
Port Francqui Dem. Rep. Congo see Ilebo
Port-Gentil Gabon 94 A4
Port Glasgow U.K. 46 E5
Port Harcourt Nigeria 92 D4
Port Harrison Canada see Inukjuak
Porthcawl U.K. 45 D7
Port Hedland Australia 104 B5
Port Henry U.S.A. 131 I1
Port Herald Malawi see Nsanje
Porthleven U.K. 45 B8
Porthmadog U.K. 45 C6
Port Hope Canada 131 F2
Port Hope Simpson Canada 119 L3
Port Hueneme U.S.A. 124 D4
Port Huron U.S.A. 130 D2
Portimão Port. 53 B5
Port Jackson Australia see Sydney
Port Jackson inlet Australia 108 E4
Port Keats Australia see Wadeye
Port Klang Malaysia see Pelabuhan Kelang
Port Láirge Rep. of Ireland see Waterford
Portland N.S.W. Australia 108 D4
Portland Vic. Australia 107 C8
Portland IN U.S.A. 130 C3
Portland ME U.S.A. 131 J2
Portland MI U.S.A. 130 C2
Portland OR U.S.A. 122 C3
Portland TN U.S.A. 130 B5
Portland, Isle of pen. U.K. 45 E8
Portland Bill hd U.K. see Bill of Portland
Portland Creek Pond l. Canada 119 K4
Portland Roads Australia 106 C2
Port-la-Nouvelle France 52 F5
Portlaoise Rep. of Ireland 47 E4
Port Lavaca U.S.A. 127 D6
Portlaw Rep. of Ireland 47 E5
Portlethen U.K. 46 G3
Port Lincoln Australia 107 A7
Port Loko Sierra Leone 92 B4
▶Port Louis Mauritius 145 L7
Capital of Mauritius.
Port-Lyautrey Morocco see Kénitra
Port Macquarie Australia 108 F3
Portmadoc U.K. see Porthmadog
Port McNeill Canada 116 E5
Port-Menier Canada 119 I4
▶Port Moresby P.N.G. 65 L8
Capital of Papua New Guinea.
Portnaguran U.K. 46 C2
Portnahaven U.K. 46 C5
Port nan Giúran U.K. see Portnaguran
Port Neill Australia 107 B7
Port Ness U.K. 46 C2
Portneuf r. Canada 119 H4
Port Nis U.K. see Port Ness
Port Noarlunga Australia 107 B7
Port Nolloth S. Africa 96 C5
Port Norris U.S.A. 131 H4
Port-Nouveau-Québec Canada see Kangiqsualujjuaq
Porto Port. see Oporto
Porto Acre Brazil 138 E5
Porto Alegre Brazil 141 A5
Porto Alexandre Angola see Tombua
Porto Amboim Angola 95 B5
Porto Amélia Moz. see Pemba
Porto Artur Brazil 139 G6
Porto Belo Brazil 141 A4
Porto de Moz Brazil 139 H4
Porto de Santa Cruz Brazil 141 C1
Porto dos Gaúchos Óbidos Brazil 139 G6
Porto Esperança Brazil 139 G7
Porto Esperidião Brazil 139 G7
Portoferraio Italy 54 D3
Porto Franco Brazil 139 I5
▶Port of Spain Trin. and Tob. 133 L6
Capital of Trinidad and Tobago.
Porto Grande Brazil 139 H3
Portogruaro Italy 54 E2
Porto Jofre Brazil 139 G7
Portola U.S.A. 124 C2
Portomaggiore Italy 54 D2
Porto Mendes Brazil 140 F2
Porto Murtinho Brazil 140 E2
Porto Nacional Brazil 139 I6
▶Porto-Novo Benin 92 D4
Capital of Benin.
Porto Novo Cape Verde 92 [inset]
Porto Primavera, Represa resr Brazil 140 F2
Port Orchard U.S.A. 122 C3
Port Orford U.S.A. 122 B4
Porto Rico Angola 95 B4
Porto Santo, Ilha de i. Madeira 92 B1
Porto Seguro Brazil 141 D2
Porto Tolle Italy 54 E2
Porto Torres Sardinia Italy 54 C4
Porto União Brazil 141 A4
Porto-Vecchio Corsica France 52 I6
Porto Velho Brazil 138 F5
Portoviejo Ecuador 138 B4
Porto Wálter Brazil 138 D5
Portpatrick U.K. 46 D6
Port Perry Canada 131 F1
Port Phillip Bay Australia 108 B7
Port Pirie Australia 107 B7
Port Radium Canada see Echo Bay
Portreath U.K. 45 B8
Portree U.K. 46 C3
Port Rexton Canada 119 L4
Port Royal U.S.A. 131 G4
Port Royal Sound inlet U.S.A. 129 D5
Portrush U.K. 47 F2
Port Safaga Egypt see Būr Safājah
Port Said Egypt 81 A4
Portsalon Rep. of Ireland 47 E2
Port Sanilac U.S.A. 130 D2
Port Severn Canada 130 F1
Port Shepstone S. Africa 97 J6
Port Simpson Canada see Lax Kw'alaams
Portsmouth U.K. 45 F8
Portsmouth NH U.S.A. 131 J2
Portsmouth OH U.S.A. 130 D4
Portsmouth VA U.S.A. 131 G5
Portsoy U.K. 46 G3
Port Stanley Falkland Is see Stanley
Port Stephens b. Australia 108 F4
Portstewart U.K. 47 F2
Port St Joe U.S.A. 129 C6
Port St Lucie City U.S.A. 129 D7
Port St Mary Isle of Man 44 C4
Port Sudan Sudan 82 E6
Port Swettenham Malaysia see Pelabuhan Kelang
Port Talbot U.K. 45 D7
Porttipahdan tekojärvi l. Fin. 40 O2
Port Townsend U.S.A. 122 C2
▶Portugal country Europe 53 C4
europe 5, 34–35
Portugália Angola see Chitato
Portuguese East Africa country Africa see Mozambique
Portuguese Guinea country Africa see Guinea-Bissau
Portuguese Timor country Asia see East Timor
Portuguese West Africa country Africa see Angola
Portumna Rep. of Ireland 47 D4
Portus Herculis Monoeci country Europe see Monaco
Port-Vendres France 52 F5
▶Port Vila Vanuatu 103 G3
Capital of Vanuatu.
Portville U.S.A. 131 F2
Port Vladimir Rus. Fed. 40 R2
Port Waikato N.Z. 109 E3
Port Washington U.S.A. 130 B2
Port William U.K. 46 E6
Porvenir Bol. 138 E6
Porvenir Chile 140 B8
Porvoo Fin. 41 N6
Posada Spain 53 D2
Posada de Llanera Spain see Posada
Posadas Arg. 140 E3
Posen Poland see Poznań
Posen U.S.A. 130 D1
Poseyville U.S.A. 130 B4
Poshekhon'ye Rus. Fed. 38 H4
Poshekon'ye-Volodarsk Rus. Fed. see Poshekhon'ye
Posht-e Badam Iran 84 D3
Poshteh-ye Chaqvīr hill Iran 84 E4
Posht-e Kūh mts Iran 84 B3
Posht-e Rūd-e Zamindavar reg. Afgh. see Zamīndāvar
Posht Kūh hill Iran 84 C2
Posio Fin. 40 P3
Poso Indon. 65 G7
Posof Turkey 87 F2
Posŏng S. Korea 71 B6
Possession Island Namibia 96 B4
Pößneck Germany 49 L4
Post U.S.A. 127 C5
Postavy Belarus see Pastavy
Poste-de-la-Baleine Canada see Kuujjuarapik
Postmasburg S. Africa 96 F5
Poston U.S.A. 125 F4
Postville Canada 119 K3
Postville U.S.A. 118 C6
Post Weygand Alg. 92 D2
Postysheve Ukr. see Krasnoarmiys'k
Pota Indon. 104 C2
Pótam Mex. 123 F8
Poté Brazil 141 C2
Poteau U.S.A. 127 E5
Potegaon India 80 D2
Potentia Italy see Potenza
Potenza Italy 54 F4
Potgietersrus S. Africa 97 I3
Poth U.S.A. 127 D6
P'ot'i Georgia 87 F2
Potikal India 80 D2
Potiraguá Brazil 141 D1
Potiskum Nigeria 92 E3
Potlatch U.S.A. 122 D3
Pot Mountain U.S.A. 122 E3
Po Toi i. Hong Kong China 73 [inset]
Potomac r. U.S.A. 131 G4
Potosí Bol. 138 E7
Potosi U.S.A. 126 F4
Potosi Mountain U.S.A. 125 F4
Potrerillos Chile 140 C3
Potrero del Llano Mex. 127 B6
Potsdam Germany 49 N2
Potsdam U.S.A. 131 H1
Potter U.S.A. 126 C3
Potterne U.K. 45 E7
Potters Bar U.K. 45 G7
Potter Valley U.S.A. 124 B2
Pottstown U.S.A. 131 H3
Pottsville U.S.A. 131 G3
Pottuvil Sri Lanka 80 D5
Potwar reg. Pak. 85 I3
Pouch Cove Canada 119 L5
Poughkeepsie U.S.A. 131 I3
Poulin de Courval, Lac l. Canada 119 H4
Poulton-le-Fylde U.K. 44 E5
Pouso Alegre Brazil 141 B3
Poŭthĭsăt Cambodia 67 C4
Poŭthĭsăt, Stœng r. Cambodia 67 D4
Považská Bystrica Slovakia 43 Q6
Povenets Rus. Fed. 38 G3
Poverty Bay N.Z. 109 F4
Povlen mt. Serb. and Mont. 55 H2
Póvoa de Varzim Port. 53 B3
Povorino Rus. Fed. 39 I6
Povorotnyy, Mys hd Rus. Fed. 70 D4
Poway U.S.A. 124 E5
Powder r. U.S.A. 122 G3
Powder, South Fork r. U.S.A. 122 G4
Powder River U.S.A. 122 G4
Powell r. U.S.A. 130 D5
Powell, Lake resr U.S.A. 125 H3
Powell Lake Canada 116 E5
Powell Mountain U.S.A. 124 D2
Powell Point Bahamas 129 E7
Powell River Canada 116 E5
Powhatan AR U.S.A. 127 F4
Powhatan VA U.S.A. 131 G5
Powo China 72 C1
Pōwrize Turkm. see Firyuza
Poxoréu Brazil 139 H7
Poyang China see Boyang
Poyang Hu l. China 73 H2
Poyan Reservoir Sing. 67 [inset]
Poyarkovo Rus. Fed. 70 C2
Pozantı Turkey 86 D3
Požarevac Serb. and Mont. 55 I2
Poza Rica Mex. 132 E4
Pozdeyevka Rus. Fed. 70 C2
Požega Croatia 54 G2
Požega Serb. and Mont. 55 I3
Pozharskoye Rus. Fed. 70 D3
Poznań Poland 43 P4
Pozoblanco Spain 53 D4
Pozo Colorado Para. 140 E2
Pozsony Slovakia see Bratislava
Pozzuoli Italy 54 F4
Prabumulih Indon. 64 C7
Prachatice Czech Rep. 43 O6
Prachi r. India 79 F6
Prachin Buri Thai. 67 C4
Prachuap Khiri Khan Thai. 67 B5
Prades France 52 F5
Prado Brazil 141 D2
▶Prague Czech Rep. 43 O5
Capital of the Czech Republic.
Praha Czech Rep. see Prague
▶Praia Cape Verde 92 [inset]
Capital of Cape Verde.
Praia do Bilene Moz. 97 K3
Prainha Brazil 139 H4
Prairie Australia 106 D4
Prairie r. U.S.A. 126 E2
Prairie Dog Town Fork r. U.S.A. 127 C5
Prairie du Chien U.S.A. 126 F3
Prairie River Canada 117 K4
Pram, Khao mt. Thai. 67 B5
Pran r. Thai. 67 C4
Pran Buri Thai. 67 B4
Prapat Indon. 67 B7
Prasonisi, Akra pt Greece 55 L7
Prata Brazil 141 A2
Prata r. Brazil 141 A2
Prat de Llobregat Spain see El Prat de Llobregat
Prathes Thai country Asia see Thailand
Prato Italy 54 D3
Pratt U.S.A. 126 D4
Prattville U.S.A. 129 C5
Pravdinsk Rus. Fed. 41 L9
Praya Indon. 104 B2
Preah, Prêk r. Cambodia 67 D4
Preăh Vihear Cambodia 67 D4
Preble U.S.A. 131 G2
Prechistoye Smolenskaya Oblast' Rus. Fed. 39 G5
Prechistoye Yaroslavskaya Oblast' Rus. Fed. 38 I4
Precipice National Park Australia 106 E5
Preeceville Canada 117 K5
Pregolya r. Rus. Fed. 41 L9
Preiļi Latvia 41 O8
Prelate Canada 117 I5
Premer Australia 108 D3
Prémery France 52 F3
Premnitz Germany 49 M2
Prentiss U.S.A. 127 F6
Prenzlau Germany 43 N4
Preparis Island Cocos Is 64 A4
Preparis North Channel Cocos Is 64 A4
Preparis South Channel Cocos Is 64 A4
Přerov Czech Rep. 43 P6
Presa San Antonio Mex. 127 C7
Prescelly Mts hills U.K. see Preseli, Mynydd
Prescott Canada 131 H1
Prescott AR U.S.A. 127 E5
Prescott AZ U.S.A. 125 G4
Prescott Valley U.S.A. 125 G4
Preseli, Mynydd hills U.K. 45 C7
Preševo Serb. and Mont. 55 I3

Presidencia Roque Sáenz Peña Arg. 140 D3
Presidente Dutra Brazil 139 J5
Presidente Eduardo Frei *research station* Antarctica 148 A2
Presidente Hermes Brazil 138 F6
Presidente Olegário Brazil 141 B2
Presidente Prudente Brazil 141 A3
Presidente Venceslau Brazil 141 A3
Presidio U.S.A. 127 B6
Preslav Bulg. *see* **Veliki Preslav**
Prešov Slovakia 39 D6
Prespa, Lake Europe 55 I4
Prespansko Ezero *l.* Europe *see* **Prespa, Lake**
Prespes *nat. park* Greece 55 I4
Prespës, Liqeni i *l.* Europe *see* **Prespa, Lake**
Presque Isle *ME* U.S.A. 128 G2
Presque Isle *MI* U.S.A. 130 D1
Pressburg Slovakia *see* **Bratislava**
Presteigne U.K. 45 D6
Preston U.K. 44 E5
Preston *ID* U.S.A. 122 F4
Preston *MN* U.S.A. 126 E3
Preston *MO* U.S.A. 126 E4
Preston, Cape Australia 104 B5
Prestonpans U.K. 46 G5
Prestonsburg U.S.A. 130 D5
Prestwick U.K. 46 E5
Preto *r. Bahia* Brazil 139 J6
Preto *r. Minas Gerais* Brazil 141 B2
Preto *r.* Brazil 141 D1
▶**Pretoria** S. Africa 97 I3
Official capital of South Africa.
Pretoria-Witwatersrand-Vereeniging *prov.* S. Africa *see* **Gauteng**
Pretzsch Germany 49 M3
Preussisch-Eylau Rus. Fed. *see* **Bagrationovsk**
Preußisch Stargard Poland *see* **Starogard Gdański**
Preveza Greece 55 I5
Prewitt U.S.A. 125 I4
Prey Vêng Cambodia 67 D5
Priaral'skiye Karakumy, Peski *des.* Kazakh. 76 B2
Priargunsk Rus. Fed. 69 L2
Pribilof Islands U.S.A. 114 A4
Priboj Serb. and Mont. 55 H3
Price *r.* Australia 104 E3
Price *NC* U.S.A. 130 F5
Price *UT* U.S.A. 125 H2
Price *r.* U.S.A. 125 H2
Price Island Canada 116 D4
Prichard *AL* U.S.A. 127 F6
Prichard *WV* U.S.A. 130 D4
Pridorozhnoye Rus. Fed. *see* **Khulkhuta**
Priekule Latvia 41 L8
Priekuļi Latvia 41 N8
Prienai Lith. 41 M9
Prieska S. Africa 96 F5
Prievidza Slovakia 43 Q6
Prignitz *reg.* Germany 49 M1
Prijedor Bos.-Herz. 54 G2
Prijepolje Serb. and Mont. 55 H3
Prikaspiyskaya Nizmennost' *lowland* Kazakh./Rus. Fed. *see* **Caspian Lowland**
Prilep Macedonia 55 I4
Priluki Ukr. *see* **Pryluky**
Přimda Czech Rep. 49 M5
Primero de Enero Cuba 129 E8
Primorsk Rus. Fed. 41 P6
Primorsk Ukr. *see* **Prymors'k**
Primorskiy Kray *admin. div.* Rus. Fed. 70 D3
Primorsko-Akhtarsk Rus. Fed. 39 H7
Primo Tapia Mex. 124 E5
Primrose Lake Canada 117 I4
Prims *r.* Germany 48 G5
Prince Albert Canada 117 J4
Prince Albert S. Africa 96 F7
Prince Albert Mountains Antarctica 148 H1
Prince Albert National Park Canada 117 J4
Prince Albert Peninsula Canada 114 G2
Prince Albert Road S. Africa 96 E7
Prince Alfred, Cape Canada 114 F2
Prince Alfred Hamlet S. Africa 96 D7
Prince Charles Island Canada 115 K3
Prince Charles Mountains Antarctica 148 E2
Prince Edward Island *prov.* Canada 119 J5
▶**Prince Edward Islands** Indian Ocean 145 K9
Part of South Africa.
Prince Edward Point Canada 131 G2
Prince Frederick U.S.A. 131 G4
Prince George Canada 116 F4
Prince Harald Coast Antarctica 148 D2
Prince of Wales, Cape U.S.A. 114 B3
Prince of Wales Island Australia 106 C1
Prince of Wales Island Canada 115 I2
Prince of Wales Island U.S.A. 116 C4
Prince of Wales Strait Canada 114 G2
Prince Patrick Island Canada 114 G2
Prince Regent Inlet *sea chan.* Canada 115 I2
Prince Rupert Canada 116 D4
Princess Anne U.S.A. 131 H4
Princess Astrid Coast Antarctica 148 C2
Princess Charlotte Bay Australia 106 C2
Princess Elizabeth Land *reg.* Antarctica 148 E2
Princess Mary Lake Canada 117 L1
Princess Ragnhild Coast Antarctica 148 C2
Princess Royal Island Canada 116 D4
Princeton Canada 116 F5
Princeton *CA* U.S.A. 124 B2
Princeton *IL* U.S.A. 126 F3
Princeton *IN* U.S.A. 130 B4
Princeton *MO* U.S.A. 126 E3
Princeton *NJ* U.S.A. 131 H3
Princeton *WV* U.S.A. 130 E5
Prince William Sound *b.* U.S.A. 114 D3
Príncipe *i.* São Tomé and Príncipe 92 D4
Prineville U.S.A. 122 C3
Prins Harald Kyst *coastal area* Antarctica *see* **Prince Harald Coast**
Prinzapolca Nicaragua 133 H6
Priozersk Rus. Fed. 41 Q6
Priozyorsk Rus. Fed. *see* **Priozersk**
Pripet *r.* Belarus/Ukr. 39 F6
also spelt Pryp"yat' (Ukraine) *or* Prypyats' (Belarus)
Pripet Marshes Belarus/Ukr. 39 E6
Prirechnyy Rus. Fed. 40 Q2
Prishtinë Serb. and Mont. *see* **Priština**
Priština Serb. and Mont. 55 I3
Pritzier Germany 49 L1
Pritzwalk Germany 49 M1
Privas France 52 G4
Privlaka Croatia 54 F2
Privolzhsk Rus. Fed. 38 I4
Privolzhskaya Vozvyshennost' *hills* Rus. Fed. 39 J6
Privolzhskiy Rus. Fed. 39 J6
Privolzh'ye Rus. Fed. 39 K5
Priyutnoye Rus. Fed. 39 I7
Prizren Serb. and Mont. 55 I3
Probolinggo Indon. 64 E8
Probstzella Germany 49 L4
Probus U.K. 45 C8
Proddatur India 80 C3
Professor van Blommestein Meer *resr* Suriname 139 G3
Progreso Hond. *see* **El Progreso**
Progreso Mex. 127 C7
Progress Rus. Fed. 70 C2
Project City U.S.A. 122 C4
Prokhladnyy Rus. Fed. 87 G2
Prokop'yevsk Rus. Fed. 68 F2
Prokuplje Serb. and Mont. 55 I3
Proletarsk Rus. Fed. 39 I7
Proletarskaya Rus. Fed. *see* **Proletarsk**
Prome Myanmar *see* **Pyè**
Promissão Brazil 141 A3
Promissão, Represa *resr* Brazil 141 A3
Prophet *r.* Canada 116 F3
Prophet River Canada 116 F3
Propriá Brazil 139 K6
Proskurov Ukr. *see* **Khmel'nyts'kyy**
Prosser U.S.A. 122 D3
Protem S. Africa 96 E8
Provadiya Bulg. 55 L3
Prøven Greenland *see* **Kangersuatsiaq**
Provence *reg.* France 52 G5
Providence *KY* U.S.A. 130 B5
Providence *MD* U.S.A. *see* **Annapolis**
▶**Providence** *RI* U.S.A. 131 J3
State capital of Rhode Island.
Providence, Cape N.Z. 109 A8
Providencia, Isla de *i.* Caribbean Sea 133 H6
Provideniya Rus. Fed. 61 T3
Provincetown U.S.A. 131 J2
Provo U.S.A. 125 H1
Provost Canada 117 I4
Prudentópolis Brazil 141 A4
Prudhoe Bay U.S.A. 114 D2
Prüm Germany 48 G4
Prüm *r.* Germany 48 G5
Prunelli-di-Fiumorbo *Corsica* France 52 I5
Pruntytown U.S.A. 130 E4
Prusa Turkey *see* **Bursa**
Prushkov Poland *see* **Pruszków**
Pruszków Poland 43 R4
Prut *r.* Europe 39 F7
Prydz Bay Antarctica 148 E2
Pryelbrusskiy Natsional'nyy Park *nat. park* Rus. Fed. 39 I8
Pryluky Ukr. 39 G6
Prymors'k Ukr. 39 H7
Prymors'ke Ukr. *see* **Sartana**
Pryp"yat' *r.* Ukr. 39 F6 *see* **Pripet**
Prypyats' *r.* Belarus 37 L5 *see* **Pripet**
Przemyśl Poland 39 D6
Przheval'sk Kyrg. *see* **Karakol**
Psara *i.* Greece 55 K5
Pskov Rus. Fed. 41 P8
Pskov, Lake Estonia/Rus. Fed. 41 O7
Pskov Oblast *admin. div.* Rus. Fed. *see* **Pskovskaya Oblast'**
Pskovskaya Oblast' *admin. div.* Rus. Fed. 41 P8
Pskovskoye Ozero *l.* Estonia/Rus. Fed. *see* **Pskov, Lake**
Ptolemaïda Greece 55 I4
Ptolemais Israel *see* **'Akko**
Ptuj Slovenia 54 F1
Pua Thai. 66 C3
Puaka *hill* Sing. 67 [inset]
Pu'an *Guizhou* China 72 E3
Pu'an *Sichuan* China 72 E2
Puan S. Korea 71 B6
Pucallpa Peru 138 D5
Pucheng *Fujian* China 73 H3
Pucheng *Shaanxi* China 73 F1
Puchezh Rus. Fed. 38 I4
Puch'ŏn S. Korea 71 B5
Puck Poland 43 Q3
Pudai *watercourse* Afgh. *see* **Dor**
Pūdanū Iran 84 D3
Pudasjärvi Fin. 40 O4
Pudimoe S. Africa 96 G4
Pudozh Rus. Fed. 38 H3
Pudsey U.K. 44 F5
Pudu China *see* **Suizhou**
Puduchcheri India *see* **Pondicherry**
Pudukkottai India 80 C4
Puebla *Baja California* Mex. 125 F5
Puebla *Puebla* Mex. 132 E5
Puebla de Sanabria Spain 53 C2
Puebla de Zaragoza Mex. *see* **Puebla**
Pueblo U.S.A. 123 G5
Pueblo Yaqui Mex. 123 F8
Puelches Arg. 140 C5
Puelén Arg. 140 C5
Puente-Genil Spain 53 D5
Pu'er China 72 D4
Puerco *watercourse* U.S.A. 125 H4
Puerto Acosta Bol. 138 E7
Puerto Alegre Bol. 138 F6
Puerto Ángel Mex. 132 E5
Puerto Armuelles Panama 133 H7
Puerto Ayacucho Venez. 138 E2
Puerto Bahía Negra Para. *see* **Bahía Negra**
Puerto Baquerizo Moreno *Galápagos* Ecuador 138 [inset]
Puerto Barrios Guat. 132 G5
Puerto Cabello Venez. 138 E1
Puerto Cabezas Nicaragua 133 H6
Puerto Carreño Col. 138 E2
Puerto Casado Para. 140 E2
Puerto Cavinas Bol. 138 E6
Puerto Coig Arg. 140 C8
Puerto Cortés Mex. 132 B4
Puerto de Lobos Mex. 123 E7
Puerto Escondido Mex. 132 E5
Puerto Francisco de Orellana Ecuador 138 C4
Puerto Frey Bol. 138 F6
Puerto Génova Bol. 138 E6
Puerto Guarani Para. 140 E2
Puerto Heath Bol. 138 E6
Puerto Huitoto Col. 138 D3
Puerto Inírida Col. 138 E3
Puerto Isabel Bol. 139 G7
Puerto Leguízamo Col. 138 D4
Puerto Lempira Hond. 133 H5
Puerto Libertad Mex. 123 E7
Puerto Limón Costa Rica 133 H6
Puertollano Spain 53 D4
Puerto Lobos Arg. 140 C6
Puerto Madryn Arg. 140 C6
Puerto Maldonado Peru 138 E6
Puerto Máncora Peru 138 B4
Puerto México Mex. *see* **Coatzacoalcos**
Puerto Montt Chile 140 B6
Puerto Natales Chile 140 B8
Puerto Nuevo Col. 138 E2
Puerto Peñasco Mex. 123 E7
Puerto Pirámides Arg. 140 D6
Puerto Plata Dom. Rep. 133 J5
Puerto Portillo Peru 138 D5
Puerto Prado Peru 138 D6
Puerto Princesa Phil. 64 F5
Puerto Rico Arg. 140 E3
Puerto Rico Bol. 138 E6
▶**Puerto Rico** *terr.* West Indies 133 K5
United States Commonwealth.
north america 9, 112–113
▶**Puerto Rico Trench** *sea feature* Caribbean Sea 144 D4
Deepest trench in the Atlantic Ocean.
Puerto Santa Cruz Arg. 140 C8
Puerto Sastre Para. 140 E2
Puerto Saucedo Bol. 138 F6
Puerto Suárez Bol. 139 G7
Puerto Supe Peru 138 C6
Puerto Vallarta Mex. 132 C4
Puerto Victoria Peru 138 D5
Puerto Visser Arg. 140 C7
Puerto Yartou Chile 140 B8
Puerto Ybapobó Para. 140 E2
Pugachev Rus. Fed. 39 K5
Pugal India 78 C3
Puge China 72 D3
Pūhāl-e Khamīr, Kūh-e *mts* Iran 84 D5
Puhiwaero *c.* N.Z. *see* **South West Cape**
Puigmal *mt.* France/Spain 52 F5
Pui O Wan *b. Hong Kong* China 73 [inset]
Puji China *see* **Puge**
Pukaki, Lake N.Z. 109 C7
Pukapuka *atoll* Cook Is 103 J3
Pukaskwa National Park Canada 118 D4
Pukatawagan Canada 117 K4
Pukchin N. Korea 71 B4
Pukch'ŏng N. Korea 71 C4
Pukekohe N.Z. 109 E3
Puketeraki Range *mts* N.Z. 109 D6
Pukeuri Junction N.Z. 109 C7
Puksubaek-san *mt.* N. Korea 70 B4
Pula China *see* **Nyingchi**
Pula Croatia 54 E2
Pula *Sardinia* Italy 54 C5
Pulap *atoll* Micronesia 65 L5
Pulaski *NY* U.S.A. 131 G2
Pulaski *VA* U.S.A. 130 E5
Pulaski *WI* U.S.A. 130 A1
Pulheim Germany 48 G3
Pulicat Lake *inlet* India 80 D3
Pulivendla India 80 C3
Pulkkila Fin. 40 N4
Pullman U.S.A. 122 D3
Pulo Anna *i.* Palau 65 I6
Pulozero Rus. Fed. 40 R2
Púlpito, Punta *pt* Mex. 123 F8
Pulu China 78 E1
Pülümür Turkey 87 E3
Pulusuk *atoll* Micronesia 65 L5
Puluwat *atoll* Micronesia 65 L5
Pulwama India 85 I3
Pumasillo, Cerro *mt.* Peru 138 D6
Puma Yumco *l.* China 79 G3
Pumiao China *see* **Yongning**
Puná, Isla *i.* Ecuador 138 B4
Punakha Bhutan 79 G4
Punch India 78 C2
Punchaw Canada 116 F4
Punda Maria S. Africa 97 J2
Pundri India 78 D3
Pune India 80 B2
P'ungsan N. Korea 70 C4
Puning China 73 H4
Punjab *state* India 78 C3
Punjab *prov.* Pak. 85 H4
Punmah Glacier China/Jammu and Kashmir 78 D2
Puno Peru 138 D7
Punta, Cerro de *mt.* Puerto Rico 133 K5
Punta Abreojos Mex. 123 E8
Punta Alta Arg. 140 D5
Punta Arenas Chile 140 B8
Punta Balestrieri *mt.* Italy 54 C4
Punta del Este Uruguay 140 F5
Punta Delgada Arg. 140 D6
Punta Gorda Belize 132 G5
Punta Gorda U.S.A. 129 D7
Punta Norte Arg. 140 D6
Punta Prieta Mex. 123 E7
Puntarenas Costa Rica 133 H6
Punxsutawney U.S.A. 131 F3
Puokio Fin. 40 O4
Puolanka Fin. 40 O4
Puqi China *see* **Chibi**
Pur *r.* Rus. Fed. 60 I3
Puracé, Volcán de *vol.* Col. 138 C3
Purcell U.S.A. 127 D5
Purcell Mountains Canada 116 G5
Purgatoire *r.* U.S.A. 126 C4
Puri India 80 E2
Purmerend Neth. 48 E2
Purna *r. Maharashtra* India 78 D5
Purna *r. Maharashtra* India 80 C2
Purnea India *see* **Purnia**
Purnia India 79 F4
Purnululu National Park Australia 104 E4
Pursat Cambodia *see* **Poŭthĭsăt**
Puruliya India 79 F5
▶**Purus** *r.* Peru 138 F4
3rd longest river in South America.
Puruvesi *l.* Fin. 40 P6
Purwodadi Indon. 64 E8
Puryŏng N. Korea 70 C4
Pusad India 80 C2
Pusan S. Korea 71 C6
Pusatlı Dağı *mt.* Turkey 81 A1
Pushchino Rus. Fed. 39 H5
Pushemskiy Rus. Fed. 38 J3
Pushkin Rus. Fed. 41 Q7
Pushkino Azer. *see* **Biläsuvar**
Pushkinskaya, Gora *mt.* Rus. Fed. 70 F3
Pushkinskiye Gory Rus. Fed. 41 P8
Pusht-i-Rud *reg.* Afgh. *see* **Zamīndāvar**
Pustoshka Rus. Fed. 38 F4
Pusur *r.* Bangl. 79 G5
Putahow Lake Canada 117 K3
Putain Indon. 104 D2
Putao Myanmar 66 B1
Puteoli Italy *see* **Pozzuoli**
Puthein Myanmar *see* **Bassein**
Putian China 73 H3
Puting China *see* **De'an**
Puting, Tanjung *pt* Indon. 64 E7
Putlitz Germany 49 M1
Putna *r.* Romania 55 L2
Putney U.S.A. 131 I2
Putoi *i. Hong Kong* China *see* **Po Toi**
Putorana, Gory *mts* Rus. Fed. 149 E2
▶**Putrajaya** Malaysia 67 C7
Administrative capital of Malaysia.
Putre Chile 138 E7
Putsonderwater S. Africa 96 E5
Puttalam Sri Lanka 80 C4
Puttalam Lagoon Sri Lanka 80 C4
Puttelange-aux-Lacs France 48 G5
Putten Neth. 48 F2
Puttershoek Neth. 48 E3
Puttgarden Germany 43 M3
Putumayo *r.* Col. 138 D4
also known as Ica (Peru)
Putuo China *see* **Shenjiamen**
Puumala Fin. 41 P6
Puuwai *HI* U.S.A. 123 [inset]
Puvurnituq Canada 118 F1
Puyallup U.S.A. 122 C3
Puyang China 73 G1
Puy de Sancy *mt.* France 52 F4
Puyehue, Parque Nacional *nat. park* Chile 140 B6
Puysegur Point N.Z. 109 A8
Puzla Rus. Fed. 38 L3
Pweto Dem. Rep. Congo 95 C4
Pwinbyu Myanmar 66 A2
Pwllheli U.K. 45 C6
Pyal'ma Rus. Fed. 38 G3
Pyalo Myanmar 66 A3
Pyamalaw *r.* Myanmar 66 A4
Pyandzh Tajik. *see* **Panj**
Pyaozero, Ozero *l.* Rus. Fed. 40 Q3
Pyaozerskiy Rus. Fed. 40 Q4
Pyapali India 80 C3
Pyapon Myanmar 66 A3
Pyasina *r.* Rus. Fed. 60 J2
Pyatigorsk Rus. Fed. 87 F1
Pyatikhatki Ukr. *see* **P"yatykhatky**
P"yatykhatky Ukr. 39 G6
Pyay Myanmar *see* **Pyè**
Pychas Rus. Fed. 38 L4
Pyè Myanmar 66 A3
Pye, Mount *hill* N.Z. 109 B8
Pyetrykaw Belarus 39 F5
Pygmalion Point India 67 A6
Pyhäjoki Fin. 40 N4
Pyhäjoki *r.* Fin. 40 N4
Pyhäntä Fin. 40 O4
Pyhäsalmi Fin. 40 N5
Pyhäselkä *l.* Fin. 40 P5
Pyi Myanmar *see* **Pyè**
Pyin Myanmar *see* **Pyè**
Pyingaing Myanmar 66 A2
Pyinmana Myanmar 66 B3
Pyle U.K. 45 D7
Pyl'karamo Rus. Fed. 60 J3
Pylos Greece 55 I6
Pymatuning Reservoir U.S.A. 130 E3
Pyŏktong N. Korea 70 B4
P'yŏnggang N. Korea 71 B5
P'yŏnghae S. Korea 71 C5
P'yŏngsong N. Korea 71 B5
P'yŏngt'aek S. Korea 71 B5
▶**P'yŏngyang** N. Korea 71 B5
Capital of North Korea.
Pyramid Hill Australia 108 B6
Pyramid Lake U.S.A. 124 D1
Pyramid Peak U.S.A. 125 J1
Pyramid Range *mts* U.S.A. 124 D2
Pyramids of Giza *tourist site* Egypt 86 C5
Pyrénées *mts* Europe *see* **Pyrenees**
Pyrenees *mts* Europe 53 H2
Pyrénées Occidentales, Parc National des *nat. park* France/Spain 52 D5
Pyrgos Greece 55 I6
Pyryatyn Ukr. 39 G6
Pyrzyce Poland 43 O4
Pyshchug Rus. Fed. 38 J4
Pytalovo Rus. Fed. 41 O8
Pyu Myanmar 66 B3
Pyxaria *mt.* Greece 55 J5

↓ Q

Qaa Lebanon 81 C2
Qaanaaq Greenland *see* **Thule**
Qabātiya West Bank 81 B3
Qabnag China 72 B2
Qabqa China *see* **Gonghe**
Qacentina Alg. *see* **Constantine**
Qacha's Nek Lesotho 97 I6
Qādes Afgh. 85 F3
Qādisīyah, Sadd *dam* Iraq 87 F4
Qadisiyah Dam Iraq *see* **Qādisīyah, Sadd**
Qa'emabad Iran 85 F4
Qagan China 69 L3
Qagan Nur China 69 K4
Qagan Nur *l.* China 70 B3
Qagan Us *Nei Mongol* China 69 K4
Qagan Us *Qinghai* China *see* **Dulan**
Qagbasêrag China 72 B2
Qagca China 72 C1
Qagcaka China 79 E2
Qagchêng China *see* **Xiangcheng**
Qahremānshahr Iran *see* **Kermānshāh**
Qaidam He *r.* China 79 H1
Qaidam Pendi *basin* China 76 H4
Qainaqangma China 79 G2
Qaisar Afgh. 85 G3
Qaisar, Koh-i- *mt.* Afgh. *see* **Qeyşār, Kūh-e**
Qakar China 78 E1
Qal'a Beni Hammad *tourist site* Alg. 53 I6
Qalā Diza Iraq 87 G3
Qalagai Afgh. 85 H3
Qala-i-Kang Afgh. *see* **Kang**
Qal'aikhum Tajik. 85 H2
Qala Jamal Afgh. 85 F3
Qalansīyah Yemen 83 H7
Qala Shinia Takht Afgh. 85 G3
Qalāt Afgh. *see* **Kalāt**
Qal'at al Ḥiṣn Syria 81 C2
Qal'at al Mu'aẓẓam Saudi Arabia 86 E6
Qal'at Bīshah Saudi Arabia 82 F5
Qal'at Muqaybirah, Jabal *mt.* Syria 81 D2
Qal'eh Dāgh *mt.* Iran 84 B2
Qal'eh Tirpul Afgh. 85 F3
Qal'eh-ye Bost Afgh. 85 G4
Qal'eh-ye Now Afgh. 85 F3
Qal'eh-ye Shūrak *well* Iran 84 E3
Qalhāt Oman 84 E6
Qalīb Bāqūr *well* Iraq 87 G5
Qalluviartuuq, Lac *l.* Canada 118 G2
Qalyūb Egypt 86 C5
Qalyûb Egypt *see* **Qalyūb**
Qamalung China 72 C1
Qamanirjuaq Lake Canada 117 M2
Qamanittuaq Canada *see* **Baker Lake**
Qamashi Uzbek. *see* **Kamashi**
Qamata S. Africa 97 H6
Qamdo China 72 C2
Qanāt as Suways *canal* Egypt *see* **Suez Canal**
Qandahar Afgh. *see* **Kandahār**
Qandarānbāshī, Kūh-e *mt.* Iran 84 B2
Qandyaghash Kazakh. *see* **Kandyagash**
Qangzê China 78 D3
Qapan Iran 84 D2
Qapshagay Kazakh. *see* **Kapchagay**
Qapshagay Bögeni *resr* Kazakh. *see* **Kapchagayskoye Vodokhranilishche**
Qapugtang China *see* **Zadoi**
Qaqortoq Greenland 115 N3
Qara Āghach *r.* Iran *see* **Mand, Rūd-e**
Qarabutaq Kazakh. *see* **Karabutak**
Qaraçala Azer. 84 C2
Qara Ertis *r.* China/Kazakh. *see* **Ertix He**
Qaraghandy Kazakh. *see* **Karaganda**
Qaraghayly Kazakh. *see* **Karagayly**
Qārah Egypt 86 B5
Qārah Saudi Arabia 87 F5
Qarah Bāgh Afgh. 85 H3
Qarak China 85 J2
Qaraqum *des.* Turkm. *see* **Kara Kumy**
Qaraqum *des.* Turkm. *see* **Karakum Desert**
Qara Quzi Iran 84 D2
Qarasu Azer. 87 H2
Qara Şū Chāy *r.* Syria/Turkey *see* **Karasu**
Qara Tarai *mt.* Afgh. 85 G3
Qarataū Kazakh. *see* **Karatau**
Qarataū Zhotasy *mts* Kazakh. *see* **Karatau, Khrebet**
Qara Tikan Iran 84 C2
Qarazhal Kazakh. *see* **Karazhal**
Qardho Somalia 94 E3
Qareh Chāy *r.* Iran 84 C3
Qareh Sū *r.* Iran 84 B2
Qareh Tekān Iran 85 F2
Qarhan China 79 H1
Qarkilik China *see* **Ruoqiang**
Qarn al Kabsh, Jabal *mt.* Egypt 86 D5
Qarnayn *i.* U.A.E. 84 D5
Qarnein *i.* U.A.E. *see* **Qarnayn**
Qarn el Kabsh, Gebel *mt.* Egypt *see* **Qarn al Kabsh, Jabal**
Qarokŭl *l.* Tajik. 85 I2
Qarqan China *see* **Qiemo**
Qarqan He *r.* China 76 G4
Qarqaraly Kazakh. *see* **Karkaralinsk**
Qarshi Uzbek. *see* **Karshi**
Qarshi Chŭli *plain* Uzbek. *see* **Karshinskaya Step'**
Qartaba Lebanon 81 B2
Qārūh, Jazīrat *i.* Kuwait 84 C4
Qārūn, Birkat *l.* Egypt 86 C5
Qârûn, Birket *l.* Egypt *see* **Qārūn, Birkat**
Qaryat al Gharab Iraq 87 G5
Qaryat al Ulyā Saudi Arabia 84 B5
Qasa Murg *mts* Afgh. 85 F3
Qāsemābād Iran 84 E3
Qash Qai *reg.* Iran 84 C4
Qasigiannguit Greenland 115 M3
Qaşr al Azraq Jordan 81 C4
Qaşr al Farāfirah Egypt 86 B6
Qaşr al Kharānah Jordan 81 C4
Qaşr al Khubbāz Iraq 87 F4
Qaşr 'Amrah *tourist site* Jordan 81 C4
Qaşr Burqu' *tourist site* Jordan 81 C3
Qaşr-e Shīrīn Iran 84 B3
Qaşr Farâfra Egypt *see* **Qaşr al Farāfirah**
Qassimiut Greenland 115 N3
Qaṭanā Syria 81 C3
▶**Qatar** *country* Asia 84 C5
asia 6, 58–59
Qaṭmah Syria 81 C1
Qaṭrūyeh Iran 84 D4
Qaṭṭāfī, Wādī al *watercourse* Jordan 81 C4
Qaṭṭâra, Râs *esc.* Egypt *see* **Qaṭṭārah, Ra's**
Qattara Depression Egypt 86 B5
Qaṭṭārah, Ra's *esc.* Egypt 86 B5
Qaṭṭīnah, Buḥayrat *resr* Syria 81 C2
Qax Azer. 87 G2
Qāyen Iran 84 E3
Qaynar Kazakh. *see* **Kaynar**
Qaysīyah, Qa' al *imp. l.* Jordan 81 C4
Qaysūm, Juzur *is* Egypt 86 D6
Qayyārah Iraq 87 F4
Qazangödağ *mt.* Armenia/Azer. 87 G3
Qazaq Shyghanaghy *b.* Kazakh. *see* **Kazakhskiy Zaliv**
Qazaqstan *country* Asia *see* **Kazakhstan**
Qazax Azer. 82 G1
Qazi Ahmad Pak. 85 H5
Qazımämmäd Azer. 87 H2
Qazvīn Iran 84 C2
Qeisûm, Gezâ'ir *is* Egypt *see* **Qaysūm, Juzur**
Qeisum Islands Egypt *see* **Qaysūm, Juzur**
Qena Egypt *see* **Qinā**
Qeqertarsuaq Greenland 115 M3
Qeqertarsuaq *i.* Greenland 115 M3
Qeqertarsuatsiaat Greenland 115 M3
Qeqertarsuup Tunua *b.* Greenland 115 M3
Qeshm Iran 84 E5
Qeydār Iran 84 C2
Qeydū Iran 84 C3
Qeys *i.* Iran 84 D5
Qeyşār, Kūh-e *mt.* Afgh. 85 G3
Qezel Owzan, Rūdkhāneh-ye *r.* Iran 84 C2
Qezi'ot Israel 81 B4
Qian'an China 70 B3
Qian Gorlos China *see* **Qianguozhen**
Qianguozhen China 70 B3
Qianjiang *Chongqing* China 73 F2
Qianjiang *Hubei* China 73 G2
Qianjin *Heilong.* China 70 D3
Qianjin *Jilin* China 70 C3
Qianning China 72 D2
Qianqihao China 70 A3
Qian Shan *mts* China 70 A4
Qianxi China 72 E3
Qiaocheng China *see* **Bozhou**
Qiaojia China 72 D3
Qiaoshan China *see* **Huangling**
Qiaowa China *see* **Muli**
Qiaowan China 76 I3
Qiaozhuang China *see* **Qingchuan**
Qibā' Saudi Arabia 87 G6
Qibing S. Africa 97 H5
Qichun China 73 G2
Qidong China 73 G3
Qidukou China 72 B1
Qiemo China 76 G4
Qijiang China 72 E2
Qijiaojing China 76 H3
Qikiqtarjuaq Canada 115 L3
Qila Ladgasht Pak. 85 F5
Qila Saifullah Pak. 85 H4
Qilian China 76 J4
Qilian Shan *mts* China 76 I4
Qillak *i.* Greenland 115 O3
Qiman Tag *mts* China 79 G1
Qimusseriarsuaq *b.* Greenland 115 L2
Qinā Egypt 82 D4
Qin'an China 72 E1
Qincheng China *see* **Nanfeng**
Qing'an China 70 B3
Qingchuan China 72 E1
Qingdao China 69 M5
Qinggang China 70 B3
Qinggil China *see* **Qinghe**
Qinghai *prov.* China 72 B1
Qinghai Hu *salt l.* China 76 J4
Qinghai Nanshan *mts* China 76 I4
Qinghe *Heilong.* China 70 C3
Qinghe *Xinjiang* China 76 H2
Qinghecheng China 70 B4
Qinghua China *see* **Bo'ai**
Qingjiang *Jiangsu* China *see* **Huai'an**
Qingjiang *Jiangxi* China *see* **Zhangshu**
Qing Jiang *r.* China 73 F2
Qingkou China *see* **Ganyu**
Qinglan China 73 F5
Qingliu China 73 H3
Qinglung China 79 G3
Qingpu China 73 I2
Qingquan China *see* **Xishui**
Qingshan China *see* **Wudalianchi**
Qingshui China 72 E1
Qingshuihe *Nei Mongol* China 69 K5
Qingshuihe *Qinghai* China 72 C1
Qingtian China 73 I2
Qingyang *Anhui* China 73 H2
Qingyang *Jiangsu* China *see* **Sihong**
Qingyuan *Gansu* China *see* **Weiyuan**
Qingyuan *Guangdong* China 73 G4
Qingyuan *Guangxi* China *see* **Yizhou**
Qingyuan *Liaoning* China 70 B4
Qingyuan *Zhejiang* China 73 H3
Qingzang Gaoyuan *plat.* China *see* **Plateau of Tibet**
Qingzhen China 72 E3
Qinhuangdao China 69 L5
Qinjiang China *see* **Shicheng**
Qin Ling *mts* China 72 E1
Qinshui China 73 G1
Qinting China *see* **Lianhua**
Qinzhou China 73 F4
Qionghai China 73 F5
Qiongjiexue China *see* **Qonggyai**
Qionglai China 72 D2
Qionglai Shan *mts* China 72 D2
Qiongxi China *see* **Hongyuan**
Qiongzhong China 73 F5
Qiongzhou Haixia *strait* China *see* **Hainan Strait**
Qiqian China 70 A1
Qiqihar China 70 A3
Qīr Iran 84 D4
Qira China 78 E1
Qirā'ya, Wādī *watercourse* Egypt *see* **Qurayyah, Wādī**
Qiryat Israel 81 B3
Qiryat Shemona Israel 81 B3
Qishan China 72 E1
Qishon *r.* Israel 81 B3
Qitab ash Shāmah *vol. crater* Saudi Arabia 81 C4
Qitaihe China 70 C3
Qiubei China 72 E3
Qiujin China 73 G2
Qixing He *r.* China 70 D3
Qiyang China 73 F3
Qizhou Liedao *i.* China 73 F5
Qızılağac Körfäzi *b.* Azer. 84 C2
Qizil-Art, Aghbai *pass* Kyrg./Tajik. *see* **Kyzylart Pass**
Qizilqum *des.* Kazakh./Uzbek. *see* **Kyzylkum Desert**
Qizilrabot Tajik. 85 I2
Qogir Feng *mt.* China/Jammu and Kashmir *see* **K2**
Qog Qi China *see* **Sain Us**
Qom Iran 84 C3
Qomdo China *see* **Qumdo**
Qomisheh Iran *see* **Shahrezā**
Qomolangma Feng *mt.* China/Nepal *see* **Everest, Mount**

Qomsheh Iran see Shahrezā
Qonāq, Kūh-e hill Iran 84 C3
Qondūz Afgh. see Kunduz
Qonggyai China 79 G3
Qong Muztag mt. China 79 E2
Qongrat Uzbek. see Kungrad
Qoornoq Greenland 115 M3
Qoqek China see Tacheng
Qorghalzhyn Kazakh. see Korgalzhyn
Qornet es Saouda mt. Lebanon 81 C2
Qorowulbozor Uzbek. see Karaulbazar
Qorveh Iran 84 B3
Qosh Tepe Iraq 87 F3
Qostanay Kazakh. see Kostanay
Qoubaiyat Lebanon 81 C2
Qowowuyag mt. China/Nepal see Cho Oyu
Qozideh Tajik. 85 H2
Quabbin Reservoir U.S.A. 131 I2
Quadra Island Canada 116 E5
Quadros, Lago dos l. Brazil 141 A5
Quaidabad Pak. 85 H3
Quail Mountains U.S.A. 124 E4
Quairading Australia 105 B8
Quakenbrück Germany 49 H2
Quakertown U.S.A. 131 H3
Quambatook Australia 108 A5
Quambone Australia 108 C3
Quamby Australia 106 C4
Quanah U.S.A. 127 D5
Quanbao Shan mt. China 73 F1
Quan Dao Hoang Sa is S. China Sea see Paracel Islands
Quân Đao Nam Du i. Vietnam 67 D5
Quan Dao Truong Sa is S. China Sea see Spratly Islands
Quang Ngai Vietnam 66 E4
Quang Tri Vietnam 66 D3
Quan Long Vietnam see Ca Mau
Quannan China 73 G3
Quan Phu Quoc i. Vietnam see Phu Quôc, Đao
Quantock Hills U.K. 45 D7
Quanwan Hong Kong China see Tsuen Wan
Quanzhou Fujian China 73 H3
Quanzhou Guangxi China 73 F3
Qu'Appelle r. Canada 117 K5
Quaqtaq Canada 115 L3
Quarry Bay Hong Kong China 73 [inset]
Quartu Sant'Elena Sardinia Italy 54 C5
Quartzite Mountain U.S.A. 124 E3
Quartzsite U.S.A. 125 F5
Quba Azer. 87 H2
Quchan Iran 84 E2
Qudaym Syria 81 D2
Queanbeyan Australia 108 D5

▶Québec Canada 119 H5
Provincial capital of Québec.

Québec prov. Canada 131 I1
Quebra Anzol r. Brazil 141 B2
Quedlinburg Germany 49 L3
Queen Adelaide Islands Chile see La Reina Adelaida, Archipiélago de
Queen Anne U.S.A. 131 H4
Queen Bess, Mount Canada 122 B2
Queen Charlotte Canada 116 C4
Queen Charlotte Islands Canada 116 C4
Queen Charlotte Sound sea chan. Canada 116 D5
Queen Charlotte Strait Canada 116 E5
Queen Creek U.S.A. 125 H5
Queen Elizabeth Islands Canada 115 H2
Queen Elizabeth National Park Uganda 94 C4
Queen Mary Land reg. Antarctica 148 F2
Queen Maud Gulf Canada 115 H3
Queen Maud Land reg. Antarctica 148 C2
Queen Maud Mountains Antarctica 148 J1
Queenscliff Australia 108 B7
Queensland state Australia 108 B1
Queenstown Australia 107 [inset]
Queenstown N.Z. 109 B7
Queenstown Rep. of Ireland see Cóbh
Queenstown S. Africa 97 H6
Queenstown Sing. 67 [inset]
Queets U.S.A. 122 B3
Queimada, Ilha i. Brazil 139 H4
Quelimane Moz. 95 D5
Quellón Chile 140 B6
Quelpart Island S. Korea see Cheju-do
Quemado U.S.A. 125 I4
Quemoy i. Taiwan see Chinmen Tao
Que Que Zimbabwe see Kwekwe
Querétaro Mex. 132 D4
Querétaro de Arteaga Mex. see Querétaro
Querfurt Germany 49 L3
Querobabi Mex. 123 F7
Quesnel Canada 116 F4
Quesnel Lake Canada 116 F4
Quetta Pak. 85 G4
Quetzaltenango Guat. 132 F6
Queuco Chile 140 B5
Quezaltenango Guat. see Quetzaltenango

▶Quezon City Phil. 65 G4
Former capital of the Philippines.

Qufu China 73 H1
Quibala Angola 95 B5
Quibaxe Angola 95 B4
Quibdó Col. 138 C2
Quiberon France 52 C3
Quiçama, Parque Nacional do nat. park Angola 95 B4
Qui Châu Vietnam 66 D3
Quiet Lake Canada 116 C2
Quilengues Angola 95 B5
Quillabamba Peru 138 D6
Quillacollo Bol. 138 E7
Quillan France 52 F5
Quill Lakes Canada 117 J5
Quilmes Arg. 140 E4
Quilon India 80 C4
Quilpie Australia 108 B1
Quilpué Chile 140 B4
Quimbele Angola 95 B4
Quimili Arg. 140 D3
Quimper France 52 B3
Quimperlé France 52 C3
Quinag hill U.K. 46 D2
Quincy CA U.S.A. 124 C2
Quincy FL U.S.A. 129 C6
Quincy IL U.S.A. 126 F4
Quincy IN U.S.A. 130 B4
Quincy MA U.S.A. 131 J2
Quincy MI U.S.A. 130 C3
Quincy OH U.S.A. 130 D3
Quines Arg. 140 C4
Quinga Moz. 95 E5
Qui Nhon Vietnam 67 E4
Quinn Canyon Range mts U.S.A. 125 F3
Quinto Spain 53 F3
Quionga Moz. 95 E5
Quipungo Angola 95 B5
Quirima Angola 95 B5
Quirindi Australia 108 E3
Quirinópolis Brazil 141 A2
Quissanga Moz. 95 E5
Quissico Moz. 97 L3
Quitapa Angola 95 B5
Quitilipi Arg. 140 D3
Quitman GA U.S.A. 129 D6
Quitman MS U.S.A. 127 F5

▶Quito Ecuador 138 C4
Capital of Ecuador.

Quitovac Mex. 123 E7
Quixadá Brazil 139 K4
Quixeramobim Brazil 139 K5
Qujiang Guangdong China 73 G3
Qujiang Sichuan China see Quxian
Qujie China 73 F4
Qujing China 72 D3
Qulandy Kazakh. see Kulandy
Qulbān Layyah well Iraq 84 B4
Qulin Gol r. China 70 A3
Qulsary Kazakh. see Kul'sary
Qulyndy Zhazyghy plain Kazakh./Rus. Fed. see Kulundinskaya Step'
Qulzum, Baḩr al Egypt see Suez Bay
Qumar He r. China 68 G6
Qumarheyan China 76 H4
Qumarlêb China see Sêrwolungwa
Qumarrabdün China 72 B1
Qumbu S. Africa 97 I6
Qumdo China 72 B2
Qumqŭrghon Uzbek. see Kumkurgan
Qumrha S. Africa 97 H7
Qumulangma mt. China/Nepal see Everest, Mount
Qunayy well Saudi Arabia 84 B6
Qundūz Afgh. see Kunduz
Qŭnghirot Uzbek. see Kungrad
Quntamari China 79 G2
Qu'nyido China 72 C2
Quoich r. Canada 117 M1
Quoich, Loch l. U.K. 46 D3
Quoile r. U.K. 47 G3
Quoin Point S. Africa 96 D8
Quoxo r. Botswana 96 G2
Qŭqon Uzbek. see Kokand
Qurama, Qatorkŭhi mts Asia see Kurama Range
Qurama Tizmasi mts Asia see Kurama Range
Qurayyah, Wādī watercourse Egypt 81 B4
Qurayyat al Milḩ l. Jordan 81 C4
Qŭrghonteppa Tajik. 85 H2
Qusar Azer. 87 H2
Qushan China see Beichuan
Qŭshrabot Uzbek. see Koshrabad
Qusmuryn Kazakh. see Kushmurun
Qusum China 78 D2
Quthing Lesotho see Moyeni
Quttinirpaaq National Park Canada 115 K1
Quwayq, Nahr r. Syria/Turkey 81 C2
Quxar China see Lhazê
Quxian Sichuan China 72 E2
Quxian Zhejiang China see Quzhou
Quyang China see Jingzhou
Quyghan Kazakh. see Kuygan
Quynh Luu Vietnam 66 D3
Quyon Canada 131 G1
Qūyūn Eshek i. Iran 84 B2
Quzhou China 73 H2
Qypshaq Köli salt l. Kazakh. see Kypshak, Ozero
Qyrghyz Zhotasy mts Kazakh./Kyrg. see Kirghiz Range
Qyteti Stalin Albania see Kuçovë
Qyzylorda Kazakh. see Kyzylorda
Qyzylqum des. Kazakh./Uzbek. see Kyzylkum Desert
Qyzyltū Kazakh. see Kishkenekol'
Qyzylzhar Kazakh. see Kyzylzhar

R

Raa Atoll Maldives see North Maalhosmadulu Atoll
Raab r. Austria 43 P7
Raab Hungary see Győr
Raahe Fin. 40 N4
Rääkkylä Fin. 40 P5
Raalte Neth. 48 G2
Raanujärvi Fin. 40 N3
Raasay i. U.K. 46 C3
Raasay, Sound of sea chan. U.K. 46 C3
Raba Indon. 104 B2
Rabang China 78 E2
Rabat Gozo Malta see Victoria
Rabat Malta 54 F7

▶Rabat Morocco 50 C5
Capital of Morocco.

Rabaul P.N.G. 102 F2
Rabbath Ammon Jordan see 'Ammān
Rabbit r. Canada 116 E3
Rabbit Flat Australia 104 E5
Rabbitskin r. Canada 116 F2
Rābigh Saudi Arabia 82 E5
Rabnabad Islands Bangl. 79 G5
Râbniţa Moldova see Rîbniţa
Rabocheostrovsk Rus. Fed. 38 G2
Racaka China see Riwoqê
Raccoon Cay i. Bahamas 129 F8
Race, Cape Canada 119 L5
Race Point U.S.A. 131 J2
Rachaïya Lebanon 81 B3
Rachal U.S.A. 127 D7
Rachaya Lebanon see Rachaïya
Rachel U.S.A. 125 F3
Rach Gia Vietnam 67 D5
Rach Gia, Vinh b. Vietnam 67 D5
Racibórz Poland 43 Q5
Racine WI U.S.A. 130 B2
Racine WV U.S.A. 130 E4
Rădăuţi Romania 39 E7
Radcliff U.S.A. 130 C5
Radde Rus. Fed. 70 C2
Radford U.S.A. 130 E5
Radisson Que. Canada 118 F3
Radisson Sask. Canada 117 J4
Radlinski, Mount Antarctica 148 K1
Radnevo Bulg. 55 K3
Radom Poland 43 R5
Radom Sudan 93 F4
Radomir Bulg. 55 J3
Radom National Park Sudan 93 F4
Radomsko Poland 43 Q5
Radoviš Macedonia 86 A2
Radstock U.K. 45 E7
Radstock, Cape Australia 105 F8
Radun' Belarus 41 N9
Radviliškis Lith. 41 M9
Radyvyliv Ukr. 39 E6
Rae Bareli India 78 E4
Rae-Edzo Canada 116 G2
Rae Lakes Canada 116 G1
Raeside, Lake salt flat Australia 105 C7
Raetihi N.Z. 109 E4
Rāf hill Saudi Arabia 87 E5
Rafaela Arg. 140 D4
Rafah Gaza see Rafiah
Rafaï Cent. Afr. Rep. 94 C3
Rafhā' Saudi Arabia 87 F5
Rafiah Gaza 81 B4
Rafsanjān Iran 84 D4
Raft r. U.S.A. 122 E4
Raga Sudan 93 F4
Rägelin Germany 49 M1
Ragged, Mount hill Australia 105 C8
Ragged Island Bahamas 129 F8
Rāgh Afgh. 85 H2
Rago Nasjonalpark nat. park Norway 40 J3
Ragösen Germany 49 M2
Ragueneau Canada 119 H4
Raguhn Germany 49 M3
Ragusa Croatia see Dubrovnik
Ragusa Sicily Italy 54 F6
Ra'gyagoinba China 72 D1
Raha Indon. 65 G7
Rahachow Belarus 39 F5
Rahad r. Sudan 82 D7
Rahaeng Thai. see Tak
Rahden Germany 49 I2
Rahimyar Khan Pak. 85 H4
Rahovec Serb. and Mont. see Orahovac
Rahuri India 80 B2
Rai, Hon i. Vietnam 67 D5
Raiatea i. Fr. Polynesia 147 J7
Raibu i. Indon. see Air
Raichur India 80 C2
Raiganj India 79 G4
Raigarh Chhattisgarh India 79 E5
Raigarh Orissa India 80 D2
Raijua i. Indon. 104 C2
Railroad Pass U.S.A. 124 E2
Railroad Valley U.S.A. 125 F2
Raimangal r. Bangl. 79 G5
Raimbault, Lac l. Canada 119 H3
Rainbow Lake Canada 116 G3
Raine Island Australia 106 D1
Rainelle U.S.A. 130 E5
Raini r. Pak. 85 H4
Rainier, Mount vol. U.S.A. 122 C3
Rainy r. Canada/U.S.A. 117 M5
Rainy Lake Canada/U.S.A. 121 I2
Rainy River Canada 117 M5
Raipur Chhattisgarh India 79 E5
Raipur W. Bengal India 79 F5
Raisen India 78 D5
Raisio Fin. 41 M6
Raismes France 48 D4
Raitalai India 78 D5
Raivavae i. Fr. Polynesia 147 K7
Raiwind Pak. 85 I4
Raja, Ujung pt Indon. 67 B7
Rajaampat, Kepulauan is Indon. 65 H7
Rajahmundry India 80 D2
Raja-Jooseppi Fin. 40 P2
Rajanpur Pak. 85 H4
Rajapalaiyam India 80 C4
Rajapur India 80 B2
Rajasthan state India 78 C4
Rajasthan Canal India 78 C3
Rajauri India see Rajouri
Rajevadi India 80 B2
Rajgarh India 78 D4
Rājijovsset Fin. see Raja-Jooseppi
Rajkot India 78 B5
Raj Mahal India 78 C4
Rajmahal Hills India 79 F4
Rajnandgaon India 78 E5
Rajouri India 78 C2
Rajpipla India 78 C5
Rajpur India 78 C5
Rajpura India 78 D3
Rajputana Agency state India see Rajasthan
Rajsamand India 78 C4
Rajshahi Bangl. 79 G4
Rājū Syria 81 C1
Rajula India 80 A1
Rajur India 80 C1
Rajura India 80 C2
Raka China 79 F3
Rakan, Ra's pt Qatar 84 C5
Rakaposhi mt. Jammu and Kashmir 78 C1
Raka Zangbo r. China see Dogxung Zangbo
Rakhiv Ukr. 39 E6
Rakhni Pak. 85 H4
Rakhshan r. Pak. 85 F5
Rakitnoye Belgorodskaya Oblast' Rus. Fed. 39 G6
Rakitnoye Primorskiy Kray Rus. Fed. 70 D3
Rakiura i. N.Z. see Stewart Island
Rakke Estonia 41 O7
Rakkestad Norway 41 G7
Rakni r. Pak. 85 H4
Rakovski Bulg. 55 K3
Rakushechnyy, Mys pt Kazakh. 87 H2
Rakvere Estonia 41 O7

▶Raleigh U.S.A. 128 E5
State capital of North Carolina.

Ralston U.S.A. 131 G3
Ram r. Canada 116 F2
Ramagiri India 80 E2
Ramah U.S.A. 125 I4
Ramalho, Serra do hills Brazil 141 B1
Ramallah West Bank 81 B4
Ramanagaram India 80 C3
Ramanathapuram India 80 C4
Ramapo Deep sea feature N. Pacific Ocean 145 R3
Ramapur India 80 D1
Ramas, Cape India 80 B3
Ramatlabama S. Africa 97 G3
Rambhapur India 78 C5
Rambouillet France 48 B6
Rambutyo Island P.N.G. 65 L7
Rame Head hd Australia 108 D6
Rame Head hd U.K. 45 C8
Rameshki Rus. Fed. 38 H4
Ramezān Kalak Iran 85 F5
Ramgarh Jharkhand India 79 F5
Ramgarh Madhya Pradesh India 78 E5
Ramgarh Rajasthan India 78 B4
Ramgarh Rajasthan India 78 C3
Ramgul reg. Afgh. 85 H3
Rāmhormoz Iran 84 C4
Ramingining Australia 104 F3
Ramitan Uzbek. see Romitan
Ramla Israel 81 B4
Ramlat Rabyānah des. Libya see Rebiana Sand Sea
Ramm, Jabal mts Jordan 81 B5
Ramnad India see Ramanathapuram
Râmnicu Sărat Romania 55 L2
Râmnicu Vâlcea Romania 55 K2
Ramon' Rus. Fed. 39 H6
Ramona U.S.A. 124 E5
Ramos r. Mex. 127 B7
Ramotswa Botswana 97 G3
Rampart of Genghis Khan tourist site Asia 69 K3
Rampur India 78 D3
Rampur Boalia Bangl. see Rajshahi
Ramree Myanmar 66 A3
Ramree Island Myanmar 66 A3
Ramsele Sweden 40 J5
Ramsey Isle of Man 44 C4
Ramsey U.K. 45 G6
Ramsey U.S.A. 131 H3
Ramsey Bay Isle of Man 44 C4
Ramsey Island U.K. 45 B7
Ramsey Lake Canada 118 E5
Ramsgate U.K. 45 I7
Rāmshīr Iran 84 C4
Ramsing mt. India 79 H3
Ramu Bangl. 79 H5
Ramusio, Lac l. Canada 119 J3
Ramygala Lith. 41 N9
Ranaghat India 79 G5
Ranai i. U.S.A. see Lanai
Rana Pratap Sagar resr India 78 C4
Ranapur India 78 C5
Ranasar India 78 B4
Rancagua Chile 140 B4
Rancharia Brazil 141 A3
Rancheria Canada 116 D2
Rancheria r. Canada 116 D2
Ranchi India 79 F5
Ranco, Lago l. Chile 140 B6
Rand Australia 108 C5
Randalstown U.K. 47 F3
Randers Denmark 41 G8
Randijaure l. Sweden 40 K3
Randolph ME U.S.A. 131 K1
Randolph UT U.S.A. 122 F4
Randolph VT U.S.A. 131 I2
Randsjö Sweden 40 H5
Råneå Sweden 40 M4
Ranérou Senegal 92 B3
Ranfurly N.Z. 109 C7
Rangae Thai. 67 C6
Rangamati Bangl. 79 H5
Rangapara North India 79 H4
Rangeley Lake U.S.A. 131 J1
Rangely U.S.A. 125 I1
Ranger Lake Canada 118 E5
Rangiora N.Z. 109 D6
Rangitata r. N.Z. 109 C7
Rangitikei r. N.Z. 109 E5
Rangke China see Zamtang
Rangkŭl Tajik. 85 I2
Rangôn Myanmar see Rangoon

▶Rangoon Myanmar 66 B3
Capital of Myanmar.

Rangoon r. Myanmar 66 B3
Rangpur Bangl. 79 G4
Rangsang i. Indon. 67 C7
Rangse Myanmar 66 A1
Ranibennur India 80 B3
Raniganj India 79 F5
Ranipur Pak. 85 H5
Raniwara India 78 C4
Rankin U.S.A. 127 C6
Rankin Inlet Canada 117 M2
Rankin's Springs Australia 108 C4
Ranna Estonia 41 O7
Rannes Australia 106 E5
Rannoch, L. U.K. 46 E4
Ranong Thai. 67 B5
Ranot Thai. 67 C6
Ranpur India 78 B5
Ranrkan Pak. 85 H4
Rānsa Iran 84 C3
Ransby Sweden 41 H6
Rantasalmi Fin. 40 P5
Rantau i. Indon. 67 C7
Rantauprapat Indon. 67 B7
Rantoul U.S.A. 130 A3
Rantsila Fin. 40 N4
Ranua Fin. 40 O4
Rānya Iraq 87 G3
Ranyah, Wādī watercourse Saudi Arabia 82 F5
Rao Go mt. Laos/Vietnam 66 D3
Raohe China 70 D3
Raoul Island Kermadec Is 103 I4
Rapa i. Fr. Polynesia 147 K7
Rapa-iti i. Fr. Polynesia see Rapa
Rapallo Italy 54 C2
Rapar India 78 B5
Raphoe Rep. of Ireland 47 E3
Rapidan r. U.S.A. 131 G4
Rapid City U.S.A. 126 C2
Rapid River U.S.A. 128 C2
Rapla Estonia 41 N7
Rapur Andhra Pradesh India 80 C3
Rapur Gujarat India 78 B5
Raqqa Syria see Ar Raqqah
Raquette Lake U.S.A. 131 H2
Rara National Park Nepal 79 E3
Raritan Bay U.S.A. 131 H3
Raroia atoll Fr. Polynesia 147 K7
Rarotonga i. Cook Is 147 J7
Ras India 78 C4
Rasa, Punta pt Arg. 140 D6
Ra's ad Daqm Oman 83 I6
Ra's al Ḩikmah Egypt 86 B5
Ras al Khaimah U.A.E. see Ra's al Khaymah
Ra's al Khaymah U.A.E. 84 D5
Ra's an Naqb Jordan 81 B4
Ras Dashen mt. Eth. see Ras Dejen

▶Ras Dejen mt. Eth. 94 D2
5th highest mountain in Africa.

Raseiniai Lith. 41 M9
Râs el Hikma Egypt see Ra's al Ḩikmah
Ra's Ghārib Egypt 86 D5
Rashad Sudan 82 D7
Rashīd Egypt see Rashīd
Rashīd Egypt 86 C5
Rashīd Qala Afgh. 85 G4
Rashm Iran 84 D3
Rasht Iran 84 C2
Raskam mts China 78 C1
Ras Koh mt. Pak. 85 G4
Raskoh mts Pak. 85 G4
Raso, Cabo c. Arg. 140 C6
Raso da Catarina hills Brazil 139 K5
Rason Lake salt flat Australia 105 D7
Rasony Belarus 41 P9
Rasra India 79 E4
Rasshua, Ostrov i. Rus. Fed. 69 S3
Rass Jebel Tunisia 54 D6
Rasskazovo Rus. Fed. 39 I5
Rastatt Germany 49 I6
Rastede Germany 49 I1
Rastow Germany 49 L1
Rasūl watercourse Iran 84 D5
Rasul Pak. 85 I3
Ratae U.K. see Leicester
Rätan Sweden 40 I5
Ratanda S. Africa 97 I4
Ratangarh India 78 C3
Rätansbyn Sweden 40 I5
Rat Buri Thai. 67 B4
Rathangan Rep. of Ireland 47 F4
Rathbun Lake U.S.A. 126 E3
Rathdowney Rep. of Ireland 47 E5
Rathdrum Rep. of Ireland 47 F5
Rathedaung Myanmar 66 A2
Rathenow Germany 49 M2
Rathfriland U.K. 47 F3
Rathkeale Rep. of Ireland 47 D5
Rathlin Island U.K. 47 F2
Rathluirc Rep. of Ireland 47 D5
Ratibor Poland see Racibórz
Ratingen Germany 48 G3
Ratisbon Germany see Regensburg
Ratiya India 78 C3
Rat Lake Canada 117 L3
Ratlam India 78 C5
Ratnagiri India 80 B2
Ratnapura Sri Lanka 80 D5
Ratne Ukr. 39 E6
Ratno Ukr. see Ratne
Raton U.S.A. 123 G5
Rattray Head hd U.K. 46 H3
Rättvik Sweden 41 I6
Ratz, Mount Canada 116 C3
Ratzeburg Germany 49 K1
Raub Malaysia 67 C7
Rauðamýri Iceland 40 [inset]
Raudhatain Kuwait 84 B4
Rauenstein Germany 49 L4
Raufarhöfn Iceland 40 [inset]
Raukumara Range mts N.Z. 109 F4
Raul Soares Brazil 141 C3
Rauma Fin. 41 L6
Raurkela India 79 F5
Rauschen Rus. Fed. see Svetlogorsk
Rausu Japan 70 G3
Rautavaara Fin. 40 P5
Rautjärvi Fin. 41 P6
Ravānsar Iran 84 B3
Rāvar Iran 84 E4
Ravat Kyrg. 85 H2
Ravels Belgium 48 E3
Ravena U.S.A. 131 I2
Ravenglass U.K. 44 D4
Ravenna Italy 54 E2
Ravenna NE U.S.A. 126 D3
Ravenna OH U.S.A. 130 E3
Ravensburg Germany 43 L7
Ravenshoe Australia 106 D3
Ravenswood Australia 106 D4
Ravi r. Pak. 85 H4
Ravnina Maryyskaya Oblast' Turkm. 85 F2
Ravnina Maryyskaya Oblast' Turkm. 85 F2
Rāwah Iraq 87 F4
Rawaki i. Kiribati 103 I2
Rawalpindi Pak. 85 I3
Rawalpindi Lake Canada 116 H1
Rawāndiz Iraq 87 G3
Rawi, Ko i. Thai. 67 B6
Rawicz Poland 43 P5
Rawlinna Australia 105 D7
Rawlins U.S.A. 122 G4
Rawlinson Range hills Australia 105 E6
Rawnina Turkm. see Ravnina
Rawson Arg. 140 C6
Rawu China 72 C2
Raxón, Cerro mt. Guat. 132 G5
Ray, Cape Canada 119 K5
Raya, Bukit mt. Indon. 64 E7
Rayachoti India 80 C3
Rayadurg India 80 C3
Rayagada India 80 D2
Rayagarha India see Rayagada
Rayak Lebanon 81 C3
Raychikhinsk Rus. Fed. 70 C2
Raydah Yemen 82 F6
Rayes Peak U.S.A. 124 D4
Rayevskiy Rus. Fed. 37 Q5
Rayleigh U.K. 45 H7
Raymond U.S.A. 131 J2
Raymond Terrace Australia 108 E4
Raymondville U.S.A. 127 D7
Raymore Canada 117 J5
Rayner Glacier Antarctica 148 D2
Rayong Thai. 67 C4
Raystown Lake U.S.A. 131 F3
Raz, Pointe du pt France 52 B2
Razan Iran 84 C3
Rāzān Iran 84 C3
Razani Pak. 85 H3
Razāzah, Buḩayrat ar l. Iraq 87 F4
Razdan Armenia see Hrazdan
Razdel'naya Ukr. see Rozdil'na
Razdol'noye Rus. Fed. 70 C4
Razeh Iran 84 C3
Razgrad Bulg. 55 L3
Razim, Lacul lag. Romania 55 M2
Razisi China 72 D1
Razlog Bulg. 55 J4
Razmak Pak. 85 H3
Raz"yezd 3km Rus. Fed. see Novyy Urgal
Ré, Île de i. France 52 D3
Reading U.K. 45 G7
Reading MI U.S.A. 130 C3
Reading OH U.S.A. 130 C4
Reading PA U.S.A. 131 H3
Reagile S. Africa 97 H3
Realicó Arg. 140 D5
Réalmont France 52 F5
Reăng Kesei Cambodia 67 C4
Reate Italy see Rieti
Rebais France 48 D6
Rebecca, Lake salt flat Australia 105 C7
Rebiana Sand Sea des. Libya 93 F2
Reboly Rus. Fed. 40 Q5
Rebrikha Rus. Fed. 68 E2
Rebun-tō i. Japan 70 F3
Recherche, Archipelago of the is Australia 105 C8
Rechitsa Belarus see Rechytsa
Rechna Doab lowland Pak. 85 I4
Rechytsa Belarus 39 F5
Recife Brazil 139 L5
Recife, Cape S. Africa 97 G8
Recklinghausen Germany 49 H3
Reconquista Arg. 140 E3
Recreo Arg. 140 C3
Rectorville U.S.A. 130 D4
Red r. Australia 106 C3
Red r. Canada 116 E3
Red r. Canada/U.S.A. 126 D1
Red r. TN U.S.A. 130 B5
Red r. U.S.A. 127 F6
Red r. Vietnam 66 D2
Redang i. Malaysia 67 C6
Red Bank NJ U.S.A. 131 H3
Red Bank TN U.S.A. 129 C5
Red Basin China see Sichuan Pendi
Red Bay Canada 119 K4
Redberry Lake Canada 117 J4
Red Bluff U.S.A. 124 B1
Red Bluff Lake U.S.A. 127 C6
Red Butte mt. U.S.A. 125 G4
Redcar U.K. 44 F4
Redcliff Canada 122 F2
Redcliffe, Mount hill Australia 105 C7
Red Cliffs Australia 107 C7
Red Cloud U.S.A. 126 D3
Red Deer Canada 116 H4
Red Deer r. Alberta/Saskatchewan Canada 117 I5
Red Deer r. Man./Sask. Canada 117 K4
Red Deer Lake Canada 117 K4
Reddersburg S. Africa 97 H5
Redding U.S.A. 124 B1
Redditch U.K. 45 F6
Rede r. U.K. 44 E3
Redenção Brazil 139 H5
Redeyef Tunisia 54 C7
Redfield U.S.A. 126 D2
Red Granite Mountain Canada 116 B2
Red Hills U.S.A. 127 D4
Red Hook U.S.A. 131 I3
Red Indian Lake Canada 119 K4
Redkey U.S.A. 130 C3
Redkino Rus. Fed. 38 H4
Redknife r. Canada 116 G2
Red Lake Canada 117 M5
Red Lake U.S.A. 125 G4
Red Lake r. U.S.A. 126 D2
Red Lake Falls U.S.A. 117 L6
Red Lakes U.S.A. 126 E1
Redlands U.S.A. 124 E4
Red Lion U.S.A. 131 G4
Red Lodge U.S.A. 122 F3
Redmesa U.S.A. 125 I3
Redmond OR U.S.A. 122 C3
Redmond UT U.S.A. 125 H2
Red Oak U.S.A. 126 E3
Redonda Island Canada 116 E5
Redondo Port. 53 C4
Redondo Beach U.S.A. 124 D5
Red Peak U.S.A. 122 E3
Red River, Mouths of the Vietnam 66 D2
Red Rock Canada 118 C4
Red Rock AZ U.S.A. 125 H5
Redrock U.S.A. 125 I5
Red Rock PA U.S.A. 131 G3
Redrock Lake Canada 116 H1
Red Sea Africa/Asia 82 D4
Redstone r. Canada 116 E1
Red Sucker Lake Canada 117 M4
Reduzum Neth. see Roordahuizum
Redwater Canada 116 H4
Redway U.S.A. 124 B1
Red Wing U.S.A. 126 E2
Redwood City U.S.A. 124 B3
Redwood Falls U.S.A. 126 E2
Redwood National Park U.S.A. 122 B4
Redwood Valley U.S.A. 124 B2
Ree, Lough l. Rep. of Ireland 47 E4
Reed U.S.A. 130 B5
Reed City U.S.A. 130 C2
Reedley U.S.A. 124 D3
Reedsport U.S.A. 122 B4
Reedsville U.S.A. 130 E4
Reedville U.S.A. 131 G5
Reedy U.S.A. 130 E4
Reedy Glacier Antarctica 148 J1
Reefton N.Z. 109 C6
Rees Germany 48 G3
Reese U.S.A. 130 D2
Reese r. U.S.A. 124 E1
Refahiye Turkey 86 E3
Refugio U.S.A. 127 D6
Regen Germany 49 N6
Regen r. Germany 49 M5
Regência Brazil 141 D2
Regensburg Germany 49 M5
Regenstauf Germany 49 M5
Reggane Alg. 92 D2
Reggio Calabria Italy see Reggio di Calabria
Reggio Emilia-Romagna Italy see Reggio nell'Emilia
Reggio di Calabria Italy 54 F5
Reggio Emilia Italy see Reggio nell'Emilia
Reggio nell'Emilia Italy 54 D2
Reghin Romania 55 K1
Regi Afgh. 85 G3

▶Regina Canada 117 J5
Provincial capital of Saskatchewan.

Régina Fr. Guiana 139 H3
Registān reg. Afgh. 85 G4
Registro Brazil 140 G2
Registro do Araguaia Brazil 141 A1
Regium Lepidum Italy see Reggio nell'Emilia
Regozero Rus. Fed. 40 Q4
Rehau Germany 49 M4
Rehburg (Rehburg-Loccum) Germany 49 J2
Rehli India 78 D5
Rehoboth Namibia 96 C2
Rehoboth Bay U.S.A. 131 H4
Rehovot Israel 81 B4
Reibell Alg. see Ksar Chellala

Reibitz Germany 49 M3
Reichenbach Germany 49 M4
Reichshoffen France 49 H6
Reid Australia 105 E7
Reidh, Rubha pt U.K. 46 D3
Reidsville U.S.A. 128 E4
Reigate U.K. 45 G7
Reiley Peak U.S.A. 125 H5
Reims France 48 E5
Reinbek Germany 49 K1
Reindeer r. Canada 117 K4
Reindeer Island Canada 117 L4
Reindeer Lake Canada 117 K3
Reine Norway 40 H3
Reinosa Spain 53 D2
Reinsfeld Germany 48 G5
Reiphólsfjöll hill Iceland 40 [inset]
Reisaelva r. Norway 40 L2
Reisa Nasjonalpark nat. park Norway 40 M2
Reisjärvi Fin. 40 N5
Reitz S. Africa 97 I4
Rekapalle India 80 D2
Reken Germany 48 H3
Reliance Canada 117 I2
Relizane Alg. 53 G6
Rellano Mex. 127 B7
Rellingen Germany 49 J1
Remagen Germany 49 H4
Remarkable, Mount hill Australia 107 B7
Remedios Cuba 129 E8
Remeshk Iran 84 E5
Remhoogte Pass Namibia 96 C2
Remi France see Reims
Remmel Mountain U.S.A. 122 C2
Remscheid Germany 49 H3
Rena Norway 41 G6
Renaix Belgium see Ronse
Renam Myanmar 72 C3
Renapur India 80 C2
Rendsburg Germany 43 L3
René-Levasseur, Île i. Canada 119 H4
Renews Canada 119 L5
Renfrew Canada 131 G1
Renfrew U.K. 46 E5
Rengali Reservoir India 79 F5
Rengat Indon. 64 C7
Rengo Chile 140 B4
Ren He r. China 73 F1
Renheji China 73 G2
Renhua China 73 G3
Reni Ukr. 55 M2
Renick U.S.A. 130 E5
Renland reg. Greenland see Tuttut Nunaat
Rennell i. Solomon Is 103 G3
Rennerod Germany 49 I4
Rennes France 52 D2
Rennick Glacier Antarctica 148 H2
Rennie Canada 117 M5
Reno r. Italy 54 E2
Reno U.S.A. 124 D2
Renovo U.S.A. 131 G3
Rensselaer U.S.A. 130 B3
Renswoude Neth. 48 F2
Renton U.S.A. 122 C3
Réo Burkina 92 C3
Reo Indon. 104 C2
Repalle India 80 D2
Repetek Turkm. 85 F2
Repetekskiy Zapovednik nature res. Turkm. 85 F2
Repolka Rus. Fed. 41 P7
Republic U.S.A. 122 D2
Republican r. U.S.A. 126 D4
▶Republic of Ireland country Europe 47 E4
europe 5, 34–35
▶Republic of South Africa country Africa 96 F5
5th most populous country in Africa.
africa 7, 90–91
Repulse Bay b. Australia 106 E4
Repulse Bay Canada 115 J3
Requena Peru 138 D5
Requena Spain 53 F4
Reşadiye Turkey 86 E2
Reserva Brazil 141 A4
Reserve U.S.A. 125 I5
Reshi China 73 F2
Reshteh-ye Alborz mts Iran see Elburz Mountains
Resistencia Arg. 140 E3
Reşiţa Romania 55 I2
Resolute Bay Canada 115 I2
Resolution Island Canada 115 L3
Resolution Island N.Z. 109 A7
Resplendor Brazil 141 C2
Restigouche r. Canada 119 I5
Resülayn Turkey see Ceylanpınar
Retalhuleu Guat. 132 F6
Retezat, Parcul Naţional nat. park Romania 55 J2
Retford U.K. 44 G5
Rethel France 48 E5
Rethem (Aller) Germany 49 J2
Réthimnon Greece see Rethymno
Rethymno Greece 55 K7
Retreat Australia 106 C5
Reuden Germany 49 M2
▶Réunion terr. Indian Ocean 145 L7
French Overseas Department.
africa 7, 90–91
Reus Spain 53 G3
Reusam, Pulau i. Indon. 67 B7
Reutlingen Germany 43 L6
Reval Estonia see Tallinn
Revda Rus. Fed. 40 S3
Revel Estonia see Tallinn
Revel France 52 F5
Revelstoke Canada 116 G5
Revigny-sur-Ornain France 48 E6
Revillagigedo, Islas is Mex. 132 B5
Revillagigedo Island U.S.A. 116 D4
Revin France 48 E5
Revivim Israel 81 B4
Revolyutsii, Pik mt. Tajik. see Revolyutsiya, Qullai
Revolyutsiya, Qullai mt. Tajik. 85 I2
Rewa India 78 E4
Rewari India 78 D3
Rexburg U.S.A. 122 F4
Rexton Canada 119 I5
Reyes, Point U.S.A. 124 B2
Reyhanlı Turkey 81 C1
Reykir Iceland 40 [inset]
Reykjanes Ridge sea feature N. Atlantic Ocean 144 F2
Reykjanestá pt Iceland 40 [inset]
▶Reykjavík Iceland 40 [inset]
Capital of Iceland.
Reyneke, Ostrov i. Rus. Fed. 70 E1
Reynoldsburg U.S.A. 130 D4
Reynolds Range mts Australia 104 F5
Reynosa Mex. 127 D7
Reẕā Iran 84 D3
Reẕā'īyeh Iran see Urmia
Reẕā'īyeh, Daryācheh-ye salt l. Iran see Urmia, Lake
Rēzekne Latvia 41 O8
Rezvān Iran 85 F4
Reẕvāndeh Iran see Reẕvānshahr
Reẕvānshahr Iran 84 C2
Rhaeader Gwy U.K. see Rhayader
Rhayader U.K. 45 D6
Rheda-Wiedenbrück Germany 49 I3
Rhede Germany 48 G3
Rhegium Italy see Reggio di Calabria
Rheims France see Reims
Rhein r. Germany 49 G3 see Rhine
Rheine Germany 49 H2
Rheinland-Pfalz land Germany 49 H5
Rheinsberg Germany 49 M1
Rheinstetten Germany 49 I6
Rhemilès well Alg. 92 C2
Rhin r. France 49 I6 see Rhine
Rhine r. Germany 49 G3
also spelt Rhein (Germany) or Rhin (France)
Rhinebeck U.S.A. 131 I3
Rhinelander U.S.A. 126 F2
Rhineland-Palatinate land Germany see Rheinland-Pfalz
Rhinkanal canal Germany 49 M2
Rhinow Germany 49 M2
Rhiwabon U.K. see Ruabon
Rho Italy 54 C2
Rhode Island state U.S.A. 131 J3
Rhodes Greece 55 M6
Rhodes i. Greece 55 M6
Rhodesia country Africa see Zimbabwe
Rhodes Peak U.S.A. 122 E3
Rhodope Mountains Bulg./Greece 55 J4
Rhodus i. Greece see Rhodes
Rhône r. France/Switz. 52 G5
Rhum i. U.K. see Rum
Rhuthun U.K. see Ruthin
Rhydaman U.K. see Ammanford
Rhyl U.K. 44 D5
Riachão Brazil 139 I5
Riacho Brazil 141 C2
Riacho de Santana Brazil 141 C1
Riacho dos Machados Brazil 141 C1
Rialma Brazil 141 A1
Rialto U.S.A. 124 E4
Riasi Jammu and Kashmir 78 C2
Riau, Kepulauan is Indon. 64 C6
Ribadeo Spain 53 C2
Ribadesella Spain 53 D2
Ribas do Rio Pardo Brazil 140 F2
Ribat Afgh. 85 H2
Ribat-i-Shur waterhole Iran 84 E3
Ribáuè Moz. 95 D5
Ribble r. U.K. 44 E5
Ribblesdale valley U.K. 44 E4
Ribe Denmark 41 F9
Ribécourt-Dreslincourt France 48 C5
Ribeira r. Brazil 141 B4
Ribeirão Preto Brazil 141 B3
Ribemont France 48 D5
Ribérac France 52 E4
Riberalta Bol. 138 E6
Rîbniţa Moldova 39 F7
Ribnitz-Damgarten Germany 43 N3
Říčany Czech Rep. 43 O6
Rice U.S.A. 131 F5
Rice Lake Canada 131 F1
Richards Bay S. Africa 97 K5
Richards Inlet Antarctica 148 H1
Richards Island Canada 114 E3
Richardson r. Canada 117 I3
Richardson U.S.A. 127 D5
Richardson Island Canada 116 G1
Richardson Lakes U.S.A. 131 J1
Richardson Mountains Canada 114 E3
Richardson Mountains N.Z. 109 B7
Richfield U.S.A. 125 G2
Richfield Springs U.S.A. 131 H2
Richford NY U.S.A. 131 G2
Richford VT U.S.A. 131 I1
Richgrove U.S.A. 124 D4
Richland U.S.A. 122 D3
Richland Center U.S.A. 126 F3
Richmond N.S.W. Australia 108 E4
Richmond Qld Australia 106 C4
Richmond Canada 131 H1
Richmond N.Z. 109 D5
Richmond Kwazulu-Natal S. Africa 97 J5
Richmond N. Cape S. Africa 96 F6
Richmond U.K. 44 F4
Richmond CA U.S.A. 124 B3
Richmond IN U.S.A. 130 C4
Richmond KY U.S.A. 130 C5
Richmond MI U.S.A. 130 D2
Richmond MO U.S.A. 126 E4
Richmond TX U.S.A. 127 E6
▶Richmond VA U.S.A. 131 G5
State capital of Virginia.
Richmond Dale U.S.A. 130 D4
Richmond Hill U.S.A. 129 D6
Richmond Range hills Australia 108 F2
Richtersveld National Park S. Africa 96 C5
Richvale U.S.A. 124 C2
Richwood U.S.A. 130 E4
Rico U.S.A. 125 I3
Ricomagus France see Riom
Riddell Nunataks Antarctica 148 E2
Rideau Lakes Canada 131 G1
Ridge r. Canada 118 D4
Ridgecrest U.S.A. 124 E4
Ridge Farm U.S.A. 130 B4
Ridgeland MS U.S.A. 127 F5
Ridgeland SC U.S.A. 129 D5
Ridgetop U.S.A. 130 B5
Ridgetown Canada 130 E2
Ridgeway OH U.S.A. 130 D3
Ridgeway VA U.S.A. 130 F5
Ridgway CO U.S.A. 125 J2
Ridgway PA U.S.A. 131 F3
Riding Mountain National Park Canada 117 K5
Riecito Venez. 138 E1
Riemst Belgium 48 F4
Riesa Germany 49 N3
Riesco, Isla i. Chile 140 B8
Riet watercourse S. Africa 96 E6
Rietavas Lith. 41 L9
Rietfontein S. Africa 96 E4
Rieti Italy 54 E3
Rifā'ī, Tall mt. Jordan/Syria 81 C3
Rifeng China see Lichuan
Rifle U.S.A. 125 J2
Rifstangi pt Iceland 40 [inset]
Rift Valley Lakes National Park Eth. see Abijatta-Shalla National Park
▶Rīga Latvia 41 N8
Capital of Latvia.
Riga, Gulf of Estonia/Latvia 41 M8
Rigain Pünco l. China 79 F2
Rīgān Iran 84 E4
Rīgas jūras līcis b. Estonia/Latvia see Riga, Gulf of
Rigby U.S.A. 122 F4
Rīgestān reg. Afgh. see Registān
Rigolet Canada 119 K3
Rigside U.K. 46 F5
Riia laht b. Estonia/Latvia see Riga, Gulf of
Riihimäki Fin. 41 N6
Riiser-Larsen Ice Shelf Antarctica 148 B2
Riito Mex. 125 F5
Rijau Nigeria 92 D3
Rijeka Croatia 54 F2
Rikā, Wādī ar watercourse Saudi Arabia 84 B6
Rikitgaib Indon. 67 B6
Rikor India 72 B2
Rikuchū-kaigan National Park Japan 71 F5
Rikuzen-takata Japan 71 F5
Rila mts Bulg. 55 J3
Rila China 79 F3
Riley U.S.A. 122 D4
Rileyville U.S.A. 131 F4
Rillieux-la-Pape France 52 G4
Rillito U.S.A. 125 H5
Rimah, Wādī al watercourse Saudi Arabia 82 F4
Rimavská Sobota Slovakia 43 R6
Rimbey Canada 116 H4
Rimini Italy 54 E2
Rîmnicu Sărat Romania see Râmnicu Sărat
Rîmnicu Vîlcea Romania see Râmnicu Vâlcea
Rimouski Canada 119 H4
Rimpar Germany 49 J5
Rimsdale, Loch l. U.K. 46 E2
Rinbung China 79 G3
Rincão Brazil 141 A3
Rindal Norway 40 F5
Ringarooma Bay Australia 107 [inset]
Ringas India 78 C4
Ringe Germany 48 G2
Ringebu Norway 41 G6
Ringhkung Myanmar 66 B1
Ringkøbing Denmark 41 F8
Ringsend U.K. 47 F2
Ringsted Denmark 41 G9
Ringtor China 79 E3
Ringvassøy i. Norway 40 K2
Ringwood Australia 108 B6
Ringwood U.K. 45 F8
Rinjani, Gunung vol. Indon. 64 F8
Rinns Point U.K. 46 C5
Rinqênzê China 79 G3
Rinteln Germany 49 J2
Rio Azul Brazil 141 A4
Riobamba Ecuador 138 C4
Rio Blanco U.S.A. 125 J2
Rio Bonito Brazil 141 C3
Rio Branco Brazil 138 E6
Rio Branco, Parque Nacional do nat. park Brazil 138 F3
Río Bravo, Parque Internacional del nat. park Mex. 127 C6
Rio Brilhante Brazil 140 F2
Rio Casca Brazil 141 C3
Rio Claro Brazil 141 B3
Río Colorado Arg. 140 D5
Río Cuarto Arg. 140 D4
Rio das Pedras Moz. 97 L2
Rio de Contas Brazil 141 C1
▶Rio de Janeiro Brazil 141 C3
3rd most populous city in South America. Former capital of Brazil.
Rio de Janeiro state Brazil 141 C3
▶Río de la Plata-Paraná r. S. America 140 E4
2nd longest river in South America.
Rio Dell U.S.A. 124 A1
Rio do Sul Brazil 141 A4
Río Gallegos Arg. 140 C8
Río Grande Arg. 140 C8
Rio Grande Brazil 140 F4
Río Grande Mex. 127 C8
Rio Grande r. Mex./U.S.A. 123 G5
also known as Río Bravo del Norte
Rio Grande City U.S.A. 127 D7
Rio Grande do Sul state Brazil 141 A5
Rio Grande Rise sea feature S. Atlantic Ocean 144 F8
Ríohacha Col. 138 D1
Río Hondo, Embalse resr Arg. 140 C3
Rioja Peru 138 C5
Río Lagartos Mex. 129 B8
Rio Largo Brazil 139 K5
Riom France 52 F4
Río Mulatos Bol. 138 E7
Río Muni reg. Equat. Guinea 92 E4
Río Negro, Embalse del resr Uruguay 140 E4
Rioni r. Georgia 87 F2
Rio Novo Brazil 141 C3
Rio Pardo de Minas Brazil 141 C1
Rio Preto Brazil 141 C3
Rio Preto, Serra do hills Brazil 141 B2
Rio Rancho U.S.A. 123 G6
Río Tigre Ecuador 138 C4
Riou Lake Canada 117 J3
Rio Verde Brazil 141 A2
Rio Verde de Mato Grosso Brazil 139 H7
Rio Vista U.S.A. 124 C2
Ripky Ukr. 39 F6
Ripley England U.K. 44 F4
Ripley England U.K. 45 F5
Ripley NY U.S.A. 130 F2
Ripley OH U.S.A. 130 D4
Ripley WV U.S.A. 130 E4
Ripoll Spain 53 H2
Ripon U.K. 44 F4
Ripon U.S.A. 124 C3
Ripu India 79 G4
Risca U.K. 45 D7
Rishiri-tō i. Japan 70 F3
Rishon Le Ẕiyyon Israel 81 B4
Rish Pish Iran 85 F5
Rising Sun IN U.S.A. 130 C4
Rising Sun MD U.S.A. 131 G4
Risle r. France 45 H9
Risør Norway 41 F7
Rissa Norway 40 F5
Ristiina Fin. 41 O6
Ristijärvi Fin. 40 P4
Ristikent Rus. Fed. 40 Q2
Risum China 78 D2
Ritchie S. Africa 96 G5
Ritchie's Archipelago is India 67 A4
Ritscher Upland mts Antarctica 148 B2
Ritsem Sweden 40 J3
Ritter, Mount U.S.A. 124 D3
Ritterhude Germany 49 I1
Ritzville U.S.A. 122 D3
Riu, Laem pt Thai. 67 B5
Riva del Garda Italy 54 D2
Rivas Nicaragua 133 G6
Rivera Arg. 140 D5
Rivera Uruguay 140 E4
River Cess Liberia 92 C4
Riverhead U.S.A. 131 I3
Riverhurst Canada 117 J5
Riverina Australia 105 C7
Riverina reg. Australia 108 B5
Riversdale S. Africa 96 E8
Riverside S. Africa 97 I6
Riverside U.S.A. 124 E5
Rivers Inlet Canada 116 E5
Riversleigh Australia 106 B3
Riverton N.Z. 109 B8
Riverton VA U.S.A. 131 F4
Riverton WY U.S.A. 122 F4
Riverview Canada 119 I5
Rivesaltes France 52 F5
Riviera Beach U.S.A. 129 D7
Rivière-du-Loup Canada 119 H5
Riviere-Pentecote Canada 119 I4
Riviere-Pigou Canada 119 I4
Rivne Ukr. 39 E6
Rivungo Angola 95 C5
Riwaka N.Z. 109 D5
Riwoqê China 72 C2
▶Riyadh Saudi Arabia 82 G5
Capital of Saudi Arabia.
Riyan India 85 I5
Riza well Iran 84 D3
Rize Turkey 87 F2
Rizhao Shandong China 73 H1
Rizhao Shandong China 73 H1
Rizokarpaso Cyprus see Rizokarpason
Rizokarpason Cyprus 81 B2
Rīzū well Iran 84 E3
Rīzū'īyeh Iran 84 E4
Rjukan Norway 41 F7
Rjuvbrokkene mt. Norway 41 E7
Rkîz Mauritania 92 B3
Roa Norway 41 G6
Roachdale U.S.A. 130 B4
Roach Lake U.S.A. 125 F4
Roade U.K. 45 G6
Roads U.S.A. 130 D4
▶Road Town Virgin Is (U.K.) 133 L5
Capital of the British Virgin Islands.
Roan Norway 40 G4
Roan Fell hill U.K. 46 G5
Roan High Knob mt. U.S.A. 128 D4
Roanne France 52 G3
Roanoke IN U.S.A. 130 C3
Roanoke VA U.S.A. 130 F5
Roanoke r. U.S.A. 128 E4
Roanoke Rapids U.S.A. 128 E4
Roan Plateau U.S.A. 125 I2
Roaring Spring U.S.A. 131 F3
Roaringwater Bay Rep. of Ireland 47 C6
Roatán Hond. 133 G5
Röbäck Sweden 40 L5
Robat r. Afgh. 85 F4
Robāṭe Tork Iran 84 C3
Robāṭ Karīm Iran 84 C3
Robāt-Sang Iran 84 E3
Robb Canada 116 G4
Robbins Island Australia 107 [inset]
Robbinsville U.S.A. 129 D5
Robe Australia 107 B8
Robe r. Australia 104 A5
Robe r. Rep. of Ireland 47 C4
Röbel Germany 49 M1
Robert Glacier Antarctica 148 D2
Robert Lee U.S.A. 127 C6
Roberts U.S.A. 122 E4
Roberts, Mount Australia 108 F2
Robertsburg U.S.A. 130 E4
Roberts Butte mt. Antarctica 148 H2
Roberts Creek Mountain U.S.A. 124 E2
Robertsfors Sweden 40 L4
Robertsganj India 79 E4
Robertson S. Africa 96 D7
Robertson, Lac l. Canada 119 K4
Robertson Bay Antarctica 148 H2
Robertson Island Antarctica 148 A2
Robertson Range hills Australia 105 C5
Robertsport Liberia 92 B4
Roberval Canada 119 G4
Robhanais, Rubha hd U.K. see Butt of Lewis
Robin Hood's Bay U.K. 44 G4
Robin's Nest hill Hong Kong China 73 [inset]
Robinson Canada 116 C2
Robinson U.S.A. 130 B4
Robinson Range hills Australia 105 B6
Robinson River Australia 106 B3
Robles Pass U.S.A. 125 H5
Roblin Canada 117 K5
Robsart Canada 117 I5
Robson, Mount Canada 116 G4
Robstown U.S.A. 127 D7
Roby U.S.A. 127 C5
Roçadas Angola see Xangongo
Rocca Busambra mt. Sicily Italy 54 E6
Rocha Uruguay 140 F4
Rochdale U.K. 44 E5
Rochechouart France 52 E4
Rochefort Belgium 48 F4
Rochefort France 52 D4
Rochefort, Lac l. Canada 119 G2
Rochegda Rus. Fed. 38 I3
Rochester Australia 108 B6
Rochester U.K. 45 H7
Rochester IN U.S.A. 130 B3
Rochester MN U.S.A. 126 E2
Rochester NH U.S.A. 131 J2
Rochester NY U.S.A. 131 G2
Rochford U.K. 45 H7
Rochlitz Germany 49 M3
Roc'h Trévezel hill France 52 C2
Rock r. Canada 116 E2
Rockall i. N. Atlantic Ocean 36 D4
Rockall Bank sea feature N. Atlantic Ocean 144 G2
Rock Creek Canada 116 B1
Rock Creek U.S.A. 130 E3
Rock Creek r. U.S.A. 122 G2
Rockdale U.S.A. 127 D6
Rockefeller Plateau Antarctica 148 J1
Rockford AL U.S.A. 129 C5
Rockford IL U.S.A. 126 F3
Rockford MI U.S.A. 130 C2
Rockglen Canada 117 J5
Rockhampton Australia 106 E4
Rockhampton Downs Australia 104 F4
Rock Hill U.S.A. 129 D5
Rockingham Australia 105 A8
Rockingham U.S.A. 129 E5
Rockingham Bay Australia 106 D3
Rockinghorse Lake Canada 117 H1
Rock Island Canada 131 I1
Rock Island U.S.A. 126 F3
Rocklake U.S.A. 126 D1
Rockland MA U.S.A. 131 J2
Rockland ME U.S.A. 128 G2
Rocknest Lake Canada 116 H1
Rockport IN U.S.A. 130 B5
Rockport TX U.S.A. 127 D7
Rock Rapids U.S.A. 126 D3
Rock River U.S.A. 122 G4
Rock Sound Bahamas 129 E7
Rock Springs MT U.S.A. 122 G3
Rocksprings U.S.A. 127 C6
Rock Springs WY U.S.A. 122 F4
Rockstone Guyana 139 G2
Rockville CT U.S.A. 131 I3
Rockville IN U.S.A. 130 B4
Rockville MD U.S.A. 131 G4
Rockwell City U.S.A. 126 E3
Rockwood MI U.S.A. 130 D2
Rockwood PA U.S.A. 130 F4
Rockyford Canada 116 H5
Rocky Harbour Canada 119 K4
Rocky Hill U.S.A. 130 D4
Rocky Island Lake Canada 118 E5
Rocky Lane Canada 116 G3
Rocky Mount U.S.A. 130 F5
Rocky Mountain House Canada 116 H4
Rocky Mountain National Park U.S.A. 122 G4
Rocky Mountains Canada/U.S.A. 120 F3
Rocourt-St-Martin France 48 D5
Rocroi France 48 E5
Rodberg Norway 41 F6
Rødbyhavn Denmark 41 G9
Roddickton Canada 119 L4
Rodeio Brazil 141 A4
Rodel U.K. 46 C3
Roden Neth. 48 G1
Rödental Germany 49 L4
Rodeo Arg. 140 C4
Rodeo Mex. 127 B7
Rodeo U.S.A. 123 F7
Rodez France 52 F4
Ródhos i. Greece see Rhodes
Rodi i. Greece see Rhodes
Roding Germany 49 M5
Rodney, Cape U.S.A. 114 B3
Rodniki Rus. Fed. 38 I4
Rodolfo Sanchez Toboada Mex. 123 D7
Rodopi Planina mts Bulg./Greece see Rhodope Mountains
Rodos Greece see Rhodes
Rodos i. Greece see Rhodes
Rodosto Turkey see Tekirdağ
Rodrigues Island Mauritius 145 M7
Roe r. U.K. 47 F2
Roebourne Australia 104 B5
Roebuck Bay Australia 104 C4
Roedtan S. Africa 97 I3
Roe Plains Australia 105 D7
Roermond Neth. 48 F3
Roeselare Belgium 48 D4
Roes Welcome Sound sea chan. Canada 115 J3
Rogachev Belarus see Rahachow
Rogätz Germany 49 L2
Rogers U.S.A. 127 E4
Rogers, Mount U.S.A. 130 E5
Rogers City U.S.A. 130 D1
Rogers Lake U.S.A. 124 E4
Rogerson U.S.A. 122 E4
Rogersville U.S.A. 130 D5
Roggan r. Canada 118 F3
Roggan, Lac l. Canada 118 F3
Roggeveen Basin sea feature S. Pacific Ocean 147 O8
Roggeveld plat. S. Africa 96 E7
Roggeveldberge esc. S. Africa 96 E7
Roghadal U.K. see Rodel
Rognan Norway 40 I3
Rögnitz r. Germany 49 K1
Rogue r. U.S.A. 122 B4
Roha India 80 B2
Rohnert Park U.S.A. 124 B2
Rohrbach in Oberösterreich Austria 43 N6
Rohrbach-lès-Bitche France 49 H5
Rohri Pak. 85 H5
Rohtak India 78 D3
Roi Et Thai. 66 C3
Roi Georges, Îles du is Fr. Polynesia 147 K6
Rois-Bheinn hill U.K. 46 D4
Roisel France 48 D5
Roja Latvia 41 M8
Rojas Arg. 140 D4
Rokeby Australia 106 C2
Rokeby National Park Australia 106 C2
Rokiškis Lith. 41 N9
Roknäs Sweden 40 L4
Rokytne Ukr. 39 E6
Rolagang China 79 G2
Rola Kangri mt. China 79 G2
Rolândia Brazil 141 A3
Rolim de Moura Brazil 138 F6
Roll AZ U.S.A. 125 G5
Roll IN U.S.A. 130 C3
Rolla MO U.S.A. 126 F4
Rolla ND U.S.A. 126 D1
Rollag Norway 41 F6
Rolleston Australia 106 E5
Rolleville Bahamas 129 F8
Rolling Fork U.S.A. 127 F5
Rollins U.S.A. 122 E3
Roma Australia 107 E5
Roma i. Indon. 104 D1
Roma Italy see Rome
Roma Lesotho 97 H5
Roma Sweden 41 K8
Romain, Cape U.S.A. 129 E5
Romaine r. Canada 119 J4
Roman Romania 55 L1
Romanâ, Câmpia plain Romania 55 J2
Romanche Gap sea feature S. Atlantic Ocean 144 G6
Romanet, Lac l. Canada 119 I2
▶Romania country Europe 55 K2
europe 5, 34–35
Roman-Kosh mt. Ukr. 86 D1
Romano, Cape U.S.A. 129 D7
Romanovka Rus. Fed. 69 K2
Romans-sur-Isère France 52 G4
Romanzof, Cape U.S.A. 114 B3
Rombas France 48 G5
Romblon Phil. 65 G4
▶Rome Italy 54 E4
Capital of Italy.
Rome GA U.S.A. 129 C5
Rome ME U.S.A. 131 K1
Rome NY U.S.A. 131 H2
Rome TN U.S.A. 130 B5
Rome City U.S.A. 130 C3
Romeo U.S.A. 130 D2
Romford U.K. 45 H7
Romilly-sur-Seine France 52 F2
Romitan Uzbek. 85 G2
Romney U.S.A. 131 F4
Romney Marsh reg. U.K. 45 H7
Romny Ukr. 39 G6
Rømø i. Denmark 41 F9
Romodanovo Rus. Fed. 39 J5
Romorantin-Lanthenay France 52 E3
Rompin r. Malaysia 67 C7
Romsey U.K. 45 F8
Romulus U.S.A. 130 D2
Ron India 80 B3
Rona i. U.K. 46 D1
Ronas Hill hill U.K. 46 [inset]
Roncador, Serra do hills Brazil 139 H6
Roncador Reef Solomon Is 103 F2
Ronda Spain 53 D5
Ronda, Serranía de mts Spain 53 D5
Rondane Nasjonalpark nat. park Norway 41 F6
Rondon Brazil 140 F2
Rondonópolis Brazil 139 H7
Rondout Reservoir U.S.A. 131 H3
Rongcheng Anhui China see Qingyang
Rongcheng Guangxi China see Rongxian
Rongcheng Hubei China see Jianli
Rong Chu r. China 79 G3
Rongelap atoll Marshall Is 146 H5
Rongjiang Guizhou China 73 F3
Rongjiang Jiangxi China see Nankang
Rongjiawan China see Yueyang
Rongklang Range mts Myanmar 66 A2
Rongmei China see Hefeng
Rongshui China 73 F3
Rongwo China see Tongren
Rongxian China 73 F4
Rongyul China 72 C2
Rongzhag China see Danba
Rönlap atoll Marshall Is see Rongelap
Rønne Denmark 41 I9
Ronneby Sweden 41 I8
Ronne Entrance strait Antarctica 148 L2
Ronne Ice Shelf Antarctica 148 L1
Ronnenberg Germany 49 J2
Ronse Belgium 48 D4
Roodeschool Neth. 48 G1
Rooke Island P.N.G. see Umboi
Roordahuizum Neth. 48 F1
Roorkee India 78 D3
Roosendaal Neth. 48 E3
Roosevelt AZ U.S.A. 125 H5
Roosevelt UT U.S.A. 125 I1
Roosevelt, Mount Canada 116 E3
Roosevelt Island Antarctica 148 I1
Root r. Canada 116 F2
Root r. U.S.A. 126 F3
Ropar India see Rupnagar
Roper r. Australia 106 A2
Roper Bar Australia 104 F3
Roquefort France 52 D4
Roraima, Mount Guyana 138 F2
Rori India 78 C3
Rori Indon. 65 J7
Røros Norway 40 G5
Rørvik Norway 40 G4
Rosa, Punta pt Mex. 123 F8
Rosalia U.S.A. 122 D3
Rosamond U.S.A. 124 D4
Rosamond Lake U.S.A. 124 D4
Rosario Arg. 140 D4
Rosário Brazil 139 J4
Rosario Baja California Mex. 123 E7
Rosario Coahuila Mex. 127 C7
Rosario Sinaloa Mex. 132 C4
Rosario Sonora Mex. 120 F6
Rosario Zacatecas Mex. 127 C7
Rosario Venez. 138 D1
Rosário do Sul Brazil 140 F4
Rosário Oeste Brazil 139 G6
Rosarito Baja California Mex. 123 E7
Rosarito Baja California Mex. 124 E5
Rosarito Baja California Sur Mex. 123 F8
Rosarno Italy 54 F5
Roscoff France 52 C2
Roscommon Rep. of Ireland 47 D4
Roscommon U.S.A. 130 C1
Roscrea Rep. of Ireland 47 E5
Rose r. Australia 106 A2
Rose, Mount U.S.A. 124 D2
Rose Atoll American Samoa see Rose Island
▶Roseau Dominica 133 L5
Capital of Dominica.
Roseau U.S.A. 126 E1
Roseau r. U.S.A. 126 D1
Roseberth Australia 107 B5
Rose Blanche Canada 119 K5
Rosebud r. Canada 116 H5
Rosebud U.S.A. 122 G3
Roseburg U.S.A. 122 C4
Rose City U.S.A. 130 C1
Rosedale U.S.A. 127 F5
Rosedale Abbey U.K. 44 G4
Roseires Reservoir Sudan 82 D7
Rose Island atoll American Samoa 103 J3
Rosenberg U.S.A. 127 E6
Rosendal Norway 41 E7

Rosendal S. Africa 97 H5
Rosenheim Germany 43 N7
Rose Peak U.S.A. 125 I5
Rose Point Canada 116 D4
Roseto degli Abruzzi Italy 54 F3
Rosetown Canada 117 J5
Rosetta Egypt see Rashîd
Rose Valley Canada 117 K4
Roseville CA U.S.A. 124 C2
Roseville MI U.S.A. 130 D2
Roseville OH U.S.A. 130 D4
Rosewood Australia 108 F1
Roshchino Rus. Fed. 41 P6
Rosh Pinah Namibia 96 C4
Roshtkala Tajik. see Roshtqal'a
Roshtqal'a Tajik. 85 H2
Rosignano Marittimo Italy 54 D3
Roşiori de Vede Romania 55 K2
Roskilde Denmark 41 H9
Roskruge Mountains U.S.A. 125 H5
Roslavl' Rus. Fed. 39 G5
Roslyakovo Rus. Fed. 40 R2
Roslyatino Rus. Fed. 38 J4
Ross N.Z. 109 C6
Ross, Mount hill N.Z. 109 E5
Rossano Italy 54 G5
Rossan Point Rep. of Ireland 47 D3
Ross Barnett Reservoir U.S.A. 127 F5
Ross Bay Junction Canada 119 I3
Ross Carbery Rep. of Ireland 47 C6
Ross Dependency reg. Antarctica 148 I2
Rosseau, Lake Canada 130 F1
Rossel Island P.N.G. 106 F1
Ross Ice Shelf Antarctica 148 I1
Rossignol, Lac l. Canada 118 G3
Rössing Namibia 96 B2
Ross Island Antarctica 148 H1
Rossiyskaya Sovetskaya Federativnaya Sotsialisticheskaya Respublika country Asia/Europe see Russian Federation
Rossland Canada 116 G5
Rosslare Rep. of Ireland 47 F5
Rosslare Harbour Rep. of Ireland 47 F5
Roßlau Germany 49 M3
Rosso Mauritania 92 B3
Ross-on-Wye U.K. 45 E7
Rossony Belarus see Rasony
Rossosh' Rus. Fed. 39 H6
Ross River Canada 116 C2
Ross Sea Antarctica 148 H1
Roßtal Germany 49 K5
Røssvatnet l. Norway 40 I4
Rossville U.S.A. 130 B3
Roßwein Germany 49 N3
Rosswood Canada 116 D4
Rostāq Afgh. 85 H2
Rostāq Iran 84 D5
Rosthern Canada 117 J4
Rostock Germany 43 N3
Rostov Rus. Fed. 38 H4
Rostov-na-Donu Rus. Fed. 39 H7
Rostov-on-Don Rus. Fed. see Rostov-na-Donu
Rosvik Sweden 40 L4
Roswell U.S.A. 123 G6
Rota i. N. Mariana Is 65 L4
Rot am See Germany 49 K5
Rotch Island Kiribati see Tamana
Rote i. Indon. 104 C2
Rotenburg (Wümme) Germany 49 J1
Roth Germany 49 L5
Rothaargebirge hills Germany 49 I4
Rothbury U.K. 44 F3
Rothenburg ob der Tauber Germany 49 K5
Rother r. U.K. 45 G8
Rothera research station Antarctica 148 L2
Rotherham U.K. 44 F5
Rothes U.K. 46 F3
Rothesay U.K. 46 D5
Rothwell U.K. 45 G6
Roti Indon. 104 C2
Roti i. Indon. see Rote
Roto Australia 108 B4
Rotomagus France see Rouen
Rotomanu N.Z. 109 C6
Rotondo, Monte mt. Corsica France 52 I5
Rotorua N.Z. 109 F4
Rotorua, Lake N.Z. 109 F4
Röttenbach Germany 49 L5
Rottendorf Germany 49 K5
Rottenmann Austria 43 O7
Rotterdam Neth. 48 E3
Rottleberode Germany 49 K3
Rottnest Island Australia 105 A8
Rottweil Germany 43 L6
Rotuma i. Fiji 103 H3
Rotumeroog i. Neth. 48 G1
Rotung India 72 B2
Rötviken Sweden 40 I5
Rötz Germany 49 M5
Roubaix France 48 D4
Rouen France 48 B5
Rough River Lake U.S.A. 130 B5
Roulers Belgium see Roeselare
Roumania country Europe see Romania
Roundeyed Lake Canada 119 H3
Round Hill hill U.K. 44 F4
Round Mountain Australia 108 F3
Round Rock AZ U.S.A. 125 I3
Round Rock TX U.S.A. 127 D6
Roundup U.S.A. 122 F3
Rousay i. U.K. 46 F1
Rouses Point U.S.A. 131 I1
Rouxville S. Africa 97 H6
Rouyn Canada 118 F4
Rovaniemi Fin. 40 N3
Roven'ki Rus. Fed. 39 H6
Rovereto Italy 54 D2
Rôviĕng Tbong Cambodia 67 D4
Rovigo Italy 54 D2
Rovinj Croatia 54 E2
Rovno Ukr. see Rivne
Rovnoye Rus. Fed. 39 J6
Rovuma r. Moz./Tanz. see Ruvuma
Rowena Australia 108 D2
Rowley Island Canada 115 K3
Rowley Shoals sea feature Australia 104 B4
Równe Ukr. see Rivne
Roxas Mindoro Phil. 65 G4
Roxas Palawan Phil. 64 F4
Roxas Panay Phil. 65 G4
Roxboro U.S.A. 128 E4
Roxburgh N.Z. 109 B7
Roxburgh Island Cook Is see Rarotonga
Roxby Downs Australia 107 B6
Roxo, Cabo c. Senegal 92 B3
Roy MT U.S.A. 122 F3
Roy NM U.S.A. 123 G5
Royal Canal Rep. of Ireland 47 E4
Royal Chitwan National Park Nepal 79 F4
Royale, Île i. Canada see Cape Breton Island
Royale, Isle i. U.S.A. 126 F1
Royal Natal National Park S. Africa 97 I5
Royal National Park Australia 108 E5
Royal Oak U.S.A. 130 D2
Royal Suklaphanta National Park Nepal 78 E3
Royan France 52 D4
Roye France 48 C5
Roy Hill Australia 104 B5
Royston U.K. 45 G6
Rozdil'na Ukr. 55 N1
Rozivka Ukr. 39 H7
Rtishchevo Rus. Fed. 39 I5
Ruabon U.K. 45 D6
Ruaha National Park Tanz. 95 D4
Ruahine Range mts N.Z. 109 F5
Ruanda country Africa see Rwanda
Ruapehu, Mount vol. N.Z. 109 E4
Ruapuke Island N.Z. 109 B8
Ruatoria N.Z. 109 G3
Ruba Belarus 39 F5

▶Rub' al Khālī des. Saudi Arabia 82 G6
Largest uninterrupted stretch of sand in the world.

Rubaydā reg. Saudi Arabia 84 C5
Rubtsovsk Rus. Fed. 76 F1
Ruby U.S.A. 114 C3
Ruby Dome mt. U.S.A. 125 F1
Ruby Mountains U.S.A. 125 F1
Rubys Inn U.S.A. 125 G3
Ruby Valley U.S.A. 125 F1
Rucheng China 73 G3
Ruckersville U.S.A. 131 F4
Rudall River National Park Australia 104 C5
Rudarpur India 79 E4
Ruda Śląska Poland 43 Q5
Rudauli India 79 E4
Rūdbār Iran 84 C2
Rudkøbing Denmark 41 G9
Rudnaya Pristan' Rus. Fed. 70 D3
Rudnichnyy Rus. Fed. 38 L4
Rudnik Ingichka Uzbek. see Ingichka
Rudnya Smolenskaya Oblast' Rus. Fed. 39 F5
Rudnya Volgogradskaya Oblast' Rus. Fed. 39 J6
Rudnyy Kazakh. 74 F1
Rudolf, Lake salt l. Eth./Kenya see Turkana, Lake

▶Rudol'fa, Ostrov i. Rus. Fed. 60 G1
Most northerly point of Europe.

Rudolph Island Rus. Fed. see Rudol'fa, Ostrov
Rudolstadt Germany 49 L4
Rudong China 73 I1
Rūdsar Iran 84 C2
Rue France 48 B4
Rufiji r. Tanz. 95 D4
Rufino Arg. 140 D4
Rufisque Senegal 92 B3
Rufrufua Indon. 65 I7
Rufunsa Zambia 95 C5
Rugao China 73 I1
Rugby U.K. 45 F6
Rugby U.S.A. 126 C1
Rugeley U.K. 45 F6
Rügen i. Germany 43 N3
Rugged Mountain Canada 116 E5
Rügland Germany 49 K5
Ruḩayyat al Ḩamr'ā' waterhole Saudi Arabia 84 B5
Ruhengeri Rwanda 94 C4
Ruhnu i. Estonia 41 M8
Ruhr r. Germany 49 G3
Ruhuna National Park Sri Lanka 80 D5
Rui'an China 73 I3
Rui Barbosa Brazil 141 C1
Ruicheng China 73 F1
Ruijin China 73 G3
Ruili China 72 C3
Ruin Point Canada 117 P2
Ruipa Tanz. 95 D4
Ruiz Mex. 132 C4
Ruiz, Nevado del vol. Col. 138 C3
Rujaylah, Ḩarrat ar lava field Jordan 81 C3
Rūjiena Latvia 41 N8
Ruk is Micronesia see Chuuk
Rukanpur Pak. 85 I4
Rukumkot Nepal 79 E3
Rukwa, Lake Tanz. 95 D4
Rulin China see Chengbu
Rulong China see Xinlong
Rum i. U.K. 46 C4
Rum, Jebel mts Jordan see Ramm, Jabal
Ruma Serb. and Mont. 55 H2
Rumāh Saudi Arabia 82 G4
Rumania country Europe see Romania
Rumbek Sudan 93 F4
Rumberpon i. Indon. 65 I7
Rum Cay i. Bahamas 129 F8
Rum Jungle Australia 104 E3
Rummānā hill Syria 81 D3
Rumphi Malawi 95 D5
Runan China 73 G1
Runaway, Cape N.Z. 109 F3
Runcorn U.K. 44 E5
Rundu Namibia 95 B5
Rundvik Sweden 40 K5
Rŭng, Kaôh i. Cambodia 67 C5
Rungwa Tanz. 95 D4
Rungwa r. Tanz. 95 D4
Runheji China 73 H1
Runing China see Runan
Runton Range hills Australia 105 C5
Ruokolahti Fin. 41 P6
Ruoqiang China 76 G4
Rupa India 79 H4
Rupat i. Indon. 67 C7
Rupert r. Canada 118 F4
Rupert ID U.S.A. 122 E4
Rupert WV U.S.A. 130 E5
Rupert Bay Canada 118 F4
Rupert Coast Antarctica 148 J1
Rupert House Canada see Waskaganish
Rupnagar India 78 D3
Rupshu reg. Jammu and Kashmir 78 D2
Ruqqād, Wādī ar watercourse Israel 81 B3
Rural Retreat U.S.A. 130 E5
Rusaddir N. Africa see Melilla
Rusape Zimbabwe 95 D5
Ruschuk Bulg. see Ruse
Ruse Bulg. 55 K3
Rusera India 79 F4
Rush U.S.A. 130 D4
Rush Creek r. U.S.A. 126 C4
Rushden U.K. 45 G6
Rushinga Zimbabwe 95 D5
Rushville IL U.S.A. 126 F3
Rushville IN U.S.A. 130 C4
Rushville NE U.S.A. 126 C3
Rushworth Australia 108 B6
Rusk U.S.A. 127 E6
Russell Man. Canada 117 K5
Russell Ont. Canada 131 H1
Russell N.Z. 109 E2
Russell KS U.S.A. 126 D4
Russell PA U.S.A. 130 F3
Russell Bay Antarctica 148 J2
Russell Lake Man. Canada 117 K3
Russell Lake N.W.T. Canada 116 H2
Russell Lake Sask. Canada 117 J3
Russell Range hills Australia 105 C8
Russell Springs U.S.A. 130 C5
Russellville AR U.S.A. 127 E5
Russellville KY U.S.A. 130 B5
Rüsselsheim Germany 49 I4
Russia country Asia/Europe see Russian Federation
Russian r. U.S.A. 124 B2

▶Russian Federation country Asia/Europe 60 I3
Largest country in the world, Europe and Asia. Most populous country in Europe and 5th in Asia.
asia 6, 58–59
europe 5, 34–35

Russian Soviet Federal Socialist Republic country Asia/Europe see Russian Federation
Russkiy, Ostrov i. Rus. Fed. 70 C4
Russkiy Kameshkir Rus. Fed. 39 J5
Rust'avi Georgia 87 G2
Rustburg U.S.A. 130 F5
Rustenburg S. Africa 97 H3
Ruston U.S.A. 127 E5
Rutanzige, Lake Dem. Rep. Congo/Uganda see Edward, Lake
Ruteng Indon. 104 C2
Ruth U.S.A. 125 F2
Rüthen Germany 49 I3
Rutherglen Australia 108 C6
Ruther Glen U.S.A. 131 G5
Ruthin U.K. 45 D5
Ruthiyai India 78 D4
Ruth Reservoir U.S.A. 124 B1
Rutka r. Rus. Fed. 38 J4
Rutland U.S.A. 131 I2
Rutland Water resr U.K. 45 G6
Rutledge Lake Canada 117 I2
Rutog Xizang China 72 B2
Rutög China 78 D2
Rutog Xizang China 79 F3
Rutul Rus. Fed. 87 G2
Ruukki Fin. 40 N4
Ruvuma r. Moz./Tanz. 95 E5
also known as Rovuma
Ruwayshid, Wādī watercourse Jordan 81 C3
Ruwayṭah, Wādī watercourse Jordan 81 C5
Ruweis U.A.E. 84 D5
Ruwenzori National Park Uganda see Queen Elizabeth National Park
Ruza Rus. Fed. 38 H5
Ruzayevka Kazakh. 74 F1
Ruzayevka Rus. Fed. 39 J5
Ruzhou China 73 G1
Ružomberok Slovakia 43 Q6
▶Rwanda country Africa 94 C4
africa 7, 90–91
Ryābād Iran 84 D2
Ryan, Loch b. U.K. 46 D5
Ryazan' Rus. Fed. 39 H5
Ryazhsk Rus. Fed. 39 I5
Rybachiy, Poluostrov pen. Rus. Fed. 40 R2
Rybach'ye Kyrg. see Balykchy
Rybinsk Rus. Fed. 38 H4
Rybinskoye Vodokhranilishche resr Rus. Fed. 38 H4
Rybnik Poland 43 Q5
Rybnitsa Moldova see Rîbniţa
Rybnoye Rus. Fed. 39 H5
Rybreka Rus. Fed. 38 G3
Ryd Sweden 41 I8
Rydberg Peninsula Antarctica 148 L2
Ryde U.K. 45 F8
Rye U.K. 45 H8
Rye r. U.K. 44 G4
Rye Bay U.K. 45 H8
Ryegate U.S.A. 122 F3
Rye Patch Reservoir U.S.A. 124 D1
Rykovo Ukr. see Yenakiyeve
Ryl'sk Rus. Fed. 39 G6
Rylstone Australia 108 D4
Ryn-Peski des. Kazakh. 37 P6
Ryukyu Islands Japan 71 B8
Ryūkyū-rettō is Japan see Ryukyu Islands
Ryukyu Trench sea feature N. Pacific Ocean 146 E4
Rzeszów Poland 39 D6
Rzhaksa Rus. Fed. 39 I5
Rzhev Rus. Fed. 38 G4

S

Sa'ādah al Barṣā' pass Saudi Arabia 81 C5
Sa'ādatābād Iran 84 D4
Saal an der Donau Germany 49 L6
Saale r. Germany 49 L3
Saalfeld Germany 49 L4
Saanich Canada 116 F5
Saar land Germany see Saarland
Saar r. Germany 48 G5
Saarbrücken Germany 48 G5
Saaremaa i. Estonia 41 M7
Saarenkylä Fin. 40 N3
Saargau reg. Germany 48 G5
Saarijärvi Fin. 40 N5
Saari-Kämä Fin. 40 O3
Saarikoski Fin. 40 L2
Saaristomeren kansallispuisto nat. park Fin. see Skärgårdshavets nationalpark
Saarland land Germany 48 G5
Saarlouis Germany 48 G5
Saatlı Azer. 87 H3
Saatly Azer. see Saatlı
Sab'a Egypt see Saba'ah
Saba'ah Egypt 81 A4
Sab' Ābār Syria 81 C3
Šabac Serb. and Mont. 55 H2
Sabadell Spain 53 H3
Sabae Japan 71 E6
Sabak Malaysia 67 C7
Sabalana i. Indon. 64 F8
Sabalana, Kepulauan is Indon. 64 F8
Sabana, Archipiélago de is Cuba 133 H4
Sabang Indon. 67 A6
Şabanözü Turkey 86 D2
Sabará Brazil 141 C2
Sabastiya West Bank 81 B3
Sab'atayn, Ramlat as des. Yemen 82 G6
Sabaudia Italy 54 E4
Sabaya Bol. 138 E7
Sabdê China 72 D2
Sabelo S. Africa 96 F6
Şabḩā Jordan 81 C3
Sabhā Libya 93 E2
Şabḩā' Saudi Arabia 84 B6
Sabhrai India 78 B5
Sabi r. India 78 D3
Sabi r. Moz./Zimbabwe see Save
Sabie Moz. 97 K3
Sabie r. Moz./S. Africa 97 K3
Sabie S. Africa 97 J3
Sabina U.S.A. 130 D4
Sabinal Mex. 123 G7
Sabinal, Cayo i. Cuba 129 E8
Sabinas Mex. 127 C7
Sabinas r. Mex. 127 C7
Sabinas Hidalgo Mex. 127 C7
Sabine r. U.S.A. 127 E6
Sabine Lake U.S.A. 127 E6
Sabine Pass U.S.A. 127 E6
Sabini, Monti mts Italy 54 E3
Sabirabad Azer. 87 H2
Sabkhat al Bardawīl Reserve nature res. Egypt see Lake Bardawil Reserve
Sable, Cape Canada 119 I6
Sable, Cape U.S.A. 129 D7
Sable, Lac du l. Canada 119 I3
Sable Island Canada 119 K6
Sabon Kafi Niger 92 D3
Sabrina Coast Antarctica 148 F2
Sabugal Port. 53 C3
Sabzawar Afgh. see Shīndand
Sabzevār Iran 84 E2
Sabzvārān Iran see Jīroft
Sacalinul Mare, Insula i. Romania 55 M2
Sacaton U.S.A. 125 H5
Sac City U.S.A. 126 E3
Săcele Romania 55 K2
Sachigo r. Canada 117 N4
Sachigo Lake Canada 117 M4
Sachin India 78 C5
Sach'on S. Korea 71 C6
Sach Pass India 78 D2
Sachsen land Germany 49 N3
Sachsen-Anhalt land Germany 49 L2
Sachsenheim Germany 49 J6
Sachs Harbour Canada 114 F2
Sacirsuyu r. Syria/Turkey see Sājūr, Nahr
Sackpfeife hill Germany 49 I4
Sackville Canada 119 I5
Saco ME U.S.A. 131 J2
Saco MT U.S.A. 122 G2
Sacramento Brazil 141 B2

▶Sacramento U.S.A. 124 C2
State capital of California.

Sacramento r. U.S.A. 124 C2
Sacramento Mountains U.S.A. 123 G6
Sacramento Valley U.S.A. 124 B1
Sada S. Africa 97 H7
Sádaba Spain 53 F2
Sá da Bandeira Angola see Lubango
Şadad Syria 81 C2
Şa'dah Yemen 82 F6
Sadao Thai. 67 C6
Saddat al Hindīyah Iraq 87 G4
Saddleback Mesa mt. U.S.A. 127 C5
Saddle Hill hill Australia 106 D2
Saddle Peak hill India 67 A4
Sa Đec Vietnam 67 D5
Sadêng China 72 B2
Sadieville U.S.A. 130 C4
Sadīj watercourse Iran 84 E5
Sadiola Mali 92 B3
Sadiqabad Pak. 85 H4
Sad Istragh mt. Afgh./Pak. 85 I2
Sa'dīyah, Hawr as imp. l. Iraq 87 G4
Sa'diyyat i. U.A.E. 84 D5
Sado r. Port. 53 B4
Sadoga-shima i. Japan 71 E5
Sadot Egypt see Sadūt
Sadovoye Rus. Fed. 39 J7
Sa Dragonera i. Spain 53 H4
Sadras India 80 D3
Sadūt Egypt 81 B4
Sadût Egypt see Sadūt
Sæby Denmark 41 G8
Saena Julia Italy see Siena
Safad Israel see Ẕefat
Safayal Maqūf well Iraq 87 G5
Safed Khirs mts Afgh. 85 H2
Safed Koh mts Afgh. 85 G3
Safed Koh mts Afgh./Pak. 85 H3
Saffānīyah, Ra's as pt Saudi Arabia 84 C4
Säffle Sweden 41 H7
Safford U.S.A. 125 I5
Saffron Walden U.K. 45 H6
Safi Morocco 50 C5
Safīdār, Kūh-e mt. Iran 84 D4
Safid Kūh mts Afgh. see Paropamisus
Safid Sagak Iran 85 F3
Safiras, Serra das mts Brazil 141 C2
Şāfītā Syria 81 C2
Safonovo Arkhangel'skaya Oblast' Rus. Fed. 38 K2
Safonovo Smolenskaya Oblast' Rus. Fed. 39 G5
Safrā' al Asyāḩ esc. Saudi Arabia 84 A5
Safrā' as Sark esc. Saudi Arabia 82 F4
Safranbolu Turkey 86 D2
Saga China 79 F3
Saga Japan 71 C6
Saga Kazakh. 76 B1
Sagaing Myanmar 66 A2
Sagami-nada g. Japan 71 E6
Sagamore U.S.A. 130 F3
Saganthit Kyun i. Myanmar 67 B4
Sagar Karnataka India 80 B3
Sagar Karnataka India 80 C2
Sagar Madhya Pradesh India 78 D5
Sagaredzho Georgia see Sagarejo
Sagarejo Georgia 87 G2
Sagar Island India 79 G5
Sagarmatha National Park Nepal 79 F4
Sagastyr Rus. Fed. 61 N2
Sagavanirktok r. U.S.A. 114 D2
Sage U.S.A. 122 F4
Saggi, Har mt. Israel 81 B4
Saghand Iran 84 D3
Saginaw U.S.A. 130 D2
Saginaw Bay U.S.A. 130 D2
Saglek Bay Canada 119 J2
Saglouc Canada see Salluit
Sagone, Golfe de b. Corsica France 52 I5
Sagres Port. 53 B5
Sagthale India 78 C5
Saguache U.S.A. 123 G5
Sagua la Grande Cuba 133 H4
Saguaro Lake U.S.A. 125 H5
Saguaro National Park U.S.A. 125 H5
Saguenay r. Canada 119 H4
Sagunt Spain see Sagunto
Sagunto Spain 53 F4
Saguntum Spain see Sagunto
Sahagún Spain 53 D2
Sahand, Kūh-e mt. Iran 84 B2

▶Sahara des. Africa 92 D3
Largest desert in the world.

Şaḩara el Gharbîya des. Egypt see Western Desert
Şaḩara el Sharqîya des. Egypt see Eastern Desert
Saharan Atlas mts Alg. see Atlas Saharien
Saharanpur India 78 D3
Sahara Well Australia 104 C5
Saharsa India 79 F4
Sahaswan India 78 D3
Sahat, Kūh-e hill Iran 84 D3
Sahatwar India 79 F4
Şahbuz Azer. 87 G3
Şahdol India see Shahdol
Sahebganj India see Sahibganj
Sahebgunj India see Sahibganj
Saheira, Wâdi el watercourse Egypt see Suhaymī, Wādī as
Sahel reg. Africa 92 C3
Sahibganj India 79 F4
Sahiwal Pak. 85 I4
Sahlābād Iran 85 E3
Şahm Oman 84 E5
Şahneh Iran 84 B3
Şahrā al Ḩijārah reg. Iraq 87 G5
Sahuaripa Mex. 123 F7
Sahuayo Mex. 132 D4
Sahuteng China see Zadoi
Sa Huynh Vietnam 67 E4
Sahyadri mts India see Western Ghats
Sahyadriparvat Range hills India 80 B1
Sai r. India 79 E4
Sai Buri Thai. 67 C6
Saïda Alg. 53 G6
Saïda Lebanon see Sidon
Sai Dao Tai, Khao mt. Thai. 67 C4
Saïdia Morocco 53 E6
Sa'īdīyeh Iran see Solṭānīyeh
Saidpur Bangl. 79 G4
Saiha India 79 H5
Saihan Tal China 69 K4
Saijō Japan 71 D6
Saikai National Park Japan 71 C6
Saiki Japan 71 C6
Sai Kung Hong Kong China 73 [inset]
Sailana India 78 C5
Saimaa l. Fin. 41 P6
Saimbeyli Turkey 86 E3
Saindak Pak. 85 F4
Sa'īndezh Iran 84 B2
Sa'in Qal'eh Iran see Sa'īndezh
St Abb's Head hd U.K. 46 G5
St Agnes U.K. 45 B8
St Agnes i. U.K. 45 A9
St Alban's Canada 119 L5
St Albans U.K. 45 G7
St Albans VT U.S.A. 131 I1
St Albans WV U.S.A. 130 E4
St Alban's Head hd U.K. 45 E8
St Albert Canada 116 H4
St Aldhelm's Head hd U.K. see St Alban's Head
St-Amand-les-Eaux France 48 D4
St-Amand-Montrond France 52 F3
St-Amour France 52 G3
St-André, Cap pt Madag. see Vilanandro, Tanjona
St Andrews U.K. 46 G4
St Andrew Sound inlet U.S.A. 129 D6
St Anne U.S.A. 130 B3
St Ann's Bay Jamaica 133 I5
St Anthony Canada 119 L4
St Anthony U.S.A. 122 F4
St-Arnaud Alg. see El Eulma
St Arnaud Australia 108 A6
St Arnaud Range mts N.Z. 109 D6
St-Arnoult-en-Yvelines France 48 B6
St-Augustin Canada 119 K4
St Augustin r. Canada 119 K4
St Augustine U.S.A. 129 D6
St Austell U.K. 45 C8
St-Avertin France 52 E3
St-Avold France 48 G5
St Barbe Canada 119 K4
St-Barthélemy i. West Indies 133 L5
St Bees U.K. 44 D4
St Bees Head hd U.K. 44 D4
St Bride's Bay U.K. 45 B7
St-Brieuc France 52 C2
St Catharines Canada 130 F2
St Catherines Island U.S.A. 129 D6
St Catherine's Point U.K. 45 F8
St-Céré France 52 E4
St-Chamond France 52 G4
St Charles ID U.S.A. 122 F4
St Charles MD U.S.A. 131 G4
St Charles MI U.S.A. 130 C2
St Charles MO U.S.A. 126 F4
St-Chély-d'Apcher France 52 F4
St Christopher and Nevis country West Indies see St Kitts and Nevis
St Clair r. Canada/U.S.A. 130 D2
St Clair, Lake Canada/U.S.A. 130 D2
St-Claude France 52 G3
St Clears U.K. 45 C7
St Cloud U.S.A. 126 E2
St Croix r. U.S.A. 118 B5
St Croix Falls U.S.A. 126 E2
St David U.S.A. 125 H6
St David's Head hd U.K. 45 B7
St-Denis France 48 C6

▶St-Denis Réunion 145 L7
Capital of Réunion.

St-Denis-du-Sig Alg. see Sig
St-Dié France 52 H2
St-Dizier France 48 E6
St-Domingue country West Indies see Haiti
Sainte Anne Canada 117 L5
Ste-Anne, Lac l. Canada 119 I4
St Elias, Cape U.S.A. 114 D4

▶St Elias, Mount U.S.A. 116 A2
4th highest mountain in North America.

St Elias Mountains Canada 116 A2
Ste-Marguerite r. Canada 119 I4
Ste-Marie, Cap c. Madag. see Vohimena, Tanjona
Sainte-Marie, Île i. Madag. see Boraha, Nosy
Ste-Maxime France 52 H5
Sainte Rose du Lac Canada 117 L5
Saintes France 52 D4
Sainte Thérèse, Lac l. Canada 116 F1
St-Étienne France 52 G4
St-Étienne-du-Rouvray France 48 B5
St-Fabien Canada 119 H4
St-Félicien Canada 119 G4
Saintfield U.K. 47 G3
St-Florent Corsica France 52 I5
St-Florent-sur-Cher France 52 F3
St Floris, Parc National nat. park Cent. Afr. Rep. 94 C3
St-Flour France 52 F4
St Francesville U.S.A. 127 F6
St Francis U.S.A. 126 C4
St Francis r. U.S.A. 127 F5
St Francis Isles Australia 105 F8
St-François r. Canada 119 G5
St-François, Lac l. Canada 119 H5
St-Gaudens France 52 E5
St George Australia 108 D2
St George r. Australia 106 D3
St George AK U.S.A. 114 B4
St George SC U.S.A. 129 D5
St George UT U.S.A. 125 G3
St George, Point U.S.A. 122 B4
St George Head hd Australia 108 E5
St George Island U.S.A. 114 B4
St George Ranges hills Australia 104 D4
St-Georges Canada 119 H5

▶St George's Grenada 133 L6
Capital of Grenada.

St George's Bay Nfld. and Lab. Canada 119 K4
St George's Bay N.S. Canada 119 J5
St George's Channel P.N.G. 102 F2
St George's Channel Rep. of Ireland/U.K. 47 F6
St Gotthard Hungary see Szentgotthárd
St Gotthard Pass Switz. 52 I3
St Govan's Head hd U.K. 45 C7
St Helen U.S.A. 130 C1
St Helena U.S.A. 124 B2
St Helena i. S. Atlantic Ocean 144 H7

▶St Helena and Dependencies terr. S. Atlantic Ocean 144 H7
United Kingdom Overseas territory. Consists of St Helena, Ascension, Tristan da Cunha and Gough Island.
africa 7

St Helena Bay S. Africa 96 D7
St Helens Australia 107 [inset]
St Helens U.K. 44 E5
St Helens U.S.A. 122 C3
St Helens, Mount vol. U.S.A. 122 C3
St Helens Point Australia 107 [inset]

▶St Helier Channel Is 45 E9
Capital of Jersey.

Sainthiya India 79 F5
St-Hubert Belgium 48 F4
St-Hyacinthe Canada 119 G5
St Ignace U.S.A. 128 C2
St Ignace Island Canada 118 D4
St Ishmael U.K. 45 C7
St Ives England U.K. 45 B8
St Ives England U.K. 45 G6
St-Jacques, Cap Vietnam see Vung Tau
St-Jacques-de-Dupuy Canada 118 F4
St James MN U.S.A. 126 E3
St James MO U.S.A. 126 F4
St James, Cape Canada 116 D5
St-Jean r. Canada 119 I4
St-Jean, Lac l. Canada 119 G4
St-Jean-d'Acre Israel see 'Akko
St-Jean-d'Angély France 52 D4
St-Jean-de-Monts France 52 C3
St-Jean-sur-Richelieu Canada 131 I1
St-Jérôme Canada 118 G5
St Joe r. U.S.A. 122 D3
Saint John Canada 119 I5
St John U.S.A. 126 D4
St John r. U.S.A. 128 H2
St John, Cape Canada 119 L4
St John Bay Canada 119 K4
St John Island Canada 119 K4

▶St John's Antigua and Barbuda 133 L5
Capital of Antigua and Barbuda.

▶St John's Canada 119 L5
Provincial capital of Newfoundland and Labrador.

St Johns AZ U.S.A. 125 I4
St Johns MI U.S.A. 130 C2
St Johns OH U.S.A. 130 C3
St Johns r. U.S.A. 129 D6
St Johnsbury U.S.A. 131 I1
St John's Chapel U.K. 44 E4
St Joseph IL U.S.A. 130 A3
St Joseph LA U.S.A. 127 F6
St Joseph MI U.S.A. 130 B2
St Joseph MO U.S.A. 126 E4
St Joseph r. U.S.A. 130 C3

St Joseph, Lake Canada 117 N5
St-Joseph-d'Alma Canada see Alma
St Joseph Island Canada 118 E5
St-Junien France 52 E4
St Just U.K. 45 B8
St-Just-en-Chaussée France 48 C5
St Keverne U.K. 45 B8
St Kilda i. U.K. 36 E4
St Kilda is U.K. 42 C2
▶St Kitts and Nevis country West Indies 133 L5
north america 9, 112–113
St-Laurent inlet Canada see St Lawrence
St-Laurent, Golfe du g. Canada see St Lawrence, Gulf of
St-Laurent-du-Maroni Fr. Guiana 139 H2
St Lawrence Canada 119 L5
St Lawrence inlet Canada 119 H4
St Lawrence, Cape Canada 119 J5
St Lawrence, Gulf of Canada 119 J4
St Lawrence Island U.S.A. 114 B3
St Lawrence Islands National Park Canada 131 H1
St Lawrence Seaway sea chan. Canada/U.S.A. 131 H1
St-Léonard Canada 119 G5
St Leonard U.S.A. 131 G4
St Lewis r. Canada 119 K3
St-Lô France 52 D2
St-Louis Senegal 92 B3
St Louis MI U.S.A. 130 C2
St Louis MO U.S.A. 126 F4
St Louis r. U.S.A. 118 B5
▶St Lucia country West Indies 133 L6
north america 9, 112–113
St Lucia, Lake S. Africa 97 K5
St Lucia Estuary S. Africa 97 K5
St Luke's Island Myanmar see Zadetkale Kyun
St Magnus Bay U.K. 46 [inset]
St-Maixent-l'École France 52 D3
St-Malo France 52 C2
St-Malo, Golfe de g. France 52 C2
St-Marc Haiti 133 J5
St Maries U.S.A. 122 D3
St Marks S. Africa 97 H7
St Mark's S. Africa see Cofimvaba

▶St-Martin i. West Indies 133 L5
Dependency of Guadeloupe (France). The southern part of the island is the Dutch territory of Sint Maarten.

St Martin, Cape S. Africa 96 C7
St Martin, Lake Canada 117 L5
St Martin's i. U.K. 45 A9
St Martin's Island Bangl. 66 A2
St Mary Peak Australia 107 B6
St Mary Reservoir Canada 116 H5
St Mary's Canada 130 E2
St Mary's U.K. 46 G2
St Mary's i. U.K. 45 A9
St Marys PA U.S.A. 131 F3
St Marys WV U.S.A. 130 E4
St Marys r. U.S.A. 130 C3
St Mary's, Cape Canada 119 L5
St Mary's Bay Canada 119 L5
St Marys City U.S.A. 131 G4
St Matthew Island U.S.A. 114 A3
St Matthews U.S.A. 130 C4
St Matthew's Island Myanmar see Zadetkyi Kyun
St Matthias Group is P.N.G. 65 L7
St Maurice r. Canada 119 G5
St Mawes U.K. 45 B8
St-Médard-en-Jalles France 52 D4
St Meinrad U.S.A. 130 B4
St Michaels U.S.A. 131 G4
St Michael's Bay Canada 119 L3
St-Mihiel France 48 F6
St-Nazaire France 52 C3
St Neots U.K. 45 G6
St-Nicolas Belgium see Sint-Niklaas
St-Nicolas, Mont hill Lux. 48 G5
St-Nicolas-de-Port France 52 H2
St-Omer France 48 C4
Saintonge reg. France 52 D4
St-Pacôme Canada 119 H5
St-Palais France 52 D5
St Paris U.S.A. 130 D3
St Pascal Canada 119 H5
St Paul r. Canada 119 K4
St-Paul atoll Fr. Polynesia see Héréhérétué
St Paul AK U.S.A. 114 A4

▶St Paul MN U.S.A. 126 E2
State capital of Minnesota.

St Paul NE U.S.A. 126 D3
St-Paul, Île i. Indian Ocean 145 N8
St Paul Island U.S.A. 114 A4
St Peter and St Paul Rocks is N. Atlantic Ocean see São Pedro e São Paulo

▶St Peter Port Channel Is 45 E9
Capital of Guernsey.

St Peter's Nova Scotia Canada 119 J5
St Peters P.E.I. Canada 119 J5
St Petersburg Rus. Fed. 41 Q7
St Petersburg U.S.A. 129 D7
St-Pierre mt. France 52 G5

▶St-Pierre St Pierre and Miquelon 119 L5
Capital of St Pierre and Miquelon.

▶St Pierre and Miquelon terr. N. America 119 K5
French Territorial Collectivity.
north america 9, 112–113

St-Pierre-d'Oléron France 52 D4
St-Pierre-le-Moûtier France 52 F3
St-Pol-sur-Ternoise France 48 C4
St-Pourçain-sur-Sioule France 52 F3
St-Quentin France 48 D5
St Regis U.S.A. 122 E3
St Regis Falls U.S.A. 131 H1
St-Rémi Canada 131 I1
St-Saëns France 48 B5
St Sebastian Bay S. Africa 96 E8
St Siméon Canada 119 H5
St Simons Island U.S.A. 129 D6
St Theresa Point Canada 117 M4
St Thomas Canada 130 E2
St-Trond Belgium see Sint-Truiden
St-Tropez France 52 H5
St-Tropez, Cap de c. France 52 H5
St-Vaast-la-Hougue France 45 F9
St-Valery-en-Caux France 45 H9
St-Véran France 52 H4
St Vincent U.S.A. 126 D1
St Vincent country West Indies see St Vincent and the Grenadines
St Vincent, Cape Australia 107 [inset]
St Vincent, Cape Port. see São Vicente, Cabo de
St Vincent, Gulf Australia 107 B7
▶St Vincent and the Grenadines country West Indies 133 L6
north america 9, 112–113
St Vincent Passage St Lucia/St Vincent 133 L6
St-Vith Belgium 48 G4
St Walburg Canada 117 I4
St Williams Canada 130 E2
St-Yrieix-la-Perche France 52 E4
Sain Us China 68 J4
Saioa mt. Spain 53 F2
Saipal mt. Nepal 78 E3
Saipan i. N. Mariana Is 65 L3
Sai Pok Liu Hoi Hap Hong Kong China see West Lamma Channel
Saiteli Turkey see Kadınhanı
Saitlai Myanmar 66 A2
Saittanulkki hill Fin. 40 N3
Sai Yok National Park Thai. 67 B4
Sajam Indon. 65 I7
Sajama, Nevado mt. Bol. 138 E7
Sājir Saudi Arabia 84 B5
Sājūr, Nahr r. Syria/Turkey 81 D1
Sajzi Iran 84 D3
Sak watercourse S. Africa 96 E5
Sakaide Japan 71 D6
Sakākah Saudi Arabia 87 F5
Sakakawea, Lake U.S.A. 126 C2
Sakami Canada 118 G3
Sakami r. Canada 118 F3
Sakami Lake Canada 118 F3
Sakar mts Bulg. 55 L4
Sakaraha Madag. 95 E6
Sak'art'velo country Asia see Georgia
Sakarya Turkey 55 N4
Sakarya r. Turkey 55 N4
Sakassou Côte d'Ivoire 92 C4
Sakata Japan 71 E5
Sakchu N. Korea 71 B4
Sakesar Pak. 85 I3
Sakhalin i. Rus. Fed. 70 F2
Sakhalin Oblast admin. div. Rus. Fed. see Sakhalinskaya Oblast'
Sakhalinskaya Oblast' admin. div. Rus. Fed. 70 F2
Sakhalinskiy Zaliv b. Rus. Fed. 70 F1
Sakhi India 78 C3
Sakhile S. Africa 97 I4
Sakht-Sar Iran 84 C2
Şäki Azer. 87 G2
Šaki Nigeria see Shaki
Saki Ukr. see Saky
Šakiai Lith. 41 M9
Sakir mt. Pak. 85 G4
Sakishima-shotō is Japan 69 M8
Sakoli India 78 D5
Sakon Nakhon Thai. 66 D3
Sakrivier S. Africa 96 E6
Sakura Japan 71 F6
Saky Ukr. 86 D1
Säkylä Fin. 41 M6
Sal i. Cape Verde 92 [inset]
Sal r. Rus. Fed. 39 I7
Sala Sweden 41 J7
Salaberry-de-Valleyfield Canada 131 H1
Salacgrīva Latvia 41 N8
Sala Consilina Italy 54 F4
Salada, Laguna salt l. Mex. 125 F5
Saladas Arg. 140 E3
Salado r. Buenos Aires Arg. 140 E5
Salado r. Santa Fé Arg. 140 D4
Salado r. Mex. 127 D7
Salaga Ghana 92 C4
Salairskiy Kryazh ridge Rus. Fed. 68 E2
Salajwe Botswana 96 G2
Şalālah Oman 83 H6
Salamanca Mex. 132 D4
Salamanca Spain 53 D3
Salamanca U.S.A. 131 F2
Salamanga Moz. 97 K4
Salamantica Spain see Salamanca
Salamat, Bahr r. Chad 93 E4
Salāmī Iran 85 E3
Salamina i. Greece 55 J6
Salamis tourist site Cyprus 81 A2
Salamis i. Greece see Salamina
Salamīyah Syria 81 C2
Salamonie r. U.S.A. 130 C3
Salamonie Lake U.S.A. 130 C3
Salang Tunnel Afgh. 85 H3
Salantai Lith. 41 L8
Salar de Pocitos Arg. 140 C2
Salari Pak. 85 G5
Salas Spain 53 C2
Salaspils Latvia 41 N8
Salawati i. Indon. 65 I7
Salawin, Mae Nam r. China/Myanmar see Salween
Salaya India 78 B5
Salayar i. Indon. 65 G8

▶Sala y Gómez, Isla i. S. Pacific Ocean 147 M7
Most easterly point of Oceania

Salazar Angola see N'dalatando
Salbris France 52 F3
Šalčininkai Lith. 41 N9
Salcombe U.K. 45 D8
Saldae Alg. see Bejaïa
Saldaña Spain 53 D2
Saldanha S. Africa 96 C7
Saldanha Bay S. Africa 96 C7
Saldus Latvia 41 M8
Sale Australia 108 C7
Saleh, Teluk b. Indon. 64 F8
Şāleḩābād Iran 84 C3
Salekhard Rus. Fed. 60 H3
Salem India 80 C4
Salem AR U.S.A. 127 F4
Salem IL U.S.A. 126 F4
Salem IN U.S.A. 130 B4
Salem MA U.S.A. 131 J2
Salem MO U.S.A. 126 F4
Salem NJ U.S.A. 131 H4
Salem NY U.S.A. 131 I2
Salem OH U.S.A. 130 E3

▶Salem OR U.S.A. 122 C3
State capital of Oregon.

Salem SD U.S.A. 126 D3
Salem VA U.S.A. 130 E5
Salen Scotland U.K. 46 D4
Salen Scotland U.K. 46 D4
Salerno Italy 54 F4
Salerno, Golfo di g. Italy 54 F4
Salernum Italy see Salerno
Salford U.K. 44 E5
Salgótarján Hungary 43 Q6
Salgueiro Brazil 139 K5
Salian Afgh. 85 F4
Salibabu i. Indon. 65 H6
Salida U.S.A. 123 G5
Salies-de-Béarn France 52 D5
Salihli Turkey 55 M5
Salihorsk Belarus 41 O10
Salima Malawi 95 D5
Salina KS U.S.A. 126 D4
Salina UT U.S.A. 125 H2
Salina, Isola i. Italy 54 F5
Salina Cruz Mex. 132 E5
Salinas Brazil 141 C2
Salinas Ecuador 138 B4
Salinas Mex. 132 D4
Salinas r. Mex. 127 D7
Salinas U.S.A. 124 C3
Salinas r. U.S.A. 124 C3
Salinas, Cabo de c. Spain see Ses Salines, Cap de
Salinas, Ponta das pt Angola 95 B5
Salinas Peak U.S.A. 123 G6
Saline U.S.A. 130 D2
Saline r. U.S.A. 126 D4
Saline Valley depr. U.S.A. 124 E3
Salinópolis Brazil 139 I4
Salinosó Lachay, Punta pt Peru 138 C6
Salisbury U.K. 45 F7
Salisbury MD U.S.A. 131 H4
Salisbury NC U.S.A. 128 D5
Salisbury Zimbabwe see Harare
Salisbury Plain U.K. 45 E7
Şalkhad Syria 81 C3
Salla Fin. 40 P3
Sallisaw U.S.A. 127 E5
Salluit Canada 149 K2
Sallum, Khalīj as b. Egypt 86 B5
Sallyana Nepal 79 E3
Salmās Iran 84 B2
Salmi Rus. Fed. 38 F3
Salmo Canada 116 G5
Salmon U.S.A. 122 E3
Salmon r. U.S.A. 122 D3
Salmon Arm Canada 116 G5
Salmon Falls Creek r. U.S.A. 122 E4
Salmon Gums Australia 105 C8
Salmon Reservoir U.S.A. 131 H2
Salmon River Mountains U.S.A. 122 E3
Salmtal Germany 48 G5
Salo Fin. 41 M6
Salome U.S.A. 125 G5
Salon India 78 E4
Salon-de-Provence France 52 G5
Salonica Greece see Thessaloniki
Salonika Greece see Thessaloniki
Salpausselkä reg. Fin. 41 N6
Salqīn Syria 81 C1
Salses, Étang de l. France see Leucate, Étang de
Sal'sk Rus. Fed. 39 I7
Salsomaggiore Terme Italy 54 C2
Salt Jordan see As Salţ
Salt watercourse S. Africa 96 F7
Salt r. U.S.A. 125 G5
Salta Arg. 140 C2
Saltaire U.K. 44 F5
Saltash U.K. 45 C8
Saltcoats U.K. 46 E5
Saltee Islands Rep. of Ireland 47 F5
Saltfjellet Svartisen Nasjonalpark nat. park Norway 40 I3
Saltfjorden sea chan. Norway 40 H3
Salt Fork Arkansas r. U.S.A. 127 D4
Salt Fork Lake U.S.A. 130 E3
Saltillo Mex. 127 C7
Salt Lake India 85 I5

▶Salt Lake City U.S.A. 125 H1
State capital of Utah.

Salt Lick U.S.A. 130 D4
Salto Brazil 141 B3
Salto Uruguay 140 E4
Salto da Divisa Brazil 141 D2
Salto Grande Brazil 141 A3
Salton Sea salt l. U.S.A. 125 F5
Salto Santiago, Represa de resr Brazil 140 F3
Salt Range hills Pak. 85 I3
Salt River Canada 117 H2
Saluda U.S.A. 131 G5
Salûm Egypt see As Sallūm
Salûm, Khalîg el b. Egypt see Sallum, Khalīj as
Saluq, Kūh-e mt. Iran 84 E2
Salur India 80 D2
Saluzzo Italy 54 B2
Salvador Brazil 141 D1
Salvador country Central America see El Salvador
Salvador, Lake U.S.A. 127 F6
Salvaleón de Higüey Dom. Rep. see Higüey
Salvation Creek r. U.S.A. 125 H2
Salwah Saudi Arabia 94 F1
Salwah, Dawḩat b. Qatar/Saudi Arabia 84 C5
Salween r. China/Myanmar 72 C5
also known as Mae Nam Khong or Mae Nam Salawin or Nu Jiang (China) or Thanlwin (Myanmar)
Salyan Azer. 87 H3
Salyan Nepal see Sallyana
Sal'yany Azer. see Salyan
Salyersville U.S.A. 130 D5
Salzbrunn Namibia 96 C3
Salzburg Austria 43 N7
Salzgitter Germany 49 K2
Salzhausen Germany 49 K1
Salzkotten Germany 49 I3
Salzmünde Germany 49 L3
Salzwedel Germany 49 L2
Sam India 78 B4
Samae San, Ko i. Thai. 67 C4
Samagaltay Rus. Fed. 76 H1
Samāh well Saudi Arabia 84 B4
Samaida Iran see Someydeh
Samaixung China 79 E2
Samakhixai Laos see Attapu
Samalanga Indon. 67 B6
Samalayuca Mex. 123 G7
Samalkot India 80 D2
Samālūţ Egypt 86 C5
Samâlût Egypt see Samālūţ
Samana Cay i. Bahamas 129 F8
Samanala mt. Sri Lanka see Adam's Peak
Samandağı Turkey 81 B1
Samangān Afgh. see Āybak
Samangān Iran 85 F3
Samani Japan 70 F4
Samanlı Dağları mts Turkey 55 M4
Samar Kazakh. see Samarskoye
Samar i. Phil. 65 H4
Samara Rus. Fed. 39 K5
Samara r. Rus. Fed. 37 Q5
Samarga Rus. Fed. 70 E3
Samarinda Indon. 64 F7
Samarka Rus. Fed. 70 D3
Samarkand Uzbek. 85 G2
Samarkand, Pik mt. Tajik. see Samarqand, Qullai
Samarobriva France see Amiens
Samarqand Uzbek. see Samarkand
Samarqand, Qullai mt. Tajik. 85 H2
Sāmarrā' Iraq 87 F4
Samarskoye Kazakh. 76 F2
Samasata Pak. 85 H4
Samastipur India 79 F4
Şamaxı Azer. 87 H2
Samba Jammu and Kashmir 78 C2
Sambaliung mts Indon. 64 F6
Sambalpur India 79 E5
Sambar, Tanjung pt Indon. 64 E7
Sambas Indon. 67 E7
Sambat Ukr. see Kiev
Sambava Madag. 95 F5
Sambha India 79 G4
Sambhajinagar India see Aurangabad
Sambhal India 78 D3
Sambhar Lake India 78 C4
Sambir Ukr. 39 D6
Sambito r. Brazil 139 J5
Sâmbor Cambodia 67 D4
Sambor Ukr. see Sambir
Samborombón, Bahía b. Arg. 140 E5
Sambre r. Belgium/France 48 E4
Samch'ŏk S. Korea 71 C5
Samch'ŏnp'o S. Korea see Sach'on
Same Tanz. 94 D4
Samer France 48 B4
Sami India 78 B5
Samīrah Saudi Arabia 82 F4
Samirum Iran see Yazd-e Khvāst
Samjiyŏn N. Korea 70 C4
Şämkir Azer. 87 G2
Şamnan va Damghan reg. Iran 84 D3
Sam Neua Laos see Xam Nua
▶Samoa country S. Pacific Ocean 103 I3
oceania 8, 100–101
Samoa Basin sea feature S. Pacific Ocean 146 I7
Samoa i Sisifo country S. Pacific Ocean see Samoa
Samobor Croatia 54 F2
Samoded Rus. Fed. 38 I3
Samokov Bulg. 55 J3
Šamorín Slovakia 43 P6
Samos i. Greece 55 L6
Samosir i. Indon. 67 B7
Samothrace i. Greece see Samothraki
Samothraki i. Greece 55 K4
Samoylovka Rus. Fed. 39 I6
Sampê China see Xiangcheng
Sampit Indon. 64 E7
Sampit, Teluk b. Indon. 64 E7
Sam Rayburn Reservoir U.S.A. 127 E6
Samrong Cambodia see Phumĭ Sâmraông
Samsang China 79 E3
Sam Sao, Phou mts Laos/Vietnam 66 C2
Samson U.S.A. 129 C6
Sâm Sơn Vietnam 66 D3
Samsun Turkey 86 E2
Samti Afgh. 85 H2
Samui, Ko i. Thai. 67 C5
Samut Prakan Thai. 67 C4
Samut Sakhon Thai. 67 C4
Samut Songkhram Thai. 67 C4
Samyai China 79 G3
San Mali 92 C3
San, Phou mt. Laos 66 C3
San, Tônlé r. Cambodia 67 D4

▶Şan'ā' Yemen 82 F6
Capital of Yemen.

Sanaa Yemen see Şan'ā'
Sanae research station Antarctica 148 B2
San Agostín U.S.A. see St Augustine
San Agustin, Cape Phil. 65 H5
San Agustin, Plains of U.S.A. 125 I5
Sanak Island U.S.A. 114 B4
Sanandaj Iran 84 B3
San Andreas U.S.A. 124 C2
San Andrés, Isla de i. Caribbean Sea 133 H6
San Andres Mountains U.S.A. 123 G6
San Angelo U.S.A. 127 C6
San Antonio Chile 140 B4
San Antonio NM U.S.A. 123 G6
San Antonio TX U.S.A. 127 D6
San Antonio r. U.S.A. 127 D6
San Antonio, Cabo c. Cuba 133 H4
San Antonio Abad Spain 53 G4
San Antonio del Mar Mex. 123 D7
San Antonio Oeste Arg. 140 D6
San Antonio Reservoir U.S.A. 124 C4
San Augustín de Valle Fértil Arg. 140 C4
San Augustine U.S.A. 127 E6
San Benedetto del Tronto Italy 54 E3
San Benedicto, Isla i. Mex. 132 B5
San Benito U.S.A. 127 D7
San Benito r. U.S.A. 124 C3
San Benito Mountain U.S.A. 124 C3
San Bernardino U.S.A. 124 E4
San Bernardino Mountains U.S.A. 124 E4
San Bernardo Chile 140 B4
San Blas Mex. 123 F8
San Blas, Cape U.S.A. 129 C6
San Borja Bol. 138 E6
Sanbornville U.S.A. 131 J2
Sanbu China see Kaiping
San Buenaventura Mex. 127 C7
San Carlos Chile 140 B5
San Carlos Equat. Guinea see Luba
San Carlos Coahuila Mex. 127 C6
San Carlos Tamaulipas Mex. 127 D7
San Carlos U.S.A. 125 H5
San Carlos Venez. 138 E2
San Carlos de Bariloche Arg. 140 B6
San Carlos de Bolívar Arg. 140 D5
San Carlos Lake U.S.A. 125 H5
Sancha China 72 E1
Sanchahe China see Fuyu
Sancha He r. China 72 E3
Sanchi India 78 D5
San Chien Pau mt. Laos 66 C2
Sanchor India 78 B4
San Clemente U.S.A. 124 E5
San Clemente Island U.S.A. 124 D5
Sanclêr U.K. see St Clears
San Cristóbal Arg. 140 D4
San Cristóbal i. Solomon Is 103 G3
San Cristóbal Venez. 138 D2
San Cristóbal, Isla i. Galápagos Ecuador 138 [inset]
San Cristóbal de las Casas Mex. 132 F5
Sancti Spíritus Cuba 133 I4
Sand r. S. Africa 97 J2
Sandagou Rus. Fed. 70 D4
Sanda Island U.K. 46 D5
Sandakan Sabah Malaysia 64 F5
Sândăn Cambodia 67 D4
Sandane Norway 40 E6
Sandanski Bulg. 55 J4
Sandaré Mali 92 B3
Sandau Germany 49 M2
Sanday i. U.K. 46 G1
Sandbach U.K. 45 E5
Sandborn U.S.A. 130 B4
Sand Cay reef India 80 B4
Sandefjord Norway 41 G7
Sandercock Nunataks Antarctica 148 D2
Sanders U.S.A. 125 I4
Sandersleben Germany 49 L3
Sanderson U.S.A. 127 C6
Sandfire Roadhouse Australia 104 C4
Sand Fork U.S.A. 130 E4
Sandgate Australia 108 F1
Sandhead U.K. 46 E6
Sand Hill r. U.S.A. 126 D2
Sand Hills U.S.A. 126 C3
Sandia Peru 138 E6
San Diego Mex. 127 B6
San Diego CA U.S.A. 124 E5
San Diego TX U.S.A. 127 D7
San Diego, Sierra mts Mex. 123 F7
Sandıklı Turkey 55 N5
Sandila India 78 E4
Sand Lake Canada 118 D5
Sand Lake l. Canada 117 M5
Sandnes Norway 41 D7
Sandnessjøen Norway 40 H3
Sandoa Dem. Rep. Congo 95 C4
Sandomierz Poland 39 D6
San Donà di Piave Italy 54 E2
Sandover watercourse Australia 106 B4
Sandovo Rus. Fed. 38 H4
Sandoway Myanmar 66 A3
Sandown U.K. 45 F8
Sandoy i. Faroe Is 40 [inset]
Sand Point U.S.A. 114 B4
Sandpoint U.S.A. 122 D2
Sandray i. U.K. 46 B4
Sandringham Australia 106 B5
Şandrul Mare, Vârful mt. Romania 55 L1
Sandsjö Sweden 41 I6
Sandspit Canada 116 D4
Sand Springs U.S.A. 127 D4
Sand Springs Salt Flat U.S.A. 124 D2
Sandstone Australia 105 B6
Sandstone U.S.A. 126 E2
Sandu Guizhou China 72 E3
Sandu Hunan China 73 G3
Sandur Faroe Is 40 [inset]
Sandusky MI U.S.A. 130 D2
Sandusky OH U.S.A. 130 D3
Sandveld mts S. Africa 96 D6
Sandverhaar Namibia 96 C4
Sandvika Akershus Norway 41 G7
Sandvika Nord-Trøndelag Norway 40 H5
Sandviken Sweden 41 J6
Sandwich Bay Canada 119 K3
Sandwich Island Vanuatu see Éfaté
Sandwich Islands N. Pacific Ocean see Hawaiian Islands
Sandwick U.K. 46 [inset]
Sandwip Bangl. 79 G5
Sandy U.S.A. 125 H1
Sandy r. U.S.A. 131 K1
Sandy Bay Canada 117 K4
Sandy Cape Qld Australia 106 F5
Sandy Cape Tas. Australia 107 [inset]
Sandy Hook U.S.A. 130 D4
Sandy Hook pt U.S.A. 131 H3
Sandy Island Australia 104 C3
Sandykachi Turkm. 85 F2
Sandykgachy Turkm. see Sandykachi
Sandykly Gumy des. Turkm. see Sundukli, Peski
Sandy Lake Alta Canada 116 H4
Sandy Lake Ont. Canada 117 M4
Sandy Lake l. Canada 117 M4
Sandy Springs U.S.A. 129 C5
San Estanislao Para. 140 E2
San Esteban, Isla i. Mex. 123 E7
San Felipe Chile 140 B4
San Felipe Baja California Mex. 123 E7
San Felipe Chihuahua Mex. 123 G8
San Felipe Venez. 138 E1
San Felipe, Cayos de is Cuba 129 D8
San Felipe de Puerto Plata Dom. Rep. see Puerto Plata
San Fernando Chile 140 B4
San Fernando Mex. 127 D7
San Fernando watercourse Mex. 123 E7
San Fernando Phil. 65 G3
San Fernando Spain 53 C5
San Fernando Trin. and Tob. 133 L6
San Fernando U.S.A. 124 D4
San Fernando de Apure Venez. 138 E2
San Fernando de Atabapo Venez. 138 E3
San Fernando de Monte Cristi Dom. Rep. see Monte Cristi
Sanford FL U.S.A. 129 D6
Sanford ME U.S.A. 131 J2
Sanford MI U.S.A. 130 C2
Sanford NC U.S.A. 128 E5
Sanford, Mount U.S.A. 114 D3
Sanford Lake U.S.A. 130 C2
San Francisco Arg. 140 D4
San Francisco U.S.A. 124 B3
San Francisco, Cabo de c. Ecuador 138 B3
San Francisco, Passo de pass Arg./Chile 140 C3
San Francisco Bay inlet U.S.A. 124 B3
San Francisco del Oro Mex. 127 B7
San Francisco de Paula, Cabo c. Arg. 140 C7
San Francisco Javier Spain 53 G4
San Gabriel, Punta pt Mex. 123 E7
San Gabriel Mountains U.S.A. 124 D4
Sangachaly Azer. see Sanqaçal
Sangameshwar India 80 B2
Sangamon r. U.S.A. 126 F3
Sangan, Koh-i- mt. Afgh. see Sangān, Kūh-e
Sangān, Kūh-e mt. Afgh. 85 G3
Sangar Rus. Fed. 61 N3
Sangareddi India 80 C2
Sangareddy India see Sangareddi
San Gavino Monreale Sardinia Italy 54 C5
Sangay, Parque Nacional nat. park Ecuador 138 C4
Sangbur Afgh. 85 F3
Sangeang i. Indon. 104 B2
Sanger U.S.A. 124 D3
Sangerfield U.S.A. 131 H2
Sangerhausen Germany 49 L3
Sang-e Surakh Iran 84 E2
Sanggarmai China 72 D1
Sanggau Indon. 64 E6
Sangilen, Nagor'ye mts Rus. Fed. 76 I1
San Giovanni in Fiore Italy 54 G5
Sangir India 78 C5
Sangir i. Indon. 65 H6
Sangir, Kepulauan is Indon. 65 G6
Sangiyn Dalay Mongolia 68 I3
Sangkapura Indon. 64 E8
Sangkulirang Indon. 64 F6
Sangli India 80 B2
Sangmai China see Dêrong
Sangmélima Cameroon 92 E4
Sangngagqoiling China 72 B2
Sango Zimbabwe 95 D6
Sangole India 80 B2
San Gorgonio Mountain U.S.A. 124 E4
Sangpi China see Xiangcheng
Sangre de Cristo Range mts U.S.A. 123 G5
Sangrur India 78 C3
Sangu r. Bangl. 79 G5
Sanguem India 80 B3
Sangutane r. Moz. 97 K3
Sangzhi China 73 F2
Sanhe China see Sandu
San Hipólito, Punta pt Mex. 123 E8
Sanhūr Egypt 86 C5
Sanhûr Egypt see Sanhūr
San Ignacio Beni Bol. 138 E6
San Ignacio Santa Cruz Bol. 138 F7
San Ignacio Santa Cruz Bol. 138 F7
San Ignacio Baja California Mex. 123 E7
San Ignacio Durango Mex. 127 C7
San Ignacio Sonora Mex. 123 F7
San Ignacio Para. 140 E3
San Ignacio, Laguna l. Mex. 123 E8
Sanikiluaq Canada 118 F2
Sanin-kaigan National Park Japan 71 D6
San Jacinto U.S.A. 124 E5
San Jacinto Peak U.S.A. 124 E5
San Javier Bol. 138 F7
Sanjeli India 78 C5
Sanjiang Guangdong China see Liannan
Sanjiang Guangxi China 73 F3
Sanjiang Guizhou China see Jinping
Sanjiangkou China 70 A4
Sanjiaocheng China see Haiyan
Sanjiaoping China 73 F2
Sanjō Japan 71 E5
San Joaquin r. U.S.A. 124 C2
San Joaquin Valley U.S.A. 124 C3
San Jon U.S.A. 127 C5
San Jorge, Golfo de g. Arg. 140 C7
San Jorge, Golfo de g. Spain see Sant Jordi, Golf de

▶San José Costa Rica 133 H7
Capital of Costa Rica.

San Jose Phil. 65 G3
San Jose CA U.S.A. 124 C3
San Jose NM U.S.A. 123 G6
San Jose watercourse U.S.A. 125 J4
San José, Isla i. Mex. 132 B4
San José de Amacuro Venez. 138 F2
San José de Bavicora Mex. 123 G7
San José de Buenavista Phil. 65 G4
San José de Chiquitos Bol. 138 F7
San José de Comondú Mex. 123 F8
San José de Gracia Mex. 123 E8
San Joséde la Brecha Mex. 123 F8
San José del Cabo Mex. 132 C4
San José del Guaviare Col. 138 D3
San José de Mayo Uruguay 140 E4
San José de Raíces Mex. 127 C7
San Juan Arg. 140 C4
San Juan r. Costa Rica/Nicaragua 133 H6
San Juan mt. Cuba 129 D8
San Juan Mex. 123 G8
San Juan r. Mex. 127 D7

▶San Juan Puerto Rico 133 K5
Capital of Puerto Rico.

San Juan U.S.A. 125 J5
San Juan r. U.S.A. 125 H3
San Juan, Cabo c. Arg. 140 D8
San Juan, Cabo c. Equat. Guinea 92 D4
San Juan Bautista Para. 140 E3
San Juan Bautista de las Misiones Para. see San Juan Bautista
San Juan de Guadalupe Mex. 127 C7
San Juan de los Morros Venez. 138 E2
San Juan Mountains U.S.A. 125 J3
San Juan y Martínez Cuba 129 D8
San Julián Arg. 140 C7
San Justo Arg. 140 D4
Sankari Drug India 80 C4
Sankh r. India 77 F7
Sankhu India 78 C3
Sankra Chhattisgarh India 80 D1
Sankra Rajasthan India 78 B4
Sankt Augustin Germany 49 H4
Sankt Gallen Switz. 52 I3
Sankt-Peterburg Rus. Fed. see St Petersburg
Sankt Pölten Austria 43 O6
Sankt Veit an der Glan Austria 43 O7
Sankt Vith Belgium see St-Vith
Sankt Wendel Germany 49 H5
Sanku Jammu and Kashmir 78 D2
Şanlıurfa Turkey 86 E3

Şanlıurfa prov. Turkey 81 D1
San Lorenzo Arg. 140 D4
San Lorenzo Beni Bol. 138 E7
San Lorenzo Tarija Bol. 138 F8
San Lorenzo Ecuador 138 C3
San Lorenzo mt. Spain 53 E2
San Lorenzo, Cerro mt. Arg./Chile 140 B7
San Lorenzo, Isla i. Mex. 123 E7
Sanlúcar de Barrameda Spain 53 C5
San Lucas Baja California Sur Mex. 123 E8
San Lucas Baja California Sur Mex. 132 C4
San Lucas, Serranía de mts Col. 138 D2
San Luis Arg. 140 C4
San Luis AZ U.S.A. 125 F5
San Luis AZ U.S.A. 125 H5
San Luis CO U.S.A. 127 B4
San Luis, Isla i. Mex. 123 E7
San Luisito Mex. 123 E7
San Luis Obispo U.S.A. 124 C4
San Luis Obispo Bay U.S.A. 124 C4
San Luis Potosí Mex. 132 D4
San Luis Reservoir U.S.A. 124 C3
San Luis Río Colorado Mex. 125 F5
San Manuel U.S.A. 125 H5
San Marcial, Punta pt Mex. 123 F8
San Marcos U.S.A. 127 D6
San Marcos, Isla i. Mex. 123 E8
▶San Marino country Europe 54 E3
europe 5, 34–35

▶San Marino San Marino 54 E3
Capital of San Marino.

San Martín research station Antarctica 148 L2
San Martín Catamarca Arg. 140 C3
San Martín Mendoza Arg. 140 C4
San Martín, Lago l. Arg./Chile 140 B7
San Martín de los Andes Arg. 140 B6
San Mateo U.S.A. 124 B3
San Mateo Mountains U.S.A. 125 J4
San Matías Bol. 139 G7
San Matías, Golfo g. Arg. 140 D6
Sanmen China 73 I2
Sanmen Wan b. China 73 I2
Sanmenxia China 73 F1
San Miguel El Salvador 132 G6
San Miguel U.S.A. 124 C4
San Miguel r. U.S.A. 125 I2
San Miguel de Huachi Bol. 138 E7
San Miguel de Tucumán Arg. 140 C3
San Miguel do Araguaia Brazil 141 A1
San Miguel Island U.S.A. 124 C4
Sanming China 73 H3
Sanndatti India 80 B3
Sanndraigh i. U.K. see Sandray
Sannicandro Garganico Italy 54 F4
San Nicolás Durango Mex. 127 B7
San Nicolás Tamaulipas Mex. 127 D7
San Nicolas Island U.S.A. 124 D5
Sannieshof S. Africa 97 G4
Sanniquellie Liberia 92 C4
Sanok Poland 39 D6
San Pablo Bol. 138 E8
San Pablo Phil. 65 G4
San Pablo de Manta Ecuador see Manta
San Pedro Arg. 140 D2
San Pedro Bol. 138 F7
San Pedro Chile 140 C2
San-Pédro Côte d'Ivoire 92 C4
San Pedro Baja California Sur Mex. 120 E7
San Pedro Chihuahua Mex. 123 G7
San Pedro Para. see San Pedro de Ycuamandyyú
San Pedro watercourse U.S.A. 125 H5
San Pedro, Sierra de mts Spain 53 C4
San Pedro Channel U.S.A. 124 D5
San Pedro de Arimena Col. 138 D3
San Pedro de Atacama Chile 140 C2
San Pedro de las Colonias Mex. 127 C7
San Pedro de Macorís Dom. Rep. 133 K5
San Pedro de Ycuamandyyú Para. 140 E2
San Pedro Martir, Parque Nacional nat. park Mex. 123 E7
San Pedro Sula Hond. 132 G5
San Pierre U.S.A. 130 B3
San Pietro, Isola di i. Sardinia Italy 54 C5
San Pitch r. U.S.A. 125 H2
Sanqaçal Azer. 87 H2
Sanquhar U.K. 46 F5
Sanquianga, Parque Nacional nat. park Col. 138 C3
San Quintín, Cabo c. Mex. 123 D7
San Rafael Arg. 140 C4
San Rafael CA U.S.A. 124 B3
San Rafael NM U.S.A. 125 J4
San Rafael r. U.S.A. 125 H2
San Rafael Knob mt. U.S.A. 125 H2
San Rafael Mountains U.S.A. 124 C4
San Ramón Bol. 138 F6
Sanrao China 73 H3
San Remo Italy 54 B3
San Roque Spain 53 B2
San Roque, Punta pt Mex. 123 E8
San Saba U.S.A. 127 D6
San Salvador i. Bahamas 129 F7

▶San Salvador El Salvador 132 G6
Capital of El Salvador.

San Salvador, Isla i. Galápagos Ecuador 138 [inset]
San Salvador de Jujuy Arg. 140 C2
Sansanné-Mango Togo 92 D3
San Sebastián Arg. 140 C8
San Sebastián Spain see Donostia - San Sebastián
San Sebastián de los Reyes Spain 53 E3
Sansepolcro Italy 54 E3
San Severo Italy 54 F4
San Simon U.S.A. 125 I5
Sanski Most Bos.-Herz. 54 G2
Sansoral Islands Palau see Sonsorol Islands
Sansui China 73 F3
Santa r. Peru 138 C5
Santa Ana Bol. 138 E7
Santa Ana El Salvador 132 G6
Santa Ana Mex. 123 F7
Santa Ana i. Solomon Is 103 G3
Santa Ana U.S.A. 124 E5
Santa Ana de Yacuma Bol. 138 E6
Santa Anna U.S.A. 127 D6
Santa Bárbara Brazil 141 C2
Santa Bárbara Cuba see La Demajagua
Santa Bárbara Mex. 127 B7
Santa Barbara U.S.A. 124 D4
Santa Bárbara, Ilha i. Brazil 141 D2
Santa Barbara Channel U.S.A. 124 C4
Santa Bárbara d'Oeste Brazil 141 B3
Santa Barbara Island U.S.A. 124 D5
Santa Catalina, Gulf of U.S.A. 124 E5
Santa Catalina, Isla i. Mex. 123 F8
Santa Catalina de Armada Spain 53 B2
Santa Catalina Island U.S.A. 124 D5
Santa Catarina state Brazil 141 A4
Santa Catarina Baja California Mex. 123 E7
Santa Catarina Nuevo León Mex. 127 C7
Santa Catarina, Ilha de i. Brazil 141 A4
Santa Clara Col. 138 E4
Santa Clara Cuba 133 I4
Santa Clara Mex. 127 B6
Santa Clara CA U.S.A. 124 C3
Santa Clara UT U.S.A. 125 G3
Santa Clarita U.S.A. 124 D4
Santa Clotilde Peru 138 D4
Santa Comba Angola see Waku-Kungo
Santa Croce, Capo c. Sicily Italy 54 F6
Santa Cruz Bol. 138 F7
Santa Cruz Brazil 139 K5
Santa Cruz Costa Rica 138 A1
Santa Cruz U.S.A. 124 B3
Santa Cruz watercourse U.S.A. 125 G5
Santa Cruz, Isla i. Galápagos Ecuador 138 [inset]
Santa Cruz, Isla i. Mex. 123 F8
Santa Cruz Cabrália Brazil 141 D2
Santa Cruz de Goiás Brazil 141 A2
Santa Cruz de la Palma Canary Is 92 B2
Santa Cruz del Sur Cuba 133 I4
Santa Cruz de Moya Spain 53 F4

▶Santa Cruz de Tenerife Canary Is 92 B2
Joint capital of the Canary Islands.

Santa Cruz do Sul Brazil 140 F3
Santa Cruz Island U.S.A. 124 D4
Santa Cruz Islands Solomon Is 103 G3
Santa Elena, Bahía de b. Ecuador 138 B4
Santa Elena, Cabo c. Costa Rica 133 G6
Santa Elena, Punta pt Ecuador 138 B4
Santa Eudóxia Brazil 141 B3
Santa Eufemia, Golfo di g. Italy 54 G5
Santa Fé Arg. 140 D4
Santa Fé Cuba 129 D8

▶Santa Fe U.S.A. 123 G6
State capital of New Mexico.

Santa Fé de Bogotá Col. see Bogotá
Santa Fé de Minas Brazil 141 B2
Santa Fé do Sul Brazil 141 A3
Santa Helena Brazil 139 I4
Santa Helena de Goiás Brazil 141 A2
Santai Sichuan China 72 E2
Santai Yunnan China 72 D3
Santa Inês Brazil 139 I4
Santa Inés, Isla i. Chile 148 L3
Santa Isabel Arg. 140 C5
Santa Isabel Equat. Guinea see Malabo
Santa Isabel i. Solomon Is 103 F2
Santa Juliana Brazil 141 B2
Santalpur India 78 B5
Santa Lucia Range mts U.S.A. 124 C3
Santa Margarita U.S.A. 124 C4
Santa Margarita, Isla i. Mex. 132 B4
Santa María Arg. 140 C3
Santa Maria Amazonas Brazil 139 G4
Santa Maria Rio Grande do Sul Brazil 140 F3
Santa Maria Cape Verde 92 [inset]
Santa María r. Mex. 123 G7
Santa María Peru 138 D4
Santa Maria U.S.A. 124 C4
Santa Maria r. U.S.A. 125 G4
Santa Maria, Cabo de c. Moz. 97 K4
Santa Maria, Cabo de c. Port. 53 C5
Santa Maria, Chapadão de hills Brazil 141 B1
Santa María, Isla i. Galápagos Ecuador 138 [inset]
Santa Maria, Serra de hills Brazil 141 B1
Santa Maria da Vitória Brazil 141 B1
Santa María de Cuevas Mex. 127 B7
Santa Maria do Suaçuí Brazil 141 C2
Santa María Island Vanuatu 103 G3
Santa Maria Madalena Brazil 141 C3
Santa Maria Mountains U.S.A. 125 G4
Santa Marta Col. 138 D1
Santa Marta, Cabo de c. Angola 95 B5
Santa Marta Grande, Cabo de c. Brazil 141 A5
Santa Maura i. Greece see Lefkada
Santa Monica U.S.A. 124 D4
Santa Monica, Pico mt. Mex. 123 E8
Santa Monica Bay U.S.A. 124 D5
Santan Indon. 64 F7
Santana Brazil 141 C1
Santana r. Brazil 141 A2
Santana do Araguaia Brazil 139 H5
Santander Spain 53 E2
Santa Nella U.S.A. 124 C3
Santanilla, Islas is Caribbean Sea see Swan Islands
Santan Mountain hill U.S.A. 125 H5
Sant'Antioco Sardinia Italy 54 C5
Sant'Antioco, Isola di i. Sardinia Italy 54 C5
Santapilly India 80 D2
Santaquin U.S.A. 125 H2
Santa Quitéria Brazil 139 J4
Santarém Brazil 139 H4
Santarém Port. 53 B4
Santa Rita Mex. 127 C7
Santa Rosa Arg. 140 D5
Santa Rosa Acre Brazil 138 D5
Santa Rosa Rio Grande do Sul Brazil 140 F3
Santa Rosa Mex. 127 C7
Santa Rosa CA U.S.A. 124 B2
Santa Rosa NM U.S.A. 123 G6
Santa Rosa de Copán Hond. 132 G6
Santa Rosa de la Roca Bol. 138 F7
Santa Rosa Island U.S.A. 124 C5
Santa Rosalía Mex. 123 E8
Santa Rosa Range mts U.S.A. 122 D4
Santa Rosa Wash watercourse U.S.A. 125 G5
Santa Sylvina Arg. 140 D3
Santa Teresa Australia 105 F6
Santa Teresa r. Brazil 141 A1
Santa Teresa Mex. 127 D7
Santa Vitória Brazil 141 A2
Santa Ynez r. U.S.A. 124 C4
Santa Ysabel i. Solomon Is see Santa Isabel
Santee U.S.A. 124 E5
Santee r. U.S.A. 129 E5
Santiago Brazil 140 F3
Santiago i. Cape Verde 92 [inset]

▶Santiago Chile 140 B4
Capital of Chile.

Santiago Dom. Rep. 133 J5
Santiago Panama 133 H7
Santiago Phil. 65 G3
Santiago de Compostela Spain 53 B2
Santiago de Cuba Cuba 133 I4
Santiago del Estero Arg. 140 D3
Santiago de los Caballeros Dom. Rep. see Santiago
Santiago de Veraguas Panama see Santiago
Santiaguillo, Laguna de l. Mex. 127 B7
Santianna Point Canada 117 P2
Santipur India see Shantipur
Sant Jordi, Golf de g. Spain 53 G3
Santo Amaro Brazil 141 D1
Santo Amaro de Campos Brazil 141 C3
Santo Anastácio Brazil 141 A3
Santo André Brazil 141 B3
Santo Angelo Brazil 140 F3

▶Santo Antão i. Cape Verde 92 [inset]
Most westerly point of Africa.

Santo Antônio Brazil 138 F4
Santo Antônio r. Brazil 141 C2
Santo Antônio São Tomé and Príncipe 92 D4
Santo Antônio, Cabo c. Brazil 141 D1
Santo Antônio da Platina Brazil 141 A3
Santo Antônio de Jesus Brazil 141 D1
Santo Antônio do Içá Brazil 138 E4
Santo Corazón Bol. 139 G7
Santo Domingo Cuba 129 D8

▶Santo Domingo Dom. Rep. 133 K5
Capital of the Dominican Republic.

Santo Domingo Baja California Mex. 123 E7
Santo Domingo Baja California Sur Mex. 123 F8
Santo Domingo country West Indies see Dominican Republic
Santo Domingo de Guzmán Dom. Rep. see Santo Domingo
Santo Hipólito Brazil 141 B2
Santorini i. Greece see Thira
Santos Brazil 141 B3
Santos Dumont Brazil 141 C3
Santos Plateau sea feature S. Atlantic Ocean 144 E7
Santo Tomás Mex. 123 E7
Santo Tomás Peru 138 D6
Santo Tomé Arg. 140 E3
Sanup Plateau U.S.A. 125 G3
San Valentín, Cerro mt. Chile 140 B7
San Vicente El Salvador 132 G6
San Vicente Mex. 123 D7
San Vicente de Baracaldo Spain see Barakaldo
San Vicente de Cañete Peru 138 C6
San Vincenzo Italy 54 D3
San Vito, Capo c. Sicily Italy 54 E5
Sanwer India 78 C5
Sanya China 73 F5
Sanyuan China 73 F1
Sanza Pombo Angola 95 B4
Sao, Phou mt. Laos 66 C3
São Bernardo do Campo Brazil 141 B3
São Borja Brazil 140 E3
São Carlos Brazil 141 B3
São Domingos Brazil 141 B1
São Felipe, Serra de hills Brazil 141 B1
São Félix Bahia Brazil 141 D1
São Félix Mato Grosso Brazil 139 H6
São Félix Pará Brazil 139 H5
São Fidélis Brazil 141 C3
São Francisco Brazil 141 B1

▶São Francisco r. Brazil 141 C1
5th longest river in South America.

São Francisco, Ilha de i. Brazil 141 A4
São Francisco de Paula Brazil 141 A5
São Francisco de Sales Brazil 141 A2
São Francisco do Sul Brazil 141 A4
São Gabriel Brazil 140 F4
São Gonçalo Brazil 141 C3
São Gonçalo do Abaeté Brazil 141 B2
São Gonçalo do Sapucaí Brazil 141 B3
São Gotardo Brazil 141 B2
São João, Ilhas de is Brazil 139 J4
São João da Barra Brazil 141 C3
São João da Boa Vista Brazil 141 B3
São João da Madeira Port. 53 B3
São João da Ponte Brazil 141 B1
São João del Rei Brazil 141 B3
São João do Paraíso Brazil 141 C1
São Joaquim Brazil 141 A5
São Joaquim da Barra Brazil 141 B3
São José Amazonas Brazil 138 E4
São José Santa Catarina Brazil 141 A4
São José do Rio Preto Brazil 141 A3
São José dos Campos Brazil 141 B3
São José dos Pinhais Brazil 141 A4
São Leopoldo Brazil 141 A5
São Lourenço Brazil 141 B3
São Lourenço r. Brazil 139 G7
São Luís Brazil 139 J4
São Luís Brazil 139 G4
São Luís de Montes Belos Brazil 141 A2
São Manuel Brazil 141 A3
São Marcos r. Brazil 141 B2
São Mateus Brazil 141 D2
São Mateus do Sul Brazil 141 A4
São Miguel i. Arquipélago dos Açores 144 G3
São Miguel r. Brazil 141 B2
São Miguel do Tapuio Brazil 139 J5
Saône r. France 52 G4
Saoner India 78 D5
São Nicolau i. Cape Verde 92 [inset]

▶São Paulo Brazil 141 B3
Most populous city in South America and 3rd in the world.

São Paulo state Brazil 141 A3
São Paulo de Olivença Brazil 138 E4
São Pedro da Aldeia Brazil 141 C3
São Pedro e São Paulo is N. Atlantic Ocean 144 G5
São Pires r. Brazil see Teles Pires
São Raimundo Nonato Brazil 139 J5
São Romão Amazonas Brazil 138 E5
São Romão Minas Gerais Brazil 141 B2
São Roque Brazil 141 B3
São Roque, Cabo de c. Brazil 139 K5
São Salvador Angola see M'banza Congo
São Salvador do Congo Angola see M'banza Congo
São Sebastião Brazil 141 B3
São Sebastião, Ilha do i. Brazil 141 B3
São Sebastião do Paraíso Brazil 141 B3
São Sebastião dos Poções Brazil 141 B1
São Simão Minas Gerais Brazil 139 H7
São Simão São Paulo Brazil 141 B3
São Simão, Barragem de resr Brazil 141 A2
São Tiago i. Cape Verde see Santiago

▶São Tomé São Tomé and Príncipe 92 D4
Capital of São Tomé and Príncipe.

São Tomé i. São Tomé and Príncipe 92 D4
São Tomé, Cabo de c. Brazil 141 C3
São Tomé, Pico de mt. São Tomé and Príncipe 92 D4
▶São Tomé and Príncipe country Africa 92 D4
africa 7, 90–91
Saoura, Oued watercourse Alg. 50 D6
São Vicente Brazil 141 B3
São Vicente i. Cape Verde 92 [inset]
São Vicente, Cabo de c. Port. 53 B5
Sapanca Turkey 55 N4
Sapaul India see Supaul
Şaphane Dağı mt. Turkey 55 N5
Sapo National Park Liberia 92 C4
Sapouy Burkina 92 C3
Sapozhok Rus. Fed. 39 I5
Sappa Creek r. U.S.A. 126 D3
Sapporo Japan 70 F4
Sapulpa U.S.A. 127 D4
Sapulut Sabah Malaysia 64 F6
Saputang China see Zadoi
Sāqī Iran 84 E3
Saqqez Iran 84 B2
Sarā Iran 84 B2
Sarāb Iran 84 B2
Sara Buri Thai. 67 C4
Saradiya India 78 B5
Saragossa Spain see Zaragoza
Saragt Akhal'skaya Oblast' Turkm. 85 F2
Saragt Akhal'skaya Oblast' Turkm. see Sarakhs
Saraguro Ecuador 138 C4
Sarahs Turkm. see Sarakhs
Sarai Afgh. 85 G3
Sarai Sidhu Pak. 85 I4

▶Sarajevo Bos.-Herz. 54 H3
Capital of Bosnia-Herzegovina.

Sarakhs Turkm. 85 F2
Saraktash Rus. Fed. 60 G4
Saraland U.S.A. 127 F6
Saramati mt. India/Myanmar 66 A1
Saran' Kazakh. 76 D2
Saranac U.S.A. 130 C2
Saranac r. U.S.A. 131 I1
Saranac Lake U.S.A. 131 H1
Saranda Albania see Sarandë
Sarandë Albania 55 I5
Sarandib country Asia see Sri Lanka
Sarangani Islands Phil. 65 H5
Sarangpur India 78 D5
Saransk Rus. Fed. 39 J5
Sara Peak Nigeria 92 D4
Saraphi Thai. 66 B3
Sarapul Rus. Fed. 37 Q4
Sarapul'skoye Rus. Fed. 70 E2
Sarāqib Syria 81 C2
Sarasota U.S.A. 129 D7
Saraswati r. India 85 H6
Sarata Ukr. 55 M1
Saratoga CA U.S.A. 124 B3
Saratoga WY U.S.A. 122 G4
Saratoga Springs U.S.A. 128 F3
Saratok Sarawak Malaysia 64 E6
Saratov Rus. Fed. 39 J6
Saratovskoye Vodokhranilishche resr Rus. Fed. 39 J5
Saravan Iran 85 F5
Saravan Laos 66 D4
Saray Turkey 55 L4
Sarayköy Turkey 55 M6
Sarayönü Turkey 86 D3
Sarbāz Iran 83 J4
Sarbāz reg. Iran 85 F5
Sarbhang Bhutan 79 G4
Sarbīsheh Iran 83 I3
Sarda r. Nepal 79 E3
Sardab Pass Afgh. 85 H2
Sardarshahr India 78 C3
Sar Dasht Iran 84 B2
Sardegna i. Sardinia Italy see Sardinia
Sardica Bulg. see Sofia
Sardinia i. Sardinia Italy 54 C4
Sardis MS U.S.A. 127 F5
Sardis WV U.S.A. 130 E4
Sardis Lake resr U.S.A. 127 F5
Sar-e Būm Afgh. 85 G3
Sareks nationalpark nat. park Sweden 40 J3
Sarektjåkkå mt. Sweden 40 J3
Sar-e Pol Afgh. 85 G2
Sar-e Pol-e Z̄ahāb Iran 84 B3
Sar Eskandar Iran see Hashtrud
Sare Yazd Iran 84 D4
Sargasso Sea N. Atlantic Ocean 147 P4
Sargodha Pak. 85 I3
Sarh Chad 93 E4
Sarhad reg. Iran 85 F4
Sārī Iran 84 D2
Saria i. Greece 55 L7
Sar-i-Bum Afgh. see Sar-e Būm
Sáric Mex. 123 F7
Sarigan i. N. Mariana Is 65 L3
Sarigh Jilganang Kol salt l. Aksai Chin 78 D2
Sarıgöl Turkey 55 M5
Sarıkamış Turkey 87 F2
Sarikei Sarawak Malaysia 64 E6
Sarikül, Qatorkŭhi mts China/Tajik. see Sarykol Range
Sarila India 78 D4
Sarina Australia 106 E4
Sarıoğlan Kayseri Turkey 86 D3
Sarıoğlan Konya Turkey see Belören
Sariqamish Kuli salt l. Turkm./Uzbek. see Sarykamyshskoye Ozero
Sarīr Tibesti des. Libya 93 E2
Sarita U.S.A. 127 D7
Sarıveliler Turkey 81 A1
Sariwŏn N. Korea 71 B5
Sarıyar Barajı resr Turkey 55 N5
Sarıyer Turkey 55 M4
Sarız Turkey 86 E3
Sark i. Channel Is 45 E9
Sarkand Kazakh. 76 E2
Şarkikaraağaç Turkey 55 N5
Şarkışla Turkey 86 E3
Şarköy Turkey 55 L4
Sarlath Range mts Afgh./Pak. 85 G4
Sarmi Indon. 65 J7
Särna Sweden 41 H6
Sarneh Iran 84 B3
Sarnen Switz. 52 I3
Sarni India see Amla
Sarnia Canada 130 D2
Sarny Ukr. 39 E6
Sarolangun Indon. 64 C7
Saroma-ko l. Japan 70 F3
Saronikos Kolpos g. Greece 55 J6
Saros Körfezi b. Turkey 55 L4
Sarova Rus. Fed. 39 I5
Sarowbī Afgh. 85 H3
Sarpa, Ozero l. Rus. Fed. 39 J6
Sarpan i. N. Mariana Is see Rota
Sarpsborg Norway 41 G7
Sarqant Kazakh. see Sarkand
Sarre r. France 48 H5
Sarrebourg France 48 H6
Sarreguemines France 48 H5
Sarria Spain 53 C2
Sarry France 48 E6
Sartana Ukr. 39 H7
Sartanahu Pak. 85 H5
Sartène Corsica France 52 I6
Sarthe r. France 52 D3
Sartu China see Daqing
Saruna Pak. 85 G5
Sarupsar India 78 C3
Şärur Azer. 87 G3
Saru Tara tourist site Afgh. 85 F4
Sarv Iran 84 D3
Sarvābād Iran 84 B3
Sárvár Hungary 54 G1
Sarwar India 78 C4
Sarygamysh Köli salt l. Turkm./Uzbek. see Sarykamyshskoye Ozero
Sary-Ishikotrau, Peski des. Kazakh. see Saryyesik-Atyrau, Peski
Sarykamyshskoye Ozero salt l. Turkm./Uzbek. 87 J2
Sarykol Range mts China/Tajik. 85 I2
Saryozek Kazakh. 76 E3
Saryshagan Kazakh. 76 D2
Sarysu watercourse Kazakh. 76 C2
Sarytash Kazakh. 87 H1
Sary-Tash Kyrg. 85 I2
Sary Yazikskoye Vodokhranilishche resr Turkm. 85 F2
Saryyesik-Atyrau, Peski des. Kazakh. 76 E2
Sarzha Kazakh. 87 H2
Sasar, Tanjung pt Indon. 104 B2
Sasaram India 79 F4
Sasebo Japan 71 C6
Saskatchewan prov. Canada 117 J4
Saskatchewan r. Canada 117 K4
Saskatoon Canada 117 J4
Saskylakh Rus. Fed. 61 M2
Saslaya mt. Nicaragua 133 H6
Sasoi r. India 78 B5
Sasolburg S. Africa 97 H4
Sasovo Rus. Fed. 39 I5
Sass r. Canada 116 H2
Sassandra Côte d'Ivoire 92 C4
Sassari Sardinia Italy 54 C4
Sassenberg Germany 49 I3
Sassnitz Germany 43 N3
Sass Town Liberia 92 C4
Sasykkol' Ozero l. Kazakh. 76 F2
Sasykoli Rus. Fed. 39 J7
Sasyqköl l. Kazakh. see Sasykkol', Ozero
Satahual i. Micronesia see Satawal
Sata-misaki c. Japan 71 C7
Satana India 80 B1
Satan Pass U.S.A. 125 I4
Satara India 80 B2
Satara S. Africa 97 J3
Satawal i. Micronesia 65 L5
Sätbaev Kazakh. see Satpayev
Satevó Mex. 127 B7
Satevo r. Mex. 123 G8
Satırlar Turkey see Yeşilova
Satkania Bangl. 79 H5
Satkhira Bangl. 79 G5
Satluj r. India/Pak. see Sutlej
Satmala Range hills India 80 C2
Satna India 78 E4
Satpayev Kazakh. 76 C2
Satpura Range mts India 78 C5
Satsuma-hantō pen. Japan 71 C7
Sattahip Thai. 67 C4
Satteldorf Germany 49 K5
Satthwa Myanmar 66 A3
Satu Mare Romania 39 D7
Satun Thai. 67 C6
Satwas India 78 D5
Sauceda Mountains U.S.A. 125 G5
Saucillo Mex. 127 B6
Sauda Norway 41 E7
Sauðárkrókur Iceland 40 [inset]
▶Saudi Arabia country Asia 82 F4
asia 6, 58–59
Sauer r. France 49 I6
Saugatuck U.S.A. 130 B2
Saugeen r. Canada 130 E1
Sāūjbolāgh Iran see Mahābād
Sauk Center U.S.A. 126 E2
Saulieu France 52 G3
Saulnois reg. France 48 G6
Sault Sainte Marie Canada 118 D5
Sault Sainte Marie U.S.A. 128 C2
Saumalkol' Kazakh. 74 F1
Saumarez Reef Australia 106 F4
Saumlakki Indon. 104 E2
Saumur France 52 D3
Saunders, Mount hill Australia 104 E3
Saunders Coast Antarctica 148 J1
Saurimo Angola 95 C4
Sautar Angola 95 B5
Sauvolles, Lac l. Canada 119 G3
Sava r. Europe 54 I2
Savage River Australia 107 [inset]
Savai'i i. Samoa 103 I3
Savala r. Rus. Fed. 39 I6
Savalou Benin 92 D4
Savanat Iran see Eṣṭahbān
Savane r. Canada 119 H4
Savanna U.S.A. 126 F3
Savannah GA U.S.A. 129 D5
Savannah OH U.S.A. 130 D3
Savannah TN U.S.A. 127 F5
Savannah r. U.S.A. 129 D5
Savannah Sound Bahamas 129 E7
Savannakhét Laos 66 D3
Savanna-la-Mar Jamaica 133 I5
Savant Lake Canada 118 C4
Savant Lake l. Canada 118 C4
Savanur India 80 B3
Sävar Sweden 40 L5
Savaştepe Turkey 55 L5
Savè Benin 92 D4
Save r. Moz./Zimbabwe 95 D6
Sāveh Iran 84 C3
Saverne France 49 H6
Saverne, Col de pass France 49 H6
Saviaho Fin. 40 P5
Savinskiy Rus. Fed. 38 I3
Savitri r. India 80 B2
Savli India 78 C5
Savoie reg. France see Savoy
Savona Italy 54 C2
Savonlinna Fin. 40 P6
Savonranta Fin. 40 P5
Savoy reg. France 52 H3
Şavşat Turkey 87 F2
Sävsjö Sweden 41 I8
Savu i. Indon. 104 C2
Savukoski Fin. 40 P3
Savur Turkey 87 F3
Savu Sea Indon. see Sawu, Laut
Saw Myanmar 66 A2
Sawai Madhopur India 78 D4
Sawan Myanmar 66 B1
Sawar India 78 C4
Sawatch Range mts U.S.A. 122 G5
Sawel Mountain hill U.K. 47 E3
Sawhāj Egypt 82 D4
Sawi, Ao b. Thai. 67 B5
Sawn Myanmar 66 B2
Sawtell Australia 108 F3
Sawtooth Range mts U.S.A. 122 C2
Sawu Indon. 104 C2
Sawu i. Indon. see Savu
Sawu, Laut sea Indon. 104 C2
Sawye Myanmar 66 B2
Sawyer U.S.A. 130 B3
Saxilby U.K. 44 G5
Saxmundham U.K. 45 I6
Saxnäs Sweden 40 I4
Saxony land Germany see Sachsen
Saxony-Anhalt land Germany see Sachsen-Anhalt
Saxton U.S.A. 131 F3
Say Niger 92 D3
Sayabouri Laos see Muang Xaignabouri
Sayak Kazakh. 76 E2
Sayanogorsk Rus. Fed. 68 G2
Sayano-Shushenskoye Vodokhranilishche resr Rus. Fed. 68 G2
Sayansk Rus. Fed. 68 I2
Sayaq Kazakh. see Sayak
Sayat Turkm. see Sayat
Sayat Turkm. 85 F2
Şaydā Lebanon see Sidon
Şayen Iran 84 D4
Sayer Island Thai. see Similan, Ko
Sayghān Afgh. 85 G3
Sayḥūt Yemen 82 H6
Sayingpan China 72 D3
Saykhin Kazakh. 37 P6
Sāylac Somalia 93 H3
Saylan country Asia see Sri Lanka
Saynshand Mongolia 69 K4
Sayn-Ust Mongolia 76 H2
Sayoa mt. Spain see Saioa
Sayot Turkm. see Sayat
Şayqal, Bahr imp. l. Syria 81 C3
Sayqyn Kazakh. see Saykhin
Sayre OK U.S.A. 127 D5
Sayre PA U.S.A. 131 G3
Sayreville U.S.A. 131 H3
Sayula Mex. 132 F5
Sayyod Turkm. see Sayat
Sazdy Kazakh. 39 K7
Sazin Pak. 85 I3
Sbaa Alg. 50 D6
Sbeitla Tunisia 54 C7
Scaddan Australia 105 C8
Scafell Pike hill U.K. 44 D4
Scalasaig U.K. 46 C4
Scalea Italy 54 F5

Shangpaihe China *see* **Feixi**
Shangqiu *Henan* China *see* **Suiyang**
Shangqiu *Henan* China **73** G1
Shangrao China **73** H2
Shangshui China **73** G1
Shangyou China **73** G3
Shangyou Shuiku *resr* China **76** F3
Shangyu China **73** I2
Shangzhi China **70** B3
Shangzhou China **73** F1
Shanhe China *see* **Zhengning**
Shanhetun China **70** B3
Shankou China **73** F4
Shannon *airport* Rep. of Ireland **47** D5
Shannon *est.* Rep. of Ireland **47** D5
Shannon *r.* Rep. of Ireland **47** D5
Shannon, Mouth of the Rep. of Ireland **47** C5
Shannon National Park Australia **105** B8
Shannon Ø *i.* Greenland **149** I1
Shan Plateau Myanmar **66** B2
Shansi *prov.* China *see* **Shanxi**
Shan Teng *hill* Hong Kong China *see* **Victoria Peak**
Shantipur India **79** G5
Shantou China **73** H4
Shantung *prov.* China *see* **Shandong**
Shanwei China **73** G4
Shanxi *prov.* China **73** F1
Shanxian China **73** H1
Shanyang China **73** F1
Shaodong China **73** F3
Shaoguan China **73** G3
Shaowu China **73** H3
Shaoxing China **73** I2
Shaoyang China **73** F3
Shap U.K. **44** E4
Shapa China **73** F4
Shaping China *see* **Ebian**
Shapinsay *i.* U.K. **46** G1
Shapkina *r.* Rus. Fed. **38** L2
Shapshal'skiy Khrebet *mts* Rus. Fed. **76** G1
Shaqrā' Saudi Arabia **82** G4
Shār, Jabal *mt.* Saudi Arabia **86** D6
Sharaf *well* Iraq **87** F5
Sharāh, Jibāl ash *mts* Jordan **81** B4
Sharan Jogizai Pak. **85** H4
Shārb Māh Iran **84** E4
Sharbulag Mongolia **76** H2
Shardara Kazakh. **76** C3
Shardara, Step' *plain* Kazakh. *see* **Chardara, Step'**
Sharga Mongolia **76** I2
Sharhulsan Mongolia **68** I4
Shari *r.* Cameroon/Chad *see* **Chari**
Shārī, Buḩayrat *imp. l.* Iraq **87** G4
Shari-dake *vol.* Japan **70** G4
Sharīfah Syria **81** C2
Sharjah U.A.E. **84** D5
Sharka-leb La *pass* China **79** G3
Sharkawshchyna Belarus **41** O9
Shark Bay Australia **105** A6
Shark Reef Australia **106** D2
Sharlyk Rus. Fed. **37** Q5
Sharm ash Shaykh Egypt **86** D6
Sharm el Sheikh Egypt *see* **Sharm ash Shaykh**
Sharon U.S.A. **130** E3
Sharon Springs U.S.A. **126** C4
Sharpe Lake Canada **117** M4
Sharp Peak *hill* Hong Kong China **73** [inset]
Sharqat Iraq *see* **Ash Sharqāṭ**
Sharqī, Jabal ash *mts* Lebanon/Syria **81** B3
Sharur Azer. *see* **Şärur**
Shar'ya Rus. Fed. **38** J4
Shashe *r.* Botswana/Zimbabwe **95** C6
Shashemenē Eth. **94** D3
Shashi China *see* **Jingzhou**
Shasta U.S.A. **124** B1
Shasta, Mount *vol.* U.S.A. **122** C4
Shasta Lake U.S.A. **124** B1
Shatilki Belarus *see* **Svyetlahorsk**
Sha Tin *Hong Kong* China **73** [inset]
Shatki Rus. Fed. **39** J5
Shaṭnat as Salmās, Wādī *watercourse* Syria **81** D2
Sha Tong Hau Shan *Hong Kong* China *see* **Bluff Island**
Shatoy Rus. Fed. **87** G2
Shatsk Rus. Fed. **39** I5
Shaṭṭ al 'Arab *r.* Iran/Iraq **87** H5
Shatura Rus. Fed. **39** H5
Shaubak Jordan *see* **Ash Shawbak**
Shaunavon Canada **117** I5
Shaver Lake U.S.A. **124** D3
Shaw *r.* Australia **104** B5
Shawangunk Mountains *hills* U.S.A. **131** H3
Shawano U.S.A. **130** A1
Shawano Lake U.S.A. **130** A1
Shawinigan Canada **119** G5
Shawnee *OK* U.S.A. **127** D5
Shawnee *WY* U.S.A. **122** G4
Shawneetown U.S.A. **126** F4
Shaxian China **73** H3
Shay Gap Australia **104** C5
Shaykh, Jabal ash *mt.* Lebanon/Syria *see* **Hermon, Mount**
Shaykh Miskīn Syria **81** C3
Shayṭūr Iran **84** D4
Shāzand Iran **84** C3
Shaẓāẓ, Jabal *mt.* Saudi Arabia **87** F6
Shazud Tajik. **85** I2
Shchekino Rus. Fed. **39** H5
Shchel'yayur Rus. Fed. **38** L2
Shcherbakov Rus. Fed. *see* **Rybinsk**
Shchigry Rus. Fed. **39** H6
Shchors Ukr. **39** F6
Shchuchin Belarus *see* **Shchuchyn**
Shchuchyn Belarus **41** N10
Shebalino Rus. Fed. **76** G1
Shebekino Rus. Fed. **39** H6
Shebergh̄an Afgh. **85** G2
Sheboygan U.S.A. **130** B2
Shebshi Mountains Nigeria **92** E4
Shebunino Rus. Fed. **70** F3
Shediac Canada **119** I5
Shedin Peak Canada **116** E4
Shedok Rus. Fed. **87** F1
Sheelin, Lough *l.* Rep. of Ireland **47** E4
Sheep Haven *b.* Rep. of Ireland **47** E2
Sheepmoor S. Africa **97** J4
Sheep Mountain U.S.A. **125** J2
Sheep Peak U.S.A. **125** F3
Sheep's Head *hd* Rep. of Ireland *see* **Muntervary**
Sheerness U.K. **45** H7
Sheet Harbour Canada **119** J5
Shefar'am Israel **81** B3
Sheffield N.Z. **109** D6
Sheffield U.K. **44** F5
Sheffield *AL* U.S.A. **129** C5
Sheffield *PA* U.S.A. **130** F3
Sheffield *TX* U.S.A. **127** C6
Sheffield Lake Canada **119** K4
Shegah Afgh. **85** G4
Shegmas Rus. Fed. **38** K2
Shehong China **72** E2
Sheikh, Jebel esh *mt.* Lebanon/Syria *see* **Hermon, Mount**
Sheikhpura India **79** F4
Shekak *r.* Canada **118** D4
Shekār Āb Iran **84** D3
Shekhawati *reg.* India **85** I5
Shekhem West Bank *see* **Nāblus**
Shekhpura India *see* **Sheikhpura**
Shekhupura Pak. **85** I4
Sheki Azer. *see* **Şäki**
Shekka Ch'ün-Tao *Hong Kong* China *see* **Soko Islands**
Shek Kwu Chau *i. Hong Kong* China **73** [inset]
Shekou China **73** [inset]
Sheksna Rus. Fed. **38** H4
Sheksninskoye Vodokhranilishche *resr* Rus. Fed. **38** H4
Shek Uk Shan *mt. Hong Kong* China **73** [inset]
Shela China **72** B2
Shelagskiy, Mys *pt* Rus. Fed. **61** S2
Shelbina U.S.A. **126** E4
Shelburn U.S.A. **130** B4
Shelburne *N.S.* Canada **119** I6
Shelburne *Ont.* Canada **130** E1
Shelburne Bay Australia **106** C1
Shelby *MI* U.S.A. **130** B2
Shelby *MS* U.S.A. **127** F5
Shelby *MT* U.S.A. **122** F2
Shelby *NC* U.S.A. **129** D5
Shelbyville *IL* U.S.A. **126** F4
Shelbyville *IN* U.S.A. **130** C4
Shelbyville *KY* U.S.A. **130** C4
Shelbyville *TN* U.S.A. **128** C5
Sheldon *IA* U.S.A. **126** E3
Sheldon *IL* U.S.A. **130** B3
Sheldrake Canada **119** I4
Shelek Kazakh. *see* **Chilik**
Shelikhova, Zaliv *g.* Rus. Fed. **61** Q3
Shelikof Strait U.S.A. **114** C4
Shell U.S.A. **126** B2
Shellbrook Canada **117** J4
Shelley U.S.A. **122** E4
Shellharbour Australia **108** E5
Shell Lake Canada **117** J4
Shell Lake U.S.A. **126** F2
Shell Mountain U.S.A. **124** B1
Shelter Bay Canada *see* **Port-Cartier**
Shelter Island U.S.A. **131** I3
Shelter Point N.Z. **109** B8
Shelton U.S.A. **122** C3
Shemakha Azer. *see* **Şamaxı**
Shemordan Rus. Fed. **38** K4
Shenandoah *IA* U.S.A. **126** E3
Shenandoah *PA* U.S.A. **131** G3
Shenandoah Mountains U.S.A. **130** F4
Shenandoah National Park U.S.A. **131** F4
Shendam Nigeria **92** D4
Shending Shan *hill* China **70** D3
Shengena *mt.* Tanz. **95** D4
Shengli China **73** G2
Shengli Feng *mt.* China/Kyrg. *see* **Pobeda Peak**
Shengping China **70** B3
Shengrenjian China *see* **Pinglu**
Shengsi China **73** I2
Shengsi Liedao *is* China **73** I2
Shenjiamen China **73** I2
Shen Khan Bandar Afgh. **85** H2
Shenkursk Rus. Fed. **38** I3
Shenmu China **69** K5
Shennong Ding *mt.* China **73** F2
Shennongjia China **73** F2
Shenqiu China **73** G1
Shenshu China **70** C3
Shensi *prov.* China *see* **Shaanxi**
Shentala Rus. Fed. **39** K5
Shenton, Mount *hill* Australia **105** C7
Shenyang China **70** A4
Shenzhen China **73** G4
Shenzhen Wan *b. Hong Kong* China *see* **Deep Bay**
Sheopur India **78** D4
Shepetivka Ukr. **39** E6
Shepetovka Ukr. *see* **Shepetivka**
Shepherd Islands Vanuatu **103** G3
Shepherdsville U.S.A. **130** C5
Shepparton Australia **108** B6
Sheppey, Isle of *i.* U.K. **45** H7
Sheqi China **73** G1
Sherabad Uzbek. **85** G2
Sherborne U.K. **45** E8
Sherbro Island Sierra Leone **92** B4
Sherbrooke Canada **119** H5
Sherburne U.S.A. **131** H2
Shercock Rep. of Ireland **47** F4
Shereiq Sudan **82** D6
Shergaon India **79** H4
Shergarh India **78** C4
Sheridan *AR* U.S.A. **127** E5
Sheridan *WY* U.S.A. **122** G3
Sheringham U.K. **45** I6
Sherman U.S.A. **127** D5
Sherman Mountain U.S.A. **125** F1
Sherobod Uzbek. *see* **Sherabad**
Sherpur *Dhaka* Bangl. **79** G4
Sherpur *Rajshahi* Bangl. **79** G4
Sherridon Canada **117** K4
's-Hertogenbosch Neth. **48** F3
Sherwood Forest *reg.* U.K. **45** F5
Sherwood Lake Canada **117** K2
Sheryshevo Rus. Fed. **70** C2
Sheslay Canada **116** D3
Sheslay *r.* Canada **116** C3
Shethanei Lake Canada **117** L3
Shetland *is* U.K. **46** [inset]
Shetpe Kazakh. **74** E2
Sheung Shui *Hong Kong* China **73** [inset]
Sheung Sze Mun *sea chan. Hong Kong* China **73** [inset]
Shevchenko Kazakh. *see* **Aktau**
Shevli *r.* Rus. Fed. **70** D1
Shexian China **73** H2
Sheyang China **73** I1
Sheyenne *r.* U.S.A. **126** D2
Sheykh Sho'eyb *i.* Iran **84** D5
Shey Phoksundo National Park Nepal **79** E3
Shiant Islands U.K. **46** C3
Shiashkotan, Ostrov *i.* Rus. Fed. **61** Q5
Shibām Yemen **82** G6
Shibar Pass Afgh. **85** H3
Shibata Japan **71** E5
Shibazhan China **70** B1
Shibh Jazīrat Sīnā' *pen.* Egypt *see* **Sinai**
Shibīn al Kawm Egypt **86** C5
Shibîn el Kôm Egypt *see* **Shibīn al Kawm**
Shibogama Lake Canada **118** C3
Shibotsu-jima *i.* Rus. Fed. *see* **Zelenyy, Ostrov**
Shicheng *Fujian* China *see* **Zhouning**
Shicheng *Jiangxi* China **73** H3
Shidād al Mismā' *hill* Saudi Arabia **81** D4
Shidao China **69** M5
Shidian China **72** C3
Shiel, Loch *l.* U.K. **46** D4
Shield, Cape Australia **106** B2
Shieli Kazakh. *see* **Chiili**
Shifa, Jabal ash *mts* Saudi Arabia **86** D5
Shifang China **72** E2
Shigatse China *see* **Xigazê**
Shiḩān *mt.* Jordan **81** B4
Shihezi China **76** G3
Shihkiachwang China *see* **Shijiazhuang**
Shijiao China *see* **Fogang**
Shijiazhuang China **69** K5
Shijiu Hu *l.* China **73** H2
Shijiusuo China *see* **Rizhao**
Shikag Lake Canada **118** C4
Shikar *r.* Pak. **85** F4
Shikarpur Pak. **85** H5
Shikengkong *mt.* China **73** G3
Shikhany Rus. Fed. **39** J5
Shikohabad India **78** D4
Shikoku *i.* Japan **71** D6
Shikoku-sanchi *mts* Japan **71** D6
Shikotan, Ostrov *i.* Rus. Fed. **70** G4
Shikotan-tō *i.* Rus. Fed. *see* **Shikotan, Ostrov**
Shikotsu-Tōya National Park Japan **70** F4
Shildon U.K. **44** F4
Shilega Rus. Fed. **38** J2
Shiliguri India **79** G4
Shilin China **72** D3
Shilipu China **73** G2
Shiliu China *see* **Changjiang**
Shilla *mt.* Jammu and Kashmir **78** D2
Shillelagh Rep. of Ireland **47** F5
Shillo *r.* Israel **81** B3
Shillong India **79** G4
Shilovo Rus. Fed. **39** I5
Shimada Japan **71** E6
Shimanovsk Rus. Fed. **70** B1
Shimbiris *mt.* Somalia **94** E2
Shimen *Gansu* China **72** D1
Shimen *Hunan* China **73** F2
Shimen *Yunnan* China *see* **Yunlong**
Shimla India **78** D3
Shimoga India **80** B3
Shimokita-hantō *pen.* Japan **70** F4
Shimoni Kenya **95** D4
Shimonoseki Japan **71** C6
Shimsk Rus. Fed. **38** F4
Shin, Loch *l.* U.K. **46** E2
Shināfīyah Iraq *see* **Ash Shanāfīyah**
Shinan China *see* **Xingye**
Shīndand Afgh. **85** F3
Shingbwiyang Myanmar **66** B1
Shing-gai Myanmar **66** B1
Shinghshal Pass Pak. **85** I2
Shingletown U.S.A. **124** C1
Shingū Japan **71** E6
Shingwedzi S. Africa **97** J2
Shingwedzi *r.* S. Africa **97** J2
Shinkai Hills Afgh. **85** H3
Shinkāy Afgh. **85** G4
Shinnston U.S.A. **130** E4
Shinshār Syria **81** C2
Shinyanga Tanz. **94** D4
Shiocton U.S.A. **130** A1
Shiogama Japan **71** F5
Shiono-misaki *c.* Japan **71** D6
Shipai China **73** H2
Shiping China **72** D4
Shipki Pass China/India **78** D3
Shipman U.S.A. **131** F5
Shippegan Island Canada **119** I5
Shippensburg U.S.A. **131** G3
Shiprock U.S.A. **125** I3
Shiprock Peak U.S.A. **125** I3
Shipu China **73** I2
Shipunovo Rus. Fed. **68** E2
Shiqian China **73** F3
Shiqiao China *see* **Panyu**
Shiqizhen China *see* **Zhongshan**
Shiquan China **73** F1
Shiquanhe *Xizang* China *see* **Ali**
Shiquanhe *Xizang* China *see* **Gar**
Shiquan He *r.* China *see* **Indus**
Shiquan Shuiku *resr* China **73** F1
Shira Rus. Fed. **68** F2
Shīrābād Iran **84** C2
Shirakawa-go and Gokayama *tourist site* Japan **71** E5
Shirane-san *vol.* Japan **71** E5
Shirase Coast Antarctica **148** J1
Shirase Glacier Antarctica **148** D2
Shīrāz Iran **84** D4
Shire *r.* Malawi **95** D5
Shireza Pak. **85** G5
Shīrīn Tagāb Afgh. **85** G2
Shiriya-zaki *c.* Japan **70** F4
Shirkala *reg.* Kazakh. **76** A2
Shīr Kūh *mt.* Iran **84** D4
Shiroro Reservoir Nigeria **92** D3
Shirpur India **78** C5
Shirten Holoy Gobi *des.* China **76** I3
Shīrvān Iran **84** E2
Shisanzhan China **70** B2
Shishaldin Volcano U.S.A. **114** B4
Shisha Pangma *mt.* China *see* **Xixabangma Feng**
Shishou China **73** G2
Shitan China **73** G3
Shitang China **73** I2
Shithāthah Iraq **87** F4
Shiv India **78** B4
Shiveluch, Sopka *vol.* Rus. Fed. **61** R4
Shivpuri India **78** D4
Shivwits U.S.A. **125** G3
Shivwits Plateau U.S.A. **125** G3
Shiwan Dashan *mts* China **72** E4
Shiwa Ngandu Zambia **95** D5
Shixing China **73** G3
Shiyan China **73** F1
Shizhu China **73** F2
Shizilu China *see* **Junan**
Shizipu China **73** H2
Shizong China **72** D3
Shizuishan China **68** J5
Shizuoka Japan **71** E6

▶**Shkhara** *mt.* Georgia/Rus. Fed. **87** F2
3rd highest mountain in Europe.

Shklov Belarus *see* **Shklow**
Shklow Belarus **39** F5
Shkodër Albania **55** H3
Shkodra Albania *see* **Shkodër**
Shkodrës, Liqeni i *l.* Albania/Serb. and Mont. *see* **Scutari, Lake**
Shmidta, Ostrov *i.* Rus. Fed. **60** K1
Shmidta, Poluostrov *pen.* Rus. Fed. **70** F1
Shoal Lake Canada **117** K5
Shoals U.S.A. **130** B4
Shōbara Japan **71** D6
Shoh Tajik. **85** H2
Shohi Pass Pak. *see* **Tal Pass**
Shokanbetsu-dake *mt.* Japan **70** F4
Sholakkorgan Kazakh. **76** C3
Sholapur India *see* **Solapur**
Sholaqorghan Kazakh. *see* **Sholakkorgan**
Shomba *r.* Rus. Fed. **40** R4
Shomvukva Rus. Fed. **38** K3
Shona Ridge *sea feature* S. Atlantic Ocean **144** I9
Shonzha Kazakh. *see* **Chundzha**
Shor India **78** D2
Shorap Pak. **85** G5
Shorapur India **80** C2
Shorawak *reg.* Afgh. **85** G4
Shorewood *IL* U.S.A. **130** A3
Shorewood *WI* U.S.A. **130** B2
Shorkot Pak. **85** I4
Shorkozakhly, Solonchak *salt flat* Turkm. **87** J2
Shoshone *CA* U.S.A. **124** E4
Shoshone *ID* U.S.A. **122** E4
Shoshone *r.* U.S.A. **122** F3
Shoshone Mountains U.S.A. **124** E2
Shoshone Peak U.S.A. **124** E3
Shoshong Botswana **97** H2
Shoshoni U.S.A. **122** F4
Shostka Ukr. **39** G6
Shouyang Shan *mt.* China **73** F1
Showak Sudan **82** E7
Show Low U.S.A. **125** H4
Shoyna Rus. Fed. **38** J2
Shpakovskoye Rus. Fed. **87** F1
Shpola Ukr. **39** F6
Shqipëria *country* Europe *see* **Albania**
Shreve U.S.A. **130** D3
Shreveport U.S.A. **127** E5
Shrewsbury U.K. **45** E6
Shri Lanka *country* Asia *see* **Sri Lanka**
Shri Mohangarh India **78** B4
Shrirampur India **79** G5
Shu Kazakh. **76** D3
Shū *r.* Kazakh./Kyrg. *see* **Chu**
Shu'ab, Ra's *pt* Yemen **83** H7
Shuajingsi China **72** D1
Shuangbai China **72** D3
Shuangcheng *Fujian* China *see* **Zherong**
Shuangcheng *Heilong.* China **70** B3
Shuanghe China **73** G2
Shuanghechang China **72** E2
Shuangjedagang China **70** C2
Shuangjiang *Guizhou* China *see* **Jiangkou**
Shuangjiang *Hunan* China *see* **Tongdao**
Shuangjiang *Yunnan* China *see* **Eshan**
Shuangliao China **70** A4
Shuangliu China **72** D2
Shuangpai China **73** F3
Shuangshipu China *see* **Fengxian**
Shuangxi China *see* **Shunchang**
Shuangyang China **70** B4
Shuangyashan China **70** C3
Shubarkuduk Kazakh. **76** A2
Shubayh *well* Saudi Arabia **81** D4
Shugozero Rus. Fed. **38** G4
Shuicheng China *see* **Lupanshui**
Shuidong China *see* **Dianbai**
Shuijing China **72** E1
Shuikou China **73** F3
Shuikouguan China **72** E4
Shuikoushan China **73** G3
Shuiluocheng China *see* **Zhuanglang**
Shuizhai China *see* **Wuhua**
Shulan China **70** B3
Shumagin Islands U.S.A. **114** B4
Shumba Zimbabwe **95** C5
Shumen Bulg. **55** L3
Shumerlya Rus. Fed. **38** J5
Shumilina Belarus **39** F5
Shumyachi Rus. Fed. **39** G5
Shunchang China **73** H3
Shuncheng China **70** A4
Shunde China **73** G4
Shuoxian China *see* **Shuozhou**
Shuozhou China **69** K5
Shuqrah Yemen **82** G7
Shūr *r.* Iran **84** D4
Shūr *r.* Iran **85** F3
Shūr *watercourse* Iran **84** D5
Shur *watercourse* Iran **84** E3
Shūr, Rūd-e *watercourse* Iran **84** E4
Shūr Āb *watercourse* Iran **84** D4
Shurchi Uzbek. **85** G2
Shūrjestān Iran **84** D4
Shūrū Iran **85** F4
Shuryshkarskiy Sor, Ozero *l.* Rus. Fed. **37** T2
Shūsh Iran **84** C3
Shusha Azer. *see* **Şuşa**
Shushtar Iran **84** C3
Shutar Khun Pass Afgh. **85** G3
Shutfah, Qalamat *well* Saudi Arabia **84** D6
Shuwaysh, Tall ash *hill* Jordan **81** C4
Shuya *Ivanovskaya Oblast'* Rus. Fed. **38** I4
Shuya *Respublika Kareliya* Rus. Fed. **38** G3
Shuyskoye Rus. Fed. **38** I4
Shwebo Myanmar **66** A2
Shwedwin Myanmar **66** A1
Shwegun Myanmar **66** B3
Shwegyin Myanmar **66** B3
Shweudaung *mt.* Myanmar **66** B2
Shyghanaq Kazakh. *see* **Chiganak**
Shymkent Kazakh. **76** C3
Shyok Jammu and Kashmir **78** D2
Shypuvate Ukr. **39** H6
Shyroke Ukr. **39** G7
Sia Indon. **65** I8
Siabu Indon. **67** B7
Siahan Range *mts* Pak. **85** F5
Sīah Chashmeh Iran **84** B2
Siahgird Afgh. **85** G2
Siah Koh *mts* Afgh. **85** G3
Sialkot Pak. **85** I3
Siam *country* Asia *see* **Thailand**
Sian China *see* **Xi'an**
Sian Rus. Fed. **70** B1
Siang *r.* India *see* **Brahmaputra**
Siantan *i.* Indon. **67** D7
Siargao *i.* Phil. **65** H5
Siau *i.* Indon. **65** H6
Šiauliai Lith. **41** M9
Siazan' Azer. *see* **Siyäzän**
Si Bai, Lam *r.* Thai. **66** D4
Sibasa S. Africa **97** J2
Sibayi, Lake S. Africa **97** K4
Sibda China **72** C2
Šibenik Croatia **54** F3
Siberia *reg.* Rus. Fed. **61** M3
Siberut *i.* Indon. **64** B7
Siberut, Selat *sea chan.* Indon. **64** B7
Sibi Pak. **85** G4
Sibidiri P.N.G. **65** K8
Sibigo Indon. **67** A7
Sibiloi National Park Kenya **94** D3
Sibir' *reg.* Rus. Fed. *see* **Siberia**
Sibiti Congo **94** B4
Sibiu Romania **55** K2
Sibley U.S.A. **126** E3
Siboa Indon. **65** G6
Sibolga Indon. **67** B7
Siborongborong Indon. **67** B7
Sibsagar India **79** H4
Sibu *Sarawak* Malaysia **64** E6
Sibut Cent. Afr. Rep. **94** B3
Sibuyan *i.* Phil. **65** G4
Sibuyan Sea Phil. **65** G4
Sicamous Canada **116** G5
Sicca Veneria Tunisia *see* **Le Kef**
Siccus *watercourse* Australia **107** B6
Sicheng *Anhui* China *see* **Sixian**
Sicheng *Guangxi* China *see* **Lingyun**
Sichon Thai. **67** B5
Sichuan *prov.* China **72** D2
Sichuan Pendi *basin* China **72** E2
Sicié, Cap *c.* France **52** G5
Sicilia *i.* Italy *see* **Sicily**
Sicilian Channel Italy/Tunisia **54** E6
Sicily *i.* Italy **54** F5
Sicuani Peru **138** D6
Siddhapur India **78** C5
Siddipet India **80** C2
Sideros, Akra *pt* Greece **55** L7
Sidesaviwa S. Africa **96** F7
Sidhauli India **78** E4
Sidhi India **79** E4
Sidhpur India *see* **Siddhapur**
Sidi Aïssa Alg. **53** H6
Sidi Ali Alg. **53** G5
Sīdī Barrānī Egypt **86** B5
Sidi Bel Abbès Alg. **53** F6
Sidi Bennour Morocco **50** C5
Sidi Bou Sa'id Tunisia *see* **Sidi Bouzid**
Sidi Bouzid Tunisia **54** C7
Sidi el Barrâni Egypt *see* **Sīdī Barrānī**
Sidi El Hani, Sebkhet de *salt pan* Tunisia **54** D7
Sidi Ifni Morocco **92** B2
Sidi Kacem Morocco **50** C5
Sidikalang Indon. **67** B7
Sidi Khaled Alg. **50** E5
Sid Lake Canada **117** J2
Sidlaw Hills U.K. **46** F4
Sidley, Mount Antarctica **148** J1
Sidli India **79** G4
Sidmouth U.K. **45** D8
Sidney *IA* U.S.A. **126** E3
Sidney *MT* U.S.A. **122** G3
Sidney *NE* U.S.A. **126** C3
Sidney *OH* U.S.A. **130** C3
Sidney Lanier, Lake U.S.A. **129** D5
Sidoktaya Myanmar **66** A2
Sidon Lebanon **81** B3
Sidr Egypt *see* **Sudr**
Siedlce Poland **39** D5
Sieg *r.* Germany **49** H4
Siegen Germany **49** I4
Siěmréab Cambodia **67** C4
Siem Reap Cambodia *see* **Siěmréab**
Si'en China *see* **Huanjiang**
Siena Italy **54** D3
Sieradz Poland **43** Q5
Sierra Blanca U.S.A. **123** G7
Sierra Colorada Arg. **140** C6
Sierra Grande Arg. **140** C6

▶**Sierra Leone** *country* Africa **92** B4
africa 7, 90–91

Sierra Leone Basin *sea feature* N. Atlantic Ocean **144** G5
Sierra Leone Rise *sea feature* N. Atlantic Ocean **144** G5
Sierra Madre Mountains U.S.A. **124** C4
Sierra Mojada Mex. **127** C7
Sierra Nevada, Parque Nacional *nat. park* Venez. **138** D2
Sierra Nevada de Santa Marta, Parque Nacional *nat. park* Col. **138** D1
Sierraville U.S.A. **124** C2
Sierra Vista U.S.A. **123** F7
Sierre Switz. **52** H3
Sievi Fin. **40** N5
Sifang Ling *mts* China **72** E4
Sifangtai China **70** B3
Sīfenī Eth. **94** E2
Sifnos *i.* Greece **55** K6
Sig Alg. **53** F6
Sigguup Nunaa *pen.* Greenland **115** M2
Sighetu Marmaţiei Romania **39** D7
Sighişoara Romania **55** K1
Siglap Sing. **67** [inset]
Sigli Indon. **67** A6
Siglufjörður Iceland **40** [inset]
Signal de Botrange *hill* Belgium **48** G4
Signal de la Ste-Baume *mt.* France **52** G5
Signal Peak U.S.A. **125** F5
Signy-l'Abbaye France **48** E5
Sigourney U.S.A. **126** E3
Sigri, Akra *pt* Greece **55** K5
Sigsbee Deep *sea feature* G. of Mexico **147** N4
Sigüenza Spain **53** E3
Siguiri Guinea **92** C3
Sigulda Latvia **41** N8
Sigurd U.S.A. **125** H2
Sihanoukville Cambodia **67** C5
Sihaung Myauk Myanmar **66** A2
Sihawa India **80** D1
Sihong China **73** H1
Sihora India **78** E5
Sihui China **73** G4
Siikajoki Fin. **40** N4
Siilinjärvi Fin. **40** O5
Siirt Turkey **87** F3
Sijawal Pak. **78** B4
Sika India **78** B5
Sikaka Saudi Arabia *see* **Sakākah**
Sikandra Rao India **78** D4
Sikanni Chief Canada **116** F3
Sikanni Chief *r.* Canada **116** F3
Sikar India **78** C4
Sikaram *mt.* Afgh. **85** H3
Sikasso Mali **92** C3
Sikaw Myanmar **66** B2
Sikeston U.S.A. **127** F4
Sikhote-Alin' *mts* Rus. Fed. **70** D4
Sikhote-Alinskiy Zapovednik *nature res.* Rus. Fed. **70** E3
Sikinos *i.* Greece **55** K6
Sikkim *state* India **79** G4
Siksjö Sweden **40** J4
Sil *r.* Spain **53** C2
Şila' *i.* Saudi Arabia **86** D6
Šilalė Lith. **41** M9
Si Lanna National Park Thai. **66** B3
Silas U.S.A. **127** F6
Silavatturai Sri Lanka **80** C4
Silawaih Agam *vol.* Indon. **67** A6
Silberberg *hill* Germany **49** J1
Silchar India **79** H4
Şile Turkey **55** M4
Sileru *r.* India **80** D2
Silesia *reg.* Czech Rep./Poland **43** P5
Sileti *r.* Kazakh. **68** C2
Siletiteniz, Ozero *salt l.* Kazakh. **75** G1
Silgadi Nepal *see* **Silgarhi**
Silgarhi Nepal **78** E3
Silghat India **79** H4
Siliana Tunisia **54** C6
Silifke Turkey **81** A1
Siliguri India *see* **Shiliguri**
Siling Co *salt l.* China **79** G3
Silipur India **78** D4
Silistra Bulg. **55** L2
Silistria Bulg. *see* **Silistra**
Silivri Turkey **55** M4
Siljan *l.* Sweden **41** I6
Silkeborg Denmark **41** F8
Sillajhuay *mt.* Chile **138** E7
Sillamäe Estonia **41** O7
Sille Turkey **86** D3
Silli India **79** F5
Sillod India **80** B1
Silobela S. Africa **97** J4
Silsby Lake Canada **117** M4
Silt U.S.A. **125** J2
Siltaharju Fin. **40** O3
Sīlūp *r.* Iran **85** F5
Šilutė Lith. **41** L9
Silvan Turkey **87** F3
Silvânia Brazil **141** A2
Silvassa India **80** B1
Silver Bank Passage Turks and Caicos Is **133** J4
Silver Bay U.S.A. **126** F2
Silver City Canada **116** B2
Silver City *NM* U.S.A. **125** I5
Silver City *NV* U.S.A. **124** D2
Silver Creek *r.* U.S.A. **125** H4
Silver Lake U.S.A. **122** C4
Silver Lake *l.* U.S.A. **124** E4
Silvermine Mts *hills* Rep. of Ireland **47** D5
Silver Peak Range *mts* U.S.A. **124** E3
Silver Spring U.S.A. **131** G4
Silver Springs U.S.A. **124** D2
Silverthrone Mountain Canada **116** E5
Silvertip Mountain Canada **116** F5
Silverton U.K. **45** D8
Silverton *CO* U.S.A. **125** J3
Silverton *TX* U.S.A. **127** C5
Sima China **79** G3
Simanggang *Sarawak* Malaysia *see* **Sri Aman**
Simao China **72** D4
Simard, Lac *l.* Canada **118** F5
Simaria India **79** F4
Simav Turkey **55** M5
Simav Dağları *mts* Turkey **55** M5
Simba Dem. Rep. Congo **94** C3
Simbirsk Rus. Fed. *see* **Ul'yanovsk**
Simcoe Canada **130** E2
Simcoe, Lake Canada **130** F1
Simdega India **80** E1
Simēn *mts* Eth. **94** D2
Simēn Mountains Eth. *see* **Simēn**
Simeulue *i.* Indon. **67** B7
Simeulue Reserve *nature res.* Indon. **67** A7
Simferopol' Ukr. **86** D1
Simi *i.* Greece *see* **Symi**
Simikot Nepal **79** E3
Similan, Ko *i.* Thai. **67** B5
Simi Valley U.S.A. **124** D4
Simla India *see* **Shimla**
Simla U.S.A. **122** G5
Şimleu Silvaniei Romania **55** J1
Simmerath Germany **48** G4
Simmern (Hunsrück) Germany **49** H5
Simmesport U.S.A. **127** F6
Simms U.S.A. **122** F3
Simojärvi *l.* Fin. **40** O3
Simon Mex. **127** C7
Simonette *r.* Canada **116** G4
Simon Wash *watercourse* U.S.A. **125** I5
Simoom Sound Canada **116** E5
Simoon Sound Canada *see* **Simoom Sound**
Simpang Indon. **64** C7
Simpang Mangayau, Tanjung *pt* Malaysia **64** F5
Simplício Mendes Brazil **139** J5
Simplon Pass Switz. **52** I3
Simpson Canada **117** J5
Simpson U.S.A. **122** F2
Simpson Desert Australia **106** B5
Simpson Desert National Park Australia **106** B5
Simpson Desert Regional Reserve *nature res.* Australia **107** B5
Simpson Islands Canada **117** H2
Simpson Park Mountains U.S.A. **124** E2
Simpson Peninsula Canada **115** J3
Simrishamn Sweden **41** I9
Simushir, Ostrov *i.* Rus. Fed. **69** S3
Sina *r.* India **80** B2
Sinabang Indon. **67** B7
Sinabung *vol.* Indon. **67** B7
Sinai *pen.* Egypt **81** A5
Sinai, Mont *hill* France **48** E5
Sinai al Janūbīya *governorate* Egypt *see* **Janūb Sīnā'**
Sinai ash Shamālīya *governorate* Egypt *see* **Shamāl Sīnā'**
Si Nakarin Reservoir Thai. **66** B4
Sinaloa *state* Mex. **123** F8
Sinalunga Italy **54** D3

Sinan China 73 F3
Sinancha Rus. Fed. see Cheremshany
Sinbo Myanmar 66 B1
Sinbyubyin Myanmar 67 B4
Sinbyugyun Myanmar 66 A2
Sincan Turkey 86 E3
Sincelejo Col. 138 C2
Sinchu Taiwan see T'aoyüan
Sinclair Mills Canada 116 F4
Sincora, Serra do hills Brazil 141 C1
Sind r. India 78 D4
Sind Pak. see Thul
Sind prov. Pak. see Sindh
Sinda Rus. Fed. 70 E2
Sindari India 78 B4
Sindelfingen Germany 49 I6
Sindh prov. Pak. 85 H5
Sindhuli Garhi Nepal 79 F4
Sindhulimadi Nepal see Sindhuli Garhi
Sındırgı Turkey 55 M5
Sindor Rus. Fed. 38 K3
Sindou Burkina 92 C3
Sindri India 79 F5
Sind Sagar Doab lowland Pak. 85 H4
Sinel'nikovo Ukr. see Synel'nykove
Sines Port. 53 B5
Sines, Cabo de c. Port. 53 B5
Sinettä Fin. 40 N3
Sinfra Côte d'Ivoire 92 C4
Sing Myanmar 66 B2
Singa Sudan 82 D7
Singanallur India 80 C4
▶Singapore country Asia 67 [inset] asia 6, 58–59
▶Singapore Sing. 67 [inset] Capital of Singapore.
Singapore r. Sing. 67 [inset]
Singapore, Strait of Indon./Sing. 67 [inset]
Singapura country Asia see Singapore
Singapura Sing. see Singapore
Singapuru India 80 D2
Singaraja Indon. 104 A2
Sing Buri Thai. 66 C4
Singhampton Canada 130 E1
Singhana India 78 C3
Singida Tanz. 95 D4
Singidunum Serb. and Mont. see Belgrade
Singkaling Hkamti Myanmar 66 A1
Singkawang Indon. 64 D6
Singkep i. Indon. 64 C7
Singkil Indon. 67 B7
Singkuang Indon. 67 B7
Singleton Australia 108 E4
Singleton, Mount hill N.T. Australia 104 E5
Singleton, Mount hill W.A. Australia 105 B7
Singora Thai. see Songkhla
Sin'gosan N. Korea see Kosan
Singra India 79 G4
Singri India 79 H4
Singu Myanmar 72 B4
Singwara India 80 D1
Sin'gye N. Korea 71 B5
Sinhala country Asia see Sri Lanka
Sinhkung Myanmar 66 B1
Sining China see Xining
Siniscola Sardinia Italy 54 C4
Sinj Croatia 54 G3
Sinjai Indon. 65 G8
Sinjār, Jabal mt. Iraq 87 F3
Sinkat Sudan 82 E6
Sinkiang aut. reg. China see Xinjiang Uygur Zizhiqu
Sinkiang Uighur Autonomous Region aut. reg. China see Xinjiang Uygur Zizhiqu
Sinmi-do i. N. Korea 71 B5
Sinn Germany 49 I4
Sinnamary Fr. Guiana 139 H2
Sinn Bishr, Gebel hill Egypt see Sinn Bishr, Jabal
Sinn Bishr, Jabal hill Egypt 81 A5
Sinneh Iran see Sanandaj
Sinoia Zimbabwe see Chinhoyi
Sinop Brazil 139 G6
Sinop Turkey 86 D2
Sinope Turkey see Sinop
Sinp'a N. Korea 70 B4
Sinp'o N. Korea 71 C4
Sinsang N. Korea 71 B5
Sinsheim Germany 49 I5
Sintang Indon. 64 E6
Sint Eustatius i. Neth. Antilles 133 L5
Sint-Laureins Belgium 48 D3
▶Sint Maarten i. Neth. Antilles 133 L5 Part of the Netherlands Antilles. The northern part of the island is the French territory of St Martin.
Sint-Niklaas Belgium 48 E3
Sinton U.S.A. 127 D6
Sintra Port. 53 B4
Sint-Truiden Belgium 48 F4
Sinŭiju N. Korea 71 B4
Sinzig Germany 49 H4
Siófok Hungary 54 H1
Sioma Ngwezi National Park Zambia 95 C5
Sion Switz. 52 H3
Sion Mills U.K. 47 E3
Siorapaluk Greenland 115 K2
Sioux Center U.S.A. 121 H3
Sioux City U.S.A. 126 D3
Sioux Falls U.S.A. 126 D3
Sioux Lookout Canada 117 N5
Siphaqeni S. Africa see Flagstaff
Siping China 70 B4
Sipiwesk Canada 117 L4
Sipiwesk Lake Canada 117 L4
Siple, Mount Antarctica 148 J2
Siple Coast Antarctica 148 I1
Siple Island Antarctica 148 J2
Siponj Tajik. see Bartang
Sipsey r. U.S.A. 127 F5
Sipura i. Indon. 64 B7
Siq, Wādī as watercourse Egypt 81 A5
Sir r. Pak. 85 H6
Sir, Dar'yoi r. Asia see Syrdar'ya
Sira India 80 C3
Sira r. Norway 41 E7
Şīr Abū Nu'āyr i. U.A.E. 84 D5
Siracusa Sicily Italy see Syracuse
Siraha Nepal see Sirha
Sirajganj Bangl. 79 G4
Sir Alexander, Mount Canada 116 F4
Şiran Turkey 87 E2
Širbāl, Jabal mt. Egypt 86 D5
Şīr Banī Yās i. U.A.E. 84 D5
Sircilla India see Sirsilla
Sirdaryo r. Asia see Syrdar'ya
Sirdaryo Uzbek. see Syrdar'ya
Sirdingka China see Lhari
Sir Edward Pellew Group is Australia 106 B2
Sirha Nepal 79 F4
Sirḥān, Wādī as watercourse Jordan/Saudi Arabia 81 C4
Sirik, Tanjung pt Malaysia 64 E6
Siri Kit Dam Thai. 66 C3
Sirina i. Greece see Syrna
Sīrjā Iran 85 F5
Sir James MacBrien, Mount Canada 116 E2
Sīrjān Iran 84 D4
Sīrjān salt flat Iran 84 D4
Sirkazhi India 80 C4
Sirmilik National Park Canada 115 K2
Şırnak Turkey 87 F3
Sirohi India 78 C4
Sirombu Indon. 67 B7
Sironj India 78 D4
Síros i. Greece see Syros
Sirpur India 80 C2
Sirretta Peak U.S.A. 124 D4
Sīrrī, Jazīreh-ye i. Iran 84 D5
Sirsa India 78 C3
Sir Sandford, Mount Canada 116 G5
Sirsi Karnataka India 80 B3
Sirsi Madhya Pradesh India 78 D4
Sirsi Uttar Pradesh India 78 D3
Sirsilla India 80 C2
Sirte Libya 93 E1
Sirte, Gulf of Libya 93 E1
Sir Thomas, Mount hill Australia 105 E6
Siruguppa India 80 C3
Sirur India 80 B2
Şirvan Turkey 87 F3
Sirvel India 80 C3
Širvintai Lith. see Širvintos
Širvintos Lith. 41 N9
Sīrwān r. Iraq 87 G4
Sir Wilfrid Laurier, Mount Canada 116 G4
Sis Turkey see Kozan
Sisak Croatia 54 G2
Sisaket Thai. 66 D4
Siscia Croatia see Sisak
Sishen S. Africa 96 F4
Sishilipu China 72 E1
Sishuang Liedao is China 73 I3
Sisian Armenia 87 G3
Sisimiut Greenland 115 M3
Sisipuk Lake Canada 117 K4
Sisŏphŏn Cambodia 67 C4
Sissano P.N.G. 65 K7
Sisseton U.S.A. 126 D2
Sistān reg. Iran 85 F4
Sīstan, Daryācheh-ye marsh Afgh./Iran 85 F4
Sisteron France 52 G4
Sisters is India 67 A5
Sit Iran 84 E5
Sitamarhi India 79 F4
Sitang China see Sinan
Sitapur India 78 E4
Siteia Greece 55 L7
Siteki Swaziland 97 J4
Sithonia pen. Greece 55 J4
Sitía Greece see Siteia
Sitidgi Lake Canada 114 E3
Sitila Moz. 97 L2
Siting China 72 E3
Sítio do Mato Brazil 141 C1
Sitka U.S.A. 116 C3
Sitka National Historical Park nat. park U.S.A. 116 C3
Sitra oasis Egypt see Sitrah
Sitrah oasis Egypt 86 B5
Sittang r. Myanmar 66 B3
Sittard Neth. 48 F4
Sittaung Myanmar 66 A1
Sittaung r. Myanmar see Sittang
Sittensen Germany 49 J1
Sittingbourne U.K. 45 H7
Sittoung r. Myanmar see Sittang
Sittwe Myanmar 66 A2
Situbondo Indon. 64 E8
Siumpu i. Indon. 65 G8
Siuri India 79 F5
Sivaganga India 80 C4
Sivakasi India 80 C4
Sivaki Rus. Fed. 70 B1
Sivan India see Siwan
Sivas Turkey 86 E3
Sivaslı Turkey 55 M5
Siverek Turkey 87 E3
Siverskiy Rus. Fed. 41 Q7
Sivers'kyy Donets' r. Rus. Fed./Ukr. see Severskiy Donets
Sivomaskinskiy Rus. Fed. 37 S2
Sivrice Turkey 87 E3
Sivrihisar Turkey 55 N5
Sivukile S. Africa 97 I4
Siwa Egypt see Sīwah
Sīwah Egypt 86 B5
Sīwah, Wāḥāt oasis Egypt 86 B5
Siwalik Range mts India/Nepal 78 D3
Siwan India 79 F4
Siwana India 78 C4
Siwa Oasis oasis Egypt see Sīwah, Wāḥāt
Sixian China 73 H1
Sixmilecross U.K. 47 E3
Siyabuswa S. Africa 97 I3
Siyäzän Azer. 87 H2
Sīyunī Iran 84 D3
Sizhan China 70 B2
Siziwang Qi China see Ulan Hua
Sjælland i. Denmark see Zealand
Sjenica Serb. and Mont. 55 I3
Sjöbo Sweden 41 H9
Sjøvegan Norway 40 J2
Skadarsko Jezero nat. park Serb. and Mont. 55 H3
Skadovs'k Ukr. 55 O1
Skaftafell nat. park Iceland 40 [inset]
Skaftárós r. mouth Iceland 40 [inset]
Skagafjörður inlet Iceland 40 [inset]
Skagen Denmark 41 G8
Skagerrak strait Denmark/Norway 41 F8
Skagit r. U.S.A. 122 C2
Skagway U.S.A. 149 A3
Skaidi Norway 40 N1
Skaland Norway 40 J2
Skalmodal Sweden 40 I4
Skanderborg Denmark 41 F8
Skaneateles Lake U.S.A. 131 G2
Skara Sweden 41 H7
Skardarsko Jezero l. Albania/Serb. and Mont. see Scutari, Lake
Skardu Jammu and Kashmir 78 C2
Skärgårdshavets nationalpark nat. park Fin. 41 L7
Skarnes Norway 41 G6
Skarżysko-Kamienna Poland 43 R5
Skaulo Sweden 40 L3
Skawina Poland 43 Q6
Skeena r. Canada 116 D4
Skeena Mountains Canada 116 D3
Skegness U.K. 44 H5
Skellefteå Sweden 40 L4
Skellefteälven r. Sweden 40 L4
Skelleftehamn Sweden 40 L4
Skellig Rocks is Rep. of Ireland 47 B6
Skelmersdale U.K. 44 E5
Skerries Rep. of Ireland 47 F4
Ski Norway 41 G7
Skiathos i. Greece 55 J5
Skibbereen Rep. of Ireland 47 C6
Skibotn Norway 40 L2
Skiddaw hill U.K. 44 D4
Skien Norway 41 F7
Skiermûntseach Neth. see Schiermonnikoog
Skiermûntseach i. Neth. see Schiermonnikoog
Skierniewice Poland 43 R5
Skikda Alg. 54 B6
Skipsea U.K. 44 G5
Skipton Australia 108 A6
Skipton U.K. 44 E5
Skirlaugh U.K. 44 G5
Skiros i. Greece see Skyros
Skive Denmark 41 F8
Skjern Denmark 41 F9
Skjolden Norway 41 E6
Skobelev Uzbek. see Fergana
Skobeleva, Pik mt. Kyrg. 85 I2
Skodje Norway 40 E5
Skoganvarre Norway 40 N2
Skokie U.S.A. 130 B2
Skomer Island U.K. 45 B7
Skopelos i. Greece 55 J5
Skopin Rus. Fed. 39 H5
▶Skopje Macedonia 55 I4 Capital of Macedonia.
Skoplje Macedonia see Skopje
Skövde Sweden 41 H7
Skovorodino Rus. Fed. 70 A1
Skowhegan U.S.A. 131 K1
Skrunda Latvia 41 M8
Skukum, Mount Canada 116 C2
Skukuza S. Africa 97 J3
Skull Valley U.S.A. 125 G4
Skuodas Lith. 41 L8
Skurup Sweden 41 H9
Skutskär Sweden 41 J6
Skvyra Ukr. 39 F6
Skye i. U.K. 46 C3
Skylge i. Neth. see Terschelling
Skyring, Seno b. Chile 140 B8
Skyros Greece 55 K5
Skyros i. Greece 55 K5
Skytrain Ice Rise Antarctica 148 L1
Slættaratindur hill Faroe Is 40 [inset]
Slagelse Denmark 41 G9
Slagnäs Sweden 40 K4
Slane Rep. of Ireland 47 F4
Slaney r. Rep. of Ireland 47 F5
Slantsy Rus. Fed. 41 P7
Slapovi Krke nat. park Croatia 54 F3
Slashers Reefs Australia 106 D3
Slatina Croatia 54 G2
Slatina Romania 55 K2
Slaty Fork U.S.A. 130 E4
Slava Rus. Fed. 70 C1
Slave r. Canada 117 H2
Slave Coast Africa 92 D4
Slave Lake Canada 116 H4
Slave Point Canada 116 H2
Slavgorod Belarus see Slawharad
Slavgorod Rus. Fed. 68 D2
Slavkovichi Rus. Fed. 41 P8
Slavonska Požega Croatia see Požega
Slavonski Brod Croatia 54 H2
Slavuta Ukr. 39 E6
Slavutych Ukr. 39 F6
Slavyanka Rus. Fed. 70 C4
Slavyansk Ukr. see Slov"yans'k
Slavyanskaya Rus. Fed. see Slavyansk-na-Kubani
Slavyansk-na-Kubani Rus. Fed. 86 E1
Slawharad Belarus 39 F5
Sławno Poland 43 P3
Slayton U.S.A. 126 E3
Sleaford U.K. 45 G5
Slea Head hd Rep. of Ireland 47 B5
Sleat Neth. see Sloten
Sleat, Sound of sea chan. U.K. 46 D3
Sled Lake Canada 117 J4
Sleeper Islands Canada 118 F2
Sleeping Bear Dunes National Lakeshore nature res. U.S.A. 130 B1
Slessor Glacier Antarctica 148 B1
Slick Rock U.S.A. 125 I2
Slide Mountain U.S.A. 131 H3
Slieve Bloom Mts hills Rep. of Ireland 47 E5
Slieve Car hill Rep. of Ireland 47 C3
Slieve Donard hill U.K. 47 G3
Slieve Gamph hills Rep. of Ireland 47 C4
Slievekimalta hill Rep. of Ireland 47 D5
Slieve Mish Mts hills Rep. of Ireland 47 B5
Slieve Snaght hill Rep. of Ireland 47 E2
Sligachan U.K. 46 C3
Sligeach Rep. of Ireland see Sligo
Sligo Rep. of Ireland 47 D3
Sligo U.S.A. 130 F3
Sligo Bay Rep. of Ireland 47 D3
Slinger U.S.A. 130 A2
Slippery Rock U.S.A. 130 E3
Slite Sweden 41 K8
Sliven Bulg. 55 L3
Sloan U.S.A. 125 F4
Sloat U.S.A. 124 C2
Sloboda Rus. Fed. see Ezhva
Slobodchikovo Rus. Fed. 38 K3
Slobodskoy Rus. Fed. 38 K4
Slobozia Romania 55 L2
Slochteren Neth. 48 G1
Slonim Belarus 41 N10
Slootdorp Neth. 48 E2
Sloten Neth. 48 F2
Slough U.K. 45 G7
▶Slovakia country Europe 36 J6 europe 5, 34–35
▶Slovenia country Europe 54 F2 europe 5, 34–35
Slovenija country Europe see Slovenia
Slovenj Gradec Slovenia 54 F1
Slovensko country Europe see Slovakia
Slovenský raj nat. park Slovakia 43 R6
Slov"yans'k Ukr. 39 H6
Słowiński Park Narodowy nat. park Poland 43 P3
Sluch r. Ukr. 39 E6
Słupsk Poland 43 P3
Slussfors Sweden 40 J4
Slutsk Belarus 41 O10
Slyne Head hd Rep. of Ireland 47 B4
Slyudyanka Rus. Fed. 68 I2
Small Point U.S.A. 131 K2
Smallwood Reservoir Canada 119 I3
Smalyavichy Belarus 41 P9
Smalyenskaya Wzvyshsha hills Belarus/Rus. Fed. see Smolensko-Moskovskaya Vozvyshennost'
Smarhon' Belarus 41 O9
Smeaton Canada 117 J4
Smederevo Serb. and Mont. 55 I2
Smederevska Palanka Serb. and Mont. 55 I2
Smela Ukr. see Smila
Smethport U.S.A. 131 F3
Smidovich Rus. Fed. 70 D2
Smila Ukr. 39 F6
Smilde Neth. 48 G2
Smiltene Latvia 41 N8
Smirnykh Rus. Fed. 70 F2
Smith Canada 116 H4
Smith Center U.S.A. 126 D4
Smithfield S. Africa 97 H6
Smithfield NC U.S.A. 128 E5
Smithfield UT U.S.A. 122 F4
Smith Glacier Antarctica 148 K1
Smith Island India 67 A4
Smith Island MD U.S.A. 131 G4
Smith Island VA U.S.A. 131 H5
Smith Mountain Lake U.S.A. 130 F5
Smith River Canada 116 E3
Smiths Falls Canada 131 G1
Smithton Australia 107 [inset]
Smithtown Australia 108 F3
Smithville OK U.S.A. 127 E5
Smithville WV U.S.A. 130 E4
Smoke Creek Desert U.S.A. 124 D1
Smoky Bay Australia 105 F8
Smoky Cape Australia 108 F3
Smoky Falls Canada 118 E4
Smoky Hill r. U.S.A. 126 C4
Smoky Hills KS U.S.A. 120 H4
Smoky Hills KS U.S.A. 126 D4
Smoky Lake Canada 117 H4
Smoky Mountains U.S.A. 122 E4
Smøla i. Norway 40 E5
Smolenka Rus. Fed. 39 K6
Smolensk Rus. Fed. 39 G5
Smolensk-Moscow Upland hills Belarus/Rus. Fed. see Smolensko-Moskovskaya Vozvyshennost'
Smolensko-Moskovskaya Vozvyshennost' hills Belarus/Rus. Fed. 39 G5
Smolevichi Belarus see Smalyavichy
Smolyan Bulg. 55 K4
Smooth Rock Falls Canada 118 E4
Smoothrock Lake Canada 118 C4
Smoothstone Lake Canada 117 J4
Smørfjord Norway 40 N1
Smorgon' Belarus see Smarhon'
Smyley Island Antarctica 148 L2
Smyrna Turkey see İzmir
Smyrna U.S.A. 131 H4
Smyth Island atoll Marshall Is see Taongi
Snæfell mt. Iceland 40 [inset]
Snaefell hill Isle of Man 44 C4
Snag Canada 116 A2
Snake r. Canada 116 C1
Snake r. U.S.A. 122 D3
Snake Island Australia 108 C7
Snake Range mts U.S.A. 125 F2
Snake River Canada 116 F3
Snake River Plain U.S.A. 122 E4
Snare r. Canada 116 G2
Snare Lake Canada 117 J3
Snare Lakes Canada see Wekweti
Snares Islands N.Z. 103 G6
Snåsa Norway 40 H4
Sneedville U.S.A. 130 D5
Sneek Neth. 48 F1
Sneem Rep. of Ireland 47 C6
Sneeuberge mts S. Africa 96 G6
Snegamook Lake Canada 119 J3
Snegurovka Ukr. see Tetiyiv
Snelling U.S.A. 124 C3
Snettisham U.K. 45 H6
Snezhnogorsk Rus. Fed. 60 J3
Snežnik mt. Slovenia 54 F2
Sniečkus Lith. see Visaginas
Snihurivka Ukr. 39 G7
Snits Neth. see Sneek
Snizort, Loch b. U.K. 46 C3
Snoqualmie Pass U.S.A. 122 C3
Snøtinden mt. Norway 40 H3
Snoul Cambodia see Snuŏl
Snover U.S.A. 130 D2
Snovsk Ukr. see Shchors
Snowbird Lake Canada 117 K2
Snowcrest Mountain Canada 116 G5
Snowdon mt. U.K. 45 C5
Snowdonia National Park U.K. 45 D6
Snowdrift Canada see Łutselk'e
Snowdrift r. Canada 117 I2
Snowflake U.S.A. 125 H4
Snow Hill U.S.A. 131 H4
Snow Lake Canada 117 K4
Snowville U.S.A. 122 E4
Snow Water Lake U.S.A. 125 F1
Snowy r. Australia 108 D6
Snowy Mountain U.S.A. 131 H2
Snowy Mountains Australia 108 C6
Snowy River National Park Australia 108 D6
Snug Corner Bahamas 129 F8
Snug Harbour Nfld. and Lab. Canada 119 L3
Snug Harbour Ont. Canada 130 E1
Snuŏl Cambodia 67 D4
Snyder U.S.A. 127 C5
Soalala Madag. 95 E5
Soalara Madag. 95 E6
Soanierana-Ivongo Madag. 95 E5
Soan-kundo is S. Korea 71 B6
Soavinandriana Madag. 95 E5
Sobat r. Sudan 82 D8
Sobernheim Germany 49 H5
Sobger r. Indon. 65 K7
Sobinka Rus. Fed. 38 I5
Sobradinho, Barragem de resr Brazil 139 J6
Sobral Brazil 139 J4
Sochi Rus. Fed. 87 E2
Sŏch'ŏn S. Korea 71 B5
Society Islands Fr. Polynesia 147 J7
Socorro Brazil 141 B3
Socorro Col. 138 D2
Socorro U.S.A. 123 G6
Socorro, Isla i. Mex. 132 B5
Socotra i. Yemen 83 H7
Soc Trăng Vietnam 67 D5
Socuéllamos Spain 53 E4
Soda Lake CA U.S.A. 124 D4
Soda Lake CA U.S.A. 124 E4
Sodankylä Fin. 40 O3
Soda Plains Aksai Chin 78 D2
Soda Springs U.S.A. 122 F4
Söderhamn Sweden 41 J6
Söderköping Sweden 41 J7
Södertälje Sweden 41 J7
Sodiri Sudan 82 C7
Sodo Eth. 94 D3
Södra Kvarken strait Fin./Sweden 41 K6
Sodus U.S.A. 131 G2
Soë Indon. 65 G8
Soekarno, Puntjak mt. Indon. see Jaya, Puncak
Soekmekaar S. Africa 97 I2
Soerabaia Indon. see Surabaya
Soerendonk Neth. 48 F3
Soest Germany 49 I3
Soest Neth. 48 F2
Sofala Australia 108 D4
▶Sofia Bulg. 55 J3 Capital of Bulgaria.
Sofiya Bulg. see Sofia
Sofiyevka Ukr. see Vil'nyans'k
Sofiysk Khabarovskiy Kray Rus. Fed. 70 D1
Sofiysk Khabarovskiy Kray Rus. Fed. 70 E2
Sofporog Rus. Fed. 40 Q4
Softa Kalesi tourist site Turkey 81 A1
Sōfu-gan i. Japan 71 F7
Sog China 72 B2
Soğanlı Dağları mts Turkey 87 E2
Sogda Rus. Fed. 70 D2
Sögel Germany 49 H2
Sogma China 78 E2
Søgne Norway 41 E7
Sognefjorden inlet Norway 41 D6
Sogruma China 72 D1
Söğüt Turkey 55 N4
Söğüt Dağı mts Turkey 55 M6
Soh Iran 84 C3
Sohâg Egypt see Sawhāj
Sohagpur India 78 D5
Soham U.K. 45 H6
Sohan r. Pak. 85 H3
Sohano P.N.G. 102 F2
Sohar Oman see Şuḥār
Sohawal India 78 E4
Sohela India 79 E5
Sohng Gwe, Khao hill Myanmar/Thai. 67 B4
Sŏho-ri N. Korea 71 C4
Sohŭksan-do i. S. Korea 71 B6
Soignies Belgium 48 E4
Soila China 72 C2
Soini Fin. 40 N5
Soissons France 48 D5
Sojat India 78 C4
Sojat Road India 78 C4
Sok r. Rus. Fed. 39 K5
Sokal' Ukr. 39 E6
Sokch'o S. Korea 71 C5
Söke Turkey 55 L6
Sokh Tajik. 85 H2
Sokhor, Gora mt. Rus. Fed. 68 J2
Sokhumi Georgia 87 F2
Sokiryany Ukr. see Sokyryany
Sokodé Togo 92 D4
Soko Islands Hong Kong China 73 [inset]
Sokol Rus. Fed. 38 I4
Sokolo Mali 92 C3
Sokolov Czech Rep. 49 M4
Sokoto Nigeria 92 D3
Sokoto r. Nigeria 92 D3
Sokyryany Ukr. 39 E6
Sola Cuba 129 E8
Sola i. Tonga see Ata
Solan India 78 D3
Solana Beach U.S.A. 124 E5
Solander Island N.Z. 109 A8
Solapur India 80 B2
Soldotna U.S.A. 114 C3
Soledad U.S.A. 124 C3
Soledade Brazil 140 F3
Solenoye Rus. Fed. 39 I7
Solfjellsjøen Norway 40 H3
Solginskiy Rus. Fed. 38 I3
Solhan Turkey 87 F3
Soligalich Rus. Fed. 38 I4
Soligorsk Belarus see Salihorsk
Solihull U.K. 45 F6
Solikamsk Rus. Fed. 37 R4
Sol'-Iletsk Rus. Fed. 60 G4
Solimões r. S. America see Amazon
Solingen Germany 48 H3
Solitaire Namibia 96 B2
Sol-Karmala Rus. Fed. see Severnoye
Şollar Azer. 87 H2
Sollefteå Sweden 40 J5
Söllichau Germany 49 M3
Solling hills Germany 49 J3
Sollstedt Germany 49 K3
Sollum, Gulf of Egypt see Sallum, Khalīj as
Solms Germany 49 I4
Solnechnogorsk Rus. Fed. 38 H4
Solnechnyy Amurskaya Oblast' Rus. Fed. 70 A1
Solnechnyy Khabarovskiy Kray Rus. Fed. 70 E2
Solok Indon. 64 C7
Solomon U.S.A. 125 I5
Solomon, North Fork r. U.S.A. 126 D4
▶Solomon Islands country S. Pacific Ocean 103 G2 4th largest and 5th most populous country in Oceania. oceania 8, 100–101
Solomon Sea S. Pacific Ocean 102 F2
Solon U.S.A. 131 K1
Solon Springs U.S.A. 126 F2
Solor i. Indon. 104 C2
Solor, Kepulauan is Indon. 104 C2
Solothurn Switz. 52 H3
Solovetskiye Ostrova is Rus. Fed. 38 G2
Solov'yevsk Rus. Fed. 70 B1
Šolta i. Croatia 54 G3
Solṭānābād Kermān Iran 84 E4
Solṭānābād Khorāsān Iran 85 E3
Solṭānābād Iran 84 C3
Solṭānīyeh Iran 84 C2
Soltau Germany 49 J2
Sol'tsy Rus. Fed. 38 F4
Solvay U.S.A. 131 G2
Sölvesborg Sweden 41 I8
Solway Firth est. U.K. 46 F6
Solwezi Zambia 95 C5
Soma Turkey 55 L5
Somain France 48 D4
▶Somalia country Africa 94 E3 africa 7, 90–91
Somali Basin sea feature Indian Ocean 145 L6
Somali Republic country Africa see Somalia
Sombo Angola 95 C4
Sombor Serb. and Mont. 55 H2
Sombrero Channel India 67 A6
Sombrio, Lago do l. Brazil 141 A5
Somero Fin. 41 M6
Somerset KY U.S.A. 130 C5
Somerset MI U.S.A. 130 C2
Somerset OH U.S.A. 130 D4
Somerset PA U.S.A. 130 F4
Somerset, Lake Australia 108 F1
Somerset East S. Africa 97 G7
Somerset Island Canada 115 I2
Somerset Reservoir U.S.A. 131 I2
Somerset West S. Africa 96 D8
Somersworth U.S.A. 131 J2
Somerton U.S.A. 125 F5
Somerville NJ U.S.A. 131 H3
Somerville TN U.S.A. 127 F5
Someydeh Iran 84 B3
Somme r. France 48 B4
Sommen l. Sweden 41 I7
Sömmerda Germany 49 L3
Sommet, Lac du l. Canada 119 H3
Somnath India 78 B5
Somutu Myanmar 66 B1
Son r. India 79 F4
Sonag China see Zêkog
Sonapur India 80 D1
Sonar r. India 78 D4
Sŏnch'ŏn N. Korea 71 B5
Sønderborg Denmark 41 F9
Sondershausen Germany 49 K3
Søndre Strømfjord Greenland see Kangerlussuaq
Søndre Strømfjord inlet Greenland see Kangerlussuaq
Sondrio Italy 54 C1
Sonepat India see Sonipat
Sonepur India see Sonapur
Songbai China see Shennongjia
Songbu China 73 G2
Sông Cau Vietnam 67 E4
Songcheng China see Xiapu
Sông Da, Hô resr Vietnam 66 D2
Songea Tanz. 95 D5
Songhua Hu resr China 70 B4
Songhua Jiang r. Heilongjiang/Jilin China 70 D3
Songhua Jiang r. Jilin China see Di'er Songhua Jiang
Songjiang China 73 I2
Songjianghe China 70 B4
Sŏngjin N. Korea see Kimch'aek
Songkan China 72 E2
Songkhla Thai. 67 C6
Songling China see Ta'erqi
Songlong Myanmar 66 B2
Sŏngnam S. Korea 71 B5
Songnim N. Korea 71 B5
Songo Angola 95 B4
Songo Moz. 95 D5
Songpan China 72 D1
Songshan China see Ziyun
Song Shan mt. China 73 G1
Songtao China 73 F2
Songxi China 73 H3
Songxian China 73 G1
Songyuan Fujian China see Songxi
Songyuan Jilin China 70 B3
Songzi China 73 F2
Sonid Youqi China see Saihan Tal
Sonid Zuoqi China see Mandalt
Sonipat India 78 D3
Sonkajärvi Fin. 40 O5
Sonkovo Rus. Fed. 38 H4
Sơn La Vietnam 66 C2
Sonmiani Pak. 85 G5
Sonmiani Bay Pak. 85 G5
Sonneberg Germany 49 L4
Sono r. Minas Gerais Brazil 141 B2
Sono r. Tocantins Brazil 139 I5
Sonoma U.S.A. 124 B2
Sonoma Peak U.S.A. 124 E1
Sonora r. Mex. 123 F7
Sonora state Mex. 123 F7
Sonora CA U.S.A. 124 C3
Sonora KY U.S.A. 130 C5
Sonora TX U.S.A. 127 C6
Sonoran Desert U.S.A. 125 G5
Sonoran Desert National Monument nat. park U.S.A. 123 E6
Sonqor Iran 84 B3
Sonsonate El Salvador 132 G6
Sonsorol Islands Palau 65 I5
Sơn Tây Vietnam 66 D2
Sonwabile S. Africa 97 I6
Soochow China see Suzhou
Soomaaliya country Africa see Somalia
Sopi, Tanjung pt Indon. 65 H6
Sopo watercourse Sudan 93 F4
Sopot Bulg. 55 K3
Sopot Poland 43 Q3
Sop Prap Thai. 66 B3
Sopron Hungary 54 G1
Sopur Jammu and Kashmir 78 C2
Sora Italy 54 E4
Sorab India 80 B3
Sorada India 80 E2
Söråker Sweden 40 J5
Sŏrak-san mt. S. Korea 71 C5
Sorak-san National Park S. Korea 71 C5
Sorel Canada 119 G5
Soreq r. Israel 81 B4
Sorgun Turkey 86 D3
Sorgun r. Turkey 81 B1
Soria Spain 53 E3
Sorkh, Kūh-e mts Iran 84 D3
Sorkhān Iran 84 E4
Sorkheh Iran 84 D3
Sørli Norway 40 H4
Soro India 79 F5
Soroca Moldova 39 F6

Sorocaba Brazil 141 B3
Soroki Moldova see Soroca
Sorol atoll Micronesia 65 K5
Sorong Indon. 65 I7
Soroti Uganda 94 D3
Sørøya i. Norway 40 M1
Sorraia r. Port. 53 B4
Sørreisa Norway 40 K2
Sorrento Italy 54 F4
Sorsele Sweden 40 J4
Sorsogon Phil. 65 G4
Sortavala Rus. Fed. 40 Q6
Sortland Norway 40 I2
Sortopolovskaya Rus. Fed. 38 K3
Sorvizhi Rus. Fed. 38 K4
Sŏsan S. Korea 71 B5
Sosenskiy Rus. Fed. 39 G5
Soshanguve S. Africa 97 I3
Sosna r. Rus. Fed. 39 H5
Sosneado mt. Arg. 140 C4
Sosnogorsk Rus. Fed. 38 L3
Sosnovka Arkhangel'skaya Oblast' Rus. Fed. 38 J3
Sosnovka Kaliningradskaya Oblast' Rus. Fed. 37 K5
Sosnovka Murmanskaya Oblast' Rus. Fed. 38 I2
Sosnovka Tambovskaya Oblast' Rus. Fed. 39 I5
Sosnovo Rus. Fed. 41 Q6
Sosnovo-Ozerskoye Rus. Fed. 69 K2
Sosnovyy Rus. Fed. 40 R4
Sosnovyy Bor Rus. Fed. 41 P7
Sosnowiec Poland 43 Q5
Sosnowitz Poland see Sosnowiec
Sos'va Khanty-Mansiyskiy Avtonomnyy Okrug Rus. Fed. 37 S3
Sos'va Sverdlovskaya Oblast' Rus. Fed. 37 S4
Sotang China 72 B2
Sotara, Volcán vol. Col. 138 C3
Sotkamo Fin. 40 P4
Sotteville-lès-Rouen France 48 B5
Souanké Congo 94 B3
Soubré Côte d'Ivoire 92 C4
Souderton U.S.A. 131 H3
Soufflenheim France 49 H6
Soufli Greece 55 L4
Soufrière St Lucia 133 L6
Soufrière vol. St Vincent 133 L6
Sougueur Alg. 53 G6
Souillac France 52 E4
Souilly France 48 F5
Souk Ahras Alg. 54 B6
Souk el Arbaâ du Rharb Morocco 50 C5
Sŏul S. Korea see Seoul
Soulac-sur-Mer France 52 D4
Soulom France 52 D5
Sounding Creek r. Canada 117 I4
Souni Cyprus 81 A2
Soûr Lebanon see Tyre
Soure Brazil 139 I4
Sour el Ghozlane Alg. 53 H5
Souris Canada 117 K5
Souris r. Canada 117 L5
Souriya country Asia see Syria
Sousa Brazil 139 K5
Sousa Lara Angola see Bocoio
Sousse Tunisia 54 D7
Soustons France 52 D5

▶South Africa, Republic of country Africa 96 F5
5th most populous country in Africa.
africa 7, 90–91

Southampton Canada 130 E1
Southampton U.K. 45 F8
Southampton U.S.A. 131 I3
Southampton, Cape Canada 115 J3
Southampton Island Canada 115 J3
South Andaman i. India 67 A5
South Anna r. U.S.A. 131 G5
South Anston U.K. 44 F5
South Aulatsivik Island Canada 119 J2
South Australia state Australia 102 D5
South Australian Basin sea feature Indian Ocean 145 P8
Southaven U.S.A. 127 F5
South Baldy mt. U.S.A. 123 G6
South Bank U.K. 44 F4
South Bass Island U.S.A. 130 D3
South Bend IN U.S.A. 130 B3
South Bend WA U.S.A. 122 C3
South Bluff pt Bahamas 129 F8
South Boston U.S.A. 131 F5
South Brook Canada 119 K4
South Cape pt U.S.A. see Ka Lae
South Carolina state U.S.A. 129 D5
South Charleston OH U.S.A. 130 D4
South Charleston WV U.S.A. 130 E4
South China Sea N. Pacific Ocean 64 F4
South Coast Town Australia see Gold Coast
South Dakota state U.S.A. 126 C2
South Downs hills U.K. 45 G8
South-East admin. dist. Botswana 97 G3
South East Cape Australia 107 [inset]
Southeast Cape U.S.A. 114 B3
Southeast Indian Ridge sea feature Indian Ocean 145 N8
South East Isles Australia 105 C8
Southeast Pacific Basin sea feature S. Pacific Ocean 147 M10
South East Point Australia 108 C7
Southend Canada 117 K3
Southend U.K. 46 D5
Southend-on-Sea U.K. 45 H7
Southern admin. dist. Botswana 96 G3
Southern Alps mts N.Z. 109 C6
Southern Cross Australia 105 B7
Southern Indian Lake Canada 117 L3
Southern Lau Group is Fiji 103 I3
Southern National Park Sudan 93 F4
Southern Ocean 148 C2
Southern Pines U.S.A. 129 E5
Southern Rhodesia country Africa see Zimbabwe
Southern Uplands hills U.K. 46 E5
South Esk r. U.K. 46 F4
South Esk Tableland reg. Australia 104 D4
Southey Canada 117 J5
Southfield U.S.A. 130 D2
South Fiji Basin sea feature S. Pacific Ocean 146 H7
South Fork U.S.A. 124 B1
South Geomagnetic Pole Antarctica 148 F1
South Georgia i. S. Atlantic Ocean 140 I8

▶South Georgia and South Sandwich Islands terr. S. Atlantic Ocean 140 I8
United Kingdom Overseas Territory.

South Harris pen. U.K. 46 B3
South Haven U.S.A. 130 B2
South Henik Lake Canada 117 L2
South Hill U.S.A. 131 F5
South Honshu Ridge sea feature N. Pacific Ocean 146 F3
South Indian Lake Canada 117 L3
South Island India 80 B4

▶South Island N.Z. 109 D7
2nd largest island in Oceania.

South Junction Canada 117 M5
▶South Korea country Asia 71 B5
asia 6, 58–59
South Lake Tahoe U.S.A. 124 C2
South Luangwa National Park Zambia 95 D5
South Magnetic Pole Antarctica 148 G2
South Mills U.S.A. 131 G5
Southminster U.K. 45 H7
South Mountains hills U.S.A. 131 G4
South New Berlin U.S.A. 131 H2
South Orkney Islands S. Atlantic Ocean 144 F10
South Paris U.S.A. 131 J1
South Platte r. U.S.A. 126 C3
South Point Bahamas 129 F8
South Pole Antarctica 148 C1
Southport Qld Australia 108 F1
Southport Tas. Australia 107 [inset]
Southport U.K. 44 D5
Southport U.S.A. 131 G2
South Portland U.S.A. 131 J2
South Ronaldsay i. U.K. 46 G2
South Royalton U.S.A. 131 I2
South Salt Lake U.S.A. 125 H1
South Sand Bluff pt S. Africa 97 J6
South Sandwich Islands S. Atlantic Ocean 144 G9
South Sandwich Trench sea feature S. Atlantic Ocean 144 G9
South San Francisco U.S.A. 124 B3
South Saskatchewan r. Canada 117 J4
South Seal r. Canada 117 L3
South Shetland Islands Antarctica 148 A2
South Shetland Trough sea feature S. Atlantic Ocean 148 L2
South Shields U.K. 44 F3
South Sinai governorate Egypt see Janūb Sīnā'
South Solomon Trench sea feature S. Pacific Ocean 146 G6
South Taranaki Bight b. N.Z. 109 E4
South Tasman Rise sea feature Southern Ocean 146 F9
South Tent mt. U.S.A. 125 H2
South Tons r. India 79 E4
South Twin Island Canada 118 F3
South Tyne r. U.K. 44 E4
South Uist i. U.K. 46 B3
South Wellesley Islands Australia 106 B3
South-West Africa country Africa see Namibia
South West Cape N.Z. 109 A8
South West Entrance sea chan. P.N.G. 106 E1
Southwest Indian Ridge sea feature Indian Ocean 145 K8
South West National Park Australia 107 [inset]
Southwest Pacific Basin sea feature S. Pacific Ocean 146 I8
Southwest Peru Ridge sea feature S. Pacific Ocean see Nazca Ridge
South West Rocks Australia 108 F3
South Whitley U.S.A. 130 C3
South Wichita r. U.S.A. 127 D5
South Windham U.S.A. 131 J2
Southwold U.K. 45 I6
Southwood National Park Australia 108 E1
Soutpansberg mts S. Africa 97 I2
Souttouf, Adrar mts W. Sahara 92 B2
Soverato Italy 54 G5
Sovetsk Kaliningradskaya Oblast' Rus. Fed. 41 L9
Sovetsk Kirovskaya Oblast' Rus. Fed. 38 K4
Sovetskaya Gavan' Rus. Fed. 70 F2
Sovetskiy Khanty-Mansiyskiy Avtonomnyy Okrug Rus. Fed. 37 S3
Sovetskiy Leningradskaya Oblast' Rus. Fed. 41 P6
Sovetskiy Respublika Mariy El Rus. Fed. 38 K4
Sovetskoye Chechenskaya Respublika Rus. Fed. see Shatoy
Sovetskoye Stavropol'skiy Kray Rus. Fed. see Zelenokumsk
Sovyets'kyy Ukr. 86 D1
Sowa China 72 C2
Soweto S. Africa 97 H4
Sōya-kaikyō strait Japan/Rus. Fed. see La Pérouse Strait
Sōya-misaki c. Japan 70 F3
Soyana r. Rus. Fed. 38 I2
Soyma r. Rus. Fed. 38 K2
Soyopa Mex. 123 F7
Sozh r. Europe 39 F6
Sozopol Bulg. 55 L3
Spa Belgium 48 F4

▶Spain country Europe 53 E3
4th largest country in Europe.
europe 5, 34–35

Spalato Croatia see Split
Spalatum Croatia see Split
Spalding U.K. 45 G6
Spanish Canada 118 E5
Spanish Fork U.S.A. 125 H1
Spanish Guinea country Africa see Equatorial Guinea
Spanish Netherlands country Europe see Belgium
Spanish Sahara terr. Africa see Western Sahara
Spanish Town Jamaica 133 I5
Sparks U.S.A. 124 D2
Sparta Greece see Sparti
Sparta GA U.S.A. 129 D5
Sparta KY U.S.A. 130 C4
Sparta MI U.S.A. 130 C2
Sparta NC U.S.A. 130 E5
Sparta TN U.S.A. 128 C5
Spartanburg U.S.A. 129 D5
Sparti Greece 55 J6
Spartivento, Capo c. Italy 54 G6
Spas-Demensk Rus. Fed. 39 G5
Spas-Klepiki Rus. Fed. 39 I5
Spassk-Dal'niy Rus. Fed. 70 D3
Spassk-Ryazanskiy Rus. Fed. 39 I5
Spata (Eleftherios Venezelos) airport Greece 55 J6
Spatha, Akra pt Greece 55 J7
Spearman U.S.A. 127 C4
Speedway U.S.A. 130 B4
Spence Bay Canada see Taloyoak
Spencer IA U.S.A. 126 E3
Spencer ID U.S.A. 122 E3
Spencer IN U.S.A. 130 B4
Spencer NE U.S.A. 126 D3
Spencer WV U.S.A. 130 E4
Spencer, Cape U.S.A. 116 B3
Spencer Bay Namibia 96 B3
Spencer Gulf est. Australia 107 B7
Spencer Range hills Australia 104 E3
Spennymoor U.K. 44 F4
Sperrin Mountains hills U.K. 47 E3
Sperryville U.S.A. 131 F4
Spessart reg. Germany 49 J5
Spétsai i. Greece see Spetses
Spetses i. Greece 55 J6
Spey r. U.K. 46 F3
Speyer Germany 49 I5
Spezand Pak. 85 G4
Spice Islands Indon. see Moluccas
Spijk Neth. 48 G1
Spijkenisse Neth. 48 E3
Spilimbergo Italy 54 E1
Spilsby U.K. 44 H5
Spīn Būldak Afgh. 85 G4
Spintangi Pak. 85 H4
Spirit Lake U.S.A. 126 E3
Spirit River Canada 116 G4
Spirovo Rus. Fed. 38 G4
Spišská Nová Ves Slovakia 39 D6
Spiti r. India 78 D3

▶Spitsbergen i. Svalbard 60 C2
5th largest island in Europe.

Spittal an der Drau Austria 43 N7
Spitzbergen i. Svalbard see Spitsbergen
Split Croatia 54 G3
Split Lake Canada 117 L3
Split Lake l. Canada 117 L3
Spokane U.S.A. 122 D3
Spoletium Italy see Spoleto
Spoleto Italy 54 E3
Spóng Cambodia 67 D4
Spoon r. U.S.A. 126 F3
Spooner U.S.A. 126 F2
Spornitz Germany 49 L1
Spotsylvania U.S.A. 131 G4
Spotted Horse U.S.A. 122 G3
Spranger, Mount Canada 116 F4
Spratly Islands S. China Sea 64 E4
Spray U.S.A. 122 D3
Spree r. Germany 43 N4
Sprimont Belgium 48 F4
Springbok S. Africa 96 C5
Springdale Canada 119 L4
Springdale U.S.A. 130 C4
Springe Germany 49 J2
Springer U.S.A. 123 G5
Springerville U.S.A. 125 I4
Springfield CO U.S.A. 126 C4

▶Springfield IL U.S.A. 126 F4
State capital of Illinois.

Springfield KY U.S.A. 130 C5
Springfield MA U.S.A. 131 I2
Springfield MO U.S.A. 127 E4
Springfield OH U.S.A. 130 D4
Springfield OR U.S.A. 122 C3
Springfield TN U.S.A. 130 B5
Springfield VT U.S.A. 131 I2
Springfield WV U.S.A. 131 F4
Springfontein S. Africa 97 G6
Spring Glen U.S.A. 125 H2
Spring Grove U.S.A. 130 A2
Springhill Canada 119 I5
Spring Hill U.S.A. 129 D6
Springhouse Canada 116 F5
Spring Mountains U.S.A. 125 F3
Springs Junction N.Z. 109 D6
Springsure Australia 106 E5
Spring Valley MN U.S.A. 126 E3
Spring Valley NY U.S.A. 131 H3
Springview U.S.A. 126 D3
Springville CA U.S.A. 124 D3
Springville NY U.S.A. 131 F2
Springville PA U.S.A. 131 H3
Springville UT U.S.A. 125 H1
Sprowston U.K. 45 I6
Spruce Grove Canada 116 H4
Spruce Knob mt. U.S.A. 128 E4
Spruce Mountain CO U.S.A. 125 I2
Spruce Mountain NV U.S.A. 125 F1
Spurn Head hd U.K. 44 H5
Spuzzum Canada 116 F5
Squam Lake U.S.A. 131 J2
Square Lake U.S.A. 119 H5
Squillace, Golfo di g. Italy 54 G5
Squires, Mount hill Australia 105 D6
Srbija aut. rep. Serb. and Mont. 55 I3
Srbinje Bos.-Herz. see Foča
Srê Âmbĕl Cambodia 67 C5
Sredets Burgas Bulg. 55 L3
Sredets Sofiya-Grad Bulg. see Sofia
Sredinnyy Khrebet mts Rus. Fed. 61 Q4
Sredna Gora mts Bulg. 55 J3
Srednekolymsk Rus. Fed. 61 Q3
Sredne-Russkaya Vozvyshennost' hills Rus. Fed. see Central Russian Upland
Sredne-Sibirskoye Ploskogor'ye plat. Rus. Fed. see Central Siberian Plateau
Sredneye Kuyto, Ozero l. Rus. Fed. 40 Q4
Sredniy Ural mts Rus. Fed. 37 R4
Srednogorie Bulg. 55 K3
Srednyaya Akhtuba Rus. Fed. 39 J6
Sreepur Bangl. see Sripur
Sre Khtum Cambodia 67 D4
Srê Noy Cambodia 67 D4
Sretensk Rus. Fed. 69 L2
Sri Aman Sarawak Malaysia 64 E6
Sriharikota Island India 80 D3

▶Sri Jayewardenepura Kotte Sri Lanka 80 C5
Capital of Sri Lanka.

Srikakulam India 80 E2
Sri Kalahasti India 80 C3

▶Sri Lanka country Asia 80 D5
asia 6, 58–59
Srinagar India 78 C2
Sri Pada mt. Sri Lanka see Adam's Peak
Sripur Bangl. 79 G4
Srirangam India 80 C4
Sri Thep tourist site Thai. 66 C3
Srivardhan India 80 B2
Staaten r. Australia 106 C3
Staaten River National Park Australia 106 C3
Stabroek Guyana see Georgetown
Stade Germany 49 J1
Staden Belgium 48 D4
Stadskanaal Neth. 48 G2
Stadtallendorf Germany 49 J4
Stadthagen Germany 49 J2
Stadtilm Germany 49 L4
Stadtlohn Germany 48 G3
Stadtoldendorf Germany 49 J3
Stadtroda Germany 49 L4
Staffa i. U.K. 46 C4
Staffelberg hill Germany 49 L4
Staffelstein Germany 49 K4
Stafford U.K. 45 E6
Stafford U.S.A. 131 G4
Stafford Creek Bahamas 129 E7
Stafford Springs U.S.A. 131 I3
Stagg Lake Canada 116 H2
Staicele Latvia 41 N8
Staines U.K. 45 G7
Stakhanov Ukr. 39 H6
Stakhanovo Rus. Fed. see Zhukovskiy
Stalbridge U.K. 45 E8
Stalham U.K. 45 I6
Stalin Bulg. see Varna
Stalinabad Tajik. see Dushanbe
Stalingrad Rus. Fed. see Volgograd
Staliniri Georgia see Ts'khinvali
Stalino Ukr. see Donets'k
Stalinogorsk Rus. Fed. see Novomoskovsk
Stalinogród Poland see Katowice
Stalinsk Rus. Fed. see Novokuznetsk
Stalowa Wola Poland 39 D6
Stamboliyski Bulg. 55 K3
Stamford Australia 106 C4
Stamford U.K. 45 G6
Stamford CT U.S.A. 131 I3
Stamford NY U.S.A. 131 H2
Stampalia i. Greece see Astypalaia
Stampriet Namibia 96 D3
Stamsund Norway 40 H2
Stanardsville U.S.A. 131 F4
Stanberry U.S.A. 126 E3
Stancomb-Wills Glacier Antarctica 148 B1
Standard Canada 116 H5
Standdaarbuiten Neth. 48 E3
Standerton S. Africa 97 I4
Standish U.S.A. 130 D2
Stanfield U.S.A. 125 H5
Stanford KY U.S.A. 130 C5
Stanford MT U.S.A. 122 F3
Stanger S. Africa 97 J5
Stanislaus r. U.S.A. 124 C3
Stanislav Ukr. see Ivano-Frankivs'k
Stanke Dimitrov Bulg. see Dupnitsa
Staňkov Czech Rep. 49 N5
Stanley Australia 107 [inset]
Stanley Hong Kong China 73 [inset]

▶Stanley Falkland Is 140 E8
Capital of the Falkland Islands.

Stanley U.K. 44 F4
Stanley ID U.S.A. 122 E3
Stanley KY U.S.A. 130 B5
Stanley ND U.S.A. 126 C1
Stanley VA U.S.A. 131 F4
Stanley, Mount hill N.T. Australia 104 E5
Stanley, Mount hill Tas. Australia 107 [inset]
Stanley, Mount Dem. Rep. Congo/Uganda see Margherita Peak
Stanleyville Dem. Rep. Congo see Kisangani
Stann Creek Belize see Dangriga
Stannington U.K. 44 F3
Stanovoye Rus. Fed. 39 H5
Stanovoye Nagor'ye mts Rus. Fed. 69 L1
Stanovoy Khrebet mts Rus. Fed. 61 N4
Stansmore Range hills Australia 104 E5
Stanthorpe Australia 108 E2
Stanton U.K. 45 H6
Stanton KY U.S.A. 130 D5
Stanton MI U.S.A. 130 C2
Stanton ND U.S.A. 126 C2
Stanton TX U.S.A. 127 C5
Stapleton U.S.A. 126 C3
Starachowice Poland 43 R5
Stara Planina mts Bulg./Serb. and Mont. see Balkan Mountains
Staraya Russa Rus. Fed. 38 F4
Stara Zagora Bulg. 55 K3
Starbuck Island Kiribati 147 J6
Star City U.S.A. 130 B3
Starcke National Park Australia 106 D2
Stargard in Pommern Poland see Stargard Szczeciński
Stargard Szczeciński Poland 43 O4
Staritsa Rus. Fed. 38 G4
Starke U.S.A. 129 D6
Starkville U.S.A. 127 F5
Star Lake U.S.A. 131 H1
Starnberger See l. Germany 43 M7
Starobel'sk Ukr. see Starobil's'k
Starobil's'k Ukr. 39 H6
Starogard Gdański Poland 43 Q4
Starokonstantinov Ukr. see Starokostyantyniv
Starokostyantyniv Ukr. 39 E6
Starominskaya Rus. Fed. 39 H7
Staroshcherbinovskaya Rus. Fed. 39 H7
Star Peak U.S.A. 124 D1
Start Point U.K. 45 D8
Starve Island Kiribati see Starbuck Island
Staryya Darohi Belarus 39 F5
Staryye Dorogi Belarus see Staryya Darohi
Staryy Kayak Rus. Fed. 61 L2
Staryy Oskol Rus. Fed. 39 H6
Staßfurt Germany 49 L3
State College U.S.A. 131 G3
State Line U.S.A. 127 F6
Staten Island Arg. see Los Estados, Isla de
Statenville U.S.A. 129 D6
Statesboro U.S.A. 129 D5
Statesville U.S.A. 128 D5
Statia i. Neth. Antilles see Sint Eustatius
Station U.S.A. 130 C4
Station Nord Greenland 149 I1
Stauchitz Germany 49 N3
Staufenberg Germany 49 I4
Staunton U.S.A. 130 F4
Stavanger Norway 41 D7
Staveley U.K. 44 F5
Stavropol' Rus. Fed. 87 F1
Stavropol Kray admin. div. Rus. Fed. see Stavropol'skiy Kray
Stavropol'-na-Volge Rus. Fed. see Tol'yatti
Stavropol'skaya Vozvyshennost' hills Rus. Fed. 87 F1
Stavropol'skiy Kray admin. div. Rus. Fed. 87 F1
Stayner Canada 130 E1
Stayton U.S.A. 122 C3
Steadville S. Africa 97 I5
Steamboat Springs U.S.A. 122 G4
Stearns U.S.A. 130 C5
Stebbins U.S.A. 114 B3
Steele Island Antarctica 148 L2
Steelville U.S.A. 126 F4
Steen r. Canada 116 G3
Steenderen Neth. 48 G2
Steenkampsberge mts S. Africa 97 J3
Steen River Canada 116 G3
Steens Mountain U.S.A. 122 D4
Steenstrup Gletscher glacier Greenland see Sermersuaq
Steenvoorde France 48 C4
Steenwijk Neth. 48 G2
Stefansson Island Canada 115 H2
Stegi Swaziland see Siteki
Steigerwald mts Germany 49 K5
Stein Germany 49 L5
Steinach Germany 49 L4
Steinaker Reservoir U.S.A. 125 I1
Steinbach Canada 117 L5
Steinfeld (Oldenburg) Germany 49 I2
Steinfurt Germany 49 H2
Steinhausen Namibia 95 B6
Steinheim Germany 49 J3
Steinkjer Norway 40 G4
Steinkopf S. Africa 96 C5
Steinsdalen Norway 40 G4
Stella S. Africa 96 G4
Stella Maris Bahamas 129 F8
Stellenbosch S. Africa 96 D7
Stello, Monte mt. Corsica France 52 I5
Stelvio, Parco Nazionale dello nat. park Italy 54 D1
Stenay France 48 F5
Stendal Germany 49 L2
Stenhousemuir U.K. 46 F4
Stenungsund Sweden 41 G7
Steornabhagh U.K. see Stornoway
Stepanakert Azer. see Xankändi
Stephens, Cape N.Z. 109 D5
Stephens City U.S.A. 131 F4
Stephens Lake Canada 117 M3
Stephenville U.S.A. 127 D5
Stepnoy Rus. Fed. see Elista
Stepnoye Rus. Fed. 39 J6
Sterkfontein Dam resr S. Africa 97 I5
Sterkstroom S. Africa 97 H6
Sterlet Lake Canada 117 I1
Sterlibashevo Rus. Fed. 37 R5
Sterling S. Africa 96 E6
Sterling CO U.S.A. 126 C3
Sterling IL U.S.A. 126 F3
Sterling KS U.S.A. 126 D4
Sterling MI U.S.A. 130 C1
Sterling UT U.S.A. 125 H2
Sterling City U.S.A. 127 C6
Sterling Heights U.S.A. 130 D2
Sterlitamak Rus. Fed. 60 G4
Stettin Poland see Szczecin
Stettler Canada 117 H4
Steubenville KY U.S.A. 130 C5
Steubenville OH U.S.A. 130 E3
Stevenage U.K. 45 G7
Stevenson U.S.A. 122 C3
Stevenson Lake Canada 117 L4
Stevens Point U.S.A. 126 F2
Stevens Village U.S.A. 114 D3
Stevensville MI U.S.A. 130 B2
Stevensville PA U.S.A. 131 G3
Stewart Canada 116 D4
Stewart r. Canada 116 B2
Stewart, Isla i. Chile 140 B8
Stewart Crossing Canada 116 B2
Stewart Island N.Z. 109 A8
Stewart Islands Solomon Is 103 G2
Stewart Lake Canada 115 J3
Stewarton U.K. 46 E5
Stewarts Point U.S.A. 124 B2
Stewiacke Canada 119 J5
Steynsburg S. Africa 97 G6
Steyr Austria 43 O6
Steytlerville S. Africa 96 G7
Stiens Neth. 48 F1
Stif Alg. see Sétif
Stigler U.S.A. 127 E5
Stikine r. Canada 116 C3
Stikine Plateau Canada 116 D3
Stikine Strait U.S.A. 116 C3
Stilbaai S. Africa 96 E8
Stiles U.S.A. 130 A1
Stillwater MN U.S.A. 126 E2
Stillwater OK U.S.A. 127 D4
Stillwater Range mts U.S.A. 124 D2
Stillwell U.S.A. 130 B3
Stilton U.K. 45 G6
Stilwell U.S.A. 127 E5
Stinnett U.S.A. 127 C5
Štip Macedonia 55 J4
Stirling Australia 104 F5
Stirling Canada 131 G1
Stirling U.K. 46 F4
Stirling Creek r. Australia 104 E4
Stirling Range National Park Australia 105 B8
Stittsville Canada 131 H1
Stjørdalshalsen Norway 40 G5
Stockbridge U.S.A. 130 C2
Stockerau Austria 43 P6
Stockheim Germany 49 L4

▶Stockholm Sweden 41 K7
Capital of Sweden.

Stockinbingal Australia 108 C5
Stockport U.K. 44 E5
Stockton CA U.S.A. 124 C3
Stockton KS U.S.A. 126 D4
Stockton MO U.S.A. 126 E4
Stockton UT U.S.A. 125 G1
Stockton Lake U.S.A. 126 E4
Stockton-on-Tees U.K. 44 F4
Stockville U.S.A. 126 C3
Stod Czech Rep. 49 N5
Stœng Trêng Cambodia 67 D4
Stoer, Point of U.K. 46 D2
Stoke-on-Trent U.K. 45 E5
Stokesley U.K. 44 F4
Stokes Point Australia 107 [inset]
Stokes Range hills Australia 104 E4
Stokkseyri Iceland 40 [inset]
Stokkvågen Norway 40 H3
Stokmarknes Norway 40 I2
Stolac Bos.-Herz. 54 G3
Stolberg (Rheinland) Germany 48 G4
Stolbovoy Rus. Fed. 149 G2
Stolbtsy Belarus see Stowbtsy
Stolin Belarus 41 O11
Stollberg Germany 49 M4
Stolp Poland see Słupsk
Stolzenau Germany 49 J2
Stone U.K. 45 E6
Stoneboro U.S.A. 130 E3
Stonecliffe Canada 118 F5
Stonecutters' Island pen. Hong Kong China 73 [inset]
Stonehaven U.K. 46 G4
Stonehenge Australia 106 C5
Stonehenge tourist site U.K. 45 F7
Stoner U.S.A. 125 I3
Stonewall Canada 117 L5
Stonewall Jackson Lake U.S.A. 130 E4
Stony Creek U.S.A. 131 G5
Stony Lake Canada 117 L3
Stony Point U.S.A. 131 G2
Stony Rapids Canada 117 J3
Stony River U.S.A. 114 C3
Stooping r. Canada 118 E3
Stora Lulevatten l. Sweden 40 K3
Stora Sjöfallets nationalpark nat. park Sweden 40 J3
Storavan l. Sweden 40 K4
Store Bælt sea chan. Denmark see Great Belt
Støren Norway 40 G5
Storfjordbotn Norway 40 O1
Storforshei Norway 40 I3
Storjord Norway 40 I3
Storkerson Peninsula Canada 115 H2
Storm Bay Australia 107 [inset]
Stormberg S. Africa 97 H6
Storm Lake U.S.A. 126 E3
Stornosa mt. Norway 40 E6
Stornoway U.K. 46 C2
Storozhevsk Rus. Fed. 38 L3
Storozhynets' Ukr. 39 E6
Storrs U.S.A. 131 I3
Storseleby Sweden 40 J4
Storsjön l. Sweden 40 I5
Storskrymten mt. Norway 40 F5
Storslett Norway 40 L2
Stortemelk sea chan. Neth. 48 F1
Storuman Sweden 40 J4
Storuman l. Sweden 40 J4
Storvik Sweden 41 J6
Storvorde Denmark 41 G8
Storvreta Sweden 41 J7
Story U.S.A. 122 G3
Stotfold U.K. 45 G6
Stoughton Canada 117 K5
Stour r. England U.K. 45 F6
Stour r. England U.K. 45 F8
Stour r. England U.K. 45 I7
Stour r. England U.K. 45 I7
Stourbridge U.K. 45 E6
Stourport-on-Severn U.K. 45 E6
Stout Lake Canada 117 M4
Stowbtsy Belarus 41 O10
Stowe U.S.A. 131 I1
Stowmarket U.K. 45 H6
Stoyba Rus. Fed. 70 C1
Strabane U.K. 47 E3
Stradbally Rep. of Ireland 47 E4
Stradbroke U.K. 45 I6
Stradella Italy 54 C2
Strakonice Czech Rep. 43 N6
Stralsund Germany 43 N3
Strand S. Africa 96 D8
Stranda Norway 40 E5
Strangford U.K. 47 G3
Strangford Lough inlet U.K. 47 G3
Strangways r. Australia 104 F3
Stranraer U.K. 46 D6
Strasbourg France 52 H2
Strasburg Germany 49 N1
Strasburg U.S.A. 131 F4
Strassburg France see Strasbourg
Stratford Australia 108 C6
Stratford Canada 130 E2
Stratford CA U.S.A. 124 D3
Stratford TX U.S.A. 127 C4
Stratford-upon-Avon U.K. 45 F6
Strathaven U.K. 46 E5
Strathmore Canada 116 H5
Strathmore r. U.K. 46 E2
Strathnaver Canada 116 F4
Strathroy Canada 130 E2
Strathspey valley U.K. 46 F3
Strathy U.K. 46 F2
Stratton U.K. 45 C8
Stratton U.S.A. 131 J1
Stratton Mountain U.S.A. 131 I2
Straubing Germany 49 M6
Straumnes pt Iceland 40 [inset]
Strawberry U.S.A. 125 H4
Strawberry Mountain U.S.A. 122 D3
Strawberry Reservoir U.S.A. 125 H1
Streaky Bay Australia 105 F8
Streaky Bay b. Australia 105 F8
Streator U.S.A. 126 F3
Street U.K. 45 E7
Streetsboro U.S.A. 130 E3
Strehaia Romania 55 J2
Strehla Germany 49 N3
Streich Mound hill Australia 105 C7
Strelka Rus. Fed. 61 Q3
Strel'na r. Rus. Fed. 38 H2
Strenči Latvia 41 N8
Streymoy i. Faroe Is 40 [inset]
Stříbro Czech Rep. 49 M5
Strichen U.K. 46 G3
Strimonas r. Greece 55 J4
also known as Struma (Bulgaria)
Stroeder Arg. 140 D6
Strokestown Rep. of Ireland 47 D4
Stroma, Island of i. U.K. 46 F2
Stromboli, Isola i. Italy 54 F5
Stromness S. Georgia 140 I8
Stromness U.K. 46 F2
Strömstad Sweden 41 G7
Strömsund Sweden 40 I5
Strongsville U.S.A. 130 E3
Stronsay i. U.K. 46 G1
Stroud Australia 108 E4
Stroud U.K. 45 E7
Stroud Road Australia 108 E4
Stroudsburg U.S.A. 131 H3

Struer Denmark 41 F8
Struga Macedonia 55 I4
Strugi-Krasnyye Rus. Fed. 41 P7
Struis Bay S. Africa 96 E8
Strullendorf Germany 49 K5
Struma r. Bulg. 55 J4
also known as Strimonas (Greece)
Strumble Head hd U.K. 45 B6
Strumica Macedonia 55 J4
Struthers U.S.A. 130 E3
Stryama r. Bulg. 55 K3
Strydenburg S. Africa 96 F5
Stryn Norway 40 E6
Stryy Ukr. 39 D6
Strzelecki, Mount hill Australia
104 F5
Strzelecki Regional Reserve
nature res. Australia 107 B6
Stuart FL U.S.A. 129 D7
Stuart NE U.S.A. 126 D3
Stuart VA U.S.A. 130 E5
Stuart Lake Canada 116 E4
Stuart Range hills Australia 107 A6
Stuarts Draft U.S.A. 130 F4
Stuart Town Australia 108 D4
Stuchka Latvia see Aizkraukle
Stučka Latvia see Aizkraukle
Studholme Junction N.Z. 109 C7
Studsviken Sweden 40 K5
Stukley, Lac l. Canada 131 I1
Stung Treng Cambodia see
Stœng Trêng
Stupart r. Canada 117 M4
Stupino Rus. Fed. 39 H5
Sturge Island Antarctica 148 H2
Sturgeon r. Ont. Canada 118 F5
Sturgeon r. Sask. Canada 117 J4
Sturgeon Bay b. Canada 117 L4
Sturgeon Bay U.S.A. 130 B1
Sturgeon Bay Canal lake channel
U.S.A. 130 B1
Sturgeon Falls Canada 118 F5
Sturgeon Lake Ont. Canada 117 N5
Sturgeon Lake Ont. Canada 131 F1
Sturgis MI U.S.A. 130 C3
Sturgis SD U.S.A. 126 C2
Sturt, Mount hill Australia 107 C6
Sturt Creek watercourse Australia
104 D4
Sturt National Park Australia
107 C6
Sturt Stony Desert Australia 107 C6
Stutterheim S. Africa 97 H7
Stuttgart Germany 49 J6
Stuttgart U.S.A. 127 F5
Stykkishólmur Iceland 40 [inset]
Styr r. Belarus/Ukr. 39 E5
Suaçuí Grande r. Brazil 141 C2
Suai East Timor 104 D2
Suakin Sudan 82 E6
Suao Taiwan 73 I3
Suaqui Grande Mex. 123 F7
Suau P.N.G. 106 E1
Subačius Lith. 41 N9
Subankhata India 79 G4
Subarnapur India see Sonapur
Sūbāshī Iran 84 C3
Subay reg. Saudi Arabia 84 B5
Şubayḩah Saudi Arabia 81 D4
Subei China 76 H4
Subi Besar i. Indon. 67 E7
Subi Kecil i. Indon. 67 E7
Sublette U.S.A. 127 C4
Subotica Serb. and Mont. 55 H1
Success, Lake U.S.A. 124 D3
Succiso, Alpi di mts Italy 54 D2
Suceava Romania 39 E7
Suchan Rus. Fed. see Partizansk
Suck r. Rep. of Ireland 47 D4
Suckling, Mount P.N.G. 106 E1
Suckow Germany 49 L1

▶Sucre Bol. 138 E7
Legislative capital of Bolivia.

Suczawa Romania see Suceava
Sud, Grand Récif du reef
New Caledonia 103 G4
Suda Rus. Fed. 38 H4
Sudak Ukr. 86 D1

▶Sudan country Africa 93 F3
Largest country in Africa.
africa 7, 90–91

Suday Rus. Fed. 38 I4
Sudayr reg. Saudi Arabia 84 B5
Sudbury Canada 118 E5
Sudbury U.K. 45 H6
Sudd swamp Sudan 82 C8
Sude r. Germany 49 K1
Sudest Island P.N.G. see
Tagula Island
Sudetenland mts Czech Rep./Poland
see Sudety
Sudety mts Czech Rep./Poland
43 O5
Sudislavl' Rus. Fed. 38 I4
Sudlersville U.S.A. 131 H4
Süd-Nord-Kanal canal Germany
48 H2
Sudogda Rus. Fed. 38 I5
Sudr Egypt 81 A5
Suðuroy i. Faroe Is 40 [inset]
Sue watercourse Sudan 93 F4
Sueca Spain 53 F4
Suez Egypt 81 A5
Suez, Gulf of Egypt 81 A5
Suez Bay Egypt 81 A5
Suez Canal Egypt 81 A4
Suffolk U.S.A. 131 G5
Sugarbush Hill hill U.S.A. 126 F2
Sugarloaf Mountain U.S.A. 131 J1
Sugarloaf Point Australia 108 F4
Suguan China 76 E4
Sūhāj Egypt see Sawhāj
Şuḩār Oman 84 E5
Suhaymī, Wādī as watercourse
Egypt 81 A4
Sühbaatar Mongolia 68 J2
Suheli Par i. India 80 B4
Suhl Germany 49 K4
Suhlendorf Germany 49 K2
Suhul reg. Saudi Arabia 84 B6
Suhūl al Kidan plain Saudi Arabia
84 D6
Şuhut Turkey 55 N5
Sui Pak. 85 H4
Sui, Laem pt Thai. 67 B5
Suibin China 70 C3
Suid-Afrika country Africa see
Republic of South Africa
Suide China 69 K5
Suidzhikurmsy Turkm. see Madau
Suifenhe China 70 C3
Suihua China 70 B3
Suileng China 70 B3
Suining Hunan China 73 F3
Suining Jiangsu China 73 H1
Suining Sichuan China 72 E2
Suippes France 48 E5
Suir r. Rep. of Ireland 47 E5
Suisse country Europe see
Switzerland
Sui Vehar Pak. 85 H4
Suixi China 73 H1
Suixian Henan China 73 G1
Suixian Hubei China see Suizhou
Suiyang Guizhou China 72 E3
Suiyang Henan China 73 G1
Suiza country Europe see Switzerland
Suizhong China 69 M4
Suizhou China 73 G2
Sujangarh India 78 C4
Sujawal Pak. 85 H5
Suk atoll Micronesia see Pulusuk
Sukabumi Indon. 64 D8
Sukagawa Japan 71 F5
Sukarnapura Indon. see Jayapura
Sukarno, Puncak mt. Indon. see
Jaya, Puncak
Sukchŏn N. Korea 71 B5
Sukhinichi Rus. Fed. 39 G5
Sukhona r. Rus. Fed. 38 J3
Sukhothai Thai. 66 B3
Sukhumi Georgia see Sokhumi
Sukhum-Kale Georgia see Sokhumi
Sukkertoppen Greenland see
Maniitsoq
Sukkozero Rus. Fed. 38 G3
Sukkur Pak. 85 H5
Sukma India 80 D2
Sukpay Rus. Fed. 70 E3
Sukpay r. Rus. Fed. 70 E3
Sukri r. India 78 C4
Sukri r. India 78 C4
Suktel r. India 80 D1
Sukun i. Indon. 104 C2
Sula i. Norway 41 D6
Sula r. Rus. Fed. 38 K2
Sula, Kepulauan is Indon. 65 H7
Sulaiman Range mts Pak. 85 H4
Sulak Rus. Fed. 87 G2
Sūlār Iran 84 C4
Sula Sgeir i. U.K. 46 C1
Sulawesi i. Indon. see Celebes
Sulaymān Beg Iraq 87 G4
Sulayyimah Saudi Arabia 84 B6
Sulci Sardinia Italy see Sant'Antioco
Sulcis Sardinia Italy see Sant'Antioco
Suledeh Iran 84 C2
Sule Skerry i. U.K. 46 E1
Sule Stack i. U.K. 46 E1
Sulingen Germany 49 I2
Sulitjelma Norway 40 J3
Sulkava Fin. 40 P6
Sullana Peru 138 B4
Sullivan IL U.S.A. 126 F4
Sullivan IN U.S.A. 130 B4
Sullivan Bay Canada 116 E5
Sullivan Island Myanmar see
Lanbi Kyun
Sullivan Lake Canada 117 I5
Sulmo Italy see Sulmona
Sulmona Italy 54 E3
Sulphur LA U.S.A. 127 E6
Sulphur OK U.S.A. 127 D5
Sulphur r. U.S.A. 127 E5
Sulphur Springs U.S.A. 127 E5
Sultan Canada 118 E5
Sultan, Koh-i- mts Pak. 85 F4
Sultanabad India see Osmannagar
Sultanabad Iran see Arāk
Sultan Dağları mts Turkey 55 N5
Sultanıye Turkey see Karapınar
Sultanpur India 79 E4
Sulu Archipelago is Phil. 65 G5
Sulu Basin sea feature
N. Pacific Ocean 146 E5
Sülüklü Turkey 86 D3
Sülüktü Kyrg. 85 H2
Sulusaray Turkey 86 E3
Sulu Sea N. Pacific Ocean 64 F5
Suluvvaulik, Lac l. Canada 119 G2
Sulyukta Kyrg. see Sülüktü
Sulzbach-Rosenberg Germany
49 L5
Sulzberger Bay Antarctica 148 I1
Sumāil Oman 84 E6
Sumampa Arg. 140 D3
Sumapaz, Parque Nacional nat. park
Col. 138 D3
Sūmār Iran 84 B3
Sumatera i. Indon. see Sumatra

▶Sumatra i. Indon. 67 B7
2nd largest island in Asia.

Šumava nat. park Czech Rep. 43 N6
Sumba i. Indon. 104 C2
Sumba, Selat sea chan. Indon.
104 B2
Sumbar r. Turkm. 84 D2
Sumbawa i. Indon. 104 B2
Sumbawabesar Indon. 104 B2
Sumbawanga Tanz. 95 D4
Sumbe Angola 95 B5
Sumbu National Park Zambia 95 D4
Sumburgh U.K. 46 [inset]
Sumburgh Head hd U.K. 46 [inset]
Sumdo China 72 D2
Sumdum, Mount U.S.A. 116 C3
Sume'eh Sarā Iran 84 C2
Sumeih Sudan 82 C8
Sumenep Indon. 64 E8
Sumgait Azer. see Sumqayıt
Sumisu-jima i. Japan 69 Q6
Summēl Iraq 87 F3
Summer Beaver Canada 118 C3
Summerford Canada 119 L4
Summer Island U.S.A. 128 C2
Summer Isles U.K. 46 D2
Summerland Canada 116 G5
Summersville U.S.A. 130 E4
Summit Lake Canada 116 F4
Summit Mountain U.S.A. 124 E2
Summit Peak U.S.A. 123 G5
Sumnal Aksai Chin 78 D2
Sumner N.Z. 109 D6
Sumner, Lake N.Z. 109 D6
Sumon-dake mt. Japan 71 E5
Šumperk Czech Rep. 43 P6
Sumpu Japan see Shizuoka
Sumqayıt Azer. 87 H2
Sumskiy Posad Rus. Fed. 38 G2
Sumter U.S.A. 129 D5
Sumur Jammu and Kashmir 78 D2
Sumy Ukr. 39 G6
Sumzom China 72 C2
Suna Rus. Fed. 38 K4
Sunaj India 78 D4
Sunam India 78 C3
Sunamganj Bangl. 79 G4
Sunart, Loch inlet U.K. 46 D4
Şunaynah Oman 84 D6
Sunburst U.S.A. 122 F2
Sunbury Australia 108 B6
Sunbury OH U.S.A. 130 D3
Sunbury PA U.S.A. 131 G3
Sunch'ŏn S. Korea 71 B6
Sun City S. Africa 97 H3
Sun City AZ U.S.A. 125 G5
Sun City CA U.S.A. 124 E5
Sunda, Selat strait Indon. 64 C8
Sunda Kalapa Indon. see Jakarta
Sundance U.S.A. 122 G3
Sundarbans coastal area Bangl./India
79 G5
Sundarbans National Park
Bangl./India 79 G5
Sundargarh India 79 F5
Sunda Shelf sea feature
Indian Ocean 145 P5
Sunda Strait Indon. see Sunda, Selat
Sunda Trench sea feature
Indian Ocean see Java Trench
Sunda Trench sea feature
Indian Ocean see Java Trench
Sunderland U.K. 44 F4
Sundern (Sauerland) Germany 49 I3
Sündiken Dağları mts Turkey 55 N5
Sundown National Park Australia
108 E2
Sundre Canada 116 H5
Sundridge Canada 118 F5
Sundsvall Sweden 40 J5
Sundukli, Peski des. Turkm. 85 F2
Sundumbili S. Africa 97 J5
Sungaipenuh Indon. 64 C7
Sungari r. China see Songhua Jiang
Sungei Petani Malaysia 67 C6
Sungei Seletar Reservoir Sing.
67 [inset]
Sungkiang China see Songjiang
Sung Kong i. Hong Kong China
73 [inset]
Sungqu China see Songpan
Sungsang Indon. 64 C7
Sungurlu Turkey 86 D2
Sun Kosi r. Nepal 79 F4
Sunman U.S.A. 130 C4
Sunndal Norway 41 E6
Sunndalsøra Norway 40 F5
Sunne Sweden 41 H7
Sunnyside U.S.A. 122 D3
Sunnyvale U.S.A. 124 B3
Sun Prairie U.S.A. 126 F3
Sunset House Canada 116 G4
Sunset Peak hill Hong Kong China
73 [inset]
Suntar Rus. Fed. 61 M3
Suntsar Pak. 85 F5
Sunwi-do i. N. Korea 71 B5
Sunwu China 70 B2
Sunyani Ghana 92 C4
Suolijärvet l. Fin. 40 P3
Suomi country Europe see Finland
Suomussalmi Fin. 40 P4
Suō-nada b. Japan 71 C6
Suonenjoki Fin. 40 O5
Suong r. Laos 66 C3
Suoyarvi Rus. Fed. 38 G3
Supa India 80 B3
Supaul India 79 F4
Superior AZ U.S.A. 125 H5
Superior MT U.S.A. 122 E3
Superior NE U.S.A. 126 D3
Superior WI U.S.A. 126 E2

▶Superior, Lake Canada/U.S.A.
121 J2
Largest lake in North America and
2nd in the world.
north america 110–111
world 12–13

Suphan Buri Thai. 67 C4
Süphan Dağı mt. Turkey 87 F3
Supiori i. Indon. 65 J7
Suponevo Rus. Fed. 39 G5
Support Force Glacier Antarctica
148 A1
Sūq ash Shuyūkh Iraq 87 G5
Suqian China 73 H1
Suquṭrá i. Yemen see Socotra
Şūr Oman 85 E6
Sur, Point U.S.A. 124 C3
Sur, Punta pt Arg. 140 E5
Sura r. Rus. Fed. 39 J4
Şuraabad Azer. 87 H2
Surabaya Indon. 64 E8
Sūrak Iran 84 E5
Surakarta Indon. 64 E8
Sūran Iran 85 F5
Şūrān Syria 81 C2
Surat Australia 108 D1
Surat India 78 C5
Suratgarh India 78 C3
Surat Thani Thai. 67 B5
Surazh Rus. Fed. 39 G5
Surbiton Australia 106 D4
Surdulica Serb. and Mont. 55 J3
Sûre r. Lux. 48 G5
Surendranagar India 78 B5
Surf U.S.A. 124 C4
Surgut Rus. Fed. 60 I3
Suri India see Siuri
Suriapet India 80 C2
Surigao Phil. 65 H5
Surin Thai. 66 C4
Surinam country S. America see
Suriname
▶Suriname country S. America
139 G3
south america 9, 136–137
Surin Nua, Ko i. Thai. 67 B5
Suriyān Iran 84 D4
Surkhan Uzbek. 85 G2
Surkhduz Afgh. 85 G4
Surkhet Nepal 79 E3
Surkhon Uzbek. see Surkhan
Sürmene Turkey 87 F2
Surovikino Rus. Fed. 39 I6
Surpura India 78 C4
Surrey Canada 116 F5
Surry U.S.A. 131 G5
Surskoye Rus. Fed. 39 J5
Surt Libya see Sirte
Surtsey i. Iceland 40 [inset]
Sürü Hormozgan Iran 84 E5
Sürü Sīstān va Balūchestān Iran 84 E5
Suruç Turkey 81 D1
Surud, Raas pt Somalia 94 E2
Surud Ad mt. Somalia see Shimbiris
Suruga-wan b. Japan 71 E6
Surulangun Indon. 64 C7
Surwold Germany 49 H2
Suryapet India see Suriapet
Şuşa Azer. 87 G3
Susah Tunisia see Sousse
Susaki Japan 71 D6
Susan U.S.A. 131 G5
Süsangerd Iran 84 C4
Susanino Rus. Fed. 70 F1
Susanville U.S.A. 124 C1
Suşehri Turkey 86 E2
Suso Thai. 67 B6
Susong China 73 H2
Susquehanna U.S.A. 131 H3
Susquehanna r. U.S.A. 131 G4
Susquehanna, West Branch r.
U.S.A. 131 G3
Susques Arg. 140 C2
Sussex U.S.A. 131 G5
Susuman Rus. Fed. 61 P3
Susupu Indon. 65 H6
Susurluk Turkey 55 M5
Sutak Jammu and Kashmir 78 D2
Sutherland Australia 108 E5
Sutherland S. Africa 96 E7
Sutherland U.S.A. 126 C3
Sutherland Range hills Australia
105 D6
Sutjeska nat. park Bos.-Herz. 54 H3
Sutlej r. India/Pak. 78 B3
Sütlüce Turkey 81 A1
Sutter U.S.A. 124 C2
Sutterton U.K. 45 G6
Sutton Canada 131 I1
Sutton r. Canada 118 E3
Sutton U.K. 45 H6
Sutton NE U.S.A. 126 D3
Sutton WV U.S.A. 130 E4
Sutton Coldfield U.K. 45 F6
Sutton in Ashfield U.K. 45 F5
Sutton Lake Canada 118 D3
Sutton Lake U.S.A. 130 E4
Suttor r. Australia 106 D4
Suttsu Japan 70 F4
Sutwik Island U.S.A. 114 C4
Sutyr' r. Rus. Fed. 70 D2

▶Suva Fiji 103 H3
Capital of Fiji.

Suvadiva Atoll Maldives see
Huvadhu Atoll
Suvalki Poland see Suwałki
Suvorov atoll Cook Is see Suwarrow
Suvorov Rus. Fed. 39 H5
Suwa Japan 71 E5
Suwałki Poland 39 D5
Suwannaphum Thai. 66 C4
Suwannee r. U.S.A. 129 D6
Suwanose-jima i. Japan 71 C7
Suwarrow atoll Cook Is 103 J3
Suwaylih Jordan 81 B3
Suwayr well Saudi Arabia 87 F5
Suways, Khalīj as g. Egypt see
Suez, Gulf of
Suweilih Jordan see Suwaylih
Suweis, Khalîg el g. Egypt see
Suez, Gulf of
Suweis, Qanâ el canal Egypt see
Suez Canal
Suwŏn S. Korea 71 B5
Suz, Mys pt Kazakh. 87 I2
Suzaka Japan 71 E5
Suzdal' Rus. Fed. 38 I4
Suzhou Anhui China 73 H1
Suzhou Gansu China see Jiuquan
Suzhou Jiangsu China 73 I2
Suzi He r. China 70 B4
Suzuka Japan 71 E6
Suzu-misaki pt Japan 71 E5
Sværholthalvøya pen. Norway 40 O1

▶Svalbard terr. Arctic Ocean 60 C2
Part of Norway.

Svappavaara Sweden 40 L3
Svartenhuk Halvø pen. Greenland
see Sigguup Nunaa
Svatove Ukr. 39 H6
Svay Chék Cambodia 67 C4
Svay Riĕng Cambodia 67 D5
Svecha Rus. Fed. 38 J4
Sveg Sweden 41 I5
Sveķi Latvia 41 O8
Svelgen Norway 40 D6
Svellingen Norway 40 F5
Švenčionėliai Lith. 41 N9
Švenčionys Lith. 41 O9
Svendborg Denmark 41 G9
Svensby Norway 40 K2
Svenstavik Sweden 40 I5
Sverdlovsk Rus. Fed. see
Yekaterinburg
Sverdlovs'k Ukr. 39 H6
Sverdrup Islands Canada 115 I2
Sverige country Europe see Sweden
Sveti Nikole Macedonia 55 I4
Svetlaya Rus. Fed. 70 E3
Svetlogorsk Belarus see
Svyetlahorsk
Svetlogorsk Kaliningradskaya Oblast'
Rus. Fed. 41 L9
Svetlogorsk Krasnoyarskiy Kray
Rus. Fed. 60 J3
Svetlograd Rus. Fed. 87 F1
Svetlovodsk Ukr. see Svitlovods'k
Svetlyy Kaliningradskaya Oblast'
Rus. Fed. 41 L9
Svetlyy Orenburgskaya Oblast'
Rus. Fed. 76 B1
Svetlyy Yar Rus. Fed. 39 J6
Svetogorsk Rus. Fed. 41 P6
Svíahnúkar vol. Iceland 40 [inset]
Svilaja mts Croatia 54 G3
Svilengrad Bulg. 55 L4
Svinecea Mare, Vârful mt. Romania
55 J2
Svintsovyy Rudnik Turkm. 85 G2
Svir Belarus 41 O9
Svir' r. Rus. Fed. 38 G3
Svishtov Bulg. 55 K3
Svitava r. Czech Rep. 43 P6
Svitavy Czech Rep. 43 P6
Svitlovods'k Ukr. 39 G6
Sviyaga r. Rus. Fed. 38 K5
Svizzera country Europe see
Switzerland
Svobodnyy Rus. Fed. 70 C2
Svolvær Norway 40 I2
Svrljiške Planine mts Serb. and
Mont. 55 J3
Svyatoy Nos, Mys c. Rus. Fed. 38 K2
Svyetlahorsk Belarus 39 F5
Swadlincote U.K. 45 F6
Swaffham U.K. 45 H6
Swain Reefs Australia 106 F4
Swainsboro U.S.A. 129 D5
Swains Island atoll American Samoa
103 I3
Swakop watercourse Namibia 96 B2
Swakopmund Namibia 96 B2
Swale r. U.K. 44 F4
Swallow Islands Solomon Is 103 G3
Swamihalli India 80 C3
Swampy r. Canada 119 H2
Swan r. Australia 105 A7
Swan r. Man./Sask. Canada 117 K4
Swan r. Ont. Canada 118 E3
Swanage U.K. 45 F8
Swandale U.S.A. 130 E4
Swan Hill Australia 108 A5
Swan Hills Canada 116 H4
Swan Islands is Caribbean Sea
133 H5
Swan Lake B.C. Canada 116 D4
Swan Lake Man. Canada 117 K4
Swanley U.K. 45 H7
Swanquarter U.S.A. 129 E5
Swan Reach Australia 107 B7
Swan River Canada 117 K4
Swansea U.K. 45 D7
Swansea Bay U.K. 45 D7
Swanton CA U.S.A. 124 B3
Swanton VT U.S.A. 131 I1
Swartbergpas pass S. Africa 96 F7
Swart Nossob watercourse Namibia
see Black Nossob
Swartruggens S. Africa 97 H3
Swartz Creek U.S.A. 130 D2
Swasey Peak U.S.A. 125 G2
Swat Kohistan reg. Pak. 85 I3
Swatow China see Shantou
Swayzee U.S.A. 130 C3
▶Swaziland country Africa 97 J4
africa 7, 90–91

▶Sweden country Europe 40 I5
5th largest country in Europe.
europe 5, 34–35

Sweet Home U.S.A. 122 C3
Sweet Springs U.S.A. 130 E5
Sweetwater U.S.A. 127 C5
Sweetwater r. U.S.A. 122 G4
Swellendam S. Africa 96 E8
Świdnica Poland 43 P5
Świdwin Poland 43 O4
Świebodzin Poland 43 O4
Świecie Poland 43 Q4
Swift Current Canada 117 J5
Swiftcurrent Creek r. Canada 117 J5
Swilly r. Rep. of Ireland 47 E3
Swilly, Lough inlet Rep. of Ireland
47 E2
Swindon U.K. 45 F7
Swinford Rep. of Ireland 47 D4
Świnoujście Poland 43 O4
Swinton U.K. 46 G5
Swiss Confederation country Europe
see Switzerland
Swiss National Park Switz. 54 D1
▶Switzerland country Europe 52 I3
europe 5, 34–35
Swords Rep. of Ireland 47 F4
Swords Range hills Australia 106 C4
Syamozero, Ozero l. Rus. Fed. 38 G3
Syamzha Rus. Fed. 38 I3
Syang Nepal 79 E3
Syas'troy Rus. Fed. 38 G3
Sychevka Rus. Fed. 38 G5
Sydenham atoll Kiribati see Nonouti

▶Sydney Australia 108 E4
State capital of New South Wales.
Most populous city in Oceania.

Sydney Canada 119 J5
Sydney Island Kiribati see Manra
Sydney Lake Canada 117 M5
Sydney Mines Canada 119 J5
Syedra tourist site Turkey 81 A1
Syeverodonets'k Ukr. 39 H6
Syke Germany 49 I2
Sykesville U.S.A. 131 F3
Syktyvkar Rus. Fed. 38 K3
Sylarna mt. Norway/Sweden 40 H5
Sylhet Bangl. 79 G4
Syloga Rus. Fed. 38 I3
Sylt i. Germany 43 L3
Sylva U.S.A. 129 D5
Sylvania GA U.S.A. 129 D5
Sylvania OH U.S.A. 130 D3
Sylvan Lake Canada 116 H4
Sylvester U.S.A. 129 D6
Sylvester, Lake salt flat Australia
106 A3
Sylvia, Mount Canada 116 E3
Symerton U.S.A. 130 A3
Symi i. Greece 55 L6
Synel'nykove Ukr. 39 G6
Syngyrli, Mys pt Kazakh. 87 I2
Synya Rus. Fed. 37 R2
Syowa research station Antarctica
148 D2
Syracusae Sicily Italy see Syracuse
Syracuse Sicily Italy 54 F6
Syracuse KS U.S.A. 126 C4
Syracuse NY U.S.A. 131 G2
Syrdar'ya r. Asia 76 C3
Syrdar'ya Uzbek. 76 C3
Syrdaryinskiy Uzbek. see Syrdar'ya
▶Syria country Asia 86 E4
asia 6, 58–59
Syriam Myanmar 66 B3
Syrian Desert Asia 86 E4
Syrna i. Greece 55 L6
Syros i. Greece 55 K6
Syrskiy Rus. Fed. 39 H5
Sysmä Fin. 41 N6
Sysola r. Rus. Fed. 38 K3
Syumsi Rus. Fed. 38 K4
Syurkum Rus. Fed. 70 F2
Syurkum, Mys pt Rus. Fed. 70 F2
Syzran' Rus. Fed. 39 K5
Szabadka Serb. and Mont. see
Subotica
Szczecin Poland 43 O4
Szczecinek Poland 43 P4
Szczytno Poland 43 R4
Szechwan prov. China see Sichuan
Szeged Hungary 55 I1
Székesfehérvár Hungary 54 H1
Szekszárd Hungary 54 H1
Szentes Hungary 55 I1
Szentgotthárd Hungary 54 G1
Szigetvár Hungary 54 G1
Szolnok Hungary 55 I1
Szombathely Hungary 54 G1
Sztálinváros Hungary see
Dunaújváros

↓ T

Taagga Duudka reg. Somalia 94 E3
Ţābah Saudi Arabia 82 F4
Tabajara Brazil 138 F5
Tabakhmela Georgia see Kazret'i
Tabalo P.N.G. 65 L7
Tabanan Indon. 104 A2
Tabankulu S. Africa 97 I6
Ţabaqah Ar Raqqah Syria see
Madīnat ath Thawrah
Ţabaqah Ar Raqqah Syria 81 D2
Tabar Islands P.N.G. 102 F2
Tabarka Tunisia 54 C6
Ţabas Iran 85 F3
Tabāsin Iran 84 E4
Tābask, Kūh-e mt. Iran 84 C4
Tabatinga Amazonas Brazil 138 E4
Tabatinga São Paulo Brazil 141 A3
Tabatinga, Serra da hills Brazil
139 J6
Tabatsquri, Tba l. Georgia 87 F2
Tabayin Myanmar 66 A2
Tabbita Australia 108 B5
Tabelbala Alg. 50 D6
Taber Canada 117 H5
Tabet, Nam r. Myanmar 66 B1
Tabia Tsaka salt l. China 79 F3
Tabiteuea atoll Kiribati 103 H2
Tabivere Estonia 41 O7
Table Cape N.Z. 109 F4
Tabligbo Togo 92 D4
Tábor Czech Rep. 43 O6
Tabora Tanz. 95 D4
Tabou Côte d'Ivoire 92 C4
Tabrīz Iran 84 B2
Tabuaeran atoll Kiribati 147 J5
Tabūk Saudi Arabia 86 E5
Tabulam Australia 108 F2
Tabuyung Indon. 67 B7
Tabwémasana, Mount Vanuatu
103 G3
Täby Sweden 41 K7
Tacalé Brazil 139 H3
Tacheng China 76 F2
Tachie Canada 116 E4
Tachov Czech Rep. 49 M5
Tacloban Phil. 65 H4
Tacna Peru 138 D7
Tacoma U.S.A. 122 C3
Taco Pozo Arg. 140 D3
Tacuarembó Uruguay 140 E4
Tacupeto Mex. 123 F7
Tadcaster U.K. 44 F5
Tademaït, Plateau du Alg. 50 E6
Tadin New Caledonia 103 G4
Tadjikistan country Asia see
Tajikistan
Tadjoura Djibouti 82 F7
Tadmur Syria 81 D2
Tadohae Haesang National Park
S. Korea 71 B6
Tadoule Lake Canada 117 L3
Tadoussac Canada 119 H4
Tadpatri India 80 C3
Tadwale India 80 C2
Tadzhikskaya S.S.R. country Asia
see Tajikistan
T'aean Haean National Park
S. Korea 71 B5
Taech'ŏng-do i. S. Korea 71 B5
Taedasa-do N. Korea 71 B5
Taedong-man b. N. Korea 71 B5
Taegu S. Korea 71 C6
Taehan-min'guk country Asia see
South Korea
Taehŭksan-kundo is S. Korea 71 B6
Taejŏn S. Korea 71 B5
Taejŏng S. Korea 71 B6
T'aepaek S. Korea 71 C5
Ta'erqi China 69 M3
Taf r. U.K. 45 C7
Tafahi i. Tonga 103 I3
Tafalla Spain 53 F2
Tafeng China see Lanshan
Tafila Jordan see Aţ Ţafilah
Tafi Viejo Arg. 140 C3
Tafresh Iran 84 C3
Taft Iran 84 D4
Taft U.S.A. 124 D4
Taftān, Kūh-e mt. Iran 85 F4
Taftanāz Syria 81 C2
Tafwap India 67 A6
Taganrog Rus. Fed. 39 H7
Taganrog, Gulf of Rus. Fed./Ukr.
39 H7
Taganrogskiy Zaliv b. Rus. Fed./Ukr.
see Taganrog, Gulf of
Tagarev, Gora mt. Iran/Turkm. 84 E2
Tagarkaty, Pereval pass Tajik. 85 I2
Tagaung Myanmar 66 B2
Tagchagpu Ri mt. China 79 E2
Tagdempt Alg. see Tiaret
Taghmon Rep. of Ireland 47 F5
Tagish Canada 116 C2
Tagtabazar Turkm. 85 F3
Tagula P.N.G. 106 F1
Tagula Island P.N.G. 106 F1
Tagus r. Port. 53 B4
also known as Tajo (Portugal) or Tejo
(Spain)
Taha China 70 B3
Tahaetkun Mountain Canada
116 G5
Tahan, Gunung mt. Malaysia 67 C6
Tahanroz'ka Zatoka b. Rus. Fed./Ukr.
see Taganrog, Gulf of
Tahat, Mont mt. Alg. 92 D2
Tahaurawe i. U.S.A. see Kahoolawe
Tahe China 70 B1
Taheke N.Z. 109 D2
Tahiti i. Fr. Polynesia 147 K7
Tahlab r. Iran/Pak. 85 F4
Tahlab, Dasht-i- plain Pak. 85 F4
Tahlequah U.S.A. 127 E5
Tahltan Canada 116 D3
Tahoe, Lake U.S.A. 124 C2
Tahoe Lake Canada 115 H3
Tahoe Vista U.S.A. 124 C2
Tahoka U.S.A. 127 C5
Tahoua Niger 92 D3
Tahrūd Iran 84 E4
Tahrūd r. Iran 84 E4
Tahtsa Peak Canada 116 E4
Tahulandang i. Indon. 65 H6
Tahuna Indon. 65 H6
Taï, Parc National de nat. park
Côte d'Ivoire 92 C4
Tai'an China 69 L5
Taibai China 72 E1
Taibai Shan mt. China 72 E1
Taibei Taiwan see T'aipei
Taibus Qi China see Baochang
T'aichung Taiwan 73 I3
Taidong Taiwan see T'aitung
Taigong China see Taijiang
Taihang Shan mts Hebei China
69 K5
Taihang Shan mts China 69 K5
Taihape N.Z. 109 E4
Taihe Jiangxi China 73 G3
Taihe Sichuan China see Shehong
Taihezhen China see Shehong
Tai Ho Wan Hong Kong China
73 [inset]
Taihu China 73 H2
Tai Hu l. China 73 I2
Taijiang China 73 F3
Taikang China 70 B3

Tailai China 70 A3
Tai Lam Chung Shui Tong resr Hong Kong China 73 [inset]
Tailem Bend Australia 107 B7
Tai Long Wan b. Hong Kong China 73 [inset]
Taimani reg. Afgh. 85 F3
Tai Mo Shan hill Hong Kong China 73 [inset]
Tain U.K. 46 F2
T'ainan Taiwan see Hsinying
T'ainan Taiwan 73 I4
Tainaro, Akra pt Greece 55 J6
Taining China 73 H3
Tai O Hong Kong China 73 [inset]
Taiobeiras Brazil 141 C1
Tai Pang Wan b. Hong Kong China see Mirs Bay
▶T'aipei Taiwan 73 I3
Capital of Taiwan.
Taiping Guangdong China see Shixing
Taiping Guangxi China see Chongzuo
Taiping Guangxi China 73 F4
Taiping Malaysia 67 C6
Taipingchuan China 70 A3
Tai Po Hong Kong China 73 [inset]
Tai Po Hoi b. Hong Kong China see Tolo Harbour
Tai Poutini National Park N.Z. see Westland National Park
Tairbeart U.K. see Tarbert
Tai Rom Yen National Park Thai. 67 B5
Tairuq Iran 84 B3
Tais P.N.G. 65 K8
Taishan China 73 G4
Taishun China 73 H3
Tai Siu Mo To is Hong Kong China see The Brothers
Taissy France 48 E5
Taitanu N.Z. 109 D6
Taitao, Península de pen. Chile 140 B7
Tai To Yan mt. Hong Kong China 73 [inset]
T'aitung Taiwan 73 I4
Tai Tung Shan hill Hong Kong China see Sunset Peak
Taivalkoski Fin. 40 P4
Taivaskero hill Fin. 40 N2
▶Taiwan country Asia 73 I4
asia 6, 58–59
T'aiwan Haihsia strait China/Taiwan see Taiwan Strait
Taiwan Haixia strait China/Taiwan see Taiwan Strait
Taiwan Shan mts Taiwan see Chungyang Shanmo
Taiwan Strait China/Taiwan 73 H4
Taixian China see Jiangyan
Taixing China 73 I1
Taiyuan China 69 K5
Tai Yue Shan i. Hong Kong China see Lantau Island
Taizhao China 72 B2
Taizhong Taiwan see T'aichung
Taizhong Taiwan see Fengyüan
Taizhou Jiangsu China 73 H1
Taizhou Zhejiang China 73 I2
Taizhou Liedao i. China 73 I2
Taizhou Wan b. China 73 I2
Taizi He r. China 70 B4
Ta'izz Yemen 82 F7
Tājābād Iran 84 E4
Tajal Pak. 85 H5
Tajamulco, Volcán de vol. Guat. 132 F5
Tajerouine Tunisia 54 C7
▶Tajikistan country Asia 85 H2
asia 6, 58–59
Tajitos Mex. 123 E7
Tajo r. Spain 53 C4 see Tagus
Tajrīsh Iran 84 C3
Tak Thai. 66 B3
Takāb Iran 84 B2
Takabba Kenya 94 E3
Takahashi Japan 71 D6
Takamatsu Japan 71 D6
Takaoka Japan 71 E5
Takapuna N.Z. 109 E3
Ta karpo China 79 G4
Takatokwane Botswana 96 G3
Takatshwaane Botswana 96 E2
Takatsuki-yama mt. Japan 71 D6
Takayama Japan 71 E5
Tak Bai Thai. 67 C6
Takefu Japan 71 E6
Takengon Indon. 67 B6
Takeo Cambodia see Takêv
Take-shima i. N. Pacific Ocean see Liancourt Rocks
Takestān Iran 84 C2
Takêv Cambodia 67 D5
Takhemaret Alg. 53 G6
Takhini Hotspring Canada 116 C2
Ta Khli Thai. 66 C4
Ta Khmau Cambodia 67 D5
Takhta-Bazar Turkm. see Tagtabazar
Takht Apān, Kūh-e mt. Iran 84 C3
Takhta Pul Post Afgh. 85 G4
Takhteh Iran 84 D4
Takht-e Soleymān mt. Iran 84 C2
Takht-i-Bakhti tourist site Pak. 85 H3
Takht-i-Sulaiman mt. Pak. 85 H4
Takijuq Lake Canada see Napaktulik Lake
Takingeun Indon. see Takengon
Takinoue Japan 70 F3
Takla Lake Canada 116 E4
Takla Landing Canada 116 E4
Takla Makan des. China see Taklimakan Desert
Taklimakan Desert China 78 E1
Taklimakan Shamo des. China see Taklimakan Desert
Takpa Shiri mt. China 72 B2
Taku Canada 116 C3
Takum Nigeria 92 D4
Talachyn Belarus 39 F5
Talaja India 78 C5
Talakan Amurskaya Oblast' Rus. Fed. 70 C2
Talakan Khabarovskiy Kray Rus. Fed. 70 D2
Talandzha Rus. Fed. 70 C2
Talangbatu Indon. 64 D7
Talara Peru 138 B4
Talar-i-Band mts Pak. see Makran Coast Range
Talas Kyrg. 76 D3
Talas Ala-Too mts Kyrg. 76 D3
Talas Range mts Kyrg. see Talas Ala-Too
Talasskiy Alatau, Khrebet mts Kyrg. see Talas Ala-Too
Ṭal'at Mūsá mt. Lebanon/Syria 81 C2
Talaud, Kepulauan is Indon. 65 H6
Talavera de la Reina Spain 53 D4
Talawgyi Myanmar 66 B1
Talaya Rus. Fed. 61 Q3
Talbehat India 78 D4
Talbīsah Syria 81 C2
Talbot, Mount hill Australia 105 D6
Talbotton U.S.A. 129 C5
Talbragar r. Australia 108 D4
Talca Chile 140 B5
Talcahuano Chile 140 B5
Taldan Rus. Fed. 70 B1
Taldom Rus. Fed. 38 H4
Taldykorgan Kazakh. 76 E3
Taldy-Kurgan Kazakh. see Taldykorgan
Taldyqorghan Kazakh. see Taldykorgan
Tālesh Iran see Hashtpar
Talgarth U.K. 45 D7
Talguppa India 80 B3
Talia Australia 107 A7
Taliabu i. Indon. 65 G7
Talikota India 80 C2
Talimardzhan Uzbek. 85 G2
Talin Hiag China 70 B3
Taliparamba India 80 B3
Talisay Phil. 65 G4
Taliş Dağları mts Azer./Iran 84 C2
Talitsa Rus. Fed. 38 J4
Taliwang Indon. 104 B2
Talkeetna U.S.A. 114 C3
Talkeetna Mountains U.S.A. 114 D3
Talkh Āb Iran 84 E3
Tallacootra, Lake salt flat Australia 105 F7
Talladega U.S.A. 129 C5
▶Tallahassee U.S.A. 129 C6
State capital of Florida.
Tall al Aḥmar Syria 81 D1
Tall Baydar Syria 87 F3
Tall-e Ḥalāl Iran 84 D4
▶Tallinn Estonia 41 N7
Capital of Estonia.
Tall Kalakh Syria 81 C2
Tall Kayf Iraq 87 F3
Tall Kūjik Syria 87 F3
Tallow Rep. of Ireland 47 D5
Tallulah U.S.A. 127 F5
Tall 'Uwaynāt Iraq 87 F3
Tallymerjen Uzbek. see Talimardzhan
Talmont-St-Hilaire France 52 D3
Tal'ne Ukr. 39 F6
Tal'noye Ukr. see Tal'ne
Taloda India 78 C5
Talodi Sudan 82 D7
Taloga U.S.A. 127 D4
Talon, Lac l. Canada 119 I3
Ta-long Myanmar 66 B2
Tāloqān Afgh. 85 H2
Talos Dome ice feature Antarctica 148 H2
Ta Loung San mt. Laos 66 C2
Talovaya Rus. Fed. 39 I6
Taloyoak Canada 115 I3
Tal Pass Pak. 85 I3
Talsi Latvia 41 M8
Tal Sīyāh Iran 85 F4
Taltal Chile 140 B3
Taltson r. Canada 117 H2
Talu China 72 B2
Talvik Norway 40 M1
Talwood Australia 108 D2
Talyshskiye Gory mts Azer./Iran see Talış Dağları
Talyy Rus. Fed. 38 L2
Tamala Australia 105 A6
Tamala Rus. Fed. 39 I5
Tamale Ghana 92 C4
Tamana i. Kiribati 103 H2
Taman Negara National Park Malaysia 67 C6
Tamano Japan 71 D6
Tamanrasset Alg. 92 D2
Tamanthi Myanmar 66 A1
Tamaqua U.S.A. 131 H3
Tamar India 79 F5
Tamar Syria see Tadmur
Tamar r. U.K. 45 C8
Tamarugal, Pampa de plain Chile 138 E7
Tamasane Botswana 97 H2
Tamatave Madag. see Toamasina
Tamaulipas state Mex. 127 D7
Tambacounda Senegal 92 B3
Tambaqui Brazil 138 F5
Tambar Springs Australia 108 D3
Tambelan, Kepulauan is Indon. 67 D7
Tambelan Besar i. Indon. 67 D7
Tambo r. Australia 108 C6
Tambohorano Madag. 95 E5
Tambora, Gunung vol. Indon. 104 B2
Tamboritha mt. Australia 108 C6
Tambov Rus. Fed. 39 I5
Tambovka Rus. Fed. 70 C2
Tambura Sudan 93 F4
Tamburi Brazil 141 C1
Tâmchekket Mauritania 92 B3
Tamdybulak Uzbek. 76 B3
Tâmega r. Port. 53 B3
Tamenghest Alg. see Tamanrasset
Tamenglong India 79 H4
Tamerza Tunisia 54 B7
Tamgak, Adrar mt. Niger 92 D3
Tamgué, Massif du mt. Guinea 92 B3
Tamiahua, Laguna de lag. Mex. 132 E4
Tamiang, Ujung pt Indon. 67 B6
Tamil Nadu state India 80 C4
Tamitsa Rus. Fed. 38 H2
Ṭāmīya Egypt see Ṭāmīyah
Ṭāmīyah Egypt 86 C5
Tam Ky Vietnam 66 E4
Tammarvi r. Canada 117 K1
Tammerfors Fin. see Tampere
Tammisaari Fin. see Ekenäs
Tampa U.S.A. 129 D7
Tampa Bay U.S.A. 129 D7
Tampere Fin. 41 M6
Tampico Mex. 132 E4
Tampin Malaysia 67 C7
Tampines Sing. 67 [inset]
Tamsagbulag Mongolia 69 L3
Tamsweg Austria 43 N7
Tamu Myanmar 66 A1
Tamworth Australia 108 E3
Tamworth U.K. 45 F6
Tana r. Fin./Norway see Tenojoki
Tana r. Kenya 94 E4
Tana Madag. see Antananarivo
Tana i. Vanuatu see Tanna
Tana, Lake Eth. 94 D2
Tanabe Japan 71 D6
Tanabi Brazil 141 A3
Tana Bru Norway 40 P1
Tanada Lake U.S.A. 116 A2
Tanafjorden inlet Norway 40 P1
Tanah, Tanjung pt Indon. 64 D8
T'ana Hāyk' l. Eth. see Tana, Lake
Tanahgrogot Indon. 64 F7
Tanah Merah Malaysia 67 C6
Tanahputih Indon. 67 C7
Tanakeke i. Indon. 64 F8
Tanami Australia 104 E4
Tanami Desert Australia 104 E4
Tân An Vietnam 67 D5
Tanana r. U.S.A. 116 A2
Tananarive Madag. see Antananarivo
Tanandava Madag. 95 E6
Tancheng China see Pingtan
Tanch'ŏn N. Korea 71 C4
Tanda Côte d'Ivoire 92 C4
Tanda Uttar Pradesh India 78 D3
Tanda Uttar Pradesh India 79 E4
Tandag Phil. 65 H5
Țăndărei Romania 55 L2
Tandaué Angola 95 B5
Tandi India 78 D2
Tandil Arg. 140 E5
Tando Adam Pak. 85 H5
Tando Alahyar Pak. 85 H5
Tando Bago Pak. 85 H5
Tandou Lake imp. l. Australia 107 C7
Tandragee U.K. 47 F3
Tandur India 80 C2
Tanduri Pak. 85 G4
Tanega-shima i. Japan 71 C7
Tanen Taunggyi mts Thai. 66 B3
Tanezrouft reg. Alg./Mali 92 C2
Tanf, Jabal aṭ hill Syria 81 D3
Tang, Ra's-e pt Iran 85 E5
Tanga Tanz. 95 D4
Tangail Bangl. 79 G4
Tanga Islands P.N.G. 102 F2
Tanganyika country Africa see Tanzania
▶Tanganyika, Lake Africa 95 C4
Deepest and 2nd largest lake in Africa.
Tangará Brazil 141 A4
Tangasseri India 80 C4
Tangdan China 72 D3
Tangeli Iran 84 D2
Tanger Morocco see Tangier
Tangerhütte Germany 49 L2
Tangermünde Germany 49 L2
Tang-e Sarkheh Iran 85 E5
Tanggor China 72 D1
Tanggulashan China 72 B1
Tanggula Shan mt. China 79 G2
Tanggula Shan mts China 79 G2
Tanggula Shankou pass China 79 G2
Tangguo China 79 F3
Tanghe China 73 G1
Tangier Morocco 53 D6
Tangiers Morocco see Tangier
Tang La pass China 79 G4
Tangla India 79 G4
Tanglag China 72 C1
Tanglin Sing. 67 [inset]
Tangmai China 72 B2
Tangnag China 72 D1
Tangorin Australia 106 D4
Tangra Yumco salt l. China 79 F3
Tangse Indon. 67 A6
Tangshan Guizhou China see Shiqian
Tangshan Hebei China 69 L5
Tangte mt. Myanmar 66 B2
Tangtse Jammu and Kashmir see Tanktse
Tangwan China 73 F3
Tangwanghe China 70 C2
Tangyuan China 70 C3
Tangyung Tso salt l. China 79 F3
Tanhaçu Brazil 141 C1
Tanhua Fin. 40 O3
Tani Cambodia 67 D5
Taniantaweng Shan mts China 72 B2
Tanimbar, Kepulauan is Indon. 104 E1
Tanintharyi Myanmar see Tenasserim
Tanintharyi Myanmar see Tenasserim
Taninthayi Myanmar see Tenasserim
Tanjah Morocco see Tangier
Tanjay Phil. 65 G5
Tanjore India see Thanjavur
Tanjung Indon. 64 F7
Tanjungbalai Indon. 67 B7
Tanjungkarang-Telukbetung Indon. see Bandar Lampung
Tanjungpandan Indon. 64 D7
Tanjungpinang Indon. 67 D7
Tanjungpura Indon. 67 B7
Tanjung Puting National Park Indon. 64 E7
Tanjungredeb Indon. 64 F6
Tanjungselor Indon. 64 F6
Tankse Jammu and Kashmir see Tanktse
Tanktse Jammu and Kashmir 78 D2
Tankuhi India 79 F4
Tankwa-Karoo National Park S. Africa 96 D7
Tanna i. Vanuatu 103 G3
Tannadice U.K. 46 G4
Tännäs Sweden 40 H5
Tanner, Mount Canada 116 G5
Tannu-Ola, Khrebet mts Rus. Fed. 76 H1
Tanot India 78 B4
Tanout Niger 92 D3
Tansen Nepal 79 E4
Tanshui Taiwan 73 I3
Ṭanṭā Egypt 86 C5
Ṭanṭa Egypt see Ṭanṭā
Tan-Tan Morocco 92 B2
Tantu China 70 A3
Tantura Israel 81 B3
Tanuku India 80 D2
Tanumbirini Australia 104 F4
Tanumshede Sweden 41 G7
▶Tanzania country Africa 95 D4
africa 7, 90–91
Tanzilla r. Canada 116 D3
Tao, Ko i. Thai. 67 B5
Tao'an China see Taonan
Taobh Tuath U.K. see Northton
Taocheng China see Daxin
Tao He r. China 72 D1
Taohong China see Longhui
Taohuajiang China see Taojiang
Taohuaping China see Longhui
Taojiang China 73 G2
Taolanaro Madag. see Tôlañaro
Taonan China 70 A3
Taongi atoll Marshall Is 146 H5
Taos U.S.A. 123 G5
Taounate Morocco 50 D5
Taourirt Morocco 50 D5
Taoxi China 73 H3
Taoyang China see Lintao
Taoyuan China 73 F2
T'aoyüan Taiwan 73 I3
Tapa Estonia 41 N7
Tapachula Mex. 132 F6
Tapah Malaysia 67 C6
Tapajós r. Brazil 139 H4
Tapaktuan Indon. 67 B7
Tapauá Brazil 138 F5
Tapauá r. Brazil 138 F5
Taperoá Brazil 141 D1
Tapi r. India 78 C5
Tapiau Rus. Fed. see Gvardeysk
Tapis, Gunung mt. Malaysia 67 C6
Tapisuelas Mex. 123 F8
Taplejung Nepal 79 F4
Tap Mun Chau i. Hong Kong China 73 [inset]
Ta-pom Myanmar 66 B2
Tappahannock U.S.A. 131 G5
Tappeh, Kūh-e hill Iran 84 C3
Taprobane country Asia see Sri Lanka
Tapuaenuku mt. N.Z. 109 D5
Tapulonanjing mt. Indon. 67 B7
Tapurucuara Brazil 138 E4
Taputeouea atoll Kiribati see Tabiteuea
Taqṭaq Iraq 87 G4
Taquara Brazil 141 A5
Taquari Mato Grosso Brazil 139 H7
Taquari Rio Grande do Sul Brazil 141 A5
Taquari r. Brazil 139 G7
Taquaritinga Brazil 141 A3
Tar r. Rep. of Ireland 47 E5
Tara Australia 108 E1
Ṭarābulus Lebanon see Tripoli
Ṭarābulus Libya see Tripoli
Tarahuwan India 78 E4
Tarai reg. India 79 G4
Tarakan Indon. 64 F6
Tarakan i. Indon. 64 F6
Tarakki reg. Afgh. 85 G3
Taraklı Turkey 55 N4
Taran, Mys pt Rus. Fed. 41 K9
Tarana Australia 108 D4
Taranagar India 78 C3
Taranaki, Mount vol. N.Z. 109 E4
Tarancón Spain 53 E3
Tarangambadi India 80 C4
Tarangire National Park Tanz. 94 D4
Taranto Italy 54 G4
Taranto, Golfo di g. Italy 54 G4
Taranto, Gulf of Italy see Taranto, Golfo di
Tarapoto Peru 138 C5
Tarapur India 80 B2
Tararua Range mts N.Z. 109 E5
Tarascon-sur-Ariège France 52 E5
Tarasovskiy Rus. Fed. 39 I6
Tarauacá Brazil 138 D5
Tarauacá r. Brazil 138 E5
Tarawera N.Z. 109 F4
Tarawera, Mount vol. N.Z. 109 F4
Taraz Kazakh. 76 D3
Tarazona Spain 53 F3
Tarazona de la Mancha Spain 53 F4
Tarbagatay, Khrebet mts Kazakh. 76 F2
Tarbat Ness pt U.K. 46 F3
Tarbert Rep. of Ireland 47 C5
Tarbert Scotland U.K. 46 C3
Tarbert Scotland U.K. 46 D5
Tarbes France 52 E5
Tarboro U.S.A. 128 E5
Tarcoola Australia 105 F7
Tarcoon Australia 108 C3
Tarcoonyinna watercourse Australia 105 F6
Tarcutta Australia 108 C5
Tardoki-Yani, Gora mt. Rus. Fed. 70 E2
Taree Australia 108 F3
Tarella Australia 107 C6
Tarentum Italy see Taranto
Ṭarfā', Baṭn aṭ depr. Saudi Arabia 84 C6
Tarfaya Morocco 92 B2
Targa well Niger 92 D3
Targan China see Talin Hiag
Targhee Pass U.S.A. 122 F3
Târgoviște Romania 55 K2
Targuist Morocco 53 D6
Târgu Jiu Romania 55 J2
Târgu Mureș Romania 55 K1
Târgu Neamț Romania 55 L1
Târgu Secuiesc Romania 55 L1
Targyailing China 79 F3
Tari P.N.G. 65 K8
Tarif U.A.E. 84 D5
Tarifa Spain 53 D5
Tarifa, Punta de pt Spain 53 D5
Tarija Bol. 138 F8
Tarikere India 80 B3
Tariku r. Indon. 65 J7
Tarīm Yemen 82 G6
Tarim Basin China 76 F4
Tarime Tanz. 94 D4
Tarim He r. China 76 G3
Tarim Pendi basin China see Tarim Basin
Tarīn Kowt Afgh. 85 G3
Taritatu r. Indon. 65 J7
Tarka r. S. Africa 97 G7
Tarkastad S. Africa 97 H7
Tarkio U.S.A. 126 E3
Tarko-Sale Rus. Fed. 60 I3
Tarkwa Ghana 92 C4
Tarlac Phil. 65 G3
Tarlo River National Park Australia 108 D5
Tarma Peru 138 C6
Tarmstedt Germany 49 J1
Tarn r. France 52 E4
Tärnaby Sweden 40 I4
Tarnak r. Afgh. 85 G4
Târnăveni Romania 55 K1
Tarnobrzeg Poland 39 D6
Tarnogskiy Gorodok Rus. Fed. 38 I3
Tarnopol Ukr. see Ternopil'
Tarnów Poland 39 D6
Tarnowitz Poland see Tarnowskie Góry
Tarnowskie Góry Poland 43 Q5
Taro Co salt l. China 79 E3
Ṭārom Iran 84 D4
Taroom Australia 107 E5
Taroudannt Morocco 50 C5
Tarpaulin Swamp Australia 106 B3
Tarq Iran 84 C3
Tarquinia Italy 54 D3
Tarquinii Italy see Tarquinia
Tarrabool Lake salt flat Australia 106 A3
Tarraco Spain see Tarragona
Tarrafal Cape Verde 92 [inset]
Tarragona Spain 53 G3
Tårrajaur Sweden 40 K3
Tarran Hills hill Australia 108 C4
Tarrant Point Australia 106 B3
Tàrrega Spain 53 G3
Tarrong China see Nyêmo
Tarso Emissi mt. Chad 93 E2
Tarsus Turkey 81 B1
Tart China 79 H1
Tärtär Azer. 87 G2
Tartu Estonia 41 O7
Ṭarṭūs Syria 81 B2
Tarumovka Rus. Fed. 87 G1
Tarung Hka r. Myanmar 66 B1
Tarutao, Ko i. Thai. 67 B6
Tarutung Indon. 67 B7
Tarvisium Italy see Treviso
Tarz Iran 84 E4
Tasai, Ko i. Thai. 67 B5
Taschereau Canada 118 F4
Taseko Mountain Canada 116 F5
Tashauz Turkm. see Dashoguz
Tashi Chho Bhutan see Thimphu
Tashigang Bhutan see Trashigang
Tashino Rus. Fed. see Pervomaysk
Tashir Armenia 87 G2
Tashk, Daryācheh-ye l. Iran 84 D4
▶Tashkent Uzbek. 76 C3
Capital of Uzbekistan.
Tashkepri Turkm. 85 F2
Tāshqurghān Afgh. see Kholm
Tashtagol Rus. Fed. 68 F2
Tashtyp Rus. Fed. 68 F2
Tasialujjuaq, Lac l. Canada 119 G2
Tasiat, Lac l. Canada 118 G2
Tasiilap Karra c. Greenland 115 O3
Tasiilaq Greenland see Ammassalik
Tasīl Syria 81 B3
Tasiujaq Canada 119 H2
Tasiusaq Greenland 115 M2
Taşkent Turkey 81 A1
Tasker Niger 92 E3
Taskesken Kazakh. 76 F2
Taşköprü Turkey 86 D2
Tasman Abyssal Plain sea feature Tasman Sea 146 G8
Tasman Basin sea feature Tasman Sea 146 G8
Tasman Bay N.Z. 109 D5
▶Tasmania state Australia 107 [inset]
4th largest island in Oceania.
Tasman Islands P.N.G. see Nukumanu Islands
Tasman Mountains N.Z. 109 D5
Tasman Peninsula Australia 107 [inset]
Tasman Sea S. Pacific Ocean 102 H6
Taşova Turkey 86 E2
Tassara Niger 92 D3
Tassialouc, Lac l. Canada 118 G2
Tassili du Hoggar plat. Alg. 92 D2
Tassili n'Ajjer plat. Alg. 92 D2
Tasty Kazakh. 76 C3
Taşucu Turkey 81 A1
Tas-Yuryakh Rus. Fed. 61 M3
Tata Morocco 50 C6
Tatabánya Hungary 54 H1
Tata Mailau, Gunung mt. East Timor 104 D2
Tataouine Tunisia 50 G5
Tatarbunary Ukr. 55 M2
Tatarsk Rus. Fed. 60 I4
Tatarskiy Proliv strait Rus. Fed. 70 F2
Tatar Strait Rus. Fed. see Tatarskiy Proliv
Tate r. Australia 106 C3
Tateyama Japan 71 E6
Tathlina Lake Canada 116 G2
Tathlīth Saudi Arabia 82 F6
Tathlīth, Wādī watercourse Saudi Arabia 82 F5
Tathra Australia 108 D6
Tatinnai Lake Canada 117 L2
Tatishchevo Rus. Fed. 39 J6
Tatkon Myanmar 66 B2
Tatla Lake Canada 116 E5
Tatla Lake l. Canada 116 E5
Tatlayoko Lake Canada 116 E5
Tatnam, Cape Canada 117 N3
Tatra Mountains Poland/Slovakia 43 Q6
Tatry mts Poland/Slovakia see Tatra Mountains
Tatrzański Park Narodowy nat. park Poland 43 Q6
Tatshenshini-Alsek Provincial Wilderness Park Canada 116 B3
Tatsinskiy Rus. Fed. 39 I6
Tatta Pak. 85 G5
Tatuí Brazil 141 B3
Tatuk Mountain Canada 116 E4
Tatum U.S.A. 127 C5
Tatvan Turkey 87 F3
Tau Norway 41 D7
Taua Brazil 139 J5
Tauapeçaçu Brazil 138 F4
Taubaté Brazil 141 B3
Tauber r. Germany 49 J5
Tauberbischofsheim Germany 49 J5
Taucha Germany 49 M3
Taufstein hill Germany 49 J4
Taukum, Peski des. Kazakh. 76 D3
Taumarunui N.Z. 109 E4
Taumaturgo Brazil 138 D5
Taung S. Africa 96 G4
Taungdwingyi Myanmar 66 A2
Taunggyi Myanmar 66 B2
Taunglau Myanmar 66 B2
Taungnyo Range mts Myanmar 66 B3
Taungtha Myanmar 66 A2
Taungup Myanmar 72 B5
Taunton U.K. 45 D7
Taunton U.S.A. 131 J3
Taunus hills Germany 49 H4
Taupo N.Z. 109 F4
Taupo, Lake N.Z. 109 E4
Tauragė Lith. 41 M9
Tauranga N.Z. 109 F3
Taurasia Italy see Turin
Taureau, Réservoir resr Canada 118 G5
Taurianova Italy 54 G5
Tauroa Point N.Z. 109 D2
Taurus Mountains Turkey 81 A1
Taute r. France 45 F9
Tauu Islands P.N.G. 103 F2
Tauz Azer. see Tovuz
Tavas Turkey 55 M6
Tavastehus Fin. see Hämeenlinna
Taverham U.K. 45 I6
Taveuni i. Fiji 103 I3
Tavildara Tajik. 85 H2
Tavira Port. 53 C5
Tavistock Canada 130 E2
Tavistock U.K. 45 C8
Tavoy Myanmar 67 B4
Tavoy r. mouth Myanmar 67 B4
Tavoy Island Myanmar see Mali Kyun
Tavoy Point Myanmar 67 B4
Tavşanlı Turkey 55 M5
Taw r. U.K. 45 C7
Tawang India 79 G4
Tawas City U.S.A. 130 D1
Tawau Sabah Malaysia 64 F6
Tawè Myanmar see Tavoy
Tawe r. U.K. 45 D7
Ṭawī Ḥafīr well U.A.E. 84 D5
Ṭawī Murra well U.A.E. 84 D5
Tawmaw Myanmar 66 B1
Tawu Taiwan 73 I4
Taxkorgan China 76 E4
Tay r. Canada 116 C2
Tay r. U.K. 46 F4
Tay, Firth of est. U.K. 46 F4
Tay, Lake salt flat Australia 105 C8
Tay, Loch l. U.K. 46 E4
Tayandu, Kepulauan is Indon. 65 I8
Taybola Rus. Fed. 40 R2
Taycheedah U.S.A. 130 A2
Tayinloan U.K. 46 D5
Taylor Canada 116 F3
Taylor AK U.S.A. 114 B3
Taylor MI U.S.A. 130 D2
Taylor NE U.S.A. 126 D3
Taylor TX U.S.A. 127 D6
Taylor, Mount U.S.A. 125 J4
Taylorsville U.S.A. 130 C4
Taylorville U.S.A. 126 F4
Taymā' Saudi Arabia 86 E6
Taymura r. Rus. Fed. 61 K3
Taymyr, Ozero l. Rus. Fed. 61 L2
Taymyr, Poluostrov pen. Rus. Fed. see Taymyr Peninsula
Taymyr Peninsula Rus. Fed. 60 J2
Tây Ninh Vietnam 67 D5
Taypak Kazakh. 37 Q6
Taypaq Kazakh. see Taypak
Tayshet Rus. Fed. 68 H1
Taytay Phil. 64 F4
Tayuan China 70 B2
Tayyebād Iran 85 F3
Taz r. Rus. Fed. 60 I3
Taza Morocco 50 D5
Tāza Khurmātū Iraq 87 G4
Taze Myanmar 66 A2
Tazewell TN U.S.A. 130 D5
Tazewell VA U.S.A. 130 E5
Tazin r. Canada 117 I2
Tazin Lake Canada 117 I3
Tāzirbū Libya 93 F2
Tazmalt Alg. 53 I5
Tazovskaya Guba sea chan. Rus. Fed. 60 I3
Tbessa Alg. see Tébessa
▶T'bilisi Georgia 87 G2
Capital of Georgia.
Tbilisskaya Rus. Fed. 39 I7
Tchabal Mbabo mt. Cameroon 92 E4
Tchad country Africa see Chad
Tchamba Togo 92 D4
Tchibanga Gabon 94 B4
Tchigaï, Plateau du Niger 93 E2
Tchin-Tabaradene Niger 92 D3
Tcholliré Cameroon 93 E4
Tchula U.S.A. 127 F5
Tczew Poland 43 Q3
Te, Prêk r. Cambodia 67 D4
Teague, Lake salt flat Australia 105 C6
Te Anau N.Z. 109 A7
Te Anau, Lake N.Z. 109 A7
Teapa Mex. 132 F5
Te Araroa N.Z. 109 G3
Teate Italy see Chieti
Te Awamutu N.Z. 109 E4
Teba Indon. 65 J7
Tébarat Niger 92 D3
Tebas Indon. 67 E7
Tebay U.K. 44 E4
Tebesjuak Lake Canada 117 L2
Tébessa Alg. 54 C7
Tébessa, Monts de mts Alg. 54 C7
Tebingtinggi Indon. 67 B7
Tébourba Tunisia 54 C6
Téboursouk Tunisia 54 C6
Tebulos Mt'a Georgia/Rus. Fed. 87 G2
Tecate Mex. 124 E5
Tece Turkey 81 B1
Techiman Ghana 92 C4
Tecka Arg. 140 B6
Tecklenburger Land reg. Germany 49 H2
Tecoripa Mex. 123 F7
Técpan Mex. 132 D5
Tecuala Mex. 132 C4
Tecuci Romania 55 L2
Tecumseh MI U.S.A. 130 D3
Tecumseh NE U.S.A. 126 D3
Tedzhen Turkm. 85 F2
Teec Nos Pos U.S.A. 125 I3
Tees r. U.K. 44 F4
Teeswater Canada 130 E1
Tefé r. Brazil 138 F4
Tefenni Turkey 55 M6
Tegal Indon. 64 D8
Tegel airport Germany 49 N2
Tegid, Llyn l. U.K. 45 D6
▶Tegucigalpa Hond. 133 G6
Capital of Honduras.
Teguidda-n-Tessoumt Niger 92 D3
Tehachapi U.S.A. 124 D4
Tehachapi Mountains U.S.A. 124 D4
Tehachapi Pass U.S.A. 124 D4
Tehek Lake Canada 117 M1
Teheran Iran see Tehrān
Tehery Lake Canada 117 M1
Téhini Côte d'Ivoire 92 C4
▶Tehrān Iran 84 C3
Capital of Iran.
Tehri India see Tikamgarh
Tehuacán Mex. 132 E5
Tehuantepec, Golfo de Mex. see Tehuantepec, Gulf of
Tehuantepec, Gulf of Mex. 132 F5
Tehuantepec, Istmo de isthmus Mex. 132 F5

Teide, Pico del vol. Canary Is 92 B2
Teifi r. U.K. 45 C6
Teignmouth U.K. 45 D8
Teixeira de Sousa Angola see Luau
Teixeiras Brazil 141 C3
Teixeira Soares Brazil 141 A4
Tejakula Indon. 104 A2
Tejen Turkm. see Tedzhen
Tejo r. Port. 53 B4 see Tagus
Tejon Pass U.S.A. 124 D4
Tekapo, Lake N.Z. 109 C6
Tekax Mex. 132 G4
Tekeli Kazakh. 76 E3
Tekes China 76 F3
Tekiliktag mt. China 78 E1
Tekin Rus. Fed. 70 D2
Tekirdağ Turkey 55 L4
Tekka India 80 D2
Tekkali India 80 E2
Teknaf Bangl. 79 H5
Tekong Kechil, Pulau i. Sing. 67 [inset]
Te Kuiti N.Z. 109 E4
Tel r. India 80 D1
Télagh Alg. 53 F6
Telanaipura Indon. see Jambi
Tel Ashqelon tourist site Israel 81 B4
Télataï Mali 92 D3
Tel Aviv-Yafo Israel 81 B3
Telč Czech Rep. 43 O6
Telchac Puerto Mex. 132 G4
Telekhany Belarus see Tsyelyakhany
Telêmaco Borba Brazil 141 A4
Teleorman r. Romania 55 K3
Telerhteba, Djebel mt. Alg. 92 D2
Telescope Peak U.S.A. 124 E3
Teles Pires r. Brazil 139 G5
Telford U.K. 45 E6
Telgte Germany 49 H3
Télimélé Guinea 92 B3
Teljo, Jebel mt. Sudan 82 C7
Telkwa Canada 116 E4
Tell Atlas mts Alg. see Atlas Tellien
Tell City U.S.A. 130 B5
Teller U.S.A. 114 B3
Tell es Sultan West Bank see Jericho
Tellicherry India 80 B4
Tellin Belgium 48 F4
Telloh Iraq 87 G5
Telluride U.S.A. 125 J3
Tel'novskiy Rus. Fed. 70 F2
Telok Anson Malaysia see Teluk Intan
Telo Martius France see Toulon
Tel'pos-Iz, Gora mt. Rus. Fed. 37 R3
Telsen Arg. 140 C6
Telšiai Lith. 41 M9
Teltow Germany 49 N2
Teluk Anson Malaysia see Teluk Intan
Telukbetung Indon. see Bandar Lampung
Teluk Cenderawasih Marine National Park Indon. 65 I7
Teluk Intan Malaysia 67 C6
Temagami Lake Canada 118 F5
Temanggung Indon. 64 E8
Têmarxung China 79 G2
Temba S. Africa 97 I3
Tembagapura Indon. 65 J7
Tembenchi r. Rus. Fed. 61 K3
Tembilahan Indon. 64 C7
Tembisa S. Africa 97 I4
Tembo Aluma Angola 95 B4
Teme r. U.K. 45 E6
Temecula U.S.A. 124 E5
Temerloh Malaysia see Temerluh
Temerluh Malaysia 67 C7
Teminabuan Indon. 65 I7
Temirtau Kazakh. 76 D1
Témiscamie r. Canada 119 G4
Témiscamie, Lac l. Canada 119 G4
Temiscaming Canada 118 F5
Témiscamingue, Lac l. Canada 118 F5
Témiscouata, Lac l. Canada 119 H5
Temmes Fin. 40 N4
Temnikov Rus. Fed. 39 I5
Temora Australia 108 C5
Temósachic Mex. 123 G7
Tempe U.S.A. 125 H5
Tempe Downs Australia 105 F6
Tempelhof airport Germany 49 N2
Temple MI U.S.A. 130 C1
Temple TX U.S.A. 127 D6
Temple Bar U.K. 45 C6
Temple Dera Pak. 85 H4
Templemore Rep. of Ireland 47 E5
Temple Sowerby U.K. 44 E4
Templeton watercourse Australia 106 B4
Templin Germany 49 N1
Tempué Angola 95 B5
Temryuk Rus. Fed. 86 E1
Temryukskiy Zaliv b. Rus. Fed. 39 H7
Temuco Chile 140 B5
Temuka N.Z. 109 C7
Temuli China see Butuo
Tena Ecuador 138 C4
Tenabo Mex. 132 F4
Tenabo, Mount U.S.A. 124 E1
Tenali India 80 D2
Tenasserim Myanmar 67 B4
Tenasserim r. Myanmar 67 B4
Tenbury Wells U.K. 45 E6
Tenby U.K. 45 C7
Tendaho Eth. 94 E2
Tende, Col de pass France/Italy 52 H4
Ten Degree Channel India 67 A5
Tendō Japan 71 F5
Tenedos i. Turkey see Bozcaada
Ténenkou Mali 92 C3
Ténéré reg. Niger 92 D2
Ténéré du Tafassâsset des. Niger 92 E2
Tenerife i. Canary Is 92 B2
Ténès Alg. 53 G5
Teng, Nam r. Myanmar 66 B3
Tengah, Kepulauan is Indon. 64 F8
Tengah, Sungai r. Sing. 67 [inset]
Tengcheng China see Tengxian
Tengchong China 72 C3
Tengeh Reservoir Sing. 67 [inset]
Tengger Shamo des. China 68 I5
Tenggul i. Malaysia 67 C6
Tengiz, Ozero salt l. Kazakh. 76 C1
Tengqiao China 73 F5
Tengréla Côte d'Ivoire 92 C3
Ten'gushevo Rus. Fed. 39 I5
Tengxian China 73 F4
Teni India see Theni
Teniente Jubany research station Antarctica see Jubany
Tenille U.S.A. 129 D6
Tenke Dem. Rep. Congo 95 C5
Tenkeli Rus. Fed. 61 P2
Tenkodogo Burkina 92 C3
Ten Mile Lake salt flat Australia 105 C6
Ten Mile Lake Canada 119 K4
Tennant Creek Australia 104 F4
Tennessee r. U.S.A. 127 F4
Tennessee state U.S.A. 130 C5
Tennessee Pass U.S.A. 122 G5
Tennevoll Norway 40 J2
Tenojoki r. Fin./Norway 40 P1
Tenosique Mex. 132 F5
Tenteno Indon. 65 G7
Tenterden U.K. 45 H7
Tenterfield Australia 108 F2
Ten Thousand Islands U.S.A. 129 D7
Tentudia mt. Spain 53 C4
Tentulia Bangl. see Tetulia
Teodoro Sampaio Brazil 140 F2
Teófilo Otôni Brazil 141 C2
Tepa Indon. 104 E1
Tepache Mex. 123 F7
Te Paki N.Z. 109 D2
Tepatitlán Mex. 132 D4
Tepehuanes Mex. 127 B7
Tepeköy Turkey see Karakoçan
Tepelenë Albania 55 I4
Tepelská Vrchovina hills Czech Rep. 49 M5
Tepequem, Serra mts Brazil 133 L8
Tepic Mex. 132 D4
Te Pirita N.Z. 109 C6
Teplá r. Czech Rep. 49 M4
Teplice Czech Rep. 43 N5
Teplogorka Rus. Fed. 38 L3
Teploozersk Rus. Fed. 70 C2
Teploye Rus. Fed. 39 H5
Teploye Ozero Rus. Fed. see Teploozersk
Tepoca, Cabo c. Mex. 123 E7
Tepopa, Punta pt Mex. 123 E7
Tequila Mex. 132 D4
Téra Niger 92 D3
Teramo Italy 54 E3
Terang Australia 108 A7
Ter Apel Neth. 48 H2
Teratani r. Pak. 85 H4
Tercan Turkey 87 F3
Terebovlya Ukr. 39 E6
Terekty Kazakh. 76 G2
Teresa Cristina Brazil 141 A4
Tereshka r. Rus. Fed. 39 J6
Teresina Brazil 139 J5
Teresina de Goias Brazil 141 B1
Teresita Col. 138 E3
Teresópolis Brazil 141 C3
Teressa Island India 67 A5
Terezinha Brazil 139 H3
Tergeste Italy see Trieste
Tergnier France 48 D5
Teriberka Rus. Fed. 40 S2
Termez Uzbek. 85 G2
Termini Imerese Sicily Italy 54 E6
Términos, Laguna de lag. Mex. 132 F5
Termit-Kaoboul Niger 92 E3
Termiz Uzbek. see Termez
Termo U.S.A. 124 C1
Termoli Italy 54 F4
Termonde Belgium see Dendermonde
Tern r. U.K. 45 E6
Ternate Indon. 65 H6
Terneuzen Neth. 48 D3
Terney Rus. Fed. 70 E3
Terni Italy 54 E3
Ternopil' Ukr. 39 E6
Ternopol' Ukr. see Ternopil'
Terpeniya, Mys c. Rus. Fed. 70 G2
Terpeniya, Zaliv g. Rus. Fed. 70 F2
Terra Alta U.S.A. 130 F4
Terra Bella U.S.A. 124 D4
Terrace Canada 116 D4
Terrace Bay Canada 118 D4
Terra Firma S. Africa 96 F3
Terråk Norway 40 H4
Terralba Sardinia Italy 54 C5
Terra Nova Bay Antarctica 148 H1
Terra Nova National Park Canada 119 L4
Terre Adélie reg. Antarctica see Adélie Land
Terrebonne Bay U.S.A. 127 F6
Terre Haute U.S.A. 130 B4
Terre-Neuve prov. Canada see Newfoundland and Labrador
Terre-Neuve-et-Labrador prov. Canada see Newfoundland and Labrador
Terres Australes et Antarctiques Françaises terr. Indian Ocean see French Southern and Antarctic Lands
Terry U.S.A. 122 G3
Terschelling i. Neth. 48 F1
Terskiy Bereg coastal area Rus. Fed. 38 H2
Tertenia Sardinia Italy 54 C5
Terter Azer. see Tärtär
Teruel Spain 53 F3
Terutao National Park Thai. 67 B6
Tervola Fin. 40 N3
Tešanj Bos.-Herz. 54 G2
Teseney Eritrea 82 E6
Tesha r. Rus. Fed. 39 I5
Teshekpuk Lake U.S.A. 114 C2
Teshio Japan 70 F3
Teshio-gawa r. Japan 70 F3
Teslin Canada 116 C2
Teslin r. Canada 116 C2
Teslin Lake Canada 116 C2
Tesouras r. Brazil 141 A1
Tessalit Mali 92 D2
Tessaoua Niger 92 D3
Tessolo Moz. 97 L1
Test r. U.K. 45 F8
Testour Tunisia 54 C6
Tetachuck Lake Canada 116 E4
Tetas, Punta pt Chile 140 B2
Tete Moz. 95 D5
Te Teko N.Z. 109 F4
Teteriv r. Ukr. 39 F6
Teterow Germany 43 N4
Tetiyev Ukr. see Tetiyiv
Tetiyiv Ukr. 39 F6
Tetlin U.S.A. 116 A2
Tetlin Lake U.S.A. 116 A2
Tetney U.K. 44 G5
Teton r. U.S.A. 122 F3
Tétouan Morocco 53 D6
Tetovo Macedonia 55 I3
Tetpur India 78 B5
Tetuán Morocco see Tétouan
Tetulia Bangl. 79 G4
Tetulia sea chan. Bangl. 79 G5
Tetyukhe Rus. Fed. see Dal'negorsk
Tetyukhe-Pristan' Rus. Fed. see Rudnaya Pristan'
Tetyushi Rus. Fed. 39 K5
Teuco r. Arg. 140 D2
Teufelsbach Namibia 96 C2
Teunom Indon. 67 A6
Teunom r. Indon. 67 A6
Teutoburger Wald hills Germany 49 I2
Teuva Fin. 40 L5
Tevere r. Italy see Tiber
Teverya Israel see Tiberias
Teviot r. U.K. 46 G5
Te Waewae Bay N.Z. 109 A8
Te Waiponamu i. N.Z. see South Island
Tewane Botswana 97 H2
Tewantin Australia 107 F5
Tewkesbury U.K. 45 E7
Têwo China 72 D1
Texarkana AR U.S.A. 127 E5
Texarkana TX U.S.A. 127 E5
Texas Australia 108 E2
Texas state U.S.A. 127 D6
Texel i. Neth. 48 E1
Texhoma U.S.A. 127 C4
Texoma, Lake U.S.A. 127 D5
Teyateyaneng Lesotho 97 H5
Teykovo Rus. Fed. 38 I4
Teza r. Rus. Fed. 38 I4
Tezpur India 79 H4
Tezu India 79 I4
Tha, Nam r. Laos 66 C2
Thaa Atoll Maldives see Kolhumadulu Atoll
Tha-anne r. Canada 117 M2
Thabana-Ntlenyana mt. Lesotho 97 I5
Thaba Nchu S. Africa 97 H5
Thaba Putsoa mt. Lesotho 97 H5
Thaba-Tseka Lesotho 97 I5
Thabazimbi S. Africa 97 H3
Thab Lan National Park Thai. 67 C4
Tha Bo Laos 66 C3
Thabong S. Africa 97 H4
Thabyedaung Myanmar 72 C4
Thade r. Myanmar 66 A3
Thagyettaw Myanmar 67 B4
Tha Hin Thai. see Lop Buri
Thai Binh Vietnam 66 D2
▶Thailand country Asia 66 C4
asia 6, 58–59
Thailand, Gulf of Asia 67 C5
Thai Muang Thai. 67 B5
Thai Nguyên Vietnam 66 D2
Thaj Saudi Arabia 84 C5
Thakurgaon Bangl. 79 G4
Thakurtola India 78 E5
Thal Germany 49 K4
Thala Tunisia 54 C7
Thalang Thai. 67 B5
Thalassery India see Tellicherry
Thal Desert Pak. 85 H4
Thale (Harz) Germany 49 L3
Thaliparamba India see Taliparamba
Thallon Australia 108 D2
Thalo Pak. 85 G4
Thamaga Botswana 97 G3
Thamar, Jabal mt. Yemen 82 G7
Thamarīt Oman 83 H6
Thame r. U.K. 45 F7
Thames r. Ont. Canada 121 K3
Thames r. Ont. Canada 130 D2
Thames N.Z. 109 E3
Thames est. U.K. 45 H7
Thames r. U.K. 45 H7
Thamesford Canada 130 E2
Thana India see Thane
Thanatpin Myanmar 66 B3
Thandwè Myanmar see Sandoway
Thane India 80 B2
Thanet, Isle of pen. U.K. 45 I7
Thăng Binh Vietnam 66 E4
Thangoo Australia 104 C4
Thangra Jammu and Kashmir 78 D2
Thanh Hoa Vietnam 66 D3
Thanh Tri Vietnam 67 D5
Thanjavur India 80 C4
Than Kyun i. Myanmar 67 B5
Thanlwin r. China/Myanmar see Salween
Thanlyin Myanmar see Syriam
Thaolintoa Lake Canada 117 L2
Tha Pla Thai. 66 C3
Thap Put Thai. 67 B5
Thapsacus Syria see Dibsī
Thap Sakae Thai. 67 B5
Tharabwin Myanmar 67 B4
Tharad India 78 B4
Thar Desert India/Pak. 85 H5
Thargomindah Australia 108 A1
Tharrawaw Myanmar 66 A3
Tharthār, Buḥayrat ath l. Iraq 87 F4
Tharwānīyyah U.A.E. 84 D6
Thasos i. Greece 55 K4
Thatcher U.S.A. 125 I5
Thât Khê Vietnam 66 D2
Thât Nôt Vietnam 67 D5
Thaton Myanmar 66 B3
Thaungdut Myanmar 66 A1
Tha Uthen Thai. 66 D3
Thayawthadangyi Kyun i. Myanmar 67 B4
Thayetmyo Myanmar 66 A3
Thazi Magwe Myanmar 66 A3
Thazi Mandalay Myanmar 79 I5
The Aldermen Islands N.Z. 109 F3
Theba U.S.A. 125 G5
▶The Bahamas country West Indies 129 E7
north america 9, 112–113
Thebes Greece see Thiva
The Bluff Bahamas 129 E7
The Broads nat. park U.K. 45 I6
The Brothers is Hong Kong China 73 [inset]
The Calvados Chain is P.N.G. 106 F1
The Cheviot hill U.K. 44 E3
The Dalles U.S.A. 122 C3
Thedford U.S.A. 126 C3
The Entrance Australia 108 E4
The Faither stack U.K. 46 [inset]
The Fens reg. U.K. 45 G6
▶The Gambia country Africa 92 B3
africa 7, 90–91
Thegon Myanmar 66 A3
The Grampians mts Australia 107 C8
The Great Oasis oasis Egypt see Khārijah, Wāḥāt al
The Grenadines is St Vincent 133 L6
The Gulf Asia 84 C4
▶The Hague Neth. 48 E2
Seat of government of the Netherlands.
The Hunters Hills N.Z. 109 C7
Thekulthili Lake Canada 117 I2
The Lakes National Park Australia 108 C6
Thelon r. Canada 117 L1
The Lynd Junction Australia 106 D3
Themar Germany 49 K4
Thembalihle S. Africa 97 I4
The Minch sea chan. U.K. 46 C2
The Naze c. Norway see Lindesnes
The Needles stack U.K. 45 F8
Theni India 80 C4
Thenia Alg. 53 H5
Theniet El Had Alg. 53 H6
The North Sound sea chan. U.K. 46 G1
Theodore Australia 106 E5
Theodore Canada 117 K5
Theodore Roosevelt Lake U.S.A. 125 H5
Theodore Roosevelt National Park U.S.A. 126 C2
Theodosia Ukr. see Feodosiya
The Old Man of Coniston hill U.K. 44 D4
The Paps hill Rep. of Ireland 47 C5
The Pas Canada 117 K4
The Pilot mt. Australia 108 D6
Thera i. Greece see Thira
Thérain r. France 48 C5
Theresa U.S.A. 131 H1
Thermaïkos Kolpos g. Greece 55 J4
Thermopolis U.S.A. 122 F4
The Rock Australia 108 C5
Thérouanne France 48 C4
The Salt Lake salt flat Australia 107 C6
▶The Settlement Christmas I. 64 D9
Capital of Christmas Island.
The Skaw spit Denmark see Grenen
The Slot sea chan. Solomon Is see New Georgia Sound
The Solent strait U.K. 45 F8
Thessalon Canada 118 E5
Thessalonica Greece see Thessaloniki
Thessaloniki Greece 55 J4
The Storr hill U.K. 46 C3
Thet r. U.K. 45 H6
The Terraces hills Australia 105 C7
Thetford U.K. 45 H6
Thetford Mines Canada 119 H5
Thetkethaung r. Myanmar 66 A4
The Triangle mts Myanmar 66 B1
The Trossachs hills U.K. 46 E4
The Twins Australia 107 A6
Theva-i-Ra reef Fiji see Ceva-i-Ra
▶The Valley Anguilla 133 L5
Capital of Anguilla.
Thevenard Island Australia 104 A5
Thévenet, Lac l. Canada 119 H2
Theveste Alg. see Tébessa
The Wash b. U.K. 45 H6
The Weald reg. U.K. 45 H7
The Woodlands U.S.A. 127 E6
Thibodaux U.S.A. 127 F6
Thicket Portage Canada 117 L4
Thief River Falls U.S.A. 126 D1
Thiel Neth. see Tiel
Thiel Mountains Antarctica 148 K1
Thielsen, Mount U.S.A. 122 C4
Thielt Belgium see Tielt
Thiérache reg. France 48 D5
Thiers France 52 F4
Thiès Senegal 92 B3
Thika Kenya 94 D4
Thiladhunmathi Atoll Maldives 80 B5
Thiladunmathi Atoll Maldives see Thiladhunmathi Atoll
Thimbu Bhutan see Thimphu
▶Thimphu Bhutan 79 G4
Capital of Bhutan.
Thionville France 48 G5
Thira i. Greece 55 K6
Thirsk U.K. 44 F4
Thirty Mile Lake Canada 117 L2
Thiruvananthapuram India see Trivandrum
Thiruvannamalai India see Tiruvannamalai
Thiruvarur India 80 C4
Thiruvattiyur India see Tiruvottiyur
Thisted Denmark 41 F8
Thistle Creek Canada 116 B2
Thistle Lake Canada 117 I1
Thityabin Myanmar 66 A2
Thiu Khao Luang Phrabang mts Laos/Thai. see Luang Phrabang, Thiu Khao
Thiva Greece 55 J5
Thívai Greece see Thiva
Thlewiaza r. Canada 117 M2
Thoa r. Canada 117 I2
Thô Chu, Đao i. Vietnam 67 C5
Thoen Thai. 72 C5
Thoeng Thai. 66 C3
Thohoyandou S. Africa 97 J2
Tholen Neth. 48 E3
Tholen i. Neth. 48 E3
Tholey Germany 48 H5
Thomas Hill Reservoir U.S.A. 126 E4
Thomas Hubbard, Cape Canada 115 I1
Thomaston CT U.S.A. 131 I3
Thomaston GA U.S.A. 129 C5
Thomastown Rep. of Ireland 47 E5
Thomasville AL U.S.A. 129 C6
Thomasville GA U.S.A. 129 D6
Thommen Belgium 48 G4
Thompson Canada 117 L4
Thompson r. Canada 116 F5
Thompson U.S.A. 125 I2
Thompson r. U.S.A. 120 I4
Thompson Falls U.S.A. 122 E3
Thompson Peak U.S.A. 123 G6
Thompson's Falls Kenya see Nyahururu
Thompson Sound Canada 116 E5
Thomson U.S.A. 129 D5
Thon Buri Thai. 67 C4
Thonokied Lake Canada 117 I1
Thôn Son Hai Vietnam 67 E5
Thoothukudi India see Tuticorin
Thoreau U.S.A. 125 I4
Thorn Neth. 48 F3
Thorn Poland see Toruń
Thornaby-on-Tees U.K. 44 F4
Thornapple r. U.S.A. 130 C2
Thornbury U.K. 45 E7
Thorne U.K. 44 G5
Thorne U.S.A. 124 D2
Thornton r. Australia 106 B3
Thorold Canada 130 F2
Thorshavnfjella reg. Antarctica see Thorshavnheiane
Thorshavnheiane reg. Antarctica 148 C2
Thota-ea-Moli Lesotho 97 H5
Thouars France 52 D3
Thoubal India 79 H4
Thourout Belgium see Torhout
Thousand Islands Canada/U.S.A. 131 G1
Thousand Lake Mountain U.S.A. 125 H2
Thousand Oaks U.S.A. 124 D4
Thousandsticks U.S.A. 130 D5
Thrace reg. Europe 55 L4
Thraki reg. Europe see Thrace
Thrakiko Pelagos sea Greece 55 K4
Three Gorges Project resr China 73 F2
Three Hills Canada 116 H5
Three Hummock Island Australia 107 [inset]
Three Kings Islands N.Z. 109 D2
Three Oaks U.S.A. 130 B3
Three Pagodas Pass Myanmar/Thai. 66 B4
Three Points, Cape Ghana 92 C4
Three Rivers U.S.A. 130 C3
Three Sisters mt. U.S.A. 122 C3
Three Springs Australia 105 A7
Thrissur India see Trichur
Throckmorton U.S.A. 127 D5
Throssell, Lake salt flat Australia 105 D6
Throssel Range hills Australia 104 C5
Thrushton National Park Australia 108 C1
Thubun Lakes Canada 117 I2
Thu Dâu Môt Vietnam 67 D5
Thuddungra Australia 108 D5
Thuin Belgium 48 E4
Thul Pak. 85 H4
Thulaythawāt Gharbī, Jabal hill Syria 81 D2
Thule Greenland 115 L2
Thun Switz. 52 H3
Thunder Bay Canada 115 J5
Thunder Bay b. U.S.A. 130 D1
Thunder Creek r. Canada 117 J5
Thüngen Germany 49 J5
Thung Salaeng Luang National Park Thai. 66 C3
Thung Song Thai. 67 B5
Thung Yai Naresuan Wildlife Reserve nature res. Thai. 66 B4
Thüringen land Germany 49 K3
Thüringer Becken reg. Germany 49 L3
Thüringer Wald mts Germany 49 K4
Thuringia land Germany see Thüringen
Thuringian Forest mts Germany see Thüringer Wald
Thurles Rep. of Ireland 47 E5
Thurn, Pass Austria 43 N7
Thursday Island Australia 106 C1
Thurso U.K. 46 F2
Thurso r. U.K. 46 F2
Thurston Island Antarctica 148 K2
Thurston Peninsula i. Antarctica see Thurston Island
Thüster Berg hill Germany 49 J2
Thuthukudi India see Tuticorin
Thwaite U.K. 44 E4
Thwaites Glacier Tongue Antarctica 148 K1
Thyatira Turkey see Akhisar
Thyborøn Denmark 41 F8
Thymerais reg. France 48 B6
Tianchang China 73 H1
Tiancheng China see Chongyang
Tianchi China see Lezhi
Tiandeng China 72 E4
Tiandong China 72 E4
T'ianet'i Georgia 87 G2
Tianfanjie China 73 H2
Tianjin China 69 L5
Tianjin municipality China 69 L5
Tianjun China 76 I4
Tianlin China 72 E3
Tianma China see Changshan
Tianmen China 73 G2
Tianqiaoling China 70 C4
Tianquan China 72 D2
Tianshan China 69 M4
Tian Shan mts China/Kyrg. see Tien Shan
Tianshui China 72 E1
Tianshuihai Aksai Chin 78 D2
Tiantai China 73 I2
Tiantang China see Yuexi
Tianyang China 72 E4
Tianzhou China see Tianyang
Tianzhu Gansu China 68 I5
Tianzhu Guizhou China 73 F3
Tiaret Alg. 53 G6
Tiassalé Côte d'Ivoire 92 C4
Tibagi Brazil 141 A4
Tibal, Wādī watercourse Iraq 87 F4
Tibati Cameroon 92 E4
Tibba Pak. 85 H4
Tibé, Pic de mt. Guinea 92 C4
Tiber r. Italy 54 E4
Tiberias Israel 81 B3
Tiberias, Lake Israel see Galilee, Sea of
Tiber Reservoir U.S.A. 122 F2
Tibesti mts Chad 93 E2
Tibet aut. reg. China see Xizang Zizhiqu
Tibi India 85 I4
Tibooburra Australia 107 C6
Tibrikot Nepal 79 E3
Tibro Sweden 41 I7
Tibur Italy see Tivoli
Tiburón, Isla i. Mex. 123 E7
Ticehurst U.K. 45 H7
Tichborne Canada 131 G1
Tichégami r. Canada 119 G4
Tîchît Mauritania 92 C3
Tichla W. Sahara 92 B2
Ticinum Italy see Pavia
Ticonderoga U.S.A. 131 I2
Ticul Mex. 132 G4
Tidaholm Sweden 41 H7
Tiddim Myanmar 66 A2
Tiden India 67 A6
Tidjikja Mauritania 92 B3
Tiefa China 70 A4
Tiel Neth. 48 F3
Tieli China 70 B3
Tieling China 70 A4
Tielongtan Aksai Chin 78 D2
Tielt Belgium 48 D4
Tienen Belgium 48 E4
Tien Shan mts China/Kyrg. 68 D4
Tientsin municipality China see Tianjin
Tiên Yên Vietnam 66 D2
Tierp Sweden 41 J6
Tierra Amarilla U.S.A. 123 G5
▶Tierra del Fuego, Isla Grande de i. Arg./Chile 140 C8
Largest island in South America.
south america 134–135
Tierra del Fuego, Parque Nacional nat. park Arg. 140 C8
Tiétar r. Spain 53 D4
Tiétar, Valle de valley Spain 53 D3
Tietê r. Brazil 141 A3
Tieyon Australia 105 F6
Tiffin U.S.A. 130 D3
Tiflis Georgia see T'bilisi
Tifton U.S.A. 129 D6
Tiga Reservoir Nigeria 92 D3
Tigen Kazakh. 87 H1
Tigh Āb Iran 85 F5
Tigheciului, Dealurile hills Moldova 55 M2
Tighina Moldova 55 M1
Tigiria India 80 E1
Tignère Cameroon 92 E4
Tignish Canada 119 I5
Tigranocerta Turkey see Siirt
Tigre r. Venez. 138 F2
Tigris r. Asia 87 G5
also known as Dicle (Turkey) or Nahr Dijlah (Iraq/Syria)
Tigrovaya Balka Zapovednik nature res. Tajik. 85 H2
Tiguidit, Falaise de esc. Niger 92 D3
Tīh, Gebel el plat. Egypt see Tīh, Jabal at
Tīh, Jabal at plat. Egypt 81 A5
Tijuana Mex. 124 E5
Tikamgarh India 78 D4
Tikanlik China 76 G3
Tikhoretsk Rus. Fed. 39 I7
Tikhvin Rus. Fed. 38 G4
Tikhvinskaya Gryada ridge Rus. Fed. 38 G4
Tiki Basin sea feature S. Pacific Ocean 147 L7
Tikokino N.Z. 109 F4
Tikopia i. Solomon Is 103 G3
Tikrīt Iraq 87 F4
Tikse Jammu and Kashmir 78 D2
Tiksheozero, Ozero l. Rus. Fed. 40 R3
Tiksi Rus. Fed. 61 N2
Tiladummati Atoll Maldives see Thiladhunmathi Atoll
Tilaiya Reservoir India 79 F4
Tilbeşar Ovasi plain Turkey 81 C1
Tilbooroo Australia 108 B1
Tilburg Neth. 48 F3
Tilbury Canada 130 D2
Tilbury U.K. 45 H7
Tilcara Arg. 140 C2
Tilden U.S.A. 127 D6
Tilemsès Niger 92 D3
Tilemsi, Vallée du watercourse Mali 92 D3
Tilhar India 78 D4
Tilimsen Alg. see Tlemcen
Tilin Myanmar 66 A2
Tillabéri Niger 92 D3
Tillamook U.S.A. 122 C3
Tillanchong Island India 67 A5
Tillia Niger 92 D3
Tillicoultry U.K. 46 F4
Tillsonburg Canada 130 E2
Tillyfourie U.K. 46 G3
Tilonia India 85 I5
Tilos i. Greece 55 L6
Tilothu India 79 F4
Tilpa Australia 108 B3
Tilsit Rus. Fed. see Sovetsk
Tilt r. U.K. 46 F4
Tilton IL U.S.A. 130 B3
Tilton NH U.S.A. 131 J2
Tim Rus. Fed. 39 H6
Ṭimā Egypt 82 D4
Timah, Bukit hill Sing. 67 [inset]
Timakara i. India 80 B4
Timanskiy Kryazh ridge Rus. Fed. 38 K2
Timar Turkey 87 F3
Timaru N.Z. 109 C7
Timashevsk Rus. Fed. 39 H7
Timashevskaya Rus. Fed. see Timashevsk
Timbedgha Mauritania 92 C3
Timber Creek Australia 102 D3
Timber Mountain U.S.A. 124 E3
Timberville U.S.A. 131 F4
Timbuktu Mali 92 C3
Timétrine reg. Mali 92 C3
Timiaouine Alg. 92 D2
Timimoun Alg. 50 E6
Timirist, Râs pt Mauritania 92 B3
Timiskaming, Lake Canada see Témiscamingue, Lac
Timişoara Romania 55 I2
Timmins Canada 118 E4
Timms Hill hill U.S.A. 126 F2
Timon Brazil 139 J5
Timor i. East Timor/Indon. 104 D2
Timor-Leste country Asia see East Timor
Timor Loro Sae country Asia see East Timor
Timor Sea Australia/Indon. 102 C3
Timor Timur country Asia see East Timor
Timperley Range hills Australia 105 C6
Timrå Sweden 40 J5
Tīn, Ra's at pt Libya 86 A4
Ţīna, Khalīg el b. Egypt see Ţīnah, Khalīj aţ
Tinah Syria 81 D1
Ţīnah, Khalīj aţ b. Egypt 81 A4
Tin Can Bay Australia 107 F5
Tindivanam India 80 C3
Tindouf Alg. 50 C6
Ti-n-Essako Mali 92 D3
Tinggi i. Malaysia 67 D7
Tingha Australia 108 E2
Tingis Morocco see Tangier
Tingo Maria Peru 138 C5
Tingréla Côte d'Ivoire see Tengréla
Tingsryd Sweden 41 I8
Tingvoll Norway 40 F5
Tingwall U.K. 46 F1
Tingzhou China see Changting
Tinharé, Ilha de i. Brazil 141 D1
Tinh Gia Vietnam 66 D3
Tinian i. N. Mariana Is 65 L4
Tini Heke is N.Z. see Snares Islands
Tinnelvelly India see Tirunelveli
Tinogasta Arg. 140 C3

Tinos Greece 55 K6
Tinos i. Greece 55 K6
Tinqueux France 48 D5
Tinrhert, Plateau du Alg. 92 D2
Tinsukia India 79 H4
Tintagel U.K. 45 C8
Țînțâne Mauritania 92 B3
Tintina Arg. 140 D3
Tintinara Australia 107 C7
Tioga U.S.A. 126 C1
Tioman i. Malaysia 67 D7
Tionesta U.S.A. 130 F3
Tionesta Lake U.S.A. 130 F3
Tipasa Alg. 53 H5
Tiphsah Syria see Dibsī
Tipperary Rep. of Ireland 47 D5
Tipton CA U.S.A. 124 D3
Tipton IA U.S.A. 126 F3
Tipton IN U.S.A. 130 B3
Tipton MO U.S.A. 126 E4
Tipton, Mount U.S.A. 125 F4
Tiptop U.S.A. 130 E5
Tip Top Hill hill Canada 118 D4
Tiptree U.K. 45 H7
Tiptur India 80 C3
Tipturi India see Tiptur
Tiracambu, Serra do hills Brazil 139 I4
Tirah reg. Pak. 85 H3

▶Tirana Albania 55 H4
Capital of Albania.

Tiranë Albania see Tirana
Tirano Italy 54 D1
Tirari Desert Australia 107 B5
Tiraspol Moldova 55 M1
Tiraz Mountains Namibia 96 C4
Tire Turkey 55 L5
Tirebolu Turkey 87 E2
Tiree i. U.K. 46 C4
Tirgoviște Romania see Târgoviște
Tîrgu Jiu Romania see Târgu Jiu
Tîrgu Mureș Romania see Târgu Mureș
Tîrgu Neamț Romania see Târgu Neamț
Tîrgu Secuiesc Romania see Târgu Secuiesc
Tiri Pak. 85 G4
Tirich Mir mt. Pak. 85 H2
Tirlemont Belgium see Tienen
Tirna r. India 80 C2
Tîrnăveni Romania see Târnăveni
Tirnavos Greece see Tyrnavos
Tiros Brazil 141 B2
Tirourda, Col de pass Alg. 53 I5
Tirreno, Mare sea France/Italy see Tyrrhenian Sea
Tirso r. Sardinia Italy 54 C5
Tirthahalli India 80 B3
Tiruchchendur India 80 C4
Tiruchchirappalli India 80 C4
Tiruchengodu India 80 C4
Tirunelveli India 80 C4
Tirupati India 80 C3
Tiruppattur Tamil Nadu India 80 C3
Tiruppattur Tamil Nadu India 80 C4
Tiruppur India 80 C4
Tiruttani India 80 C3
Tirutturaippundi India 80 C4
Tiruvallur India 80 C3
Tiruvannamalai India 80 C3
Tiruvottiyur India 80 D3
Tiru Well Australia 104 D5
Tisa r. Serb. and Mont. 55 I2
also known as Tisza (Hungary), Tysa (Ukraine)
Tisdale Canada 117 J4
Tishomingo U.S.A. 127 D5
Ţisīyah Syria 81 C3
Tissemsilt Alg. 53 G6
Tisza r. Hungary see Tisa
Titalya Bangl. see Tetulia
Titan Dome ice feature Antarctica 148 H1
Titao Burkina 92 C3
Tit-Ary Rus. Fed. 61 N2
Titawin Morocco see Tétouan
Titicaca, Lago Bol./Peru see Titicaca, Lake

▶Titicaca, Lake Bol./Peru 138 E7
Largest lake in South America.
south america 134–135

Tititea mt. N.Z. see Aspiring, Mount
Titlagarh India 80 D1
Titograd Serb. and Mont. see Podgorica
Titova Mitrovica Serb. and Mont. see Kosovska Mitrovica
Titov Drvar Bos.-Herz. 54 G2
Titovo Užice Serb. and Mont. see Užice
Titovo Velenje Slovenia see Velenje
Titov Veles Macedonia see Veles
Titov Vrbas Yugo. see Vrbas
Ti Tree Australia 104 F5
Titu Romania 55 K2
Titusville FL U.S.A. 129 D6
Titusville PA U.S.A. 130 F3
Tiu Chung Chau i. Hong Kong China 73 [inset]
Tiumpain, Rubha an hd U.K. see Tiumpan Head
Tiumpan Head hd U.K. 46 C2
Tiva watercourse Kenya 94 D4
Tivari India 78 C4
Tiverton Canada 130 E1
Tiverton U.K. 45 D8
Tivoli Italy 54 E4
Ṭīwī Oman 84 E6
Ti-ywa Myanmar 67 B4
Tizi El Arba hill Alg. 53 H5
Tizimín Mex. 132 G4
Tizi N'Kouilal pass Alg. 53 I5
Tizi Ouzou Alg. 53 I5
Tiznap He r. China 78 D1
Tiznit Morocco 92 C2
Tiztoutine Morocco 53 E6
Tjaneni Swaziland 97 J3
Tjappsåive Sweden 40 K4
Tjeukemeer l. Neth. 48 F2
Tjirebon Indon. see Cirebon
Tjolotjo Zimbabwe see Tsholotsho
Tjorhom Norway 41 E7
Tkibuli Georgia see Tqibuli
Tlahualilo Mex. 127 C7
Tlaxcala Mex. 132 E5
Tl'ell Canada 116 D4
Tlemcen Alg. 53 F6
Tlhakalatlou S. Africa 96 F5
Tlholong S. Africa 97 I5
Tlokweng Botswana 97 G3
Tlyarata Rus. Fed. 87 G2
To r. Myanmar 66 B3
Toad r. Canada 116 E3
Toad River Canada 116 E3
Toamasina Madag. 95 E5
Toana mts U.S.A. 125 F1
Toano U.S.A. 131 G5
Toa Payoh Sing. 67 [inset]
Toba China 72 C2
Toba, Danau l. Indon. 67 B7
Toba, Lake Indon. see Toba, Danau
Toba and Kakar Ranges mts Pak. 85 G4
Toba Gargaji Pak. 85 I4
Tobago i. Trin. and Tob. 133 L6
Tobelo Indon. 65 H6
Tobermorey Australia 106 B4
Tobermory Australia 108 A1
Tobermory Canada 130 E1
Tobermory U.K. 46 C4
Tobi i. Palau 65 I6
Tobin, Lake salt flat Australia 104 D5
Tobin, Mount U.S.A. 124 E1
Tobin Lake Canada 117 K4
Tobin Lake l. Canada 117 K4
Tobi-shima i. Japan 71 E5
Tobol r. Kazakh./Rus. Fed. 74 F1
Tobol'sk Rus. Fed. 60 H4
Tô Bong Vietnam 67 E4
Tobruk Libya see Tubruq
Tobseda Rus. Fed. 38 L1
Tobyl r. Kazakh./Rus. Fed. see Tobol
Tobysh r. Rus. Fed. 38 K2
Tocache Nuevo Peru 138 C5
Tocantinópolis Brazil 139 I5
Tocantins r. Brazil 141 A1
Tocantins state Brazil 141 A1
Tocantinzinha r. Brazil 141 A1
Toccoa U.S.A. 129 D5
Tochi r. Pak. 85 H3
Töcksfors Sweden 41 G7
Tocopilla Chile 140 B2
Tocumwal Australia 108 B5
Tod, Mount Canada 116 G5
Todd watercourse Australia 106 A5
Todi Italy 54 E3
Todoga-saki pt Japan 71 F5
Todos Santos Mex. 132 B4
Toe Head hd U.K. 46 B3
Tofino Canada 116 E5
Toft U.K. 46 [inset]
Tofua i. Tonga 103 I3
Togatax China 78 E2
Togian i. Indon. 65 G7
Togian, Kepulauan is Indon. 65 G7
Togliatti Rus. Fed. see Tol'yatti
▶Togo country Africa 92 D4
africa 7, 90–91
Togtoh China 69 K4
Togton He r. China 79 H2
Togton Heyan China see Tanggulashan
Tohatchi U.S.A. 125 I4
Toholampi Fin. 40 N5
Toiba China 79 G3
Toibalewe India 67 A5
Toijala Fin. 41 M6
Toili Indon. 65 G7
Toi-misaki pt Japan 71 C7
Toivakka Fin. 40 O5
Toiyabe Range mts U.S.A. 124 E2
Tojikiston country Asia see Tajikistan
Tok U.S.A. 116 A2
Tokar Sudan 82 E6
Tokara-rettō is Japan 71 C7
Tokarevka Rus. Fed. 39 I6
Tokat Turkey 86 E2
Tŏkchok-to i. S. Korea 71 B5
Tokdo i. N. Pacific Ocean see Liancourt Rocks

▶Tokelau terr. S. Pacific Ocean 103 I2
New Zealand Overseas Territory.
oceania 8, 100–101

Tokmak Kyrg. see Tokmok
Tokmak Ukr. 39 G7
Tokmok Kyrg. 76 E3
Tokomaru Bay N.Z. 109 G4
Tokoroa N.Z. 109 E4
Tokoza S. Africa 97 I4
Toksun China 76 G3
Tok-tō i. N. Pacific Ocean see Liancourt Rocks
Toktogul Kyrg. 76 D3
Tokto-ri i. N. Pacific Ocean see Liancourt Rocks
Tokur Rus. Fed. 70 D1
Tokushima Japan 71 D6
Tokuyama Japan 71 C6

▶Tōkyō Japan 71 E6
Capital of Japan. Most populous city in the world and in Asia.

Tokzār Afgh. 85 G3
Tolaga Bay N.Z. 109 G4
Tôlañaro Madag. 95 E6
Tolbo Mongolia 76 H2
Tolbukhin Bulg. see Dobrich
Tolbuzino Rus. Fed. 70 B1
Toledo Brazil 140 F2
Toledo Spain 53 D4
Toledo IA U.S.A. 126 E3
Toledo OH U.S.A. 130 D3
Toledo OR U.S.A. 122 C3
Toledo, Montes de mts Spain 53 D4
Toledo Bend Reservoir U.S.A. 127 E6
Toletum Spain see Toledo
Toliara Madag. 95 E6
Tolitoli Indon. 65 G6
Tol'ka Rus. Fed. 60 J3
Tolleson U.S.A. 125 G5
Tollimarjon Uzbek. see Talimardzhan
Tolmachevo Rus. Fed. 41 P7
Tolo Dem. Rep. Congo 94 B4
Tolo Channel Hong Kong China 73 [inset]
Tolochin Belarus see Talachyn
Tolo Harbour b. Hong Kong China 73 [inset]
Tolosa France see Toulouse
Tolosa Spain 53 E2
Toluca Mex. 132 E5
Toluca de Lerdo Mex. see Toluca
Tol'yatti Rus. Fed. 39 K5
Tom' r. Rus. Fed. 70 B2
Tomah U.S.A. 126 F3
Tomakomai Japan 70 F4
Tomales U.S.A. 124 B2
Tomali Indon. 65 G7
Tomamae Japan 70 F3
Tomanivi mt. Fiji 103 H3
Tomar Brazil 138 F4
Tomar Port. 53 B4
Tomari Rus. Fed. 70 F3
Tomarza Turkey 86 D3
Tomaszów Lubelski Poland 39 D6
Tomaszów Mazowiecki Poland 43 R5
Tomatin U.K. 46 F3
Tomatlán Mex. 132 C5
Tomazina Brazil 141 A3
Tombador, Serra do hills Brazil 139 G6
Tombigbee r. U.S.A. 129 C6
Tomboco Angola 95 B4
Tombouctou Mali see Timbuktu
Tombstone U.S.A. 123 F7
Tombua Angola 95 B5
Tom Burke S. Africa 97 H2
Tomdibuloq Uzbek. see Tamdybulak
Tome Moz. 97 L2
Tomelilla Sweden 41 H9
Tomelloso Spain 53 E4
Tomi Romania see Constanța
Tomingley Australia 108 D4
Tomini, Teluk g. Indon. 65 G7
Tominian Mali 92 C3
Tomintoul U.K. 46 F3
Tomislavgrad Bos.-Herz. 54 G3
Tomkinson Ranges mts Australia 105 E6
Tømmerneset Norway 40 I3
Tommot Rus. Fed. 61 N4
Tomo r. Col. 138 E2
Tomóchic Mex. 123 G7
Tomortei China 69 K4
Tompkinsville U.S.A. 130 C5
Tom Price Australia 104 B5
Tomra China 79 F3
Tomsk Rus. Fed. 60 J4
Toms River U.S.A. 131 H4
Tomtabacken hill Sweden 41 I8
Tomtor Rus. Fed. 61 P3
Tomur Feng mt. China/Kyrg. see Pobeda Peak
Tomuzlovka r. Rus. Fed. 39 J7
Tom White, Mount U.S.A. 114 D3
Tonalá Mex. 132 F5
Tonantins Brazil 138 E4
Tonb-e Bozorg, Jazīreh-ye i. The Gulf see Greater Tunb
Tonb-e Kūchek, Jazīreh-ye i. The Gulf see Lesser Tunb
Tonbridge U.K. 45 H7
Tondano Indon. 65 G6
Tønder Denmark 41 F9
Tondi India 80 C4
Tone r. U.K. 45 E7
Toney Mountain Antarctica 148 K1
▶Tonga country S. Pacific Ocean 103 I4
oceania 8, 100–101
Tongaat S. Africa 97 J5
Tongariro National Park N.Z. 109 E4
Tongatapu Group is Tonga 103 I4

▶Tonga Trench sea feature S. Pacific Ocean 146 I7
2nd deepest trench in the world.

Tongbai Shan mts China 73 G1
Tongcheng China 73 H2
T'ongch'ŏn N. Korea 71 B5
Tongchuan Shaanxi China 73 F1
Tongchuan Sichuan China see Santai
Tongdao China 73 F3
Tongde China 72 D1
Tongduch'ŏn S. Korea 71 B5
Tongeren Belgium 48 F4
Tonggu China 73 G2
Tonggu Zui pt China 73 F5
Tonghae S. Korea 71 C5
Tonghai China 72 D3
Tonghe China 70 C3
Tonghua Jilin China 70 B4
Tonghua Jilin China 70 B4
Tongi Bangl. see Tungi
Tongjiang Heilong. China 70 D3
Tongjiang Sichuan China 72 E2
Tongking, Gulf of China/Vietnam 66 E2
Tongle China see Leye
Tongliang China 72 E2
Tongliao China 69 M4
Tongling China 73 H2
Tonglu China 73 H2
Tongo Australia 108 A3
Tongo Lake salt flat Australia 108 A3
Tongren Guizhou China 73 F3
Tongren Qinghai China 72 D1
Tongres Belgium see Tongeren
Tongsa Bhutan see Trongsa
Tongshan China 73 H1
Tongshi China 73 F5
Tongta Myanmar 66 B2
Tongtian He r. Qinghai China 72 B1
Tongtian He r. Qinghai China 72 C1
see Yangtze
Tongue U.K. 46 E2
Tongue r. U.S.A. 122 G3
Tongue of the Ocean sea chan. Bahamas 129 E7
Tongxin China 68 J5
T'ongyŏng S. Korea 71 C6
Tongzi China 72 E2
Tónichi Mex. 123 F7
Tonk India 78 C4
Tonkābon Iran 84 C2
Tonkin reg. Vietnam 66 D2
Tônlé Repou r. Laos 67 D4
Tônlé Sab l. Cambodia see Tonle Sap

▶Tonle Sap l. Cambodia 67 C4
Largest lake in Southeast Asia.

Tonopah AZ U.S.A. 125 G5
Tonopah NV U.S.A. 124 E2
Tønsberg Norway 41 G7
Tonstad Norway 41 E7
Tonto Creek watercourse U.S.A. 125 H5
Tonvarjeh Iran 84 E3
Tonzang Myanmar 66 A2
Tonzi Myanmar 66 A1
Toobeah Australia 108 D2
Toobli Liberia 92 C4
Tooele U.S.A. 125 G1
Toogoolawah Australia 108 F1
Tooma r. Australia 108 D6
Toompine Australia 108 B1
Toora Australia 108 C7
Tooraweenah Australia 108 D3
Toorberg mt. S. Africa 96 G7
Toowoomba Australia 108 E1
Tooxin Somalia 94 F2
Top Afgh. 85 H3
Top Boğazı Geçidi pass Turkey 81 C1

▶Topeka U.S.A. 126 E4
State capital of Kansas.

Topia Mex. 123 G8
Töplitz Germany 49 M2
Topoľčany Slovakia 43 Q6
Topolobampo Mex. 123 F8
Topolovgrad Bulg. 55 L3
Topozero, Ozero l. Rus. Fed. 40 R4
Topsfield U.S.A. 128 H2
Tor Eth. 93 G4
Tor Baldak mt. Afgh. 85 G4
Torbalı Turkey 55 L5
Torbat-e Heydarīyeh Iran 84 E3
Torbat-e Jām Iran 85 F3
Torbay Bay Australia 105 B8
Torbert, Mount U.S.A. 114 C3
Torbeyevo Rus. Fed. 39 I5
Torch r. Canada 117 K4
Tordesillas Spain 53 D3
Tordesilos Spain 53 F3
Töre Sweden 40 M4
Torelló Spain 53 H2
Torenberg hill Neth. 48 F2
Toretam Kazakh. see Baykonyr
Torgau Germany 49 M3
Torghay Kazakh. see Turgay
Torgun r. Rus. Fed. 39 J6
Torhout Belgium 48 D3
Torino Italy see Turin
Tori-shima i. Japan 71 F7
Torit Sudan 93 G4
Torkamān Iran 84 B2
Torkovichi Rus. Fed. 38 F4
Tornado Mountain Canada 116 H5
Torneå Fin. see Tornio
Torneälven r. Sweden 40 N4
Torneträsk l. Sweden 40 K2
Torngat, Monts mts Canada see Torngat Mountains
Torngat Mountains Canada 119 I2
Tornio Fin. 40 N4
Toro Spain 53 D3
Toro, Pico del mt. Mex. 127 C7
Torom Rus. Fed. 70 D1

▶Toronto Canada 130 F2
Provincial capital of Ontario and 5th most populous city in North America.

Toro Peak U.S.A. 124 E5
Toropets Rus. Fed. 38 F4
Tororo Uganda 94 D3
Toros Dağları mts Turkey see Taurus Mountains
Torphins U.K. 46 G3
Torquay Australia 108 B7
Torquay U.K. 45 D8
Torrance U.S.A. 124 D5
Torrão Port. 53 B4
Torre mt. Port. 53 C3
Torreblanca Spain 53 G3
Torre Blanco, Cerro mt. Mex. 123 E6
Torrecerredo mt. Spain 53 D2
Torre del Greco Italy 54 F4
Torre de Moncorvo Port. 53 C3
Torrelavega Spain 53 D2
Torremolinos Spain 53 D5

▶Torrens, Lake imp. l. Australia 107 B6
2nd largest lake in Oceania.

Torrens Creek Australia 106 D4
Torrent Spain 53 F4
Torrente Spain see Torrent
Torreón Mex. 127 C7
Torres Brazil 141 A5
Torres Mex. 123 F7
Torres del Paine, Parque Nacional nat. park Chile 140 B8
Torres Islands Vanuatu 103 G3
Torres Novas Port. 53 B4
Torres Strait Australia 102 E2
Torres Vedras Port. 53 B4
Torreta, Sierra hill Spain 53 G4
Torrevieja Spain 53 F5
Torrey U.S.A. 125 H2
Torridge r. U.K. 45 C8
Torridon, Loch b. U.K. 46 D3
Torrijos Spain 53 D4
Torrington Australia 108 E2
Torrington CT U.S.A. 128 F3
Torrington WY U.S.A. 122 G4
Torsby Sweden 41 H6

▶Tórshavn Faroe Is 40 [inset]
Capital of the Faroe Islands.

Tortilla Flat U.S.A. 125 H5
Törtköl Uzbek. see Turtkul'
Tortolì Sardinia Italy 54 C5
Tortona Italy 54 C2
Tortosa Spain 53 G3
Tortum Turkey 87 F2
Ţorūd Iran 84 D3
Torugart, Pereval pass China/Kyrg. see Turugart Pass
Torul Turkey 87 E2
Toruń Poland 43 Q4
Tory Island Rep. of Ireland 47 D2
Tory Sound sea chan. Rep. of Ireland 47 D2
Torzhok Rus. Fed. 38 G4
Tosa Japan 71 D6
Tosbotn Norway 40 H4
Tosca S. Africa 96 F3
Toscano, Arcipelago is Italy 54 C3
Tosham India 78 C3
Tōshima-yama mt. Japan 71 F4
Toshkent Uzbek. see Tashkent
Tosno Rus. Fed. 38 F4
Toson Hu l. China 79 I1
Tostado Arg. 140 D3
Tostedt Germany 49 J1
Tosya Turkey 86 D2
Totapola mt. Sri Lanka 80 D5
Tôtes France 48 B5
Tot'ma Rus. Fed. 38 I4
Totness Suriname 139 G2
Tottenham Australia 108 C4
Totton U.K. 45 F8
Tottori Japan 71 D6
Touba Côte d'Ivoire 92 C4
Touba Senegal 92 B3
Toubkal, Jbel mt. Morocco 50 C5
Toubkal, Parc National nat. park Morocco 50 C5
Touboro Cameroon 93 E4
Tougan Burkina 92 C3
Touggourt Alg. 50 F5
Tougué Guinea 92 B3
Touil Mauritania 92 B3
Toul France 48 F6
Touliu Taiwan 73 I4
Toulon France 52 G5
Toulon U.S.A. 126 F3
Toulouse France 52 E5
Toumodi Côte d'Ivoire 92 C4
Toungoo Myanmar 66 B3
Toupai China 73 F3
Tourane Vietnam see Đa Năng
Tourcoing France 48 D4
Tourgis Lake Canada 117 J1
Tourlaville France 45 F9
Tournai Belgium 48 D4
Tournon-sur-Rhône France 52 G4
Tournus France 54 A1
Touros Brazil 139 K5
Tours France 52 E3
Tousside, Pic mt. Chad 93 E2
Toussoro, Mont mt. Cent. Afr. Rep. 94 C3
Toutai China 70 B3
Touwsrivier S. Africa 96 E7
Toužim Czech Rep. 49 M4
Tovarkovo Rus. Fed. 39 G5
Tovil'-Dora Tajik. see Tavildara
Tovuz Azer. 87 G2
Towada Japan 70 F4
Towak Mountain hill U.S.A. 114 B3
Towanda U.S.A. 131 G3
Towaoc U.S.A. 125 I3
Towcester U.K. 45 G6
Tower Rep. of Ireland 47 D6
Towner U.S.A. 126 C1
Townes Pass U.S.A. 124 E3
Townsend U.S.A. 122 F3
Townsend, Mount Australia 108 D6
Townshend Island Australia 106 E4
Townsville Australia 106 D3
Towot Sudan 93 G4
Towr Kham Afgh. 85 H3
Towson U.S.A. 131 G4
Towyn U.K. see Tywyn
Toy U.S.A. 124 D1
Toyah U.S.A. 127 C6
Toyama Japan 71 E5
Toyama-wan b. Japan 71 E5
Toyohashi Japan 71 E6
Toyokawa Japan 71 E6
Toyonaka Japan 71 D6
Toyooka Japan 71 D6
Toyota Japan 71 E6
Tozanlı Turkey see Almus
Tozê Kangri mt. China 79 E2
Tozeur Tunisia 50 F5
Tozi, Mount U.S.A. 114 C3
Tqibuli Georgia 87 F2
Traben Germany 48 H5
Trâblous Lebanon see Tripoli
Trabotivište Macedonia 55 J4
Trabzon Turkey 87 E2
Tracy CA U.S.A. 124 C3
Tracy MN U.S.A. 126 E2
Trading r. Canada 118 C4
Traer U.S.A. 126 E3
Trafalgar U.S.A. 130 B4
Trafalgar, Cabo c. Spain 53 C5
Traffic Mountain Canada 116 D2
Trail Canada 116 G5
Tràille, Rubha na pt U.K. 46 D5
Traill Island Greenland see Traill Ø
Traill Ø i. Greenland 115 P2
Trainor Lake Canada 116 F2
Trajectum Neth. see Utrecht
Trakai Lith. 41 N9
Tra Khuc, Sông r. Vietnam 66 E4
Trakiya reg. Europe see Thrace
Trakt Rus. Fed. 38 K3
Trakya reg. Europe see Thrace
Tralee Rep. of Ireland 47 C5
Tralee Bay Rep. of Ireland 47 C5
Trá Lí Rep. of Ireland see Tralee
Tramandaí Brazil 141 A5
Tramán Tepuí mt. Venez. 138 F2
Trá Mhór Rep. of Ireland see Tramore
Tramore Rep. of Ireland 47 E5
Tranås Sweden 41 I7
Trancas Arg. 140 C3
Trancoso Brazil 141 D2
Tranemo Sweden 41 H8
Tranent U.K. 46 G5
Trang Thai. 67 B6
Trangan i. Indon. 104 F1
Trangie Australia 108 C4
Transantarctic Mountains Antarctica 148 H2
Trans Canada Highway Canada 117 H5
Transylvanian Alps mts Romania 55 J2
Transylvanian Basin plat. Romania 55 K1
Trapani Sicily Italy 54 E5
Trapezus Turkey see Trabzon
Trapper Peak U.S.A. 122 E3
Trappes France 48 C6
Traralgon Australia 108 C7
Trashigang Bhutan 79 G4
Trasimeno, Lago l. Italy 54 E3
Trasvase, Canal de Spain 53 E4
Trat Thai. 67 C4
Traunsee l. Austria 43 N7
Traunstein Germany 43 N7
Travellers Lake imp. l. Australia 107 C7
Travers, Mount N.Z. 109 D6
Traverse City U.S.A. 130 C1
Tra Vinh Vietnam 67 D5
Travnik Bos.-Herz. 54 G2
Trbovlje Slovenia 54 F1
Tre, Hon i. Vietnam 67 E4
Treasury Islands Solomon Is 102 F2
Trebbin Germany 49 N2
Trebević nat. park Bos.-Herz. 54 H3
Třebíč Czech Rep. 43 O6
Trebinje Bos.-Herz. 54 H3
Trebišov Slovakia 39 D6
Trebizond Turkey see Trabzon
Trebnje Slovenia 54 F2
Trebur Germany 49 I5
Tree Island India 80 B4
Trefaldwyn U.K. see Montgomery
Treffurt Germany 49 K3
Treffynnon U.K. see Holywell
Trefyclawdd U.K. see Knighton
Trefynwy U.K. see Monmouth
Tregosse Islets and Reefs Australia 106 E3
Treinta y Tres Uruguay 140 F4
Trelew Arg. 140 C6
Trelleborg Sweden 41 H9
Trélon France 48 E4
Tremblant, Mont hill Canada 118 G5
Trembleur Lake Canada 116 E4
Tremiti, Isole is Italy 54 F3
Tremont U.S.A. 131 G3
Tremonton U.S.A. 122 E4
Tremp Spain 53 G2
Trenance U.K. 45 B8
Trenary U.S.A. 128 C2
Trenche r. Canada 119 G5
Trenčín Slovakia 43 Q6
Trendelburg Germany 49 J3
Trêng Cambodia 67 C4
Trenque Lauquén Arg. 140 D5
Trent Italy see Trento
Trent r. U.K. 45 G5
Trento Italy 54 D1
Trenton Canada 131 G1
Trenton FL U.S.A. 129 D6
Trenton GA U.S.A. 129 C5
Trenton KY U.S.A. 130 B5
Trenton MO U.S.A. 126 E3
Trenton NC U.S.A. 129 E5
Trenton NE U.S.A. 126 C3

▶Trenton NJ U.S.A. 131 H3
State capital of New Jersey.

Treorchy U.K. 45 D7
Trepassey Canada 119 L5
Tres Arroyos Arg. 140 D5
Tresco i. U.K. 45 A9
Três Corações Brazil 141 B3
Tres Esquinas Col. 138 C3
Tres Forcas, Cabo c. Morocco see Trois Fourches, Cap des
Três Lagoas Brazil 141 A3
Três Marias, Represa resr Brazil 141 B2
Tres Picachos, Sierra mts Mex. 123 G7
Tres Picos, Cerro mt. Arg. 140 D5
Três Pontas Brazil 141 B3
Tres Puntas, Cabo c. Arg. 140 C7
Três Rios Brazil 141 C3
Tretten Norway 41 G6
Tretyy Severnyy Rus. Fed. see 3-y Severnyy
Treuchtlingen Germany 49 K6
Treuenbrietzen Germany 49 M2
Treungen Norway 41 F7
Treves Germany see Trier
Treviglio Italy 54 C2
Treviso Italy 54 E2
Trevose Head hd U.K. 45 B8
Tri An, Hô resr Vietnam 67 D5
Triánda Greece see Trianta
Triangle U.S.A. 131 G4
Trianta Greece 55 M6
Tribal Areas admin. div. Pak. 85 H3
Tri Brata, Gora hill Rus. Fed. 70 F1
Tribune U.S.A. 126 C4
Tricase Italy 54 H5
Trichinopoly India see Tiruchchirappalli
Trichur India 80 C4
Tricot France 48 C5
Trida Australia 108 B4
Tridentum Italy see Trento
Trier Germany 48 G5
Trieste Italy 54 E2
Trieste, Golfo di g. Europe see Trieste, Gulf of
Trieste, Gulf of Europe 54 E2
Triglav mt. Slovenia 54 E1
Triglavski Narodni Park nat. park Slovenia 54 E1
Trikala Greece 55 I5
Trikkala Greece see Trikala

▶Trikora, Puncak mt. Indon. 65 J7
2nd highest mountain in Oceania.

Trim Rep. of Ireland 47 F4
Trincomalee Sri Lanka 80 D4
Trindade Brazil 141 A2
Trindade, Ilha da i. S. Atlantic Ocean 144 G7
Trinidad Bol. 138 F6
Trinidad Cuba 133 I4
Trinidad i. Trin. and Tob. 133 L6
Trinidad Uruguay 140 E4
Trinidad U.S.A. 123 G5
Trinidad country West Indies see Trinidad and Tobago
▶Trinidad and Tobago country West Indies 133 L6
north america 9, 112–113
Trinity U.S.A. 127 E6
Trinity r. CA U.S.A. 124 B1
Trinity r. TX U.S.A. 127 E6
Trinity Bay Canada 119 L5
Trinity Islands U.S.A. 114 C4
Trinity Range mts U.S.A. 124 D1
Trinkat Island India 67 A5
Trionto, Capo c. Italy 54 G5
Tripa r. Indon. 67 B7
Tripkau Germany 49 L1
Tripoli Greece 55 J6
Tripoli Lebanon 81 B2

▶Tripoli Libya 93 E1
Capital of Libya.

Trípolis Greece see Tripoli
Tripolis Lebanon see Tripoli
Tripunittura India 80 C4
Tripura state India 79 G5

▶Tristan da Cunha i. S. Atlantic Ocean 144 H8
Dependency of St Helena.

Trisul mt. India 78 D3
Triton Canada 119 L4
Triton Island atoll Paracel Is 64 E3
Trittau Germany 49 K1
Trittenheim Germany 48 G5
Trivandrum India 80 C4
Trivento Italy 54 F4
Trnava Slovakia 43 P6
Trobriand Islands P.N.G. 102 F2
Trochu Canada 116 H5
Trofors Norway 40 H4
Trogir Croatia 54 G3
Troia Italy 54 F4
Troisdorf Germany 49 H4
Trois Fourches, Cap des c. Morocco 53 E6
Trois-Ponts Belgium 48 F4
Trois-Rivières Canada 119 G5
Troitsko-Pechorsk Rus. Fed. 37 R3
Troitskoye Altayskiy Kray Rus. Fed. 68 E2
Troitskoye Khabarovskiy Kray Rus. Fed. 70 E2
Troitskoye Respublika Kalmykiya - Khalm'g-Tangch Rus. Fed. 39 J7
Trollhättan Sweden 41 H7
Trombetas r. Brazil 139 G4
Tromelin, Île i. Indian Ocean 145 L7
Tromelin Island Micronesia see Fais
Tromen, Volcán vol. Arg. 140 B5
Tromie r. U.K. 46 E3
Trompsburg S. Africa 97 G6
Tromsø Norway 40 K2
Trona U.S.A. 124 E4
Tronador, Monte mt. Arg. 140 B6
Trondheim Norway 40 G5
Trondheimsfjorden sea chan. Norway 40 F5
Trongsa Bhutan 79 G4
Troödos, Mount Cyprus 81 A2
Troödos Mountains Cyprus 81 A2
Troon U.K. 46 E5
Tropeiros, Serra dos hills Brazil 141 B1

Uluru National Park Australia *see* **Uluṟu - Kata Tjuṯa National Park**
Ulutau Kazakh. *see* **Ulytau**
Ulutau, Gory *mts* Kazakh. *see* **Ulytau, Gory**
Uluyatır Turkey **81** C1
Ulva *i.* U.K. **46** C4
Ulvenhout Neth. **48** E3
Ulverston U.K. **44** D4
Ulvsjön Sweden **41** I6
Ul'yanov Kazakh. *see* **Ul'yanovskiy**
Ul'yanovsk Rus. Fed. **39** K5
Ul'yanovskiy Kazakh. **76** D1
Ul'yanovskoye Kazakh. *see* **Ul'yanovskiy**
Ulysses *KS* U.S.A. **126** C4
Ulysses *KY* U.S.A. **130** D5
Ulytau Kazakh. **76** C2
Ulytau, Gory *mts* Kazakh. **76** C2
Uma Rus. Fed. **70** A1
Umaltinskiy Rus. Fed. **70** D2
'Umān *country* Asia *see* **Oman**
Uman' Ukr. **39** F6
Umarao Pak. **85** G4
'Umarī, Qa' al *salt pan* Jordan **81** C4
Umaria India **78** E5
Umarkhed India **80** C2
Umarkot India **80** D2
Umarkot Pak. **85** H5
Umaroona, Lake *salt flat* Australia **107** B5
Umarpada India **78** C5
Umatilla U.S.A. **122** D3
Umba Rus. Fed. **38** G2
Umbagog Lake U.S.A. **131** J1
Umbeara Australia **105** F6
Umboi *i.* P.N.G. **65** L8
Umeå Sweden **40** L5
Umeälven *r.* Sweden **40** L5
Umfolozi *r.* S. Africa **97** K5
Umfreville Lake Canada **117** M5
Umhlanga Rocks S. Africa **97** J5
Umiiviip Kangertiva *inlet* Greenland **115** N3
Umingmaktok Canada **149** L2
Umirzak Kazakh. **87** H2
Umiujaq Canada **118** F2
Umkomaas S. Africa **97** J6
Umlaiteng India **79** H4
Umlazi S. Africa **97** J5
Umm ad Daraj, Jabal *mt.* Jordan **81** B3
Umm al 'Amad Syria **81** C2
Umm al Jamājim *well* Saudi Arabia **84** B5
Umm al Qaiwain U.A.E. *see* **Umm al Qaywayn**
Umm al Qaywayn U.A.E. **84** D5
Umm ar Raqabah, Khabrat *imp. l.* Saudi Arabia **81** C5
Umm at Qalbān Saudi Arabia **87** F6
Umm az Zumūl *well* Oman **84** D6
Umm Bāb Qatar **84** C5
Umm Bel Sudan **82** C7
Umm Keddada Sudan **82** C7
Umm Lajj Saudi Arabia **82** E4
Umm Nukhaylah *hill* Saudi Arabia **81** D5
Umm Qaṣr Iraq **87** G5
Umm Quṣur *i.* Saudi Arabia **86** D6
Umm Ruwaba Sudan **82** D7
Umm Sa'ad Libya **86** B5
Umm Sa'id Qatar **84** C5
Umm Shugeira Sudan **82** C7
Umm Wa'āl *hill* Saudi Arabia **81** D4
Umm Wazīr *well* Saudi Arabia **84** B6
Umnak Island U.S.A. **114** B4
Um Phang Wildlife Reserve *nature res.* Thai. **66** B4
Umpqua *r.* U.S.A. **122** B4
Umpulo Angola **95** B5
Umraniye Turkey **55** N5
Umred India **80** C1
Umri India **78** D4
Umtali Zimbabwe *see* **Mutare**
Umtata S. Africa **97** I6
Umtentweni S. Africa **97** J6
Umuahia Nigeria **92** D4
Umuarama Brazil **140** F2
Umvuma Zimbabwe *see* **Mvuma**
Umzimkulu S. Africa **97** I6
Una *r.* Bos.-Herz./Croatia **54** G2
Una Brazil **141** D1
Una India **78** D3
'Unāb, Jabal al *hill* Jordan **81** C5
'Unāb, Wādī al *watercourse* Jordan **81** C4
Unaí Brazil **141** B2
Unai Pass Afgh. **85** H3
Unalaska Island U.S.A. **114** B4
Unapool U.K. **46** D2
'Unayzah Saudi Arabia **82** F4
'Unayzah, Jabal *hill* Iraq **87** E4
Uncia Bol. **138** E7
Uncompahgre Peak U.S.A. **125** J2
Uncompahgre Plateau U.S.A. **125** I2
Undara National Park Australia **106** D3
Underberg S. Africa **97** I5
Underbool Australia **107** C7
Underwood U.S.A. **130** C4
Undur Indon. **65** I7
Unecha Rus. Fed. **39** G5
Ungama Bay Kenya *see* **Ungwana Bay**
Ungarie Australia **108** C4
Ungava, Baie d' *b.* Canada *see* **Ungava Bay**
Ungava, Péninsule d' *pen.* Canada **118** G1
Ungava Bay Canada **119** I2
Ungava Peninsula Canada *see* **Ungava, Péninsule d'**
Ungeny Moldova *see* **Ungheni**
Unggi N. Korea **70** C4
Ungheni Moldova **55** L1
Unguja *i.* Tanz. *see* **Zanzibar Island**
Unguz, Solonchakovyye Vpadiny *salt flat* Turkm. **84** E2
Üngüz Angyrsyndaky Garagum *des.* Turkm. *see* **Zaunguzskiye Karakumy**
Ungvár Ukr. *see* **Uzhhorod**
Ungwana Bay Kenya **94** E4
Uni Rus. Fed. **38** K4
União Brazil **139** J4
União da Vitória Brazil **141** A4
União dos Palmares Brazil **139** K5
Unimak Island U.S.A. **114** B4
Unini *r.* Brazil **138** F4
Union *MO* U.S.A. **126** F4
Union *WV* U.S.A. **130** E5
Union, Mount U.S.A. **125** G4
Union City *OH* U.S.A. **130** C3
Union City *PA* U.S.A. **130** F3
Union City *TN* U.S.A. **127** F4
Uniondale S. Africa **96** F7
Unión de Reyes Cuba **129** D8

▶**Union of Soviet Socialist Republics**
Divided in 1991 into 15 independent nations: Armenia, Azerbaijan, Belarus, Estonia, Georgia, Kazakhstan, Kyrgyzstan, Latvia, Lithuania, Moldova, the Russian Federation, Tajikistan, Turkmenistan, Ukraine and Uzbekistan.

Union Springs U.S.A. **129** C5
Uniontown U.S.A. **130** F4
Unionville U.S.A. **131** G3
▶**United Arab Emirates** *country* Asia **84** D6
asia 6, 58–59
United Arab Republic *country* Africa *see* **Egypt**

▶**United Kingdom** *country* Europe **42** G3
3rd most populous country in Europe.
europe 5, 34–35

United Provinces *state* India *see* **Uttar Pradesh**

▶**United States of America** *country* N. America **120** F3
Most populous country in North America and 3rd in the world. 3rd largest country in the world and 2nd in North America.
north america 9, 112–113

United States Range *mts* Canada **115** L1
Unity Canada **117** I4
Unjha India **78** C5
Unna Germany **49** H3
Unnao India **78** E4
Ŭnp'a N. Korea **71** B5
Ŭnsan N. Korea **71** B4
Ŭnsan N. Korea **71** B5
Unst *i.* U.K. **46** [inset]
Unstrut *r.* Germany **49** L3
Untari India **79** E4
Untor, Ozero *l.* Rus. Fed. **37** T3
Unuk *r.* Canada/U.S.A. **116** D3
Unuli Horog China **79** G2
Unzen-dake *vol.* Japan **71** C6
Unzha Rus. Fed. **38** J4
Upalco U.S.A. **125** H1
Upar Ghat *reg.* India **79** F5
Upemba, Lac *l.* Dem. Rep. Congo **95** C4
Uperbada India **79** F5
Upernavik Greenland **115** M2
Upington S. Africa **96** E5
Upland U.S.A. **124** E4
Upleta India **78** B5
Upoloksha Rus. Fed. **40** Q3
Upolu *i.* Samoa **103** I3
Upper Arlington U.S.A. **130** D3
Upper Arrow Lake Canada **116** G5
Upper Chindwin Myanmar *see* **Mawlaik**
Upper Fraser Canada **116** F4
Upper Garry Lake Canada **117** K1
Upper Hutt N.Z. **109** E5
Upper Klamath Lake U.S.A. **122** C4
Upper Lough Erne *l.* U.K. **47** E3
Upper Marlboro U.S.A. **131** G4
Upper Mazinaw Lake Canada **131** G1
Upper Missouri Breaks National Monument *nat. park* U.S.A. **126** A2
Upper Peirce Reservoir Sing. **67** [inset]
Upper Red Lake U.S.A. **126** E1
Upper Sandusky U.S.A. **130** D3
Upper Saranac Lake U.S.A. **131** H1
Upper Seal Lake Canada *see* **Iberville, Lac d'**
Upper Tunguska *r.* Rus. Fed. *see* **Angara**
Upper Volta *country* Africa *see* **Burkina**
Upper Yarra Reservoir Australia **108** B6
Uppinangadi India **80** B3
Uppsala Sweden **41** J7
Upsala Canada **118** C4
Upshi Jammu and Kashmir **78** D2
Upton U.S.A. **131** J2
'Uqayqah, Wādī *watercourse* Jordan **81** B4
'Uqayribāt Syria **81** C2
Uqlat al 'Udhaybah *well* Iraq **87** G5
Uqturpan China *see* **Wushi**
Uracas *vol.* N. Mariana Is *see* **Farallon de Pajaros**
Urad Houqi China *see* **Sain Us**
Ūrāf Iran **84** E4
Urakawa Japan **70** F4
Ural *hill* Australia **108** C4
Ural *r.* Kazakh./Rus. Fed. **74** E2
Uralla Australia **108** E3
Ural Mountains Rus. Fed. **37** S2
Ural'sk Kazakh. **74** E1
Ural'skaya Oblast' *admin. div.* Kazakh. *see* **Zapadnyy Kazakhstan**
Ural'skiye Gory *mts* Rus. Fed. *see* **Ural Mountains**
Ural'skiy Khrebet *mts* Rus. Fed. *see* **Ural Mountains**
Urambo Tanz. **95** D4
Uran India **80** B2
Urana Australia **108** C5
Urana, Lake Australia **108** C5
Urandangi Australia **106** B4
Urandi Brazil **141** C1
Uranium City Canada **117** I3
Uranquity Australia **108** C5
Uraricoera *r.* Brazil **138** F3
Urartu *country* Asia *see* **Armenia**
Ura-Tyube Tajik. *see* **Ŭroteppa**
Uravakonda India **80** C3
Uravan U.S.A. **125** I2
Urawa Japan **71** E6
'Urayf an Nāqah, Jabal *hill* Egypt **81** B4
Uray'irah Saudi Arabia **84** C5
'Urayq ad Duḥūl *des.* Saudi Arabia **84** B5
'Urayq Sāqān *des.* Saudi Arabia **84** B5
Urbana *IL* U.S.A. **126** F3
Urbana *OH* U.S.A. **130** D3
Urbino Italy **54** E3
Urbinum Italy *see* **Urbino**
Urbs Vetus Italy *see* **Orvieto**
Urdoma Rus. Fed. **38** K3
Urdyuzhskoye, Ozero *l.* Rus. Fed. **38** K2
Urdzhar Kazakh. **76** F2
Ure *r.* U.K. **44** F4
Ureki Georgia **87** F2
Uren' Rus. Fed. **38** J4
Urengoy Rus. Fed. **60** I3
Uréparapara *i.* Vanuatu **103** G3
Urewera National Park N.Z. **109** F4
Urfa Turkey *see* **Şanlıurfa**
Urfa *prov.* Turkey *see* **Şanlıurfa**
Urga Mongolia *see* **Ulan Bator**
Urgal *r.* Rus. Fed. **70** D2
Urganch Uzbek. *see* **Urgench**
Urgench Uzbek. **76** B3
Ürgüp Turkey **86** D3
Urgut Uzbek. **85** G2
Urho China **76** G2
Urho Kekkosen kansallispuisto *nat. park* Fin. **40** O2
Urie *r.* U.K. **46** G3
Uril Rus. Fed. **70** C2
Urisino Australia **108** A2
Urjala Fin. **41** M6
Urk Neth. **48** F2
Urkan Rus. Fed. **70** B1
Urkan *r.* Rus. Fed. **70** B1
Urla Turkey **55** L5
Urlingford Rep. of Ireland **47** E5
Urluk Rus. Fed. **69** J2
Urmā aş Şughrá Syria **81** C1
Urmai China **79** F3
Urmia Iran **84** B2
Urmia, Lake *salt l.* Iran **84** B2
Urmston Road *sea chan.* Hong Kong China **73** [inset]
Uromi Nigeria **92** D4
Uroševac Serb. and Mont. **55** I3
Ŭrosozero Rus. Fed. **38** G3
Ŭroteppa Tajik. **85** H2
Urru Co *salt l.* China **79** F3
Urt Moron China **76** H4
Uruáchic Mex. **120** F6
Uruaçu Brazil **141** A1
Uruana Brazil **141** A1
Uruapan *Baja California* Mex. **123** D7
Uruapan *Michoacán* Mex. **132** D5
Urubamba *r.* Peru **138** D6
Urucara Brazil **139** G4
Urucu *r.* Brazil **138** F4
Uruçuca Brazil **141** D1
Uruçuí Brazil **139** J5
Uruçuí, Serra do *hills* Brazil **139** I5
Urucuia Brazil **141** B2
Urucurituba Brazil **139** G4
Uruguai *r.* Arg./Uruguay *see* **Uruguay**
Uruguaiana Brazil **140** E3
Uruguay *r.* Arg./Uruguay **140** E4
also known as Uruguai
▶**Uruguay** *country* S. America **140** E4
south america 9, 136–137
Uruhe China **70** B2
Urumchi China *see* **Ürümqi**
Ürümqi China **76** G3
Urundi *country* Africa *see* **Burundi**
Urup, Ostrov *i.* Rus. Fed. **69** S3
Urusha Rus. Fed. **70** A1
Urutaí Brazil **141** A2
Uryl' Kazakh. **76** G2
Uryupino Rus. Fed. **69** M2
Uryupinsk Rus. Fed. **39** I6
Ürzhar Kazakh. *see* **Urdzhar**
Urzhum Rus. Fed. **38** K4
Urziceni Romania **55** L2
Usa Japan **71** C6
Usa *r.* Rus. Fed. **38** M2
Uşak Turkey **55** M5
Usakos Namibia **96** B1
Usarp Mountains Antarctica **148** H2
Usborne, Mount *hill* Falkland Is **140** E8
Ushakova, Ostrov *i.* Rus. Fed. **60** I1
Ushant *i.* France *see* **Ouessant, Île d'**
Üsharal Kazakh. *see* **Ucharal**
Ush-Bel'dyr Rus. Fed. **68** H2
Ushtobe Kazakh. **76** E2
Ush-Tyube Kazakh. *see* **Ushtobe**
Ushuaia Arg. **140** C8
Ushumun Rus. Fed. **70** B1
Usingen Germany **49** I4
Usinsk Rus. Fed. **37** R2
Usk U.K. **45** E7
Usk *r.* U.K. **45** E7
Uskhodni Belarus **41** O10
Uskoplje Bos.-Herz. *see* **Gornji Vakuf**
Üsküdar Turkey **55** M4
Uslar Germany **49** J3
Usman' Rus. Fed. **39** H5
Usmanabad India *see* **Osmanabad**
Usmas ezers *l.* Latvia **41** M8
Usogorsk Rus. Fed. **38** K3
Usol'ye-Sibirskoye Rus. Fed. **68** I2
Uspenovka Rus. Fed. **70** B1
Ussel France **52** F4
Ussuri *r.* China/Rus. Fed. **70** D2
Ussuriysk Rus. Fed. **70** C4
Ust'-Abakanskoye Rus. Fed. *see* **Abakan**
Usta Muhammad Pak. **85** H4
Ust'-Balyk Rus. Fed. *see* **Nefteyugansk**
Ust'-Donetskiy Rus. Fed. **39** I7
Ust'-Dzheguta Rus. Fed. **87** F1
Ust'-Dzhegutinskaya Rus. Fed. *see* **Ust'-Dzheguta**
Ustica, Isola di *i. Sicily* Italy **54** E5
Ust'-Ilimsk Rus. Fed. **61** L4
Ust'-Ilimskiy Vodokhranilishche *resr* Rus. Fed. **61** L4
Ust'-Ilych Rus. Fed. **37** R3
Ústí nad Labem Czech Rep. **43** O5
Ustinov Rus. Fed. *see* **Izhevsk**
Üstirt *plat.* Kazakh./Uzbek. *see* **Ustyurt Plateau**
Ustka Poland **43** P3
Ust'-Kamchatsk Rus. Fed. **61** R4
Ust'-Kamenogorsk Kazakh. **76** F2
Ust'-Kan Rus. Fed. **76** F1
Ust'-Koksa Rus. Fed. **76** G1
Ust'-Kulom Rus. Fed. **38** L3
Ust'-Kut Rus. Fed. **61** L4
Ust'-Kuyga Rus. Fed. **61** O2
Ust'-Labinsk Rus. Fed. **87** E1
Ust'-Labinskaya Rus. Fed. *see* **Ust'-Labinsk**
Ust'-Lyzha Rus. Fed. **38** M2
Ust'-Maya Rus. Fed. **61** O3
Ust'-Nera Rus. Fed. **61** P3
Ust'-Ocheya Rus. Fed. **38** K3
Ust'-Olenek Rus. Fed. **61** M2
Ust'-Omchug Rus. Fed. **61** P3
Ust'-Ordynskiy Rus. Fed. **68** I2
Ust'-Penzhino Rus. Fed. *see* **Kamenskoye**
Ust'-Port Rus. Fed. **60** J3
Ustrem Rus. Fed. **37** T3
Ust'-Tsil'ma Rus. Fed. **38** L2
Ust'-Uda Rus. Fed. **68** I2
Ust'-Umalta Rus. Fed. **70** D2
Ust'-Undurga Rus. Fed. **69** L2
Ust'-Ura Rus. Fed. **38** J3
Ust'-Urgal Rus. Fed. **70** D2
Ust'-Usa Rus. Fed. **38** M2
Ust'-Vayen'ga Rus. Fed. **38** I3
Ust'-Voya Rus. Fed. **37** R3
Ust'-Vyyskaya Rus. Fed. **38** J3
Ust'ya *r.* Rus. Fed. **38** I3
Ust'ye Rus. Fed. **38** H4
Ustyurt, Plato *plat.* Kazakh./Uzbek. *see* **Ustyurt Plateau**
Ustyurt Plateau Kazakh./Uzbek. **74** E2
Ustyurt Platosi *plat.* Kazakh./Uzbek. *see* **Ustyurt Plateau**
Ustyuzhna Rus. Fed. **38** H4
Usulután El Salvador **132** G6
Usumbura Burundi *see* **Bujumbura**
Usvyaty Rus. Fed. **38** F5
Utah *state* U.S.A. **122** F5
Utah Lake U.S.A. **125** H1
Utajärvi Fin. **40** O4
Utashinai Rus. Fed. *see* **Yuzhno-Kuril'sk**
'Utaybah, Buḩayrat al *imp. l.* Syria **81** C3
Utena Lith. **41** N9
Uterlai India **78** B4
Uthai Thani Thai. **66** C4
Uthal Pak. **85** G5
'Uthmānīyah Syria **81** C2
Utiariti Brazil **139** G6
Utica *NY* U.S.A. **131** H2
Utica *OH* U.S.A. **130** D3
Utiel Spain **53** F4
Utikuma Lake Canada **116** H4
Utlwanang S. Africa **97** G4
Utrecht Neth. **48** F2
Utrecht S. Africa **97** J4
Utrera Spain **53** D5
Utsjoki Fin. **40** O2
Utsunomiya Japan **71** E5
Utta Rus. Fed. **39** J7
Uttaradit Thai. **66** C3
Uttarakhand *state* India *see* **Uttaranchal**
Uttaranchal *state* India **78** D3
Uttar Kashi India *see* **Uttarkashi**
Uttarkashi India **78** D3
Uttar Pradesh *state* India **78** D4
Uttoxeter U.K. **45** F6
Uttranchal *state* India *see* **Uttaranchal**
Utubulak China **76** G2
Utupua *i.* Solomon Is **103** G3
Uummannaq Greenland *see* **Dundas**
Uummannaq Fjord *inlet* Greenland **149** J2
Uummannarsuaq *c.* Greenland *see* **Farewell, Cape**
Uurainen Fin. **40** N5
Uusikaarlepyy Fin. *see* **Nykarleby**
Uusikaupunki Fin. **41** L6
Uutapi Namibia **95** B5
Uva Rus. Fed. **38** L4
Uvalde U.S.A. **127** D6
Uval Karabaur *hills* Kazakh./Uzbek. **87** I2
Uval Muzbel' *hills* Kazakh. **87** I2
Uvarovo Rus. Fed. **39** I6
Uvéa *atoll* New Caledonia *see* **Ouvéa**
Uvinza Tanz. **95** D4
Uvs Nuur *salt l.* Mongolia **76** H1
Uwajima Japan **71** D6
'Uwayriḍ, Ḩarrat al *lava field* Saudi Arabia **82** E4
Uwaysiţ *well* Saudi Arabia **81** D4
Uweinat, Jebel *mt.* Sudan **82** C5
Uwi *i.* Indon. **67** D7
Uxbridge Canada **130** F1
Uxbridge U.K. **45** G7
Uxin Qi China *see* **Dabqig**
Uyaly Kazakh. **76** B3
Uyar Rus. Fed. **68** G1
Üydzin Mongolia **68** J4
Uyo Nigeria **92** D4
Uyu Chaung *r.* Myanmar **66** A1
Uyuni Bol. **138** E8
Uyuni, Salar de *salt flat* Bol. **138** E8
Uza *r.* Rus. Fed. **39** J5
▶**Uzbekistan** *country* Asia **76** B3
asia 6, 58–59
Üzbekiston *country* Asia *see* **Uzbekistan**
Uzbekskaya S.S.R. *country* Asia *see* **Uzbekistan**
Uzbek S.S.R. *country* Asia *see* **Uzbekistan**
Uzen' Kazakh. *see* **Kyzylsay**
Uzhgorod Ukr. *see* **Uzhhorod**
Uzhhorod Ukr. **39** D6
Užhorod Ukr. *see* **Uzhhorod**
Užice Serb. and Mont. **55** H3
Uzlovaya Rus. Fed. **39** H5
Üzümlü Turkey **55** M6
Uzun Uzbek. **85** H2
Uzunköprü Turkey **55** L4
Uzynkair Kazakh. **76** B3

↓ V

Vaaf Atoll Maldives *see* **Felidhu Atoll**
Vaajakoski Fin. **40** N5
Vaal *r.* S. Africa **97** F5
Vaala Fin. **40** O4
Vaalbos National Park S. Africa **96** G5
Vaal Dam S. Africa **97** I4
Vaalwater S. Africa **97** I3
Vaasa Fin. **40** L5
Vaavu Atoll Maldives *see* **Felidhu Atoll**
Vabkent Uzbek. **85** G1
Vác Hungary **43** Q7
Vacaria Brazil **141** A5
Vacaria, Campo da *plain* Brazil **141** A5
Vacaville U.S.A. **124** C2
Vachon *r.* Canada **119** H1
Vad Rus. Fed. **38** J5
Vad *r.* Rus. Fed. **39** I5
Vada India **80** B2
Vadla Norway **41** E7
Vadodara India **78** C5
Vadsø Norway **40** P1

▶**Vaduz** Liechtenstein **52** I3
Capital of Liechtenstein.

Værøy *i.* Norway **40** H3
Vaga *r.* Rus. Fed. **38** I3
Vågåmo Norway **41** F6
Vaganski Vrh *mt.* Croatia **54** F2
Vágar *i.* Faroe Is **40** [inset]
Vägsele Sweden **40** K4
Vágur Faroe Is **40** [inset]
Váh *r.* Slovakia **43** Q7
Vähäkyrö Fin. **40** M5

▶**Vaiaku** Tuvalu **103** H2
Capital of Tuvalu, on Funafuti atoll.

Vaida Estonia **41** N7
Vaiden U.S.A. **127** F5
Vail U.S.A. **120** F4
Vailly-sur-Aisne France **48** D5
Vaitupu *i.* Tuvalu **103** H2
Vajrakarur India *see* **Kanur**
Vakhsh Tajik. **85** H2
Vakhsh *r.* Tajik. **85** H2
Vakhstroy Tajik. *see* **Vakhsh**
Vakīlābād Iran **84** E4
Valbo Sweden **41** J6
Valcheta Arg. **140** C6
Valdai Hills Rus. Fed. *see* **Valdayskaya Vozvyshennost'**
Valday Rus. Fed. **38** G4
Valdayskaya Vozvyshennost' *hills* Rus. Fed. **38** G4
Valdecañas, Embalse de *resr* Spain **53** D4
Valdemārpils Latvia **41** M8
Valdemarsvik Sweden **41** J7
Valdepeñas Spain **53** E4
Val-de-Reuil France **48** B5

▶**Valdés, Península** *pen.* Arg. **140** D6
Lowest point in South America.
south america 134–135

Valdez U.S.A. **114** D3
Valdivia Chile **140** B5
Val-d'Or Canada **118** F4
Valdosta U.S.A. **129** D6
Valdres *valley* Norway **41** F6
Vale Georgia **87** F2
Vale U.S.A. **122** D3
Valemount Canada **116** G4
Valença Brazil **141** D1
Valence France **52** G4
Valencia Spain **53** F4
València Spain *see* **Valencia**
Valencia *reg.* Spain **53** F4
Valencia Venez. **138** E1
Valencia, Golfo de *g.* Spain **53** G4
Valencia de Don Juan Spain **53** D2
Valencia Island Rep. of Ireland **47** B6
Valenciennes France **48** D4
Valensole, Plateau de France **52** H5
Valentia Spain *see* **Valencia**
Valentin Rus. Fed. **70** D4
Valentine U.S.A. **126** C3
Våler Norway **41** G6
Valera Venez. **138** D2
Vale Verde Brazil **141** D2
Val Grande, Parco Nazionale della *nat. park* Italy **54** C1
Valjevo Serb. and Mont. **55** H2
Valka Latvia **41** O8
Valkeakoski Fin. **41** N6
Valkenswaard Neth. **48** F3
Valky Ukr. **39** G6
Valkyrie Dome *ice feature* Antarctica **148** D1
Valladolid Mex. **132** G4
Valladolid Spain **53** D3
Vallard, Lac *l.* Canada **119** H3
Vall de Uxó Spain **53** F4
Valle Norway **41** E7
Vallecillos Mex. **127** D7
Vallecito Reservoir U.S.A. **125** J3
Valle de la Pascua Venez. **138** E2
Valledupar Col. **138** D1
Vallée-Jonction Canada **119** H5
Valle Fértil, Sierra de *mts* Arg. **140** C4
Valle Grande Bol. **138** F7
Valle Hermoso Mex. **127** D7
Vallejo U.S.A. **124** B2
Vallenar Chile **140** B3

▶**Valletta** Malta **54** F7
Capital of Malta.

Valley *r.* Canada **117** L5
Valley U.K. **44** C5
Valley City U.S.A. **126** D2
Valleyview Canada **116** G4
Valls Spain **53** G3
Val Marie Canada **117** J5
Valmiera Latvia **41** N8
Valmy U.S.A. **124** E1
Valnera *mt.* Spain **53** E2
Valognes France **45** F9
Valona Albania *see* **Vlorë**
Valozhyn Belarus **41** O9
Val-Paradis Canada **118** F4
Valparai India **80** C4
Valparaíso Chile **140** B4
Valparaiso U.S.A. **130** B3
Valpoi India **80** B3
Valréas France **52** G4
Vals, Tanjung *c.* Indon. **65** J8
Valsad India **80** B1
Valspan S. Africa **96** G4
Val'tevo Rus. Fed. **38** J2
Valtimo Fin. **40** P5
Valuyevka Rus. Fed. **39** I7
Valuyki Rus. Fed. **39** H6
Vammala Fin. **41** M6
Van Turkey **87** F3
Van, Lake *salt l.* Turkey **87** F3
Vanadzor Armenia **87** G2
Van Buren *AR* U.S.A. **127** E5
Van Buren *MO* U.S.A. **127** F4
Van Buren *OH* U.S.A. *see* **Kettering**
Vanceburg U.S.A. **130** D4
Vanch Tajik. *see* **Vanj**
Vancleve U.S.A. **130** D5
Vancouver Canada **116** F5
Vancouver U.S.A. **122** C3
Vancouver, Mount Canada/U.S.A. **116** B2
Vancouver Island Canada **116** E5
Vanda Fin. *see* **Vantaa**
Vandalia *IL* U.S.A. **126** F4
Vandalia *OH* U.S.A. **130** C4
Vandekerckhove Lake Canada **117** K3
Vanderbijlpark S. Africa **97** H4
Vanderbilt U.S.A. **130** C1
Vandergrift U.S.A. **130** F3
Vanderhoof Canada **116** E4
Vanderkloof Dam *resr* S. Africa **96** G6
Vanderlin Island Australia **106** B2
Vanderwagen U.S.A. **125** I4
Van Diemen, Cape *N.T.* Australia **104** E2
Van Diemen, Cape *Qld* Australia **106** B3
Van Diemen Gulf Australia **104** F2
Van Diemen's Land *state* Australia *see* **Tasmania**
Vändra Estonia **41** N7
Väner, Lake Sweden *see* **Vänern**

▶**Vänern** *l.* Sweden **41** H7
4th largest lake in Europe.

Vänersborg Sweden **41** H7
Vangaindrano Madag. **95** E6
Van Gölü *salt l.* Turkey *see* **Van, Lake**
Van Horn U.S.A. **123** G7
Vanikoro Islands Solomon Is **103** G3
Vanimo P.N.G. **65** K7
Vanino Rus. Fed. **70** F2
Vanivilasa Sagara *resr* India **80** C3
Vaniyambadi India **80** C3
Vanj Tajik. **85** H2
Vanna *i.* Norway **40** K1
Vännäs Sweden **40** K5
Vannes France **52** C3
Vannes, Lac *l.* Canada **119** I3
Vannovka Kazakh. *see* **Turar Ryskulov**
Van Rees, Pegunungan *mts* Indon. **65** J7
Vanrhynsdorp S. Africa **96** D6
Vansant U.S.A. **130** D5
Vansbro Sweden **41** I6
Vansittart Island Canada **115** J3
Van Starkenborgh Kanaal *canal* Neth. **48** G1
Vantaa Fin. **41** N6
Van Truer Tableland *reg.* Australia **105** C6
Vanua Lava *i.* Vanuatu **103** G3
Vanua Levu *i.* Fiji **103** H3
▶**Vanuatu** *country* S. Pacific Ocean **103** G3
oceania 8, 100–101
Van Wert U.S.A. **130** C3
Vanwyksvlei S. Africa **96** E6
Vanwyksvlei *l.* S. Africa **96** E6
Văn Yên Vietnam **66** D2
Van Zylsrus S. Africa **96** F4
Varadero Cuba **129** D8
Varahi India **78** B5
Varakļāni Latvia **41** O8
Varalé Côte d'Ivoire **92** C4
Varāmīn Iran **84** C3
Varanasi India **79** E4
Varandey Rus. Fed. **38** M1
Varangerfjorden *sea chan.* Norway **40** P1
Varangerhalvøya *pen.* Norway **37** L1
Varangerhalvøya *pen.* Norway **40** P1
Varaždin Croatia **54** G1
Varberg Sweden **41** H8
Vardar *r.* Macedonia **55** J4
Varde Denmark **41** F9
Vardenis Armenia **87** G2
Vardø Norway **40** Q1
Varel Germany **49** I1
Varėna Lith. **41** N9
Varese Italy **54** C2
Varfolomeyevka Rus. Fed. **70** D3
Vårgårda Sweden **41** H7
Varginha Brazil **141** B3
Varik Neth. **48** F3
Varillas Chile **140** B2
Varkana Iran *see* **Gorgān**
Varkaus Fin. **40** O5
Varna Bulg. **55** L3
Värnamo Sweden **41** I8
Värnäs Sweden **41** H6
Varnavino Rus. Fed. **38** J4
Várnjárg *pen.* Norway *see* **Varangerhalvøya**
Varpaisjärvi Fin. **40** O5
Várpalota Hungary **54** H1
Varsaj Afgh. **85** H2
Varsh, Ozero *l.* Rus. Fed. **38** J2
Varto Turkey **87** F3
Várzea da Palma Brazil **141** B2
Vasa Fin. *see* **Vaasa**
Vasai India **80** B2
Vashka *r.* Rus. Fed. **38** J2
Vasht Iran *see* **Khāsh**
Vasilkov Ukr. *see* **Vasyl'kiv**
Vaskna rva Estonia **41** O7
Vaslui Romania **55** L1
Vassar U.S.A. **130** D2
Vas-Soproni-síkság *hills* Hungary **54** G1
Vastan Turkey *see* **Gevaş**
Västerås Sweden **41** J7
Västerdalälven *r.* Sweden **41** I6
Västerfjäll Sweden **40** J3
Västerhaninge Sweden **41** K7
Västervik Sweden **41** J8
Vasto Italy **54** F3
Vasyl'kiv Ukr. **39** F6
Vatan France **52** E3
Vaté *i.* Vanuatu *see* **Éfaté**
Vatersay *i.* U.K. **46** B4
Vathar India **80** B2
Vathí Greece *see* **Vathy**
Vathy Greece **55** L6

▶**Vatican City** Europe **54** E4
Independent papal state, the smallest country in the world.
europe 5, 34–35

Vaticano, Città del Europe *see* **Vatican City**
Vatnajökull *ice cap* Iceland **40** [inset]
Vatoa *i.* Fiji **103** I3
Vatra Dornei Romania **55** K1
Vätter, Lake Sweden *see* **Vättern**
Vättern *l.* Sweden **41** I7
Vaughn U.S.A. **123** G6
Vaupés *r.* Col. **138** E3
Vauquelin *r.* Canada **118** F3
Vauvert France **52** G5
Vauxhall Canada **117** H5
Vavatenina Madag. **95** E5
Vava'u Group *is* Tonga **103** I3
Vavitao *i.* Fr. Polynesia *see* **Raivavae**
Vavoua Côte d'Ivoire **92** C4
Vavozh Rus. Fed. **38** K4
Vavuniya Sri Lanka **80** D4
Vawkavysk Belarus **41** N10
Växjö Sweden **41** I8
Vây, Đao *i.* Vietnam **67** C5
Vayenga Rus. Fed. *see* **Severomorsk**
Vazante Brazil **141** B2
Vazáš Sweden *see* **Vittangi**
Veaikevárri Sweden *see* **Svappavaara**
Veal Vêng Cambodia **67** C4
Vecht *r.* Neth. **48** G2
also known as Vechte (Germany)
Vechta Germany **49** I2

Vechte r. Germany 49 G2
also known as Vecht (Netherlands)
Veckerhagen (Reinhardshagen) Germany 49 J3
Vedaranniyam India 80 C4
Vedasandur India 80 C4
Veddige Sweden 41 H8
Vedea r. Romania 55 K3
Veedersburg U.S.A. 130 B3
Veendam Neth. 48 G1
Veenendaal Neth. 48 F2
Vega i. Norway 40 G4
Vega U.S.A. 127 C5
Vegreville Canada 117 H4
Vehkalahti Fin. 41 O6
Vehoa Pak. 85 H4
Veinticinco de Mayo Buenos Aires Arg. see 25 de Mayo
Veinticinco de Mayo La Pampa Arg. see 25 de Mayo
Veirwaro Pak. 85 H5
Veitshöchheim Germany 49 J5
Vejle Denmark 41 F9
Vekil'bazar Turkm. 85 F2
Velbert Germany 48 H3
Velbŭzhdki Prokhod pass Bulg./Macedonia 55 J3
Velddrif S. Africa 96 D7
Velebit mts Croatia 54 F2
Velen Germany 48 G3
Velenje Slovenia 54 F1
Veles Macedonia 55 I4
Vélez-Málaga Spain 53 D5
Vélez-Rubio Spain 53 E5
Velhas r. Brazil 141 B2
Velibaba Turkey see Aras
Velika Gorica Croatia 54 G2
Velika Plana Serb. and Mont. 55 I2
Velikaya r. Rus. Fed. 38 K4
Velikaya r. Rus. Fed. 41 P8
Velikaya r. Rus. Fed. 61 S3
Velikaya Kema Rus. Fed. 70 E3
Veliki Preslav Bulg. 55 L3
Velikiye Luki Rus. Fed. 38 F4
Velikiy Novgorod Rus. Fed. 38 F4
Velikiy Ustyug Rus. Fed. 38 J3
Velikonda Range hills India 80 C3
Veliko Tŭrnovo Bulg. 55 K3
Velikoye Rus. Fed. 38 H4
Velikoye, Ozero l. Rus. Fed. 39 I5
Veli Lošinj Croatia 54 F2
Velizh Rus. Fed. 38 F5
Vella Lavella i. Solomon Is 103 F2
Vellar r. India 80 C4
Vellberg Germany 49 J5
Vellmar Germany 49 J3
Vellore India 80 C3
Velpke Germany 49 K2
Vel'sk Rus. Fed. 38 I3
Velsuna Italy see Orvieto
Velten Germany 49 N2
Veluwezoom, Nationaal Park nat. park Neth. 48 F2
Velykyy Tokmak Ukr. see Tokmak
Vel'yu r. Rus. Fed. 38 L3
Vemalwada India 80 C2
Vema Seamount sea feature S. Atlantic Ocean 144 I8
Vema Trench sea feature Indian Ocean 145 M6
Vembe Nature Reserve S. Africa 97 I2
Vempalle India 80 C3
Venado Tuerto Arg. 140 D4
Venafro Italy 54 F4
Venceslau Bráz Brazil 141 A3
Vendinga Rus. Fed. 38 J3
Vendôme France 52 E3
Venegas Mex. 127 C8
Venetia Italy see Venice
Venetie Landing U.S.A. 114 D3
Venev Rus. Fed. 39 H5
Venezia Italy see Venice
Venezia, Golfo di g. Europe see Venice, Gulf of

▶Venezuela country S. America 138 E2
5th most populous country in South America.
south america 9, 136–137

Venezuela, Golfo de g. Venez. 138 D1
Venezuelan Basin sea feature S. Atlantic Ocean 144 D4
Vengurla India 80 B3
Veniaminof Volcano U.S.A. 114 C4
Venice Italy 54 E2
Venice U.S.A. 129 D7
Venice, Gulf of Europe 54 E2
Vénissieux France 52 G4
Venkatapalem India 80 D2
Venkatapuram India 80 D2
Venlo Neth. 48 G3
Vennesla Norway 41 E7
Venray Neth. 48 F3
Venta r. Latvia/Lith. 41 M8
Venta Lith. 41 M8
Ventersburg S. Africa 97 H5
Ventersdorp S. Africa 97 H4
Venterstad S. Africa 97 G6
Ventnor U.K. 45 F8
Ventotene, Isola i. Italy 54 E4
Ventoux, Mont mt. France 52 G4
Ventspils Latvia 41 L8
Ventura U.S.A. 124 D4
Venus Bay Australia 108 B7
Venustiano Carranza Mex. 127 C7
Venustiano Carranza, Presa resr Mex. 127 C7
Vera Arg. 140 D3
Vera Spain 53 F5
Vera Cruz Brazil 141 A3
Vera Cruz Mex. see Veracruz
Veracruz Mex. 132 E5
Veraval India 78 B5
Verbania Italy 54 C2
Vercelli Italy 54 C2
Vercors reg. France 52 G4
Verdalsøra Norway 40 G5
Verde r. Goiás Brazil 141 A2
Verde r. Goiás Brazil 141 A2
Verde r. Goiás Brazil 140 B2
Verde r. Minas Gerais Brazil 141 A2
Verde r. Mex. 123 G8
Verde r. U.S.A. 125 H5
Verden (Aller) Germany 49 J2
Verde Pequeno r. Brazil 141 C1
Verdi U.S.A. 124 D2
Verdon r. France 52 G5
Verdun France 48 F5
Vereeniging S. Africa 97 H4
Vereshchagino Rus. Fed. 37 Q4
Vergennes U.S.A. 131 I1
Véria Greece see Veroia
Verín Spain 53 C3
Veríssimo Brazil 141 A2
Verkhneimbatsk Rus. Fed. 60 J3
Verkhnekolvinsk Rus. Fed. 38 M2
Verkhnespasskoye Rus. Fed. 38 J4
Verkhnetulomskiy Rus. Fed. 40 Q2
Verkhnetulomskoye Vdkhr. res. Rus. Fed. 40 Q2
Verkhnevilyuysk Rus. Fed. 61 N3
Verkhneye Kuyto, Ozero l. Rus. Fed. 40 Q4
Verkhnezeysk Rus. Fed. 69 N2
Verkhniy Vyalozerskiy Rus. Fed. 38 G2
Verkhnyaya Khava Rus. Fed. 39 H6
Verkhnyaya Salda Rus. Fed. 37 S4
Verkhnyaya Tunguska r. Rus. Fed. see Angara
Verkhnyaya Tura Rus. Fed. 37 R4
Verkhoshizhem'ye Rus. Fed. 38 K4
Verkhovazh'ye Rus. Fed. 38 I3
Verkhov'ye Rus. Fed. 39 H5
Verkhoyansk Rus. Fed. 61 O3
Verkhoyanskiy Khrebet mts Rus. Fed. 61 N2
Vermand France 48 D5
Vermelho r. Brazil 141 A1
Vermilion Canada 117 I4
Vermilion Bay U.S.A. 127 F6
Vermilion Cliffs AZ U.S.A. 125 G3
Vermilion Cliffs UT U.S.A. 125 G3
Vermilion Cliffs National Monument nat. park U.S.A. 125 H3
Vermilion Lake U.S.A. 126 E2
Vermillion U.S.A. 126 D3
Vermillion Bay Canada 117 M5
Vermont state U.S.A. 131 I1
Vernadsky research station Antarctica 148 L2
Vernal U.S.A. 125 I1
Verner Canada 118 E5
Verneuk Pan salt pan S. Africa 96 E5
Vernon Canada 116 G5
Vernon France 48 B5
Vernon AL U.S.A. 127 F5
Vernon IN U.S.A. 130 C4
Vernon TX U.S.A. 127 D5
Vernon UT U.S.A. 125 G1
Vernon Islands Australia 104 E3
Vernoye Rus. Fed. 70 C2
Vernyy Kazakh. see Almaty
Vero Beach U.S.A. 129 D7
Veroia Greece 55 J4
Verona Italy 54 D2
Verona U.S.A. 130 F4
Versailles France 48 C6
Versailles IN U.S.A. 130 C4
Versailles KY U.S.A. 130 C4
Versailles OH U.S.A. 130 C3
Versec Serb. and Mont. see Vršac
Versmold Germany 49 I2
Vert, Île i. Canada 119 H4
Vertou France 52 D3
Verulam S. Africa 97 J5
Verulamium U.K. see St Albans
Verviers Belgium 48 F4
Vervins France 48 D5
Verwood Canada 117 J5
Verzy France 48 E5
Vescovato Corsica France 52 I5
Vesele Ukr. 39 G7
Veselyy Rus. Fed. 39 I7
Veshenskaya Rus. Fed. 39 I6
Vesle r. France 48 D5
Veslyana r. Rus. Fed. 38 L3
Vesontio France see Besançon
Vesoul France 52 H3
Vesselyy Yar Rus. Fed. 70 D4
Vessem Neth. 48 F3
Vesterålen is Norway 40 H2
Vesterålsfjorden sea chan. Norway 40 H2
Vestertana Norway 40 O1
Vestfjorddalen valley Norway 41 F7
Vestfjorden sea chan. Norway 40 H3
Véstia Brazil 141 A3
Vestmanna Faroe Is 40 [inset]
Vestmannaeyjar Iceland 40 [inset]
Vestmannaeyjar is Iceland 40 [inset]
Vestnes Norway 40 E5
Vesturhorn hd Iceland 40 [inset]
Vesuvio vol. Italy see Vesuvius
Vesuvius vol. Italy 54 F4
Ves'yegonsk Rus. Fed. 38 H4
Veszprém Hungary 54 G1
Veteli Fin. 40 M5
Veteran Canada 117 I4
Vetlanda Sweden 41 I8
Vetluga Rus. Fed. 38 J4
Vetluga r. Rus. Fed. 38 J4
Vetluzhskiy Kostromskaya Oblast' Rus. Fed. 38 J4
Vetluzhskiy Nizhegorodskaya Oblast' Rus. Fed. 38 J4
Vettore, Monte mt. Italy 54 E3
Veurne Belgium 48 C3
Vevay U.S.A. 130 C4
Vevey Switz. 52 H3
Vexin Normand reg. France 48 B5
Veyo U.S.A. 125 G3
Vézère r. France 52 E4
Vezirköprü Turkey 86 D2
Vialar Alg. see Tissemsilt
Viamao Brazil 141 A5
Viana Espírito Santo Brazil 141 C3
Viana Maranhão Brazil 139 J4
Viana do Castelo Port. 53 B3
Vianen Neth. 48 F3
Viangchan Laos see Vientiane
Viangphoukha Laos 66 C2
Vianópolis Brazil 141 A2
Viareggio Italy 54 D3
Viborg Denmark 41 F8
Viborg Rus. Fed. see Vyborg
Vibo Valentia Italy 54 G5
Vic Spain 53 H3
Vicam Mex. 123 F8
Vicecomodoro Marambio research station Antarctica see Marambio
Vicente, Point U.S.A. 124 D5
Vicente Guerrero Mex. 123 D7
Vicenza Italy 54 D2
Vich Spain see Vic
Vichada r. Col. 138 E3
Vichadero Uruguay 140 F4
Vichy France 52 F3
Vicksburg AZ U.S.A. 125 G5
Vicksburg MS U.S.A. 127 F5
Viçosa Brazil 141 C3
Victor, Mount Antarctica 148 D2
Victor Harbor Australia 107 B7
Victoria Arg. 140 D4
Victoria r. Australia 104 E3
Victoria state Australia 108 B6

▶Victoria Canada 116 F5
Provincial capital of British Columbia.

Victoria Chile 140 B5
Victoria Malaysia see Labuan
Victoria Malta 54 F6

▶Victoria Seychelles 145 L6
Capital of the Seychelles.

Victoria TX U.S.A. 127 D6
Victoria VA U.S.A. 131 F5
Victoria prov. Zimbabwe see Masvingo

▶Victoria, Lake Africa 94 D4
Largest lake in Africa and 3rd in the world.
africa 88–89
world 12–13

Victoria, Lake Australia 107 C7
Victoria, Mount Fiji see Tomanivi
Victoria, Mount Myanmar 66 A2
Victoria, Mount P.N.G. 65 L8
Victoria and Albert Mountains Canada 115 K2
Victoria Falls Zambia/Zimbabwe 95 C5
Victoria Harbour sea chan. Hong Kong China see Hong Kong Harbour

▶Victoria Island Canada 114 H2
3rd largest island in North America.

Victoria Land coastal area Antarctica 148 H2
Victoria Peak Belize 132 G5
Victoria Peak hill Hong Kong China 73 [inset]
Victoria Range mts N.Z. 109 D6
Victoria River Downs Australia 104 E4
Victoriaville Canada 119 H5
Victoria West S. Africa 96 F6
Victorica Arg. 140 C5
Victorville U.S.A. 124 E4
Victory Downs Australia 105 F6
Vidalia U.S.A. 127 F6
Vidal Junction U.S.A. 125 F4
Videle Romania 55 K2
Vidisha India 78 D5
Vidlin U.K. 46 [inset]
Vidlitsa Rus. Fed. 38 G3
Viechtach Germany 49 M5
Viedma Arg. 140 D6
Viedma, Lago l. Arg. 140 B7
Viejo, Cerro mt. Mex. 123 E7
Vielank Germany 49 L1
Vielsalm Belgium 48 F4
Vienenburg Germany 49 K3

▶Vienna Austria 43 P6
Capital of Austria.

Vienna MO U.S.A. 126 F4
Vienna WV U.S.A. 130 E4
Vienne France 52 G4
Vienne r. France 52 E3

▶Vientiane Laos 66 C3
Capital of Laos.

Vieques i. Puerto Rico 133 K5
Vieremä Fin. 40 O5
Viersen Germany 48 G3
Vierzon France 52 F3
Viesca Mex. 127 C7
Viesīte Latvia 41 N8
Vieste Italy 54 G4
Vietas Sweden 40 K3
Viêt Nam country Asia see Vietnam
▶Vietnam country Asia 66 D3
asia 6, 58–59
Viêt Tri Vietnam 66 D2
Vieux Comptoir, Lac du l. Canada 118 F3
Vieux-Fort Canada 119 K4
Vieux Poste, Pointe du pt Canada 119 J4
Vigan Phil. 65 G3
Vigevano Italy 54 C2
Vigia Brazil 139 I4
Vignacourt France 48 C4
Vignemale mt. France 50 D3
Vignola Italy 54 D2
Vigo Spain 53 B2
Vihanti Fin. 40 N4
Vihari Pak. 85 I4
Vihti Fin. 41 N6
Viipuri Rus. Fed. see Vyborg
Viitasaari Fin. 40 N5
Vijayadurg India 80 B2
Vijayanagaram India see Vizianagaram
Vijayapati India 80 C4
Vijayawada India 80 D2
Vik Iceland 40 [inset]
Vikajärvi Fin. 40 O3
Vikeke East Timor see Viqueque
Viking Canada 117 I4
Vikna i. Norway 40 G4
Vikøyri Norway 41 E6
Vila Vanuatu see Port Vila
Vila Alferes Chamusca Moz. see Guija
Vila Bittencourt Brazil 138 E4
Vila Bugaço Angola see Camanongue
Vila Cabral Moz. see Lichinga
Vila da Ponte Angola see Kuvango
Vila de Aljustrel Angola see Cangamba
Vila de Almoster Angola see Chiange
Vila de João Belo Moz. see Xai-Xai
Vila de María Arg. 140 D3
Vila de Trego Morais Moz. see Chókwè
Vila Fontes Moz. see Caia
Vila Franca de Xira Port. 53 B4
Vilagarcía de Arousa Spain 53 B2
Vila Gomes da Costa Moz. 97 K3
Vilalba Spain 53 C2
Vila Luísa Moz. see Marracuene
Vila Marechal Carmona Angola see Uíge
Vila Miranda Moz. see Macaloge
Vilanandro, Tanjona pt Madag. 95 E5
Vilanculos Moz. 97 L1
Vila Nova de Gaia Port. 53 B3
Vilanova i la Geltrú Spain 53 G3
Vila Pery Moz. see Chimoio
Vila Real Port. 53 C3
Vilar Formoso Port. 53 C3
Vila Salazar Angola see N'dalatando
Vila Salazar Zimbabwe see Sango
Vila Teixeira de Sousa Angola see Luau
Vila Velha Brazil 141 C3
Vilcabamba, Cordillera mts Peru 138 D6
Vil'cheka, Zemlya i. Rus. Fed. 60 H1
Viled' r. Rus. Fed. 38 J3
Vileyka Belarus see Vilyeyka
Vil'gort Rus. Fed. 38 K3
Vilhelmina Sweden 40 J4
Vilhena Brazil 138 F6
Viliya r. Belarus/Lith. see Neris
Viljandi Estonia 41 N7
Viljoenskroon S. Africa 97 H4
Vilkaviškis Lith. 41 M9
Vilkija Lith. 41 M9
Vil'kitskogo, Proliv strait Rus. Fed. 61 K2
Vilkovo Ukr. see Vylkove
Villa Abecia Bol. 138 E8
Villa Ahumada Mex. 123 G7
Villa Ángela Arg. 140 D3
Villa Bella Bol. 138 E6
Villa Bens Morocco see Tarfaya
Villablino Spain 53 C2
Villacañas Spain 53 E4
Villach Austria 43 N7
Villacidro Sardinia Italy 54 C5
Villa Cisneros W. Sahara see Ad Dakhla
Villa Constitución Mex. see Ciudad Constitución
Villa Dolores Arg. 140 C4
Villagarcía de Arosa Spain see Vilagarcía de Arousa
Villagrán Mex. 127 D7
Villaguay Arg. 140 E4
Villahermosa Mex. 132 F5
Villa Insurgentes Mex. 123 F8
Villajoyosa Spain see Villajoyosa - La Vila Joíosa
Villajoyosa - La Vila Joíosa Spain 53 F4
Villaldama Mex. 127 C7
Villa Mainero Mex. 127 D7
Villa María Arg. 140 D4
Villa Montes Bol. 138 F8
Villa Nora S. Africa 97 I2
Villanueva de la Serena Spain 53 D4
Villanueva de los Infantes Spain 53 E4
Villanueva-y-Geltrú Spain see Vilanova i la Geltrú
Villa Ocampo Arg. 140 E3
Villa Ocampo Mex. 127 B7
Villa Ojo de Agua Arg. 140 D3
Villaputzu Sardinia Italy 54 C5
Villa Regina Arg. 140 C5
Villarrica Para. 140 E3
Villarrica, Lago l. Chile 140 B5
Villarrica, Parque Nacional nat. park Chile 140 B5
Villarrobledo Spain 53 E4
Villas U.S.A. 131 H4
Villasalazar Zimbabwe see Sango
Villa San Giovanni Italy 54 F5
Villa Sanjurjo Morocco see Al Hoceima
Villa San Martín Arg. 140 D3
Villa Unión Arg. 140 C3
Villa Unión Coahuila Mex. 127 C6
Villa Unión Durango Mex. 127 B8
Villa Unión Sinaloa Mex. 132 C4
Villa Valeria Arg. 140 D4
Villavicencio Col. 138 D3
Villazon Bol. 138 E8
Villefranche-sur-Saône France 52 G4
Ville-Marie Canada see Montréal
Villena Spain 53 F4
Villeneuve-sur-Lot France 52 E4
Villeneuve-sur-Yonne France 52 F2
Villers-Cotterêts France 48 D5
Villers-sur-Mer France 45 G9
Villerupt France 48 F5
Villeurbanne France 52 G4
Villiers S. Africa 97 I4
Villingen Germany 43 L6
Villuppuram India see Villupuram
Villupuram India 80 C4
Vilna Canada 117 I4
Vilna Lith. see Vilnius

▶Vilnius Lith. 41 N9
Capital of Lithuania.

Vil'nyans'k Ukr. 39 G7
Vilppula Fin. 40 N5
Vils r. Germany 49 L5
Vils r. Germany 49 N6
Vilvoorde Belgium 48 E4
Vilyeyka Belarus 41 O9
Vilyuy r. Rus. Fed. 61 N3
Vilyuyskoye Vodokhranilishche resr Rus. Fed. 61 M3
Vimmerby Sweden 41 I8
Vimy France 48 C4
Vina r. Cameroon 93 E4
Vina U.S.A. 124 B2
Viña del Mar Chile 140 B4
Vinalhaven Island U.S.A. 128 G2
Vinaròs Spain 53 G3
Vinaroz Spain see Vinaròs
Vincelotte, Lac l. Canada 119 G3
Vincennes U.S.A. 130 B4
Vincennes Bay Antarctica 148 F2
Vinchina Arg. 140 C3
Vindelälven r. Sweden 40 K5
Vindeln Sweden 40 K4
Vindhya Range hills India 78 C5
Vindobona Austria see Vienna
Vine Grove U.S.A. 130 C5
Vineland U.S.A. 131 H4
Vinh Vietnam 66 D3
Vinh Linh Vietnam 66 D3
Vinh Long Vietnam 67 D5
Vinh Thuc, Đao i. Vietnam 66 D2
Vinita U.S.A. 127 E4
Vinjhan India 78 B5
Vinland i. Canada see Newfoundland
Vinnitsa Ukr. see Vinnytsya
Vinnytsya Ukr. 39 F6
Vinogradov Ukr. see Vynohradiv

▶Vinson Massif mt. Antarctica 148 L1
Highest mountain in Antarctica.

Vinstra Norway 41 F6
Vinton U.S.A. 126 E3
Vinukonda India 80 C2
Violeta Cuba see Primero de Enero
Vipperow Germany 49 M1
Viqueque East Timor 104 D2
Virac Phil. 65 G4
Viramgam India 78 C5
Viranşehir Turkey 87 E3
Virawah Pak. 85 H5
Virchow, Mount hill Australia 104 B5
Virdel India 78 C5
Virden Canada 117 K5
Virden U.S.A. 125 I5
Vire France 52 D2
Virei Angola 95 B5
Virgem da Lapa Brazil 141 C2
Virgilina U.S.A. 131 F5
Virgin r. U.S.A. 125 F3
Virginia Rep. of Ireland 47 E4
Virginia S. Africa 97 H5
Virginia U.S.A. 126 F4
Virginia state U.S.A. 130 F5
Virginia Beach U.S.A. 131 H5
Virginia City MT U.S.A. 122 F3
Virginia City NV U.S.A. 124 D2
Virginia Falls Canada 116 E2

▶Virgin Islands (U.K.) terr. West Indies 133 L5
United Kingdom Overseas Territory.
north america 9, 112–113

▶Virgin Islands (U.S.A.) terr. West Indies 133 L5
United States Unincorporated Territory.
north america 9, 112–113

Virgin Mountains U.S.A. 125 F3
Virginópolis Brazil 141 C2
Virkkala Fin. 41 N6
Virôchey Cambodia 67 D4
Viroqua U.S.A. 126 F3
Virovitica Croatia 54 G2
Virrat Fin. 40 M5
Virton Belgium 48 F5
Virtsu Estonia 41 M7
Virudhunagar India 80 C4
Virudunagar India see Virudhunagar
Virunga, Parc National des nat. park Dem. Rep. Congo 94 C4
Vis i. Croatia 54 G3
Visaginas Lith. 41 O9
Visakhapatnam India see Vishakhapatnam
Visalia U.S.A. 124 D3
Visapur India 80 B2
Visayan Sea Phil. 65 G4
Visbek Germany 49 I2
Visby Sweden 41 K8
Viscount Melville Sound sea chan. Canada 115 G2
Visé Belgium 48 F4
Vise, Ostrov i. Rus. Fed. 60 I2
Viseu Brazil 139 I4
Viseu Port. 53 C3
Vishakhapatnam India 80 D2
Vishera r. Rus. Fed. 37 R4
Vishera r. Rus. Fed. 38 L3
Viški Latvia 41 O8
Visnagar India 78 C5
Viso, Monte mt. Italy 54 B2
Visoko Bos.-Herz. 54 H3
Visp Switz. 52 H3
Visselhövede Germany 49 J2
Vista U.S.A. 124 E5
Vista Lake U.S.A. 124 D4
Vistonida, Limni lag. Greece 55 K4
Vistula r. Poland 43 Q3
Vitebsk Belarus see Vitsyebsk
Viterbo Italy 54 E3
Vitichi Bol. 138 E8
Vitigudino Spain 53 C3
Viti Levu i. Fiji 103 H3
Vitimskoye Ploskogor'ye plat. Rus. Fed. 69 K2
Vitória Brazil 141 C3
Vitória da Conquista Brazil 141 C1
Vitoria-Gasteiz Spain 53 E2
Vitória Seamount sea feature S. Atlantic Ocean 144 F7
Vitré France 52 D2
Vitry-en-Artois France 48 C4
Vitry-le-François France 48 E6
Vitsyebsk Belarus 39 F5
Vittangi Sweden 40 L3
Vittel France 52 G2
Vittoria Sicily Italy 54 F6
Vittorio Veneto Italy 54 E2
Viveiro Spain 53 C2
Vivero Spain see Viveiro
Vivo S. Africa 97 I2
Vizagapatam India see Vishakhapatnam
Vizcaíno, Desierto de des. Mex. 123 E8
Vizcaíno, Sierra mts Mex. 123 E8
Vize Turkey 55 L4
Vizhas r. Rus. Fed. 38 J2
Vizianagaram India 80 D2
Vizinga Rus. Fed. 38 K3
Vlaardingen Neth. 48 E3
Vlădeasa, Vârful mt. Romania 55 J1
Vladikavkaz Rus. Fed. 87 G2
Vladimir Primorskiy Kray Rus. Fed. 70 D4
Vladimir Vladimirskaya Oblast' Rus. Fed. 38 I4
Vladimiro-Aleksandrovskoye Rus. Fed. 70 D4
Vladimir-Volynskiy Ukr. see Volodymyr-Volyns'kyy
Vladivostok Rus. Fed. 70 C4
Vlakte S. Africa 97 I3
Vlasotince Serb. and Mont. 55 J3
Vlas'yevo Rus. Fed. 70 F1
Vlieland i. Neth. 48 E1
Vlissingen Neth. 48 D3
Vlora Albania see Vlorë
Vlorë Albania 55 H4
Vlotho Germany 49 I2
Vlotslavsk Poland see Włocławek
Vltava r. Czech Rep. 43 O5
Vöcklabruck Austria 43 N6
Vodlozero, Ozero l. Rus. Fed. 38 H3
Voe U.K. 46 [inset]
Voerendaal Neth. 48 F4
Vogelkop Peninsula Indon. see Doberai, Jazirah
Vogelsberg hills Germany 49 I4
Voghera Italy 54 C2
Vohburg an der Donau Germany 49 L6
Vohémar Madag. see Iharaña
Vohenstrauß Germany 49 M5
Vohibinany Madag. see Ampasimanolotra
Vohimarina Madag. see Iharaña
Vohimena, Tanjona c. Madag. 95 E6
Vohipeno Madag. 95 E6
Vöhl Germany 49 I3
Võhma Estonia 41 N7
Voinjama Liberia 92 C4
Vojens Denmark 41 F9
Vojvodina prov. Serb. and Mont. 55 H2
Vokhma Rus. Fed. 38 J4
Voknavolok Rus. Fed. 40 Q4
Vol' r. Rus. Fed. 38 L3
Volcano Bay Japan see Uchiura-wan

▶Volcano Islands Japan 65 K2
Part of Japan.

Volda Norway 40 E5
Vol'dino Rus. Fed. 38 L3
Volendam Neth. 48 F2
Volga Rus. Fed. 38 H4

▶Volga r. Rus. Fed. 39 J7
Longest river and largest drainage basin in Europe.
europe 32–33

Volga Upland hills Rus. Fed. see Privolzhskaya Vozvyshennost'
Volgodonsk Rus. Fed. 39 I7
Volgograd Rus. Fed. 39 J6
Volgogradskoye Vodokhranilishche resr Rus. Fed. 39 J6
Völkermarkt Austria 43 O7
Volkhov Rus. Fed. 38 G4
Volkhov r. Rus. Fed. 38 G3
Völklingen Germany 48 G5
Volkovysk Belarus see Vawkavysk
Volksrust S. Africa 97 I4
Vol'no-Nadezhdinskoye Rus. Fed. 70 C4
Volnovakha Ukr. 39 H7
Vol'nyansk Ukr. see Vil'nyans'k
Volochanka Rus. Fed. 60 K2
Volochisk Ukr. see Volochys'k
Volochys'k Ukr. 39 E6
Volodars'ke Ukr. 39 H7
Volodarskoye Kazakh. see Saumalkol'
Volodymyr-Volyns'kyy Ukr. 39 E6
Vologda Rus. Fed. 38 H4
Volokolamsk Rus. Fed. 38 G4
Volokovaya Rus. Fed. 38 K2
Volos Greece 55 J5
Volosovo Rus. Fed. 41 P7
Volot Rus. Fed. 38 F4
Volovo Rus. Fed. 39 H5
Volozhin Belarus see Valozhyn
Volsinii Italy see Orvieto
Vol'sk Rus. Fed. 39 J5

▶Volta, Lake resr Ghana 92 D4
5th largest lake in Africa.

Volta Blanche r. Burkina/Ghana see White Volta
Voltaire, Cape Australia 104 D3
Volta Redonda Brazil 141 B3
Volturno r. Italy 54 E4
Volubilis tourist site Morocco 50 C5
Volvi, Limni l. Greece 55 J4
Volzhsk Rus. Fed. 38 K5
Volzhskiy Samarskaya Oblast' Rus. Fed. 39 K5
Volzhskiy Volgogradskaya Oblast' Rus. Fed. 39 J6
Vondanka Rus. Fed. 38 J4
Vontimitta India 80 C3
Vopnafjörður Iceland 40 [inset]
Vopnafjörður b. Iceland 40 [inset]
Vörå Fin. 40 M5
Voranava Belarus 41 N9
Voreioi Sporades is Greece 55 J5
Voriai Sporádhes is Greece see Voreioi Sporades
Voring Plateau sea feature N. Atlantic Ocean 144 I1
Vorjing mt. India 79 H3
Vorkuta Rus. Fed. 60 H3
Vormsi i. Estonia 41 M7
Vorona r. Rus. Fed. 39 I6
Voronezh Rus. Fed. 39 H6
Voronezh r. Rus. Fed. 39 H6
Voronov, Mys pt Rus. Fed. 38 I2
Vorontsovo-Aleksandrovskoye Rus. Fed. see Zelenokumsk
Voroshilov Rus. Fed. see Ussuriysk
Voroshilovgrad Ukr. see Luhans'k
Voroshilovsk Rus. Fed. see Stavropol'
Voroshilovsk Ukr. see Alchevs'k
Vorotynets Rus. Fed. 38 J4
Vorozhba Ukr. 39 G6
Vorpommersche Boddenlandschaft, Nationalpark nat. park Germany 43 N3
Vorskla r. Rus. Fed. 39 G6
Võrtsjärv l. Estonia 41 N7
Võru Estonia 41 O8
Vorukh Tajik. 85 H2
Vosburg S. Africa 96 F6
Vose Tajik. 85 H2
Vosges mts France 52 H3
Voskresensk Rus. Fed. 39 H5
Voskresenskoye Rus. Fed. 38 H4
Voss Norway 41 E6
Vostochno-Sakhalinskiy Gory mts Rus. Fed. 70 F2
Vostochno-Sibirskoye More sea Rus. Fed. see East Siberian Sea
Vostochnyy Kirovskaya Oblast' Rus. Fed. 38 L4
Vostochnyy Sakhalinskaya Oblast' Rus. Fed. 70 F2
Vostochnyy Chink Ustyurta esc. Uzbek. 76 A3
Vostochnyy Sayan mts Rus. Fed. 68 G2

▶Vostok research station Antarctica 148 F1
Lowest recorded screen temperature in the world.

Vostok Primorskiy Kray Rus. Fed. 70 D3
Vostok Sakhalinskaya Oblast' Rus. Fed. see Neftegorsk
Vostok Island Kiribati 147 J6
Vostroye Rus. Fed. 38 J3
Votkinsk Rus. Fed. 37 Q4
Votkinskoye Vodokhranilishche resr Rus. Fed. 37 R4
Votuporanga Brazil 141 A3
Vouziers France 48 E5
Voves France 52 E2
Voyageurs National Park U.S.A. 126 E1
Voynitsa Rus. Fed. 40 Q4
Vöyri Fin. see Vörå
Voyvozh Rus. Fed. 38 L3
Vozhayel' Rus. Fed. 38 K3
Vozhe, Ozero l. Rus. Fed. 38 H3
Vozhega Rus. Fed. 38 I3
Vozhgaly Rus. Fed. 38 K4
Voznesens'k Ukr. 39 F7
Vozonin Trough sea feature Arctic Ocean 149 F1
Vozrozhdeniya, Ostrov i. Uzbek. 76 A3
Vozzhayevka Rus. Fed. 70 C2

Vrangel' Rus. Fed. 70 D4
Vrangelya, Mys pt Rus. Fed. 70 E1
Vranje Serb. and Mont. 55 I3
Vratnik pass Bulg. 55 L3
Vratsa Bulg. 55 J3
Vrbas Serb. and Mont. 55 H2
Vrede S. Africa 97 I4
Vredefort S. Africa 97 H4
Vredenburg S. Africa 96 C7
Vredendal S. Africa 96 D6
Vresse Belgium 48 E5
Vriddhachalam India 80 C4
Vries Neth. 48 G1
Vrigstad Sweden 41 I8
Vršac Serb. and Mont. 55 I2
Vryburg S. Africa 96 G4
Vryheid S. Africa 97 J4
Vsevidof, Mount vol. U.S.A. 114 B4
Vsevolozhsk Rus. Fed. 38 F3
Vu Ban Vietnam 66 D2
Vučitrn Serb. and Mont. 55 I3
Vukovar Croatia 55 H2
Vuktyl' Rus. Fed. 37 R3
Vukuzakhe S. Africa 97 I4
Vulcan Canada 116 H5
Vulcan Island P.N.G. see Manam Island
Vulcano, Isola i. Italy 54 F5
Vu Liêt Vietnam 66 D3
Vulture Mountains U.S.A. 125 G5
Vung Tau Vietnam 67 D5
Vuohijärvi Fin. 41 O6
Vuolijoki Fin. 40 O4
Vuollerim Sweden 40 L3
Vuostimo Fin. 40 O3
Vurnary Rus. Fed. 38 J5
Vushtri Serb. and Mont. see Vučitrn
Vvedenovka Rus. Fed. 70 C2
Vyara India 78 C5
Vyarkhowye Belarus see Ruba
Vyatka Rus. Fed. see Kirov
Vyatka r. Rus. Fed. 38 K5
Vyatskiye Polyany Rus. Fed. 38 K4
Vyazemskiy Rus. Fed. 70 D3
Vyaz'ma Rus. Fed. 39 G5
Vyazniki Rus. Fed. 38 I4
Vyazovka Rus. Fed. 39 J5
Vyborg Rus. Fed. 41 P6
Vychegda r. Rus. Fed. 38 J3
Vychegodskiy Rus. Fed. 38 J3
Vyerkhnyadzvinsk Belarus 41 O9
Vyetryna Belarus 41 P9
Vygozero, Ozero l. Rus. Fed. 38 G3
Vyksa Rus. Fed. 39 I5
Vylkove Ukr. 55 M2
Vym' r. Rus. Fed. 38 K3
Vynohradiv Ukr. 39 D6
Vypin Island India 80 C4
Vypolzovo Rus. Fed. 38 G4
Vyritsa Rus. Fed. 41 Q7
Vyrnwy, Lake U.K. 45 D6
Vyselki Rus. Fed. 39 H7
Vysha Rus. Fed. 39 I5
Vyshhorod Ukr. 39 F6
Vyshnevolotskaya Gryada ridge Rus. Fed. 38 G4
Vyshniy-Volochek Rus. Fed. 38 G4
Vyškov Czech Rep. 43 P6
Vysokaya Gora Rus. Fed. 38 K5
Vysokogorniy Rus. Fed. 70 E2
Vystupovychi Ukr. 39 F6
Vytegra Rus. Fed. 38 H3
Vyya r. Rus. Fed. 38 J3
Vyžuona r. Lith. 41 N9

↓ W

Wa Ghana 92 C3
Waal r. Neth. 48 E3
Waalwijk Neth. 48 F3
Waat Sudan 82 D8
Wabag P.N.G. 65 K8
Wabakimi Lake Canada 118 C4
Wabasca r. Canada 116 H3
Wabasca-Desmarais Canada 116 H4
Wabash U.S.A. 130 C3
Wabash r. U.S.A. 130 A5
Wabasha U.S.A. 126 E2
Wabassi r. Canada 118 D4
Wabatongushi Lake Canada 118 D4
Wabē Gestro r. Eth. 74 D6
Wabē Shebelē Wenz r. Eth. 94 E3
Wabigoon Lake Canada 117 M5
Wabowden Canada 117 L4
Wabrah well Saudi Arabia 84 B5
Wabu China 73 H1
Wabuk Point Canada 118 D3
Wabush Canada 119 I3
Waccasassa Bay U.S.A. 129 D6
Wächtersbach Germany 49 J4
Waco Canada 119 I4
Waco U.S.A. 127 D6
Waconda Lake U.S.A. 126 D4
Wad Pak. 85 G5
Wadbilliga National Park Australia 108 D6
Waddān Libya 51 H6
Waddell Dam U.S.A. 125 G5
Waddeneilanden Neth. see West Frisian Islands
Waddenzee sea chan. Neth. 48 E2
Waddington, Mount Canada 116 E5
Waddinxveen Neth. 48 E2
Wadebridge U.K. 45 C8
Wadena Canada 117 K5
Wadena U.S.A. 126 E2
Wadern Germany 48 G5
Wadesville U.S.A. 130 B4
Wadeye Australia 104 E3
Wadgassen Germany 48 G5
Wadhwan India see Surendranagar
Wadi India 80 C2
Wādī as Sīr Jordan 81 B4
Wadi Halfa Sudan 82 D5
Wad Medani Sudan 82 D7
Wad Rawa Sudan 82 D6
Wadsworth U.S.A. 124 D2
Waenhuiskrans S. Africa 96 E8
Wafangdian China 69 M5
Wafra Kuwait see Al Wafrah
Wagenfeld Germany 49 I2
Wagenhoff Germany 49 K2
Wagga Wagga Australia 108 C5
Wagner U.S.A. 126 D3
Wagoner U.S.A. 127 E4
Wagon Mound U.S.A. 123 G5
Wah Pak. 85 I3
Wahai Indon. 65 H7
Wāhāt Jālū Libya 93 F2
Wahemen, Lac l. Canada 119 H3
Wahiawa HI U.S.A. 123 [inset]
Wahlhausen Germany 49 J3
Wahpeton U.S.A. 126 D2
Wahran Alg. see Oran
Wah Wah Mountains U.S.A. 125 G2
Wai India 80 B2
Waialua HI U.S.A. 123 [inset]
Waiau N.Z. see Franz Josef Glacier
Waiau r. N.Z. 109 D6
Waiblingen Germany 49 J6
Waidhofen an der Ybbs Austria 43 O7
Waigeo i. Indon. 65 I7
Waiheke Island N.Z. 109 E3
Waikabubak Indon. 104 B2
Waikaia r. N.Z. 109 B7
Waikari N.Z. 109 D6
Waikerie Australia 107 B7
Waikouaiti N.Z. 109 C7
Wailuku HI U.S.A. 123 [inset]
Waimangaroa N.Z. 109 C5
Waimarama N.Z. 109 F4
Waimate N.Z. 109 C7
Waimea HI U.S.A. 123 [inset]
Wainganga r. India 80 C2
Waingapu Indon. 104 C2
Wainhouse Corner U.K. 45 C8
Waini Point Guyana 139 G2
Wainwright Canada 117 I4
Wainwright U.S.A. 114 C2
Waiouru N.Z. 109 E4
Waipahi N.Z. 109 B8
Waipaoa r. N.Z. 109 F4
Waipara N.Z. 109 D6
Waipawa N.Z. 109 F4
Waipukurau N.Z. 109 F4
Wairarapa, Lake N.Z. 109 E5
Wairau r. N.Z. 109 E5
Wairoa N.Z. 109 F4
Wairoa r. N.Z. 109 F4
Waitahanui N.Z. 109 F4
Waitahuna N.Z. 109 B7
Waitakaruru N.Z. 109 E3
Waitaki r. N.Z. 109 C7
Waitangi N.Z. 103 I6
Waite River Australia 104 F5
Waiuku N.Z. 109 E3
Waiwera South N.Z. 109 B8
Waiyang China 73 H3
Wajima Japan 71 E5
Wajir Kenya 94 E3
Waka Indon. 104 C2
Wakasa-wan b. Japan 71 D6
Wakatipu, Lake N.Z. 109 B7
Wakaw Canada 117 J4
Wakayama Japan 71 D6
Wake Atoll terr. N. Pacific Ocean see Wake Island
WaKeeney U.S.A. 126 D4
Wakefield N.Z. 109 D5
Wakefield U.K. 44 F5
Wakefield MI U.S.A. 126 F2
Wakefield RI U.S.A. 131 J3
Wakefield VA U.S.A. 131 G5

▶Wake Island terr. N. Pacific Ocean 146 H4
United States Unincorporated Territory.

Wakema Myanmar 66 A3
Wakhan reg. Afgh. 85 I2
Wakkanai Japan 70 F3
Wakkerstroom S. Africa 97 J4
Wakool Australia 108 B5
Wakool r. Australia 108 A5
Wakuach, Lac l. Canada 119 I3
Waku-Kungo Angola 95 B5
Wałbrzych Poland 43 P5
Walcha Australia 108 E3
Walcott U.S.A. 122 G4
Walcourt Belgium 48 E4
Wałcz Poland 43 P4
Waldburg Range mts Australia 105 B6
Walden U.S.A. 131 H3
Waldenbuch Germany 49 J6
Waldenburg Poland see Wałbrzych
Waldkraiburg Germany 43 N6
Waldo U.S.A. 130 D3
Waldoboro U.S.A. 131 K1
Waldorf U.S.A. 131 G4
Waldport U.S.A. 122 B3
Waldron U.S.A. 127 E5
Waldron, Cape Antarctica 148 F2
Walebing Australia 105 B7
Walêg China 72 D2
Wales admin. div. U.K. 45 D6
Walgaon India 78 D5
Walgett Australia 108 D3
Walgreen Coast Antarctica 148 K1
Walhalla MI U.S.A. 130 B2
Walhalla ND U.S.A. 126 D1
Walikale Dem. Rep. Congo 93 F5
Walingai P.N.G. 65 L8
Walker r. Australia 106 A2
Walker watercourse Australia 105 F6
Walker MI U.S.A. 130 C2
Walker MN U.S.A. 126 E2
Walker r. U.S.A. 124 D2
Walker Bay S. Africa 96 D8
Walker Creek r. Australia 106 C3
Walker Lake Canada 117 L4
Walker Lake U.S.A. 124 D2
Walker Pass U.S.A. 124 D4
Walkersville U.S.A. 131 G4
Walkerton Canada 130 E1
Walkerton U.S.A. 130 B3
Wall, Mount hill Australia 104 B5
Wallaby Island Australia 106 C2
Wallace ID U.S.A. 122 D3
Wallace NC U.S.A. 129 E5
Wallace VA U.S.A. 130 D5
Wallaceburg Canada 130 D2
Wallal Downs Australia 104 C4
Wallangarra Australia 108 E2
Wallaroo Australia 107 B7
Wallasey U.K. 44 D5
Walla Walla Australia 108 C5
Walla Walla U.S.A. 122 D3
Walldürn Germany 49 J5
Wallekraal S. Africa 96 C6
Wallendbeen Australia 108 D5
Wallingford U.K. 45 F7
Wallis, Îles is Wallis and Futuna Is 103 I3

▶Wallis and Futuna Islands terr. S. Pacific Ocean 103 I3
French Overseas Territory.
oceania 8, 100–101

Wallis et Futuna, Îles terr. S. Pacific Ocean see Wallis and Futuna Islands
Wallis Islands Wallis and Futuna Is see Wallis, Îles
Wallis Lake inlet Australia 108 F4
Wallops Island U.S.A. 131 H5
Wallowa Mountains U.S.A. 122 D3
Walls U.K. 46 [inset]
Walls of Jerusalem National Park Australia 107 [inset]
Wallumbilla Australia 107 E5
Walmsley Lake Canada 117 I2
Walney, Isle of i. U.K. 44 D4
Walnut Creek U.S.A. 124 B3
Walnut Grove U.S.A. 124 C2
Walnut Ridge U.S.A. 127 F4
Walong India 79 I3
Walpole U.S.A. 131 I2
Walsall U.K. 45 F6
Walsenburg U.S.A. 123 G5
Walsh U.S.A. 127 C4
Walsrode Germany 49 J2
Waltair India 80 D2
Walterboro U.S.A. 129 D5
Walters U.S.A. 127 D5
Walter's Range hills Australia 108 B2
Walthall U.S.A. 127 F5
Waltham U.S.A. 131 J2
Walton IN U.S.A. 130 B3
Walton KY U.S.A. 130 C4
Walton NY U.S.A. 131 H2
Walton WV U.S.A. 130 E4
Walvisbaai Namibia see Walvis Bay
Walvisbaai b. Namibia see Walvis Bay
Walvis Bay Namibia 96 B2
Walvis Bay b. Namibia 96 B2
Walvis Ridge sea feature S. Atlantic Ocean 144 H8
Wama Afgh. 85 H3
Wamba Equateur Dem. Rep. Congo 93 F5
Wamba Orientale Dem. Rep. Congo 94 C3
Wamba Nigeria 92 D4
Wampum U.S.A. 130 E3
Wampusirpi Hond. 133 H5
Wamsutter U.S.A. 122 G4
Wana Pak. 85 H3
Wanaaring Australia 108 B2
Wanaka N.Z. 109 B7
Wanaka, Lake N.Z. 109 B7
Wan'an China 73 G3
Wanapitei Lake Canada 118 E5
Wanbi Australia 107 C7
Wanbrow, Cape N.Z. 109 C7
Wanda Shan mts China 70 D3
Wandering River Canada 117 H4
Wandersleben Germany 49 K4
Wandlitz Germany 49 N2
Wando S. Korea 71 B6
Wandoan Australia 107 E5
Wanganui N.Z. 109 E4
Wanganui r. N.Z. 109 E4
Wangaratta Australia 108 C6
Wangcang China 72 E1
Wangda China see Zogang
Wangdain China 79 G3
Wangdue Phodrang Bhutan 79 G4
Wanggamet, Gunung mt. Indon. 104 C2
Wanggao China 73 F3
Wang Gaxun China 79 I1
Wangiwangi i. Indon. 65 G8
Wangkui China 70 B3
Wangmo China 72 E3
Wangqing China 70 C4
Wangwu Shan mts China 73 F1
Wangying China see Huaiyin
Wangziguan China 72 E1
Wanham Canada 116 G4
Wan Hsa-la Myanmar 66 B2
Wanie-Rukula Dem. Rep. Congo 94 C3
Wankaner India 78 B5
Wankie Zimbabwe see Hwange
Wanlaweyn Somalia 94 E3
Wanna Germany 49 I1
Wanna Lakes salt flat Australia 105 E7
Wannian China 73 H2
Wanning China 73 F5
Wanroij Neth. 48 F3
Wanshan China 73 F3
Wanshan Qundao is China 73 G4
Wansheng China 72 E2
Wanshengchang China see Wansheng
Wantage U.K. 45 F7
Wanxian Chongqing China see Shahe
Wanxian Chongqing China 73 F2
Wanyuan China 73 F1
Wanzai China 73 G2
Wanze Belgium 48 F4
Wapakoneta U.S.A. 130 C3
Wapawekka Lake Canada 117 J4
Wapello U.S.A. 126 F3
Wapikaimaski Lake Canada 118 C4
Wapikopa Lake Canada 118 C3
Wapiti r. Canada 116 G4
Wapusk National Park Canada 117 M3
Waqên China 72 D1
Waqf aș Şawwān, Jibāl hills Jordan 81 C4
War U.S.A. 130 E5
Warab Sudan 82 C8
Warangal India 80 C2
Waranga Reservoir Australia 108 B6
Waratah Bay Australia 108 B7
Warbreccan Australia 106 C5
Warburg Germany 49 J3
Warburton Australia 105 D6
Warburton watercourse Australia 107 B5
Warburton Bay Canada 117 I2
Warche r. Belgium 48 F4
Ward, Mount N.Z. 109 B6
Warden S. Africa 97 I4
Wardenburg Germany 49 I1
Wardha India 80 C1
Wardha r. India 80 C2
Ward Hill hill U.K. 46 F2
Ward Hunt, Cape P.N.G. 65 L8
Ware Canada 116 E3
Ware U.S.A. 131 I2
Wareham U.K. 45 E8
Waremme Belgium 48 F4
Waren Germany 49 M1
Warendorf Germany 49 H3
Warginburra Peninsula Australia 106 E4
Wargla Alg. see Ouargla
Warialda Australia 108 E2
Warin Chamrap Thai. 66 D4
Warkum Neth. see Workum
Warkworth U.K. 44 F3
Warli China see Walêg
Warloy-Baillon France 48 C4
Warman Canada 117 J4
Warmbad Namibia 96 D5
Warmbad S. Africa 97 I3
Warmbaths S. Africa see Warmbad
Warminster U.K. 45 E7
Warminster U.S.A. 131 H3
Warmond Neth. 48 E2
Warm Springs NV U.S.A. 124 E2
Warm Springs VA U.S.A. 130 F4
Warmwaterberg mts S. Africa 96 E7
Warner Canada 117 H5
Warner Lakes U.S.A. 122 D4
Warner Mountains U.S.A. 122 C4
Warnes Bol. 138 F7
Warning, Mount Australia 108 F2
Waronda India 80 C2
Warora India 80 C1
Warra Australia 108 E1
Warragamba Reservoir Australia 108 E5
Warragul Australia 108 B7
Warrambool r. Australia 108 C3
Warrandirinna, Lake salt flat Australia 107 B5
Warrandyte Australia 108 B6
Warrawagine Australia 104 C5
Warrego r. Australia 108 B3
Warrego Range hills Australia 106 D5
Warren Australia 108 C3
Warren AR U.S.A. 127 E5
Warren MI U.S.A. 130 D2
Warren MN U.S.A. 126 D1
Warren OH U.S.A. 130 E3
Warren PA U.S.A. 130 F3
Warren Hastings Island Palau see Merir
Warren Island U.S.A. 116 C4
Warrenpoint U.K. 47 F3
Warrensburg MO U.S.A. 126 E4
Warrensburg NY U.S.A. 131 I2
Warrenton S. Africa 96 G5
Warrenton GA U.S.A. 129 D5
Warrenton MO U.S.A. 126 F4
Warrenton VA U.S.A. 131 G4
Warri Nigeria 92 D4
Warriners Creek watercourse Australia 107 B6
Warrington N.Z. 109 C7
Warrington U.K. 44 E5
Warrington U.S.A. 129 C6
Warrnambool Australia 107 C8
Warroad U.S.A. 126 E1
Warrumbungle National Park Australia 108 D3

▶Warsaw Poland 43 R4
Capital of Poland.

Warsaw IN U.S.A. 130 C3
Warsaw KY U.S.A. 130 C4
Warsaw MO U.S.A. 126 E4
Warsaw NY U.S.A. 131 F2
Warsaw VA U.S.A. 131 G5
Warshiikh Somalia 94 E3
Warstein Germany 49 I3
Warszawa Poland see Warsaw
Warta r. Poland 43 O4
Warwick Australia 108 F2
Warwick U.K. 45 F6
Warwick U.S.A. 131 J3
Warzhong China 72 D2
Wasaga Beach Canada 130 E1
Wasatch Range mts U.S.A. 122 F5
Wasbank S. Africa 97 J5
Wasco U.S.A. 124 D4
Washburn ND U.S.A. 126 C2
Washburn WI U.S.A. 126 F2
Washim India 80 C1
Washimeska r. Canada 119 G4

▶Washington DC U.S.A. 131 G4
Capital of the United States of America.

Washington GA U.S.A. 129 D5
Washington IA U.S.A. 126 F3
Washington IN U.S.A. 130 B4
Washington MO U.S.A. 126 F4
Washington NC U.S.A. 128 E5
Washington NJ U.S.A. 131 H3
Washington PA U.S.A. 130 E3
Washington UT U.S.A. 125 G3
Washington state U.S.A. 122 C3
Washington, Cape Antarctica 148 H2
Washington, Mount U.S.A. 131 J1
Washington Court House U.S.A. 130 D4
Washington Island U.S.A. 128 C2
Washington Land reg. Greenland 115 L2
Washir Afgh. 85 F3
Washita r. U.S.A. 127 D5
Washpool National Park Australia 108 F2
Washtucna U.S.A. 122 D3
Washuk Pak. 85 G5
Wasi India 80 B2
Wasi' Saudi Arabia 84 B5
Wasi' well Saudi Arabia 84 C6
Waskaganish Canada 118 F4
Waskaghegnish Canada see Waskaganish
Waskaiowaka Lake Canada 117 L3
Waskey, Mount U.S.A. 114 C4
Wassenaar Neth. 48 E2
Wasser Namibia 96 D4
Wasserkuppe hill Germany 49 J4
Wassertrüdingen Germany 49 K5
Wassuk Range mts U.S.A. 124 D2
Wasua P.N.G. 65 K8
Wasum P.N.G. 65 L8
Waswanipi r. Canada 118 F4
Waswanipi, Lac l. Canada 118 F4
Watam P.N.G. 65 K7
Watampone Indon. 65 G7
Watapi Lake Canada 117 I4
Watarrka National Park Australia 105 E6
Watenstadt-Salzgitter Germany see Salzgitter
Waterbury CT U.S.A. 131 I3
Waterbury VT U.S.A. 131 I1
Waterbury Lake Canada 117 J3
Water Cays i. Bahamas 129 E8
Waterdown Canada 130 F2
Wateree r. U.S.A. 129 D5
Waterfall U.S.A. 116 C4
Waterford Rep. of Ireland 47 E5
Waterford PA U.S.A. 130 F3
Waterford WI U.S.A. 130 A2
Waterford Harbour Rep. of Ireland 47 F5
Watergrasshill Rep. of Ireland 47 D5
Waterhen Lake Canada 117 L4
Waterloo Australia 104 E4
Waterloo Belgium 48 E4
Waterloo Ont. Canada 130 E2
Waterloo Que. Canada 131 I1
Waterloo IA U.S.A. 126 E3
Waterloo IL U.S.A. 126 F4
Waterloo NY U.S.A. 131 G2
Waterlooville U.K. 45 F8
Waterton Lakes National Park Canada 116 H5
Watertown NY U.S.A. 131 H2
Watertown SD U.S.A. 126 D2
Watertown WI U.S.A. 126 F3
Waterval-Boven S. Africa 97 J3
Water Valley U.S.A. 127 F5
Waterville ME U.S.A. 131 K1
Waterville WA U.S.A. 122 C3
Watford Canada 130 E2
Watford U.K. 45 G7
Watford City U.S.A. 126 C2
Wathaman r. Canada 117 K3
Wathaman Lake Canada 117 K3
Watheroo National Park Australia 105 A7
Wathlingen Germany 49 K2
Watino Canada 116 G4
Watīr, Wādī watercourse Egypt 81 B5
Watkins Glen U.S.A. 131 G2
Watling Island Bahamas see San Salvador
Watmuri Indon. 104 E1
Watonga U.S.A. 127 D5
Watrous Canada 117 J5
Watrous U.S.A. 123 G6
Watseka U.S.A. 130 B3
Watsi Kengo Dem. Rep. Congo 93 F5
Watson r. Australia 106 C2
Watson Canada 117 J4
Watson Lake Canada 116 D2
Watsontown U.S.A. 131 G3
Watsonville U.S.A. 124 C3
Watten U.K. 46 F2
Watterson Lake Canada 117 L2
Watton U.K. 45 H6
Watts Bar Lake resr U.S.A. 128 C5
Wattsburg U.S.A. 130 F2
Watubela, Kepulauan is Indon. 65 I7
Wau P.N.G. 65 L8
Wau Sudan 82 C8
Waubay Lake U.S.A. 126 D2
Wauchope N.S.W. Australia 108 F3
Wauchope N.T. Australia 104 F5
Waukaringa Australia 107 B7
Waukarlycarly, Lake salt flat Australia 104 C5
Waukegan U.S.A. 130 B2
Waukesha U.S.A. 130 A2
Waupaca U.S.A. 126 F2
Waupun U.S.A. 126 F3
Waurika U.S.A. 127 D5
Wausau U.S.A. 126 F2
Wausaukee U.S.A. 128 C2
Wauseon U.S.A. 130 C3
Wautoma U.S.A. 126 F2
Wave Hill Australia 104 E4
Waveney r. U.K. 45 I6
Waverly IA U.S.A. 126 E3
Waverly NY U.S.A. 131 G2
Waverly OH U.S.A. 130 D4
Waverly TN U.S.A. 128 C4
Waverly VA U.S.A. 131 G5
Wavre Belgium 48 E4
Waw Myanmar 66 B3
Wawa Canada 118 D5
Wawalalindu Indon. 65 G7
Wāw al Kabīr Libya 93 E2
Wawasee, Lake U.S.A. 130 C3
Wawo Indon. 65 G7
Waxahachie U.S.A. 127 D5
Waxü China 72 D1
Waxxari China 76 G4
Way, Lake salt flat Australia 105 C6
Waycross U.S.A. 129 D6
Wayland KY U.S.A. 130 D5
Wayland MI U.S.A. 130 C2
Wayne NE U.S.A. 126 D3
Wayne WV U.S.A. 130 D4
Waynesboro GA U.S.A. 129 D5
Waynesboro MS U.S.A. 127 F6
Waynesboro TN U.S.A. 128 C5
Waynesboro VA U.S.A. 131 F4
Waynesburg U.S.A. 130 E4
Waynesville MO U.S.A. 126 E4
Waynesville NC U.S.A. 128 D5
Waynoka U.S.A. 127 D4
Waza, Parc National de nat. park Cameroon 93 E3
Wāzah Khwāh Afgh. see Wazi Khwa
Wazi Khwa Afgh. 85 H3
Wazirabad Pak. 85 I3
W du Niger, Parcs Nationaux du nat. park Niger 92 D3
We, Pulau i. Indon. 67 A6
Weagamow Lake Canada 117 N4
Weam P.N.G. 65 K8
Wear r. U.K. 44 F4
Weare U.S.A. 131 J2
Weatherford U.S.A. 127 D5
Weaver Lake Canada 117 L4
Weaverville U.S.A. 122 C4
Webb, Mount hill Australia 104 E5
Webequie Canada 118 D3
Weber, Mount Canada 116 D4
Weber Basin sea feature Laut Banda 146 E6

▶Webi Shabeelle r. Somalia 94 E3
5th longest river in Africa.

Webster IN U.S.A. 130 C4
Webster MA U.S.A. 131 J2
Webster SD U.S.A. 126 D2
Webster City U.S.A. 126 E3
Webster Springs U.S.A. 130 E4
Wecho Lake Canada 116 H2
Wedau P.N.G. 106 E1
Weddell Abyssal Plain sea feature Southern Ocean 148 A2
Weddell Island Falkland Is 140 D8
Weddell Sea Antarctica 148 A2
Wedderburn Australia 108 A6
Weddin Mountains National Park Australia 108 D4
Wedel (Holstein) Germany 49 J1
Wedge Mountain Canada 116 F5
Wedowee U.S.A. 129 C5
Weedville U.S.A. 131 F3
Weenen S. Africa 97 J5
Weener Germany 49 H1
Weert Neth. 48 F3
Weethalle Australia 108 C4
Wee Waa Australia 108 D3
Wegberg Germany 48 G3
Węgorzewo Poland 43 R3
Weichang China 69 L4
Weida Germany 49 M4
Weidenberg Germany 49 L5
Weiden in der Oberpfalz Germany 49 M5
Weidongmen China see Qianjin
Weifang China 69 L5
Weihai China 69 M5
Wei He r. Shaanxi China 72 F1
Wei He r. China 73 G1
Weilburg Germany 49 I4
Weilmoringle Australia 108 C2
Weimar Germany 49 L4
Weinan China 73 F1
Weinheim Germany 49 I5
Weining China 72 E3
Weinsberg Germany 49 J5
Weipa Australia 106 C2
Weiqu China see Chang'an
Weir r. Australia 108 D2
Weir River Canada 117 M3
Weirton U.S.A. 130 E3
Weiser U.S.A. 122 D3
Weishan China 72 D3
Weishan Hu l. China 73 H1
Weishi China 73 G1
Weiße Elster r. Germany 49 L3
Weißenburg in Bayern Germany 49 K5
Weißenfels Germany 49 L3
Weißkugel mt. Austria/Italy 43 M7
Weissrand Mountains Namibia 96 D3
Weiterstadt Germany 49 I5
Weitzel Lake Canada 117 J3
Weixi China 72 C3
Weixin China 72 E3
Weiya China 76 H3
Weiyuan Gansu China 72 E1
Weiyuan Sichuan China 72 E2
Weiyuan Yunnan China see Jinggu
Weiyuan Jiang r. China 72 D4
Weiz Austria 43 O7
Weizhou China see Wenchuan
Weizhou Dao i. China 73 F4
Wejherowo Poland 43 Q3
Wekilbazar Turkm. see Vekil'bazar
Wekusko Canada 117 L4
Wekusko Lake Canada 117 L4
Wekweti Canada 116 H1
Welatam Myanmar 66 B1
Welbourn Hill Australia 105 F6
Welch U.S.A. 130 E5
Weld U.S.A. 131 J1
Weldiya Eth. 94 D2
Welford National Park Australia 106 C5
Welk'īt'ē Eth. 94 D3
Welkom S. Africa 97 H4
Welland Canada 130 F2
Welland r. U.K. 45 G6
Welland Canal Canada 130 F2
Wellesley Canada 130 E2
Wellesley Islands Australia 106 B3
Wellesley Lake Canada 116 B2
Wellfleet U.S.A. 131 J3
Wellin Belgium 48 F4
Wellingborough U.K. 45 G6
Wellington Australia 108 D4
Wellington Canada 131 G2

▶Wellington N.Z. 109 E5
Capital of New Zealand.

Wellington S. Africa 96 D7
Wellington England U.K. 45 D8
Wellington England U.K. 45 E6
Wellington CO U.S.A. 122 G4
Wellington IL U.S.A. 130 B3
Wellington KS U.S.A. 127 D4
Wellington NV U.S.A. 124 D2
Wellington OH U.S.A. 130 D3
Wellington TX U.S.A. 127 C5
Wellington UT U.S.A. 125 H2
Wellington, Isla i. Chile 140 B7
Wellington Range hills N.T. Australia 104 F3
Wellington Range hills W.A. Australia 105 C6
Wells Canada 116 F4
Wells U.K. 45 E7
Wells U.S.A. 122 E4
Wells, Lake salt flat Australia 105 C6
Wellsboro U.S.A. 131 G3
Wellsburg U.S.A. 130 E3
Wellsford N.Z. 109 E3
Wells-next-the-Sea U.K. 45 H6
Wellston U.S.A. 130 C1
Wellsville U.S.A. 131 G2
Wellton U.S.A. 125 F5
Wels Austria 43 O6
Welshpool U.K. 45 D6
Welsickendorf Germany 49 N3
Welwitschia Namibia see Khorixas
Welwyn Garden City U.K. 45 G7
Welzheim Germany 49 J6
Wem U.K. 45 E6
Wembesi S. Africa 97 I5
Wembley Canada 116 G4
Wemindji Canada 118 F3
Wenatchee U.S.A. 122 C3
Wenatchee Mountains U.S.A. 122 C3
Wenbu China see Nyima
Wenchang Hainan China 73 F5
Wenchang Sichuan China see Zitong
Wenchow China see Wenzhou
Wenchuan China 72 D2
Wendelstein Germany 49 L5
Wenden Germany 49 H4
Wenden Latvia see Cēsis
Wenden U.S.A. 125 G5
Wendover U.S.A. 125 F1
Weng'an China 72 E3
Wengshui China 72 C2
Wengyuan China 73 G3
Wenhua China see Weishan
Wenlan China see Mengzi
Wenling China 73 I2
Wenlock r. Australia 106 C2
Wenping China see Ludian
Wenquan Guizhou China 72 E2
Wenquan Henan China see Wenxian
Wenquan Hubei China see Yingshan

▶Wenquan Qinghai China 79 G2
Highest settlement in the world.

Wenquan Xinjiang China 76 F3
Wenshan China 72 E4
Wenshui China 72 E2
Wensum r. U.K. 45 I6
Wentorf bei Hamburg Germany 49 K1
Wentworth Australia 107 C7
Wenxi China 73 F1
Wenxian Gansu China 72 E1
Wenxian Henan China 73 G1
Wenxing China see Xiangyin
Wenzhou China 73 I3
Wenzlow Germany 49 M2
Wepener S. Africa 97 H5
Wer India 78 D4
Werben (Elbe) Germany 49 L2

Werda Botswana 96 F3
Werdau Germany 49 M4
Werdër Eth. 94 E3
Werder Germany 49 M2
Werdohl Germany 49 H3
Werl Germany 49 H3
Wernberg-Köblitz Germany 49 M5
Werne Germany 49 H3
Wernecke Mountains Canada 116 B1
Wernigerode Germany 49 K3
Werra r. Germany 49 J3
Werris Creek Australia 108 E3
Wertheim Germany 49 J5
Wervik Belgium 48 D4
Wesel Germany 48 G3
Wesel-Datteln-Kanal canal Germany 48 G3
Wesenberg Germany 49 M1
Wesendorf Germany 49 K2
Weser r. Germany 49 I1
Weser sea chan. Germany 49 I1
Wesergebirge hills Germany 49 I2
Weslaco U.S.A. 127 D7
Weslemkoon Lake Canada 131 G1
Wesleyville Canada 119 L4
Wessel, Cape Australia 106 B1
Wessel Islands Australia 106 B1
Wesselsbron S. Africa 97 H4
Wesselton S. Africa 97 I4
Wessington Springs U.S.A. 126 D2
Westall, Point Australia 105 F8
West Allis U.S.A. 130 A2
West Antarctica reg. Antarctica 148 J1
West Australian Basin sea feature Indian Ocean 145 O7

▶West Bank terr. Asia 81 B3
Territory occupied by Israel.
asia 6

West Bay Canada 119 K3
West Bay inlet U.S.A. 129 C6
West Bend U.S.A. 130 A2
West Bengal state India 79 F5
West Branch U.S.A. 130 C1
West Bromwich U.K. 45 F6
Westbrook U.S.A. 131 J2
West Burke U.S.A. 131 J1
West Burra i. U.K. 46 [inset]
Westbury U.K. 45 E7
West Caicos i. Turks and Caicos Is 129 F8
West Cape Howe Australia 105 B8
West Caroline Basin sea feature N. Pacific Ocean 146 F5
West Chester U.S.A. 131 H4
Westcliffe U.S.A. 123 G5
West Coast National Park S. Africa 96 D7
West End Bahamas 129 E7
Westerburg Germany 49 H4
Westerholt Germany 49 H1
Westerland Germany 43 L3
Westerlo Belgium 48 E3
Westerly U.S.A. 131 J3
Western r. Canada 117 J1
Western Australia state Australia 105 C6
Western Cape prov. S. Africa 96 E7
Western Desert Egypt 86 C6
Western Dvina r. Europe see Zapadnaya Dvina
Western Ghats mts India 80 B3
Western Port b. Australia 108 B7

▶Western Sahara terr. Africa 92 B2
Disputed territory (Morocco).
africa 7, 90–91

Western Samoa country S. Pacific Ocean see Samoa
Western Sayan Mountains reg. Rus. Fed. see Zapadnyy Sayan
Westerschelde est. Neth. 48 D3
Westerstede Germany 49 H1
Westerville U.S.A. 130 D3
Westerwald hills Germany 49 H4
West Falkland i. Falkland Is 140 D8
West Fargo U.S.A. 126 D2
West Fayu atoll Micronesia 65 L5
Westfield IN U.S.A. 130 B3
Westfield MA U.S.A. 131 I2
Westfield NY U.S.A. 130 F2
Westfield PA U.S.A. 131 G3
West Frisian Islands Neth. 48 E1
Westgat sea chan. Neth. 48 G1
Westgate Australia 108 C1
West Glacier U.S.A. 122 E2
West Grand Lake U.S.A. 128 H2
West Hartford U.S.A. 131 I3
Westhausen Germany 49 K6
West Haven U.S.A. 131 I3
Westhill U.K. 46 G3
Westhope U.S.A. 126 C1
West Ice Shelf Antarctica 148 E2
West Indies is Caribbean Sea 133 J4
West Island India 67 A4
Westkapelle Neth. 48 D3
West Kazakhstan Oblast admin. div. Kazakh. see Zapadnyy Kazakhstan
West Kingston U.S.A. 131 J3
West Lafayette U.S.A. 130 B3
West Lamma Channel Hong Kong China 73 [inset]
Westland Australia 106 C4
Westland National Park N.Z. 109 C6
Westleigh S. Africa 97 H4
Westleton U.K. 45 I6
West Liberty U.S.A. 130 D5
West Linton U.K. 46 F5
West Loch Roag b. U.K. 46 C2
Westlock Canada 116 H4
West Lorne Canada 130 E2
West Lunga National Park Zambia 95 C5
West MacDonnell National Park Australia 105 F5
West Malaysia pen. Malaysia see Peninsular Malaysia
Westmalle Belgium 48 E3
Westmar Australia 108 D1
West Mariana Basin sea feature N. Pacific Ocean 146 F4
West Memphis U.S.A. 127 F5
Westminster U.S.A. 131 G4
Westmoreland Australia 106 B3
Westmoreland U.S.A. 130 B5
Westmorland U.S.A. 125 F5
Weston OH U.S.A. 130 D3
Weston WV U.S.A. 130 E4
Weston-super-Mare U.K. 45 E7
West Palm Beach U.S.A. 129 D7
West Plains U.S.A. 127 F4
West Point pt Australia 107 [inset]
West Point CA U.S.A. 124 C2
West Point KY U.S.A. 130 C5
West Point MS U.S.A. 127 F5
West Point NE U.S.A. 126 D3
West Point VA U.S.A. 131 G5
West Point Lake resr U.S.A. 129 C5
Westport Canada 131 G1
Westport N.Z. 109 C5
Westport Rep. of Ireland 47 C4
Westport CA U.S.A. 124 B2
Westport KY U.S.A. 130 C4
Westport NY U.S.A. 131 I1
Westray Canada 117 K4
Westray i. U.K. 46 F1
Westray Firth sea chan. U.K. 46 F1
Westree Canada 118 E5
West Rutland U.S.A. 131 I2
West Salem U.S.A. 130 D3
West Siberian Plain Rus. Fed. 60 J3
West-Skylge Neth. see West-Terschelling
West Stewartstown U.S.A. 131 J1
West-Terschelling Neth. 48 F1
West Topsham U.S.A. 131 I1
West Union IA U.S.A. 126 F3
West Union IL U.S.A. 130 B4
West Union OH U.S.A. 130 D4
West Union WV U.S.A. 130 E4
West Valley City U.S.A. 125 H1
Westville U.S.A. 130 B3
West Virginia state U.S.A. 130 E4
Westwood U.S.A. 124 C1
West Wyalong Australia 108 C4
West York U.S.A. 131 G4
Westzaan Neth. 48 E2
Wetar i. Indon. 104 D1
Wetar, Selat sea chan. East Timor/Indon. 104 D2
Wetaskiwin Canada 116 H4
Wete Tanz. 95 D4
Wetter r. Germany 49 I4
Wettin Germany 49 L3
Wetumpka U.S.A. 129 C5
Wetwun Myanmar 66 B2
Wetzlar Germany 49 I4
Wewahitchka U.S.A. 129 C6
Wewak P.N.G. 65 K7
Wewoka U.S.A. 127 D5
Wexford Rep. of Ireland 47 F5
Wexford Harbour b. Rep. of Ireland 47 F5
Weyakwin Canada 117 J4
Weybridge U.K. 45 G7
Weyburn Canada 117 K5
Weyhe Germany 49 I2
Weymouth U.K. 45 E8
Weymouth U.S.A. 131 J2
Wezep Neth. 48 G2
Whakaari i. N.Z. 109 F3
Whakatane N.Z. 109 F3
Whalan Creek r. Australia 108 D2
Whale r. Canada see La Baleine, Rivière à
Whalsay i. U.K. 46 [inset]
Whampoa China see Huangpu
Whangamata N.Z. 109 E3
Whanganui National Park N.Z. 109 E4
Whangarei N.Z. 109 E2
Whapmagoostui Canada 118 F3
Wharfe r. U.K. 44 F5
Wharfedale valley U.K. 44 F4
Wharton U.S.A. 127 D6
Wharton Lake Canada 117 L1
Wha Ti Canada 116 G2
Wheatland IN U.S.A. 130 B4
Wheatland WY U.S.A. 122 G4
Wheaton IL U.S.A. 130 A3
Wheaton MN U.S.A. 126 D2
Wheaton-Glenmont U.S.A. 131 G4
Wheeler U.S.A. 127 C5
Wheeler Lake Canada 116 H2
Wheeler Lake resr U.S.A. 129 C5
Wheeler Peak NM U.S.A. 123 G5
Wheeler Peak NV U.S.A. 125 F2
Wheelersburg U.S.A. 130 D4
Wheeling U.S.A. 130 E3
Whernside hill U.K. 44 E4
Whinham, Mount Australia 105 E6
Whiskey Jack Lake Canada 117 K3
Whitburn U.K. 46 F5
Whitby Canada 131 F2
Whitby U.K. 44 G4
Whitchurch U.K. 45 E6
Whitchurch-Stouffville Canada 130 F2
White r. Canada 118 D4
White r. Canada/U.S.A. 116 B2
White r. AR U.S.A. 121 I5
White r. AR U.S.A. 127 F5
White r. CO U.S.A. 125 I1
White r. IN U.S.A. 130 B4
White r. MI U.S.A. 130 B2
White r. NV U.S.A. 125 F3
White r. SD U.S.A. 126 D3
White r. VT U.S.A. 131 I2
White watercourse U.S.A. 125 H5
White, Lake salt flat Australia 104 E5
White Bay Canada 119 K4
White Butte mt. U.S.A. 126 C2
White Canyon U.S.A. 125 H3
White Cloud U.S.A. 130 C2
Whitecourt Canada 116 H4
Whiteface Mountain U.S.A. 131 I1
Whitefield U.S.A. 131 J1
Whitefish r. Canada 116 E1
Whitefish U.S.A. 122 E2
Whitefish Bay U.S.A. 130 B1
Whitefish Lake Canada 117 J2
Whitefish Point U.S.A. 128 C2
Whitehall Rep. of Ireland 47 E5
Whitehall U.K. 46 G1
Whitehall NY U.S.A. 131 I2
Whitehall WI U.S.A. 126 F2
Whitehaven U.K. 44 D4
Whitehead U.K. 47 G3
White Hill hill Canada 119 J5
Whitehill U.K. 45 G7

▶Whitehorse Canada 116 C2
Territorial capital of Yukon.

White Horse U.S.A. 125 J4
White Horse, Vale of valley U.K. 45 F7
White Horse Pass U.S.A. 125 F1
White House U.S.A. 130 B5
White Island Antarctica 148 D2
White Island N.Z. see Whakaari
White Lake Ont. Canada 118 D4
White Lake Ont. Canada 131 G1
White Lake LA U.S.A. 127 E6
White Lake MI U.S.A. 130 B2
Whitemark Australia 107 [inset]
White Mountain Peak U.S.A. 124 D3
White Mountains U.S.A. 131 J1
White Mountains National Park Australia 106 D4
Whitemouth Lake Canada 117 M5
Whitemud r. Canada 116 G3
White Nile r. Sudan/Uganda 82 D6
also known as Bahr el Abiad or Bahr el Jebel
White Nossob watercourse Namibia 96 D2
White Oak U.S.A. 130 D5
White Otter Lake Canada 117 N5
White Pass Canada/U.S.A. 116 C3
White Pine Range mts U.S.A. 125 F2
White Plains U.S.A. 131 I3
White River Canada 118 D4
Whiteriver U.S.A. 125 I5
White River U.S.A. 126 C3
White River Valley U.S.A. 125 F2
White Rock Peak U.S.A. 125 F2
White Russia country Europe see Belarus
Whitesail Lake Canada 116 E4
White Salmon U.S.A. 122 C3
Whitesand r. Canada 116 H2
White Sands National Monument nat. park U.S.A. 123 G6
Whitesburg U.S.A. 130 D5
White Sea Rus. Fed. 38 H2
White Stone U.S.A. 131 G5
White Sulphur Springs MT U.S.A. 122 F3
White Sulphur Springs WV U.S.A. 130 E5
Whitesville U.S.A. 130 E5
Whiteville U.S.A. 129 E5
White Volta r. Burkina/Ghana 92 C4
also known as Nakambé or Nakanbe or Volta Blanche
Whitewater U.S.A. 125 I2
Whitewater Baldy mt. U.S.A. 125 I5
Whitewater Lake Canada 118 C4
Whitewood Australia 106 C4
Whitewood Canada 117 K5
Whitfield U.K. 45 I7
Whithorn U.K. 46 E6
Whitianga N.Z. 109 E3
Whitland U.K. 45 C7
Whitley Bay U.K. 44 F3
Whitmore Mountains Antarctica 148 K1
Whitney Canada 131 F1
Whitney, Mount U.S.A. 124 D3
Whitney Point U.S.A. 131 H2
Whitstable U.K. 45 I7
Whitsunday Group is Australia 106 E4
Whitsunday Island National Park Australia 106 E4
Whitsun Island Vanuatu see Pentecost Island
Whittemore U.S.A. 130 D1
Whittlesea Australia 108 B6
Whittlesey U.K. 45 G6
Whitton Australia 108 C5
Wholdaia Lake Canada 117 J2
Why U.S.A. 125 G5
Whyalla Australia 107 B7
Wiang Sa Thai. 66 C3
Wiarton Canada 130 E1
Wibaux U.S.A. 122 G3
Wichelen Belgium 48 D3
Wichita U.S.A. 126 D4
Wichita r. U.S.A. 127 D5
Wichita Falls U.S.A. 127 D5
Wichita Mountains U.S.A. 127 D5
Wick U.K. 46 F2
Wick r. U.K. 46 F2
Wickenburg U.S.A. 125 G5
Wickes U.S.A. 127 E5
Wickford U.K. 45 H7
Wickham r. Australia 104 E4
Wickham, Cape Australia 107 [inset]
Wickham, Mount hill Australia 104 E4
Wickliffe U.S.A. 127 F4
Wicklow Rep. of Ireland 47 F5
Wicklow Head hd Rep. of Ireland 47 G5
Wicklow Mountains Rep. of Ireland 47 F5
Wicklow Mountains National Park Rep. of Ireland 47 F4
Widerøe, Mount Antarctica 148 C2
Widerøefjellet mt. Antarctica see Widerøe, Mount
Widgeegoara watercourse Australia 108 B1
Widgiemooltha Australia 105 C7
Widnes U.K. 44 E5
Wi-do i. S. Korea 71 B6
Wied r. Germany 49 H4
Wiehengebirge hills Germany 49 I2
Wiehl Germany 49 H4
Wielkopolskie, Pojezierze reg. Poland 43 O4
Wielkopolski Park Narodowy nat. park Poland 43 P4
Wieluń Poland 43 Q5
Wien Austria see Vienna
Wiener Neustadt Austria 43 P7
Wierden Neth. 48 G2
Wieren Germany 49 K2
Wieringerwerf Neth. 48 F2
Wiesbaden Germany 49 I4
Wiesenfelden Germany 49 M5
Wiesentheid Germany 49 K5
Wiesloch Germany 49 I5
Wiesmoor Germany 49 H1
Wietze Germany 49 J2
Wietzendorf Germany 49 J2
Wieżyca hill Poland 43 Q3
Wigan U.K. 44 E5
Wiggins U.S.A. 127 F6
Wight, Isle of i. England U.K. 45 F8
Wignes Lake Canada 117 J2
Wigston U.K. 45 F6
Wigton U.K. 44 D4
Wigtown U.K. 46 E6
Wigtown Bay U.K. 46 E6
Wijchen Neth. 48 F3
Wijhe Neth. 48 G2
Wilberforce, Cape Australia 106 B1
Wilbur U.S.A. 122 D3
Wilburton U.S.A. 127 E5
Wilcannia Australia 108 A3
Wilcox U.S.A. 131 F3
Wilczek Land i. Rus. Fed. see Vil'cheka, Zemlya
Wildberg Germany 49 M2
Wildcat Peak U.S.A. 124 E2
Wild Coast S. Africa 97 I6
Wilderness National Park S. Africa 96 F8
Wildeshausen Germany 49 I2
Wild Horse Hill mt. U.S.A. 126 C3
Wildspitze mt. Austria 43 M7
Wildwood FL U.S.A. 129 D6
Wildwood NJ U.S.A. 131 H4
Wilge r. S. Africa 97 I4
Wilge r. S. Africa 97 I3
Wilgena Australia 105 F7

▶Wilhelm, Mount P.N.G. 65 L8
5th highest mountain in Oceania.

Wilhelm II Land reg. Antarctica see Kaiser Wilhelm II Land
Wilhelmina Gebergte mts Suriname 139 G3
Wilhelmina Kanaal canal Neth. 48 F3
Wilhelmshaven Germany 49 I1
Wilhelmstal Namibia 96 C1
Wilkes-Barre U.S.A. 131 H3
Wilkesboro U.S.A. 128 D4
Wilkes Coast Antarctica 148 G2
Wilkes Land reg. Antarctica 148 G2
Wilkie Canada 117 I4
Wilkins Coast Antarctica 148 L2
Wilkins Ice Shelf Antarctica 148 L2
Wilkinson Lakes salt flat Australia 105 F7
Will, Mount Canada 116 D3
Willand U.K. 45 D8
Willandra Billabong watercourse Australia 108 B4
Willandra National Park Australia 108 B4
Willapa Bay U.S.A. 122 B3
Willard Mex. 123 F7
Willard NM U.S.A. 123 G6
Willard OH U.S.A. 130 D3
Willcox U.S.A. 125 I5
Willcox Playa salt flat U.S.A. 125 I5
Willebadessen Germany 49 J3
Willebroek Belgium 48 E3

▶Willemstad Neth. Antilles 133 K6
Capital of the Netherlands Antilles.

Willeroo Australia 104 E3
Willette U.S.A. 130 C5
William, Mount Australia 107 C8
William Creek Australia 107 B6
William Lake Canada 117 L4
Williams AZ U.S.A. 125 G4
Williams CA U.S.A. 124 B2
Williamsburg KY U.S.A. 130 C5
Williamsburg OH U.S.A. 130 C4
Williamsburg VA U.S.A. 131 G5
Williams Lake Canada 116 F4
William Smith, Cap c. Canada 119 I1
Williamson NY U.S.A. 131 G2
Williamson WV U.S.A. 130 D5
Williamsport IN U.S.A. 130 B3
Williamsport PA U.S.A. 131 G3
Williamston U.S.A. 128 E5
Williamstown KY U.S.A. 130 C4
Williamstown NJ U.S.A. 131 H4
Willimantic U.S.A. 131 I3
Willis Group atolls Australia 106 E3
Williston S. Africa 96 E6
Williston ND U.S.A. 126 C1
Williston SC U.S.A. 129 D5
Williston Lake Canada 116 F4
Williton U.K. 45 D7
Willits U.S.A. 124 B2
Willmar U.S.A. 126 E2
Willoughby, Lake U.S.A. 131 I1
Willow Beach U.S.A. 125 F4
Willow Bunch Canada 117 J5
Willow Hill U.S.A. 131 G3
Willow Lake Canada 116 G2
Willowlake r. Canada 116 F2
Willowmore S. Africa 96 F7
Willowra Australia 104 F5
Willows U.S.A. 124 B2
Willow Springs U.S.A. 127 F4
Willowvale S. Africa 97 I7
Wills, Lake salt flat Australia 104 E5
Wilma U.S.A. 129 C6
Wilmington DE U.S.A. 131 H4
Wilmington NC U.S.A. 129 E5
Wilmington OH U.S.A. 130 D4
Wilmore U.S.A. 130 C5
Wilmslow U.K. 44 E5
Wilno Lith. see Vilnius
Wilnsdorf Germany 49 I4
Wilpattu National Park Sri Lanka 80 D4
Wilseder Berg hill Germany 49 J1
Wilson watercourse Australia 107 C5
Wilson atoll Micronesia see Ifalik
Wilson KS U.S.A. 126 D4
Wilson NC U.S.A. 128 E5
Wilson NY U.S.A. 131 F2
Wilson, Mount CO U.S.A. 125 J3
Wilson, Mount NV U.S.A. 125 F2
Wilson, Mount OR U.S.A. 122 C3
Wilsonia U.S.A. 124 D3
Wilson's Promontory pen. Australia 108 C7
Wilson's Promontory National Park Australia 108 C7
Wilsum Germany 48 G2
Wilton r. Australia 104 F3
Wilton U.S.A. 131 J1
Wiltz Lux. 48 F5
Wiluna Australia 105 C6
Wimereux France 48 B4
Wina r. Cameroon see Vina
Winamac U.S.A. 130 B3
Winbin watercourse Australia 107 D5
Winburg S. Africa 97 H5
Wincanton U.K. 45 E7
Winchester Canada 131 H1
Winchester U.K. 45 F7
Winchester IN U.S.A. 130 C3
Winchester KY U.S.A. 130 C5
Winchester NH U.S.A. 131 I2
Winchester TN U.S.A. 129 C5
Winchester VA U.S.A. 131 F4
Wind r. Canada 116 C1
Wind r. U.S.A. 122 F4
Windau Latvia see Ventspils
Windber U.S.A. 131 F3
Wind Cave National Park U.S.A. 126 C3
Windermere U.K. 44 E4
Windermere l. U.K. 44 E4
Windham U.S.A. 116 C3

▶Windhoek Namibia 96 C2
Capital of Namibia.

Windigo Lake Canada 117 N4
Windlestraw Law hill U.K. 46 G5
Wind Mountain U.S.A. 123 G6
Windom U.S.A. 126 E3
Windom Peak U.S.A. 125 J3
Windorah Australia 106 C5
Window Rock U.S.A. 125 I4
Wind Point U.S.A. 130 B2
Wind River Range mts U.S.A. 122 F4
Windrush r. U.K. 45 F7
Windsbach Germany 49 K5
Windsor Australia 108 E4
Windsor N.S. Canada 119 I5
Windsor Ont. Canada 130 D2
Windsor U.K. 45 G7
Windsor NC U.S.A. 128 E4
Windsor NY U.S.A. 131 H2
Windsor VA U.S.A. 131 G5
Windsor VT U.S.A. 131 I2
Windsor Locks U.S.A. 131 I3
Windward Islands Caribbean Sea 133 L5
Windward Passage Cuba/Haiti 133 J5
Windy U.S.A. 114 D3
Winefred Lake Canada 117 I4
Winfield KS U.S.A. 127 D4
Winfield WV U.S.A. 130 E4
Wingate U.K. 44 F4
Wingen Australia 108 E3
Wingene Belgium 48 D3
Wingen-sur-Moder France 49 H6
Wingham Australia 108 F3
Wingham Canada 130 E2
Winisk Canada 118 D3
Winisk r. Canada 118 D3
Winisk Lake Canada 118 D3
Winkana Myanmar 66 B4
Winkelman U.S.A. 125 H5
Winkler Canada 117 L5
Winlock U.S.A. 122 C3
Winneba Ghana 92 C4
Winnebago, Lake U.S.A. 130 A1
Winnecke Creek watercourse Australia 104 E4
Winnemucca U.S.A. 124 E1
Winnemucca Lake U.S.A. 124 D1
Winner U.S.A. 126 C3
Winnett U.S.A. 122 F3
Winnfield U.S.A. 127 E6
Winnibigoshish, Lake U.S.A. 126 E2
Winnie U.S.A. 127 E6
Winning Australia 105 A5

▶Winnipeg Canada 117 L5
Provincial capital of Manitoba.

Winnipeg r. Canada 117 L5
Winnipeg, Lake Canada 117 L5
Winnipegosis Canada 117 L5
Winnipegosis, Lake Canada 117 K4
Winnipesaukee, Lake U.S.A. 131 J2
Winona AZ U.S.A. 125 H4
Winona MN U.S.A. 126 F2
Winona MO U.S.A. 127 F4
Winona MS U.S.A. 127 F5
Winschoten Neth. 48 H1
Winsen (Aller) Germany 49 J2
Winsen (Luhe) Germany 49 K1
Winsford U.K. 44 E5
Winslow AZ U.S.A. 125 H4
Winslow ME U.S.A. 131 K1
Winsop, Tanjung pt Indon. 65 I7
Winsted U.S.A. 131 I3
Winston-Salem U.S.A. 128 D4
Winterberg Germany 49 I3
Winter Haven U.S.A. 129 D6
Winters CA U.S.A. 124 C2
Winters TX U.S.A. 127 D6
Wintersville U.S.A. 130 E3
Winterswijk Neth. 48 G3
Winterthur Switz. 52 I3
Winterton S. Africa 97 I5
Winthrop U.S.A. 131 K1
Winton Australia 106 C4
Winton N.Z. 109 B8
Winton U.S.A. 128 E4
Winwick U.K. 45 G6
Wirral pen. U.K. 44 D5
Wirrulla Australia 107 A7
Wisbech U.K. 45 H6
Wiscasset U.S.A. 131 K1
Wisconsin r. U.S.A. 126 F3
Wisconsin state U.S.A. 130 A1
Wisconsin Rapids U.S.A. 126 F2
Wise U.S.A. 130 D5
Wiseman U.S.A. 114 C3
Wishaw U.K. 46 F5
Wisher U.S.A. 126 D2
Wisil Dabarow Somalia 94 E3
Wisła r. Poland see Vistula
Wismar Germany 43 M4
Wistaria Canada 116 E4
Witbank S. Africa 97 I3
Witbooisvlei Namibia 96 D3
Witham U.K. 45 H7
Witham r. U.K. 45 H6
Witherbee U.S.A. 131 I1
Withernsea U.K. 44 H5
Witjira National Park Australia 107 A5
Witmarsum Neth. 48 F1
Witney U.K. 45 F7
Witrivier S. Africa 97 J3
Witry-lès-Reims France 48 E5
Witteberg mts S. Africa 97 H6
Wittenberg Germany see Lutherstadt Wittenberg
Wittenberge Germany 49 L2
Wittenburg Germany 49 L1
Wittingen Germany 49 K2
Wittlich Germany 48 G5
Wittmund Germany 49 H1
Wittstock Germany 49 M1
Witu Islands P.N.G. 65 L7
Witvlei Namibia 96 D2
Witzenhausen Germany 49 J3
Wivenhoe, Lake Australia 108 F1
Władysławowo Poland 43 Q3
Włocławek Poland 43 Q4
Wobkent Uzbek. see Vabkent
Wodonga Australia 108 C6
Wœrth France 49 H6
Wohlthat Mountains Antarctica 148 C2
Woippy France 48 G5
Wōjjā atoll Marshall Is see Wotje
Wokam i. Indon. 65 I8
Woken He r. China 70 C3
Wokha India 79 H4
Woking U.K. 45 G7
Wokingham watercourse Australia 106 C4
Wokingham U.K. 45 G7
Woko National Park Australia 108 E3
Wolcott IN U.S.A. 130 B3
Wolcott NY U.S.A. 131 G2
Woldegk Germany 49 N1
Wolea atoll Micronesia see Woleai
Woleai atoll Micronesia 65 K5
Wolf r. Canada 116 C2
Wolf r. TN U.S.A. 127 F5
Wolf r. WI U.S.A. 126 F2
Wolf Creek MT U.S.A. 122 E3
Wolf Creek OR U.S.A. 122 C4
Wolf Creek Pass U.S.A. 123 G5
Wolfen Germany 49 M3
Wolfenbüttel Germany 49 K2
Wolfhagen Germany 49 J3
Wolf Lake Canada 116 D2
Wolf Point U.S.A. 122 G2
Wolfsberg Austria 43 O7
Wolfsburg Germany 49 K2
Wolfstein Germany 49 H5
Wolfville Canada 119 I5
Wolgast Germany 43 N3
Wolin Poland 43 O4
Wollaston Lake Canada 117 K3
Wollaston Lake l. Canada 117 K3
Wollaston Peninsula Canada 114 G3
Wollemi National Park Australia 108 E4
Wollongong Australia 108 E5
Wolmaransstad S. Africa 97 G4
Wolmirstedt Germany 49 L2
Wolong Reserve nature res. China 72 D2
Wolseley Australia 107 C8
Wolseley S. Africa 96 D7
Wolsey U.S.A. 126 D2
Wolsingham U.K. 44 F4
Wolvega Neth. 48 G2
Wolvegea Neth. see Wolvega
Wolverhampton U.K. 45 E6
Wolverine U.S.A. 130 C1
Wommelgem Belgium 48 E3
Womrather Höhe hill Germany 49 H5
Wonarah Australia 106 B3
Wondai Australia 107 E5
Wongalarroo Lake salt l. Australia 108 B3
Wongarbon Australia 108 D4
Wong Chuk Hang Hong Kong China 73 [inset]
Wong Leng hill Hong Kong China 73 [inset]
Wong Wan Chau Hong Kong China see Double Island
Wŏnju S. Korea 71 B5
Wonowon Canada 116 F3
Wŏnsan N. Korea 71 B5
Wonthaggi Australia 108 B7
Wonyulgunna, Mount hill Australia 105 B6
Woocalla Australia 107 B6
Wood, Mount Canada 116 A2
Woodbine GA U.S.A. 129 D6
Woodbine NJ U.S.A. 131 H4
Woodbridge U.K. 45 I6
Woodbridge U.S.A. 131 G4
Wood Buffalo National Park Canada 116 H3
Woodburn U.S.A. 122 C3
Woodbury NJ U.S.A. 131 H4
Woodbury TN U.S.A. 127 G5
Wooded Bluff hd Australia 108 F2
Wood Lake Canada 117 K4
Woodlake U.S.A. 124 D3
Woodland CA U.S.A. 124 C2
Woodland PA U.S.A. 131 F3
Woodland WA U.S.A. 122 C3
Woodlands Sing. 67 [inset]
Woodlark Island P.N.G. 102 F2
Woodridge Canada 117 L5
Woodroffe watercourse Australia 106 B4
Woodroffe, Mount Australia 105 E6
Woodruff UT U.S.A. 122 F4
Woodruff WI U.S.A. 126 F2
Woods, Lake salt flat Australia 104 F4
Woods, Lake of the Canada/U.S.A. 121 I2
Woodsfield U.S.A. 130 E4
Woodside Australia 108 C7
Woodstock N.B. Canada 119 I5
Woodstock Ont. Canada 130 E2
Woodstock IL U.S.A. 126 F3
Woodstock VA U.S.A. 131 F4
Woodstock VT U.S.A. 131 I2
Woodsville U.S.A. 131 I1
Woodville Canada 131 F1
Woodville MS U.S.A. 127 F6
Woodville OH U.S.A. 130 D3
Woodville TX U.S.A. 127 E6
Woodward U.S.A. 127 D4
Woody U.S.A. 124 D4
Wooler U.K. 44 E3
Woolgoolga Australia 108 F3
Wooli Australia 108 F2
Woollard, Mount Antarctica 148 K1
Woollett, Lac l. Canada 118 G4
Woolyeenyer Hill hill Australia 105 C8
Woomera Australia 107 B6
Woomera Prohibited Area Australia 105 F7
Woonsocket RI U.S.A. 131 J2
Woonsocket SD U.S.A. 126 D2
Woorabinda Australia 106 E5
Wooramel r. Australia 105 A6
Wooster U.S.A. 130 E3
Worbis Germany 49 K3
Worbody Point Australia 106 C2
Worcester S. Africa 96 D7
Worcester U.K. 45 E6
Worcester MA U.S.A. 131 J2
Worcester NY U.S.A. 131 H2
Wörgl Austria 43 N7
Workai i. Indon. 65 I8
Workington U.K. 44 D4
Worksop U.K. 44 F5
Workum Neth. 48 F2
Worland U.S.A. 122 G3
Wörlitz Germany 49 M3
Wormerveer Neth. 48 E2
Worms Germany 49 I5
Worms Head hd U.K. 45 C7
Wortel Namibia 96 C2
Wörth am Rhein Germany 49 I5
Worthing U.K. 45 G8
Worthington IN U.S.A. 130 B4
Worthington MN U.S.A. 126 E3
Wotje atoll Marshall Is 146 H5
Wotu Indon. 65 G7
Woudrichem Neth. 48 E3
Woustviller France 48 H5
Wowoni i. Indon. 65 G7
Wozrojdeniye Oroli i. Uzbek. see Vozrozhdeniya, Ostrov
Wrangel Island Rus. Fed. 61 T2
Wrangell Island U.S.A. 116 C3
Wrangell Mountains U.S.A. 149 B3
Wrangell-St Elias National Park and Preserve U.S.A. 116 A2
Wrath, Cape U.K. 46 D2
Wray U.S.A. 126 C3
Wreake r. U.K. 45 F6
Wreck Point S. Africa 96 C5
Wreck Reef Australia 106 F4

acknowledgements

Maps and data

General

Maps designed and created by HarperCollins Reference, Glasgow, UK
Design: One O'Clock Gun Design Consultants Ltd, Edinburgh, UK
Cross-sections (pp32–33, 56–57, 88–89, 98–99, 110–111, 134–135) and globes (pp14–15, 142–143): Alan Collinson Design, Llandudno, UK

The publishers would like to thank all national survey departments, road, rail and national park authorities, statistical offices and national place name committees throughout the world for their valuable assistance, and in particular the following:
British Antarctic Survey, Cambridge, UK
Tony Champion, Professor of Population Geography, University of Newcastle upon Tyne, UK

Mr P J M Geelan, London, UK
International Boundary Research Unit, University of Durham, UK
The Meteorological Office, Bracknell, Berkshire, UK
Permanent Committee on Geographical Names for British Official Use, London, UK

Data

Antarctica (p148): Antarctic Digital Database (versions 1 and 2), © Scientific Committee on Antarctic Research (SCAR), Cambridge, UK (1993, 1998)
Bathymetric data: The GEBCO Digital Atlas published by the British Oceanographic Data Centre on behalf of IOC and IHO, 1994

Earthquakes data (pp14–15): United States Geological S[...]
National Earthquakes Information Center, Denver, USA
Coral reefs data (p18): UNEP World Conservation Monitor[...]
Cambridge, UK and World Resources Institute (WRI), Wa[...]
USA
Desertification data (p18): U.S. Department of Agriculture [...]
Resources Conservation Service
Population data (pp20–21): Center for International Earth Sc[...]
Information Network (CIESIN), Columbia University; Internati[...]
Policy Research Institute (IFPRI); and World Resources Instit[...]
2000. Gridded Population of the World (GPW), Version 2. Pa[...]
NY: CIESIN, Columbia University.
http://sedac.ciesin.columbia.edu/plue/gpw

Photographs and images

Page	Image	Satellite/Sensor	Credit
1	Canada	Shuttle	NASA/CORBIS
5	The Alps	MODIS	MODIS/NASA
	Amsterdam	IKONOS	Space Imaging Europe/Science Photo Library
	Italy	AVHRR	Earth Satellite Corporation/Science Photo Library
6	Ganges Delta	SPOT	CNES, 1987 Distribution Spot Image/Science Photo Library
	Cyprus	MODIS	MODIS/NASA
	Indian subcontinent	AVHRR	Earth Satellite Corporation/Science Photo Library
7	Victoria Falls		Roger De La Harpe, Gallo Images/CORBIS
	Madagascar	MODIS	MODIS/NASA
	Sinai Peninsula	Shuttle	NASA
8	Canberra		The aerial photograph on page 8 courtesy Geoscience Australia, Canberra. Crown Copyright ©. All rights reserved. www.ga.gov.au/nmd
	New Zealand	Landsat	M-SAT Ltd/Science Photo Library
	Mt Cook		Mike Schroder/Still Pictures
	Bora Bora	SPOT	CNES, Distribution Spot Image/Science Photo Library
	Ayers Rock		ImageState
	Sydney	IKONOS	IKONOS satellite imagery provided by Space Imaging, Thornton, Colorado, www.spaceimaging.com
9	The Pentagon	IKONOS	IKONOS satellite imagery provided by Space Imaging, Thornton, Colorado, www.spaceimaging.com
	Panama Canal	Landsat	Clifton-Campbell Imaging Inc. www.tmarchive.com
	Cuba	MODIS	MODIS/NASA
10–11	Dili	SPOT	CNES, Distribution Spot Image/Science Photo Library
	Vatican City	IKONOS	IKONOS satellite imagery provided by Space Imaging, Thornton, Colorado, www.spaceimaging.com
12–13	Greenland	MODIS	MODIS/NASA
	Nile Valley	MODIS	MODIS/NASA
14–15	Kocaeli (Izmit)		ABC AJANSI/CORBIS SYGMA
	Mt Etna		Bernhard Edmaier/Science Photo Library
16–17	Tropical Cyclone Dina	MODIS	MODIS/NASA/GSFC
	Annual precipitation map	Microwave infrared	NASA/Goddard Space Flight Centre
	Climate change maps		Met. Office, Hadley Centre for Climate Prediction and Research
18–19	Snow and ice		Klaus Andrews/Still Pictures
	Urban		Ron Giling/Still Pictures
	Forest		Wolfgang Kaehler/CORBIS
	Aral Sea	Landsat	Data available from the U.S. Geological Survey, EROS Data Center, Sioux Falls, SD
	Barren/Shrubland		Simon Fraser/Science Photo Library
20–21	Kuna Indians		Royalty-Free/CORBIS
	Masai Village		Yann Arthus-Bertrand/CORBIS
22–23	Los Angeles	SRTM/Landsat 5	NASA
	Tōkyō		Cities Revealed aerial photography © The GeoInformation Group, 1998
24–25	International telecommunications traffic map		Telegeography, Inc., Washington D.C., USA
	Fibre optics		Sanford/Agliolo/CORBIS
26–27	Water		Harmut Schwarzbach/Still Pictures
	Education		Moacyr Lopes Junior/UNEP/Still Pictures
28–29	Sudan Village		Mark Edwards/Still Pictures
	The City		London Aerial Photo Library/CORBIS
30–31	Egypt/Gaza border		Marc Schlossman/Panos Pictures
	Spratly Islands	IKONOS	IKONOS satellite imagery provided by Space Imaging, Thornton, Colorado, www.spaceimaging.com
	Kosovo		Andrew Testa/Panos Pictures
32–33	Iceland	MODIS	MODIS/NASA
	Danube delta	MODIS	MODIS/NASA
	Caucasus	MODIS	MODIS/NASA
34–35	Paris	IKONOS	Space Imaging Europe/Science Photo Library
	Bosporus	SPOT	CNES, 1991 Distribution Spot Image/Science Photo Library
	Belgrade	SIR-C/X-SAR	NASA JPL
56–57	Kamchatka Peninsula	MODIS	MODIS/NASA
	Caspian Sea	MODIS	MODIS/NASA
	Yangtze	MODIS	MODIS/NASA
58–59	Timor	MODIS	MODIS/NASA
	Beijing	IKONOS	IKONOS satellite imagery provided by Space Imaging, Thornton, Colorado, www.spaceimaging.com
	Gaza/Egypt/Israel border	Shuttle	Digital image ©1996 CORBIS; Original image courtesy of NASA/CORBIS
88–89	Congo	Shuttle	NASA
	Lake Victoria	MODIS	MODIS/NASA
	Kilimanjaro	Landsat	USGS/NASA
90–91	Cape Verde	MODIS	MODIS/NASA
	Cairo	IKONOS	IKONOS satellite i[...] provided by Space Thornton, Colorad[...] www.spaceimaging[...]
	Cape Town	IKONOS	IKONOS satellite i[...] provided by Space Thornton, Colorad[...] www.spaceimagin[...]
98–99	Lake Eyre	Shuttle	NASA
	New Caledonia and Vanuatu	SeaWiFS	Image provided b[...] ORBIMAGE © C[...] Imaging Corpor[...] processing by N[...] Goddard Spac[...] Center.
	Banks Peninsula		Institute of Geol[...] Nuclear Sciences[...] New Zealand
100–101	Wellington		NZ Aerial Mapping L[...] www.nzam.com
	Tasmania	SeaWiFS	Image provided by ORBIMAGE. © Orbital Imaging Corporation an[...] processing by NASA Goddard Space Flight Center.
	Tahiti and Moorea	SPOT	CNES, Distribution Spot Image/Science Photo Library
110–111	Mississippi	ASTER	ASTER/NASA
	Grand Canyon	SPOT	CNES, 1996 Distribution Spot Image/Science Photo Library
	Yucatan	MODIS	MODIS/NASA
112–113	The Bahamas	MODIS	MODIS/NASA
	El Paso	Shuttle	NASA
	Washington DC		US Geological Society/Science Photo Library
134–135	Lake Titicaca	Shuttle	NASA
	Tierra del Fuego	MODIS	MODIS/NASA
	Amazon/Rio Negro	Terra/MISR	NASA
136–137	Galapagos Islands	SPOT	CNES, 1988 Distribution Spot Image/Science Photo Library
	Falkland Islands	MODIS	MODIS/NASA
	Rio de Janeiro	SPOT	Earth Satellite Corporation/Science Photo Library
142–143	Arctic sea ice concentration	SSM/I	Data provided by the EOS Distributed Active Archive Center (DAAC) at the National Snow and Ice Data Center, University of Colorado, Boulder, CO.
	Antarctica	AVHRR	NRSC Ltd/Science Photo Library
	Novaya Zemlya	Landsat ETM	NASA